Schirmer History of Music

SCHIRMER HISTORY OF MUSIC

Léonie Rosenstiel, General Editor

The Middle Ages, Charlotte Roederer
The Ars Nova and the Renaissance, Alejandro Enrique
Planchart
The Baroque Era, Lowell Lindgren
From Preclassic to Classic, Gordana Lazarevich
The Romantic and Post-Romantic Eras, L. Michael Griffel
The Twentieth Century, Faye-Ellen Silverman
The New World, Léonie Rosenstiel

Margaret Ross Griffel, Consulting Editor

SCHIRMER BOOKS
A Division of Macmillan Publishing Co., Inc.
NEW YORK

Collier Macmillan Publishers
LONDON

Copyright © 1982 by Schirmer Books
A Division of Macmillan Publishing Co., Inc.

Schirmer Books
A Division of Macmillan Publishing Co., Inc.
866 Third Avenue, New York, N.Y.   10022

Collier Macmillan Canada, Inc.

Library of Congress Catalog Card Number: 81-51061

Printed in the United States of America

printing number
1 2 3 4 5 6 7 8 9 10

BOOK DESIGN BY RON FARBER

Library of Congress Cataloging in Publication Data
Main entry under title:

Schirmer history of music.

Includes bibliographies and index.
Contents: The Middle Ages / Charlotte Roederer—
The ars nova and the Renaissance / Alejandro
Enrique Planchart—The baroque era / Lowell
Lindgren—[etc.]
1. Music—History and criticism. I. Rosenstiel,
Léonie.
ML160.S32   780'.9   81-51061
ISBN 0-02-872190-X   AACR2

Contents

PART TWO
THE ARS NOVA AND THE RENAISSANCE

PART THREE
THE BAROQUE ERA

PART FIVE
THE ROMANTIC AND POST-ROMANTIC ERAS

PART SIX
THE TWENTIETH CENTURY

PART SEVEN
THE NEW WORLD

Preface

Ranging from antiquity to the twentieth-century avant-garde, the Western music tradition confronts students with a complex assortment of styles. Any of these styles may be said to owe its characteristics not simply to the inventive genius of the composers, performers, and theorists of a given period but to a variety of extramusical influences—wars, political and religious beliefs, philosophical trends, social and technological conditions—that serve to remind one that music-making is and always has been inextricably linked to the great endeavors of human thought and activity. In writing the *Schirmer History of Music,* therefore, we have attempted to discuss the intrinsic qualities of the music of each period while taking pains at the same time to place the music in its larger historical and cultural context.

We have tried as well to present the Western music tradition in a balanced fashion. Having decided to work as a team, with each of us an expert in one era, we agreed to allot equal consideration to each period. As a result, we have devoted more attention to the early Middle Ages and to the twentieth century than is customary in such texts. Furthermore, at the close of the book we have added a unique section on the music of the New World. This section, which traces music history in the Americas from the Renaissance to the present, attests to the fact that musical and cultural ideas have long traveled in *both* directions across the Atlantic.

Throughout the book the history of music is discussed as the history of a performing art. In recent years musicians have attempted to recreate the performance practices of their forebears, seeking to understand the ways in which earlier music was actually interpreted and performed. Although it seems obvious that this process of reconstruction bears directly on the historical study of musical style, many music scholars have shown no special interest in investigating the history of performance. Because each of us regularly performs many of the compositions we discuss, we believe we have made a contribution toward examining this neglected area.

We presume that our readers are familiar with the terms of harmony but have defined other terms as they are introduced in the text. Photographs and musical examples serve pedagogical purposes, illustrating or emphasizing important points; when we discuss works found in the standard anthologies of music, such as *HAM,* we cite them in the text. In addition, a complete list of the anthologies used can be found on page xvii. Each chapter ends with a summary of its contents and a selective bibliography of books and scores for further study.

Anthologies Used in the Text

ABRAHAM, GERALD, ed. *The History of Music in Sound,* 8 vols. New York: Oxford University Press, 1953–1958. (*HMS*)

BURKHART, CHARLES, ed. *Anthology for Musical Analysis,* 3rd ed. New York: Holt, Rinehart and Winston, 1978. (*AMA*)

CHASE, GILBERT, ed. *The American Composer Speaks.* Baton Rouge: Louisiana State University Press, 1966. (*ACS*)

CLARO VALDÉS, SAMUEL, ed. *Antologia de la música colonial en América del Sur.* Santiago de Chile: Universidad de Chile, 1974. (Claro)

DAVISON, ARCHIBALD T., and APPEL, WILLI, eds. *Historical Anthology of Music.* Cambridge, Mass.: Harvard University Press, 1946. (*HAM*)

HARDY, GORDON, and FISH, ARNOLD, eds. *Music Literature: A Workbook for Analysis,* 2 vols. New York: Harper & Row, 1963–1966. (*ML*)

KAMIEN, ROGER, ed. *The Norton Scores,* expanded ed., 2 vols. New York: W. W. Norton, 1970. (Kamien)

KAMIEN, ROGER, ed. *The Norton Scores: An Anthology for Listening,* 3rd ed. New York: W. W. Norton, 1977. (*NS*; S represents the one-volume Standard edition, and E the two-volume Expanded edition)

KIRBY, F. E., ed. *Music in the Classic Period: An Anthology with Commentary.* New York: Schirmer Books, 1979. (*MCP*)

LERNER, EDWARD R., ed. *Study Scores of Musical Styles.* New York: McGraw-Hill, 1968. (Lerner)

MARROCCO, W. THOMAS, and GLEASON, HAROLD, eds, *Music in America.* New York: W. W. Norton, 1964, reprint 1974. (*MA*)

MARROCCO, W. THOMAS, and SANDON, NICHOLAS, eds. *Medieval Music* (The Oxford Anthology of Music). London: Oxford University Press, 1977. (*OxMM*)

PALISCA, CLAUDE V., ed. *Norton Anthology of Western Music,* 2 vols. New York: W. W. Norton, 1980. (*NAWM*; S represents the one-volume Shorter edition)

PARRISH, CARL, and OHL, JOHN F., eds. *Masterpieces of Music before 1750.* New York: W. W. Norton, 1951. (*MM*)

RIEMANN, HUGO, ed. *Johann Schobert Ausgewählte Werke,* vol. 39 in *Denkmäler Deutscher Tonkunst.* Wiesbaden: Breitkopf & Härtel, 1958. (*DDT*)

SCHERING, ARNOLD, ed. *Geschichte der Musik in Beispielen.* Wiesbaden: Breitkopf & Härtel, 1931. (*GMB*)

STARR, WILLIAM J., and DEVINE, GEORGE F., eds. *Music Scores Omnibus,* 2 vols. Englewood Cliffs, N.J.: Prentice-Hall, 1964; vol. 1, 2nd ed., 1974. (*MSO* or *Omnibus*)

VAN DEN BORREN, CHARLES, ed. *Polyphonia Sacra: A Continental Miscellany of the*

Fifteenth Century. London: Plainsong and Mediaeval Music Society, 1932; reprint, College Park: Pennsylvania State University Press, 1963. (*PS*)

WARD-STEINMAN, DAVID, and WARD-STEINMAN, SUSAN L., eds. *Comparative Anthology of Musical Forms,* 2 vols. Belmont, Calif.: Wadsworth Publishing Co., 1976. (*CAMF* or Ward-Steinman)

PART
ONE

*The
Middle
Ages*

I

Medieval Music: The Historical Background and Cultural Sources

C.S. LEWIS has said that "there are more ways than one of reading old books."[1] There also are more ways than one of appreciating old music. We can seek to transport ourselves back into the period when the work was created and to re-create as closely as possible the historical experience. Or we can approach the music more intuitively, reveling in it primarily as present experience. Neither approach, however, can stand totally alone, for even the most ardent historicists function in the present, and even the most sensitive artists are helpless until the manuscripts they wish to transform into sound are deciphered. Thus some combination of objective and subjective, outside and inside, approaches is necessary. Or, as Professor Lewis so aptly put it: "That anything which takes us outside the poem [or the music] and leaves us there is regrettable, I fully agree. But we may have to go outside it in order that we may presently come inside it again, better equipped. . . . And what we find inside will always depend a great deal on what we have brought in with us."[2] The material that follows is directed primarily toward equipping students to "presently come inside again."

The designation "Middle Ages" originated with writers of the fourteenth and fifteenth centuries, who looked upon their age as a remarkable revival of the glories of ancient Greece and Rome and therefore gave their own period the name "Renaissance," or "rebirth." To the centuries that intervened between this "Renaissance" and its classical prototypes, they gave the name "Middle Ages." For the historian of written music, the medieval period begins somewhat later than it does for the linguist, the philosopher, or the political historian. Musical notation is not found extensively in manuscript sources until the ninth century, and it is only sources of the eleventh century (and later) that can as yet be transcribed into modern notation without the aid of later manuscripts that happen to preserve the same piece. For information about the music of centuries before the ninth, we are dependent upon more indirect types of evidence: non-notated liturgical manuscripts, the writings of music theorists, and scattered historical, literary, and pictorial references.

"Middle Ages"

Theorists of the Middle Ages emphasized that music is to be understood as an integral part of the natural world. It is to be designed in such a way as to reflect in its own realm—the realm of audible sound—the patterns and proportions that pervade the natural world as a whole. This concept was not new to the Middle Ages; it was rooted in classical Greek thought, and thus, through this link, this shared central idea, Western music history can be said to begin with classical Greece.

Pythagoras   The Greek mathematician and experimental scientist Pythagoras (c. 550 B.C.) is credited with having demonstrated that simple numerical ratios produce all the intervals necessary to create a musical scale. He showed, for example, that two lengths of string in the ratio of 2:1 produce notes an octave apart, and that lengths of string in other small whole-number ratios produce other important intervals, such as the fifth (3:2), the fourth (4:3), and the whole tone (9:8). The philosopher Plato, writing about 380 B.C., envisioned the entire universe created according to musical proportion and showed how all the basic intervals are related mathematically. These ideas were echoed throughout the Middle Ages and lived on in the writings of various thinkers —not only music theorists, but also theologians and theorists of art and architecture.

St. Augustine   St. Augustine, writing in the first decades of the fourth century A.D., was a major force in "Christianizing" these "pagan" ideas. Drawing upon the Biblical passage, "You have ordered all things by measure, number, and weight," (Wisdom of Solomon 11: 20b), he applied the mystical, number-theoretical, approach of Plato and Pythagoras to establish a cosmology that was the dominant philosophy in the West until the rise of Aristotelianism in the late Middle Ages. In the first quarter of the sixth century the music theorist Anicius Manlius Severinus Boethius (c. 480–524) affirmed Plato's **Boethius: three types of music** musically proportioned universe in his division of *musica* into three hierarchical but interrelated levels: *musica mundana* (the music of the universe, or the music of the spheres), *musica humana* (the music of the human body and soul, including vocal music), and *musica instrumentalis* (music produced on instruments by plucking, blowing, or striking). Boethius also transmitted highly technical schemes of tuning and temperament closely related to those described in classical Greek sources, and the Boethian measurements were copied repeatedly in later theoretical manuscripts, even those of the eleventh, twelfth, and thirteenth centuries. (See Chapter 2 for further discussion.)

Several centuries after Boethius, Plato's division of the "world soul" (an intelligent principle that organizes the cosmos in accord with the ratios of Pythagoras) was newly fused with the Augustinian idea of a universe ordered "by measure, number, and weight," so that the Creation appeared as a "symphonic" composition. This idea was articulated in the ninth century by the Irish-born Carolingian scholar Johannes Scotus Erigena (c. 810–877) and later adopted and developed by the School of Chartres. Peter Abelard (1079–1142), for example, identified the Platonic world soul with the Holy Spirit: both create and order matter, and the order is that of musical consonance.

Aesthetics of medieval art

The *aesthetics* of sounding music, of architecture, or of any other art form flowed logically from such an underlying philosophy. On the one hand, the beauty of a work of art was said to arise from its *analogical* nature; that is, it was beautiful to the extent that it was in harmony with, or partook of, the proportions and design of the mystical prototype. On the other hand, the purpose of such art was *anagogical,* to raise the mind to the perception of ultimate truth. In other words, music, architecture, and the other arts were the bridge between the order of the cosmos and the order of humanity. And for art to accomplish its purpose of raising the individual to a realization of the Infinite, the connection had to be right at both ends of the artistic work. At one end, where it was connected with the Creator, it had to be exactly proportioned, but those proportions had to be modulated (in music, expressed through sound) in such a way that when they were transmitted to the individual at the other end, he could relate to them. Thus, a gradation of artistic standards developed: a purer, more unadorned type of art for those more spiritually attuned and more able to comprehend the esoteric aspects; and a more decorated, but still properly proportioned, type of art for those at more elementary levels of artistic development. This dichotomy was reflected, for example, in different standards for monastic and cathedral architecture. It may also have been reflected in varying levels of purity in musical composition and performance.

European civilization in the Middle Ages. (From *Historical Atlas of the World.* Copyright © 1962 by J. W. Cappelens Forlag A/S. Reprinted by permission of J. W. Cappelens Forlag A/S)

Philosophical and Musical Background

Music in medieval Western Europe has its roots in three major sources: (1) classical Greek culture, influenced by still older Near Eastern traditions, which left considerable imprint through its ideas, both philosophical and music-theoretical; (2) Jewish culture, whose poetry, liturgy, and music were the direct source for Christian usage; and (3) Eastern Orthodox, or Byzantine, practice—an overwhelming element, since it was not until A.D. 1054 that Eastern and Western Christianity irrevocably went their separate theological and administrative ways.

Classical Greek Culture

Plato and Aristotle

Plato (427–347 B.C.) and his student Aristotle (384–322 B.C.) are two of the greatest figures in classical Greek philosophy. Both developed comprehensive systems of thought, but because they disagreed fundamentally on first principles, the resulting systems were of opposing design. So well constructed were these systems, though, that they have inspired philosophical speculation ever since.

Music formed an essential part of life in both systems. Plato's views on this are expressed primarily in two of his writings, *The Republic* and *Timaeus*. In the first, he is concerned with music as a builder of character. In the second, he relates a vision of the creation of a universe regulated by musical proportions.

Plato: *The Republic*

In *The Republic,* Plato examines extensively the various musical modes, with an eye toward their practical application. Each one, he says, has its own unique attributes; and only those melodies should be used that contribute to the building of good moral character. Through general discussions of the modes and through specific examples of music's ability to modify an individual's behavior, Plato implies that various types of melodies can be used with great precision to achieve their intended results. Furthermore, those who are being influenced by music in this way need not understand why they are being so trained, nor do they need to know why specific melodies are chosen for them. Essentially, the process is automatic. The result is achieved subconsciously, without active participation by the listener's intellect.

Such formative training is sufficient for most people, says Plato, but the rulers of the State must master a higher form of musical knowledge. They must see beyond specific compositions and practical effect to the underlying truths. Central to this process is mastery of the mathematical arts—arithmetic, geometry, astronomy, and music—disciplines that constitute different manifestations of the general art and science of numbers. For it is through the mathematical laws in sound that music can guide the mind to higher philosophical truths.

The result of Plato's own effort at such a breakthrough is recorded in *Ti-*   *Timaeus*
maeus. He describes how the Creator of the universe designed a perfect,
spherical body from the matter of the four elements—earth, air, fire, and
water—and gave it life by giving it a soul by which it would be ruled. Since
the model for this universe is the eternal Idea of a perfect creature, Plato
maintains that the ruling world soul must be of the same nature.

After describing the creation of such a universe, Plato divides the substance of the soul into parts that produce this series: 1, 2, 3, 4, 8, 9, and 27. If
these proportions are viewed as relative string lengths, the series yields the
pattern of intervals shown on the left of Figure 1.1. If they are seen as frequency ratios, the reverse pattern emerges, as shown on the right. One is just
the mirror image of the other, and the calculations are the same viewed from
either perspective.

Plato then speaks of filling up the intervals in the series of the powers of 2

Figure 1.1.   Plato's musical universe

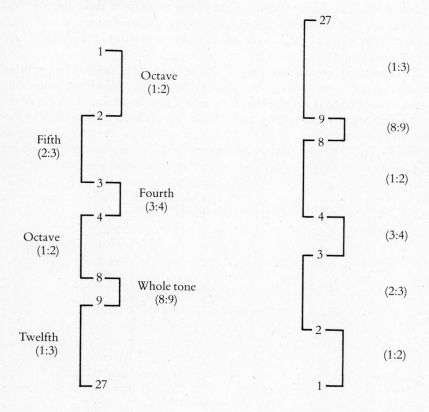

The number series   The number series
viewed as string lengths   viewed as frequencies

and the intervals in the series of the powers of 3. This strategy is puzzling until we realize that the division just outlined can also be expressed as the first four elements of each of these two power series:

2 to the zero power equals 1.   3 to the zero power equals 1.
2 to the first equals 2.   3 to the first equals 3.
2 squared equals 4.   3 squared equals 9.
2 cubed equals 8.   3 cubed equals 27.

Derivations of the basic intervals

The next step, says Plato, is to place two means, that is, two types of mid-point—the arithmetic mean and the harmonic mean—between each interval generated by the series. Consider, for example, the octave (1:2). The arithmetic mean between any two numerical extremes is the number that falls exactly midway between them, e.g., the arithmetic mean between 1 and 2 is 1½. Now, 1½ minus 1 has the same numerical value as 2 minus 1½: both equal ½. Expressed proportionally, the arithmetic mean between two notes an octave apart is 1:1½:2. Multiplied by two to eliminate the fractions, it is 2:3:4. Musically interpreted, using the string-length version of the model (see Figure 1.2), this proportion indicates that when an octave is divided by its arithmetic mean, the intervals created are a perfect fifth on top and a perfect fourth on the bottom. Using the frequency version of the model, the fourth would be on top, the fifth on the bottom.

The harmonic mean between any two numerical extremes is the number that divides the distance between them into segments of the same proportion as that of the extremes themselves. Consider again the octave (1:2). Since the smaller extreme is half the larger, the harmonic mean will be a number between 1 and 2 half as far from 1 as it is from 2. Thus the harmonic mean between 1 and 2 is 1⅓; 1⅓ minus 1 is ⅓, and 2 minus 1⅓ is ⅔; and the proportion of ⅓ to ⅔ is the same as that of the original interval 1:2. Ex-

Figure 1.2.   Schematic diagram of the arithmetic mean

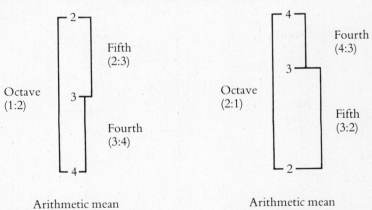

Arithmetic mean
Ratio of string lengths
         Arithmetic mean
Ratio of frequencies

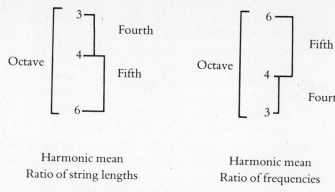

Harmonic mean
Ratio of string lengths

Harmonic mean
Ratio of frequencies

Figure 1.3.   Schematic diagram of the harmonic mean

pressed as a continuous ratio, the harmonic mean between two notes an octave apart is $1:1\frac{1}{3}:2$. Multiplied by three to eliminate the fractions, it is
$3:4:6$. Musically interpreted, using the string-length version of the model,
this indicates that when an octave is divided by its harmonic mean, the intervals created are a perfect fourth on top and a perfect fifth on the bottom, just
the reverse of the pattern yielded by the arithmetic mean in the same version
of the model. Using the frequency version, the fifth would be on top, the
fourth on the bottom (again, just the reverse of the pattern yielded by the
arithmetic mean in the same model).

Similar calculations for the next interval in Plato's series, the fifth $(2:3)$,
yield the following results:

$$\text{arithmetic mean}\quad 2:2\frac{1}{2}:3$$
$$\text{or}\quad 4:5:6$$
$$\text{harmonic mean}\quad 2:2\frac{2}{5}:3$$
$$\text{or}\quad 10:12:15$$

Figure 1.4.   Schematic diagram of the relationship between the arithmetic and
harmonic means

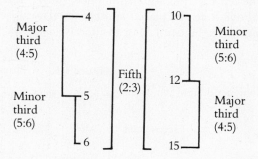

Arithmetic division

Harmonic division

Ratio of string lengths

Musically, the arithmetic mean produces a major third on top and a minor third below; the harmonic mean produces the reverse.

In the same way, calculations for the major third (4:5) yield two whole-tone ratios, including the most commonly used one (8:9).

In this manner, all the intervals larger than a semitone are derived and defined in terms of whole-number, single-integer ratios: octave (1:2), fifth (2:3), fourth (3:4), major third (4:5), minor third (5:6), and whole tone (8:9). In the more specifically music-theoretical sources from classical Greece, these intervals are combined to form two major tonal systems: the Greater Perfect and the Lesser Perfect. (See the following section for an introduction to these systems.)

Aristotle   These views, both philosophical and music-theoretical, constituted the intellectual atmosphere surrounding Aristotle. He agreed with Plato that various modes have distinct ethical effects, and he also valued music's contribution to the education and moral betterment of mankind, but his reasoning was different. It is not the power of number, he said, that is at the root of this phenomenon, nor is it the fact that both music and mankind somehow reflect the same Ideal. Rather, music is one of the imitative arts, and a piece of music can be formed in such a way that it imitates the character of man as it manifests itself in some action or state of mind. When a particular musical form is repeated, it can, if it is a true representation, arouse a similar or related action or emotion in a person who might not otherwise be so aroused.

The Platonic view of music became embodied in the medieval notion of "the music of the spheres," but since the Renaissance, Western musical practice, like Western culture in general, has tended to favor Aristotle's views. Only recently, as part of the general reawakening of Western minds to Eastern thinking and musical culture, have ideas similar to those of Plato begun to gain renewed currency.

The Greater and Lesser Perfect Systems of Classical Greece

The basic unit of both the Greater Perfect and the Lesser Perfect systems is the tetrachord. The central tetrachord is bounded by two notes called the *mese* and the *hypate*. Above it can be placed another tetrachord joined either conjunctly (*synemmenon*) (see Figure 1.5) or disjunctly (*diezeucmenon*) (see Figure 1.6).

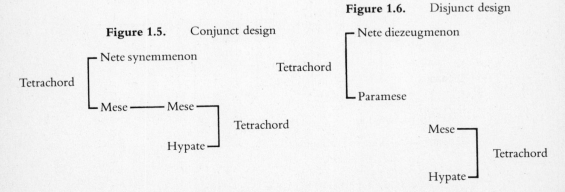

Figure 1.6.   Disjunct design

Figure 1.5.   Conjunct design

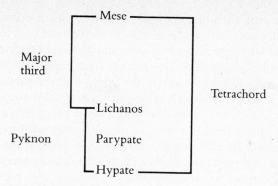

Figure 1.7.   Enharmonic genus

These are the fixed notes of the system, its structural skeleton, within this part of its range. Each of these tetrachords is then filled in with two notes that are movable. These two movable notes can be arranged in three different ways, according to the three melodic *genera* (sing.: *genus*). To illustrate, take the tetrachord bounded by the mese and hypate.

In the *enharmonic* genus (Figure 1.7), the higher movable note, called the *lichanos,* lies a major third below the mese. The remaining interval, called the *pyknon,* appears to be divided by the lower movable note, the *parypate.*

In the *chromatic* genus (Figure 1.8), the lichanos lies a minor third below the mese, and the pyknon, divided by the parypate, is therefore larger.

In the *diatonic* genus (Figure 1.9), the lichanos is a whole tone below the mese, and the parypate is a whole tone below the lichanos.

As we can see from the diagrams of the three genera, the inner notes change frequency from one tuning to the next, but the names by which they are designated do not change; they simply are modified by having the name of the genus added to them. The Greek names thus do not refer to pitches

Figure 1.8.   Chromatic genus

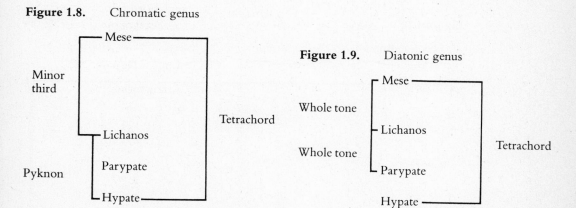

Figure 1.9.   Diatonic genus

directly, but rather to functions, such as the higher movable note, or the lower movable note, or the upper or lower fixed note of a tetrachord. One part of the system, the tetrachordal skeleton, remains fixed, while the other part, the interior construction of the tetrachord in each genus, changes.

In the tetrachord(s) lying above the mese, the corresponding movable notes are called *paranete* (instead of lichanos), and *trite* (instead of parypate). Tetrachords are joined to cover the whole range of a piece in two different ways. The Greater Perfect System (Figure 1.10) consists of two conjunct tetrachords separated by a disjunctive tone, plus a bottom note (*proslambanomenos*) added to complete the overall range of a double octave.

The Lesser Perfect System (Figure 1.11) consists of three conjunct tetrachords and the proslambanomenos. This partly fixed, partly movable tetrachordal design opens up fascinating possibilities for melodic construction by means of various types of modulation.

Greek Hymns: Surviving Musical Fragments

Only about forty fragments of ancient Greek music have been found to date. Some were probably written in the third or second centuries B.C.; others date from the first centuries A.D.; and at least a third may be forgeries. Three of the most impressive remains are engraved on stone. The most extensive is **Delphic** the "First Delphic Hymn," addressed to Apollo and dating from the second **hymns** century B.C. Presumably it was the prizewinner at the Pythian festival (held every four years at Delphi), a prestigious competition that tested the skills of both musicians and athletes. A "Second Delphic Hymn" survives as well, dating from 128–7 B.C., composed by one Limenius of Athens. Finally, we have the "Epitaph of Seikilos," a piece engraved on a tombstone from Aydin, in Turkey, which probably dates from the first century A.D.

From late antiquity, an extensive set of music notational signs is pre-**Notation:** served, together with an explanation of their meaning and use. The Greek **Alypian** writer Alypius (c. 360 A.D.) distinguishes two systems of notation, designat-**tables** ing one "vocal" and the other "instrumental." Such a simple dichotomy does

Figure 1.10.   Greater perfect system

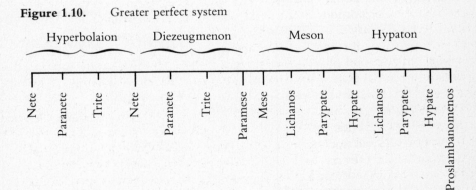

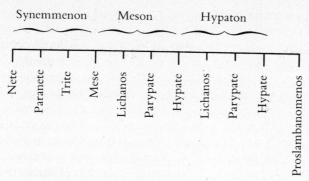

Figure 1.11.   Lesser perfect system

not hold, however, when tested against the use of these signs in actual musical examples. Not only do vocal pieces employ "instrumental" signs, but there also is a rich mixture of signs to indicate the theoretically complex interval of a third.

    Although this repertory is fragmentary and incompletely deciphered, certain generalizations can still be made about its musical style. Classical Greek music is monophonic; it consists of one pure, unencumbered melodic line. If the composition is vocal, the text is poetic, written in one of the classical metrical patterns. And the fragments on papyrus consist largely of excerpts from literary works: the poetry of Greek tragedies and dramatic monologues. **Style characteristics**

Jewish Tradition

    In terms of repertory, melodic style, and performance practice, the greatest influence upon European medieval liturgical music was exercised first by the Jewish and then by the Byzantine religious traditions. The synagogue service, in which most early Christians were brought up, consisted of prayers, both biblical and newly composed, as well as the singing of psalms and the reading of other portions of Scripture, particularly the first five books of the Old Testament. By the second and third centuries A.D., a rich variety of performing patterns had been recorded in sources derived from the Talmud, a written compilation of Jewish oral legal tradition. These sources describe both responsorial singing (one singer alternating with a group) and antiphonal singing (two halves of a group alternating with each other). **Music in the synagogue**

    Independent, or direct, performances by a soloist were in one of two rather opposing styles: either a very simple speechlike singing, used for the biblical prayers and readings, or an elaborate improvisation that at times must have bordered on the ecstatic. During at least the first five hundred years A.D., the formulas used for reading Scripture were transmitted orally with the help of an instructional system involving specific finger and hand motions. Only **Soloistic repertory** during the second half of the millennium did the *lection tones* used for biblical cantillation begin to be fixed in a written notation.

Jews of biblical times and medieval Christians believed that there should be a professional body of priests and musicians whose sole obligation was to prepare and conduct religious services. In the temple tradition of classical Judaism this role had been performed by the Levites, and in medieval Christianity, an important part of the Church's work came to be the training of singers and the education of clerics. This training was carried on inside the monastery walls, in contrast to the education of laymen, which, when undertaken at all, was carried on outside those walls. Also common to both religions was the practice of arranging texts and music into liturgical cycles. For example, in Judaism, certain psalms were associated with specific days of the week. These designations were not only familiar to the early Christians, who were Jews themselves, but were carried over to the Gentile segment of the new Church when titles referring to this association were retained in the Septuagint, the first Greek translation of the Old Testament, begun in the third century B.C. Similarly, readings from the Pentateuch, the first five books of the Old Testament, were chosen so that the entire corpus of the law would be read twice in a seven-year period.

Liturgical cycles

In short, the early Church, both East and West, inherited from Judaism much that was critical to the establishment of its own liturgy. It adopted the concept of a yearly cycle of services, with each day ranked according to its importance, and retained Bible reading and psalm singing as major constituents of worship. The performance techniques of antiphonal and responsorial singing, and of soloistic virtuosity in an improvisatory style, were all put to use. Even some of the actual melodic formulas, particularly those used in psalm singing, can be found in parallel Jewish and Christian versions. Finally, like the Jews of the synagogue, the Christians of East and West generally employed only vocal music within their liturgy.

Byzantine Tradition

Early Christianity had no strong centralized ecclesiastical authority. But gradually a Church administration evolved that paralleled the civil administration of the Byzantine state. Above the ordinary bishops rose the metropolitans (bishops of the more important jurisdictions), and first in precedence were the patriarchs, singled out as the inheritors of the five apostolic sees (bishoprics): Jerusalem, Antioch, Alexandria, Constantinople, and Rome. The civil and Church hierarchies met loosely at the top in the person of the emperor. Disputed questions of Church doctrine and practice were resolved by authority of regional or general Church councils at which the patriarchs presided, but each one only as "first among equals." Therefore as long as orthodoxy was observed, the liturgy and music of each region was allowed to develop more or less according to its own inspiration.

In addition to developing an elaborate system of lection tones for reciting the sacred texts, the Eastern Christians cultivated responsorial and antiphonal psalmody. The monasteries and churches of Syria were particularly important in the development of antiphonal singing and in the cultivation of a new type of liturgical composition—the hymn. This performance practice and this new genre of composition both probably spread from Syria by way of Byzantium (Constantinople) to Milan and to other Western centers.

Lection tones

The Byzantine hymn developed from the short responses traditionally sung between verses of a psalm. These responses grew gradually until they became established as separate pieces, independent of the psalm. Hymns were of two principal kinds: the earlier version, the *kontakion,* dating from around the sixth century, and the later type, the *kanon,* dating from the eighth to tenth centuries. These hymns had a more elaborate structure than the simple strophic pattern of most Western hymns. A kanon usually consisted of eight *odes,* each of which had several strophes. Each ode corresponded to a specific biblical canticle, such as the Song of Mary, *Magnificat anima mea Dominum* ("My soul magnifies the Lord," Luke 1: 46–55), or the Song of Simeon, *Nunc dimittis servum tuum Domine* ("Lord, now you can let your servant depart in peace," Luke 2: 29–32). Most of these canticles were retained in the Western liturgy and assigned to one of the Daily Offices. (For an example of the kontakion for Christmas Day, *He parthenos semeron* ["The Virgin today gives birth to the Almighty"], see *OxMM,* 1, pp. 14–15.)[3]

Hymns

The melodies of both the Jewish synagogues and the Byzantine churches were taught and learned by oral tradition for centuries before they were written down. These melodies were highly formulaic; i.e., they were built up from smaller units of short melodic motives. Soloists used standard ornamental flourishes of many notes in their virtuoso improvisations. For clarity in constructing the chants, these melodic turns were grouped into various families. For example, they were classified according to their position in the chant (beginning, middle, or end) and according to their pitch and intervallic structure. This latter classification was called *mode* in the synagogue chants and *echos* in the Byzantine. The system of eight Byzantine *echoi* grouped into four pairs associated with the notes D, E, F, and G, respectively, was a grouping that many Western theorists carried over into discussions of their chant as well.

Oral tradition

Just exactly how the Jewish system of modes, the Byzantine system of echoi, and the classical Greek system of *tonoi* relate to each other and to Western chant theory and practice is a problem of enormous dimensions. Individual interconnections have been established. In general, however, investigation into these matters is hampered by the long period of time over which the Jewish and Byzantine repertories were transmitted only orally, by difficulties in deciphering the notation of the earliest preserved sources, and by the relatively few classical Greek compositions that still survive. Nonetheless, continuing comparative studies will undoubtedly provide more insight into this very important cultural interchange.

Summary

The music of medieval Western Europe is rooted in three major sources: (1) classical Greek culture, which left considerable imprint through its ideas, both philosophical and music-theoretical; (2) Jewish culture, within whose poetic, liturgical, and musical traditions early Christian usage first developed; and (3) Eastern Orthodox, or Byzantine, practice—a dominant factor, since it was not until 1054 that Eastern and Western Christianity irrevocably went their separate ways.

The Greek theorist and mathematician Pythagoras demonstrated that simple numerical ratios produce all the intervals necessary to create a musical scale. Later the philosopher Plato envisioned the entire universe created according to musical proportions and demonstrated how all the basic musical ratios are related through arithmetic and harmonic means. He argued that the only modes and melodies used should be those that contribute to the building of good moral character.

Aristotle agreed that various modes have distinct ethical effects and also valued the potential contribution of music to education and moral betterment; but he asserted that music is one of the imitative arts and that, properly formed, a piece of music can imitate the character of man as manifest in an action or a state of mind. When this particular musical piece is then recreated, it can, if it is a true representation, arouse a similar or related action or emotion in someone who would not otherwise be so aroused. The Platonic view of music can be found in the Middle Ages in the idea known as "the music of the spheres"; but since the Renaissance, Western musical practice, like Western culture in general, has tended to favor Aristotle's view.

Relatively few examples of classical Greek music survive, although brief excerpts from literary works have been identified. All the music is monophonic, consisting of one unencumbered melodic line. If the composition is vocal, the text is poetic, designed according to one of the quantitative meters.

In repertory, melodic style, and performance practice, Jewish tradition exercised a great influence upon Byzantine practice, and both of these traditions interacted repeatedly with European medieval liturgy and music. Early Christian worship, like the Jewish synagogue service, consisted of biblical and newly composed prayers, of psalm singing, and of readings of other portions of Scripture. The most elaborate music of all three traditions was sung by highly trained virtuoso soloists, who took the basic psalmodic structures and built upon them according to an exuberant, orally transmitted, improvisational tradition.

Like the Jews, the Byzantines arranged both the sacred texts and music into extended liturgical cycles; and both Eastern and Western Christianity followed Judaism in its extensive use of antiphonal and responsorial psalmody. The Byzantines also developed and cultivated the hymn and imparted it to the West.

Notes

1. C. S. Lewis, "'De audiendis poetis,'" *Studies in Medieval and Renaissance Literature.* Cambridge: Cambridge University Press, 1966, p. 1.
2. Ibid.
3. W. Thomas Marrocco and Nicholas Sandon, *Medieval Music (The Oxford Anthology of Music).* London: Oxford University Press, 1977. (*OxMM*)

Bibliography

Guide to Bibliographies

Books and Articles

HUGHES, ANDREW. *Medieval Music: The Sixth Liberal Art.* Toronto: University of Toronto Press, 1974.

Books, Articles, and Recordings

STERNFELD, F. W., ed. *Music from the Middle Ages to the Renaissance.* New York: Praeger, 1973, pp. 431–486.

Chant Recordings

BERRY, MARY. "Gregorian Chant—The Restoration of the Chant and Seventy-five Years of Recording." *Early Music* 7 (1979): 197–217.

Recordings in General

COOVER, JAMES B. *Medieval and Renaissance Music on Long-Playing Records.* Detroit: Information Service, 1964; supplement, 1962–1971, Information Coordinators, 1973.

General Reading and Reference

BULLOUGH, DONALD. *The Age of Charlemagne.* London: Paul Elek, 1965.

CARPENTER, NAN COOKE. *Music in the Medieval and Renaissance Universities.* Norman: University of Oklahoma Press, 1958.

HASKINS, CHARLES H. *The Renaissance of the Twelfth Century.* Cambridge, Mass.: Harvard University Press, 1927.

HOLLANDER, JOHN. *The Untuning of the Sky.* Princeton, N.J.: Princeton University Press, 1961.

KNOWLES, DAVID. *The Monastic Order in England: A History of Its Development from the Times of St. Dunstan to the Fourth Lateran Council 943–1216.* Cambridge, England: The University Press, 1941.

LOPEZ, ROBERT S. *The Birth of Europe.* English translation published in London: J. M. Dent, 1966.

PANOFSKY, ERWIN. *Gothic Architecture and Scholasticism.* Latrobe, Pa.: Archabbey Press, 1951.

SIMSON, OTTO VON. *The Gothic Cathedral: Origins of Gothic Architecture and the Medieval Concept of Order*. New York: Pantheon Books, 1956.

SOUTHERN, R. W. *Western Society and the Church in the Middle Ages*. Middlesex, England: Penguin Books, 1970.

————. *The Making of the Middle Ages*. London: Hutchinson, 1967.

WEINBERG, JULIUS R. *A Short History of Medieval Philosophy*. Princeton, N.J.: Princeton University Press, 1964.

General Musical Reference

SADIE, STANLEY, ed. *The New Grove Dictionary of Music and Musicians,* 20 vols. London: Macmillan, 1980.

Specialized Reading

HENDERSON, ISOBEL, and WULSTAN, DAVID. "Introduction: Ancient Greece," in *Music from the Middle Ages to the Renaissance,* ed. F. W. Sternfeld. New York: Praeger, 1973, pp. 27–58.

McCLAIN, ERNEST G. *The Pythagorean Plato: Prelude to the Song Itself*. New York: Nicolas Hayes, 1978.

PÖHLMANN, EGERT. *Denkmäler altgriechischer Musik,* Sammlung, Übertragung und Erläuterung aller Fragmente und Fälschungen (Monuments of Ancient Greek Music; Collection, Translation, and Transcription of, and Commentary on all Fragments and Forgeries). Nürnberg: Verlag Hans Carl, 1970.

SENDREY, ALFRED. *Music in the Social and Religious Life of Antiquity*. Madison, N.J.: Fairleigh Dickinson University Press, 1974.

STRUNK, OLIVER. *Essays on Music in the Byzantine World*. New York: Norton, 1977.

————, ed. *Source Readings in Music History*. New York: Norton, 1950; *Antiquity and the Middle Ages* issued in paperback as a separate volume, 1965.

WELLESZ, EGON. "Byzantine Music and Its Place in the Liturgy." *Proceedings of the Royal Musical Association for the Investigation and Discussion of Subjects Concerned with the Art and Science of Music* 59 (1932–33): 1–22; and 81 (1954–55): 13–28.

————. "Music of the Eastern Churches." *New Oxford History of Music,* vol. 2 (*Early Medieval Music up to 1300*). London: Oxford University Press, 1954, pp. 14–57.

2

The Repertory and Theory
of Medieval Chant

I T would be difficult to overestimate the importance of monophonic chant to the history of musical life in the Middle Ages. A large repertory of melodies existed not only for the Mass but also for the Daily Offices. This year-long cycle of music was copied and recopied in hundreds of manuscripts dating not only from the ninth to the thirteenth centuries, but into the Renaissance as well.

By the time the chant melodies used in the daily services began to be recorded extensively in manuscripts, some of the monasteries had developed into very elaborate organizations. A remarkable model for one such "planned community" exists in the design laid out for the monastery of St. Gall, a foundation of great musical importance as well. It was an ideal plan and never fully executed, but many of its features were characteristic of the way the larger, better-ordered communities lived.

St. Gall: model monastery

The physical and spiritual center of the community was the church, much larger than any of the other buildings grouped around it. Nearby was an arcaded cloister, a wonderful place to enjoy the out-of-doors in all types of weather. Living quarters for the monks included a dining hall and kitchen, supplied by a food cellar, brewery, and bakery. The dormitory was well designed, with the sleeping area on the upper level and the heating apparatus on the lower. The novices had their own quarters, and the abbot his own house. Visitors of various ranks stayed in the guest houses, sometimes for extended periods of time; all who came were to be welcomed graciously as children of God.

A farm surrounded and supported the establishment. Orchards and vineyards, vegetable and herb gardens, were planted. There also were coops for chickens and geese, stables for horses, pens for sheep, and a sty for pigs. In fact, monasteries were often leaders in agriculture, building up the land and developing new breeds of animals and methods of crop cultivation.

Near the church were the library and the rooms where manuscripts were

19

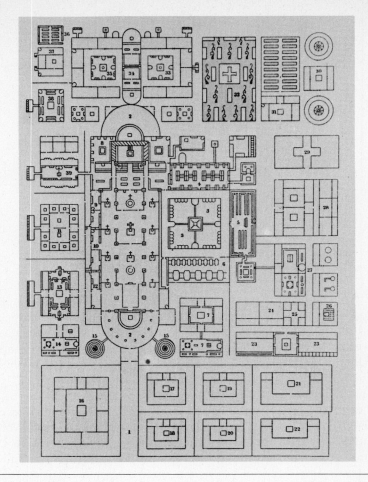

copied. From the end of the ninth century on, St. Gall was famous throughout Europe for its high-quality production of manuscripts and for its manuscript collection.

Monastic artworks Elsewhere on the grounds were workshops for other monastic craftsmen, e.g., goldsmiths, blacksmiths, saddlers, dyers, woodcarvers, and turners. Just about everything needed was at hand, and provision for the needs of everyday life often went hand in hand with the creation of objects of great aesthetic value. A sheep could be a source not only of wool but also of meat and hide. Depending upon its quality, the fleece might be spun and woven into rough monastic habits or used to create beautifully refined altar cloths and liturgical vestments. A fine sheepskin might end up as a manuscript. Metalworkers provided hinges for books and reliquaries for the safekeeping and proper display of precious relics. These artisans could also fashion many items necessary for corporate worship, such as crosses, candlesticks, thuribles for the burning of incense, and various sacramental cups and plates. It was within such well-planned and self-sufficient communities that the great body of medieval chant evolved.

The mastery of such an extensive repertory posed an enormous challenge

This ground plan is taken from the ninth-century handwritten original preserved in the present monastery (St. Gall, Switzerland) library. It represents an ideal Benedictine house, and was probably not carried out in complete detail. The enclosure, surrounded by a wall, was about four hundred feet long by about three hundred wide. 1. Entrance to the church from outside the walls. 2. Church with two apses and numerous altars. 3. Main cloister, showing arches. 4. Dormitory above; room with heating apparatus below. 5. Refectory below; wardrobe above. 6. Cellar with storehouses above. 7. House for pilgrims and poor travellers, with brewery and bakery adjoining. 8. Writing-room below; library above. 9. Living-room and dormitory for visiting monks. 10. School-master's lodging. 11. School-room for ordinary pupils with lodgings for the teachers. 12. Porter's lodge. 13. Quarters for guests of higher rank. 14. Brewery and bakery belonging to quarters for guests of higher rank. 15. Towers with spiral staircases, overlooking the whole place. 16. Large building of unknown use. 17. Sheep-stall. 18. Servants' quarters. 19. Goat-stall with goatherds' quarters. 20. Swine-stall with swineherds' quarters. 21. Cattle-shed with cowherds' quarters. 22. Horse barn with grooms' quarters. 23. Stable for mares and oxen with hay-lofts above and quarters for servants in the middle. 24. Workshops of coopers and turners. 25. Storehouse for brewery-grain. 26. Fruit-drying house. 27. Brewery and bakery for the resident monks, showing mortars and hand-mills. 28. Workshops of shoemakers, saddlers, sword and shield-makers, carvers, turners, goldsmiths, blacksmiths, fullers. 29. Granary and threshing-floor. 30. House of poultry-keeper; hen-house and goose-pen adjoining. 31. House of the gardener; kitchen-garden adjoining. The original gives names of vegetables on the several beds. 32. Burying-ground. 33. Cloister and living-rooms of the *oblati* and their teacher, and of convalescents. 34. Church for the novices and the ill. 35. Cloister and living-rooms, especially for the seriously ill. 36. Hospital-garden. 37. Physician's quarters, apothecary-shop, and rooms for patients. 38. Additional building for surgical purposes. 39. Abbot's house, showing entrance to church and to main cloister. (From William R. Shepherd, *Shepherd's Historial Atlas,* 9th ed., p. 101. Copyright © 1964 by Barnes & Noble, Inc., a division of Harper & Row, Publishers, Inc. Reprinted by permission of Harper & Row, Publishers, Inc.)

Mono-phonic chant

to medieval musicians. Clearly, it was essential to organize the chants so that singers would not encounter each one as a totally unfamiliar phenomenon but would recognize it as characteristic of a whole group of melodies. As modern students of the repertory with a similar problem, we will turn to the writings of medieval theorists for guidance through the maze of chants and for help in answering two major questions. First, how were the pitches of the melodies derived, selected, and organized? Second, how were the chants arranged rhythmically?

Various approaches to the chant

To understand the chant as sounding music might seem enough to us, but to the medieval mind, matters of pitch and rhythm were thought to be significant on more than one level. Of course, they were the indispensable tools of the singer's craft. But the true musician not only had to understand this practical application but also had to see beyond it to the underlying mathematical and philosophical principles. Only by developing this deeper insight could he understand how his discipline fitted together with the other subjects of learned inquiry, and how music ultimately tied into the overall order of the cosmos.

This highly integrative tendency in medieval thinking may be difficult for us to appreciate, for we have a tendency to prefer apparently clear-cut definitions. A mode is either this or that, we say. If one theorist describes it one way and another theorist another, our tendency is to accept one and reject the other, unless the definitions are readily reconcilable. Likewise, when chant is treated on the one hand as presenting a vocal repertory to be mastered, and on the other as a key to understanding the music of the spheres, our tendency is to be skeptical of the idea we find less familiar. The medieval drive, however, was always to harmonize and interrelate, to approach a problem from all sides. A medieval person's instinctive reaction, when presented with two definitions or two treatments of a concept, would have been to say something like "Well, it must be both."

Origins of the chant

Gregory the Great

The origins and early development of medieval chant are obscured by the lack of a precise written record. Iconography and legend attribute its creation to divine inspiration, transmitted through Pope Gregory I, who was often pictured with a dove, representing the Holy Spirit, perched on his shoulder next to his ear. Gregory came from a wealthy Roman senatorial family and served as prefect of Rome in 573. In the years following, he founded several monasteries in Sicily as well as St. Andrew's in Rome, to which he withdrew to live as a monk. But he was not to be allowed the contemplative life for long. From 579 to 586, he was sent to Constantinople as an envoy; after his return he was elected bishop of Rome (Pope), apparently against his will. Nonetheless, he was well prepared for the position, for he had not only the cosmopolitan tradition of his family background to call upon, but also his own practical experience as envoy to the East and as abbot of St. Andrew's. As Pope, Gregory was a vigorous but fair administrator; through his dedication and skill, he substantially expanded the influence of his office.

The Early Tradition
(Sixth to Tenth Centuries)

It is not surprising that Gregory I, who accomplished so much, was widely credited with establishing the musical tradition of the Western Church. He had not only an aura of comprehensive leadership, but also, because of his seven years in Constantinople, an opportunity to become thoroughly familiar with Eastern liturgy and chant. It is virtually impossible to document his legendary activity, however, because the time gap is great between Gregory's pontificate and the first written chant sources. Clearly, though, a long tradition of oral transmission lies behind the first major

Improvisation and oral transmissions

written chant repertories, such as the one copied during the ninth and tenth centuries at the monastery of St. Gall. Although the notation is not yet fully understood by modern scholars, the repertory is very extensive, and the craftsmanship of parchment preparation and calligraphy is of extremely high quality. This repertory does not appear to be tentative or experimental. Instead, it is part of a tradition that already was highly developed by the time it was notated.

How did this repertory evolve? Since documentary evidence is lacking, stylistic analysis of the melodies is the primary means by which various theories are constructed. Yet this approach is hampered by the fact that the earliest manuscripts remain largely unfathomed except to the extent that their contents have been retained in later (already deciphered) copies. The most likely hypothesis is that before they were notated, chants were improvised according to orally transmitted stylistic norms. The essential features of such performances were traditional, well-established melodic structures. Some of these were associated with particular seasons in the liturgical year; others were determined according to the type of chant being sung. These melodic progressions, organized into or flowing from complex theoretical systems of *modes* and *tonoi,* provided the basic framework of a piece, upon which the singer hung detailed embellishments.

These features, similar to those in the music of many other cultures with highly developed melodic styles, were present in classical Greek music and in Jewish liturgical practice. The same features permeated the repertory of medieval Byzantine chant, and today are most familiar in the traditions of Indian, Islamic, and other non-Western cultures, where they have been preserved more extensively than in the West.

If scholars are correct in assuming that before the ninth century chant was transmitted orally by means of a highly developed system of melodic improvisation, we can easily understand why the early sources vary from one geographical area to another. The most important of these regional chant dialects are the *Gallican* in France, the *Mozarabic* in Spain, and the *Ambrosian* in Milan. Yet even the most disparate of these sources are more alike than different, both in their choice of texts for a particular service and in the basic designs of the melodies they transmit. Indeed, the degree of similarity among the hundreds of service books copied all over Western Europe from the ninth century on is remarkable.

Pepin and Charlemagne

The ecclesiastical explanation advanced for this similarity was that all chant flowed from one true source, the divine inspiration of Pope Gregory, but the practical impetus behind it came largely from Charlemagne (reg. 800–814). He energetically sought to unify his inherited lands and subdue his barbarous neighbors into a modern revival of the Roman Empire in the West. To help establish cohesiveness in his patchwork domain, Charlemagne sent envoys throughout his territories with detailed instructions on every aspect of life related to public order. For example, all the clergy were directed to correct the psalms, the *notas,* and the calendar, because, as Charlemagne explained, people often desire to pray to God properly but do so badly for lack of correct books. It is tempting to interpret what he called the *notas* to mean musical notation, for medieval tables listing and naming the signs employed to record chant melodies are sometimes entitled *nomina notarum.* And although the earliest of the surviving service books with music date from at least a generation or two after Charlemagne's death, the Frankish king might well have been instrumental in causing previously orally transmitted chant traditions to be converted to written form. Such activity would have been consistent with his practice of codifying other orally transmitted repertories, such as tribal laws and epic poetry.

Against this background, it seems hardly coincidental that writers of the eighth and ninth centuries vigorously advanced the theory of one true, divinely inspired, "Gregorian" chant. Nothing could fit better with Charlemagne's plan of political unification backed by spiritual justification. Accordingly, in 789 Charlemagne ordered his envoys to ensure that all the clergy taught the Roman chant and celebrated the services according to the uniform liturgical books, "as our father Pepin, of blessed memory, ordered done when he suppressed the Gallican use for the sake of unity with the apostolic see and the peaceful harmony of the Holy Church of God."

Regional Chant Traditions

Gallican   The venerable *Gallican* practice included both Celtic and Byzantine elements, but since it was the closest geographically to the center of Carolingian power, it was the first to be suppressed. The few elements that did survive did so either by adoption as an integral part of the Roman-Carolingian model or by entry among the less strictly codified chants of the repertory, such as processional pieces. One of the most famous Gallican survivals is the refrain *Crux fidelis* ("Faithful cross"), together with the hymn *Pange lingua* ("Sing, my tongue"). Originally these were used on feasts of the Holy Cross, but when taken over into the Roman rite, they were transferred to the afternoon liturgy on Good Friday. (See *OxMM*, 2, pp. 15–16.)

In Spain the native liturgy also incorporated Eastern practices brought from Syria and Byzantium in the fifth century. This liturgy had been codified by the Council of Toledo in 633, and in the eighth century, after the Islamic **Mozarabic**   conquest of much of the Iberian Peninsula, it was given the name *Mozarabic*. The Muslims proved to be tolerant of the native practice, and for a time the local liturgy flourished. Because of the geographical protection afforded by the Pyrenees Mountains, and because much of the imperial energy was spent on the Aquitanians, whose territory lay closer to Frankish lands, the Mozarabic rite was not replaced until the third quarter of the eleventh century. Even then, the changeover was not total; elements of local usage persisted in several areas, including Toledo and Salamanca. A number of manuscripts dating from the ninth to the eleventh centuries preserve this repertory, but their musical notation cannot presently be read. Therefore the only Mozarabic melodies currently known are the approximately two dozen transmitted in later concordances. (See *OxMM*, 3a and 3b, pp. 16–17, for two chants from the Office for the Dead.)

Ambrosian   Longest-lived of all the non-Gregorian traditions is the *Ambrosian*, fostered in Milan and named after that city's great fourth-century bishop, St. Ambrose (credited with introducing antiphonal psalmody to the West). During his episcopate, Milan had extensive ties with the East; in fact, it was the seat of the Western division of the Empire. The Ambrosian liturgy and its extensive body of melodies maintained a separate identity throughout the Middle Ages, one that has been preserved even into modern times.[1]

Medieval Music Theory

The Philosophy of Music

In the Middle Ages, sounding music, whether vocal or instrumental, was not considered something apart from the rest of the natural world, isolated from the rest of human experience. Rather, it was regarded as a manifestation of the universal law that governs all of life. The leading early exponent of this philosophy of music was Anicius Manlius Severinus Boethius (c. 480–524), a highly educated Roman aristocrat who combined the pursuit of scholarship with the discharge of heavy political responsibilities.

Boethius

Boethius learned Greek and therefore was able to read the works of Plato and Aristotle in their original language. He also studied the seven liberal arts. Of the three lower-ranking disciplines called the *trivium* — grammar, dialectic, and rhetoric — Boethius seems to have been particularly interested in the second. He not only translated the four works that comprise Aristotle's *Organon* ("Instrument," a body of treatises on logic) and wrote commentaries on two of them, but he also wrote five essays of his own on the subject, thereby influencing the whole method of inquiry and mode of discourse used by thinkers in the Middle Ages. In addition, Boethius wrote books on three of the four higher disciplines constituting the *quadrivium* — arithmetic, geometry, and music — and probably a book on the fourth discipline as well, astronomy. These were to become standard texts in medieval schools.

Boethius became consul in 510, and by his early forties he had advanced to the position of Master of the King's Offices, one of the highest positions in the Western Empire. In 523, however, he suffered sudden political reversals that led to disgrace, exile, and execution. While in prison he wrote his masterpiece, *De consolatione philosophiae* ("The Consolation of Philosophy"), in which he draws upon his own experience to develop a powerful statement of moral philosophy — that the pursuit of riches, honors, power, fame, and pleasure is legitimate, but only as a means toward the attainment of the perfect good.

"The Consolation of Philosophy"

Clearly, Boethius' great authority in music was only part of the strong impact he had on the intellectual life of the Middle Ages. Furthermore, in Boethius' writing, music is in no sense an isolated discipline but is thoroughly integrated with the other linguistic and mathematical arts. This point is vital, for if these integrative theories actually accord with the laws of nature, they relate to music of any period, including our own.

In *De institutione musica* ("Principles of Music"), Boethius transmits Greek ideas about music's ability to ennoble or corrupt character. Echoing Plato, he observes that the soul of the universe is united by musical concord and that people are attracted to whatever arrangement of musical sounds reflects the order or lack of order within their own characters. Because human beings are linked with audible sound by a type of sympathetic vibration, music can be used to influence behavior and shape character.

Music's omnipresent influence

Boethius also maintains that the investigation of the ethical potential of music does not proceed merely from idle curiosity, for the existence of music and its attendant effect is an inescapable fact of human life. What does it mean, Boethius asks, that when a person's ears and mind are pleased by a melody he involuntarily keeps time by some bodily motion, and afterwards the melodic strain keeps running through his head? From this and many other commonplace examples of human responsiveness to music, Boethius concludes that music is so much a part of our nature that we cannot do without it, even if we might want to. Therefore we should attempt to understand by scientific investigation what is inherent in the nature of music, for real musicians are not content just to be delighted by melodies. They also must know by what proportions sounds are interrelated.

Musicus and cantor
    In fact, without this higher knowledge, one is not even to be called a *musicus,* but merely a *cantor.* For, as Boethius explains, every art or discipline has two aspects—that of a craft, produced by the hands and labor of a craftsman, and that of a science, whereby the rules of the craft and their relationship to the other liberal arts are understood by reason. To know what someone else does, Boethius continues, is far nobler than to accomplish what someone else knows, because physical skill "obeys like a handmaid" whereas reason "rules like a mistress." In further illustration of the relationship between a cantor and a musicus, Boethius points out that craftsmen dealing with physical objects take their names not from their discipline but rather from their instruments, e.g., the player of the cithara, or the player of the aulos. But the one who understands the science of singing by virtue of "study and contemplation" is given the name *musicus.* This distinction is observable, he notes, in other human endeavors as well, such as construction or war; for we name the monuments after and attribute the victories to those by whose "rule and reason" they were begun, not to those by whose "labor and servitude" they were completed.

The Three Kinds of Music
    In *De institutione musica,* Boethius also explains the three kinds of music: *musica mundana, musica humana,* and *musica instrumentalis.* The music of the universe, he says, is especially to be studied in the combination of the elements and the variety of constellations observable in the heavens. The planets and other heavenly bodies move so swiftly and their orbits are so intricately interwoven that proportion and an established order of interacting according to proportion, or modulation, cannot be lacking. Musica mundana is seen on

Musica mundana
earth, as well, in the orderly sequence of seasons, each not only bringing forth its own fruit but also helping the others to bring forth theirs. What winter binds, spring releases; what summer warms, autumn ripens. Altogether the seasons form a unity, a harmony which could not exist if any one of the parts were absent. The importance of the music of the universe to the medieval Church can be gauged when we realize that the movable portion of the temporal cycle of feasts, as well as the daily cycle of services, was regulated according to these seasonal cycles.

Musica humana
    Just as musica mundana rules in the macrocosmos, musica humana is the

characteristic order of the microcosmos, the human being. This harmony has several aspects: the proportions of the physical body, the consonance or dissonance of the soul, and the interrelationship between body and soul. In fact, Boethius asserts, the soul and body are united by the same proportions found in sounding music. Musica instrumentalis, says Boethius, is that which exists in instruments of three types: those that produce sound by tension, such as strings; those sounded by blowing, such as wind instruments or water organs; and those sounded by being struck, such as percussion.

Musica in-strumentalis

These ideas were reiterated by theorists throughout the Middle Ages and were considered indispensable to any comprehensive treatment of music. Of many later commentators, three especially will be called upon for their insights into the nature of sounding music. The earliest is Aurelian of Réôme, whose *Musica disciplina* was compiled in the 840s. This work is an important representative of the grammatical or rhetorical approach to church music, whereby grammar was seen to present models adaptable to the discussion of individual works of art. The tenth-century treatise *Enchiridion musices* ("Handbook of Music"), or *Dialogus de musica* ("Dialogue about Music") is usually attributed to Odo and features a format frequently used by writers in this period—a dialogue between a kindly master and an eager student. The subject, as stated by the master, is "the science of singing correctly and the easy road to perfection in singing."

Aurelian

Odo

But even more influential than these two treatises were the writings of Guido of Arezzo (c. 995–1050), dating from the first quarter of the eleventh century. His *Micrologus* (c. 1030) was so widely copied and circulated that it still exists, entire or in part, in almost eighty manuscripts. Nor was its importance restricted to the century of its origin. Copies were made in the twelfth, thirteenth, fourteenth, and even the fifteenth centuries as well.

Guido

Musica Humana: Harmonics, Rhythmics, and Metrics

After echoing Boethius' definition of the three types of music, Aurelian offers a more extensive discussion of musica humana which indicates that for him it not only consists of a speculative type of music, but also includes the audible repertory of liturgical chant melodies. Musica humana, he says, has three parts: harmonics, rhythmics, and metrics. "Harmonics" he defines as that part of musical science which distinguishes the high and low in sound. Harmonics does not include pitches sounding simultaneously (a usage of the word deriving from later, polyphonic styles); rather, it is the study of the relative frequencies of successive pitches in a melody. "Rhythmics" is defined as the inquiry into whether words in combination sound well or badly together. Finally, "metrics" refers to the rhythmic patterns of chant, which should be so ordered as to correspond to the arrangement of metrical feet in poetry.

Although the pitch aspects of medieval chant practice are better understood than the rhythmic, both are still debated among scholars. Therefore the treatment that follows will approach the issues by posing two questions. (1) What are the theoretical possibilities? (2) Which of the options theoretically available seem to have been used in practice? The second question is more difficult to answer, because the quality of usage probably varied greatly from one church or monastery to another.

The Pitch Structure of Chant Melodies

The first problem confronting a medieval singer was to determine which sounds would constitute his pitch palette. Out of the infinite gradations of high and low that the human voice can produce, which was he to use, and how was he to arrange them? The traditional device for deriving pitches was the *monochord,* an instrument consisting of a single string stretched over a long wooden resonator. A movable fret was attached so that the vibrating length of the string could be varied to yield the desired intervals. The monochord was said to have been invented by Pythagoras and remained the starting point for most medieval discussions of how to derive pitches.

The most rigorous type of training for a singer began with mastering the individual intervals. It continued on into groupings of several intervals, then whole phrases, and finally entire chants. The more common procedure, as described by Guido, seems to have consisted largely of rote imitation. The singer was to sound the letters of each melodic turn, or each neume, on the monochord. Then, by listening, he would be able to learn the melody. *Dialogus de musica* describes a similar procedure, and both master and student make amusing observations about the virtues of the monochord. The master is impressed that the student may learn from such a mechanical master. The student marvels over the typically medieval paradox that the monochord, though made by him, teaches him; and, though teaching him, knows nothing. The machine further endears itself to the student because it never beats or abuses him when he is slow to learn. One requirement remains, however, which the master stresses: the student must be a very diligent listener. This diligence is to be directed at the combinations of sounds that form the various intervals used in chant melodies:

1. A *semitone,* defined by a number of theorists as any interval less than a tone
2. A *tone*
3. Two sounds that are separated by a tone and a semitone, or a *minor third*
4. Two sounds that are separated by two tones, or a *major third*
5. A *diatessaron,* or a fourth
6. A *diapente,* or a fifth

These are the melodic building blocks on the intervallic level.

On the larger structural level, *Dialogus de musica* indicates several possibilities. In response to the student's question concerning the number of sounds proper to form a melody, the master replies that some say eight, others nine, and still others ten. Eight results when a *tetrachord* (four notes related by a whole tone, whole tone, and semitone) is joined with a *pentachord* (segment of five notes) into a *diapason* (the octave). Nine results when a pentachord is

Marginal notes:

The monochord

Six basic intervals

Eight-, nine-, and ten-note melodies

joined *conjunctly* with another pentachord, that is, when the last note of one pentachord is the same as the first note of the next one. Ten results when three tetrachords are joined conjunctly. For example, when G is used as the lowest note, the following three patterns emerge:

Eight Notes	Nine Notes	Ten Notes
G–A–B–C or G–A–B–C–D	G–A–B–C–D	G–A–B–C
C–D–E–F–G D–E–F–G	D–E–F–G–A	C–D–E–F
		F–G–A–B$^\flat$

Fewer notes may be used, but they should center around a single tetrachord or pentachord. There also are some chants containing "excessive ascents and descents," but these highly melismatic melodies are excused from conformity by "universal usage."

    The next step in understanding the melodic organization of chants is to group them into modes. A *mode,* according to *Dialogus de musica,* is a rule which classes every melody according to its *final,* the note that is the pitch center of the piece and on which it usually, but not always, ends. The Greek names of the four chief modes according to the final are *Protus* (First) (D), *Deuterus* (Second) (E), *Tritus* (Third) (F), and *Tetrardus* (Fourth) (G). Each of these in turn is divided into two subcategories according to the behavior of the rest of the melody in relation to the final. (See Figure 2.1.) The higher, or *authentic,* version of each mode ascends as many as eight notes above the final but descends no more than one note below it. (For example, the authentic

Melodic modes

Figure 2.1.   Names of modes used by Greek and Latin theorists

			Used by many Latin theorists	
		Used by Greek and some Latin theorists		
D	Protus	authentic	I	Dorian
		plagal	II	Hypodorian
E	Deuterus	authentic	III	Phrygian
		plagal	IV	Hypophrygian
F	Tritus	authentic	V	Lydian
		plagal	VI	Hypolydian
G	Tetrardus	authentic	VII	Mixolydian
		plagal	VIII	Hypomixolydian

Protus would have D as its final and would include the notes D–E–F–G–A–B–C–D and also the C below the final.) The lower, or *plagal,* version of each mode places the final in the center of the overall *tessitura* of the chant. The usual range is a fifth above and a fifth below the final (for example, the plagal Protus would have D as its final and would range through the notes G–A–B–C–D–E–F–G–A).

The exact range of each mode depends, of course, upon which structural combination of tetrachords and pentachords is used. The most elaborate chants sometimes combined the plagal and authentic versions of the same mode into one sweeping virtuoso range.

Aurelian's grammatical approach

Another critical aspect of modal design is highlighted by the earlier theorist Aurelian of Réôme, who stressed that each mode is distinguished by characteristic melodic turns. Just as letters and syllables cannot be joined randomly to produce coherent words, so notes must be carefully ordered into intervals, and intervals into melodic turns and phrases, so that the results are intelligible according to the requirements of each "mode" of musical structure.

Both approaches to modal design—Aurelian's concern for the proper construction and use of characteristic melodic turns, and the later focus on finals and ranges—continued to be treated by theorists. But from the eleventh century on, more attention was given to what might be termed "choirmaster's basic musicianship." The purpose of this type of writing was to enable performers to sight-sing without undergoing extensive theoretical instruction. The practical dilemma was the same one that choir directors face today. The most elementary type of teaching still entails rote imitation, which Guido dismissed as "childish, good indeed for beginners, but very bad for pupils who have made some progress." The ideal type of procedure is for singers to understand so completely the theoretical structure and modulatory pattern of a piece that they can sight-read it flawlessly. But most choral groups fall somewhere in the middle, and it was to help such intermediately trained singers that Guido developed his system of *solmization.* Naming the degrees of the scale by syllables—ut, re, mi, fa, sol, la—instead of letters is a sight-reading method that has been used in various forms ever since.

Guido: solmization, the hexachord

Guido explained his general idea like this:

If you wish to memorize any note or melodic turn so that you can promptly remember it whenever you wish, in any melody whatsoever, whether known to you or not, so that you will be able to sing it at once and with full confidence, you must mentally mark that note or melodic turn at the beginning of some especially well known melody; and in order to remember each and every note, you must have at your command a familiar melody which begins with that note. For example, let it be this melody which, in teaching boys, I use not only at the beginning but right through to the very end [see Example 2.1]: Don't you see how, in this melody, each of the six phrases begins with a different note? If, trained as I have described, you know the beginning of each phrase so that you can quickly and confidently begin whichever one you wish, you will be able easily to sing these notes correctly wherever you see them.[2]

Ex. 2.1   Guido of Arezzo, *Ut queant laxis*

Ut que-ant lax - is *re* - so - na-re fib-ris *mi* - ra ges - to - rum *fa*-mu - li tu - o - rum,

sol - ve pol - lu - ti *la* - bi - i re - a - tum, sanc - te Io - han - nes.

"So that your servants may openly sing forth the wonders of your deeds, remove all restraints of guilt from their unclean lips, O St. John."

From Guido of Arezzo, *Epistola de ignoto cantu,* transcribed from Gerbert, *Scriptores ecclesiastici de musica,* II, p. 45, St. Blasien, 1784; reprinted Georg Olms, Hildesheim, 1963.

These beginning notes include all the basic intervals used in chant melodies:

1. Semitone: mi–fa
2. Tone: ut–re, re–mi, fa–sol, sol–la
3. Minor third: re–fa, mi–sol
4. Major third: ut–mi, fa–la
5. Perfect fourth: ut–fa, re–sol
6. Perfect fifth: ut–sol, re–la

Therefore, by building hexachords on G and C, or C and F, or on all three, any piece in any mode can be understood and sung in terms of only one six-note pattern.

To go from one hexachord to another, the singer has only to pivot out of one into the other on a pitch that occurs in both. For example, in Figure 2.2, if after arriving at G "sol" (the second G from the bottom) from pitches below

Figure 2.2.   Hexachord modulation

							(etc.)
	G					sol	
	F					fa	
	E				la	mi	
	D				sol	re	
C					fa	ut	
B					mi		
A				la	re		
G	G			sol	ut		
	F			fa			
	E		la	mi			
	D		sol	re			
C			fa	ut			
B			mi				
A			re				
G			ut				

G, the singer has to go still higher, he simply establishes in his mind that G functions no longer as "sol," but as "ut." That is, while staying on the same pitch, he substitutes one function for the other. Then, with G established as "ut," he can continue, for he already knows how to get from "ut" to any of the notes above it in the hexachord.

The "Guidonian hand"

As a further aid, Guido developed the idea known as the "Guidonian hand," a system of visual and tactile associations between the pitch syllables (ut, re . . . la) and prominent parts of the hand such as joints and fingertips. A choirmaster could thereby point out or a singer feel, literally, the course of a melody. Finally, Guido championed the practice of writing neumes on a staff, one where certain notes were identified by characteristic colors. As he explains in *Prologus antiphonarii sui* ("Prologue to His Antiphoner," c. 1025), yellow is to be associated with C, whether on a line or a space, and red with F. This color coding, he thought, would facilitate learning to which mode or melodic formula and to what letter(s) of the monochord each neume belonged.

In general, then, the medieval theorists' concerns ranged from the cosmic to the everyday practical. And, according to their temperament and interests, modern readers will find one level or the other more satisfying intellectually and musically. But our predispositions should not blind us to the fact that medieval writers believed the various levels to be integrally related.

The Rhythmic Structure of Chant Melodies

Grammatical analogies

Many discussions of music, both medieval and modern, draw upon linguistic models or analogies. The grammatical element may be introduced in one of at least two different ways, however, and it is important to distinguish them. Guido of Arezzo uses this approach in *Micrologus,* when he observes that a melodic phrase is structured like a verbal phrase. In language, he points out, the smallest unit is a letter; in music, the smallest is a *sonus*. One, two, or three of these *soni* constitute a *syllaba,* the musical equivalent of the linguistic syllable; one or more of these *syllabae* make up a *neuma,* a musical word; and one or more *neumae* make up the musical phrase, a *distinctio*. Like linguistic units, these structural units of music are set off from one another—perhaps by lengthening the last sonus of each larger unit. The working of this musical punctuation, this *tenor,* as Guido calls it, is not yet clear to modern scholars.

The second type of grammatical reference consists of drawing conclusions about the rhythm of a particular melody not from grammatical rules but from the metrical or accentual behavior of the specific text to which the music has been set.

Notational evidence of rhythm

Not only do the theorists speak of a rhythmic practice, but the musical manuscripts themselves provide ample evidence of a rhythmic tradition. St. Gall neumatic notation is particularly rich in this respect. Above the neumes appear letters which, according to the explanation offered by a medieval writer, refer to details of pitch, rhythm, and vocal quality. These letters are said to have been introduced by the Roman singer Romanus near the end of the eighth century. The most frequently encountered of these so-called "Romanian letters" are *t* and *c*. They stand for *trahere* or *tenere* ("stretch out," "hold") and *cito* or *celeriter* ("fast," "quickly"). Also present in some of the manuscripts written in heighted notations are systematic, though not quite so obvious, rhythmic indications.

And, if Guido is to be taken literally, the very shape of the neume and its position within the musical phrase also convey rhythmic information.

Yet, the conclusions drawn from this discussion are varied. The "accentualists" point out that after the fifth century Latin syllables were no longer measured quantitatively, but were rendered equally, and that an accent or stress on a given syllable became the governing rhythmic element. This approach, they believe, carried over into the chant, and accents on words in the text became the primary source of rhythmic impetus in the music. In performance, the accentualists stress the primary accent of the word in syllabic and neumatic chants. In melismatic settings, the first note of each neume is stressed. The result is a nonmetered accentual rhythm imparted to notes of basically equal time value.

The accentualists

The theory proposed by the monks of Solesmes,[3] who have been responsible for the restoration of chant within the Roman Catholic Church during the late nineteenth and the twentieth centuries, is sympathetic to the accentualists' idea of free rhythm and essential equality of note lengths in the chant. They reject, however, the centrality of the verbal accent of the text and instead have developed an elaborate system of rhythmic interpretation based on a single, indivisible pulse as the fundamental unit. These pulses are grouped in twos and threes and freely mixed into larger rhythmic divisions. In so grouping the notes, the monks are in accord with Guido's concept of soni being combined to make syllabae and neumae. However, they attribute particular rhythmic importance not to the last note of these groupings but to the first, which they call the *ictus*. The ictus articulates the rhythmic flow, which alternates between a rising phrase (*arsis*) and a falling phrase (*thesis*) but is independent of the text-accentual pattern. In their modern reconstructions of chant, such as are found in the *Liber usualis* and the *Graduale romanum,* the Solesmes editors use four different rhythmic indications: the vertical *episema* ('), which marks the ictus; the horizontal episema (-), which marks a retard; the dot (.), which doubles the value of the note it follows; and the comma (,), which indicates a breath.

The monks of Solesmes

The "mensuralists" begin with the proposition that two basic note values exist—a long and a short in the proportion of 2 to 1. These are variously arranged in the different mensural systems that have been proposed.

The mensuralists

None of these rhythmic theories adequately accounts for all the evidence found in medieval notation and theoretical writings, but each seems to have grasped some important aspect of the problem. And each has a certain aesthetic appeal regardless of its historical authenticity.

Summary

Monophonic chant is of central importance to the history of musical life in the Middle Ages. The year-long cycle of vocal music for both the Mass and the Offices was copied repeatedly; it survives in hundreds of manuscripts dating from the ninth through the thirteenth centuries and from the Renaissance as well.

Iconography and legend attribute the origin of Western chant to divine inspiration transmitted through Gregory I, Pope from 590 to 604. However, the practical impetus behind a uniform liturgy and chant came largely from the efforts of Pepin and Charlemagne to unify the Frankish Empire in the late eighth and early ninth centuries.

In addition to the Roman practice as imported, adapted, and imposed by the Franks, there were important regional repertories as well: the Gallican in France, the Mozarabic in Spain, and the Ambrosian in Milan. The essential feature of all these was a traditional set of well-established melodic designs, embellished improvisationally in performance, according to orally transmitted stylistic norms.

The first manuscripts with extensive musical notation date from the ninth and tenth centuries, but the notation is neumatic and not yet fully understood by modern scholars. These neumes may have served to prompt singers already extensively trained in the oral tradition. A singer could master the basic intervals with the aid of a monochord, said to have been invented by Pythagoras. Then he could continue his training by learning to group the intervals into various types of phrases and then into whole chants.

Early chant theorists stressed that each mode is distinguished by characteristic melodic turns. Just as letters and syllables cannot be joined randomly to produce coherent words, so notes must be carefully ordered into intervals, and intervals into melodic turns and phrases, intelligible according to the requirements of the various modes. Later theorists categorized modes by their ranges and finals. Each of the four historic modes—with finals on D, E, F, and G—was subdivided into two categories according to range and tessitura. The higher was known as the authentic, the lower as the plagal. This system of four modes subdivided later came to be known as a system of eight modes, numbered I (D authentic) through VIII (G plagal).

Medieval theorists also described the rhythmic structure of chant by means of verbal analogies. Units of chant melodies were combined just as letters were combined into syllables, syllables into words, and words into phrases. Furthermore, just as pitches could not be joined randomly, neither could the rhythms.

Notes

1. The standard twentieth-century edition of music for the Ambrosian rite is the *Antiphonale missarum iuxta ritum Sanctae Ecclesiae Mediolensis*. Rome, 1935.

2. Dom Gregory Suñol, *Text Book of Gregorian Chant*. Tournai, 1930.
3. For example, J. W. A. Vollaerts, *Rhythmic Proportions in Early Medieval Ecclesiastical Chant*. Leiden: E. J. Brill, 1960.

Bibliography

ADKINS, CECIL. "The Technique of the Monochord." *Acta musicologica* 39 (1967): 34–43.

ANGLÈS, HIGINI. "Latin Chant Before St. Gregory." *New Oxford History of Music,* vol. 2 (*Early Medieval Music up to 1300*). London: Oxford University Press, 1954, pp. 58–91.

CROCKER, RICHARD A. "Pythagorean Mathematics and Music." *Journal of Aesthetics and Art Criticism* 22 (1963–1964): 189–198, 325–335.

GUSHEE, LAWRENCE A. "Questions of Genre in Medieval Treatises on Music." In *Gattungen der Musik in Einzeldarstellungen,* vol. 1 (Festschrift for Leo Schrade). Berlin and Munich: Francke Verlag, 1973, pp. 365–433.

RAYBURN, JOHN. *Gregorian Chant: A History of the Controversy Concerning Its Rhythm.* New York, 1964.

TREITLER, LEO. "Homer and Gregory: The Transmission of Epic Poetry and Plainchant." *Musical Quarterly* 60 (1974): 333–372

Music Theory in Translation

BABB, WARREN, trans., and PALISCA, CLAUDE, ed. *Hucbald, Guido, and John on Music: Three Medieval Treatises.* New Haven: Yale University Press, 1978. Hucbald, *Melodic Instruction* [*De harmonica institutione*], pp. 13–44; Guido of Arezzo, *Micrologus,* pp. 57–83; John, *On Music* [*De musica*], pp. 101–187.

PONTE, JOSEPH, trans. *Aurelian of Réôme: The Discipline of Music* [*Musica disciplina*]. Colorado Springs: Colorado College Music Press, Translations no. 3, 1968.

STRUNK, OLIVER, ed. *Source Readings in Music History.* New York: Norton, 1950; *Antiquity and the Middle Ages* issued in paperback as a separate volume, 1965.

3

The Style and Liturgical Function
of Medieval Chant

I N the eleventh century, several types of notation appeared that are carefully heighted and therefore relatively easy to read without resort to later concordances. Unheighted neumes continued to be used in some parts of Europe, particularly the Germanic areas, but heighted notation became predominant. Thus, from the eleventh century on, historians can work directly with primary sources.

This music is to be sung. In a medieval monastery, it was not intended to entertain listeners, if in fact there were any. It was a spiritual exercise, designed to increase the receptivity and awareness of the members of the community. Of course, a cathedral or parish church did have a congregation, but the farther back we go in the history of the Mass, the more concern there is that the congregation be actively involved in its celebration. The people joined their voices in acclamations and responses. They watched the precisely meaningful ecclesiastical ritual. They tasted the communion elements and smelled the incense. In short, the Mass was a multisensory, participatory experience.

Quite apart from its historical importance, however, the chant is highly gratifying to sing because of the sounds of the Latin text and the sensitive shaping of the melodic line. Even though the chant is monophonic, it consists of a counterpoint in sound, for the basic aural vibratory pattern is set up by the text. In fact, medieval theorists had a separate category of study called "rhythmics," devoted to a consideration of whether words sounded well or badly together; music scribes indicated certain vowel and consonantal combinations by distinctive notation. Time and again, the music speaks for itself, as extensive melismatic flourishes occur over vocally rewarding sounds such as the *a* of "allelu-*ia*" or the *om* of "*dom*-inus" and "*om*-nes."

In the West we have pursued a polyphonic tradition for so long that we have largely lost our ear for very subtle modulations of pitch and rhythm in a single musical line, but renewed interest in various non-Western repertories has at least made us more aware that such nuances exist.

A full appreciation of the subtlety and power of chant can be gained only

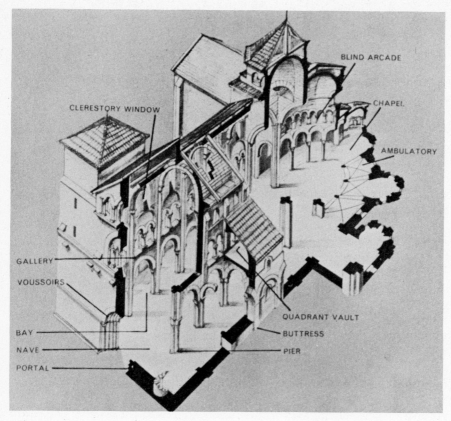

"Analytical perspective of St. Etienne at Nevers." This structure, Romanesque in style, was completed in 1097. (From *Larousse Encyclopedia of Byzantine and Medieval Art,* ed. René Huyghe. Copyright © 1958 by Angé, Gillon, Hollier-Larousse, Moreau et Cie [Librairie Larousse, Paris]. Reprinted by permission of Librairie Larousse, Paris)

through total immersion in the repertory. But for now, our aims are more modest. They consist primarily of becoming familiar with the basic styles of chant melody, and developing an understanding of how these styles were used in the Mass.

Eleventh-Century Chant Style

Musical-Textual Relationships

One of the most important characteristics of monophonic vocal music is the relationship of the music to the text. This relationship has many aspects, but two of the most basic are: (1) the amount of melody associated with given textual units, and (2) the degree to which this association is exclusive. A setting usually reflects the practical situation for which the music was designed: the liturgical function it served, the person(s) who ordinarily sang it, and the intended aesthetic or spiritual effect.

Lection tones   The simplest type of musical-textual relationship is that of the *lection tone,* or *reciting tone.* This consists of basically a single pitch upon which are recited long sections of prose texts, such as the Old Testament lessons, the Epistles, and the Gospels. At appropriate spots, the reciting tone is inflected by raising or lowering the pitch, a kind of musical punctuation that normally coincides with places in the text where modern verbal punctuation would fall, that is, at the ends of phrases and sentences. Musical notation in the manuscript occurs only at the points of inflection, which are marked by strokes resembling linguistic accents. In fact, musical notation is thought to have grown out of this type of textual marking. These lection signs resemble the early neumes, but a continuous path of development from sparsely annotated scriptural manuscripts to complete Graduals and Antiphoners filled with musical inscriptions has yet to be documented.

The lection tone is similar in structure to the text it conveys. Prose is essentially linear, and the lection tone consists of essentially one ongoing pitch. Different formulas are preserved, however, each of which is associated with a particular type of biblical text. For example, one tonal pattern is used only for readings from the Epistles and another is reserved for passages from the Gospels. Acoustically, reciting the Scripture lesson is a good way to project the sound of the text over the entire congregation, even in large churches. Besides, merely speaking the texts against a background of sung liturgy creates a substantial aesthetic and atmospheric letdown. And, as the church fathers repeatedly observed in their discussions of the role of music, melody flows more directly into the heart and soul of the listener than does mere speech.

Psalm tones   A more elaborate type of setting is the *psalm tone,* designed as a multipurpose vehicle for singing this beautiful Old Testament poetry. The psalm tones are probably the most important musical structures of the entire liturgy. If a monastery observed the full complement of services, the entire Book of Psalms, all 150 of them, would be sung in a single week. Not surprisingly, the most fundamental intellectual requirement for those who sought to be accepted as members of a religious community was to know the Psalter by heart. *Psalmody* was important not only because it was used so extensively but also because it formed the structural foundation of many of the more elaborate chants.

In psalmody, as in Scripture reading, the heart of the music is a reciting tone. But in psalmody the tone is more rigidly structured than in Scripture reading: shorter in length, and punctuated by a highly developed system of intonations and cadences, i.e., beginnings and endings. This structure reflects the more regular design of the poetic text itself. Typically, a psalm verse consists of two balanced phrases: a statement and a response. For example, two verses of a psalm that are used for the Christmas Mass proceed as in Example 3.1.

The first half of the psalm tone begins with an *intonation* that marks unmistakably the mode of the piece. It continues with a reciting tone, longer or shorter according to the length of the text to be set, and concludes with a medial cadence—one that provides a sense of pause but not of finality.

Ex. 3.1   v. *Cantate Domino*

1a.	Can	-	ta	-	te	domino		can	- ti - cum no - vum
2a.	No		tum		fecit	dominus	sa - lu	- ta - re su - um	

1b.	qui	- a	mi - ra	-	bi	-	li - a	fe	- cit
2b.	in	con -	spectu gentium relevavit iu - sti	-			ti - am su	- am	

"Sing to the Lord a new song,/for he has performed wonders./The Lord has made known his salvation./In the sight of all the peoples, he has revealed his justice."

Christmas Introit verse set to the psalm tone for Mode VII as transcribed from Paris, B. N. latin 1121, f. 206v.

The second half of the psalm tone continues similarly, but in reverse order of complexity. Again, there is an intonation, but a simpler one; then the reciting tone, upon which most of the text is sung. Finally, there is the cadence, characteristically one that returns to the basic note of the mode, the final, and gives the chant a feeling of completion.

This structure can also be modified to accommodate a text with three phrases, such as the *Gloria Patri* (known also as the Lesser Doxology) that is sung at the end of each psalm (see Example 3.2). The first and last phrases are identical to the first and last phrases of the psalm verse setting. The middle phrase is begun with the mediant intonation, continued with the reciting tone, and closed with the mediant cadence. The practice of concluding the psalms by singing the *Gloria Patri* predates the notated sources and may have

Ex. 3.2   *Gloria Patri*

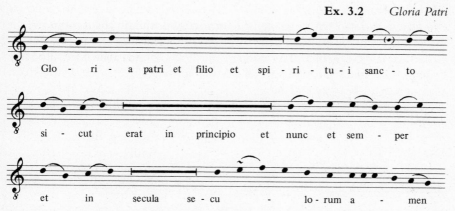

Glo - ri - a patri et filio et spi - ri - tu - i sanc - to

si - cut erat in principio et nunc et sem - per

et in secula se - cu - lo - rum a - men

"Glory to the Father, the Son, and the Holy Spirit: As it was in the beginning, is now, and will be forever, even throughout the ages of ages."

Gloria Patri set to the psalm tone for Mode VII as transcribed from Paris, B.N. latin 1121, f. 206v.

been prompted by a desire to allow the whole congregation to participate. Having heard the psalm tone pattern sung for several verses, they could apply it to a text common to all psalms, added on as a final refrain.

Since the psalm tones are formulaic, they were written out in full only once or twice in a given manuscript, just to establish the pattern. Thereafter, the intonation, the beginning of the reciting tone, and the final cadence were sufficient written reminder. In Example 3.1, verses 1 and 2 are written out in full, since Christmas was the first time in the Church year when this particular psalm tone was used in this liturgical position. But for the *Gloria Patri,* only the first-word intonation and the beginning of the reciting tone are indicated, followed by the cadence over the last two words, *seculorum amen*. When this same psalm tone came to be used later in the year, the psalm verses, too, were notated only in abbreviated form, and the *Gloria Patri* text was signaled only by the vowels of its last two words, *seculorum amen*: EUOUAE.

The three remaining melodic styles—syllabic, neumatic, and melismatic—are distinguished from the lection tone and psalm tone in that the music was always written out in full and was used with only one text at any one time. These styles were not designed to be adjustable during performance. Instead, each musical-textual pairing was normally worked out and notated in full prior to being sung.

Guido of Arezzo

Syllabic and neumatic styles

As mentioned before, Guido of Arezzo discusses basic elements of chant style by drawing an analogy between musical lines and poetic lines. This analogy can be quite helpful in understanding how a chant melody is put together.

For instance, *syllabic style* features one note per syllable of text. *Neumatic* chants usually are more elaborate, such as the famous Introit antiphon for Christmas, *Puer natus est nobis* ("A boy is born for us"), presented in Example 3.3. Guido's musical unit of the *neuma* corresponds in practice to the amount of music associated with each syllable of text in neumatic chants. But the division between syllabic and neumatic styles is not always clear-cut. For, as Guido explains, a neuma may contain only one *syllaba,* which in turn may contain only one *sonus*. When this occurs, some parts of a neumatic chant may appear to be very syllabic.

Melismatic style

The most elaborate melodic style in the chant repertory is *melismatic,* in

Ex. 3.3   *Puer natus est nobis*

Pu - er na - tus est no - bis

"A boy is born for us. . . ."

From the Christmas Introit antiphon as transcribed from Paris, B.N. latin 903, f. 9v.

Ex. 3.4   *Viderunt omnes — v. Notum fecit Dominus*

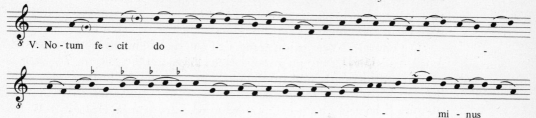

"The Lord has made known [his salvation]."

From the Christmas Gradual responsory verse as transcribed from Paris, B.N. latin 776, ff. 13v.

which certain syllables of the text are singled out for elaborate melodic treatment, with flourishes of twenty, thirty, or even more notes ornamenting them. See the verse *Notum fecit Dominus* ("The Lord has made known . . .") from the Christmas Gradual responsory *Viderunt omnes fines terrae* ("All the ends of the earth have seen . . ."), illustrated in Example 3.4. Especially striking is the exuberant melisma over the first syllable of the third word, "*do*-minus." Not surprisingly, chants such as this Gradual verse were performed by highly skilled soloists and constituted the purely musical highlight of the service.

The fact that syllabic, neumatic, and melismatic chants were designed as a special joining of text and melody for any specific occasion did not, however, preclude reuse of either text or melody in different circumstances. As is apparent from Examples 3.1 and 3.4, the same text could appear in different parts of the service. *Notum fecit Dominus* serves both as an Introit verse and as the verse of the Gradual responsory. In its first role, it is sung to a psalm tone; in the second, it is set melismatically. Thus the style of the setting depends upon the liturgical context and function of the chant.

Similarly, preexistent melodies could be provided with new words, so as to relate lesser feasts to the greater feast preceding them. Such is the case, for example, with the melismatic Gregorian Alleluia verse for Christmas, *Dies sanctificatus illuxit nobis* ("The holy day has shined upon us"), which is basically a highly ornamented psalm tone. The melody was rewritten only slightly in order to adapt it to different texts, and thus it appears as the Alleluia verse for the feasts of St. Stephen (December 26), St. John (December 27), and the Epiphany (January 6), as well as for Christmas.

All these ways of distributing music over a text constitute a palette of chant styles, so to speak, combined and recombined in accord with the liturgical requirements and aesthetic design of each service. Each service then takes its place in a larger order: the cycle of Masses and Daily Office Hours. And each day contributes to the realization of the grand design that is the liturgical year.

Reuse of melodies

The Church Calendar and Clock

The Liturgical Year (The Calendar)

Temporal and sanctoral cycles

The Liturgical Year, which orders all aspects of Church life including the music, consists of two interlocked cycles of festivals. One, the *temporal,* is partly fixed and partly movable (in terms of secular calendar dates); the other, the *sanctoral,* is totally fixed. The most important festivals in the fixed part of the temporal cycle are Christmas, celebrated every year on December 25, and the Epiphany, observed on January 6. The sanctoral cycle marks the feast days of the saints. The movable part of the temporal cycle includes those feasts that occur every year on different dates because they are determined in relation to Easter, the first Sunday following the first full moon after the spring equinox.

The Church year opens with Advent, a three- to four-week period of fasting in preparation for the coming of Jesus. It begins on the fourth Sunday before Christmas and constitutes the first segment of a three-part season which is the most important one in the fixed part of the temporal cycle. The second segment of the season is Christmastide, from December 25 until January 5, and the third is the octave of the Epiphany, the week from January 6 until January 13. (It is interesting to note that the liturgical usage of the word "octave" is the same as its musical usage; both denote cycles in which the eighth element corresponds to the first, e.g., Sunday to Sunday, D to d.) The other major liturgical seasons are associated with Easter; they are the movable part of the temporal cycle. Ash Wednesday marks the beginning of Lent, a forty-day period of penance in preparation for the celebration of Christ's Resurrection. The Sunday before Easter is Palm Sunday, the day of His triumphal entry into Jerusalem. Between Palm Sunday and Easter is Holy Week, which includes Maundy Thursday (Holy Thursday), the day of the Last Supper, and Good Friday, the day of the Crucifixion. Eastertide is the fifty-day period of Easter, highlighted after forty days by the Feast of the Ascension, which marks the end of Jesus' physical ministry on earth. Ten days after the Ascension, the Easter season ends with the dramatic Feast of Pentecost, which recalls the outpouring of the Holy Spirit upon the apostolic Church.

Interaction of the two cycles

Since Christmas is fixed but Easter is movable, two parts of the Church year expand or contract accordingly: the time between the Epiphany and Ash Wednesday, and the time between Pentecost and the beginning of Advent. Thus in one year a given saint's day might occur before the beginning of Lent, whereas in another year it might come afterward. Such variables require musical accommodation. For example, in the Mass, the Alleluia and its verses are replaced during penitential seasons by the Tract. Thus, musicians had to know how the cycles related to each other not just generally, but specifically—in that particular year. Accordingly, the interaction of the temporal and sanctoral cycles made the rhythm of the Church year not merely a mechanical repetition of dates but rather an organic counterpoint through which the seasonal cycles of the natural world were experienced in relation to the fixed reference point of the Incarnation.

The Daily Offices (The Clock)

There are basically two types of Western medieval Christian service: the Mass and the Daily Offices (also called Daily Hours or Office Hours). The Mass is uniquely important, for it incorporates the celebration of the Eucharist, the Christian Church's central sacrament, which has its origin in the Last Supper of Jesus and his disciples. The Office Hours are less important theologically, for they are devotional rather than sacramental, consisting primarily of prayers, readings, and, especially, psalm singing. Nonetheless, the practical influence of the Offices was great, especially in the early Middle Ages. "Low Mass," spoken by a single priest and server, did not exist until later on, and "High Mass," sung by various orders of singers and priests, was so demanding that the Office Hours were by far the most frequently held services.

The eight Daily Hours include Matins, Lauds, Prime, Terce, Sext, None, Vespers, and Compline. Matins is the traditional midnight service. Lauds, one of the oldest services, was timed to coincide with the appearance of the morning star. Prime, Terce, Sext, and None are observed at the first, third, sixth, and ninth hours, respectively, after daybreak (therefore around 6:00 A.M., 9:00 A.M., noon, and 3:00 P.M.). The Mass was usually celebrated between Terce and Sext. Vespers began at the rising of the evening star, and Compline originally consisted of the prayers of members of a monastic community, said in the dormitory just before retiring. Just as the movable part of the temporal cycle of feasts was measured by the seasonal rhythms of the equinoxes, the daily cycle of services was ordered by the rhythms of night and day.

The eight Daily Hours

Liturgically, the Offices consisted primarily of a weekly cycle of psalms, some of which were sung daily. The music was of two types: (1) elaborately ornamented excerpts of psalm texts and other Scripture, and (2) simpler, more formulaic treatments of the whole Psalter. The first resembled the Gradual responsories of the Mass; the second were unornamented psalm tones, like Introit or Communion verses. The latter were also furnished with appropriate antiphons, set neumatically, which served at first as recurring refrains, framing each psalm verse, and sung by either the ordinary members of a monastic community or by the lay congregation. Eventually, the antiphons came to be sung only before the first verse and after the *Gloria Patri*.

In addition to the psalms, the Offices were enriched by the inclusion of other poetic texts called *canticles*. Three principal ones, used throughout the year, were the Song of Zachariah, *Benedictus Dominus Deus Israel* ("Blessed be the Lord God of Israel," Luke 1: 68–79), sung at Lauds; the Song of Mary, *Magnificat anima mea Dominum* ("My soul magnifies the Lord," Luke 1: 46–

The canticles

55), sung at Vespers, and the Song of Simeon, *Nunc dimittis servum tuum Domine* ("Lord, now you may let your servant depart in peace," Luke 2: 29–32), sung at Compline. Like the psalms, the canticles were sung to psalm tones; and they, too, had their own antiphons.

The history of these daily sung services is one of gradual elaboration. The two original exercises of morning and evening prayer developed into eight Offices, and various appendages were added to each Hour. The principle seems to have been not to disturb the shape of the basic service, but to add preparations at the beginning and devotions at the end. An example of this practice, of much moment for the history of liturgical polyphony, was the introduction of *Marian antiphons*. Why the term "antiphon" was used in this context is a bit of a mystery, for these pieces were not associated with psalm verses, but it can be thought of in the sense of its modern English cognate, "anthem."

Marian antiphons

These Marian antiphons, too, followed a yearly cycle. *Alma redemptoris mater* ("Sweet Mother of the Redeemer") was sung from Advent to February 1. From February 2, the Purification of the Virgin Mary, until Wednesday of Holy Week, *Ave regina caelorum* ("Hail, Queen of Heaven") was used. *Regina caeli laetare* ("Rejoice, Queen of Heaven") was sung from Easter to the Friday after Pentecost, and *Salve regina* ("Hail, O Queen") was used from the Feast of the Trinity, the first Sunday after Pentecost, until the Saturday before the first Sunday of Advent, when the whole cycle began once more. These antiphons were appended to Compline and thus became the last musical act before the religious community retired to sleep. Gradually, these pieces developed such a hold over musicians that by the Renaissance, they overshadowed completely the more venerable liturgical sections of Compline.

The Mass

Introduction

The *Mass,* the most important service of the Roman Catholic Church, is divided into two parts: the Liturgy of the Word and the Liturgy of the Eucharist. In the first part, prayers and readings from Scripture prepare worshippers for the sacrament of Communion. Originally, the Liturgy of the Word was a more distinct service, called the Mass of the Catechumens, for not only the initiated were allowed to attend but also the catechumens, who were still receiving instruction in the tenets of Christianity. They were formally dismissed at its completion, however, for only those already baptized were allowed to participate in the second part, the Liturgy of the Eucharist. It consisted of three successive ritual acts: the Offering of bread and wine, the Consecration of the elements, and the Communion, at which point the sacred offering was received by being eaten and drunk.

Musically, the Mass incorporates many melodic styles from the medieval palette. How they interact with one another within their liturgical context can be highlighted by pursuing a two-part inquiry. First, how are the separate pieces arranged into the liturgical whole? Second, how is the melodic style and structure of each piece suited to its function within the Mass?

Each Mass has, as a rule, a musical core of five chants that are assigned especially to it (which are, in other words, "proper" to it). Accordingly, these five chants—the Introit, the Gradual responsory, the Alleluia, the Offertory, and the Communion—are known as the *Proper of the Mass.* They are performed with other chants that do not change from one service to the next, but are used more or less on a seasonal basis. Known collectively as the *Ordinary of the Mass,* these other chants are the Kyrie, the Gloria (also known as the Laudes), the Credo (not sung in the Roman rite until late in the Middle Ages), the Sanctus, and the Agnus Dei. When the sung elements of the Mass are integrated with the major spoken or recited prayers and Scripture readings, the overall order of the service is as shown in Figure 3.1.

The Proper

The Ordinary

The reason a Mass needs to be reconstructed is that no single medieval source preserves all the elements of a service, written out just as it would have been celebrated. While the exact content and organization of a particular type of service book varied from region to region, each was responsive to two very practical considerations. First, which participants—clerics, and/or singers—were involved? For example, a soloist might well have his own little book, while the choir would have a larger manuscript, an *antiphonale mis-*

Liturgical books used at Mass

Figure 3.1. Parts of the Mass

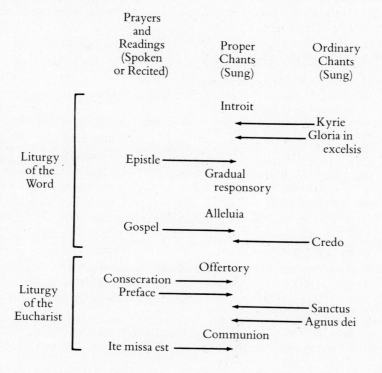

sarum, from which a number of singers could perform at once. The chief celebrant would have his own book, too, a compilation of prayers known as a
sacramentary.

Another practical consideration was how the most efficient use could be
made of two valuable resources: parchment and skilled copyists. Just as a
psalm tone was usually indicated only by its incipit, an Ordinary chant was
not copied repeatedly for each service. Rather, settings of the Kyrie, the
Gloria, and so forth were grouped separately, and participants went back and
forth between the items of the Proper and the Ordinary by following written
directions, called rubrics. (See Figure 3.2.)

The more elaborate the celebration, the greater the challenge to coordinate the participants and the contents of the various service books. Accordingly, in connection with the most highly developed practices—those of an
important monastery, a major cathedral, or the papal chapel—a particular
Ordines   type of document known as an *ordo* (pl., *ordines,* "order") was developed. Its
simplest function was to identify and list in order the chants, prayers, and
readings to be used for each service (see Figure 3.2). But more extensive ordines included instructions about appropriate liturgical vestments and detailed the choreography of processions and other ceremonial matters. These
ordines are very helpful in providing a background against which the music
of the Mass can be more readily understood.

The formal design and melodic style of individual chants of the Mass are
intimately intertwined with their liturgical functions. To illustrate this point,
we will "set the scene" for several chants by using the descriptions of an espe-

Figure 3.2.   Medieval liturgical books

   I. Books with Spoken or Recited Texts
   1. *Evangelarium* (evangeliary)—contains Scripture readings from the Gospels, Matthew,
      Mark, Luke, and John.
   2. *Lectionarium* (lectionary)—contains other Scripture readings which are used as lessons
      in the services.
   3. *Sacramentarium* (sacramentary)—contains the texts spoken or recited by the officiating
      priest, primarily prayers and prefaces for the Canon of the Mass, the most sacred
      part of the Liturgy, during which the bread and wine are consecrated.

   II. Books with Sung Texts
   1. *Antiphonale missarum* (gradual)—contains chants for use during the Mass (later called
      graduale).
   2. *Antiphonale officii* (antiphoner)—contains chants for use during the Daily Offices (later
      called *antiphonale*).
   3. *Cantatorium* (cantatory)—contains the soloistic chants of the Mass.
   4. *Troparium* (troper)—contains tropes.

   III. Theoretical source
     Tonarium (tonary)—a theoretical source containing just chant incipits; it indexes all
      the chants first according to the eight modes and then according to more subtle
      stylistic traits within each mode.

cially elaborate twelfth-century ordo from Laon, in present-day northern France. It is of particular interest to musicians, for it not only describes the pomp of a Mass celebrated by a bishop but also records an event that undoubtedly was eagerly anticipated: the episcopal distribution of a Christmas bonus in "good coin." **The Laon ordo**

The ordo will be presented virtually in its entirety, section by section. In that way the reader will be able to get a "feel" for the ceremony as described in a firsthand source. Each major section of the ordo will be followed by a brief explanation of the contents. The chief purpose of these *glosses* will be to point out a few of the close relationships between musical style and liturgical function in various chants, and to highlight some of the more important turning points in their historical development.

Structure

The Christmas service detailed in the Laon ordo begins with the entrance of the sacred ministers from the *sacristy* (the room where the liturgical vestments, vessels, and utensils are kept and where the clergy put on their vestments) into the sanctuary (or presbytery), the part of the church around the altar. The party includes members of all four higher orders of ecclesiastical office—a bishop, priests, deacons, and subdeacons—as well as a monastic head, an abbot. Also present are four *acolytes,* members of the lower order of ecclesiastical office, assigned to assist the higher orders in their service at the altar. The exact number of deacons and subdeacons involved depends upon the interaction of Christmas with the movable part of the temporal cycle that year. If both cycles are at their peak—that is, if Christmas falls on Sunday—then seven of each are required. This procession is accompanied by the singing of the Introit (*introitus* means "a going into," "an entering"), which for the Third Mass for Christmas Day is *Puer natus est nobis*. (See Examples 3.3, 3.1, and 3.2, in that order, as you read the following section of the ordo.) **The Introit**

At the Mass, the cantor and subcantor begin *Puer natus est nobis*. Meanwhile, the bishop leaving the sacristy stands before the door of the presbytery with the procession ordered in this manner: There proceed two acolytes with candles, two with thuribles; four subdeacons two by two, then a fifth carrying the text; after him four deacons two by two, followed by a fifth, by whom the Gospel will be read, and if the day is Sunday there are seven deacons and seven subdeacons; at the end the bishop proceeding with two priests. When the psalm *Cantate Domino* ("Sing to the Lord") IIc is begun, thus ordered, they go up into the presbytery. The acolytes put down the candles. The bishop remains in front of the altar, with the abbot, the priest, and the deacons and subdeacons standing by on the right and left. The confession said, the deacon standing farthest on the right side kisses the bishop first, then another deacon to the left, and similarly all in their turn—then the priests, and finally the abbot. While these things are going on, the bishop, bowing his head, turns to the clerics. This completed, the deacons and subdeacons withdraw. The bishop with the priests and abbot proceeds to the altar. After *Gloria Patri* ("Glory to the Father"). . . . Cantor *Kyrie eleison* ("Lord, have mercy on us").

The central part of the Introit is the psalm. For the Third Mass of Christmas Day, its text begins, "Sing to the Lord a new song, for he has performed wonders," Psalm 97 in the Vulgate edition (96 in other editions). Potentially, all the verses could be used, but in practice, only one, two, or occasionally three were set. These verses are sung to a psalm tone by part of the choir. The other part of the choir sings the antiphon, a neumatic setting of material which often comes from a psalm too, but which for this particular festival draws on a more specifically appropriate text, the prophecy of Isaiah 9: 6: "A boy is born for us, and a son is given to us." The antiphon introduces the first verse of the psalm, then alternates regularly with the rest of the verses and the *Gloria Patri*.

Introit

Part of the choir sings the same antiphon each time.	Part of the choir sings each verse and the *Gloria Patri* to the same psalm tone.

Ant. *Puer natus est nobis* [see Example 3.3]
   Ps. V. 1: *Cantate Domino canticum novum* [see Example 3.1]
Ant. *Puer natus est nobis*
   Ps. v. 2: *Notum fecit Dominus salutare* [see Example 3.1]
Ant. *Puer natus est nobis*
    Gloria Patri et Filio
    et Spiritui Sancto [see Example 3.2]
Ant. *Puer natus est nobis*

According to the Laon ordo, the Introit is begun by the cantor and the subcantor; probably each one was responsible for leading his side of the choir in this antiphonal chant. In such a setting, there is double flexibility. On the smaller scale, the psalm tone is designed to expand and contract in order to accommodate different verses and the *Gloria Patri*. On the larger scale, the whole Introit can vary in length by incorporating just as many verses as the procession and its accompanying ceremony require. This same type of musical structure is found again toward the end of the service in the Communion.

The Kyrie The Kyrie is the only sung part of the Mass entirely in Greek, a reminder of the Eastern roots of the Western church. Its text is the threefold, or thrice threefold, invocation:

Kyrie eleison.	Lord, have mercy on us.
Kyrie eleison.	Lord, have mercy on us.
Kyrie eleison.	Lord, have mercy on us.
Christe eleison.	Christ, have mercy on us.
Christe eleison.	Christ, have mercy on us.
Christe eleison.	Christ, have mercy on us.
Kyrie eleison.	Lord, have mercy on us.
Kyrie eleison.	Lord, have mercy on us.
Kyrie eleison.	Lord, have mercy on us.

In the simplicity of its ternary (three-part) design, the Kyrie resembles two other chants of the Ordinary: the Sanctus and the Agnus Dei. In fact, these three chants alone constituted the earliest body of the Ordinary, which only later was expanded to include the Gloria and the Credo. The Kyrie, Sanctus, and Agnus Dei also shared a common early function as congregational acclamations.

As a congregational chant, the Kyrie was simple to sing and easy to remember. Judging by the litanies that have been preserved, it was set syllabically and covered only a narrow melodic range. When the chant was transferred from the congregation to the choir, it became more involved, both musically and textually. This does not mean that older melodies did not continue to be used, or that simple melodies suitable for congregational use did not continue to be newly composed; after all, grand musical establishments were the exception then as now. But in those monasteries and cathedrals that did pay particular attention to the musical elaboration of the liturgy, the Kyrie began to assume lengthy texts from at least the ninth century on, and some newer settings may have included these colorful phrases from the very beginning of their notation for use in the liturgy. Quotations from only the first one-third of a well-known Christmas composition will suggest how expansive this form was:

> *Tibi Christe supplices exoramus cunctipotens,*
>   *ut nostri digneris eleison.*
> *Kyrie . . .*   *. . . eleison.*
> *Tibi laus decet cum tripudio iugiter atque*
>   *tibi petimus dona et eleison.*
> *Kyrie . . .*   *. . . eleison.*
> *O bone rex qui super astra sedes et Domine*
>   *qui cuncta gubernas eleison.*
> *Kyrie . . .*   *. . . eleison.*

> We humbly entreat you, Christ, all-powerful Lord,
>   that you grant us mercy.
> Lord . . .   . . . have mercy on us.
> It is fitting continually to praise you with dancing;
>   grant what we ask of you and have mercy.
> Lord . . .   . . . have mercy on us.
> O good king, you who sit beyond the stars; O Lord,
>   you who govern all things, have mercy.
> Lord . . .   . . . have mercy on us.

The first line of each pair was set syllabically. The second line repeated the same melody but was highly melismatic because it was set with just two words: *Kyrie eleison*. Sometimes only the texted (syllabic) version of the melody was used, sometimes only the two-word (melismatic) version, and sometimes both. In any version, the intricacies of such an elaborate text, or the extensive melismas that resulted when just the words *Kyrie eleison* were sung, clearly transformed the chant into one suitable only for trained singers.

After the Kyrie, the service described in the Laon ordo continues in this manner:

After the *Kyrie eleison* is sung, the cantor intones *Gloria in excelsis* ("Glory to God in the highest"). Getting up, two canons wearing silk copes sing the Laudes [the rest of the Gloria] to the bishop, the cantor and subcantor standing next to the cathedram [the bishop's chair], and this as prescribed. The Laudes finished, they go to the bishop and he gives each of them twelve pieces of good coin.

The Gloria   The Gloria is an ancient hymn of praise, consisting of a chain of several elements. Beginning with the song of the angels to the shepherds announcing the birth of Christ, as recorded in Luke 2: 14, it continues with a series of acclamations addressed first to God the Father, then to God the Son.

> *Gloria in excelsis Deo,*
> *Et in terra pax hominibus bonae voluntatis.*
> > Glory to God in the highest,
> > And on earth peace to men of good will.
> *Laudamus te, benedicimus te,*
> *Adoramus te, glorificamus te,*
> *Gratias agimus tibi propter magnam gloriam tuam.*
> > We praise you, we bless you,
> > We worship you, we glorify you,
> > We give thanks to you because of your great glory.
> *Domine Deus, rex caelestis,*
> *Deus Pater omnipotens,*
> *Domine Fili unigenite, Jesu Christe.*
> > Lord God, heavenly king,
> > God the Father almighty,
> > Son of the Father, only-begotten, Jesus Christ.
> *Domine Deus, Agnus Dei, Filius Patris,*
> *qui tollis peccata mundi, miserere nobis.*
> > Lord God, Lamb of God, Son of the Father,
> > you who take away the sins of the world,
> > have mercy on us.
> *Qui tollis peccata mundi,*
> *suscipe deprecationem nostram.*
> *Qui sedes ad dexteram Patris,*
> *miserere nobis.*
> > You who take away the sins of the world,
> > receive our prayer.
> > You who sit at the right hand of God the
> > Father, have mercy on us.
> *Quoniam tu solus sanctus, tu solus Dominus,*
> *tu solus altissimus, Jesu Christe,*
> *cum Sancto Spiritu in gloria Dei Patris, Amen.*
> > For you only are holy, you only are the Lord,
> > you only are most high, Jesus Christ,
> > with the Holy Spirit, in the glory of God the Father, Amen.

The Gloria was used liturgically from at least the fourth century on; it is found as a morning prayer in both Greek and Syrian sources. By the sixth century, it had become part of the Christmas Mass in Rome. Until as late as the eleventh century, however, the Roman rite restricted its use to bishops. Rubrics in some tenth- and eleventh-century musical sources indicate that the bishop himself sang the "Laudes" (i.e., the Gloria). Here, in the twelfth-century ordo, its episcopal connection is retained, although the actual performance is delegated to members of the bishop's staff: two canons, who might have been appointed more for their musical ability than the bishop himself would have been. For by this time he had assumed vast temporal (worldly) administrative responsibilities, ones that might even be termed governmental. Indeed, the coins delivered by the bishop were stamped in his own mint, because the ordo specifically calls for "good coin," that is, the pure silver of ecclesiastical issue, not the debased coinage of the French king, who issued "silver" heavily mixed with copper.

The original melodies of the Gloria were simple and highly formulaic, as was the text. The power of the terse acclamations was built up through repetition of very compact melodic phrases. The later chants became more verbose, and eventually the Gloria was subjected to interlinear additions of text and music. The practical opportunity for this development is apparent from the ceremony described in the ordo. It would be a simple matter for the cantor not only to sing the intonation but also to continue in dialogue throughout the piece. The practice of intoning the first phrase, then leaving the rest of the chant to be sung by others, was retained well into the Renaissance and beyond. Thus most later polyphonic settings begin not with *Gloria in excelsis* ("Glory in the highest"), but with *Et in terra pax* ("And peace on earth").

The Epistle

After the Gloria comes the reading of the Epistle, an excerpt from one of the New Testament letters. For Christmas, it is taken from the first chapter of Hebrews: "God speaking long ago to our fathers in many diverse ways through the Prophets now in these last days has spoken to us in his Son."

A subdeacon ascends into the pulpit on the left, bearing the book and a silver spoon, and reads the Epistle *Multipharie*. Two subdeacons, wearing silk copes, sing in the same place R. [respond], *Viderunt omnes*, v. [verse], *Notum fecit* (R. "All the ends of the earth have seen"; v., "The Lord has made known"). Meanwhile, the subdeacon remaining in the choir, bowing his head to the right and left, goes to the bishop for coins. Two deacons sing *Alleluia, Dies sanctificatus* ("Alleluia," "The holy day"). The response sung, the first two go for coins, similarly the others after the Alleluia.

The Gradual responsory and Alleluia

The Gradual responsory, which follows the Epistle, and the Alleluia, which introduces the Gospel, are the two most virtuoso musical portions of the Mass. Both chants are responsorial, performed by the choir and a soloist in alternation. The soloistic parts are highly melismatic, and the choral parts hardly less so. (See Examples 3.4 and 3.5.)

A full presentation of each consists of the soloist's singing of the Gradual respond or the Alleluia, followed by a choral repetition of the same. The soloist then sings the verse, and the choir returns with the Gradual respond or the Alleluia after the verse.

Gradual Responsory

(soloist) R. *Viderunt omnes*
(choir)   R. *Viderunt omnes*
(soloist)   v. *Notum fecit*
(choir)   R. *Viderunt omnes*

Alleluia

(soloist) *Alleluia*
(choir)   *Alleluia*
(soloist)   v. *Dies sanctificatus*
(choir)   *Alleluia*

The word "Gradual" evidently comes from the location in the church from which the responsory originally was performed—the *gradus,* or step, of the ambo, a raised place between the church's sanctuary and its nave, designed especially for the reading of the lessons and for soloistic chants. By the later Middle Ages the ambo had evolved into a pulpit, but its function remained the same, as can be seen from the ordo, which directs the subdeacon to ascend into the pulpit on the left to read the Epistle, and then directs the two subdeacons to sing the responsory from the same place.

Like the antiphonal chants, the responsorial chants were sung at times in abbreviated form. In such a case, the soloist would intone only the opening phrase; performance of the whole Gradual respond or the full Alleluia was left to the choir. Then, after the verse, the choral return was eliminated, and the choir simply joined with the soloist on the last several phrases of the

The Tract   verse. The Tract replaced the Alleluia on more solemn occasions, such as during Lent or in a Requiem Mass (Mass for the Dead). It contained two to fourteen psalm verses and was sung without an antiphon or response.

The fact that the Gradual responsory and the Alleluia required the most highly skilled singers had important implications for their future stylistic development. For the Gradual responsory and the Alleluia were two chants that received extensive elaboration in the newest polyphonic styles, especially

Ex. 3.5   *Alleluia —v. Dies sanctificatus*

Al - le - lu - ia

V. Di   -   -   es   sanc - ti - fi - ca - tus

"Alleluia. The holy day [has shined upon us]."

From the Alleluia and verse as transcribed from Paris, B.N. latin 776, f. 14r.

those of the twelfth- and thirteenth-century composers associated with the Cathedral of Notre-Dame de Paris.

The Alleluia, as mentioned before, introduces the reading of the Gospel, **The Gospel** the point at which the following section of the ordo begins:

> The Gospel is read in the pulpit: *In principio erat verbum* ("In the beginning was the Word"). While the Gospel is being read, the bishop with the aforementioned goes to the altar; the Gospel read, the deacon cries out in a loud voice *Humiliate vos ad benedictionem* ("Bow down to receive the blessing"); the choir responds with *Deo gratias* ("Thanks be to God"). The bishop gives the blessing over the clerics and the people. The blessing given, the bishop turns to the altar and says *Credo in unum Deum* ("I believe in one God"). Then the deacon, cantor, subcantor, and other servers receive coins from the bishop. Offertory *Tui sunt caeli* ("Yours are the heavens").

The Credo

Like the Introit and Communion, the Offertory is a functional piece that **The** originally accompanied the Offertory Procession, during which the people **Offertory** and clergy brought gifts in kind, including the bread and wine to be consecrated for use during Communion. The early form of the chant may have been antiphonal, like the other two processional pieces. But the early manuscripts preserve multi-verse Offertories seemingly more closely related to the responsorial chants. The Offertory antiphons tend to be predominantly neumatic, but the verses include some very melismatic sections. Like the Introit and the Communion, the Offertory was curtailed as the ceremony itself was abbreviated. By the twelfth century, the verses usually had been dropped altogether, leaving only the antiphon to accompany an offering ritual deprived of its symbolic depth. The Offertory marks the beginning of the Eucharistic part of the Mass, which then continues as the bishop prepares for the Consecration. As described in the ordo:

> Two of the processing subdeacons administer water and a towel to the
>   bishop.
> The Christmas preface is said. . . .
> [Sanctus] ("Holy")
> [Agnus Dei] ("Lamb of God")
> Communion: *Viderunt omnes fines terrae*
>   ("All the ends of the earth have seen")
> Postcommunion [prayer], *Praesta quesumus*
>   ("Here we seek")

Like the Kyrie, the Sanctus and the Agnus Dei originally functioned as **The Sanctus** congregational acclamations. Charlemagne's *Admonitio generalis* of 789, for example, directs that the Sanctus be sung by the whole congregation. The liturgy itself has language that suggests a congregational response. In the preface, the celebrant introduces the Sanctus with words such as: "Therefore, with angels and archangels, and with all the company of heaven, we laud and magnify your Holy Name, evermore praising you and saying. . . ." How appropriate it would be for the earthly company, in fact, to join in proclaiming:

Sanctus, sanctus, sanctus,
Dominus Deus sabaoth.
Pleni sunt caeli et terra gloria tua.
Hosanna in excelsis.
Benedictus qui venit in nomine Domini.
Hosanna in excelsis.
> Holy, holy, holy,
> Lord God of hosts.
> Heaven and earth are full of your glory.
> Hosanna in the highest.
> Blessed is He who comes in the name
> of the Lord.
> Hosanna in the highest.

Congregational singing of the Sanctus and the Agnus Dei largely predate the earliest notated sources, but stylistic analyses of the first recorded melodies, together with verbal prescriptions for and descriptions of liturgical practice, provide a reasonably accurate picture of the early tradition. Just as the texts are highly formulaic and therefore easy to remember, the earliest melodies are also quite accessible, for the Sanctus and Agnus Dei are limited in range and set neumatically.

The Sanctus and Agnus Dei changed less drastically than the Kyrie in their conversion from "popular" acclamations to choral chants, probably because they occur at the most sacred part of the service. There they would be more likely to retain a conventional cast, even when other parts of the service were undergoing extensive modernization. The basic units of text and music in the Sanctus were retained, but they were separated by interpolated lines of newly composed text and music designed to fit harmoniously with the older core. For example, the beginning of a commonly used Sanctus for Christmas is shown in Example 3.6. By comparing it with the text given above, we can see the additions. We also can see that the melodic style of the piece is quite unified, neumatic throughout.

The Agnus Dei   Like the Kyrie, the Agnus Dei has its liturgical roots in the litanies. Biblically, it is founded on John 1: 29, which records John the Baptist's proclamation as he baptized Jesus in the river Jordan: "Behold, the Lamb of God, who takes away the sins of the world." The form of the Agnus Dei that eventually became standard is this threefold invocation:

Agnus Dei qui tollis peccata mundi,
miserere nobis.
> O Lamb of God, you who take away the sins
> of the world, have mercy on us.
Agnus Dei qui tollis peccata mundi,
miserere nobis.
> O Lamb of God, you who take away the sins
> of the world, have mercy on us.
Agnus Dei qui tollis peccata mundi,
suscipe deprecationem nostram.
> O Lamb of God, you who take away the sins
> of the world, receive our prayer.

Ex. 3.6　　*Sanctus*

Sanc - tus

De - us pa - ter in - ge - ni - tus

Sanc - tus

Fi - li - us e - ius u - ni - ge - ni - tus

Sanc - tus , do - mi - nus

Spi - ri - tus pa - ra - cli - tus ex u - tro - que pro - ce - dens

De - us sa - ba - oth

"Holy/God, un-begotten Father/Holy/His only-begotten Son/Holy Lord/Spirit, para-
clete proceeding from each/God of hosts."

From the Sanctus as transcribed from Paris, B.N. latin 903, f. 177r.

Many medieval settings, however, were much freer than this one. One
Agnus Dei commonly used for Christmas employs only the first third of the
"standard" text, plus a repetition of *miserere nobis*. The introductory line of
the chant recalls John's identification of Jesus as the *Agnus Dei*. (See Example
3.7.) Therefore, even when it was well settled as an independent piece in the
Mass, the Agnus Dei retained an elusiveness of form that is characteristic of
the congregational acclamations during the earlier stages of their use in the
liturgy.

The Communion parallels the Introit in structure and style; psalm verses
alternate with a neumatically set antiphon. As with the Introit, some sources

**The Com-
munion**

Ex. 3.7   *Agnus Dei*

"This is the true Lamb, of whom John exclaimed, saying/O Lamb of God, you who take away the sins of the world/You who sit at the right hand of the Father, the one invisible King/Have mercy on us./King of kings, God, joy of the angels/Have mercy on us."

Agnus Dei as transcribed from Paris B.N. latin 903, f. 179r.

preserve two or even three verses, but the most common transmission is of only one. Relatively early, the laity were restricted to communing in only one "kind," taking the bread but not the wine; and this ceremonial abbreviation probably caused the musical brevity. In addition, the antiphon usually does not return in its entirety, but only the last half or so is brought back after the verse(s) and after the *Gloria Patri*. The service ends with a dismissal of the congregation by the deacon: *Ite missa est* ("Go, you are dismissed"). This phrase is the source of the name given to the entire celebration: *Missa*, or Mass.

Ite missa est

Summary

In the eleventh century, several varieties of carefully heighted notation began to be used in musical manuscripts. These can be read or sung from directly, without consulting later concordances.

The particular type of musical-textual setting used for a given chant reflects the practical situation for which the music was designed—its liturgical function, the singer(s) who were to perform it, and the aesthetic or spiritual effect intended. The simplest was the *lection tone,* for singing long sections of prose texts. More elaborate was the *psalm tone,* for singing the poetry found in the psalms. These psalm tones are formulas consisting of a *reciting tone* punctuated by an elaborate system of intonations and cadences grounded in the eight melodic modes. Psalmody was the backbone of medieval worship, especially of the Offices.

The more elaborate musical-textual relationships—*syllabic, neumatic,* and *melismatic*—are distinguished from lection tones and psalm tones in that when they are employed, the music is written out in full and is associated with only one text at a time. Among these styles the simplest settings are the syllabic chants, and the most important of the early ones are the hymns. Neumatic chants are more elaborate, and the most characteristic of them are the Mass and Office antiphons. Melismatic settings are the most complex, and were usually performed by highly skilled soloists.

That syllabic, neumatic, and melismatic chants were designed as a unique joining of text and melody for a specific occasion did not preclude reuse of either the text or the melody in different circumstances. The same text could appear in different parts of the service, its setting dependent upon its liturgical function. Similarly, preexistent melodies could be provided with new words. Such newly texted chants were sometimes used to relate lesser feast days to the greater feast that preceded them.

Each Mass has, as a rule, a musical core of five chants assigned especially to it and thus known as the *Proper*—the Introit, the Gradual responsory, the Alleluia, the Offertory, and the Communion. These are joined by other chants that change less frequently, that are used more or less on a seasonal basis. They are the Kyrie, the Gloria, the Credo, the Sanctus, and the Agnus

Dei—known collectively as the *Ordinary*. The formal design and melodic style of individual chants are intimately intertwined with their liturgical functions. The Mass itself closes with a brief dialogue between the deacon and the congregation, from which the entire service takes its name: *Ite missa est,* says the deacon, and the congregation responds, *Deo gratias.*

Bibliography

ANGLÈS, HIGINI. "Gregorian Chant." *New Oxford History of Music,* vol. 2 (*Early Medieval Music up to 1300*). London: Oxford University Press, 1954, pp. 92–127.

APEL, WILLI, *Gregorian Chant.* Bloomington: Indiana University Press, 1958.

BERRY, MARY. "Gregorian Chant—The Restoration of the Chant and Seventy-five Years of Recording." *Early Music* 7 (1979): 197–217.

JUNGMAN, JOSEF A. *The Mass of the Roman Rite,* 2 vols. New York, 1951–1955.

McKINNON, JAMES W. "Representations of the Mass in Medieval and Renaissance Art." *Journal of the American Musicological Society* 31 (1978): 21–52.

PLUMMER, JOHN. *Liturgical Manuscripts for the Mass and the Divine Office.* New York: Pierpont Morgan Library, 1964.

ROEDERER, CHARLOTTE. *Festive Troped Masses.* New Haven: Yale Collegium Musicum, n.d.

WAGNER, PETER. *Einführung in die gregorianischen Melodien,* 3 vols. Leipzig, 1895–1921. First volume translated as *Origin and Development of the Forms of Liturgical Chant.* London: The Plainsong and Medieval Music Society, 1907(?).

WELLESZ, EGON. *Eastern Elements in Western Chant.* Copenhagen: Munksgaard, 1947.

4
New Liturgical and Secular Monophony

LITURGICAL dramas—especially the *Play of Daniel*, the *Play of Herod* (see *OxMM*, 12, pp. 47–60), and different versions of the Easter dialogue *Quem queritis* ("Whom do you seek?")—have been most popular both with audiences and with historians of music, liturgy, and drama. The real impetus behind their growth was pinpointed by two thoughtful questions posed by a liturgist. Why, he wanted to know, did they spring up only in the Roman rite, and why did they grow up only where that rite had recently supplanted another?[1] The answer was apparent from an examination of the texts used in the displaced rites. These texts are exuberant, highly dramatic, and, to an outsider, almost embarrassingly literal. By contrast, the Roman rite achieves its power through the reserve, balance, and objectivity of its rhetoric. When the Frankish-Roman rite was imposed, it often resulted in a serious mismatch between the congregation affected and the mode of expression prescribed for them. So the poetic vitality, the creative impulse that had generated the development of regional styles, was redirected into genres other than the most central chants of the Mass and Office.

Of these new genres, "liturgical drama" is the most widely known. There also were smaller pieces of new text and music, the *tropes,* which served both as introductions to and expansions of chants already well established in the liturgy. Especially numerous were tropes for Introits, Offertories, and Communions.

Sequences, although probably rooted in liturgical Alleluias, soon grew beyond them into large independent pieces that pursued their own line of development.

Elaborate chants were made easier to remember by adding words to long melismatic flourishes. By this process sequences became *proses,* and melismas from various sources, such as Alleluia or Offertory verses, became *prosulas.* Favorite old chants were disguised as "new" tropes, and "retired" pieces were saved by being integrated into repertories still flexible enough to expand, such as processional chants.

59

Also new during this period were the repertories of *conductus* and *versus* (both terms are the same in the singular and in the plural), settings of poetical texts, cast in easily recognizable, regular metrical patterns. These could be used during a service as well as in extraliturgical or even totally secular contexts. The conductus originated as processional songs, and the versus were often associated with the elaborate ritual of important feast days.

Because these repertories constitute the "growing edge" of the monophony that was added to or associated with the liturgy in the ninth, tenth, and eleventh centuries, it is in these pieces especially that we can feel the pulse of the period's immediate religious concerns: the joy of highly emotional spiritual expression, the delicacy of more private devotional supplications, the battle to preserve doctrinal orthodoxy, and the desire to make the liturgical mysteries more comprehensible by recasting them in words and images both literal and immediate.

In studying the development of these new texts and their music, however, we should not be overly rigid in differentiating between sacred and secular. Such dualism did not exist in medieval thinking. All varieties of manifestation, properly understood, were seen to emerge from the same source. For example, love could be expressed in many ways: the love of Christ for His Church, the devotion of the believer to the saints, the attraction of a man to his mistress, and the love of a mother for her child. All were but different reflections of the same basic reality, namely, the love of God.

Then as now, this deep interconnection was often misunderstood or forgotten. But not until the Renaissance did it become the norm consciously to deny it. Therefore, when approaching the more "secular" side of medieval poetry and music, we perhaps should first try to understand it not as something opposed to the "sacred" but as an extension of it, a manifestation of it on another plane.

Monophonic Additions to the Liturgy

Within the Mass, tropes and sequences were two especially prominent additions. The heart of the trope repertory consisted of newly composed texts and melodies inserted into and used together with antiphonal chants: the Introit, Offertory, and Communion. Tropes often seem to have been motivated textually as much as musically. They might be exclamations of praise or heightened expressions of the contents of the liturgical text. Or the new lines might be doctrinal in nature, *glossing* the basic text and paralleling, although in a more "popular" way, the functions of various levels of biblical interpretation.

Introductory and interlinear tropes

Formally, tropes were of two types: introductory and interlinear, or intercalated. The first are independent pieces of varying size sung directly before and leading directly into the antiphon; the antiphon is then sung in its entirety as usual. The intercalated type is introduced into an antiphon broken up into its phrases, resulting in a constant alternation between one line of trope and one phrase of the antiphon. Typically, tropes were sung by a soloist. They were not especially difficult musically, but the choir already was involved in an antiphonal performance of the underlying chant. Therefore, one musical effect of troping was to mix responsorial and antiphonal performances in the same piece, but without the typically florid soloistic melodies of the "true" responsorial chants.

Musically, the introductory tropes are usually more interesting, for the longer ones present an opportunity to develop a complete melodic idea in the newest style of composition. The interlinear tropes, on the other hand, are more restricted in their possibilities for independent expression, for they must flow relatively unobtrusively from one piece of preexistent melody to another.

Occasionally, chants other than the Introit, Offertory, and Communion were troped as well, but such unusual procedures have sometimes proved to be merely subterfuge. For example, one way to preserve favorite old melodies for the Alleluia verses of the Christmas season, after the new Frankish-Roman melodies were imposed, was to shift them out of the *antiphonale missarum* into the *troparium* and use them as tropes. Similarly, other sets of tropes have been found upon closer examination to be based on familiar old hymn melodies that were saved by being disguised as tropes.

The other major new chant was the sequence, or prose, a large independent piece sung after the Alleluia in the Mass. (See *HAM*[2] I, 16, pp. 13–14; and *OxMM*, 11h, pp. 34–35.) Originally, it gathered up stylistic elements already existing in the repertory, but in size and complexity it soon outgrew them completely. Still extant is a ninth-century, first-person account of the origin of at least one important collection of proses. Notker (c. 840–912), a monk at St. Gall, wrote that as a young man he had sung the very long melismas attached to the Alleluia, but because of their complexity he had had trouble memorizing them. Then, he continued, a monk came to St. Gall who was fleeing from his monastery of Jumièges, in northern France, because it had been destroyed by the Normans. With him he brought a book of chants, including *sequentiae* to which words had been fitted, apparently in the form of poetic verse. Even though he was not satisfied with the quality of the poetry, Notker immediately saw how much easier the melodies would be to remember if they were texted. So with the advice and encouragement of his teacher Iso, he decided to write better verses. Thus Notker explains the origin of his own works.

Sequences (proses)

Notker's Proses

The characteristic design of the texted sequence, or prose, consists of paired lines of text and music, an overall form that typically is A1A2, B1B2, C1C2, and so on. The internal structure of the paired lines may vary considerably from one pair to the next, both in length and in phrase and accentual pattern; contrast pairs A and C in Example 4.1. Variations could be introduced on a higher level as well. Pairs could be grouped into larger units so that although the text was not repeated, the entire structure would be rounded off musically.

Proses sometimes begin with an isolated phrase that stands outside the

Ex. 4.1   *Alleluia celebranda*

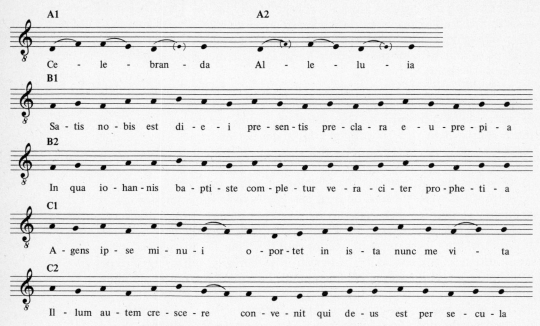

A1   A2

Ce - le - bran - da   Al - le - lu - ia

B1

Sa - tis no - bis est di - e - i pre - sen - tis pre - cla - ra e - u - pre - pi - a

B2

In qua io - han - nis ba - pti - ste com - ple - tur ve - ra - ci - ter pro - phe - ti - a

C1

A - gens ip - se mi - nu - i   o - por - tet in is - ta nunc me vi - ta

C2

Il - lum au - tem cre - sce - re   con - ve - nit qui de - us est per se - cu - la

"Celebrate/Alleluia/These goodly events are sufficient for us on this wonderful day/On which the prophecy of John the Baptist is fulfilled truly,/A prophecy in which he says, "It is right that I should now decrease in this life./It is proper that he increase who is God forever."

From the Sequence as transcribed from Paris, B.N. latin 903, f. 182rv.

rest of the pattern of paired lines. Such an introduction may be very brief and related melodically to the first pair, or it may be longer and melodically independent. Its only text may be "Alleluia," and very occasionally it has some connection with a Gregorian Alleluia melody. By around A.D. 900, the total repertory of proses numbered perhaps seventy-five. Composition of texts outstripped that of melodies, for *contrafacta*—new texts to old melodies—became fairly common. Like the tropes, the sequences included several types of textual content: joyful praise, the piling up of devotional superlatives, and doctrinal arguments and clarifications, with contrafacta of the same melody sometimes railing against opposite heresies.

Prosulas   A smaller type of piece made from preexistent melismas provided with new texts was known as a *prosula*. Typically, a prosula appeared either after an Alleluia but before its verse, or after an Alleluia or Offertory verse that ended with a large cadential flourish. The pitches of the original chant melody were retained, but instead of being sung melismatically over a single syllable of text, they were provided with enough new text so that each of the original notes of the melisma received its own syllable or word. (See Example 4.2.)

Ex. 4.2   *Alleluia—Natus est nobis*

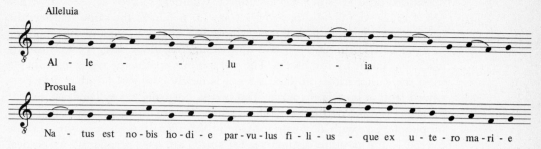

"A little son has been born for us today from the womb of Mary."

From the Alleluia and prosula as transcribed from Paris, B.N. latin 776, f. 14r.

Conductus, Versus, and Goliard Songs

So far the discussion has focused entirely upon music associated with the liturgy, but surely the medievals had other types of music as well. Unfortunately, however, before the eleventh century there is virtually no written record of it, neither the pieces themselves nor theoretical commentary. Thus we are left with only isolated circumstantial references in literature and occasional remarks in Church decrees. Once again we are reminded of how dependent historians are upon a rather narrowly circumscribed type of evidence.

Music undoubtedly flourished outside the Church. Indeed, it would be hard to imagine a culture in which people did not sing and play instruments and dance. But those who were able to create historical artifacts—those who could write and notate music—did not document this side of life. They might simply have been unaware of it, but it seems more likely that it was just taken for granted. Everyone knew about it, and many participated in it, but no one bothered to write it down. Just as only the sumptuous feasts of royalty and high nobility (but not everyday menus) were recorded in cookbooks and chronicles, and just as liturgical vestments (but not everyday dress)—how they were made, what they meant, and how they were used—were the subject of written notice, so only the music of the liturgy was preserved by being systematically notated.

One of the most important types of new Latin composition to appear in the eleventh century was the *conductus,* a processional piece used both within the services and outside them. Not having the established liturgical position of processional pieces such as the Introit, the conductus was used to fill in smaller spaces of silence when the Mass celebrant or the cleric-actor in a liturgical drama was "conducted" from one place to another. The texts were metrical and the music newly composed, usually independently of any liturgical melodies surrounding it. By the twelfth century, the term *conductus* was being

The conductus

applied more generally to any song of similar character or use that had a Latin poetic text dealing with a serious subject, whether "sacred" or "secular." (See *HAM* I, 17a–d, pp. 14–15; and *OxMM,* 13, p. 62.) In the same century, the conductus underwent polyphonic elaboration, appearing first in the repertory of the Parisians about 1170 and flourishing for about sixty years, until its place was taken by the motet. The polyphonic conductus is distinguishable from the earlier motet in that its tenor is newly composed, rather than borrowed from a liturgical source. The text is normally set syllabically, except for the last or next-to-last syllable of a line. The texture is predominantly homophonic, i.e., with all voices moving in a similar rhythmic pattern. And the overall sound is quite distinctive, for thirds are used frequently as vertical consonances. (See *HAM* I, 38–39, pp. 41–42; and *OxMM,* 51–55, pp. 111–117.) That these progressive musical procedures should be found in processional music is quite in character, for that repertory has been unusually flexible, able to absorb the chants of different, even competing traditions and to support stylistic innovation.

The versus   The eleventh century also saw the flourishing of a new style of religious verse—monophonic settings of regular rhyming, scanning poetry. One of the most important collections of these *versus* comes from St. Martial of Limoges, a monastery already famous for its contributions to the new liturgical repertories of tropes and proses. *Versus* embraced a wealth of designs, but focused on exploring the possibilities of strophic form. Some were very complex; others were virtually one-line musical strophes (or stanzas), simply repeated again and again. The St. Martial collection also contains some of the earliest lyrics in the vernacular of the region. The poem *In hoc anni circulo* is macaronic (written in a mixture of languages), with alternate verses in Latin and the vernacular. Another Latin poem has the Provençal refrain "We poor unfortunate ones have slept too long." Finally, we find a versus addressed to the Virgin, *O Maria Deu maire* ("O Mary, mother of God"), sung to the tune of the famous Latin Marian hymn *Ave maris stella* ("Hail, star of the sea"); the versus is a vernacular *contrafactum* of the Latin hymn. All of these pieces probably date from the second half of the eleventh century.

Goliard songs   The student culture of the eleventh and twelfth centuries expressed itself in the *Goliard* songs, writings of wandering scholars and footloose clerics who had begun to collect in various urban centers, drawn by outstanding masters at the cathedral schools. The atmosphere of student life seems to have been very colorful; not surprisingly, their songs strike the same note of youthful exuberance. Literate and intelligent, the Goliards nonetheless had no lifetime institutional commitment. So they spent their literary and musical talents not on the preparation of liturgical manuscripts but on works of religious and political satire, on poems in praise of wine and women. One of the earliest collections of Goliard songs is an eleventh-century manuscript now at Cambridge, England. Perhaps the most famous collection is in a thirteenth-century manuscript now in Munich, widely known under its nineteenth-century editor's title, *Carmina burana.* The poetry is lively and comes in varying shades of delicacy, but unfortunately only a few of the texts are notated, and that usually in unheighted neumes. Therefore the musical realization of Goliard poetry is left largely to the imagination, but undoubtedly these songs were great fun.

The Troubadours and Trouvères

The *troubadours* and *trouvères* were poets and poet-musicians who, during the eleventh, twelfth, and thirteenth centuries, created an extensive repertory

Medieval knight in falcon headdress. (Universitätsbibliothek Heidelberg, Codex Manesse, Cod. Pal. Germ. 848, fol 104v.)

of at least five thousand vernacular poems. Melodies have been preserved for about a third of them. Toward the middle of the thirteenth century, when these songs were first collected and written down in the *chansonniers,* the area that constitutes modern-day France had no uniform language with standardized spelling and pronunciation, but only a number of regional and local dialects. These can be divided roughly into two major groups: Old Provençal, or *langue d'oc,* used in the southern half of the country and occasionally in the northern parts of present-day Italy and Spain as well; and Old French, or *langue d'oïl,* used in the north. (The names of these two languages, incidentally, are derived from the way people in each region said "yes": *oc* or *oïl*.) Both languages seem to have been literary creations to some extent; that is, they do not reflect exactly the linguistic usage of any one area. But in general, Old Provençal is modeled on the dialect of Toulouse, and Old French on that of Paris.

Langue d'oc and langue d'oil

The literary and musical movement associated with these languages started first in the south, where the poet-musicians were called troubadours. By the last third of the twelfth century, however, the activity of the troubadours had spread to the north, where it was carried on and developed further by the trouvères. Both designations for the poet-musicians derive from related words: *trobar* and *trouver,* meaning "to find," "to invent," or "to make up." The names were appropriate, for the troubadours and trouvères sought out and passed on traditional poems and melodies, and when the need arose for new ones, they invented them.

The social position of the troubadours seems to have varied considerably, but their activity was centered at the courts of the nobility. Of the approximately one hundred southern poets for whom biographical information exists, about half seem to have been noblemen of various ranks themselves; at least seven were women, and about one-third are said to have been *jongleurs* as well as troubadours. Jongleurs were general entertainers, who juggled, danced, told stories, played instruments, and performed with trained animals.

Duke William IX of Aquitaine

The title "first troubadour" is usually given to Guillaume (William) IX, duke of Aquitaine and Poitou, who was singled out by those who knew him as an especially accomplished singer; the designation is appropriate figuratively, even if not absolutely true historically. He is not the author of the oldest songs preserved, nor is he the only one of his generation specifically named as a writer of verse. But because of his social prominence, his work, like his life, is the first of any troubadour's to be well documented. He was born in 1071 and lived until 1126. His poetic works are not only preserved but also identified as his. Unfortunately, however, only the poetry and not the music has survived.

Duke William is also the first to have established a strong family tradition of encouraging others at court to contribute to this new repertory of vernacular song. Successors like his son Guillaume X, who were not themselves poets or musicians, nonetheless patronized others who were so gifted, such as the troubadour Macabru (d. 1150). (See *HAM* I, 18a, p. 15.) Therefore, as a representative of the rich, long-lived cultural tradition of the south that gave birth to this new genre of song, none could serve better than Duke William IX, one of a long line of colorful personalities from that region, not the least of whom was the duke's own granddaughter, the fabled Eleanor of Aquitaine (c. 1122–1204).

Eleanor of Aquitaine

Eleanor, in fact, played a considerable part in the spread of the troubadour tradition northward, both personally and through her offspring. Her marriage in 1137 to Louis VII of France (reg. 1137–1180) strengthened the political ties between the south and north of present-day France, and she brought to Louis' court the flourishing southern tradition of poetry and song as well. Fifteen years and two daughters later, Louis procured an annulment of this marriage, complaining of the "flirtatious habits" of his wife; but whatever the truth of those allegations, Louis' actions were probably grounded in the considerably more grievous "failure" of Eleanor to produce a male heir.

Eleanor promptly married another northerner, Henry of Anjou, duke of Normandy and future king of England (reg. 1154–1189). To the court of Normandy she brought one of the most famous troubadours of the day, Bernart de Ventadorn (d. 1195). (See *HAM* I, 18b, p. 15; and *OxMM,* 14, pp. 62–63.) She also bore Henry a son, Richard, known to history as "the Lion-Hearted." Richard (reg. 1189–1199) wrote this type of poetry himself, and he is the subject of a favorite trouvère legend. Blondel de Nesle (c. 1150–1200) is said to have served his master not only musically but also quite practically, for after Richard had been captured on a military campaign, the faithful trouvère located him by singing one of Richard's own songs outside the castle where the king was imprisoned.

Marie, one of Eleanor's daughters by Louis, became the countess of Champagne, where she carried on her family tradition of artistic patronage. One of her favorite protégés was Chrétien de Troyes, writer of many chivalric poems such as *Lancelot* and *Perceval.* Although his literary fame lies largely outside the area of lyric poetry, he may have authored a number of *chansons* as well, converting the sentiments and figures of southern poetry into the language of the north. Even more important, for the trouvère repertory in particular, is the work of Marie's grandson, Thibaut (1201–1253), who succeeded his father and grandfather as count of Champagne and later also became king of Navarre (reg. 1234–1253) in what is present-day Spain. Thibaut was one of the most gifted and prolific of all the trouvères. (See *OxMM,* 25 and 26, pp. 73–75.) So admired were his works that they served as models for both literary scholars and music theorists of the next several generations. By the time of his death, however, the trouvère tradition had begun to drift from its historical moorings at court and to become an activity of the urban middle class. During the second half of the thirteenth century, a number of guilds (or "brotherhoods") of poets and singers were established that fostered this type of compositional activity by sponsoring public contests as a forum for the best new songs. These guilds were based in the newly flourishing towns and cities of northern France.

Thibaut of Champagne and Navarre

L'amour courtois

The central subject of both troubadour and trouvère poetry is love, particularly the type known as *l'amour courtois,* usually translated, not entirely satisfactorily, as "courtly love." Eager to see love as something more elevated than mere physical attraction, the poet often speaks of an obligation to the concept of love itself. This obligation requires that a man not surrender to his natural inclinations. Indeed, the truly worthy lover does not betray his feelings to anyone, even his friends, and certainly not to the lady in question. Yet in the end his love is so great and his suffering so profound that it cannot go unnoticed. Accompanying this highly disciplined behavior of the lover is high praise for the lady. In such poetry, she is always beautiful and "courtly," and usually of high social standing. Envious rivals surround her, creating ad-

The Love Scene. (Universitätsbibliothek Heidelberg, Codex Manesse, Cod. Pal. Germ. 848, fol 249v.)

ditional obstacles to the lover's course. The poet repeatedly despairs, but if his love is true, the well-bred lady will respond, though with benevolence and self-control rather than passion.

Our attitude toward the idea of courtly love is most likely a reflection of our own experiences with love. On one level, the sentiments expressed in these poems may seem little more than adolescent excess; on another, they may seem to be merely lust, thinly disguised; and on still another, they may be understood as attempts to express more profoundly the subtler nature of love. Or, as the troubadour Uc de St. Circ expressed it, "To be in love is to stretch toward Heaven through a woman."[3.]

Since the Middle Ages, the ideals of romantic love have become so ingrained in Western culture that it may be difficult to remember just how unusual they must have seemed at the time. Romantic love would not have been an appropriate prerequisite to seeking out a marriage partner, for among the propertied classes marriage was first of all an economic and political alliance between families. Nor would it have been appropriate for a man to direct such love toward his wife. Even in the unlikely event that she came from a higher social class than he, after marriage she was little more than a property — greatly loved and highly valued perhaps, but hardly in a position to be celebrated with such ardor in public. Indeed, just about the only social situation that could support an open and idealistic expression of romantic love was one in which the lady was situated safely outside the social circle of the suitor and was already married to someone else.

In addition to courtly love lyrics, the chansonniers of the troubadours preserve lighthearted *pastourelles* and the more serious *albas*. In the former the main characters are a shepherdess of uncertain innocence and a young nobleman, who either observes a dalliance or pursues one of his own. In an alba, the participants are social equals who have consummated their love. Warned of the approach of dawn, the poet sings of the sorrows of parting, and his beloved voices her concern for his safe return home. Other poems may consist of dialogues on the relative merits of loving a lady or taking a nice young girl. Still others are discussions between a man and a woman, or between two men, of the myriad details of social etiquette. **Other poetic subjects**

Northern poets especially seem to have enjoyed narrative songs. Their pastourelles surround the dalliance scene with detailed descriptions of both the countryside and the customs and manners of its natives. These poets wrote other types of dramatic ballads as well. Earlier works were usually monologues, but later pieces often involved several characters and lent themselves to dramatization. In the genre known as *chansons de toile* ("pictorial songs"—a *toile* is an artist's canvas) the verbal picture is painted not by the poet, but by the lady of the song herself. Before voicing her complaint—that her lover is absent, or her husband present, or that she cannot marry the one she loves—the lady describes her setting. She may, for example, be lost in wistful thought over her needlework or seeking solace in an orchard beside a little stream.

A troubadour is bound with the gold thread of love. (f. 251r.)

From her window a lady hoists (or lowers) her lover. (f. 71v.)

A lover invites his coy mistress to walk in the woods. (f. 395v.)

Repairing his armor, a knight is offered refreshment. (f. 256v.)

(Universitätsbibliothek Heidelberg, Codex Manesse, Cod. Pal. Germ. 848)

These songs are not difficult to sing. Both troubadour and trouvère settings are generally syllabic, with only occasional short melismatic flourishes
at the beginnings and endings of phrases. The melodies rarely range beyond a
sixth, or at most an octave. Their modal construction is usually straightforward, with a clear-cut phrase structure. Yet despite this simplicity, or perhaps
because of it, the music can be very compelling. We are not carried away by
overwhelming bursts of virtuosity, but we can be almost mesmerized by the
repetitiveness of the numerous refrains, and drawn in by the intricate poetic
structures, so tightly woven and turned in upon themselves.

Musical style

Many of the troubadour and trouvère songs are strophic. That is, they
consist of several stanzas of text, each sung to the same melody. Otherwise,
the stanzas of different songs are of various and often ingenious design.
Wordplay, double entendres, and an almost musical counterpoint among the
sounds of the text itself enliven these poetic forms, which, when described in
the abstract, may seem rather rigid.

Poetic forms

One of the most popular stanzaic patterns is the form that was called a
canzo in the south and that developed even more extensively in the north as
the *ballade*. In these works the stanza is bipartite. The first part, the *frons,* is
subdivided into two identical sections each called a *pes,* which consists of two
or three lines. (*Pes* in Latin means "foot"; *pedes* is the plural.) The second part
of the stanza—the *cauda,* or tail—varies in length, but most often it is three to
six lines long. Overall, then, each verse is a large three-part AAB form, consisting of pes, pes, and cauda. The AAB form—also known as the *Bar form*—
was immensely popular among the German Minnesingers and Meistersingers
(see below).

The trouvères were especially given to the creation of elaborate poetic
structures, and in their work can be found early examples of several procedures that eventually developed into the *formes fixes,* or "fixed forms," so
characteristic of later French poetry (and, therefore, song). The first of these
forms, the ballade, was already anticipated by the troubadours in their *canzos.*
(See *HAM* I, 18b–c, p. 15; 19a–c, p. 16.) Another form is the *rondeau,* a word
which originally referred to various types of round dances in which refrains
sung by the whole group alternated with solo lines sung by the dance leader.
Many thirteenth-century *rondeaux* contain only six lines, but by the end of the
century the more standard eight-line version was well established. The text of
a rondeau includes a two-line refrain (AB) that appears both at the beginning
and at the end of a poem (i.e., as lines 1 and 2, and as lines 7 and 8). The usual
structure of the poem is that the first half of the refrain also appears internally,
as line 4. Thus the poet has to create a refrain not only complete in itself but
also divisible so that the first part can function as a free-standing line. Lines 3
and 5 rhyme with the first half of the refrain, line 6 with the second half. The
music consists of only the two phrases to which the refrain is set. A schematic
diagram of rondeau form is: ABaAabAB. (See *HAM* I, 19d–e, p. 17.) The
refrain, whether whole or fragmented, is indicated by capital letters. Lines
indicated as "a" rhyme with the first half of the refrain, but are identical neither to it nor to each other. The line labeled "b" rhymes with the second half

Formes fixes

of the refrain. All of the "a" or "A" lines are set to the same music, and all of the "b" or "B" lines also are set to their own melody.

A third fixed form, the *virelai,* did not really become established until the fourteenth century. It consisted of a verse structure summarizable as AbbaA. When more than one stanza was to be sung, the closing refrain of the first served as the opening refrain of the next, so that the overall strophic pattern of the virelai is AbbaAbbaAbbaA, etc. (See *HAM* I, 19f–g, p. 17; also, see Chapter 8 for a monophonic example from the fourteenth century.)

Other poetic and musical designs were employed as well, and although less readily categorized, they constitute a considerable part of the repertory. A song written in a freer form, *L'amours dont sui espris,* by Blondel de Nesle (c. 1150–1200), Richard the Lion-Hearted's resourceful trouvère, exhibits the main stylistic and interpretive features of these songs. Each stanza of the poem is eleven lines long, with only two sets of rhymes. The rhyme pattern of the first verse is laid out in Figure 4.1, along with the pattern of melodic repetition.

While most medieval chansonniers are ambiguous in their notation of musical rhythm, *L'amours dont sui espris* is one of the few pieces for which the manuscripts give clear rhythmic indications. While some scholars suggest that, as a rule, an underlying triple meter is best, others argue that the presentation should be basically declamatory, reflecting the rhythms and accents of the text. Blondel's chanson, however, is notated so that it can be read according to the rhythmic modes of Notre-Dame polyphony (see Chapter 5), the solution offered in Example 4.3.

The piece is subtle in its use of the melodic modes. It appears to lie completely within the Dorian authentic range, and for the first four lines the melody proceeds quite regularly. But line 5 ends unusually, on the third degree of the mode, F. And by the end of line 6, the melody has clearly modulated so that F is now the final of the new sound space. Line 7 remains firmly in F, and lines 8 and 9 exploit the modal ambiguity created by using only notes common to both modes. Here also the regular rhyme scheme of the text starts to

Figure 4.1.   Rhyme pattern of verse

Line		Melody
1	espris	a
2	chanter	b
3	soupris	a
4	amender	b
5	conquis	c
6	vanter	d
7	apris	e
8	amer	f
9	penser	c
10	dis	d
11	oster	g

Ex. 4.3   Blondel de Nesle, *L'Amours dont sui espris*

1. L'a - mours, dont sui es - pris, 2. Me se - mont de chan - ter, 3. Si chant com hom sou - pris, 4. Qui ne puet a - men - der. 5. Pe - tit i ai con - quis, 6. Mais bien me puis van - ter: 7. Se li plaist, j'ai a - pris 8. Loi - au - ment a a - mer. 9. A cel sunt mi pen - ser 10. Et se - ront a tous dis; 11. Ja nes en quier os - ter.

"The love I feel compels me to sing; and I am like a man taken by surprise, who cannot resist. Yet I have gained so much that I can be proud of it: for I learned long ago to love loyally. My thoughts are always of her, and always will be, for I never wish to have them elsewhere."

Transcription of the first verse of the chanson by Blondel de Nesle; from Hendrik van der Werf, *The Chansons of the Troubadours and Trouvères* (Utrecht: A. Oosthoek's Uitgevs-maatschaapij NV, 1972), pp. 100–103. Used by permission.

become interestingly varied. Line 10 is strongly in F mode; line 11 begins there but then returns to the original D mode to close the piece.

The vocal qualities most consistently praised among the singers of these songs were strength and clarity. Some tunes are preserved in a number of different versions and individual singers probably felt free to rework a famil-

**Perfor-
mance
practice**

iar piece in their own particular styles. They may have been accompanied instrumentally, but there is surprisingly little evidence to support this surmise. There is no musical notation in the chansonniers to indicate an accompaniment, but at least two literary references hint that one might, upon occasion, have been improvised. In the famous French allegory of courtly love, *Le Roman de la rose* ("The Romance of the Rose"), the author recounts a lady's singing of a new *chansonnette* together with a jongleur playing the *vielle,* the most popular bowed string instrument of the time. And a German literary source advises vielle players to join the sounds of their instruments to the songs of others. Little pictorial evidence suggests instrumental participation in either troubadour or trouvère performances. As extensive as the courtly literature is, and as imaginatively illustrated as it was, it seems strange that so little trace remains of instrumental accompaniments, if, indeed, they were in general use. To the extent that instruments were used, they probably would have provided *drones* (long, held notes, usually in the lowest part), or doubled the voice, or improvised preludes, interludes, and codas.

Minnelieder, Cantigas, and Laude

Minnelieder

Among other nonliturgical repertories of the time were works produced in German, Spanish, and Italian. The *Minnesingers* (*minne* means "courtly love") were a group of nobly born German poet-musicians of the twelfth through the fourteenth centuries, who were probably inspired by the French troubadours. Their rise to importance is usually dated from the marriage in 1156 of Frederick Barbarossa to Beatrix of Burgundy. Among the Minnesingers are two made famous by Richard Wagner in two of his nineteenth-century operas: Walther von der Vogelweide (d. 1230) and Tannhäuser (mid-thirteenth century). Another was Neidhardt von Reuenthal (c. 1180–1240). The texts of the *Minnelieder* ("Songs of courtly love") were usually narratives, and modal melodies were the norm. Two forms commonly employed were Bar form (AAB) and the *Leich* ("lay"), which was similar to the liturgical sequence.

Cantigas

Other monophonic works influenced by the troubadours were the Spanish *cantigas,* thirteenth-century songs mostly in honor of the Virgin Mary. The chief form used was the virelai, and the texts often told of miracles performed by the Virgin. A collection of some four hundred such works, the *Cantigas de Santa Maria* ("Songs of Saint Mary"), was assembled for Alfonso the Wise (1221–1284), ruler of Castile and León and a great devotee of the arts.

Laude

The Italian *laude spirituali* ("spiritual praises") were monophonic hymns of devotion and praise. Their development is attributed to St. Francis of Assisi (c. 1182–1226) and to the penitential fraternities of Italy during the thirteenth and fourteenth centuries. These works, which showed some troubadour influence as well, used a poetic structure of several stanzas, each of four to six lines, in alternation with a refrain, usually of two lines.

Summary

Liturgical texts used in regional rites tended to be exuberant, dramatic, and highly pictorial. By contrast, the Roman rite achieved its power of expression through the reserve, balance, and objectivity of its rhetoric. Therefore, where the Roman rite displaced local usage, the poetic vitality and creative impulse that had generated the development of regional styles in the first place led to the development of genres other than the most central chants of the Mass and Office.

The most plentiful of the new pieces were *tropes:* newly composed texts and melodies inserted into and used primarily with antiphonal chants, the Introit, Offertory, and Communion. There were two main types of trope—introductory and interlinear, or intercalated. The impetus behind these additions to the liturgy seems often to have been as much poetic or doctrinal as musical.

The other most important new type of Latin chant was the *sequence,* or *prose,* a large, independent piece sung after the Alleluia in the Mass. It consisted of paired lines of text and music sometimes introduced by a single unpaired line. Smaller new chants were the *prosulas,* created entirely by providing new texts for preexistent melismas. The pitches of the original chant melody were retained, but instead of being sung melismatically over a single syllable of text, they were provided with enough new text so that each note of the original melisma received its own syllable or word.

The *conductus* was a processional piece used both within the liturgy and outside it—for example, in liturgical drama. The texts were metrical, and the music, whether monophonic or polyphonic, was newly composed, not based on liturgical melodies. *Versus,* which also flourished during the eleventh century, were monophonic settings of regular rhyming, scanning poetry in strophic form. The student culture of the eleventh and twelfth centuries expressed itself in the *Goliard* songs.

Troubadours and *trouvères* were poets and poet-musicians who, during the eleventh, twelfth, and thirteenth centuries, created an extensive new repertory of poems in the vernacular—*langue d'oc* and *langue d'oïl;* melodies have been preserved for about one-third of this output. The activity of these poet-musicians centered around the courts of the nobility, and in fact the nobility itself often contributed to the repertory. The central subject was love, especially "courtly love."

Troubadour and trouvère chansons are not difficult to sing. The settings are generally syllabic and often strophic, consisting of several stanzas of text, each sung to the same melody. Wordplays, double entendres, and counterpoint among the sounds of the text enliven the complex poetic forms. Overall, there is surprisingly little evidence of instrumental participation in these songs; but to the extent that vielles or other instruments might have been used, they probably would have provided drones, doubled the voice, or improvised preludes, interludes, and codas. Monophonic songs in other languages included the *Minnelieder* in Germany, the Spanish *cantigas,* and the Italian *laude.*

Notes

1. C. Clifford Flanigan, "The Roman Rite and the Origins of Liturgical Drama." *University of Toronto Quarterly* 43 (1974): 263–284.
2. Archibald T. Davison and Willi Apel, *Historical Anthology of Music.* Cambridge, Mass.: Harvard University Press, 1946. (*HAM*)
3. Meg Bogin, *The Women Troubadours.* London: Paddington Press, 1976, p. 37.

Bibliography

ATKINSON, CHARLES M. "The Earliest Agnus Dei Melody and Its Tropes." *Journal of the American Musicological Society* 30 (1977): 1–19.

BOGIN, MEG. *The Women Troubadours.* London: Paddington Press, 1976.

CROCKER, RICHARD. *The Early Medieval Sequence.* Berkeley: University of California Press, 1977.

———. "The Troping Hypothesis." *The Musical Quarterly* 52 (1966): 183–203.

EVANS, PAUL. *The Early Trope Repertory of St. Martial de Limoges.* Princeton: Princeton University Press, 1970.

FLANIGAN, C. CLIFFORD. "The Roman Rite and the Origins of Liturgical Drama." *The University of Toronto Quarterly* 43 (1974): 263–284.

HARDISON, O. B. *Christian Rite and Christian Drama in the Middle Ages.* Baltimore: The Johns Hopkins Press, 1965.

HOLOMAN, D. KERN. "Staging the *Play of Daniel.*" *Early Music* 4 (1976): 159–163.

KELLY, THOMAS FORREST. "New Music from Old—The Structuring of Responsory Proses." *Journal of the American Musicological Society* 30 (1977): 366–390.

LEWIS, C. S. *The Allegory of Love.* New York: Oxford University Press, 1958.

PARKER, IAN. "The Performance of Troubadour and Trouvère Songs: Some Facts and Conjectures." *Early Music* 5 (1977): 184–207.

STEINER, RUTH. "Some Melismas for Office Responsories." *Journal of the American Musicological Society* 26 (1973): 108–31.

WERF, HENDRIK VAN DER. *The Chansons of the Troubadours and Trouvères.* Utrecht: A Oosthoek's Uitgeversmaatschappij Nv, 1972.

YOUNG, KARL. *The Drama of the Medieval Church,* 2 vols. London: Oxford University Press, 1933.

5

The Rise of Polyphony

DURING the eleventh and twelfth centuries, music created for liturgical use expanded to include not only horizontal elaboration, i.e., tropes, sequences, and the like, but also vertical elaboration, known as "polyphony," in which one or more new melodic lines were invented to be sung simultaneously with the original chant tune. These two types of expansion (horizontal and vertical) were complementary, in that they affected different parts of the repertory. Troping, or linear ornamentation, was introduced most commonly in connection with choral, or antiphonal, chants, especially the Introit, Offertory, and Communion of the Mass; whereas vertical ornamentation, or polyphony, typically was associated with the soloistic, or responsorial, chants, especially the responsories for both the Mass and Office and the Alleluias of the Mass.

Throughout the Middle Ages, polyphony was a soloist's art, a bold new style in which only the most highly skilled professionals could be expected to perform. The repertory was also elite, found in a relative handful of manuscripts associated with only a few of the leading ecclesiastical institutions. In short, it was the very dramatic, avant-garde, ear-catching tip of the repertorial iceberg, which in most monasteries and churches continued to consist primarily of the familiar old chants, sung monophonically.

Avant-garde soloistic repertory

The rise of polyphony marks the point at which the history of Western music sets off in a decisively different direction from that of many non-Western cultures. It opened up vast new opportunities for stylistic development, particularly of a more exterior sort that could be appreciated not just by performers and a few other initiates, but by the musical laity as well. It is probably no accident that the largest and best understood of the early polyphonic repertories, that of Notre-Dame de Paris, arose in a secular cathedral setting, that is, in a cathedral staffed by secular clergy—a dean and canons—rather than by monks.

Secular cathedral setting

The bishop and his staff not only served liturgical and pastoral functions, but also conducted the business of the diocese, exercising many functions that

77

later would be termed governmental. Many chapters established a cathedral school. Ecclesiastical courts administered justice, and their jurisdiction extended not just to the clergy in general, but to the laity as well in matters such as the probate of wills. (The reader may recall that the coins given the singers during the Christmas service described in the Laon *ordo* had been struck at the bishop's mint.) Therefore the atmosphere around the Cathedral of Notre-Dame de Paris would not have been one of withdrawal, but rather one of openness to and participation in the life of this cosmopolitan city where intellectual experiment and expansion were the order of the day.

Cathedral schools   During these same centuries, a critical shift of the educational role took place as well, from the monastery to the cathedral schools, from the more contemplative atmosphere of the cloister to the bustle of the developing urban centers. These schools were run by their respective cathedral chapters primarily to educate choristers and young clerics, secondarily to educate a rising civil servant class. Young men flocked to these centers, where instruction was given in both the *trivium* and *quadrivium,* and, in some cities, in professional subjects as well, such as law and medicine. Pressed beyond their capacity by the influx of students, the chapters ultimately had to establish a licensing system, whereby masters other than members of the chapter were allowed to set up a classroom in the neighborhood of the cathedral and lecture on their chosen subjects. Individual lecturers often established substantial reputations, and students crisscrossed Europe in search of intellectual stimulation and an agreeable life-style. By the year 1215, the model of a centralized institution with a relatively stable student population began to crystalize.

Universities   Typically, the central organizational body of a medieval university was the guild of masters, but this group was by no means unitary or monolithic. Among both students and masters there were traditional patterns of loyalty or animosity based upon one's geographical origin or social background or affiliation with a religious order. Within these traditional bounds, each master competed with the others for students and the attendant fees. The primary method of teaching was for the master to read aloud (hence "lecture," from *lectare,* the Latin verb "to read aloud") the basic authority in the field, such as Boethius in music. Then the master would comment upon the material, pass on traditional glosses by earlier commentators, and perhaps add insights of his own. This procedure was the most efficient available, given the technology of the time. Individual texts were prohibitively expensive. If a student wanted one, he had to rent a master copy of the desired book from a bookseller, then purchase parchment and all the accessories necessary to make his own handwritten copy. He might save a little money by purchasing paper instead of parchment, for paper was introduced into western Europe by way of Spain in the twelfth century. And he might save some effort by hiring one of the professional lay copyists who had begun to gather around the universities. But even under the best of circumstances, making a new copy of a text was cumbersome and expensive. Therefore a real premium was placed on developing a quick and perceptive aural ability. It was very much to a student's advantage to be able to hear and understand material on the spot, without necessarily ever seeing it written out. This aural alacrity must have carried over into music, and we can reasonably assume that the medieval university student could make more sense out of a new musical pattern or remember an old one more accurately than his twentieth-century counterpart, who has been trained so overwhelmingly by means of visual rather than aural techniques.

All students began by mastering the subjects of the trivium—grammar, dialectic, and rhetoric—which gave them the technical tools for approaching the more substantive disciplines. Since language is the primary medium of intellectual communication, understanding its structure was considered critical. Hence the study of grammar. Dialectic enabled a student to perceive how an argument is constructed, and then to detect its logical weaknesses or fallacies. Thereafter, he could construct a counterposition, which in turn had to be examined for its own dialectical soundness. Rhetoric concentrated on how to fashion material most effectively, given the particular forum in which it was to be presented. The ability to recognize and thus to combat the twisted use of language, the ability to distinguish the essential from the superfluous or intentionally misleading in an argument—these were essential skills, the foundation of all later study. And the rhetorical forum in which these skills were most frequently displayed within the university was the public disputation, where the ability to be articulate and persuasive under the pressure of a well-informed, contentious audience was developed to a high degree.

Centrality of the trivium

The Earliest Repertories

The first evidence of the new polyphonic practice is believed to be found in a theoretical treatise of the late ninth century, *Musica enchiriadis* ("Music Manual"), which has been understood to describe several ways of producing this new complex of sound called *organum*. The first type, referred to as *parallel organum*, simply duplicates the chant at one of the most consonant intervals, a fourth or a fifth. To illustrate, the anonymous author of this treatise writes out a setting of the phrases *Sit gloria Domini in saecula, laetabitur Dominus in operibus suis* as they would sound with the *vox principalis* ("principal voice") singing the chant and the *vox organalis* ("organal voice," i.e., the added voice in this organum) shadowing it at the interval of a fifth below. Adding to this pair a third voice singing the chant an octave below the vox principalis and a fourth voice duplicating the vox organalis an octave above resulted in a broad, full, four-voiced sound. (See *HAM* I, 25b-1, p. 22; and *OxMM,* 37c, p. 84.) Yet so simple was this type of setting that the extra voices seem not to have been written down but merely added improvisatorily.

Musica enchiriadis also describes what appears to be a second, more flexible type of organum, which employs not only parallel motion between the

Musica enchiriadis

Parallel organum

**Oblique and
contrary
motion**

voices but also oblique motion, in which one voice stays on the same pitch while the other moves. (See *HAM* I, 25b-2, p. 22; and *OxMM*, 37d, p. 84.) Another treatise, *Ad organum faciendum* ("How to Construct Organum"), describes a style that features contrary motion, in which both voices move simultaneously but in opposite directions. These three basic interlinear vertical relationships laid the groundwork for later styles of polyphonic composition. No matter what the details of melodic behavior, whether elaborately melismatic or more reserved, the basic harmonic idea was to move from one point of consonance between the voices to another. Simple, basic consonances were used at a piece's most important structural points, less stable consonances at secondary points. More unstable combinations, even dissonances, could be used in between, ornamentally.

Liturgical settings in organal style, as distinguished from examples in treatises showing how to improvise organum, date from the first part of the eleventh century. Repertories composed according to these new principles have been found in manuscripts from several centers: the Cathedral of Notre-Dame de Chartres, a spiritual crossroads 60 miles from Paris; the Abbey of St. Martial de Limoges in south-central France; the Cathedral of Santiago de Compostela, a great pilgrimage center in northwest Spain; and Winchester Cathedral in England.

**Polyphony
as layered
composition**

It is critical to understand that medieval polyphony is primarily a layered type of composition. One voice, the *tenor,* usually preexists independently as a monophonic entity, and the strong linear identity it originally had is never lost, although it may be tempered by the interweaving of a second voice. When another line is added, it constitutes a separate strand woven around the tenor, or a second layer placed upon the foundation of the tenor. Vertical fit is important, but the fundamental concept is of two or more melodies interacting. Even when the tenor was newly fashioned, as in many conductus, the composer began by making a tenor, then added the upper voice(s). Not until as late as the fifteenth century is it reported that composers wrote the various voices of a polyphonic composition simultaneously (rather than one after the other).

Chartres

The Chartres repertory consists of two manuscripts that preserve a cycle of Alleluias for the main feasts of the Church year: Christmas, Easter, Ascension, and Pentecost. Unlike the practice understood to be described in *Musica enchiriadis,* the Chartres style uses the chant in the lower voice, and the newly added voice is placed on top of the chant tune. The melodic style is generally note-against-note in the two voices, a style described by the Latin phrase *punctus contra punctum,* from which the term "counterpoint" comes.

St. Martial

The St. Martial repertory dates from around the first half of the twelfth century and features an elaborate new style of writing. The added voice, the *duplum,* no longer moves simply note-against-note with the tenor, but undertakes sweeping melismatic flourishes over a single note in the tenor. This technique lengthens the setting substantially, for the tenor must literally "hold" for the duration of the duplum's melisma. (The noun "tenor" was derived from the Latin verb *tenere,* "to hold.") Sections in this bold new style are combined with others in which the duplum is more reserved, moving neumatically or even syllabically in relation to the tenor. The styles are not distributed in clear-cut sections, but tend to flow freely from one into the other. Of the some sixty-five or seventy polyphonic pieces in these manuscripts, most are settings of what were then the newest types of monophonic composition: versus, sequences, conductus, and *Benedicamus Domino* tropes. (See *OxMM,* 40, p. 87.) Thus the St. Martial repertory is distinctly different from that of either Winchester or Notre-Dame de Paris, for both of those cathedral centers concentrated on liturgical settings for the Mass and Offices.

Santiago de Compostela

The repertory of Santiago de Compostela is contained in one manuscript, the *Liber Sancti Jacobi* ("The Book of St. James"), also known as the Codex Calixtinus, which is still housed in the library of the cathedral for which it was copied. The fame of Compostela and its popularity as the goal of numerous pilgrims rested on the belief that it was in possession of the relics of James the Apostle. And this manuscript, devoted to promoting his cult, contains an unusual collection of both musical and nonmusical material. One section, for example, preserves the services of the Vigil and Feast of the saint, complete with all the necessary music. Another section serves as a twelfth-century "tourist guide" for pilgrims. It describes the main roads to Compostela, points out major "sights" along the way, and even offers advice about people the pilgrims might meet, extolling the virtues or warning of the vices of the natives of various regions.

Twenty-one pieces of polyphony are contained in the *Liber Sancti Jacobi.* One-third are *Benedicamus* settings, both troped and untroped. Several are conductus, and others are elaborations of well-known Kyrie tropes. (See *HAM* I, 276, p. 23; and *OxMM,* 42, p. 90.) Six are settings of responsorial chants: one Gradual and Alleluia from the Mass and four Office responsories. Repertorially, then, Compostela stands midway between St. Martial and the two other cathedral centers, for while it includes polyphonic arrangements based on the newer types of monophony, it does not neglect to set the traditional liturgical chants as well. Stylistically, though, the Compostela pieces are almost indistinguishable from those of St. Martial.

Winchester

The Winchester repertory, dating from the last part of the tenth and first part of the eleventh centuries, consists of some 170 pieces. The majority of these settings are of pieces that, even as chants, would have been sung by soloists: about fifty Alleluias, about fifty responsories, and about twenty Tracts.

In addition, a wide variety of other chants are set. From the Ordinary of the Mass, there are Kyries and Glorias, as well as newer types of compositions like sequences. Processional antiphons, settings of both Mass and Office antiphons, and even tropes to the Easter Introit antiphon are included. Two of the organa are for chants with Greek versions of the text: one *Gloria in excelsis* and the *Alleluia Dies sanctificatus* for Christmas. This repertory, then, is very significant, even though until recently it was considered undecipherable with respect to both its pitch and its rhythm, for the notation consists of un-heighted neumes, an Anglo-Saxon version of the type of notation used at St. Gall for its monophonic repertory.

The School of Notre-Dame de Paris

The twelfth- and thirteenth-century repertory of Notre-Dame polyphony is of unique importance, for it not only is the largest collection of early multi-voiced settings, but it also is the most accessible. Although the notation can sometimes suggest more than one reasonable rhythmic interpretation, the music can readily be transcribed, both the pitch and the rhythm.

Manuscript sources   The three most important manuscript sources are Wolfenbüttel, Herzog August Bibliothek 677 (W₁); Wolfenbüttel, Herzog August Bibliothek 1206 (W₂); and Florence, Biblioteca Laurenziana, Pluteus 29.1(F). One of the features that distinguishes these sources from those transmitting earlier poly-phonic repertories is that they are devoted exclusively to settings in the new multivoiced styles; this is a significant historical "first."

Melody   Melodically, Notre-Dame notation presents few problems. A two-part piece typically is written on two staves, the upper one consisting of 5 lines and 4 spaces, the lower one of 4 lines and 3 spaces (as would be appropriate for a chant line). C-clefs and F-clefs are used in various positions, and may be moved in the course of the piece to accommodate the range of the musical line.

Rhythm   The rhythm of Notre-Dame notation is relational. Individual notes do not have independent rhythmic significance, but they derive their meaning from their context, and the meanings change accordingly. The first level of organi-zation consists of arranging the notes into ligatures. The most common groupings are a single note, ❜ ; a *binaria,* two notes arranged like this ♩ or like this ▐▪ , for example; and a *ternaria,* three notes joined like this ▐▶ or this ♩ or this ▐▪ . The second level of rhythmic organization, that of mode, gives the ligatures their meaning when grouped into larger patterns. For example, a common pattern in one mode is 3 + 2 + 2; a common pat-tern in another mode is 1 + 3 + 3; but the ternaria (the 3) in each of the two patterns has two entirely different rhythms because its context is different.

Poetic analogies   It was not easy to decipher this complicated system, but one approach that did prove helpful was to apply principles enunciated in the late fourth or early fifth century by St. Augustine in his treatise *De musica*. Although the time gap is great between Augustine and the Notre-Dame repertory, more nearly contemporary writers such as Guido of Arezzo also stressed that there are certain principles of rhythmic or metric organization that transcend individual disciplines. Thus, poetic analogies are directly relevant to the question of how music is organized rhythmically.

In classical poetic scansion, there are two values for the syllables, long and short. These are combined into patterns of feet which range in length from two to four syllables. These feet, in turn, are combined into poetic lines, and the lines into whole literary pieces.

By the end of the twelfth century, the musical codification of this general poetic-metric theory resulted in a system of six rhythmic modes:

Six rhythmic modes

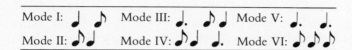

Three of these, I, II, and VI, are equivalent to three poetic patterns of metrical feet known as the *trochee* (long-short), the *iamb* (short-long), and the *tribach* (short-short-short). In these three patterns, the basic relationship between the long and the short is duple; musically speaking, the *longa* ("long" in English) has twice the value of the *brevis* ("breve" or "short" in English). To describe the longs and breves in these three modes, theorists used the term *recta,* meaning "correct."

Mode I seems to have been the first to have come into general use, and even after the other modes were introduced, Mode I continued to dominate. Mode VI may have originated as an ornamented version of either of the first two before it came to be recognized as a separate mode in its own right. At any rate, by the next century, such a procedure, whereby notes in a modal pattern are subdivided into smaller values, had a name of its own: *fractio modi,* or "fracturing the mode."

The other three modes, III, IV, and V, can be seen to be equivalent to three other patterns of metrical feet, the *dactyl* (long-short-short), *anapest* (short-short-long), and *spondee* (long-long), but only if the long and breve have basically a three-to-one, rather than a two-to-one, relationship. These modes are not found in Augustine's basic system of measurement, and their unusual character was sensed by medieval theorists, who described the longs of these modes as *ultra mensuram,* or "beyond the unit of measure."

The origin of Mode V seems to have been in styles of music where a single note in the lower voice of a two-part composition was set against an entire foot of Mode I or Mode II in the upper voice. The historical development of Modes III and IV is more problematic. Theorists explain that these two do consist of long-short-short and short-short-long patterns respectively, but in addition to the longs being "ultra mensuram," some of the breves are also unusual. The first in a succession of two is recta, or correct, but the second is *altera,* or "altered," so that it has twice the length of a correct breve. Like Mode V, Modes III and IV may have resulted from combining more fundamental rhythmic patterns, specifically those of Mode II, into longer note values and longer patterns. Such a process is the reverse of fracturing the mode and is known as *extensio modi,* or "extending the mode."

Ordines

In order to establish any one of these six modes as a pattern, it must be repeated at least once. Accordingly, the basic unit of composition was an *ordo,* consisting of at least two feet of any given rhythmic mode. For example, a two-foot ordo in Mode I would be long-breve, long-breve, the last breve being a rest. The role of the rest was to set this pattern off from the following one. *Ordines* could be much longer, too—four, five, or even six feet.

In sum, then, several levels of rhythmic organization exist, all interrelated and interdependent. Notes became rhythmically intelligible when grouped into ligatures, and ligatures derive their meaning from their positions in modal patterns of varying lengths. The modal patterns can be analyzed as musical expressions of classical poetic procedures, which consist of combining metrical feet into ever larger and more intricate patterns.

The difficulties encountered in understanding the Notre-Dame rhythmic tradition probably arise from attempting to describe as a single coherent system a tradition that was still in flux, one that had developed over a long period of time and was not at all clearly documented in the various stages of its development. But the two-to-one long-breve relationships of Modes I, II, and VI, and the three-to-one long-breve relationships together with the correct and altered breves of Modes III, IV, and V are compatible conceptually, and they can be codified into a single rather simple logical system, something that was done in the thirteenth century by the theorist Franco of Cologne (see Chapter 6).

Notre-Dame polyphony was primarily a liturgical repertory. The earliest practice was to add a second voice, a duplum, above certain parts of a chant melody. The most likely place for polyphony to appear in the Mass and Offices was in connection with those chants that already were sung soloistically —the responsories and Alleluias—for only the most highly trained singers would have been called upon to perform in this venturesome new style. Not all the original chant was set polyphonically, however, only certain sections. Throughout these polyphonic sections, the usual chant melody constituted the lower voice, the tenor. The rest of the chant was sung monophonically, as before. So the original chant melody was kept intact and in order, although it may have been extended rhythmically. (See *HAM* I, 29, pp. 27–30.)

This type of polyphony, as in the repertories discussed earlier, is known generally as organum. Notre-Dame organum is subdivided into two more specific substyles: *organum purum* ("pure organum"), or simply organum, and *discantus,* or discant style. Organum purum is a florid, melismatic type of writing in which the tenor moves only occasionally in comparison to the duplum. This elaborate type of setting is usually reserved for the more simple sections of the chant. On the other hand, those syllables and words in the chant that are set melismatically in the monophonic versions are set in a more reserved polyphonic style, in discant. In these sections the two voices move much more nearly together rhythmically. The practicality of this procedure is clear: piling a melismatic duplum upon a tenor segment that was itself melismatic would have overextended the piece. (See *HAM* I, 29, pp. 27–30.)

The way in which polyphony flows into and out of monophony in this type of composition raises interesting questions about the rhythmic performance of the chant that was being set polyphonically. Organum purum style so stretches the notes of the chant that a feeling of rhythmic pulsation is lost in the tenor, though not in the upper voice. In discant, both the tenor and the duplum are clearly and vigorously rhythmic. It might seem a bit incongruent aesthetically to couple such a strong polyphonic rhythmic style with anything less vigorous in the monophonic segments of the same piece. In differ-

Organum (both melismatic and discant style) for Christmas Gradual responsory verse *Viderunt omnes,* Wolfenbüttel 1099 (1206), ff. 63rv.

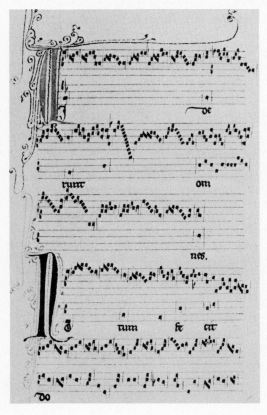
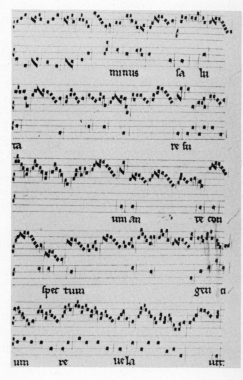

ent polyphonic settings, however, the same snippet of chant that was being used as a tenor was cast in a whole series of different rhythmic patterns, as was the duplum. What happened to the surrounding monophonic parts of the chant then? Were they different for different polyphonic elaborations, or were they designed to be the perfect multipurpose setting for each polyphonic gem? These perplexing and stimulating questions still await solutions.

The manuscripts that preserve the Notre-Dame repertory contain a substantial number of "complete" polyphonic settings—complete in the sense that all the segments of the chant which were to be "organized," i.e., set in organum, are included. In addition, there are even larger collections of *substitute clausulae,* alternative polyphonic settings which could be used in connection with one of the more prominent subsections of the piece. Each clausula represents a newly fashioned piece of counterpoint for the tenor, and each demonstrates different ways of elaborating polyphonically upon the same basic snippet of chant melody. (See *HAM* I, 29 and 30, pp. 27–30.)

Substitute clausulae

Despite the striking stylistic innovations within this repertory, the personalities behind it are never identified in the musical manuscripts themselves. Were it not for the report of an Englishman who studied at the University of Paris about 1280, we would know nothing of the two leading Notre-Dame composers: Léonin, who pioneered in the style, probably during the 1160s; and Pérotin, his successor, who flourished around the turn of the century (1190–1220). (The Latin versions of their names are Leoninus and Perotinus.) Ironically, the Englishman himself remains unidentified, but scholars have come to know him and refer to him rather affectionately as Anonymous IV.[1] He reports the following:

Léonin and Pérotin

Anonymous IV

Magister Leoninus was the best composer of organum, who made the *Magnus liber organi de Gradali et Antiphonario* in order to increase the divine service. This was in use until the time of the great Perotinus who shortened this book and made many better *clausulae* or *puncta* [substitute sections], since he was the best composer of discantus and better than Leoninus, although he cannot be said to reveal the subtlety of [Leonin's] organum. This Magister Perotinus wrote the best *quadrupla* [four-part organa] such as *Viderunt* and *Sederunt* with an abundance of "colors" in the art of harmonic music, as well as many most noble *tripla* [three-part organa] such as *Alleluia, Posui adjutorium; Nativitas,* etc. He also made conductus in three parts, such as *Salvatoris hodie;* and two-part conductus, such as *Dum sigillum summi patris;* and simple conductus together with many others, such as *Beata viscera; Justitia,* etc. The book or books of Magister Perotinus were in use both in the choir of the church of Notre-Dame in Paris until the time of Magister Robertus de Sabilone, and from his time until the present day.[2]

Of the categories of composition cultivated by Léonin and Pérotin, two-part organum and discant have already been discussed. (For an example of three-part organum, see *HAM* I, 31, pp. 31–32.) One of the largest works that Anonymous IV actually names—the quadruplum, or four-part organum, *Viderunt*—is a flamboyant setting of the Christmas Gradual responsory. The aural effect of this dramatic piece must have been stunning when it was sung for the first time, probably in 1198, according to an ordinance issued by the archbishop of Paris, Eudes de Sully. Long stretches of highly ac-

Pérotin's quadruplum *Viderunt*

Substitute clausulae for *Dominus,* from Christmas Gradual responsory verse, Florence, Biblioteca Mediceo–Laurenziana, Pluteus 29.1, f. 149v.

tive rhythmic movement in the upper three voices are suspended over a static tonal foundation provided by the tenor, and striking contrasts from one section to the next result from the succession of vowel sounds slowly unfolding in the text.

Also identified by name is Pérotin's conductus *Salvatoris hodie* ("Today the blood of the Savior"), a through-composed polyphonic setting of three stanzas, written in a lively trochaic pattern with alternate lines ending on strong and weak beats. In reading the first verse, shown below, note that the

Pérotin's conductus *Salvatoris hodie*

Ex. 5.1 Pérotin, *Salvatoris hodie*

Sal - va - to - ris ho - di - e

Sal - va - to - ris ho - di - e

san - guis pre - gu - sta - - -

san - guis pre - gu - sta - - -

- - - -

- - - -

Ex. 5.1   cont.

Ex. 5.1   cont.

First stanza of Pérotin's conductus; from Janet Knapp, *Thirty-Five Conductus for Two and Three Voices* (New Haven: Yale Collegium Musicum, 1965), pp. 1–3. Used by permission.

symbol ¯ indicates a long (stressed) syllable, and the symbol ˘ refers to a short (unstressed) syllable.

Sālvătōrĭs hŏdĭē	Today, the blood of the
Sānguĭs prēgŭstātŭr	Savior is foretasted,
Īn quŏ Sўŏn fīlĭē	By which the daughter of
Stōlă cāndīdātŭr.	Zion is dressed in a shining
	robe [i.e., redeemed].

This piece was composed for the Christmas season; it was performed during the Mass of the Feast of the Circumcision, on January 1. This is the same feast for which the archbishop of Paris had decreed that a four-part setting of the Gradual responsory (probably *Viderunt omnes*) should be sung in Paris.

In setting the text *Salvatoris hodie*, Pérotin follows closely its poetical design (see Example 5.1). Each line is set off from the following one by a long musical *cauda*, or "tail," so that the amount of music used to set the text is matched in length by the ornamental flourish which occurs on the last stressed syllable of every line, i.e., "Hodi-*e*," "pregus-*ta*-tur," "fili*e*," and "candi-*da*-tur." The predominant rhythmic pattern of the musical setting is also long-short (♩ ♪), sometimes "merged" into "longer" longs (♩.). Thus the music parallels the rhythmic pattern of the text but does not coincide with it. Rather, the syllables of the text have been spread out to cover the entire long-short metrical foot of musical Mode I, creating a pattern of intertwined accents. The textual stresses coincide with the first part of every other musical foot.

Although this particular conductus was used liturgically, many were sung in more casual settings. Because such a piece was independent of the liturgy both textually and musically, it became the most avant-garde of the polyphonic genres during the first half of the thirteenth century. Even though the voices of a conductus were conceived one at a time, as were pieces based on a preexistent tenor, the style of combining the lines was more "popular." There was a stronger sense of vertical integration; the voices tended to move together homophonically.

The conductus was also very progressive harmonically in its admission of less perfect intervals, especially thirds, as consonances. Textually, the conductus—both monophonic and polyphonic—soon branched out from liturgically inspired texts to political commentary and love poetry.

The sound of *Salvatoris hodie* is one of "close harmony," for the voices share one another's tonal space. The duplum overlaps or coincides with the tenor fairly often, and the duplum and triplum interweave as well. Consequently no single voice always has the "melody" in the overall sound complex, and no single voice always provides the foundation. Such a setting is ideal ensemble music, for it both requires and rewards three equally skilled singers.

Summary

Linear ornamentation, or *troping,* was introduced most commonly in connection with choral antiphonal chants, especially the Introit, Offertory, and Communion of the Mass. Vertical ornamentation, or *polyphony,* typically was associated with soloistic responsorial chants, especially the responsories for both the Mass and Office and the Alleluias of the Mass. Early polyphony was a soloist's art, reserved for highly skilled professionals singing an elite repertory that is found in only a few manuscripts associated with a small number of the leading ecclesiastical institutions.

Liturgical settings in organal style (organum), from the first part of the eleventh century on, are preserved in practical service books from Chartres, St. Martial, Compostela, and Winchester. Early polyphony was a layered type of composition. One voice, the tenor, was preexistent, an independent monophonic entity, and it never entirely lost this separate identity. When a second or third line was added, each additional voice constituted a separate strand woven around the tenor, or another layer placed upon its foundation.

The St. Martial repertory, dating from the first half of the twelfth century, features an elaborate new style of writing. The *duplum* not only proceeds note against note with the tenor but also undertakes sweeping melismatic flourishes over a single note in the tenor, thereby lengthening the overall setting considerably. Most of the St. Martial polyphonic pieces are settings of what were then the newest types of monophonic composition: *versus, sequences, conductus,* and *Benedicamus Domino* tropes.

At Notre-Dame de Paris, by contrast, the repertory was primarily liturgical. It grew up at first by the addition of a second voice above selected parts of a chant melody, one usually already being sung by a soloist. In these polyphonic sections the chant melody was retained in the lower voice; where no new voice was added, the chant was sung monophonically as before.

This type of Notre-Dame polyphony, in which upper and lower voices share the same liturgical text, is known generally as *organum*. It was further subdivided into *organum purum* and *discantus*. Organum purum is a florid, melismatic type of writing in which the duplum has long flourishes over individual notes in the tenor. This style was usually reserved for those sections of the chant that were set simply to begin with. In discantus, the two voices move much more nearly in tandem.

The Notre-Dame repertory is quite extensive; three major manuscripts are devoted entirely to it, and there are numerous other fragmentary sources. Léonin pioneered in the style, probably in the 1160s, and was said to have been the best composer of organum in the florid style. Pérotin, his successor, flourished around the turn of the century and excelled at discantus. Notre-Dame polyphony presents some rhythmic problems to readers of its manuscripts. Nonetheless, it is the first body of polyphonic music whose rhythmic notation is clear enough to permit relatively easy transcription.

Notes

1. Anonymous theorists of the Middle Ages were given numerical designations by their nineteenth-century editors to enable scholars to distinguish one from the other when referring to them. Anonymous IV is found in E. de Coussemaker, *Scriptorum de Musica Medii Aevi,* 4 vols. Paris: Durand, 1864–1876, reprinted 1931, 1961, vol. 1, pp. 327–365.
2. William G. Waite, *The Rhythm of Twelfth-Century Polyphony: Its Theory and Practice.* New Haven: Yale University Press, 1954, pp. 3–4. Used by permission.

Bibliography

ANDERSON, GORDON A. "Clausulae or Transcribed-Motets in the Florence Manuscript?" *Acta musicologica* 42 (1970): 109–128.

BALZER, REBECCA. "Thirteenth-Century Illuminated Miniatures and the Date of the Florence Manuscript." *Journal of the American Musicological Society* 25 (1972): 1–18.

ROESNER, EDWARD H. "The Origins of W_1." *Journal of the American Musicological Society* 29 (1976): 337–380.

———. "The Performance of Parisian Organum." *Early Music* 7 (1979): 174–189.

SANDERS, ERNEST H. "Polyphony and Secular Monophony: Ninth Century–c. 1300." In *Music from the Middle Ages to the Renaissance,* ed. F. W. Sternfeld. New York: Praeger, 1973, pp. 89–143.

SMITH, NORMAN E. "Inter-relationships Among the Alleluias of the *Magnus liber organi.*" *Journal of the American Musicological Society* 25 (1972): 175–202.

TISCHLER, HANS. "How Were Notre-Dame Clausulae Performed?" *Music and Letters* 50 (1969): 273–277.

WAITE, WILLIAM G. *The Rhythm of Twelfth-Century Polyphony: Its Theory and Practice.* New Haven: Yale University Press, 1954.

The Development of the Motet

IN the thirteenth century, the leading polyphonic genre was the *motet*. It consisted of a *tenor,* borrowed traditionally from a well-known chant melody, over which a second voice was added, called the *duplum* or *motetus,* and often a third voice as well, called the *triplum.* A motet is customarily identified by the first few words of each of the upper vocal parts, top down, plus either the *incipit* of the tenor text or the words of the chant from which the tenor melody is taken. For example, the motet title *O mitissima (Quant voi)—Virgo virginum—Haec dies* indicates a three-part piece. The triplum is in Latin and begins with the words *O mitissima;* the duplum is also in Latin and begins with the words *Virgo virginum;* and the tenor is derived from the melody of the Gradual responsory for Easter, *Haec dies.* The part of the title in parentheses *(Quant voi)* indicates that this piece also has an alternative triplum with a French text (see Example 6.3).

Originally rooted in the substitute clausula, the motet became, in the course of the thirteenth century, the all-purpose polyphonic genre; and as the distance between the liturgy and the motet increased, so did the freedom with which the motet underwent stylistic change. At first, such innovations consisted primarily of treating traditional elements in nontraditional ways: putting new words under old melodies, substituting new texts for old, and recasting old melodies into new rhythmic and formal patterns. As time went on, more and more material was newly composed.

Together with the secularization of the motet came equally important changes in aesthetic attitudes. Not only traditional liturgical melodies, but also fundamental matters of musical style were subject to alteration and eventual abandonment. The most important of these to be undermined was the triple-based rhythmic system which had been central to the *Ars antiqua* style. The *Ars nova* ("new art") currents of the late thirteenth and early fourteenth centuries put forth as equally valid a duple-based system.

Significantly, proponents of the new trends appealed primarily to practical considerations, such as ease of performance and aural attractiveness, and dismissed as largely irrelevant to sounding music the more philosophical and mathematical considerations that had constituted the foundation of the older systems. From the fourteenth century on, then, the concept of one totally integrated musical cosmos—measurable on its vertical axis as pitch and on its horizontal axis as rhythm—became a philosophical ideal remembered and connected with practice by only a few.

From Clausula to Motet

The way in which polyphonic clausulas metamorphosed into motets, and motets in turn expanded independently of the liturgy, cannot be outlined with chronological precision. Only a few pieces can be dated, and there probably was a certain ebb and flow as more complex types of settings developed at different rates in different geographical areas. But general trends can be traced, and there are logical interrelationships among the various stages.

From the time of the substitute clausulas to the middle of the thirteenth century, the motet underwent significant expansion. The likely first step was that the duplum of a clausula no longer simply echoed the liturgical words of the tenor; instead, it was given its own new text.

A second major step was the addition of a third voice, a triplum, above the duplum. Among these two- and three-part settings there seems to have been constant interchange. New texts could be substituted for use with old music in the duplum or triplum, and these contrafacta might be in either Latin or French. The texts of the two upper voices might be the same, or they might be different. They might even be in different languages—the duplum in Latin and the triplum in French was a typical arrangement. One voice might be stripped away from a polyphonic complex and another written in with entirely new text and music. The time was one of free borrowing and extensive remodeling—a profuseness of activity that conveys the vitality of the repertory.

By about 1260, the motet had become such an all-inclusive genre, both in textual subject matter and in musical style, that it absorbed and united two previously independent polyphonic strains: the liturgically related tradition of the texted clausula and the more independent repertory of the newly composed conductus. During the Ars antiqua, the three-voiced, double-texted motet (with different texts in each of the upper two voices) was the predominant type cultivated. Development turned inward, away from exterior characteristics such as the number of voices and the language of the text to more interior concerns, such as rhythmic interrelationships among the voices and subtler matters of formal design.

Examples 6.1 and 6.2 demonstrate the decisive step in the development of the motet. Example 6.1 is a clausula in which the tenor melody is the melisma over "Dominus" from the Gradual verse for Christmas, *Notum fecit Dominus*. In the clausula, the chant melisma has been laid out in a regular Mode V rhythmic pattern consisting of two-foot ordines.

Ex. 6.1   *Viderunt omnes — v. Notum fecit Dominus*

From a clausula setting of the word "Dominus" from the Christmas Gradual responsory verse, as transcribed from Wolfenbüttel 1099 (1206), ff. 63r.

Motet, Factum est salutare

In Example 6.2 this *Dominus* clausula appears with a new text in the duplum, *Factum est salutare* ("Salvation has been made known"). The upper voice no longer is simply vocalized on the same extended vowel sound as the tenor, that is, on "*Do*-minus"; now it has its own text. Indeed, the name of the new genre, "motet," came from the French term for "word," "mot." The Latin equivalent, *motetus,* was used in two ways: (1) as a synonym for "duplum," the upper voice of a two-part motet, and (2) as the generic name for this type of piece, for the whole polyphonic structure of two, three, or even four voices. The duplum text of Example 6.2 is closely related to the liturgical content of the tenor. It paraphrases the Gradual verse from which the *Dominus* melisma is taken and then elaborates upon the same idea.

Gradual verse:
Notum fecit Dominus salutare suum;
ante conspectum gentium relevavit
iusticiam suum.
    The Lord has made known his salvation;
    in the sight of all peoples he has
    revealed his justice.

Duplum of the motet:
Factum est salutare conspectu notum gentium.
A rege mundus cesare describitur;
factor omnium, rex nascitur salvare quod periit.
Ergo Lazare, post triduum iam compare.
Tardare nimis fatuum, sanare quartum mortuum
numquam voluit Dominus.
Salvation has been made known
in the sight of all peoples.
By the king, by the Caesar, the
world is regulated.
[But] the maker of all, our king,
has been born to save it, because it
is perishing.
Therefore, Lazarus, after three days,
appear. To remain too long in death,
to heal the dead after four days,
this the Lord never intended.

The new text glossed the meaning of the tenor source and expanded upon its importance, as had the tropes. And the compositional device used, a simple texting out of a preexisting melisma, was also an old one, used, for example, in the prosulas.

Ex. 6.2   *Factum est salutare*

Ex. 6.2   cont.

Motet created from the "Dominus" clausula of Ex. 6.1. Transcribed from Florence, Bibliotheca Mediceo–Laurenziana, Pluteus 29.1, f. 408v.

This initial step, seemingly so simple, had a profound impact on one crucial aspect of the music: the notation of the rhythm of the duplum. Since the intelligibility of the Notre-Dame system depended so heavily upon the interrelationships among groups of notes, the destruction of these groups, the breaking up of ligatures by spreading the notes out one by one over the new syllables of text, dealt a serious blow to the conceptual foundations of the system. As these syllabic motets grew in popularity not only within the liturgy but also independently as devotional pieces or as commentaries on more worldly affairs, a new way of notating rhythm had to be developed so that each individual note could communicate its own nature: whether it was a short or a long. The system that gradually emerged is the one codified and authoritatively explained by Franco of Cologne around the year 1260.

Breaking up of ligatures

The motetus texts of these earliest two-part settings sometimes interacted with the tenor not just conceptually but also poetically. For example, the vowel sound of the extended tenor syllable could be echoed in the duplum by words carefully chosen not only for their meaning but also for their sound.

Soon the subject matter of the motetus expanded to include general moralizing, unrelated to any particular liturgical expression. In *Error populus—*

New subject matter

Beginning of the two-part motet *Adveniam pervenian/Tamquam,* Wolfenbüttel 1099 (1206), f. 145r. The illuminated "A" with which the series begins probably is an accurate representation of the performance practice of these motets. The one soloist stands before a lectern, which holds the book out of which he sings the upper voice of the two-voice motet.

Dominus, for example, the same rhythmic version of the tenor is used as in *Factum est salutare* — *Dominus.* But a later stage of stylistic development is evident in that the tenor is repeated, thus doubling the length of the piece. The Latin duplum laments the corruption prevalent among those in high places, a sentiment that must have found widespread resonance, for when a French contrafactum was written for the duplum, it just paraphrased the Latin text.

The Later Styles

Most clausulas and motets dating up to and through the first half of the thirteenth century are anonymous. The stock of melodies, both tenors and upper parts, seems to have been considered to be in the public domain. Accordingly, they could be used and altered freely by anyone. In this respect, the motet repertory from the first half of the thirteenth century represents the end of an important facet of the medieval tradition of musicianship: the sub-

Beginning of motet *O mitissima* — *Virgo virginum* — *Hec dies,* Bamberg, Ms. Ed. IV.6, ff. 60r.

ordination of the personality who created the work, either visually or aurally, to the work itself. From the mid-thirteenth century on, increasing emphasis is placed on individual styles, on cultivating the type of awareness that Anonymous IV demonstrated in comparing the talents of Léonin and Pérotin. By the next century, anonymity seems more and more to be the result not of policy, but accidents of historical preservation.

One lovely example of the anonymous tradition is the motet *O mitissima (Quant voi)—Virgo virginum—Hec dies* ("O most gentle" ["When I see"]—"Virgin of virgins"—"This day") (see Example 6.3). It is a double-texted, three-part motet, preserved with Latin in the upper two voices in the Bamberg manuscript, and with an alternative French triplum in the Montpellier source. The rhythmic movement in all three voices is predominantly Mode I. Melodically, the duplum and triplum are closely interwoven to create a composite "upper voice." The phrasing in all the voices is regular and parallel. Conservative cadences of open fifths are the rule; fifths also open the phrases. The more dissonant intervals, fourths and thirds, are reserved for the weak part of the Mode I foot, the short of the long-short pattern. The overall harmonic design is a complex of Dorian, transposed Dorian (to G), and Mixolydian. **An anonymous motet**

The tenor is liturgical. The motetus addresses Mary and recalls not only the birth of the Christ-child but also its miraculous circumstances. Theologically, these two voices are closely connected, for Christmas marks the beginning of the series of events that culminates in Easter. The Latin triplum also addresses Mary, not in a formal liturgical way, but devotionally, invoking her aid more personally. The French triplum sighs for the secular Marion and rejoices in the delights of this season of new birth, the time of the spring equinox, of Easter.

In these early thirteenth-century motets, the duplum and triplum are similar in character. But later in the century, composers began to introduce distinctions in style not only between the tenor and the upper voices, but also between the upper voices themselves. This type of setting is usually called *Franconian,* after Franco of Cologne, a composer and theorist active from about 1250 to about 1280. One good example of the style is the motet *Pucelete —Je languis—Domino.* (See Example 6.4.) A hint of its freer form is given by the tenor itself, which is drawn not from the Proper of the Mass but from the dismissal *Benedicamus Domino,* a refrain that was first set polyphonically at St. Martial, home of the most loosely liturgical of the early organum repertories. **A Franconian motet**

Both of the upper voices are in French. The duplum is predominantly in a Mode II (♩ ♪) rhythmic pattern; the triplum is in the quicker Mode VI (♩ ♩ ♩), with the first short regularly subdivided into still more rapid movement (♪♩ ♩ ♩). In the slower duplum, which in range generally nestles in the interior of the piece, the lover languishes much as he had in numerous troubadour and trouvère texts. In the most exposed position, the triplum, he displays the charming, lively, and debonair face appropriate to offer publicly; but in the last line, desire overcomes even the triplum.

Ex. 6.3   *O mitissima—Virgo virginum—Hec dies*

O mi - tis - si - ma   Vir - go Ma - ri -

Vir - go vir - gi - num   Lu - men lu - mi -

[Hec   dies

a   Pos - ce   tu - um   fi - li - um

num   Re - for - ma - trix   ho - mi - num

Ut   no - bis   au - xi - li - um

Que   por - ta - sti   do - mi - num

Det   et   re - me - di - um   Con - tra   de - mo -

Per   te   Ma - ri -, a   De - tur   ve - ni -

Ex. 6.3   cont.

Triplum: "O most gentle Virgin Mary, intercede with your son to give us help and assistance against the deceiving tricks of the demons and their evil doings." Duplum: "Virgin of virgins, light of lights, transformer of men, who bore the Lord: through thee, O Mary, let grace be given, as the angel announced, 'You are a virgin before and after.'"

Transcription of the motet from Bamberg, Ms. Ed. IV.6, ff. 60rv.

The phrase structure of *Pucelete*—*Je languis*—*Domino* is more complex than that of *O mitissima* and seems to have been designed for dramatic effect. All three voices frequently overlap; the most usual pattern is that while two voices are cadencing, the third carries on, propelling the whole piece forward. Therefore, when all three lines do cadence simultaneously, a striking contrast is created. This combination occurs only once, just before the lover's final despairing appeal for mercy from his beloved.

As in *O mitissima*, the sharpest dissonances in *Pucelete* tend to appear on the second half of the modal foot. But since the basic modal pattern here is Mode II, short–long, rather than Mode I, long–short, the dissonances in *Pucelete* are considerably accented (since they occur on the longer part of the metrical foot).

In addition to lending his name to a style of motet composition, Franco contributed substantially to musical developments in the second half of the thirteenth century by accomplishing a major codification of rhythmic notation. Written about 1260 and entitled *Ars cantus mensurabilis* ("The Art of Mensurable Music"), Franco's treatment was so comprehensive and clear that it exerted great authority well into the next century. He understood the importance of an internally logical notational scheme but also was realistic in recognizing the weight of existing practice.

The treatise begins by acknowledging the authority of Boethius on the theory of monophonic chant, and of Guido on its practice. Franco's treatment of polyphony starts by dividing it into two types: wholly mensurable and partly mensurable. Discant is an example of the former, since it is measured in all its parts. Organum belongs to the latter category, for the tenor in organum purum is stretched beyond the measure of the modal system.

Moving on to more modern topics, he takes up notational developments prompted by the motet repertory. The system he describes grew out of the

practice of the rhythmic modes, and is based on the principle of ternary subdivision. Like the earlier Guidonian approach to rhythm, Franco's system is pyramidal in structure. The three principal rhythmic signs are the *long* ⌐ , the *breve* ▪ , and the *semibreve* ◆ . Conceptually, these are related to each other entirely by threes. The long normally has three breves, and the breve normally has three semibreves. Lengths of time are measured in *tempora*. One *tempus* is the usual duration of a breve. Three tempora constitute a *perfection*, the usual duration of a long. (See Figure 6.1.)

Ex. 6.4   *Pucelete bele et avenant—Je languis—Domino*

Ex. 6.4   cont.

Ex. 6.4   cont.

Triplum: "Chaste maiden, beautiful and comely; pretty one, refined and pleasing; the delightful one whom I desire so much makes me joyous, gay and loving. In May there is no nightingale so merrily singing. I shall love my pretty one, my fair brunette, with all my heart. Sweet friend, to you who so long have held my life at your command I cry mercy, sighing."

Duplum: "I languish from the malady of love. Far rather would I have this kill me than any other illness, for such death is very pleasant. Relieve me, sweet friend, of this malady, lest love kill me."

Motet excerpt transcribed from Montpellier, Bibliothèque de la Faculté de Médecine, Ms. H 196, ff. 193v–195r.

Starting from this basic pattern of ternary relations throughout, variations can be introduced. For example, if two longs are separated by a breve ⌐ ▪ ⌐, the first long is said to be imperfected by the following breve. So instead of lasting its normal length of one perfection, or three tempora, the long gives up one tempus to the breve, and lasts only two tempora itself (♩ ♩ ♩.). If two longs are separated by two breves, ⌐ ▪ ▪ ⌐, the grouping of perfections is thought of as one long plus two breves plus one long. Since a complete perfection consists of three tempora, which must, in this situation, be distributed over only two breves, the first breve is assigned one tempus and the second receives two. It becomes an *altered breve* (♩. ♪ ♩ ♩.).

In Franconian Notation

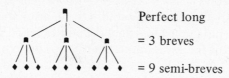

Perfect long

= 3 breves

= 9 semi-breves

Figure 6.1.   Franco's triple subdivision

Note that in absolute length, the imperfected long of the first pattern and the altered breve of the second pattern have exactly the same duration, two tempora. Thus, in the Franconian system of triple subdivision, a singer can pivot from a higher rhythmic level to a lower one, or vice versa, by means of alteration and imperfection, just as in the pitch system, the singer can pivot from a higher hexachord to a lower, or vice versa, by means of solmization. **Pivoting**

Just as "G" can be both "sol" in the C hexachord and "ut" in the G hexachord, so also the time duration of two tempora can be either a breve, if altered, or a long, if imperfected. Thus it acts as a "pivot rhythm," so to speak. An analogous interrelationship exists between the breve and semibreve levels as well.

The normal process of imperfection can be halted if, in the first pattern, for example, a dot is placed after the first long to indicate the end of a perfection (◖• ◼ ◖). Since the breve cannot intrude upon the long when blocked by this point of division, it will have to imperfect the following long. Then the resulting rhythmic pattern will be three tempora plus one plus two (♩. ♩ ♪) instead of the more usual two plus one plus three. With longer patterns of breves uninterrupted by a long, the principles are the same. The breves should be grouped into perfections for as long as there are multiples of three breves. When only one is left over, the first long is imperfected; when two are left, both the first and last longs are imperfected.

Post-Franconian motet developments during the last quarter of the thirteenth century included the use of liturgical tenors from a wider variety of sources than the Notre-Dame repertory had drawn upon: Kyries, hymns, and antiphons were added to the collection of available tunes. The trend toward using a secular tenor, traceable since the mid-thirteenth century, also gathered momentum.

Thus, by the end of the century, two fairly distinct styles emerged. One featured a fast, sometimes almost speechlike triplum, a slower duplum, and a chant-derived tenor in a strict rhythmic pattern. The other usually employed a French secular tenor, and all the voices tended to proceed in more nearly equal rhythmic patterns. The first remained highly stratified rhythmically, whereas the second had the tendency to be more integrated in that respect. In both styles, each voice tended to move predominantly in its own tonal space. **A Petronian**

The first type of motet is often called *Petronian,* after Petrus de Cruce, or, **motet** in French, Pierre de la Croix, who was active from about 1270 until the end of the century. His motet *Aucun—Lonc tans—Annun[tiantes]* is a good example of the rhythmic subdivision introduced into the triplum. The transcription, Example 6.5, presents about a fourth of the piece. (See *HAM* I, 34, pp. 36–37, for a transcription of the entire motet. For details on Petronian notation, see Chapter 8.)

New rhythms   The tenor melody of the Petronian motet is the concluding melisma of the Gradual responsory for the Feast of the Epiphany, on January 6. It is laid out

Petrus de Cruce, beginning of motet *Aucun—Lonc tans —Annun[tiantes]*, Montpellier H 196, ff. 273r.

in an old-fashioned regular Mode V scheme of two-foot ordines. The duplum moves primarily in the long-short pattern of Mode I, with the second part of the foot occasionally subdivided. The triplum is a heavily fractured Mode VI, with three or four, sometimes even six or seven, syllables worked into a space usually occupied by a single short. Compared with the stately-moving lower lines, it is almost a patter-type triplum.

It should also be noted that the overall modal color of the piece changes more rapidly than it did in earlier motets. For example, over the duplum text *Mes or ai raison de joie mener* ("But now I have reason to be joyful") the three voices pass through a different modal configuration with each ternary long, transcribed here as lasting a measure. *Mes or ai* uses Lydian on C, *raison* moves to Dorian, *de joi* (the first syllable of *joi-e*) shifts up to Dorian on A, and *-e me-* goes back to Lydian, this time at its basic pitch level F, with a twist on the last third of the measure toward Lydian on C, preparatory to going to Lydian on G, or Mixolydian, for the final cadence over *-ner*. Thus the agitated rhythmic movement in the triplum is accompanied by a similarly restless shifting about of the modal center defined by all three voices.

In works like this, the old motet framework was stretched so far both rhythmically and modally that further stylistic development virtually required intrusion into and alteration of the most fundamental aspects of motet structure. Indeed, the most characteristic innovation of the newer type of late-thirteenth-century motet is the abandonment of the traditional hierarchical roles of the several voices. This change constitutes a vital shift in the overall balance of the composition, because up to this point, the horizontal, linear aspects had been predominant. The tenor, duplum, and triplum all had their own well-defined functions, as well as considerable freedom to develop within their own individual bounds. But a tenor could never be mistaken for a triplum, for the traditional requirements of each role were so different that the same type of line could not satisfy both. **Stylistic tradeoffs**

In other words, up to this point the individual line had been the primary "module" of construction. Had it not been so, the tenors, and even upper voices, could not have been so freely "mixed and matched" among various compositions. But by the end of the thirteenth century, the motet became less of a layered type of composition and more of a vertically blended one. And like so many stylistic developments, this one involved a tradeoff among various musical goals. By making the various lines more homogeneous, the motet as a whole gained vertical cohesiveness. But at the same time, each line lost something of its previous individual strength and character.

Instrumental Music

Any discussion of medieval instruments and instrumental music is necessarily spotty, for in contrast to the vast amount of precise manuscript information we have concerning vocal music, most of our knowledge about the instrumental side of medieval life is based on indirect literary or pictorial evi-

Ex. 6.5 Petrus de Cruce, *Aucun—Lonc tans—Annun*[*tiantes*]

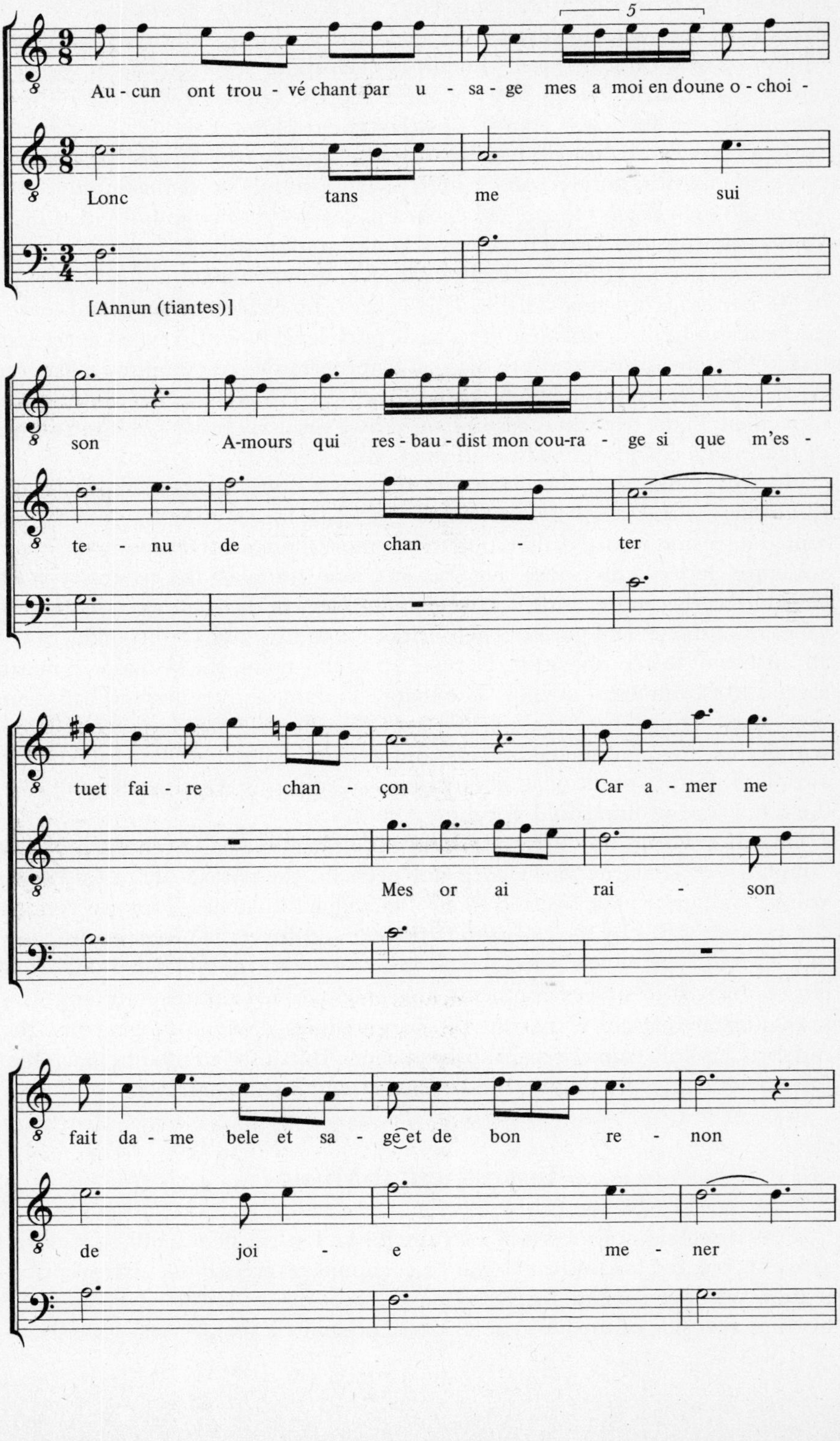

Ex. 6.5   cont.

Et je qui li ai fait houma-ge pour li ser - vir tout mon a - ge de loi -

Car bou - ne a - mour

al cuer sans pen-ser

me fait de - si - rer La mieus

Translation of transcribed portion (first quarter of piece)
Triplum: "Some write songs by convention; but it is love that inspires me, making my heart rejoice so that I must write a song.
For a lovely and wise lady of good renown has won my love.
And I, who have sworn to serve her all my life with loyal heart and no betray-ing. . . ."
Duplum: "For a long time I have held back from singing; but now I have reason to be joyful, for true love makes me long for. . . ."

Motet excerpt transcribed from Montpellier H 196, ff. 273rv.

dence. The first preserved polyphonic repertory that scholars generally agree was intended for instrumental performance is a group of untexted settings in motet style of the familiar *In seculum* tenor from the Easter Gradual *Haec dies.* (See *HAM* I, 32e, pp. 34–35.)

One of these settings carries the inscription *In seculum viellatoris,* which, to-gether with the fact that none of the musical lines has any text, has been taken to imply that these works should be played rather than sung. The instrument referred to, the *vielle,* is the most important string instrument of the twelfth and thirteenth centuries. It was held to the chest and played with a bow. Of its five strings, four could be stopped with the fingers in order to change their pitches, while one was a drone.

No music theorist before Johannes de Grocheo (c. 1300) deals specifically

*In seculum
settings*

with music to be played on any type of instrument, but it seems most unlikely that a lively, orally transmitted repertory of music for dancing and other occasions was not available. According to *Conseils aux jongleurs* ("Advice to Jongleurs"), written by Guirauc de Calanson in 1210, jongleurs were expected to be sufficiently versatile to perform on as many as ten instruments. The earliest medieval dance, whose name doubles as the name of a

Estampie and ductia
particular instrumental form, is the *estampie,* which consists of several sections, each repeated. The first statement ends on an "open," or incomplete, cadence; the repetition, on a "closed," or final, cadence. According to Grocheo, the estampie proper consists of five to seven sections, or *puncti,* while a shorter version of the same dance type is called a *ductia.* (See *HAM* I, 40, pp. 42–43.) The thirteenth-century *Chansonnier du Roy* ("Song book of the King") contains eight monophonic examples of these purely instrumental estampies.

Instrumental music was sometimes said to have inspired troubadours to create a suitable poem. The story is told that the text of *Kalenda maya* ("The Month of May") was written by the troubadour Raimbaut de Vaqueiras (fl. 1180–1207) to the melody of an *estampida* played by two *joglar de Fransa,* or French jongleurs, on their vielles. Another troubadour song, *Chanterai d'aquetz trobadors* by Pierre d'Auvergne, mentions at the end of its text that it was composed to the bagpipes amidst games and laughter.

A number of medieval instruments have their roots in antiquity. The

Kithara, lyra, and harp
leading instrument of classical Greece was the *kithara,* which consisted of a wooden soundbox, two curved lateral arms, and a crossbar. Across these were stretched varying numbers of strings, from five to eleven. The *lyra* was a lighter version of the kithara, whose soundbox was usually made from the shell of a turtle. The *harp* originated in the Middle East and made its first European appearance in Ireland, where it still is used as the national heraldic symbol. There is much scholarly controversy concerning the development and use of these two types of instrument during the Middle Ages, and about the development of new instruments with confusingly similar names.

What has prompted much of this attention is the fact that these instruments figure prominently in one of the most common iconographical themes of the entire period—one that was illustrated again and again in sculpture and manuscript illuminations: "King David and His Harp," or was it his Lyre? Another theme that prompted artistic depiction of many instruments was set forth in these magnificent lines from Psalm 150: "Praise him in the sound of the trumpet, praise him upon the lute and harp. Praise him in the timbrels and dances, praise him upon the strings and pipe. Praise him upon the well-tuned cymbals, praise him upon the loud cymbals." Since the pictures used to illustrate such themes are one of our chief sources of information about medieval instruments, we must make sure when studying them to try to establish whether the artist is (a) depicting an instrument actually in use at the time; (b) copying from a historical model long abandoned in practice; or (c) picturing some idealized form of an instrument that may never have existed. Even if the artist is clearly working from "real life," the question remains as to how technically accurate his representation is.

In addition to the harp, the lyre, and the vielle, other instruments that art-ists depicted include the *organistrum,* the *psaltery,* and the *lute.* The organis-trum was a three-stringed vielle that usually was held across the knees, and its strings were made to vibrate by a revolving wheel turned by a crank, rather than by a bow. The organistrum was quite large, and playing it sometimes required the cooperation of two people. The psaltery is similar to the zither. It consists of a flat soundboard over which a number of strings are stretched and is played by plucking the strings with the fingers. The lute entered Europe through Spain, where it had been introduced by the Arabs as early as the ninth century. The instrument then spread to other parts of the continent but did not become widely popular until the Renaissance.

Orga-nistrum, psaltery, and lute

Flutes existed as well. The older, more common version was the end-blown, or recorder, type, which was made of wood. Its distinctive tone qual-ity was due in part to the size and shape of the wind passage, or internal bore, usually larger near the mouthpiece than at the opposite end. Its pitches were determined primarily by the placement of the finger-holes when the flute was constructed; only slight variations could be introduced by altering the man-ner of blowing. The transverse wood flute also existed by at least the end of the twelfth century. Throughout the Middle Ages it was primarily a fife-like military instrument, particularly popular in Germanic areas. Medieval *drums* were plentiful and came in a variety of shapes and sizes. Some were in the form of a barrel; others were cylindrical. They were suspended around the player's neck or set on the ground. One famous thirteenth-century miniature from Spain even shows a drum shaped like an hourglass carried on the player's shoulder.

Flutes and drums

The historical roots of the *organ* were in a Greek invention, the *hydraulis,* which had a loud and penetrating sound. In Rome, it was used chiefly to ac-company public entertainments such as gladiator fights. In Byzantium the organ was used to enhance imperial ceremonies and spectacles. The Byzan-tine version of this instrument came to the West by at least the middle of the eighth century, when the Eastern Emperor presented one to King Pepin of the Franks, Charlemagne's father.

Organs

In the tenth century, the English monk Wulfstan reports a huge organ at Winchester, whose wind supply had to be generated by seventy men pump-ing twenty-six bellows, "working with their arms, covered with perspira-tion, each inciting his companions to drive the wind up with full strength, so that [the organ] can speak with its four hundred pipes." The instrument was played not by pressing down keys, but by activating one of twenty slider mechanisms. Two organists were needed to cover the two keyboards. Wulf-stan observes that the sound of the organ, once "revved up," was so powerful that everyone held his hands over his ears.

Up until the thirteenth century, an organ was constructed as a single tonal unit. Organs varied in size, from one rank (one set of pipes covering the entire range of the keyboard) to twenty, but on any given instrument all of the ranks had to be used at once. No stop mechanism was available by which one rank could be singled out now and another chosen later on. In other words, a large organ could not be sounded softly. Therefore an instrument's tonal subtlety or flexibility came primarily from voicing contrasts built into the different pitch registers. The lower sounds tended to have a penetrating string-like tone, and the higher sounds a lighter flute-like tone.

The Winchester installation was exceptional, of course, and two smaller types of organ were far more common. The *portative* consisted of only a single rank of pipes and was small enough to be managed by only one person. The organist would play the music with his right hand and pump the bellows with his left. The *positive* was a somewhat larger variety. It, too, could be carried, but had to be placed on a table in order to be played, and the organist required an assistant to pump the bellows.

In sum, there was a fairly wide variety of instruments in the Middle Ages, and undoubtedly they were used to create lively improvised and orally transmitted repertories. But documentary recognition was slow in coming. Instrumental music was not written down extensively until the Renaissance, and not until the Baroque period would it be treated, both in theory and in practice, as the equal of vocal music.

Summary

The motet was the leading polyphonic genre of the thirteenth century. Rooted in Notre-Dame substitute clausulas, it consisted of a tenor line, borrowed from a well-known chant melody, over which a second voice was added, and often a third as well.

Critical to the development of the motet repertory was a shift in compositional focus. No longer was a whole chant the unit of reference; now one little melisma governed the musical composition. Eventually this focus became so concentrated that the melisma drifted loose entirely from its liturgical moorings. Once established as an independent entity, it then expanded to a size more appropriate for a free-standing piece.

As the distance between the liturgy and the motet increased, so did the freedom with which the motet underwent stylistic change. The first step was that the upper voice no longer simply echoed the liturgical words of the tenor; instead, it was given a whole new text, and thus the piece became a motet. Another major step was the addition of a third voice, or triplum, above the duplum. New texts could be substituted for use with old music in the duplum or triplum (contrafacta in either Latin or French) or new lines of both music and text could be fashioned into alternate upper voices.

By about 1260 the motet had become such an all-inclusive genre, both textually and musically, that it absorbed and united two previously independent polyphonic strains: the liturgically related tradition of the texted clausula and the independently composed repertory of conductus.

By the end of the thirteenth century, two distinct styles had emerged. One, named after its best-known practitioner, Petrus de Cruce (Petronian style), featured a fast, almost speechlike rhythm in the triplum, a slower duplum, and a chant-derived tenor in strict rhythmic patterns. The other usually employed a French secular tenor, and all the voices, including the tenor, tended to proceed in more nearly equal rhythmic patterns.

Together with the secularization of the motet came important changes in aesthetic attitudes. The alteration and eventual abandonment of traditional liturgical melodies was accompanied by other changes in fundamental matters of musical structure and style. Among the most important to be undermined was the concept of a triple-based rhythmic system, central to the *Ars antiqua* style, as codified by Franco of Cologne in his 1260 treatise *Ars cantus mensurabilis*. The *Ars nova* proponents of the late thirteenth and early fourteenth centuries put forth as equally valid a duple-based rhythmic system. Significantly, they appealed primarily to practical considerations, such as ease of performance and aural attractiveness, and dismissed to a great extent the more philosophical and mathematical considerations that had constituted the foundation of the older systems. In a sense, then, the end of the Ars antiqua also marks the end of the medieval age, for from the fourteenth century on, the concept of one totally integrated musical cosmos became a philosophical ideal that was connected with musical practice by only a few.

Bibliography

BOWLES, EDMUND A. "The Role of Musical Instruments in Medieval Sacred Drama." *The Musical Quarterly* 45 (1959): 67–84.

———. "The Symbolism of the Organ in the Middle Ages: A Study in the History of Ideas." In *Aspects of Medieval and Renaissance Music: A Birthday Offering to Gustave Reese*. New York: W. W. Norton, 1966; reprinted, New York: Pendragon Press, 1978, pp. 27–39.

———. "Tower Musicians in the Middle Ages." *Brass Quarterly* 5 (1961–1962): 91–103.

CRANE, FREDERICK. "On Performing the *Lo estampies*." *Early Music* 7 (1979): 25–33.

McKINNON, JAMES W. "Musical Instruments in Medieval Psalm Commentaries and Psalters." *Journal of the American Musicological Society* 21 (1968): 3–20.

PAGE, CHRISTOPHER. "Biblical Instruments in Medieval Manuscript Illustration." *Early Music* 5 (1977): 299–309.

RANDEL, DON M. "AL-FARABI and the Role of Arabic Music Theory in the Latin Middle Ages." *Journal of the American Musicological Society* 29 (1976): 173–188.

REMNANT, MARY. "The Diversity of Medieval Fiddles." *Early Music* 3 (1975): 47–51.

STRUNK, OLIVER, ed. *Source Readings in Music History*. New York: W. W. Norton, 1950; *Antiquity and the Middle Ages* issued in paperback as a separate volume, 1965.

PART
TWO

*The Ars Nova
and the
Renaissance*

7

Ars Nova and Renaissance
Music in Society

THOSE who live through times of unrest seldom appreciate all the implications of the turmoil around them. Occasionally, however, the changes are so stunning as to be unmistakable.

Such is the case with the first decades of the fourteenth century. To be sure, the seeds of political, economic, and intellectual change had been sown in the last half of the previous century, as the rise of secular political power conflicted with the papacy. In addition, the population growth and economic expansion that had characterized European society since the tenth century came to a halt in the last three decades of the thirteenth, and Europe, at least north of the Alps, slid into a depression that lasted until the fifteenth century and created bitter social discontent and rebellion.

Most important, the supranational influences in Europe weakened. The Church declined, and the Holy Roman Empire became merely a German federation. At the same time a spirit of nationalism flourished—if not always in politics, at least in the arts, as was shown, for example, in the rise of vernacular literatures: Dante, Petrarch, and Boccaccio in Italy; Guillaume de Machaut, Christine de Pisan, and Charles d'Orleans in France; Jorge Manrique and Juan Ruiz in Spain; Chaucer and the Gawain poet in England. Indeed, it was partially this nationalist feeling, this search for the past glories of Rome, that led to the humanistic pursuits of Petrarch and Boccaccio. In music this tide was reflected in the three different styles of the fourteenth century, from France, England, and Italy. To be sure, the fifteenth century saw an apparent reversal of this trend, as humanism itself became an international force and a single style, the so-called Franco-Netherlandish style, became the musical lingua franca of continental Europe. But nationalism reasserted itself strongly in the sixteenth century amid a welter of variations on the central musical language as well as a profusion of music reflecting the Italian, French, English, or German cultures.

Nationalism

119

The Transition of the Fourteenth Century

Political change   Initial change resulted from the onset of hostilities between England and France in 1294, which shattered nearly a century of peace in transalpine Europe. Meanwhile, fierce attacks on the papacy staged by ministers of Philip the Fair led to the abduction of Pope Boniface VIII in 1303. Anglo-French hostilities eventually created the Hundred Years War, an era when outright warfare alternated with periods of "peace" and rampant brigandage. The attacks on the papacy finally brought about the so-called Babylonian Captivity of the Church in Avignon (1305–1378) as well as the Great Schism (1378–1417), which all but destroyed the moral authority of the Church and brought a wave of anticlericalism and a resurgence of popular heresy.

Literature   A mood of pessimism was already apparent in the second part of the late-thirteenth-century *Roman de la rose*. Dante's *Inferno,* begun in 1302, reflects the poet's severe judgment of his times. But such despair appears harshest in one of the earliest poetic and musical monuments of the fourteenth century, the *Roman de Fauvel,* a long satirical poem written between 1310 and 1314 by Gervaise de Bus, and expanded with musical interpolations by Chaillou de Pesstain in 1316 (see Chapter 8).

Musicians and Their Music

Composers of the fourteenth and fifteenth centuries generally worked as members of one of the royal or noble chapels, the papal chapel, or one of the choirs connected with a cathedral. In addition, the new independence of the cities gave rise to a number of musicians' guilds. These were, in a sense, the true inheritors of the trouvère tradition, even if the new guilds, with the exception of the German guilds of *Meistersinger,* consisted of instrumentalists rather than singers and composers. Guild musicians were usually laymen, while members of the chapels were clerks who had taken at least minor orders.

Chapels   The main function of the chapel was to perform music for the Mass and the Daily Office, and for those ceremonial occasions that required sacred music. During the fifteenth century, the chapel became one of the prime organizations of the court, as kings, lords, and popes eagerly sought the ablest singers and composers, as well as new works by the famous musicians of other courts. Nevertheless, the daily life of the chapel centered around the services that were sung (most often) in chant.

Musicians in Society

Chaplains   Court musicians were of two categories: the chaplains and the minstrels. The chaplains, as noted above, were all clerics or at least clerks in minor

Chaplains singing the Mass. Chantilly, Musèe Condé, 1284, Très Riches Heures de Jean de Berry.

orders, but the minstrels were laymen. It is among the chaplains that we find the important composers of the fourteenth and fifteenth centuries, for they were generally educated men, trained either in a cathedral school or in one of the choir schools connected with noble chapels. They were trained primarily as singers, and only the most gifted became composers. Although some chaplains could probably play an instrument such as the vielle, the recorder, or the lute, until the sixteenth century the only instrument with a place in the chapel was the organ. Chaplains were usually the gifted children of commoners, sent to choir school as an avenue for advancement, but their number also included members of the minor nobility and landed gentry. Composers who showed musical gifts as well as intellectual and administrative abilities accumulated wealth and privileges and had easy access to powerful rulers.

Minstrels   Minstrels were essentially instrumentalists, although occasionally one is listed as a *menestrel de voix* ("singing minstrel"). Like the chaplains, minstrels were commoners. But also like the chaplains, they earned a substantial living from their musical skill. They learned their art by being apprenticed to other minstrels, and were seldom educated musicians in the same sense as the chaplains. Indeed, many evidently could not read music. Such inability, however, did not preclude extraordinary virtuosity, often on several families of instruments. If minstrels learned their music by rote, they must have had at least as good an ear and memory as the numerous folk and country musicians today who cannot read music either.

Travels   Chaplains and minstrels were allowed leaves of absence that permitted them to temporarily join other establishments. And just as the lords borrowed singers from a cathedral choir, so did they lend their own singers to other chapels and choirs, although there was always the danger that an extremely gifted musician might be lured away permanently. Such envoys, however, were not always purely musical. A famous, learned musician was a

Minstrels of Emperor Maximilian. From *Triumphzug Maximilians* by Hans Brugkmair.

useful ambassador, since the entree to high places that his art permitted him enabled him to glean valued information.

Payment to the minstrels was recorded less systematically than that to the chaplains, but both received money, clothes, and food for their work. The court itself paid for the acquisition and repair of the instruments, as well as for the copying and care of the chant and polyphonic music books.

Financial support

The Cathedral Chapter

A cathedral chapter was not organized very differently from a private chapel. The canons received income from one or more prebends (stipends from income of the cathedral chapter), some of which entailed specific duties or perquisites. Although all canons could perform the Mass and the Offices in chant, only a small number participated in the singing of polyphony. French cathedral records reveal a surprisingly consistent number of polyphonic singers throughout the fourteenth and fifteenth centuries. At Cambrai, for example, the polyphonic choir fluctuated between thirteen and sixteen men. To these, of course, we must add the six or so choirboys who sang only on special occasions. In any case, there were usually about as many singers of polyphonic music at a major cathedral as there were at a large court chapel.

Choirs

The cathedrals maintained schools for boys with more consistency than did the noble chapels, and often the instructor was himself a distinguished composer. Nicholas Grenon, for example, was master of the choirboys at Cambrai in the early fifteenth century. Cathedrals also provided a sinecure for aging masters, so that when Simon le Breton retired from the Burgundian chapel in 1465 he was given a full year's pay and a prebend at Cambrai.

Schools

Music in the Towns and Cities

In the towns and cities, instrumental music was provided by members of the guild of musicians. Occasionally guild musicians joined with cathedral singers for the performance of a Mass or ceremonial motet. One such rare instance is recorded in Paris in 1412, when a Mass was sung "with a large number of soft instruments." More common was a motet performance outside the church, as with Dufay's *Nuper rosarum flores* ("Lately the rosebush"), written for the consecration of Santa Maria del Fiore in Florence by Pope Eugenius IV in 1436. Instruments were also used in processions like that for Corpus Christi, but we cannot always determine from the chronicles whether the instrumentalists played with the choir or rendered a separate piece. Joint performances, however, became far more common after 1500, when instruments were employed even in the performance of liturgical works.

Town guilds

One aspect of the city-bred trouvère tradition preserved by the minstrels was the creation of schools and fairs, where musicians could trade profes-

Minstrels' schools and fairs

sional secrets and learn new songs. The schools provided a place of contact between the city minstrels, grouped in musicians' guilds, and the court minstrels sent by their lords. But after about 1400 attendance by court minstrels at these schools declined because the courts themselves were offering similar opportunities. In the many "courts of love," the minstrels of the assembled nobles, besides entertaining the company, traded songs and knowledge.

Religion and Music

The perspective of an essentially secular age may make it difficult to understand the extent to which religion permeated daily life in the Middle Ages and even in the Renaissance. The day was measured by the sound of the church bells, and in many towns the evening peal indicated the end of the working day. Sudden storms, plagues, bountiful crops, uncommonly mild weather, the onset of and recovery from illness, and the many small accidents and happenings of life were regarded as continuing messages from Heaven. And these could be answered through prayer, either private or public (in the form of liturgy), or more violently through oath and blasphemy.

Interpenetration of sacred and secular

One consequence of this world view is the interpenetration of the sacred and secular worlds in medieval art, literature, and music. It is responsible for the grotesqueries that adorn the capitals of the columns in many a cathedral, as well as the margins of illuminated books of hours. This intermingling also influenced the language of traditional prayers such as the Marian antiphon *Ave regina caelorum,* which is practically a love-letter addressed to the Virgin. Therefore we should not be surprised that in the thirteenth and fourteenth centuries a motet or a conductus with what may seem to be a secular text could be sung in church and understood in a homiletic or allegorical manner. Or that in the fifteenth and sixteenth centuries songs of courtly love were transformed into sacred works by the substitution of a new text or simply by the change of a few key words.

The Hundred Years War and Music

Cultural exchanges

Despite the dire economic consequences of the Hundred Years War and the religious upheavals of the fourteenth century, such turmoil had positive consequences as well. The invasions and changing alliances of the war brought many French, Italian, and English courts, both episcopal and secular, into close contact, providing poets and musicians opportunity to learn the work of their counterparts in other countries. These cultural exchanges were crucial during the Councils of Constance (1414–1418) and Basel (1431–1449).

Another effect of the wars was the exaltation of national feelings, and the fourteenth and fifteenth centuries saw an enormous increase in the composition of political works, usually motets or ballades, celebrating a coronation, a dynastic marriage, a peace treaty, or a military victory. Others simply praise a ruler or hurl invective at an enemy. The best known work of this type is perhaps the carol *Deo gratias anglia* ("England, God be thanked"), celebrating the English victory over the French at Agincourt (1415).

Political music

Court and Cathedral Music, Liturgical and Ceremonial Music

Music demanded by the court chapel was not very different from that required by a cathedral chapter: liturgical music for religious festivals and, from time to time, a large ceremonial work to celebrate an important occasion. In addition, however, the court composer had to write many songs for the entertainment of his patrons, and these usually dealt with courtly love.

In considering the fourteenth and fifteenth centuries we should draw a distinction between purely liturgical works, generally conceived on a modest scale, and ceremonial pieces in liturgical garb, in which the composer sought to produce a brilliant, deliberately learned work. An example is Guillaume Dufay's *Missa Ave regina caelorum,* written for the consecration of the Cambrai Cathedral in 1472. The tradition behind such ceremonial pieces is not purely liturgical and harks back to the political motets of the fourteenth century as well as the ceremonial ballades and madrigals of the early fifteenth century. The texts of these ceremonial works, particularly the motets, are curious hybrids of sacred and secular: they simply describe the event celebrated, then conclude with a short prayer. Not until the later fifteenth century did the ceremonial pieces begin to become more liturgical, as the cantus firmus Mass replaced the motet in this function. But the tradition of the secular motet remained, albeit diminished, particularly in funeral pieces. Thus we encounter hybrids of motet and chanson, such as Ockeghem's lament on the death of Binchois or Josquin Des Prés's lament on the death of Ockeghem. In addition, some purely secular motets were composed, such as Josquin's setting of Vergil's *Fama malum.*

Migrations to Italy

One of the most notable consequences of the council movement in the early fifteenth century was that just about the time when the internal energy of the Italian music of the *trecento* (fourteenth century) was spent, there descended upon northern Italy the various delegations to the Church councils — cardinals and bishops, who often brought retinues that included their own singers and composers. To be sure, some Italian musicians had traveled north during the years of the Avignon exile and the Great Schism, and a few northerners had been in Italy in the closing decades of the fourteenth century, such

Church councils

as Johannes Ciconia of Liège, who ended his days as a canon in Padua. But the reasons for such travels were clearly political.

At any event, descriptions of musical performances in the council meetings show that the Italian prelates were dazzled by the intricate art of the northerners, particularly the English and the Franco-Flemish musicians. The northern composers were receptive as well to the graceful, flowing melodic style of late trecento music and sought to adapt it to their own music. The new international style, simpler than that of the late French Ars nova, was essentially the product of a generation of northern composers influenced by both the melodic style of the Italian trecento and the harmonic sound of English music. These must have been heard at council ceremonies. The music of the northerners was suddenly very much in demand, but with the possible exceptions of Burgundy and Paris no northern court could offer the musicians the artistic and intellectual stimulus of the north Italian courts. As a result, a massive number of composers and singers emigrated from France and the Low Countries to Italy, a movement which lasted for over a century and threatened to engulf the entire musical life of the peninsula.

Universities   Another influential migration to Italy was that of the students who attended the great universities of Padua, Bologna, and Florence. Essentially they sought to study law or hear the lectures of the new humanists who were beginning to spread the cult of classical antiquity. But these travelers also encountered new music. German students in particular brought this repertory back to their own lands and to centers that were removed from the court music tradition, such as universities and monasteries.

Humanism

The shift in political, social, and intellectual patterns that distinguishes the Renaissance from the Middle Ages was not only very gradual but took place at different times in different countries. Even within a particular country it did not affect all areas of thought at once, so that "medieval" and "Renaissance" elements coexisted side by side in European society for nearly two centuries.

Perhaps the most important cultural development of the new age was the emergence of humanism. At its core lay a reevaluation of the culture of classical antiquity. Initially only the literary and philosophical culture of Greece and Rome were revived, but later the entire surviving artistic and intellectual heritage of the ancient world was reaffirmed.

Revival of   Early humanists exaggerated in stating that the Middle Ages had allowed
antiquity   this heritage to lie dormant. After all, whatever Roman literature and philosophy they rediscovered survived because it had been copied and preserved by medieval scribes. But medieval scholars admittedly had a restricted knowledge of this legacy, and they used it entirely differently than did the humanists. On the whole, the Greek heritage survived better, because the Byzantine

Empire had never broken from its classical past with the abruptness that the barbarian invasions had caused in the West. The Greek heritage also reached the West at precisely the time when Europe was ready to accept it eagerly, in the decades immediately before and after the fall of Constantinople in 1453.

The aesthetics—and even more, the ethos—of the classical world were essentially foreign to the Middle Ages. Although medieval rhetoricians did know Quintilian, Porphyry, and Cicero, their goal was to write a very different kind of Latin. They wrote the living Latin of their own time, with all the accretions that later humanists considered barbarisms but that were essential to express ideas and patterns foreign to the classical world. In contrast, Renaissance humanists viewed a knowledge of the classics as a worthy goal in itself, although even while disseminating that knowledge they effectively froze the Latin tongue into dead language. It was also important that this dissemination came in an age of increased secularism, when most preserved works were not tracts of systematic philosophy, but poetry, moral philosophy, and reflections on the secular life—all concerns of the lay leaders of the Renaissance. The invention of printing in the fifteenth century also helped immeasurably to spread the new learning, as well as to create its new, essentially secular, public. The need to edit and publish the ancient texts gave birth to the sciences of philology and text criticism, both of which contributed to undermining medieval reverence for the authority of the written word.

Despite some reservations about the new movement, both popes and cardinals competed with secular princes and humanists in collecting manuscripts and starting enormous libraries that are the foundation of some of the most important contemporary European collections. These include the Vatican Library, the Biblioteca Mediceo-Laurenziana in Florence, and the Bibliotheca Vadiana in St. Gall. **Church support**

As humanism spread north of the Alps, its concerns turned more toward philosophy and religion, as evidenced by the works of Johannes Reuchlin, Desiderius Erasmus, and Thomas More. Here the humanist tendency to place man ever closer to the center of intellectual inquiry paved the way for the individualistic views of theological and doctrinal matters that pervaded the thinking of the northern Reformation. **Northern humanism**

Music Teaching and Music Printing

The training of young musicians probably varied little throughout Europe from 1300 to 1600. Most young singers began as choirboys in a cathedral school or a princely chapel, where they learned grammar, Latin, and music, and encountered the liturgy simply by singing the Mass and the Office repeatedly over a number of years. The range of music instruction probably varied with the talent and interest of the master and the children, but a sample of the students' living arrangements survives in a charter of Philip the Good, who established a choir school in Dijon in 1424. Four children lived with the **Teaching choirboys** master and were taught the art of music: singing, counterpoint, and discant. Similar institutions existed in virtually every cathedral and collegiate church, and throughout the fifteenth century the schools of Liège, Bruges, and Cambrai were famous for the number of great composers who received an education there.[1]

We know virtually nothing of the actual method of instruction. But the teacher in a cathedral school had access to a number of the famous music books of his day and probably expounded their contents, so that the children learned the Church modes, the methods of solmization, the basic rules of note-against-note discant, and other essentials. Years of sight-singing, improvising counterpoint on a given chant, and other performance skills preceded any attempts at composition. Much could be learned as well by the constant exposure to the new pieces composed and sung at the church.

After their voices changed, some of the boys attended a university to study the liberal arts with the expectation of entering the clergy. Some continued further into canon law and theology. Others took orders, joined a chapel as clerks, and eventually became chaplains. The basic musical profession of all these men was singing; composition was a special, extra skill.

Music printing   The advent of music printing, beginning with Ottaviano Petrucci's edition of the *Odhecaton* (1501), did considerably more than make multiple copies of music easily available. Soon thereafter the best music publishers began to adopt many of the editorial procedures of the text publishers, as well as correcting and polishing editions in subsequent printings. Furthermore,

The first print of polyphonic music, Ottaviano Petrucci's *Odhecaton* (1501).

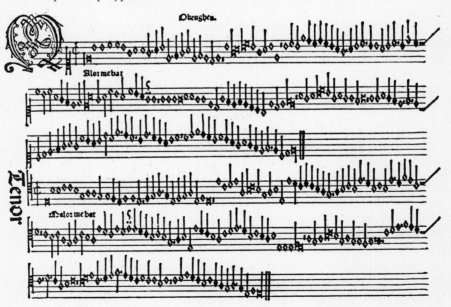

their effect upon the creation of a large secular music public was like that of the humanistic editors, who helped to create a large lay readership for literature. In addition to promoting the rapid expansion of what can best be called "commercial music"—that is, the arrangements of popular *chansons* and madrigals for every conceivable medium, as well as editions of dance music —printing accelerated the spread of new music throughout the Continent. Publishers freely pirated one another's editions as long as they could publish the version in a locale where a competitor's letters patent or monopoly was invalid or unenforceable. **A new public**

Also significant is that at this time we encounter the first books of self-instruction, with which an amateur could hope to learn to play the lute, recorder, or guitar. There also appeared the first mass-printed dance manual, Thoinot Arbeau's *Orchesographie* (1589). The spirit of these new works is embodied in the title of Thomas Morley's treatise *A Plaine and easie Introduction to Practicall Musicke* (1597). The new urban, secular public eagerly bought edition after edition of madrigal and chanson prints, and would eventually grow into the paying audience that flocked to the opera houses of the seventeenth century. **Self-tutors**

Humanism and Music

Humanism did not affect music quite so directly as it affected literature and the plastic arts, for unlike the other arts, the music of antiquity had

perished almost entirely. Indeed, most of the few scraps of ancient music extant today were known and eagerly discussed in the sixteenth century, but they are simply too meager to permit even a hypothetical reconstruction of the music that enveloped the plays of the great Athenian dramatists or carried forward the Homeric epic poetry.

The fourteenth century

One cannot speak of a humanistic influence on music in the fourteenth century. The French Ars nova and the Italian trecento, despite the self-awareness of Johannes de Muris, Philippe de Vitry, and Marchetto of Padua as the heralds of a new era, belong clearly to the world of the Middle Ages. And the music of Machaut, Landini, and their followers is still essentially "number made perceptible in sound." Even the music of the generations of Dufay and Ockeghem remains a Janus-faced art, blending the new sonorities taken from English music with the same concern for abstract structure, often pervaded by number symbolism, that had ruled the music of the fourteenth century.

The fifteenth century

Nevertheless, a change occurred in the middle of the fifteenth century. As the German musicologist Friederich Blume notes, at the root of the change was a new awareness of music as an autonomous art, subject to its own rules and evolution.[2] If a new era was implied in the titles that Vitry and Muris gave to their treatises, Johannes Tinctoris makes his own awareness of a new style absolutely explicit in the preface of his *Liber de arte contrapuncti* (1477): "It is a matter of great surprise that there is no composition written over forty years ago that is thought of by the learned as worthy of performance."[3] He defines the origins of the change in the sound of English music and calls the first generation of the new style that of Dunstaple, Dufay, and Binchois. This need to point to the beginning of a new age, to separate the ancients from the moderns, and to distinguish between the different generations is a new phenomenon, and it reappears in the writings of many men after Tinctoris. Of course, the generation that is seen as the first practitioners of the "new music" changes.

Effects on poetry

Humanism also altered music indirectly by affecting the poetry of the Renaissance. Not only did it produce a return to classical Latin style in the works of poets such as Pietro Bembo, but it also spurred a resurgence of vernacular poetry, first in Italy and later in France, Spain, and England. Such poetry owed its style not only to antiquity but also to Petrarch, the prime mover of the Italian literary Renaissance. New concerns arose for correct, flexible, and graceful versification.

Declamation

The first effects of these forces upon music are modest and almost outside the mainstream of the art. They appear in the efforts of German humanists to set classical odes to simple musical patterns, with strict attention to rhythm and the quantities of the verse lines. A similar attitude, although far less self-conscious, pervades the Italian *frottola* and Spanish *villancico* repertories of the turn of the sixteenth century. These concerns are also reflected in the simple text settings characteristic of the early-sixteenth-century madrigal, as well as the efforts of late-sixteenth-century French musicians to set verse to music with absolutely strict application of the metric quantities of the text (*vers mesuré*). An example is the vers mesuré settings of Claude le Jeune.

Concern with correct text setting also affects the prose texts of the Latin liturgy. In the late works of Josquin Des Prés we encounter time and again motives that are rhythmically derived from the sound of spoken words. The theorists of the generation immediately after Josquin are also the first to treat underlay in a systematic manner. These concerns have two consequences. First, they tend to eliminate the very long, often irrational, melismas that appear in the music of Dufay, Ockeghem, and their contemporaries. As musical phrase structure becomes shorter and more closely tied to the prosody of the text, it brings the music nearer to the measure of a human element—words —rather than the abstract numerical proportions that regulated the long melismatic filigrees of the fifteenth century. This trend is also reflected in Tinctoris' definition of consonance. He abandons the medieval definition based on mathematical proportion and focuses instead on congruence of sound pleasing to the human ear.

The second consequence is perhaps even more momentous. From paying careful attention to the rhythm and sound of the words it was but a small step to express their meaning through music. Such *word painting* by means of musical analogs was already present in the music of Josquin, but the madrigal composers took up this approach in greater earnest, so that the device has also become known as *madrigalism*. In the end it led to depiction of not just isolated words but the emotional content of entire phrases. When such a technique became commonplace, the classical scholars could then point to accounts of the enormous emotional power of music in ancient Greek tragedy. A group of cultivated amateurs in Florence entered into imaginary correspondence with Roman scholars in attempts to revive such musical expression. This group, known as the *Florentine Camerata,* correctly guessed that emotional expression required not only that the text be clearly audible to the listener, but also that the words take precedence over the music. Ultimately this attitude led to the *recitative* of the early Baroque era (see Chapter 14).

Text expression

Summary

The sharp political and economic break with the past represented by the early fourteenth century took some time to be felt in music, even though political concerns are reflected in the texts of the fourteenth-century motets. Humanism, primarily a literary and philosophical movement, was also slow in influencing music, as its effects do not show directly in that art until the sixteenth century. The religious upheavals of the Great Schism and the subsequent conciliar movement, however, brought a large number of foreign musicians to northern Italy and helped to create an international style in the fifteenth century, a style that benefited as well from the invention of printing.

But it eventually dissolved into new national styles as political and religious divisions brought about by the Reformation further separated the European courts in the sixteenth century.

The upbringing and employment of musicians throughout the period was almost exclusively clerical for the singers and lay for the instrumentalists. A sharp division between the chaplains and the minstrels persisted until the sixteenth century, when the prestige of secular music brought the madrigal composer, the instrumentalist, and the instrumental composer into a position of greater social prestige.

Notes

1. Jeanne Marix, *Histoire de la musique et des musiciens de la cour de Bourgogne sous le regne de Philippe le Bon* [1420–1467] (Strasbourg, 1939), pp. 162–163.
2. *Renaissance and Baroque Music: A Comprehensive Survey,* trans. M. D. Herter Norton (New York: W. W. Norton, 1967), pp. 1–2.
3. *The Art of Counterpoint,* trans. Albert Seay. Musicological Studies and Documents, 5 (Rome: American Institute of Musicology, 1961), p. 61.

Bibliography

Studies of the Social and Intellectual History of the Period

HUIZINGA, JOHANN. *The Waning of the Middle Ages.* Garden City, N.Y.:Doubleday, 1954. First published in 1924.
KRISTELLER, PAUL OSKAR. *Renaissance Thought,* 2 vols. New York: Harper & Row, 1961–1965.
PANOFSKY, ERWIN. *Renaissance and Renascences in Western Art.* New York: Harper & Row, 1969.

General Studies of Ars nova and Renaissance Music

BLUME, FRIEDERICH. *Renaissance and Baroque Music: A Comprehensive Survey,* trans. M. D. Herter Norton. New York: W. W. Norton, 1967.
The New Oxford History of Music. Vol. 3, *Ars Nova and the Renaissance, 1300–1540,* ed. Anselm Hughes. Vol. 4, *The Age of Humanism, 1540–1630,* ed. Gerald Abraham. London: Oxford University Press, 1960–1968.
REESE, GUSTAVE. *Music in the Renaissance,* rev. ed. New York: W. W. Norton, 1959.

Musical Life and the Employment of Musicians

D'ACCONE, FRANK A. "The Singers of San Giovanni in Florence in the Fifteenth Century." *Journal of the American Musicological Society* 14 (1961): 307–358.
———. "The Musical Chapels at the Florentine Cathedral and Baptistry During the First Half of the Sixteenth Century." *Journal of the American Musicological Society* 24 (1971): 1–50.
SEAY, ALBERT. "The Fifteenth-Century Cappella at Santa Maria del Fiore." *Journal of the American Musicological Society* 11 (1958): 45–55.

WRIGHT, CRAIG. "Dufay at Cambrai: Discoveries and Revisions." *Journal of the American Musicological Society* 28 (1975): 175–229.

Music Printing

HEARTZ, DANIEL. *Pierre Attaignant: Royal Printer of Music.* Berkeley: University of California Press, 1969.

KING, A. HYATT. *Four Hundred Years of Music Printing,* 2nd ed. London: British Museum, 1968.

POGUE, SAMUEL. *Jacques Moderne: Lyons Music Printer of the Sixteenth Century.* Geneva: Librairie Droz, 1969.

8

The Ars Nova and the Trecento

AS indicated in the previous chapter, cultural changes between the thirteenth and the fourteenth centuries manifested themselves in music only gradually, and the seeds of fourteenth-century style go back to the music composed in and around Paris between 1280 and 1300. Most of these innovations concerned the expansion of the rhythmic language to include shorter notes and duple time, with the consequent expansion of notational systems to indicate the new rhythms with some clarity.

The Breakdown of Franconian Notation

During the late decades of the thirteenth century the motet, particularly its rhythmic structure, underwent a series of changes that pushed the older Franconian notation to its limits. These bespoke the final dissolution of the older rhythmic modes as an organizing force in music.

Petronian notation   Nothing in the music of Petrus de Cruce and his contemporaries—or even that of his immediate successors—cannot be notated using the system propounded by Franco of Cologne in the thirteenth century. Yet their music placed a severe strain on the older notation and finally led to its replacement by the notations proposed in the *Ars nova* of Philippe de Vitry and the *Pomerium* of Marchetto of Padua. Petrus extended the divisions of the *brevis* (in English, "breve") and therefore had to rely on an increased use of the *punctum divisionis* ("dot of division"). With his rhythmic subdivision Petrus created a new note-value. At first it was called *semibrevis minima* ("the smallest semibrevis"), later simply *minima* (in English, "minim"). As the use of *minimae* spread, the Franconian system could not clarify their relationship with the minor (unaltered) and major (altered) *semibreves*. In other words, as composers realized that the minima was indeed a new note, a systematic codification of its relationship to the other notes became necessary, and this

134

the Franconian system did not provide. In the transitional stages, around 1300, the groups of semibreves were apparently interpreted as follows:

■ · ♦ ♦ ♦ ♦ · ■ = ♩ ♫₃ ♫₃ ♩, and   ■ · ♦ ♦ ♦ ♦ · ■ = ♩ ♫₃

♫₃ ♩. Finally, around 1320, a new note-shape for the minima was introduced, ↓, which clarified the internal divisions of the brevis. Now the Franconian system needed major revision, or replacement by a notational system that would account for the new rhythmic divisions.

French *Ars nova* Notation

Vitry and Muris

The earliest theoretical expositions of the new notation in France were the *Ars novae musicae* ("The Art of New Music," 1319) by Johannes de Muris and the *Ars nova* ("The New Music," c. 1320) by Philippe de Vitry. A detailed account of their writings goes beyond what can be attempted here, but the notational hierarchies they established can be summarized.

Both held that any note longer than the minima could be subdivided into two or three equal values, thus placing duple time (*tempus imperfectum*) on the same plane of usability as triple time (*tempus perfectum*). The interrelationship between the *longa* (English, "long") and the brevis—the crucial relationship in the old rhythmic modes—was governed by the *modus,* which could be major (¶ = ■ ■ ■) or minor (¶ = ■ ■). The relationship between the brevis and the semibrevis was governed by the *tempus,* which could be perfect (■ = ♦ ♦ ♦) or imperfect (■ = ♦ ♦). And the relationship between the semibrevis and the minima was governed by the *prolatio,* which could be major (♦ = ↓ ↓ ↓) or minor (♦ = ↓ ↓). Any combination of the three levels was possible. By the early fourteenth century, however, the longa moved so slowly that the modus was virtually imperceptible, and affected only the notation of the slow-moving tenors. The crucial relationships were those of tempus and prolatio, and among them four combinations were possible:

1. Tempus perfectum, prolatio maior	■ = ♦ ♦ ♦ = ↓↓↓ ↓↓↓ ↓↓↓	9/8
2. Tempus perfectum, prolatio minor	■ = ♦ ♦ ♦ = ↓↓ ↓↓ ↓↓	3/4
3. Tempus imperfectum, prolatio maior	■ = ♦ ♦ = ↓↓↓ ↓↓↓	6/8
4. Tempus imperfectum, prolatio minor	■ = ♦ ♦ = ↓↓ ↓↓	2/4

Mensuration signs

Philippe de Vitry proposed two signs to indicate the tempus: O for tempus perfectum, and C for tempus imperfectum. Other writers added prolatio signs, so that the four combinations of tempus and prolatio listed above could be indicated as follows:

	System A	System B	Modern Equivalent
1. Perfect—major	⊙	⊙	$\frac{9}{8}$
2. Perfect—minor	⊙	○	$\frac{3}{4}$
3. Imperfect—major	⊙	₵	$\frac{6}{8}$
4. Imperfect—minor	⊙	C	$\frac{2}{4}$

These signs were little used during Philippe's time, but by the end of the fourteenth century and the beginning of the fifteenth, those in System B had become standard. They are the ancestors of our modern time signatures (e.g., C = $\frac{4}{4}$ today).

In the triple division of the brevis (tempus perfectum) or the semibrevis (prolatio maior) all the old contextual rules for short notes taking some of the value from the longer ones were still in force; now, however, a brevis could be imperfected not only by a semibrevis (○ ■ ♦ = $\frac{3}{4}$ ♩ ♩) but even by a minima (○ ■ ♩ = $\frac{3}{4}$ ♩ ♫). Also, such passages as ○ ■ ■ ■ could mean only: $\frac{3}{4}$ ♩. | ♩. | ♩. |, and in order to write the rhythm $\frac{3}{4}$ ♩ ♩ | ♩ ♩ | the composer had to write the three breves in red rather than black ink. This was known as *coloration*. In tempus imperfectum, or prolatio minor, duple values could be extended 50 percent by the addition of a dot, as is still the practice in modern notation, and triplet subdivision could be achieved by the use of coloration.

Italian Trecento Notation

The music of the early fourteenth century in Italy differed in a number of ways from that of France. Italian composers favored a two-voice texture in which one part was a simple tenor and the other an ornamented voice with elaborate *coloraturas*. This style was fundamentally dependent on a steady metric pulse and strongly influenced the shape of Italian notation.

Division of the brevis

Unlike the French, the Italians considered the brevis an inalterable note that could be divided into a number of semibreves by the use of *puncta divisionis*. In this respect Italian notation was similar to the late Franconian notation used by Petrus de Cruce and his followers. The division of the brevis took place at several levels:

Brevis

1st division	*binaria* (2 notes)	*ternaria* (3 notes)
2nd division	*quaternaria* $\left(4 \text{ notes; } 2 \times 2 = \frac{2}{4}\right)$	*senaria perfecta* $\left(6 \text{ notes; } 3 \times 2 = \frac{3}{4}\right)$
	senaria imperfecta $\left(6 \text{ notes; } 3 \times 2 = \frac{6}{8}\right)$	*novenaria* $\left(9 \text{ notes; } 3 \times 3 = \frac{9}{8}\right)$
3rd division	*octonaria* (8 notes; 2×4)	*duodenaria* (12 notes; 3×4)

The first division was usually theoretical, however, and among the groups of the third division the duodenaria (i.e., division of the brevis into twelve notes) was rarely used. In the few cases when the duodenaria was used it appeared either as indicated above or in an alternate version: 4×3.

The four groups in the second division correspond roughly to the four combinations of tempus and prolatio found in the French notation. The third-division groups represent a fundamental acceleration of the speed of the semibrevis, so that the octonaria is $\frac{2}{4}$, but with ♦ = ♪ rather than ♪, and and duodenaria represents $\frac{3}{4}$, with the same rate of speed for the semibrevis as the octonaria. Divisions were indicated by the use of a letter—q. (quaternaria), p. (senaria perfecta), i. (senaria imperfecta), n. (novenaria), o. (octonaria), and d. (duodenaria).

The music itself seldom contained the full complement of semibreves in any division. In these cases the shorter notes came at the beginning of the division; thus, for example: q. ♦♦♦ = $\frac{2}{4}$ ♫ ♩, or p. ♦♦♦♦ = $\frac{3}{4}$ ♫ ♩ ♩. These internal arrangements of the division did hark back to thirteenth-century rules that had become traditional and were therefore called *via naturae* ("the natural way"). Composers who wanted the shorter notes at the end, or separated by a long note, had to resort to the addition of upward stems to the short notes—for example, q. ♦ ♪♪ = $\frac{2}{4}$ ♩ ♫, or p. ♦ ♪ ♪ = $\frac{3}{4}$ ♩ ♪♩ ♪, and so on. Such divisions were called the *via artis* ("the artificial way") and led to the creation of a host of note-shapes with absolutely fixed meanings. These could be used in the artificial divisions to contain, so to speak, the more ambiguous semibreves in their proper place in the measure.

The most common of these were:

1. ♦ Minima = ½ semibreve
2. ♦ Dragma = ♦ ♦ (used in i. [$\frac{6}{8}$] to indicate hemiola)
3. ♪ — = ♦ ♦ ♦
4. ♪ — = ♪ ♪ ♪
5. ♪ Semiminima = ½ minima

Triplets of minimae were indicated by void notes, i.e., ♩ ♩ ♩ = ♩ ♩, and triplets of semiminimae by turning the flags around, i.e., ♪ ♪ ♪ = ♪ ♪.

As the music of the fourteenth century became rhythmically more intricate, composers in France and Italy developed elaborate variations of these note-shapes and used coloration extensively. In the fifteenth century, with the return of a simpler style, composers realized that their music could be adequately notated with the note-shapes of the French Ars nova alone. Around 1430, copyists began writing the notes in outline, i.e., ■ = □ , ■ = □ , ◆ = ◇ , and ♩ = ♩, leaving ♩ to indicate an even shorter value. Around 1600 the note-heads became rounded (e.g., ◆ = ♩), giving rise to modern note-shapes.

The Isorhythmic Motet

As motets in the new style developed in the early fourteenth century, tenors consisting of a simple series of longs, favored by the composers of the late thirteenth century, obviously could not adequately articulate the structure of the new pieces. This deficiency led composers to adopt *isorhythm,* that is, the partitioning of the tenor melody into a series of segments that had the same rhythmic pattern. In a sense, this innovation was simply an extension of the older principle of modal *ordines,* but fulfilled on a much larger, more complex plane. Examples 8.1 and 8.2 show two examples of isorhythmic tenor.

Colores and taleae   Each repetition in the tenor was called a *color* by the medieval theorists. This term, borrowed from rhetoric, meant a repetition of any kind. Later, however, a distinction was made between melodic repetition, which retained the name "color," and a purely rhythmic repetition, called *talea,* a word meaning "measuring rod." Thus Example 8.1 has one color and five taleae, but Example 8.2 has two colores and six taleae (three in each color).

Another trait of Example 8.2 is that the rhythms of the second color move twice as fast as those of the first. This procedure, called *diminution,* creates the effect of a formal speeding up of the piece, an effect that fourteenth-century composers found exciting.

Ex. 8.1   Tenor of a motet in *Le Roman de Fauvel*

Ex. 8.2   Tenor of a motet by Philippe de Vitry

Le Roman de Fauvel

The earliest extant collection containing motets in the style of the Ars nova is *Le Roman de Fauvel,* the long, satirical poem written between 1310 and 1314 by Gervaise de Bus, with musical interpolations by Chaillou de Pestain. *Fauvel* is essentially an anticlerical satire. The poem's hero is a golden stallion whose name is an anagram of the most common vices of the medieval clergy—*Flatterie, Avarice, Vilanie, Variété* ("faithlessness"), *Envie,* and *Lascheté* ("lechery")—and the miniatures in the manuscript represent him as a horse in clerical garb. In adding the musical interpolations, Chaillou incorporated motets from the old Notre-Dame repertory, Franconian motets, and a number of modern motets including a few by Philippe de Vitry. In addition, Chaillou also included a large number of monophonic interpolations: fifty-four short liturgical chants, fourteen French secular songs, twenty-four conductus, four lais, and thirty-one refrains. Many of the older works were revised to make them appropriate to their new surroundings. Thus the motet *Ad solitum—Regnat,* a moral piece from c. 1220 that ended with *hoc seculum* ("in this day and age"), is provided with a few extra bars of music and extra text: "in this day and age, when Fauvel wears a bishop's ring and a crozier." In sum, the interpolations in *Fauvel* provide a comprehensive picture of the repertory, old and new, sung in Paris around 1300.

Philippe de Vitry

The most important French composer of the early fourteenth century was Philippe de Vitry (1291–1361). A poet, diplomat, musician, and ecclesiastic, Philippe was one of the most learned men of his age. A friend of Petrarch, he was an officer of the French royal household from 1322 to 1351, when he became bishop of Meaux, a title he held until his death. Famed as the virtual creator of the new motet style of the fourteenth century, Vitry is reputed also to have had great influence on secular song. Unfortunately, only one ballade, without music, has survived among his secular songs, and in the case of the motets we have but a fragment of his probable output. Seven motets are ascribed to him, either in manuscripts or by fourteenth-century writers. Eight more are probably his, either because they are very close to his style or

Ex. 8.3   Philippe de Vitry, *Douce playsence—Garison—Neuma*

Ex. 8.3   cont.

Triplum: "It is a sweet pleasure to love loyally, for otherwise lovers could not well suffer that burning pain born of love, when these glances, through their subtle attraction in glancing. . . ."
Motetus: "Relief, naturally, is sought from pain. . . ."
Tenor: Melody of the fifth mode.

because he makes use of them in the *Ars nova*. One motet survives without music, and two others are considered of doubtful authenticity by some scholars.

Vitry's motets show an extraordinary concern for clarity, in both their rhythmic structure and their contrapuntal flow. As in all *cantus firmus* works, the contrapuntal flow is regulated by the tenor. The tenor and the upper voices form a fundamental framework of perfect consonances that is ornamented by the figuration in the upper voices and given cogency and tonal direction by the slower motion of the tenor. Example 8.3 shows the beginning of a motet (*Douce playsence—Garison—Neuma*) that was composed c. 1317–1320 and is ascribed to Vitry. Although the tenor moves so slowly that almost any note could be used to support a cadence, Vitry so plans his cadences that they fall on the *final* or on one of the *cofinals* of the mode, with an occasional cadence on the note above the final for contrast. Similarly, in his choice of tenors Vitry preferred chants with finals on F, C, or G; that is, finals where the normal medieval *gamut* would provide him with a major third above the final.

In comparison with thirteenth-century motets, Vitry's display greater range in the voices and a consequent increase in sonority. In his late motets he often added a fourth voice, which worked with the tenor as part of the slow-moving foundation of the piece. Hence its name: *contratenor*.

Of the texts of Vitry's motets, only one is in French, and so they represent a departure from the prevailing pattern of the previous century. Vitry's texts tend to be moral and admonishing, and his works begin the tradition in which the motet became the learned piece par excellence. Throughout the fourteenth and early fifteenth centuries, composers turned to the motet as the music for important ceremonial occasions.

The Motets of Guillaume de Machaut

The motets of Guillaume de Machaut (c. 1300–1377), the most important composer of the generation after Philippe de Vitry, are clearly part of the tradition begun by Vitry, but they also recall an earlier concept of the motet as an amatory secular genre. Unlike Vitry's works, Machaut's poetry and music are preserved virtually in their entirety, in a series of manuscripts copied under his supervision.

Of Machaut's twenty-three motets, seventeen have French texts and only six have Latin texts. Thus Machaut turns away from Vitry's precedent and looks toward an earlier tradition. In contrast, the musical style of the motets follows Vitry's closely, but even musically Machaut seems to delight in beclouding the tenor structure as much as Vitry had delighted in clarifying it. In addition, Machaut often uses incomplete taleae that throw off the periodic structure of the tenor. His motet *S'il estoit nulz—S'amours—Et gaudebit* ("If there is anyone—If love were—And your heart will rejoice"; *HAM* I, 47), for instance, follows Vitry's style on the surface but presents the listener with all the irregularities typical of his own motet style.

Nevertheless, Machaut extended Vitry's concern for the periodicity of the upper voices toward complete isorhythm in all parts, not only in a few of the motets but also in the motet-like sections of his Mass of Notre-Dame. Here the composer points to the late-fourteenth-century motet.

With their French amatory texts and their curious mixture of archaic and progressive traits, Machaut's motets are essentially outside the mainstream of fourteenth-century music, and very few survive outside the Machaut manuscripts. Apparently they are mostly early works, and clearly they were not his most popular in his time. Machaut realized that polytextual motets were not the best genre for the courtly love texts to which he was so devoted, and he turned his attention instead to the composition of polyphonic songs, using the strophic forms inherited from the trouvères. In these genres his influence and popularity were extraordinary.

Late-Fourteenth-Century Motets

French motet composers of the generations after Machaut followed the tradition of Philippe de Vitry both in their choice of ceremonial, devotional, or admonishing texts and in their preference for Latin, although a few French motets survive as well. The late motets also carry the concern for periodicity one step further and show isorhythm in all voices. The result, however, is not always an increase in structural clarity; the tenor of some of the late motets is at times extraordinarily intricate, with colores presented in *retrograde* motion for some sections. In addition, the rigid isorhythm of the upper parts cannot always accommodate the shifting word accents of the poetry, and the results are some of the most problematic pieces in the entire repertory, such as *Alpha vibrans—Coetus—(Contra)—Amicus* (*OxMM*, no. 59). In short, the totally isorhythmic motets of the late fourteenth century are more schematic, but not necessarily more clearly organized, than those of Philippe de Vitry or Guillaume de Machaut. Nevertheless, in the hands of a skilled composer the totally isorhythmic motet can combine audible clarity with complex rhythmic and formal schemes to splendid effect.

Song Forms

Although Philippe de Vitry composed ballades, lais, and rondeaux, the extensive cultivation of polyphonic song in France began with Machaut. To be sure, Adam de la Halle had written a number of polyphonic rondeaux in the late thirteenth century, and the Ivrea codex shows a few works that seem to represent one of the earliest stages of polyphonic secular song in France. These are three-part unison canons with texts that describe hunting or rustic scenes, and make use of hockets imitating hunting cries or bird songs. Appropriately, they are called *chaces* ("hunts").

The chace

The popularity of the chace in France was apparently short-lived, but its lively textures survived in a number of later virelais that have rustic texts and make use of bird-call imitations. In addition, Italian composers adapted the chace by making it a two-part canon supported by an instrumental tenor and dealing with the same topics as the chace. The *caccia*, as the Italians called their form, was cultivated throughout the fourteenth century.

Machaut's songs

Machaut's first steps were the elimination of the motet's *triplum* and the replacement of the plainsong tenor by a freely composed voice that mainly supported the vocal part. This innovation led to a tenor that moved considerably faster than that of the motet and was far more closely tied to the texted vocal part by the rules of *discant*. To these structural voices Machaut added in subsequent pieces an instrumental triplum. An even later development was the elimination of this triplum and the use instead of a *contratenor*, a voice that was as active as the older tripla but did not interfere with the range of the uppermost voice, or *cantus*. Some of the songs—for example, the ballade *De petit po*—have alternate parts; some sources transmit a triplum and others a contratenor. Although a few manuscripts have both, these voices clearly were not meant to be performed simultaneously. Later sources show that in a few other songs, an old contratenor was replaced by a new one. Finally, Machaut did write a few four-part songs, such as the rondeau *Tant doulcement* ("So sweetly"; *OxMM,* no. 71); these are among his most elaborate works. By the end of the fourteenth century, however, the standard texture for the secular song was fixed as cantus, tenor, and contratenor—a combination that endured until the end of the fifteenth century.

Formal traits   In the absence of a slow-moving plainsong tenor to regulate the overall shapes of the music, this function was fulfilled by the forms of the poetry itself. Most of the poetic forms required the repetition of one or two sections of the music, and different cadences made clear the difference between the first and second statement. By the middle of the fourteenth century, as the song style had crystallized, the favored ending tones were the note above the final for the *ouvert,* or first ending, and the final itself for the *clos,* or second ending.

The ballade   The principal poetic forms that Machaut and later composers set to music were the *ballade,* the *virelai,* and the *rondeau.* Each was characterized by a specific interaction between music and poetry, but within each there were a number of possible variations, particularly in respect to the number of verses and the rhyme schemes. The following patterns, however, can be taken as typical of each form.

As a poetic form, the ballade usually consisted of two to three stanzas of seven or eight lines each. The text of the last line, or sometimes of the last two lines, constituted the refrain and was repeated in each stanza. The rhyme scheme of the first four lines was usually ab ab, but thereafter the ballades varied from poem to poem. The last two lines, at least in the early and middle fourteenth century ballades, usually have the same rhyme. An example of the poetic and musical structure of the ballade is the first stanza of Machaut's *Se quanque amours:*

Music	Line	Rhyme	Text
A	1	a	*Se quanque amours puet doner a ami,*
	2	b	*Et quanque cuer d'ami puet desirer,*
A	3	a	*Et quanque dame y porroit mettre aussi*
	4	b	*De bien, de pais, par loyaument amer,*
B	5	c	*Estoient entièrement*
	6	c	*En un suel cuer, je scay certeinement*
	7	d	*Qu'il sentiroit grief, tristesse et esmay*
	8	d	*Contre le bien e la joie que j'ay.* (refrain)
			(If all that love can give a lover,
			And all that a lover's heart could wish,
			And all that a lady could also add
			Of happiness, of peace, for loving loyal,
			Were all contained
			In a single heart, I know certainly
			That it would still feel grief, sadness, and dismay,
			Compared with the joys I have.)

The most common variant of this scheme is a seven-line stanza, ab ab b cc. In some ballades, such as Machaut's *De toutes flours* ("Of all flowers"), the music at the end of lines 2 and 4 is repeated to end the final line.

The virelai
The *virelai,* or *chanson balladée,* is a poem in which a refrain, usually of two lines, alternates with a series of stanzas. A stanza consists of two rhyming lines, plus two more that rhyme with the refrain. The result is the following scheme:

	Refrain	Stanza	Refrain
Text rhyme:	aa	bb aa	aa
Music:	A	BB A	A

Several textual expansions of this scheme, which could alter the rhymes of the stanza and the number of lines for each section, were also used. Two common variants are:

Music:	A	B B	A	A
Text rhyme:	ab ab	ca ca	ab ab	ab ab
Text rhyme:	aa	bc bc	ca	aa

Rhyme variation and the change in the number of lines are more frequent in the virelais than in the ballades. A popular subgenre of the virelai was one in which texts incorporated bird-songs, often set to elaborate hockets. An example (see Example 8.4) is Jean Vaillant's *Par maintes fois.*

The rondeau
The *rondeau* is the most stable of the musico-poetic forms of the fourteenth century. At its simplest it consists of an eight-line poem set to two strains of music as follows: AB aA ab AB. In this diagram, capital letters indicate a refrain text set to the two strains of music; lower-case letters indicate new text set to the same music. Expansions of the rondeau were achieved by substituting two, three, or more lines of text for each of the eight lines of the simpler basic scheme.

The lai
One additional category of secular song became important in the fourteenth century, only because it was extensively cultivated by Machaut. This was the *lai,* which was probably derived from the medieval *prose* and had been cultivated by thirteenth-century poets and composers. Its structure is far less stable than that of the other forms, but its salient trait is the chainlike succession of monorhymic stanzas of two, three, or four lines that follow no definite pattern and can change in number within a given piece. Each group of lines is set to the same music. For instance:

Music:	AA′	BB′	C	DDD′	EE′	etc.
Text:	aa	bb	c	ddd	ee	etc.

Ex. 8.4   Jean Vaillant, *Par maintes fois*

"Fi, oci, oci, oci, fi, fi. Fie on any cuckoo who wants to speak of love."

As the example indicates, an occasional single line was also used. Most of Machaut's lais are monophonic, though a few make use of polyphony. With one or two exceptions, no composers after Machaut wrote lais.

Machaut's Songs

Machaut left a song repertory considerably larger than that of any of his contemporaries, probably because of the care with which he had his works copied and edited. We have forty-two ballades, thirty-three virelais, twenty-one rondeaux, nineteen lais, one *complainte* (lament), and one *chanson royal* (royal, or kingly, song).

The complainte, the chanson royal, and most of the lais and virelais are monophonic, and despite their "modern" rhythmic language they hark back to the art of the thirteenth-century trouvères (see the lai *J'aim la flour* ["I love the flower"], *OxMM*, no. 69). Two of the lais, the *Lai de la fontaine* and the *Lai de confort,* alternate between monophonic sections and three-part canons. Two more have also been found to be polyphonic in that each pair of lines can be sung simultaneously.

Much shorter than the lais, the virelais recall even more the trouvère songs, with their simple declamatory style and very clear melodic shapes. Those of *Douce dame jolie* ("Sweet beautiful lady," Example 8.5) seem to approach folk music. Seven of Machaut's virelais are polyphonic, but their polyphony is extremely simple, as in *Se je souspir* ("If I sigh"; *OxMM,* no. 69) or *Plus dure* ("Harder"; *HAM* I, no. 46b).

In contrast, the rondeaux show an extraordinary variety of textures. Two are for two voices, two are for four voices, and the others are for three voices. The two-voice rondeaux, such as *Douce dame jolie* (a different text from that of Example 8.5), seem early and may represent the first stages of the adaptation of motet polyphony to the secular song. In the three- and four-part rondeaux, particularly in such works as *Tant doulcement* Machaut achieves rhythmic textures of great variety and subtlety, as well as a rich sonority characteristic of the ballades.

The ballades are Machaut's most elaborately composed song forms. Most **Machaut's** of the first sixteen are bipartite, and their tenors recall the slow-moving motet **ballades** tenors. But the later ballades are invariably in three or four parts. The early three-part works usually have an instrumental triplum, suggesting again the adaptation of traditional motet texture, but later ballades have instead a contratenor.

Ex. 8.5   Guillaume de Machaut, *Douce dame jolie*

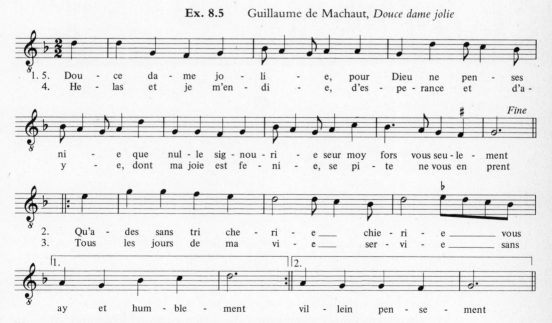

"Sweet and beautiful lady, for God's sake, do not think that anyone else has any claims on me except you alone. For always, without trickery, I have cherished you humbly. All the days of my life I have served you without evil thought. Alas, I beg in hope and anguish, since my joy is ended if you do not take pity. Sweet and beautiful lady. . . ."

Nature presenting her children Sensibility, Rhetoric, and Music to Guillaume de Machaut. (Français 1584 [Machaut MS A], fol. E; Bibliothèque Nationale, Paris)

In the late ballades, as well as in the more elaborate rondeaux, Machaut's rhythmic and melodic ornamentation of the two-voice framework reaches a level of extraordinary complexity and sophistication. Rhythmic displacements and accented dissonances produce a pungent, colorful harmonic style that veils the contrapuntal framework without obscuring its basic drive. In the absence of large-scale tenor patterns, the cadences, governed by the text structure, become extremely important, and Machaut takes extreme care to create patterns consistent with the internal cadences.

Italian Song Forms

The flowering of secular polyphony in Italy during the fourteenth century also produced its own distinctive forms. Although some are related to the French forms, the resemblances are often incidental. The principal Italian song forms are the madrigal, the *caccia,* and the *ballata.*

The madrigal was the earliest to be set extensively to polyphony. Madrigal texts deal not only with courtly love, but also with mythological, moral, and ceremonial topics, and they tend to be both serious and expressive.

The madrigal

Poetically, the madrigal consists of two to four stanzas of three lines each, with lines of seven or eleven syllables, followed by a two-line *ritornello.* Despite the implication of its name, the ritornello does not return; it is simply a concluding section. Rhyme patterns vary not only from poem to poem but even from one stanza to another within a single madrigal. But the two lines of the ritornello usually rhyme. The stanzas are sung to the same music, with a new strain for the ritornello, giving the form AAB to the two-stanza madrigal, and AAAB to the three-stanza composition. Occasionally madrigals have two *ritornelli,* e.g., AAA BB.

Madrigals were usually composed for two voices, with an elaborate upper part over a simpler tenor. Both voices were probably intended to be sung, although instrumental performance of the tenor, not always given the full text, was also possible. The coloraturas in the upper voice could be very elaborate. Example 8.6, from a madrigal by Donato da Firenze (fl. 1380), is typical. The few surviving three-voice madrigals are all exceptional works. They are canonic, like the caccia; tri-textual, like Jacopo da Bologna's *Aquil' al tera —Creatura gentil—Uccel di dio* (*OxMM,* no. 76); or share the isorhythmic structure of the motet, like Landini's famous *Si dolce non sono* ("So sweetly did not Orpheus sound"; *HAM* I, no. 54).

The caccia resembles the French *chace* in its canonic structure, the rustic nature of the texts, and the use of hockets and onomatopoeia, but unlike the chace, the caccia is a two-part canon supported by a free tenor. The texts vary from blank verse to rhymed verse in the manner of the madrigal, and conclude with a ritornello that is usually set to a new canon. Therefore the musical shape of the caccia—Canon A, Canon B—resembles that of the canonic madrigal.

The caccia

The ballata is an exact counterpart of the French virelai. Like the virelai, it consists of a stanza (subdivided into two *pedes* and a *volta*) surrounded by a refrain (*ripresa*). Also like the virelai, the ballata may have several stanzas. Its simplest form is as follows:

The ballata

Ballata text and music:	R	P P	V	R
Virelai text and music:	A	B b	a	A

Ex. 8.6   Donato da Firenze, *L'aspido sordo*

L'a - - - - - - - pi - do ___ sor - do e'l tir - el - lo scor - zo - - - - - - - - ne

"The deaf adder and the bark worm. . . ."

Each formal element in this scheme may occupy from one to three lines. A common trait, however, is that the pedes are shorter than the ripresa or the volta (e.g., AAA BB bb AAA AAA). The ballata repertory is divided between two- and three-part works.

Chronology of forms   Madrigals were favored by the early trecento composers. Most stem from the decades around 1350 and are for two voices. With Landini's music there is a shift toward the ballata and also toward three-part writing. Some of the later composers wrote almost exclusively ballate. Virtually every composer also wrote caccie, but no one produced more than one or two of them except for Maestro Piero (fl. 1340), who cultivated this form more extensively.

Composers of the middle generations of the trecento cultivated secular song almost to the exclusion of the motet. Only one motet survives, and it is an atypical one, by Jacopo da Bologna: *Lux purpurata—Diligite iustiam/* (Tenor). We also have a few fragments of some by Landini.

Trecento Composers

The earliest generation of trecento composers is dominated by three figures. Of Maestro Piero, probably the oldest, we know only that his works are dominated by canonic technique. Johannes de Florentia (known also as Giovanni da Cascia) was organist at the Florentine cathedral of Santa Maria del Fiore from 1329 to 1351. His works include eighteen madrigals, two caccie, and one ballata, and he was the first of the trecento composers to achieve wide fame. Jacopo da Bologna, a contemporary of Johannes and probably also the teacher of Landini, has left us thirty-one madrigals, one caccia, one motet, and one *lauda* in ballata form.

Johannes and Jacopo are among the finest composers of the century. In their work the madrigal is crystallized as a serious and reserved genre with remarkable subtlety and expressive power. Jacopo's *Non al suo amante* ("Not did Diana ever please her lover"; *HAM* I, no. 49), one of his best works, is perhaps the earliest surviving setting of a Petrarch poem. Two other composers of this time were Bartolino da Padova and Lorenzo da Firenze, capable of writing extraordinary works, even if less consistently than Jacopo and Johannes.

The figure of Francesco Landini (c. 1325–1397) dominates the middle generation. Blind from childhood as a result of smallpox, Landini developed not only extraordinary musical skills but those of a poet and a philosopher as well. In Landini's music we also see incipient French influence in such devices as hockets and in the isorhythm of works like *Si dolce non sono*.

Together with Landini, some composers of the generation remained faithful to the older style, albeit with greatly expanding coloratura writing. An example is Donato da Cascia (fl. 1380), who left sixteen very intricate madrigals (see Example 8.6 above) and one ballata. Slightly earlier is Gherardello da Firenze (d. 1364), whose works continued the tradition of Johannes and Jacopo.

Later composers include Niccolò da Perugia, Paolo da Firenze (also known as Paolo Tenorista), and Andrea dei Servi (d. 1415). Paolo was a traditional composer whose works sustained the madrigal tradition, but in Niccolò and Andrea we find a shift to the ballata and the pervading influence of French music.

Marginal notes:
Maestro Piero

J. de Florentia and J. da Bologna

Landini

Later composers

Francesco Landini playing the *organetto,* and the cantus and tenor of his madrigal Musica son. (Palatinus 87 [squarcialupi Codex], fol. 122v; Biblioteca Medicea Laurenziana, Florence)

The Late Ars nova and the Transition in France and Italy

Composers
During the last thirty years of the fourteenth century, an important group of composers began to move away from the formal clarity of the motets of Philippe de Vitry and the songs of Machaut. These composers seem to have been more interested in twisting the basic frameworks of the style to achieve expressive ends. Some, like Solage (fl. 1380), used extreme chromaticism to obscure the contrapuntal framework (see Example 8.7). Others, like Matteo da Perugia (d. 1411) and Jacob de Senleches (fl. 1380), overlaid the basic con-

Ex. 8.7 Solage, *Fumeux*

"Fu - - - meux _____"

"Smoky smokes. . . ."

trapuntal structure with layers of cross-rhythms (see Example 8.8). Most of these extremely complex works are *grandes ballades,* in which the composers display their learning and subtlety. A fine example of the genre is Senleches's *En attendant esperance* ("While waiting, hope"; *HAM* I, no. 47). The virelais and rondeaux of these composers, however, show a much simpler style.

In northern France and what is today Belgium, composers preserved the simpler style of Machaut and subjected it to further harmonic purification. The earliest of these northerners is Johannes Ciconia (c. 1370–1411), from Liège, who traveled south and died in Padua as a cathedral canon. Ciconia's works reflect the mixture of styles at the turn of the fifteenth century. *I cani sono fuora* is a classic madrigal in the Italian manner; *Sus une fontaine* ("Under a fountain"; *OxMM,* no. 73) is fiercely complex, and his later motets and Mass sections (see *HAM* I, no. 55) reveal the clarity and balance of northern music at the beginning of the fifteenth century.

The northern school

By the end of the fourteenth century, the northern school began to make its influence felt, not only in France but also in Italy. Composers such as Baude Cordier, Johannes Carmen, Johannes Tapissier, and Johannes Cesaris (see Chapter 9) shifted to a simpler rhythmic style (see Cordier's *Amans ames* ["Lovers, love"], *HAM* I, no. 48).

Ex. 8.8   Matteo da Perugia, excerpt from a ballade

"Except in appearance. . . ."

Italy   In Italy, probably through the influence of Ciconia and men like Cordier, who met the Italian composers at Avignon, the northern influence began to exert itself, and such works as Andrea dei Servi's *Sotto candido vel* (Example 8.9) could well pass for a piece by a northerner.

Liturgical Music

Despite the papal bull of 1324–1325 condemning the use of the modern style in Church music, composers in the second half of the fourteenth century

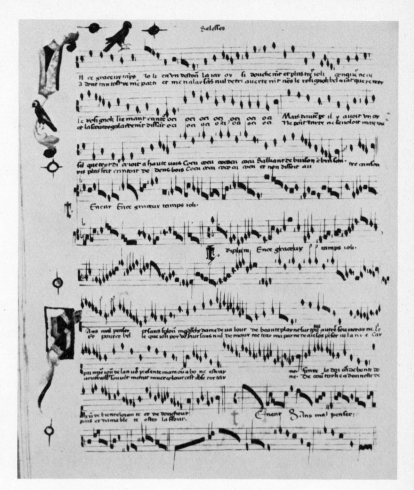

Virelai: *En ce gracieux tamps,* by Jacob de Selesses, a sample of *Ars subtilior* notation. (M. 5, fol. 25v; Biblioteca Estense, Modena)

turned their attention again to music for the liturgy, which had taken second place to secular music during the thirteenth and early fourteenth centuries. In contrast to the Notre-Dame composers, who had chosen to set the responsorial Propers of the Mass, Ars nova composers devoted themselves to the Ordinary of the Mass.

The composition of unified cycles of five or six movements, however, was not a concern of fourteenth-century musicians, and rarely have more than one or two Mass sections by any one composer survived. The famous Mass of Notre-Dame by Guillaume de Machaut is the exception. In addition, we have four cycles apparently compiled by scribes. These are the so-called Masses of Tournai (probably the earliest), Barcelona, Besançon, and Toulouse—often the only polyphonic Mass music in the sources that transmit them as a cycle. In sources rich in this kind of repertory, however, the Mass sections are grouped by category; that is, all Kyries, all Glorias, etc., are copied together.

Mass sections

Ex. 8.9   Andrea dei Servi, *Sotto candido vel*

"Under a white veil. . . ."

Style   Most fourteenth-century Mass settings are stylistically derived from other music categories, principally the old conductus and the isorhythmic motet. In this sense the Machaut Mass is typical. The long texts, Gloria and Credo, are set in simultaneous (i.e., conductus) style with little ornamentation, but the Kyrie, Sanctus, Agnus Dei, and *Ite missa est* are elaborate isorhythmic motets with appropriate Mass chants as their tenors. In addition, the *Amen* section of both the Gloria and Credo are in motet style. A few Mass sections by Machaut's contemporaries, particularly those set to the *Ite missa est,* carry the motet style to the point of having trope texts in the upper voices. Composers also turned to secular forms for models, and we have a number of Mass sections in chanson style, such as the Agnus Dei in Example 8.10.

English Fourteenth-Century Music

Early in the century   Extant English polyphony prior to the fourteenth century is characterized by (1) the extensive use of *exchange of voices;* (2) a preference for interval combinations that include a third above the bass; (3) the use of repeating tenors

Ex. 8.10   From an Agnus Dei in the Apt manuscript

"Lamb of God. . . ."

that border on the *ostinato*—the English *pes;* and (4) the virtual avoidance of vernacular texts and secular topics from the motet repertory. These traits, accompanied by a conservative attitude toward the rhythmic surface of the music, were carried over into the fourteenth century, albeit with some modifications. These, however, were essentially expansions of older traits. And as the range of the polyphonic framework extended beyond one octave, exchange of voices became more problematic and therefore less frequent. Some works, however, contain enormously long phrases with exchange of voices.

Styles

The expansion of the contrapuntal frame also led to an increase in the use of such interval combinations as $\frac{6}{3}$ and $\frac{10}{5}$ instead of the simpler $\frac{5}{3}$ of the earlier music. These combinations not only increased the sonority and variety of the music, but the $\frac{6}{3}$, far less stable than the other combinations, also increased the melodic drive and contrapuntal tension of the English style. The $\frac{6}{3}$ was used most frequently in simple settings in *cantilena* style, the English counterpart of the chanson style in continental music. In the uses of the *cantus firmus,* the pes technique was expanded in motets that combine repeated tenor patterns with variation technique in the upper voices.

Far more important from the point of view of later developments was the English practice of placing the tenor in the middle voice, providing it with a note-against-note "counter" below and a voice variously called *triplex* or *mean* above (see Example 8.11). This format permitted a harmonic reinterpretation of any given tenor note, and thus the composer was allowed to control the harmonic flow of the music even more effectively than by the continental procedure of placing the tenor at the bottom of the texture.

Isorhythm

Isorhythm made few inroads in England in the early and middle fourteenth century, although such isorhythmic pieces as *O homo considera*—*O homo de pulvere*—(Contra)—*Filiae Jerusalem* (*OxMM,* no. 50) survive in a very archaic style. Most English fourteenth-century motets are isoperiodic instead; that is, they use tenor phrases of the same length but with different internal rhythmic organizations. In the late fourteenth century, however, we do encounter elaborate English isorhythmic works, such as the fiercely complex isorhythmic motets and Mass sections of the Old Hall Manuscript.

Ex. 8.11 Leonel Power, *Beata progenies*

"O holy offspring. . . ."

Sources of English Music

Old Hall   Apart from the Old Hall Manuscript (now British Library, Add. MS. 57,950), most sources are simply fragments of manuscripts preserved in bindings, the scattered remains of a once-rich tradition. Far more complete is the Old Hall Manuscript, a well-preserved collection of sacred and devotional music copied in the early fifteenth century and containing a vast amount of music from c. 1370 to c. 1430. It is not only the best source for the late English fourteenth century but also preserves the works of the English generation that ushered in the new sound which was to change the course of musical development in Europe in the fifteenth century. The fourteenth-century works in Old Hall reveal a combination of rhythmic and melodic styles, with some traits seemingly imported from the Continent, but the combination remains a uniquely English version of the late-fourteenth-century style.

Summary

The fourteenth century in France is characterized by the emergence of isorhythm as a structural principle in motet composition; by the rise of polyphonic secular song in fixed forms, probably as a result of Machaut's influence; and by the first attempts since the eleventh century to compose polyphonic music for the Ordinary of the Mass. As the center of musical life shifted from the north to the southern courts, an extremely complex rhythmic style evolved, which finally spent itself around 1400, when the northern style resumed prominence.

In Italy an extraordinary flowering of secular music contained florid vocal ornamentation and utilized its own individual notational procedures and poetic forms. The uniquely Italian style barely survived past the turn of the fifteenth century. It was absorbed by an international style that originated in northern France.

In England the fourteenth century witnessed far less drastic musical changes. Traditional forms and procedures were expanded and combined with techniques imported from abroad, to be examined presently.

Bibliography

Books and Articles

General

The New Oxford History of Music. Vol. 3, *Ars Nova and the Renaissance, 1300–1540,* ed. Anselm Hughes. London: Oxford University Press, 1960.
STRUNK, OLIVER. *Source Readings in Music History from Classical Antiquity Through the Romantic Era.* New York: W. W. Norton, 1950.

Franconian and Ars Nova Notation

APEL, WILLI. *The Notation of Polyphonic Music, 900–1600,* 5th rev. ed. Cambridge, Mass.: Medieval Academy of America, 1961.
PARRISH, CARL. *The Notation of Medieval Music.* New York: W. W. Norton, 1959.

Philippe de Vitry and Guillaume de Machaut

GOMBOSI, OTTO. "Machaut's Messe Nostre Dame." *The Musical Quarterly* 36 (1950): 204–224 (errata, p. 466).
HOPPIN, RICHARD H. "Notational Licenses of Guillaume de Machaut." *Musica disciplina* 14 (1960): 13–27.
PERLE, GEORGE. "Integrative Devices in the Music of Machaut." *The Musical Quarterly* 34 (1948): 169–176.
REANEY, GILBERT. "A Chronology of the Ballades, Rondeaux, and Virelais Set to Music by Guillaume de Machaut." *Musica disciplina* 6 (1952): 33–38.
————. "Fourteenth Century Harmony and the Ballades, Rondeaux, and Virelais of Guillaume de Machaut." *Musica disciplina* 7 (1953): 129–146.
————. *Guillaume de Machaut.* Oxford Studies of Composers, 9. London: Oxford University Press, 1971.
————. "Machaut's Influence on Late Medieval Music. I: France and Burgundy. II: The Non-Gallic Countries." *Monthly Musical Record* 88 (1958): 50–58, 96–101.
————. "The Ballades, Rondeaux, and Virelais of Guillaume de Machaut: Melody, Rhythm, and Form." *Acta musicologica* 27 (1955): 40–58.
————. "The *Lais* of Guillaume de Machaut and Their Background." *Proceedings of the Royal Musical Association* 82 (1955–1956): 15–32.
————. "The Poetic Form in Machaut's Works." *Musica disciplina* 13 (1959): 21–41.
————. "Voices and Instruments in the Music of Guillaume de Machaut." *Revue belge de musicologie* 10 (1956): 3–17, 93–104.
SANDERS, ERNEST H. "The Early Motets of Philippe de Vitry." *Journal of the American Musicological Society* 28 (1975): 24–45.
————. "Vocal Scoring in the Works of Guillaume de Machaut." *Journal of the American Musicological Society* 21 (1968): 251–257.

French Song Forms

REANEY, GILBERT. "Concerning the Origins of the Rondeau, Virelai, and Ballade Forms." *Musica disciplina* 6 (1952): 155–166.
————. "The Development of the Rondeau, Virelai, and Ballade Forms from Adam de la Halle to Guillaume de Machaut." *Festschrift Karl Gustav Fellerer zum 60. Geburstag,* ed. Heinrich Huschen. Regensburg: Gustav Bosse, 1962. Pp. 421–427.
WILKINS, NIGEL, ed. *One Hundred Ballades, Rondeaux, and Virelais from the Late Middle Ages.* Cambridge, Eng.: Cambridge University Press, 1969.
————. "The Structure of Ballades, Rondeaux, and Virelais in Froissart and Christine de Pisan." *French Studies* 23 (1969): 337–348.

The Italian Trecento

ELLINWOOD, LEONARD. "Francesco Landini and His Music." *The Musical Quarterly* 22 (1936): 190–216.
FISCHER, KURT VON. "On the Technique, Origin, and Evolution of Italian Trecento Music." *The Musical Quarterly* 47 (1961): 41–57.

MARROCCO, W. THOMAS. "The Ballata: A Metamorphic Form." *Acta musicologica* 31 (1959): 32–37.

———. "The Fourteenth-Century Madrigal: Its Form and Content." *Speculum* 26 (1951): 449–457.

SCHACHTER, CARL. "Landini's Treatment of Consonance and Dissonance: A Study in Fourteenth-Century Counterpoint." *Music Forum* 2 (1970): 130–186.

The Late Ars Nova

GÜNTHER, URSULA. "The Fourteenth-Century Motet and Its Development." *Musica disciplina* 12 (1958): 27–58.

REANEY, GILBERT. "The Isorhythmic Motet and Its Social Background." *Gesellschaft für Musikforschung, Bericht über den Internationalaen Musikwissenschaftlichen Kongress, Kassel, 1962,* ed. Georg Reichert and Martin Just. Kassel: Barenreiter, 1963. Pp. 25–27.

Liturgical Music

JACKSON, ROLAND. "Musical Interrelationships Between Fourteenth-Century Mass Movements." *Acta musicologica* 29 (1957): 54–64.

STÄBLEIN-HARDER, HANNA. *Fourteenth-Century Mass Music in France.* Musicological Studies and Documents, 7. Rome: American Institute of Musicology, 1962.

English Music, Cypriot Music

BENT, MARGARET. "Sources of the Old Hall Manuscript." *Proceedings of the Royal Musical Association* 94 (1967–1968): 19–35.

BUKOFZER, MANFRED. *Studies in Medieval and Renaissance Music.* New York: W. W. Norton, 1950.

HARRISON, FRANK LL. *Music in Medieval Britain.* London: Routledge & Kegan Paul, 1958.

SANDERS, ERNEST H. "Cantilena and Discant in Fourteenth-Century England." *Musica disciplina* 19 (1965): 7–52.

Editions and Facsimiles

APEL, WILLI, ed. *French Secular Compositions of the Fourteenth Century;* ed. of the literary texts by Samuel N. Rosenberg. 3 vols. Corpus mensurabilis musicae, 53. Rome: American Institute of Musicology, 1970–1972.

———. *French Secular Music of the Late Fourteenth Century.* Cambridge, Mass.: Medieval Academy of America, 1950.

AUBRY, PIERRE. *Le Roman de Fauvel.* Paris: Société des Anciens Textes Français, 1907. Facsimile.

ELLINWOOD, LEONARD. *The Works of Francesco Landini.* Cambridge, Mass.: Medieval Academy of America, 1939.

GASTOUÉ, AMÉDÉE. *Le Manuscrit de musique du trésor d'Apt.* Publications de la Société Française de Musicologie, ser. 1, vol. 10. Paris: Droz, 1936.

GUNTHER, URSULA. *The Motets of Manuscripts Chantilly, Musée Condé, 564 (olim 1047) and Modena, Biblioteca Estense, a. M. 5. 24* (olim lat. 568). Corpus mensurabilis musicae, 39. Rome: American Institute of Musicology, 1965.

HOPPIN, RICHARD H. *The Cypriot French Repertory of the Manuscript Torino, Biblioteca Nazionale, J. II. 9,* 4 vols. Corpus mensurabilis musicae, 21. Rome: American Institute of Musicology, 1960–1963.

HUGHES, ANDREW, and BENT, MARGARET. *The Old Hall Manuscript,* 3 vols. (in 4). Corpus mensurabilis musicae, 46. Rome: American Institute of Musicology, 1969–1973.

LUDWIG, FRIEDERICH, and BESSELER, HEINRICH. *Guillaume de Machaut, Musikalische Werke,* 4 vols. Leipzig: Breitkopf & Hartel, 1926–1929, 1954. Vol. 4 was published by Besseler in 1954 from Ludwig's papers.

MARROCCO, W. THOMAS. *Fourteenth-Century Italian Cacce,* 2nd ed. Cambridge, Mass.: Medieval Academy of America, 1961.

————. *The Music of Jacopo da Bologna.* University of California Publications in Music, 5. Berkeley and Los Angeles: University of California Press, 1954.

PIRROTTA, NINO. *The Music of Fourteenth-Century Italy,* 5 vols. Corpus mensurabilis musicae, 8. Rome: American Institute of Musicology, 1954–1964.

REANEY, GILBERT. *The Manuscript London, British Museum Additional 29 987,* Musicological Studies and Documents, 13. Rome: American Institute of Musicology, 1965. Facsimile.

SCHRADE, LEO; HARRISON, FRANK LL.; and VON FISCHER, KURT, general eds. *Polyphonic Music of the Fourteenth Century.* Monaco: Editions de L'Oiseau Lyre, 1956–   . Eventually to be 24 vols. The following have appeared: 1. *The Roman de Fauvel, The Works of Philippe de Vitry, French Cycles of the Ordinarium Missae,* ed. Schrade (1956). 2–3. *The Works of Guillaume de Machaut,* ed. Schrade (1956). 4. *The Works of Francesco Landini,* ed. Schrade (1958). 5. *Motets of French Provenance,* ed. Harrison; French texts ed. Elizabeth Ritson; notes on Latin texts by A. G. Rigg (1968). 6–11. *Italian Secular Music,* ed. W. Thomas Marrocco (1967–1978). 12. *Italian Sacred Music,* ed. von Fischer and F. Alberto Gallo (1976). 14. *English Music of the Thirteenth and Early Fourteenth Centuries,* ed. Ernest H. Sanders (1979). 15. *Motets of English Provenance,* ed. Frank Ll. Harrison, texts edited and translated by Peter Lefferts (1980).

STÄBLEIN-HARDER, HANNA. *Fourteenth-Century Mass Music in France.* Corpus mensurabilis musicae, 29. Rome: American Institute of Musicology, 1962.

VECCHI, GIUSEPPE. *Il canzoniere musicale del Codice Vaticano Rossi 215, con uno studio sulla melodica italiana del Trecento,* Monumenta lyrica medii aevi Italica, III. Mensurabilia, 2. Bologna: Università degli Studi, 1966. Facsimile.

WILKINS, NIGEL. *A Fourteenth-Century Repertory from the Codex Reina (Paris, Bibl. Nat. Nouv. Aqu. Fr. 6771).* Corpus mensurabilis musicae, 36. Rome: American Institute of Musicology, 1966.

WOLF, JOHANNES. *Der Squarcialupi Codex, Pal. 87 der Biblioteca Mediceo Laurenziana zu Florenz.* Lippstadt: Fr. Kistner and C. F. W. Siegel, 1955. This is a posthumous work, fraught with problems.

9
The Early Renaissance

$\mathcal{S}$PECIFIC innovations of the early fourteenth century did not affect music as dramatically as those of the turn of the fifteenth century. Most likely these later changes resulted from meetings of continental and English composers at the Church councils, and from the continental composers' fascination with the mellifluous sound of the otherwise old-fashioned style of the English art. The adaptation of this sound by continental composers ushered in that new era which Tinctoris mentions in his *Liber de arte contrapuncti*. And the change appeared so drastic to contemporary ears that, as Tinctoris pointed out, music written before it no longer seemed worthy. The name given the new sound by the poet Martin le Franc was *la contenance angloise* ("the English countenance"), an appropriate sobriquet that may well serve as the central theme of this chapter.

Forms and Styles in the Old Hall Manuscript

Three styles   In the course of the fourteenth century three distinct styles evolved in England. The first, known as *English discant,* sets an unornamented plainsong with a note-against-note counter below and a slightly ornamented triplex above (see Chapter 8, Example 8.11). In the second style, known as *chanson style,* an ornamented triplex is set against a simple tenor and provided with a contratenor to fill in the harmonies. In its bare essentials the chanson style is, as its name implies, similar to that of the secular songs of the second half of the fourteenth century. In addition, English composers cultivated a mixture of discant and chanson styles in works where the triplex is still the main melodic voice but where other parts are smoother and more active than in the discant settings. The *mixed style* avoids the melodic angularity of discant settings and the rhythmic extravagances of some of the works in chanson style.

If the tenor in a chanson–style piece is a plainsong, the piece lends itself to complex isorhythmic treatment. Many such pieces were freely composed, some with a second or third triplex, often canonically derived from the first.

162

Many chanson-style and mixed-style pieces contain an alternation of duets with three- or four-voice passages.

All these styles are present in the main surviving source of early fifteenth-century English music, the Old Hall Manuscript. This codex, copied in the first quarter of the fifteenth century, transmits a repertory of forty Glorias, thirty-five Credos, twenty-seven Sanctus, nineteen Agnus Dei, seventeen votive antiphons, and nine isorhythmic motets that date from c. 1370 to c. 1420. The older works, apart from simple discant settings, include some that reflect the complexities of the late Ars nova. Such is true particularly of the highly complicated pieces by Pycard, as well as those by Byttering and Queldryk, composers about whose lives we know virtually nothing. An apparently later generation of composers in Old Hall consists of Chirbury (fl. 1421–1437), Cooke (fl. 1400–1430), Thomas Damett (fl. 1413–1437), John Forest (d.

Repertory and composers

Score notation: a Sanctus in discant style by Chirbury in the Old Hall Manuscript. (Add. 57950, fol. 88r; reproduced by permission of the British Library, London)

1446), Leonel Power (d. 1445), and Nicholas Sturgeon (d. 1454). These composers gradually turned from the strict discant style and the more extravagant forms of chanson style toward music in which all voices shared in the melodic ornamentation. Still, rhythmic layering was preserved, with the tenor and contratenor more active than the upper parts, particularly in the isorhythmic works.

Paired Mass movements

In later repertory in Old Hall, composers tend to pair off Mass movements, either into Gloria–Credo or Sanctus–Agnus Dei groups. The procedures for such pairing range from the use of liturgically related cantus firmi to the choice of clef combinations and a general stylistic similarity. The final step, the composition of all movements on the same cantus firmus, is not present in Old Hall, but is the creation of English composers of the generation of Leonel and John Dunstaple, whose tenor Masses survive in continental sources.

Compositions dating from the later layers of Old Hall show a marked

Choirbook notation: a Credo from the Old Hall Manuscript. Note the double texts in the cantus, denoting the canonic derivation of several voices of it. (Add. 57950, fols. 62v–63r; reproduced by permission of the British Library, London)

increase first in the preparation of dissonances, as well as concern for full sonorities that virtually always include an imperfect consonance. The writing is fluid and smoothly rhythmic, particularly in the upper voices. This style became widely known on the Continent, since the conciliar movement and the English victory at Agincourt (1415) brought to Italy and northern France a large number of English lords and prelates with their chaplains. The English style had a profound influence on continental composers. Martin le Franc, writing in approximately 1440 about the best continental composers of his generation, Gilles Binchois and Guillaume Dufay, tells us:

The spread of the English style

> *Car ilz ont nouvelle pratique*
> *de faire frisque concordance*
> *en haulte et en basse musique,*
> *en fainte, en pause et en muance,*
> *et ont pris de la contenance*
> *angloise et ensuy Dunstaple,*
> *por quoy merveilleuse plaisance*
> *rend leur chant joyeux et notable.*[1]
> (For they have the new way
> of making sweet concords
> in loud and soft music,
> with accidentals, rests, and tonal shifts,
> and have taken the English countenance,
> and followed Dunstaple,
> and for that reason such marvelous pleasingness
> makes their music joyful and famous.)

English Composers

Among the composers represented in the Old Hall Manuscript, Thomas Damett, Leonel Power, and John Dunstaple[2] represent the transition to the new style of the fifteenth century. In their late works, both Leonel and Dunstaple bring this style to its first full flowering, and in the early works of Leonel or the few extant pieces of Damett the transitional style appears. These transitional pieces include simple discant settings and mixtures of the discant and chanson styles, such as are found in Damett's *Beata Dei genitrix* ("Blessed mother of God"; *HAM* I, no. 64). Many of Leonel's works match the complexity and dissonant counterpoint of Pycard or Byttering; see, for instance, Leonel's Credo (in *OxMM,* no. 66), or the following excerpt from a Gloria (Example 9.1). Damett's most forward-looking works retain a large number of dissonances, some on accented beats; but in Leonel's late music, such as the extraordinary *Gloriosae virginis* ("Of the glorious virgin"), dissonances are prepared carefully or restricted to the short notes on the offbeats.

Stylistic transition

Leonel's Mass settings evolved similarly. Many earlier works found in Old Hall are isorhythmic motets in the old style, and the paired movements have little in common beyond the same number of voices. Early in the fifteenth century, continental composers such as Arnold de Lantins (c. 1400–?)

Leonel and Dunstaple

Ex. 9.1   Leonel Power, *Gratias agimus/tibi propter magnam gloriam tuam*

"We give thee thanks for thy great glory."

had resorted to using a *motto* beginning, that is, starting each movement of the Mass with the same motive in order to signal the listener that the different movements are related. Leonel pursued a different and ultimately more fruitful path in the *Missa Alma redemptoris mater,* by basing each movement on the same cantus firmus. This procedure, initiated apparently by Leonel, Dunstaple, and a number of other English composers, was combined later with motto beginnings to produce the classic cantus firmus Mass cycles of the mid-fifteenth century.

Leonel's music, even in such late works as the *Missa Alma redemptoris mater,* still shows a fair number of dissonant frictions between voices, but the music of his younger contemporary, John Dunstaple, is almost devoid of dissonance. More than any of his contemporaries, Dunstaple was the master of the *frisque concordance* mentioned by Martin le Franc. The older, relatively harsh, style of the Old Hall composers is absent from his works. Even his most complex isorhythmic pieces, such as the motet *Veni sancte spiritus — Veni creator spiritus* ("Come holy spirit—Come spirit of God"), are smooth and flowing, often dominated by the treble, in which parts frequently outline triads in their melodic motion. This style can be observed quite clearly in the opening of his motet *Sancta Maria, non est similis* ("Holy Mary, none like thee"; *HAM* I, no. 62), in which all three parts have essentially the same melodic construction, even though the treble is the most ornamented.

In his treatment of the cantus firmus, Dunstaple utilized all the techniques found in the works of his contemporaries, but his most notable achievement was the total absorption of the plainsong into the rhythmic and melodic texture of the music through ornamentation. The plainsong's appearance in one of the lower voices, which traditionally moved in slower note values, posed little challenge, but when the plainsong appeared in the treble (as in Example 9.2) Dunstaple seemed to delight in ornamenting it so as to render it indistinguishable from a freely composed part.

A number of cantus firmus Mass settings are ascribed to Dunstaple. These range from rigidly isorhythmic works such as the Gloria–Credo pairs on *Jesu Christe Fili Dei* ("Jesus Christ, Son of God") and *De gaudiorum praemia* to the very flexible *Missa Rex saeculorum* (a work probably by Leonel), whose cantus firmus is reworked rhythmically and ornamented differently in each movement.

Later contemporaries of Dunstaple, such as John Benet (fl. 1450), John Bedyngham (fl. 1450), John Forest (d. 1446), John Plummer (fl. 1440), and Walter Frye (d. 1475), continued the English tradition, even if some, such as Bedyngham and Frye, seem to have worked on the Continent as well as in England. As with Dunstaple, the majority of their works survive in continental manuscripts, and the continental influence is felt in their use of motto beginnings and isomelic variations in the upper voices of their cantus firmus settings. ("Isomelic" means having the same melody recurring cyclically in one or more voices.) Such techniques are also present in their occasional settings of French or Italian texts.

Later composers

Ex. 9.2   John Dunstaple, *Ave maris stella*

"Hail, star of the sea. . . . Did receive the salutation. . . ."

The Early Cantus Firmus Mass

The English
repertory

As noted before, the idea of relating different movements of the Mass by composing them on the same cantus firmus probably originated with the English composers of the early fifteenth century. This idea was a logical outgrowth of the isorhythmic Mass setting of the late fourteenth century and of the desire for a larger structural unity, as manifested in the practice of composing paired movements.

Unifying
devices

On the Continent the drive for unity manifested itself first in the use of motto beginnings, which clearly signal to the listener the relationship among the movements of the work. Equally common, and structurally more satisfactory than the motto beginning, is reliance on similar structures, both in terms of the number of voices used and the succession of mensurations. This practice is found on both sides of the Channel. It appears in the *Missa Sine nomine* and the *Missa Sancti Jacobi* of Guillaume Dufay, as well as in a pair of elaborate Mass sections by Dunstaple. Composers also continued to use the cantus firmus in its traditional role as the voice regulating the structure of the music. The next logical step, after writing movements with the same outward structure, was to create them on the same cantus firmus, as Dunstaple did in the Gloria–Credo pair on *Jesu Christe Fili Dei*.

Masses after
Dunstaple

The Masses of the generation after Dunstaple, notably those of John Bedyngham and Walter Frye, present a later stage in the development of the cantus firmus Mass. Both composers ornament the cantus firmus, and in Frye's *Missa Nobilis et pulchra* ("Nobility and beauty") the tenor alternates between the plainsong cantus firmus and long stretches of freely composed music. Both composers have left Masses based on secular cantus firmi. Bedyngham's used Binchois's ballade *Dueil angoisseus* ("Deep sorrow"), and Frye's used his own ballade *So ys emprentyd*.[3]

The final crystallization of the English cantus firmus Mass is represented by a group of four-part works, most of which survive anonymously in Italian and French sources. They probably date from the decades between 1440 and 1460. The best known is the splendid *Missa Caput* ("Head," c. 1445), which, until recently, was attributed to Dufay. The *Missa Caput* takes its cantus firmus from the final melisma of the antiphon *Venit ad petrum* ("He came to Peter") for Maundy Thursday, a chant that belongs to the English Salisbury rite and is not found in Roman books. The composer laid out the cantus firmus twice in each movement with an almost isorhythmic regularity, and also made use of a motto beginning and isomelic returns in the upper voices to create a subtle network of correspondences between movements.

Carols and Later English Polyphony

Apart from the Mass cycles and a group of smaller liturgical works that survive in the Egerton and Pepys manuscripts,[4] the most remarkable form of mid-fifteenth-century English polyphony is the *carol*. As a literary form, the carol consists of a number of regular stanzas with a *burden* ("refrain") that begins the piece and is sung after every stanza. Thus the carol is related to refrain forms such as the virelai and the ballata, and, like them, probably had its beginnings as a dance song. Carols are devotional or ceremonial works, and the texts may be English (or Anglo-French), Latin, or a mixture of languages (*macaronic*). They were connected not only with Christmas but also with Easter, and a number of other feasts and important occasions. Early carols show a simple alternation of a choral burden with a number of solo verses, but later ones have more intricate structures, such as double burdens (choir and solos) or short choral interpolations in the verse. The burdens of the earlier carols, often simply composed in parallel motion between the top and bottom voices, lend themselves to the improvised filling out of the harmony, and, indeed, to extemporaneous harmonization of the burden's melody. To this extent they may be considered a form of "popular polyphony," as opposed to such elaborately composed music as that of Old Hall.

Even though carols could be described as popular polyphony, there were other, even simpler forms of improvised polyphony that developed in fifteenth-century England. One, called *faburden,* was clearly derived from English discant. One singer took the plainsong and another improvised a part below by a series of imagined *transpositions* (*sights*) of the same plainsong. The resultant line was always a third or a fifth below the plainsong note; since two consecutive fifths were unacceptable, this line consisted mostly of parallel thirds below the chant. A third singer improvised a line a perfect fourth above the plainsong, thus producing the texture given in Example 9.3. Continental composers adopted a similar procedure, with an ornamented plainsong as the top voice; a composed part, mostly in parallel sixths, at the bottom; and an improvised middle part in fourths below the plainsong. This technique they called *fauxbourdon*. The relationship between faburden and fauxbourdon remains a matter of argument among historians, but the generally held view is that fauxbourdon is a continental version of faburden.

The music of the late fifteenth century, such as the works in the Eton Choirbook,[5] shows an expansion of texture from four to five, six, and more voices. The chief genres of this period (Masses, votive antiphons, and Magnificats) are large-scale works. Thus John Sutton's seven-voice *Salve regina* runs to 235 measures in the modern edition. These works carry to an extreme the love of the English for full sonorities that was first demonstrated in the four-

Ex. 9.3   Faburden from a Kyrie

Lux et o - ri - go____ lu - cis sum - me de - us e - lei - son

"Light and source of light, O highest God, have mercy."

teenth century with their preference for imperfect consonances. The works are, in a sense, the final flowering of the *contenance angloise,* with an incredibly busy but wholly consonant texture, which had already become something of an anachronism on the Continent.

Continental Music in the Early Fifteenth Century

Continental style

Continental composers of the early fifteenth century faced stylistic problems different from those of the English. The complex style of the late Ars nova had run its course by about 1410. Yet the simpler styles cultivated on the Continent did not have the harmonic richness that allowed English composers to support a simple melody with a contrapuntal texture rich in imperfect consonances that impelled the music forward. Supported by a leaner texture based on perfect consonances, the simpler continental melodies tend to sound static. Composers sought to counter this by resorting to a lively rhythmic style that avoided the extravagant syncopations of the late Ars nova but

Ex. 9.4 Johannes Cesaris, excerpt from a Sanctus

"Holy, Holy, Holy. . . ."

exploited the rhythmic ambiguities inherent in the mensurations $\mathbb{C}$ $\binom{6}{8}$ $\bigcirc$ $\binom{3}{4}$ and used a larger number of unprepared dissonances. See Example 9.4 by Johannes Cesaris.

Continental composers also began to turn more frequently to liturgical music, in particular the Ordinary of the Mass, votive antiphons, and hymns. The early-fifteenth-century approach to Mass composition is perfectly illustrated by Arnold de Lantins's *Missa Verbum incarnatum* ("The Word made flesh"; *PS,*[6] nos. 1–5). In this freely composed work, movements are related only by a motto beginning and a general structural plan in which duets alternate with trios, a method of organization that is applied to each movement. These alternations are made even clearer by directions in the manuscript indicating that the duos are to be sung by soloists and the trios by a small choir.

Liturgical music

In the field of secular music, where the late-fourteenth-century composers had produced their most intricate works, we find a turning away from the ballade, with its serious or ceremonial texts and elaborate music. Instead, composers began to cultivate the simpler tradition of the rondeau.

Secular music

The transitional generation on the Continent is completely dominated by northern composers. Some—like Baude Cordier (fl. 1400), Johannes Cesaris (fl. 1410), Johannes Carmen (fl. 1400), Johannes Tapissier (fl. 1408), and Richard de Loqueville (d. 1418)—seem to have worked mostly in the north, even though Cordier and Tapissier were in Avignon. But many—including Nicholas Grenon (d. 1454), Guillaume and Johannes Legrant (fl. 1430), Arnold and Hugo de Lantins (fl. 1430), and Johannes de Lymburgia (fl. 1430)—pursued careers in Italy as well as in their native lands. These northern émigrés established a pattern that was to persist into the sixteenth century.

Transitional composers

English Influence

English influence on the works of continental composers becomes noticeable around 1430 in the works of those born near the turn of the century. The most important among these are Guillaume Dufay and Gilles Binchois. Binchois probably met a number of English musicians during his years of service to William Pole, earl of Suffolk (c. 1424–1430), and Dufay must have come into contact with English works circulated in northern Italy in the 1420s and 1430s.

The most pervasive sign of English influence is a shift away from the relatively dissonant counterpoint of the northern school and toward a flowing style pervaded by the sound of imperfect consonances. The change can be seen clearly in a comparison of the following Kyrie, written by Dufay about 1430 (see Example 9.5), with the Sanctus in Example 9.4. Here Dufay paraphrases the plainsong in the top voice. What is new is that the other structural voice, the tenor, is so constructed that it ensures an almost continuous flow of imperfect consonances with the plainsong. The only perfect consonances are at the start of the phrase and at the cadential point, and Dufay is careful to use

A more consonant style

Ex. 9.5   Guillaume Dufay, excerpt from a Kyrie

"Lord, have mercy."

an octave in measure 7 to give weight to the start of his most extended ornament of the chant.

Cantus firmus Masses   The other important sign of English influence on the Continent is the
adoption of the cantus firmus Mass (also known as *tenor Mass*). This innovation seems to have taken longer to be accepted by continental composers,
since the earliest extant continental cycles come from the middle of the century. These are Johannes Ockeghem's *Missa Caput* (c. 1450), Dufay's *Missa Se
la face ay pale* ("If the face is pale," 1452), and the two Masses on *L'Homme armé*
("The armed man") by Dufay and Ockeghem (1455). Significantly, what
may well be the earliest of these Masses, Ockeghem's *Missa Caput,* is modeled directly on the anonymous English *Missa Caput* (once ascribed to Dufay)

of the 1440s. Indeed, even Dufay's *Missa Se la face ay pale* shows the influence of the English style in its use of mensurations and in many of the internal cadences of the work.

The differences between these pieces and the English Masses are also telling. Both Ockeghem and Dufay break with the English tradition in their selection of secular songs, rather than plainsongs, for the tenors. Indeed, by about 1450 the stylistic leadership on the Continent had passed from the English to the hands of Dufay and Ockeghem.

Secular cantus firmi

Guillaume Dufay

Guillaume Dufay was the most important composer of the first half of the fifteenth century. Born about 1400 near Cambrai, he was a choirboy at the cathedral there. In approximately 1420 he entered the service of the Malatesta family and went to Italy, where he stayed, with a few interruptions, until 1439. His Italian patrons, besides the Malatestas, included the popes and the dukes of Savoy. Having become a canon at Cambrai in 1436, Dufay returned there in 1439. Two further sojourns in Savoy followed, one in 1450 and another from 1452 to 1458, the year of his final return to Cambrai, where he died in 1474.

Dufay encountered every style of music of his time, and he absorbed and fused these styles into a unified musical language that became the lingua franca of European music in the fifteenth century. As a man trained in the north, his early works, such as the ballade *Resveillez vous* ("Wake up," 1423), show the nervous rhythms and dissonant counterpoint of the northern school. But by 1430 Dufay had adopted the full triadic texture and the smooth melodic style of the English. These he combined with his own deep concern for melodic direction and clarity of phrase structure to produce such lucid works as the rondeau *Craindre vous vueil* (see Example 9.6).

Musical style

Dufay's small liturgical and devotional pieces closely parallel the style of the songs. In the large ceremonial works Dufay continued the old tradition of the isorhythmic motet, at least until the middle of the century. But by 1430 the texture of his large motets had changed considerably. In *Nuper rosarum flores,* written in 1436 for the consecration of the Florentine church Santa Maria del Fiore, Dufay sets in a canon at the fifth two isorhythmic tenors taken from a Gregorian Introit for the Mass for the Dedication of a Church. The tempos, regulated by shifts in mensuration, produce a work in four sections related in the proportion 6:4:2:3. Numerous other details suggest that the proportions of the piece are derived from the architectural proportions of the church building itself. Number symbolism aside, the two rigid tenors support two flowing lines that weave a series of variations over the tenor repetitions. These parts, occasionally divided into doubled notes to increase sonority, hide the rigidity of the tenor structure in a continuous flow of melody and supple rhythms.

Ex. 9.6   Guillaume Dufay, *Craindre vous vueil*

"I want to fear you, sweet and worthy lady, to love, doubt. . . ."

Masses   Dufay's Mass settings follow essentially the pattern of his other works. The early pieces—mostly isolated movements, pairs, and trios—are firmly rooted in the northern tradition. Dufay wrote at least nine cycles of the Ordinary, seven of which survive. The first three—*Missa Sine nomine* (c. 1420), *Missa Sancti Jacobi* (1425–1427), and *Missa Sancti Anthonii* (c. 1445)—are unified by any of the following devices: short motivic repetitions, the occasional use of opening mottos, similar changes of textures, or similar mensuration series in each movement. They remain essentially within the northern tradition, even though the Communion of the *Missa Sancti Jacobi* is written in fauxbourdon, and the rhythms of the *Missa Sancti Anthonii* show the new flowing style.

The last four Masses—the *Missa Se la face ay pale* (1452), *Missa L'Homme armé* (c. 1455), *Missa Ecce ancilla* ("Behold, the handmaiden," c. 1463), and *Missa Ave regina* (1472)—are all cantus firmus Masses in the English manner. In the first two, however, Dufay alters the English tradition by using secular songs rather than chants for the tenor. *Se la face ay pale* is based on the tenor of his own ballade of the same title (c. 1430), and *L'Homme armé* is based on a popular tune that eventually became the single most popular Renaissance cantus firmus. Both Masses are in essence gigantic motet cycles that set the

The cathedral of Cambrai before its demolition in 1795.

Mass texts. In fact, *Se la face ay pale* has a rigidly isorhythmic tenor pattern in the Gloria and Credo. In *L'Homme armé* the tenor treatment is much freer, with ornamentation occasionally added. Both Masses represent the "classic" stage of the continental cantus firmus cycle (see the Kyrie and Agnus Dei of *L'Homme armé* in *HAM* I, no. 66). The last two Masses, as well as a setting of the *Ave regina caelorum* antiphon (c. 1464), show further development. These works are written in the a cappella tradition of Cambrai, a cathedral where unaccompanied singing was the norm, since it did not even have an organ until the latter part of the sixteenth century. The pieces preserve a vestige of the separation between the tenor and the other voices by using the cantus firmus text of the antiphons rather than that of the Mass, or of the personal prayer in the motet. Otherwise the plainsong is ornamented to sound like a freely composed fifteenth-century line. In addition, the motivic material of the tenor is often imitated by the other voices, producing a homogeneous contrapuntal texture, as shown in Example 9.7.

Ex. 9.7   Guillaume Dufay, Gloria from *Missa Ave regina*

Ex. 9.7   cont.

"And on earth peace to men of good will. We praise thee. We bless thee. We worship thee."
"Hail, queen of heaven."

In the *Missa Ave regina caelorum* Dufay also derived much of the motivic material for the free voices from the music of a motet of his written around 1464. This procedure points the way to the elaboration of a polyphonic model that became a common practice in the sixteenth century and has become known today as *parody*.

Gilles Binchois

Dufay's most famous contemporary is Gilles Binchois (c. 1400–1460). In contrast to Dufay's peripatetic life, that of Binchois appears almost provincial. Born at Mons, he was a soldier in his youth, but by 1424 he was a singer for the earl of Suffolk. Around 1430 he joined the chapel of the court of Burgundy, where he remained to the end of his life.

Binchois was primarily a secular composer. Since secular music was in many ways the most conservative type of the day, he appears as a traditional composer despite such new traits in his music as the extensive use of imitation or the richness of his harmonic writing. His sacred works are modest settings of plainchant, either in fauxbourdon or in a closely related style. They resemble the pieces Dufay wrote in the 1430s and 1440s. Binchois wrote no large Mass cycles, either free or on a cantus firmus.

His chansons show a fastidious, refined attitude toward the literary text seldom found among his contemporaries. They are delicate works, with the melodic interest concentrated in the treble, which tends to move in short and well-defined phrases (see Example 9.8). Most of the chansons are rondeaux, with a few ballades and one free chanson, *Files à marier* ("Girls to be married"; *HAM* I, no. 70), based on a popular tune set in the tenor.

Ex. 9.8   Gilles Binchois, *Marguerite, fleur de valeur*

"Marguerite, O worthy flower, sovereign above all others. . . ."

The Later Fifteenth Century

Johannes Ockeghem

Unlike Dufay, Johannes Ockeghem never left the north and had little contact with Italy. He may have been a student of Binchois, and his early years were spent in Antwerp and Moulins. From about 1452 until his death he was a member of the French royal chapel. Around 1459 he was appointed treasurer of the Abbey of St. Martin of Tours, one of the highest ecclesiastical offices that the kings of France could confer. In the sixteenth century his fame as a learned composer and teacher was legendary to the point of blinding later historians to Ockeghem's merits as a lyrical composer.

Despite his enormous fame, Ockeghem was not prolific. He left only two three-voice Masses, nine four-voice Masses (one incomplete), two five-voice Masses (both incomplete), a Requiem, a Credo, ten motets, a lamentation on the death of Binchois, and some twenty-six chansons. Beyond these works we know of about four more lost Masses.

Ockeghem's most traditional works are his chansons. Most show the typical late-fifteenth-century texture: a duo between the treble and the tenor, often in imitation, with an ornamental contratenor. This texture can be seen most clearly in his *bergerette* (a one-stanza virelai) *Ma Bouche rit* ("My mouth laughs"; *HAM* I, no. 75). Unlike Dufay, Ockeghem did not use a clear phrase structure, preferring instead to veil phrase endings or to extend them with sudden, capricious melismatic passages. Compare, for instance, the opening of Dufay's song in Example 9.6 with the opening of Ockeghem's *Ma Maîtresse* (Example 9.9). Ockeghem's melodic line has reached its goal by measure 5, but precisely at this point the supporting voices become active and lead to a

Secular works

Ex. 9.9 Johannes Ockeghem, *Ma Maîtresse*

"My mistress and my greatest friend. . . ."

two-measure extension quite unlike anything that came before. The opening of the song is also typical of Ockeghem's attitude toward formal processes. The treble and the tenor have the same motive a fifth apart; however, both begin together, and the extension of the first tenor note by one beat transforms the passage into a short canonic entry.

Motets   Ockeghem's motets are diverse. Although most are cantus firmus settings, with the borrowed voice elaborated and blended into the texture, each is unique. Ockeghem repeats himself less than any other composer of his time. One of his best motets is a setting of the *Alma redemptoris mater,* with the plainsong paraphrased in the alto rather than in the tenor. Example 9.10 shows the opening duet of the motet, given without bar lines (as the parts

Johannes Ockeghem and his choir. (Français 1587, fol. 58v; Bibliothèque Nationale, Paris)

Ex. 9.10   Johannes Ockeghem, *Alma redemptoris mater*

"Gracious. . . ."

stand in the manuscript) in order to show most clearly Ockeghem's rhythmic inventiveness.

Beautiful as his songs and motets are, it is in the Masses that Ockeghem **Masses** reveals the full extent of his genius. Most are cantus firmus cycles; *Caput* and *L'Homme armé* use the cantus firmus straightforwardly, with only modest ornamentation in *L'Homme armé* (Kyrie and Agnus Dei III in *HAM* I, no. 73). *De plus en plus* ("More and more"), based on a Binchois chanson, and *Ecce* *ancilla,* based on an antiphon, extensively ornament and paraphrase the cantus firmus. *Ma Maîtresse* and *Fors seulement,* based on his own chansons, use several voices from each song as cantus firmi in ways that point toward the parody Mass of the sixteenth century. The Requiem and the five-voice *Missa Sine nomine* use the appropriate plainsongs rather than a single cantus firmus. These are set mostly in the tenor in the *Missa Sine nomine,* and in the treble in the Requiem, though occasionally they appear in other voices. Since Dufay's Requiem is lost, Ockeghem's is the earliest extant polyphonic setting of the Mass for the Dead. The *Missa Au Travail suis,* barely employing a cantus firmus beyond the Kyrie, is almost wholly a free Mass.

The freely composed Masses—*Quinti toni; Sine nomine a 3; Mi-mi; Cuiusvis toni;* and the *Missa Prolationum* ("Prolation")—present the most complex side of Ockeghem's musical personality. In these works we encounter a constantly changing contrapuntal texture of voices that seldom have a definite melodic profile. Indeed, the profile is often so complex as to be beyond the immediate grasp of the listener. Phrases and sections melt into each other without apparent seams; yet the whole is carefully structured, even if that structure is not always easily perceived. This kind of texture is exemplified by the opening of the Gloria of the *Missa Mi-mi* (see Example 9.11).

The bass sounds the opening motto of the work, the fifth E–A (*mi* in the natural hexachord and *mi* in the hard hexachord). The few snatches of imitation, such as those in measures 7–8, pass so quickly as to be hardly noticeable, yet they do unify the voices. As a major cadence point approaches in measure 11, the music grows active rhythmically and very complex texturally. This *drive to the cadence* becomes even more extended and intricate in the approach to the final cadence, and can be taken as a mannerism of Ockeghem.

The *Missa Cuiusvis toni* and the *Missa Prolationum* are both tours de force. The first is notated without clefs and so written that with the addition of the appropriate accidentals and clefs it may be sung in any of the four *maneriae* (combinations of the authentic and plagal modes): Dorian, Phrygian, Lydian, and Mixolydian. The second Mass is even more complex. It consists of a series of canons, from the unison to the seventh, many of which are *mensuration canons.* In these the two written parts generate four parts, one in each mensuration. Thus one part is sung simultaneously in ○ and ₵ (tempus perfectum and imperfectum, respectively), and the other in ⊙ and ₵̇. All four parts start simultaneously, and those in tempus imperfectum gain on those in tempus perfectum until a suitable distance is reached. Then Ockeghem shifts to either short inalterable values or to black notation, and the movement ends as a straightforward double canon. The sheer intellectual feats in these works are staggering, but even more important is the great beauty of their flowing and graceful melodies.

Antoine Busnois

Antoine Busnois is as different from Ockeghem as Binchois is from Dufay. Indeed, Busnois, like Binchois, is primarily a composer of secular

Ex. 9.11 Johannes Ockeghem, Gloria from *Missa Mi-mi*

"And on earth peace to men of good will."

music, and it is probably no coincidence that both composers spent most of their working lives at the court of Burgundy. Busnois's sacred and ceremonial music includes three Masses, seven motets, two hymns, and two Magnificats. In these works he is closer than Ockeghem to the formal clarity of Dufay, even if his melodic writing can be at times as intricate as anything by Ockeghem. Nevertheless, in contrast to Ockeghem's music, Busnois's sacred works seem to be more harmonically conceived (see Example 9.12).

At least two of his motets also deserve special mention. *In hydraulis,* a long work in praise of Ockeghem, has a tenor derived from the intervals mentioned in the text (a fifth and an octave). The other piece, *Anthoni usque ad limina,* has a cantus firmus consisting of a single note, D, which was most likely intended to be played by a bell. These tenors point toward a later tradition of artificial cantus firmi, derived from solmization patterns, or derived, through the solmization syllables, from the vowels in the name of a person.

Ex. 9.12   Antoine Busnois, Kyrie from *Missa L'Homme armé*

Ex. 9.12   cont.

"Lord, have mercy."

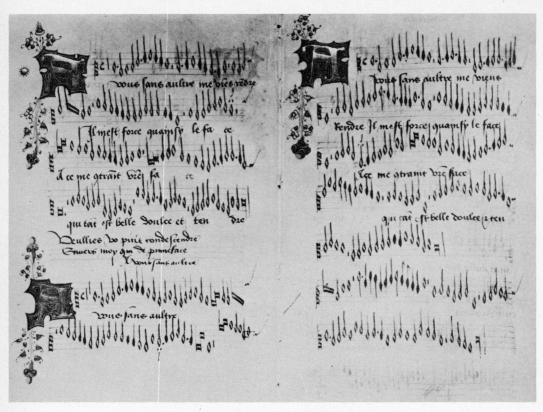

A rondeau of Antoine Busnois from the Mellon Chansonnier. (MS 91, fols. 55v–56r; The Beinecke Rare Book Manuscript Library, Yale University)

Chansons

Busnois's sixty-three chansons contain what is arguably his best music. Like those of Binchois, they show a discerning taste in poetry, and, indeed, Busnois himself was considered a very good poet. The chansons contain some of the finest melodic writing of the late fifteenth century. Busnois's melodies combine Dufay's clarity with Ockeghem's flexibility. Most of the chansons are treble-tenor duets in imitation, with a free contratenor, but in several the contratenor also takes part in the imitative texture.

Contemporaries of Ockeghem and Busnois

Around Ockeghem and Busnois we encounter a host of minor composers, some of whom combined the stylistic traits of the two masters in different ways. At the Burgundian court, Robert Morton (d. 1475) and Hayne van Ghizeghem (d. 1472?) composed very fine chansons. Around Cambrai Cathedral clustered Johannes Regis (c. 1430–1485), who was for a time secretary to Dufay; Philippe Caron (fl. 1490s); and Johannes Tinctoris (c. 1435–1511). Caron and Tinctoris eventually went to Italy, where Tinctoris served in the court of King Ferrante of Naples (reg. 1458–1490). The output of these three was small, but in the case of Tinctoris it was complemented by a number of important theoretical treatises, which provide the most thorough contemporary view of late-fifteenth-century musical thought. A slightly older contemporary was Vincent Faugues (fl. 1460), a composer of Masses, one of which was ascribed for a time to Ockeghem.

Summary

The fifteenth century saw the end of the extremely complex style of the late Ars nova known as *subtilior,* as well as the end of the extraordinary flowering of an indigenous Italian musical style. Both were supplanted by a new manner of writing that combined northern French contrapuntal practice, English harmonic style, and flowing melodic and rhythmic writing that resulted in smooth vocal lines.

In sacred music the period saw the end of the isorhythmic motet and the rise of the *cantus firmus Mass cycle* under English influence. Toward the middle of the century secular cantus firmi were first used, and the ornamentation of the tenor started to produce a blend of all voices into a homogeneous texture. This trend was carried further through the use of motivic imitation among the voices. Around 1440 the normal three-part texture of the Mass expanded to four, and toward the end of the fifteenth century five-part writing began to appear on the Continent, while in England writing in more than five parts was common. The smaller liturgical forms used a treble-dominated style, including *fauxbourdon,* that was eventually absorbed into the more complex style of the cyclic Mass.

In secular music, the *ballade* became obsolete by about 1440 except among the English, and most songs from the fifteenth century are either *rondeaux* or *virelais,* with a few free song forms. The texture of secular music was also influenced by the use of imitation, and songs tended to become treble-tenor duets with a free *contratenor*. In a few songs the normal texture was expanded to four parts.

The music of the fifteenth century was dominated by composers from the north, with the schools of Liège, Cambrai, and Antwerp, as well as the English school, being by far the most prominent. Many northerners, however, worked for long periods in Italy, either in the north Italian courts or in the papal chapel, and thus they dominated the art of the peninsula. After a period of wide influence in the early part of the century, the English remained essentially isolated from continental influence and charted a course of their own that was to last until the end of the sixteenth century.

Notes

1. Cited in Gustave Reese, *Music in the Renaissance* (New York: W. W. Norton, 1954), p. 13.
2. Though usually spelled Dunstable, his name, from most sources and his epitaph,

was Dunstaple. See Margaret Bent, *Dunstaple,* Oxford Studies of Composers, No. 17 (London: Oxford University Press, 1981).

3. Only a fragment of the Kyrie of this Mass has survived.

4. London, British Library, Egerton 3307, see Gwynn McPeek, *The British Museum Manuscript Egerton 3307* (Chapel Hill: University of North Carolina Press, 1963), and Cambridge, Magdalene College, Pepys 1236, see Sidney Charles, ed., *The Music of the Pepys MS 1236,* Corpus mensurabilis musicae, 40 (Rome: American Institute of Musicology, 1967).

5. Windsor, Eton College Library, MS 178, see Frank Ll. Harrison, ed., *The Eton Choirbook,* 3 vols., Musica Britannica, vols. 10–12 (London: Stainer & Bell, 1965–1968).

6. *Polyphonia Sacra: A Continental Miscellany of the Fifteenth Century,* ed. Charles van den Borren (London: Plainsong and Mediaeval Music Society, 1932; reprinted, College Park: Pennsylvania State University Press, 1963). *(PS)*

Bibliography

Books and Articles on Composers and Styles

BENT, MARGARET. *Dunstaple*. Oxford Studies of Composers, No. 17. London: Oxford University Press, 1981.

BROOKS, CATHERINE. "Antoine Busnois, Chanson Composer." *Journal of the American Musicological Society* 6 (1953): 111–135.

BROWN, HOWARD M. *Music in the French Secular Theater, 1400–1550*. Cambridge, Mass.: Harvard University Press, 1963.

BROWN, SAMUEL E. "New Evidence of Isomelic Design in Dufay's Isorhythmic Motets." *Journal of the American Musicological Society* 10 (1957): 7–13.

BUKOFZER, MANFRED. "John Dunstable: A Quincentenary Report." *The Musical Quarterly* 40 (1954): 24–49.

———. *Studies in Medieval and Renaissance Music*. New York: W. W. Norton, 1950.

CAZEAUX, ISABELLE, *French Music in the Fifteenth and Sixteenth Centuries*. New York: Praeger, 1975.

CHEW, GEOFFREY. "The Early Cyclic Mass as an Expression of Royal and Papal Supremacy." *Music and Letters* 53 (1972): 254–269.

COHEN, JUDITH. *The Six Anonymous "L'Homme armé" Masses in Naples, Biblioteca Nazionale, MS. VI. E. 40*. Musicological Studies and Documents, 21. Rome: American Institute of Musicology, 1968.

FINSCHER, LUDWIG. *Loyset Compère and His Works*. Musicological Studies and Documents, 12. Rome: American Institute of Musicology, 1964.

GOSSETT, PHILIP. "Techniques of Unification in Early Cyclic Masses and Mass Pairs." *Journal of the American Musicological Society* 19 (1966): 205–231.

HAMM, CHARLES. "A Catalogue of Anonymous English Pieces in Fifteenth-Century Continental Manuscripts." *Musica disciplina* 22 (1968): 47–76.

———. *A Chronology of the Works of Guillaume Dufay Based on a Study of Mensural Practice*. Princeton Studies in Music, vol. 1. Princeton, N.J.: Princeton University Press, 1964.

———. "A Group of Anonymous English Pieces in Trent 88." *Music and Letters* 41 (1960): 211–215.

———. "The Motets of Lionel Power." In *Studies in Music History: Essays for Oliver Strunk,* ed. Harold Powers. Princeton, N.J.: Princeton University Press, 1968. Pp. 125–136.

HARRISON, FRANK LL. "Faburden in Practice." *Musica disciplina* 16 (1962): 11–34.

———. *Music in Medieval Britain*. London: Routledge & Kegan Paul, 1958.

HUGHES, ANDREW. "Mass Pairs in the Old Hall and Other English Manuscripts." *Revue Belge de musicologie* 19 (1965): 15–27.

––––––. "Mensural Polyphony for Choir in Fifteenth-Century England." *Journal of the American Musicological Society* 19 (1966): 352–369.

––––––. "Some Notes on the Early-Fifteenth-Century Contratenor." *Music and Letters* 50 (1969): 376–387.

––––––. "The Choir in Fifteenth-Century English Music: Non-Mensural Polyphony." *Essays in Musicology in Honor of Dragan Plamenac on His Seventieth Birthday,* ed. Gustave Reese and Robert J. Snow. Pittsburgh: University of Pittsburgh Press, 1969. Pp. 127–145.

KENNEY, SYLVIA. "English Discant and Discant in England." *The Musical Quarterly* 45 (1959): 26–48.

––––––. *Walter Frye and the Contenance Angloise.* Yale Studies in Music, vol. 3. New Haven: Yale University Press, 1964.

LERNER, EDWARD R. "The Polyphonic Magnificat in Fifteenth-Century Italy." *The Musical Quarterly* 50 (1964): 44–58.

LOCKWOOD, LEWIS. "Dufay at Ferrara." In *Papers Read at the Dufay Quincentenary Conference, Brooklyn College, December 6–7, 1974,* ed. Allan W. Atlas. Brooklyn, N.Y.: Brooklyn College, 1975. Pp. 1–25.

MANIATES, MARIA RIKA. "Combinative Chansons in the Dijon Chansonnier." *Journal of the American Musicological Society* 23 (1970): 228–281.

––––––. "Combinative Chansons in the Escorial Chansonnier." *Musica disciplina* 29 (1975): 61–125.

PERLE, GEORGE. "The Chansons of Antoine Busnois." *The Music Review* 11 (1950): 89–97.

PIRROTTA, NINO. "Music and Cultural Tendencies in Fifteenth-Century Italy." *Journal of the American Musicological Society* 19 (1969): 127–161.

––––––. "On Text Forms from Ciconia to Dufay." In *Aspects of Medieval and Renaissance Music: A Birthday Offering to Gustave Reese,* ed. Jan La Rue. New York: W. W. Norton, 1966. Pp. 673–682.

PLANCHART, ALEJANDRO ENRIQUE. "Guillaume Dufay's Masses: Notes and Revisions." *The Musical Quarterly* 58 (1972): 1–23.

––––––. "Guillaume Dufay's Masses: A View of the Manuscript Traditions." In *Papers Read at the Dufay Quincentenary Conference, Brooklyn College, December 6–7, 1974,* ed. Allan W. Atlas. Brooklyn, N.Y.: Brooklyn College, 1975. Pp. 26–60.

REESE, GUSTAVE. *Music in the Renaissance,* rev. ed. New York: W. W. Norton, 1959.

SCOTT, ANN B. "English Music in Modena, Biblioteca Estense a. X. 1. 11, and Other Italian Manuscripts." *Musica disciplina* 26 (1972): 145–160.

SPARKS, EDGAR. *Cantus Firmus in Mass and Motet, 1420–1520.* Berkeley and Los Angeles: University of California Press, 1963.

––––––. "The Motets of Antoine Busnois." *Journal of the American Musicological Society* 6 (1953): 216–226.

TREITLER, LEO. "Tone System in the Works of Guillaume Dufay." *Journal of the American Musicological Society* 18 (1965): 131–169.

TROWELL, BRIAN. "Faburden and Fauxbourdon." *Musica disciplina* 13 (1959): 43–78.

––––––. "Some English Contemporaries of Dunstable." *Proceedings of the Royal Musical Association* 81 (1954–1955): 77–92.

TRUMBLE, ERNEST. *Fauxbourdon: An Historical Survey,* vol. 1. Musicological Studies, vol. 3. Brooklyn, N.Y.: Institute of Medieval Music, 1959.

WARD, TOM R. "The Polyphonic Hymn and the Liturgy of Fifteenth-Century Italy." *Musica disciplina* 26 (1972): 161–188.

WARREN, CHARLES. "Brunelleschi's Dome and Dufay's Motet." *The Musical Quarterly* 59 (1973): 92–105.

WRIGHT, CRAIG. "Dufay at Cambrai: Discoveries and Revisions." *Journal of the American Musicological Society* 28 (1975): 175–230.

Music Editions and Facsimiles

ADLER, GUIDO; KOLLER, OSWALD; VON FICKER, RUDOLF, et al., eds. *Sechs (Sieben) Trienter Codices, erste-sechste Auswahl,* 6 vols. Of the series Denkmaler der Tonkunst in Osterreich, these are vols. 14–15 (1900), 22 (1904), 28 (1912), 53 (1920), 76 (1933). Vienna. Reprinted Graz: Akademische Druk und Verlaganstalt, 1959–1960. A series of anthologies of music from the Trent Codices, in the old clefs and unreduced note-values. Much of it superseded, but still the only available edition of a number of important works.

BENT, MARGARET, ed. *Fifteenth Century Liturgical Music, II: Four Anonymous Masses.* Early English Church Music, vol. 22. London: Stainer & Bell, 1979. An exemplary edition of four major English works from the first half of the fifteenth century.

BINCHOIS, GILLES. *Die Chansons von Gilles Binchois,* ed. Wolfgang Rehm. Musikalische Denkmaler, vol. 2. Mainz: B. Schott's Sohne, 1957.

CARON, PHILIPPE. *Les Oeuvres complètes de Philippe (?) Caron,* 2 vols., ed. James Thomson. Brooklyn: Institute of Medieval Music, 1971–1976.

CARVER, ROBERT. *Collected Works,* ed. Denis Stevens. Corpus mensurabilis musicae, 14. Rome: American Institute of Musicology, 1959.

CHARLES, SYDNEY R., ed. *The Music of the Pepys Manuscript, 1236.* Corpus mensurabilis musicae, 40. Rome: American Institute of Musicology, 1967.

COMPÈRE, LOYSET. *Opera omnia,* 6 vols., ed. Ludwig Finscher, Corpus mensurabilis musicae, 15. Rome: American Institute of Musicology, 1958–1973.

DROZ, EUGÉNIE; THIBAULT, GENEVIÈVE, and ROKSETH, YVONNE, eds. *Trois Chansonniers français du XVe siècle,* vol. 1. Documents artistiques du XVe siècle, vol. 4. Paris: Droz, 1927.

DUFAY, GUILLAUME. *Opera omnia,* 6 vols., ed. Heinrich Besseler. Corpus mensurabilis musicae, 1. Rome: American Institute of Musicology, 1949–1966.

DUNSTABLE, JOHN. *Complete Works,* ed. Manfred Bukofzer; 2nd edition revised by Ian and Margaret Bent, Brian Trowell. Musica Britannica, vol. 8. London: Stainer & Bell, 1970.

FEINIGER, LAURENCE, ed. *Documenta polyphoniae liturgicae sanctae ecclesiae Romanae,* 13 vols. in three series. Rome: Societas Universalis Sanctae Ceciliae, 1957–1961.

———. *Monumenta polyphoniae liturgicae sanctae ecclesiae Romanae,* 5 vols. (1–4 in 16 fascicles), in two series. Rome-Trent: Societas Universalis Sanctae Ceciliae, 1947–1965.

FRYE, WALTER. *Collected Works,* ed. Sylvia Kenney. Corpus mensurabilis musicae, 19. Rome: American Institute of Musicology, 1960.

HARRISON, FRANK LL., ed. *The Eton Choirbook,* 3 vols. Musica Britannica, vol. 22. London: Stainer & Bell, 1965–1968.

MARIX, JEANNE, ed. *Les Musiciens de la cour de Bourgogne au XVe siècle: messes, motets, chansons.* Monaco: Oiseau Lyre, 1937.

OCKEGHEM, JOHANNES. *Collected Works,* ed. Dragan Plamenac, 3 vols. New York: American Musicological Society, 1947–1977. Vol. 1, first published in Leipzig, 1927. Vol. 2, 2nd ed. 1959.

PLANCHART, ALEJANDRO ENRIQUE, ed. *Missae Caput.* Collegium Musicum, vol. 5. New Haven: Yale Graduate School, 1964. The three *Caput* Masses: (1) Anonymous ("Dufay"); (2) Ockeghem; (3) Obrecht.

POWER, LEONEL. *Opera omnia,* ed. Charles Hamm. Corpus mensurabilis musicae, 50. Rome: American Institute of Musicology, 1969–   (1 vol. by 1977).

REANEY, GILBERT, ed. *Early Fifteenth Century Music,* 8 vols. Corpus mensurabilis musicae, 11. Rome: American Institute of Musicology, 1955–

REGIS, JOHANNES. *Opera omnia,* 2 vols., ed. Cornelis Lindenburg. Corpus mensurabilis musicae, 9. Rome: American Institute of Musicology, 1956.

SMIJERS, ALBERT, ed. *Van Ockeghem tot Sweelinck,* 7 vols. Amsterdam: Alsbach, 1949–1956.

STAINER, SIR JOHN, J. F. R., and CECIE, eds. *Dufay and His Contemporaries.* London: Plainsong and Medieval Music Society, 1898.

STEVENS, JOHN, ed. *Music at the Court of Henry VIII.* Musica Britannica, vol. 18. London: Stainer & Bell, 1962. Rev. ed., 1969.

———. *Medieval Carols,* 2nd ed. Musica Britannica, vol. 4. London: Stainer & Bell, 1958.

TROWELL, BRIAN, ed. *Four Motets by John Plummer.* Banbury, England: Plainsong and Medieval Music Society, 1968.

VAN DE BORREN, CHARLES, ed. *Pièces polyphoniques de provenance Liègeoise (XVᵉ siècle).* Brussels: Editions de la Librairie Encyclopédique, 1950. The collected secular works of the Lantins and the Gremblacos.

———. *Polyphonia sacra: A Continental Miscellany of the Fifteenth Century.* London: Plainsong and Medieval Music Society, 1932. Reprinted, College Park: Pennsylvania State University Press, 1963.

WILKINS, NIGEL. *A Fifteenth-Century Repertory from the Codex Reina (Paris, Bibl. Nat. nouv. acqu. fr. 6771).* Corpus mensurabilis musicae, 37. Rome: American Institute of Musicology, 1966.

10

The High Renaissance:
National Styles

THE stylistic changes in the music of the last two decades of the fifteenth century and the first two of the sixteenth were less dramatic than the rise of the *contenance angloise* around 1420. Nevertheless, these changes were profound. The musical language created by the generations of Dufay and Ockeghem had become sufficiently clear and efficient to permit its expansion by a generation of extraordinarily gifted composers who made it more flexible and expressive. Significantly, as often happens when a musical language has established but not yet exhausted itself, the writing became less problematic, and the output of composers rose dramatically. This pattern will become obvious if one compares the total production of composers in the generation of Josquin Des Prés and Jacob Obrecht with that of the generation of Ockeghem and Busnois.

The new style was an interaction of two forces: (1) the northern tradition, now a combination of northern and southern traits, but still stemming from the great cathedral schools of the north; and (2) the "popular" art of Italy and of the French court under Louis XII and Francis I. It was an art based on simple harmonic procedures, dominated by melodiousness and immediacy. In clear declamation of text this new art also reflected the concerns of the humanists. Nevertheless, the most important composers of this new style were still northerners, albeit northerners who, like Josquin, worked for a long time in Italy.

The Rise of the Polyphonic Style

The drive toward a polyphonic texture in which all voices have the same melodic importance can be observed in the late works of Dufay and in those of the generation of Ockeghem and Busnois. This spirit was brought to its first full flowering by a generation of composers born around 1450—a group dominated, at least in our perspective, by Josquin Des Prés (c. 1440–1521). As we have seen, the drive began with the gradual absorption of the cantus

192

firmus into the texture, first by ornamentation of the borrowed melody, then through the imitation of its motivic substance by other voices. This trend naturally led to the deliberate breaking of the cantus firmus into small melodic segments that could be imitated in the other parts, and eventually to the use of such motives as the basic formal units of the music. Thus a long work could be composed that consisted of interlocked segments, each built on a motive imitated in all parts and expanded into free counterpoint. As one phrase would come to a close, some of the voices would introduce a new motive, the germ of the next phrase. Hence the work would consist of a series of *points of imitation,* each freely expanded according to the composer's whim. This element can be observed, in its classical sixteenth-century formulation, in the illustrated work of Philippe Verdelot (d. c. 1552), which was composed about 1523 (see Example 10.1).

Such a technique can be combined with a preexistent cantus firmus in a number of ways. Example 10.1 shows one possibility, since all the motives in the work are derived from a famous plainsong sequence (*LU*, 780).[1] But the procedure itself does not depend on the presence of a cantus firmus and can be used to produce music entirely independent of borrowed material. In addition, it demands a different approach to the composition of a work; unlike the old cantus firmus pieces, the new works cannot be written one voice at a time; rather, all parts must be conceived simultaneously. To be sure, such a manner of composing began to take hold in the late fifteenth century, but it is in the work of Josquin's generation that we encounter it with the most consistency. Composers who worked in this new style were also helped immeasurably by their contact with the simpler musical types cultivated in Italy and at the French court—a background that gave their work a greater "chordal" orientation and contributed to the clarification of the polyphonic fabric.

In the decades around 1500 there were, in addition to Josquin, a host of excellent and prolific composers. They included Jacob Obrecht (c. 1450–1505), Alexander Agricola (1446–1506), Gaspar van Weerbecke (c. 1445–1514), Heinrich Isaac (c. 1450–1518), Loyset Compère (c. 1450–1518), Pierre de la Rue (c. 1460–1518), Antoine Brumel (c. 1450–1520), Antoine de Févin (c. 1460–1512), and Jean Mouton (c. 1459–1522). But it is Josquin who seems to tower over them all—a judgment that, if not entirely current in his lifetime, became accepted very soon after his death.

Josquin Des Prés

Josquin's career shows some similarities to that of Dufay. Born about 1440 in Picardy, he may have been a choirboy at Saint-Quentin. By 1459 he was in Milan, where he remained until 1479, and even after that date he retained connections with the Sforza family, particularly with Cardinal Ascanio Sforza (d. 1505). About 1486 Josquin joined the papal chapel, where he remained until 1494. In 1503 he entered the service of the duke of Ferrara, but he left Ferrara for the north before 1505. He spent his last years as provost of the Chapter of Condé-sur-l'Escaut, where he died in 1521.

Ex. 10.1   Philippe Verdelot, *Victimae paschali*

"Let Christians offer praises to the Paschal victim. . . ."

Josquin's surviving works are eighteen Masses, about a hundred motets, and some seventy-five secular works. As a rule, the Masses show the more conservative side of Josquin's music, and the motets the more advanced and even experimental side; but as with Dufay and Ockeghem, his greatness illuminates every one of his works, and we should be wary of attaching any aesthetic value to such terms as "conservative" or "advanced."

All but two of Josquin's Masses, the *Missa Ad fugam* and the *Missa Sine nomine* (both canonic cycles), make use of borrowed material, but its treatment is almost as varied as the works that employ it. Josquin uses cantus firmi derived from plainsongs (*Ave maris stella; Gaudeamus* ["Let us rejoice"]; *Pange Lingua*), popular monophonic tunes (*L'Ami baudichon; L'Homme armé*), or polyphonic chansons (*Faysant regretz; Fortuna desperata; Malheur me bat; Missa Di dadi; Una Musque de buscaya; D'Ung aultre amer*). He also uses artificial cantus firmi, called *sogetti cavati delle vocali*—that is, melodies derived from a phrase or a name through correspondence between the vowels of the phrase and those of the solmization syllables (*Hercules, dux Ferrariae* ["Ercole, Duke of Ferrara"], *La sol fa re mi*). One work, the *Missa De Beata Virgine,* uses the appropriate plainsongs of the Ordinary as cantus firmi. Another, the *Missa Mater patris et fili,* is a full-fledged, if crude, parody Mass on a motet by Brumel. Some of the chanson Masses—for example, *Fortuna desperata* and *Malheur me bat* ("Misfortune strikes me")—approach parody in that they employ material from several voices of the models.

In his use of cantus firmus Josquin reaches from the relatively rigid and traditional settings found in his two *L'Homme armé* Masses, the *Missa Hercules,* and the *Missa L'Ami baudichon* to the near parody of the chanson Masses and the extremely free use of borrowed material found in the plainsong Masses. These, particularly *Ave maris stella* and *Pange lingua,* are essentially two sets of five polyphonic *fantasias* based on motives derived from the plainsong. This technique can be seen in the first Kyrie of the *Missa Pange lingua* (Example 10.2). The first double-phrase (measures 1–8) is based on the first segment of the chant, with the cantus firmus migrating from the tenor to the soprano (fragments of it are also present in the alto and the bass). Josquin seizes upon the similarity of the intervals in the chant settings of *Pange lingua* and *corporis* to duplicate the opening figure on *c* at the start of the final phrase (measures 9–16). Again, the tenor and soprano have two different elaborations of the chant melody, this time sung simultaneously, starting in close imitation. The approach to the cadence of the final Kyrie (Example 10.3) shows an even more elaborate expansion of a cantus firmus motive. The chant phrase, a–b–G–a–F, is broken into cells, a–b–G / G–a–F, and used sequentially in the soprano and the bass. The final drive to the cadence is merely a repetition of this cell in the soprano and bass. Here only the most general shape and direction of the chant melody itself survives in the soprano. Clearly the cantus firmus is no longer a scaffolding voice but rather a source of melodic and motivic material that lends its own profile to the whole Mass.

Josquin's chansons, apart from a few Italian frottole such as *In te, Domine, speravi* (*HAM* I, no. 95b), are for the most part an elaboration of the tradi-

Masses

Chansons

Ex. 10.2   Josquin Des Prés, first Kyrie from *Missa Pange lingua*

Ex. 10.2 cont.

Chant: "Sing, O tongue, of the mystery of the glorious body. . . ."
Polyphony: "Lord, have mercy."

tional framework of the French chanson of the period of Ockeghem and Busnois. The opening of the five-voice *Plusieurs regretz* ("Many regrets") serves
as an illustration (see Example 10.4). In this chanson the imitative duet of the
older chanson has become a two-part canon between the *tenor* and *altus,* expanded by an imitative voice, the *superius.* The role of the contratenor in the
old chanson is taken by the *quintus* and the *bassus,* but their countermotive (see
measures 1–3) is also imitated by the superius in measures 5–7. As a rule, in
Josquin's five-part chansons, many of which make use of canon, the voices
are paired as two canonic voices, two freely imitative voices, and a filler part,
usually the quintus, which resembles the older contratenor. In the four-part
songs, such as the famous *Mille regretz* ("A thousand regrets"), Josquin often
writes freely imitative counterpoint, with all voices sharing equally in the
texture.

    The motets offer the most varied picture of Josquin's output. In these he **Motets**
ranges over the entire spectrum of polyphonic composition in his day, from
strict cantus firmus settings, such as *Praeter rerum series* or *Miserere mei Deus,*
through chant-paraphrase works and freely invented pieces. In some of the
chant-paraphrase settings, particularly when Josquin sets psalms, he uses the
recitation formulas as a source of motivic material, and he shows extraordinary inventiveness in clothing the essentially monotone recitations in the
most elaborate contrapuntal figuration. Throughout this repertory the most
notable traits are Josquin's ability to invent fresh, expressive figures, his concern for the clarity of the text setting, and his vertical control of the polyphonic fabric. In some early works, such as *Tu solus qui facis mirabilia* ("You
alone who may create miracles"), his concern for declamation leads him to
write simple homophony, occasionally relieved by modest figuration. But
the same concern also accounts for the very clear declamation in many of Jos-

Ex. 10.3   Josquin Des Prés, final Kyrie from *Missa Pange lingua*

Chant: "[Blood] shed by the king of all people."
Polyphony: "Lord, have mercy."

quin's middle and late motets, where the musical rhythms seem to be deliberately derived from the rhythm of the words. Such is the case, for example, in the splendid *In exitu Israel* and *Dominus regnavit*. At the end of the first part of *Dominus regnavit,* his concern for text expression goes beyond correct declamation, and the music paints an expressive image of the text: *elevaverunt flumina fluctus suum* ("the rivers have lifted their waters") (see Example 10.5). Such outright word-painting became far more common in the music of later composers, but it can be found frequently in Josquin's late works, too.

Agricola and Obrecht

Among Josquin's contemporaries, Alexander Agricola and Jacob Obrecht represent the most conservative side of the new style. Agricola's career was divided between his service in Italy (Milan and Florence) and the north. His later years were spent in the service of Philip the Handsome, duke of Burgundy, and like Binchois and Busnois before him, most of Agricola's output is secular, although eight Masses and some two dozen motets by him also survive. His music is extremely intricate contrapuntally, since he favored

Ex. 10.4   Josquin Des Prés, *Plusieurs regretz*

Ex. 10.4   cont.

sur   la   ter - - - re   sont

qui   sur   la   ter - re   sont

qui   sur   la   ter - re   sont

- re   sont

sur   la   ter - - re   sont

"Most sorrows that are found on earth. . . ."

florid lines, which he could fit together with extraordinary skill. Many of his secular works survive only with text incipits, and are so complex as to suggest that they were meant as instrumental music.

Obrecht spent most of his life in the north, despite two journeys to Ferrara (where he died in 1505). His music has the same contrapuntal complexity found in Agricola's, but Obrecht is far clearer harmonically, and the figurations tend to run in sequences or in *ostinati*. Most of his production is sacred music: twenty-five Masses, twenty motets, and some thirty secular works. Some of the motets, particularly the extraordinary five-voice *Salve crux,* are among the best works written at the time, but it is in the Masses that Obrecht reveals his full genius as a master of the cantus firmus technique. Such works as the *Missa Sub tuum praesidium* and the *Missa Graecorum* show his command of this old-fashioned technique: cantus firmi are laid out in extremely ingenious ways in the latter piece and there are multiple cantus firmi in the former.

La Rue, Mouton, Isaac

In contrast to Obrecht and Agricola, Pierre de la Rue, Jean Mouton, and Heinrich Isaac represent the newer tendencies of the age. La Rue, composer to Marguerite of Austria, never left the north. He applies imitative procedures in the manner of Josquin to a rigorous contrapuntal texture that resembles Ockeghem's on occasion, as in the *Missa L'Homme armé* (*HAM* I, no. 92). Unlike the older master, La Rue uses the short motives and ostinati found in Obrecht's music but seldom in Ockeghem's.

Ex. 10.5   Josquin Des Prés, *Dominus regnavit*

Ex. 10.5   cont.

a   vo - ci bus   a - qua - rum mul - ta - rum

os   a   vo - ci - bus   a - qua - rum mul - ta - rum

vo - ci - bus   a - qua - rum   mul - ta - rum

a   vo - ci - bus   a - qua - rum mul - ta - rum

"The rivers raised their voice; the rivers raised their flow in the voice of many waters."

Mouton is in many ways the most progressive of the composers mentioned above. His music shows enormous contrapuntal skill and he shares Josquin's fondness for canon. Mouton's textures are clearer than those of La Rue or Obrecht and were probably the foundation of the later French style. Among his Masses is one of the earliest full parody Masses, based on the motet *Quem dicunt homines* ("What men will say") by Johannes Richafort (c. 1480–1547). Among the earliest parody Masses are also those of an extraordinary composer, Antoine de Févin, who died too young to reveal his full potential, but whose Masses *Ave Maria* and *Mente tota* (Agnus Dei, *HAM* I, no. 106) are among the finest of the period.

Josquin's most famous contemporary was Heinrich Isaac, who worked first in Florence under the Medici and later at the court of Emperor Maximilian. Isaac was as versatile as Josquin and even more prolific. His most extraordinary work, the *Choralis Constantinus* (commissioned in 1508), is a cycle of settings of the Propers for the Sundays and major feasts throughout the year—something no one had attempted since Léonin's *Magnus liber organi*. Besides the *Choralis Constantinus* Isaac wrote a large number of Masses, including several plainsong settings in which sections in polyphony alternate either with sections in chant or with organ paraphrases of the chant (*alternatim* Masses). He also used plainsong settings in Masses built according to all the traditional cantus firmus procedures. His secular works are similar to those of Josquin, but they also include many purely instrumental compositions clearly modeled on the chanson genre. To be sure, Josquin and Obrecht also wrote such works (see, for example, *HAM* I, no. 78), but it is in Isaac and Agricola that we find their most eloquent exponents.

Now that the complete works of Isaac are becoming available in a consistent edition, the *Choralis Constantinus* seems less of an isolated monument in

Isaac's production, although it remains in many ways his crowning achievement. The settings of the *Choralis Constantinus* are a veritable compendium of Netherlandish contrapuntal practice at the time, and Isaac's obvious facility is everywhere apparent. As in his other music, he favors textures that are generally thicker and busier than those of Josquin, and this tendency was transmitted through Isaac and Agricola to the composers of the German school in the sixteenth century.

The Diffusion of the Netherlands Style, 1520–1550

Willaert

Among Josquin's successors the most influential was Adrian Willaert (c. 1490–1562), a student of Mouton who was chapel master at St. Mark's Cathedral in Venice (1527–1562), where he taught several generations of Italian and northern composers. Like Josquin, Willaert was a master of every genre of composition, and his Masses (mostly parodies of Mouton's motets), madrigals, and instrumental *ricercari* are among the best examples of each genre written between 1530 and 1560. In his motets, however, Willaert shows his most advanced style. He favors a five-voice texture, sometimes expanded to six, which under his influence became the standard texture by the middle of the century. The thick writing is sometimes relieved by passages in three or four voices, though less frequently than in Josquin's music. Furthermore, Willaert has a relaxed approach to imitation, and the voices often share only a very general shape rather than a specific motive. This quality can be seen in the motet *Sub tuum praesidium,* published in 1559 as part of the *Musica nova,* a collection of motets, madrigals, and instrumental pieces that had a seminal influence on the master's contemporaries and successors (see Example 10.6).

The motet in this example uses no borrowed material, but a number of others do have cantus firmi, often in canon (e.g., see *HAM* I, no. 113). In his motets and madrigals, Willaert takes special care in setting the words to the music to preserve their proper accentuation—a concern that reflects his contact with the new humanistic ideals and that he transmitted to his disciples. Humanist influence is also reflected in his choice of madrigal texts. All but one madrigal in the *Musica nova* are settings of Petrarch's sonnets. Each is divided into two parts: one for the two quatrains and another for the two tercets, a division that was to become standard.

Beyond these achievements Willaert also gained fame for strengthening in Italy the tradition of *cori spezzati:* that is, the antiphonal use of two polyphonic choirs situated in different parts of the church. This technique was not invented by Willaert, but he used it brilliantly, probably under the inspiration of the architecture of St. Mark's which had two choir galleries, each with its own organ. And the practice became a Venetian specialty under Willaert's successors, Andrea and Giovanni Gabrieli.

Cori spezzati

Ex. 10.6   Adrian Willaert, *Sub tuum praesidium*

"Under your rule we take refuge. . . ."

Gombert

Nicholas Gombert (c. 1500–1556), a singer in the chapel of Emperor Charles V from 1526 to c. 1540, is often regarded as the classical exponent of the style of imitative polyphony. Like Willaert, Gombert is clearly a follower of Josquin. But his melodies, unlike those of Josquin, which are often composed of short and well-articulated segments, are usually long, florid lines that seem to hark back to the style of Ockeghem. Despite its relative thickness, Gombert's texture tends to be clearer than that of Ockeghem because it is far more controlled by vertical sonorities. Nevertheless, he also shares Ockeghem's fondness for low tessituras and unprepared dissonances—the latter a surprising element in what is probably some of the most euphonious music written in the early sixteenth century. Gombert favors a consistent texture with no apparent breaks and virtually no passages in reduced scoring, organized as a series of tightly interlocked points of imitation and propelled by the constantly changing melodic shape of the lines.

Few composers display Gombert's melodic inventiveness and sense for vocal line. More than any other music of his generation, his is a singer's art. The beautifully ordered, dense polyphony of his music is seen in the motet *Super flumina* ("By the rivers of Babylon"; *HAM* I, no. 114). Nine of Gombert's ten Masses are parody Masses. The exception is the *Missa Da pacem,* a plainsong fantasy in the manner of Josquin's *Missa Pange lingua.* In his parody Masses Gombert follows a loose set of conventions for borrowing material from polyphonic models that later became widely accepted. The beginning and the end of the model usually start and close each Mass movement. Themes from the model tend to appear in the Mass in the same order, and major subdivisions of the Mass movements are based on those in the model, particularly when the model is a motet or a madrigal in several parts. But the ways in which the original material is transformed are often unique to each work, and parody remains one of the least classifiable procedures in a style that is already hard to define in terms of structure or shape. The beginning of Gombert's six-voice motet *Media vita,* and that of the five-voice Mass based upon it, are given in Examples 10.7 and 10.8.

The general shape of the motet opening, with its leisurely entrances, is preserved in the Mass, albeit transposed up an octave. This motion allows Gombert to substitute a very effective bass entrance (Kyrie, measure 8) for the almost inaudible entrance of the sixth voice in the motet (*altus,* measure 9). The parody, of course, goes well beyond the altering of relationships between parts and includes new contrapuntal patterns spun out of the motives. Note that Gombert, unlike Josquin and Willaert, is not too concerned with the proper declamation of the text. To be sure, each text phrase is set to a new musical phrase, but the words are often "misaccented."

Clemens non Papa

In contrast with the relatively cosmopolitan lives of Willaert and Gombert, Jacob Clement (c. 1510–c. 1556)—known as Clemens non Papa, a humorous nickname that may date from his student days, when the memory of Pope Clement VII (d. 1534) was still fresh—led the life of a provincial church musician in the Low Countries. But his enormous output—15 parody Masses, a Requiem, 15 Magnificats, 90 chansons, 150 *souterliedekens* (Dutch psalms), and more than 230 motets—as well as the extraordinary quality of his music make him clearly the third major composer of the post-Josquin generation. Like Gombert, he favors very thick textures, but rhythmically his music is often far more active than that of Gombert. In a few of his works

Ex. 10.7   Nicholas Gombert, Motet *Media vita*

"In the midst of life. . . ."

Ex. 10.8   Nicholas Gombert, Kyrie from parody Mass

"Lord, have mercy."

Clemens seems to have composed the parts so that if the singers were to follow the rules for the addition of accidentals known as *musica ficta* with absolute consistency (and courage), they would produce a chromatic version of
the work that could go as far afield as the use of C-flat and F-flat. Examples of
this kind of music, though few in number, were composed by Clemens, Willaert, and others. Some scholars have thought that such "secret chromat-

icism" was symbolic of the composers' sympathies for religious reform,[2] but most likely it reflects the age-old delight with arcane beauty accessible only to the highly skilled.

Other Composers

Besides the three composers mentioned above, the numbers of brilliant composers active in the early sixteenth century were legion. In the north Johannes Richafort (c. 1480–1547) and Claudin de Sermisy (c. 1490–1562) continued the tradition of Mouton, and a number of Italianized northerners—notably Philippe Deslouges, known as Verdelot (d.c. 1552); Jacob Arcadelt (c. 1504–1568); and Cipriano de Rore (1516–1565), the outstanding student of Willaert—composed Masses and motets in the new style. Like Sermisy in France, however, they devoted their best efforts to secular music. Their work will be discussed later. In Germany Ludwig Senfl (c. 1486–1543), a student of Isaac, also continued his teacher's tradition of elaborate counterpoint and florid writing.

Italy

Throughout the fifteenth century, northern composers wrote occasional settings of Italian texts. We have Dunstaple's *O rosa bella* ("Oh, beautiful rose," possibly a contrafactum), a handful of works by Dufay (including his setting of Petrarch's *Vergine bella*), and a number of anonymous settings and some contrafacta of French songs in the later chansonniers. Composers of Josquin's generation, particularly Isaac, added to the Italian repertory, sometimes with pieces having only an Italian title, such as Isaac's *La morra (Mora, donna gentile)* or Josquin's *La Bernardina,* and at other times with settings of complete Italian texts, such as Johannes Martini's *Fortuna d'un gran tempo,* Josquin's and Compère's *Scaramella,* and Josquin's famous frottola *Il grillo* ("The cricket").

Italian composers   By the last decade of the fifteenth century, however, a native school of Italian composers began to emerge in the north Italian courts, particularly that of Mantua under the patronage of Isabella d'Este (1474–1539). These included Marchetto Cara (d.c. 1530) and Bartolomeo Tromboncino (d.c. 1535) in Mantua, Michele Pesenti (d. after 1521) in Verona, Antonio Caprioli (fl. 1510) in Brescia, and Francesco d'Ana (d.c. 1503) in Venice. Their music springs from a tradition of improvised song, usually with the accompaniment of a lute or a *lira da braccio* (a violin-like instrument with seven strings—five on the fingerboard and two drones—that was cultivated in Italy during the fifteenth century). The few samples of such improvised songs that were committed to writing show a simple chordal pattern supporting a declamatory melody, which was probably used as the basis for further elaborations by the performer. With their irregular meter, dependent entirely upon the structure of the text, their repetitive strophic forms, their simple declamatory style, and their fundamentally chordal accompaniments, these pieces are far removed from the contrapuntal polyphony of the north. The Italian composers of the late fifteenth and early sixteenth centuries carried this style one step beyond mere improvisation into a fully composed style of simple but carefully structured and often very delicate music. Composers of this generation are usually called "the frottolists." This title is an oversimplification, since their output included not only frottole but also other poetic and "popular" types of songs (e.g., *villotte, strambotti, capitoli*), sonnets, odes, and, in the case of Pesenti, motets.

The frottola proper, or *barzelletta,* is a fixed form related to the old Italian ballata. It consists of a four-line *ripresa* and a six-line stanza set to music as follows:

The frottola

	Ripresa				Stanza					
Music:	A	B	C	D	A	B	A	B	C	D
Rhyme:	a	b	b	a	c	d	c	d	d	a

The ripresa is sung before each stanza, and the number of stanzas is not fixed. Occasionally composers wrote a shorter ripresa to be sung between the stanzas, and it takes the musical form of A–B–coda. Frottole and the settings of the other poetic forms, copied together in the manuscript anthologies, also appear together in the eleven books of frottole printed by Ottaviano Petrucci between 1504 and 1514.

The style of these works shows its debt to the earlier improvisatory style in its repetitive structures, its patterned rhythms, and its texture, an essentially ornamented homophony with only occasional passages of contrapuntal figuration, as in measures 15–17 of the frottola by Marchetto Cara shown in Example 10.9.

The evolution of the frottola toward the madrigal was not only a musical process but a literary one. The texts of most frottole are charming but ephemeral poems of no great literary merit. The turn toward more serious

From frottola to madrigal

Ex. 10.9   Marchetto Cara, *O mia cieca e dura sorte*

Ex. 10.9   cont.

tri - ta,   O   mi - se - ria   di   mia   vi - ta   tri sto a -

nuntio a la _____ mi - a   mor - te   a la mia _____ mor - te

"O my blind and harsh fate, fed always by sorrow, O misery of my life, sad pre-
monition of my death. . . ."

Bernardo Pisano

texts took place largely because of the influence of Cardinal Pietro Bembo
(1470–1547), a poet and literary scholar who turned Italian men of letters to
the works of Petrarch and initiated the Petrarchist school. In 1520 Petrucci
issued the *Musica di messer Bernardo Pisano sopra le canzone del Petrarca.* Bernardo Pisano (1490–1548), a Florentine musician, goes beyond the frottola in
these works and approaches the style of the madrigal, not only in his choice
of serious and expressive texts, but also in his restrained application of motet-
like polyphony to his settings. In these works Pisano was writing what
Alfred Einstein has called "polyphonically animated homophony."[3] Other
influences seem to have affected Italian musicians. Most prominent was the
new *Parisian chanson,* a genre cultivated by composers such as Claudin de Sermisy, whose works began to appear in the collections of the Parisian printer
Pierre Attaingnant in 1528.

Early madrigalists

Early madrigal collections began to appear in the 1530s and are dominated by the works of northern composers active in Florence, namely Verdelot and, slightly later, Arcadelt. To them we should add the name of the Italian composer who along with Verdelot must be considered one of the earliest true madrigalists, Costanzo Festa (d. 1545; active in Rome). Around them cluster a number of lesser composers such as Francesco Corteccia (d. 1571), Francesco de Layolle (d. 1540), and Domenico Ferrabosco (1513–1574). Only later was this group joined by the great master of northern polyphony Adrian Willaert, who essentially changed the texture of the madrigal from four to five voices and established the careful treatment of the words characteristic of the next generation of composers.

The texture typical of the classic Florentine madrigal is not much different, however, from that found in the more complex settings of Pisano. Little in Festa's *Quando ritrova* ("When I find my shepherdess"; *HAM* I, no. 129) or in Arcadelt's *Voi ve n'andate* ("You go heavenward"; *HAM* I, no. 130) could not be found in Pisano's music, although in Arcadelt's work we begin to encounter a concern for text expression through word-painting that is typical of the later madrigal. The normal texture of the early madrigal is four voices, even though Verdelot and Arcadelt also composed five-voice works. The writing is barely one step beyond homophony, despite the use of imitation. But in a few works, such as Verdelot's *Madonna il tuo bel viso* (see Example 10.10), a fully developed contrapuntal style appears. Madrigals of this type were usually composed to the more serious and expressive texts.

As noted above, in the works of Willaert the texture changed to five voices and became more intricate and contrapuntally conceived. The major change, however, came with a second generation of madrigal composers, **Second-** dominated by Willaert's brilliant disciples Cipriano de Rore (1516–1565) and **generation** Andrea Gabrieli (c. 1520–1586), but also including Annibale Padovano **madrigalists** (1527–1575), Costanzo Porta (c. 1529–1601), Vincenzo Ruffo (1510–1587), and others. Even though the very best composer of this generation, Cipriano de Rore, was a northerner, the generation was dominated by Italian composers.

In Rore's and Gabrieli's madrigals we encounter the same attention to **Rore** proper prosody and text declamation as in the music of Willaert, but Rore goes even further in his desire to express the meaning of every word and the sense of the whole poem through musical means. His extraordinary setting of *Da le belle contrade* ("From the fair regions"; *HAM* I, no. 131) is a compendium of his techniques, from the simple word-painting in giving to a single voice the words *sola mi lasci* ("you are leaving me alone") to the realistic setting of the sighs and exclamations of sorrow in the text. There are also serpentine lines that describe the embrace of the two lovers as the entwining of ivy or acanthus. But far more subtle is the series of chromatic shifts that set a passionate plaint by one of the lovers, and move from near hysteria to emotional exhaustion in a few measures. As the direct speech ends and the original narrative tone of the madrigal resumes, the opening tonal center of F reappears, seemingly out of nowhere (see Example 10.11).

In his concern for text expression Rore pushed the musical framework of

Ex. 10.10   Philippe Verdelot, *Madonna il tuo bel viso*

"Lady, your lovely visage, that is my guide in the great sea of love. . . ."

the madrigal near the breaking point. And, not surprisingly, those composers who finally went beyond the Renaissance style toward what was later called the *seconda pratica,* the "second style" of the Baroque period, looked upon Rore as the founder of the new manner. The art of the great madrigalists of the end of the sixteenth century—Luca Marenzio, Giaches de Wert, and above all Claudio Monteverdi (see Chapter 14)—rests on the foundations created by Rore.

Other genres   Along with the madrigal, composers in Italy continued cultivating the lighter genres, direct descendants of the *villotta* and the carnival songs. High-spirited and irreverent, these pieces either use texts in dialect—*villanella* from Naples, *giustiniana* from Venice, *bergamasca* from Bergamo—or poke fun at foreign accents. The more lyrical *canzonetta* and *balletto* (a dance song) were also made popular by such composers as Domenico da Nola, Giovanni Giacomo Gastoldi, Willaert, and Marenzio.

France

The tradition of French secular song reached its most elaborate expression in the chansons of Josquin. But the genre underwent a period of simplification in the years between the three great anthologies published by Petrucci in 1501 and 1504 and the first collections that were published in Paris by Pierre Attaingnant in 1528. Significantly, the few sources of chansons between Petrucci and Attaingnant contain virtually no works of Josquin, and his compo-

Sources of the French style

Ex. 10.11   Cipriano de Rore, *Da le belle contrade*

Ex. 10.11   cont.

mo pia - cer fi - nisc'_____ in pian - to

mo pia - cer fi - nisc' in pian - to ne po-ten - do dir

cer fi - nisc' in pian - to

cer fi - nisc' in pian - to ne po - ten - to dir piu

cer fi - nisc' in pian - to ne po- ten -do dir piu

"Alas, cruel Love, your pleasures are certainly dubious and short, for you take pleasure in making the greatest pleasure end in tears."

sitions do not reappear until the publication of collections by Tylman Susato in Antwerp in 1543 and 1544.

The origins of the musical style found in the Parisian collections of the 1530s remain unclear. To be sure, the chansons of Jean Mouton and Antoine de Févin are immediate predecessors of the new style, and just how influential Josquin's chansons were is uncertain. Beautiful as they are, these elaborate works seem to represent a bypath that found no immediate followers. The change found in the works of Claudin de Sermisy (c. 1490–1562). Clément Jannequin (c. 1485–c. 1560), Pierre Certon (d. 1572), and others is not just a matter of a simpler style but of the texts as well. The influence of Clément **Early** Marot (1496–1544) was decisive, for Marot turned from the artificial rhetoric **chansons** of the late fifteenth century toward a plainer, more direct poetry. At their best, the poems of Marot and his circle are delicate, elegant, and sentimental. In addition, Marot cultivated a genre of the picaresque that often consisted of extremely lewd texts set in elegant verse. Both varieties of poetry were set to music by the Parisian composers, and the texture of the songs was generally four voices. In the sentimental songs, we often encounter a simple and tuneful soprano, which declaims the text with a few melismas, supported by a tenor that is almost as tuneful, a harmonically conceived bass, and an alto that serves essentially as harmonic filler. This structure occurs even in the chansons that use imitative entries once all voices are singing. The typical texture appears in the opening of Sermisy's *Amour partes* (see Example 10.12).

The obscene chansons followed essentially the same pattern but tended to use rapid *patter-song,* particularly in the lewder sections. A related genre, which also used something like patter-song, was the descriptive chanson, into which bird calls, battle cries, or street noises were incorporated. The master of this genre was Jannequin, whose works *La Guerre* ("War"), *Le Chant des oiseaux* ("Song of the birds"), and *L'Alouette* ("The lark"; *HAM* I, no. 107) gained immense favor. Except for the descriptive chansons, which often follow a pattern of strophic variations, the typical chanson pattern is AA B CC, although a number of variants are also found. *Amour partes,* cited above, has the form Ax B C Axx; that is, the final phrase of A is sung twice at the end.

The French chanson, as cultivated by Netherlandish composers of the generation of Gombert and Clemens non Papa, had a more rigorously contrapuntal texture. By the middle of the century, however, the more complex style of the Netherlanders had begun to spread in France, partly in response to a new change in literary tastes there. A group of poets known as La

Midcentury chansons

Cipiriano de Rore. (Bayerische Staatsbibliothek, Munich)

Pléiade, led by Pierre Ronsard (1524–1585), advocated a return to lofty subjects and a rhetorical style modeled on ancient poetry. The new texts were set to more contrapuntal music by composers such as Arcadelt, Claude Goudimel (c. 1520–1572), Claude le Jeune (c. 1525–1600), and Guillaume Costeley (c. 1531–1606). In addition to the contrapuntal settings, however, some composers experimented with settings of poems by Antoine de Baïf and his circle, called *vers mesuré à l'antique,* in which the poetry adhered to classical meters and the music rigidly followed the long and short syllables of the text. Le Jeune's *Revecy venir le printemps* ("Here comes spring again") and *D'une Coline* ("As I walk upon a hill"; *HAM* I, no. 138) are among the most notable examples of this musical style, known as *musique mesurée.*

Other genres   Just as the Italian composers cultivated the lighter genres, the French also cultivated simple homophonic settings of popular songs called *voix de ville* ("vaudevilles"), often for solo voice and lute. This genre eventually gave rise to the *airs de cour,* solo songs that point toward the Baroque.

The sacred music of Sermisy, Certon, and the other Parisian composers of the second quarter of the sixteenth century is clearly derived from the style of Mouton, but the Masses and motets of the Parisians, affected as they were

Anonymous painter: *The Prodigal Son.* Performance of a chanson by a singer, lute, and flute. Howard Brown (*JAMS,* XXIV [1971], 215–219) points out that the piece performed is Sermisy's *Au pres de vous* and the depiction is so realistic that the music written in the painting and the fingerings of lute and flute point to m. 11 of the piece. (Musée Carnevalet, Paris)

Ex. 10.12   Claudin de Sermisy, *Amour partes*

"Love, depart! I chase you away. . . ."

also by the chanson style, are more declamatory and simpler than those of Willaert, Gombert, Clemens non Papa, or Rore. The French style even influenced such Italian exiles as Francesco de Layolle, who worked at Lyons for Jacques Moderne, a printer who issued numerous collections devoted to Netherlandish, Italian, and Parisian composers, as well as to provincial French musicians.

Germany

German music of the fifteenth and sixteenth centuries is often associated in the popular mind with the guilds of *Meistersinger* ("mastersingers"), primarily because of Richard Wagner's well-known opera, which presents a his-

The mastersingers

torically accurate account of the Nuremberg guild and of the singing contests sponsored by the mastersingers. Their guilds, which flourished from about 1450 to 1600, were societies of amateur musicians who modeled themselves on the medieval minnesingers. Elaborate rules were devised for the composition of their songs, monophonic pieces mostly in bar form (AAB) and based on texts that paraphrased the Bible. These texts were set syllabically to notes of equal value; the occasional melismas that were used were called *Blumen* ("flowers"). The mastersingers had little direct effect on polyphonic music in Germany, but they did influence the musical education of the bourgeoisie. The most famous of the mastersingers, and the hero of Wagner's opera, was Hans Sachs of Nuremberg (1494–1576), who wrote more than six thousand songs.

Sources of the music   Our picture of fifteenth-century polyphonic music in Germany is derived mainly from a number of collections copied during the second half of the century. These sources contain many songs from the Dufay and Ockeghem generations, most without words or with the original French texts supplanted by Latin contrafacta. In addition to the imported works, however, the *Liederbucher* ("songbooks") have a considerable number of seemingly local pieces. Some have no text but fancy titles such as *Dy Katzen Pfothe* ("The cat's paw") or *Der Ratten Schwancz* ("The rat's tail"); these are the ancestors of instrumental music. Others do have full German texts. Among the latter we encounter the earliest examples of what was to become a distinctive German genre, the *Tenor-Lied,* in which a simple tenor line with text was accompanied by two or more instrumental parts, often more florid than the vocal line.

The Tenor-Lied   The last decade of the fifteenth century and the early part of the sixteenth saw a great flowering of the Tenor-Lied, particularly in the works of Heinrich Isaac, Paul Hofhaimer (1459–1537), Heinrich Finck (1447–1527), and Ludwig Senfl (c. 1486–1543). These composers brought to the Tenor-Lied the techniques of Netherlandish polyphony, including the use of imitation, which inevitably brought about a more homogeneous texture. Nevertheless, the polarity between the tenor and the other parts remained. Occasionally a second voice, usually the *superius,* formed a structural duet with the tenor, and a few songs show an added text in the superius. The classical stage of the Tenor-Lied can be seen in Hofhaimer's *Herzliebstes Bild* (see Example 10.13). The tenor and superius form a parallel-motion duet in the first half (some sources have text also in the superius), but at the beginning of the *Abgesant* the other voices start a modest imitation. In Senfl's *Gott hat sein Wort* (see Example 10.14), imitative texture pervades the entire piece.

Still, in Senfl's work the older duet polarization appears at the beginning between the bass and tenor, but even such a small distinction between parts is absent in Isaac's *Zwischen Berg und tiefen Tal* ("Between the mountain and the deep valley"; *HAM* I, no. 87). Simple chordal settings, such as Isaac's famous *Innsbruck, ich muss dich lassen* ("Innsbruck, I must leave thee"), also persisted, as did the purely instrumental settings of popular tunes. Isaac and Finck were particularly prolific in this genre.

Ex. 10.13 Paul Hofhaimer, *Herzliebstes Bild*

"A loving image you present me with your love and favor. In the same manner, I will to you, when, with pleasure and desire I give you my heart."

Ex. 10.14   Ludwig Senfl, *Gott hat sein Wort*

"God has maintained his word in many places, free from tyranny. . . ."

Sacred music   The sacred music of the German composers derives from the style of Isaac, for Senfl and Finck were fully at home in the dense, florid counterpoint of the older master. The typical midcentury style, in which Catholic and Protestant works appear side by side, can be seen in a series of publications printed by Petreius, Ott, and Georg Rhaw. These pieces continued the tradition of florid counterpoint, at least in the Latin settings of Sixtus Dietrich (1492–1548) and Benedictus Ducis (d. 1544), while Hans Leo Hassler cultivated a more transparent style indebted essentially to the Italian composers.

Spain

Netherlands style in Spain   Throughout the fifteenth century, Netherlandish polyphony was cultivated in Spain by native as well as foreign composers. The oldest known

Spanish Renaissance master is Johannes Cornago (fl. 1455–1475), of the chapel of Alfonso I of Aragon. Cornago worked in Italy and Spain, and his works are preserved in sources from both countries. These works show him to be a gifted composer in the style prevalent at the time of Ockeghem. Indeed, Ockeghem chose to pay homage to Cornago by reworking and adding an extra voice to his *villancico* called *Que's mi vida preguntays?*

The marriage of Ferdinand of Aragon and Isabella of Castile in 1469 ushered in the most brilliant period in the cultural history of Spain. Ferdinand and Isabella maintained a musical chapel in the last decades of the fifteenth century that included Juan de Anchieta (c. 1462–1523) and Francisco de Peñalosa (c. 1470–1528). Emperor Charles V, who grew up in the Netherlands, brought a Flemish chapel with him to Spain, but in 1529 he also established a Spanish chapel to serve his wife, Isabel of Portugal. Both chapels coexisted until 1636, when they were united.

Composers in the different cathedrals included Pedro de Escobar (d. 1514) in Tarazona, and Martin de Rivaflecha (d. 1527) in Palencia. They all wrote sacred music, and Peñalosa's *Missa Nunca fué pena mayor* (based on a villancico by Johannes Wreede), Escobar's *Clamabat autem mulier,* and Rivaflecha's *Salve regina* are among the finest works of the period. Nevertheless, the richest collections of Spanish music of the late fifteenth and early sixteenth centuries are the *cancioneros,* large anthologies of secular works.

The earliest cancioneros contain a number of foreign works—frottole and villotte—as well as villancicos by foreign masters, such as Johannes Wreede (or Urrede, fl. 1475), whose villancico *Nunca fué pena mayor,* on a poem by the duke of Alba, opens the *Cancionero de Palacio.* But the repertory is dominated by villancicos and romances (long poems with four-line stanzas about legendary or historical subjects). The villancico and the closely related *canción* are fixed forms derived from the French virelai or the Italian ballata. Their scheme is as follows:

Villancicos

		Copla (stanza)	
	Estribillo (refrain)	mudanza	vuelta
Music:	A	B B	A
Rhyme:			
1. Canción:	a a	b b	a a
2. Villancico:	a a	b b	b a

Note the similarities to the ballata's *piedi* and *volta* in the stanza. The divisions, however, are not always so clear as the above diagram suggests. The manuscripts list as villancicos many pieces with canción texts—a practice that is particularly prevalent in the early cancioneros.

The early villancico is stylistically close to the Italian frottola. The simplest pieces are merely homophonic settings based on the chord schemes that were emerging in instrumental music as dance-tune progressions: the *Passamezzo* and *Romanesca.*

Juan del Encina   The composer whose work dominates the early repertory is Juan del Encina (c. 1467–1529). Apparently he wrote most of his music in his early youth, when he was in the service of the duke of Alba. Three of his villancicos—*Congoxa mas que cruel; Pues que jamas olvidaros;* and *Mas vale trocar placer*—appear in *HAM* (I, nos. 98a, b, and c) and demonstrate his style, fundamentally homophonic but enlivened by some delicately balanced contrapuntal sections. The last of these villancicos is probably a theatrical piece, for Encina's duties included running the ducal theater.

Italian influence   Italian poetry, which influenced the poetry of Juan Boscán (c. 1493–1542) and Garcilaso de la Vega (1503–1536), effected a subtle change in the character of the Spanish villancico, which became more Italianate and madrigal-like. This shift is already noticeable in the pieces of the *Cancionero de Medinaceli* set to Garcilaso's poetry, but it reaches its apex in the two collections of Juan Vásquez (c. 1500–1560), published in 1551 and 1560 respectively. Villancicos

Ex. 10.15   Juan Vásquez, *Si no os hubiera mirado*

"If I had not seen you, would to God that I had not. . . ."

such as *Si no os hubiera mirado* (Example 10.15) are essentially madrigals set to Spanish words. The same tendencies are present in the slightly more conservative repertory of the *Cancionero de Upsala,* which includes one work by Cristóbal de Morales, *Si no os hubiera mirado* (a different text from that of Vásquez), and one by Gombert (the only composer named in the print), *Dezidle al caballero.* Also noteworthy are works by Mateo Flecha the Elder (c. 1481– 1553), particularly two brilliant pieces, *Que farem del pobre Joan* and *Teresica hermana* (see Example 10.16), in which a traditional villancico text is set in the manner of a Parisian chanson. Flecha and his nephew, Mateo Flecha the Younger (c. 1520– 1604), also produced a number of elaborate *quodlibets,* in which several popular tunes, or fragments of tunes, are played in counterpoint with each other. These are similar to the descriptive chansons, which the Flechas called *ensaladas* (salads).

Just as the frottola repertory was often intabulated for solo voice and lute, the Spanish secular repertory—even contrapuntal works like Flecha's villancicos—was intabulated for voice and *vihuela de mano,* a guitarlike instrument tuned like the lute. A number of virtuoso *vihuelistas* published extensive collections of intabulations that included not only purely instrumental music of great complexity but also parodies and outright transcriptions of polyphonic vocal music.

Intabulations

Ex. 10.16   Mateo Flecha, *Teresica hermana*

Ex. 10.16   cont.

de   la fa ra ri ri - ra   de   la fa ra   ri   ri   ra, her - 'ma - na Te - re - sa

fa ra ri ri ra   de   la fa ri ra   la   fa ra - ri - ra, her - ma - na Te - re - sa

Te - re-si - ca her - ma - na   de   la   fa ra ri ri - ra, her - ma - na Te - re - sa

si - ca her ma - na   de   la fa ra ri ri - ra - ri - ra, her - ma - na Te - re - sa

"Teresica, sister (of the *farariri rá*), sister Teresa. . . ."

Morales   The most important Spanish composer of the post-Josquin generation, a master fully the equal of Gombert or Clemens non Papa, is Cristóbal de Morales (c. 1500–1553). Ironically, Morales never served in the Spanish royal chapel and wrote virtually no secular music. But he produced twenty-two Masses, sixteen *alternatim* Magnificats (one for the odd and one for the even verses in each of the eight modes), and more than a hundred motets. His career took him to Rome and to a number of Spanish cathedrals, including Avila, Toledo, Palencia, Marchena, and Malaga.

Morales favored a dense texture reminiscent of Gombert and Clemens, but his treatment of dissonance already points to the controlled style of Palestrina. Typical of his dense but euphonious music is the motet *Emendemus in melius* ("Let us make amends"; *HAM* I, no. 128), set to an *ostinato* cantus firmus with its own text. In his Masses, Morales cultivated every technique of the time — cantus firmus, paraphrase, and parody — using secular and sacred models. In the motets, particularly those that were freely composed, he used canon extensively — a device he also used to increase the number of voices in the final Agnus Dei of the Masses and in the final verse of the Magnificats (see Example 10.17). Morales was the first Spanish master to achieve truly international fame, a fact reflected by his designation as "a Netherlander" in the Spanish theorist Juan Bermudo's *Declaracion de instrumentos musicales* ("Declaration on Musical Instruments," 1544).

England

Early Tudor music   English music in the early part of the sixteenth century changed less than did continental music. On the Continent the last decades of the fifteenth century and the early part of the sixteenth witnessed an enormous surge in secu-

lar music, but in England sacred music continued to be the most vital genre.
Rather than turning to the new kinds of motet texts found in continental
works, English composers continued setting the Mass, the Magnificat, and
votive antiphons in the florid style of the older generation. William Cornysh
(d. 1523), Robert Fairfax (1464–1521), John Redford (d. 1547), Nicholas Ludford (c. 1485–c. 1557), Robert Carver (c. 1491–c. 1550), and above all John
Taverner (c. 1495–1545) continued the tradition of Dunstaple and his followers.

Taverner's music can be taken almost as a summation of the early six-   **Taverner**
teenth-century English style. He wrote three festal Masses *a 6*, three *a 5*—one
of which (the *Missa Mater Christi*) is a parody Mass, a genre not normally
cultivated in England—and one Mass *a 4, The Western Wynde*. His other
works include votive antiphons, Magnificats, responsories, sequences,
Tracts, a *Te Deum,* and a prose. *The Western Wynde* is the earliest work based
on this particular cantus firmus (there are two others, by Christopher Tye
and John Shepherd). The Benedictus, found in *HAM* I, no. 112, shows the
great harmonic clarity that Taverner imposed on the florid style. More than
most of his contemporaries, Taverner valued structural clarity, and his music
makes considerable use of imitation, canon, and repeated patterns: traits that
go counter to the almost irrational melodic lines of the older English style.
But the enormous rhythmic activity and expansive lines of the older style remain an essential part of Taverner's work.

Ex. 10.17   Cristóbal de Morales, Magnificat

Ex. 10.17   cont.

"As it was in the beginning, is now, and ever shall be. . . ."

English secular music from this period is scarce. The published court **Sources of** songs consist of simple settings that reflect the influence of the French chan- **the music** son. A few are attributed to Henry VIII, a competent amateur, whose songs, usually two lines in thirds over a simple bass, are among the clearest examples of the basic procedures underlying this repertory. Those by Cornysh and Fairfax are artistically superior settings, particularly Cornysh's *Ah, Robin, Gentle Robin,* and *Adew, Adew (HAM* I, no. 86).

The religious upheavals that followed Henry VIII's break with Rome in 1534 did not affect English church music so much as the reforms during the **Church** reign of his son, Edward VI (1547–1553), which nearly extinguished all **music** music in English churches. Mary's short reign (1553–1558) and her futile res- toration of Catholicism, as well as Elizabeth's love for music and for ritual, repaired some of the damage, but the great English tradition of florid church music died with the composers who lived through these changes: William Mundy (c. 1529–1591), Robert Parsons (d. 1570), John Shepherd (c. 1520– 1563), Christopher Tye (c. 1520–1573), Robert White (1535–1574), and, above all, Thomas Tallis (c. 1505–1585) and his disciple William Byrd (1543– 1623). These composers wrote not only Latin church music but also music for the new English liturgy. We should be wary, however, of the generaliza- tion that Latin works were intended for the Roman liturgy only. With the exception of the long Marian antiphons of Mundy, probably written during Mary's reign, the complete Latin Ordinaries, and Byrd's two books of the *Gradualia,* many Latin works could have been used in the Anglican services after Elizabeth restored the use of Latin for parts of the service in 1559 (a res- toration that met with great resistance, however).

William Byrd's Latin sacred music belongs stylistically with that of Lasso, Palestrina, and Victoria, and will be discussed in the next chapter. Tallis, on **Tallis** the other hand, may be viewed more properly as the last representative of the older style. Although he was a master of every technique of composition, his taste favored the traditional cantus firmus settings. Some early works written without a cantus firmus show a rather stiff use of imitation; but among the pieces that may be considered late works, published in the *Cantiones sacrae* ("Sacred songs") of 1575 (together with Byrd, who perhaps influenced him), Tallis produced masterpieces of imitative polyphony, with expansive and stately expositions, such as the motet *O sacrum convivium,* the responsory *Au- divi vocem* ("I heard a voice"; *HAM* I, no. 127), or the dramatic *In jejunio et fletu.* A similarly impressive display of skill appears in Tallis' famous motet for forty voices, *Spem in alium.*

The secular music of the second and third quarters of the sixteenth cen- tury is dominated by a genre that has aptly been called *consort song* by Philip **The consort** Brett.[4] It is as different from the early songs as they are from the music that **song** preceded them. These works, which consist of a solo voice accompanied by four instruments, were apparently sung by a choirboy accompanied by four viols. When two parts were provided with text, the second was sung by one of the viol players. The texts are often strophic poems, many of which appear in a miscellany compiled by Richard Edwards, *The Paradise of Dainty Devices* (London, 1576), or else form part of the "choirboy plays" performed by the children of the Chapel Royal, St. Paul's Cathedral, and Westminster Abbey.

Byrd's songs   Among the composers of consort songs were John Shepherd and Robert Parsons, but it was William Byrd who brought this genre to its highest peak and continued to cultivate it after the new vogue for Italianate madrigals supplanted it. Indeed, Byrd's first secular publication, *Psalmes, Sonets and Songs of Sadness and Pietie* (1588), consists mostly of consort songs with words added to the viol parts, as Byrd himself states in the preface: "If thou delight in music of great compasse, heere are divers songs being originally made for instruments to express the harmonie, and one voice to pronounce the dittie, are now framed in all parts for voices to sing the same."[5]

The texture and style of the music, even when it comes close to the French chanson, as in *Susanna faire,* is far from that of continental secular music. Rather, it approaches the counterpoint of the older English school, with perhaps some influence of the midcentury Netherlands school. Some imitation is present, but the accompanying parts are so vague as to be unnoticeable as lines, throwing the main singing voices into greater relief. This phenomenon can be observed in one of Byrd's finest songs, the elegy for the death of Tallis, *Ye Sacred Muses* (see Example 10.18).

To be sure, Byrd could write in the most modern Italianate style, as shown in *This Sweet and Merry Month of May,* commissioned by Thomas Watson for his anthology of 1590, *Italian Madrigals Englished.* Byrd also combined the consort-song technique and the choral responsory to create a new genre, the *verse anthem,* in works such as the famous *Christ Rising* of 1611 (*HAM* I, no. 152).

The Late Madrigal in Italy

In the years following the death of Cipriano de Rore (1565), there arose in Italian music tendencies that led to the disintegration of the Renaissance style. Their roots, like those of past changes, lay in the humanistic attitude toward music and in a change in literary tastes that began to make itself felt after approximately 1560.

Literary and musical changes   By 1550 literati and musical scholars had arrived at a relatively unified view of the role of music in antiquity, a view dependent largely on descriptions of this music's effect on listeners and upon increased knowledge of the sources of Greek harmonic theory. Such scholars as Heinrich Glarean (1488–1563), Gioseffo Zarlino (1517–1590), and Nicola Vicentino (1511–1572) considered that sixteenth-century music had reached a state of near perfection, even if it could not elicit the extreme passions ancient music had supposedly produced in its listeners. Yet other scholars—notably Vincenzo Galilei, Antonio Francesco Doni, and a group of musical amateurs that met under the auspices of the Florentine count Giovanni de' Bardi (1534–1612) and called

Ex. 10.18   William Byrd, *Ye Sacred Muses*

themselves the *Camerata* —held that the music of their day was vastly inferior to that of antiquity. Aided in understanding Greek music by correspondence with the Roman philologist Girolamo Mei, Galilei and the Florentines concluded that the power of ancient music lay in the proper declamation of a uniquely apt setting of the words, a goal unachievable in a polyphonic setting. Their experiments, particularly those of the two professional singers among the Florentines, Jacopo Peri and Giulio Caccini, led to monodic settings with a simple chordal accompaniment and in a highly declamatory style that became the essential style of the Baroque era (see Chapter 14).

Just as important as these attempts to recover the expressive power of antique music was the shift in literary tastes away from the poetry of Petrarch's school and toward the far more emotionally charged poetry of Torquato Tasso (1544–1595) and Lodovico Ariosto (1474–1533), or the pathos of Gianbattista Guarini (1537–1612). The shift influenced the traditional composers as much as the innovators.

The new interest in chromaticism, already present in the works of Rore, is as much a consequence of the new humanist interest in Greek music as of the heightened expressivity demanded by the new texts. But the scholarly efforts of Vicentino to revive the Greek chromatic and enharmonic *genera* had little influence on the development of the new style.

The Virtuoso Madrigalists

Typical of the secular composers of the final decades of the sixteenth century are a group that Alfred Einstein has called "the virtuoso madrigalists,"[6] De Wert namely Giaches de Wert (1535–1599), Luca Marenzio (1553–1599), Carlo Gesualdo (c. 1560–1612), and Claudio Monteverdi (1557–1643). Wert, the oldest and the only Netherlander in the group, began in the tradition of Rore. Most of his activity took place at the Gonzaga court in Mantua, but he also was closely connected with Ferrara, where a group of virtuoso singers, the celebrated "ladies of Ferrara" (one of whom had an unhappy liaison with Wert), spurred the composition of a number of complex madrigals, often for three female voices or for three female and two male voices.

Wert's works after 1580, however, became very declamatory settings. Starkly chordal passages, virtually "ensemble recitative," alternated with passages that anticipated the melodic elaboration eventually to become typical of the Baroque style (see *Giunto a la tomba* ["Together at the tomb"]; no. 69 in Einstein, *The Italian Madrigal,* vol. 3).

Marenzio Within the fundamentally romantic and highly charged style of the late madrigal, Luca Marenzio appears as a classicist, "the Schubert of the madrigal," as Denis Arnold has aptly put it.[7] As in his own time, Marenzio is now best known for his early works, brilliant and exquisitely crafted pieces, whose attention to text painting is so extreme that it almost interferes with musical continuity. That it never does so is a mark of Marenzio's extraordinary taste and skill. In his first six books of madrigals *a 5*, the first five books *a 6*, and his only book *a 4*, all published between 1581 and 1593, Marenzio favors pastoral texts, perhaps due to the influence of the conservative Roman milieu in which he worked, as opposed to the northern centers where Wert and Monteverdi were active.

Marenzio's approach to a text can be seen in his setting of Petrarch's *Due rose fresche* (Example 10.19). The "two fresh roses" call forth a duet (incidentally, a quotation from an earlier setting by Andrea Gabrieli). The phrase *tra duo minori egualmente diviso* ("divided equally between two younger ones") is allotted to a set of duos, with a homophonic passage for the word *egualmente* ("equally") that is separated by a rest from the word *diviso* ("divided"). The word *paradiso* ("paradise") is set to an ascending line. The mention of the first day of May calls forth a stylized fragment of a maypole-dance song, and the *si dolce parlar e con un riso* ("sweet words and a smile") are set to a gently rising chromatic line with a florid ending on *riso* ("smile"). Nevertheless, the music surges forward in a convincing, continuous flow, neither because of these devices nor in spite of them, but independently, for the devices are simply surface ornaments. Yet because they are generated by the words, they are expressive ornaments as well.

Toward the end of his life Marenzio turned from pastoral poetry and text painting alike, and the music of the last three books *a 5*, and the sixth book *a 6* is austere to the point of severity. Indeed, as Marenzio himself stated, the texts of these works were chosen for a certain *mesta gravità* ("melancholy gravity"). An example, *O fere stelle,* appears as no. 80 in Einstein, *The Italian Madrigal,* vol. 3. These works are, in many respects, Marenzio's finest and most subtly expressive music.

Carlo Gesualdo

Carlo Gesualdo, prince of Venosa, has become something of a romantic figure because of a violent episode in his life, the murder of his adulterous wife and her lover in 1590. This scandal, in combination with the extreme chromaticism of some of his late madrigals, has made him a cult figure in recent years. In his first four books of madrigals (1594–1596), Gesualdo shows himself to be a very good composer of pieces no different in style and manner from those produced by his contemporaries, although already in Book IV we find the first of his chromatic madrigals, *Moro, e mentre spiro* ("While I hope, I die"). Experiments with extreme chromaticism, albeit under tight contrapuntal control, pervade the pieces in Books V and VI (1611). The chromaticism, coupled with violent changes in texture and rhythm, give his pieces the almost neurotic expressivity found in his famous *Moro, lasso* (see Example 10.20). Gesualdo's expressivity, however, does not really exceed Marenzio's, except that where Marenzio's text painting is essentially objective and descriptive, Gesualdo's is subjective and expressionistic. In *Moro, lasso* the concern for the emotional content of each phrase results in the destruction of the musical flow, at least in terms the Renaissance understood. Thus the product, although a magnificent work, is no longer a Renaissance madrigal. In his attitude toward the text Gesualdo also differs from the

Ex. 10.19   Luca Marenzio, *Due rose fresche*

"Two fresh roses, gathered in paradise, born the other day, on the first day of
May, are the beautiful gift of a lover. . . . Divided equally between two younger
ones, with such sweet words and with a smile. . . ."

Ex. 10.19   cont.

Trà   duo mi - no - ri e - gual-

Trà   duo mi - no - ri   e - gual-

Trà duo mi - no - ri,   trà   duo mi - no - ri e - gual-

Trà   duo mi - no - ri   e - gual-

Trà   duo mi - no - ri   e - gual-

men - te   di - vi - so con si dol - ce par -

men - te   di - vi - so   con_____ si dol -

men - te   di - vi - so   con_____ si dol -

men - te   di - vi - so

men - te   di - vi - so

lar   e con un ri   - so

ce par - lar_____ e con_____ un ri   - so

ce par - lar_____ e con_____ un ri   - so

other madrigalists by his lack of concern for literary values and for the structural integrity of the poems set. For instance, Marenzio's pictorialisms never disrupt the literary flow, and Monteverdi's audacities underscore the dramatic structure of the entire poem. Gesualdo, in contrast, tears his texts apart with repetitions of odd phrases, and he even mutilates poems by omitting lines or sections. Gesualdo's sacred music, published in 1603 and 1611, is considerably more conservative than his madrigals, although such emotional texts as the famous *O vos omnes* still inspire intricately chromatic settings.

Ex. 10.20   Carlo Gesualdo, *Moro, lasso*

Ex. 10.20   cont.

"Alas, I die of my sorrow, and who can give me life, alas, kills me."

Claudio Monteverdi

The dissolution of the Renaissance style takes a more radical form in the works of Claudio Monteverdi. In his first four books of madrigals, Monteverdi follows Cipriano de Rore with such works as *Baci soavi* (Book I) and shows himself a master of the virtuoso madrigal in pieces like *Quel augellin che canta* (Book IV). Here long coloraturas alternate with homophonic passages that are virtually ensemble recitatives. In all these works Monteverdi shows his concern not only for the expression of the text but also for its overall dramatic structure. This care leads him to superimpose contrasting motives and to make extraordinarily free use of unprepared dissonances. Both procedures are evident in the opening of *Ohimè se tanto amate* (see Example 10.21).

The treatment of dissonance in Book IV was the object of a violent attack by the theorist Giovanni Maria Artusi,[8] and Monteverdi responded with a brief preface to his Book V (1605), later glossed by his brother Giulio Cesare in the preface to *Scherzi musicali* (1607).[9] In their answer the Monteverdis distinguish between a *prima pratica* ("first practice"), in which music rules the words, and a *seconda pratica* ("second practice"), in which words dominate the music. They not only explain but justify the harmonic and motivic procedures used by Claudio. Their list of composers of the seconda pratica is instructive, for it includes Rore, Gesualdo, Marco Ingegneri (c. 1545–1592, Monteverdi's teacher), Marenzio, Wert, Luzzaschi, Peri, and Caccini—indeed, the entire constellation of major secular composers of the last two decades of the sixteenth century, with Rore as their patron saint.

In the last six madrigals of Book V, Monteverdi also provided a part for a *basso continuo,* an explicit admission that harmonic control of the texture was now preeminent, and that purely contrapuntal thinking could no longer explain much of this music. Between Book V and Book VI (1614), Monteverdi wrote his two great Mantuan operas *L'Orfeo* (1607) and *L'Arianna* (1608; most of it is now lost), the *Missa In illo tempore* (based on a Gombert motet), and the magnificent Vespers of 1610. In the Mass, as in some madrigals of Book VI, he again demonstrated his absolute mastery of the prima pratica, but in the other works he firmly established the new Baroque style and provided its first masterpieces.

Ex. 10.21   Claudio Monteverdi, *Ohimè se tanto amate*

Ex. 10.21   cont.

"Alas! If you so love to hear me say 'Alas!' . . ."

Other Composers

The Italian musical scene at the end of the sixteenth century presents a picture of great vitality and diversity. In Rome, Palestrina (see Chapter 11) was writing madrigals in a style several decades out of date, while in Ferrara, Luzzaschi was writing complex madrigals for one, two, or three voices and continuo that belong essentially to the early Baroque. In Venice, Andrea and Giovanni Gabrieli continued the tradition of Rore, albeit in a lighter vein, but devoted their best efforts to monumental polychoral works (see Chapter 11). Madrigal cycles arranged around a loose plot such as *L'amfiparnasso* (1597) by Orazio Vecchi (1550–1605), or works filled with droll imitations of animal cries, such as the *Festina nella sera del Giovedi grasso* (1608), served as court entertainments in the northern cities. Modern and old-fashioned traits continued side by side, and so the changes from the Renaissance to the Baroque were gradual, contradictory, and often imperceptible. Only a few extraordinarily lucid minds, such as Monteverdi's, were really aware of the profound extent of stylistic change (see Chapter 14).

The English Madrigal

The publication of *Musica Transalpina* ("Music from beyond the Alps") by Nicholas Yonge in 1588 inaugurated one of the most brilliant periods in the history of English music. The madrigals in this print, particularly those of Marenzio, became enormously popular, and in 1590 Thomas Watson published a second anthology, *Italian Madrigals Englished,* dominated by Maren-

Musica Transalpina

zio's work. Between these two publications, almost as a reaction, fall the two secular collections of William Byrd (see Chapter 11), *Psalmes, Sonets and Songs* (1588) and *Songs of Sundrie Natures* (1589), devoted to the older consort song, albeit dressed in madrigalian garb.

Morley   If Byrd resisted the new fashion, no other English composer did, and Byrd's pupil Thomas Morley (1557–1602) brought out not only further collections of Italian works but also his own very popular collections of Italianate settings. The most important were the *First Booke of Balletts* (1595), issued in an English and an Italian edition, and *The Triumphes of Oriana* (1601), an anthology of English works commissioned by him in honor of Queen Elizabeth. Morley's example prompted a flood of similar publications in the last years of the sixteenth century and the first two decades of the seventeenth.

Morley was interested primarily in the light madrigal, and many of his works, such as the famous *Now Is the Month of Maying* or *My Bonnie Lass, She Smileth* (*HAM* I, no. 170), follow the example of the *balletti* of Giovanni Giacomo Gastoldi. (These latter works were dance songs whose patterned rhythms and harmonies point toward the harmonically oriented music of the Baroque.) Other composers, however, turned increasingly to the serious madrigal, derived essentially from Marenzio. Among these were Thomas **Weelkes**   Weelkes (c. 1575–1628) and John Wilbye (1574–1638), the best Elizabethan madrigalists. Weelkes did cultivate some light madrigals, such as *Hark All Ye Lovely Saints,* as well as the serious ones. His works include pieces with extreme chromatic experiments, such as the opening of the second part of *O Care Thou Wilt Dispatch Me:* "Hence, care, thou art too cruell." But the influence of the light madrigal was so pervasive that even in such a mournful work as this a section is set to the conventional *fa-la-la* typical of the *ballets*.

Wilbye   Wilbye's madrigals tend to be organized more rigorously along purely musical lines than those of most of his contemporaries, and in works such as *When Shall My Wretched Life* (see Example 10.22) the writing is not markedly different from that found in the motet or instrumental fantasy of the time.

The English madrigal school shone brightly but briefly. It was, after all, an anachronistic movement that disappeared rapidly as the Baroque style took hold in England. Even at its beginnings the groundwork for the English Baroque was being laid down in the *ayres* for solo voice and lute of John Dowland and Thomas Campion (see Chapter 14).

Summary

The sixteenth century saw the culmination of an international style based on imitative techniques. It originated with Netherlandish composers, then spread to Italy, Germany, and Spain. Cantus firmus procedures were gradually replaced either by free composition or parody techniques, in which a work was based upon a polyphonic model rather than a single cantus firmus

Ex. 10.22   John Wilbye, *When Shall My Wretched Life Give Place to Death?*

melody. In Italy, France, Germany, and Spain, national styles rooted in popular forms began to emerge, and the Italian and French styles, influenced by humanistic tendencies, eventually merged with the international style to produce the madrigal and the French court chanson. These genres in turn affected the style of sacred music in both Italy and France.

England, isolated from the Continent, retained its individual traditions longer than countries affected by the international style, but toward the end of the sixteenth century the Italian madrigal spurred a brief but brilliant development of the Italianate English madrigal school.

In the last decades of the sixteenth century, the concerns for expression of the text that had initially been felt around 1500 were integrated with the humanist revival of interest in classical antiquity. These forces led theorists and composers to seek means of communicating the emotions of the text through musical devices: word painting, the affective use of chromaticism, and ultimately the rejection of polyphony in favor of the monodic, highly declamatory style characteristic of the early Baroque.

Notes

1. *Liber usualis missae et officii* [Paris, Tournai: Desclée (No. 780), 1954]. The paginations in the numerous editions of the *Liber usualis* vary somewhat; the only identification of each edition is the number given on the half-title page. (*LU*)
2. Edward E. Lowinsky, *Secret Chromatic Art in the Netherlands Motet* (New York: Columbia University Press, 1946). Lowinsky's interpretation of the evidence has been severely criticized.
3. *The Italian Madrigal,* 3 vols. (Princeton, N.J.: Princeton University Press, 1949), vol. 1, p. 153.
4. Philip Brett, "The English Consort Song, 1570–1625," *Proceedings of the Royal Musical Association,* 88 (1961–1962): 73–88.
5. William Byrd, *Collected Works,* vol. 12, ed. Edmund Fellowes, rev. Philip Brett (London: Stainer & Bell, 1969), xxxvi.
6. *The Italian Madrigal,* vol. 2, p. 608.
7. *Marenzio,* Oxford Studies of Composers, No. 2 (London: Oxford University Press, 1965), p. 2.
8. See Oliver Strunk, ed., *Source Readings in Music History from Classical Antiquity through the Romantic Era* (New York: W.W. Norton, 1950), pp. 393–404.
9. Ibid., pp. 404–405.

Bibliography

Books and Articles

Josquin and His Contemporaries

BROWN, HOWARD MAYER. *Music in the French Secular Theater, 1450–1550.* Cambridge, Mass.: Harvard University Press, 1963. Treats the theatrical works of Josquin and his generation.

Davison, Nigel. "The Motets of Pierre de la Rue." *The Musical Quarterly* 48 (1962): 19–35.

Haar, James, ed. *Chanson and Madrigal, 1480–1530.* Cambridge, Mass.: Harvard University Press, 1964.

Lowinsky, Edward E., and Blackburn, Bonnie J., eds. *Josquin des Prez: Proceedings of the International Festival-Conference Held at the Juilliard School at Lincoln Center in New York City, 21–25 June 1971.* London: Oxford University Press, 1976.

Perkins, Leeman, L. "Mode and Structure in the Masses of Josquin." *Journal of the American Musicological Society* 26 (1973): 190–239.

Picker, Martin, ed. *The Chanson Albums of Marguerite of Austria, MSS 228 and 11239 of the Bibliothèque Royale de Belgique, Brussels.* Berkeley and Los Angeles: University of California Press, 1965.

Salop, Arnold. "Jacob Obrecht and the Early Development of Harmonic Polyphony." *Journal of the American Musicological Society* 17 (1964): 288–309.

Sparks, Edgar H. *Cantus Firmus in Mass and Motet, 1420–1520.* Berkeley and Los Angeles: University of California Press, 1963.

The Successors of Josquin

Arnold, Denis. "The Significance of Cori Spezzati." *Music and Letters* 40 (1959): 4–14.

Bernet Kembers, K. Ph. "Jacobus Clemens non Papa's Chansons in Their Chronological Order." *Musica disciplina* 15 (1961): 187–189.

Cuyler, Louise. *The Emperor Maximilian and Music.* London: Oxford University Press, 1973.

Lenaerts, René Bernard. "The Sixteenth-Century Parody Mass in the Netherlands." *The Musical Quarterly* 36 (1950): 410–421.

Lockwood, Lewis L. "A View of the Early-Sixteenth-Century Parody Mass." In *Twenty-fifth Anniversary Festschrift (1937–1962)* [of Queens College], ed. Albert Mell. Flushing, N.Y.: Queens College Department of Music, 1964. Pp. 55–81.

————. "On 'Parody' as Term and Concept." In *Aspects of Medieval and Renaissance Music: A Birthday Offering to Gustave Reese,* ed. Jan La Rue. New York: W. W. Norton, 1966. Pp. 560–575.

Lowinsky, Edward E. *Secret Chromatic Art in the Netherlands Motet.* New York: Columbia University Press, 1946.

Meier, Bernhard. "The Musica Reservata of Adrianus Petit Coclico and Its Relationship to Josquin." *Musica disciplina* 10 (1956): 67–105.

From Frottola to Early Madrigal

D'Accone, Frank A. "Bernardo Pisano: An Introduction to His Life and Works." *Musica disciplina* 20 (1966): 151–174.

————. "Traditional Text Forms and Settings in an Early-Sixteenth-Century Florentine Manuscript." In *Words and Music: The Scholar's View; a Medley of Problems and Solutions Compiled in Honor of A. Tillman Merritt by Sundry Hands,* ed. Lawrence Berman. Cambridge, Mass.: Music Department, Harvard University, 1972. Pp. 29–58.

Einstein, Alfred. *The Italian Madrigal,* 3 vols. Princeton, N.J.: Princeton University Press, 1949. Reprinted 1971.

Haar, James, ed. *Chanson and Madrigal, 1480–1530.* Cambridge, Mass.: Harvard University Press, 1964.

Harran, Don. "Verse Types in the Early Madrigal." *Journal of the American Musicological Society* 22 (1969): 27–53.

Mace, Dean T. "Pietro Bembo and the Literary Origins of the Italian Madrigal." *The Musical Quarterly* 55 (1969): 65–86.

PIRROTTA, NINO. "Music and Cultural Tendencies in Fifteenth-Century Italy." *Journal of the American Musicological Society* 19 (1969): 121–161.

ROCHE, JEROME. *The Madrigal*. London: Hutchinson, 1972.

RUBSAMEN, WALTER H. *Literary Sources of Secular Music in Italy (c. 1500)*. Berkeley and Los Angeles: University of California Press, 1943. Reprinted, New York: Da Capo, 1972.

Midcentury Music in Italy

KAUFMANN, HENRY W. *The Life and Works of Niccolò Vincentino (1511–c. 1576)*. Musicological Studies and Documents, 11. Rome: American Institute of Musicology, 1966.

MILLER, CLEMENT A. "The Dodecachordon: Its Origin and Influence on Renaissance Musical Thought." *Musica disciplina* 15 (1961): 156–168.

France

BERNSTEIN, LAWRENCE F. "Claude Gervaise as Chanson Composer." *Journal of the American Musicological Society* 18 (1965): 359–381.

———. "*La Courone et fleur des chansons à troys:* A Mirror of the French Chanson in Italy During the Years Between Ottaviano Petrucci and Antonio Gardano." *Journal of the American Musicological Society* 26 (1973): 1–68.

———. "The Cantus-Firmus Chansons of Tylman Susato." *Journal of the American Musicological Society* 22 (1969): 197–240.

HEARTZ, DANIEL. "*Au près de vous*—Claudin's Chanson and the Commerce of Publisher's Arrangements." *Journal of the American Musicological Society* 24 (1971): 193–235.

LESURE, FRANÇOIS. *Musicians and Poets of the French Renaissance,* trans. Elio Gianturco and Joseph Rosenwald. New York: Merlin Press, 1955.

WALKER, D. P., and LESURE, FRANÇOIS. "Claude le Jeune and *musique mesurée*." *Musica disciplina* 3 (1949): 151–170.

WALKER, D. P. "Some Aspects and Problems of *musique mesurée à l'antique*." *Musica disciplina* 14 (1950): 163–186.

———. "The Aims of Baïf's *Académie de Poésie et de Musique*." *Journal of Renaissance and Baroque Music* 1 (1946): 91–100.

Spain

POPE, ISABEL. "Musical and Metrical Form of the Villancico." *Annales musicologiques* 2 (1954): 189–214.

RANDEL, DON. "Sixteenth-Century Spanish Polyphony and the Poetry of Garcilaso." *The Musical Quarterly* 60 (1974): 61–79.

STEVENSON, ROBERT. "Cristóbal de Morales (c. 1500–1553): A Fourth Centenary Biography." *Journal of the American Musicological Society* 6 (1953): 3–42.

———. *Spanish Cathedral Music in the Golden Age*. Berkeley and Los Angeles: University of California Press, 1961.

———. *Spanish Music in the Age of Columbus*. The Hague: Nijhof, 1960.

England

BAILLIE, HUGH. "Nicholas Ludford (c. 1465–c. 1557)." *The Musical Quarterly* 44 (1958): 196–208.

BENHAM, HUGH. "The Formal Design and Construction of Taverner's Works." *Musica disciplina* 26 (1972): 189–209.

BERGSAGEL, JOHN D. "An Introduction to Ludford." *Musica disciplina* 14 (1960): 105–130.

BRETT, PHILIP. "The English Consort Song." *Proceedings of the Royal Musical Association* 88 (1961–1962): 73–88.

DAVISON, NIGEL. "The *Western Wind* Masses." *The Musical Quarterly* 57 (1971): 429–443.

DOE, PAUL. *Tallis.* Oxford Studies of Composers, No. 4. London: Oxford University Press, 1968.

EINSTEIN, ALFRED. "The Elizabethan Madrigal and the 'Musica Transalpina.'" *Music and Letters* 25 (1944): 66–77.

FELLOWES, EDMUND. *English Cathedral Music,* 5th ed., rev. J. A. Westrup. New York: Barnes and Noble, 1969.

HARRISON, FRANK LL. *Music in Medieval Britain.* London: Routledge & Kegan Paul, 1958.

HUGHES, ANSELM. "An Introduction to Fairfax." *Musica disciplina* 6 (1952): 83–104.

KERMAN, JOSEPH. "Byrd, Tallis, and the Art of Imitation." *Aspects of Medieval and Renaissance Music: A Birthday Offering to Gustave Reese,* ed. Jan La Rue. New York: W. W. Norton, 1966.

———. *The Elizabethan Madrigal.* New York: American Musicological Society, 1962.

MORLEY, THOMAS. *A Plain and Easy Introduction to Practical Music (London, 1597),* ed. R. A. Harman. New York: W. W. Norton, 1952.

STEVENS, DENIS. *Tudor Church Music.* New York: W. W. Norton, 1961.

The Late Madrigal in Italy

ARNOLD, DENIS. *Marenzio.* Oxford Studies of Composers, No. 2. London: Oxford University Press, 1965.

KENTON, EGON. *The Life and Works of Giovanni Gabrieli.* Musicological Studies and Documents, 16. Rome: American Institute of Musicology, 1967.

LOWINSKY, EDWARD E. *Tonality and Atonality in Sixteenth-Century Music.* Berkeley and Los Angeles: University of California Press, 1961.

MACCLINTOCK, CAROL. *Giaches de Wert (1535–1596): Life and Works.* Musicological Studies and Documents, 17. Rome: American Institute of Musicology, 1966.

SCHRADE, LEO. *Monteverdi, Creator of Modern Music.* New York: W. W. Norton, 1950.

STEELE, JOHN. "The Late Madrigals of Luca Marenzio." *Studies in Music* 3 (1969): 17–24.

WATKINS, GLENN. *Gesualdo: The Man and His Music.* Chapel Hill: University of North Carolina Press, 1973.

Music Anthologies

ANGLÉS, HIGINI, and FIGUEROA, JOSÉ, eds. *La musica en la corte de los reyes católicos,* 4 vols. (in 5). Monumentos de la música española, vols. 1, 5, 10, 14 (parts 1 and 2). Barcelona: Consejo Superior de Investigaciones Científicas, 1941–1965.

BRETT, PHILIP, ed. *Consort Songs.* Musica Britannica, vol. 22. London: Stainer & Bell, 1967.

BROWN, HOWARD M., ed. *Theatrical Chansons of the Fifteenth and Early Sixteenth Centuries.* Cambridge, Mass.: Harvard University Press, 1963.

CESARI, G.; MONTEROSO, R.; and DISERTORI, B., eds. *Le frottole nell'edizione principe di Ottaviano Petrucci, I (Libri I, II, e III).* Cremona: Athenaeum Cremonese, 1954.

D'ACCONE, FRANK A., ed. *Music of the Florentine Renaissance,* 6 vols. Corpus mensurabilis musicae, 32. Rome: American Institute of Musicology, 1966–1973.

FELLOWES, EDMUND H., ed. *The English Madrigal School,* 36 vols. London: Stainer & Bell, 1913–1924. Rev. ed., Thurston Dart, Philip Brett, et al. London: Stainer & Bell, 1958–   .

———et al., eds. *Tudor Church Music,* 10 vols. London: Stainer & Bell, 1922–1929. Reprinted, New York: Broude, 1969.

GERBER, RUDOLF, and FINSCHER, LUDWIG, eds. *Der Mensuralkodex des Nikolaus Apel (MS 1494 der Universitatsbibliothek, Leipzig),* 3 vols. Das Erbe Deutscher Musik, vols. 32–34. Kassel: Bärenreiter, 1956–1975.

HEWITT, HELEN, ed. *Ottaviano Petrucci, Canti B numero cinquanta.* Monuments of Renaissance Music, vol. 2. Chicago: University of Chicago Press, 1967.

———. *Ottaviano Petrucci, Harmonice Musices Odhecaton A (Venice, 1501).* Cambridge, Mass.: Medieval Academy of America, 1942. Reprinted, New York: Da Capo, 1978.

LESURE, FRANÇOIS. *Anthologie de la chanson Parisienne au XVIe siècle.* Monaco: Oiseau Lyre, 1953.

LOWINSKY, EDWARD E., ed. *The Medici Codex of 1518,* 3 vols. Monuments of Renaissance Music, vols. 3–5. Chicago: University of Chicago Press, 1968.

MITJANA, RAFAEL; BAL Y GAY, JESUS; and POPE, ISABEL, eds. *Cancionero de Upsala.* México: El Colegio de México, 1944.

QUEROL GAVALDÁ, MIGUEL, ed. *Cancionero de la Casa de Medinaceli,* 2 vols. Monumentos de la música española, vols. 8–9. Barcelona: Consejo Superior de Investigaciones Científicas, 1949–1950.

SLIM, H. COLIN, ed. *A Gift of Madrigals and Motets,* 2 vols. Chicago: University of Chicago Press, 1972.

SMIJERS, ALBERT, and MERRITT, A. TILLMAN, eds. *Treize Livres de motets parus chez Attaingnant en 1534 et 1535,* 14 vols. Monaco: Oiseau Lyre, 1934–1964.

STEVENS, JOHN, ed. *Early Tudor Songs and Carols.* Musica Britannica, vol. 36. London: Stainer & Bell, 1975.

———. *Music at the Court of Henry VIII.* Musica Britannica, vol. 18. London: Stainer & Bell, 1962.

Collected Works of Composers

AGRICOLA, ALEXANDER. *Opera omnia,* ed. Edward R. Lerner, 5 vols. Corpus mensurabilis musicae, 22. Rome: American Institute of Musicology, 1961–1970.

ARCADELT, JACOB. *Opera omnia,* ed. Albert Seay, 10 vols. Corpus mensurabilis musicae, 31. Rome: American Institute of Musicology, 1965–1970.

BRUMEL, ANTOINE. *Opera omnia,* ed. Barton Hudson, 6 vols. Corpus mensurabilis musicae, 5. Rome: American Institute of Musicology, 1951–1972.

CERTON, PIERRE. *Chansons polyphoniques publiées par Pierre Attaingnant: Livre I (1533–1539), Livre III (1546–1550),* ed. Henri Expert and Aimé Agnel. Paris: Heugel, 1967–1968.

CLEMENT, JACOB (CLEMENS NON PAPA). *Opera omnia,* ed. K. Ph. Bernet Kempers and Chris Maas, 21 vols. Corpus mensurabilis musicae, 4. Rome: American Institute of Musicology, 1951–1976.

DESPREZ (DES PRÉS), JOSQUIN. *Werken,* ed. Albert Smijers, Miroslav Antonoaycz, and Willem Elders, 55 vols. Amsterdam: Alsbach, 1922–1969.

FAUGUES, VINCENT. *Collected Works,* ed. George Schuetze. Brooklyn, N.Y.: Institute of Medieval Music, 1967.

FESTA, CONSTANZO. *Opera omnia,* ed. Alexander Main and Albert Seay, 2 vols. Corpus mensurabilis musicae, 25 (in progress). Rome: American Institute of Musicology, 1962–   .

FINCK, HEINRICH. *Ausgewählte Werke,* vol. 1, ed. Lothar Hoffman Erbrecht. Das Erbe Deutscher Musik, vol. 57. Frankfurt: C. F. Peters, 1962.

GABRIELI, GIOVANNI. *Opera omnia,* ed. Denis Arnold, 6 vols. Corpus mensurabilis musicae, 12. Rome: American Institute of Musicology, 1956–1977.

GOMBERT, NICHOLAS. *Opera omnia,* ed. Joseph Schmidt Gorg, 10 vols. Corpus mensurabilis musicae, 6. Rome: American Institute of Musicology, 1951–1970.

GUERRERO, FRANCISCO. *Opera omnia,* ed. Miguel Querol Gavaldá, Vicente García, and José Maria Llorens Cisteró, 3 vols., Monumentos de la música española, vols. 16, 19, 36. Barcelona: Consejo Superior de Investigaciones Científicas, 1955–   .

ISAAC, HEINRICH. *Choralis Constantinus,* vol. 1, ed. Emil Bezecny and Walter Rabl. Denkmäler der Tonkunst in Österreich, vol. 10. Vienna, 1898. Reprinted, Graz: Akademische Druck und Verlagansthalt, 1960.

———. *Choralis Constantinus,* vol. 2, ed. Anton von Webern. Denkmäler der Tonkunst in Österreich, vol. 32. Vienna, 1900. Reprinted, Graz: Akademische Druck und Verlagansthalt, 1960.

———. *Choralis Constantinus,* vol. 3, ed. Luise Cuyler. Ann Arbor: University of Michigan Press, 1950.

———. *Five Polyphonic Masses,* ed. Luise Cuyler. Ann Arbor: University of Michigan Press, 1956.

———. *Messen,* ed. Martin Staehelin. Musikalische Denkmäler, vol. 7. Mainz: B. Schott's Söhne, 1970.

———. *Opera omnia,* ed. Edward R. Lerner, 5 vols. Corpus mensurabilis musicae, 65. Rome: American Institute of Musicology, 1974–1977.

———. *Weltliche Werke,* ed. Johannes Wolf. Denkmäler der Tonkunst in Österreich, vol. 28. Vienna, 1907. Reprinted, Graz: Akademische Druck und Verlagansthalt, 1960.

JANNEQUIN, CLÉMENT. *Chansons polyphoniques,* ed. A. Tillman Merritt and François Lesure, 5 vols. Monaco: Oiseau Lyre, 1965–1968.

LA RUE, PIERRE DE. *Drei Messen,* ed. René Bernard Lenaerts and Josef Robijns. Monumenta musicae Belgicae, vol. 8. Antwerp: Vereeniging voor Muziekgeschiedenis te Antwerpen, 1960.

MARENZIO, LUCA. *The Secular Works,* ed. Steven Ledbetter and Patricia Myers, 2 vols. New York: Broude Brothers, 1977. Two volumes out of a projected twenty had appeared by 1980.

———. *Opera omnia,* ed. Bernhard Meier and Roland Jackson, 4 vols. Corpus mensurabilis musicae, 72. Rome: American Institute of Musicology, 1976–   .

———. *Sämtliche Werke,* ed. Alfred Einstein, 2 vols. Publikationen alterer Musik, vol. 4, part 1, and vol. 6. Leipzig: Breitkopf & Härtel, 1929–1931. Only two volumes, with the first six books of madrigals, were issued.

MONTE, PHILIPPE DE. *Opera omnia,* ed. Charles van de Borren, Julius van Nuffel, and G. van Doorslaer, 31 vols. Bruges: Deslcée de Brouwer, 1927–1939. Reprinted, New York: Broude, 1965. An incomplete edition.

———. *Opera: New Complete Edition,* ed. Milton Steinhardt, 2 vols. Leuwen: Leuwen University Press, 1975–   .

MONTEVERDI, CLAUDIO. *Il primo libro de madrigali a 5 voci,* ed. Bernard Bailly de Surcy, 5 vols. Paris and New York: Les Editions Renaissantes, 1972. Facsimile.

———. *Il primo libro de madrigali a 5 voci,* ed. Bernard Bailly de Surcy. Paris and New York: Les Editions Renaissantes, 1972.

———. *Tutte le opere di Claudio Monteverdi,* ed. Gian Francesco Malipiero, 12 vols. Vienna: Universal Edition, 1926–1942. Reprinted, 1967–1968.

MORALES, CRISTÓBAL DE. *Opera omnia,* ed. Higini Anglés and Miguel Querol Gavaldá, 8 vols. Monumentos de la música española, vols. 9, 13, 15, 17, 20, 21, 24, 34. Barcelona: Consejo Superior de Investigaciones Científicas, 1952–   .

MOUTON, JEAN. *Opera omnia,* ed. Andrew Minor, 4 vols. Corpus mensurabilis musicae, 43. Rome: American Institute of Musicology, 1967–   .

OBRECHT, JACOB. *Werke,* ed. Johannes Wolf, 7 vols. Amsterdam: Alsbach, 1912–1921. Reprinted, Farnborough, England: Gregg, 1968.

————. *Opera omnia,* ed. Albert Smijers and Marcus van Crevel, 6 vols. Amsterdam: Alsbach, 1959–   .

RORE, CIPRIANO DE. *Opera,* ed. Bernhard Meier, 8 vols. Corpus mensurabilis musicae, 14. Rome: American Institute of Musicology, 1959–   .

SERMISY, CLAUDIN DE. *Opera omnia,* ed. Gaston Allaire and Isabelle Cazeaux, 5 vols. Corpus mensurabilis musicae, 52. Rome: American Institute of Musicology, 1970–   .

SILVA, ANDREAS DE. *Opera omnia,* ed. Winifred Kirsch, 3 vols. Corpus mensurabilis musicae, 49. Rome: American Institute of Musicology, 1970–1974.

VASQUEZ, JUAN. *Recopilación de sonetos y villancicos a quatro y a cinco* (Seville, 1560), ed. Higini Anglés. Monumentos de la música española, vol. 4. Barcelona: Consejo Superior de Investigaciones Científicas, 1946.

VERDELOT, PHILIPPE. *Opera omnia,* ed. Anne-Marie Bragard, 2 vols. Corpus mensurabilis musicae, 28. Rome: American Institute of Musicology, 1966–

WERT, GIACHES DE. *Opera omnia,* ed. Carol MacClintock and Melvin Bernstein, 17 vols. Corpus mensurabilis musicae, 24. Rome: American Institute of Musicology, 1961–   .

WILLAERT, ADRIAN. *Musica nova,* ed. H. Colin Slim. Monuments of Renaissance Music, vol. 1. Chicago: University of Chicago Press, 1965.

————. *Opera omnia,* ed. Hermann Zenck, 9 vols. Corpus mensurabilis musicae, 3. Rome: American Institute of Musicology, 1950–   .

11

Reformation and Counter-Reformation

THE Reformation brought to European civilization a wave of anticlericalism and complaints against corruption in the Church. The attendant reaction of the Roman Church in the Counter-Reformation movement inevitably affected the course of music history deeply, all the more so because until the eve of the Reformation music had remained firmly tied to the Church. This connection had barely been loosened by the interest in secular music shown by composers in the late fifteenth century, but the reform movements of the early sixteenth century so disturbed it that the new secularism of the humanist movement found fertile soil among musicians. In the late sixteenth century the most important area of production for most composers was secular music. Exceptions like Palestrina and Orlando di Lasso come to mind, but as a rule, the connection of music and the Church was fatally weakened by the Reformation.

We must also remember that the Reformation was not a single movement but rather a series of movements often closely tied to the personality of a reformer and to the national origins of the movement. Accordingly, the Reformation encouraged and at the same time took strength from the rising national consciousness that was sweeping Europe in the early sixteenth century. As a result, the rise of music for the reformed Church parallels closely the rise of national styles discussed in the previous chapter, and the music of the Reformation may best be considered country by country.

Germany: Lutheran Music

As Martin Luther was proposing changes within the Church of Rome, one of his most cherished aims was to make the liturgy more accessible to a lay congregation that no longer knew Latin. As the rift with Rome became permanent, Luther tried to provide his new congregation with precisely such a liturgy. This task required a thorough examination of the role of music within the Church, as well as the composition of music for the new liturgy. Unlike some of the more radical reformers, who sought to severely limit or even suppress the role of music in the divine service, Luther, a musical man with a deep admiration for Josquin, sought to preserve as much as possible of the musical heritage of the old Church. He had the close cooperation of Johann Walther (1496–1570), as well as the advice of several notable composers, including Ludwig Senfl.

The chorales

Luther and his associates set out to collect, adapt, or compose music for the new service. At the core of their production lies a body of sacred songs in the vernacular, known as *chorales,* which were simple enough to be sung by the congregation. Also essential was a new rite, the *Deudsche Messe und Ordnung Gottesdiensts* ("German Mass and Order of Service"), published in 1526, in which samples of plainsong with German words and two hymns — *Ich will der Herren loben* and *Jesaia dem Prophetem* — were included. Some of the chorale melodies, such as *Christ lag in Todesbanden,* are adaptations of chants (in this case, *Victimae paschali laudes*). Others are adaptations of popular songs, and a few, notably *Ein feste Burg* ("A mighty fortress"), were composed by Luther himself.

Before the publication of the *Deudsche Messe,* a number of hymn collections had already appeared: the *Achtliederbuch* (1524), two collections entitled *Enchiridion* (both 1524), and, more important, Johann Walther's *Gesang Buchleyn* (1524), with a preface by Luther himself. In Walther's collection the dual nature of the Lutheran musical tradition was apparent. It contains simple chorale settings, composed virtually note-against-note, such as *Aus tiefer Not* (see Example 11.1), and also includes more elaborate contrapuntal settings, in which each chorale phrase is paraphrased polyphonically, such as *Christ lag in Todesbanden* (Example 11.2). In both cases, however, the chorale melody in its simplest form appears most of the time in the tenor rather than in the superius. In addition to German works, Walther's collection contains Latin motets in the traditional style of Netherlandish polyphony, for Luther never set out to exclude Latin completely from the liturgy. In the second half of the sixteenth century, the two traditions continued side by side, with perhaps an increase in the production of the more elaborate settings, in Latin as well as in German. Composers like Lucas Ossiander (1534–1604), in his *Geistliche Lieder und Psalmen* (1586), continued the chorale tradition, but others, like Hans Leo Hassler, wrote elaborate as well as simple settings, contributing to the Latin as well as the German repertory. Among the latter group is Seth Calvisius (1556–1615), cantor of the Church of St. Thomas in Leipzig, who concentrated on German settings, but whose works are in both the simpler and more florid styles. It is the florid settings that set the stage for the most impressive achievements of the early German Baroque in the music of Michael Praetorius and Heinrich Schütz.

France and Switzerland: Calvinist Music

Ulrich Zwingli (1484–1531) was probably the most learned man among the early reformers, and like Luther, he was an amateur musician. Neverthe-

Ex. 11.1   Johann Walther, *Aus tiefer Not*

"Out of the depths I have cried unto thee, O Lord. God, hear my voice. . . ."

less, his radical religious views allowed no place for music in Christian worship, and he condoned the wanton destruction of the organs in the Swiss churches. After his death in 1531, the Swiss reform movement was essentially leaderless until the emergence of the Frenchman John Calvin (1509–1564) in Geneva in 1541. Calvin was hardly less suspicious of music than Zwingli, but from 1538 to 1541 he had been in Strasbourg, where he had heard the congregational singing under Matthias Greiter (1490–1550), and on his arrival at Geneva he sought to compile a suitable corpus of monophonic settings of the French Psalter for his congregation. In fact, as early as 1539 he had published the *Alcuns Pseaulmes et cantiques mys en chant* ("Some psalms and canticles put into song form"). After returning to Geneva, from which he had been banished in 1538, Calvin set to work on a metrical translation of the Psalter with Clément Marot (1496–1544), who had sought refuge in Geneva shortly after

The Genevan Psalter

Ex. 11.2   Johann Walther, *Christ lag in Todesbanden*

"Christ lies in the bonds of death, sacrificed for our sin. . . ."

Calvin's return. The *Alcuns Pseaulmes* of 1539 already contained some of Marot's translations, written for the court of Francis I, but the witty and urbane Marot could not work smoothly with Calvin, and their collaboration lasted less than two years. The Genevan Psalter was completed in 1562 by Théodore de Bèze (1519–1605) and others. Besides the Genevan Psalter, other French translations appeared also in Strasbourg and Antwerp, where a Flemish Psalter was also published.

Calvinist polyphony   Although Calvin disapproved of polyphony in the church—the Genevan Psalter was set to single-line melodies—as early as 1547 one of his associates, Louis Bourgeois (c. 1510–c. 1561), published in Lyons the *Cinquante Pseaumes de David roy et prophète,* set in simple four-part polyphony. Bourgeois's later publications, including the *Quatre vingt Psaumes de David en musique* (Paris,

Ex. 11.3   Claude Goudimel, *Non Point à nous*

"Not unto us, O Lord, not unto us. . . ."

1561), also contained chanson-like or motet-like settings of the psalms for four, five, and six voices.

However, the most important composer to concern himself with the Calvinist Psalter was Claude Goudimel (c. 1510–1572). Following Calvin's strictures against polyphony, Goudimel expressly stated that his polyphonic settings were to be sung only at home. From 1551 onward, Goudimel also issued a series of psalms set to music "in the manner of motets." In these works, such as Psalm 115, *Non Point à nous,* from Book I (1551), he follows the graceful polyphonic style of Claudin de Sermisy (see Example 11.3).

Goudimel

But his most famous settings by far were those in which the entire Psalter was set in note-against-note style, the music following the declamation of the words in the manner of the *vers mesuré* (see, for instance, Psalm 42, *Ainsi qu'on oit,* Example 11.4).

Goudimel's collections of the entire Psalter were published in 1564 and 1565 by Le Roy and Ballard in Paris, and also in Geneva in 1566. These simple settings, which often use the tunes of the Genevan Psalter, became immensely

Ex. 11.4   Claude Goudimel, *Ainsi qu'on oit*

"As the hart panteth for the fountains of water. . . ."

popular in France and also in Germany, where they began appearing in German translation from 1573 onward. To this day they represent the core of the Huguenot tradition. Although most of Goudimel's music consists of settings of the French psalms, he also wrote a considerable number of Latin motets and five Masses published between 1552 and 1558, in which he followed the Parisian traditions.

Like Goudimel, the last Renaissance composer of French Protestant polyphony, Jan Pieterzoon Sweelinck (1562–1621), set not only the vernacular psalms but also Latin texts in elaborate, florid counterpoint, such as his famous *Hodie Christus natus est*. But the collection in which this work was published, the *Cantiones sacrae* of 1619, also marks the beginning of the northern European Baroque in the use of an organ *continuo* for a number of motets.

England: Anglican Church Music

The English Reformation
    For some time before Henry VIII's final break with Rome in 1534, the Oxford humanists (John Colet, Erasmus, and Sir Thomas More) had proposed reforms in the English Church which included a biting satirical pamphlet by Erasmus against the choral foundations. In addition, the ideas of Luther and John Wycliffe circulated freely in England in the 1520s, despite Henry's known animosity. Nevertheless, the Henrician reform and the dissolution of the monasteries (1540–1541) did not greatly affect the liturgy, which continued to be sung in Latin despite the publication of the English Litany in 1534. However, the reforms of Edward VI and the publication of the first *Book of Common Prayer* in 1549 had a more far-reaching effect in banning Latin from the English liturgy.

The twin pillars on which later Anglican music was based were the publications of John Day, *Certaine Notes Set Forthe in Foure and Three Partes* (1560) and *The Whole Booke of Psalmes* (1563). The first of these was also reissued in 1565 as *Mornyng and Evenyng Praier and Communion*. The second contained settings of the enormously influential metrical translations of the psalms by Theodore Sternhold and John Hopkins, whose work reflected the Calvinist side of the English Reformation. Among the composers of music for the Anglican Church in this period we encounter virtually all those already listed in the section on Latin church music, particularly Tallis, Tye, Shepherd, and Mundy. But the most important composer of music for the new English rite, William Byrd, not only belonged to a later generation but was himself a devout Catholic. He nevertheless enjoyed the protection of Queen Elizabeth, who clearly distinguished between recusancy (refusal of Catholics to attend Church of England services) and treason when she referred to one of Byrd's noble patrons as "a stiff papist and a good subject."[1]

Byrd
    Byrd includes English psalm settings in all of his vernacular collections, in which sacred and secular works stand side by side. The first one, *Psalmes, Sonets and Songs* (1588), opens with an extraordinary setting of Hopkins' metrical version of Psalm 55, *O God, Give Ear*. In *Songs of Sundrie Natures* (1589)

and *Psalmes, Songs, and Sonnets* (1611), Byrd includes some of the most impressive works of a new genre, the *verse anthem,* which combines the soloistic tradition of the consort song with the motet tradition in works such as *Christ Rising* (*HAM* I, no. 151). Byrd's two services, particularly the enormously complex *Great Service,* which survives only in manuscript, transcend all the categories of English church music. They are neither in the style of the full anthem for choir nor in that of the verse anthem, with a soloist or soloists alternating with the choir. Instead they are virtually *concerted* works with elaborate alternations of forces and textures in a constantly changing manner.

The church music of Morley, Weelkes, and Tomkins follows Byrd's tradition, although Tomkins lived so long that most of his production belongs rightfully to the early Baroque. Morley and Weelkes, on the other hand, remain well within the Renaissance style, and Weelkes's anthems show a considerable influence of the madrigal tradition, both in their texture and in their treatment of words. The same can be said of the anthems of Orlando Gibbons (1583–1625), two of which—the full anthem *O Lord Increase My Faith* and the verse anthem *This Is the Record of John*—are given in *HAM* I (nos. 171–172).

Later composers

The Counter-Reformation

The Council of Trent

During the second quarter of the sixteenth century the Roman Church, partly in reaction to the outside forces of the Reformation and partly in answer to the demands of an increasing number of Catholic ecclesiastics, began the task of internal reform. Calls for a general council were finally answered when, after some delays, sessions began in the north Italian city of Trent in 1545 (they were continued, with some interruptions, until 1563). The role of music in the Church was finally taken up by the prelates in 1562 and 1563. A commission of cardinals was appointed to study the matter, and it met in Rome in 1564 and 1565. Among the most active of the reforming cardinals was Carlo Borromeo (1530–1584), bishop of Milan, whose interest in musical and liturgical matters has been particularly well documented.[2]

Neither the Council of Trent nor the commission produced specific directives about the kind of church music that should be written; rather, they offered general guidelines. These included the primacy of chant over polyphony and the necessity for the text to be clearly intelligible in polyphonic settings. The Council never seriously considered banning polyphony from the Church, as the legend that has grown around Palestrina and his Pope Marcellus Mass would have us believe. To be sure, one or two cardinals, influenced by Reformation ideals, proposed such a step, and the members of the commission indeed tested a number of polyphonic works as to their intelligibility in an effort to arrive at a suitable liturgical style. But the guidelines proposed by the Council were very much the product of the cultural movements of its time; that is, they were humanistic and antihistorical. For example, the

The Council and music

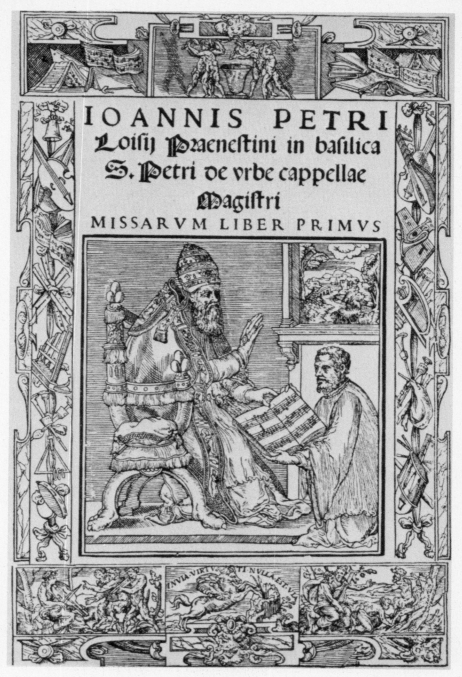

Palestrina presenting his Masses to the Pope, from the frontispiece of his first book of Masses (1554). In fact the plate was taken from the first book of Masses by Morales (1544), with the faces of the pope and the composer changed.

commendation of correct Latin declamation and the discouragement of excessive melismas were applied not only to polyphony but to the chant as well. The chant, which was considered to have been corrupted, was then revised accordingly, and the Medicean edition of 1614 was prepared by two disciples of Palestrina, Felice Anerio (c. 1560–1614) and Francesco Soriano (1549–c. 1621), after Palestrina himself had begun and abandoned the project. This 1614 edition gives versions of the Gregorian melodies with "correct" accentuation, shortened melismas (often moved so as to fall on an accented syllable), and other marks of the newly awakened humanistic concern for proper declamation and text expression.

Beyond these reforms, the commission also demanded the elimination of secular influences in sacred music. The reference was probably to the very popular parody Masses built on chansons or madrigals rather than to the older cantus firmus Masses, which by then were old-fashioned and little sung. Some composers, notably Vincenzo Ruffo (c. 1510–1587), who was *maestro di cappella* ("chapel-master") in Milan under Carlo Borromeo, adapted their music to the new requirements, and they produced Masses that were a virtual embodiment of the Council's reforms. Others, including Palestrina, adopted many of these reforms willingly, probably because they coincided with their own artistic direction. But their adoption of the Council's tenets was by no means total or consistent, and in numerous works the florid counterpoint that the Council deplored appeared as luxuriant as ever, while tame names, such as *Missa Quarti toni* and *Missa Sine nomine,* simply hid Masses built upon a madrigal or a chanson. Nevertheless, the Council's influence was felt not only in the simpler and more declamatory style of much of the sacred music of the 1570s and 1580s, but also in a sudden increase in the production of "spiritual madrigals," that is, madrigalian works with sacred or moral texts. These were either simple contrafacta of secular works or newly composed pieces with moral texts (sometimes themselves parodies of secular poems). Among these were the *Canciones y villanescas espirituales* of Francisco Guerrero and the famous *Lagrime de San Pietro* ("Saint Peter's tears") by Orlando di Lasso. The similar publications that appeared in Lyons in the 1560s as *chansons spirituelles,* however, were a product not of the Counter-Reformation but of the Huguenot movement in France.

Effect of the reforms

The Roman School

Latin church music in Italy during the second and third quarters of the sixteenth century was already moving toward the tightly controlled style now associated with Palestrina. This tendency was already noticeable in the motets of Arcadelt and Festa as well as in the late works of Willaert, but it became even more pronounced in the works of the Roman composers, and in particular in those of their chief representative, Giovanni Pierluigi da Palestrina (c. 1525–1594).

Palestrina's life was externally uneventful, without the extended travels that characterized the lives of many of his contemporaries. Most of his career

Palestrina

was spent in Rome, either in the papal chapel or in the choir of one or another of the great basilicas. But unlike a number of the papal singers, Palestrina never became a priest. At the death of his first wife in 1580, he briefly toyed with the idea of the priesthood, but in 1581 he married the widow of a furrier and took charge of her business while maintaining his own career as a singer and a composer.

The musical language evolved by Palestrina is so regular and controlled that it lends itself easily to systematic description and classification: in other words, it can be easily taught. Therefore, in the eighteenth century the Viennese court *Kapellmeister* ("chapel-master") Johann Joseph Fux based his famous counterpoint treatise, the *Gradus ad Parnassum* (1725), on the practice of Palestrina as he understood it. That Fux distorted the contrapuntal practice of the sixteenth century is undeniable, but his textbook was useful and effective, and virtually all major composers in the next hundred and fifty years learned their trade with it.

A far more accurate description of Palestrina's style was published by Knud Jeppesen in 1925, *The Style of Palestrina and the Dissonance*.[3] Jeppesen carefully noted that the foundation of Palestrina's style is melodic and contrapuntal. The even flow of the music is seldom disturbed by drastic changes in rhythmic density or harmonic texture. Palestrina seldom uses chromatic inflections in the manner of the late-madrigal composers. Thus, for example, in his motet *Sicut cervus* ("As the hart"; *HAM* I, no. 141), the single E-flat on the word *lachrymae* ("tears") becomes enormously expressive in contrast to the total diatonicism of the rest of the work. The melodies of Palestrina's music are often long-breathed, particularly in the pieces with short texts, such as the Kyrie, Sanctus, and Agnus Dei, and the phrases are carefully balanced. Large leaps, which for him mean anything above a third, are immediately followed by a change in direction, so that the long-range drive of the melody is never damaged.

In his text setting and treatment of dissonance, Palestrina is extremely careful. All dissonances that occur on a strong beat are prepared by a consonant interval, and the preparation is always longer than or at least the same length as the dissonance. Thus a suspended quarter note will always be prepared by a quarter or half note tied over. Passing tones and other dissonant combinations appear only on weak beats or in the off-beats of the pulse, but they are approached and left by step, with the exception of the *nota cambiata* patterns, in which Palestrina allows himself a small liberty. Otherwise the turning point in any of his melodies, even if it occurs on a weak beat, is virtually always a consonant tone.

This careful and systematic approach to treatment of dissonance is matched by an equally careful approach to the setting of the text. Accented syllables are always provided with either a strong beat or a small melisma, and long melismas virtually never occur over an unaccented syllable. Syllables seldom change after notes shorter than a half note (a minim in the original notation) in order to avoid sharp accents on any syllable. The clarity of the musical language achieved also affects the formal construction, and so Palestrina's compositions are often laid out in an almost self-analytical manner.

A prolific composer, Palestrina wrote more than 105 Masses, 250 motets, and 120 madrigals divided equally between secular and spiritual ones. The Masses present us with a summary of every means of composing a Mass cycle known in the sixteenth century: cantus firmus, paraphrase, parody, canon cycles, and free cycles. All are found in his work, but parody Masses predominate. Palestrina's motets, like his Masses, present virtually every known technique of the genre, even though their language is less colorful than that of his northern contemporaries. In his madrigals, several of which were immensely popular (see, for example, *HAM* I, no. 142), he is very conservative and harks back to the delicate writing of Arcadelt and the early Florentine madrigalists.

Among Palestrina's contemporaries, none achieved the same heights except his own student, Tomás Luis de Victoria (c. 1548–1611). Born in Avila, Victoria spent most of his early maturity in Rome before returning permanently to Spain in 1586. Like the other two famous Spaniards, Morales and Guerrero, Victoria was a composer of sacred music, and no secular works by him were published or have come to light. His output is considerably smaller than Palestrina's: twenty Masses and about sixty motets and other liturgical works. Victoria's music is as clear and carefully wrought as Palestrina's, but the Spaniard shows considerably more concern for the *affective* setting of the text than his master. This care is particularly true of the motets, and in his famous *O vos omnes* ("All ye"; *HAM* I, no. 149) Victoria does not hesitate to use a fair amount of chromaticism to interrupt the flow of the music in order to convey the pathos of the words. In the Masses, most of which are parody works, he subjects the model to drastic revisions right from the start, as can be seen in the Mass *Quam pulchri sunt,* based on his own motet (see Examples 11.5 and 11.6).

Victoria

In some of his late works, particularly those written for two and three choirs, Victoria provided the texture with an organ accompaniment, usually doubling one of the choirs in the manner of a *basso seguente*. In his nine-voice *Missa pro victoria,* based on Jannequin's *La Guerre* (Victoria's only Mass based on a secular model), Victoria experimented with the new *concertato* style (see Chapter 17) and with highly declamatory passages reminiscent of the style of the Venetian composer Giovanni Gabrieli.

Side by side with Victoria, and in many ways the third most illustrious member of the "Roman" school, is Francisco Guerrero (c. 1527–1599), a student of Morales. Unlike Morales and Victoria, Guerrero received his training entirely in Spain and spent only a short time in Italy, when he was already a mature composer. Virtually his entire career was spent in Andalusia, but his music belongs in every way with that of the Roman composers. His works were printed in Italy and were spread widely throughout Europe. Far too few of his works are available in modern editions, but those that are, such as the *alternatim* antiphon *Salve regina* (*HAM* I, no. 139), show that Guerrero is

Guerrero

Ex. 11.5   Tomás Luis de Victoria, *Quam pulchri sunt*

"How beautiful are thy steps. . . ."

Ex. 11.6   Tomás Luis de Victoria, Kyrie from parody Mass

"Lord have mercy."

closer to the clarity and balance of Palestrina than to the style of either of the other two Spanish masters, even at the price of a certain blandness in Guerrero's music. In a way Guerrero simply refined and clarified the already careful idiom of Morales, and he did retain something of Morales' enormous rhythmic vitality in his music.

Northern Italy: The Gabrielis

In the north of Italy the Venetian composers, under the leadership of Andrea Gabrieli (1520–1586) and his nephew Giovanni Gabrieli (1555–1612), developed a style of sacred music that relied on the juxtaposition of different choirs, often accompanied by wind instruments and organ. This *cori spezzati* practice, which sharply contrasted with the Roman style, had been cultivated by their teacher Adrian Willaert.

The Gabrieli compositions, despite their often-madrigalian treatment of the text, seem to rely more for their effect on sheer brilliance of sound and on what amounts to abstract interplay of textures: the answering back and forth of two or three choirs; the movement of motives from choir to choir in intri-

A Mass celebrated with two choirs and instruments. Engraving by Adrian Collaert after a drawing by Johannes Stradarus, 1595.

cate traceries; the production of massive sonorities by the entire ensemble. The Gabrielis' music, particularly that of Giovanni, seems to move outside the standard "Counter-Reformation" style, and spiritually it harks back to the grand style of the ceremonial music of earlier centuries, even if clothed in the most advanced musical idiom of the sixteenth century. Indeed, in their concern with the interplay of contrasting forces, the Gabrielis prefigure the Baroque *concerted style,* and some of Giovanni's late works, such as the motet *In ecclesiis* ("Praise the Lord in the congregation"; *HAM* I, no. 157), belong to the emerging Baroque style. The Venetian style had an enormous influence in the north, particularly in Germany, where contemporaries and successors of Giovanni Gabrieli eagerly imitated the polychoral writing and brilliant effects of the Venetian school.

The Northern School

Although Orlando di Lasso[4] is usually linked with Palestrina, few composers of the late sixteenth century could be more different from the Roman master. Born in Mons (now in southwest Belgium) in 1532, Lasso spent much of his youth and early manhood in Italy and traveled widely before becoming a member of the Bavarian court chapel in 1566. He stayed in Bavaria the rest of his life, not only becoming maestro di cappella but also earning a patent of nobility from Emperor Maximilian II (reg. 1562–1576). Even during his years in Bavaria, Lasso continued to travel occasionally, and his letters to Duke Wilhelm V, written in a mixture of several languages, show him to be a warm and witty man, with a bit of *commedia dell'arte* humor. In addition, Lasso was something of a prodigy: At twenty-one he was already maestro di cappella at St. John Lateran in Rome, and by the age of twenty-four, when he published a famous collection of motets in Antwerp (1556), he had evolved a personal and fully mature musical language. Unlike many prodigies, however, Lasso continued his extraordinary production all his life, and we have of his work some 70 Masses, 176 madrigals, 135 chansons, 93 German lieder, and 520 motets.

Lasso

Lasso's mastery of virtually every genre of music written in his time is overwhelming, though his treatment of each varies both in quality and variety. The Masses are his most traditional works. Most are parody Masses, but often all references to the model disappear after the Kyrie and a few bars of each of the successive movements. There are, however, some extraordinary Masses—for example, the *Missa Douce mémoire* ("Sweet memory"), which is based on a chanson of Pierre Sandrin, and the *Missa In te Domine speravi,* which is based on Lasso's own motet and has six voices that are often treated like a double choir.

Lasso's Masses

In his secular works, particularly those composed in the 1560s and 1570s, Lasso experimented with the chromaticism of Cipriano de Rore and his followers, and took great pains with the setting of the text. This conscientiousness is apparent not only in the madrigals but also in the chansons and the German lieder, and thus some chansons become very Italianate and madrigalian in their textures. In his late works, however, Lasso returned to a simple

Lasso's secular works

Orlando di Lasso (at the keyboard) with the musicians of the Bavarian court. (Bayerische Staatsbibliothek, Munich, Mus. MS. A.II, fol. 187r)

style that recalls the music of the early sixteenth century. The contrast may be observed in the openings of *La Nuict froide et sombre* (1576) and *Gallans qui par terre* (1584). The earlier work, with its homophonic opening and chromatic shifts, sounds more like a contemporary Italian madrigal, while the later one could easily be taken for a Parisian chanson of the 1530s (see Examples 11.7 and 11.8).

Lasso's motets   Lasso's most important works, standing above the rest, are his motets. They present a bewildering variety of textures and compositional procedures, from the wildly chromatic *Prophetiae Sybillarum* ("Prophecies of the Sybil"), whose *tonal* center of gravity is difficult to discern, to the spacious settings of the penitential psalms made in 1584 (three verses of one of them are found in *HAM* I, no. 144) and the complex polychoral works reminiscent of the music of the Gabrieli-era Venetians. Few of the motets are well known today, however, because they pose enormous performance problems. Much of Lasso's music is dense and intricate, a texture favored by German masters since the days of Isaac, and they demand virtuoso singers. Even Lasso's very late motets are extremely complicated, since he returned to an austere style that harks back to the music of the 1520s.

The other great Netherlander active in Germany at the end of the sixteenth century was Philippe de Monte (1521–1603), who became maestro di cappella to Emperor Maximilian II in 1568. Monte was an extremely cultivated man, fluent in several languages. In his youth he studied in Naples and Rome, and later he visited Spain and England in the service of Philip II of Spain. By the time he joined the Austrian chapel, he was already a famous composer of madrigals who had published five books of them—two *a 6*, two *a 5*, and one *a 4*—but had written little sacred music. Secular music remained the most important part of Monte's output, and he published nine books of madrigals *a 6*, nineteen books *a 5*, four books *a 4*, two *a 7*, and one *a 3*, as well as five books of spiritual madrigals for five and six voices. He eventually also published ten books of motets for four, five, and six voices, each containing twenty-nine motets, as well as twenty-four Masses. Virtually all of his sacred music, however, was written after 1568.

Monte

Stylistically, Monte stands between Palestrina and Lasso. His polyphony is neither so smooth as Palestrina's—he favors a more disjunct melodic style —nor so dense as Lasso's. Monte's Masses and motets are clearly influenced by his madrigalian style, which is sensitive but rather conservative, and he eschews the extremes of Cipriano, Marenzio, or Monteverdi. The Sanctus of Monte's Mass based on Wert's *Cara la mia vita* ("My dear life"; *HAM* I, no. 146b) shows his skill in altering the model drastically, yet retaining its harmonic clarity and much of its madrigalian feeling.

Ex. 11.7   Orlando di Lasso, *La Nuict froide et sombre*

"The cold and somber night, covering with dark shadow. . . ."

Ex. 11.8   Orlando di Lasso, *Gallans qui par terre*

"O gallants, who by land and sea go to the weddings and feasts. . . ."

William Byrd: English Recusant

The Counter-Reformation in England was a clandestine movement, fed from within the country by the resistance of the recusant community and from without by a steady stream of missionaries, mostly Jesuits, trained at the English college in Douai. Public celebration of the Catholic Mass was forbidden under Elizabeth and James, and even private Masses were considered virtual treason. Nevertheless, a closely knit recusant community that included a good number of noble households survived well into the seventeenth century. William Byrd, although organist of Lincoln Cathedral and later of the Chapel Royal, remained a Catholic all his life and enjoyed the patronage of several recusant lords as well as the tolerance of Elizabeth. This freedom permitted him to publish several collections of Latin church music, including liturgical works clearly intended for the Catholic service.

To be sure, many of Byrd's Latin motets found in the *Cantiones sacrae* of 1575 (published jointly with Tallis), 1589, and 1591 could easily be used in the Anglican service as well, particularly after Elizabeth's injunctions of 1559 and the issuance of a Latin version of the *Book of Common Prayer*. But, as Joseph Kerman has suggested,[5] a number of motets, such as the monumental *Deus invenerunt gentes* of 1589, are but thinly veiled laments for the fate of the recusant community in England. Others, such as the *Salve regina* of 1591, are distinctly Catholic works with texts that run counter to the Anglican doctrine of the time. In all, the three sets of *Cantiones sacrae* contain fifty-two motets by Byrd, and eighteen more survive in manuscript copies.

Besides the *Cantiones sacrae*, Byrd published three collections devoted exclusively to music for the Catholic liturgy. The first, issued without a title page, probably between 1592 and 1595, contains three settings of the Ordinary of the Mass for three, four, and five voices. The other two, Books I and II of the *Gradualia* (1605 and 1607), contain complete cycles of polyphonic

Byrd's Latin music

The Sistine Chapel in the early seventeenth century. Anonymous engraving.

Propers for the major feasts of the year and for the Lady Masses, as well as a few motets without a definite liturgical function. The circumstances under which these extraordinary, complex works for a forbidden liturgy may have been performed can be ascertained from the memoirs of a Jesuit missionary, Father William Weston. He reports a clandestine celebration of a very elaborate liturgy in a country house in 1586, at which Byrd himself was present.[6] Nevertheless, it is still extraordinary that these works were ever published and sold in England.

Byrd's Masses and motets, particularly those of the *Gradualia,* reflect the Counter-Reformation in their concern with liturgical propriety and with the correct and clear declamation of the texts (despite the density of the textures). Both standards were demanded by the Trent commission. These works are products of the Counter-Reformation for another reason too: Byrd's gradual abandonment, after 1575, of the old English rite of Salisbury in favor of Roman versions, both in his choice of melodies for the cantus firmi and in the selection of Propers texts for several feasts. This choice, of course, was probably a reflection of the situation within the recusant community, which came to be dependent on liturgical books imported from Rome and Douai that reflected the post–Council of Trent Roman usage rather than the rite of Salisbury. And still another break with the essentially conservative English tradition was Byrd's preference for freely composing his liturgical music, rather than using cantus firmi.

The continental repertory known in England in the late sixteenth century was dominated by the works of Lasso, whose music had been published in England and was also avidly copied by the recusant musicians. In his variety of textures and compositional procedures, Byrd is closest to Lasso. Both men share a preference for dense, intricate contrapuntal textures, but Byrd's works are, if anything, better controlled harmonically. As a result Byrd's music seldom poses the fierce performance problems of Lasso's works, and his Latin motets tend to sound more transparent than those of the Netherlander. In some of the *Cantiones sacrae* of 1575 Byrd still uses the rather neutral counterpoint of the earlier English composers, but in those of 1589 and 1591 his concern for text expression borders on the madrigalian. This attention is particularly noticeable in the opening piece of the 1591 set, *Laudibus in sanctis* (see Example 11.9).

In this piece, as in most of the *Cantiones sacrae,* Byrd writes in the grand manner, allowing himself time to present and recombine the motives of each point of imitation at leisure. In addition, the majority of his motets tend to be exceptionally lengthy and spacious. In the Masses and the *Gradualia,* however, the music is far more compressed, and Byrd at times achieves textures of such density and intricacy that they approach the very elaborate concerted style of the Venetian school.

Not only is Byrd the equal of Palestrina, Victoria, and Lasso as a representative of the late sixteenth century, but he also had a versatility matched only by Lasso among the continental composers. Lasso, however, wrote little in-

Ex. 11.9   William Byrd, *Laudibus in sanctis*

"Praise the supreme Lord in his saints, let the heavens resound with his mighty deeds. . . ."

strumental music, while Byrd must be considered as one of the founders of the modern keyboard style of the seventeenth century.

In his Latin church music Byrd is almost unique in England. His contemporaries and successors, Alfonso Ferrabosco and Thomas Morley, wrote Latin motets but no Masses. Indeed, the three Byrd Masses stand as the only examples of this genre from the late English Renaissance.

Summary

The ultimate effect of the Reformation, particularly in Germany but also in France and England, was to strengthen the separate national identities of the countries affected. The movement also influenced the musical culture of these countries, and Protestant church music in Germany, France, and England became German, French, and English music in a way that the earlier liturgical style did not—a way that paralleled the development of the national styles in the secular field. It is no coincidence that Protestant composers looked to the secular tradition for their inspiration.

Counter-Reformation music, in contrast, remained a refinement of the international style that by the end of the sixteenth century had become associated with the conservative schools in central Italy. Only a few great masters, Lasso and Byrd in particular, and to some extent Victoria, were able to transcend this style and produce music that did not sound Italianate. The great master of the Italian style was Palestrina, whose name in later centuries came to be almost synonymous with Renaissance counterpoint.

Notes

1. Edmund H. Fellowes, *William Byrd,* 2nd ed. (London: Oxford University Press, 1948), p. 36.
2. Lewis Lockwood, "Vincenzo Ruffo and Musical Reform After the Council of Trent," *The Musical Quarterly* 43 (1957): 342–371.
3. 2nd ed., trans. Edward J. Dent (London: Oxford University Press, 1946).
4. His name was originally Roland de Lassus, but the composer himself adopted the Italian form and used it quite consistently.
5. In "England: c. 1540–1610," *Music from the Middle Ages to the Renaissance,* ed. F. W. Sternfeld. Praeger History of Western Music, vol. 1 (New York: Praeger, 1973), pp. 320–321.
6. Fellowes, *Byrd,* p. 42.

Bibliography

Books and Articles

Reformation and Counter-Reformation

BLUME, FRIEDERICH. *Protestant Church Music: A History.* London: Gollancz, 1975.
CLIVE, H. P. "The Calvinist Attitude to Music, and Its Literary Aspects and Sources." *Bibliothèque d'humanisme et Renaissance* 19 (1957): 80–102, 294–319; 20 (1958): 79–107.
LE HURAY, PETER. *Music and the Reformation in England, 1549–1660.* London: Oxford University Press, 1967.
LOCKWOOD, LEWIS. *The Counter-Reformation and the Masses of Vincenzo Ruffo.* Venice: Fondazione Giorgio Cini, 1970.
————. "Vincenzo Ruffo and Musical Reform After the Council of Trent." *The Musical Quarterly* 43 (1957): 342–371.

The German Reformation

NETTL, PAUL. *Luther and Music,* trans. Frida Best and Ralph Wood. Philadelphia: Muhlenberg, 1948. Reprinted, New York: Russell & Russell, 1967.

Huguenot Music

GARSIDE, CHARLES. "Calvin's Preface to the Psalter: A Reappraisal." *The Musical Quarterly* 37 (1951): 566–577.

——. *Zwingli and the Arts*. New Haven: Yale University Press, 1966.

GEROLD, THÉODORE. *Psaumes de Clément Marot avec les mélodies*. Strasbourg: Université de Strasbourg, 1919.

PIDOUX, PIERRE. *Le Psautier Huguenot du XVIe siècle. Mélodies et documents*. Basel: Bärenreiter, 1962.

English Reformation Music

DANIEL, RALPH, and LE HURAY, PETER. *The Sources of English Church Music, 1549–1660*, 2 vols. London: Stainer & Bell, 1974.

LE HURAY, PETER. *Music and the Reformation in England, 1549–1660*. London: Oxford University Press, 1967.

STEVENSON, ROBERT. "John Marbeck's 'Noted Booke' of 1550." *The Musical Quarterly* 37 (1959): 220–233.

The Counter-Reformation in Italy and Spain

ANDREWS, HILDA K. *An Introduction to the Technique of Palestrina*. London: Novello, 1958.

BOYD, MALCOLM. *Palestrina's Style: A Practical Introduction*. London: Oxford University Press, 1973.

FELLERER, KARL GUSTAV. "Church Music and the Council of Trent." *The Musical Quarterly* 39 (1953): 576–594.

JEPPESEN, KNUD. "The Recently Discovered Mantova Masses of Palestrina." *Acta Musicologica* 22 (1950): 36–47.

——. *The Style of Palestrina and the Dissonance*, 2nd ed., trans. Edward J. Dent. London: Oxford University Press, 1946. Reprinted, 1970.

LOCKWOOD, LEWIS. "Vincenzo Ruffo and Musical Reform After the Council of Trent." *The Musical Quarterly* 43 (1957): 342–371.

——. *The Counter-Reformation and the Masses of Vincenzo Ruffo*. Venice: Fondazione Giorgio Cini, 1970.

MARSHALL, ROBERT. "The Paraphrase Technique of Palestrina in His Masses Based on Hymns." *Journal of the American Musicological Society* 16 (1963): 347–372.

ROCHE, JEROME. *Palestrina*. London: Oxford University Press, 1971.

The Counter-Reformation in Northern Europe and England

ANDREWS, HILDA K. *The Technique of Byrd's Vocal Polyphony*. London: Oxford University Press, 1966.

BOETTICHER, WOLFGANG. "New Lasso Studies." In *Aspects of Medieval and Renaissance Music: A Birthday Offering to Gustave Reese,* ed. Jan La Rue. New York: W. W. Norton, 1966. Pp. 17–26.

BRETT, PHILIP. "Homage to Taverner in Byrd's Masses," *Early Music* 9 (1981): 169–191.

FELLOWES, EDMUND H. *William Byrd,* 2nd ed. London: Oxford University Press, 1948.

JACKMAN, JAMES L. "Liturgical Aspects of Byrd's Gradualia." *The Musical Quarterly* 49 (1963): 17–37.

KERMAN, JOSEPH. "Byrd's Motets: Chronology and Canon." *Journal of the American Musicological Society* 14 (1961): 359–382.

————. "On Byrd's *Emendemus in melius*." *The Musical Quarterly* 49 (1963): 431–449.

————. "The Elizabethan Motet: A Study of Texts for Music." *Studies in the Renaissance* 9 (1962): 273–308.

Music Editions

BYRD, WILLIAM. *Collected Works,* ed. Edmund H. Fellowes, 22 vols. London: Stainer & Bell, 1937–1950. Rev. ed., Thurston Dart et al. London: Stainer & Bell, 1962–   .

GOUDIMEL, CLAUDE. *Oeuvres complètes,* ed. Pierre Pidoux and Maire Egan, 13 vols. Brooklyn, N.Y.: Institute of Medieval Music, 1967–1974.

LASSO, ORLANDO DI. *Samtliche Werke,* ed. Franz X. Haberl and A. Sandberger, 21 vols. Leipzig: Breitkopf & Härtel, 1894–1927.

————. *Sämtliche Werke,* ed. Wolfgang Boetticher, 12 vols. Kassel: Bärenreiter, 1956–   .

PALESTRINA, GIOVANNI PIERLUIGI DA. *Le opere complete,* ed. Raffaele Casimiri, Lucio Virgili, and Knud Jeppesen, 31 vols. Rome: Istituto Italiano per la Historia de la Musica, 1935–1965.

VICTORIA, TOMÁS LUIS DE. *Opera omnia,* ed. Higini Anglés, 4 vols. Monumentos de la música española, vols. 25, 26, 30, 31. Barcelona: Consejo Superior de Investigaciones Científicas, 1965–1968.

WALTHER, JOHANN. *Sämtliche Werke,* ed. Otto Schroder and Max Schneider, 6 vols. Kassel: Bärenreiter, 1943–1970. Vol. 1 reprinted 1953.

12

Instrumental Music and Performance Practice

THE period 1300 to 1600 and even beyond was an age of vocal rather than instrumental music. This probably reflects the different social status of singers and instrumentalists—that is, of chaplains and minstrels—discussed in Chapter 7. And it is no coincidence that the rise of instrumental music in the sixteenth century coincided with the secularization of the entire field of music composition. Nevertheless, even when instrumental music became an accepted and widely cultivated subdivision of learned composition in the sixteenth century, vocal music still dominated. To consider the total output of the major composers of the sixteenth and seventeenth centuries, or even that of J. S. Bach and George Frideric Handel, is to realize that vocal music remained the most important type of composition until the very end of the Baroque period.

Since so much instrumental music of the thirteenth, fourteenth, and fifteenth centuries was closely tied to the practice of improvisation, a discussion of this repertory should lead to analysis of performance practices in those times. This topic is, to be sure, a slippery one, where idle speculation has often taken the place of accurate scholarship.

Instrumental Music

The Fourteenth and Fifteenth Centuries

Even though the literature of the late Middle Ages and the early Renaissance contains numerous references to instruments and instrumental performance, very little music for instruments written prior to the fifteenth century has survived. The reason is clear. Medieval and early Renaissance instrumentalists, with the consistent exception of organists, were by and large minstrels, who were seldom trained to read their music, much less write it down. When required to play composed part-music, they most likely learned their parts by ear. Thus it is not surprising that most early collections of written-down instrumental music are keyboard anthologies, since organists were the only "learned" instrument-performers.

Instrumentalists

271

**Division of
instruments**

By the fourteenth century the division of the instruments into two classes, *haut* and *bas* —literally "high" and "low" but meaning "loud" and "soft"— was well established. The loud instruments included the trumpets, the wood or ivory cornets (wind instruments that were either straight or curved and had a trumpet-like mouthpiece), the double-reed family of the shawms (wind instruments akin to modern oboes), and eventually the sackbuts (early trombones). Some of these were signal instruments, used in battle or in the hunt; others were used to play out-of-doors music, including some of the early dance pieces. The soft instruments included the recorders, the many varieties of plucked and bowed string instruments, and eventually the capped-reed instruments such as the crumhorns, instruments where a free-standing double reed was covered by a small wooden cap with a blow-hole on the top. The soft instruments were probably used to perform written music in the accompaniment of *chansons*. Nevertheless, no hard and fast rules can be drawn, particularly for the fourteenth and fifteenth centuries. The evidence for the use of instruments is at best ambiguous, and it is well to remember that all modern performances of medieval and Renaissance music, even those that claim to use the "authentic instruments," are hypothetical reconstructions of this music.

The manuscripts of the late thirteenth, fourteenth, and early fifteenth centuries which transmit an important repertory of instrumental music are:

1. Instrumental motet-like compositions
   Bamberg, Staatsbibliothek, Lit. 115
2. Monophonic dances
   London, British Library, Add. 29987 (late 13th-cent. France)
3. Keyboard music
   London, British Library, Add. 28350 (early 14th-cent. France or England)
   Paris, Bibliothèque Nationale, n.a.fr. 6771 (early 15th-cent. Italy)
   Faenza, Biblioteca Communale, 117 (early 15th-cent. Italy)

The instrumental works in the Bamberg manuscript are copied at the very end of the collection. Although they differ little from the vocal motets that precede them, doubtless the scribe considered them a different kind of music. They appear in score and have no text other than the incipit of the tenor. The last five pieces in the set are based on the tenor *In seculum,* from the Gradual *Haec dies* (*LU,* 778). Four of the *In seculum* settings form two pairs, for they have essentially the same music, set in one case over a tenor in longs (mode 5) and in the other over a tenor in longs and shorts (mode 1). Therefore one is labeled *In seculum longum* and the other *In seculum breve.*

The first piece of the second pair is labeled *In seculum d'Amiens longum,* but its short counterpart is simply labeled *In seculum.* The extra setting, however, has the most interesting label, for it is called *In seculum viellatoris,* that is, "*In seculum* of the vielle player." This could mean that the piece was composed by a vielle player, or that it was meant to be played on vielles. If the second conjecture is the case, this would be the earliest known indication of a specific instrument in the history of Western music.

All these pieces use extensive *hocketing,* in which a rhythmic line is divided between two voices, so that when one voice has a rest the other sings. It would thus appear that hockets were considered particularly appropriate for instrumental performance. Indeed, the only textless piece among the works of Machaut, and therefore possibly his one purely instrumental work, is also a hocket, which is simply labeled *Hoquetus David* in the manuscripts.

Hockets

To be sure, the hockets in the Bamberg Codex go back well into the thirteenth century. But they also represent the kind of polyphonic instrumental music that was still in vogue at the beginning of the Ars nova, as Machaut's *David* testifies. The same continuation of older forms is apparent in the

The earliest surviving keyboard music from the Robertsbridge Codex (Add. 28550, f. 43r.; reproduced by permission of the British Library)

monophonic *estampies* (instrumental pieces similar to vocal sequences) in London (British Library, Add. 29987), which do not differ from those found in much earlier trouvère manuscripts.

The Roberts-bridge Codex

A new style, however, appears in the keyboard intabulations found in London (British Library, Add. 28350) and known as the Robertsbridge Codex. Here the right hand is notated on a staff, and the left is notated in the form of a letter tablature. The fragment contains three estampies (one incomplete) and three intabulations of vocal pieces (also one incomplete). Two are arrangements of motets by Philippe de Vitry from the *Roman de Fauvel* and therefore must date from after 1316. In these works we begin to find a distinctive keyboard style, as the voices of the model are elaborated into small *figuration* groups. The nature of the figuration, however, is little different

Ex. 12.1   Philippe de Vitry, *Tribum quem non abhorruit—Quoniam secta—Merito hec patimur*

Merito hec pati -

Ex. 12.1   cont.

Triplum: "The group who does not avoid an unseemly ascent. . . ."
Motetus: "As a crew of thieves. . . ."
Tenor: "The virtue hereby shown. . . ."

from that used in the vocal versions of the pieces, except that it becomes far more plentiful in the intabulations (Example 12.1). In addition, the three voices of the model are often reduced to two in the intabulations.

The same style, albeit more developed, appears in the Faenza Codex, an extraordinary collection of keyboard pieces with a repertory that clearly goes back to the second half of the fourteenth century. The Faenza intabulations are notated in a "modern" keyboard score, with Italian notation, on two staves. They include arrangements of works by Machaut, Landini, Jacopo da Bologna, and others, as well as plainsong settings in which one hand has the cantus firmus and the other spins out elaborate, quasi-improvisatory figurations over it. The two keyboard pieces in the Reina Codex (Paris, Bibliothèque Nationale, n.a.fr. 6771) show the same style as the work in the Faenza manuscript.

The Faenza Codex

The Later Fifteenth Century

Although the Faenza Codex was copied in the fifteenth century, its repertory goes back to the second half of the fourteenth. Similar collections survive from the middle decades of the fifteenth century in Germany. These include, in addition to a number of fragments, the tablature of Adam Ileborgh (copied c. 1448), the *Fundamentum organisandi* ("Basis of organization") of Conrad Paumann (written c. 1452), and the *Buxheimer Orgelbuch* (copied c. 1470).

Ileborgh's tablature, which contains a number of preludes notable for their rhythmic flexibility, as well as intabulations of some German songs, is

Ileborgh's tablature

among the earliest sources to indicate the specific use of the organ pedals. Intriguing as it is, however, the Ileborgh tablature is too small a sample to provide more than a glimpse of the composer's personality.

The case of Paumann (1410–1473), the famous blind organist of Munich, is different, for his music survives in several collections, including the *Buxheimer Orgelbuch*. The *Fundamentum organisandi* is a methodical approach to the spinning out of melodic figuration over a bass progression. This emphasis on ornamentation carries over to Paumann's intabulations of vocal pieces and makes him the predecessor of the school of organists known as the *colorists,* because of their interest in figural ornamentation of the melodies. But Paumann's use of ornamentation is by no means as pervasive as that of the later composers.

**The
*Buxheimer
Orgelbuch***

The intabulations in the *Buxheimer Orgelbuch* show essentially the same style as Paumann's. They include a considerable number of German lieder as well as French chansons by the Lantins, Binchois, Dunstaple, Frye, and Dufay. Like the Faenza manuscript, this collection also includes plainsong settings, although here they are more numerous and elaborate.

**Hofhaimer
and the
colorists**

The generation of composers following Paumann is dominated by two very different figures, Paul Hofhaimer (1459–1537) and Arnold Schlick (c. 1640–c. 1517). Very little of Hofhaimer's instrumental music has survived other than in the arrangements of his disciples and followers, known as "the Paulomines" or "the colorists": men such as Konrad Buchner (d. 1541), Hans Buchner (1483–1538), Hans Kotter (1480–1541), Fridolin Sicher (1490–1546), and Leonhard Kleber (1495–1556). Furthermore, the few authentic surviving Hofhaimer works are without his disciples' tendency to ornament lines to the point of obscuring the melodic shapes. Hofhaimer's style of ornamentation is remarkably sober, and the large shapes of the melodies are clearly audible, as shown, for instance, in Example 12.2.

Schlick

Schlick's music differs drastically from that of Hofhaimer and the Paulomines in that he has little taste for ornamentation and relies on a long-breathed linear drive very similar to that in the vocal music of the generation of Josquin Des Prés. His *Tabulaturen etlicher Lobgesang und Liedlein uff die Orgeln und Lauten* ("Tablatures on some psalms and little songs for the organ and lute," 1518) is the earliest printed tablature available. It shows Schlick to be far more interested in contrapuntal interplay than in the brilliant instrumental effects of the Hofhaimer school.

Improvised Ensemble Music

A minute fragment of what must have been a vast repertory of improvised instrumental music has survived because it was written down in a few scattered manuscripts. It consists of a few settings of a dance category known

**The basse
danse**

as *basse danse.* These pieces were improvised upon a tenor set in notes of equal value that regulated the dancers' movements. The common basse danse ensemble was two shawms and a sackbut (or slide trumpet). Several of the tenors were derived from fifteenth-century chansons and given the appropriate names. Others seem to have had an independent existence as cantus firmi,

Ex. 12.2   Paul Hofhaimer, setting of *Salve regina*

among them the famous tenor known as *La Spagna,* used not only as a basse danse tenor but also as the foundation for Masses and motets by several composers.

    A number of French sources, such as the anonymous print *L'Art et instruction de bien danser* ("The art and directions for dancing well," before 1494) and the sumptuous manuscript 9085 in the Royal Library of Brussels, contain collections of tenors with a shorthand notation for the dance steps. The Italian sources, such as the *Trattato dell'arte del ballo* (Treatise on the art of dancing," c. 1463) by Guglielmo Ebreo, and the *Libro dell'arte del danzare* ("Book on the art of dance," c. 1465) by Antonio Cornazano, also contain elaborate choreographies. A three-part setting, written by Francisco de la Torre and based on the same tenor, is printed in *HAM* I (no. 102).

Composed Ensemble Music

    Toward the end of the fifteenth century, many textless compositions appeared in the chansonniers. The growth of this repertory, little understood for a long time, has now been charted by several scholars. Louise Litterick[1] has shown that the vocal-instrumental chanson of northern France, when it

**Chanson-
niers
from Italy**

An open-air ensemble of three shawms. (Français 12574, fol. 181v; Bibliothèque Nationale, Paris)

was imported into Italy with the influx of French composers, became a purely instrumental composition. The chansonniers copied in France show the full text in the top voice and sometimes in the tenor as well, but those copied in Italy have only a title or the incipits of the text.

The process goes further than the mere stripping of texts from earlier chansons. As French composers worked in Italian courts, they exceeded the simple adaptation of vocal pieces and began to write chanson-like works that despite frequent French titles were never intended to be anything other than instrumental works. This trend applies even more to the polyphonic settings of popular tunes, settings that in the north spawned the *combinative chanson*. In this form, the text of the popular tune, as found in some of the voices, was sung simultaneously with a rondeau text in the top voice. In Italy such pieces were completely instrumental, and indeed, the three great collections issued by Petrucci in the early sixteenth century were probably intended primarily for instrumental performance. As this repertory grew, a subtle stylistic change took place in the music itself. Composers began to employ more often such devices as sequential passages and short *ostinati,* and also repeated motives that were largely absent from the earlier chanson repertory but helped make the flow of a purely instrumental piece easier to comprehend. Among the composers represented in the Italian collections, either by arrangements or original works, the majority were still Franco-Netherlanders: Ockeghem, Josquin, Caron, Busnois, De Orto, and Brumel.

In Germany, developments were not very different from those in Italy, except that the rise of purely instrumental music took place a little earlier. The relationship between German instrumental music of the late fifteenth century and the Franco-Italian development discussed above is made clear by the composers who dominate the repertory. Alexander Agricola and Heinrich Isaac both worked extensively in Italy and produced many instrumental pieces with French chanson titles. Their fondness for purely abstract figuration is, if anything, stronger than that of the composers who remained in Italy. In their settings of popular tunes, the German composers also took special delight in combining several snatches of them in elaborate pieces called *quodlibets.* Also revealing are a large number of pieces by Heinrich Finck—who preferred German titles or the Latin title *carmen* ("poem")—and by Jacob Obrecht, whose pieces include settings of Dutch popular tunes as well (see *HAM* I, no. 78).

German music

The Early Sixteenth Century

The sixteenth century witnessed not only the emergence of distinctive instrumental genres, but also a veritable explosion in the production and publication of instrumental music. The advent of printing made music more readily available to a larger audience, and this development coincided with the growing wealth and importance of the merchant class, which was eager to imitate and adopt the cultural conventions of the nobility. It is scarcely surprising, then, that most of the new repertory was for the two household instruments capable of producing polyphony, the lute and the harpsichord, or for instruments closely related to them, such as the Spanish *vihuela de mano.*

For the sake of convenience, sixteenth-century instrumental ensemble music can be divided into four categories: (1) dance music; (2) transcriptions of vocal works; (3) settings of popular tunes; and (4) "free" compositions. To be sure, these categories often overlap. Tylman Susato published dances based on Josquin's chanson *Mille Regretz* and Sermisy's *Dont vient cela,* and Francesco da Milano published an intabulation of Richafort's *De mon Triste Desplaisir,* as well as a ricercare based upon the themes of the chanson. Nevertheless, the four categories might well be discussed separately, in order to trace their development as well as their interrelationships.

Categories of instrumental music

Dance Music

The cantus firmus dances of the fifteenth century evolved into sets of dances that made use of an extension of the cantus firmus principle, that is,

Ex. 12.3   Bass patterns for dances

Passamezzo antico

Romanescca

Folia

Passamezzo moderno

Bass patterns   the pattern-bass. Bass patterns were clearly present in much of the frottola and villancico repertory in the late fifteenth century, and they lent themselves readily to extension and improvisation. The names of some of them, such as the *passamezzo* (*pass'e mezzo;* "step and a half"), suggest their close connection with dance music. Most involve only the simplest harmonic relationships, clearly interrelated (see Example 12.3).

These bass patterns were often accompanied by standard trebles that helped to clarify the harmonic implications of the bass. Among the most famous trebles were *Greensleeves* in England and *Guárdame las vacas* ("Watch the cows for me") in Spain. Note the elaboration of one pattern in a polyphonic dance in a basse danse published by Attaingnant in 1530 (Example 12.4).

Ex. 12.4   Basse dance based on the passamezzo antico

In addition to abstract bass patterns, dance composers also used the harmonic and melodic framework of well-known songs. In the adaptation of a complex imitative piece like Josquin's *Mille regretz,* the texture was simplified and "squared off," as can be observed by comparing the first phrase of the original chanson (Example 12.5) with the pavane based upon it by the German publisher and composer Tylman Susato (c. 1500–c. 1561) (see Example 12.6). Toward the end of the century, particularly in England, such arrangements became extremely subtle. The countless pavanes based on Dowland's song *Flow, My Tears,* commonly called *Lachrymae pavan,* attest to the popularity of this kind of dance composition.

The early sixteenth-century dances were published not just for instrumental ensemble but in arrangements for keyboard and lute as well. It is difficult to determine today how such arrangements were used—that is, whether

Arrangements

Ex. 12.5   Josquin Des Prés, *Mille regretz*

"Leaving you causes me a thousand sorrows. . . ."

Ex. 12.6   Tylman Susato, pavane based on *Mille regretz*

they were employed by professional musicians or else intended as simplified versions for amateurs who lacked the improvisatory skills of the professionals. The most important publishers of dance music were those who published the bulk of the French chanson repertory: Attaingnant and Le Roy and Ballard in Paris, Jacques Moderne in Lyons, Tylman Susato in Antwerp, and Pierre Phalèse in Louvain.

Dance pairs   Early in the sixteenth century, dances began to be grouped in pairs of two. By far the most common pair was that of the *pavane* (in duple meter) and the *galliard* (in triple meter), called in Germany *Tanz* and *Nachtanz* (the Nachtanz was also called *Tripla, Proporz,* or *Hupauff*), and in Italy *passamezzo* and *saltarello*. Similar pairing developed later between the *allemande* and the *courante*. Often the pairs contrasted in meter and tempo, the first piece often being a slow gliding dance and the second a fast leaping one. But frequently both members of a pair used the same thematic material.

Although the tendency to build dances on abstract patterns or preexistent songs continued until the seventeenth century, the rhythmic surface of the individual dances became so stereotyped that it was possible to compose a completely free piece that would be immediately recognizable as a particular dance type. Such is the case with the exquisitely crafted keyboard dances of the English virginalists, particularly those of Orlando Gibbons and William Byrd. Byrd also wrote out the ornamented repeats for each strain of the piece, ornaments that had most likely been left for improvisation in the earlier repertory. These pieces do not seem to have been conceived as actual dance music but rather as stylizations of the dance forms. In a few instances, however, the pieces may well have been intended for dancing as well as for simple listening. This was probably true, for example, of the elaborate dance arrangements for broken consort published by Thomas Morley in 1599.

Transcriptions of Vocal Music
As noted above, French chansons, when imported into Italy and Germany in the late fifteenth and early sixteenth centuries, became essentially instru-

mental music. The tendency toward outright transcription, however, did not abate in the sixteenth century, and we therefore encounter a large repertory of intabulations of vocal originals for lute or for keyboard. The models, however, were not only chansons but also madrigals, motets, and Mass movements. These intabulations go beyond mere transcriptions of vocal polyphony for a single instrument, as they involve figural ornament of the vocal lines, hardly different from that used by the German organists. An example is the following chanson by Claudin de Sermisy, transcribed for keyboard in Pierre Attaingnant's *Dixneuf Chansons musicales reduictes en la tablature des orgues, espinettes, manicordions, et telz semblables instruments musicaulx* ("Nineteen musical songs reduced to tablature for organs, harpsichords, clavichords, and similar musical instruments," Paris, 1530) (see Example 12.7).

Similar intabulations are found in the Spanish *vihuela* repertory, as well as in that of the English virginalists, such as the intabulation of Lasso's *Bon jour mon coeur* ("Good day, my heart") by Peter Philips (see *HAM* I, no. 145). In both the Spanish and English intabulations, however, the ornamentation is more elaborate than in the Attaingnant example above. It begins to approach the kind of free fantasia based upon a vocal model that became particularly popular in Spain, Italy, and England during the middle and late years of the sixteenth century.

Settings of Monophonic Tunes

These works had essentially two formats. One consisted of settings of plainsong assigned to one polyphonic voice, while the others weaved a contrapuntal fabric around the plainsong. Such settings, particularly for organ, were popular throughout Europe. The English composers John Redford and Thomas Preston set a considerable number of hymns and other Office chants in this manner, as did the Spaniard Antonio de Cabezón (1510–1566). In the other format the monophonic tune is treated as a source for the thematic material of the work, in much the same manner as the vocal composers after Josquin paraphrased monophonic cantus firmi.

Plainsong settings

Far more important, however, were the settings of Mass and Office chants in *alternatim*. This is a performance style in which the organ elaborates every other verse of the plainsong in polyphony, while the choir sings the remaining verses either in chant or in figural polyphony. Such *organ Masses* and *organ Magnificats* were composed by Girolamo Cavazzoni (c. 1520–1560; see *HAM* I, no. 117), Cabezón, and the Gabrielis, and in their hands these relatively simple works acquired great sophistication. The chant was treated not simply as a cantus firmus but rather in a polyphonic paraphrase similar to the vocal paraphrases found in the music of Josquin, Morales, and other composers of the first half of the sixteenth century.

Organ masses

Equally important, particularly among Spanish and English composers, were variation sets based upon popular tunes. Some, such as *Guárdame las vacas* or *John Come Kisse Me Now,* were simply some of the traditional trebles of the *romanesca* or passamezzo patterns. But others, like the *Canto llano del caballero,* set by Cabezón (see *HAM* I, no. 134), or *The Carman's Whistle,* set

Variation sets

Ex. 12.7   Keyboard intabulation of Claudin de Sermisy's *Amour, partez*

"Love, go away, I chase you off. . . ."

by Byrd, seem to be independent tunes unrelated to any bass pattern. Such tunes were set not only for keyboard, but for lute and vihuela as well. The Spanish composers also included variation sets on plainsongs in their vihuela collections, such as the *diferencias* ("variations") on *O gloriosa Domina* by Luis de Narváez (see *HAM* I, no. 122). The most famous and numerous of these chant variations, however, were the English *In nomine* settings for keyboard, lute, or viol consort.

The variation technique, which simply used instrumental figuration to embellish the melodic line, is also present, as noted above, in the simple settings of dance pieces or of songs in the works of the English virginalists. These techniques of melodic embellishment, known as *diminuation* or *glosas,* were also explored more or less systematically in a number of treatises on ornamentation, such as Diego Ortiz's *Tratado de glosas* (1553) and Silvestro Ganassi's *Opera intitulata fontegara* (1535).

Free Instrumental Music

In the early sixteenth century, instrumental music independent of vocal models or dance patterns took the form of *ricercari* and *fantasias* for lute, keyboard, or, more rarely, for a string instrument such as the viol. Differences between the ricercare and the fantasia were never pronounced, and composers seem to have used the terms interchangeably.

Early ricercari and fantasias, such as those found in Vincenzo Capirola's **Ricercari** lute book (c. 1517) or in Luis de Milan's *El Maestro* (1535), are sectional works **and** consisting almost entirely of quasi-improvisatory instrumental figuration **fantasias** with little or no imitation (see *HAM* I, no. 121). Later in the century, however, both types evolved into contrapuntal pieces resembling the midcentury vocal motet in texture and technique. This similarity is particularly the case with the organ ricercari, as well as with those written for instrumental ensemble (e.g., pieces in Willaert's *Musica nova* of 1559; see *HAM* I, no. 115) and those of Andrea Gabrieli (*HAM* I, no. 136). The contrapuntal style of the ensemble ricercare was less suited to the lute, and to the end of the century the ricercari and fantasias for this instrument remained closer to the improvisatory style of pieces from the early sixteenth century than did those for keyboard or ensemble. Yet in the hands of Miguel de Fuenllana (b.c. sixteenth century), Francesco da Milano, and John Dowland, the lute fantasia became a far more contrapuntal piece than those found in Milan's *El Maestro*.

The close stylistic and technical similarities between the ensemble ricer- **Parody** care and the motet also anticipated the use of parody in the instrumental **ricercare** pieces, so that by the 1540s a considerable number of such works were instrumentally conceived parodies of vocal models. They differed from mere intabulations in the freedom with which the thematic material was transformed, as well as in the actual reworking of the textures and points of imitation.

In both the ricercare and the fantasia, the differences between the lute, keyboard, and ensemble pieces are a function of the medium rather than an inherent element of the style. The ensemble works simply carry out explicitly the implied polyphony found in the lute and keyboard works. Similarly, in

England, the apparent preference for the homogeneous, smooth sound of the viol consort for ensemble music lent to the ensemble fantasy a characteristically smooth and complex contrapuntal texture. This was absent from continental works intended to be performed by strings, winds, or a combination of the two, possibly because the louder wind instruments were not capable of the viols' agility and delicacy of phrasing.

The canzona   Related to the later ricercare and the fantasia was the *canzon da suonare* ("song for playing") or *canzon francese* ("French song"), later simply called *canzona*. This genre was not, as its early names imply, derived from the chanson-like instrumental works produced by French composers in Italy during the late fifteenth and early sixteenth centuries. The source, rather, is the Parisian vocal chanson of the 1520s and 1530s, which probably reached Italy through the diplomatic contacts between the French court and the Medici. The canzona retained the conventional dactylic rhythmic opening found in many French chansons (♩ ♫ ♩), but it borrowed from the motet-like ricercare its contrapuntal texture and the reliance upon successive points of imitation. Nevertheless, instead of following the relatively loose structure of the ricercare and the fantasia, the canzona did incorporate some of the formal traits of the French chanson. Most notable was the return of the opening phrase group at the end to produce an ABA structure, or else the immediate repeat of the first or the last phrase group, leading to an AAB or an ABB form.

Like the ricercare and the fantasia, the canzona remained essentially a chamber-music genre throughout the sixteenth century. Consider the early *canzone* of Marc'Antonio Ingenieri (1579); those of Florentio Maschera (1584), Battista Guami (1588), and Viadana (1590); and even those as late as Giovanni Batista Grillo (1608). With the appearance of Giovanni Gabrieli's *Sacrae symphoniae* in 1597, however, the canzona was turned into a monumental work, as Gabrieli composed such pieces for eight, twelve, or sixteen parts divided into antiphonal choirs employing mostly the louder instruments. In these works not only the dynamic levels but also the textures are full of sharp contrasts and brilliant effects. Understandably, contrapuntal considerations here are subordinate to the sheer brilliance of the sound and the contrast of different rhythms and textures. Typical of these works is the *Sonata pian' e forte* ("Piece for playing soft and loud"; *HAM* I, no. 173), a composition which also anticipates the transformation of the canzona into what would become the Baroque ensemble sonata. Indeed, Gabrieli's canzone of 1597, and espcially those published in 1615, belong no longer to the Renaissance but rather to the beginnings of the Baroque style.

Performance Practice

Sketchy Notation

The notion of writing music to be performed not only by a composer's contemporaries but also by musicians several generations later did not become current until the nineteenth century. Composers of previous eras seldom considered such a possibility. An exception could be Guillaume de Machaut, who, as we have seen, had all of his works collected and copied in a series of sumptuously illuminated manuscripts, but even in this case his primary aim was most likely to offer them as a gift to several of his noble patrons.

In any case, not even the most precise musical notation can convey all the necessary information to allow a performer totally unfamiliar with the musical tradition of a given work to produce a faithful performance. And in the Middle Ages and the Renaissance, composers relied heavily upon musical tradition. Therefore the performer of medieval or Renaissance music today is faced with a written notation that provides only the barest hints about how the work should sound. Missing are such fundamental matters as the number of singers or instruments employed, the nature of the instruments themselves, the tone color of the voice or the instruments, the pitch and tunings, the tempo and phrasing, the addition of unwritten accidentals, the placement of the text syllables under the music, and the addition of melodic embellishment to the lines.

Ways of complementing and understanding the information provided by music manuscripts can be gathered from a number of other sources. Among these are literary accounts, historical records, theoretical treatises, paintings, sculptures, and manuscript illuminations, as well as the evidence of the surviving instruments from the period.

Literary Sources

No detailed study of this kind of evidence has been made, although both Craig Wright and Maria Fowler have begun such a task, and scattered examples have been cited again and again.[2] Most evidence consists of musical performances described in poems or stories, often containing no more than vague general references to a performance, but occasionally with long lists of the instruments employed. The problem with the instrumental enumerations is that rather than representing descriptions of actual performances, they often fall prey to a medieval desire for inclusiveness, so that all instruments known to the author may be simply listed haphazardly.

A few accounts, however, such as those found in Boccaccio's *Decameron* and in the writings of a few other trecento authors, notably Giovanni da Prato, Franco Sachetti, and Simone Prodenzani, do seem to describe actual performances. Or at least they describe a performance in relatively realistic terms. Typical of these is the following description in a sonnet by Prodenzani:[3]

> *Quella sera cantaro ei madrigali,*
> *Cancon del Cieco a modo perugino,*
> *Rondel franceschi de Fra Bartolino,*
> *Strambotti de Sicilia a la reale.*
>
> *D'ogni cosa Sollazzo e principale,*
> *Comme quel che de musica era pino;*
> *El tenor gli tenea Frate Agustino,*
> *E'l contra maestro Pier de Giuvenale.*

That evening they sang madrigals,
Songs by the blind one[4] in the Perugian manner,
French rondels by Fra Bartolino,
Strambotti of Sicily in the royal way.

In each Sollazzo was the leader,
As the one who was full of music,
The tenor was taken by Fra Agustino,
And the contratenor by master Pier de Giuvenale.

The description has the ring of plausibility, but in fact it raises more questions than it answers. It tells us that trecento polyphony is essentially a soloistic art, but it also states that the tenor and the contratenor were sung rather than played on an instrument, since most poets enjoyed exhibiting their knowledge of the instruments and would mention them whenever possible. Furthermore, we wonder whether "the Perugian manner" and "the royal way" were specific traditions of performance or simply conceits of the poet. If the former, then they represent something now apparently totally lost and possibly not recoverable. The passage also seems to suggest different ways of singing a given piece, something about which we have today very little, if any, information.

Historical Records

Chronicles   Such records are essentially of two kinds: chronicles and account books. The chronicles sometimes contain descriptions of musical performances on important occasions. As with the literary accounts, unless the writer had some musical knowledge, these tend to be relatively superficial. But at least they seem to give more genuine lists of the instruments used than do the literary accounts.

Account books   Account books, indicating the payments to a court's singers and minstrels, or to a cathedral's canons and vicars, contain the best information about forces available for the performance of music in a given court or church. In addition, they sometimes provide a wealth of other information, including payments made for the repair of instruments and the copying of music books. Ancillary sources such as testament records also provide extraordinarily detailed accounts of the music performed at funerals and commemorative ceremonies for dead dignitaries.

The combined study of chronicles and account records sometimes provides a clear picture of music performance at a given establishment. For most of the medieval and early Renaissance period, it also indicates a definite stratification of musicians into chaplains and minstrels, as reflected in the repertories they played or sang. The chaplains performed no secular music and the minstrels performed no sacred music (except on a very few ceremonial occasions). The studies also show that whatever music was available to a given establishment was simply adapted to the forces at hand, with little or no concern for the original intention of the composer (i.e., for the present-day notion of "authenticity").

Theoretical Treatises

Theoretical treatises of the Middle Ages and the Renaissance contain occasional references to performance, but as a rule these are incidental to the main purpose of the treatises. Nevertheless, a number are invaluable in two fields that directly concern performance: (1) the rhythmic interpretation of the notation and the mensuration and proportional signs used from the fourteenth century onward; and (2) the use of *musica ficta,* that is, the accidentals added by the performers but seldom notated in the manuscripts.

Notation

Musica ficta

How extemporized accidentals in the Middle Ages and the Renaissance were used is relatively well known. They were usually added in order to avoid tritones, imperfect fifths, and imperfect octaves between the parts; or were added in cadential patterns in order to expand or contract the final imperfect consonance. Thus the final perfect octave, fifth, or unison would be approached from the imperfect consonance nearest to it in size (see Example 12.8).

Toward the end of the fifteenth century and during the early decades of the sixteenth, theorists were also concerned with proper declamation of text. In their works are sets of rules on how to set the syllables of the text to the music—rules that are particularly useful when dealing with the extremely

Ex. 12.8   Examples of musica ficta

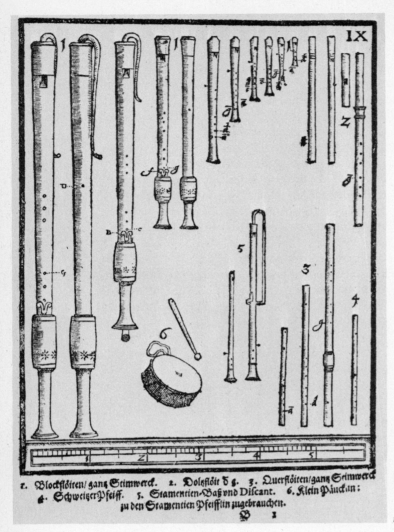

1. Blockflöten/gantz Stimwerck. 2. Dolsflöit d s. 3. Querflöiten/gantz Stimwerck
4. Schweitzerpfeiff. 5. Stamentien-Baß vnd Discant. 6. Klein Plöcklin:
zu den Stamentien Pfeifflin zugebrauchen.
B I

Recorders and transverse flutes drawn to scale in Michael Praetorius, *Syntagma musicum* (1619).

melismatic style of sacred music from the late fifteenth and early sixteenth centuries.

Descriptions of instruments

Similarly, descriptions of musical instruments, including woodcuts depicting them, appear in the treatises, particularly those of the German writers. Indeed, among the earliest instrumental descriptions we have is Sebastian Virdung's *Musica getutscht* ("Music Germanized") of 1511, the very first published treatise to deal not only with the technique of playing instruments but with their manufacture. This tradition culminates at the very end of the Renaissance in Michael Praetorius' monumental *Syntagma musicum* of 1619, with its extensive lists of plates and descriptions of virtually every instrument in use.

A third group of sixteenth-century treatises, such as those by Ortiz and

Ganassi mentioned earlier, also deals with the problem of the addition of melodic embellishments. To be sure, these seem to represent a relatively late and specialized tradition, but they appear in connection not only with instrumental music but also with vocal works. The nature of the ornaments themselves suggests that their origin was the written-out ornamentation of early intabulations of vocal works at the beginning of the sixteenth century.

Summary

Instrumental music throughout the Middle Ages and the Renaissance was largely improvised. What was set down was usually closely derived from vocal models. The exception is the relatively small repertory of monophonic and elementary polyphonic dances that survives in a few manuscripts and probably represents the written-out versions of works that were normally improvised.

The first large collections of instrumental music in the fourteenth and fifteenth centuries are keyboard tablatures, for among the instrumentalists the organist normally had access to the more elaborate art-music tradition of "learned" musicians, a tradition associated with sacred music. Therefore the use of written notation does represent, to some extent, the keyboard player's special status among instrumentalists.

The fifteenth century, particularly in ensemble music, saw the growth of an independent instrumental repertory, albeit still tied stylistically to vocal music. The growing importance of the commercial bourgeoisie during the early sixteenth century gave further impetus to this growth, particularly as the lute became a popular instrument among amateurs who sought to emulate the great lute virtuosos. This direction gave rise to the first truly independent forms of abstract instrumental music, the *ricercare* and the *fantasia,* and also reflected the higher social status of the instrumentalists in the sixteenth century.

The proper execution of medieval and Renaissance music, notated without indication of instrumentation, tempo, dynamics, and the like, requires the most careful understanding of the notation itself as well as comprehension of the unwritten traditions that gave rise to it. These can be gleaned from a number of sources, including literary and historical records and theoretical treatises. To be sure, all sources of evidence should be collated and treated with care, as they often raise their own problems. Ultimately, no single performance of a piece of early music can be judged "correct," but many may be considered plausible.

Notes

1. "Performing Franco-Netherlandish Secular Music of the Late Fifteenth Century: Texted and Untexted Parts in the Sources," *Early Music* 8 (1980): 474–485.
2. Wright, "Performance Practices," *The Musical Quarterly* 64 (1978): 295–328;

Fowler, "Women Musicians in Medieval France," in *Women Making Music,* ed. Jane Bowers and Judith Tick (Berkeley and Los Angeles: University of California Press, in press).

3. Cited by Leonard Ellinwood in "The Fourteenth Century in Italy," in *The New Oxford History of Music,* vol. 3, ed. Anselm Hughes and Gerald Abraham (London: Oxford University Press, 1960), p. 36.

4. The "blind one" is Francesco Landini.

Bibliography

Books and Articles

Instrumental Music

APEL, WILLI. *The History of Keyboard Music to 1700,* trans. Hans Tischler. Bloomington: University of Indiana Press, 1972.

———. "Solo Instrumental Music." In *The New Oxford History of Music,* vol. 4, *The Age of Humanism, 1540–1640,* ed. Gerald Abraham. London: Oxford University Press, 1968. Pp. 602–708.

HEARTZ, DANIEL. "The Basse Dance." *Annales musicologiques* 6 (1958–1963): 287–340.

HOWELL, ALMONTE C. "Cabezón: An Essay in Structural Analysis." *The Musical Quarterly* 50 (1964): 18–30.

MEYER, ERNEST. "Concerted Instrumental Music." In *The New Oxford History of Music,* vol. 4, *The Age of Humanism, 1540–1640,* ed. Gerald Abraham. London: Oxford University Press, 1968. Pp. 550–601.

MUNROW, DAVID. *Instruments of the Middle Ages and the Renaissance.* London: Oxford University Press, 1976.

REESE, GUSTAVE. "The Origin of the English 'In nomine.'" *Journal of the American Musicological Society* 2 (1949): 7–22.

SACHS, CURT. *The History of Musical Instruments.* New York: W. W. Norton, 1940.

SLIM, H. COLIN. "Francesco da Milano: A Bio-Bibliographical Study." *Musica disciplina* 18 (1964): 63–84; 19 (1965): 109–128.

———. "Keyboard Music at Castell'Arquato by an Early Madrigalist." *Journal of the American Musicological Society* 15 (1962): 35–47.

SOUTHERN, EILEEN. *The Buxheim Organ Book.* Musicological Studies, vol. 6. Brooklyn, N.Y.: Institute of Medieval Music, 1963.

———. "Some Keyboard Basse Dances of the Fifteenth Century." *Acta musicologica* 35 (1963): 114–124.

WARD, JOHN M. "The Use of Borrowed Material in Sixteenth-Century Instrumental Music." *Journal of the American Musicological Society* 5 (1952): 88–98.

YOUNG, WILLIAM. "Keyboard Music to 1600." *Musica disciplina* 16 (1962): 115–150; 17 (1963): 163–193.

Performance Practice

This topic is as vast as it is confused. The best guide to it is Mary Vinquist and Neal Zaslaw, *Performance Practice: A Bibliography* (New York: W. W. Norton, 1971), which covers not just the Middle Ages and the Renaissance but the entire field of European music history.

ARBEAU, THOINOT. *Orchesographie (Langres, 1589),* trans. Mary Stewart Evans, with an introduction by Julia Sutton. New York: Dover, 1967.

BANK, J. A., *Tactus, Tempo and Notation in Mensural Music from the Thirteenth to the Seventeenth Century.* Amsterdam: Annie Bank, 1972.

BROWN, HOWARD MAYER. *Embellishing Sixteenth-Century Music.* Early Music Series, vol. 1. London: Oxford University Press, 1976.

———. "On the Performance of Fifteenth-Century Chansons." *Early Music* 1 (1973): 3–10.

GANASSI, SILVESTRO. *La Fontegara,* trans. D. S. Swaingson; ed. Hildemarie Peter. Berlin: R. Lienau, 1925. Reprinted, London: Novello, 1969.

HARRAN, DON. "New Light on the Question of Text Underlay Prior to Zarlino." *Acta musicologica* 45 (1973): 24–56.

HUGHES, ANDREW. *Ficta in Focus: Manuscript Accidentals, 1530–1450.* Musicological Studies and Documents, 27. Rome: American Institute of Musicology, 1972.

KOTTICK, EDWARD L. "Flats, Modality, and Musica Ficta in Some Early Renaissance Chansons." *Journal of Music Theory* 12 (1968): 264–280.

KOVARIK, EDWARD. "The Performance of Dufay's Paraphrase Kyries." *Journal of the American Musicological Society* 28 (1975): 230–244.

LITTERICK, LOUISE. "Performing Franco-Netherlandish Secular Music of the Late Fifteenth Century: Texted and Untexted Parts in the Sources." *Early Music* 8 (1980): 474–485.

LOWINSKY, EDWARD E. "A Treatise on Text Underlay by a German Disciple of Francesco da Salinas." *Festschrift Heinrich Besseler.* Leipzig: Breitkopf & Härtel, 1961. Pp. 231–251.

PERKINS, LEEMAN L. "Towards a Rational Approach to Text Placement in the Secular Music of Dufay's Time." *Papers Read at the Dufay Quincentenary Conference, Brooklyn College, December 6–7, 1974,* ed. Allan W. Atlas. Brooklyn, N.Y.: Brooklyn College, 1975. Pp. 102–114.

POLK, KEITH. "Ensemble Performance in Dufay's Time." *Papers Read at the Dufay Quincentenary Conference, Brooklyn College, December 6–7, 1974,* ed. Allan W. Atlas. Brooklyn, N.Y.: Brooklyn College, 1975. Pp. 61–75.

RANDEL, DON M. "Emerging Triadic Tonality in the Fifteenth Century." *The Musical Quarterly* 57 (1971): 73–86.

SACHS, CURT. *Rhythm and Tempo.* New York: W. W. Norton, 1953.

Scores and Facsimiles

AMELN, KONRAD, ed. *Locheimer Liederbuch und Fundamentum organisandi des Conrad Paumann.* Berlin, 1925. Reprinted, Documenta musicologica, ser. 2, no. 3. Kassel: Bärenreiter, 1972.

ANGLÈS, HIGINI, ed. *La música en la corte de Carlos V, con la transcripción del "Libro de cifra nueva para tecla, arpa y vihuela" de Luys Vegas de Henestrosa (1557),* 2 vols. Monumentos de la música española, vol. 2 (parts 1 and 2). Barcelona: Consejo Superior de Investigaciones Científicas, 1944–1965.

APEL, WILLI, ed. *Keyboard Music of the Fourteenth and Fifteenth Centuries.* Corpus of Early Keyboard Music, 1. Rome: American Institute of Musicology, 1963.

ATTAINGNANT, PIERRE. *Preludes, Chansons, and Dances for Lute,* ed. Daniel Heartz. Neuilly-sur-Seine: Société de Musique d'Autrefois, 1964.

———. *Transcriptions of Chansons for Keyboard,* ed. Albert Seay. Corpus mensurabilis musicae, 20. Rome: American Institute of Musicology, 1961.

BULL, JOHN. *Keyboard Music I,* ed. J. Steele, F. Cameron, and T. Dart. Musica Britannica, vol. 14. London: Stainer & Bell, 1960. Revised, 1967.

———. *Keyboard Music II,* ed. T. Dart. Musica Britannica, vol. 19. London: Stainer & Bell, 1963. Revised, 1970.

BYRD, WILLIAM. *Keyboard Music,* ed. Allan Brown, 2 vols. Musica Britannica, vols. 27, 28. London: Stainer & Bell, 1969–1971.

————. *My Lady Nevells Booke,* ed. Hilda K. Andrews. London: J. Curwen, 1925. Reprinted, New York: Dover, 1969.

CABEZÓN, ANTONIO DE. *Obras de musica para tecla, arpa y vihuela,* 3 vols., ed. Higini Anglès. Monumentos de la música española, vols. 27, 29. Barcelona: Consejo Superior de Investigaciones Científicas, 1966.

CANOVA DA MILANO, FRANCESCO. *The Lute Music of Francesco Canova da Milano,* ed. J. Arthur Ness, 2 vols. (in one). Harvard Publications in Music, vols. 3, 4. Cambridge: Harvard University Press, 1970.

CAPIROLA, VINCENZO. *Compositione de Meser Vincenzo Capirola. Lute Book (circa 1517),* ed. Otto Gombosi. Neuilly-sur-Seine: Société de Musique d'Autrefois, 1955.

CARAPETYAN, ARMEN, ed. *An Early-Fifteenth-Century Italian Source of Keyboard Music, the Codex Faenza, Biblioteca Comunale 117.* Musicological Studies and Documents, 10. Rome: American Institute of Musicology, 1961.

DALLA LIBERA, SANDRO, ed. *Antologia organistica Italiana.* Milan: Ricordi, 1957.

DISERTORI, BENVENUTO, ed. *Le frottole par canto e liuto intabulate de Franciscus Bossinensis.* Instituzioni e monumenti dell'arte musicale Italiana, nuova serie, vol. 3. Milan: Ricordi, 1964.

ENRIQUEZ DE VALDERRABANO, ENRIQUE. *Libro de música de vihuela intitulado Silva de sirenas,* 2 vols., ed. Emilio Pujol. Monumentos de la música española, vols. 22, 23. Barcelona: Consejo Superior de Investigaciones Científicas, 1965.

GABRIELI, ANDREA. *Tre Messe per organo,* ed. Sandro dalla Libera. Milan: Ricordi, 1958.

GABRIELI, GIOVANNI. *Canzoni e sonate per sonar con ogni sorte de instrommenti,* ed. Michel Sanvoisin. Le Pupitre, no. 27. Paris: Heugel, 1971.

————. *Composizioni per organo,* 2 vols., ed. Sandro dalla Libera. Milan: Ricordi, 1957.

————. *Works for Keyboard Instruments,* ed. G. S. Bedbrook. Kassel: Bärenreiter, 1957.

GIESBERT, F. J., ed. *Pariser Tanzbuch (1530),* 2 vols. Mainz: B. Schott's Söhne, 1950.

MERULO, CLAUDIO. *Toccate per organo,* 3 vols., ed. Sandro dalla Libera. Milan: Ricordi, 1958–1959.

MILAN, LUYS DE. *El maestro,* ed. Charles Jacobs. University Park: Pennsylvania State University Press, 1971.

————. *Libro de musica de vihuela de mano intitulado El Maeastro,* ed. Leo Schrade. Publikationen älterer Musik, vol. 2. Leipzig: Breitkopf & Härtel, 1927. Reprinted, Hildesheim: Olms, 1967.

MODERNE, JACQUES. *Musique de Joye (c. 1550),* ed. F. J. Giesbert. Kassel: Nagel's Verlag, 1934.

MUDARRA, ALONSO. *Tres libros de musica en cifra para vihuela (1546),* ed. Emilio Pujol. Monumentos de la música española, vol. 7. Barcelona: Consejo Superior de Investigaciones Científicas, 1949.

NARVÁEZ, LUYS DE. *Los seis libros del delphin de música de cifra para taner vihuela (1538),* ed. Emilio Pujol. Monumentos de la música española, vol. 3. Barcelona: Consejo Superior de Investigaciones Científicas, 1945.

ORTIZ, DIEGO. *Tratado de glosas . . . (Rome, 1553),* ed. Max Schneider. Kassel: Bärenreiter, 1936.

PLAMENAC, DRAGAN, ed. *Keyboard Music of the Late Middle Ages in Codex Faenza 117.* Corpus mensurabilis musicae, 57. Rome: American Institute of Musicology, 1972.

ROMANO, EUSTACHIO. *Musica duarum, Rome 1521,* ed. from the literary estate of Hans T. David by Howard M. Brown and Edward E. Lowinsky. Monuments of Renaissance Music, vol. 6. Chicago: University of Chicago Press, 1975.

SICHER, FRIDOLIN. *Ein altes Spielbuch,* 2 vols. ed. F. J. Giesbert. Mainz: B. Schott's Söhne, 1936.

SLIM, H. COLIN, ed. *Musica nova, accomodata per cantar et sonar . . . Venice, 1540.* Monuments of Renaissance Music, vol. 1. Chicago: University of Chicago Press, 1964.

STEVENS, DENIS, ed. *The Mulliner Book.* Musica Britannica, vol. 1. London: Stainer & Bell, 1951, rev. 1954.

SUSATO, TYLMAN. *Danserye "zeer lustich ende bequaem om spelen op alle musicale instrumenten" (1551),* 2 vols., ed. F. J. Giesbert. Mainz: B. Schott's Söhne, 1936.

WALLNER, BERTHA A., ed. *Das Buxheimer Orgelbuch.* Documenta musicologica, ser. 2, vol. 1. Kassel: Bärenreiter, 1955.

———. *Das Buxheimer Orgelbuch,* 3 vols. Das Erbe deutscher Musik, vols. 37–39. Kassel: Bärenreiter, 1958–1959.

PART
THREE

The Baroque Era

13

The Age and Its Musical Artisans and Artists

THE Baroque era in music spans one and a half centuries (c. 1580–1750) and encompasses a rich variety of musical genres in each of the main European states. This great diversity is unified by a typical scoring in which one or two treble melodies are placed above an instrumental bass part serving as both a melody and a foundation for chordal harmony. The harmony is completed by a chord-playing instrument, such as the organ, harpsichord, lute, or guitar. This characteristic scoring was introduced as a novelty by song composers working in Florence about 1580, but it was abandoned (for a texture in which the bass was not a melody) as outmoded by opera composers working throughout Italy after about 1720. During this 140-year period, Italians—especially northern Italians—created most of the important innovations in Baroque musical style. Italian works were enthusiastically received throughout Europe, and many composers in transalpine countries eagerly adapted their own styles to accord with the prevailing Italian mode. As might be expected, they sometimes lagged a generation behind the fashion in Italy, and consequently the era did not end in northern lands until around 1750—with the works of Bach in Leipzig, Handel in London, and Rameau in Paris.

Italian musical domination

Baroque writers distinguished three arenas for musical performances: chamber,[1] theater, and church (the subjects of chapters 15, 16, and 17, respectively). In establishing this division, they gave recognition to the role that social function played in determining style. They also identified the chief patrons of Baroque music as (1) the Church and (2) the courtly class, which commissioned much of the theater and chamber music for use in noble and royal residences. Throughout the era, Church and court maintained their traditional, paternalistic systems of patronage, in which musicians were servants. They did not, however, maintain their former ascendancy, because an ever-widening musical public began to support musicians by studying with them, buying printed music, and paying admission at public opera houses and occasionally at public concerts.

Characteristics of the Age

The sudden upsurge in public patronage of music is only one of many significant societal changes during the Baroque era. War was one of the chief means by which changes were wrought. In the seventeenth century, only seven calendar years passed without war among European states, and the next century began with the widespread War of the Spanish Succession (1701–1713), in which France was at length somewhat humbled. Throughout the period France was the most powerful country, and the aggressor in most wars. By means of shrewd restructurings of her government, Henry IV (reg. 1589–1612) and the cardinal-ministers Richelieu (1624–1642) and Mazarin (1642–1661) built France into the first modern nation, a state so centralized that the reign of Louis XIV (1661–1715) is considered the apex of an "age of absolutism." These leaders also established the first modern diplomatic corps, which did far more to maintain French glory than did her old-fashioned military corps, and which was so influential that even the language of international diplomacy was changed from Latin to French during the era. Of all the transalpine countries, only France was powerful enough to withstand the Italian musical "invasion" and to maintain a distinctive Baroque style.

French political domination

In many wars of the period, political objectives were inextricably mixed with religious goals. Although religious freedom-seekers often seemed to be hardly more than pawns in the political wrangles between kings, queens, and knights, their ideals were, nevertheless, sometimes realized. The Puritans, for example, defeated the royalists in the English Civil War (1642–1646), then beheaded King Charles I in 1649 and maintained middle-class rule all during the 1650s. In retrospect, their revolt was a harbinger of the many later bourgeois revolutions. Lutherans and other Protestants in Germany secured religious liberty by means of the devastating Thirty Years War (1618–1648), which is of great importance to musical and intellectual history as well. Like other extensive wars, it forced the spread of new musical ideas by compelling many musicians (e.g., Heinrich Schütz) to move and to adapt their styles to extraordinary conditions. Largely for reasons of self-protection, many Protestant and Catholic rulers (the latter were assisted by the Jesuits) broadened the base of education and founded universities in their small realms; as a result, higher education became easily accessible throughout Germany, a country noted for excellence in scholarship ever since.

Religious wars

Intellectual activity was centered in the many learned societies that flourished during the era. To spread ideas, their members, a virtual pan-European "republic of letters," published the first modern newspapers, journals, dictionaries, and encyclopedias. Many Baroque concepts that shattered age-old ways of thinking were developed by great philosopher-scientists, who depended far less on newly invented tools like the microscope and telescope than on new, frequently mathematical paths of reasoning. These individuals were of two groups: those whose theories were partly derived from observa-

Ideas

tions of the natural world, including Francis Bacon (1561–1626), Galileo Galilei (1564–1642), William Harvey (1578–1657), John Locke (1632–1704), and Isaac Newton (1642–1727); and those whose conclusions were based on intellectual axioms, including Johannes Kepler (1571–1630), René Descartes (1596–1650), Blaise Pascal (1623–1662), Baruch Spinoza (1632–1677), and Gottfried Wilhelm Leibnitz (1646–1716).

In painting, sculpture, and architecture, Baroque artists tried to over- **Visual arts** whelm viewers emotionally by exaggerating even more the expressive dis- tensions employed by sixteenth-century Mannerists. This intention is most apparent in their extreme contrast of light and shade, and in the dynamic, often violent, movement of their figures, as is evident in superb works by seventeenth-century artists like Peter Paul Rubens (1577–1640), Giovanni Lorenzo Bernini (1598–1680), Diego Velásquez (1599–1660), Rembrandt van Rijn (1606–1669), and Christopher Wren (1632–1723). By the end of the era, such affective exaggerations had been emulated everywhere. The style was exhausted, preserving little of its original emotional power, and around

View of the Interior of the Basilica of St. Peter in the Vatican, from the Principal Entrance, etched in 1766 by Domenico Montaigu, after a design by Francesco Pannini (c. 1720– c. 1794). Bernini's baldachin, with its four twisting columns, stands over the tomb of St. Peter. (Courtesy, Museum of Fine Arts, Boston)

1750 it was dubbed *Baroque* to indicate that it was distorted and unnatural (the Portuguese word *barroco* means "a misshapen pearl"). The label retained this negative connotation until around 1900, when art critics' acceptance of similar exaggerations (especially lighting effects) in impressionism opened the door to a reevaluation of the dramatic art of the Baroque era. Since then, *Baroque* has been a convenient label for a remarkable creative age in many fields of human endeavor (certainly including music).

Drama　　　The Baroque age is among the greatest in the history of dramatic literature. Baroque exaggerations are plentiful in the works of those who wrote most convincingly of the tragicomedy of human existence. Seventeenth-century masters include Lope de Vega (1562–1635), William Shakespeare (1564–1616), Pedro Calderón de la Barca (1600–1681), Pierre Corneille (1606–1684), John Milton (1608–1674), Molière (Jean-Baptiste Poquelin, 1622–1673), and Jean Racine (1639–1699). At least equally representative of the age is the multitude of minor dramatic works, written chiefly by Italians, known as *libretti* ("little books"). Here exaggerations are plentiful. Librettists developed the new genres of opera, cantata, and oratorio in collaboration with composers who set them to music and visual artists who provided stage decor.

Opera　　　Opera, which required the most intricate interaction of the arts, best satisfied humanity's incurable craving for pomp and pathos during the Baroque era. Because each production was ephemeral, it is difficult, even when libretto, music, and drawings of the decor have survived, to understand today why the Baroque age lavished its funds and tears upon opera. The answer must lie partly in the era's extraordinary concern with the expressive power of music. In music, as in literature, the visual arts, philosophy, and science, powerful new styles and productive new paths were discovered, and the result was an age of great creative and intellectual activity, today known as the Baroque era.

Musical Artisans and Artists

Composers

Composers, performers, instrument makers, and music printers were regarded primarily as artisans during the era. Yet many composers and performers, especially Italians, demanded and received consideration as artists. As previously mentioned, the influence of Italians was enormous during the entire Baroque period, and because of the great demand throughout Europe for good Italian musicians they became valuable commodities in an international market, commanding princely salaries and treatment from their employers, often to the chagrin of local musicians.

The mobility and liberal treatment of Italian musicians greatly helped to hasten the downfall of the old, paternalistic order, in which artisans supplied their lifetime employer with everything from music to cake. Under this old

Giuseppe Maria Crespi (1665–1747), *The Lute Player* (c. 1700). Its Baroque features include the extreme contrast of light with shade and the contorted posture. The player is tuning her instrument. (Courtesy, Museum of Fine Arts, Boston; Charles Potter Kling Fund)

order, all artisans were liveried servants (e.g., Monteverdi at Mantua), receiving food, clothing, lodging, and sometimes money. Despite its constraints, the old order had some great virtues. Composers wrote for a small audience whose taste they knew well, and their music served a practical purpose: to solemnify the many celebrations of the Church and the nobility. The frequency of such events forced composers to produce a large—indeed, often prodigious—amount of music in a variety of Baroque genres.

Nearly all music at the time was "occasional"; like baked goods, it was to be enjoyed when "fresh." In most instances the manuscript copy used for performance has been long since consumed by the elements, so that much of the music written by Baroque composers is now irretrievably lost. Fortunately, however, owing to the prevailing artisan-like practice of refashioning old musical works to make "new" ones, the actual loss of works is far less than at first appears. Bach and Handel are the best-known "refreshers" of works, including ones originally written by others. Indeed, there seems to have been little concept of a "finished" work, because a piece was reworked whenever a composer found an occasion to perform it again.

Music printing   Publication remained the exception rather than the rule. It was, nevertheless, one of the chief means of manifesting composers' worth and spreading their fame. During the seventeenth century, the printing of music from movable type flourished as never before, but type-setting was gradually supplanted by copper-plate engraving, a process that flourished first in Italy and allowed for the creation of exquisitely wrought works whose beauty has rarely been surpassed.

The mercantile art of printing enabled a composer to live independently of a noble patron or to find new patrons, and was one of many important factors in the breakdown of the old social system. The traditional system of education was, however, retained throughout the era. Composers often received their first training from a father who was a professional musician. Many were students in choir schools. Nearly all were trained in orchestras, because once they had become "masters" they were expected to play violin and harpsichord well enough to direct an orchestra from either instrument. Usually they had obtained an estimable position by the age of twenty, and teaching was commonly an integral part of their position as concertmaster or chapel-master. Thus they were responsible for the training of those intending to become professional musicians, and the cycle continued. Noble amateurs who patronized noted "masters" often studied with them as well, while poorer amateurs learned from the many printed self-tutors as well as from the myriad performers who called themselves "masters" in order to attract students.

Instrument Makers and Instrumentalists

Most instruments changed significantly during the era, and thus Baroque makers are to an incalculable degree responsible for many changes in style of composition and performance.

Violins and harpsichords   Innovative sixteenth-century makers, especially Italians, produced instruments in a multitude of sizes and shapes, many of which are illustrated in volumes by Michael Praetorius and Marin Mersenne. The typical Baroque chamber or orchestral group required instruments of the violin family, invented in sixteenth-century Italy, and a harpsichord, developed at the same time in Italy. Great violins made in Germany by Jacob Stainer (1617?–1683) as well as great harpsichords made in Antwerp by the Ruckers family were based on Italian models. Although individual instruments were often partly rebuilt in the Baroque and succeeding eras, the early-seventeenth-century harpsichords by the Ruckers and violins by Nicola Amati (1596–1684), Giovanni Paolo Maggini (c. 1581–c. 1632), and Stainer were generally considered unsurpassable through the time of Leopold Mozart (1719–1787), who, like Bach, owned and played a Stainer violin. These early Baroque instruments lost favor only around 1800, when larger concert halls and orchestras

Gerard Terborch (1617–1681), *A Lesson on the Lute* (c. 1670). The lute is a theorbolute, with two peg-boxes and eleven (?) courses, a favorite instrument of mid-seventeenth-century lutenists. A gamba lies on the table. (Isabella Stewart Gardner Museum, Boston)

proved better suited to the more powerful late Baroque instruments: violins of Antonio Stradivari (1644–1737) and Giuseppe Guarneri (1698–1744); and pianofortes of Bartolommeo Cristofori (1655–1731), Gottfried Silbermann (1683–1753), and later builders.

In the second half of the seventeenth century, the direct ancestors of the modern woodwinds and horn appeared. The Hotteterre family seems to have been responsible for most of the innovations in woodwind construction, beginning in the 1650s. Previously the recorder, transverse flute, oboe (or shawm), and bassoon (or curtal) had been made in a single piece; afterward they were made in three to five pieces, with tenon and socket joints, an altered bore, and added keys (one on the flute, two or three on the oboe, and three on the bassoon). These changes altered both playing techniques and tone quality. The new woodwind instruments probably first appeared in orchestras conducted by Jean-Baptiste Lully, whose concern with orchestral sound quality might have influenced the innovations. By 1700 they were

Winds

being made and played throughout Europe. Johann Denner (1655–1707) of Nuremberg, a fine maker of woodwinds, reportedly invented the clarinet — at first a two-keyed instrument — about 1700. At that time, the finest brass instruments were produced by members of the Ehe and Haas families, who also worked in Nuremberg. Although the trumpet and trombone underwent no significant changes during the Baroque era, by 1680 the horn had been transformed — probably first in France — from a helical, closely coiled instrument to a circular or hooplike instrument with only one or two coils. Trombones mainly doubled voices in church music, but trumpets and horns had independent parts in many Baroque scores. Parts such as Bach's for trumpets and Handel's for horns reflect the great virtuosity then required of brass players, especially in Germany.

Eighteenth-century woodwinds, made of ivory with a conoidal (conical) bore. From top to bottom: *treble recorder* made in three principal parts: head (including mouthpiece), body, and foot-joint. Seven finger-holes are in front, and a thumb-hole is in the rear. *Oboe* made in France in three parts: two body-joints and a bell. Six finger-holes are in front (the third and fourth are double), and two vent-holes are on the bell. The three square keys are made of brass. Shown without reed. *Transverse flute* made in Rome c. 1724 in four principal parts: head, two body joints, and foot-joint. It includes an elliptical embouchure, six finger holes, and a square key made of silver. *Practice chanter* made in Ireland. It includes seven finger-holes in front, a thumb-hole in the rear, and a vent-hole on each side. A chanter is the melody-playing part of a bagpipe. (Courtesy, Museum of Fine Arts, Boston; L. L. Mason Collection)

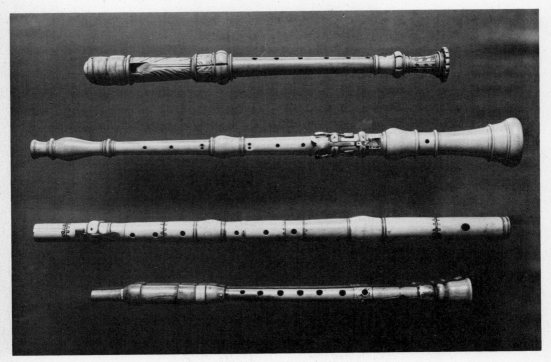

Virtuosos on brass or the new woodwind instruments were rarely of more than local importance during the Baroque era, whereas keyboard and especially string virtuosos often became well known in several countries for their skills. Monteverdi, Lully, Corelli, and Vivaldi were primarily string players, and Schütz, Purcell, Scarlatti, Rameau, Bach, and Handel were primarily keyboard players. Italian instrumentalists were in demand everywhere. They were even welcomed in France, where Italian singers were rarely heard during the era, and some French instrumentalists were trained in Italy. French and German instrumentalists, on the other hand, were seldom employed outside of their native country, which is also typical of the age.

Keyboard and string virtuosos

Among the strings the gamba and lute were going out of fashion during this period. Their finest exponents were in France, the country that most successfully resisted the new Italian fashions. Two other string instruments were enjoying their heyday: the theorbo—a bass lute—was a favorite accompanying instrument, while the guitar was the favored instrument for courtiers of both sexes as well as for members of the humbler classes. The guitarist Francesco Corbetta (c. 1615–1681) entranced the principal rulers of Europe, and when he was in England one of his sarabands was so beloved that all the guitar players at court tried their hand at it.

The traveling virtuoso with his "hit tune" was, therefore, already a common figure in the Baroque era. Each one had his "bag of tricks" that were exhibited to the multitudes mainly during church services or theater performances. For instance, when the French gambist André Maugars (c. 1580–c. 1645) was in Rome in about 1638, he revealed his improvisational ability at a festival Mass in honor of St. Louis. According to his own report, he was applauded when he went up to the musician's gallery. After the third Kyrie, he was given a subject of fifteen to twenty notes on which he improvised variations to the accompaniment of a small organ. Those present were so greatly pleased that the thirty-three participating cardinals asked him to play again after the Agnus Dei. A century later, Vivaldi exhibited similarly virtuosic feats on the violin during performances of his operas. Vivaldi typically accompanied one aria per opera, adding near the end a cadenza or fantasy that astonished the audience.

Singers

Despite the prevalence of string and keyboard virtuosi, most of the virtuosic display in churches and theaters was by singers, for instrumentalists were merely occasional attractions here. Italian singers were unequaled during the era, and the development of their art closely parallels that of the Italian violin: both were perfected for expressive sweetness from the late 1500s to the late 1600s, then developed for brilliance. A new style of singing with exquisite embellishments appeared in the 1570s, apparently invented by Giulio Caccini (c. 1550–1618), a tenor virtuoso at the court in Florence. The best-known repository of works with embellishments written in is Caccini's *Le nuove musiche* ("The New Music") of 1602. Caccini himself brought the style

Italian singers

to France when he and his family sang at the French court in 1604 and 1605, while it was made known in England by an anonymous translator of the discourse on singing by Caccini that prefaced his *Nuove musiche*. This discourse was reprinted from 1664 to 1694 in several editions of John Playford's *Introduction to the Skill of Musick*.

Castrati   Although northern Europeans were thus acquainted with the new vocal style, only the Italians castrated many promising boy singers in order to develop their treble voices to the ultimate degree. *Castrati* were accepted into Catholic church choirs from about the 1560s on in ever increasing numbers, and during the Baroque age they conventionally portrayed female as well as male characters in Italian operas and oratorios. During the entire age, women were prohibited from performing in churches, and in Rome and some other Catholic cities they were not allowed to sing in theaters either. For castrati in one of the four Neapolitan conservatories largely responsible for training them, the full daily schedule included theory, composition, and keyboard exercises as well as singing. Consequently, the best castrati were excellent musicians in every respect, although very few became known as composers or teachers.

Writers on Music

Baroque authors are the teachers whose precepts, concerning everything from ancient to innovative ideas, are still discoverable today. In the following chronologically ordered list, writings published over a 151-year span by the most notable Italian, German, and French writers are briefly characterized.

Twenty Baroque Classics of Music Literature

1. VINCENZO GALILEI (c. 1520–1591), *Dialogo della musica antica e della moderna* (Venice, 1581). A student of Gioseffo Zarlino (1517–1590), Galilei treats many theoretical issues in this "Dialogue of Ancient and Modern Music" and declares that the "modern" Renaissance contrapuntal style codified by Zarlino is far less expressive than the "ancient" Greek monodic style codified by Girolamo Mei (1519–1594).

2. MICHAEL PRAETORIUS (1571–1621), *Syntagma musicum* (Wittenberg and Wolfenbüttel, 1614–1620). The three volumes of this "Musical Compendium" concern: (1) liturgical and secular monophony; (2) modern instruments, especially the organ; and (3) modern, especially Italian, genres, terms, and performance problems.

3. GIOVANNI DONI (1594–1647), *Compendio del trattato de' generi e de' modi della musica* (Rome, 1635). In this "Compendium Treating Genera and Modes of Music" and in other writings, Doni shows his fine understanding of ancient Greek music and of the varieties of early-seventeenth-century monody.

Gaspar Netscher (1639–1684), *Lady Playing a Guitar*. Music books lie on the table. (Courtesy, Museum of Fine Arts, Boston)

4. MARIN MERSENNE (1588–1648), *Harmonie universelle* (Paris, 1636–1637). Mersenne's deductive and inductive "propositions" manifest "Universal Harmony" in the realms of music; his information on instruments, e.g., their tuning and temperament, has been of great use.

5. ATHANASIUS KIRCHER (1602–1680), *Musurgia universalis* (Rome, 1650). Equal to Mersenne's work in encyclopedic scope and frequency of theological analogies. Kircher's "Universal Science of Music" was severely attacked in 1652 by the Dutch philologist Marcus Meibom (in his edition of ancient writers on music), who lambasted Kircher's ignorance of Greek sources.

6. GIOVANNI MARIA BONONCINI (1642–1678), *Musico prattico* (Bologna, 1673). "The Practical Musician" is herein taught elements of notation and rules of counterpoint. Although Zarlino's rules are somewhat modernized, the book represents a retreat to Renaissance precepts for the purpose of instruction.

7. ANGELO BERARDI (c. 1636–1694), *Miscellanea musicale* (Bologna, 1689). A student of Marco Scacchi, Berardi in his "Musical Miscellany" and in other treatises includes both speculative and practical theory; his categorizations, such as five species of counterpoint and three arenas for musical performance, were adopted by many later writers.

8. WOLFGANG PRINTZ (1641–1717), *Historische Beschreibung der edelen Sing- und Kling-Kunst* (Dresden, 1690). The first print intended solely as a history of music from earliest times to the present is this "Historical Description of the Noble Vocal and Instrumental Art," largely anecdotal and largely based on Kircher's work.

9. GIOVANNI BONTEMPI (1624–1705), *Historia musica* (Perugia, 1695). This first "Music History" in Italian concerns mainly theoretical aspects of ancient and modern practice, and is ordered by "corollaries," in the manner of a geometry treatise.

10. SÉBASTIEN DE BROSSARD (1655–1730), *Dictionnaire des termes grecs, latins et italiens* (Paris, 1701). Brossard's main purpose for compiling his musical "Dictionary of Greek, Latin and Italian Terms" was to define for French musicians the terms encountered in Italian music.

11. FRANÇOIS RAGUENET (c. 1660–1722), *Paralèle des italiens et des françois, en ce qui regarde la musique et les opéra* (Paris, 1702). Concisely draws a "Parallel" between aspects of French and Italian opera, and prefers the latter in most cases.

12. JEAN LE CERF DE LA VIÉVILLE de Freneuse (1674–1707), *Comparaison de la musique italienne et de la musique françoise* (Brussels, 1704–1706), Verbosely makes a "Comparison" of Italian music (for which he has no appreciation) with French music, for which he develops intriguing aesthetic ideals of taste and beauty.

13. JOHANN MATTHESON (1681–1764), *Das neu-eröffnete Orchestre* (Hamburg, 1713). Mattheson's "Newly Begun Orchestra," the first of his more than eighty treatises on music, is a compendium, for amateurs as well as professionals, of the latest approaches to all kinds of music.

14. PIERRE BOURDELOT (1610–1685), and PIERRE (d. 1708) and JACQUES (d. 1724) BONNET, *Histoire de la musique et de ses effets* (Paris, 1715). This first "History of Music" in French examines critically many anecdotes about the "effects" of music from its origins to 1715.

15. BENEDETTO MARCELLO (1686–1739), *Il teatro alla moda* (Venice, c. 1720). The "Theater à la Mode" in Baroque Italy produced operas, and most of the funny human foibles of the participants are still "à la mode." The treatise is delightfully satirical.

16. JEAN-PHILIPPE RAMEAU (1683–1764), *Traité de l'harmonie* (Paris, 1722). Chord inversion and the primacy of tonic, subdominant, and dominant chords are among the concepts introduced and grounded on acoustical principles in this "Treatise of Harmony," the cornerstone of modern harmonic theory.

17. MATTHESON (see above), *Critica musica* (Hamburg, 1722–1725, in twenty-four issues). "The Music Critic" was the first periodical devoted to music.

18. JOHANN FUX (1660–1741), *Gradus ad Parnassum* (Vienna, 1725). These "Steps to Parnassus" are exercises that lead a student to facility in Palestrina-style counterpoint. Haydn, Mozart, and Beethoven are among those who have used this treatise.

19. JOHANN HEINICHEN (1683–1729), *Der General-Bass in der Composition* (Dresden, 1728). In "The Thoroughbass in Composition," Heinichen treats all aspects of composition from a "modern" viewpoint, i.e., one opposed to contrapuntal complexity.

20. JOHANN WALTHER (1684–1748), *Musicalisches Lexicon* (Leipzig, 1732). Begun as a supplement to the dictionary of Brossard, this excellent "Music Lexicon" includes biographies as well as definitions that tell much about compositional and performance practices of the time.

Reasonings and Polemics

Several Baroque authors were polemical aestheticians, eager to abolish what they considered outmoded practices. It is striking that writers forcefully attacked contrapuntal music (whether Palestrina's or Bach's) at either end of the Baroque period, thus in a sense signaling the start and finish of that era. A beginning point for the Baroque was polemically provided by Galilei (father of the astronomer Galileo) in 1581, when he declared that the consummate artifices of late Renaissance style were worthless:

Aesthetics

Consider every rule of the modern contrapuntists by itself, or, if you like, consider them all together. Their goal is nothing other than the delight of the ears, if it can truly be called delight. As for the manner of expressing the concepts of the spirit, or of impressing them with the greatest possible effectiveness upon the minds of listeners, no book that these contrapuntists have for their use and convenience deals with such matters. So they only think, as they have thought since inventing such counterpoint, of how to mangle music as much as possible whenever possible. Indeed, today they never think of the manner of expressing the concepts of the words with the affect that is required, except in that ridiculous way [i.e., madrigalisms] that I will describe shortly, which is a sure sign that their practices and rules comprise nothing more than a way of harmonizing musical intervals, of making a piece into a game of varied chords, according to the precepts described above, without otherwise taking into account the concept and sense of the words.[2]

The artifices of late Baroque style were similarly attacked in 1728 by Heinichen, who thus provided an ending point for the Baroque era:

As is known, musicians in the past selected two judges for music: *reason* and the *ear*. . . . Unfortunately, they badly explained the word *reason,* and in those simple times (when nothing of the present taste and brilliance in music was known, and every crude harmony seemed beautiful) they thought *reason* could be no better employed than in the supposedly learned and speculative artificialities of musical notation. Therefore, they began (as if out of idleness) *theoretically* to measure out innocent notes with a mathematical ruler and a proportional yardstick, then *practically* to extend them on lines (just as if they were on a rack), draw them out (which is expressed in counterpoint as *to augment*), turn them upside down, repeat them, and transform them, until finally they arrived at a *practice* containing innumerable superfluous contrapuntal features, and a *theory* glutted with metaphysical contemplations of the soul and mind. Thus, in *practice* one no longer had cause to ask whether written music sounded well and pleased listeners, but only whether it looked good on paper. . . . This extremely great injustice to the musical sovereign, *the ear,* is requited by present more than by past practitioners. . . . For we all now understand that for us the goal of music is to stir the affects and to please the true musical object, the ear.[3]

Doctrines of Expression

Throughout the era, writers such as Galilei and Heinichen were preoccupied with the aesthetic question of how music moves or *affects* the listener— that is, how it moves the *affections*. Discourses on the power of music over human passions have been written in all ages, but Baroque writers constructed what is perhaps the most elaborately systematized explanation. They

**Affekten-
lehre**

formulated a doctrine of the affections—often termed *Affektenlehre,* because it was developed mainly by Germans such as Kircher, Mattheson, Heinichen, and Walther—for each musical category: intervals, modes and keys, rhythmic patterns, tempos, meters, instruments, dance types, and so on. Each interval, mode, or key was said to possess an affective character. For example, Mattheson in 1713 described D minor as devout, calm, contented, noble, and gently flowing. Rameau characterized it more generally in 1722 as sweet and tender, while Marc Antoine Charpentier in about 1692 had already defined it as serious and pious. Heinichen cogently objected to such descriptions by asserting that the affect was determined more by the context than by the key itself, which changes its character according to the composer, the work, and the pitch level and temperament employed. This objection is as pertinent to other musical categories as it is to keys, preventing the wholesale application of the doctrine of any writer to even his own music.

**Figuren-
lehre**

Just as Baroque writers tried to codify the affective character of each element of the music of their time in the Affektenlehre, so, too, did they try to codify the melodic figures that rendered their music affective, in the *Figurenlehre.* This doctrine applied Greek and Latin names for rhetorical devices (figures of speech that enhance ordinary language) to the melodic figures that intensified late Renaissance and Baroque music, thus establishing a musical rhetoric that focused on the categories of *hypotyposis* (pictorialism) and *em-*

phasis. Included in the techniques of hypotyposis are late Renaissance figures like *katabasis,* a stepwise descent to picture the concept of descending, and new Baroque figures like the *saltus duriusculus,* a harsh leap such as that of the diminished seventh.

Emphasis is the more important category for an understanding of Baroque music, and sequential repetition, or *epizeuxis,* is the chief means of emphasis in this music. Although emphasis is significant in all music, the typically through-composed pieces of the late Renaissance limited its role, whereas the sovereign Baroque principle of *Fortspinnung,* or "spinning out" material based on the opening figure, allowed it ample scope. The doctrine of melodic figures thus tends to confirm that Baroque musicians determined the affect of a piece from the opening figure (which in turn contained intervals and was in a key or meter of classifiable affects) and rhetorically emphasized it as the piece progressed.

Summary

Like any other historical era, the Baroque is far from easy to categorize in a few words, but many of the developments during the period have become conspicuous elements in the modern world. Any current mixed-media art form (such as the musical or film) is a byproduct of the Baroque fascination with a dramatic interaction of the arts, especially in opera. And opera, a Baroque invention, was the first art form to flourish chiefly because of public patronage as we know it.

Baroque artists, writers, and composers freely employed *emphasis* and other exaggerations in order to stir the emotions of viewers, readers, and listeners. At the same time, they achieved remarkable formal clarity and balance within a great many genres. In order to perceive their works at least somewhat as their age did, it is necessary to study first the formal conventions of Baroque style.

Notes

1. "Chamber" will refer throughout the five chapters on the Baroque period to any room or hall that is neither a theater nor a church. "Chamber music" will therefore include not only works for a small ensemble of soloists (its meaning in the classical period and later), but pieces written for any number of performers, from a single soloist to a large orchestral group.
2. *Dialogo della musica antica e della moderna,* pp. 85–86. This passage is cited within its context in Oliver Strunk, *Source Readings in Music History: The Renaissance* (New York: W. W. Norton, 1965), pp. 122–123.
3. *Der General-Bass in der Composition,* pp. 3n–4n. This passage is cited within its context in George Buelow, *Thorough-Bass Accompaniment According to Johann David Heinichen* (Berkeley: University of California Press, 1966), pp. 265–266.

Bibliography

Books and Articles

The Age

CLARK, GEORGE. *The Seventeenth Century,* 2nd ed. London: Oxford University Press, 1947.

FRIEDRICH, CARL J. *The Age of the Baroque: 1610–60.* New York: Harper & Brothers, 1952.

HAUSER, ARNOLD. *The Social History of Art,* trans. Stanley Godman. New York: Alfred A. Knopf, 1951.

HAZARD, PAUL. *The European Mind: 1680–1715,* trans. J. Lewis May. London: Hollis & Carter, 1953.

OGG, DAVID. *Europe in the Seventeenth Century,* 8th ed. London: Adam & Charles Black, 1960.

WILLEY, BASIL. *The Seventeenth Century Background.* London: Chatto & Windus, 1934.

Music — in General

BLUME, FRIEDRICH. *Renaissance and Baroque Music,* trans. M. D. H. Norton. New York: W. W. Norton, 1967.

BUKOFZER, MANFRED. *Music in the Baroque Era.* New York: W. W. Norton, 1947.

PALISCA, CLAUDE. *Baroque Music,* 2nd ed. Englewood Cliffs, N.J.: Prentice-Hall, 1981.

Singers

HERIOT, ANGUS. *The Castrati in Opera.* London: Secker & Warburg, 1956; reprinted, New York: Da Capo, 1975.

Printers

KING, A. HYATT. *Four Hundred Years of Music Printing,* 2nd ed. London: British Museum, 1968.

Instruments

MARCUSE, SYBIL. *Musical Instruments: A Comprehensive Dictionary,* corrected ed. New York: W. W. Norton, 1975.

Writers

ALLEN, WARREN D. *Philosophies of Music History: A Study of General Histories of Music: 1600–1960,* 2nd ed. New York: Dover, 1962.

COHEN, ALBERT, et al. "National Predilections in Seventeenth-Century Music Theory: A Symposium." *Journal of Music Theory* 16 (1972): 4–73.

REESE, GUSTAVE. *Fourscore Classics of Music Literature.* New York: Liberal Arts Press, 1957; reprinted, New York: Da Capo, 1970.

STRUNK, OLIVER. *Source Readings in Music History: The Baroque Era.* New York: W. W. Norton, 1965.

14

Concepts of Musical Style

THIS chapter describes the principal changes made in the texture and structure of music in the Baroque era, when Italians were responsible for the main modifications in European style. Italian music was in fashion everywhere. As a lasting proof of its widespread influence, the musical terms introduced by Baroque-era Italians have remained in common use throughout the Western world. (Examples are *cantata, concerto, opera, oratorio, sonata,* and other names of genres; *adagio, andante, allegro, forte, piano, legato, staccato,* and many other terms used as interpretative guides for performers.) *Aria* ("air" in English and French) may be considered the most important Italian term, because an understanding of the origin and development of Baroque style can be gained from a study of changes in the texture and structure of pieces called arias.

The following discussion of Baroque style will concentrate on (1) the rise to prominence of elements of the aria, in music from 1580 to 1620; (2) the texture of the melodic solo or duet over a "walking" bass, in music from 1620 to 1680; and (3) the structure of the *ritornello* form with a tonal arch, in music from 1680 to 1720. To the aria-like basis of early Baroque music, the typical texture and structure of the two later phases were added.

Elements of the *Aria da Cantar*, 1540–1740

In the sixteenth century, the word *aria* was employed for vocal or instrumental pieces with (1) a tuneful top part, (2) lively and often dancelike rhythms, (3) chordal texture, and (4) *variation* structure (a result of adding embellishments when a section was repeated). These four elements are basic to Baroque style.

These components were first joined in the *aria da cantar* ("air for singing") that flourished in early-sixteenth-century Italy. Any of a number of related eight-chord patterns could accompany the singing of each strophe of its long text (usually a romance or ballad). Around 1540, one of these chord patterns

r. del.   N. Bonnart, rue St Jaques, à l'aigle. avec. priuil.

Italienne chantante, et recitant à l'opera.
du Carnaval de Venize, Representé à Paris.

An Italian Character Singing and Reciting in an Opera, "Le Carnaval de Venise" ("The Carnival of Venice"; Paris, 1699), engraved by Nicolas Bonnart (c. 1636–1718). The accompanying instrument is an archlute (bass lute) or chitarrone. (Harvard Theatre Collection)

became a favorite basis for instrumental music, for both dance pieces and sets of variations. Called the *passamezzo antico,* this pattern included only the tonic and dominant chords from a minor key and from its relative major key (see Example 14.1).

Tonality exists in a rudimentary state in this pattern and in related ones. Two close relatives of the passamezzo antico were especially prominent in Baroque music: the *romanesca* and the *folia.* The best-known folia is Arcangelo Corelli's set of twenty-two variations for violin, Op. 5 (1700), No. 12.

Its theme has the two-part structure—   ‖:8 m.——▶V :‖: 8m.——▶i :‖

Ex. 14.1   Passamezzo antico

—and the rhythmic character— ♩ ♩. ♪│♩   ♩—of a dance called the *saraband*.

In 1741–1742, two hundred years after the first appearance of instrumental variations on dance-like aria patterns, J. S. Bach published what is perhaps the greatest of such sets: the *Goldberg* Variations. His set clearly demonstrates that the basic elements of Baroque style in its most refined state were still those of the aria da cantar. Its theme, in saraband rhythm, is unnamed in a collection of harpsichord pieces that Bach assembled for his wife in 1725, but he named it "aria" when he published his thirty variations upon it.

The aria theme is in binary form— ‖: 16m.——▶V :‖‖: 16m.——▶I :‖

Every eight measures contains one statement of the eight-chord pattern,

‖:I V⁶ IV♯⁶ V I⁶ IV V I :‖, which is subjected to several chord and key changes.

The Early Baroque, Stage 1:
Imitative Polyphony Incorporates Elements
of the Aria (1580–1600)

The Popular Arias Around 1600

By 1612, an airy, chordal texture was in great favor in England and France as well as Italy, and the intricate, imitative Renaissance texture was rapidly losing favor. In England, the new *ayre* was favored over the old madrigal; the new genre was so popular that from 1597 through 1612 twenty-two collections by fifteen different composers were printed, e.g., those of John Dowland (1563–1626). The ayre generally had a homophonic, four-voice texture. Its "ayre," or tune, was sung by the top voice, and the accompanying three parts were sung or, preferably, played on a chord-playing instrument like the lute, sometimes with the bass part doubled by a viol.   **Ayre**

The chief model for the English ayre was the French *air de cour,* which likewise had a strophic text, a chordal texture, and a sung or played accompaniment. French airs de cour continued to flourish far into the seventeenth century: the largest anthology of them, in sixteen volumes, was printed with lute accompaniment in 1608–1643. Many of these pieces were heard in the *ballet de cour.* This genre was first exemplified by *Le Balet comique de la royne* ("The   **Air de cour**

Queen's Dramatic Ballet," performed in Paris in 1581), perhaps the first modern Western stage-work that consciously combined dance, poetry, and music into a unified whole. Italians played many roles in the creation of this ballet, which was planned by a violinist—Baldassare de Belgioioso (known in France as Balthasar de Beaujoyeulx)—who had settled in Paris together with other Italian musicians and dancers about 1555. Therefore even the characteristically French genre of ballet de cour owes much to the Italians.

The *Balet comique* includes several song texts set in *musique mesurée,* that is, with long notes for long, stressed syllables and shorter notes for short, unstressed syllables. The exponents of "measured music" had hoped to bring poetry and music into a closer relationship and thereby reactivate the ancient power of song over human affections. Their settings are in neither duple nor triple meter, and many seventeenth-century airs de cour retain some of this metric ambiguity. The end of one "measured song" from the ballet is given in Example 14.2. Although all five parts are texted in the print, there was only one singer (a castrato); seven others accompanied the three strophes on "flûtes."

Aria   The Italian aria antedates both the French air and the English ayre. Italians developed the chordally accompanied aria throughout the sixteenth century, at the same time that northerners from Josquin to Wert were working in Italy to perfect imitative polyphony. Italian arias were often printed in collections entitled *frottole* in the early 1500s and *villanelle* in the mid-1500s. From 1580 to **Canzonetta**   1620, *canzonetta* was the most common name for an aria, and countless examples were written by such composers as Orazio Vecchi (1550–1605) and Claudio Monteverdi (1567–1643). An aria from the famous collection of

Ex. 14.2   Lambert de Beaulieu or Jacques Salmon, *O Pan, Diane irritée*

Ex. 14.2   cont.

"[The wood-nymphs] who accentuated their dance by trampling the grass in time with the sweet sound of their voices."

From *Le Balet comique de la royne*, ed. Carol and Lander MacClintock. American Institute of Musicology, Musicological Studies and Documents, No. 25. Copyright 1971 by Armen Carapetyan. Used by permission.

"new music" by Giulio Caccini exhibits the melodious, dancelike character that typifies these pieces (see Example 14.3). Its text is by Ottavio Rinuccini.

Elements of the Aria

The infectious tunefulness of such arias was the first of their elements to affect imitatively textured genres in late-sixteenth-century Italy, and the term *arioso*, meaning "aria-like," was occasionally applied to imitative works that were distinctly melodious. For example, each of the four keyboard works titled *Ricercar arioso* by Andrea Gabrieli is airy and spirited, rather than severe and somber like his other ricercari. Anthologies called *Madrigali ariosi* appeared in the 1550s, and Andrea's nephew Giovanni Gabrieli wrote two eight-voice madrigals that were published in an anthology—*Dialoghi musicali* ("Musical Dialogues"; Venice, 1590)—with the title *Aria. Per sonar* ("Air. To be played"). They are dialogues in the sense that one homophonic, four-voice group answers another, and their title indicates they can be played as well as sung. Another performance method was to sing the top, tuneful part of each group while the lower three parts were played—the usual way that an aria or air was performed.

This aria-like method of performance is a second trait that infiltrated imi-

Tunefulness

Ex. 14.3   Giulio Caccini, *Udite udite amanti*

Ex. 14.3 cont.

do - glio, Pian - ge - te al mio_____ cor - do - glio.

"Hear ye, lovers; listen, oh errant beasts, heaven, stars, moon, sun, young ladies and lords, to my words; and if my suffering seems reasonable, weep for my deep sorrow."

From *Le nuove musiche* (Florence, 1602), ed. H. Wiley Hitchcock. Madison: A-R Editions, 1970. Used by permission.

The Concert, an anonymous Bolognese-school painting of the seventeenth century. A woman plays the figured bass part on a virginal. One boy and four men are singing; a fifth man plays a cornett (perhaps doubling a sung part), while a sixth conducts with a rolled-up page of music. (Courtesy, Fogg Art Museum, Harvard University; Purchase—Francis H. Burr Memorial, Alpheus Hyatt, Louis Haskell Daly, and Richard Norton Funds and Gifts for special uses fund)

Instrumental accompaniment

tative polyphony. Praetorius recommended this method for Venetian polychoral motets, often called *concertato* motets because voices are "in concert with" instruments. *Concerto* was a fashionable term during the entire Baroque era. Giovanni Gabrieli may have begun its popularity with his *Concerti* (Venice, 1587) for voices and instruments, and he helped continue it by using a Greek equivalent, *symphoniae,* for his two collections of *Sacrae symphoniae* (Venice, 1597 and 1615).

Beginning in 1575, church compositions were sometimes printed in Italy with a *basso seguente* ("following bass"), an organ part consisting of the lowest-pitched vocal note at any given point throughout a piece, above which the organist played the chords of the piece, easily filling in for any part that was not being sung. Any keyboard, lute, or theorbo player who thus accompanied ensembles must have thought in terms of chords, and the increasing use of chord-playing instruments in the late sixteenth century was closely related to increased triadic, rather than intervallic, thinking.

Tonality

The triad was first recognized as a theoretical entity by Zarlino in the 1550s, but tonal progressions of triads were not theoretically recognized before Rameau's treatise of 1722. Yet many chordal arias of the sixteenth century already contained repeated tonal progressions. In his works, Giovanni Gabrieli often incorporated such progressions in sequences moving by fifths, thus lending a sense of order to a work.

By 1600, according to Ludovico Grossi da Viadana (1564–1627), organists frequently filled in for several missing voice parts during the performance of Renaissance motets. However, the imitative texture of Renaissance motets permits each part to rest as often as it sings, and thus any performance with less than all parts sung tends to be unsuccessful. Therefore Viadana began to write motets for one to four singers over a melodic bass part for the organ. He called these motets a "new invention" when he published them in his *Cento concerti ecclesiastici* ("One Hundred Church Concertos"; Venice, 1602).

Chord-playing instruments

Viadana had "invented" a motet in which the lowest part can properly be performed only by a chord-playing instrumentalist, and in fact he asserted that "the effect will never be good" if this part is sung. Viadana did not invent the bass part that must be played rather than sung. It had first appeared in prints of 1600–1601, containing dramatic works by Cavalieri, Caccini, and Peri, and it must have already been an integral part of the arias (e.g., Example 14.3) written by Caccini and his circle from the 1570s on. Viadana's contribution was to combine the chord-bearing, instrumental bass part of the "new music" with the melodic style and imitative texture of Renaissance polyphony, a combination that soon became commonplace in Baroque church music.

In other words, Viadana incorporated the bass part of the Baroque aria into imitative polyphony. This part is not merely a basso seguente (simply reproducing the lowest vocal part). It is, instead, an independent line, and it

Figured bass

is called the *basso continuo, thoroughbass,* or *figured bass* because it is continuous, plays throughout, and is supplemented by figures (i.e., numbers and accidentals) that specify notes in the chord above the bass. It soon became an integral part of almost all concerted pieces (that is, pieces for more than one performer) until well into the Classic period. In the following excerpt with a text from a responsory (Example 14.4), the bass has only a single figure (a sharp in measures 39 and 42, indicating that the third above the bass is to be raised to a B♮) and a single, brief motivic imitation (measures 34–35). In this example the small notes printed for the player's right hand are editorial suggestions, generally known as a *realization* of the chordal implications of the bass part.

Ex. 14.4   Ludovico Grossi da Viadana, *Decantabat populus Israel*

"And David with the singers plucked the lyre in the house of the Lord."

From *Cento concerti ecclesiastici,* Part 1, ed. Claudio Gallico. Copyright 1964 by Bärenreiter, Kassel. Used by permission.

**Embellish-
ment**   The final element of the aria that was incorporated into imitative polyphony is clearly shown in Viadana's church concerto (Example 14.4, measures
40–41): the basic chordal motion in half notes, and occasionally in quarters,
has been embellished by *diminutions* or *divisions* in the vocal part. When a
chordally accompanied soloist added florid diminutions, the tune was aptly
made more distinct from the accompaniment. On the other hand, if a singer
in an imitative texture did the same, havoc could result. Yet the fascination
with virtuosic diminutions grew so strong in late-sixteenth-century Italy that
they were even applied to imitative textures in a cult-like, manneristic way.

The ensuing craze for virtuoso vocal embellishments at concert performances played an important role in the formation of Baroque melodic style.
Because of the growing fondness for diminutions, many late-sixteenth-century instruction books for vocal and instrumental soloists discussed how
diminutions could be applied almost mechanically to smooth Renaissance
melodic lines. Sometimes the result was grotesque: half notes inexplicably alternating with sixteenths or even thirty-seconds. To prevent such disfigure-
ment of their melodies, composers like Viadana began to write in a modicum
of figuration and to request that performers add no more. Although such embellishment was at first rather unconvincingly written, its "figures" became
the basis of Baroque melodic style and were later codified in the Baroque
doctrine of *Figurenlehre*.

The Early Baroque, Stage 2: Monody Replaces
Polyphony as the Chief Bearer of Expression
in the Second Practice (1600–1620)

When early Baroque composers were no longer moved by imitative polyphony, they became preoccupied with the expressive capabilities of music.
In 1581, Galilei declared that imitative texture was suitable for instrumental
music only; in his opinion, the staggered entrances of voice parts in different
pitch ranges mangled vocal music. He recommended instead the homophonic texture of the simplest arias as ideal for achieving a powerful effect.
The French poets and composers of musique mesurée had the same homophonic ideal. They were indeed avant-garde, on the radical fringe of the gradual incorporation of aria-like traits into imitative polyphony during the late
sixteenth century. At this time the most noted Italian composers were instead
trying to deepen the affective power of Renaissance polyphony. Perhaps
partly because the strictures of the Counter-Reformation tended to inhibit
textural and harmonic complexities in works written for the Catholic
Church, the Italian attempts were made chiefly in the madrigal.

Dissonance   Chromaticism and dissonance were the most potent intensifiers employed
by composers. Gesualdo was the most notorious purveyor of the former,
while Monteverdi was the most controversial master of the latter. In 1605
Monteverdi claimed credit for having coined the expression "second prac-

tice," in which dissonances were employed to underscore affective words. Indeed, such words impelled Monteverdi to use freer dissonance treatment than Renaissance practice allowed, because his aim was to move listeners' emotions as deeply as possible.

The New Solo Madrigal and Monody

One of the most impressive younger contemporaries of Monteverdi, who applied dissonance and chromaticism affectively to the madrigal, was Sigismondo d'India (c. 1582–1629). He did so primarily in madrigals set for one solo voice with a chord-playing instrumentalist. By 1600 this aria-like texture had become so popular that the solo madrigal soon supplanted the many-voiced madrigal. From 1602 to 1635, more than two hundred collections of secular pieces set for one or more vocal parts over a figured bass were published in Italy. These collections were often simply titled "Music" or "Arias." Later Doni used the term *monody* (Greek for "solo song") to refer to any piece in them. The name held, and more recent scholars have given the analogous name *pseudo-monody* to the many-voiced madrigals and motets sung in the late sixteenth century as solos over an instrumental accompaniment. While any vocal genre could be written as a monody in the early 1600s, most monodies were secular: either madrigals, which had nonstrophic texts, or arias, which had strophic texts. More madrigals than arias were included in secular monodic collections published up to 1618, but afterward arias predominated. Another rich source of monodic madrigals and arias was opera of the early seventeenth century.

Monody

Around 1600, northern Italians experimented widely with the dramatic, representational power of music. For example, Orazio Vecchi's *L'amfiparnaso* ("Two Peaks of Parnassus," i.e., poetry and music; published in Venice in 1597), the masterpiece of the genre called *madrigal comedy*, demonstrated that a series of fourteen tuneful and homophonic madrigals for five voices (plus a parody of a madrigal by Rore) could wittily tell a comic tale (see *GMB*, no. 164, and Lerner, no. 59).[1] At least some of these madrigals could easily be performed as pseudo-monody. Meanwhile, the poet Ottavio Rinuccini (1562–1621) and the composer Jacopo Peri (1561–1623) explored the dramatic capabilities of a series of monodic madrigals and arias in the first *opera*, their *Dafne* (premiered in Florence in 1598). Only a few selections from *Dafne* survive.

Because monodic madrigals were well-suited to narration, they became the main ingredient of early opera. In a book published in 1640, Doni identified three types of monody in early-seventeenth-century dramatic works. The first is *narrative monody*, perfected by Peri (see *GMB*, no. 171b), in which a speechlike continuity is achieved with vocal lines of small melodic range, longer notes for stressed syllables, long bass notes that support the voice but do not form a melody, and infrequent V–I cadences.

Narrative monody

Doni's second type is *expressive monody*. He exemplified it with Monteverdi's *Lamento d'Arianna* ("Lament of Arianna") (Example 14.5), which has a

Expressive monody

Ex. 14.5   Claudio Monteverdi, *Lamento d'Arianna*

"Let me die. And which of you could wish to comfort me, abandoned so cruelly, in such great tribulation. Let me die."

From the opera *Arianna,* in Monteverdi, *Tutte le opere,* ed. G. Francesco Malipiero, Vol. 11. Copyright 1966 by Universal Edition A. G., Vienna. Used by permission.

reflective rather than narrative text. This piece appeared first as a monodic madrigal in Monteverdi's opera *Arianna* (1608), then as a five-voice madrigal in his sixth book of madrigals (Venice, 1614). In this monody Monteverdi employed a highly irregular succession of note values and phrase lengths in order to express Arianna's volatile mood. The intensity of her sorrow is made apparent by her unexpected return to the opening music (in measures 12–15), as well as by dissonance and chromaticism.

Ex. 14.6   Claudio Monteverdi, *Possente spirto*

While narrative monody (which resembles later recitative) and expressive monody (which resembles later arioso) both have madrigalian texts, Doni's third type of monody has a strophic text. He named it *special recitation monody*, because its strophes were "recited" in a speechlike manner over a repeated chordal pattern. He probably avoided the name "aria" because its characteristically dancelike melody and bass were not used in special recitation. This final type of dramatic monody seems to have been a very special genre in early-seventeenth-century Italy. For example, in 1600 Giulio Caccini set the final piece of his *Il rapimento di Cefalo* ("The Abduction of Cefalo") as a recitation monody. He then printed it as the centerpiece of his *Le nuove musiche* (Florence, 1602). In this piece each strophe is differently embellished and is sung by a different singer. A choral *ritornello* ("refrain") is sung before and between the strophes, and a related ritornello follows them.

Special recitation monody

Caccini's splendid composition is surpassed by the special recitation that Monteverdi placed at the affective high point of his opera *Orfeo* (1607). In this third-act monody, *Possente spirto* ("Powerful Spirit"), five of the six text strophes and the ritornellos after each of the first three strophes are composed over the bass pattern given in Example 14.6 (the complete piece is in Lerner, no. 63, and *Omnibus* I, pp. 91–100).[2] The notes marked with an asterisk are the bass notes of the *folia* pattern. The melody for each strophe is very differently embellished in order to portray Orfeo's changes in emotion as he sings of his great love for Euridice. Likewise, the instruments and their figuration are changed at the beginning of each new strophe. This practice, known as *strophic variation*, is a marvelous way to merge the virtues of madrigal and aria. As in the madrigal, it allows for a musical change at each variation in mood; yet, as in the aria, it maintains a repetitive structure.

Strophic variation

The Middle Baroque: *Bel Canto* Arias for One or Two Soloists over a Lively Bass (1620–1680)

The New Texture and Bass Patterns

About 1618, the speechlike madrigal began to disappear from Italian songbooks. In the middle Baroque, its offspring, speechlike recitative, replaced it as the opposing pole to the dancelike aria, and nearly every passage written in the middle or late Baroque, whether vocal or instrumental, can be loosely categorized as either recitative-like or aria-like. Growing out of light-

Hendrick ter Brugghen (1588–1629), *A Boy Singing* (1627). (Courtesy, Museum of Fine Arts, Boston; Ernest Wadsworth Longfellow Fund)

hearted canzonettas of the early Baroque (such as Example 14.3), the aria became the bearer of an ever-widening range of affects from 1620 on. By the end of the Baroque, it had achieved true grandeur of proportion and had been employed to express every emotion then conceivable.

Bel canto

In the middle Baroque, aria melodies had an urbanity that earned them the name *bel canto*—perhaps best translated as "elegant song." One soloist could sing smoothly over a figured bass, but even more suave were two soloists over a bass, for they could produce a long series of sweet thirds or sixths as their voices paralleled each other or intertwined imitatively. This typical middle Baroque setting of two melodies of equal importance and range over a

Trio texture

bass is called either *trio texture* or *chamber duet*. It had become "the rage" just before 1620, as is clearly evident in Monteverdi's seventh book of madrigals (1619), entitled *Concerto* because of its combination of voices with instruments. It contains twenty-nine pieces: fifteen are for two equal voices over an instrumental bass, and four others are for two equal voices over a vocal bass that generally doubles the instrumental bass. One of the fifteen (see Example

14.7) is a "canzonetta for two voices in concert with two violins and a chitar-rone [a large lute or theorbo] or a harpsichord," in which the "walking" bass has a four-bar pattern that is interrupted only for expressive purposes. (See the interruption at *ancidete,* i.e., "wound," in measures 33–38.) The complete form (R = ritornello, S = strophe) is:

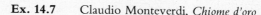

m.	1	5	9	13	17	21	25	29	38	42	46	50
‖: R1 :‖: R2 :‖: R3 :‖			S1	R1	S2	R3	S3	R2	S4	R1	S5 ‖

Any obstinately repeated bass pattern is called a *basso ostinato* or *ground bass.* During the middle Baroque, such patterns frequently helped to structure aria-like music, in which the bass was often "walking" or "dancing," that is, constantly moving in even or in long-short note values. Relatively few works had an unchanging pattern, but nearly the same effect can be achieved by a bass with traces of a pattern (a *quasi-ostinato*). The effect can be hypnotic, especially when a brief ostinato in triple meter is heard countless times under melodic phrases that embellish it in myriad ways. Two such brief bass and chord patterns were in great favor in Italy during the 1630s and 1640s: the

Basso ostinato

Ex. 14.7   Claudio Monteverdi, *Chiome d'oro*

BASIC PATTERN (for ritornellos)

Vi - ve stel-le che si bel-le e si vaghe ri - splen-de - te

Vi - ve stel - le che si bel-le e si vaghe ri - splen-de - te

VARIED PATTERN (for text strophes)

Ex. 14.7   cont.

"Lively stars [i.e., eyes], that shine so fair and bright, if you gaze on me you wound me."

From Monteverdi, *Tutte le opere,* ed. G. Francesco Malipiero, Vol. 7. Copyright 1966 by Universal Edition A. G., Vienna. Used by permission.

passacaglia and *ciaccona* (in French, *passacaille* and *chaconne*). The first was apparently of Spanish origin, while the second may have come from Mexico (see Chapter 37).

The pattern of the passacaglia (from *passer caille,* "promenade")— **Passacaglia** ‖: i (VII) iv₆ V :‖ —began as a chordal prelude or interlude (ritornello) for strophic arias of the 1500s. It first appeared as an ostinato basis for keyboard variations in a set of thirty that Girolamo Frescobaldi (1583–1643) published in 1627. In 1630 he published an *Aria di Passacaglia,* in which text strophes 1, 3, and 5 are sung over the pattern, while strophes 2 and 4 are set in recitative. And in 1637 he published *Cento partite sopra passacagli* ("One Hundred [and Three] Variations on Passacaglias") for keyboard. In these works Frescobaldi established the distinctive character of Baroque passacaglias, both vocal and instrumental; they are usually in minor keys and often have a chord between i and iv. The inserted chord allows the pattern to form a scale that descends from tonic to dominant. As Example 14.8 shows, Frescobaldi embellished the scale (d–c–b^b–a, circled in Example 14.8) through the use of figuration and chromaticism, and constantly varied the chord between i and iv.

The ciaccona pattern—‖: I V vi (iii IV) V :‖—entered Europe **Ciaccona** about 1600 as the accompaniment for a sung Spanish dance. It is usually in the major mode, as in Monteverdi's *Zefiro torna* ("Gentle breeze return") (Example 14.9). As might be expected, Monteverdi twice interrupts the pattern with speechlike recitative for an expressive purpose: to convey the mournful emotion of the final lines of the sonnet text. The example begins just after the first interruption (which occurs after the two-bar pattern has been stated fifty-six times!) and includes the second one (measures 141–145).

Ex. 14.8   Girolamo Frescobaldi, *Cento partite sopra passacagli*

Ex. 14.8   cont.

From *Toccate d'intavolatura di cimbalo et organo,* Vol. 1 (1637). Reprinted from Frescobaldi, *Orgel- und Klavierwerke,* ed. Pierre Pidoux, Vol. 3. Copyright 1949 by Bärenreiter, Kassel, Edition No. 2203. Used by permission.

The Blend of Speech and Song

In its inclusion of both aria-like and recitative-like textures, Monteverdi's *Zefiro* demonstrates an important element of middle-Baroque style: a suppleness that allows an aria-like passage to become recitative-like at any moment, and vice versa. Indeed, the ideal for church music written in the new style was a blend or hybrid of the virtues of both aria and recitative, according to Marco Scacchi's *Breve discorso sopra la musica moderna* ("Brief Discourse on Modern Music"; Warsaw, 1649). This ideal was best realized by Heinrich Schütz (1585–1672), a friend of Scacchi, in his five collections of sacred symphonies and concertos (1629–1650). He published them after he had visited Monteverdi at Venice in 1628–1629, and they have the same supple suaveness found in Monteverdi's middle-Baroque works. In one piece (*Es steh Gott auf,* "Let God arise") from the 1647 collection, Schütz honored his great model by incorporating elements of two of Monteverdi's chamber duets of 1632: *Armato il cor* ("Arm the Heart") at the beginning and *Zefiro torna* at the end.

Cantata   A flexible mixture of aria and recitative likewise typifies the *cantata* of 1620–1680, which grew out of the chordally accompanied aria. Although the term was used infrequently during the middle Baroque, composers like Alessandro Grandi (d. 1630), Giovanni Berti (d. 1638), Giovanni Sances (d. 1679), and Schütz's pupil Caspar Kittel (d. 1639) applied it to various vocal solos and duets over a lively bass. These pieces frequently employed strophic variations or brief ostinato patterns as structural devices, but the genre also included works that contained other structures current at the time. Almost any vocal solo or duet written in middle-Baroque Italy could therefore be called a cantata.

Two of the finest composers of such works during the middle Baroque worked in Rome: Luigi Rossi (1598–1653), who wrote at least 300 cantatas, and Giacomo Carissimi (1605–1674), who wrote at least 150. The following strophic-variation cantata by Carissimi illustrates his extraordinary ability to write both aria-like passages that capture subtle speech inflections (see Exam-

Ex. 14.9   Claudio Monteverdi, *Zefiro torna*

Ex. 14.9   cont.

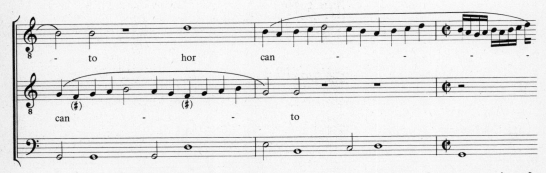

". . . sometimes I sing. Just as my fate moves me, sometimes I weep, sometimes I sing."

From Monteverdi, *Scherzi musicali* (Venice, 1632), No. 9, text by Ottavio Rinuccini. Reprinted from Monteverdi, *Tutte le opere,* ed. G. Francesco Malipiero, Vol. 9. Copyright 1966 by Universal Edition A. G., Vienna. Used by permission.

ple 14.10a, measures 1–4) and recitative-like passages that are intensely melodic (see measures 21–23). The refrain for each of the three strophes ends with a splendid melisma on *piangere* ("to weep"), intricately ornamented in the second strophe. The expressive Neapolitan sixth chord (II♭$^{\flat6}_{\flat3}$ in Example 14.10b, measure 75, beat 3), common in Italian music after 1650, occurs here in a smooth cadential chord progression that displays Carissimi's grasp of the principles of tonality.

Opera   Most of the same characteristics can be seen in the operas of midcentury composers, e.g., Francesco Cavalli (1602–1676), who wrote more than forty operas, and Antonio Cesti (1623–1669), who apparently wrote twelve.

Sonata   The middle-Baroque *sonata* was in many respects the instrumental equivalent of the cantata. It simply replaced voices with violins (or, occasionally, with other instruments). Indeed, many cantatas and arias included instrumental ritornellos that were much like sections of contemporary sonatas. From 1620 to 1680 the generic terms "cantata" and "sonata" were infrequently

Ex. 14.10 Giacomo Carissimi, *In un mar di pensieri*

Strophe 1: "In a sea of thoughts, the solitary soul wanders. . . . Because the fate of anyone damned by fortune [*Refrain:* cannot be broken, I must always weep]."
Strophe 2: "Never respite or peace is felt by my anxious heart. . . . Because the vile and cruel stars of fate [*Refrain*]."
Strophe 3: "Like the rock of Sisyphus is my desire. . . . This bitter misfortune, ever harsher [*Refrain*]."

used. Both were applied mainly to pieces written for one or two soloists over a lively bass and can therefore include almost any such piece. The stylistic difference between cantatas and sonatas is partly a result of their different ancestries: the cantata derived from the chordal aria, while the sonata grew out of the imitative canzona and ricercare. Frescobaldi never used the title "sonata," but Giovanni Gabrieli did.

During the middle Baroque, "canzona" and "sonata" were virtually interchangeable titles. Indeed, the rather common title *canzon da sonar* ("canzona to be played") includes both terms. When Frescobaldi or Giovanni Gabrieli based an entire canzona or ricercare on its opening theme, they divided it into sections, varying the theme, the figuration, or the meter from section to section. These imitative works, called *variation canzonas* or *variation ricercari,* are the principal models for middle-Baroque sonatas (and canzonas). The composers of these sonatas were mainly northern Italians. Two of the finest were Maurizio Cazzati (c. 1620–1677) and Giovanni Legrenzi (1626–1690). One of Cazzati's later sonatas (see Example 14.11) displays both the imitative texture and variation structure that were derived from the variation canzona. All four movements are based on the notes $e-f-e-d-e$ or $a-b^b-a-g-a$ (see the bracketed passages). The slow, second movement is recitative-like; its seriousness is clear from the descending diminished fourths and minor ninths as well as from the syncopations.

The Formal Ideal: Variation on One Affect

The variation principle

The musicologist Manfred Bukofzer wrote that "variation appears so consistently as an element of Baroque music that the whole era may justly be called one of variation."[3] The works just discussed, as well as the Corelli and Bach sets mentioned near the beginning of this chapter, are masterly examples of the art of variation. Of course, few arias, cantatas, or sonatas are so tautly and neatly constructed as these. They have been chosen to illustrate as clearly as possible that Baroque works, at least those written after the early Baroque, usually present variations on one affect, or emotional state. The affect may be interrupted, and it may then be continued by themes seemingly unrelated to earlier ones in their outlines. Although they may often be ignored today, the affections seem to have been of paramount importance to the Baroque composer and his audience. For example, Monteverdi wrote in the preface to his *Madrigali guerrieri et amorosi . . . libro ottavo* ("Madrigals of War and Love . . . Book Eight"; Venice, 1638): "I have reflected that the principal passions or affections of our mind are three, namely, anger, moderation, and humility or supplication."[4] Although he had never heard angry, warlike, agitated (*concitato*) music, he knew from reading Plato that it had once existed. Hence he applied himself to its rediscovery in the 1620s and knew that it could greatly move the affections, which was "the purpose which all good music should have." To move all the affections, he included agitated songs of war as well as moderate and supplicating songs of love in his eighth book.

Although most middle-Baroque composers were not nearly so bent on rediscovery and theorizing as Monteverdi, they, too, usually wrote variations on one affect in each piece. In this regard the strophic-variation form they favored became a good example of combining the elements of unity and variety. Little wonder that other genres featuring variation were likewise popular with composers, e.g., the variation canzona mentioned earlier and the *variation suite* of dances. Excellent examples of the latter can be found in a collection by Johann Schein (1586–1630): the *Banchetto musicale* ("Musical Ban-

Ex. 14.11   Maurizio Cazzati, Sonata, Op. 55, No. 1: *La pellicana*

Ex. 14.11   cont.

From Franz Giegling, *The Solo Sonata.* Anthology of Music, Vol. 15. Copyright 1960 by Arno Volk Verlag, Cologne. Used by permission.

quet"; Leipzig, 1617; see *Omnibus* I, pp. 112–116, and Lerner, no. 67). Even *toccatas,* the most improvisatory-sounding pieces of the era, were often constructed as variations on chord patterns. Since instrumental pieces have no text to provide continuity, variation forms became a staple provider of that requirement, and fine sets of variations exist from the beginnings of independent instrumental music. For the early Baroque, the set for keyboard by Jan Pieterszoon Sweelinck (1562–1621) on *Mein junges Leben hat ein End* ("My

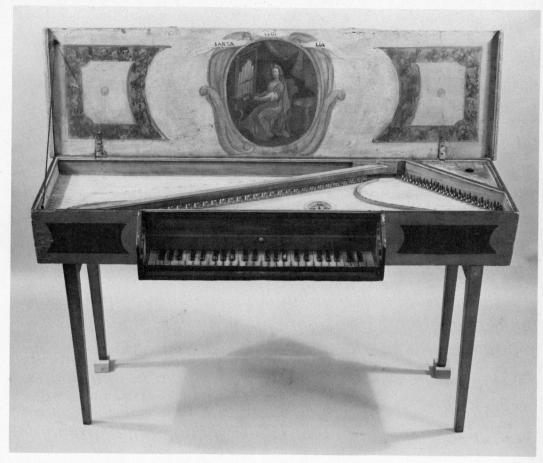

This early seventeenth-century Italian virginal has boxwood keys, birchwood bridges, pearwood sound-board, maplewood jacks, crow-quill plectrums, and a three-tiered rose of parchment. The range is from C to f³; the lowest octave is "short" (i.e., the lowest E, F, F♯, G, A♭ sound C, F, D, G, E, respectively). In the cover medallion, St. Cecilia, the patron saint of music, is shown at an organ. (Courtesy, Museum of Fine Arts, Boston; L. L. Mason Collection)

Young Life Has an End") can serve as a model. For the middle Baroque, a virtual "catalog" of the art was provided by Sweelinck's student Samuel Scheidt (1587–1654) in his *Tabulatura nova* ("New [Keyboard] Tablature"; Hamburg, 1624; see *HAM* II, no. 196, *GMB,* no. 185, and Lerner, no. 66). It contains sets on twenty-two chorales, hymns, secular songs, and dances. In these, as in the numberless other middle-Baroque works that employed variation techniques, the melodic figures introduced as embellishments in the early Baroque were exhaustively treated in sequence after sequence until they became an integral part of melodic style—the style of the late Baroque.

The Late Baroque: Tonality and the Ritornello as Formal Principles (1680–1720)

Binary Form

In order to convey an affect in the most powerful way conceivable, Italian composers of the 1680s and 1690s expanded old forms and evolved new ones, basing them on two principles: (1) tonality, and (2) repetition or return after minimal contrast. They intensified the affect by "spinning out" the piece from the opening "threads" and introducing only closely related themes, textures, and keys as contrasting material. If the contrast was long and sharp enough to diverge from the main affect, the composer immediately reinforced it by repeating part or all of the opening section.

In the following discussion, we will treat three of the Italians' most influential forms, which became common throughout Europe in the early eighteenth century. The first is the old *binary* dance form, called *rounded binary* if the opening section returns near the end (and *simple binary* if it does not). The other forms are new: the *da capo,* usually associated with arias for one or more voices; and the *ritornello,* associated mainly with fast movements of concertos.

Corelli's binary forms
The binary forms used by Arcangelo Corelli (1653–1713) have served subsequent ages as models of spinning-out and of sequential tonal progressions in which every chord is convincingly placed. In attaining such consistency, Corelli limited himself to highly polished versions of a very few of the chord progressions, textures, and forms developed by his predecessors. All of his works except Op. 5 employ the typical middle-Baroque trio texture, consisting of a tuneful duet over a lively bass. In the second half of one of his binary dances (see Example 14.12, measures 12–22), he limited himself to a spinning-out of the melodic figures introduced in the opening bars (measures 1–3), to closely related keys (d–F–g–F–d), and to standard tonal progressions (mainly IV–V–I). The spinning-out is mainly accomplished by sequences, which smoothly extend phrases to the unequal lengths characteristic of late-Baroque music (four plus seven in measures 12–22).

Da Capo Aria Form

Like most Baroque binary forms, the example by Corelli includes no contrast that is either sharp or long enough to require a "rounding" repetition of the opening bars. The da capo and ritornello forms, on the other hand, are founded on such contrast and repetition. The da capo aria is based on a text strophe that states the motto or affect in the opening line(s), elaborates upon it in the remaining lines, then restates it for dramatic emphasis at the end. Such strophes became popular in Italian operas of the 1680s, when arias began to be sung more frequently at the end rather than at the beginning of scenes. In a typical late-Baroque opera scene, a character learns in narrative recitative that he or she is trapped in an emotion-charged situation, then discharges the emotion in a da capo aria. In attempting to match the intensity of the recitative, composers gradually increased the length of the aria. Since the musical

Ex. 14.12   Arcangelo Corelli, *Allemanda*

From Arcangelo Corelli, *Sonate da camera a tre,* Op. 2 (1685), No. 2.

setting of even a single text strophe had already become quite long by the 1690s, the multiple text strophes that had characterized the aria since its inception soon disappeared. What remained was a strophe divided into A and B sections, the A section being repeated *da capo*—that is, "from the head, or top."

Such bipartite strophes conveyed the widest possible range of affects during a century when several hundred European composers, many of whom wrote thousands of da capo arias, only infrequently included other text forms in their operas, oratorios, secular cantatas, sacred cantatas, or related genres. Nearly half of the vocal pieces in Mozart's *La clemenza di Tito* (1791) still have two-section texts, but all of his settings diverge from the "ideal" late-Baroque form given in Figure 14.1.

Ritornello Forms

One of the clearest and simplest ritornello forms is the A section of the da capo aria, in which three instrumental ritornellos frame two vocal solos. It served as a model for the first composers who organized concerto movements by means of a recurrent ritornello.

Concerto texture   Corelli did not use this form as a model, however. His concertos (Op. 6) have the same forms, mainly binary and imitative ones, as his trio sonatas (Ops. 1–4), and basically the same texture as well. The *concertino* (solo group) consists of two violins and basso continuo that play throughout, while the *ripieno* (orchestral group) includes two violins, viola, and continuo that double and thus reinforce the concertino at various points, especially at cadences. The orchestral group used by Corelli was standard for the late Baroque, but other composers often varied the solo group. In the twelve *Concerti grossi* ("Grand Concertos," Op. 8; Bologna, 1709) of Giuseppe Torelli (1658–1709), six have only one violin and continuo in the concertino. In the twelve concertos of *L'estro armonico* ("Harmonic Whimsy," Op. 3; Amsterdam, 1711) by Antonio Vivaldi (1678–1741), four have four violins, four have two, and four have one (and continuo) in the concertino. These con-

Fig. 14.1.   Standard da capo aria form

sections	A					B	(A)
performers	instruments	+ voice(s)	instruments	+ voice(s)	instruments	+ voice(s)	da capo al 𝄐
subsections	complete ritornello	complete A text	partial ritornello	complete A text	complete ritornello	complete B text	
major-mode aria	I-I	I-V	V-V	V-I	I-I	vi-iii	
minor-mode aria	i-i	i-III	III-III	III-I	i-i	III-V	

certos of Torelli and Vivaldi are among the first and most influential to have a ritornello structure.

Ritornello forms are often fascinating to analyze, because they were limited only by their own musical material. They did not have an "ideal" from which they might vary, as did the da capo form. Nevertheless, they often adhered to a ritornello principle, which may be described as follows: A movement begins and ends with complete statements of the ritornello in the tonic key, played by everyone (*tutti*); throughout the movement, whenever any passage for the concertino has provided sufficient contrast, the ritornello recurs in part or in full to reinforce the opening affect. Since each passage for the concertino generally modulates to a key that is closely related to the tonic, all ritornellos from the second through the penultimate are ordinarily in keys other than the tonic. The movement is thus ordered as a tonal arch, frequently employing most or all of the five closely related keys (i.e., those no more than a sharp or flat away) before returning to the tonic. Torelli's movements are often clear-cut models of the ritornello principle; for examples, see his Op. 8, No. 9, movements 1 and 3, each of which has six ritornellos framing five solo passages. The same structure is found in the first movement of the well-known Concerto in the Italian Style (1735) for harpsichord by Johann Sebastian Bach (1685–1750), in which one player must give the effect of "orchestral" solos and tuttis through contrasting registrations.

Bach's ritornello forms are rarely clear-cut, however, partly because one **Bach** of his chief models was Vivaldi, who characteristically supplanted the expected with the bizarre. This great Italian master of the late-Baroque concerto strove constantly to surprise the listener, and the alternation of ritornellos with solos is sometimes so little in evidence that the tonal arch seems to be the only form-producing element. In Bach's concertos, the ritornello–solo alternations are sometimes assimilated into a larger-scale variation structure. For example, in the first movement of his *Brandenburg* Concerto No. 2 (1721), the solo passages are so frequently interrupted or accompanied by the ripieno playing the ritornello that the resulting structure (shown below) consists of seven varied statements of the opening ritornello. The tonal arch stresses all five closely related keys. (The complete concerto is in Kamien I, no. 23.)[5]

ritornellos:	R1	R2	R3	R4	R5	R6	R7
length in measures:	8	20	11	20	24	19	16
keys:	I–1	I–V	I–vi	vi–IV	IV–ii	ii–iii	I–I

Bach was fond of this structure, which resembles the strophic-variation aria form that had been valued, perhaps above all other forms, by many early- and middle-Baroque composers. To all the advantages of the earlier form, Bach's adds the great advantage of tonal order. Bach likewise employed it for arias, even though their texts were far from strophic. Consider, for example, *Nun du wirst mein Gewissen stillen* ("Now thou wilt appease my conscience") from Cantata No. 78: *Jesu der du meine Seele* (1724). It has the structure shown below. (The complete cantata is in Lerner, no. 86.)

ritornellos:	R1	R2	R3	R4	R5	R6	R7 (= R1)
length in measures:	8	8	8	8	8 + 2	1½ + 8 + 1½	8
text lines:		1–2	1–4		5–7	5–7	
keys:	i–i	i–i	i–v	v–v	v–iv	i–i	i–i

Thus the late Baroque formed its grand vocal and instrumental movements by combining the ritornello principle with a tonal arch. This structure even pervaded binary forms, producing the rounded binary, and ultimately the Classic-period sonata form. It likewise permeated imitative forms, ultimately resulting in the famed "Bach fugue," in which statements of the subject (acting like ritornellos) alternate with episodes (serving as solos) that provide contrast. The structure served as an ideal way to explore an affect thoroughly, the main goal of a late-Baroque movement. The closely related modulations in episodes or solos could probe the entire tonal area surrounding the affect of the opening subject or ritornello, which frequently returned to remind the listener of the affect being examined.

By 1720, Italian Baroque style was ripe, and the century-old partnership of a lively bass (usually demanding a new chord on almost every beat) with an equally lively solo or duet above (generally consisting of phrases of unequal lengths) began to give way to a new partnership, in which a subservient bass and a slow chordal motion joined a symmetrically phrased, sovereign melody. At the same time, the Baroque equilibrium of major and minor keys gave way to a preponderance of the major mode, symbolizing a turning away from Baroque explorations of all conceivable affects in favor of a Preclassic concentration on tender sentiments (see Part Four). Italian composers, including Vivaldi, were the first to turn away from the mature Italian style, allowing foreigners—including Bach, Handel, and Rameau—to produce the ripest fruit.

Summary

From 1580 to 1600 the tuneful, dancelike, chordally textured aria was so popular and considered so expressive that its elements were incorporated into imitative polyphony. As a result, madrigals and motets as well as arias written after 1600 frequently consisted only of a "tune" with chordal accompaniment, that is, a "figured" melody and a figured bass. Six elements—tunefulness, instrumental accompaniment, chord-playing instruments, tonality, figured bass, and embellishment—were crucial to the transformation of the Renaissance into the Baroque (or second) practice. While the figured bass was realized by a chord-playing instrumentalist, a "figured" melodic line was heard in each upper part. Bass figures were merely numbers or accidentals that represented notes above the bass, but melodic "figures," which could be improvised if not written, ranged from brief ornaments to extended divisions.

From 1600 to 1620, arias were still very popular, but the "tunes" then thought to be most expressive were much more speechlike than dancelike, in accord with the text-based ideal of the second practice. The Italian experiments with affective speech-settings were soon imitated in the French air de cour and in the English ayre. These works often reveal their experimental character by a certain awkwardness in their melodic leaps, harmonic astringencies, and rhythmic contrasts. So far as is known, the composers of these speech-settings made no attempt to categorize their "experiments," but in 1640 Doni tried to do so. His narrative, expressive, and special-recitation types of dramatic monody are loosely identifiable with later recitative, arioso, and ritornello-form (especially da capo) aria, respectively. To the new musical style, these experiments thus contributed speech-settings of a variety wide enough to support the varied needs and moods of an entire drama, i.e., a music drama or opera.

In the early 1600s, the "new music" was monody, and its expressive "centerpiece" was the strophic-variation aria over a slowly moving bass. In the mid-1600s, the great novelty was bel canto, embodied in the strophic-variation aria over a lively bass, which was renamed "cantata" and sometimes "sonata." (The sonata also had imitative ancestors, chiefly the variation canzona.) The aria discarded its old strophic form in the late 1600s, taking on a da capo form that developed a conventional scheme of ritornellos and keys, and served as the bearer of every conceivable affect. Consequently instrumental forms ordered by ritornellos and tonal arches developed in the early 1700s.

Throughout the era Italians were the avant-garde who instigated stylistic innovations. These then served as a stylistic basis for composers in other lands. Thus Schütz developed innovations by Giovanni Gabrieli, Viadana, and Monteverdi; Lully adopted much from Cavalli and similar composers; and Purcell learned much from composers like Cazzati. In each of the next three chapters, we will concentrate on one of the arenas in which Baroque music was performed and discuss each national tradition separately.

Notes

1. Arnold Schering, *Geschichte der Musik in Beispielen* (Wiesbaden: Breitkopf & Härtel, 1931) (*GMB*); and Edward R. Lerner, *Study Scores of Musical Styles* (New York: McGraw-Hill, 1968). (Lerner)
2. William J. Starr and George F. Devine, *Music Scores Omnibus,* Part 1, 2nd ed. (Englewood Cliffs, N.J.: Prentice-Hall, 1974). (*Omnibus*)
3. *Music in the Baroque Era* (New York: W. W. Norton, 1947), p. 352.
4. Cited in Oliver Strunk, *Source Readings in Music History: The Baroque Era* (New York: W. W. Norton, 1965), p. 53.
5. Roger Kamien, *The Norton Scores,* expanded ed., 2 vols. (New York: W. W. Norton, 1970). (Kamien)

Bibliography

Books and Articles

1580–1600

BROWN, HOWARD M. *Sixteenth-Century Instrumentation: The Music for the Florentine Intermedii.* [Rome:] American Institute of Musicology, 1973.

HOLLANDER, JOHN. *The Untuning of the Sky: Ideas of Music in English Poetry, 1500–1700.* Princeton: Princeton University Press, 1961; reprinted, New York: W. W. Norton, 1970.

HORSLEY, IMOGENE. "The Diminutions in Composition and Theory of Composition." *Acta musicologica* 35 (1963): 124–153.

HUDSON, RICHARD. "The Ripresa, the Ritornello, and the Passacaglia." *Journal of the American Musicological Society* 24 (1971): 364–394.

1600–1620

FORTUNE, NIGEL. "Italian Secular Monody from 1600 to 1635: An Introductory Survey." *Musical Quarterly* 39 (1953): 171–195.

PALISCA, CLAUDE. "The Artusi-Monteverdi Controversy." In *The Monteverdi Companion,* ed. D. Arnold and N. Fortune, pp. 133–166. New York: W. W. Norton, 1968.

1620–1680

HUDSON, RICHARD. "Further Remarks on the Passacaglia and Ciaccona." *Journal of the American Musicological Society* 23 (1970): 302–314.

PALISCA, CLAUDE. "Marco Scacchi's Defense of Modern Music." In *Words and Music: The Scholar's View,* ed. Laurence Berman, pp. 189–235. Cambridge, Mass.: Harvard University Department of Music, 1972.

WALKER, THOMAS. "Ciaccona and Passacaglia: Remarks on Their Origin and Early History." *Journal of the American Musicological Society* 21 (1968): 300–320.

Scores

BACH, JOHANN SEBASTIAN, *Werke,* ed. Bach-Gesellschaft, 61 vols. in 47 parts. Leipzig: Breitkopf & Härtel, 1851–1926.

———. *Neue Ausgabe,* ed. Bach-Institut, Göttingen, and Bach-Archiv, Leipzig. Kassel: Bärenreiter, 1954–   .

BEAULIEU, LAMBERT DE, and JACQUES SALMON. *Le Balet comique de la royne,* ed. Carol and Lander MacClintock. [Rome:] American Institute of Musicology, 1971.

CACCINI, GIULIO. *Le nuove musiche,* ed. H. Wiley Hitchcock. Madison, Wisc.: A-R Editions, 1970.

CARISSIMI, GIACOMO. *Six Solo Cantatas,* ed. Gloria Rose. London: Faber Music, 1969.

CESTI, ANTONIO. [Seven Solo Cantatas,] ed. David Burrows. Wellesley, Mass.: Wellesley Edition, 1963.

CORELLI, ARCANGELO. *Les oeuvres,* ed. Joseph Joachim and Friedrich Chrysander, 5 vols. London: Augener, 1888–1891.

———. *Gesamtausgabe,* ed. Hans Oesch. Cologne: Arno Volk Verlag, 1976–

DOWLAND, JOHN. *Ayres for Four Voices,* trans. Edmund Fellowes and ed. Thurston Dart and Nigel Fortune. Musica Britannica, vol. 6. London: Stainer & Bell, 1953.

FRESCOBALDI, GIROLAMO. *Orgel- und Klavierwerke,* ed. Pierre Pidoux, 5 vols. Kassel: Bärenreiter, 1949–1954.

GABRIELI, ANDREA. *Canzonen und Ricercari ariosi,* ed. Pierre Pidoux. Kassel: Bärenreiter, 1943.

GABRIELI, GIOVANNI. *Opera omnia,* ed. Denis Arnold. Corpus mensurabilis musicae, ser. 12. [Rome:] American Institute of Musicology, 1956– .

GESUALDO, CARLO. *Sämtliche Madrigale für fünf Stimmen,* ed. Wilhelm Weismann, 6 vols. Hamburg: Ugrino, 1957–1962.

D'INDIA, SIGISMONDO. *Il primo libro di musiche,* ed. Federico Mompellio. Cremona: Athenaeum Cremonense, 1970.

MONTEVERDI, CLAUDIO. *Tutte le opere,* ed. G. Francesco Malipiero, 17 vols. Bologna, Vienna, and Venice: 1926–1966.

––––––. *Opera omnia,* ed. Fondazione Claudio Monteverdi. Cremona: Athenaeum Cremonense, 1970– .

SCHEIDT, SAMUEL. *Tabulatura nova,* ed. Max Seiffert, rev. Hans Joachim Moser. Denkmäler Deutscher Tonkunst, vol. 1. Wiesbaden: Breitkopf & Härtel, 1958.

SCHEIN, JOHANN HERMANN. *Neue Ausgabe sämtlicher Werke,* ed. Adam Adrio. Kassel: Bärenreiter, 1963– .

SCHÜTZ, HEINRICH. *Sämtliche Werke,* ed. Philipp Spitta et al., 18 vols. Leipzig: Breitkopf & Härtel, 1885–1927.

––––––. *Neue Ausgabe sämtlicher Werke,* ed. Neue Schütz-Gesellschaft. Kassel: Bärenreiter, 1955– .

SWEELINCK, JAN PIETERSZOON. *Opera omnia,* ed. Max Seiffert, 10 vols. Amsterdam: Vereniging voor Nederlandse Muziekgeschiedenis, 1894–1901.

––––––. *Opera omnia,* new ed., ed. Gustav Leonhardt et al. Amsterdam: Vereniging voor Nederlandse Muziekgeschiedenis, 1957– .

TORELLI, GIUSEPPE. *Concerto,* Op. 8, No. 9, ed. Piero Santi. Milan: Suvini Zerboni, 1959.

VECCHI, ORAZIO. *L'Amfiparnaso,* ed. Cecil Adkins. Chapel Hill: University of North Carolina Press, 1977.

VIADANA, LUDOVICO GROSSI DA. *Cento concerti ecclesiastici,* part 1, ed. Claudio Gallico. Kassel: Bärenreiter, 1964.

VIVALDI, ANTONIO. *Le opere,* ed. G. Francesco Malipiero. Milan: Ricordi, 1947–1972. Contains 530 instrumental works.

15

Baroque Chamber Music and Performance Practice

P UBLIC performances were generally presented only in the church and theater until the end of the Baroque era. Hardly any chamber music was intended for public concerts, which were first given in London in 1672, when the English violinist and composer John Banister (1630–1679) organized a successful series in a tavern. Most Baroque chamber works were written for music-lovers to perform at home, at convivial clubs, or wherever a "chamber" could be found. Baroque chamber music can be divided into works for voice, instrumental ensemble, and solo instrumentalists. In this chapter, we shall discuss each of these categories in the context of performance practice.

Notation and Performance Practice

General Principles

The expressive art of Baroque performers was largely based upon conventional practices that were ordinarily *not* clearly indicated in the notation. No composer gave precise instructions for all the practices discussed below.

Performer as re-creator Baroque composers indeed expected performers to alter or even to "re-create" a piece spontaneously every time they performed it. Such alterations are feasible only when there is one person to a part, and Baroque music is largely soloistic. Even in most pieces that require a choral or orchestral group, many passages or even entire movements are reserved for soloists (the *concertino* in Italian music and the *petit choeur* in French music). We cannot know the precise extent of the interpretive "graces" added at any given performance, but we do know that performers added whatever they thought would move listeners to the desired affect.

Importance of context The way that any passage was altered depended upon its *context,* within both the era and a particular piece. From careful study of musical notation, instrument construction, pictorial representation, and writings on music, scholars have learned much about regional and temporal differences in per-

348

formance practices. They have subsequently made many generalizations which enable them to distinguish styles of performance, e.g., French from Italian, or early from late Baroque. These distinctions are valuable guidelines for the present-day performer, but they should be followed only if they make good (Baroque or modern) musical sense within a piece itself. Baroque musicians were well aware of the necessity of adapting conventions to suit a particular piece. For example, Praetorius wrote: "C is slow and ₵ is fast, but look at the music to discover exactly how slow or how fast it should be."[1] In other words, if performers today want to "re-create" a Baroque piece, they must try to obtain a Baroque soloist's understanding of both the piece itself and the conventional practices of the age.

Jacob Toorenvliet (c. 1635–1719), *A Concert*. It includes a violin, transverse flute (made in one piece, with a cylindrical bore), cello, and five-course guitar. The woman in the center is singing and beating time. As in most Baroque chamber performances, there was no audience (except for a dog). (Courtesy, Museum of Fine Arts, Boston; Bequest of Mrs. Arthur Croft)

Conventions

Tempo

In late Renaissance style, a time signature theoretically determined the *tactus* ("beat"), and hence the *tempo* of a piece. This correlation was, in general, not preserved by seventeenth-century composers (as Praetorius intimated in his above-cited remark). Instead, they introduced words like *grave* and *vivace* to indicate the prevailing mood, affect, and tempo of a piece. Among the pieces that they left without such specifications are many based on the rhythmic patterns of dances. According to the composer Georg Muffat (1653–1704), "knowledge of the art of dance" is a great help toward finding "the true tempo" of a dance-based piece, in which this tempo must be kept "exactly constant for as long as the same piece is played."[2] A constant tempo that allows for expressive but temporary fluctuations is indeed the norm for all Baroque music that is arialike or dancelike.

Recitative-like music is at the opposite pole. In monodic madrigals, according to Bardi, the singer "may contract or expand the time at will."[3] These works are clearly the ancestors of recitative style, in which the singer, in Doni's words, "is not in the habit of confining himself to any beat."[4] Indeed, anyone who slavishly follows the notated values misses the entire point of the style, in which every change of mood or affect should be dramatized by a change in speed.

French composers from Lully through Rameau tried to notate some of this desired fluidity with frequent changes of time signature in their recitative passages. The same fluidity of tempo was transferred to the performance of organ toccatas by Frescobaldi,[5] and many Baroque ensemble sonatas included "declamatory" movements that were to be "recited" without any regular beat. The Baroque concept of this impassioned style was summed up in Monteverdi's instruction for the performance of his *Lamento della ninfa* ("Lament of the Nymph") from his *Eighth Book of Madrigals* (Venice, 1638): *a tempo dell'affetto dell'animo*" ("the tempo is determined by the affect of your soul").

Artic-
ulation

After determining a proper tempo, a performer must find a feasible and suitable *articulation* for each motive or phrase of a piece. For a Baroque instrumentalist, the normal method of playing required that each note be articulated, resulting in an overall detached or *non-legato* style; it was freely intermixed with *legato* and *staccato* playing in order to give each motive a distinctive, affective character.

In most cases, Baroque composers did not provide the slurs and dots (or wedges) employed today to specify articulation, because performers considered it their prerogative (and responsibility) to give character to a theme. Bach, however, provided a great number of slurs and dots for the trio sonata in his *Musical Offering;* the fourth-movement theme is shown in Example 15.1. Although exceptions are shown in this example, Baroque slurs generally do not cross bar lines, and they cover only a few notes, most often going in stepwise motion. (Longer slurs usually indicate phrase structure rather than articulation.) Although the articulation chosen for the first statement of a

Ex. 15.1 J. S. Bach, Sonata for Flute, Violin, and Continuo

theme should ordinarily be retained for all subsequent statements, expressive variants can be incorporated during a performance. When a piece is performed again, its affective character can be changed by altering the articulation (or any other category of performance practice).

The third category of performance practice is *dynamics*. Although indications of loudness are not unknown in Baroque music, most pieces have few, if any. *Crescendo* and *decrescendo* markings are especially rare, but we know from Caccini and many later Baroque musicians that gradual increases and decreases in volume were common—except, of course, on harpsichord and organ, where they were practically impossible. Present-day instruments have, in general, a far greater dynamic range than Baroque ones, but performers striving to restrict their range accordingly should avoid any limitation that supplants robustness with a lackluster quality. The standard opening dynamic is *forte*, whether notated or not. When a *piano* is marked after a *forte*, the context must be examined in order to determine whether a gradual or an abrupt dynamic change is preferable. Abrupt contrasts are especially apt for the repetition of passages, because echo effects are among the most common and affective ingredients of Baroque performance practice.

Rhythm and the other categories yet to be discussed are areas in which Baroque conventions invited or even required alterations of the written score. Performers were expected to change notated rhythmic values in order to heighten one of three effects: smoothness, crispness, or lilt. When a composer notated two notes against three, performers usually maintained smoothness by assimilating the less common beat division into the ruling one (thus ♪♪♪

Dynamics

Rhythm

and became when a triple division prevailed, as in the Larghetto by Handel included in Burkhart, pp. 76–77). When dotted notes were written, performers could intensify crispness by overdotting (so that became approximately , the rest contributing as much as the shortened note to the crisper effect).

Such assimilation and overdotting were presumably common throughout Europe, while the unequal performance of pairs of equal-valued notes seems to have been a standard practice only in France. Rhythmic inequality provides a lilt, and in French music it was applied almost obligatorily to any stepwise pair of notes having the shortest note-value commonly found in a slow or moderately fast piece. Any note-pair played unequally must be slurred, while a staccato marking prevents inequality as well as slurring.

Signs for Ornaments, and Their Meaning, from Jean Henri d'Anglebert, *Pièces de Clavecin,* 2nd edition (Paris, 1703). The ornaments shown in line 1 (top) are: a plain trill, prepared (leaned-on) trill, upper turn, lower turn, lower double turn, upper double turn, upper turn without a trill, and turn on a third. Those in line 2 are: a mordent, another mordent, trill and mordent, ascending appoggiatura, descending appoggiatura, appoggiatura and mordent, upward slide, downward slide, and slide on two successive notes (3 examples). Those in line 3 are: an appoggiatura on one note, the same on two notes, double appoggiatura for a third, the same for one note, arpeggio (4 examples), rest before a trill, and rest before a mordent. (By permission of the Houghton Library, Harvard University)

The execution of melodic *ornaments,* or *embellishments,* likewise depends largely on the taste of a performer, who must decide how much rhythmic give-and-take is required in each case in order to make the work sound both spontaneous and affective. Such rhythmic *rubato* is essential to the performance of all Baroque embellishments, including those notated by composers. The shortest were usually indicated by symbols, which were developed chiefly by seventeenth-century French composers of lute and harpsichord pieces. They often prefaced their published collections with tables that listed note-equivalents for each symbol.

Such tables are invaluable guides to the proper execution of brief ornaments, but they indicate neither the rate of speed nor the amount of rubato, both of which varied according to context. Two brief ornaments were so commonly employed by performers that composers rarely notated them. The first was the long *appoggiatura* in recitative, which adds both a dissonant "bite" and melodic smoothness. The second was the *cadential trill,* which also begins with a stress on the dissonant upper note, and then continues in a more or less rapid alternation with the given or main note. This trill was obligatory at all main cadences and was sometimes fully written out in early Baroque pieces. Cadential trills clearly delineated the structure of a Baroque piece by providing an energetic end to almost every phrase.

Florid Baroque embellishments, i.e., those not notated by symbols, were an outgrowth of the Renaissance practice of diminution, which was still applied at pre-cadential points in many early Baroque works. Such *divisions* are basically consonant and were therefore shunned by modernists like Caccini, who sought greater affectivity by stressing strong dissonances. A dissonant, energetic "bite" is indeed a characteristic element of Baroque ornamentation.

Some composers wrote in nearly all the florid embellishments they wanted played or sung. Most late-Baroque Italian and Italianate composers did not. In their da capo arias, a singer had to supply the B section and especially the da capo section with florid ornaments, ending each section with a scintillating *cadenza* that could be performed in a single breath. In their instrumental works, soloists had to view Adagio movements in particular as mere outlines. Examples of how a solo violinist might elaborate upon the Adagios in Corelli's Op. 5 were given in a print of about 1715 (see *HAM* II, no. 252),[6] but the printer's claim that Corelli himself played the given ornaments is doubtful. A floridly embellished slow movement by George Frideric Handel (1685–1759) gives some idea of how a quarter-note framework (here: $\|d-c^\sharp-d-a|b^\flat-c^\natural-a-a\|$) might be elaborated upon by a harpsichordist (Example 15.2).

A *continuo accompaniment* is required for all Baroque music except unaccompanied solos for keyboard, string, or wind instruments. In festive church or theater performances, the continuo group often included about a dozen members: two or three keyboard instruments and two or three plucked-string instruments played the written bass line and added improvised chordal figuration above it, while an assortment of cellos, viols, bassoons, and trombones played only the bass line. In small chamber performances, one

Ex. 15.2   G. F. Handel, Suite No. 3 in D minor

Air

chord-playing instrument together with a cello or gamba usually sufficed. The cellist (or gambist) played the bass line with rhythmic incisiveness and occasionally added tasteful diminutions or other ornaments. The harpsichordist (or organist or theorbist) played the bass line and "realized" its chordal implications; the result was often a succession of mainly four-part chords. According to Francesco Geminiani (1687–1762), however, a harpsichordist "who has no other Qualities than that of playing the Notes in Time, and placing the Figures, as well as he can, is but a wretched Accompanyer." Indeed, the bass figures as often as not represent only the pitches written in the solo part(s), which the harpsichordist "should by no means play . . . unless with an Intention to instruct or affront" the soloist(s).[7] A fine accompanist, on the other hand, added immense vitality by constantly varying the fullness and frequency of chords, by improvising melodic motives wherever they helped to maintain melodic interest, and by providing variegated arpeggiations and colorful *acciaccaturas* in slow movements.

Instru-
ments   In Baroque music, the most common groupings of *instruments* are treble–treble–bass (TrTrB) and treble–treble–alto–bass (TrTrAB). The parts above the basso continuo were usually played by strings of the violin family. Whenever oboes doubled the treble-clef parts, bassoons were customarily added to the bass line. A penetrating sound and transparent texture were achieved by having no more than perhaps four violins and two oboes on each treble part. Composers, however, rarely indicated preference for either the instruments or the number of performers to be employed, and their TrTrB or TrTrAB scores often served whatever instruments were at hand, whether a single harpsichord or a gala orchestra of 150 players. Such extreme flexibility

in scoring and numbers was, however, only one reason why the sound of a given Baroque piece could vary significantly. "Standard" instruments did not exist, and many, especially woodwinds, underwent great and frequent changes during the era. Improvements in construction required alteration of playing techniques, which already differed greatly from region to region. Pitch was not at all constant; it often varied from one church to another, and church organs were generally tuned to a pitch that was a major second or a minor third higher than that used in theaters or chambers. (Some performers today have nevertheless fixed upon a half-step below standard pitch—in which $a^1 = 440$ c.p.s.—as an all-purpose "Baroque pitch," partly because it was the most common pitch in France around 1700, as still evidenced by many Hotteterre woodwind instruments.) Temperament was likewise not standardized, but keyboard instruments were often tuned according to some variant of the *mean-tone* system (based on almost perfect fifths), which worked well for keys ranging from two flats to three sharps. In such a temperament, sequential passages (which are ubiquitous in most Baroque pieces) have a different sound-color at each pitch-level because the semitones vary in size.

In summary, the expressive "colorings" of any Baroque piece changed significantly from one performance to another, and the choice of "hues" was left largely up to performers. For each of the seven categories we have discussed, the editorial freedoms and responsibilities were so great that a piece was truly re-created whenever it was performed. Musicians today who wish to reinstate Baroque performance practices have the same freedoms—and responsibilities.[8]

The performer's role

Vocal Music

The Early Baroque

The monodic madrigal, the favorite genre of Italians who wanted to explore affective extremes from about 1600 to 1620, allowed both composer and performer what seemed to be unprecedented expressive freedoms. In order to intensify the affects, the performer made free use of rubato and was expected to introduce many short crescendos and decrescendos. Trills were used, and they may be re-created either as a present-day trill or, preferably, as the *trillo* of Caccini, which consists of rapid reiterations of one pitch. For optimum flexibility, the accompaniment should be played by the singer. One instrument, e.g., harpsichord or guitar, is sufficient; a cello or gamba was not customarily included in performances of early-Baroque melody.

Monody

The Middle Baroque

Italian writers of the seventeenth century consistently named sweetness as the vocal quality to be prized above all, and it ideally suits the suave bel canto arias that flourished during the middle Baroque. Around 1620 the monodic

Italy: the cantata

madrigal rapidly lost favor to the new aria for one or two voices over a lively, often patterned bass. Some of the new works were called *cantatas*. During the middle phase, cantata texts typically employed the marvelous metaphorical language of the poet Giambattista Marini (1569–1625) and his followers, and the usual subject was unrequited love. Diverse structures were employed, ranging from strophic poems to a series of contrasting verse units, each set as a section in aria, arioso, or recitative style.

A great many cantatas, written by many different composers, survive from the middle Baroque; yet a far greater number have doubtless disappeared. Manuscript copies are the only sources for most of those that have survived, since relatively few were printed after the 1630s. Among the notable exceptions are those of the renowned Venetian singer Barbara Strozzi

To Stimulate a Nightingale into Song, etched by Domenico Tempesta (1555–1630). In the foreground, from left to right, are a tenor viol, trombone, harpsichord, cornett, harp, lute, and viola da gamba. In the background is a *whole consort* consisting of six shawms (ancestors of the oboe); the players are reading from the partbooks lying on the table. (Courtesy, Museum of Fine Arts, Boston)

(1619–1664?), who from 1651 to 1664 published at least five volumes containing her cantatas. In sharp contrast, her noted contemporaries Luigi Rossi, Carissimi, Mario Savioni (1608–1685), and Cesti did not publish a single volume of their many cantatas. Example 15.3 shows Strozzi's highly expressive style. The melismatic middle section (measures 63–70), a rewritten version of the opening section of the cantata, is an intense lament that powerfully conveys the ruling affect of the work. Yet even the long appoggiaturas and diminished melodic intervals seem suave, especially when compared with the harsher gestures favored by the monodists. The performance should certainly stress sweetness, although the lamenting tone might well be heightened with harpsichord acciaccaturas.

In place of the expansive Italian middle-Baroque cantata, French seventeenth-century vocal chamber music featured brief *airs,* usually in binary form with only two or three text lines in each half. Some were dancelike *chansons à boire* ("drinking songs"), and others were based more or less on dance rhythms, chiefly those of the *gavotte* and *sarabande.* But the *air* proper usually employed a nonmetrical combination of long and short note-values, and in that sense was an outgrowth of late-sixteenth-century musique me-

**France:
the air**

Ex. 15.3   Barbara Strozzi, *Lagrime mie*

Ex. 15.3   cont.

-gri - me   mi - e   à   che, à che   vi trat - te - ne - te.

Adagio

Lidia, ahi - mè,   veg - go   man - car - mi,   Li - dia, ahi - mè,   veg - go   man -

car - mi,   l'i - dol   mio, che tan - to   ado - - - ro

"And you, sorrowing eyes, do not weep. My tears, what holds you back?" Aria: "Lydia, alas, is not here. My beloved, whom I much adore. . . ." Note that the transcription preserves the coloration (♦ = ○) employed in Strozzi's collection.

From Barbara Strozzi, *Diporte di Euterpe overo cantate et ariette a voce sola* ("Diversions of Euterpe or Cantatas and Ariettas for Solo Voice"), Op. 7, No. 4; Venice, 1659; text by Pietro Dolfino. Reprinted in Jan Racek, *Stilprobleme der italienischen Monodie* (Prague: Státní pedagogické nakladatelství). Used by permission of the author.

surée. Until the 1640s it was called an *air de cour* ("courtly air"), and was furnished with a written-out lute accompaniment. Afterward it was known as the *air sérieux* ("serious air"), and was provided with only a continuo bass line. In airs de cour, composers like Pierre Guédron (c. 1570–c. 1620) and Antoine Boësset (c. 1586–1643) purposely disregarded the correspondence between syllable and note lengths that had characterized musique mesurée in order to produce manneristic misaccentuations—one type of preciosity that resulted, perhaps almost inevitably, from the intense cultivation of this small-scale art form by a highly restricted society of courtiers.

Another type of preciosity was manneristic embellishment. This intricate performance practice is preserved in written-out examples, such as those published in 1660 by Michel Lambert (1610–1696), perhaps the best composer of middle-Baroque airs sérieux, and those published in 1668 by Bénigne de Bacilly (c. 1625–1690). Bacilly codified the practice of the air sérieux in his *Remarques curieuses sur l'art de bien chanter* ("Meticulous Comments on the Art of Singing Well"; Paris, 1668), which remained a standard guide for nearly a century. As shown in Example 15.4, the first strophe (*simple*) of an air was ordinarily printed with few ornaments. In performance the singer was expected to add a few more. Ornamentation in the second strophe (*double*) was profuse, and it was determined entirely by the singer, who diligently planned and practiced all embellishments, because the success of any performance depended largely upon them. Bacilly recommended a flexible interpretation of all rhythmic values, and he preferred the theorbo as an accom-

Ex. 15.4 Bénigne de Bacilly, *Vous savez donner de l'amour*

Strophe 1: "You know how to inflame love, the power of your eyes bears witness to that. . . ."
Strophe 2: "By your craft of charming all, you could just as easily be charmed. . . ."

From Bénigne de Bacilly, *Les trois livres d'airs* ("Three Books of Airs"; Paris, 1668). Reprinted in Hellmuth Christian Wolff, *Original Vocal Improvisations from the Sixteenth–Eighteenth Centuries,* trans. A. C. Howie. Anthology of Music, Vol. 41, p. 100. Copyright 1972 by Arno Volk Verlag, Cologne. Used by permission.

panying instrument. He cautioned theorbists, though, against confusing singers by playing a plethora of notes.

French and Italian elements were freely intermingled with native traditions in the many songs with continuo accompaniment written by German and English composers from the 1630s on. The most notable masters of the strophic Baroque *lied* were Heinrich Albert (1604–1651) and Adam Krieger (1634–1666). In his eight collections of *Arien* ("Arias"; Königsberg, 1638–1650; see *HAM* II, no. 205, and *GMB,* no. 193), Albert included a great diversity of both religious and secular works suitable for home music-making. Krieger generally captured a folk-like quality in his superbly crafted works, ranging from drinking songs (see *GMB,* no. 209) to formal laments (see *HAM* II, no. 228).

Germany: the lied

England: songs and catches

English song in the middle Baroque had an equally wide range. The "intellectual" side was represented by experimental "recitative musick," in which fine verse was set to the declamatory rhythms and pitch inflections that a great orator might have employed. Composed mainly by Nicholas Lanier (1588–1666), John Wilson (1595–1674), Henry Lawes (1596–1662), and his brother William Lawes (1602–1645), these accompanied songs suffer from a lack of both harmonic direction and tunefulness—qualities present in abundance in the excellent songs written by Pelham Humfrey (1647–1674), John Blow (1649–1708), and especially Henry Purcell (1659–1695). The great Purcell had an uncanny ability to write enchanting melodies that declaimed English texts convincingly, and he manifested it in pieces as diverse as religious songs, Italianate cantatas, and drinking songs. The last category consisted largely of *catches,* i.e., rounds, usually ribald and most often for three vocal parts. The first printed collections of catches were the three compiled by Thomas Ravenscroft (c. 1582–c. 1635) in 1609–1611. The genre continued to flourish in the hands of such composers as William Lawes, John Hilton (1599–1657), who published *Catch as Catch Can* in 1652, and Purcell. Although the round is not a genre that can be claimed by any time or place, it certainly reached a convivial highpoint in middle-Baroque England. (See *GMB,* no. 248; Burkhart, p. 64; and Ward-Steinman II, nos. 121–122.)[9]

Late-Baroque Cantatas

Italy

Native song traditions in England, Germany, and France lost most of their momentum during the late Baroque, when Italian cantatas were the vocal chamber pieces in favor everywhere. The more than eight hundred extant cantatas by Alessandro Scarlatti (1660–1725) clearly demonstrate the standardization of the genre that occurred by the late 1690s. His earlier works include a variable number of arias in a variety of structures (including binary, basso ostinato, da capo, and through-composed), while those written from the 1690s on fall within a structural norm of recitative 1–da capo aria 1–recitative 2–da capo aria 2 (e.g., *HAM* II, no. 258). In some works, recitative 1 was preceded by an arioso (*GMB,* no. 260), while in others aria 1 opened the cantata (Lerner, no. 73). A third recitative–aria pair could be added whenever

Dirck van Baburen (c. 1595–1624), *The Procuress* (1622). A seven-course lute is shown. (Courtesy, Museum of Fine Arts, Boston)

the usual plaint concerning unrequited love had a "twist" that could propel it beyond aria 2. When divine rather than human love was the subject of the works, they were called *moral* or *spiritual cantatas*. The great majority of late-Baroque cantatas were written for one voice, usually a soprano, and continuo. But some have a fuller accompaniment, and others are scored for two or three singers. The *chamber duet*—the vocal equivalent of the trio sonata—was cultivated most notably by Agostino Steffani (1654–1728; see *GMB,* no. 242). It was an exceptional kind of cantata in that it often had neither recitatives nor da capo arias, but instead consisted of a series of dulcet ariosos, the epitome of Baroque bel canto.

In a small chamber, subtleties of expression have far greater force than in a large church or theater, a consideration that influenced both the composition and performance of cantatas. Expressive details abound in the many fine cantatas written by Scarlatti, Francesco Gasparini (1661–1727), Giovanni Bononcini (1670–1747), Francesco Mancini (1672–1737), Handel, Benedetto

Marcello (see *TEM,* no. 49), and numerous other composers. They usually wrote recitatives with great care, because the judicious audience for cantatas took "vast Delight" in them, according to the composer and singer Pier Francesco Tosi (c. 1654–1732). In his *Opinioni de' cantori antichi e moderni o sieno osservazioni sopra il canto figurato* ("Opinions on Ancient and Modern Singers, or Observations on the Florid Song"; Bologna, 1723), Tosi carefully distinguished church, theater, and chamber singing styles, and provided an excellent guide to the affective style of singing that had flourished in Italy around 1700. By 1720 it was rapidly losing favor to the "modern" *galant* style, in which volubility was greatly preferred over pathos. For Tosi, the "pathetick" style was the touchstone of "true Taste in Singing," and this style predominated only in cantatas, whose texts were, "for the most part, adapted to move the most violent Passions of the Soul." Tosi focused his discussion on ornaments (especially the appoggiatura and trill) but also touched on countless other aspects of "true Taste in Singing." Among the more fascinating is the subtle art of rubato, employed only in the "pathetick" style: "The stealing of Time . . . is an honourable Theft in one that sings better than others, provided he makes a Restitution with Ingenuity."[10]

Perhaps the best indication of the pan-European rage for Italian cantatas from about 1700 to about 1730 (when they rapidly fell from fashion) is the offshoot that thrived in France during these years. Indeed, performances of cantatas (and sonatas) by both Italian and French composers were so frequent **France and** in France that many French writers complained of a deluge. Louis Nicolas **Germany** Clérambault (1676–1749) was the most noted among several fine composers. Secular cantatas flourished somewhat later in Germany, where, for example, Bach wrote about fifty, while Georg Philipp Telemann (1681–1767) wrote hundreds. German cantatas occasionally featured native elements in both text and music (as in Bach's so-called *Peasant* Cantata, BWV 212, 1742), but a German structure distinct from the Italian one was never developed.

Instrumental Ensemble Music

The Early Baroque

Until about 1620, when the middle phase of the Baroque began, com-
The consort posers of instrumental ensemble music mainly continued late-Renaissance
tradition traditions. They favored performing groups consisting of "whole consorts" (of viols, flutes, double reeds, or brasses) that required no continuo instrument. They continued to write homophonic dances (singly, in pairs, or in suites) and motivically imitative works. Dance music was the basis for most of the instrumental chamber works written throughout the Baroque era, and ensemble dances reached an early-Baroque culmination in the suites by Paul Peuerl (1570–c. 1625; see *GMB,* no. 157) and Johann Schein. Imitative genres were rather uncommon in early-Baroque chamber music. In Italy, such types as the ricercare and canzona were intended for church use, while in France and England only one such genre was cultivated: the *fantasy,* or *fancy.*

In France, the first printed ensemble collections of the seventeenth century contained fantasies by Claude Le Jeune, Eustache Du Caurroy (1549–1609), and Charles Guillet (d. 1654); even though these works were issued in part-book format in 1610–1612, they were intended primarily for church organists. The English fancy, on the other hand, was exclusively a chamber genre, written for a consort of from two to six viols. It flourished throughout the seventeenth century, in works by composers such as Orlando Gibbons (1583–1625), Matthew Locke (1622–1677), and Henry Purcell (see *HMS* IV, pp. 53–54;[11] and *HAM* II, nos. 230 and 256).

The Middle Baroque

By 1620, whole consorts were outmoded in Italy. The new mode, which remained in fashion during the rest of the Baroque era, favored trio texture. It first appeared in the instrumental ritornellos of Monteverdi's vocal *Scherzi musicali* (Venice, 1607) and in the *Sinfonie e gagliarde* ("Sinfonias and Galliards"; Venice, 1607) of Salamone Rossi (1570–c. 1630). These two collections feature dancelike pieces, and their composers recommended arm-held instruments of the violin family (*viole da braccio*) for the treble parts. The development of the extraordinarily expressive violin by craftsmen in northern Italy in the 1600s is inextricably bound up with the development of a new mode of ensemble music by north Italian composers during the middle Baroque. The only treble instrument mentioned as an alternative by Rossi and many other early-seventeenth-century composers is the *cornett,* a woodwind with a cup-shaped mouthpiece.

Salamone Rossi's four instrumental collections (1607, 1608, 1622, and 1623) apparently served as models for the many collections of miscellaneous pieces published between 1618 and 1655 by Biagio Marini (c. 1598–1663), a virtuoso violinist. Marini's innovative works suggest that he did more than any other early-seventeenth-century composer to develop both violin technique and a newly affective type of chamber music. In his Op. 8, Marini provided many performance instructions, such as: *forte* and *piano* for dynamics, *tardo* and *presto* ("slow" and "fast") for tempo, *groppo* and *t* for trills, and *affetti* for ad libitum affective ornamentation (such as tremolos or arpeggios). Among the new technical devices that Marini included in his Op. 8 were double stops, triple stops, and *scordatura.* His contemporary Carlo Farina (c. 1600–1640) wrote a *Capriccio stravagante* ("Extravagant Caprice"; Dresden, 1627) in which other new techniques are required: *vibrato, pizzicato, col legno, sul ponticello,* and *glissando.* A focus on novel violinistic effects was characteristic of only a few works of the 1620s. Special effects are infrequently called for in later Italian Baroque works.

Two main types of ensemble music in middle-Baroque Italy were clearly distinguished in Marini's Op. 22, *Diversi generi di sonate, da chiesa, e da camera* ("Diverse Kinds of Sonatas: For Church, and for Chamber"; Venice, 1655), the distinction being both a functional and a musical one. A typical church sonata consisted of contrasting sections, each of them through-composed. Sections were often structured and animated by motivic imitation, just as

Italy

Sonata da chiesa

they had been in the canzona, the parent of the church sonata. Indeed, these two generic terms were often used interchangeably around 1650, as in Tarquinio Merula's Op. 12: *Canzoni, overo sonate concertate per chiesa, e camera* ("Canzonas, or Ensemble Sonatas for Church and Chamber"; Venice, 1637; see *GMB*, no. 184). By his title, Merula (1595–1665) also implied that all the works in the print were written for church use but were apt for chambers as well. Many such works were probably played chiefly in chambers.

One year after Marini distinguished the two chief genres in his Op. 22, Legrenzi did likewise in his Op. 4: *Suonate da chiesa, e da camera, correnti, balletti, allemande, e sarabande* ("Sonatas for Church, and for Chamber, Corants, Ballets, Allemands, and Sarabands"; Venice, 1656). The chamber sonatas in his Op. 4 consist of a single movement in binary form, to which any dances in the volume could be added ad libitum. Such flexibility in content was characteristic of the middle-Baroque *sonata da camera* or *suite*. In printed collections, the most common suite was a duple-meter *balletto, allemanda,* or *aria* followed by a triple-meter *corrente,* the most popular dance of the seventeenth century. Sometimes composers made larger groupings, as Marini did in the *Balletto secondo* of his Op. 22: *entrata* ("entrance"), *balletto, gagliarda, corrente,* and *retirata* ("exit").

Sonata da camera or suite

The middle-Baroque chamber sonata had its final flowering at the court in Modena, where the newest French fashions were rapidly incorporated into the repertory by composers such as Marco Uccellini (c. 1603–1680), Giovanni Battista Vitali (1632–1692), and Giovanni Maria Bononcini. The difference between the "pointed" (i.e., dotted) French style and the flowing, more virtuosic Italian style is succinctly summed up in the openings of six dances that constitute two suites in Bononcini's Op. 4 (see Example 15.5). Its French movements form a *variation suite,* in which the *corrente* and *sarabanda*

Ex. 15.5   Giovanni Maria Bononcini, Six dances

(a) Aria in stil Francese: La Palavicina

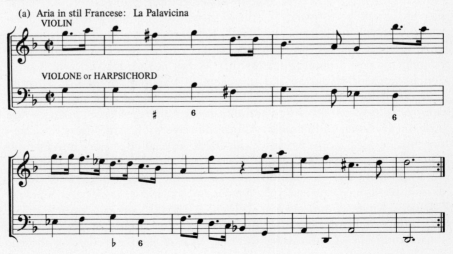

Ex. 15.5 cont.

(b) Corrente in stil Francese: La Strozza

(c) Sarabanda in stil Francese

(d) Aria: La Pozza

Ex. 15.5   cont.

(e) Corrente: La Montanara

(f) Sarabanda

The titles for the arias and corants are perhaps names of patrons or friends of the composer.

From Giovanni Maria Bononcini, Op. 4: *Arie, correnti, sarabande, gighe, et allemande a violino, e violone, over spinetta* ("Arias, Corants, Sarabands, Jigs, and Allemands for Violin and Violone or Spinet"; Bologna, 1671), Nos. 3–5 and 7–9.

(*courante* and *sarabande* in French) have the typical French rhythmic patterns of ♩. ♪♪♩♩. ♪ and ♩ ♩. ♪|♩. ♫, respectively. The customary ³⁄₂ ⁶⁄₄ metrical fluidity of a courante can be heard from the first measure of Example 15.5b. (In the late Baroque, the courante was supplanted by the French *minuet,* which first appeared in an Italian print in 1692: Vitali's Op. 14.) The sarabanda was originally a very fast dance, and the speed of Example 15.5f should be in accord with its origin. The French often converted it into a slow dance, which a performance of Example 15.5c should reflect.

The ad libitum designation "violone or spinet" (i.e., cello or harpsichord) given for the bass part of Bononcini's Op. 4 was at the time common for chamber sonatas. A chord-playing continuo instrument was apparently often considered optional at chamber performances, perhaps because two or three string players in a small room preferred to perform without the percussive brilliance of a plucked keyboard instrument. Ad libitum scorings in suites extended to treble parts, too. Bononcini's Op. 7 (1674) is an extreme example, written to be performed on a single violin, a violin and violone, two violins and a violone, or two violins, viola, and violone. Such reductions in the written number of parts are feasible only when the principal melody is contained in the first treble part and the texture is generally homophonic. These are two prominent traits of chamber sonatas, which in comparison with church sonatas have relatively little motivic imitation or crossing of treble lines.

Very little middle-Baroque chamber music from France is known, but a large amount survives from Germany and England. Much of this incorporates Italian innovations while retaining distinctive national traits. Among the most notable Germans were five whose first name was Johann: Vierdanck (c. 1605–1646), Kindermann (1616–1655), Rosenmüller (c. 1619–1684), Schmelzer (c. 1623–1680), and Pezel (1639–1694). Rosenmüller, in his *Sonate da camera* (Venice, 1667; reprinted Nuremberg, 1670), manifested the German preference for five-part texture by scoring for two violins, two violettas (violas, which are termed optional), and bass (see *GMB,* no. 220). Kindermann's trio sonatas of 1643 attest to his countrymen's favoring of wind instruments; he listed cornett, recorder, or violin for the treble parts and trombone, bassoon, or cello for the bass part. Both five-part texture and a wind ensemble are characteristic of the distinctively German *Turmsonaten* ("tower sonatas"), which were played in towers of town halls and churches by "town pipers" at appointed hours. Those by Pezel for two cornetts and three trombones are the best known (see *GMB,* no. 221).

In middle-Baroque England, the traditional fantasy for viols remained popular, but the new Italian violin and trio texture were sometimes intermixed with native traditions in distinctive ways. The most notable example was the *fantasy-suite* for one or two violins, a bass viol, and a fully written out organ part. It consisted of a contrapuntal fantasy followed by two somewhat imitative dance airs, usually an *almain* (an Anglicization of *allemande*) and a *galliard*. The probable originator of this genre was John Cooper (c. 1570–1626), who Italianized his name to Giovanni Coperario. It was continued by his pupil William Lawes, and by Matthew Locke and John Jenkins (1592–1678). The end-products of the middle-Baroque combination of English counterpoint, which stressed poignant dissonances and cross-relations, with Italian suavity were Purcell's trio sonatas (twelve published in 1683, and ten more printed posthumously in 1697). Like Cazzati and Legrenzi, Purcell favored fugal fast movements, often giving them the title "canzona." Although

Germany and England

none of the movements has a dance title, most are suffused with dance rhythms, by means of which Purcell achieved great rhythmic drive in his works.

The Late Baroque

Trio sonatas

Powerful rhythmic propulsion is a feature of most late-Baroque music, in which the main propellants are clear tonal progressions that both give direction to sequential melodies and provide a basis for dissonance control. The model works are those by Corelli, who published two volumes of trio sonatas for the church (Op. 1 of 1681 and Op. 3 of 1689) and two for the chamber (Op. 2 of 1685 and Op. 4 of 1694). Those for the church have a typical structure, which was also characteristically used by many of Corelli's younger contemporaries, e.g., Tomaso Antonio Vitali (1663–1745) and Evaristo Felice dall'Abaco (1675–1742). (For examples of Corelli's church sonatas, see Op. 3, No. 2 in Lerner, no. 76; and Op. 3, No. 7 in *MM*, no. 39,[12] and in Kamien, no. 16. Examples of the same genre by Vitali and Dall'Abaco are in *GMB*, no. 241, and *HAM* II, nos. 263 and 269.)

The structure can be outlined as follows:

Movement	Tempo	Meter	Stylistic characteristics
1	slow	$\frac{4}{4}$	chain suspensions above a moving bass
2	fast	$\frac{4}{4}$ or $\frac{2}{2}$	fugal imitation
3	slow	$\frac{3}{2}$	lyrical, often based on the rhythmic patterns of the saraband or galliard
4	fast	any duple or triple	usually more homophonic than fugal, and often with the rhythms and the binary form of the gigue, minuet, corrente, or gavotte

Corelli clearly differentiated between church and chamber sonatas in the titles of his trio publications. Stylistically, however, these categories were not clearly distinguished. The last two movements of his church sonatas are often infused with dance elements of the chamber, and his chamber sonatas often have the slow–fast–slow–fast structure of the church works, as well as elements of their contrapuntal texture. This fusion of church and chamber traits continued in the works of other composers, who generally employed the title *sonata* without qualifying it by *da chiesa* or *da camera*. Trio sonatas gradually lost favor after 1700, as the solo sonata gained ever more prominence. The Baroque trio sonata reached ripeness in those published by Handel in London, Jean-Marie Leclair (1697–1764) in Paris, and Bach in Leipzig.

Solo sonatas

Corelli's Ops. 1–4 established a standard for the late-Baroque trio sonata, and his Op. 5 (1700) did the same for sonatas written for a solo instrument with continuo accompaniment (called *solo sonatas* even though more than one performer is needed). Corelli's Op. 5 solos (see, e.g., *HAM* II, no. 252) have both significantly longer movements and more difficult passagework than do his trios. Increased breadth and virtuosity are typical of solo sonatas written after 1700, as is a three-movement structure (fast–slow–fast, or slow–fast–fast) that was apparently established by Venetian composers, especially Tomaso Albinoni (1671–1751) and Vivaldi.

During the late Baroque, the violin was by far the most popular solo instrument in ensemble sonatas; yet a large number did feature the trumpet, cello, or flute. In the late 1600s, trumpet and cello sonatas were cultivated mainly in Bologna, the former most notably by Torelli and the latter by Domenico Gabrielli (1651–1690) and his pupil Giuseppe Jacchini (c. 1663–1727). Few cello sonatas were printed, however, until the 1730s and 1740s, when sets of six each by Benedetto Marcello, Vivaldi, and Geminiani were among the many issued in either London or Paris.

Instruments

The transverse flute first became popular north of the Alps, beginning in the early 1700s. Its widespread use by 1730 is attested to by title pages that specify flute as an alternative for the violin: e.g., trio sonatas by Johann Quantz (1697–1773) (Op. 3; Paris, 1728), Giuseppe Sammartini (1695–1750) (London, 1730), and Handel (Op. 5; London, 1739). The first instruction book for the transverse flute was published in 1707 by Jacques Hotteterre (1674–1763). In a companion volume, *Pièces* (1708), he helpfully notated most of the ornaments that were ordinarily left up to the performer's "good taste."

The *concerto grosso* and *solo concerto*—offspring of trio and solo sonatas, respectively—originated in the late Baroque. *Concerti grossi* first appeared in Rome, and the first published examples are in Georg Muffat's *Armonico tributo, cioè sonate di camera commodissime a pocchi, o a molti stromenti* ("Harmonic Tribute, That Is, Chamber Sonatas Very Suitable for Few or for Many Instruments"; Salzburg, 1682). In the preface, Muffat described how these five-voiced sonatas could be converted into the "new genre" called concertos: a concertino of two violins and continuo plays throughout, while the concerto grosso, or ripieno, group (including more than one performer for each of the five parts) enters for the passages marked *tutti* but is silent during those marked *solo*. The resulting texture is that of a trio sonata with selected passages, e.g., cadences, greatly reinforced. Most Italian concerti grossi were written for use in large churches, where such textural contrasts are especially effective. Corelli's set, Op. 6 of 1714, contains eight for the church and four for the chamber, all scored for a concertino of two violins and basso continuo and an "optional" concerto grosso of two violins, viola, and continuo.

Concerto grosso

Characteristic concerto grosso texture—that of an intermittently reinforced concertino—was varied in two ways: (1) in some sections the entire orchestra played throughout; (2) in other sections individual instruments rather than the concertino group as a whole played solos, a rare occurrence in Corelli's works.

If the entire orchestra plays throughout every section, allowing at most some very brief passages for soloists, the work should be called a *ripieno concerto* or *sinfonia* rather than a concerto grosso. Ripieno concertos are found in

Torelli's Op. 5 (1692) and Op. 6 (1698), Albinoni's Op. 2 (1700) and Op. 5 (1707), and Bach's *Brandenburg* Concertos (1721), Nos. 3 and 6. Sinfonias were typically placed before and within dramatic vocal works. In his *Florilegia* (2 vols., Augsburg, 1695, and Passau, 1698; see *GMB*, no. 251), Muffat made suites out of the orchestral pieces typically found in French opera, and Bach did the same in his four well-known Overtures (BWV 1066–69, early 1720s; see Kamien I, no. 25).

Vivaldi   Corelli's younger contemporaries, especially Vivaldi and Handel, often split up both concertino and concerto grosso groups in order to obtain a seemingly limitless variety of textures. (See the examples from Vivaldi's Op. 3 of 1711 in Lerner, no. 77; *HAM* II, no. 270; Kamien I, no. 18; and *Omnibus* I, pp. 144–157; and from Handel's Op. 6 of 1739 in Burkhart, pp. 80–86.) The second movement of Vivaldi's Op. 3, No. 2 for string orchestra—with a concertino of two violins, and a ripieno of two violins, two violas, and basso continuo—is a good example (in Lerner, no. 77), because each solo passage introduces a new, unexpected texture. The movement is in ritornello form. Some of its stylistic features are more characteristic of Preclassic than of Baroque style, e.g., violins in unison (rather than in two-part dialogue) and syncopated rhythm (♪ ♩ ♪) in the opening ritornello. (For more on Preclassic texture, see Part Four.)

Dramatic surprises are a hallmark of Vivaldi's concerto movements, and they result from unexpected formal as well as textural twists. Like most early-eighteenth-century concerto composers, Vivaldi favored ritornello form, and he frequently used it to set up, then frustrate, the listener's expectations. In the second movement of Op. 3, No. 2 he sequentially develops motivic figuration in each of the first three solos, employing a motive from the ritornello only in the middle of solo 2. A listener accordingly expects solo 4 to contain similar sequences and is therefore startled when the solo first violin plays instead the first half of the ritornello in the tonic key. This caprice robs the orchestra of its customary closing tonal gesture, and a subdued coda is heard in place of a forceful ritornello.

Vivaldi sometimes depicts "realistic" occurrences—as in the well-known concertos (*The Seasons*) from Op. 8 (1725), and in *La notte* ("The Night") from Op. 10 (c. 1729). *La notte* features flute and bassoon soloists, and the addition of winds to the usual string orchestra serves to increase immensely the number of possible textures. Glorious results can also be heard in Albinoni's oboe concertos in his Op. 7 (1715) and Op. 9 (1722), in Handel's oboe concertos in his Op. 3 (1734), and especially in Bach's *Brandenburg* Concertos, Nos. 1, 2, 4, and 5. No. 5 has a concertino group consisting of flute, violin, and harpsichord, and it includes one prominent trait of solo concertos in its first movement: a cadenza (in this case written out by the composer) for the harpsichordist.

Solo   Although the solo sonata had in many places supplanted the trio sonata by
concerto about 1710, its offspring, the solo concerto, did not attain a similar ascendancy over the concerto grosso until the *galant* style became predominant

around 1730. Perhaps many Baroque composers were reluctant to reduce the concertino to a single instrument because this reduction would have severely limited the possibilities for textural variety. Any loss in variety could, however, be amply compensated for by a gain in dramatic focus: the astonishing virtuosity of a single instrumentalist could be pitted against the massed weight of an orchestral group. The first notable solo concertos are the six for violin in Torelli's Op. 8 of 1709 (see *HAM* II, no. 246; and *GMB*, no. 257). Vivaldi's require far more virtuosity, and sometimes include written-out cadenzas; yet even they generally lack the tortuous difficulties found quite often in galant concertos by composers like Giuseppe Tartini and Pietro Locatelli (both discussed in Chapter 21). Vivaldi wrote many solo concertos, including at least 222 for violin, 39 for bassoon, 27 for cello, 15 for flute, 10 for oboe, and several for various other instruments. Many of the ones for violin were written for his own use, and the same may be said of the harpsichord concertos by Bach, organ concertos by Handel, and flute concertos by Quantz. These masters undoubtedly interpolated many fresh embellishments, including cadenzas, every time they played a concerto. The most comprehensive guide to such performance practices is Quantz's famous treatise, *Versuch einer Anweisung die Flöte traversiere zu spielen* ("Essay of a Method for Playing the Transverse Flute"; Berlin, 1752).

Music for a Solo Instrumentalist

Plucked Strings

Unaccompanied Baroque chamber works were written almost exclusively for instruments capable of playing chords: the lute and guitar, the gamba and cello, the violin, and the harpsichord. Among these, only the lute had a magnificent solo repertory created for it during the late Renaissance. Sixteenth-century traditions were culminated by numerous lutenist-composers of the early seventeenth century: e.g., Englishmen such as John Dowland and Robert Johnson (c. 1583–1633). Meanwhile, the rather different Baroque traditions were formed in France by such lutenists as Robert Ballard (c. 1575–c. 1650), René Mesangeau (d. 1638), and the Gaultiers. Their favorite instrument was apparently a theorbo-lute with six stopped courses (pairs of strings) attached to one peg-box and from four to six bass courses attached to another. The repertoire consisted mainly of dances (especially courantes), which were often grouped by tuning and key (and sometimes by melodic relationships) into *suites*. In performance, a suite was frequently preceded by an improvised prelude that served to test the tuning and establish the key.

The predominant texture was *style brisé* ("broken [-chord] style"), in which imaginatively arpeggiated chords combined with nonharmonic tones to maintain sonorousness, provide animation, and create the illusion of several rhythmically independent voices. In Example 15.6 by Denis Gaultier (1603–1672) some arpeggiations are written out, while others are merely in-

Lute

dicated by diagonal lines. Trills (notated by ⌁)add further complexity, and lute suites were just as mannered and "precious" as contemporary airs de cour. Example 15.6 is a *tombeau,* a lament or funeral oration, for the lutenist Henry de L'Enclos (d. 1649). French composers often indicated the subject of an "oration" by means of mood-setting titles for their pieces (e.g., *La Solitude*).

French lute practices were adopted in Germany and England. The chief German representatives were Esaias Reusner the Younger (1636–1679), who introduced the French style into Germany, and Sylvius Weiss (1686–1750), who infused it with much contrapuntal artifice. Reusner is noted for his highly expressive suites (see *HAM* II, no. 233, and *GMB,* no. 216), while Weiss is admired for the almost Bachian craftsmanship of both his suites and his abstract works (e.g., the Fantasia in Lerner, no. 82). Baroque England produced no comparable lutenist-composers, but a "monument" to the French tradition was contributed by the Englishman Thomas Mace (1613?–1706?).

Ex. 15.6   Denis Gaultier, *Allemande grave*

From Denis Gaultier, *Pièces de luth* ("Lute Pieces"), I, Paris, c. 1670. Used by permission of the Société Française de Musicologie.

Antoine Watteau (1684–1721), *Italian Comedians* (London, 1720). The troupe is apparently taking a curtain call. The enigmatic Pierrot (Gilles) is in the center, while Mezzetin poses brilliantly at the left with his ever-present five-course guitar. (National Gallery of Art, Washington; Samuel H. Kress Collection)

In *Musick's Monument* (London, 1676) he provided a wealth of information for the beginning lutenist, perhaps hoping to stem the rapidly declining popularity of the instrument. But by 1750, the lute was outmoded everywhere.

In Italy, the five-course Spanish guitar (usually tuned $A-d-g-b-e^1$) had far surpassed the lute in popularity by the early 1600s. It was much easier to play, and it rapidly became the main instrument of "the people" and of popular entertainments like the *commedia dell'arte*.

Guitar

During the course of the seventeenth century, composers intermixed its basic *rasgueado* (chord-strumming) style with *punteado* (note-plucking) techniques learned from the French lutenists, and thus produced attractive and refined dance suites. The leading Italian composers were Francesco Corbetta (c. 1615–1681), Giovanni Battista Granata (who published seven collections in Bologna between 1646 and 1684), and Ludovico Roncalli (who published his fine collection in Bergamo in 1692). Corbetta was the greatest guitarist-composer of the age, according to an informative guitar tutor published by the Spaniard Gaspar Sanz (1640?–1710) at Saragossa in 1674. Corbetta's most notable pupil was a Frenchman, Robert de Visée (c. 1660–c. 1720).

Bowed Strings

Like the guitar, the viola da gamba, or bass viol, is a fretted instrument tuned in fourths except for one third ($[A^1] D-G-c-e-a-d^1$). Chord playing is easier on the viol than on violin-family instruments because the bridge is wider and less arched. During the early and middle Baroque, most gamba solos consisted of improvised variations on a short melody, or *ground,* that was played by the continuo. Not until the late Baroque did small but distin-

Gamba and cello

guished repertories of unaccompanied solos for gamba and cello come into being. The earliest solo pieces for the cello were ricercari, written by Giovanni Battista Degli Antoni (Op. 1, Bologna, 1687) and Domenico Gabrielli (manuscript of 1689; see *GMB,* no. 228); these works include several sections or movements, thus resembling canzonas and sonatas. The first solo pieces for gamba were printed more than a hundred and forty years earlier: two ricercari in Sylvestro Ganassi's *Regola Rubertina* ("Rules for Ruberto"; Venice, 1542–1543), which already feature the double stops characteristic of the late Baroque solo repertory (see *HAM* I, no. 119). The most outstanding gambist-composer of the late Baroque was Marin Marais (1656–1728), who published 555 solo pieces in five volumes, and issued continuo accompaniments for them in separate part-books. Although all his pieces are thus accompanied, in many of them the gamba part has frequent chords, and the continuo part mainly doubles the lowest note of each. For such pieces, the continuo seems to be dispensable. August Kühnel (1645–c. 1700) did indicate that it was optional for similar pieces in his collection (Kassel, 1698), and Jan Schenck (1660–c. 1712) did the same for many in two of his collections (Ops. 6 and 9; Amsterdam, 1698 and 1703–1704, respectively). These French, German, and Dutch gamba suites were superbly crafted (see the fugue by Schenck in *GMB,* no. 245), and therefore seem to be possible models for the six great cello suites by Bach (BWV 1007–12; Cöthen, c. 1720; a courante is in Hardy and Fish II, pp. 12–13).[13] In any case, a knowledge of the performance practices of gambists can give cellists many fresh ideas about possible articulations for Bach's suites, and much information about such practices can be found in the meticulously edited publications of Marais.[14]

Violin

Polyphonically conceived gamba and cello suites were largely based on the lutenists' style brisé, and so were polyphonic violin solos. Although a few Italian composers wrote unaccompanied violin pieces, the chief seventeenth-century examples are by German virtuosos: Thomas Baltzar (c. 1630–1663) of Lübeck, who wrote several short works (see *GMB,* no. 237); Heinrich Biber (1644–1704), whose last Mystery Sonata is an unaccompanied passacaglia consisting of sixty-five variations on the pattern ($g-f-e^b-d$); and Johann Paul Westhoff (1656–1705), who published one solo suite in a Parisian periodical of 1683 and dedicated six others to the Dresden Electress in 1696. These are the main precedents known for Bach's magnificent set of three sonatas and three suites (BWV 1001–06; Cöthen, 1720; the suites are called "partitas"). A rather Bachian sonata by Johann Georg Pisendel (1687–1755) and another by Geminiani probably postdate Bach's set. (Telemann's set of twelve fantasies, composed c. 1735, certainly does; see *TEM,* no. 48.) Bach's works for solo violin include some of his most stupendous achievements: the third sonata has a fugue of 354 measures, and the second suite closes with a "ciaccona" of 256 (in Burkhart, pp. 90–96). The latter, in fact a passacaglia on the simple pattern of four stepwise descending notes, is a culminating example of the Baroque art of variation.

Harpsichord

During the first half of the seventeenth century, variation form had an especially prominent place in pieces written for harpsichord and related keyboard instruments such as the virginal. Much of the metric figuration that Baroque composers employed in motivic sequences first appeared in variation sets written by English virginalist-composers on well-known tunes or dance patterns. (Some examples based on tunes are in *HAM* I, no. 177; *GMB,* no. 147; Lerner, no. 55; and *MM,* no. 29. Some based on dances, in which each strain is repeated with written-out variations, are in *HAM* I, no. 179; *TEM,* no. 30; and *Omnibus* I, pp. 79–80.) The finest virginalist-composers were William Byrd, John Bull (c. 1563–1628), and Orlando Gibbons, the only composers included in the first keyboard collection printed in England: *Parthenia or the Maydenhead of the First Musicke that ever was printed for the Virginalls* (London, 1613). Thirty-three additional composers are named in the largest of the many manuscript collections, *The Fitzwilliam Virginal Book* (compiled 1609–1619), which contains 297 pieces. This English repertory served as a basis for excellent variation sets written by northern European composers, most notably Sweelinck and his student Scheidt. Their sets usually have a clear-cut structure, with a distinctive rhythmic motive for each variation, and a definite rhythmic or textural climax in the last one. Similar sets, titled *partite* ("parts"), were written in southern Europe by Ascanio Mayone (d. 1627), Giovanni Maria Trabaci (d. 1647), and Frescobaldi, who were contemporaries of Gibbons and Scheidt. Their partite are often based on chord patterns and sometimes seem whimsical or impetuous in their succession of motives (see Example 14.8, and *HAM* II, no. 192). English sets based on chord or bass patterns were called *grounds* (see Ward-Steinman II, no. 96; and *MM,* no. 38).

In France, Baroque pieces for *clavecin* (harpsichord) had basically the same style traits as those for lute. Indeed, some of the earliest known examples of Baroque clavecin music are attributed to lutenists, e.g., Mesangeau. The first great composer was Jacques Champion de Chambonnières (c. 1602–1672), a contemporary of Denis Gaultier; Chambonnières succeeded his father as

1600–1650

France

harpsichordist to the king in 1640. Three of his students became noted composers: Louis Couperin (c. 1626–1661), Jean Henri d'Anglebert (1628–1691), and Nicolas Le Bègue (1631–1702). The traditions they established were carried to their ultimate refinement in the early 1700s by François Couperin (1668–1733, nephew of Louis) and by Rameau.

Brilliant-sounding ornaments and motivic figuration were an integral part of the clavecin style. The early and middle Baroque pieces may have had a rather transparent texture; at least there were few ornaments specified in the sources that preserve them (chiefly the Bauyn manuscript compiled c. 1660; see *HAM* II, nos. 212 and 229). But they were undoubtedly performed with many more ornaments. When Chambonnières published two collections in 1670, he included many ornaments (see *GMB*, no. 218). D'Anglebert prefaced his volume of 1689 with a list of twenty-nine ornamental signs (see illustration, page 352, and *HAM* II, no. 232). François Couperin provided a similar list in his first book (1713), then discussed fingerings, ornamentation, and other performance problems in *L'Art de toucher le clavecin* ("The Art of Playing the Harpsichord"; Paris, 1716). He declared in the preface to his third book (1722) that his placement of ornaments was "not at all arbitrary," and that those who (through "unpardonable negligence") ignored any of them would "never make a proper impression on persons possessing true taste." Rameau similarly prefaced his second collection (1724) with an essay on playing technique and a table of ornaments.

Such great concern with the manner in which any single piece was to be performed was paired with an apparent lack of concern for the number and choice of pieces to be played as a unit; harpsichordists were presumably free to combine whichever ones struck their fancy. Like the lutenists, clavecin composers grouped their works into suites consisting of from three to more than twenty-three pieces in the same key (occasionally including some in relative or parallel keys). Traditionally, these pieces were nearly all binary-form dances, some of which bore descriptive titles. However, beginning with **François** François Couperin's first collection in 1713, the predominant type became the **Couperin** descriptive piece that was not clearly related to any dance. Indeed, in the preface to his first collection, Couperin termed his pieces "portraits," declaring that listeners had sometimes found them to resemble the subject portrayed when he had played them. He published 226 pieces (or more if we count the divisions of some compound ones), grouped in 27 suites, which he called *ordres*. Almost one-fifth of these pieces are in rondeau form: refrain–couplet 1–refrain–couplet 2, etc. (see *HAM* II, no. 265b, and Burkhart, pp. 70–73). Rondeau form had been employed by seventeenth-century clavecinists most notably for chaconnes (see *HAM* II, no. 212), and it became the predominant form in Rameau's collection of 1724.

Froberger The first great German composer of keyboard suites was Johann Jakob Froberger (1616–1667). Like the clavecinists, he typically employed style brisé and often began the first and second strains of a binary-form dance with contrasting motives. He used little artifice (e.g., figuration and phrase extension) in sarabands, but employed it lavishly in allemandes, some of which are tombeaux (see *HAM* II, no. 216). The tombeau that he wrote on the death of the lutenist Blancheroche (d. 1657?) is to be played "without maintaining any beat," and perhaps such rhythmic freedom was often employed in order to intensify a mournful affect. In contrast with French works, each of Froberger's twenty-seven extant suites includes only three or four pieces, placed in the following order: allemande, gigue (not included in his early works), courante, and saraband.

The standard late-Baroque German suite is represented by works of Dietrich Buxtehude (c. 1637–1707), Johann Krieger (1651–1735), Johann Pachelbel (1653–1706; see *HAM* II, no. 250, and Lerner, no. 83), Johann Kuhnau (1660–1720), Georg Böhm (1661–1733; see *GMB*, no. 253), and Bach. Their works sometimes include one or more additional movements (placed after the courante, saraband, or gigue). Handel usually replaced or omitted at least one of the standard four movements in his suites, which were for the most part written in Germany in the early 1700s. His finest ones are the eight "lessons" that he reworked for his London publication of 1720 (a prelude is in *GMB*, no. 279; see also Example 15.2). Johann Kaspar Ferdinand Fischer (c. 1670–1746) wrote suites that included none of the standard movements; for example, one from his 1696 collection consists of a prelude, passacaille (in rondeau form), bourrée, and menuet (in *HAM* II, no. 248). Both Fischer and Kuhnau typically prefaced their suites with preludes.

Late-Baroque German suites

Kuhnau, Bach's predecessor as cantor in Leipzig, published two collections of suites, which he called *partitas,* under the title of *Neue Clavier Übung* ("New Keyboard Practice"; Leipzig, 1689 and 1692). Bach emulated him by publishing six partitas as his *Clavier-Übung,* Op. 1 (Leipzig, 1731), "composed for music lovers, to give their spirits recreation." This set of suites, written in Leipzig between approximately 1725 and 1730, was preceded by two others, which likewise contain six works each: the so-called "English" and "French" suites, which were completed, respectively, in Weimar about 1715 and in Cöthen about 1723. The "French" ones (BWV 812–817) are the most concise; they include only dance movements (see Suite No. 1 in Hardy and Fish II, pp. 74–84). The "English" suites (BWV 806–811) and the partitas (BWV 825–830) are each prefaced by a lengthy prelude. The preludes in the earlier set all mingle Italian exuberance with German craftsmanship. For example, the prelude to Suite No. 3 in G minor has the ritornello form of an Italian concerto. The ritornello begins with a motive treated in lively *stretto*-like imitation by six "voices," and each of the three solos begins with a second motive that becomes the subject of a fugal exposition, in which the first motive serves as countersubject. For the sarabands in Suites No. 2 and 3, Bach provided both mildly and floridly ornamented versions, thus giving clear examples of his own manner of embellishing the repetition of strains in slow movements. The two gavottes and the gigue from Suite No. 3 show his

Bach

typical use of the same motive to begin each half of a binary-form dance. In the gigue, the motive is introduced in a three-voiced fugal exposition, then inverted at the beginning of the second half.

The partitas are longer and more concentrated than the "English" suites, and their preludial movements are much more diverse. The one opening Partita No. 4 in D major (given complete in *Omnibus,* I, pp. 157–167) is a French overture, consisting of a Grave in which the dotted notes should be overdotted, followed by a long three-voiced fugue in which most of the opening section is recapitulated a fifth lower at the end. Nonstandard movements are included in this partita both before and after the saraband, an excellent example of rounded binary form. As in *sonata form,* the recapitulation of this saraband presents both the first and second subjects in the tonic key. In 1735 Bach's last keyboard suite, entitled *Overture nach französischer Art* ("Overture in the French Style," BWV 831), was published together with his Concerto in the Italian Style as part 2 of his *Clavier-Übung.* Like Partita No. 4, this suite is prefaced by a monumental French overture. The final two parts of the *Clavier-Übung* (1739 and c. 1741) contained, respectively, organ works and the superb set of *Goldberg* Variations.

Bach's published harpsichord works are among his most finely polished, and they were obviously intended for "music lovers" who had mastered most of the elements of keyboard playing. In other words, they represent an advanced stage of "keyboard practice," and Bach presumably employed them for this purpose when he gave lessons. Although he wrote various harpsichord works (most notably his toccatas, BWV 910–916, and Chromatic Fantasy, BWV 903) apparently intended mainly for display of his own virtuosity, he is best known for those that he wrote for pedagogical purposes. As he taught his eldest son, Wilhelm Friedemann Bach (1710–1784), at Cöthen in 1720–1722, he created the *Inventions,* the first book of *The Well-Tempered Clavier,* and the "French" suites as stepping-stones on the road to a mastery of much more than keyboard technique. He made his intention clear when he inscribed a copy (dated 1723) of the *Inventions* with a statement concerning their purpose: "a straightforward primer" for playing in two, then in three obbligato parts, which will further help students "not only to acquire good ideas (*inventions*) but also to work them out well, and—most important of all—to attain a singing (*cantabile*) style of playing, and moreover to receive a solid foretaste of composition." In each of these works, fifteen in two parts and fifteen in three, one motivic idea ("invention") is developed, chiefly by imitation and inversion.

The Well-Tempered Clavier   The first book of *The Well-Tempered Clavier* contains the next steps for a student. Like the second book (compiled in Leipzig by 1742), it includes twenty-four preludes and fugues, one in each major and minor key, thus demanding a well-tempered tuning that approximates *equal temperament.* Its contents are often called "etudes," because each piece embraces a limited number of figural difficulties, but by the same token each is a concise exploration of one affect and, in this respect, a masterpiece of Baroque art. The affect is so sharply etched in the opening motive that each piece could be interpreted as a *character piece* by the performer. As with all Baroque music, the performer's primary responsibility is to identify, then convey, an affective character for the piece. The great diversity of moods in *The Well-Tempered Clavier* makes it an ideal stepping-stone toward an understanding of Baroque music in general.

An entirely different kind of etude was written by Domenico Scarlatti (1685–1757), an exact contemporary of Bach, in his *sonatas* for the harpsichord. Nearly all of these 555 harpsichord pieces are in binary form, and at least 400 are apparently to be played in pairs or, rarely, in groups of three. None can be dated before the late 1730s, and most first appeared in manuscripts dated 1752–1757. They are therefore both post-Baroque and Preclassic works, thriving in their own distinctive, and extremely witty, stylistic world. They have little to do with Classic-period sonatas, which derive principally from Baroque ensemble sonatas and harpsichord suites.

Sonatas: Domenico Scarlatti

Summary

In this chapter we have surveyed the music written for performance in Baroque "chambers." The chief vocal genre was the *cantata,* which grew out of monody in early-seventeenth-century Italy and flourished throughout Europe during the early eighteenth century. The principal genres for instrumental ensemble were the *trio sonata* and its reinforced relative, the *concerto grosso.* The standard models for both were written by Corelli in the late seventeenth century, by which time these trio-texture genres were gradually giving way to *solo sonatas* and *solo concertos.* Instrumental ensemble music written for the chamber (rather than the church) typically consisted of a series of dance movements, and the same was true of works written for instrumental soloists unaccompanied by a continuo part. The most significant and extensive repertory for such soloists was that for harpsichord.

Baroque instrumentalists as well as singers were expected to arouse and still passions in their listeners, sometimes gently but more often impetuously, and always by conveying musical affects with unmistakable clarity. In vocal music, the focus of the remaining two chapters on the Baroque, this goal is relatively easy to achieve, because a verbal text underpins the musical discourse. In instrumental music, the principal focus of the present chapter, listeners can much more easily lose sight of the prevailing affect, as one Frenchman (reputedly the Baroque essayist and librettist Bernard Le Bovier de Fontenelle) apparently did when he cried out despairingly in the midst of a performance: *Sonate, que me veux-tu?* ("Sonata, what do you want of me?"). That protest may have been uttered only because the players were conveying none of the affections contained in the score. In order to avoid comparable objections, today's performers of Baroque music should unleash the full range of passions, remembering that the range was bridled only during the ensuing Classic era.

Notes

1. *Syntagma musicum* (1614–1620), cited in Thurston Dart, *The Interpretation of Music* (London: Hutchinson, 1954), p. 107.
2. Treatise of 1698, cited in "Georg Muffat's Observations on the Lully Style of Performance," trans. Kenneth Cooper and Julius Zsako, *Musical Quarterly* 53 (1967): 231.
3. Count Giovanni de' Bardi, treatise of c. 1580, cited in Oliver Strunk, *Source Readings in Music History: The Renaissance* (New York: W. W. Norton, 1965), p. 109.
4. Treatise of c. 1635, cited in Robert Donington, *The Interpretation of Early Music,* new version (London: Faber & Faber, 1974), p. 642.
5. Frescobaldi's performance instructions are summarized in Dart, *The Interpretation of Music,* pp. 110–111 and 117.
6. Six of the embellished movements are given in Hans-Peter Schmitz, *Die Kunst der Verzierung im 18. Jahrhundert* (Kassel: Bärenreiter, 1955), ex. IIa.
7. Treatise of c. 1745, cited in Dart, *The Interpretation of Music,* pp. 63–64.
8. For a trenchantly written summary of editorial responsibilities, see [Thurston Dart et al.] *Editing Early Music: Notes on the Preparation of Printer's Copy* (London: Novello, Oxford University Press, and Stainer & Bell, 1963).
9. David and Susan L. Ward-Steinman, *Comparative Anthology of Musical Forms,* 2 vols. (Belmont, California: Wadsworth, 1976). (Ward-Steinman)
10. The passages cited are from John Ernest Galliard's translation: *Observations on the Florid Song,* 2nd ed. (London, 1743; reprinted, New York: Johnson Reprint, 1968), pp. 67–68, 156, 180, and 182.
11. Gerald Abraham, ed., *The History of Music in Sound,* 8 vols. (New York: Oxford University Press, 1953–1958). (*HMS*)
12. Carl Parrish and John F. Ohl, *Masterpieces of Music before 1750* (New York: W. W. Norton, 1951). (*MM*)
13. Gordon Hardy and Arnold Fish, *Music Literature: A Workbook for Analysis,* 2 vols. (New York: Dodd, Mead & Co., 1963–1966).
14. See especially Gordon J. Kinney, "Marin Marais as Editor of His Own Compositions," and Karl Neumann, "The Slur Marks in Bach's 'Cello Suites," in the *Journal of the Viola da Gamba Society of America* 3 (1966): 5–16 and 34–51, respectively.

Bibliography

Books and Articles

Performance Practice

The standard guide to sources of information is Mary Vinquist and Neal Zaslaw, eds., *Performance Practice: A Bibliography,* New York: W. W. Norton, 1971. Supplements to this book have been printed in *Current Musicology,* no. 12 (1971): 129–149, and no. 15 (1973): 126–136.

DART, THURSTON. *The Interpretation of Music.* London: Hutchinson, 1954.

DONINGTON, ROBERT. *A Performer's Guide to Baroque Music.* London: Faber & Faber, 1973.

————. *The Interpretation of Early Music,* new version. London: Faber & Faber, 1974.

Vocal Music

FORTUNE, NIGEL. "Italian Seventeenth-Century Singing." *Music and Letters* 35 (1954): 206–219.

HITCHCOCK, H. WILEY. "Vocal Ornamentation in Caccini's *Nuove musiche.*" *The Musical Quarterly* 56 (1970): 389–404.

ROSE, GLORIA. "The Italian Cantata of the Baroque Period." In *Gattungen der Musik in Einzeldarstellungen: Gedenkschrift Leo Schrade,* vol. 1, pp. 655–677. Berne: Francke, 1973.

TUNLEY, DAVID. *The Eighteenth-Century French Cantata.* London: Dennis Dobson, 1974.

Instrumental Ensemble Music

BECK, HERMANN. *The Suite,* trans. Robert Kolben. Anthology of Music, vol. 26. Cologne: Arno Volk Verlag, 1966.

BOYDEN, DAVID D. *The History of Violin Playing from Its Origins to 1761, and Its Relationship to the Violin and Violin Music.* London: Oxford University Press, 1965.

ENGEL, HANS. *The Concerto Grosso,* trans. Robert Kolben. Anthology of Music, vol. 23. Cologne: Arno Volk Verlag, 1964.

SCHENK, ERICH. *The Italian Trio Sonata* and *The Trio Sonata Outside Italy,* trans. Robert Kolben. Anthology of Music, vols. 7 and 35. Cologne: Arno Volk Verlag, 1955 and 1970, respectively.

Music for a Solo Instrumentalist

COWLING, ELIZABETH. *The Cello.* London: B. T. Batsford, 1975.

FERGUSON, HOWARD, ed. *Style and Interpretation: An Anthology of Keyboard Music,* vols. 1–2: Early Keyboard Music. London: Oxford University Press, 1963.

KEITH, RICHARD. *"La Guitarre Royale:* A Study of the Career and Compositions of Francesco Corbetta." *Recherches sur la musique française classique* 6 (1966): 73–93. See also Keith's "The Guitar Cult in the Courts of Louis XIV and Charles II." *Guitar Review* 26 (1962): 3–9.

KIRKPATRICK, RALPH. *Domenico Scarlatti.* Princeton, N.J.: Princeton University Press, 1953.

Scores

For composers not listed here, see the bibliography of scores in Chapter 14.

ALBERT, HEINRICH. *Arien,* ed. Eduard Bernouilli, rev. Hans Joachim Moser. Denkmäler Deutscher Tonkunst, vols. 12–13. Wiesbaden: Breitkopf & Härtel, 1958.

ALBINONI, TOMASO. *Concerti,* Ops. 5 and 7, selections ed. Martin L. Shapiro. Bryn Mawr: Theodore Presser, 1976.

————. *Concerti,* Op. 7, selections ed. Walter Kolneder. Zurich: Eulenberg, 1975.

D'ANGLEBERT, JEAN HENRI. *Pièces de clavecin,* ed. Marguerite Roesgen-Champion. Paris: Société Française de Musicologie, 1934.

BALLARD, ROBERT. *Premier livre* and *Deuxième livre,* ed. André Souris and Sylvie Spycket, 2 vols. Paris: Centre National de la Recherche Scientifique, 1963–1964.

BOËSSET, ANTOINE. In *Airs de cour pour voix et luth (1603–1643),* ed. André Verchaly. Paris: Heugel, 1961. Also contains airs by Pierre Guédron and other composers.

BONONCINI, GIOVANNI MARIA. In William Klenz, *Giovanni Maria Bononcini of Modena.* Durham, N.C.: Duke University Press, 1962. The musical supplement also contains works by Maurizio Cazzati and other composers.

CAZZATI, MAURIZIO. *Sonatas,* Op. 35, Nos. 10–12, for trumpet and strings, ed. Robert P. Block and Edward H. Tarr. London: Musica Rara, 1972.

CHAMBONNIÈRES, JACQUES CHAMPION DE. *Les Deux Livres de clavecin,* ed. Thurston Dart. Monaco: Oiseau Lyre, 1969.

CLÉRAMBAULT, LOUIS NICOLAS. *Orphée,* ed. David Tunley. London: Faber Music, 1972.

————. *Pièces de clavecin,* ed. Paul Brunold, rev. Thurston Dart. Monaco: Oiseau Lyre, 1964.

CORBETTA, FRANCESCO. *La guitarre royale,* facsimile reprint of the edition of 1674. Bologna: Forni, 1971.

————. *Varii capricci,* selections ed. Alexander Bellow. New York: Colombo, 1967.

COUPERIN, FRANÇOIS. *Pièces de clavecin,* ed. Kenneth Gilbert, 4 vols. Paris: Heugel, 1969–1972.

COUPERIN, LOUIS. *Pièces de clavecin,* ed. Alan Curtis. Paris: Heugel, 1970.

FARINA, CARLO. *Capriccio stravagante,* ed. Nikolaus Harnoncourt. New York: Peters, 1970.

FROBERGER, JOHANN JAKOB. *Orgel- und Klavierwerke,* ed. Guido Adler. Denkmäler der Tonkunst in Österreich, vols. 8, 13, and 21. Vienna: Artaria, 1897–1903; reprinted, Graz: Akademische Druck- und Verlaganstalt, 1959.

GAULTIER, DENIS. *La Rhétorique des dieux et autres pièces de luth,* ed. André Tessier, 2 vols. (facsimile and transcription). Paris: Société Française de Musicologie, 1932–1933.

GEMINIANI, FRANCESCO. *Concerti grossi,* Op. 3, ed. Robert Hernried. Leipzig: Eulenberg, 1935.

————. *Cello Sonatas,* Op. 5, ed. Walter Kolneder. Leipzig: Peters, 1964.

GRANATA, GIOVANNI BATTISTA. *Novi capricci,* facsimile reprint of the edition of 1674. Bologna: Forni, 1971.

————. *Soavi concenti,* selections ed. Alexander Bellow. New York: Colombo, 1968.

GUÉDRON, PIERRE: see Boësset.

HANDEL, GEORGE FRIDERIC. *Werke,* ed. Friedrich Chrysander, 95 vols. Leipzig: Breitkopf & Härtel, 1858–1902.

————. *Halische Händel Ausgabe,* ed. Händel-Gesellschaft. Kassel: Bärenreiter, 1955–

HOTTETERRE, JACQUES. *Deuxième Suite* (1708). Reproduced in facsimile in Hans-Peter Schmitz, *Die Kunst der Verzierung im 18. Jahrhundert.* Kassel: Bärenreiter, 1955.

JENKINS, JOHN. *Consort Music of Four Parts,* ed. Andrew Ashbee. Musica Britannica, vol. 26. London: Stainer & Bell, 1969.

————. *Fancies and Ayres,* ed. Helen Joy Sleeper. Wellesley, Mass.: Wellesley Edition, 1950.

KINDERMANN, JOHANN. *Ausgewählte Werke,* pt. 2, ed. Felix Schreiber and Bertha Wallner. Denkmäler Deutscher Tonkunst, vol. 32. Augsburg: Benno Filser, 1924.

KRIEGER, ADAM. *Arien,* ed. Alfred Heuss, rev. Hans Joachim Moser. Denkmäler Deutscher Tonkunst, vol. 19. Wiesbaden: Breitkopf & Härtel, 1958.

KUHNAU, JOHANN. *Klavierwerke,* ed. Carl Päsler, rev. Hans Joachim Moser. Denkmäler Deutscher Tonkunst, vol. 4. Wiesbaden: Breitkopf & Härtel, 1958.

LAWES, HENRY and WILLIAM. *Dialogues,* ed. Roy Jesson. University Park: Pennsylvania State University Press, 1964.

LAWES, WILLIAM. *Select Consort Music,* 2nd ed., ed. Murray Lefkowitz. Musica Britannica, vol. 21. London: Stainer & Bell, 1971.

LE BÈGUE, NICOLAS. *Oeuvres de clavecin,* ed. Norbert Dufourcq. Monaco: Oiseau Lyre, 1956.

LECLAIR, JEAN-MARIE. *Sonatas for Violin and Continuo,* ed. Robert E. Preston, 4 vols. New Haven and Madison: A–R Editions, 1968–1971.

LEGRENZI, GIOVANNI. *Cantatas and Canzonets for Solo Voice,* ed. Albert Seay, 2 vols. Madison: A–R Editions, 1972.

––––––. *Sonate da chiesa,* Ops. 4 and 8, selections ed. Albert Seay. Paris: Heugel, 1968.

LOCKE, MATTHEW. *Chamber Music,* ed. Michael Tilmouth. Musica Britannica, vols. 31–32. London: Stainer & Bell, 1971–1972.

MARAIS, MARIN. *Pièces de viole,* bks. 3–4, selections ed. Gordon J. Kinney. Madison: A–R Editions, 1976.

MERULA, TARQUINIO. *Opere complete,* ed. Adam Sutkowski. Brooklyn: Institute of Medieval Music, 1974– .

MUFFAT, GEORG. *Armonico tributo,* ed. Erich Schenk. Denkmäler der Tonkunst in Österreich, vol. 89. Vienna: Österreichische Bundesverlag, 1953.

––––––. *Florilegium primum* and *Florilegium secundum,* ed. Heinrich Rietsch. Denkmäler der Tonkunst in Österreich, vols. 2 and 4. Vienna: Artaria, 1894–1895; reprinted, Graz: Akademische Druck- und Verlagsanstalt, 1959.

PACHELBEL, JOHANN. *Klavierwerke,* ed. Max Seiffert. Denkmäler der Tonkunst in Bayern, vol. 2. Leipzig: Breitkopf & Härtel, 1901; reprinted, 1968.

PEZEL, JOHANN. *Turmmusik und Suiten,* ed. Arnold Schering. Denkmäler Deutscher Tonkunst, vol. 63. Leipzig: Breitkopf & Härtel, 1928; reprinted, 1959.

PISENDEL, JOHANN GEORG. *Sonate für Violine allein ohne Bass,* ed. Günter Hausswald. Mainz: Schott, 1954.

PURCELL, HENRY. *The Works,* ed. Purcell Society, 32 vols. London: Novello, 1878–1965.

RAVENSCROFT, THOMAS. *Pammelia, Deuteromelia, Melismata,* facsimile reprint of the editions of 1609–1611, ed. MacEdward Leach. Philadelphia: American Folklore Society, 1961.

REUSNER, ESAIAS. In *Lautenmusik des 17./18. Jahrhunderts,* ed. Hans Neemann. Das Erbe Deutscher Musik, vol. 12. Frankfurt: Henry Litolff, 1939. Also contains music by Sylvius Weiss.

ROSENMÜLLER, JOHANN. *Sonate da camera,* ed. Karl Nef, rev. Hans Joachim Moser. Denkmäler Deutscher Tonkunst, vol. 18. Wiesbaden: Breitkopf & Härtel, 1957.

ROSSI, SALAMONE. *Sinfonie et gagliarde,* bks. 1–2, ed. Fritz Rikko and Joel Newman, 3 vols. New York: Mercury Music, 1965–1971.

––––––. *Sinfonie et gagliarde,* bk. 3, selections ed. Alfred Mann and Fritz Rikko. New Brunswick, N.J.: Rutgers University Press, 1965.

SCARLATTI, ALESSANDRO. Cantatas *Io son pur solo* and *Lontan dalla sua Clori,* ed. Malcolm Boyd. Kassel: Bärenreiter, 1972.

SCARLATTI, DOMENICO. *Complete Keyboard Works in Facsimile from the Manuscript and Printed Sources,* ed. Ralph Kirkpatrick, 18 vols. New York: Johnson Reprint, 1972.

––––––. *Sonatas,* ed. Kenneth Gilbert, 11 vols. Paris: Heugel, 1971–1978.

––––––. *Sixty Sonatas,* ed. Ralph Kirkpatrick, 2 vols. New York: G. Schirmer, 1953.

SCHENCK, JAN. *Le Nymphe de Rheno* and *L'Echo du Danube,* ed. Karl Heinz Pauls. Das Erbe Deutscher Musik, vols. 44 and 67. Kassel: Nagel, 1956 and 1973, respectively.

––––––. *Scherzi musicali,* ed. Hugo Leichtentritt. Vereniging voor Nederlandse Muziekgeschiedenis, vol. 28. Amsterdam: Alsbach, 1907.

STEFFANI, AGOSTINO. *Ausgewählte Werke,* pt. 1, ed. Alfred Einstein and Adolf Sandberger. Denkmäler der Tonkunst in Bayern, vol. 11. Leipzig: Breitkopf & Härtel, 1905.

STROZZI, BARBARA. In *The Solo Song: 1580–1730,* ed. Carol MacClintock. New York: W. W. Norton, 1973. This excellent anthology contains 75 works by 60 composers.

TELEMANN, GEORG PHILLIPP. *Musikalische Werke,* ed. Gesellschaft für Musikforschung. Kassel: Bärenreiter, 1950–   .

VISÉE, ROBERT DE. *Oeuvres complètes pour guitare,* ed. Robert W. Strizich. Paris: Heugel, 1969.

WEISS, SYLVIUS: see Reusner.

WESTHOFF, JOHANN PAUL. *Sechs Suiten für Violine Solo,* facsimile reprint of the edition of 1696, ed. Wolfgang Reich, plus transcription by Manfred Fechner. Leipzig: Peters, 1974.

16

Theater Music

ITALIAN opera was the principal genre of theatrical entertainment throughout much of Europe during the Baroque era. Its frequent employment as the costliest spectacle at princely weddings and coronations was only partly responsible for its preeminence. From its inception, opera was also the concern of literary and musical academicians who hoped that it could move the affections of an audience. Their hopes were certainly fulfilled. From all reports, opera had a surprising power over those who saw it, and it consequently became a truly popular genre in Italy.

This chapter will trace the development of Italian opera, its diffusion throughout Western Europe, and its influence upon the distinctive genres of musical theater in other lands. These genres—French opera, Spanish *zarzuela,* and English dramatic opera—arose in countries that had a flourishing spoken theater in the 1600s. Because of the ravages of the Thirty Years War (1618–1648), Germany had no chance to develop any theatrical traditions, and therefore the musical theater cultivated there after 1650 consisted largely of imports, chiefly Italian operas.

Italy

The Early Baroque

From about 1650 until far beyond the end of the Baroque era, opera was an essential ingredient of almost every Italian festivity, most notably of the carnival season that extends from just after Christmas to just before Lent. In the following pages, we will trace the development of Italian opera by focusing on representative works by a few composers: Peri, Monteverdi, and Gagliano in the early Baroque; Monteverdi, Cesti, and Cavalli in the middle Baroque; and Alessandro Scarlatti in the late Baroque.

Opera began in Florence in 1598 as an outgrowth of musico-dramatic experiments, including the 1589 entertainment given for the wedding of Grand Duke Ferdinand de' Medici and Christine of Lorraine. Its six musical *interme-*

Precursors of opera

385

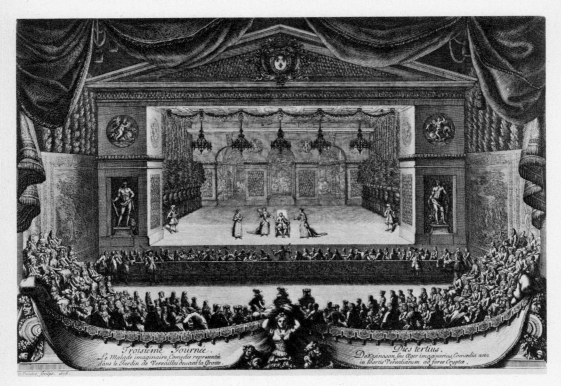

Le Malade imaginaire, a comedy, as produced in the Garden of Versailles on August 21, 1674, engraved by Jean Le Pautre (1618–1682). The play was by Molière (1622–1673), the music by Marc-Antoine Charpentier (1634–1704). It is probably Charpentier who is conducting with a roll of music paper. There are about 20 performers on either side; those closest to the conductor are playing bass lutes. Many of the courtiers seem to be paying little attention to the proceedings onstage. Louis XIV has the best seat. (Harvard Theatre Collection)

dii ("interludes") were devised by Count Giovanni de' Bardi around one theme: the power of music. This theme fascinated Bardi, his protégé Vincenzo Galilei, and many other Florentine academicians, including Ottavio Rinuccini, who wrote the text of the third *intermedio,* describing the combat of the god of music, Apollo, with the Python. Music for these interludes was composed mainly by Cristofano Malvezzi (1547–1597) and Luca Marenzio. Additional settings were by Bardi, Giulio Caccini (another of Bardi's protégés), Malvezzi's student Jacopo Peri, the singer Vittoria Archilei's husband Antonio (d. after 1610), and the Florentine superintendent of spectacles, Emilio de' Cavalieri (c. 1550–1602).

The first opera: *Dafne*   By about 1594, Rinuccini had written the text of *Dafne* ("Daphne"), a pastoral drama destined to be the first *opera,* or *dramma per musica* —i.e., a drama sung throughout. It includes a prologue, a new version of his combat scene of 1589, and four scenes concerning Apollo's vain pursuit of the nymph Dafne. Choral pieces modeled after those of ancient Greek tragedy end all scenes (sometimes called "acts") except the third. This play was an "academic" experiment, which Rinuccini wrote to test the affect-inducing capabilities of "modern" music. His patron, Jacopo Corsi (1561–1602), composed a few "arias" (perhaps melodies only) for it, then engaged the singer-composer Peri to complete the music. With Peri singing the role of Apollo, *Dafne* was performed at Corsi's house during the 1597–1598 carnival season. Only five or six numbers written for the work have survived, but judging by them it seems likely that Peri's setting included all three kinds of dramatic monody and used dance-like canzonettas in scenes of solo or choral rejoicing. This first opera was received with such great enthusiasm that it was revived with revisions during several subsequent years.

The ensuing scramble to get an opera into print in 1600 is further evidence of the great success of *Dafne*. Cavalieri had his *Rappresentatione* (Chapter 17) performed in a church at Rome and had it published in September. In October, Rinuccini's new opera libretto, *Euridice* ("Eurydice") was performed for princely wedding festivities in Florence. The music was by Peri, except for some pieces that Caccini managed to replace with others he himself had composed. Caccini apparently felt that Peri's *Euridice* was far more impressive than his own *Il rapimento di Cefalo,* because, instead of publishing his *Cefalo,* he hurriedly composed his own setting of *Euridice.* Closely modeling it after Peri's setting, Caccini had it printed in December 1600 (although it was not performed until December 1602). Peri's setting, not printed until February 1601, has far greater dramatic power than those composed by his rivals.

Three rival composers

Like his *Dafne,* Peri's *Euridice* is a pastoral drama consisting of a prologue and five acts, with a plot drawn from Greek mythology. Marvelous, supernatural events are central to both plots: Dafne is transformed into a laurel tree, while Orfeo wrests a mortal (Euridice) from Hades. Since Euridice's release is obtained by the power of Orfeo's singing, the plot was obviously ideal for the Florentines who wished to demonstrate the dramatic power of their new music (monody) and of their new genre (opera).

Peri's Euridice

For them, Peri's setting successfully demonstrated both. As in *Dafne,* he set the strophic prologue as a special-recitation monody without written variation for successive strophes. Most of the text of each act is set in narrative monody, but expressive monody is used when the text demands it, chiefly in Orfeo's moving appeal to the ruler of Hades. The four- and five-voice settings of the choruses that end each of the five acts also differ in construction in order to suit their texts.

Dafne and *Euridice* are the direct ancestors of three operas performed at Mantua: Monteverdi's *Orfeo* ("Orpheus," 1607), a new setting of *Dafne* (1608) by the Florentine composer Marco da Gagliano (1582–1643), and Monteverdi's *Arianna* (1608). The text of *Orfeo,* by Alessandro Striggio (1573–1630), retells the story of *Euridice,* and Monteverdi's setting follows the outline of Peri's model, from special-recitation monody for the strophic prologue to five-voice choruses at the end of each of the five acts. But Monteverdi achieved an even greater dramatic intensity through his written-in melodic variations for strophic texts, clear melodic goals for phrases, power-

Monteverdi's Orfeo

ful choral writing, and musico-dramatic organization resulting from the repetition of pieces, especially instrumental ones.

On an allegorical level, the power of music is the subject of *Orfeo*. The
five-strophe prologue is sung by Music personified, who affirms her power
to move the affections. The instrumental ritornello (see Example 16.1a)
played before and after each of her strophes represents her power whenever it
is employed later in the opera. The ritornello returns in unaltered form before
acts III and V, in which her supernatural power is needed. Within act III, its
distinctive cadence returns twice in the low-pitched *sinfonia* (Example 16.1b)
that sets an otherworldly mood for Orfeo's great aria of incantation, *Possente
spirto*. The first three strophes of this aria are addressed to Charon, whose
boat transports spirits across the River Styx to Hades. But in strophe 4 Orfeo
turns inward (*Orfeo son io* — "Orpheus am I"), and the distinctive cadence immediately returns in the instruments (Example 16.1c) — the clearest possible
indication of Music's support for the greatest mortal musician-poet in his
hour of need.

Ex. 16.1   Claudio Monteverdi, *Orfeo*

(a)   Ritornello for *La Musica*

Ex. 16.1   cont.

(b)   Sinfonia preceding *Possente spirto*

(c)   *Possente spirto*

From Monteverdi, *Tutte le opere,* ed. G. Francesco Malipiero, Vol. 11. Copyright 1966 by Universal Edition A. G., Vienna. Used by permission.

Orfeo is a true music drama because Monteverdi's setting interprets the text. Without understanding the interpretive role of the music, we cannot fully understand the drama. Only if we appreciate, for example, that the solemn sinfonia (in Example 16.1b) represents the intervention of the god of music, who has been invoked in strophe 6 of *Possente spirto,* can we then understand who puts Charon to sleep, so that Orfeo can enter Hades and obtain Euridice. Since Orfeo is human, a species that by nature cannot completely master its passions, he is destined to lose control of them, as happens in act IV, when Music consequently does not support him, and he once again loses Euridice. Only at the end of the opera does Apollo state the moral that has already been made clear by the music: Orfeo the artist is immortal, but Orfeo the passionate human is a failure.

Gagliano's
Dafne

The texts of the two Mantuan operas of 1608 are both by the first opera librettist, Rinuccini, who wrote his new libretto, *Arianna* ("Ariadne"), for Monteverdi and revised his *Dafne* for a new setting by Gagliano. Like Rinuccini's earlier librettos, *Arianna* is a pastoral drama with roles for mythological gods and with the widest possible range of emotions. It plumbs the depths of sorrow in Arianna's lament, the only extended selection that survives. Many of the additions that Rinuccini made to his *Dafne* of 1608 are expressive rather than narrative. The chief example is the new lament that Gagliano set in expressive monody, first as a solo, then as a duet (see Example 16.2), and finally as a five-voice chorus. Making his dramatic points musically, Gagliano opens the work with a strophic prologue for Ovid and ends the drama with a strophic piece for Apollo. These are the only two pieces in the opera set as special-recitation monodies, symbolizing the relationship between these two great poets. Only Apollo's aria, however, is set with strophic variations, making it the focal point of the opera.

The Middle Baroque

Roman
opera

In the middle Baroque, opera underwent a great transformation as it emerged from academies and courts and became a popular genre. Its transformation began in Rome, the next important operatic center after Mantua, and continued at commercial theaters throughout Italy, especially in Venice. The practice of basing opera plots on pastoral mythology continued in Roman operas from *La morte d'Orfeo* ("The Death of Orpheus," 1619), set to music by Stefano Landi (c. 1586–1639), to *La Diana schernita da Amore* ("Diana Scorned by Cupid," 1629), with music by Giancinto Cornachioli (1599–c. 1673). To this pastoral basis were gradually added the entertaining aspects of

Comedy
enters
opera

the popular theater of Italy, the *commedia dell'arte* (which had borrowed many of these elements from Spanish plays): entangled plots with many characters (often disguised and sometimes transvestite), many scene changes, magical metamorphoses, and broad comedy often approaching the level of bedroom farce. In the 1619 *Orfeo,* the boatman Charon is a coarsely comic character. The 1629 *Diana* has an almost outrageous plot: Diana scorns Cupid, and he retaliates by convincing Endymion, Diana's beloved, to take the form of a hunter and watch over her. When the "hunter" is discovered watching Diana undress to bathe, she transforms him into a stag, has him pursued and killed, then has him wafted to heaven on a machine emblazoned with the heraldic arms of the papal family.

From 1623 to 1644, when Maffeo Barberini ruled as Pope Urban VIII, opera flourished in Rome. The papal family included three nephews whom the pope endowed with much "good fortune." They spent a great deal of money on lavish operatic entertainments during carnival seasons. Approximately a dozen librettos were written for them by Monsignor Giulio Rospigliosi (1600–1669), who became Pope Clement IX in 1667. *Il San Alessio* ("Saint Alexis") was the first of several he wrote about saints. Set to music by Landi for performance in 1631, it was revived with revisions during the next

Ex. 16.2   Marco da Gagliano, *Piangete, ninfe* from *Dafne*

"Alas, eclipsed and extinguished is the vibrant splendor of her serene eyes. Weep, nymphs, and with you let love weep."

three carnivals in a huge hall seating three thousand spectators. Such a large theater almost demands spectacle, and therefore the revised *Alessio* included magnificent stage sets and machinery, ballets, and impressive act-ending choruses.

In order to provide relief from the morose recitatives of the serious char-

La Décoration du Palais d'Apolon.
Representé et Inventé par Iaques Torelli de Fano en Italie, et gravé par Aveline. auec Priuil. du Roy.

Decor for the Palace of Apollo, engraved by Pierre Aveline (1654–1722), after the stage set and machines designed by Giacomo Torelli (1608–1678) for *Le nozze di Peleo e di Theti* ("The Marriage of Peleus and Thetis"; Paris, 1654). Fourteen musicians are seated in the foreground of the uppermost cloud machine, accompanying a celestial ballet of cupids. Deities have descended in other clouds in order to watch the rustic festivities onstage. The ingenious stage designer Torelli worked mainly in Venice and Paris. (Harvard Theatre Collection)

Comic servants acters, Rospigliosi added comic servants to the cast of *San Alessio,* thus introducing a practice that flourished in Italian opera until the early 1700s. He borrowed stereotypes for servants from the commedia dell'arte, and his opera *Il falcone,* or *Chi soffre speri* ("The Falcon, or Who Suffers May Hope," 1637), to music by Virgilio Mazzocchi (1597–1626) in collaboration with Marco Marazzoli (c. 1602–1662), is so full of their antics that it is often called the first comic opera. The servants sometimes poke fun at the impracticality of the endless moralizing and lamentation of the serious characters, but usually they merely state carefree and eminently practical views, often in dancelike arias.

Venetian opera In the 1630s, Roman operatic spectacles were imitated in northern Italian productions, which included many performers imported from Rome. One such production was *Ermiona,* with music by Sances, given at Padua with spectacular stage machinery in April 1636. Its stage effects and its Roman singers reappeared in *Andromeda,* performed at neighboring Venice during the carnival of 1637. *Andromeda,* the first opera to be performed in Venice, had a text by the theorbist Benedetto Ferrari (1597–1681) and music by the singer Francesco Manelli (1595–1667). During the next few years the Ferrari–Manelli troupe performed operas in other northern Italian cities as well, but they returned to Venice for every carnival season, and soon they faced competition there. A second Venetian theater began offering carnival-season operas in 1639, a third in 1640, and a fourth in 1641. Many additional theaters opened in the following years. From the 1640s until long after the end of the Baroque era, several Venetian theaters offered competing operas during almost every carnival season—when crowds flocked to Venice from all over Europe—and sometimes during other parts of the year as well.

In Venice, opera was a commercial enterprise. Although Venetian theaters were owned by noble families that often helped to pay for operating costs, they were managed by businessmen who either profited or lost money by their endeavors. Admission was collected at each performance, even from those who had rented a "box" for the season. Therefore the success of the enterprise depended upon the size of the audiences and the number of performances for each opera. When the Venetian season ended, the profit motive led impresarios and musicians to mount operas in other cities, many of which built opera houses based on Venetian models in the second half of the seventeenth century. The rapid growth in the number of commercial opera houses was a great boon to musicians seeking employment outside the traditional paths of court and Church patronage, and it consequently played a large role in breaking up these paternalistic systems. Although the best opera singers earned far more than the best opera composers, even the latter could amass a fortune by simultaneously working inside and outside the traditional systems. During the middle Baroque, the two most noted opera composers, Francesco Cavalli and Antonio Cesti, did just that.

Between 1640 and 1680, Italian opera underwent many changes in text and musical structure. These can be seen in four representative operas written for Venice: two by Monteverdi and one each by Cesti and Cavalli. The first is *Il ritorno d'Ulisse in patria* ("The Homecoming of Ulysses"; carnival, 1640), with a text by Giacomo Badoaro and music by Monteverdi, who was then in his seventy-third year.

Monteverdi's Ulisse

The opera opens with Penelope's lament about the continued absence of her husband, Ulysses, which Monteverdi set as expressive monody in duple meter. This emotion is immediately and sharply contrasted with a joyous love scene for two servants, which Monteverdi set mainly in the flowing triple meter of the relatively new *ciaccona.* The harmonic pattern of the ciaccona is present in a somewhat altered form in many triple-meter passages of the opera (see especially the closing duet, *Non si rammenti,* "Do not remember"). As a symbol of joy, it serves to interpret the drama musically, and it is even parodied by the joyless comic servant in act III, scene 1. Example 16.3

shows how Monteverdi sets narrative portions of a scene in duple-meter recitative and inserts triple-meter passages for expressions of joy. In the next scene, Ulysses' joyful phrase is developed into a strophic aria (one of only three in the opera), followed by a ritornello that clearly states the ciaccona pattern.

Monteverdi's *Poppea*   Monteverdi's last opera, *L'incoronazione di Poppea* ("The Coronation of Poppea"; carnival, 1643), has a libretto by Giovanni Francesco Busenello (1598–1659). The story is taken from the Roman historian Tacitus, but Busenello treated it merely as a skeleton upon which he could weave an exciting plot about the overwhelming power of love. The sexual love that Emperor Nero has for the voluptuous Poppea causes him to eliminate all obstacles to her coronation: he orders the death of the philosopher Seneca and the exile of the Empress Octavia. Poppea suggests these merciless actions to Nero out of her ambition to become empress. However, Poppea is merely an earthly personification of Love, and Cupid himself descends to protect her from her jilted lover Ottone in act II, scene 14. As in *Orfeo,* the plot thus moves on two levels: one of intense human passions, the other of allegory.

Poppea is a masterpiece of music drama because the setting by Monteverdi exquisitely interprets both levels of the plot, an extraordinary achievement for a composer in his seventy-sixth year. On the human level, his wonderfully expressive music ranges from the many laments of the rejected Ottone and Octavia to the joyous love scenes between Nero and Poppea. The latter scenes, as well as love scenes including servants, derive their passionate char-

Ex. 16.3   Claudio Monteverdi, *Il ritorno d'Ulisse in patria,* act I, scene 8

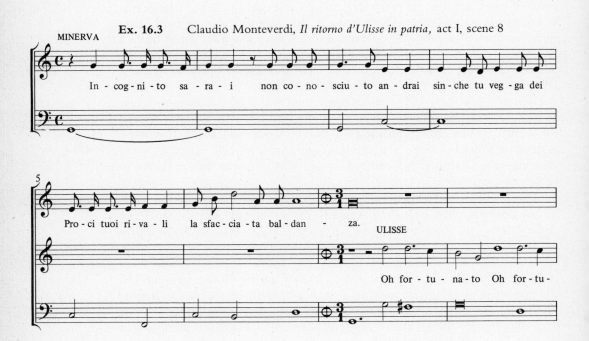

Ex. 16.3   cont.

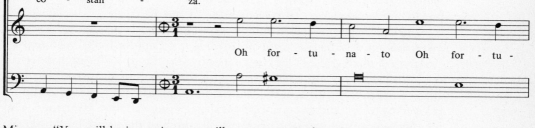

Minerva: "You will be incognito, you will go unrecognized until you see in the suitors, your rivals, their shameless pride; in chaste Penelope, her immutable constancy."
Ulysses: "O fortunate Ulysses!"

acter from Monteverdi's frequent insertion of triple-meter passages (sometimes based on the ciaccona pattern) and from his "loving" expansion of these passages by text repetition.

On the allegorical level, Monteverdi indicated the presence and power of Love with the relatively new *passacaglia* pattern. In the prologue, Fortune and Virtue join in a duet built over this pattern when they state the "moral" of the opera: Neither a human nor a divine heart can withstand Love. The pattern reappears in two other vocal duets: at about the midpoint of the opera (act II, scene 6) in *Bocca, ahi destin,* when Nero wonders at his "destiny," which is to be "wounded" by Love (i.e., Poppea); and in the closing duet, when he and Poppea marvel at their love for each other (*GMB*, no. 178). Earlier in the final scene, Monteverdi wrote the word "passacaglia" where an instrumental piece was to be inserted. Perhaps he intended that Love himself should appear triumphant during this piece.

Cesti's Orontea

Orontea (1649) was Cesti's first opera, set to a text by Giacinto Andrea Cicognini (1606–1651), and even though Cesti was a priest, he apparently sang the leading male role of Alidoro in several theaters. Three ladies (Queen Orontea, Silandra, and Giacinta, who is disguised as a boy) fall madly in love with him, and he responds affectionately to each in turn, without giving preference to any one over the others—a rather bizarre role for a priest to play. His score contains twelve strophic arias (many more than the three in *Ulisse* or the seven in *Poppea*) and five long nonstrophic ones. When these are added to the many arioso or aria-like passages, the result is an opera—perhaps the first one—in which the focus is clearly on the *bel canto* aria rather than on the recitative. The principal characters, who close the opera with an aria for four voices, all make their first entrance while singing an aria or arioso, then exit after some recitative dialogue. Exit arias are infrequent in *Orontea*. One aria sung by Alidoro in the midst of an action (that is, it is neither an entrance nor an exit aria) is an excellent example of Cesti's bel canto style (see Example 16.4). Its vocal range is less than an octave, its rhythm is a lilting triple with hemiola (see measures 13–14), and his harmonic motion is suave with expressive inflections (e.g., in measures 14–15 and 18).

Cavalli's Erismena

The final phase of Italian middle-Baroque opera is represented by a revised version of *Erismena* (carnival, 1670; first version in 1655), with text by Aurelio Aureli (fl. 1652–1708) and music by Cavalli. In 1670 Aureli deleted a few characters and some lewd scenes for servants, but the remaining nine characters provide sufficient foolishness. For example, the beautiful Aldimira is loved by a king and two princes, but she jilts them all for a "warrior," who is really a disguised woman (Erismena) in search of the prince by whom she has been abandoned. The revision of the *Erismena* music was probably done by Cavalli; if so, it may well have been his penultimate operatic composition.

Ex. 16.4   Antonio Cesti, *Destin placati un dì* from *Orontea*

Ex. 16.4   cont.

"Destiny, be placated one day. Most pure is my heart, innocent the desires of my soul. Most cruel destiny, be placated one day."

Used by permission of The Wellesley Edition.

For each new production, a Baroque opera was revised for the new cast and theater, and all revising was usually done by local hacks who had nothing to do with the original librettist and composer. By means of such revisions, any opera could incorporate the latest fashions, which were dutifully followed in the hope of promoting a commercial success. By the early 1670s, it was modish to include many arias, and the revised *Erismena* has sixty-one. Nearly half of them are strophic, and most strophes have an ABB structure, in which A and B each represent one or more lines of text. The B-section text states the main point of the strophe, which is stressed not only by repetition of this text, but also by an ensuing instrumental ritornello based on the musical motives of the B section.

Arias at exits   Both the ABB structure and the reinforcing ritornello were already common in the 1650s—for example, in *Orontea* and in the first version of *Erismena*. What is new in the 1670 version of the latter is the emphasis on exit arias: There are thirty-four of them, compared with only thirteen entrance and fourteen mid-action arias. After singing either of the latter two types, characters remain on stage, and the intensity of the mood stressed in their aria is soon lost. But when a character exits immediately after "discharging" his emotion in an aria, the aria serves to "charge" the drama. Not only does the character leave the scene in a highly emotional state, but he also leaves any characters remaining onstage in a similar condition.

The Late Baroque

Exit arias are therefore ideally suited to the serious dramas that were prevalent in the late Baroque. The farcical middle-Baroque dramas rapidly fell from favor in the 1680s and 1690s, and after about 1690 the nobler qualities were greatly stressed (partly owing to the growing influence of French dramatic ideals), while comedy was confined to separate scenes for two or three servants. Such comic scenes customarily occurred as *intermezzi* (i.e., intermissions) on the "apron," or front part, of the stage during a change of set. Venetian librettists of the 1690s were so eager to disown the farcical plots hitherto associated with their city that they often had their works printed without any comic scenes, even when such scenes were included in performances.

Scarlatti's penultimate opera   A fine, representative late-Baroque libretto is *Marco Attilio Regolo,* written by the Venetian Matteo Noris (d. 1714) and first set to music by Giovanni Pagliardi (1637–1702) in 1693. Alessandro Scarlatti reset it for the Roman carnival season of 1719. The text is typical of its time in that it has six noble characters and two servants. The voices required are equally typical, in that seven characters are youthful, and are consequently portrayed by sopranos and altos. Tenors infrequently appeared in Italian Baroque opera, and basses played only old servants (as in this opera) or old kings (as in *Erismena*). In late-Baroque opera, love remains the controlling passion, but instead of being opposed to virtue (as in *Poppea*) it is always allied with it in a happy ending, no matter how unconvincingly the alliance is brought about. Each character is a stereotype who seems unsurpassable: e.g., Attilio seems to be the noblest of all Romans, Amilcare the fiercest of all dictators, and Eurilla the greatest of all teases. In Noris' libretto, the servant pair develop their love affair in five comic scenes (cut to three in Scarlatti's setting), which occur during set changes within the acts and at the ends of acts I and II.

Marco Attilio Regolo is the penultimate of Scarlatti's seventy or more operas, and its traits are those of the final phase of Baroque opera in Italy. Its plot is narrated in *secco* recitative, which includes many expressive subtleties but consists mainly of conventional rhythms, chord progressions, and cadences. It thus provides some welcome relief from the intensity of the rest of the setting. A few of the most emotional situations, such as Attilio's prison scene and Fausta's two laments over the presumed death of Attilio, are set in *recitativo accompagnato* ("accompanied recitative"), which came into use about 1650 and includes parts for two violins and sometimes a viola in addition to the ever-present continuo.

The remaining vocal music includes forty-three arias for noble characters, eight for servants, and two choruses (which begin and end the opera). Although a small chorus may have been employed for this opera, the few "choral" pieces that appear in the commercial Italian Baroque operas written after 1650 were ordinarily sung by an ensemble consisting only of the soloists. The scenes for two comic servants have their typical structure in late-Baroque opera: each servant sings a solo, then joins in an exit duo. The pieces are usually in da capo form. Pieces for noble characters are almost always in da capo form, are usually placed at exits, and are generally solos.

In seventeenth-century opera arias (as in recitatives), the upper strings were occasionally added to the usual continuo accompaniment in order to intensify the dramatic effect. In *Marco Attilio Regolo,* every aria includes treble instruments. The violins play in unison or are divided into two groups, while the violas play a separate part or double the continuo part. Sometimes oboes double the violin part(s), but they have separate parts in only a few pieces. A bassoon may have played along with the bass instruments whenever the oboes were playing. Two trumpets appear only in military contexts, while two cornetts (presumably played by the trumpeters) and two French horns are called for only in crowd scenes.

Scarlatti's orchestra of trumpets, horns, oboes, bassoon, and strings is typical of the late Baroque and early Classic periods. His opening *sinfonia* is likewise typical in its fast–slow–fast construction: first a Presto in duple meter with many arpeggios and stepwise flourishes, then an Adagio interlude, then a Presto in a dancelike triple meter. Such late-Baroque opera sinfonias are thought to be the chief forerunners of the later *symphony*. In Italian Baroque operas, the only independent orchestral pieces were the opening sinfonias and the infrequent pieces accompanying some extraordinary action onstage, e.g., a dance or the descent of a machine. Throughout the Baroque era, the main function of the orchestra was to play the ritornellos associated with arias.

The sinfonia

Marco Attilio Regolo is one among thousands of Italian late-Baroque

Temple of Victory in Rome, engraved by Mathäus Küsel (1629–1681), after the stage design by Ludovico Burnacini (1636–1707) for act III, scene 2 of *Il fuoco eterno* ("The Eternal Fire"; Vienna, 1674), an opera with text by Nicolò Minato (c. 1630–1698) and music by Draghi. Onstage are trumpets and drums, sixteen name characters, and a large chorus of Roman citizens. This festive opera celebrated the birth of a daughter to Emperor Leopold I and his second wife, Claudia Felicitas. (Harvard Theatre Collection)

operas, almost all of which followed the same basic recipe. The ingredients were devised in order to maintain a high degree of dramatic intensity, but they lost much of their effectiveness through overexposure and an increasing lack of variety. Yet, largely because the recipe had an almost incredible success in an international market, it continued to be used well into the Preclassic era.

Germany and Austria

The South

Many German-speaking cities, especially Catholic cities in the south, were cultural satellites of Italy during the Baroque era. But Italian composers and operatic traditions were often active in northern, Protestant cities as well.

For example, Steffani wrote his first five operas for the southern city of Munich (1681–1688), his next seven for the northern city of Hanover (1689–1696), and his last three for the west-central city of Düsseldorf (1707–1709). By far the most illustrious tradition was maintained in Vienna, where the emperors Leopold I (d. 1705), Joseph I (d. 1711), and Charles VI (d. 1740) themselves composed Italianate music and employed hundreds of Italian composers, librettists, singers, and stage designers. Four of their principal composers were Antonio Draghi (1635–1700), who provided the court with about 175 secular dramatic works (operas and shorter theatrical pieces) from 1669 to 1699; Giovanni Bononcini, who provided about 20 from 1699 to 1737; Francesco Conti (1681–1732), who contributed about 25 from 1711 to 1732; and Antonio Caldara (c. 1670–1736), who wrote about 55 from 1714 to 1736. The two best-known Italian librettists of the late Baroque, Apostolo Zeno (1668–1750) and Pietro Metastasio (1698–1782), were likewise employed for many years in Vienna.

Vienna

The North
The influx of Italians into southern Germany left little opportunity for the native Germans there. Johann Fux was one of the few non-Italians to write musico-dramatic pieces for Vienna; from 1702 to 1731 he provided eighteen of them, all sung to Italian texts. In the north, the situation was different. Operas composed by Germans and sung in the native language were produced for special occasions in a number of northern cities during the seventeenth century. Hamburg was the only German-speaking city that had a flourishing public opera house—established on the Venetian model—during the era. It opened in 1678 with an opera, *Adam und Eva,* set by Schütz's pupil Johann Theile (1646–1724). Several other biblical stories were likewise represented on the Hamburg stage during its first fifteen years. During this time, all but two of the forty-five operas produced were composed by five Germans: Theile, Nikolaus A. Strungk (1640–1700), Johann W. Franck (1644–c. 1710), Johann P. Fortsch (1652–1732), and Johann G. Conradi (d. 1699). The two exceptions were French operas with music by Lully, performed at Hamburg in German. The French tradition was continued there from 1693 to 1695, when five operas were produced with music by Johann S. Cousser (or Kusser, 1660–1727), who had spent six years in Paris, where he had studied with Lully.

Hamburg

The predominant foreign influence, however, was Italian rather than French. From the beginning, Hamburg librettos were usually more or less modeled after Italian ones. From 1693 until the Hamburg theater closed in 1738, many works by Italian composers were performed. Sometimes they were sung in German—as were, for example, six operas that Steffani had originally written for Hanover. From 1703 on, a common practice was to translate only the recitatives (which tell the story), leaving the arias in Italian. The Hamburg theater was thus basically Italianate when three famous Germans worked there: Reinhard Keiser (1674–1739), who wrote about sixty operas for it from 1693 to 1734; Mattheson, who served there as a singer, harpsichordist, director, and composer from 1696 to 1711; and Telemann, who served as composer and director from 1721 to 1738.

Hamburg operas were usually full of varied delights because they retained the "vulgarities" that were purged from Italian operas in the 1680s and 1690s. *Der hochmütige, gesturzte und wieder erhobene Croesus* ("The Strong-Willed, Captured, and Then Released Croesus") is an excellent example. Its text is a 1684 reworking by Lucas von Bostel (1649–1716) of an Italian *Creso* of 1678. It kept its middle-Baroque characteristics when reset by Keiser in 1711, even when he revised it for a new production in 1730. Its middle-Baroque traits include a large number of characters (twelve), comic servants who ridicule their masters, infrequent exit arias, and infrequent da capo arias. Keiser's 1730 score is "modern" in its full orchestral accompaniment for arias; only three are accompanied by continuo alone. Its chief German features are the absence of castrati, the singing of all male roles by tenors and basses, and the prominence of dancelike songs, frequently in binary form, that sound like "folk songs." One such piece (see Example 16.5; for another example, see Lerner, no. 78) resembles middle-Baroque arias in its brevity and strophic form (each strophe being in binary form).

France

The Middle Baroque

French opera officially began when the librettist Pierre Perrin (c. 1620–1675) obtained a patent to found an Académie d'Opéra, or public opera house, at Paris in 1669. French opera incorporated much from French tragedy, the ballet de cour, and the commedia dell'arte plays given in Paris, with much music interspersed, from 1603 on. However, the chief models for French operas were Roman ones of the 1630s and Venetian ones of the 1640s and 1650s. The prime minister and virtual ruler of France from 1642 to 1661 was Cardinal Mazarin, an Italian who became a naturalized Frenchman in 1639. Six notable operas were performed in Italian under Mazarin's protection from 1645 to 1662. Their plots are full of farcical incidents, but the chief attraction was clearly the elaborate stage machinery designed by Italians. The first work was *La finta pazza* ("The Feigned Madwoman), with text by Giulio Strozzi (1583–1660) and music by Francesco Sacrati (1605–1650). It included some spoken dialogue in the manner of the commedia dell'arte, a feature that probably made it the first opera to have great commercial success throughout Italy as well as a prime position in French operatic history. The last two had music by Cavalli and were given to celebrate the wedding of Louis XIV and Maria Theresa of Spain: *Xerse* ("Xerxes," 1660) and *Ercole amante* ("Hercules in Love," 1662), the latter with text by Francesco Buti (d. 1682).

Because ballet had become an integral part of court spectacles in France, elaborate dances were added to these operas. In the opera of 1654 (see illustra-

Italian ancestors

Ex. 16.5   Reinhard Keiser, *Croesus,* Arietta from act I, scene 2

"Two hearts truly in love feel the same pains without talking about them."

From Denkmäler Deutscher Tonkunst, vol. 37, ed. Max Schneider and Hans-Joachim Moser. Copyright 1958 by Breitkopf & Härtel, Wiesbaden. Used by permission.

tion on page 392), the dancers included the sixteen-year-old Louis XIV and the twenty-two-year-old Jean-Baptiste Lully (1632–1687), a Florentine who had just entered the king's service. Lully provided the ballet music for the operas of 1660–1662 and became a naturalized Frenchman in 1661. In the 1660s he was the favored composer of court ballets, and he collaborated with Molière on *comédies-ballets*. During this time he also became acquainted with French tragedy. With his firsthand knowledge of theatrical practices in both Italy and France, he was probably better suited to the task of creating a French operatic tradition than anyone else in the country.

Lully's chief librettist was Philippe Quinault (1635–1688). Chief among his eleven *tragédies lyriques* were *Thésée* ("Theseus," 1675) and *Armide* (1686). *Thésée* held the stage longer than any other opera by Lully. It kept the Quinault–Lully tradition alive through twenty Parisian productions from 1675 to 1779 (nearly up to the time of the French Revolution). In sharp contrast, operatic fashions in Italy changed so rapidly that a musical setting was rarely

Lully's
Thésée

produced more than once in any city. Quinault's *Thésée* was also translated into German by Von Bostel, who added coarse comedy to it in the Italian manner. Strungk set it for a production at Hamburg in 1683. It was later "converted," by Nicola Haym (1679–1729) and Handel, into an Italian late-Baroque opera that was produced at London in 1715. Three more settings of the French version were made in the late 1700s, ending the remarkable history of this fine libretto.

Thésée includes four noble characters and three servants, and, as in Italian opera, Love rules them all. In comparison with Italian librettos of the 1670s, *Thésée* has a straightforward plot that treats the noble aspects of each character extensively. Indeed, French taste was unsympathetic to anything but nobility on the stage, and after *Thésée* Quinault wrote no more roles for comic servants.

Lully's musical setting is like that of an Italian opera of about 1640, in that

Thésée (1675), the climactic scene (act V, scene 4), engraved as the frontispiece to the libretto by François Chaveau (1613–1676), after the stage design by Carlo Vigarani (1623–1713?). The principal characters are, from left to right, Æglé, Thésée, Egée, and Médée. Médée has just seen her plot frustrated and has begun to flee. (Harvard Theatre Collection)

it consists chiefly of duple-meter recitative, with triple-meter insertions that lyrically stress chosen lines of text. As in Monteverdi's late operas, these lyrical passages occur in the midst of an action; they are not customary at entrances and exits, as arias were in Italian operas of the 1670s. Most are in the ABB form prevalent in Italian middle-Baroque opera, but in Lully's operas the A section of arias with this form is usually recitative-like. In his ABA or ABACA arias, the B and C sections are usually recitative-like.

The spectacle of machines, choruses, and ballets was as much a part of Lully's operas as it had been of earlier Italian operas, especially those performed in Paris. About 25 performers (10 singers and 15 instrumentalists) ordinarily sufficed for an Italian opera of the 1670s, but *Thésée* had about 130: 46 singers (10 women plus 36 tenors and basses; castrati did not appear in French opera); 33 dancers (all male, since women dancers were not allowed on the stage at Paris until 1681); and about 51 instrumentalists. The chorus comments on the action and also sings in some of the *divertissements* ("diversions"). Each prologue or act has one diversion, which usually consists of a dance air, a vocal piece, a second dance air, and a second vocal piece. Dancers appear only in the diversions and perform during the vocal pieces as well as the instrumental airs. Often the vocal pieces are merely the instrumental ones with text added—demonstrating, incidentally, the usual lack of stylistic difference between Lully's vocal and orchestral writing.

The orchestra begins the opera with Lully's typical overture, called a **The French overture**: a slow, dotted-note, duple-meter section; then a fast, fugal one in either duple or triple meter; and sometimes a recall of the opening slow section at the end. The overture, prelude-like movements within the opera, dance airs, and choral accompaniments are scored in five orchestral parts. Oboes and bassoons double the strings and continuo on the outer parts, while the three inner parts, played by strings alone, are considered "fillers." The ritornellos and accompaniments for bass solos are written in trio texture, and were played by a group of soloists called the *petit choeur*. All other solos, duets, and trios were accompanied only by the continuo. Contemporaries of Lully nevertheless complained that even this accompaniment was too loud.

The Late Baroque

After Lully's death in 1687, the Académie languished, largely because it was ignored by the aging king, who suffered several crushing military defeats in the early 1700s. The hero of Lully's tragédies lyriques had symbolically glorified the victorious Louis XIV, a glorification that had a hollow ring during the king's declining years. Nevertheless, new works continued to be produced in the heroic tradition that Lully had firmly established. *Thétis et Pélée* ("Thetis and Peleus," 1689), written by Bernard Le Bovier de Fontenelle (1657–1757) and set to music by Lully's student Pascal Collasse (1649–1709), was, however, the only unqualified success until Rameau's *Hippolyte* was produced in 1733.

During the intervening years, the most popular genre at the Académie

The opéra-ballet

was a "modern" one (that is, one without precedent in antiquity) called the *opéra-ballet*. Its success was considered a victory for the "moderns" in their literary battles with the "ancients." Sixteen opéras-ballets had been produced by 1733, the first one being *L'Europe galante* (1697), written by Houdar de La Motte (1672–1731) and set to music by André Campra (1660–1744). La Motte's characters are gallant, modern Europeans rather than ancient heros. He replaced the ancient five-act structure with a separate dramatic sketch for each act. The sketch served mainly to set the scene for an entry of the ballet corps. Campra's setting was especially modern in its inclusion of da capo arias in the newest Italian fashion; the full score (printed in 1724) included two arias in Italian and a note that several other Italian arias had been performed in the stage version. Campra's third opéra-ballet, *Les Fêtes vénitiennes* ("Venetian Festivals," 1710), on a text by Antoine Danchet (1671–1740), included several French airs written in the Italian style, in addition to three arias in Italian. Perhaps the subject, a Venetian carnival, justified both the Italianate music and the commedia-like characters, who have a notoriously pragmatic attitude toward life and love (see *GMB,* no. 261). Opéras-ballets featured lighthearted comedy only until the 1720s, when they began to favor the ancient heroes characteristic of lyric tragedies, thus preparing the way for Rameau's great works.

Charles Nicolas Cochin the Younger (1715–1790), *The Triumph of Rameau*. Rameau with a roll of music paper in hand, appears to be conducting the musicians who follow him. An angel meanwhile descends (on a cloud-machine) to his triumphal chariot and crowns him. (Courtesy, Fogg Art Museum, Harvard University; Gift—Twelve friends in memory of Alice James [Mrs. William] through Gifts for special uses fund)

While in his fifties, Jean-Philippe Rameau wrote his first stage works, including an opéra-ballet, a pastoral opera, and three lyric tragedies: *Hippolyte et Aricie* (1733), *Castor et Pollux* (1737), and *Dardanus* (1739). Campra reportedly said that *Hippolyte* had enough music for ten similar works, and the same may be said of all Rameau's theater pieces. *Hippolyte* might be the best of them, partly because of its gripping plot. Simon Joseph Pellegrin (1663–1745) based his libretto on Racine's great tragedy *Phèdre* ("Phaedra," 1677), which was in turn based primarily upon a tragedy of Euripides. Partly because much time was allotted to the customary diversions (the prologue and five acts each having one), Pellegrin's characters cannot compare with Racine's in psychological complexity, but Rameau's expressive setting largely compensates for this deficiency.

Rameau's music is unmistakably in the French tradition founded by Lully: nothing of it could fit into an Italian opera. Rameau, however, extended Lully's model in every way in order to heighten the dramatic effect. His lyrical outbursts or airs, choruses (especially *Que ce rivage* in act III, scene 8), and dance airs were often much longer. He used a wider range of keys and chords, and he much more frequently employed the full orchestra in accompaniments for recitatives and airs. The intensification is particularly effective in tragic situations. When Phèdre last appears, at the end of act IV, the thunder of the gods is vividly represented in the orchestra, her fervent prayer is greatly strengthened by an exceptionally full and widely spaced string accompaniment, and the choral comment is set as starkly as possible in order to convey the superfluity of words. Any Italian opera written after about 1650 would have had a virtuoso aria at the end of an act, but for Rameau recitative was still the expressive core of the drama. Even in solo airs for the principal characters (in contrast with airs in diversions), Rameau's vocal lines are declamatory rather than florid. Thus the focus never veers from the drama but always remains on the plight of the characters. Whether they are portrayed by singers with incredible vocal prowess is relatively unimportant, especially in comparison with the great importance of such prowess in contemporary Italian operas.

Spain

Italianate Works

Completely sung stage works were rare in Baroque Spain. The three about which something is known were commissioned by Philip IV (reg. 1621–1665) from two of the great playwrights of the "Golden Age" of Spanish drama, Lope de Vega and Pedro Calderón de la Barca. The texts survive, but music is extant for only the first act of the final work. The earliest-known work, written by Vega in 1629, is a brief pastoral drama whose composer is unidentified. In his preface Vega stressed the novelty of both the stage machinery, designed by a Florentine, and the music, which reportedly expressed all the affects that were in the text. Calderón's two operatic works were written in 1660 and 1662. The second one is *Celos aun del aire matan* ("Jealousy, Even from the Air, Kills"), set to music by Juan Hidalgo (d. 1685). This work resembles Italian operas of the 1630s and 1640s in its mythological plot (featuring gods and pastoral characters), magical transformations (utilizing stage machinery), and musical style (including expressive recitative; brief airs, usually in triple meter; and short choruses). Some of the airs, however, have the flavor of Spanish songs.

Hidalgo's opera

Native Traditions

Native art songs—such as the *villancico* and *seguidilla*—were frequently heard as *incidental music* in Spanish Baroque plays. Indeed, during the reign of Philip IV, the spectacle of song and dance occurred so often in plays presented at court that time was available for only one or two rather than the customary three acts. From the 1650s on, a two-act play that combined spoken dialogue with musical interludes was called a *zarzuela,* after the name of a palace near Madrid, one of the royal residences in which these works were given. Calderón created this genre, which intermixed ancient heroes and contemporary rustics just as Italian middle-Baroque opera did. Throughout the Baroque era, it remained a courtly genre. The three outstanding late-Baroque composers of zarzuelas were all members of the royal chapel at Madrid: Sebastián Durón (1660–1716), Antonio Líteres Carrión (1670–1747), and José de Nebra (1702–1768). Their king was a Frenchman, Philip V (reg. 1700–1746), whose two wives were Italians, and so it is hardly surprising that their works are more notable for their quasi-French spectacle and quasi-Italian musical style than for their native Spanish traits.

The zarzuela

England

The Early and Middle Baroque

In seventeenth-century England, as in Spain, the strong tradition of spoken drama at first allowed only incidental music, but plays produced after 1650 sometimes incorporated extensive musical interludes, so that these works became semi-operas. Such interludes had their origin in the court *masques* that flourished during the reigns of James I (1603–1625) and Charles I (1625–1649). The main ancestors of the masque were the Italian *mascherata* (a type of *villanella* to be sung at a procession or masked ball) and *intermedio* and the French *ballet de cour,* all of which typically consisted of a series of loosely related dances. By comparison, the *Balet comique de la royne* performed in Paris in 1581 was exceptionally well unified, and it was a direct influence on Ben Jonson (1573–1637), who wrote twenty-five masque texts from 1605 to 1631. He created a distinctive structure for the masque, consisting of: (1) a prologue, in which an allegorical plot is introduced; (2) an anti-masque, in which costumed commoners (who were professional dancers) depict some aspects of disorder and vice in undignified dances; (3) a spectacular scene

The masque

transformation; (4) the masque proper, in which costumed noblemen depict some aspects of order and virtue in dignified figure dances; (5) the revels, or masked ball, in which the noble spectators join; and, sometimes, (6) an epilogue. The essential element was the dance. Next in importance was the staging, the sets and machines, which were invented by Inigo Jones (1573–1652) after Italian models. The text was third in importance. The music served to accompany the other three elements and consisted mainly of instrumental dance pieces in binary form and of ayres or other songs performed by soloists or chorus. The allegorical plot was usually developed in spoken dialogue, but exceptions did exist: Jonson's preface to *Lovers Made Men* (1617) relates that "the whole Masque was sung after the Italian Manner, *stylo recitativo.*"

English court and public theaters were closed from the beginning of the Civil War in 1642 until a few years before the end of the Commonwealth in 1660. During this time a few masques were given for instructive purposes at schools. One example is *Cupid and Death* (1653), written by James Shirley (1596–1666), composed by Christopher Gibbons (1615–1676), and revived in 1659 with additional music by Matthew Locke, the most important English theater composer in the generation before Purcell.

Locke

The Late Baroque

The only two extant operas by seventeenth-century English composers are *Venus and Adonis* (c. 1684), set to music by John Blow, and *Dido and Aeneas* (1689), with text by Nahum Tate (1652–1715) and music by Henry Purcell. Although both are exceptionally fine works, they are somewhat peripheral to the main English theater tradition, having been privately performed: Blow's at court as "a Masque for the Entertainment of the King," and Purcell's at Josias Priest's school for gentlewomen in Chelsea. Because the court masque was an important model for both, dancing takes up much time in these works, since not only instrumental pieces but also vocal airs and choruses were often danced to, just as in the diversions of Lully's operas.

Operas by Blow and Purcell

Both Blow and Purcell began their works with a French overture and continued by intermingling French, Italian, and English elements. French and English ones are heard in the instrumental pieces, vocal ensembles, and choruses, except that the closing chorus of lament in each opera is perhaps based on Italian models. Italian middle-Baroque arias of lamentation over a basso ostinato were models for Dido's two great airs (the first is given in Lerner, no. 72; the second in *HAM* II, no. 255), and Purcell clearly imitated the Italian late-Baroque aria in *Pursue thy conquest, Love*. Recitative is relatively infrequent in these and all English seventeenth-century dramatic works, but when it occurs it is usually very expressive. For example, when Aeneas is ordered by the gods to leave Dido (see Example 16.6), he musically shakes his fist at them (measures 27–28) in the midst of his lamentation. The utterly convincing and endlessly varied speech-rhythms in Purcell's recitatives are totally unlike those in Italian or French recitative; the "Scotch snap" (♪♩) is one distinctively English trait (see measures 21, 22, and 25).

Dido and Aeneas was first publicly performed as "a Mask in Four Musical

Entertainments" at a London theater in 1700. Thus broken up, revised, and rearranged, it formed four diversions within a performance of Shakespeare's *Measure for Measure,* which was also broken up, revised, and rearranged. Even in their altered states, the two works were completely unrelated, but that was no hindrance to a Restoration theater manager who found that extraordinary "Musical Entertainments" were the best way to draw crowds. During the Restoration period (1660–c. 1710), plenty of "ordinary" music was available to be performed with a spoken play. A small orchestra played four instrumental dances and an overture before the first act, an "act tune" before each subsequent act, and mood-setting music here and there. It also accompanied

Ex. 16.6   Henry Purcell, *Dido and Aeneas,* act II, closing recitative

Ex. 16.6 cont.

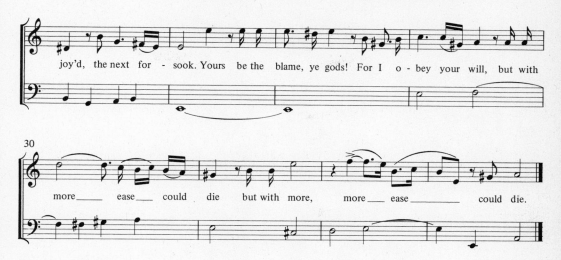

songs and dances. Many plays also included several "extraordinary" interludes featuring song and dance; they are called *dramatic operas,* and the finest
examples are the four written by Purcell from 1690 to 1695.

Around 1700, many of the musical entertainments that drew crowds to a
play in London featured Italian music performed by Italians, and from 1705
on, Italian opera was the principal kind of musical theater there. The London
opera house, unlike its counterparts in Italy, was open most of the year.
Therefore it could offer a regular and rather generous salary to musicians,
who consequently lived free from the restrictions of court and Church patronage. No wonder, then, that the London opera attracted the finest Italian
singers, the best European instrumentalists, and the greatest composer of Italian late-Baroque opera, George Frideric Handel.

Between 1711 and 1741, Handel composed thirty-six Italian operas for
London. All have the typical late-Baroque structure of recitatives alternating
with da capo exit arias, and all manifest Handel's uncanny ability to write
arias in which the precise emotion needed in any dramatic situation is conveyed as forcefully as possible. Since he had many of the greatest living singers and instrumentalists at his disposal, his usual scoring is rather thin and
"airy" in order to allow performers ample room to embellish and thus to
deepen the affectiveness of his forceful music. At some dramatic highpoints,
however, he intensified the mood greatly by dazzling scorings. For instance,
when Cleopatra sings *V'adoro, pupille* ("I adore you, eyes") in order to capti-
vate Caesar in *Giulio Cesare* (1724; libretto by Haym), her languishing melodic line unfolds over the plushest orchestral carpet Handel could envision:
muted strings, viola da gamba, theorbo, harp, oboe, and bassoons playing
offstage, echoed by muted strings and continuo in the pit. Likewise, when
battle-ready Rinaldo sings *Or la tromba* ("Now the trumpet") near the end of

**Handel's
operas**

William Hogarth (1697–1764), *The Laughing Audience* (1733). In the foreground the etching shows two bassoonists and an oboist playing in the orchestra. The audience might be viewing a comic pantomime or a ballad opera. (Courtesy, Museum of Fine Arts, Boston)

Rinaldo (1711; libretto by Aaron Hill, 1685–1750, and Giacomo Rossi), his heroic line concertizes with the loudest combination Handel could muster, including parts for four trumpets and timpani in addition to the usual complement of oboes, bassoons, strings, and continuo.

The great richness of Handel's operas results from textual as well as musical considerations, because his librettos include much that was either long outmoded in, or foreign to, the Italian mainstream. His *Serse* (1738) is based on an eighty-four-year-old Italian libretto, while his *Teseo* (1715) is modeled after a forty-year-old French one. French-style diversions, including scene transformations, ballets, and choruses, are featured in his *Alcina* (1735; libretto by Antonio Fanzaglia). However, spectacular scenic effects also played a prominent role in English dramatic operas, which were clearly the basis for the many visual extravagances in *Rinaldo,* the first opera Handel wrote for London.

English influence on Handel   English influence is, however, much more apparent in Handel's twenty-four theater works with English texts. Most are oratorios based on biblical subjects, even though they were written to be performed in the opera house rather than in a church. Five are based on secular dramatic texts and may consequently be called Handel's English operas, even though all except the first were originally done "in the manner of an oratorio," that is, in a concert version without costumes or acting. The texts of all except the last work are by renowned English Baroque poets and playwrights: *Acis and Galatea* (1718) is probably by John Gay (1685–1732); *Alexander's Feast* (1736) is by John Dryden (1631–1700); *L'Allegro ed il Penseroso* (1740), by John Milton (1608–1674); *Semele* (1744), by William Congreve (1670–1729); and *Hercules* (1745), by Thomas Broughton (1704–1774). In all these works, just as in seventeenth-century English masques and dramatic operas, vocal ensembles and choruses are as common as solos. Thus the texture is extremely well varied, and the drama moves compellingly. In sum, Handel's English oratorios stand with his English operas as the finest results of his fusion of international styles at the culmination of the Baroque era.

Summary

During the Baroque era, music was an essential ingredient of most theatrical spectacles, and much of the finest music by the best composers was written for them. In most theatrical genres, however, music did not play an essential, dramatic role. It never had much more than a decorative function in the early-Baroque Italian *intermedio,* French *ballet,* English *masque,* or Spanish *play*. The same holds true for their late-Baroque, semi-operatic descendants: French *opéra-ballet,* English *dramatic opera,* and Spanish *zarzuela*. Here music, like painted scenery, was needed to establish moods, and like machines and dances it was part of the entertainment.

In opera, however, music played a crucial dramatic role. It elucidated and stressed meanings and emotions that otherwise might have gone unnoticed, and one unusual rhythm, chord, or melodic interval was often enough to reveal the unexpected. The composer thereby interpreted the drama through his music. The international acceptance of this dramatic role for music in the new genre of opera is one of the most important musical developments of the Baroque era. An understanding of opera is the key to an understanding of the several church and chamber genres (e.g., sacred and secular cantatas) that emulated it. But understanding Baroque opera may be difficult, because its many conventions, literary and theatrical as well as musical, are unfamiliar to us.

Such conventions may be understood best by following them through three phases of Italian opera: an experimental, academic one in the early Baroque; a commedia-like, commercial one in the middle Baroque; and a "reformed" pan-European one in the late Baroque. German opera in Hamburg, French opera in Paris, and the very few Spanish and English seventeenth- and early eighteenth-century operas were all based chiefly on Italian middle-Baroque conventions, to which each also added some distinctive national traits. It was indeed the Italian middle-Baroque tradition, developed mainly outside of Italy, that became the basis for many post-Baroque developments in opera.

Bibliography

Books and Articles

General

GROUT, DONALD J. *A Short History of Opera,* 2nd ed. New York: Columbia University Press, 1965.

Italy: Origins of Opera

BROWN, HOWARD M. "How Opera Began: An Introduction to Jacopo Peri's *Euridice* (1600)." In *The Late Italian Renaissance, 1525–1630,* ed. Eric Cochrane, pp. 401–443. New York: Harper & Row, 1970.

PIRROTTA, NINO. "Temperaments and Tendencies in the Florentine Camerata." *Musical Quarterly* 40 (1954): 169–189.

Italy: Early to Middle Baroque

PIRROTTA, NINO. "Commedia dell'arte and Opera." *Musical Quarterly* 46 (1955): 305–324.

———. "Early Opera and Aria." In *New Looks at Italian Opera: Essays in Honor of Donald J. Grout,* ed. William Austin, pp. 39–107. Ithaca: Cornell University Press, 1968.

WORSTHORNE, SIMON TOWNELEY. *Venetian Opera in the Seventeenth Century.* Oxford: Clarendon Press, 1954.

Italy: Middle to Late Baroque

BURT, NATHANIEL. "Opera in Arcadia." *Musical Quarterly* 41 (1955): 145–170.

———. "Plus ça change." In *Studies in Music History: Essays for Oliver Strunk,* ed. Harold Powers, pp. 325–339. Princeton: Princeton University Press, 1968.

POWERS, HAROLD S. "Il Serse trasformato." *Musical Quarterly* 47 (1961): 481–492; 48 (1962): 73–92.

———. "L'Erismena travestita." In *Studies in Music History: Essays for Oliver Strunk,* ed. Harold Powers, pp. 259–324. Princeton: Princeton University Press, 1968.

France

ANTHONY, JAMES R. *French Baroque Music from Beaujoyeulx to Rameau,* rev. ed. New York: W. W. Norton, 1978.

GIRDLESTONE, CUTHBERT. *Jean-Philippe Rameau,* rev. ed. New York: Dover, 1969.

Spain

CHASE, GILBERT. *The Music of Spain,* 2nd ed. New York: Dover, 1959.

England

DENT, EDWARD J. *Foundations of English Opera: A Study of Musical Drama in England During the Seventeenth Century.* Cambridge, Eng.: Cambridge University Press, 1928.

MOORE, ROBERT E. *Henry Purcell and the Restoration Theatre.* Cambridge, Mass.: Harvard University Press, 1961.

Scores

For works by Handel, Monteverdi, and Purcell, see the bibliographies of scores in Chapters 14 and 15.

BLOW, JOHN. *Venus and Adonis,* ed. Anthony Lewis. Monaco: Oiseau Lyre, 1949.

CAMPRA, ANDRÉ. *L'Europe galante.* Paris: Ballard, 1724; reprinted, Farnborough, Eng.: Gregg, 1967.

———. *Les Fêtes vénitiennes,* ed. Max Lütolf. Paris: Heugel, 1971.

CESTI, ANTONIO. *Orontea,* ed. William Holmes. Wellesley, Mass.: Wellesley Edition, 1973.

GAGLIANO, MARCO DA. *Dafne* (excerpts), ed. Robert Eitner. Leipzig: Breitkopf & Härtel, 1881.

HIDALGO, JUAN. *Celos aun del aire matan,* ed. José Subirá. Barcelona: Biblioteca de Catalunya, 1933.

KEISER, REINHARD. *Croesus,* ed. Max Schneider, rev. Hans Joachim Moser. Denkmäler Deutscher Tonkunst, vol. 37. Wiesbaden: Breitkopf & Härtel, 1958.

LANDI, STEFANO. *San Alessio* (excerpts). In Hugo Goldschmidt, *Studien zur Geschichte der italienischen Oper im 17. Jahrhundert,* vol. 1, pp. 202–257.

LOCKE, MATTHEW. *Cupid and Death,* 2nd ed., ed. Edward J. Dent. Musica Britannica, vol. 2. London: Stainer & Bell, 1965.

LULLY, JEAN-BAPTISTE. *Les oeuvres complètes,* ed. Henry Prunières, 10 vols. (incomplete). Paris: Revue musicale et al., 1930–1939.

———. *Thésée* (piano-vocal score), ed. Théodore de Lajarte. Paris: Théodore Michaelis [1878].

PERI, JACOPO. *Euridice,* facsimile edition of the print of 1601, ed. Enrico Magni Dufflocq. Rome: Reale Accademia d'Italia, 1934.

RAMEAU, JEAN-PHILIPPE. *Oeuvres complètes,* ed. Camille Saint-Saëns et al., 18 vols. (incomplete). Paris: Durand, 1895–1924.

SCARLATTI, ALESSANDRO. *The Operas,* ed. Donald J. Grout et al. Cambridge, Mass.: Harvard University Press, 1974–   . Vol. 2 is *Marco Attilio Regolo,* ed. Joscelyn Godwin (1975).

For other works, see especially the list "Modern Editions of Operas or Excerpts from Operas Composed before 1800" in Grout, *A Short History of Opera,* pp. 769–786.

17

Church Music

SHATTERED by the Reformation, European Christendom had by the mid-sixteenth century split into Catholics, Lutherans, Anglicans, and Calvinists, and these groups were either aggressively or defensively militant during the Baroque era. While the last group ascetically restricted its music to block-chordal settings of psalm texts, the other three developed their musical traditions in splendid ways, and a staggering amount of church music was written. The churches provided the only elaborate music heard by most Europeans, for only a small percentage of persons heard the music performed in Baroque theaters and chambers. Church music had a far greater stylistic variety than that heard elsewhere, because it retained and revivified traditions consecrated by decades or centuries of use and at the same time incorporated the latest fashions. Almost all Baroque composers wrote church music, and for many, if not most, their chief goal was to be named *chapel-master* (*maestro di cappella* in Italian or *Kapellmeister* in German) or Lutheran *cantor* at any church that was a musical center. In this chapter, whenever feasible, we will discuss music in the context of its placement within a liturgical service, thereby manifesting a relationship between church function and musical style.

Italy

Liturgical Vocal Music

The nerve center for Catholic church music during the Baroque era was undoubtedly Italy, the site of the revivifying Council of Trent (1545–1563) and the spearhead of the consequent Counter-Reformation. Revisions of texts and of chant melodies occurred throughout the Baroque era. In some melodies, for example, melismas were eliminated, shortened, or shifted to accented syllables (for "proper" declamation). Accidentals were added and phrase beginnings and endings altered in order to achieve a "proper" modal-

416

Pier Leone Ghezzi (1674–1755), *Padre Giambattista Martini (1706–1784) of Bologna Conducting the Choir at the Basilica of the Twelve Apostles in Rome* (drawn May 1753). The work being performed, perhaps one in the stile antico by Martini, has a contrabass doubling the vocal bass. (Courtesy, Fogg Art Museum, Harvard University; Bequest—Meta and Paul J. Sachs)

ity. Some entirely new chant melodies were written. But chant was so frequently supplanted by vocal or instrumental polyphony during the era that its neglect was lamented by church synods from about 1690 onwards.

Liturgical polyphony written according to the precepts of the Counter-Reformation was supposed to induce pious thoughts appropriate to its liturgical placement. In vocal music, the words were to be clearly perceiv-

Stile antico

able and the pace gravely devout rather than gaily secular. Palestrina's six-voice Pope Marcellus Mass was regarded by many Baroque musicians as the chief model of the old church style, or *stile antico,* also known as the *stile da cappella* ("choral"), *grave* ("severe"), or *osservato* ("strict"). This style required only voices (at least four, and many more if a piece included two or more choruses), but they were sometimes supported in performance by a continuo part for organ. During the Baroque era, the choir of the Sistine Chapel (the private chapel of the popes) sang only works written in the stile antico, so that this style came to be identified especially with Rome. Such works were, however, performed throughout Italy, particularly during seasons of fasting, when the organ and other instruments were ordinarily prohibited by ecclesiastical authorities.

Because of a continuing demand, new works in the stile antico were written by many Italian composers, including Monteverdi, Gregorio Allegri (1582–1652), Orazio Benevoli (1605–1672), Giuseppe Ottavio Pitoni (1657–1743), Alessandro Scarlatti, and Antonio Lotti (1667–1740). The Baroque thus became the first stylistically self-conscious era—the first era to consciously cultivate an out-of-date polyphonic style alongside its own. The stile antico was not completely outmoded because Baroque composers updated it, much as they did chant. In comparison with Renaissance style, the Baroque stile antico is more homophonic, metric, tonal, and motivically sequential in construction. In performance, the Baroque probably included many more improvised ornaments and a far greater dynamic range, especially for a piece like Allegri's *Miserere* (c. 1638; see Example 17.1). For a long time this was the most celebrated piece in the repertory of the papal choir, which regarded the score as its own exclusive property.[1] Allegri's piece is for two choirs, one five-part (SATTB) and one four-part (SSAB), which sing Psalm 50 responsively, joining only for the final half-verse.

Falso-bordone

Allegri's work is written in the Renaissance style called *falsobordone,* in which a reciting tone (marked with X's in Examples 17.1 and 17.2) is clothed polyphonically. Not surprisingly, such settings reached their height of popularity during the early Baroque, because they exemplify both its ideal of aria-like texture and the contemporaneous Counter-Reformation ideal of homophonic declamation. When such stile antico pieces were performed, divisions were often added improvisatorily in at least the top voice. Similar ornaments are written into many of the *falsibordoni* composed around 1600 in the *stile moderno,* i.e., for solo voice(s) with continuo accompaniment. An excerpt from one, a setting of the Magnificat by Giovanni Luca Conforti (b.c. 1560), is given in Example 17.2.

Few-voiced concertato style

Like much other Baroque church music, Conforti's work is thus based on a Renaissance practice, yet written in the modern *concertato* style, which required at least one instrumental and one vocal performer. Few-voiced concertato church works—intended for only one soloist on each vocal or instrumental part—were extremely popular in the 1600s, because they satisfied both the general craze for solo singing and the desire to include vocal polyphony in services at churches that could not afford to maintain a choir.

Ex. 17.1   Gregorio Allegri, *Miserere*

"Have mercy upon me, O God, according to thy lovingkindness" (Psalm 50 [51], vs. 1).

In musical style and structure, solo and few-voiced concertato motets, such as Viadana's influential "church concertos" of 1602, resembled the monodic aria up to 1620 and the secular cantata from 1620 on. Early examples are therefore often in a ritornello (i.e., rondo-like) or strophic-variation form, while later ones usually alternate arias and recitatives. Their secular style may have violated Counter-Reformation precepts, but their employment of nonliturgical texts in the liturgy was a far more outrageous violation. Although many motets were written mainly for devotional purposes outside a liturgical service, any motet could be sung in a service, usually in place of chant during the Proper of the Mass (sometimes as an Introit, Gradual, or Alleluia, most often as an Offertory, rarely as a Communion) or during Vespers (as an antiphon, psalm, hymn, or Magnificat). Papal remonstrances—e.g., an edict of 1665 that banned both nonliturgical texts and soloistic motets from liturgical services—apparently had no effect. Vocal church music continued to be written in the most up-to-date secular style as well as in a modernized Renaissance style—the few-voiced concertato and antico styles, respectively.

Ex. 17.2   Giovanni Luca Conforti, *Magnificat*

". . . world without end, Amen."

From Conforti, *Passaggi sopra tutti li salmi* ("Divisions for all the Psalms"; Venice, 1607), reprinted in Jeffrey Kurtzman, "Some Historical Perspectives on the Monteverdi Vespers," *Analecta Musicologica* 15 (1975): 59. Copyright 1975 by Arno Volk Verlag, Cologne. Used by permission.

Many-voiced concertato style

When the vocal and instrumental soloists of the few-voiced style and the choruses of the antico style were combined in a single piece, the result was the many-voiced *stile concertato* ("concerted style") or *stile misto* ("mixed style"). It was feasible only at festive Mass or Vespers services in the most sumptuously endowed churches and is mainly associated with St. Mark's in Venice and St. Petronius in Bologna. The three leading composers at each church and their principal works are listed below.

St. Mark's in Venice

Giovanni Gabrieli, employed 1585–1612. *Symphoniae sacrae* ("Sacred Symphonies"; I, 1597; II, 1615): 72 motets and 5 Mass (Ordinary) movements in stile concertato, and 16 instrumental canzonas and sonatas.

Claudio Monteverdi, employed 1613–1643. *Sanctissimae Virgini* ("Most Holy Virgin," 1610); *Selva morale e spirituale* ("Moral and Spiritual Forest," 1641); and *Messa . . . et salmi* ("Mass . . . and Psalms," 1650): 3 Masses and 3 motets in stile da cappella, 2 Mass movements and 55 motets in stile concertato, and 5 moralistic Italian madrigals.

Francesco Cavalli, employed 1616–1676. *Musiche sacre* ("Sacred Music," 1656) and *Vesperi* ("Vespers," 1675): a Mass and 39 motets in stile concertato, and 6 instrumental sonatas.

St. Petronius in Bologna

Maurizio Cazzati, employed 1657–1671. From 1641 to 1678, he published 45 collections that include about 20 Masses and several hundred motets. About 5 collections employ the stile da cappella exclusively.

Giovanni Paolo Colonna, employed 1659–1695. His 12 published collections (1681–1694) contain only religious vocal music, mainly in stile concertato. Fifteen Masses by him in this style survive only in manuscripts.

Giacomo Antonio Perti, employed 1696–1756. He published only one collection, in 1735, but over 500 church works by him survive in manuscripts in the archive of San Petronius. They represent nearly 80 years (1678–1756) of composing for the church.

The many-voiced concertato works performed at these two churches are among the main representatives of what is often called the "colossal Baroque." By present-day standards, however, the number of performers employed is not great. Around 1600 St. Mark's had about fifteen to thirty singers, six to twenty instrumentalists (strings and winds), and two or three organists. (The larger numbers were employed for the most festive occasions.) A typical group in any one of Gabrieli's works for two to four groups or "choruses" consisted of both vocal and instrumental *soloists*. According to Praetorius, a vocal *chorus* was required only when a group was marked "cappella." Gabrieli's most famous motet, *In ecclesiis* ("In the Congregation," 1615; in *HAM* I, no. 157), uses three groups: SATB soloists with organ, SATB chorus (marked "cappella"), and a six-part instrumental ensemble (three cornetts, viola, and two trombones). The contrast of ornamental vocal and instrumental *solo* writing with plain *choral* writing is evident in such works, and a solo sound versus a ripieno or full sound is structurally as important in them as it is in late-Baroque instrumental concertos.

Refrains and solo–ripieno contrasts continued to be vital structural elements in the church music written by Gabrieli's successors. Monteverdi's most famous collection, that of 1610, includes fourteen concertato motets for Vespers of the Blessed Virgin: the opening choral response, five psalms, five motets that substitute for the antiphons ordinarily sung after each psalm (the last substitute is the *Sonata sopra Sancta Maria*), a hymn, and two Magnificats (one of which could be sung at First Vespers, the other at Second Vespers). Except for the antiphon substitutes, each setting is closely based on the ap-

Venice

Giovanni Antonio Canale called Canaletto (1697–1768), *View of the Piazza of San Marco in Venice, Facing the Basilica* (c. 1730–1735). The painter captured beautifully the radiant effect of the sunlight. (Courtesy, Fogg Art Museum, Harvard University; Grenville L. Winthrop Bequest)

propriate liturgical chant melody. Because psalm and Magnificat melodies have reciting tones, the polyphonic recitational style of falsobordone is pervasive. The opening response consists only of falsobordone alternating with three alleluia refrains, and the falsobordone is brilliantly accompanied by the opening toccata from Monteverdi's opera *Orfeo* (1607). Here is one indication that Monteverdi's secular and concertato church works are stylistically similar.

In comparison with Gabrieli, Monteverdi and Cavalli favored starker textural contrasts, introduced for dramatic effect. Such contrasts, like polychoral writing, are Baroque exaggerations designed to astound the listener. In the Credo of Cavalli's Mass, the effect is stunning when declamatory falsobordone for eight choral parts alternates with passages of fluent imitation for four soloists. Monteverdi's *Dixit Dominus* (1610) has equally startling contrasts: flowing, imitative passages over a bass that sings the chant (see Example 17.3, measures 71–76) alternate with falsobordone enlivened by fantastic ornamentation (measures 77–81; compare with Example 17.2). The combination of each imitative and ensuing falsobordone passage constitutes a strophe, so that *Dixit* is in strophic-variation form, including four such strophes (the first three followed by instrumental ritornellos) and a coda (the *Gloria Patri*). Example 17.3 shows part of strophe 3.

The monumental stile misto tradition begun at St. Mark's reached its Italian culmination at San Petronius, which had splendid church music during the seventeenth century, when Cazzati, Colonna (1637–1695), and Perti (1661–1756) served successively as its chapel-masters. Although Cazzati was

Ex. 17.3   Claudio Monteverdi, *Dixit Dominus*

Ex. 17.3   cont.

"You are a priest forever after the order of Melchizedek. The Lord is at your right hand."

From Monteverdi, *Tutte le opere,* ed. G. Francesco Malipiero, Vol. 14. Copyright 1966 by Universal Edition A. G., Vienna. Used by permission.

principally an instrumental composer he was also a prolific composer of vocal church music. In his works and in those by his successor Colonna, aspects of middle and late Baroque style are intermingled. Perti, in contrast, wrote entirely in late-Baroque style, favoring vocal solos that are stylistically indistinguishable from opera arias.

Liturgical Instrumental Music

Nearly every genre of Baroque instrumental music was developed mainly within the Church. (The chief exception is the dance suite.) During the Renaissance, the organ was the only instrument that ordinarily played solos during church services. But in the Baroque, the organ was often combined with string or wind instruments in order to further solemnify any festive occasion.

The development of instrumental ensemble music, like that of concertato vocal music, was centered successively at St. Mark's and St. Petronius, and some printed collections, such as those listed above by Giovanni Gabrieli (1597) and Cavalli (1656), included both instrumental and vocal works in the same partbooks, because they were used at the same services.

Organ solos and instrumental pieces played during Baroque church services usually replaced parts of the liturgy, yet the liturgical position for instrumental pieces was rarely indicated on Baroque scores, probably because it was obvious to composers and was also flexible. Such substitution had become common during the Renaissance, and it was officially recognized in the *Caeremoniale Episcoporum* ("Episcopal Ceremonial"; Rome, 1600), which specified the parts that could be replaced. Theologically, it made no difference whether vocal or instrumental polyphony was heard in place of recitation by the celebrant or priest in charge of a service, because the celebrant always recited the entire text (sometimes inaudibly) and thereby satisfied liturgical requirements. Any polyphony was therefore ornamental rather than an integral part of a service, and instrumental polyphony might even have been preferred for an important though negative reason: it could not introduce a nonliturgical text into the liturgy, as so many vocal works then did, including many of Giovanni Gabrieli's motets and all five antiphon-substitutes in Monteverdi's *Vespers* (1610).

According to age-old custom, the length of a piece of liturgical music was to vary according to its position within a service and according to the solemnity of the feast. Therefore if a single piece was to be suitable for various positions and feasts, it had to consist of independent and varied sections, any of which could be played separately or combined according to the needs of a particular service. The practice of separating the sections of a single piece was twice sanctioned by Frescobaldi: for toccatas in his *Toccate* (Rome, 1615) and for ricercari and canzonas in his *Fiori musicali* ("Musical Flowers"; Venice, 1635). Most seventeenth-century Italian instrumental music designed or at least suitable for church use is likewise composed of brief, contrasting sections. Four good examples are in *GMB,* nos. 183–184, 229, and 241: a violin sonata by Biagio Marini, a trio canzona by Tarquinio Merula, a trio sinfonia by Alessandro Stradella (1644–1682), and a trio sonata by Tommaso A. Vitali. After about 1650, the sections were usually written as separate movements, as in Corelli's well-known sonate da chiesa.

The five separable sections of one toccata by Frescobaldi (Example 17.4) are clearly marked by five long-held pedal points. Toccatas and intonations are two Baroque genres written almost exclusively for keyboard instruments, and many of these pieces preserve for us a sample of organists' skill at improvising over a cantus firmus. The usual cantus firmus for these genres is a psalm tone, as often indicated in their titles. Consider the toccatas by Claudio Merulo (1533–1604) in *TEM,* no. 29, and *GMB,* no. 149. The psalm-tone basis is clearest in works by Venetians such as Merulo, the Gabrielis, and their followers. It is rarely clear in toccatas by Frescobaldi, although his may simi-

Ex. 17.4   Girolamo Frescobaldi, Toccata No. 5

From Frescobaldi, *Il secondo libro di toccate* ("The Second Book of Toccatas"), Rome, 1627; reprinted in Edward Lerner, *Study Scores of Musical Styles*. Copyright 1968 by McGraw-Hill, New York. Used by permission.

larly ornament long-held "tones" (e.g., the *b* in Example 17.4). Although the first section of Example 17.4 sounds improvisatory, it is tautly constructed around one motive, *d–e–b–c,* and its variant, *d–e–f#–g.*

Devotional Vocal Music

Devotional services, which have no fixed (liturgical) texts, were instituted in several Roman *oratories* (i.e., places customarily reserved for prayer) by St. Filippo Neri (1515–1595), and his services of sermons and sacred songs called *laudas* quickly became models for others held throughout Italy. A work consisting of many laudas strung together to make a drama was performed at one of Neri's oratories with scenery, costumes, and dances shortly before Lent of 1600, and is consequently often called the first *oratorio,* even though this term was commonly applied to musical works only after 1650. This drama was Cavalieri's *Rappresentatione di anima e di corpo* ("Representation of the Soul and the Body"; Rome, 1600), the first work published in the new, monodic style of the Baroque era (see excerpts in *HAM* II, no. 183; *GMB,* no. 169; and *TEM,* no. 37).

Dialogues   From 1600 to 1650, *dialogue* was the usual designation for monodic or concertato church music in which characters responded dramatically to one another. Viadana employed it for one motet, *Fili, quid fecisti?* ("Son, why have you done this?"), in his influential collection of 1602. In this work Mary and Joseph question Jesus (see Luke 2:48–49), and then they all join in a closing trio. The structure of a dramatic conversation followed by a closing ensemble was common; it can also be seen in Giovanni F. Capello's motet for

Abraham, Isaac, and an Angel, published in his *Motetti e dialoghi* ("Motets and Dialogues"; Venice, 1615; see *GMB,* no. 180). Such dialogue-motets could be performed in liturgical as well as devotional services, while dialogues in the vernacular (sometimes called dialogue-madrigals) were heard only at the latter. After Cavalieri, the most notable early-Baroque composer of vernacular dialogues was Giovanni Francesco Anerio (c. 1567–1630). His *Teatro armonico spirituale* ("Harmonic Spiritual Theater"; Rome, 1619) is a collection of such works, including *La conversione di S. Paolo* ("The Conversion of St. Paul"), which has parts for Saul (i.e., Paul), a divine voice, Ananias, a *testo* (narrator), and an eight-voice chorus. The works by Capello and Anerio include instrumental sinfonias and ritornellos, some of which depict dramatic actions, such as the combat of Saul's followers with the Christians in Anerio's work.

Both early and middle Baroque dialogues blend tunefulness with the ex-

Bernardo Cavallino (1622–1654), *St. Cecilia.* The Saint's music book appears to be resting on a virginal. The undulating drapery conveys a feeling of graceful, and even ethereal, movement. (Courtesy, Museum of Fine Arts, Boston; Bigelow Collection)

pressivity of recitative. Giacomo Carissimi was an outstanding middle-Baroque composer of dialogue-motets, and he undoubtedly wrote many more than the approximately thirty-five that are extant. At least ten are long enough to be divisible into two parts; today they are generally called oratorios, because a two-section structure was characteristic of the late-Baroque oratorio. This partition had a practical origin, in that music was performed both before and after the sermon in the devotional meetings of Neri and his followers.

Carissimi's oratorios

Carissimi's masterpiece is *Jephte,* which was already described in glowing terms by Kircher in 1650. In this oratorio the tragic story of Jephthah and his daughter (see Judges 11:29–40) is rewritten as a drama for two soloists (S and T). The narration is sung by five other soloists (SSATB), either separately or in ensembles (see Example 17.5). Carissimi's ensemble texture is usually homophonic, and so the words are clearly intelligible. Words are rhetorically emphasized by unexpected rhythms or pitches: e.g., the syncopation on *filia* ("daughter") in measures 2–3, or the b^b on *plorabat* ("bewailed") in measure 5 of Example 17.5. Sequence, the favorite Baroque means of emphasis, is very common. For example, compare measures 1–2 with 3–4, or 10–12 with 12–14. Carissimi's oratorio style was conservative in that it stressed early- rather

Jephte

Ex. 17.5   Giacomo Carissimi, *Jephte*

Ex. 17.5   cont.

Narrator: "Then went the daughter of Jephthah into the mountains and, with her companions, bewailed her virginity, saying:
Daughter: 'Weep, ye valleys, lament, ye mountains, and resound with the affliction of my heart.'"
Echo: "Resound."

From William J. Starr and George F. Devine, *Music Scores Omnibus,* Part 1, 2nd edition. Copyright 1974 by Prentice-Hall, Englewood Cliffs, N.J. Used by permission.

than middle-Baroque traits. Narrative and expressive monody are two of Doni's categories for early-Baroque music (see chapter 14), but they also suit most of the passages in Carissimi's oratorios. In his oratorios, Carissimi rarely includes triple-meter bel canto arias, which were frequent in the middle-Baroque operas of such contemporaries as Cavalli and Cesti.

In late-Baroque Italy, most oratorios were written in the vernacular in the latest operatic style, and they were performed throughout the country on

Late-Baroque oratorios

many religious occasions, especially during Lent, and ordinarily without action or scenery. Because they were basically operas on religious subjects, they were frequently termed *sacred* or *spiritual dramas,* while similar but shorter works were called *sacred* or *moral cantatas.* Italian oratorios were written by nearly every librettist and composer who wrote operas, and those set by Stradella, Bernardo Pasquini (1637–1710), and Alessandro Scarlatti are especially noteworthy. Some works, especially those performed in a nobleman's home, were apparently staged with at least a modicum of action and scenery; an example is Handel's *La resurrezione* ("The Resurrection"), which was staged at Rome on Easter Sunday, 1708.

Other Catholic Lands

Southern Germany and Austria

Stylistic innovations in Italian church music during the 1600s were adopted first in German-speaking lands, by Lutherans as readily as by Catholics. South German and Austrian church music differed from that of Baroque Italy mainly in that it incorporated many Lutheran practices in an attempt to counterattack the Reformation musically. Thus many devotional songs,

Hymns in German

psalms, or hymns in German were printed for use by Catholics. By 1600 German hymns were permitted in many Catholic churches as substitutes for Proper chants, and by 1700 they were also allowed as replacements for Ordinary chants. A Mass in which the pieces specified for chorus are sung as hymns by the congregation to organ accompaniment is called a *Singmesse* ("Song-Mass"). German Catholics may have been the first to provide similar accompaniments for medieval liturgical chants, even those sung by priests. Such accompaniments became common throughout Europe after 1700, so that the organ was played almost continuously in many services.

Italian influences

Distinctively German Catholic traditions were maintained only in provincial areas. Cosmopolitan centers, which had imported musicians from northern Europe in the late Renaissance, continued to import Italian musicians throughout the Baroque era. For example, during the late Baroque the Viennese court chapel produced more oratorios by Italians than did any Italian church. The stile antico also flourished outside Italy; two especially notable exponents were Giuseppe Bernabei (1649–1732) in Munich and Fux in Vienna. Fux wrote more than 415 church works, including 85 Masses, which range from the strict stile antico (see *GMB,* no. 271) to the then-fashionable mixed or concertato style.

Organ music

Organ music written for German Catholic churches also followed Italian models. Venetian traditions were perpetuated in Augsburg, where Hans Leo Hassler (1562–1612), who had studied with Andrea Gabrieli, and Christian Erbach (1573–1635) wrote toccatas, ricercari, canzonas, and versets for Mass and Vespers services. Frescobaldi's manner was carried on in Vienna by two of his followers: Froberger and Johann Kaspar Kerll (1627–1693). Kerll's *Modulatio organica* ("Organ Music"; Munich, 1686) consists of a set of seven brief pieces for each of the eight Magnificat tones. Each set includes a prelude and five fugues that replace alternate verses of the Magnificat, and a toccata-like finale that replaces the ensuing antiphon. Strikingly similar liturgical collections were published by other composers, including the *Octi-Tonium* ("Eight Tones"; Augsburg, 1696) by Kerll's student Franz Xaver Murschhauser (1663–1738) and the *Blumenstrauss* ("Bouquet of Flowers"; Augsburg, n.d.) by J. K. F. Fischer. Fischer is best known for his *Ariadne musica* (1702), which includes exquisite, brief preludes and fugues for organ in twenty keys (see *HAM* II, no. 247; or *GMB*, no. 265). It served as a model for *The Well-Tempered Clavier* of J. S. Bach.

Of the German Catholic composers who wrote ensemble music for church use, the most distinctive is Heinrich Biber. His best-known church sonatas are the sixteen Rosary or Mystery Sonatas, which were presumably intended for devotional meetings held in honor of the Rosary each October in Salzburg. He obtained new sonorities by employing *scordatura,* or nonstandard tunings, for one or more strings in all but two of these sonatas. The scordatura also served to convey a sense of "mystery," which is sometimes conveyed in the music as well. For example, in the sonata depicting the Crucifixion (see Example 17.6) the opening theme is shaped like a cross: , while the following theme seems to reiterate the word *Kreuzigung* ("crucifixion").

Biber's sonatas

Ex. 17.6   Heinrich Biber, Sonata No. 10: *Die Kreuzigung Christi*

From Edward Lerner, *Study Scores of Musical Styles,* copyright 1968 by McGraw-Hill, New York. Used by permission.

Spain and Portugal

Organ music

Spain's political power declined markedly during the Baroque as Portugal declared independence in 1640 and Naples was lost to Austria in 1707. Her ties with southern Italy, however, remained very close throughout the era. As a result, organ compositions written in Naples by Giovanni de Macque (c. 1550–1614) and his students Mayone and Trabaci became models for those written by three great Spanish organ composers: Sebastian Aguilera de Heredia (c. 1565–1627), Francisco Correa de Arauxo (c. 1576–1654), and Juan Cabanilles (1644–1712). In addition to versets and sets of variations (see *HAM* II, no. 239), they wrote ricercare-like *tientos,* which included motet-like imitation, virtuoso display, and striking chromaticism and dissonance in the manner of the Neapolitans. Their sharp contrasts, introduced for affective purposes, sometimes exceed even those of Frescobaldi. The same characteristics are found in the works of the great Portuguese organ composer Manuel Rodrigues Coelho (c. 1555–c. 1635), except that he avoids chromaticism and unprepared dissonance (see *HAM* II, no. 200).

In vocal church music, Spanish composers like Juan Bautista Comes (1568–1643), Juan Pablo Pujol (1573–1626), Carlos Patiño (d. 1675), and Juan Cererols (1618–1676) usually followed Victoria as a model, and consequently wrote in the stile antico (see *GMB,* no. 179, by Pujol). Like Baroque Italians, they usually divided the performers into several "choruses," at least one ordinarily consisting of soloists, and accompanied them with basso continuo.

The villancico

Their distinctive genre was the villancico. During the Baroque era, it had a religious text in Spanish and was sung in both devotional and liturgical services. In the latter, it functioned as a motet. In a typical example (*HAM* II, no. 227, by Cererols), a choral *estribillo* (refrain) in duple meter alternates with *coplas* (couplets) for a soloist in triple meter, the whole accompanied by continuo.

France

If the insertion of nonliturgical motet texts into a liturgical service of the Catholic Church was an offense, then the greatest offender during the Baroque era must have been the "Sun King," Louis XIV. According to Pierre Perrin's preface to his *Cantica pro Capella Regis* ("Motet Texts for the Chapel Royal"; Paris, 1665), the usual Mass in Louis's chapel at Versailles was recited for the most part inaudibly while those present listened to a virtual concert: A *grand motet* was performed from the beginning of Mass up to the Elevation, a *petit motet* from the Elevation to the Post-Communion, and a third motet after the Post-Communion. The last motet was invariably a setting of the final verse of Psalm 19 (20): *Domine salvum fac regem* ("Give victory to the king, O Lord"). It obviously reflected the glory as well as the taste of the king, and *Domine* motets were heard at the close of church services throughout Baroque France; we have sixteen such settings by Marc-Antoine Charpentier (c. 1645–1704) alone. The *petits motets* usually had newly written poetic texts by Perrin or others, while *grands motets* were generally based on psalms, and the more splendid the latter were, the more they, too, reflected the glory and taste of Louis.

The grand motet

Partly because a sizeable group is required in order to perform a grand motet properly, it was cultivated primarily at the royal chapel in Versailles and from 1725 at the Concerts Spirituels in Paris. A typical group includes three five-part "choirs": a *petit choeur* of vocal soloists (SATTB), a *grand choeur* or chorus (SATTB), and an instrumental choir (including continuo). The instrumental ensemble doubles the grand choeur and plays brief *symphonies* (i.e., preludes) and *ritournelles* (interludes). The texture is strikingly varied for every verse or two of text; for example, it may begin with an arioso passage for two vocal soloists accompanied by continuo, proceed to kaleidoscopic juxtapositions of the petit choeur with the grand choeur, and then move to homophonic phrases in which the three choirs double the same five parts. Lully established the genre with seven works written between 1664, the year of his *Miserere,* and 1677, the year of his *Te Deum.* It was further developed in the twenty grands motets (1678–1684) by Henry Du Mont (1610–1684), the eighty-six by Charpentier, the seventy-one (1684 on) by Michel Richard de La Lande (1657–1726), and the thirty-one (mainly written from 1723 on) by Campra. The late-Baroque grand motet generally consists of extended movements ranging from Italianate arias, sometimes with obbligato instrumental accompaniment, to elaborate contrapuntal choruses, sometimes with much affective dissonance.

The petit motet

The petit motet was the favored genre of church music throughout Baroque France because it could be inserted at several points in church services and required only one to four vocal soloists and a continuo player. This eminently practical, few-voiced concertato genre was established in Italy by Viadana's motet collection of 1602 and in France by Du Mont's *Cantica sacra* ("Sacred Songs") of 1652. French church-music composers thus adopted it only half a century after their counterparts in Italy (and Germany) had done so. The earliest petits motets—those of Du Mont, Guillaume Nivers (1632–1714), and others—are sectional but have little textural variety. Those written after 1700, however, often feature the sharp late-Baroque contrast of aria with recitative, as in fine examples by Brossard, Campra (see *HAM* II, no. 257), François Couperin (see *HAM* II, no. 266), Nicolas Bernier (1665–1734), and Jean-Baptiste Morin (1677–1754).

Charpentier's motets

The best composer of petits motets, however, may well have been Charpentier, who was certainly the most prolific. One tally of his surviving church works, none of which was printed in his lifetime, lists 86 grands motets, 130 petits motets, 14 *historiae* (oratorios), 11 Masses, and various instrumental works. A fine dramatic sense is evident in Charpentier's motets. His many settings of the Tenebrae Lessons for Holy Week combine introspective drama with expansive lyricism. Polyphonic settings of these Lessons were traditionally written for virtuoso vocal soloists in middle- and late-Baroque Paris, and the annual performances of them at Matins services were among the most famous musical events in the city. Charpentier's settings include elaborately ornamented versions of two basic chant melodies: one for Hebrew letters (*a–a–g–f–g–f,* see Example 17.7) and a related one for Latin verses (see the *Liber usualis,* pp. 631 ff).

Organ music

Profusely ornamented melodic solos are also characteristic of French Baroque organ music. French organs typically included distinctive solo stops, such as the *cornet* and the *cromorne* (crumhorn), and composers featured these stops in their pieces entitled *Récit, Echo,* or *Dialogue.* Their printed collections grouped these pieces by tone or mode, together with others called *Fugue, Duo, Trio,* or *Plein-jeu* (mixture-stop). Since none of these pieces was based on a cantus firmus that tied it to a specific liturgical position, each could be employed as a verset anywhere in a service, so long as it was in the same tone or mode as the sung chant with which it was alternated. Collections of versets were published by many composers, including Nivers, Le Bègue, Nicolas Gigault (1625–1707), André Raison (d. 1719), and Nicolas de Grigny (1672–1703).

Lutheran Germany

The Chorale

The Baroque is the greatest age of Lutheran church music. The foundation of much of its repertory is the *chorale,* which consists of a tune and a strophic, hymn-like text. During the Baroque era, a great number of new chorale texts were written; the outstanding poets were Paul Gerhardt (1607–1676) and Johann Rist (1607–1667). Many new tunes were written as well, and composers provided a considerable variety of vocal and instrumental settings for both old and new tunes. Until about 1650 they provided many *cantional* settings, i.e., block chordal settings with the tune in the top part, for congregational singing. The accompanying parts were usually intended for performance by a choir, as in collections by Praetorius (see *GMB,* no. 162), Schein, Schütz (see *GMB,* no. 189), and Johann Crüger (1598–1662). Scheidt, however, intabulated his one hundred harmonizations of 1650 for organists, and his are worthy forerunners of the masterly chorale harmonizations by J. S. Bach (see *GMB,* no. 285; *MM,* no. 46; and Example 17.8).

Cantional settings

Schein and Crüger both included a figured-bass part for organists, who gradually took over the responsibility of accompanying congregational singing during the seventeenth century. From about 1650 until the end of the Baroque era (which coincides with the end of the main tradition of chorale writing), only a tune and a figured bass were customarily provided in chorale anthologies. The two most influential collections, intended less for church than for home use, were Crüger's *Praxis pietatis melica* ("The Practice of Piety Through Song"; Berlin, 1647) and the *Geist-reiches Gesang-Buch* ("Richly Spirited Songbook"; Halle, 1704) of Johann A. Freylinghausen (1670–1739). Church authorities, objecting to the "many hopping dactyls" in Freylinghausen's books, found then "almost licentious." A secular basis was, however, nothing new for the chorale; Luther himself had willingly "usurped tunes

Secular tunes

Ex. 17.7   Marc-Antoine Charpentier, *Première Leçon de Ténèbres du Mercredi Saint*

"She weepeth sore in the night, and her tears are on her cheeks" (The Lamentations of Jeremiah 1, vs. 2).

From the edition by Guy-Lambert.

from the Devil," saying that he didn't deserve all the good ones. A famed Baroque borrowing from the secular repertory is given in Example 17.8. Its text is strophe 9 of Gerhardt's *O Haupt voll Blut und Wunden* ("O Sacred Head Now Wounded")—a far cry from "I've Lost My Mind over a Tender Young Maid," the text with which the tune appeared in the *Lustgarten* ("Garden of Delight"; Nuremberg, 1601) of Hans Leo Hassler. Hassler's "hopping" $\frac{6}{8}$ and $\frac{3}{4}$ rhythms were converted to a sober succession of quarter notes in the chorale, as shown in Bach's marvelously expressive setting.

Gospel Commentaries

Most of the Lutheran motets, vocal concertos, and cantatas written during the Baroque era were Gospel commentaries, ordinarily sung immediately after the Gospel at Mass but sometimes also during the Communion at Mass, or at Vespers. A Mass could thus include two such pieces (or a two-section piece), one sung before and one sung after the sermon (which was likewise a commentary on the Gospel for the day). The Reformation tradition of Gospel-motet writing was enlivened in the early Baroque by a madrigalian concern for text expression, which infuses motets by the incredibly prolific Praetorius. Between 1605 and 1611, in addition to a great many liturgical pieces in Latin, Praetorius published 1,244 German chorale settings for from two to twelve voice-parts, thus providing a virtual encyclopedia of motet-like chorale settings (see, e.g., *GMB,* nos. 161–162; *HAM* I, no. 167; and *Omnibus* I, pp. 59–61). The most notable among the later motet collections—those by Schein (1615), Scheidt (1620), and Schütz (1625 and 1648)—are mainly based on biblical rather than chorale texts, and only Scheidt includes a number of chorale settings. Schütz's *Geistliche Chormusik* ("Spiritual Choir Music"; Dresden, 1648)—the culmination of the tradition—is a collection of twenty-nine motets, ten of which are settings of Gospel texts. It was written for the choir of St. Thomas's Church in Leipzig, whose noted Baroque cantors included Schein (1616–1630) and J. S. Bach (1723–1750). By Bach's

Motets *(margin)*

Ex. 17.8   J. S. Bach, Passion chorale from *St. Matthew Passion*

SOPRANOS (FL., OB., VLN. I)
ALTOS (VLN. II)

Wenn ich ein - mal soll schei - den, so schei - de nicht von mir!
Wenn ich den Tod soll lei - den, so tritt du dann her - für!

TENORS (VLA.)
BASSES (CONTINUO)

Ex. 17.8 cont.

"When I must go from hence, then don't leave me! When I must suffer death, then stand by me. When I'm most full of fear in my heart, then tear me away from the terrors of fear and pain by Thy strength."

From William J. Starr and George F. Devine, *Music Scores Omnibus,* Part 1, 2nd edition. Copyright 1974 by Prentice-Hall, Englewood Cliffs, N.J. Used by permission.

time, however, motets were written only for very special occasions; for example, four of Bach's six motets were written for graveside ceremonies. (An excerpt from one, *Jesu meine Freude* ["Jesus, My Joy"], is in Burkhart, pp. 65–73).

The composers who represent the last phase of the Gospel motet also represent the first phase of the Gospel concerto, which began to supplant the motet in Lutheran services around 1620. The new genre was based on such Italian models as the church concertos of Viadana (1602) and Giovanni Gabrieli (1615). Lutheran concertos that included chorales as an integral part of their structure were published in Schein's *Opella nova* ("A Little New Collection," 2 vols.; Leipzig, 1618 and 1626), Praetorius' *Polyhymnia* (2 vols.; Wolfenbüttel and Frankfurt, 1619–1620), and Scheidt's *Newe geistliche Concerten* ("New Spiritual Concertos," 4 vols.; Leipzig and Halle, 1631–1640). Schein clearly favored trio texture and was in general the most Italianate of these three composers (see *GMB,* no. 188, and *TEM,* no. 38).

Concertos

Where Schein left off Schütz began, collecting his exceptionally fine church concertos in five volumes published from 1629 to 1650. In sharp contrast to other Lutheran composers, Schütz hardly ever incorporated long, strophic chorales into his concertos. He preferred brief texts that progressed dramatically and were rich in imagery. His setting of the Gospel text *Meister, wir wissen, dass du wahrhaftig bist* ("Master, we know that you are true," Matthew 22:16–21) is an excellent example of how his mixed style could bring out inherent drama. The words of Jesus are sung by a tenor soloist: individual words are musically pictured—e.g., *Schalkheit* ("malice"), *Heuchler* ("hypocrite")—and so is the dramatic situation: e.g., one Pharisee hands a coin *down* to Jesus in measures 39–40. But the glorious final touch is reserved for the all-important last line (Example 17.9), at which point the dramatic energy is dissolved into the "divinely" flowing triple meter (symbolic of the Trinity) favored by the bel canto composers of the middle Baroque.

Gospel motets and concertos were usually based on a single-unit text, ordinarily a scriptural passage or a chorale, and were generally set as a single movement, with affective contrasts of texture, theme, and meter. The only notable multimovement motets and concertos were those that consisted of a series of chorale variations, one variation per strophe, the final one often set in cantional style. Two early examples are in Scheidt's motet collection of 1620, and a late example is Bach's concerto based on *Christ lag in Todesbanden* ("Christ Lay in Bonds of Death," BWV 4, c. 1708; excerpts in *MM,* nos. 46 and 48).

Even though Bach and most other Lutheran composers retained the traditional designation of "motet" or "concerto" for any Gospel commentary written during the Baroque era, many modern scholars have indiscriminately

Cantatas   applied the term "cantata" to any such piece (e.g., BWV 4) that includes several movements. Other scholars have limited the genre of Lutheran cantatas to those with variegated texts, consisting of several separate sections related by one affective idea. This narrower definition fits the Italian secular cantata that flourished contemporaneously with the Lutheran cantata, i.e., between about 1650 and 1750. The Italian model, however, generally included only newly written verse for recitatives and arias. Erdmann Neumeister (1671–1756), a German pastor who wrote and published texts for four year-long cycles of Gospel cantatas between 1700 and 1717, followed the Italian model strictly in his first two cycles, including only newly written verse, which usually commented (indeed "sermonized") upon the Gospel for the day. His other cycles, however, like most Lutheran cantatas written between 1650 and 1750, intermixed biblical and chorale texts with newly written poetry.

An immense number of Lutheran cantatas were written, but relatively few of these "occasional" works survive. For example, of the hundreds pre-

Buxte-
hude's
cantatas   sumably written by Dietrich Buxtehude, the most outstanding composer of Lutheran cantatas before 1700, only about a hundred survive, all of them dating from the years 1675–1687. Many of Buxtehude's cantata texts are intensely subjective and therefore apt for devotional purposes. His many through-composed settings of newly written strophic texts are known as *aria*

Ex. 17.9   Heinrich Schütz, *Meister, wir wissen . . .* , from *Symphoniae sacrae*

"Render therefore to Caesar the things that are Caesar's, and to God the things that are God's."

From Heinrich Schütz, *Meister wir wissen,* ed. Rudolf Holle. Copyright 1955 by Bärenreiter, Kassel, Edition No. 1486. Used by permission.

cantatas or *ode cantatas;* some of them include biblical and/or chorale texts as well (e.g., the cantata printed in part in *HAM* II, no. 235, which consists of a psalm verse and a seven-strophe aria). Some of his cantatas are dramatic dialogues, which had both Italian and German models. Those written by Andreas Hammerschmidt (1611–1675) were by far the most popular dialogues in Germany (see *HAM* II, no. 213).

After Buxtehude, the outstanding cantata composers were Johann Philipp Krieger (1649–1725), Friedrich Wilhelm Zachow (1633–1727), Christoph Graupner (1683–1760), Telemann, and Bach. Krieger remained rather close to Italian secular models in many of his more than two thousand cantatas. Telemann and Graupner each wrote about fifteen hundred cantatas, mostly in the Italian Preclassic style that began to predominate about 1720 (see Part Four). In 1723 these composers were respectively the first and second choices for the position of cantor at Leipzig, which was given to Bach after they turned it down.

Bach's cantatas

Bach was not at all like his contemporaries who wrote in the *galant* style. While they composed dozens and even hundreds of cantatas in whatever stereotyped formal structures were in fashion, he, like Monteverdi and Schütz, sought (and usually found) for each text a unique and utterly convincing musico-dramatic solution. In so doing, he often combined late-Baroque conventions like the da capo and ritornello forms with old-fashioned chorale tunes and polyphonic intricacies. Even in his earliest cantatas Bach manifested an extraordinary ability as a musical dramatist. For example, in *Gottes Zeit ist die allerbeste Zeit* ("God's Time Is the Best Time," BWV 106; Mühlhausen, c. 1707) the key progression symbolically descends to five flats as the body dies, then ascends back to three flats when Christ redeems the soul. The crux of the drama is at the point of death (Example 17.10). A jagged theme set in stile antico counterpoint for the lower three voices represents the stern *alte Bund* ("old law"). When first introduced, it receives a long and powerful development (measures 131–145). But then the soprano, representing the dying one, enters with a plea to the Redeemer, supported by a chorale played on recorders (measures 145–156). The stern theme returns, but greatly weakened by the ever-increasing encroachment of the forces pleading for redemption (measures 156–174). When it is heard for the last time (measure 174; see Example 17.10), only two voices manage to state its jagged

Ex. 17.10   J. S. Bach, *Gottes Zeit*

Ex. 17.10   cont.

Ex. 17.10   cont.

No. 2: "This is the old law: Man, thou must die. Yes, come, Lord Jesus."
No. 3: "Into Thy hands I commit my spirit."

Edition Eulenburg G.m.b.H. Adliswil/Zurich. Used by permission.

opening, and the remainder is easily "overcome"—first, by the last chorale phrase in the recorders (measures 179–182); second, surprisingly, by a phrase (bracketed in Example 17.10) that the soprano had introduced in measures 146–148, which also begins the chorale *O Haupt voll Blut und Wunden* shown in Example 17.8; and finally, by the soprano at the mention of the name Jesus. The passage has no cadence, because death is not an end for the Christian soul, and the bass climbs stepwise throughout the next aria as the soul flies into the hands of Christ in Heaven. The bass pattern in this aria, as in the tenor aria heard earlier in the cantata, is a ciaccona.

Gottes Zeit is made up of biblical passages and chorale texts. It contains no newly written verse, which became the basis of Bach's cantatas written in Weimar and Leipzig. He usually set such verse as intense recitatives and arias. A fine example from Weimar, where he wrote about one cantata a month from 1714 to 1716, is *Komm du süsse Todesstunde* ("Come, Sweet Hour of Death," BWV 161, 1715; text by Salomo Franck). Here the opening aria as well as the closing cantional setting are built on the passion chorale (Example 17.8). As cantor at Leipzig, Bach provided virtually complete cantata cycles for the years 1723–1724 and 1724–1725, incomplete cycles for the years 1725–1726 and 1726–1727, and only occasional cantatas thereafter. In all, he wrote at most three hundred church cantatas (of which nearly two hundred survive), many of which he must have revived every few years in Leipzig.

His cycle for 1724–1725 consists mainly of *chorale cantatas,* in which strophe 1 of a chorale is heard in an opening choral movement, the texts of the ensuing strophes are paraphrased in the next movements, and the final strophe is heard in the last movement. An excellent example is the seven-movement *Jesu der du meine Seele* ("Jesus, Thou Hast My Soul," BWV 78, 1724; in Lerner, no. 86), based on a text by Rist. Both the first and fourth movements represent dramatic struggles. In the opening chorus, Christ snatches man out of Hell (*herausgerissen*) in measures 75–80, after which a major key is heard for the first time and the chromatically descending passacaglia ostinato disappears for the first time (measures 85–95).[2] In most of its subsequent reappearances, the descending pattern is accompanied by victoriously rising anapests, and in one passage the descent even changes direction in midstream (measures 107–118). In the fourth movement, the centerpiece of the cantata, Bach follows the standard da capo form through the middle of the A section. Then, instead of repeating the A section text, he chooses to state the B text twice, because it contains the dramatic struggle: "The lord of Hell calls me to battle, but Jesus stands by my side so that I will be brave and victorious." The tenor twice (measures 32–36 and 46–56) battles the Devil, represented by the flute, which is twice vanquished by the name of Jesus. After presenting the innocence of childhood in a soprano–alto duet (no. 2) and the troubles of youth in a tenor solo (no. 4), Bach depicts the sublime assurance of the mature Christian in a bass aria that departs from its eight-measure units only to stress the closing concept: no enemy can ever rob a believer from Christ's hands. The symbolic drama in nos. 2–6 thus carries the listener convincingly from the turbulence of the opening chorus to the repose of the closing chorale, "Lord, I believe." Bach's cantatas, in short, are truly works of magisterial dramatic power.

Passions

The special genre of Gospel commentary performed during Holy Week is the Passion. Its history during the Baroque era largely parallels that of the commentaries just discussed. In the early Baroque, then, a complete Passion text could be set as a motet, as is Leonhard Lechner's St. John Passion (1593). However, in the more common and "realistically" dramatic type, motet texture is reserved for passages spoken by a group of persons, while an expressive recitative is employed for individual speakers, including the "evangelist," or narrator. This dramatic genre, based exclusively on the texts of the Gospels, reached its apogee in three Passions composed by Schütz in the 1650s and 1660s. In an earlier Gospel commentary for Holy Week, the *Sieben Worte am Kreuz* ("Seven Words on the Cross," c. 1640), Schütz accompanied each speaker (Jesus, two thieves, and the evangelist) with continuo, and added a "halo" of two violins for the words of Jesus, so that this work is comparable to his vocal concertos. But in his Passions, Schütz austerely renounced all instrumental accompaniment in order to gain greater solemnity (cf. *GMB,* nos. 191 and 192).

Passions began to incorporate versified commentaries on their biblical texts about 1650, at the same time that cantatas including similar commentaries first appeared. About 1700, Christian Hunold (called Menates; 1681–1721) began to write Passion texts containing only versified paraphrases of the biblical story. The vivid, indeed gory, imagery employed by Hunold was widely imitated, most notably by his Hamburg compatriot Barthold Brockes (1680–1747), whose famous Passion text was first set to music by Keiser in 1712, then by both Handel and Telemann in 1716, and by Mattheson in 1718.

Bach's Passions

Bach incorporated some of Brockes's verse into his *Johannes-Passion* (St. John Passion, 1724), which includes the entire Gospel text (rather than a paraphrase of it) and chorales as well as versified commentary. This work is relatively fast-paced and dramatically stunning in comparison to Bach's more contemplative *Matthäus-Passion* (St. Matthew Passion, 1727?), for which the verse commentaries were written by his friend Christian Friedrich Henrici (called Picander; 1700–1764).

St. Matthew Passion

The St. Matthew Passion is in many ways the grandest work Bach ever wrote. Its foundation is Matthew 26–27, which Bach set dramatically, as in Schütz's Passions, and accompanied, as in Schütz's *Sieben Worte.* Reflections upon this biblical basis are provided by Picander's thirty-two ariosos, arias, and choruses, and by sixteen chorale strophes. The former convey the often-excruciating sorrow of individuals viewing each scene, while the latter express the collective strength and grief of the Christian congregation. The juxtaposition of biblical with newly written and chorale texts is made into a dramatic whole by Bach's profound musical setting, which is overwhelming in every sense. It requires a much larger group of performers than he customarily had for a service (i.e., about sixty-four, divided into two orchestras of seventeen each, two choirs of twelve each, and a third choir of about six boys to sing the chorale in the opening chorus), and takes well over three hours to perform—not counting either the undoubtedly long sermon that divided it or the other music that surrounded it at Bach's performances on Good Friday afternoons. The overpowering effect of his setting is well illustrated by the pieces surrounding Christ's death (nos. 68–73; in *Omnibus* I, pp. 208–216). An individual's reaction to the crucifixion scene is given in an arioso and an aria for alto accompanied by two *oboi da caccia* (tenor oboes with a broadly flared metal bell) and a walking bass. The unbearably anguished arioso is leaden, like a tolling bell, with an incessant two-beat accompaniment pattern and seventh chords that lead downward into regions of five and six flats. The aria, in sharp contrast, is serenely confident, with all melodic lines climbing upward into the outstretched arms of Christ, and is even thrilling, as a chorus unexpectedly enters and punctuates with excited questions the alto's visionary leaps up. Christ is then forsaken for the first time by the Father (and consequently also by the "halo" of two violins that Bach had previously provided for him) and dies. The congregation reacts by singing a strophe of the Passion chorale for the fifth and final time in the work, and for this supreme moment Bach provided what is probably the most affecting chorale harmonization ever written (see Example 17.8 above).

Bach's cantatas and Passions represent the culmination of Lutheran Baroque church music, and they were largely written during an immensely productive few years at Leipzig, 1723–1727. After this period, Bach wrote only two vocal works comparable in scope to his Passions. The first is the Christmas Oratorio (BWV 248; 1734), consisting of six cantatas, one for each major feast-day from Christmas through Epiphany. As in the Passions, biblical texts, newly written texts, and chorale texts are juxtaposed. The first and last chorale heard in the work is (surprisingly) the Passion chorale. The ariosos, arias, and choruses set to newly written texts are mainly jubilant in mood, and many are borrowed from three secular cantatas (BWV 213–215 of 1733–1734), thus manifesting the close interrelationship between church and secular music that prevailed during the Baroque era. The second monumental work written after 1727 is the Mass in B minor (BWV 232; 1733–c. 1749), which consists of a Kyrie and Gloria written for the new Elector of Saxony in 1733 and of other movements added during the last years of Bach's life. That he completed this great work apparently without any hope of hearing it performed clearly illustrates the incredible striving for wholeness, fullness, and perfection that amazes us in Bach's works.

Christmas Oratorio

Mass in B minor

Organ Solos

Although many different instruments were heard in the Gospel concertos, cantatas, and Passions that were performed in Lutheran services, apparently only the organ customarily played solo pieces. Most of these solos were brief, usually improvised preludes, which could preface almost any part of a service. Others were brief versets played in alternation with the choir (especially during the Kyrie, Gloria, and Magnificat), or chorale settings played in alter-

Function in the service

nation with chorale strophes sung by either the choir or the congregation. The long and frequently virtuoso preludes, toccatas, and fugues written by many Lutheran organist-composers may have been played during Communion, but they were probably ordinarily reserved for church concerts, which sometimes immediately followed a service. (For examples, see *HAM* II, nos. 215, 234, and 237; and *GMB,* nos. 249 and 283.) In all the genres that they cultivated, these composers attained heights of expressive brilliance, and the crowning achievements in nearly every one of these genres were written by J. S. Bach.

Lutheran organ music was largely founded on Italian models. Italian works together with variation patterns developed by English keyboard composers were made known to many Lutherans by a Dutch Calvinist: Jan Pieterszoon Sweelinck, whose many Lutheran students carried his teachings directly to Bach. For example, two of them—Jacob Praetorius (1586–1651) and Heinrich Scheidemann (1596–1663; see *HAM* II, no. 195)—obtained employment at churches in Hamburg, as did two of their students: Matthias Weckmann (1619–1674) and Jan Adam Reincken (1623–1722). When Bach was between the ages of sixteen and eighteen, he traveled several times to Hamburg in order to learn from the playing of the then nearly eighty-year-old Reincken. Almost twenty years later, in 1720, Reincken in turn listened to Bach improvise at great length upon a chorale tune and then exclaimed: "I thought that this art was dead, but I see that in you it still lives."[3]

Chorale settings   Sweelinck's art of making sets of patterned *chorale variations* was most rigorously developed by his student Samuel Scheidt, in his *Tabulatura nova*. Scheidt presented the tune in any one of three ways: in long notes as a cantus firmus, with *coloration* by ornamental passagework, or with each phrase treated in motet-like imitation. This last type, called a *chorale fantasy,* became ever more virtuoso and rhapsodic in the hands of later north-German composers, like Reincken and Buxtehude; and Bach developed it to its fullest (see, e.g., his *Ein' feste Burg,* "A Mighty Fortress," BWV 720, 1709, in *Omnibus* I, pp. 167–168). Central Germans, on the other hand, favored the *chorale fugue,* which began with a fugue based on the first chorale phrase and continued with a complete statement of the chorale in long notes. Pachelbel wrote the finest examples (see *GMB,* no. 243, which employs the tune of Example 17.8). Pachelbel's brief fugues are exquisite, especially the ninety-four that he intended for performance in alternation with sung verses of the Magnificat (see *HAM* II, no. 251).

Chorale prelude   The last type of chorale setting that became popular during the Baroque was the *chorale prelude,* which consisted of one complete, straightforward statement of the tune in the top part. The first masters of this genre were Buxtehude and Pachelbel, and they presumably utilized it as a prelude to the singing of a chorale. For added effectivity, the tune was sometimes ornamented, and each phrase of the tune could be stated "in anticipation" by one or more of the accompanying parts. Bach, however, usually avoided both methods in his well-known collection of chorale preludes, the *Orgelbüchlein*

("Little Organ Book"). He preferred to symbolize the main concepts of the chorale text in his motivic accompaniment, as in *Durch Adams Fall* ("Through Adam's Fall," BWV 637; in Hardy and Fish II, pp. 72–73); the sinuous steps in the alto part apparently represent the serpentine Devil that causes Adam's excruciating Fall in the pedal part. (For other chorale preludes, see *HAM* II, no. 190; *MM*, no. 47; *TEM*, no. 41; Lerner, no. 85; and *Omnibus* I, pp. 129–131 and 169–170.)

England

The Church of England

The chief musical services of the Church of England during the Baroque **Services** era were Morning Prayer and Evening Prayer, which (like their Catholic ancestors, Matins and Vespers) were built around psalm singing and Scripture reading. In parish churches, the only musical activity was congregational psalm singing, accompanied by an organ in the few places that had one. In cathedrals, a choir, typically including sixteen men and eight boys, chanted the psalms in harmonized settings, and sang at least two canticles and an anthem at each service. The usual setting for a pair of canticles was homophonic, and such a pair formed a "short" service; a pair that employed extensive motivic imitation was called a "long" or "great" service. (See the mixed example by Blow in *TEM*, no. 43.) The cathedral organist accompanied the choir, sometimes playing versets in alternation with sung psalm verses, and sometimes playing a *voluntary*, or improvised piece, at the end of the psalms or at the end of the service.

The most elaborate musical genre was the *anthem*, which was ordinarily **Anthems** based on a psalm text. In the early Baroque, the completely choral type called the *full anthem*, written in the style of a late-Renaissance motet, was largely supplanted by the new *verse anthem*, written in the style of a concertato motet. In this type, each "verse," or text line, was sung by one or two soloists accompanied by a quartet of viols, the entire choir joining the ensemble only for the final line of each section. (See the examples by Byrd and Orlando Gibbons in *HAM* I, nos. 151 and 172, and in Lerner, no. 58.) Attempts to incorporate the declamatory style of Italian monody in the 1630s were interrupted by the advent of the Commonwealth (1642–1660), during which cathedral choirs were prohibited. Under Charles II, the old traditions were revived by Humfrey (see *HAM* II, no. 242), Blow, and Purcell. Their many anthems are distinguished by a tonal harmony "spiced" with unorthodox dissonance and chromaticism—especially cross-relations. In emulation of the royal chapel in France, Charles II introduced instruments of the violin family into his chapel, and many anthems with introductory symphonies and intermediary ritornellos were written for him. But this "string band" was disbanded after the Glorious Revolution of 1688, and later anthems—written, for example, by William Croft (1678–1727) and Maurice Greene (1696–1755)—are accompanied only by organ continuo. While Croft's best works are in an antiquated style, those by Greene incorporate solos in the style of late-Baroque Italian opera (see *HAM* II, nos. 268 and 279).

The most splendid Baroque anthems were those written by Purcell and Handel for special occasions. Both composed magnificent coronation anthems: Purcell wrote *My Heart Is Inditing* for James II (1685; excerpt in *GMB,* no. 246), while Handel wrote *Zadok the Priest* and three others for George II (1727). Both likewise made extraordinarily festive settings of a pair of canticles, *Te Deum* and *Jubilate,* for Morning Prayer. Purcell's were composed for a service honoring St. Cecilia at Westminster Abbey (1694), while Handel's were for the celebration of the Peace of Utrecht at St. Paul's Cathedral (1713). Handel's *Jubilate* subsequently became the basis for the first of twelve multipartite anthems (the Chandos Anthems, c. 1717–1719) that he composed for the private chapel of the duke of Chandos.

Handelian Oratorios

Handel's compositions for the duke's chapel culminated in 1720 with a dramatic work. Since its text was an English adaptation of Racine's *Esther,* a classical French drama employing the format of ancient Greek tragedy to relate a biblical story, a wealth of literary traditions had been used by the librettist before Handel added musical elements of Italian opera, English anthem, and German Lutheran Gospel commentary. When Handel's *Esther* was revived at the opera house in 1732, it was referred to as "an oratorio in English," the first of twenty such *English oratorios* that Handel produced at London theaters. Elaborate choruses are integral parts of each, making them vastly different from Italian late-Baroque oratorios, which were like contemporary operas in that they had no chorus and featured only da capo arias.[4] The finest choral traditions of the age—those of Lutheran cantatas and Passions and of Anglican anthems—formed the foundation for Handel's marvelously effective choral writing. The integration of these traditions with those of Italian opera was accomplished in his oratorios, and the resultant grandeur in design combined with vividness in expression render them comparable to some of the stunningly huge canvases of Peter Paul Rubens.

Choral grandeur

Each Handelian oratorio gains its special character from the literary and musical elements stressed within it. *Saul* (1739) and *Samson* (1743) are patriotically stirring dramas about militant Israelites, who are portrayed by a chorus that participates in the action. *Semele* (1744) and *Hercules* (1745) are like ancient tragedies in operatic form, and they are generally called *secular oratorios* or *English operas* because they concern Greek rather than biblical heroes. The final two works, *Theodora* (1750) and *Jephtha* (1752), portray intense individual suffering, and thus are inward-looking dramas concerning profound spiritual matters. *Israel in Egypt* (1739; excerpt in *Omnibus* I, pp. 217–220) and *Messiah* (1742; excerpts in Kamien I, no. 20) stand apart from the others in that they are based firmly on biblical prose (rather than on newly written poetic versions of biblical stories) and are essentially like anthems of epic proportions. Even though they have neither characters nor a plot, they are intensely dramatic in character and build up to a great climax in each act. This facet is especially clear in act I of *Messiah*, constructed in six units, each of which ends with a grand chorus. The first four units, each consisting of recitative + air + chorus, begin with three units that steadily increase our longing for Christ's birth by relating God's promises concerning the Messiah, and end with a fourth that dissolves the tension in its culminating chorus, "For unto us a child is born." The instrumental piece known as the "Pastoral Symphony" then sets a mood of serene peacefulness for the joyous, "pastoral" message that ends the act: The angels announce Christ's birth to shepherds, and he is proclaimed the good shepherd.

Handel's great skill as both master architect and expert dramatist is likewise beautifully exemplified by his oratorio *Solomon* (1749). Its central chorus —"From the east unto the west, who so wise as Solomon?"—occurs immediately after the king has heard and wisely judged the famous case in which two harlots each claim that a child is her own son (I Kings 3). This chorus, in A major, is the one with the most sharps in its key signature, and it leads down through D and G in both "eastward" and "westward" directions. Indeed, it is framed by seven choruses on either side, which may well symbolize the seven pillars of the house of wisdom (Proverbs 9:1), as well as the seven years that it took Solomon to build the temple (I Kings 6:38).[5]

The first act begins majestically, with opening choruses that ring out in honor of the newly completed temple, and it ends peacefully, with a closing chorus that provides the gentlest possible support for the love of Solomon and his bride (Lerner, no. 81). The tranquility of act I contrasts sharply with the agonized claims of the harlots in act II, which Handel depicts with indelible poignancy. Then act III pithily combines both tender and violent passions, as Solomon displays the power of music in a golden age. One serene passage that exquisitely shows Handel's mastery of affective nuance occurs in an air for Solomon, when the young king pauses, lost in amazement, both before and after gravely contemplating "Jehovah's power" (Example 17.11, measures 9–12).

Ex. 17.11   George Frideric Handel, *What thought I trace,* from *Solomon,* act I

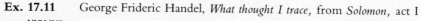

Ex. 17.11   cont.

Summary

From this chapter we can draw three important conclusions about the style of Baroque church music: (1) it corresponded to its liturgical function; (2) it usually differed not at all from that of secular music; and (3) like secular music, it was primarily soloistic (rather than choral or orchestral). The length, style, and mode (or key) of any piece of liturgical music ordinarily varied according to its function within a service and according to the solemnity of the feast for which it was intended. Unfortunately, the liturgical function of many vocal and instrumental pieces can only be hypothesized now, for it was rarely indicated by composers, perhaps because it was too obvious to their age, or because they did not want to restrict their compositions to a single function.

Indeed, with the exception of church music written in the stile antico or stile misto, any church piece could be employed as a secular piece, and vice versa. The practice of providing religious texts for secular pieces was common throughout the period. Instrumental music, which underwent great development within the Church during the Baroque era, could serve for both secular and religious occasions without any alteration at all. Yet an understanding of the stylistic development of instrumental music largely depends upon an understanding of what forms and styles were needed for church use. For eminently practical reasons, the great preponderance of Baroque church music was written for one person per part. Even works that seem colossal, such as some polychoral motets of Giovanni Gabrieli and some oratorio choruses of Carissimi, were so written.

The religious zeal that resulted from the Reformation and Counter-Reformation continued to inflame Europeans during the entire Baroque era. It imbued the church music written throughout the Continent with a fervent character that is now recognized as a signal trait of the age in general—and especially of its musical works, which are typically impassioned orations on a single theme. At the beginning of the era, the Church was the only "public" arena in which elaborate music could be heard; therefore it retained much of its former sway over the development of both vocal and instrumental genres. But public theaters for operas and public chambers for concerts were founded during the middle and late Baroque, respectively, and by the end of the era these arenas had totally eclipsed the Church in terms of musical leadership. The Baroque was thus the last great age dedicated to Western church music, and at the same time the first era in which a large number of musical artisans deserted their feudal employers, both in church and at court, in order to set themselves up as musical artists in the commercial culture of modern times.

Notes

1. The work was greatly revised about 1730, and both Mozart and Mendelssohn "illegally" copied out the new version after hearing it performed.
2. The same ostinato underlies the *Crucifixus* of Bach's Mass in B minor; see Kamien I, no. 27.
3. From the "Obituary of Bach" (1754), trans. in Hans David and Arthur Mendel, *The Bach Reader,* rev. ed. (New York: W. W. Norton, 1966), p. 219.
4. Handel's *La resurrezione* (Rome, 1708) is typical of the Italian genre in this respect.
5. The second, third, and fourth choruses in the work are printed as a single, three-section chorus.

Bibliography

Books and Articles

General. In addition to references in Chapter 12, see:

FELLERER, KARL GUSTAV. *The History of Catholic Church Music,* 2nd ed., trans. Francis Brunner. Baltimore: Helicon, 1961.

Catholic Vocal, Liturgical Polyphony

ANTHONY, JAMES R. *French Baroque Music from Beaujoyeaulx to Rameau,* rev. ed. New York: W. W. Norton, 1978.

ARNOLD, DENIS. "Formal Design in Monteverdi's Church Music." In *Claudio Monteverdi e il suo tempo,* ed. Raffaele Monterosso, pp. 187–216. Verona: Valdonega, 1969.

BONTA, STEPHEN. "Liturgical Problems in Monteverdi's Marian Vespers." *Journal of the American Musicological Society* 20 (1967): 86–106.

Catholic Instrumental, Liturgical Polyphony

BONTA, STEPHEN. "The Uses of the Sonata da Chiesa." *Journal of the American Musicological Society* 22 (1969): 54–84.

BRADSHAW, MURRAY. *The Origin of the Toccata.* [Rome:] American Institute of Musicology, 1972.

SELFRIDGE-FIELD, ELEANOR. *Venetian Instrumental Music from Gabrieli to Vivaldi.* Oxford: Basil Blackwell, 1975.

The Devotional Oratorio

HITCHCOCK, H. WILEY. "The Latin Oratorios of Marc-Antoine Charpentier." *Musical Quarterly* 41 (1955): 41–63.

MASSENKEIL, GÜNTHER. *The Oratorio,* trans. A. C. Howie. Anthology of Music, vol. 37. Cologne: Arno Volk Verlag, 1970.

SMITHER, HOWARD E. *The Oratorio in the Baroque Era.* A History of the Oratorio, vols. 1–2. Chapel Hill: University of North Carolina Press, 1977.

German Lutherans

GEIRINGER, KARL. *Johann Sebastian Bach: The Culmination of an Era.* New York: Oxford University Press, 1966.

HERZ, GERHARD. "The Place of Bach's Cantatas in History." In his edition of Bach, *Cantata No. 4,* pp. 3–20. New York: W. W. Norton, 1967.

————. "The New Chronology of Bach's Vocal Music." In his edition of Bach, *Cantata No. 140,* pp. 3–50. New York: W. W. Norton, 1972.

English Protestants

DEAN, WINSTON. *Handel's Dramatic Oratorios and Masques.* London: Oxford University Press, 1959.

DEARNLEY, CHRISTOPHER. *English Church Music: 1650–1750.* London: Barrie & Jenkins, 1970.

Scores

For works by composers not listed here, see the bibliographies of scores in Chapters 14–16.

ALLEGRI, GREGORIO. *Miserere*. In Julius Amann, *Allegris Miserere und die Aufführungspraxis in der Sixtina nach Reiseberichten und Musikhandschriften,* pp. 3–9. Regensburg: Pustet, 1935.

BIBER, HEINRICH. *Sechzehn Violinsonaten,* ed. Erwin Luntz. Denkmäler der Tonkunst in Österreich, vol. 25. Vienna: Artaria, 1905; reprinted, Graz: Akademische Druck- und Verlagsanstalt, 1959.

BUXTEHUDE, DIETRICH. *Werke,* ed. Wilibald Gurlitt et al. 8 vols. Klecken and Hamburg: Ugrino, 1925–1958.

———. *Sämtliche Orgelwerke,* ed. Klaus Beckmann, 2 vols. Wiesbaden: Breitkopf & Härtel, 1971–1972.

CABANILLES, JUAN. *Opera omnia,* ed. Higini Anglès, 4 vols. Barcelona: Biblioteca de Catalunya, 1927–1956.

CARISSIMI, GIACOMO. *Le opere complete,* ed. Lino Bianchi et al. Rome: Istituto Italiano per la Storia della Musica, 1951– .

———. *Historia di Jephte,* ed. Gottfried Wolters. Wolfenbüttel: Möseler, 1969.

CAVALIERI, EMILIO DE'. *Rappresentatione di anima e di corpo,* facsimile reprint of the edition of 1600. Rome: Casa Editrice Claudio Monteverdi, 1912.

CAVALLI, FRANCESCO. *Laetatus sum, Laudate Dominum,* Magnificat, Mass, and *Salve Regina.* In *Musiche sacre,* ed. Raymond Leppard. London: Faber Music, 1966–1973.

CAZZATI, MAURIZIO. Motets, Op. 65, Nos. 8, 9, and 11, ed. Rudolf Ewerhart. Cantio sacra, vols. 19, 55, and 60. Cologne: Edmund Bieler, 1960–1971.

CEREROLS, JUAN. *Obres completes,* ed. David Pujol, 4 vols. Montserrat: Monestir de Montserrat, 1930–1975.

CHARPENTIER, MARC-ANTOINE. *Four Elevations,* ed. Rudolf Ewerhart. Cantio sacra, vol. 26. Cologne: Edmund Bieler, 1960.

———. *Judicium Salomonis,* ed. H. Wiley Hitchcock. New Haven: A–R Editions, 1964.

———. *Midnight Mass for Christmas Eve,* ed. H. Wiley Hitchcock. St. Louis: Concordia, 1973.

———. *Première Leçon de Ténèbres du Mercredy Saint: Plorans Ploravit,* ed. Guy-Lambert. Paris: Editions de la Lyre d'Or, 1952.

COELHO, MANUEL RODRIGUES. *Flores de musica,* ed. Macario Santiago Kastner, 2 vols. Lisbon: Fundação C. Gulbenkian, 1959–1961.

COLONNA, GIOVANNI PAOLO. *Messa a nove voci concertata con stromenti,* ed. Anne Schnoebelen. Madison: A–R Editions, 1974.

CORREA DE ARAUXO, FRANCISCO. *Facultad organica,* ed. Macario Santiago Kastner, 2 vols. Barcelona: Instituto Español de Musicologia, 1948–1952.

COUPERIN, FRANÇOIS. *Oeuvres complètes,* ed. Maurice Cauchie, 12 vols. Paris: Oiseau Lyre, 1932–1933.

FISCHER, J. K. F. *Sämtliche Werke für Klavier und Orgel,* ed. Ernst von Werra. Leipzig: Breitkopf & Härtel, 1905; reprinted, New York: Broude, 1965.

FUX, JOHANN. *Sämtliche Werke,* ed. Johann-Joseph-Fux-Gesellschaft, Graz. Kassel: Bärenreiter, 1959– .

KERLL, JOHANN KASPAR. *Modulatio organica,* ed. Rudolf Walter. Altöttling: Alfred Coppenrath, 1956.

LA LANDE, MICHEL RICHARD DE. *Regina coeli (grand motet),* ed. Sylvie Spycket. Paris: Durand, 1951.

LE BÈGUE, NICOLAS. *Oeuvres complètes d'orgue,* ed. Alexandre Guilmant. Paris: Durand, 1909; reprinted, New York: Johnson Reprint, 1972.

MAYONE, ASCANIO. *Secondo libro di diversi capricci per sonare,* ed. Macario Santiago Kastner, 2 vols. Paris: Schola Cantorum, 1964–1965.

PACHELBEL, JOHANN. *Orgelkompositionen,* ed. Max Seiffert. Denkmäler der Tonkunst in Bayern, vol. 6. Leipzig: Breitkopf & Härtel, 1903.

PERTI, GIACOMO ANTONIO. *Laudate pueri,* ed. Jean Berger. University Park: Pennsylvania State University Press, 1966.

PRAETORIUS, MICHAEL. *Gesamtausgabe,* ed. Friedrich Blume et al., 21 vols. Wolfenbüttel: G. Kallmeyer, 1928–1960.

PUJOL, JUAN PABLO. *Opera omnia,* ed. Higini Anglès, 2 vols. Barcelona: Biblioteca de Catalunya, 1926–1932.

RAISON, ANDRÉ. *Livres d'orgue,* ed. Norbert Dufourcq et al. Paris: Schola Cantorum, c. 1963.

SCHEIDT, SAMUEL. *Werke,* ed. Gottlieb Harms and Christhard Mahrenholz. Hamburg: Ugrino, and Leipzig: Deutscher Verlag für Musik, 1923– .

STRADELLA, ALESSANDRO. *Gli oratori,* ed. Lino Bianchi. Rome: Istituto Italiano per la Storia della Musica, 1969– .

TRABACI, GIOVANNI MARIA. *Composizioni per organo e cembalo,* ed. Oscar Mischiati, 2 vols. Kassel: Bärenreiter, 1964–1969.

PART
FOUR

From Preclassic to Classic

18

Music in
Eighteenth-Century Society

THE eighteenth century fluctuated between two forces: an ideal of cosmopolitanism and an awakening sense of nationalism. It was an age of contradictions, in which the ideals of the Enlightenment, or Age of Reason, coexisted with *Sturm und Drang*. Similarly, we sense an overlap of musical styles, in the coexistence of the older, Baroque tendencies and the newer, Preclassic features. The end of the century witnessed a synthesis of these traditions, in the perfection of style known as Classicism.

Italy

In the eighteenth century Italy was a mosaic of city-states, republics, duchies, and kingdoms. Culturally and economically, it gradually developed closer ties with the European community. Italian music, specifically comic opera, spread throughout Europe. Italian musicians, who had assumed a prominent position in the evolution of musical styles during the Baroque era, continued to dominate the European musical world. As composers, teachers, and maestri di cappella, they carried Italian musical tastes as far north as St. Petersburg and Moscow.

Musical prominence

As part of Italy's political, economic, and cultural integration with Europe, the Italian intellectual acquired a taste for the French language and customs. During the first half of the century, Italian literature and drama were influenced by Molièresque motifs, while in the second half the focus shifted to the works of the *Encyclopédistes,* especially Diderot, Rousseau, and D'Alembert. Even such volumes as the *Mémoires* (Paris, 1787) of the Venetian playwright Carlo Goldoni (1707–1793) and those of the famous playboy and adventurer Giovanni Casanova (1725–1798) were first printed in Paris, in French, then circulated in Italy in that language.

French intellectual influences

The Italian populace was satirized in plays and comic operatic libretti, which reflected and preserved for posterity the tastes, mores, and social codes

The "democratization" of art

of an entire era. The height of popularity attained by the comic genre in the eighteenth century is indicative of the extent of the process of "democratization" of art. The works of Goldoni, for example, not only fulfilled artistic and social functions, but also skillfully depicted the whole Venetian system of values, combining the older commedia dell'arte techniques with lively character depiction of the middle classes. Goldoni, the genius of the Italian Enlightenment, thus created a new living theater, which appealed to the Italian public.

The Neapolitan conservatories

The most active musical centers included Naples, Bologna, Venice, Milan, and Florence. Music was everywhere: in churches and monasteries, in public and court theaters, in court ballrooms and private homes, in learned *accademie* (academies) and conservatories, and even in the streets. Naples, in particular, was an inexhaustible source of musical activity, at whose center were the four conservatories: San Onofrio a Capuana, Santa Maria di Loretto, Santa Maria della Pietà dei Turchini, and Poveri di Gesù Cristo. Protected by the Church, these institutions served initially as orphanages for boys, educating those who otherwise would have remained street urchins. The lessons, taught by rote, included solfeggio, singing, figured bass, counterpoint, gram-

Royal Palace of Caserta. The grand staircase was constructed between 1752 and 1754, and designed by Luigi Vanvitelli. As summer residence of the Neapolitan monarchs, the Palace was the location of a number of musical performances.

mar, and catechism. During their student years the boys earned money for the conservatories by singing throughout the city on secular and sacred occasions.

While most boys had to contend with conditions that were far from luxurious, those selected to be eunuchs (*castrati*) received special attention. The money they earned singing soprano roles was a substantial source of revenue for the conservatories. Consequently they enjoyed private rooms full of light and warmth; they were well fed and generally protected. In the first half of the century Naples seems to have been the center for the castrati. Of those who attained international fame, many were of Neapolitan origin and were trained in these conservatories.

Teachers in the conservatories were frequently the products of these same institutions. Such famous composer-teachers as Alessandro Scarlatti, Nicola Porpora, and Francesco Durante trained new generations of Neapolitan composers, who in turn disseminated their musical style to other major European centers: Domenico Scarlatti in Vienna, Nicolò (Niccolò) Jommelli in Stuttgart, and Nicola (Niccolò) Piccinni at the Russian court. Pergolesi's *La serva padrona* (1733) and *Stabat mater* (1736) were particularly popular in Paris in the 1750s, where they were considered the epitome of the Italian musical style.

The dissemination of the Neapolitan style

The many churches of Naples were also centers of intense musical activity. Large choirs and the organ of the Cathedral of San Gennaro, for example, were part of the splendid celebrations that usually extended over several days and included brilliant displays of fireworks.

Venice was the home of another, somewhat different group of conservatories. The four charitable institutions, degli Incurabili, dell'Ospedaletto, della Pietà, and dei Mendicanti, were schools for girls. Instructed in music by the best composers of the era, such as Galuppi, Sacchini and Porpora, the girls quickly acquired a long-lasting reputation as musicians of the highest caliber. The Venetian conservatories were considered a musical wonder of the eighteenth century. Unlike their counterparts in Naples, however, which trained talented boys as future musical leaders, the Venetian schools gave their girls a thorough education without providing any specific goals or encouraging them to have a professional career in music. The conservatories acted as their guardians until they were given away in marriage by the state. One of the products of the Mendicanti was the violinist and composer Maddalena Lombardini Sirmen, who, after her studies with Tartini in Padua, attained international acclaim as a violin virtuoso.

The Venetian conservatories

France

The intellectual life of mid-eighteenth-century France was dominated by the *philosophes,* staunch upholders of liberty, which to them implied freedom from domination by the Church, freedom from intolerance, and freedom from ignorance. They were skeptical of tradition, and although they recog-

The philosophes

nized religion as a viable power, they opposed dogma, belief in mysteries and miracles, and superstitious fear of the unknown—in short, everything that seemed irrational. Politically, they believed in an enlightened government that would eliminate feudal privileges, propagate equality of the bourgeoisie with the nobility, and foster both social reforms and mass education.

The main proponents of this movement in France were François-Marie Arouet de Voltaire (1694–1778), Jean-Jacques Rousseau (1712–1778), and the group called the *Encyclopédistes*. The term "Encyclopédistes" referred to the group working to compile the most comprehensive encyclopedia in France up to that time. Its thirty-five volumes contained a compendium of knowledge in politics, science, the arts, and philosophy, and the authors addressed themselves to a reading public that by the mid-eighteenth century had grown significantly. Written between the years 1751 and 1772 under the general directorship of Denis Diderot (1713–1784) and Jean Lerond d'Alembert (1717–1783), the *Encyclopédie* catered to the contemporary demand for overall surveys of knowledge.

Jean-Jacques Rousseau

In contrast to the Encyclopédistes, Rousseau (one of the most original thinkers of his generation, not only a man of letters but also a musician and composer) believed in the value of the nonrational, in a greater reliance on impulse over judgment. Through his doctrine "Back to Nature," he concluded that Nature alone makes people happy, good, and free, while the artificialities and restrictions of society corrupt them and add to their misery. In his view, there was a basic conflict between Nature and Society. He judged all the positive aspects of human beings, such as kindness, honesty, and understanding, to be products of Nature, while he attributed the negative aspects to conditioning by society. This philosophic system became extremely influential among artists and intellectuals all over Europe, forming part of the doctrine of Romanticism.

Paris

The center of French intellectual and cultural life was Paris—and the Paris of the second half of the century was the musical capital of the world. In the intensity of its concert life, the variety of its programs, and the size of its audience, Paris had no equal.

Music was performed everywhere: in the *salons*, in a variety of concert halls, at court, and in the theaters. The private salons provided occasions for discourses on politics, arts, letters, and other topics of intellectual interest; the object of such discourses was intellectual pleasure, and the predominant tone was polite. The *Théâtre de l'Opéra* (later known as the *Académie Royale de Musique*, the "Royal Academy of Music") mounted large opera productions of a serious nature (specifically, *tragédies lyriques*). Concert halls existed for public and semipublic performances of music, and series were presented by the *Concert Spirituel* ("Sacred Concert"), as well as by numerous other organizations, such as the *Concert des Amateurs* ("Concert of Amateurs"), the *Concert d'Amis* ("Concert of Friends"), and the *Concert des Associés* ("Concert of Associates").

By far the most famous of these organizations was the Concert Spirituel. Founded in 1725 by Anne Danican Philidor (1681–1728), it presented its series in the Tuileries.[1] Much of the music initially performed was religious and based on a Latin text, often with motets sung by soloists. Increasingly, however, instrumental music, symphonies, concertos, and *symphonies concertantes* alternated with the vocal works.

Toward the end of the century, half a million people lived in Paris, including many composers who had come seeking glory and fortune. Parisian concert life and the private gatherings in the salons of the nobility were responsible for a proliferation of musical culture rivaled only by similar developments in contemporary London. While monarchs resided in both cities, they were by no means the primary patrons of music. The "democratization" of art attained in London and Paris paved the way for the artistic climate of the nineteenth century.

The German-Speaking Lands

Like Italy, Germany in the eighteenth century was a conglomeration of independent geographic entities. Most musical activity took place at the courts, where musicians were employed, and wealthy aristocrats, statesmen, and rulers served as patrons. Among the most active centers were Leipzig, Dresden, Berlin, Hamburg, Munich, Mannheim, and the smaller courts along the banks of the Rhine, including Cologne, Coblenz, Darmstadt, and Ludwigsburg. In Austria, Salzburg and Vienna were leaders. **Music at the courts**

The German-speaking courts of the eighteenth century exuded splendor, elegance, and wealth, and their patrons of art were intellectuals, fluent in several languages, and musically accomplished. Music at the various German courts was a regular pastime, as both intellectual pursuit and entertainment. On a small scale, as a chamber activity, patrons frequently joined their musicians in performance. On a larger scale, the patrons treated music, especially opera, as a full evening's entertainment to which they invited other members of the aristocracy and visiting dignitaries. The best orchestras—especially those at Mannheim and Dresden—were admired for their full sound, their sense of ensemble, and their ability to project a variety of dynamic ranges.

Many larger courts took up summer residence in nearby palaces, where up to fifteen hundred people, including musicians, friends, and servants, spent the summer months. Music-making thus continued all year round. The main, or winter, court residences usually contained opera houses for the performance of large Italian operas, and the summer courts had small theaters for the performance of shorter comic works: *intermezzi* and *burlettas* (light, sometimes vulgar, comic operas).

While much musical activity was sponsored by the courts, public concerts did take place, although not as often as in France and England. Two of the **Public concerts**

Schönbrunn Palace and grounds, Vienna, by Bellotto. The summer residence of the Austro-Hungarian monarchs, completed in 1750. Johann Fischer von Erlach (1656–1723) was the architect. (Courtesy, Kunsthistorisches Museum, Vienna)

best-known series were the weekly *Liebhaberkonzerte,* begun in Berlin in 1770, and the *Gewandhaus* concerts in Leipzig, formally founded in 1763 by Johann Adam Hiller (1728–1804), a composer of German *Singspiel* (see Chapter 20). A frequent event at the Liebhaberkonzerte was the performance of Handel's oratorios.

Private concerts were also in vogue. One particularly famous example is the series held in the house of Baron Gottfried van Swieten in Vienna, now famous because the concerts provided the young Mozart with exposure to the music of Handel and Bach. On those occasions Van Swieten sang tenor, while Mozart sang alto and played the viola or piano.

Despite its vitality, artistic and musical life in the German cities, duchies, and kingdoms was affected by contemporary political situations. The Seven Years War (1756–1763), for instance, caused irreparable damage

Dresden and Leipzig

in Dresden and Leipzig and weakened musical life in both cities. Yet each court had its golden period when musical and cultural activities were at their height. The culmination of the glory of the Dresden court occurred before 1756, under the musical leadership of Johann Hasse (1699–1783), Kapellmeister to the Elector of Saxony. With Hasse, the royal theater achieved a reputation as one of the best in Germany. In Leipzig, the Gewandhaus concerts, interrupted by the Seven Years War, resumed and began to flourish. By 1781 a building was constructed to house the concerts. Under the directorship of J. A. Hiller these assumed a prominent position in the city's cultural life.

Berlin

In Berlin, the Prussian court reached the apogee of its musical development during the forty-year reign of Frederick the Great (reg. 1740–1780). A statesman and diplomat who successfully led his armies into battle against the Hapsburg rule in Austria, an avid reader who was well versed in many academic disciplines, and a keen lover of music, the king devoted four hours of his highly structured day to its study, practice, and performance—employing at his court a contingent of musicians whose sole purpose was to cater to his musical needs. Johann Joachim Quantz (1697–1773), the composer and flute player, wrote close to three hundred flute compositions for Frederick's use.

Among his court Kapellmeisters were such men as Carl Heinrich Graun (1703/4–1759); Johann Friedrich Agricola (1720–1774), who was also the music director of the court opera; and Johann Friedrich Reichardt (1752–1814). Three of the most important treatises that remain today as accounts of eighteenth-century performance practices were published by musicians from the court of Frederick of Prussia: Quantz's *Versuch einer Anweisung die Flöte traversiere zu spielen* ("An Essay on Instruction in Performance on the Transverse Flute," 1752), C. P. E. Bach's *Versuch über die wahre Art das Clavier zu spielen* ("Essay on the True Art of Playing a Keyboard Instrument," 1753 and 1775), and Agricola's *Arte del canto figurato* ("The Art of the Florid Song," 1723), translated into German by Agricola in 1757.

Perform-ance-practice treatises

The writing and translations of these didactic manuals were allied with the spirit of the Enlightenment, which encouraged the systematization of all knowledge. There was a general interest in northern Germany in publishing histories and theories of music, compiling dictionaries, and writing music criticism. Some of these major works represent the nation's earliest attempts at music criticism. Friedrich Wilhelm Marpurg (1718–1795), associated with the court of Prussia, was a theorist of great importance and a true child of the Age of Reason. In an attempt to systematize musical knowledge, he wrote critical treatises on theoretical matters, on fugue and counterpoint, the history of the organ, the history of music, and even books on temperament and tuning. During his stay in Paris in 1746 he met Voltaire and d'Alembert, and his works are in the best tradition of the Encyclopédistes. Especially famous are his *Der critische Musicus an der Spree* ("The Critical Musician as a Speaker,"[2] Berlin, 1750) and *Kritische Briefe über die Tonkunst* ("Critical Letters About Music," 1760–1764).

The rise of music criticism

Among the refined thinkers whose polemical writings laid the foundations of modern music criticism were Johann Mattheson (1681–1764) of Hamburg, whose *Critica musica* ("The Criticism of Music," 1722–1725) was the first periodical to discuss music from a critical point of view; Johann Adolf Scheibe (1708–1776), whose Hamburg paper *Der critische Musicus* ("The Critical Musician," 1737–1740) attacked the musical style of J. S. Bach; Johann Georg Sulzer (1720–1779), who edited the *Allgemeine Theorie der schönen Künste* ("The Complete Theory of the Beautiful Art," 1771–1774); and Johann Philipp Kirnberger (1721–1783), known for his two-volume treatise *Die Kunst des reinen Satzes* ("Art of Pure Composition," 1771, 1779). Hiller and Reichardt both contributed articles to magazines, and the latter even edited the journal *Musikalisches Kunstmagazin* ("The Journal of Musical Art," 1782–1791). Reichardt was one of the most important writers and critics of the century.

Like eighteenth century Paris, Vienna was a continually boiling cultural cauldron. And like the other German-speaking cities, Vienna underwent

Vienna and Maria Theresa cycles of intense musical activity alternating with those of relative cultural stagnation. Maria Theresa, eldest daughter of the Holy Roman emperor Charles VI, assumed the Hapsburg throne in 1740 (the same year that her archenemy, Frederick II, ascended the throne of Prussia). Some of those years were spent in wars with Frederick, especially the period between 1740 and 1763, when a minimum of opera was performed in Vienna. The general tempo of musical activities gathered momentum in the last three decades of the century.

Joseph II Joseph II, son of Maria Theresa, and ruler of Hungary, Bohemia, and the Hapsburg lands for a decade after her death (1780–1790), shared in the spirit of the Enlightenment through the reforms in which he sought to improve the condition of his people. The emperor sang well and played the harpsichord and cello. He took a lively interest in the theater, for he considered it a means of encouraging a national expression, and by lowering admission prices, he

Jacopo Amigoni (1675–1752), *Portrait Group* (Oil on canvas, 172.8 × 245.1 cm, Felton Bequest 1949/50). In this oil painting Metastasio is on the left, singers Teresa Castellini and Farinelli in the middle, Amigoni and an Austrian archduke to the right. (Reproduced by permission of the National Gallery of Victoria, Melbourne)

made the theater more accessible to a larger number of people. He encouraged performances of the Singspiel as a manifestation of the specifically Austrian type of comic opera which involved the use of Austrian folk elements. Perhaps most important, Joseph appointed Mozart, whom he had known since 1762, his private musician in 1787.

As we saw in Chapter 16, Vienna was the adopted home of the renowned Italian Pietro Trapassi (1698–1782), who was known as Metastasio. The texts of this poet and prolific librettist were set to music by composers throughout the century. Some of his libretti were set repeatedly; *Demofoonte,* for example, was set by forty-eight different composers within a span of fifty years. For over half a century Metastasio lived in Vienna. He assumed the post of imperial court poet of Austria and was an important figure in Viennese cultural life. Mozart met him in 1768 and later set several Metastasian texts to music. As an example of the poet's widespread fame in Europe, we need only cite Mozart's famous visit to Count Joseph von Firmian in Milan in 1770, when the young composer was given texts to arias from three Metastasian operas and asked to set them to music within several days. The finished product was performed at a *soirée* (evening party) with Mozart at the keyboard. As recompense the composer received from his host a complete set of Metastasio's works.

Metastasio

England

Socially, politically, and economically, the period in England up to approximately 1760 was one of relative stability. Men of letters came primarily from the bourgeoisie, the same social class that provided audiences and the reading public. While in much of Europe music was subsidized by the courts, in England it was almost entirely in the hands of the middle class. Public concerts were widely available, and London in the last quarter of the century easily supported three different series of orchestral concerts and two rival opera houses. Yet English musical taste remained dominated by Italian comic opera.

Middle-class culture

The increasing prominence of the middle class helped foster a new interest in literature. During the first two decades of the century, political patronage of literary activity was not uncommon. Writers were rewarded by politicians on the basis of the service they rendered their political party. Thus Joseph Addison (1679–1719), who edited the *Spectator,* a weekly periodical established in 1711, became secretary of state. The novelist Daniel Defoe (1660–1731), whose novel *Robinson Crusoe* (1719) was a poignant social satire, also received a variety of political missions. The English novelist Samuel Richardson (1689–1761) attained great popularity both in England and on the Continent. His emphasis on subjectivity, sentimentality, and the depiction of middle-class life, as well as his moralizing tone, matched the temper of the times. By midcentury, Richardson's moral novel *Pamela, or Virtue Rewarded*

Literature and politics

(1740) had already served as the basis of an opera libretto by Goldoni, and the Abbé Prévost (1697–1763) had translated Richardson's works into French.

Russia and Other Courts

Russia's cultural position in the age of Enlightenment was that of assimilator rather than imitator; it acted as a recipient of French culture even though Italian operatic tastes prevailed at court. French, and to a lesser extent German, became the official languages of the court. The upper classes became thoroughly Westernized in dress, values, and cultural tastes, considerably exacerbating an already existing spiritual schism between them and the peasants, who retained their traditional ways.

Catherine II, known as Catherine the Great, ruled Russia from 1762 until 1796. Her ascension to the throne and subsequent long rule marked the end of a thirty-seven-year period of instability. Born in Germany, Catherine was a woman of tremendous industry and energy. Her personal life was even more colorful than her political life, as she lived openly through a variety of amorous adventures. Her support of religious toleration, her disapproval of torture as a punitive measure, and her legal codifications earned her the praise of the philosophes as an Enlightened monarch. She maintained contact with Voltaire, and especially F. M. von Grimm, with whom she corresponded until her death.

Although Catherine was a cultured woman, she seemed to care little for music. Nevertheless, she was a patron of the arts who employed in her theater an Italian opera company, and at times an entire *corps de ballet*. Since the fourth decade of the eighteenth century, the court at St. Petersburg had employed Italian musicians and composers as maestri di cappella. These men wrote and directed compositions exclusively for the Russian court. Italian *intermezzi* enjoyed special popularity at the court, and throughout the 1730s, still during the reign of Empress Anna Ioannovna (d. 1740), a number of Italian troupes entertained Russian nobility with their comic repertoire. Although the intermezzi were sung in Italian, the texts were translated into Russian and German. The printed libretti (booklets containing the text) were distributed to the audiences, who followed the performance by reading the translations. During Domenico Cimarosa's tenure (1789–1792) the court librettist, F. Moretti, provided the nobility with Italian comic opera texts.

Italian musicians in Spain   The proliferation of Italian music affected the Spanish court as well. Domenico Scarlatti spent much of his life in Madrid, where he composed several hundred harpsichord sonatas. The famous castrato Carlo Broschi (1705–1782), known under the stage name Farinelli, was another Italian expatriate in Spain. As musician to King Philip V from 1737 onward, he eventually became director of the Madrid opera house, assuming an active role in performances of Italian operas in that city.

Summary

Many of the music-making activities in the eighteenth century took place at the courts, where rich and educated aristocratic patrons supported composers and performers alike. In at least two large cities, however—Paris and London—the social status and role of the artist began to change. The large number of public concerts given there enabled musicians to support themselves as freelance artists.

By the last quarter of the eighteenth century the enjoyment of art music was no longer exclusive to the upper classes. The public came from all social strata—especially the middle class—and was affected by an interpenetration of values fostered by the ideals of the Enlightenment. The members of these audiences were largely the same people who constituted the reading public, and whose new interests triggered a literary and journalistic explosion. Members of the middle and lower classes were increasingly represented as protagonists in comic opera plots, and the opera libretto thus became a reflection of the tastes and values of the society. Italian composers and performers were dispersed throughout Europe, and their music enjoyed widespread popularity.

The audiences that filled the concert halls combined their literary and musical interests, and sought guidance in their newly acquired musical tastes in the form of music criticism. The eighteenth-century spirit of rationalism is thus in part responsible for the rise of music criticism.

The first three-quarters of the century exude a spirit of cosmopolitanism, but the last quarter points to an increasing national awareness. More important, the rational, liberal, humanitarian, and scientific ideas promulgated by the Encyclopédistes and Rousseau, and adopted by Frederick II, Catherine II, and Maria Theresa, penetrated all aspects of eighteenth-century life, to create a more enlightened society. Its art and music performed a variety of social functions, and above all, was accessible to a wider spectrum of that society than was music of any preceding period. In the chapters that follow, we shall examine the various consequences of these changes.

Notes

1. The Philidor family included several generations of French musicians, of whom André Danican Philidor (l'aîné; the elder, 1647–1730) was perhaps the best known. He was composer, performer, and music librarian to the French king. Anne was one of his three children. Both F. J. Fétis, in his *Biographie Universelle des Musiciens* (Paris, 1875), vol. 7, p. 28, and J. Rushton, in his article on the family in *The New Grove's Dictionary of Music and Musicians* (London: Macmillan, 1980), vol. 14, p. 627, refer to Anne as male, and as founder of the Concert Spirituel. Other sources offer contradictory information by naming André Danican Philidor as the founder of the concert series.
2. Not a literal translation of the title, since the word *Spree* is an old north German expression, and as such is not found in current dictionaries. The word is related to *sprechen,* i.e., "to speak."

Bibliography

Books and Articles

General

ANDERSON, MATTHEW SMITH. *Europe in the Eighteenth Century, 1713–1783*. London: Longmans, Green, 1961.

MOWAT, ROBERT BALMAIN. *The Age of Reason: The Continent of Europe in the Eighteenth Century*. London: Harrap, 1934.

Italy

ARNOLD, DENIS. "Orphans and Ladies: The Venetian Conservatories (1680–1790)." *Proceedings of the Royal Musical Association* 89 (1962–1963): 31–47.

LEE, VERNON. *Studies of the Eighteenth Century in Italy,* 2nd ed. London: F. Fisher Unwin, 1907.

SALVATORELLI, LUIGI. *A Concise History of Italy.* Translated by Bernard Miall. London: Allen & Unwin, 1940.

France

PIERRE CONSTANT VICTOR. *Histoire du Concert Spirituel, 1725–1790.* Paris: Société Française de Musicologie, 1975.

German-Speaking Countries

MITFORD, NANCY. *Frederick the Great.* New York: Harper & Row, 1970.

YORKE-LONG, ALAN. *Music at Court: Four Eighteenth-Century Studies.* London: Weidenfeld & Nicolson, 1954.

England

BURNEY, CHARLES. *The Present State of Music in France and Italy,* 2nd ed. London: T. Becket, 1773. Reprinted in *Monuments of Music and Music Literature in Facsimile,* vol. 70. New York: Broude Bros., 1969.

MARSHALL, DOROTHY. *Eighteenth-Century England,* 2nd ed. London: Longmans, Green, 1974.

19

The Preclassic Style: Syntax and Structural Concepts

THE period between 1720 and 1770 presents a complex picture of intermingling and overlapping stylistic orientations. J. S. Bach completed his Mass in B minor about 1747. This work, which stands at the apex of Baroque style in northern Europe, is preceded by about fourteen years by Pergolesi's *La serva padrona* ("The Maid Mistress"), which, as a musical product of the south, is a prime example of the newer, more lighthearted homophonic style that was shortly to engulf all of Europe. In the first half of the eighteenth century this stylistic dichotomy is felt even in the creative output of the same composer. Alessandro Scarlatti, François Couperin, and Jean-Marie Leclair are but a few of the composers whose music fluctuated between older and newer features.

This chapter will summarize the techniques and elements of the Preclassic style and consider those aspects of the new idiom developed by the French, Italians, and Germans that created the regional variants. Our discussion of three stylistic subdivisions—French *style galant* (graceful style), German *empfindsamer Stil* (sensitive style), and the Italian insrumental *buffo* (comic opera) style—will reflect the multiplicity of musical tastes that existed during this short transitional period. However, we cannot really categorize such stylistic phenomena, since the history of musical styles in this period is not conducive to neat compartmentalization. For example, even though Carl Philipp Emanuel Bach (1714–1788), J. S. Bach's second oldest son, will be discussed within the context of the Berlin empfindsamer Stil, not all of his compositions are examples of that particular stylistic variant. He was active at the court of Frederick the Great, which was heavily influenced by French taste and where Italian operas were also performed. Thus his compositions inevitably reflect different styles.

Since the evolution of the Preclassic idiom parallels the development of solo instrumental music, specifically the sonata, in which the new stylistic features are most clearly recognizable, this chapter will draw from the instrumental sonata repertoire to illustrate evolving stylistic tendencies. We must remember, however, that all musical genres increasingly adopted the Preclassic idiom.

Descriptions of Nascent Sonata
(or First-Movement) Form

The Preclassic epoch witnessed not only the evolution of a musical language (with important regional variants) but also the formation of the concept of *sonata form,* which was applied to the composition of symphonies, solo instrumental music, chamber music, and concertos, and was an extremely important compositional concept well into the nineteenth century.

Sonata form was both a structure and a compositional process, usually applied (although not exclusively restricted) to the first movement of a multi-movement composition. While no single source can be pointed out as its genesis or forerunner, there is a correlation between the newer ternary structure that became the basis for sonata form, and the older, Baroque, expanded binary form influenced by dance form. Both syntactic and structural changes affected the evolution of sonata form. In their discussions of cadence points, phraseology, harmonic rhythm, and periodicity, theorists reflect on the nascent structural changes. The earliest references to larger structures (i.e., sonata form) appear in the works of two late-eighteenth-century theorists: Heinrich Christoph Koch's *Versuch einer Anleitung zur Composition* ("An Introduction to Composition," 1782–1793) and Francesco Galeazzi's *Elementi teoretico-pratici di musica* ("Theoretico-Practical Elements in Music," 1791–1796).

Koch's eigh- teenth- century view Koch divides first-movement form into two sections, suggesting that he still thinks in terms of a binary, rather than a ternary, movement. The first section, he says, may contain two or three thematic "ideas." The initial idea modulates toward and cadences in a new key, which may be the dominant or a relative minor (or major); the secondary idea, presented in this new key, is more lyrical and less forceful than the primary idea. In more modern terminology, these ideas and their tonal structure form the *first and second subject areas.* According to Koch, a third melodic idea (the equivalent of a *closing theme*) takes up a considerable portion of this first section, which ends with a repeat sign. In his definition of the first section, Koch has indeed described what nineteenth-century theorists called the *exposition.*

The second section, Koch continues, contains two parts. The first (equivalent to today's *development* section) may begin with a statement of either the main or the secondary theme, or parts of one of the themes. This material may be quoted precisely, shortened, extended, and reworked, and the harmonic motion may travel through a series of keys that are at times remote from the tonic, until the dominant, relative, or home key is reached. The second division of the second section (known today as the *recapitulation*) usually reintroduces the home key and may begin with the main theme or some other melodic idea. It then proceeds as a parallel to the first section in the original key. Koch thus described what are, in essence, the three components of the first-movement sonata form: exposition, development, and recapitulation.

It is important to remember, however, that Koch's descriptions are ideal constructs or generalizations. Not all movements in sonata form contain all the elements he mentioned. For instance, although modulations and changes of mood may be present in ample quantities within the exposition, only a single theme may be used by the composer, as in C. P. E. Bach's sonatas. Franz Joseph Haydn, too, frequently adheres to monothematic construction in a movement that may be mostly derived melodically or rhythmically from an opening motive (*head motive*).

Italy: Genesis of the Preclassic Style

Syntactic changes preceded those changes in musical idiom in larger structural concepts that are evident in Italian music in the first decades of the 1700s, especially in the vocal line that accompanied a humorous text in a *scena buffa* or intermezzo. Accents and textual inflections guided the rhythmic patterns of the musical line and determined the length of the musical phrase. Nonsense syllables, multiple repetitions of such syllables as *si* and *no,* and imitations of such sounds as a heartbeat or the tick of a clock (onomatopoeia) molded the humorous features within a musical line. The comic text, therefore, was largely responsible for syntactic changes in the vocal line. No sooner was it generated than the new phraseology was transferred from the vocal to the accompanying instrumental line.

Changes in Musical Structure

Along with the developments of the new stylistic idiom, or elements of a new language, so to speak, the eighteenth century witnessed the evolution of new structural concepts, such as sonata form. The Classic concept of sonata form as developed by Haydn and Mozart will be discussed in Chapter 22. We must mention at this point, however, the structural changes found in the works of the Preclassic composers.

The familiar Baroque binary movement contained in its initial section the main idea, followed by a passage that led to the dominant or relative key. It cadenced in the new tonality at the double bar. The second section began with a repeat of the main idea (always preserving the single affect of the movement), which reappeared in the dominant or relative key. After some modulations, the general movement toward the tonic recommenced. With the exception of the tonal directions, the musical events of the second division paralleled those of the first.

Syntactic and structural changes are noticeable in the harpsichord sonatas of Domenico Scarlatti, son of the Neapolitan opera composer Alessandro Scarlatti. Although the majority of his one-movement sonatas are still binary, some do present two themes of contrasting affect: for example, the transitional Sonata in D major, K. 29 (L. 461).[1] Noticeable here are both the older processes of sequential repetition of a single figure and the newer divisions into short phrase units and contrasting affects. Such techniques as trills on

D. Scarlatti

internal pedal points, thickening of the texture with a sudden *sforzando,* or the creation of a dissonance through *acciaccaturas* are also typical of Scarlatti's keyboard style.

    Other interesting examples of the Preclassic Italian sonata in its formative **B. Galuppi** stages are the more than fifty keyboard sonatas of Baldassare Galuppi. While Galuppi at times introduces a second subject in a contrasting key, as in the Sonata No. 6 in E-flat major,[2] he is just as likely to work out a whole movement in a single affect, a monothematic idea, as in the Sonata No. 5 in C major. Perhaps the most clearly defined second theme is evidenced in Sonata

Ex. 19.1   Baldassare Galuppi, Sonata No. 6 in E-flat major

No. 6, in which the entrance of the second subject is anticipated harmonically by the half cadence in B-flat at measure 9. The second theme contrasts with the first in its rhythmic configuration (it uses triplets), in key, and in texture. Some contrapuntal imitation occurs, while in the first subject the texture is that of a melody and accompaniment (see Example 19.1).

Galuppi's concern with smaller motivic units is exemplified in measures 5–7, in which the four-note motive is derived from the initial two-and-a-half-measure statement. Although the Classic symmetry of periodicity and the "antecedent-consequent" phrase structure is not yet found here, some feeling for symmetry is created through the repetition of the initial idea in a lower range at measures 3–4.

Sonata No. 5 in C major is based on a monothematic idea in which the so-called Alberti bass persists throughout almost the entire movement (see Example 19.2). This device typifies the technique of chordal prolongation as a conscious attempt to slow the harmonic rhythm. This lefthand figure, a type of accompaniment introduced by the keyboard composer Domenico Alberti (c. 1710–1739), was popular with Preclassic and Classic composers. The sweet, simple lyricism of the melodic line even anticipates Mozart's style. **Alberti bass**

While most of Galuppi's sonatas are in three movements, some are in two, and in at least two sonatas (No. 2 in C minor, No. 7 in G minor) the first movement ends on the dominant instead of the tonic. The sonatas do not always follow the common fast–slow–fast cyclical scheme of the Italian opera overture, as may be seen in No. 7, whose order of movements is Largo–Presto–Allegretto. Some of Galuppi's compositional techniques still reveal their origin in the Baroque style processes, but the major influence on his works is Italian comic opera. His development sections, though abbreviated, contain skillful modulation and at times introduce new material.

Other Italian keyboard composers of note whose works show Preclassic tendencies include Antonio Ferradini (c. 1718–1779), Giovanni Maria Rutini (1723–1797), Giovanni Benedetto Platti (c. 1700–1763), Giovanni Battista Pescetti (1704–1766), Pietro Domenico Paradisi (1707–1791), and one of Mozart's contemporaries who was best known for his *opere buffe*—Domenico Cimarosa. **Other Italian keyboard composers**

Ex. 19.2 Baldassare Galuppi, Sonata No. 5 in C major

Italian Style Abroad

J. C. Bach and Mozart

The one composer whose keyboard figurations bear perhaps the closest resemblance to those of Mozart is Johann Christian Bach, who settled in England in 1762, where he spent the last two decades of his life. Thoroughly Italianate in his tastes, J. C. Bach was a composer of operas, symphonies, and chamber works, with a special interest in the keyboard concerto. His other keyboard works include sonatas for four hands as well as two published sets of solo sonatas: Op. 5 (1768) and Op. 17 (1779).

He wrote specifically for the pianoforte and thoroughly understood the capabilities of the new instrument. Bach's lyricism resembles that in Mozart's sonatas, and Mozart, in turn, both loved and respected Bach. (At age eight, Mozart played some of Bach's sonatas in London, and in 1778 he used them as teaching material in Mannheim.) J. C. Bach frequently uses two-movement sonatas, and his finales are often a minuet (and trio) or a rondo. At least one sonata (Op. 5, No. 3, in G major) has a theme and variations as its last movement. Although his sonatas are generally longer than Galuppi's, Bach adheres mostly to a binary first-movement form and rarely uses an extended development section.

France: Rococo and the *Style Galant*

Rococo: definition

The French Preclassic style variant—the *style galant*—paralleled in music features exhibited by rococo art and architecture. The term *rococo* is applied to a specific style in painting, architecture, interior design, and other decorative arts in France in the period between the Regency and the death of Louis XV, spanning approximately the years 1715–1774. The style was an accurate reflection of French court society, whose primary objective was entertainment and whose values were comfort, elegance, pleasure, and beauty. Style galant

François Couperin

was most clearly expressed in the keyboard music of François Couperin (1668–1733) and the works of other clavecin composers: Jean-François Dandrieu (1682–1738), Louis-Nicolas Clérambault (1676–1749), Francois d'Agincourt (1684–1758), and Louis-Claude Daquin (1694–1772). To a lesser extent, it was also present in the violin sonata. The music of the style galant was that of connoisseurs, performed in the salons of the aristocracy. It was witty, elegant, graceful, highly ornamented, and often harmonically colorful.

Couperin composed four volumes of harpsichord (clavecin) music, totaling over two hundred compositions. Arranged in suite format to which he assigned the name *Ordre,* each contained a large number of dance pieces as well as character pieces with descriptive titles. Many titles refer in flattering and elegant terms to contemporary figures; some exhibit Couperin's sense of humor. For example, *Les Fastes de la grande et anciénne Ménestrandise* ("The Pageantries of the Stately and Ancient Ménestrandise"), from Ordre No. 11, is a satire on a guild of entertainers.

Although Couperin's music evokes the sensual paintings of Antoine Watteau (1684–1721) and is thus a product of the contemporary French aesthetic, structurally his compositions must be viewed as expressions of the neo-Baroque spirit.

During the eighteenth century and until the Classic era, the term "sonata" in France was applied equally to instrumental compositions for one or for several (three or four) instruments. The number of movements ranged customarily from three to five. Another characteristic of the period is the continuation of the Baroque interchangeability of instruments. Rameau's *Pièces de clavecin en concert avec violon ou une flûte et une viole ou un 2e violon* ("Concerted Pieces for Harpsichord and a Violin or a Flute, and a Gamba or Second Violin," published 1741) shows this. Rameau also indicates in the preface to the edition that the pieces can be played by the harpsichord alone.

Inter-changeable instruments

Front page of Jean-Joseph de Mondonville's *Pièces de clavecin* (composed 1734–1738). (Courtesy, H. Baron, London)

A flute can substitute for the violin in some of the seventeen books of sonatas for solo violin and basso continuo written by Jean-Marie Leclair (1697–1764). Especially noteworthy for its expressiveness is his Op. 9, No. 7. The four-movement composition, with its Andante, Allegro ma non troppo, Aria, and Giga, is reminiscent of the Baroque church sonata in the alteration of slow and fast tempos; however, the overall impression is that of the evolving style galant. The first and second movements contain some unexpected, piquant harmonic turns, while the Aria is a dignified gavotte. The delightful, lighthearted fourth movement exudes humor through its use of large skips.

Mondonville and Gaviniès

The evolution from the neo-Baroque to the Preclassic style in France is particularly evidenced in the works of later composers: Jean-Marie Leclair, Jean-Joseph Cassanéa de Mondonville (1711–1772), Pierre Gaviniès (1728–1800), and Johann Schobert (c. 1735–1767). Mondonville and Gaviniès were involved in the composition of instrumental *duets,* a genre that attained great popularity in Paris around the middle of the century. Instrumental combinations in these works included the violin and keyboard, as well as two violins. The sonatas of Gaviniès are usually in three movements, and their finales at times use the technique of the melodic variation.

New roles for supporting instruments

In the mid-eighteenth century the relationship of the solo and accompanying instruments in a sonata changed. The Baroque concept of a solo sonata with the solo instruments supported by a basso continuo was gradually replaced by several new possibilities. Mondonville and Schobert both experimented with new sonata formats. In Mondonville's *Pièces de clavecin en sonates avec accompagnement de violon,* Op. 3 ("Sonatas for Harpsicord with Violin Accompaniment," 1734–1738) the violin, rather than doubling the keyboard part, has independent and complementary melodic material.

Schobert

The new relationship between the keyboard and the violin was further developed in Johann Schobert's sonatas for violin and harpsichord, in which the string rather than the keyboard was the accompanying instrument. Schobert, especially, cultivated chamber music with keyboard obbligato. The Violin Sonata Op. 14, No. 3 is of interest, because the first movement is entirely for keyboard solo. In the second movement the violin accompanies the keyboard, while in the Trio of the Minuet movement the violin carries the main melodic material. The Minuet, which begins in a minor key (an unusual feature for a dance movement), is very effective in its simplicity and melodiousness (*DDT,* vol. 39).[3] The simplicity of Schobert's instrumental lines, however, is representative of Italianate tastes and the Mannheim school of composition and of the style galant as it was to evolve after the middle of the century.

Developments in the German–Speaking Lands

The term style galant was also known and used by theorists outside France. Marpurg's *Kritische Briefe über die Tonkunst* refers to the *galanter Stil,* in which cadences appear freely and are not confined merely to the conven-

The mirror room in Amalienburg (1734–1739, Nymphenburg Castle, near Munich), designed by François Cuvilliés the Elder (1695–1768). This is an excellent example of the interior decor and rococo tastes in design. Cuvilliés also designed the Residenz Theatre (1751–1752) in Munich. (Courtesy, Bayerische Verwaltung der Staatlichen Schlösser, Garten und Seen)

tional places, as in the Baroque style of composition. Sulzer's *Allgemeine Theorie der Schönen Künste* refers to the same style and mentions the composer's newly acquired ability to express a greater variety of feelings through the use of shorter phrases and smaller melodic units.

The Germans' use of the term galant, while recognizing the emergence of newer (i.e., post-Baroque) stylistic features, differs from the neo-Baroque style galant as exhibited in the works of François Couperin. The expressiveness of German music was in direct opposition to the ideals of restraint and formality intrinsic to the early eighteenth-century style galant. The Preclassic style variant in the German-speaking countries is best classified as the *empfindsamer Stil,* manifested in the feelings of unrestrained emotionalism and sentimentalism expressed in the performance of musical compositions. A literary parallel to the musicians' new inclination toward emotional expression is found in the writings of the *Sturm und Drang* ("Storm and Stress") movement. Subjectivity and emotionalism, combined with a passionate exuberance, may be found in the novels of Friedrich Maximilian von Klinger (1752–

Empfind-samer stil: definition

1831) and in the works of the young Johann Wolfgang von Goethe (1749–1832).

The search for the expression of emotions characterized by the empfindsamer Stil was also embodied by the *Affektenlehre* ("doctrine of affections"), a culmination of an aesthetic philosophy that had been evolving throughout the Baroque era. In his *Das neu-eröffnete Orchestre* ("The Newly Founded Orchestra") of 1713, Johann Mattheson (1681–1764) includes instruments in his discussion of the Affektenlehre and assigns such qualities to them as "magnificence" for the trombones, "pomposity" for the horns, "pride" for the bassoons, "harshness" for the cornets, "modesty" for the flutes, and "heroism" for the kettledrums.

Aesthetic doctrines   The expression of emotion was the essential goal of musical interpretation, and Quantz actually enumerates those elements which constitute correct interpretation. In the eleventh chapter of his *Versuch* of 1752 Quantz explains that a good performance must contain variety; light and shade must alternate. In order to move the listener the sounds must not always be equally strong or equally weak.[4] His recommended spectrum of dynamic shadings ranges from *ppp*. to *fff*. Later in the same chapter, Quantz describes the necessity that each piece contain an alternation of affects. He discusses the variety of nuances and the attention to detail so typical of his epoch. According to Quantz, some emotions that may be expressed through music are flattery, sadness, tenderness, happiness, seriousness, and impudence. Notes separated by small intervals and slurred generally suggest sadness, tenderness, and flattery. Dotted notes represent happiness, while long-held dotted notes suggest a serious and pathetic mood; dissonances denote passion. The choice of major and minor keys is also important in the expression of emotion.

Dynamic shadings and expressive details of each minute phrase were crucial to this style variant. Melodic ornamentation included essential ornaments such as trills, mordents, and turns, as well as optional embellishments. In the empfindsamer Stil essential ornaments were used in moderation and were frequently written out. The practice of improvising optional embellishments was particularly applicable to Adagio movements of a sonata and included a variety of methods: filling in large melodic intervals; subdividing long notes into shorter ones; replacement of duplets with triplets; adding passing and neighboring tones; and improvising short cadenzas.

C. P. E. Bach   Carl Philipp Emanuel Bach was the main proponent of the Empfindsamkeit. In his treatise *Versuch über die wahre Art, das Clavier zu spielen* ("Essay on the True Art of Playing a Keyboard Instrument," 1753–1775), Bach stresses the need for the performer to understand the essence of each composition. Through the expression of each work's nuances, the player must appeal to the emotions of the audience and convey the composer's intentions. Bach's **Instrumental uses of vocal style** search for expression and drama resulted in experimentation with the transfer of idiom, such as that of the recitative from the vocal to the instrumental. This is perhaps best exemplified in the second movement of his *Prussian* Sonata No. 1. The opening *andamento* (motion) in F minor over repeated bass notes is suggestive of an aria whose regular pulse is interrupted by a free recitative abounding in sudden harmonic changes. This alternation of aria and recitative occurs several more times throughout the short movement, ending with a cadenza improvised by the performer just before the penultimate note (see Example 19.3).

Through his feeling for harmonic color and the creation of idiomatic keyboard figurations, C. P. E. Bach stands as one of the founders of the expressive style which influenced Haydn, Mozart, and even Beethoven. At times Bach's bold harmonic progressions and broad range of expression suggest Romantic tendencies. He wrote more than 200 solo keyboard works, 52 keyboard concertos, 18 symphonies, and a considerable amount of church music, chamber music, and songs. The keyboard works include the six *Prussian* Sonatas, Op. 1 (1742), the six *Württemberg* Sonatas, Op. 2 (1744), and six volumes of *Sonaten, freie Fantasien und Rondos für Kenner und Liebhaber* ("Sonatas, Free Fantasias, and Rondos for Connoisseurs and Amateurs," 1779–1787). Of the last-mentioned collection, five sets are written expressly for the forte-piano.

His sonatas are in three movements, a large number of them in a minor key—a hallmark of the *empfindsamer Stil*. In his sonata-form movements the introduction of a second subject is an exception rather than a regular occurrence, and he is likely to employ a repeat of the initial idea in a related key instead of using new thematic material. In those movements which utilize sonata form, Bach recapitulates the whole exposition. Of the musicians at the court of Frederick the Great, C. P. E. Bach stands out as the most individualistic and innovative.

The circle of eighteenth-century intellectuals, poets, writers, and composers around Frederick II is today known as the Berlin school. It included **The Berlin school**

Ex. 19.3   C. P. E. Bach, *Prussian* Sonata No. 1

theorists like Mattheson, Marpurg, Agricola, and Kirnberger; musicians like Quantz, Carl Heinrich Graun and Johann Gottlieb Graun (1702?–1771), Franz (Frantisek) and Georg Anton (Jiří Antonín) Benda (1709–1786 and 1722–1795, respectively), and C. P. E. Bach; and poets and writers like Gotthold Lessing (1729–1781) and Christoph Friedrich Nicolai (1733–1811).

These north German intellectuals were united by their adherence to the aesthetic of the Empfindsamkeit, and "emotion" was their key word. While they felt that emotion could best be conveyed through instrumental compositions (particularly keyboard works), some nevertheless experimented with combining text and music, even to the point of adding a text to a keyboard composition. North German poets, in particular, studied the relationship between words and tone. Their experiments with melodrama and the instrumental recitative stand as examples of their search for expressiveness. One poet in particular experimented with the addition of a dramatic text to an already existing instrumental composition. In an attempt to heighten the expressive element in music, poet and playwright Heinrich Wilhelm von Gerstenberg (1737–1829) added Hamlet's soliloquy "To be or not to be" and his own version of the death of Socrates to C. P. E. Bach's Fantasia in C minor. The work itself was initially composed as part of the *Achtzehn Probestücke in sechs Sonaten* ("Eighteen Trial Pieces in Six Sonatas," 1753) and published in a supplement to volume 1 of Bach's keyboard treatise. Gerstenberg added the text at a later date. This experiment was all the more novel in light of the improvisatory nature of the purely idiomatic clavichord Fantasia.

The *Sturm und Drang*

Definition   Another intellectual phenomenon related to the aesthetic and philosophical endeavors of prominent German literary and musical figures was the *Sturm und Drang*. Although predominantly a literary movement, the term denotes a synthesis of musical trends with aesthetic, philosophic, and general social ideas over a span of approximately two decades (c. 1760–1780). It was preceded by the poetry of Johann Christoph Gottsched (1700–1766) and Friedrich Gottlieb Klopstock (1724–1803), as well as the dramas of Lessing and other north German writers from the Berlin–Hamburg–Leipzig areas. The aesthetics of the movement were in general conflict with the prevailing rationalistic tendencies in the earlier part of the eighteenth century.

Leading literary exponents   Johann Gottfried von Herder (1744–1803), Friedrich von Schiller (1759–1805), and the young Goethe were its leaders, while the name of the movement itself actually derives from the title of a drama written in 1776 by Maximilian von Klinger. Goethe's semiautobiographical novel *Die Leiden des jungen Werthers* ("The Sufferings of Young Werther," 1774) exemplifies the literary tendencies of the movement. Written as a series of letters, it tells the story of an artist who, disappointed in love and disillusioned with the hypocrisy of society, journeys to his place of birth in an attempt to seek his identity.

He sees himself as a pilgrim guided by the passion of his heart. The Romantic concept of love, the need for confession, and the desire to seek consolation in Nature are elements of nineteenth-century Romantic literature already evident here and in other writings of the eighteenth century. The literary products of the Sturm und Drang, like the writings of Rousseau, may be seen as antecedents of the Romantic movement.

Emotional intensity, passion, and violent outbursts in music begin to parallel the intensity of the literary Sturm und Drang at the point at which the empfindsamer Stil, especially in the works of C. P. E. Bach, reaches the climax of its emotional excesses. Musical Sturm und Drang is manifested in the increased use of the minor mode, sudden modulations, instrumental recitatives, extreme and abrupt contrasts, and a greater contrapuntal interaction of lines in an attempt to create a greater depth of musical perspective. An important treatise by the Swabian Christian Friedrich Daniel Schubart (1739–1791) —*Ideen zu einer Aesthetik der Tonkunst* ("Thoughts on Musical Aesthetics," 1784–1785)—summarizes the musical aesthetics of the movement. Included are chapters on genius, musical expression, and the relationship between key and "color" or "emotion." Schubart comments on the tendency to use flat keys for the expression of melancholy, and sharp keys for the depiction of wild and stormy emotions. To him the key of C major is suggestive of purity; A minor, of softness of character; G minor, of discontent and disgust.

> **Musical charac- teristics**

> **Schubart's treatise**

The chart on page 482 summarizes some of the most obvious aspects of the French, German, and Italian Preclassic style variants as evidenced in the instrumental sonata, so that they may be more easily compared.

Summary

As the eighteenth century progressed, the works of all Preclassic composers underwent syntactic changes. Three style variants are especially noticeable: The French style galant, the German empfindsamer Stil, and the Italian Preclassic style influenced by the comic opera. Each reflected prevalent regional and social tastes, which were also mirrored in the other arts: literature, architecture, and painting. In France, the elegant and graceful, highly ornamented instrumental music of F. Couperin, Leclair, and Mondonville made use of smaller forms and was influenced by the ever-popular operatic dance music. In north Germany, activities at the Berlin court of Frederick II, especially those of C. P. E. Bach, gave rise to the empfindsamer Stil, a highly sensitive style of performance aimed at arousing audiences' emotions. The clavichord and, later, pianoforte were the instruments most appropriate to the expression of these emotions, because they were able to produce a variety of nuances and dynamics. Poets, dramatists, and other intellectuals in Frederick's entourage, as well as those in other north German centers, created a type of literature which paralleled the musical "sensitive style"—the rebellious works of the Sturm und Drang. In its impassioned and antirational tone, the

Comparison of Preclassic Style Variants

	Style Galant	Empfindsamer Stil	Italian Style
Ornaments:	profusion of small decorative notes within a melodic line	ornaments used in moderation	ornaments used in moderation
	symbols placed over the notes indicate type of ornament to be applied	ornaments are written out; use of symbols not so frequent	most popular among ornaments is the appoggiatura
	they decorate the melodic line and bear little relation to the general harmonic fabric	ornaments incorporated into the harmonic fabric of the piece	most likely to be found in a slow movement; incorporated into the harmonic fabric
Phrase structure:	attention to detail disruptive to melodic continuity	small melodic and rhythmic units aim at a variety of contrasting dynamic shadings	motives are lively and humorous, characteristic of those used in opera buffa
Melody:	melodies are symmetrical	melodies are asymmetrical	melodies are well-balanced, predictably symmetrical
Texture:	predominantly homophonic; thin	thick; slow movements at times contrapuntal	clear; entirely homophonic; thin
Harmony:	simple; motion in secondary dominants; occasional altered chord	chromatic; powerful, particularly in slow movements; complex modulation occurs through wide range of keys	simple; occasional flatted sixth or Neapolitan sixth chord
Aesthetic goal:	restraint, objectivity, formality	subjectivity, emotionalism, passion	sentimentalism, simplicity, melodiousness
	music must entertain	music must move listener, communicate to the very soul of each individual	music must please

Sturm und Drang resembled the Romantic movement of the nineteenth century.

The eighteenth century proved fertile ground for the development of the thematic and harmonic dualism inherent in sonata form, although an actual written description of sonata form was not encountered before the end of the century, and the term itself was not in use until the nineteenth century.

Koch's treatise on composition (published in 1793) points to the eighteenth-century view of sonata form as an expansion of the already long-existent binary structure.

The concept of sonata form appears not only in eighteenth-century keyboard sonatas but also in symphonies, quartets, and other chamber music. Frequently more than one movement displays the harmonic and structural dualism of this theoretical concept.

The sonata, taken in its literal meaning, i.e., a piece to be played (as opposed to a piece to be sung), filled an important function in eighteenth-century musical society. It was composed for both amateurs and professionals, and intended for public and private concerts. An increasing phenomenon as the century progressed was the facility with which large numbers of sonatas were composed.

In Italy all musical genres were influenced by the operatic idiom, especially by that of comic opera. As the international activities of the Italian composers resulted in a diffusion of their works throughout western Europe, it was the Italian style which attained popularity everywhere. Because eighteenth-century opera and church music show these developments, both regional and national, on a larger scale, it is to them that we shall next turn our attention.

Notes

1. The initials refer to two different systems of cataloging Scarlatti's sonatas: the Kirkpatrick (K) and the Longo (L) numberings.
2. All the numbers used here for Galuppi sonatas are taken from the edition by Giacomo Benvenuti, Bologna.
3. *Denkmäler Deutscher Tonkunst* (Wiesbaden: Breitkoph & Härtel, 1958), vol. 39: *Johann Schobert Ausgewählte Werke,* ed. by Hugo Riemann. (*DDT*)
4. *Versuch einer Anweisung die Flöte traversiere zu spielen,* translated by Edward R. Reilly as *On Playing the Flute* (with an introduction by Reilly), (New York: Schirmer Books, 1966), p. 124.

Bibliography

Eighteenth-Century Treatises on Style

BACH, CARL PHILIPP EMANUEL. *Essay on the True Art of Playing a Keyboard Instrument.* Trans. W. J. Mitchell. New York: W. W. Norton, 1949.

MARPURG, FRIEDRICH WILHELM. *Historisch-Kritische Beyträge zur Aufnahme der Musik,* 5 vols. Berlin, 1754–1778.

MOZART, LEOPOLD. *A Treatise on the Fundamental Principles of Violin Playing.* Trans. Editha Knocker, Preface by Alfred Einstein. London: Oxford University Press, 1948.

QUANTZ, JOHANN JOACHIM. *On Playing the Flute.* Trans., Introduction, and Notes by Edward R. Reilly. New York: Schirmer Books, 1966.

Schubart, Christian Friedrich Daniel. *Ideen zu einer Aesthetik der Tonkunst.* Vienna, 1784–1785.
Strunk, Oliver, ed. *Source Readings in Music History: The Classic Era.* New York: W. W. Norton, 1965.

Articles

Dent, Edward J. "Italian Opera in the Eighteenth Century and Its Influence on the Music of the Classical Period." *Sammelbände der Internationalen Musikgesellschaft.* 14 (1912–1913): 500–509
Lazarevich, Gordana. "The Neapolitan Intermezzo and Its Influence on the Symphonic Idiom." *The Musical Quarterly* 57, no. 2 (April 1971): 294–313.
Helm, Eugene. "The Hamlet Fantasy and the Literary Element in C. P. E. Bach's Music." *The Musical Quarterly* 58, no. 2 (April 1972): 277–296.
Ratner, Leonard G. "Eighteenth-Century Theories of Musical Period Structure." *The Musical Quarterly* 42, no. 4 (Oct. 1956): 439–454.
Sheldon, David. "The Galant Style Revisited and Re-Evaluated." *Acta musicologica* 43, fasc. 2 (July–Dec. 1975): 240–270.

Scores

In addition to scores by Rameau and Couperin cited in Chapters 16 and 17, the following works may be consulted:

Bach, C. P. E. *The Prussian and Württemberg Sonatas.* New York: Kalmus (n.d.)
———. *18 Probestücke in Sechs Sonaten,* ed. Lothar Hoffmann-Erbrecht. Leipzig: Breitkopf & Härtel, 1957.
———. *Die Sechs Sammlungen von Sonaten, freien Fantasien und Rondos für Kenner und Liebhaber,* ed. Carl Krebs. Leipzig: Breitkopf & Härtel, 1895. Newly revised by Lothar Hoffmann-Erbrecht. Leipzig: Breitkopf & Härtel, 1953.
Bach, J. C. *Zehn Klavier Sonaten* (opp. 5/1–5 and 17/1–5), ed. Ludwig Landshoff. Leipzig: C. F. Peters, 1925.
Galuppi, Baldassare. *Dodici sonate per il cembalo,* ed. Giacomo Benvenuti. Bolona: Edizioni Bongiovanni, 1920.
———. Sonata in D major, first and second movements. In *Anthology of Music,* Vol. 1, ed. by Walter Georgii: 31–38. Cologne: Arno Volk Verlag, 1959–   .
Scarlatti, Domenico. *Opere complete per clavicembalo,* 10 vols. plus supplement, ed. Alessandro Longo. Milan: Ricordi, 1906.
———. *Sixty Sonatas,* 2 vols., ed. Ralph Kirkpatrick. New York: G. Schirmer, 1953.
———. Works in anthologies: Sonata in E-flat major (K. 380), in *AMA;* Sonata in A minor (L. 429), in *HAM* II, No. 274; Sonata in B-flat major (L. 498), in *HMS,* vol. 6; Sonata in D major (K. 119/L. 415) and Sonata in D minor (K. 120/L. 215), in F. E. Kirby, *Music in the Classic Period: An Anthology with Commentary.* New York: Schirmer Books, 1978.

20

Eighteenth-Century Opera and Religious Music

THE influence of two Italian genres pervaded much eighteenth-century European musical activity: the *opera seria* and the comic opera, with its related types. Both were disseminated by native Italian composers and by foreign-born but Italian-trained composers employed as maestri di cappella at various European courts. In the field of serious opera Italy was the undisputed leader, with its master-librettist Metastasio. The impact of the opera seria (everywhere but in France) thwarted any attempt at a national serious opera in England and the German-speaking lands. Not until the last quarter of the eighteenth century was a reaction against this Italian domination manifested in these regions. It occurred first in a nationalistically oriented part of northern Germany—Mannheim—where an attempt was made to produce a German-language opera based on events from German history. France, continuing the tradition of the tragédie lyrique, remained relatively unreceptive to developments in opera seria.

Rarely are twentieth-century audiences exposed to the pre-Mozartian opera seria. While comic operas and intermezzi are occasionally revived, eighteenth-century *opere serie* have not become part of the contemporary operatic repertoire. Yet eighteenth-century audiences loved them, and the period experienced a proliferation of serious operas whose popularity did not diminish until the end of the century.

Two main reasons may be offered for today's attitude toward the Italian opera seria: the unavailability of music because of a dearth of published scores; and the inherent problems in the relationship of music and drama. These difficulties exist on several different levels: the nature of the text; contemporary operatic conventions; and the attitudes of the singers.

This chapter examines eighteenth-century operatic conventions shaped to a great extent by the serious libretti of Metastasio. Operatic developments outside the Italian sphere of influence will also be investigated, including the phenomenon of comic opera with its various national types. Finally, another important branch of vocal activity, church music, will be discussed, especially from the point of view of the interrelationships and stylistic crossovers between secular and sacred vocal genres. Emphasis will be placed on the ways in which they fulfilled the needs and desires of their audiences.

Opera Seria

Conventions: Opera in Italy

Types of aria

The opera seria abounded in conventions to the extent that the position of every aria was prearranged according to a rational, logical plan. In his *Letters on Italian Opera* (2nd ed., 1791), John Brown, a Scottish painter and scholar active in the second half of the century, gives an account of the various aria types. The *aria cantabile* was of a sentimental nature, abounding in pathos and elegance. The *aria di portamento* consisted of long, drawn-out notes, and its main affect was one of dignity and grandeur. The *aria di mezzo carattere,* slow in pace, was sung by subordinate characters. The *aria parlante* (or *aria agitato*) served as an expression of passion. Its rapid tempo allowed for few embellishments. Finally, the *aria di bravura* existed primarily for virtuoso vocal displays.

Dramatic structure and aesthetic aims

The strictness of operatic conventions also affected the number of characters used in a libretto (usually not more than seven). When Goldoni first read his serious libretto *Amalasunta* (1735) to a private gathering in a Venetian salon in the presence of the male soprano Gaetano Majorano Caffarelli (1710–1783), the play was met with derision because it did not conform to the expectations of the audience. Goldoni reports in his *Mémoires* that his host took him aside afterward and explained the facts of operatic life:

> You are not aware of the fact that a music drama is an imperfect work, subjected to rules and usages which, although it is true [that they] do not make sense, one has to follow to the letter. If you were in France you could take great pains to please the public; but here, one must please the composer of the music; one must consult the stage painter and decorator. There are rules for everything: it would be an outrage against dramaturgy if one dared to transgress [against them], if one failed to observe them. . . .
>
> The three principal characters of the drama should each sing five arias: two in the first act, two in the second and one in the third. The supporting actor and actress may only have three, while the minor roles must content themselves with one or two at the most. The author of the words must furnish the musician with different nuances which form the contrasting shades [*clair-obscur*] of the music, and take note that two pathetic airs do not succeed each other; one must distribute with equal care the arias of bravura, arias of action, arias of *mezzo carattere,* minuets, and rondos.
>
> Above all, one must be careful not to relegate the arias of passion or bravura, or the rondos, to secondary characters.[1]

The aesthetic goal of eighteenth-century opera seria, therefore, was not the creation of a musico-dramatic unit, but rather the creation of a vehicle to glorify the contemporary singers for whom this hierarchy of rules was primarily intended. Opera seria roles were written for high voices. The principal characters were usually two male sopranos, two female leads, and one or two tenors. The bass voice was not considered to be that of a gentleman. Because of its "crudity" it was relegated to the comic opera, in which the lower social classes were represented.

Metastasian Dramatic Conventions and Operatic Traditions

The major librettist of the contemporary opera seria started his career in Naples, where in 1724 his *Didone abbandonata* ("Dido Abandoned"), set to music by Domenico Sarri (Sarro, 1679–1744), received major acclaim. He later continued his work as Viennese court poet. Through his libretti Metastasio created a drama which, in conjunction with its musical setting, gave rise to the archetypical eighteenth-century Italian opera seria. There was scarcely a composer in Europe from Pergolesi to Mozart who did not set at least one of the poet's dramas to music. Mozart used his texts in several concert arias and at least two operas: *La clemenza di Tito* ("The Clemency of Titus," 1791) and *Il Rè pastore* ("The Shepherd King," 1775). *Metastasio's popularity*

Frequently Metastasio's dramas have a happy ending and involve such elements as patriotism, loyalty, and friendship. His characters are noble and elegant; they are abstractions or stereotypes rather than individual human beings. Although Metastasian heroes are drawn from classical mythology or Roman history, they represent an abstraction of eighteenth-century morality and ethics. Each drama exalts virtues through a depiction of the characters' inner conflicts and external trials, situations that are eventually resolved according to the expectations of Metastasio's society. The hero and his beloved, driven by opposing forces—whether external circumstances or Fate—find themselves torn between their love and the demands of eighteenth-century values. Therefore the action is guided by a very rigid, rationalistic set of rules. At the verge of ruin and despair, a sudden twist in the plot saves the protagonists from destruction and leads to a happy ending. Usually two sets of lovers are involved, and each pair is united in marriage at the end. *The plots*

Metastasio's dramas consist of three acts, each containing as many as fifteen scenes. These serve as vehicles for passages in recitative, concluding with an aria that also serves as an opportunity for the character who sings it to make a dramatic exit. The occasional vocal duet or terzet may present itself, although ensemble numbers are rare. A chorus usually ends the drama, followed by a *licenza* (a statement in praise of the monarch to whom the libretto is dedicated). *Structure and style*

Metastasian drama emphasized a polarization of dramatic structure: the recitatives contained the action, the arias served as stationary expressions of sentiment. Musical structure was similarly polarized in that highly organized arias alternated with loosely structured recitatives, giving rise to sudden transitions of mood and musical pace rather than continuous dramatic evolution.

Metastasio's verse is elegant, his language flowery and mannered, abounding in metaphors and other figures of speech. A typical aria, usually consisting of two rhymed quatrains and preceded by a lengthy instrumental ritornello, may be represented as follows: *The aria: text and form*

$$
\begin{aligned}
&A \begin{cases}
\text{ritornello I} \\
\text{A-1} \\
\text{ritornello II} \\
\text{A-2} \\
\text{concluding ritornello}
\end{cases} \\
&B \begin{cases} B \end{cases} \\
&A\ da\ capo \begin{cases}
\text{ritornello I} \\
\text{A-1} \\
\text{ritornello II} \\
\text{A-2} \\
\text{concluding ritornello}
\end{cases}
\end{aligned}
$$

The overall design is ternary, and the B section is much shorter than the A section. The opening ritornello sets the mood and establishes the main key. Although A-1 and A-2 are usually based on the same text and share some melodic material, their harmonic functions differ: A-1 modulates to a related key, while A-2 modulates back to the tonic. The B section modulates through several different keys and functions as a contrasting middle section. The opening and closing ritornellos provide the aria with a feeling of symmetry and create a structurally closed unit.

The usual orchestral accompaniment of an early-eighteenth-century aria cantabile included only strings: the first and second violins frequently played in unison or parallel thirds, while the violas often doubled the continuo line. In addition, the first violins frequently doubled the vocal line. Such orchestration created a thin texture that showed off the singers' vocal prowess to the best possible advantage. In a clear, homophonic texture, there was nothing to distract from or compete with the singer's vocal line, so that he or she could easily be the focal point of attention in the aria.

Text underlay Composers took great liberties in underlaying aria texts. Word repetitions are frequent, resulting in multiple recurrences of the opening quatrain. These are the types of "abuses" to which the Italian author and literary critic Francesco Algarotti (1712–1764) referred in his treatise on operatic dramaturgy, *Saggio sopra l'opera in musica* ("A Critical Essay on the Opera," 1755). He complained that there was no correspondence between music and text; that the composer did not express the meaning of the aria as a whole text, but rather that of individual words; and, finally, that the repetition of the *da capo* was artificial and totally opposed to the natural dictates of the text.

Types of recitative *Recitativo secco* (simple recitative) and *recitativo accompagnato* (accompanied recitative) were both critically important to opera seria. Accompanied recitative was generally reserved for key dramatic moments, and its harmonic changes were more poignant and bolder than those of simple recitative. Frequent changes of mood in the text were paralleled in the music by changes of texture and tempo. Single chords punctuated the cadential pauses of the melodic line wherever the character had a question or exclamation. Diminished chords, scale passages, dotted notes, and runs in thirty-second–note values constituted the musical material of accompanied recitatives. Short, exclama-

A page from the libretto to Act II of *Demofoonte,* printed in the *Complete Works* of Metastasio by Antonio Zatta in Venice, 1781.

tory phrases in the vocal line alternated with orchestral passages, creating both a give-and-take in the musical texture and a fluctuating metric pulse.

Simple recitative was by far the most frequent mode of setting the active portions of the drama. The vocal line was set syllabically to a rapidly moving text, and the cadences occurred at such points of articulation in the text as commas, semicolons, and periods. The voice was accompanied only by a basso continuo, and the harmonies were improvised by the harpsichord player. The recitative was devoid of passages of strong emotional content. Its irregular phrases were separated by frequent rests and supported by continually changing harmonies.

Opera in the second half of the century shows a trend toward a reduction in length of the passages in recitative, a practice current especially among the operatic "radicals" such as Niccolò Jommelli, Tommaso Traëtta, and Christoph Willibald von Gluck. Gluck, for example, employs no recitativo secco in his 1762 Vienna version of *Orfeo ed Euridice,* while Jommelli has only a minimal amount in his *Demofoonte* (1764).

The cult of the singer   Italian opera was regarded primarily as a vehicle for the display of the singers' vocal acrobatics, and audiences perpetuated this attitude through their idolatry of favorite singers, especially the castrati. The powerful lungs of these male sopranos and altos were capable of great sustaining power, and their vocal range was usually extensive. The improvised embellishments to the composers' arias that were expected of the singers in the da capo portions showed not only inventiveness on the part of the singers but also considerable physical endurance in technically difficult passages. Charles Burney (1726–1814), the British humanist whose extensive travels through Europe resulted in the publication of a history of music, and whose diaries today serve as important documents on eighteenth-century musical customs, reports that the castrato Farinelli was such an expert technician that composers were unable to invent passages difficult enough to display his powers and orchestras were unable to keep up with him.[2]

Vanity, displays of temperament, and rivalry among the singers are well depicted in Benedetto Marcello's operatic satire *Il teatro alla moda* ("The Fashionable Theater"). Although this work was written in 1720, its skillful satire remained applicable to operatic practices past the middle of the eighteenth century.

Composers

Because of audiences' demand for new operas each season, composers' productivity in this area was extensive. More than one thousand works were written for Italian performances. Both Naples and Venice were active operatic centers, although Naples in the first half of the century seems to have been the home of a larger number of younger composers, products of the four conservatories (see Chapter 18), who later traveled all over Europe disseminating the Neapolitan operatic style.

J. A. Hasse   Although born in Germany and active at the court of Dresden for almost three decades, Johann Adolf Hasse (1699–1783) is considered one of the most famous representatives of the Italian school of opera composers. His works are regarded as ideal settings of Metastasian libretti, and he set almost all of the poet's dramas to music. Hasse's operatic style was known primarily for its elegance and clarity of melodic line, as well as the beauty of its bel canto. From 1764 on, Hasse and his wife, the renowned opera singer Faustina Bordoni (1700–1781), lived in Vienna, the adopted city of their great friend Metastasio. Among Hasse's approximately fifty operas is *Ruggiero,* composed for the wedding celebrations in Milan in 1771 of Archduke Ferdinand of the Hapsburgs (1754–1806) and Princess Marie Beatrice from the House of Este (1750–1829). It was for the same occasion that young Mozart was commissioned to write the *serenata* called *Ascanio in Alba,* a short dramatic work involving costumes and scenery. The two works were performed on two consecutive days, and the composition of the fifteen-year-old boy triumphed over the work of the seasoned opera composer of seventy-two.

Hasse's *Ruggiero* affords us an opportunity to study his style and, more generally, the style of the eighteenth century opera seria. Although the orchestra includes oboes, horns, trumpets, timpani, and strings, the homophonic texture is clear, and at times even transparent, because of the frequent doubling of parts. Only occasionally are all instruments used together, primarily in the opening sinfonia and the final chorus. The strings, which frequently double the vocal line, play the most prominent role in the orchestral texture, although additional instrumental combinations appear in different arias. Act II, scene 6, for example, introduces two flute parts, an additional oboe (making three separate oboe parts), and one bassoon (which appears at no other place in the opera). By his use of wind instruments, Hasse added color to the general texture, but he always took care not to overshadow his singers by creating an overly thick sound.

The "radicals" Jommelli and Traëtta, whose roots were in the Neapolitan operatic tradition but whose works differed markedly from typical eighteenth-century Italian operas, also deserve discussion. Niccolò Jommelli (1714–1774), a student of Leonardo Leo (1694–1744) and Francesco Feo (1691–1761) at the Neapolitan conservatories, was profoundly influenced by French ballet and music drama while in the service of the Duke of Württemberg at Stuttgart (1753–1769). The dramatic aspect of opera was Jommelli's primary concern, and his *Fetonte* (1768) has a dramatic unity, rich orchestral sonority, and polyphonic texture that made it quite different from the operas of his contemporaries.

The Neapolitan radicals

Jommelli's works are spectacles in which pantomime and ballet are given a new importance. In *Fetonte,* he integrates the chorus into the musical texture so that the opening of the opera is a homogeneous, unified scene. In the short sinfonia that serves as an overture, an Allegro in D major leads directly into a choral section in D minor, which is followed by another section that reiterates the original tonality. From the very beginning, the instruments contribute significantly in establishing structural cohesion. This technique differs from the prevailing Italian practice, in which the sinfonia had no direct connection with the rest of the opera.

Fetonte contains relatively few simple recitatives and proportionately more dramatic, or accompanied, recitatives. The closer the music and drama to the climax, the greater the frequency of accompanied recitatives. While duets, trios, and concerted numbers are rare in Italian serious opera, *Fetonte* has examples of each. The French predilection for elaborate spectacle and pomp shows in the large numbers of characters who fill Jommelli's stage: Moors, guards, citizens, soldiers, and priests. *Olimpiade* (1761), *Didone abbandonata* (1763) and *Demofoonte* (1764)—all three set to Metastasian libretti—are among his most successful works.

Tommaso Traëtta (1727–1779), who was active at the court of Parma (1758–1765), combined French with Italian models to an even greater extent than Jommelli. The subjects for his libretti are reminiscent of Rameau's, and pictorial details such as storms, battle scenes, and spectacular ballets are prominent in his operas. *Sofonisba* (1762), written for Vienna, is one of his best-known works.

Jommelli, Gluck, and Traëtta typify the reform elements of eighteenth-century opera, the principles of which were laid down in Gluck's famous preface to *Alceste* (1767; see below).

Stage Design and Theaters

Stage design   Opera seria was as much a stage spectacle as a vehicle for the glorification of the singers. The verisimilitude with which streets, cities, colonnades, palace interiors, ports, ships, and forests were depicted was a cause for wonder. As a typical example of architectural splendor in operatic stagecraft, we need only remember the directions of Metastasio's libretto for Domenico Sarro's *Achille in Sciro* (1737). The scene represents a "magnificent temple with two sets of spacious stairways surrounded by porticos which form a large square." Showing through the colonnades on one side are the sacred woods of Diana; on the other is the navy. The designer for that opera was Pietro Righini (1683–1742). Among the prominent names of stage architects we find the brothers Ferdinando Bibiena (1657–1743) and Francesco Galli Bibiena (1659–1739), the Galliari brothers (Bernardino, 1707–1794; Fabrizio, 1709–1790), and Luigi Vanvitelli (1700–1773), stage designer and architect of the royal summer palace at Caserta.

Theaters, audiences, attitudes   By midcentury, Venice had seven theaters for the production of opere serie, two for comic operas, and three for the spoken comedy. Of the several different theaters in Naples, the San Carlo had the most magnificent stage for serious works, while the Teatro dei Fiorentini was best equipped for comic operas. In his *Reminiscences* (London, 1827), the Irish singer Michael Kelly describes the San Carlo as having an immense stage "capable of bearing any working machinery." In the vast edifice there were seven tiers of boxes; in front of each box was a mirror and before each mirror were large wax candles. These, multiplied by reflection and aided by the flood of lights from the stage, were dazzling.

According to Kelly, each box contained twelve people. At the back of the principal tiers was a small room "where the confectioner and pages of the

Pietro Righini's design of a stage set which makes use of colonnades. (From Francesco Mancini, *Scenografia Napoletana dell'Età Barocco* [1964], pl. 33; by permission of Edizione scientifiche Italiane, Naples)

proprietor wait and distribute sweetmeats and ices to the company in the boxes and any of their friends in the pit whom they choose to recognize." The pit had sixteen rows of seats with forty seats in each row. Eighteenth-century audiences were frequently "rude" by modern standards. In Bologna they played cards in the loges. In Florence they left the hall any time they pleased, or while still in the hall gave their servants the sign to light the lanterns, thus disturbing the surrounding audience. In Naples they are reported to have laughed and talked, sometimes so loudly that they drowned out the voices of the singers.

If we bear in mind singers' free attitude toward the music, composers' "mistreatment" of the words in order to make an aria suitable for performance, and audiences' total disregard for the musical and dramatic unity in an opera, we gain a new insight into the nature of Italian opera seria and its function within the context of eighteenth-century society.

Serious Opera in Other Countries

Throughout the first half of the century, Italian opera dominated the London scene. Leading Italian singers appeared on the stage of the Haymarket Theater, and leading Italian composers performed and composed operas in Italian for English audiences. For example, during the first seven years of the

England

Royal Academy of Music at the Haymarket Theater (the Academy was initiated by Handel in 1720), productions included 245 performances of operas by Handel, 108 by Giovanni Bononcini, 55 by Attilio Ariosti, and 79 by others.[3] By the third decade of the century, the English audiences were openly hostile to the use of Italian, to the artificial subject matter of the opera, and to that idol of Italian audiences—the castrato.

Few English composers wrote opera. However, the typically English ballad opera developed gradually and on a modest scale as the century progressed, and the tradition of the opera seria was continued by such composers as Thomas Arne (1710–1778), whose *Artaxerxes* was based on a Metastasian libretto, and Stephen Storace (1762–1796), who was English-born but trained in Naples.

The German- speaking lands

Among the Germans, Hasse and at least two others stand out as being Italianized in their operatic compositions: Johann Christian Bach, known for his *Lucio Silla* (performed in Mannheim, 1774), and Karl Heinrich Graun, the Kapellmeister at the court of Frederick II, whose *Montezuma* was performed in Berlin in 1755. The libretto to *Montezuma* was written by Frederick II himself in French, then translated into Italian. Its plot is a prime example of the idea of the "noble savage." Graun wrote it in the Italian opera seria tradition, although his texture is more contrapuntal and the instrumental parts at times more complex than those in contemporary works. He was the first to make consistent use of the *cavatina,* a short, simple, binary aria usually free of extensive embellishment.

By the last quarter of the century, Mannheim had become a patriotically oriented community employing German poets, composers, and singers. The elector Karl Theodor actively encouraged the development of a German national opera to replace the Italian. An important step in this direction was taken by the poet Christoph Wieland (1733–1813) and the composer Anton Schweitzer (1735–1787), who produced a German-language opera, *Alcestis,* in 1773. Although its libretto closely resembled Metastasian models, the great success of this work led to the production of another opera, this one based on an episode from German history: *Günther von Schwarzburg* (1777). The music, by Ignaz Holzbauer, impressed Mozart when he heard it the same year. Mannheim was also the location for the construction of a German national theater and a society for the fostering of the German language.

Another composer active in Germany, Georg Benda, experimented with *melodrama,* a stage piece in which the action is spoken and mimed to a musical background. At times the music and the spoken text overlap. Benda's melodrama *Ariadna auf Naxos* ("Ariadne on Naxos," 1775) remains an experiment, but the compositional technique was later incorporated into the German Singspiel.

Gluck and His Reforms

Operatic developments in the field of serious opera in France were dominated by Rameau and Gluck, whose reforms were to have long-lasting influences. The career of Christoph Willibald von Gluck (1714–1787) shows an interesting stylistic metamorphosis. Starting as an operatic composer in the best Italian tradition, he moved away from the conventions of eighteenth-century opera seria toward a music drama with an unprecedented unity of text and music, and finally toward a renewal of the French operatic tradition of the tragédie lyrique. Gluck's early operas, some of which are based on Metastasian libretti, are stylistically similar to those of Leo and Hasse. In 1754 Gluck was appointed Kapellmeister at the Viennese court, where he and Count Jacomo Durazzo (1717–1794) initiated a reform movement against Metastasian ideals and operatic conventions.

By the time Gluck's *Orfeo ed Euridice* (1762) and *Alceste* (1767) had been performed, these reformers had succeeded in ending the long reign of Italian opera seria in Vienna. Among the first glimpses of a genuinely new type of libretto and opera was his *L'Innocenza giustificata* ("Innocence Justified," 1755), on a text by Durazzo. A further influence on Gluck's dramatic development was Jean-Georges Noverre's *Lettres sur la danse et sur les ballets* ("Letters on the Dance and Ballets," 1760). It advocated a return to Nature in ballet pieces, as well as the creation of works that were not stylized but were filled with expression, vitality, and truth. Noverre further espoused the belief that ballet should depict the manners and customs of all people, not just those of one nationality. Noverre's ideas inspired the choreography of Gasparo Angiolini's ballet *Don Juan,* for which Gluck composed the music in 1761. Thus Noverre, Angiolini, Durazzo, and Gluck formed an artistic group opposed to the aesthetics of Metastasio, the powerful and popular imperial court poet.

Just as Hasse was the musical counterpart of Metastasio, so Gluck was the musical counterpart of the librettist Raniero de'Calzabigi (1714–1795). Although the fruits of their partnership did not even approximate in volume those of Hasse and Metastasio, their stylistic affinity gave rise to the *reform opera,* whose characteristics were described in a manifesto written by Gluck as his preface to *Alceste.*[4]

Gluck's manifesto

His primary goal, as he declared in the manifesto, was to divest the music of abuses that singers and composers of the past had been inflicting on Italian opera. More specifically, he outlined the following points: (1) the vocal line must be freed of superfluous ornaments; (2) the music must be formulated according to the dictates of the drama; (3) artificial restrictions to the free expression of emotion, such as orchestral ritornelli, which break up the continuity of the poetic and musical thought must be abolished; (4) the stereotyped repetition of the da capo aria contradicts the continuity of the text and must not be used; (5) the mood of the overture should conform to the predominant mood of the drama; (6) simplicity and clarity should be sought at all times. In keeping with his theory, Gluck linked the overture to *Alceste* with the opening of the opera. He thereby set an example for other composers such as Jommelli (in *Fetonte,* which premiered in 1768, a year after *Alceste*).

Orfeo ed Euridice

Reform ideas were already present in Gluck's setting of Calzabigi's *Orfeo,* performed in Vienna in 1762, five years before *Alceste. Orfeo*'s three acts are divided into two scenes each, and the whole is called a *festa teatrale* (i.e., a court opera presenting a ballet with a jubilant chorus at the end). Because it was presented as part of a celebration in honor of the name-day of Emperor Francis I, the tragic ending of the original myth would have been inappropriate.

The opera opens with the death of Euridice. The choral-lament scene at her grave is typical of the *tombeaux* (tomb scenes) favored in French opera, of which the funeral ceremony in Rameau's *Castor et Pollux* is a good example. Orfeo, surrounded by a chorus, laments the death of his wife. Encouraged by Amor, the god of love, he proceeds to the Underworld to save her. There he faces the Furies, convinces them through his music-making to allow him entry (cf. Monteverdi's *Orfeo*), and manages to get hold of Euridice. In the process of taking her back, he disobeys the divine command not to look at her. He therefore loses her and is forced to return alone. Amor takes pity on Orfeo, however, and acts once more on his behalf by reviving Eridice. Stressing the central theme of the ability of human passion and love to overcome death, Gluck and Calzabigi created a simple, uncomplicated drama.

Aside from the chorus and the dancers the opera has only three singers — Orfeo, Euridice, and Amor. Originally the part of Orfeo was sung by the castrato Gaetano Guadagni. Euridice and Amor are both soprano roles. The recitatives are accompanied by the whole orchestra, and the basso continuo is no longer needed to fill in the texture. Perhaps the most striking aspect of this opera is its sense of dramatic continuity, which is demonstrated throughout the opening scene. The standard practice of the Italian *number opera* (which has a series of integral, separate musical pieces) was recitativo secco alternating with exit arias. Here, however, the opening scene, structured around the chorus, ballet numbers, and Orfeo's recitative and aria, achieves an organic unity through its choice of keys and its tightly interwoven, continuous musical action. It is predominantly in C minor, with one short excursion into its relative major and another into its tonic minor.

The two scenes in the second act juxtapose the infernal and pastoral moods. In the orchestral introduction to *Che puro ciel* ("How clear the sky") in act II, scene 1, an oboe solo is accompanied by triplets in the first violins, and decorated by filigree-like figures tossed back and forth among the cellos, second violins, and flutes. Here the texture and pastoral effect are so similar to those of the second movement of Beethoven's Symphony No. 6 (*Pastoral*) in F major (see Chapter 25) that they make us wonder whether Beethoven was actually influenced by this passage. As a fifteen-year-old boy in Bonn, Beethoven is known to have studied Gluck's score.

Gluck and the tragédie lyrique   Both *Orfeo* and *Alceste* were revised by Gluck for Parisian performances in 1774 and 1776 respectively. The castrato part of *Orfeo* was rewritten as a tenor role. Both libretti were translated into French, ballet scenes were added, and sections were reorchestrated. The Paris version of *Orfeo* (*Orphée*) acquired a ballet, the "Dance of the Furies" ("borrowed" from the composer's ballet *Don Juan*), and an exquisite, new orchestrally accompanied flute solo inserted at the beginning of act II, scene 2. *Alceste* was considerably more reworked than *Orfeo,* and an additional aria was added (possibly composed by François-Joseph Gossec, 1734–1829).

While *Orfeo ed Euridice* and *Alceste* are reform operas, *Iphigénie en Aulide* (1774) and *Iphigénie en Tauride* (1779) are examples of Gluck's French style. He was not consistent in his propagation of reform ideas. In the two *Iphigénie* operas Gluck introduced features he knew would appeal to French audiences, such as *divertissements* (as in *Armide,* 1777). In *Iphigénie en Tauride* he re-created the French classical tragedy with an emphasis on inner psychological developments. In these French operas he frequently reused material from his earlier operas. Gluck stands in the direct line of French operatic developments that leads through Luigi Cherubini and Gasparo Spontini to Hector Berlioz.

Comic Opera in Italy

Developments of *Opera Buffa* Conventions

Eighteenth-century comic genres emerged out of a reaction against the complexity and artificiality of opera seria and became a mirror of the Enlightened society. Through their satire of contemporary mores and social codes, the *intermezzo, scena buffa,* and comic opera libretto present a microcosm of society. From literary and musical standpoints, eighteenth-century musical comedy evolved gradually out of Baroque ethics to the championing of the Enlightenment's battle cry "Back to Nature."

Origin and philosophy of the comic genres

The Italian comic musical style evolved through three stages: (1) the comic scenes, or *scene buffe* (slapstick action interspersed with scenes of serious opera, common throughout the seventeenth century); (2) *intermezzi* (comic interludes longer than scene buffe, placed between the acts of a serious opera, and primarily an early-eighteenth-century practice); and (3) the comic opera, or *opera buffa.*

Italian comic genres (scene buffe, intermezzi, comic operas) differed from serious opera on every level. Their texts were simple, presenting places and everyday situations quite familiar to eighteenth-century audiences. Frequent use of Italian dialects and colloquialisms contributed to the humor and realism of the texts. These simpler, more realistic texts were set to a musical line that was equally uncomplicated, and structured according to the dictates of the text, so that it gradually abandoned the da capo mold. In contrast to the static delivery of arias in an opera seria, the comic works demanded stage action and movement from their performers. The element of slapstick, introduced from the commedia dell'arte, was also an essential ingredient. Furthermore, the bass voice, all but eliminated from serious opera, became an integral part of the comic plot. The *basso buffo* (comic bass) voice, ranging anywhere from a baritone to a low bass, was a favorite means of characterizing a comic servant or peasant singing in a local dialect. The castrato seldom appeared in the comic genre.

Comparison of opera seria and comic genres

Scenery was much simpler than that for the opera seria. Frequently the comic plot took place out-of-doors: on Venetian canals, or in a street, garden, or marketplace—a much more "natural" environment than the idealized opulence of the palace hall, grand staircase, or colonnades so prevalent in serious opera.

The characters for the comic casts were drawn from all walks of life, especially the middle and lower classes, thus presenting still another contrast to the elitism of the opera seria, with its nobles and allegorical figures. The comic plots introduced a popular element representative of the folk characters onstage, who intermingled with the more refined middle classes.

Scene buffe experienced a great proliferation between 1685 and 1710, especially in the two main centers of Italian operatic activity, Naples and Venice. Very early examples of this practice are found in Monteverdi's *L'incoronazione di Poppea* (act II, scene 5), where the encounter between the *damigella* and the *valetto* (the maid and the valet) is extraneous to the main dramatic developments of the opera. As a result of the textual reforms of Apostolo Zeno at the turn of the eighteenth century, the Venetian opera libretto was purged of such comic scenes. In Naples, however, operatic preferences called for the interpolation of five or six humorous scenes in most serious operas. One of the duties of a Neapolitan court composer such as Alessandro Scarlatti was to supply substitute arias and duets for existing scene buffe or to write an entirely new set of scenes to be added to performances of new operas.

Taken out of their operatic context, these scene buffe formed a dramatic continuum. Performed within an opera seria, their normal environment, they constituted a subplot that was totally independent of the main opera plot. Since they were accretions to a previously composed work rather than part of the original whole, they were easily transferable from one opera to another.

The protagonists in these comic units were two stock characters: the *vecchia,* or the toothless old woman, and the page many years her junior. Each played a minor role within the main plot of the opera: the vecchia was the nurse or confidante of the heroine, and the page was the servant of the leading male character. The only contact between these two figures occurred in a humorous context, usually in a set of stereotyped situations in which the vecchia, yearning for amorous adventure, pursued the page, who then made her the object of ridicule.

The Intermezzo

The eighteenth-century intermezzo differs entirely in concept from the sixteenth- and seventeenth-century *intermedio*—a grandiose spectacle that employed elaborate stage machinery and allegorical characters much like those of the Baroque opera seria. Unlike the intermedio, the eighteenth-century genre provided through its realism, humor, and economy of scenery total contrast to and comic relief from the main opera. In its early stages the intermezzo resembled the scena buffa. Frequently it was a mere compilation, or *pasticcio,* of two or three comic scenes taken from several different operas. During the classical phase of the intermezzo, the first four decades of the

Scene buffe (margin note)

Intermedio and intermezzo compared (margin note)

eighteenth century, the genre was developed by such composers as Sarro, Feo, Leo, Leonardo Vinci (c. 1690–1730), Giuseppe Maria Orlandini (1675–1760), Hasse, Pergolesi, Giuseppe Sellitti (1700–1777), and later Galuppi. Its structure is that of a three-unit (or three-act) short chamber opera. Each unit took between ten and fifteen minutes to perform. The first two were given immediately after the end of the first and second acts of the opera, while the third unit was presented two scenes before the end of the third act of the opera. Like the scena buffa, the intermezzo had a plot that was totally unrelated to the main action of the opera. It was therefore easily separable and was performed on different occasions with different opera seria.

Intermezzi of this period were generally of small proportions, employing two singers and a small chamber orchestra. The role of the female protagonist, usually a soprano, was that of a domineering young woman in her teens, who forces the male lead into marriage through physical coercion. The simple plot consisted of a series of jokes, tricks, and slapstick actions carried out through the use of disguise. Various nonsinging roles were included for actors who did pantomime, further heightening the elements of slapstick and the commedia dell'arte tradition. Very rarely was a chorus included in an intermezzo. Each act of the intermezzo usually contained two arias (one for each of the protagonists) and a duet. While some of the arias conformed to the stereotyped da capo pattern, others, especially those for the basso buffo, had a simpler structure shaped according to the dramatic dictates of the text. This stylistic feature is already evident in the intermezzi of the period composed by Pergolesi, Hasse, and Sellitti.

Of the hundreds of intermezzi written in this period, and the dozens that have survived in manuscript, very few have been published in modern editions and made available for present-day musicians. Hasse's *Larinda e Vanesio* and Pergolesi's *La serva padrona* and *Livietta e Tracollo* (1734) are exceptions.[5] In addition to genuine musical humor, all three works share a grace in their recitatives and an emotional warmth in their arias.

Recitatives in the intermezzi were predominantly secco, so that the speed of declamation varied according to the dramatic situation. These rather lengthy, constantly cadencing recitatives had to move at a considerable clip, sounding almost improvisatory in their emulation of the flexibility and cadences of speech.

Unlike duets in the serious opera, those in the intermezzi frequently contained two conflicting emotions simultaneously, thereby anticipating the ensemble finales of later comic operas.

Elements of musical humor in these intermezzi were manifold. The most obvious was the patter phrase in which the vocal line was set syllabically (see Example 20.1). A quick repetition of one syllable such as "yes," "no," or "you," combined with reiteration of the same pitches, often heightened a humorous moment, as in the duet shown in Example 20.2. This example also shows another technique popular in the comic intermezzo—that of multiple cadential repetitions of a melodic segment. Other musical means

Ex. 20.1   Duet, *Son ragazza, son bellina,* from Giuseppe Sellitti's *Drusilla e Strabone*

"You are pretty, you are graceful, you are spirited and so tasteful, you are brilliant and so charming, you are positively darling, yes, signora. . . ."

used for comic effect include seemingly endless sequential repetitions of a melodic pattern, the use of falsetto, the melodic octave jump, and the instrumental imitation of certain sounds like the croaking of frogs or "fluttering" of the heart. For instance, the heartbeat is imitated in a mocking fashion in the following passage from act I of Sellitti's *Drusilla e Strabone* (1735; see Example 20.3).

Opera Buffa

Intermezzo and opera buffa   Many of the features developed for the intermezzo in the first half of the century—from the multiple repetition of the same musical phrase at the cadence to the patter phrase—were adopted as standard humorous devices in the comic opera of the second half of the century. The recitativo accompagnato was reserved primarily for humorous moments, while the secco carried most of the dialogue. As the century progressed, a two–act structure became characteristic of comic operas. Da capo arias all but disappeared, and in their place were substituted a variety of simple, melodious, songlike numbers, in-

Ex. 20.2 Duet from Johann Adolf Hasse's *Larinda e Vanesio*

Larinda: "You're handsome, you, you," etc.
Vanesio: "You're dear, you, you," etc.

From *L'Artigiano Gentiluomio* or *Larinda e Vanesio*, ed. Gordana Lazarevich. Madison: A–R Editions, Inc., 1979. Recent Researches in the Music of the Classical Era, Vol. 9.

cluding the strophic aria, the two-part cavatina, and the sectionalized aria in which changes of meter mirrored the changes in mood expressed by the text. Although the formalized, structured hierarchy of opera seria affects was not adopted by the comic genre, a variety of aria types nevertheless existed: the *aria buffa* (humorous, sung by the comic bass), *aria cantabile* (lyrical, usually sung by a soprano), and *aria di bravura* (which included a variety of emotions; mock rage was a frequent occurrence).

Folk influences were also evident. For example, Leo introduced Neapolitan folk flavor into his *Alidoro* (1740) through the imitation of the strumming of a *colascione,* a Neapolitan stringed folk instrument.

Stylistic elements

It is interesting to study the treatment of the concerted finale throughout the evolution of comic opera. The pace of the drama quickens, and the composers' abilities at musical characterization are put to the test as the characters are juxtaposed and the humor of the situation emphasized. Piccinni's *La buona figliola* ("The Good Little Girl," 1760), for instance, shows well-planned and comparatively long finales. He attempts to unify the various sections through recurring musical themes (the rondo finale) and through a series of related tonal centers for each section. His harmonies in the finales are clear; the pedal point is used frequently. Highly symphonic in nature, these finales prefigure Mozart's, especially in *Le nozze di Figaro* ("The Marriage of Figaro").

Ex. 20.3   *Leimi guarda,* from Sellitti's *Drusilla e Strabone.*

"Poor sad creature, poor sad creature, your heart beats tic, tic, toc, tic, tic, tic, toc, tic, tic, tic, toc."

Among the most prolific eighteenth-century Italian composers of comic operas were Pergolesi and Vinci, whose comedies in the Neapolitan dialect attained great popularity in that city. Other composers of comic operas include Leo, Galuppi, Giovanni Paisiello (1740–1816), Antonio Salieri (1750–1825), Domenico Cimarosa (1749–1801), and Niccolò Zingarelli (1752–1837).

Comic Opera in Other Countries

France

Parisian audiences were accustomed to mythological fables, *opéras-ballets,* and *tragédies lyriques*—all spectacles that filled the imposing stage of the Académie de Musique. While Rameau's tragédies lyriques dominated French operatic developments, a parallel comic opera originated in the popular the-

Origins of the French genre

ater of the seventeenth century. The *théâtres de la foire,* or fair theaters, were small comic groups that played at the two major fairs in Paris. They presented primarily spoken comic scenes, interspersed with vaudeville tunes (simple syllabic songs for dancing, drinking, and satire), acrobatics, and puppet shows. These entertainments for the populace contained an element of crudeness derived from the commedia dell'arte.

Their major rival in the first half of the century was the Théâtre Italien at the Hôtel de Bourgogne, where the Italians, comedians of the king of France, presented parodies of the then-popular French and Italian operas. Much of the text in their comedies (highly influenced by Italian improvised comedy) was a mixture of French and Italian, and the airs that were intermingled with the text consisted of parodies of original music as well as newly composed songs. The playwright Charles Simon Favart (1710–1792) was greatly responsible for raising the quality of the comedy: he introduced airs from contemporary opera and raised vaudeville to a new level. In his libretti he created the idealized shepherd—as in *Rose et Colas* (1764), set to music by Pierre Alexandre Monsigny (1729–1816)—who was equivalent in pastoral elegance to the paintings of the period by François Boucher.

One event that stimulated the development of French comic opera was the two-year guest residence in Paris of a group of Italian *buffo* singers, the company directed by Eustachio Bambini (1697–1770). The "Bouffons" performed thirteen Italian comic works—intermezzi, comic operas, and pasticcios—by such leading Italian composers as Pergolesi, Orlandini, Gaetano Latilla (1711–1788), Rinaldo da Capua (c. 1705–c. 1780), Gioacchino Cocchi (c. 1720–after 1788), Jommelli, Sellitti, Vincenzo Ciampi (?1719–1762), and Leo.

The Italian works presented were for the most part modifications or pasticcios of the originals, with added arias, ensembles, and sometimes choral numbers. They were given in the Italian language, while the audience followed the text from libretti that contained both Italian and French. They were performed in the Académie de Musique with ballets between the acts of larger dramatic works, or as unified entities preceding French divertissements.

The Bouffons, in essence a mediocre company, soon found themselves at the center of the pamphlet war now known as the *Querelle [guerre] des Bouffons* ("Quarrel [war] of the Buffoons," 1752–1754). This dispute, which affected most Parisian intellectuals, did not revolve around the quality of the company's singing or their repertoire, but rather evolved on a theoretical and aesthetic level. Baron Friedrich Melchior von Grimm's *Le Petit Prophète de Boehmischbroda* ("The Little Prophet of Boehmischbroda") was a thinly disguised attack on various aspects of French opera, such as its extensive use of pageantry, which, he said, merely contributed to the artificialities of the drama. He also objected to its heavy texture, its monologues, and the poor quality of the opera orchestra. On the other hand, Grimm praised Pergolesi as a herald of a new kind of music. Rousseau, in his *Lettre sur la musique française*

Querelle des Bouffons

("Letter on French Music"),[6] added his praise for Italian melody, which, he felt, had a wealth of expression as compared to the French air. He felt that the Italian language was better suited to music than the French, and that Italian music generally enhanced the poetry.

The Italian partisan Rousseau himself composed an intermezzo in French, as proof that the French language could be adapted to the Italian style. This work, *Le Devin du village* ("The Village Soothsayer," 1753), was promptly parodied by Favart under the title *Les Amours de Bastien et Bastienne* ("The Loves of Bastien and Bastienne"), and it was a German translation of this libretto that Mozart set to music in 1768.

In any case, French and Italian elements were inextricably intertwined in the development of French comic opera. As mentioned before, shortly after their first appearance in Paris Italian comic works were translated into French and performed at the Théâtre Italien as parodies. At times the original music was retained, but the recitative was replaced by spoken dialogue. On occasion, additional French vaudeville airs were added, and others were newly **Duni and** composed by André Philidor (1726–1795), Egidio Duni (1708–1775) and **his** Charles Sodi (c. 1715–1788). Duni, an important Italian influence on French **successors** comic opera, came to Paris in 1757 and was one of the earliest composers in the new French genre. His *La Fille mal gardée* ("The Poorly Guarded Girl," 1758) and *L'Ecole de jeunesse* ("School for Youth," 1765) are among his better-known works.

The Italian intermezzi and opere buffe that the Bambini company introduced to their French audiences were for the most part pasticcios. These works were further changed by the French into a form acceptable to the French comic tradition. In the new combined genre, Italian arias intermingled with freshly added vaudeville airs. These potpourris constituted the comic musical fare of French audiences between 1755 and 1765. The Paris appearance of the Italian works and the controversy that surrounded them in 1752 gave French comic opera the necessary stimulus for its change of character: the existing genre was converted from a play with songs into a viable comic opera whose development was fostered by such composers as Duni, André Philidor, Monsigny, and Grétry. The new genre was called *comédie en prose mêlée d'ariettes* ("prose comedy intermingled with songs"). The new literary motifs treated in the libretti shared the sentimentalism of Goldoni's text for Piccinni's *La buona figliola,* with its themes of the honest and pure but naive heroine, oppressed peasants, and virtue extolled and ultimately triumphant. Many works in the new genre were criticisms of the existing social order.

Gluck and Gluck also played a role in the development of the French genre. He **Grétry** added airs to such pieces as Philidor's *Le Diable à quatre* ("The Four-legged Devil," 1756) for a performance at the Schönbrunn palace in Vienna, and composed *La Rencontre imprévue* ("The Unexpected Encounter," 1764). While Gluck's *Rencontre imprévue* is a mere collection of tuneful, simple, short airs, with an occasional trio and an ensemble at the end of the second and third acts, Grétry's *Richard Coeur de Lion* ("Richard the Lion-Hearted," 1784) has much more musical substance and is a more dramatically unified composition. The libretto is based on the romanticized story of Richard, the famous troubadour-king, who is rescued from prison by his faithful minstrel Blondel. In addition to the introduction of a chorus, the work displays a variety of musical structures: the *chanson à couplet* (a strophic poem in which the same music is repeated several times to a different text), air, *ariette, romance,* and ballade. Although the musical forms vary, all numbers are similar in character, on account of their utter naturalness and the simplicity of their tunes. The second and third acts of this opera are preceded by an orchestral *entr'acte,* and the third is almost entirely made up of ensembles. All these features point ahead to the nineteenth century.

While much French comic theater in Favart's time consisted of parodies of the Italian comic repertoire and the interpolation of ariettes and vaudeville airs into spoken comedies, by the last quarter of the century the *opéra comique* of Philidor and Grétry assumed much more musical and dramatic substance. This form became the new French national opera.

Germany and Austria

The *Singspiel* was a spoken play, usually a farce with interpolated tunes that were simple, strophic, and above all melodious. These farces used coarse language at times. The Singspiel attained instant popularity as a German national manifestation, as confirmed by the hundreds of performances in Berlin in the 1780s alone. Even Goethe wrote texts in an attempt to elevate the literary quality of the genre.

The north German Singspiel

In its early stages this genre was related to the English ballad opera, the French opéra comique, and the Italian opera buffa. It was frequently an adaptation of a text or music or both from other operas. The history of musical comedy in mid-eighteenth-century Europe assumes complex dimensions because of three contemporary customs: translation of an Italian comic libretto into the language of the country in which the work was to be performed; parody; and pasticcio. The custom of translation presents the fewest difficulties. In the case of parody (or free adaptation), the original music was retained without changes, and performed to a text that was an adaptation of the original text in translation. The technique resulting in a pasticcio consisted of the adoption of musical numbers from a variety of comic works and the addition of a totally new text. The more popular a work, the more often it was translated, parodied, and used in a pasticcio. For example, the Italian pasticcio *Bertoldo, Bertoldino e Cacasseno,* presented by the Bambini company in Paris in 1752, was parodied in French by Favart in his *Ninette à la cour* ("Ninette at the Court," 1755), which in turn is the source of one of the earliest German *Singspiele,* Hiller's *Löttchen am Hofe* ("Löttchen at the Court," 1767).

The initial stages of the north German Singspiel were thus bound up with other existing contemporary operatic genres. Therefore the three types of comic opera—French, Italian, and German—that were to develop distinct national characteristics later on in the century shared common roots in their formative stages.

North Germany developed the school of "Berlin" songwriters, who also

The Berlin school

shared in the development of the regional Singspiel. In addition to Hiller, the genre was cultivated by such composers as Reichardt, Georg Benda, and Beethoven's teacher Christian Gottlob Neefe (1748–1798), and by writers such as the poet Christoph Felix Weisse (1726–1804).

The Viennese Singspiel

The Viennese Singspiel, although initially influenced by the Italian opera buffa, grew out of a totally different tradition from its northern namesake; it developed from improvised comedy, with its elements of sorcery, magic, and stage machines. It was a mixture of many elements: parody of comic and serious Italian opera arias, folksongs, and popular songs. Although the Viennese Singspiel had spoken dialogue and accompanied recitatives, music predominated. Orientalisms (or "Turkisms")—stories or subjects from the Middle or Far East—were favorite topics, as were fairy tales. The Viennese especially liked to see the comic character called "Kasperl" on stage. Kasperl, a direct descendent of Hannswurst (Jack Sausage, in turn related to Pulcinella of the commedia dell'arte), was portrayed as a gourmand of somewhat less than average intelligence.

Singspiel development in Vienna was greatly encouraged by Joseph II, who founded a national opera theater, the Burghtheater, which opened with a production by Ignaz Umlauff (or Umlauf, 1746–1796) called *Die Bergknappen* ("The Miners," 1778). At that time the emperor abolished the performance of Italian opera and costly ballets.

Mozart and other composers

Mozart's *Die Entführung aus dem Serail* ("The Abduction from the Seraglio," 1782), on a "Turkish" subject, elevated the Singspiel to a new artistic level. The usual mixture of styles is in evidence here, but the greatness of the music lends the traditionally incongruous elements an inner coherence. Along with the folk-like music, there is a full-fledged concert aria, *Martern aller Arten* ("Tortures of every kind"), sung by the heroine, Constanze. This is a bravura display piece, a concerto for voice and four solo instruments (flute, oboe, violin, and cello). It was composed by Mozart to display the vocal powers and talents of his lead singer, Mlle. Cavalieri. Another notable moment is the bass Osmin's third-act bravura number, which shows off the singer's ability to produce low notes. This piece, *Ha, wie will ich triumphieren* ("Ha, how I will triumph"), is in the Italian buffo style (see Example 20.4). The work's finale is a vaudeville tune, where each character sings a verse to the same tune, followed by the refrain in the chorus.

Mozart's opera *Die Zauberflöte* ("The Magic Flute," 1791) is a direct outgrowth of this tradition. Its librettist, Emanuel Schikaneder (1751–1812), who was also the director of a troupe of actors, drew his material from *Lulu,* a fairy tale by Wieland, and from the magic opera *Oberon* (1780), written by Karl Ludwig Giesecke (1761–1833) and set to music by Paul Wranitzky (1756–1808) (see page 574).

Other composers of the Austrian Singspiel included Karl Ditters von Dittersdorf (1749–1799), whose *Doktor und Apotheker* ("The Doctor and the Apothecary," 1786) was especially well known, and Johann Schenk (1753–1836), whose works include *Der Dorfbarbier* ("The Village Barber," 1796).

Ex. 20.4 *Ha, wie will ich triumphieren,* from W. A. Mozart's *Die Entführung aus dem Serail*

Schleicht nur säu - ber - lich und lei - se, ihr ver - damm-ten Ha - rems Maü - se,

un - ser Ohr ent - deckt euch schon, ent - deckt euch schon, ent - deckt euch schon.

"Steal away neatly and softly, you damned mice of the harem, our ear will discover. . . ."

England and Spain

In the second half of the eighteenth century, London had two winter playhouses—Drury Lane (whose manager since 1750 had been the actor David Garrick) and Covent Garden—and one that was used after 1767 for productions during the summer, the Little Theatre in the Haymarket. The most popular forms of entertainment at Covent Garden were pantomimes: musical compositions with continuous orchestral accompaniment, interspersed with songs and ensembles. Music for the mimes was called *comic tunes,* and some were arranged for keyboard accompaniment. **London pantomimes**

The *ballad opera* is the closest that England came to a national comic musical theater. One of the most popular examples of the genre was *The Beggar's Opera* (1728, on a libretto by John Gay, 1685–1732). The protagonists were rogues, pickpockets, and street people, as depicted through caricature in the engravings of William Hogarth (1697–1764). The day-to-day lives, however, of the ordinary people of England were more frequent topics in all of these works. John Christopher Pepusch (1667–1752)—the composer of the overture to *The Beggar's Opera* and arranger of the ballads, songs from contemporary operas, and other musical numbers familiar to the audiences that constituted the music of a ballad opera—was musical director of Lincoln's Inn Fields Theatre. **The English ballad opera**

Another popular ballad opera was Charles Coffey's *The Devil to Pay* (1731). Thomas Arne, Thomas Linley, Sr. (1733–1795), and Stephen Storace composed English comic operas that contained spoken dialogue and musical techniques influenced by opera buffa. Arne's *Thomas and Sally* (1760) and *Love in a Village* (a pasticcio with music of sixteen different composers, first performed in 1762) were among the most popular.

Spanish operatic genres included the *zarzuela* and the *tonadilla*. The two-act zarzuela increasingly showed the influence of the Italian opera, especially in the hands of José de Nebra (c. 1688–1768). At the same time, the tonadilla grew into a short comic opera approximately twenty minutes in length. The **The Spanish zarzuela and tonadilla**

THE ENRAGED MUSICIAN.

William Hogarth (1697–1764), *The Enraged Musician*. This is a satire on a foreign musician who finds the competition with London street sounds too much for him. Notice the playbill on the left which announces John Gay's *The Beggar's Opera,* first performed in 1728. (From Sean Shesgreen [ed.], *Engravings by Hogarth* [New York: Dover Publications, 1973]; by permission of Dover Publications)

latter was originally performed as an interlude, like the intermezzo, but its structure and subject matter bore no resemblance to the Italian form. Luis Misón (d. 1766), one of the earliest composers in this genre, liberated it from its intermezzo-like functions and made it an independent work, complete in itself. Important later composers of tonadillas include Pablo Esteve y Grimau (d. 1794) and Blas de Laserna (1751–1816). The early tonadilla shared with the ballad opera an emphasis on folk-like melody and everyday subject matter, in contrast to the more formal zarzuela, with its mythological plots. Soon, however, ever-greater Italian influence permeated the genre, to the extent that not only Italian-style arias and recitative but even Italian texts were included. By the end of the century, therefore, both the zarzuela and the tonadilla had lost their "Spanish" character and absorbed that of the Italian comic genres instead.

Sacred Music

The musical center of gravity of the Age of Enlightenment was to be found in the evolution of instrumental and operatic music. While church music incorporated some contemporary operatic tendencies, it remained one of the most conservative and hybrid musical categories of the century. Because of the function of the text within a church service, composers were confined to strict limits, and they had to adhere to compositional rules proper to a religious service. For example, the text of the Gloria lends this whole section of the Mass an aura of dignity, exaltation, and splendor. Certain natural divisions of the text, such as *laudamus Te, benedicamus Te, adoramus Te,* and *glorificamus Te* ("we praise Thee," "we bless Thee," "we adore Thee," "we glorify Thee") suggest musical divisions. The musical setting had to be such that it emphasized the meaning of the words. Usually the last words of the Gloria, *Cum Sancto Spiritu in gloria Dei Patris, Amen* ("Glory be to the Father and the Holy Ghost, Amen"), were treated fugally. Such is the case particularly with Mozart's Masses. **[Religious music and the Enlightenment]** **[Mass texts]**

Categories of sacred music composed throughout the century include: Mass, Requiem, motet, Vesper psalms, Magnificat, Te Deum, Stabat Mater, litanies, and oratorio. The repertoire of the Lutheran Church, which was similar to that of the Catholic Church, also included cantatas and Passions. Both the *Missa brevis* (Short Mass) and the *Missa longa* or *solemnis* (Long or Solemn Mass) were in use. The *Missa brevis* existed in different forms: as a through-composed, simplified setting, in which the five Ordinary portions appeared as connected musical movements and with little subdivision of text, or as a setting of just the Kyrie and Gloria. Bach, for example, left four Masses of this kind. **[Missa brevis]**

The *Missa solemnis,* reserved for solemn occasions, was an elaborate Mass, whose performance required a considerable length of time. In a *Missa solemnis* the composer usually treated each separate section as an independent piece with ample alternations of solo and chorus. **[Missa solemnis]**

The performance of liturgical music was not confined to churches. Such works were also heard in the Concert Spirituel in Paris, the schools in Venice —especially the Incurabili—and the monasteries. These works were performed during Church holidays that were also public holidays (oratorios, for example, were heard during Lent) and were also performed for the entertainment of visiting Church dignitaries. As in earlier eras, the monasteries were repositories of a great deal of liturgical music. Austrian monasteries, in particular (although the Oratory of San Filippo Neri in Naples and the Abbey of Montecassino fall into the same category), contained sumptuous libraries, and their holdings still serve as places of frequent pilgrimages and study for today's students of liturgical music.

Protestantism reigned in England and northern Germany, specifically Berlin and Hamburg, while Bavaria, Austria, France, Italy, and Spain were Roman Catholic lands. However, the main dichotomy in eighteenth-century music was found not so much in the difference between Protestant and Catholic music as in the difference between *stile antico* and *stile moderno*. It was a stylistic dichotomy between the learned, contrapuntal, neo-Palestrina (a cappella) style and the newer Preclassic, more homophonous one.

Stile antico vs. stile moderno

In the first half of the century, J. S. Bach, among others, brought the Baroque liturgical style to its culmination. Coexistent with Bach were other composers whose sacred music—especially their oratorios and to a certain extent their Masses—contained more obvious operatic elements. As the century progressed, a compromise between the two styles was attained by the composers of the Austrian school, including Haydn and Mozart.

The Italian Tradition

Early-eighteenth-century proponents of the conservative stile antico in Venice included Antonio Lotti, Antonio Vivaldi, and Benedetto Marcello. Lotti's short a cappella settings of the Mass are expressive, mellifluous, and highly contrapuntal. The newer Italian style was created initially by the Neapolitan composers. Since most of those who wrote motets, oratorios, and Masses were also prolific opera composers, the imitation of operatic style in the liturgical genres was inevitable. Southern oratorios became extremely operatic. In fact, as a result of Metastasio's reforms of operatic texts, they became the sacred equivalent of the opera seria. With a focus on the solo singers, closed musical numbers, and (some) bravura passages, the oratorio acquired the same Metastasian conventions as the opera. The chorus, used minimally, at times had fugal finales.

Hasse's oratorio *La conversione di Sant' Agostino* ("The Conversion of St. Augustine"), performed in Dresden in 1750, is a case in point. The story of this Neapolitan *dramma sacro,* which opens at the time when St. Augustine is still a sinner enjoying a secular life, revolves around the saint, his parents, and a friend, and aims at teaching a moral lesson through a dramatization of the manner in which the hero eventually abandons earthly pleasures for the sake of divine love. The comparatively large orchestra consists of flutes, oboes, strings, and bassoons (the latter used for continuo purposes). The musical texture is made up entirely of solo arias, many in the grand da capo manner, separated by passages in recitativo secco as well as recitativo accompagnato. The chorus, used sparingly, rounds off the composition.

The bittersweet, sentimental, and highly lyrical southern Italian Church style, of which Hasse was a proponent, was already well defined in the works of Pergolesi and Leo. It was because of Pergolesi's *Stabat Mater,* so well received in Paris some ten years after his death, that the Parisians referred to the composer as the "divine Pergolesi." Although it was a Good Friday hymn,

Pergolesi's Stabat Mater

this composition was probably written as a *duetto spirituale,* a sacred duet, for the edification of a group of religiously inclined Neapolitan nobles who commissioned the work. Its vocal parts were sung by two male singers, one possibly a castrato capable of producing a sustained tone. The piece contains twelve individual numbers, solo arias and duets, accompanied by a string chamber orchestra. The texture is homophonic throughout, and the most "contrapuntal" example may be found at the opening of the piece, where gentle dissonances are created through overlapping melodic lines.

Similar in style, but more interspersed with contrapuntal devices are Leo's two most famous oratorios: *La morte di Abele* ("Abel's Death," 1738) and *Sant' Elena al Calvario* ("St. Helen at Calvary," 1734), both on texts by Metastasio. Much sacred music was written throughout the eighteenth century for the women of the Venetian schools, primarily the Incurabili. The maestri di cappella at these institutions included some of the most illustrious contemporary musicians—Hasse, Porpora, Jommelli, Ciampi, Cocchi, and Galuppi—whose oratorios, Misereres, Salve Reginas, and motets at times employed as many as four choruses, soloists, and orchestra.

Other works and composers

Other Catholic Centers

In Vienna, the most famous representatives of the older style were Johann Joseph Fux (1660–1741), director of music at the imperial court from 1715 on and the most prolific composer of religious music in that city, and Antonio Caldara (1670–1737). Fux's Masses are of two kinds: (1) *a cappella,* carrying out the traditions of Renaissance polyphony with all canonic and imitative contrapuntal artifices in the best Palestrinian tradition (e.g., Fux's *Missa canonica*); and (2) the *concertato* Mass.

Austria

Church music in Austria showed varying degrees of compromise between the older, contrapuntal treatments and operatic, lyric homophony. The dominance of one or the other style depended on the local peculiarities of the liturgy and the tastes of Church authorities. Church music in Salzburg in the second half of the century was fostered by Archbishop Sigismund Christoph, Count of Schrattenbach (r. 1753–1771), then Hieronymus, Count of Colloredo (r. 1772–1803), Mozart's one-time patron and himself a violinist. The archbishop had his own choristers, some of whom had received their musical training in Italy, and an orchestra that consisted of strings, wind instruments, and timpani. The custom of playing Masses with full orchestra, chorus, and soloists prevailed in Austrian cathedrals in the second half of the century.

The Salzburg cathedral organist was Anton Cajetan Adlgasser (1728–1777), and other musicians and composers employed by the archbishop of Salzburg included Johann Ernst Eberlin (1702–1762); Antonio Lolli (c. 1730–1802), who was Kapellmeister; Leopold Mozart (1719–1787), Wolfgang's father, who was Vice-Kapellmeister (assistant music director); and Michael Haydn (1737–1806), brother of Franz Joseph Haydn.

Like England, Spain remained on the periphery of the prevalent liturgical styles. The contrapuntal Masses of Don Francisco Valls (1665–1747) were in-

The Iberian Peninsula

terspersed with canticles, in the vernacular, in honor of the Eucharist and the Blessed Virgin. Other composers included: Louis Serra (d. 1759), Don Antonio Ripa (c. 1720–1795), and Don Pascual Fuentes (d. 1768).

France   Church music in France continued to follow its own tradition, quite separately from that of other western European countries, and was the least influenced by Italian operatic music. Only toward the end of the century, with Mondonville, did the *grand motet* begin to show the influence of the Italian aria. The outstanding composer was Italian-born Luigi Cherubini (1760–1842), who settled in Paris in 1787. His two Requiems and his *Missa solemnis in D major* are masterpieces that stand in their stylistic development halfway between the works of Mozart and those of Beethoven.

Toward the end of the century, the development of the oratorio in France had just about ended, while in Germany it was becoming increasingly more affected by the Italian style. In Italy it was entirely operatic. Two masterpieces of the genre composed in Vienna during this period—Haydn's *The Creation* (1798) and *The Seasons* (1801)—were both inspired by Handel.

Protestant Religious Music

Germany   In contrast to the southern (Catholic) oratorio, the north German (Protestant) oratorio still retained its direct connections with the Church. In keeping with its Lutheran tradition, it contained chorale settings, elaborate choral sections, and above all, its German text. Protestant oratorios were usually dramatic presentations of Old Testament subjects and were more devotional in nature than the Catholic works in this genre. The Passion story was still frequently set to music by Protestant composers. Karl Heinrich Graun's *Der Tod Jesu* ("Jesus' Death," 1755), for example, became very popular. Under Frederick II, the court at Berlin and Potsdam was a stronghold of German Protestantism. In addition to Graun, C. P. E. Bach was also active in the field of church music, and his Magnificat (1749) is perhaps his most famous liturgical composition.

Other north German composers actively writing for the Protestant Church include Christoph Graupner (1683–1760), Johann Mattheson, and Georg Philipp Telemann (1681–1767). Telemann alone wrote twelve complete cycles of cantatas and motets, as well as more than forty Passions.

The English Tradition

Liturgical music in England was primarily propagated by such personages as John Christopher Smith (1712–1795), James Nares (1715–1783), Benjamin Cooke (1734–1793), and Jonathan Battishill (1738–1814). Their cantatas, oratorios, and anthems constituted the main body of new Anglican liturgical music of the eighteenth century. Their conservative efforts in the field of the oratorio were overshadowed by the dominant influence of Handel, whose oratorios were performed in England throughout the century.

Summary

Two types of opera dominated the eighteenth-century stage: the serious and the comic. Opera was a popular form of entertainment in all western European countries, and it was Italian opera that dominated European stages. Only France was capable of resisting the lure of Italian opera, although in 1752 a furor was created by polemics on the aesthetic merits of French versus Italian opera. This period in French musical history, known as the "Quarrel of the Buffoons," revolved around performances of Italian comic operas and intermezzi rather than serious opera.

The direction of the *opera seria* was formulated by three major forces: (1) singers, who used opera as a means of displaying their vocal prowess in a field that encouraged a competition of egos; (2) audiences, who sought the musical theater as a means of easy entertainment, and to whom a singer's interpretation of a favorite aria was of greater relevance than the unity of the drama displayed in the libretto and the music; and (3) one librettist in particular—Pietro Metastasio—whose popularity in Italy resulted in innumerable settings of each of his libretti by different composers. The versions of *Demofoonte* and *Olimpiade* exuded a new eloquence of literary style and a new pathos.

Guiding each opera seria plot was a series of strict conventions as to the number and type of arias each character was to sing. The casting hierarchy of first lady, first man, and subordinate cast (*mezzo carattere*) distinguished very strictly among the leading and the subordinate singers.

The Italian settings of Metastasian opera gave rise to an opera form structured around recitatives (the active portion of the libretto) and arias (the reflective portion). A recitative was generally followed by an aria, which in turn was followed by the exit of the character from the stage. Ensemble, choral, or ballet numbers were infrequent. However, at least one duet involving the two leading characters was expected. The predominant number of recitatives were of the *secco* type, accompanied by a harpsichord continuo, but several accompanied recitatives were introduced at climactic moments in the drama. The arias were, for the most part, in the *da capo* form, in which the singer was expected to embellish the repeat of the first section. The extent of the embellishments depended on the affect and tempo of the particular aria.

The opera seria, dominated by *castrati,* was predominantly enjoyed by the upper classes: the nobility, and the royalty. Theaters were equipped to handle the machinery necessary for the creation of spectacular stage effects, and each Italian city had a theater specifically reserved for the performance of opera seria (and at least one in which only comic operas were performed).

Opera reform gradually took shape under the leadership of Gluck and his librettist Calzabigi. Their aim was to eliminate the liberties the singer took with the composer's music and to create a greater sense of unity between text and music.

French operatic taste differed sharply from that of the Italians. The variety of operatic types developed by Lully, Rameau, and their contemporaries— the *comédie ballet, tragédie lyrique,* and so forth—stressed ballet and large ensemble scenes and employed a large orchestra in which woodwind instruments were frequently used for coloristic purposes. Thick texture and rich harmonies predominated. Various kinds of short airs, frequently based on dance motifs, were introduced, and these were antithetical to the concept of range and breadth as shown by the castrati in their arias.

The spirit of the Enlightenment which pervaded mid-eighteenth-century Europe, with its affinity for the more natural and simpler aspects of life, was suitable to the comic opera: its protagonists reflected the mores and life-styles of the middle classes, its libretti were closer to the colloquialisms of daily speech, and its satirical topics made it easy for the audiences to laugh at their own foibles. Italian *buffo* style, developed first in short *intermezzi* and later in the *opera buffa,* was to influence the growing symphonic idiom. It also gave other countries the necessary impetus for the formation of their own individual types of musical comedy, primarily the *Singspiel* in German-speaking lands and the *opéra-comique* in France. The *ballad opera* in England and the *tonadilla* in Spain have no direct relation to the opera buffa, since their emergence was primarily a reaction against the performance of Italian opera seria in England and against the infiltration of Italian elements into the *zarzuela* in Spain. Around the middle of the century, the intermezzo, comic opera, opéra-comique, and Singspiel shared common musical material, which resulted from the practices of free adaptation, *pasticcio,* and parody.

Eighteenth-century church music shows a dichotomy between the polyphonic style and the operatic style. This conflict was treated by various composers in different ways: from the total acceptance of Italian secular operatic practices, as with the Italian oratorio composers, to the more contrapuntal style of the north German composers. Austrians adopted a compromise position, and the French showed a comparative lack of interest in the Italian style.

While church music remained the most conservative of eighteenth-century musical categories and showed less individuality than operatic and instrumental music, it shared with other Preclassic and Classic music two major qualities: expressiveness and sentimentalism. The stylistic features of eighteenth-century symphonic and chamber music will be explored in Chapter 21.

Notes

1. This and all subsequent translations are by the author of this section. The quotation is from the French version of Goldoni's *Mémoires* (Paris, 1787), Chapter 29, p. 127.
2. For an interesting example of Farinelli's art of embellishment, see *The New Oxford History of Music* (London: Oxford University Press, 1973), vol. 7, p. 15.
3. Paul Henry Lang, *George Frideric Handel* (New York: W. W. Norton, 1966), p. 188.
4. This preface is translated in Oliver Strunk, *Source Readings in Music History* (New York: W. W. Norton, 1950), p. 673.

5. Three additional Hasse intermezzi, ed. by Gordana Lazarevich, are soon to be published: *La serva scaltra* ("The Astute Servant"), *Il Tutore* ("The Tutor"), and *La Contadina* ("The Peasant Girl"). They will form part of the *Concentus musicus series* (Cologne: Arno Volk Verlag), under the general editorship of Friedrich Lippmann. Pergolesi's two intermezzi—*La serva padrona* ("The Maid Mistress," ed. by Helmuth Hucke) and *Livietta e Tracollo* (ed. by Gordana Lazarevich) are scheduled for publication in the collected works of Pergolesi by Pendragon Press, New York, under the general editorship of Barry S. Brook and Marvin Paymer. Another eighteenth-century intermezzo is available, albeit in facsimile: *Bacocco e Serpilla* by Orlandini, included as vol. 68 of Series Two of the *Italian Opera 1640–1770*, ed. H. M. Brown and Eric Weimer.
6. Both Grimm's and Rousseau's pamphlets may be found in Strunk, *Source Readings*, Chapter 14.

Bibliography

Books and Articles

In addition to those items cited in Chapter 13, see also:

ALGAROTTI, FRANCESCO. *Saggio sopra l'opera in musica*. Naples, 1755. Part of it is reprinted in an English translation in Oliver Strunk, *Source Readings in Music History: The Classic Era*. New York: W. W. Norton, 1965.

DENT, EDWARD. "Ensembles and Finales in Eighteenth-century Italian Opera." *Sammelbände der Internationalen Musikgesellschaft* 11 (1909–1910): 543–561; 12 (1910–1911): 112–138.

DOWNES, EDWARD. "Secco Recitatives in Early Classical Opera Seria (1720–1780)." *Journal of the American Musicological Society* 14 (1961): 50–68.

LAZAREVICH, GORDANA. "Eighteenth-century Pasticcio: The Historian's Gordian Knot." *Analecta musicologica* 17 (1976): 121–145.

———. "The Eighteenth-century Intermezzo as Repertory for Opera Workshops." *Current Musicology* 26 (1978): 74–82.

LOWENBERG, ALFRED. "Gluck's *Orfeo* on Stage." *Musical Quarterly* 26 (July 1940): 311–339.

ROBINSON, MICHAEL F. *Naples and Neapolitan Opera*. Oxford: Clarendon Press, 1972.

WELLECZ, EGON, AND STERNFELD, FREDERICK, eds. *The New Oxford History of Music*. Vol. 7, *The Age of Enlightenment, 1745–1790*. London: Oxford University Press, 1973.

Scores

Opera in Italy

CIMAROSA, DOMENICO. *Il matrimonio segreto*. Milan: Ricordi, 1966. Piano-vocal score.

GALUPPI, BALDASSARE. *Il filosofo di campagna*, ed. Wolf Ferrari. Milan: Ricordi, c. 1954. Piano-vocal score.

HASSE, JOHANN ADOLF. *L'artigiano gentiluomo* or *Larinda e Vanesio*, ed. Gordana Lazarevich. Wisconsin: A–R Editions. *Recent Researches in the Music of the Classical Era*, 1979, vol. 9.

———. *Arminio*, ed. Rudolf Gerber. In *Das Erbe Deutscher Musik*, vol. 27. Mainz: Schott's Söhne, 1957–1966.

————. *Ruggiero ovvero l'Eroica Gratitudine,* ed. Klaus Hortschansky. In *Concentus Musicus,* vol. 1. Cologne: Arno Volk Verlag, 1973.

————. *Siroe rè di Persia,* facsimile, Intro. by Howard Mayer Brown. In *Italian Opera 1640–1770,* Series One, vol. 33. New York and London: Garland Publishing Inc., 1980.

————. *Alcide al bivio,* facsimile, Intro. by Howard Mayer Brown and Eric Weimer. In *Italian Opera 1640–1770,* Series Two, vol. 81.

————. *Il trionfo di Clelia.* In *Italian Opera 1640–1770,* Series Two, vol. 83.

JOMMELLI, NICCOLÒ. *Demofoonte,* facsimile, Intro. by Howard Mayer Brown. In *Italian Opera 1640–1770,* Series One, vol. 48.

————. *L'Olimpiade.* In *Italian Opera 1640–1770,* Series One, vol. 46.

JOMMELLI, NICCOLÒ. *Fetonte,* ed. Hermann Abert. In *Denkmäler Deutscher Tonkunst* vols. 32, 33. Wiesbaden: Breitkopf & Härtel, 1958.

PICCINNI, NICCOLO. *La Cocchina ossia, La buona figliola,* trans., ed., and Intro. by Howard Mayer Brown and Eric Weimer. In *Italian Opera 1640–1770,* Series Two, vol. 80. New York and London: Garland Publishing Inc., 1981.

SCARLATTI, ALESSANDRO. *Operas of Alessandro Scarlatti.* Cambridge, Mass.: Harvard University Press, Publications in Music. Operas published so far: *L'Eraclea, Marco Attilio Regolo,* ed. Joscelyn Godwin, 1975; *La Griselda,* ed. D. J. Grout and Elizabeth B. Hughes, 1975; *La principessa fedele,* ed. D. J. Grout, 1977; *Il Tigrane,* ed. D. T. Grout, 1979.

————. *Telemaco,* ed. Howard Mayer Brown. In *Italian Opera 1640–1770.* Garland Publishing Inc., 1978.

Opera in England

The Ballad Opera, ed. Walter Rubsamen, 28 vols. New York: Garland Publishing Inc., 1974. A collection of 171 original texts of musical plays in facsimile.

GAY, JOHN. *The Beggar's Opera,* ed. E. J. Dent. London: Oxford University Press, 1954.

Opera in Germany

GRAUN, KARL HEINRICH. *Montezuma,* ed. A. Mayer-Reinach. *Denkmäler Deutscher Tonkunst* 15 (1904).

HOLZBAUER, IGNAZ. *Günther von Schwarzburg,* ed. Hermann Kretzschmar. *Denkmäler Deutscher Tonkunst* 7–9 (1902).

UMLAUF, IGNAZ. *Die Bergknappen,* ed. R. Haas. *Denkmäler der Tonkunst in Österreich* 18, part I (1911).

Opera in France

GLUCK, CHRISTOPH WILLIBALD. *Orfeo ed Euridice,* ed. Hermann Abert. *Denkmäler der Tonkunst in Österreich* 21 (1914). This is the Vienna version of 1762.

————. *Alceste,* ed. Rudolf Gerber. In *Sämtliche Werke.* Kassel: Bärenreiter, 1957, Series I, vol. 7. This is the French version of 1776.

GRÉTRY, ANDRÉ ERNEST MODEST. *Collection complète des oeuvres de Grétry.* 44 vols in 39. Leipzig: Breitkopf & Härtel, 1884–1924. Also, excerpt from *Richard Coeur de Lion: HAM* II, 306.

PICCINNI, NICCOLÒ. *Roland.* In *Chefs d'oeuvre classiques de l'opéra français.* Leipzig: Breitkopf & Härtel, 1880, vol. 29. Both this score and the Salieri below are in piano-vocal reduction only.

SALIERI, ANTONIO. *Les Danaïdes.* In *Chefs d'oeuvre classiques de l'opéra français.* Leipzig: Breitkopf & Härtel, 1880.

Church Music

BACH, CARL PHILIPP EMANUEL. *Magnificat*, W. 215. Stuttgart: Hänssler, 1971.

BACH, JOHANN CHRISTOPH FRIEDRICH. *Oratorios*, ed. Georg Schönemann. *Denkmäler Deutscher Tonkunst* 61 (1917).

CALDARA, ANTONIO. *Motets, Stabat mater, Te Deum*, ed. Eusebius Mandyczewski. *Denkmäler der Tonkunst in Österreich* 26 (1906).

HASSE, JOHANN ADOLF. *La conversione di Sant' Agostino*, ed. Arnold Schering. *Denkmäler Deutscher Tonkunst* 20 (1905).

21

The Preclassic Symphony, Concerto, and Instrumental Ensemble

As the eighteenth-century symphony evolved, so did sonata form, which became a basic structural concept not only in the symphony but also in the solo concerto and in chamber music. The solo concerto, in particular, encouraged increasingly idiomatic writing for a large variety of instruments, including violoncello, violin, keyboard, trumpet, clarinet, bassoon, flute, harp, viola, oboe, horn, and guitar. The concerto was a means of experimenting with the capacities, textures, and ranges of the individual instrument, and the growing use of pyrotechnics ushered in the era of the instrumental virtuoso.

Music in the eighteenth century was synonymous with entertainment. It is not surprising, then, that a variety of chamber music ensembles developed to perform a number of different social functions. Smaller instrumental ensembles increased in popularity. Trios, quartets, and quintets served for music that was written for and often involved performances by rich patrons within their private chambers. Ensembles involving more than five players generally served as background entertainment during a banquet, wedding, or other social occasion. A predominance of wind instruments suggested that a given piece may have been written for a performance out-of-doors, while the more intimate sounds of the strings indicated that a work had been intended for indoor performances. The most innovative compositional process may be found within the medium of the orchestral ensemble as this constituted the backbone of contemporary music making. The emerging symphony was to become a major genre in the eighteenth and the nineteenth centuries.

Orchestral Music

The Development of the Orchestra

In the 18th century, orchestras appeared in the opera theater, the concert room or private home, and the church. In German-speaking countries, in particular, every larger household—royal, aristocratic, or ecclesiastical—had its

518

own group of musicians, and this situation brought about a decentralization and proliferation of musical and orchestral activity.

Size of orchestra

The size of the orchestra corresponded to that of the room in which it performed. An opera orchestra was usually large, while the early symphony, because it was performed in the private quarters of members of the aristocracy, was of chamber proportions. The size of the mid-eighteenth-century orchestra fluctuated between about twenty-three players (as in Haydn's early days at Eszterháza) and about forty (as at Dresden under Hasse's leadership). The exact size of the musical forces depended on the wealth of the patrons and on the number of musicians they could support at court. Average string sections numbered four to six first violins, four to six second violins, two or three violas, two or three cellos, and two double bases.

Changes in texture and instrumentation

An integral part of the symphonic texture up to approximately the last quarter of the century was the harpsichord continuo line, which functioned as a harmonic filler and a support for the texture. It is impossible to establish the exact date by which composers stopped using the basso continuo, although according to Adam Carse,[1] Johann Friedrich Reichardt, Kapellmeister in Berlin, was one of the first to abolish the use of the continuo in the early 1780s.

Even today questions arise as to "correct" performance of a symphony written in the 1770s by J. C. Bach or Mozart—whether a harpsichord continuo would or would not have been used at the time, and therefore, whether or not it should be included today. In general, due to the increased size of the ensemble, the more contrapuntal texture of the music, and a more idomatic use of wind instruments, the additional harmonic support of the harpsichord became increasingly less necessary toward the end of the century.

Among the woodwind instruments, two oboes and two bassoons were adopted as standard additions to the traditional string ensemble. In later symphonies the oboes became more independent from the strings, as is evidenced in the slow movement of the overture to J. C. Bach's opera *Lucio Silla* (1774), in which the oboe has a beautiful solo passage supported by accompanying strings.

The bassoon was at times used as a continuo instrument doubling the bass line. It, too, received an increasingly independent treatment as part of a woodwind choir in the second half of the century. Flutes were at times interchangeable with the oboes. Even though the recorder was still in use, the transverse, or German, flute was more frequently employed within the orchestral ensemble. Clarinets seldom appeared in the symphony. They were most frequently used in military bands and opera, although some major centers, specifically Mannheim and Paris, did incorporate clarinets into the orchestra in the second half of the century. Mozart, for example, used the instruments in some of his late symphonies, and he often incorporated them into the orchestral accompaniment of his piano concertos.

Wind instruments

Because of the difference in the physical qualities of eighteenth-century wind instruments, and those used today, the sound produced by an orchestral ensemble in the eighteenth century differed considerably from that of today's orchestra playing the older repertoire. The eighteenth-century oboe had two or three keys and a range from middle C to D above the treble clef, and included all the semitones. The flutes at first had only one key, with a lower range extending to the low D. Only toward the end of the century were chromatic and two-foot keys added to the flute, and its lower range was extended to low C.

Clarinets experienced a slow and gradual emancipation within the late-eighteenth-century orchestra. We often encounter scores from the middle of the century in which the clarinet and oboe are used interchangeably, the two instruments to be played by the same person.

Horns were included as standard members of the orchestra early in the development of the symphony. Natural horns were capable of producing only a small number of pitches, and the demand for a wider spectrum of notes played by the horn resulted in the introduction of crooks. Virtuosi in the second half of the century produced a variety of sounds by "stopping" (blocking the bell by inserting a hand into it, thus varying the length of the tube).

Trumpets and drums reached the orchestra via the military band and were common by the last quarter of the century. The addition of these instruments to the orchestral texture usually signified an occasion on which color and brilliance were to be displayed. Trombones were reserved for church music and did not become a standard orchestral (symphonic) instrument until the nineteenth century.

Methods of keeping time   The concept of a conductor as a person who stands in front of an orchestra to direct the performance was foreign to most ensembles in eighteenth-century Europe. Yet the concept of beating time on the floor (even with a stick) had been familiar since the period of Lully. Eighteenth-century travelers remarked on the noise that this custom created during a performance, yet even this system was not always successful in getting musicians to play in time. The ensemble was trained by the Kapellmeister—often the composer himself—who directed either from the harpsichord or from within the string section of the orchestra. This points up another function of the harpsichord within the orchestral ensemble—as an instrument at which the composer was able to keep time. When the Kapellmeister played the keyboard continuo part, the concertmaster was expected to be in close touch with him throughout the performance, so that he could direct the other players.

The Italian Opera Overture

Origins   The history of the symphony in the early part of the eighteenth century is bound up with that of the Italian opera overture. Alessandro Scarlatti's overtures, or *sinfonie,* for example, generally contained the following arrangements of tempi: an Allegro (the use of the full orchestra lent it a brilliant effect), an Andante (a lyrical section with reduced scoring, which was at times only several measures in length), and a Presto (usually shorter than the opening Allegro, played with the full orchestra). The Italian opera *sinfonia,* which may be viewed as the early stage of the Italian symphony, eventually expanded into a three-movement unit. It was frequently transferred from one

A page from the third movement of Leonardo Leo's *sinfonia* to his opera *Amor vuol sofferenze* (1739).

opera to another and later even performed as a genre independent of its operatic context. A case in point is J. C. Bach's overture to *Lucio Silla*, which was later performed as Symphony No. 2 in B-flat major, Op. 18, No. 2.

Of the early composers, Hasse, Leo, and Sarro were perhaps those whose works contained the greatest differentiation of thematic material within the first part, i.e., the Allegro section. The overture to Hasse's *Astarto* (1726, printed with his intermezzo *L'Arinda e Vanesio* [see Bibliography]) is an example of the coexistence of the concerto grosso's ritornello concept and the newer, Preclassic concept of thematic dualism. Here the two themes that form the basis of the movement differ from each other in character. Once this initial dualism is introduced, however, the composer does little more with it structurally than to repeat both themes twice more: in the dominant major and in the tonic.

Leo's overture to *Amor vuol sofferenze,* written in 1739 (included in the volume of Neapolitan opera overtures to be published in *The Symphony 1720–1840* [see Bibliography]), has a clearly defined three-movement structure. The first movement, in strict binary form, shows an even sharper definition of the tonal areas of the first and second thematic groups than does Hasse's. The opening motif shows its derivation from the musical idiom of the intermezzo and opera buffa (see Example 21.1). A modulatory bridge follows, leading to a new motif in the dominant key. A second subject, lyrical in nature, appears in the dominant minor instead of the more common dominant major. This short, temporary detour into the minor was a favored stylistic trait among Neapolitan composers. The rest of the motivic material continues in the major.

The two typical Neapolitan overtures discussed above show that basic structural procedures that were later to be incorporated into sonata form—

Ex. 21.1   Overture to Leonardo Leo's *Amor vuol sofferenze*

i.e., thematic dualism, as well as motivic, textural, and key contrasts within the first movement of the sinfonia—took place as early as the second decade of the eighteenth century. Other examples of contemporary Neapolitan overtures are those by Domenico Sarro to his *Valdemaro* (1726), *Artemisia* (1731), *La Ginevra* (1720), and *La Didone* (1724).[2]

Jommelli   Neapolitan-trained Niccolò Jommelli, like many early Neapolitan opera composers, took great care to indicate dynamics and other performance directions in his scores. His overtures use orchestral techniques derived from his serious operas. The modulatory section between his first and second subjects often begins with a tremolo in the violins, while the motivic material is relegated to the bass line. The device of the tremolo, used in the orchestral accompaniment of a rage aria or for some similar affect, was thus transferred from an operatic to an instrumental context. (See, for example, his overture to *Fetonte*.)

After the middle of the century, the evolutions of the overture and that of the symphony were no longer parallel. While the symphony assumed larger proportions and was infused with new ideas by composers active in Germany, Austria, and France, the opera overture, specifically that of the Italian comic opera, settled into a one-movement sonata-allegro form. The overture to Cimarosa's *Il mercato di Malmantile* ("The Marketplace of Malmantile," 1784) serves as a readily available example.[3]

The Symphony

Italy

Sammartini   Giovanni Battista Sammartini (1700 or 1701–1775) was important in the development of the Preclassic symphony not only because of his use of the newer idiom, but also because of the incipient sonata form and the other new structural concepts manifested in his symphonies. His phrases are formulated by means of small motives, and his manipulation of these motives is the basis for the syntax of the new idiom. Sammartini's use of tonal centers to delineate structure constitutes another basic tenet in the development of the sonata-form concept. A prolific composer, he wrote seventy-seven symphonies and more than two hundred sonatas.

Sammartini's symphonies are orchestrated more modestly than are contemporary opera overtures and generally call for only a string quartet. Several of his *sinfonie a 3* resemble trio sonatas in texture but are more intricate in form. His symphonies are in two or three movements (e.g., the Symphony for Strings in D major, J.-C. 15).[4] In some cases, the second movement is so short that it is little more than a link between the outer movements. In other instances, the second movement is cast in the flowing, expressive Siciliana meter, which lends it a lyrical and slightly melancholy character. The first movements of his symphonies are either binary or expanded binary in form. An example of the composer's structural approach can be seen in his Symphony No. 13 in G major, in which a clear distinction is made (in the *exposition* of the first movement) between the primary thematic material, the modulatory material, the secondary, tonally contrasting motivic group, and the closing passage. The *development,* though short, modulates sequentially and contrapuntally. The *recapitulation* is a rather straightforward parallel repetition of the exposition. Although most of Sammartini's first-movement structures are still in binary form, this particular first-movement structure contains all the basic ingredients of the ternary sonata form.

Other symphony composers in Italy include Rinaldo da Capua, Galuppi, and Jommelli. Perhaps the most prolific of the later Italian symphonists was Luigi Boccherini (1743–1805), who spent a considerable portion of his life in Madrid. He is now best remembered for his cello concertos and sonatas and his chamber music, which includes over one hundred string quartets.

Other symphonists

Germany

From the fourth decade onward, several German centers assumed an important role in the development of the symphony—primarily Berlin, Hamburg, and Mannheim. Among the important Berlin symphonists were Karl Heinrich Graun and Johann Gottlieb Graun as well as Franz Benda and Anton Benda. Their symphonies were based on the three-movement Italian overture, but unlike the Italians they expanded the development section of first-movement sonata form to broader proportions.

Preclassic symphonists

Perhaps the most imaginative and harmonically innovative of the Berlin school was C. P. E. Bach. Although he was active as a symphonist while still in Berlin, his best examples of the genre were composed in Hamburg, i.e., after he left the court of Frederick II in 1768. Particularly interesting are the six symphonies (1773) dedicated to the Viennese baron Gottfried van Swieten, and the four *Orchester-Sinfonien* ("Orchestral Symphonies") completed in 1776.

C. P. E. Bach

Several stylistic features typical of C. P. E. Bach during this period are found in his Symphony No. 3 in C major (W. 182, No. 3, 1773).[5] Vestiges of the tutti-solo contrast in texture, a remnant of the concerto grosso's compositional techniques, are still evident. Quite striking is the feeling of development and manipulation of the opening motive. Example 21.2, showing his reworking of the first two measures, points to Bach's newer stylistic tendencies.

C. P. E. Bach was one of the great symphonic craftsmen of the Preclassic era, especially in his imaginative motivic manipulation. He frequently linked his movements, thereby creating a feeling of cohesion and inner unity. And

Ex. 21.2   C. P. E. Bach, Symphony No. 3 in C major, first movement

his search for expressiveness sometimes resulted in unorthodox harmonic progressions. The second movement of the 1773 Symphony in C major, for example, obscures the opening E minor tonality through the introduction of four measures of unresolved dissonances (see Example 21.3). Since clarity of harmonic intention and the use of closely related keys in modulatory sections were standard stylistic features of this period, this symphony contains musical elements contrary to the then prevalent Italian musical aesthetics. The reduction of texture, contrapuntal treatment of material, chromatically descending bass line, and striking use of dissonances all contribute to this movement's expressiveness. Its contrasting and carefully indicated dynamic gradations constitute further examples of the rampant emotionalism of the empfindsamer Stil.

Sulzer   J. G. Sulzer's definition of "symphony" in his *Allgemeine Theorie der Schönen Künste* may be directly applicable to the stylistic developments of the north German school of symphonists. He states that the chamber symphony (as opposed to the opera overture) must have a full sound and be brilliant and fiery in nature. The Allegro of such a work must contain big and bold thoughts, present what seems to be melodic and harmonic disorder, have strongly marked rhythms, make ample use of passages in unison, contain free imitation (even a fugal texture), modulate to distant keys, and show pronounced dynamic contrasts. Such an Allegro, according to Sulzer, is comparable to an ode by the ancient Greek poet Pindar: it elevates and stirs the soul of the listener. Similarly, the Andante (or Largo) must not deal with inconsequential material, but must aim to appeal to the senses. This article actually defines the essence of the north German empfindsamer Stil as applied to symphonic writing around 1770.

The "Mannheim school"   The orchestra of Duke Karl Theodor of Mannheim was famed as one of the best European ensembles. Karl Theodor was a patron of arts and letters, and during his reign he sponsored scientific institutions, museums, libraries, and a large number of actors, architects, sculptors, and musicians. Among the last were Johann Stamitz (1717–1757), Franz Xaver Richter (1709–1789), Ignaz Holzbauer (1711–1783), Anton Filtz (c. 1733–1760), the Italian-born Carl Joseph Toeschi (1731–1788), Johann Toeschi (c. 1735–1800), Christian

Cannabich (1731–1798), Franz Beck (1734–1809), and Carl Stamitz (1745–1801). Many were teachers and composers, as well as performers.

    The orchestra's first leader, and the founder of the Mannheim school, was the composer and violinist Johann Stamitz. Several features in his sym- **J. Stamitz** phonies were eventually to become mannerisms and clichés in the hands of the Mannheim symphonists: a threefold repetition of the opening chord; the carefully calculated orchestral crescendo, which, in Stamitz's case, was used as a means of dynamic animation but also was an integral part of the design of the movement; and the "steamroller" ostinato motive. These devices are found in the first movement of Stamitz's Symphony, Op. 5, No. 2 (see *HAM* II, No. 294).

    The Mannheim composers tended to slow down the harmonic motion of one or both of the main subjects (noticeable at the start of Stamitz's Op. 5, No. 2). Their use of repeated bass notes created organ points over which new themes were sometimes introduced. This compositional technique is espe- cially evident in Anton Filtz's *Symphonie périodique*, No. 2,[6] in which the last **Filtz** movement has a tonic pedal point that lasts for almost one-quarter of the movement.

    Christian Cannabich's music is free from the earlier mannerisms em- **Cannabich** ployed by Johann Stamitz's generation of players, and his symphonies reflect an Italianate vivacity and freshness. In his Symphony in B-flat major[7] he con- trasts the color of the woodwind section with that of the strings. The the- matic material in the second subject area of the opening movement is played entirely by woodwinds. The third movement introduces an effective fugato passage.

    The Mannheimers translated into the instrumental idiom the vocal style of the Italians. They introduced more counterpoint into the symphonic tex- ture, and contributed to the growth of the sonata-form principle by giving

Ex. 21.3   C. P. E. Bach, Symphony No. 3 in C major, second movement

greater emphasis to contrasting tonal areas and subsidiary themes. Thus they occupy an important position both in the history of eighteenth-century performance practice and in the development of the symphony.

Vienna

Preclassic sym-phonists   The Viennese symphonists of the Preclassic era established the tradition that Franz Joseph Haydn, Mozart, and Beethoven were directly to inherit. They include, among others, Matthias Georg Monn (1717–1750), Georg Christoph Wagenseil (1715–1777), Florian Leopold Gassmann (1729–1774), Michael Haydn (1737–1806), and Carl Ditters von Dittersdorf (1739–1799). These composers adopted the Italian concept of thematic dualism and sonata form. Monn's twelve surviving symphonies, for example, show the early sonata form, in which the first and at times the last movements present compact but clearly defined structural units. Their development sections usually begin with the first subject in the dominant key. Then, using material introduced in the exposition, they modulate through a circle of fifths. The recapitulations at times parallel the events of the exposition, while at other times they omit a repetition of the first subject.

Monn   Monn's minuets acquired an earthier, more folk-like character than the previous, stylized examples of the genre, which had its roots in the court dance. As example is the minuet of Monn's Symphony in D major, written in 1740 (last movement only in *HAM* II, No. 295).[8] The A-section consists of two four-measure phrases and a two-measure ending. The B-section is exactly double the length of the previous one, with which it shares motivic material. Monn's symphony is one of the earliest to contain four movements, which were to become the standard number several decades later.

Wagenseil   Christoph Wagenseil, whose symphonic output exceeds eighty works, exhibits an Italian influence in the vivaciousness of his predominantly three-movement works, which generally follow the Allegro–Andante–Presto or Allegro–Andante–Minuet scheme. When the minuet is used as a last movement, it may include a contrasting trio, and occasionally folk motives appear. The three movements of his symphonies are frequently in the same key. In his Symphony in D major of 1746,[9] the orchestra includes oboes, horns, and timpani—an instrumentation used in the first and last movements, with a contrasting texture in the middle movement scored for flute and strings.

Dittersdorf   The symphonic works of Carl Ditters von Dittersdorf reveal two outstanding features: a proclivity for programmatic titles and, particularly in his later symphonies, idiomatic symphonic writing closer in spirit to the broad scope of the Classic symphony than to the concise forms used by Preclassic composers. Dittersdorf, who wrote more than a hundred such works, was especially popular in Vienna for his Singspiel entitled *Doktor und Apotheker*. He skillfully combined elements of both Italian and French comic operas and furnished his operatic and orchestral works with a wealth of melodic invention. His music had an easygoing character suffused with a genuinely Ger-

Ex. 21.4   Karl Ditters von Dittersdorf, Symphony in F major

manic flavor. Example 21.4, taken from his Symphony in F major, suggests a folk theme, straight out of a Singspiel.

His symphonies on Ovid's *Metamorphoses* were also well received by the Austrian public in 1785. The group is made up of twelve programmatically titled works (such as *The Fall of Phaëton, The Transformation of Acteon into a Stag,* and *The Salvation of Andromeda by Perseus*), each of which has four movements. In some, like *The Fall of Phaëton,* the first movement (an Allegro) is preceded by a slow introduction—a device frequently adopted by Joseph Haydn in his symphonies. The programmatic titles, however, do not affect the musical content, beyond some very elementary evidences of tone painting.

Dittersdorf's late symphonies, especially the one in D major, written in 1778,[10] are representative of the mature Viennese symphonic style. The content of the first and last movements is much expanded, and the two become equal in both length and structural importance. Its second movement consists of a theme and variations, the third of a minuet and trio, the fourth of a rondo. Of particular interest is the first movement's sonata-form structure, with its expanded tonal areas and multiplicity of thematic material within each subject group. Dittersdorf especially expands the bridge between the first and second subject group. The second thematic area (i.e., subject group) of the Symphony in D major consists of two clearly stated separate themes, while the codetta that ends the exposition reintroduces some of the material from the bridge.

With the late works of Dittersdorf, each new element of sonata form assumes greater importance. His two thematic areas contain a multiplicity of themes, and the bridge sections carry motivic material that becomes functional in other (closing) passages throughout the first movement, such as the *codetta* at the end of the exposition and the *coda* at the end of the movement. In the first-movement development sections, his techniques include thematic manipulation, augmentation, and diminution. In Dittersdorf's hands the development of the symphony reaches new heights.

In the long list of composers belonging to the Viennese symphonic school, we must also include the Czech Johann Wanhall (also spelled Vanhal, 1739–1813), and Joseph Haydn's brother, Michael Haydn. Especially noteworthy is the latter's three-movement Symphony in G major (1783), performed by Mozart with the addition of a slow introduction that he composed specifically for that performance. (The entire symphony was until recently attributed to Mozart. It is now known as K. 444, or K. 425a in the revised edition of Köchel's catalog.)

Generally, the Viennese symphony represented the most mature phase of Preclassic symphonic development, and we find examples of both the three-movement and four-movement form. The Allegro movements contain several themes, with frequent soloistic treatment of wind instruments in the contrasting subject areas. Closing passages, including codas and codettas, assume greater prominence, and periodic structure is clearly defined. Counterpoint becomes important in the texture of the development sections of movements in sonata form. The first movements are usually in sonata form, while the last movements are frequently in sonata or rondo form. Minuets, when used, are folk-like, especially in the trio sections, where the winds frequently play soloistically.

France

Public concerts and performance practice   The two major influences on the development of symphonic music in France were public concerts and the proliferation of music publishers. The large number of public concerts, such as the Concert Spirituel, provided composers with ample opportunity to write works for public performances, while the demand for symphonic works helped spark the intense activity of music publishers who issued not only works by French composers, but also symphonies by Austrian, German, and Italian artists.

Paris had excellent instrumental ensembles. Their superior quality and high performance standards, and the number and type of instruments used, inevitably influenced the development of the symphony. In 1769 the Concert des Amateurs, for example, boasted an orchestra of forty violins, twelve cellos, and eight basses in addition to flutes, oboes, clarinets, bassoons, horns, and trumpets: eighty players in all! Contributing to the excellence of symphonic composition and performance in France was the fact that frequently orchestras were conducted by the composers of the works performed. The orchestra at the Concert Spirituel, particularly under Alexandre-Jean-Joseph de La Pouplinière (1693–1762), employed clarinets on a regular basis, thereby setting a precedent for the use of that instrument within an orchestral work. Stamitz probably introduced the instrument into Mannheim's orchestra as a result of his year of conducting in Paris.

F. Martin   During the first period of Parisian symphonic activity, the three-movement Italian symphony exerted considerable influence. The most remarkable composer of this period is François Martin (1727–1757), whose works show a sensitivity for orchestral sonority and whose treatment of sonata form delineates thematic dualism. His overtures differ from his symphonies in that occasionally the first movements of an overture are modeled after Lully's type of French overture: slow introduction followed by a fugal Allegro. This slow introduction to a symphonic structure may well have provided a source for the later-eighteenth-century custom of prefacing the first movement of a symphony with a slow section.

The second period of the French symphony is pervaded by a stylistic cosmopolitanism. Composers from all parts of Europe settled in France, as did, for example, Moravian-born Franz Xaver Richter, who moved from Mannheim to Strasbourg. More "foreign" music became available for performances at the public concerts. François-Joseph Gossec was active during this second period of French symphonic development, although because of his long and productive career his works may be seen as examples of the stylistic metamorphoses in the French symphony of the eighteenth century. Born within a few years of Haydn, Gossec outlived him by twenty. A master of orchestration—for example, in his effective use of trombones in *Messe des morts* (1760)—he was perhaps the most prolific French symphonist.

Gossec

By the third period of symphonic development, the use of the basso continuo had practically disappeared from the scene. Perhaps the best representative of this period was Simon Le Duc the Elder (1745–1777), an excellent violinist whose sensitive uses of orchestral sonority resulted in extraordinary textures. He occasionally subdivided the second violins and even the violas. The same period (1768–1777) witnessed the birth of the *symphonie concertante*, an orchestral work written for at least two solo instruments and orchestra. It represented a cross between the symphony and the concertato principle and was to become a highly popular genre in the last quarter of the century, not only in Paris but throughout all of Europe. Mozart's Sinfonia Concertante in E-flat major, K. 364, for violin, viola, and orchestra, is an excellent and readily available example. Long solo passages and multiple cadenzas are traits of this hybrid genre.

The symphonie concertante

Jean-Baptiste Davaux (1742–1822) and François Devienne (1759–1803) are but two of the many prolific composers of the French symphonies. Le Chevalier Joseph de Saint-Georges (1739–1799; see Chapter 38), Giuseppe Cambini (1746–1825), and Jean-Baptiste Bréval (1753–1823) are among the major composers of the symphonie concertante. All are representative of the late stages of symphonic development in France.

England

English symphonic developments were neither so innovative nor so prolific as those of the major European centers already discussed. Two of the most noteworthy composers active in England between 1762 and 1782 were Johann Christian Bach and Carl Friedrich Abel, both foreigners on English soil. Johann Christian spent some time after his father's death with his brother C. P. E. Bach in Berlin, then went to study in Milan and in Bologna with the great teacher Padre Giovanni Battista Martini (1706–1784). J. C. Bach converted to Catholicism, thus abandoning the Bach family's long Protestant tradition. Because of his one-time activities as organist in the cathedral at Milan, he was known as the "Milan Bach," a nickname later changed to the "London Bach" upon his move to the English city. Johann

J. C. Bach

Christian was steeped in the Neapolitan operatic tradition and wrote a considerable number of operas in the Italian style.

A gifted composer in his own right, J. C. Bach holds an especially important position in music history because of his influence on the style of the young Mozart. The two composers met in London in 1764 and again in Paris in 1778. Mozart wrote to his father on August 18, 1778: "Mr. Bach from London has been here for the last fortnight. He is going to write a French opera and has only come to hear the singers. . . . I love him (as you know) and respect him with all my heart."[11] The close artistic understanding and deep personal friendship that inspired this tribute was evident as early as 1764. As one of Mozart's biographers put it:

> He [J. C. Bach] liked to play with the boy; he took him upon his knee and went through a sonata with him, each in turn playing a bar with so much precision that no one would have suspected two performers. He began a fugue, which Wolfgang took up and completed when Bach broke off.[12]

J. C. Bach's works include more than fourteen operas, sixty symphonies, numerous keyboard sonatas, and various types of chamber music. Particularly expressive are his cantabile themes, both in his Allegros and in his slow movements. His six symphonies Op. 3 (1765) represent a continuation of the Italian opera overture, especially those works in the genre by Leo and Sammartini. The Italianate second movements are operatic in their melodiousness. His six symphonies Op. 6 (1767), of three movements each, are based on the Italian model of four-part string texture with two oboes and two horns supplying harmonic reinforcement.

The three symphonies of Bach's Op. 9 (1773) show an increased use of counterpoint in the development sections, and experimentation with solo woodwinds for contrasting color. The symphonies of Op. 18 (1781) include three for double orchestra, while the other three are overtures to operas. The overture to *Temistocle* (No. 4) employs in its slow movement three *clarinetti d'amore*. These bell-shaped instruments, which belong to the same family as the *oboe d'amore,* were used originally in Mannheim and their popularity was short-lived. In Bach's overture the three separate *clarinetto d'amore* parts, along with the flute and bassoon, form a small wind band that is juxtaposed against the strings.

Bach's Symphony in G Minor, Op. 6, No. 6   Bach's Symphony in G minor, Op. 6, No. 6, is unusual because of its emotional depth. One of his rare works to have all three movements in a minor key, it seems a true musical counterpart to the parallel Sturm und Drang literary movement in Germany. The first movement is rich in thematic material in that each of the two subject groups and the codetta contain two germinal ideas. The rhythm of the opening motive also figures prominently in several other places throughout the first movement, primarily the bridge passages between the first and second subject groups in the exposition, recapitulation, and coda. The second subject, in B-flat major, contrasts with the first in orchestration and character, for here the winds and the strings engage in a leisurely dialogue. Motivic manipulation and transformation are very much part of Johann Christian's symphonic style. The concept of sonata form is clearly developed. Even the standard repeat marks that traditionally separated the exposition from the rest of the first movement are eliminated in this "through-composed" movement. The slow movement of this work, in C minor, is especially worth studying because of its affinity with the first part of Mozart's keyboard Fantasy in C minor, K. 475, written eighteen years later in Vienna. Both works are in the same key, and they share the same somber tone and dark colors. Compare the opening antecedent and consequent motives in the excerpts shown in Examples 21.5 and 21.6. Especially prominent in both is the motivic outline: C, E-flat, A-flat. Both works share a descending linear pull, the triple repetition of the opening motive.

Like J. C. Bach, Carl Friedrich Abel (1723–1787) also "adopted" England. He left his native Dresden in 1759 to assume the post of chamber musician to Queen Charlotte. Shortly after J. C. Bach's arrival in London (1762), the two joined forces in the organization of the first public concert series in that city—the Bach-Abel concerts, which were continued for almost two decades, until Bach's death. It was at these events that both composers' symphonies were performed. Abel composed about thirty-six symphonies, on the whole more conservative than Bach's. Intended for performances by amateurs, these works were scored for oboes, horns, and strings, and the horn parts were such that they could be omitted entirely without damaging the texture. Similarly, the parts for oboes could be played by any other treble wind instruments or left out completely if none were available. **J. C. Bach and C. F. Abel**

When the symphonies of the Mannheimers infiltrated England in the 1760s, many conservative Englishmen were dismayed at the "foreign" influence. Generally, the home-grown English symphony retained three movements, with the first frequently the longest and most elaborate of the three. **The "English" symphony**

Ex. 21.5   J. C. Bach, Symphony No. 6 in G minor

Ex. 21.6   W. A. Mozart, Fantasy in C minor

Rondo finales were favored by English audiences, especially those based on English dance tunes or popular melodies. A number of native English composers warrant mention: Thomas Arne, William Boyce (1711–1779), John Stanley (1712–1786), and Stephen Storace. Both Arne and Boyce incorporated Handelian elements into their style. Arne's Eight Overtures in Eight Parts (1743) are in the Italian and French styles and originally preceded his theatrical works.

The Solo Concerto and Chamber Music

The Solo Concerto

With the rise of public concert series in the large European cities, a profusion of concertos, sonatas, and symphonies competed for a place in the repertory. The history and main attributes of the solo concerto will next be considered.

The violin concerto   The violin concerto was not as forward-looking as the symphony during the Preclassic era. The concerto retained its Baroque characteristics well into the eighteenth century. Pietro Locatelli (1695–1764), Giuseppe Tartini (1692–1770), and his pupil Pietro Nardini (1722–1793) figure prominently in the propagation of the violin concerto. In Germany and Italy, interest in the genre dropped off during the 1750s, while in France it was abandoned from 1734 to 1764, i.e., in the two decades between Leclair and Gaviniès. Composers contributing to the violin concerto repertoire include Antonio Lolli (c. 1725–1802), Maddalena Lombardini Sirmen (c. 1735–1785), Johann Stamitz, Johann Gottlieb Benda from the Berlin school, and two later composers—Giovanni Mane Giornovichi (c. 1740–1804) and Giovanni Battista Viotti (1755–1824).

Tartini   Giuseppe Tartini was a violin virtuoso who wrote more than 120 concertos for that instrument. A teacher of renown, his *Trattato di musica* ("Treatise on Music," Padua, 1754) is a classic among eighteenth-century works on contemporary methods, techniques, and practices. Tartini's concertos show the traditional Baroque trait of solo–ritornello alternation. In the Concerto in E minor, D. 56, for example, the almost monothematic material of the opening tutti is treated as a ritornello. More in keeping with newer stylistic concepts is the work's beautiful second movement, with its lilting Siciliana meter. Here the solo violin is supported only by chords in the orchestra, and the resultant homophonic texture, in which the basso continuo is omitted, offers a dramatic contrast to the ritornello structures of the outer movements.

Later violin concertos, for example those of Giornovichi, distinguish clearly among several contrasting themes that are presented as the basic musical ideas of the concerto in the opening tutti and solo sections. These works show little motivic play, however, and surprisingly little influence of contemporary symphonic techniques. Giornovichi was among the first composers to cast his slow movements in the mold of a *Romance*. Song-like and sentimental in nature, the Romance, which first appeared in conjunction with Italian and French opera, is a simple movement in a slow, 2/4 meter. It was to be used subsequently in instrumental music with greater frequency. Mozart has a Romance in his Piano Concerto in D minor, K. 466 (the middle movement), and Beethoven later composed two Romances for violin and orchestra.

The cello concerto

The violoncello concerto literature, although not so abundant as that of the violin, was developed by such composers as Leonardo Leo and Luigi Boccherini. Leo's concertos have Baroque four-movement designs, with one concerto even adding a fugue as a fifth movement. Leo was a pioneer, however, in his treatment of the solo cello as a deeply expressive instrument, and the melodies of his slow movements, frequently Sicilianas, resemble those of his operas.

Boccherini

Boccherini, an important late-eighteenth-century composer of music for the cello, was responsible for sparking the enormous enthusiasm for the instrument that gripped Madrid during his years there. His Cello Concerto in B-flat major, (No. 9), is still widely known and performed by cellists today.[13] The composer's rich harmonies and melodious themes bear a stylistic resemblance to those of Mozart and Haydn.

The clarinet concerto

Johann Stamitz composed some of the earliest solo concertos for the clarinet. It was in Mannheim that Mozart, who had previously heard the instrument in London in 1764, reacquainted himself with the clarinet as an expressive orchestral solo instrument.

The theories of Koch

One major treatise of the era summarizes the typical Preclassic concept of concerto form: Heinrich Christoph Koch's comprehensive treatise *Versuch einer Anleitung zur Komposition,* which has already been mentioned in Chapter 19 in connection with the concept of sonata form. This same source gives the following description of the first (Allegro) movement of a concerto: Its three main periods or sections are performed by the solo instrument; alternating with these are four secondary sections that act as ritornelli and are performed by the full orchestra. The three solo sections function within a concerto in the same way as do the three major sections within the first movement of a sonata. (In current terminology, these would correspond to the exposition, development, and recapitulation sections.) Graphically, Koch's description of concerto structure in the first movement may be found as follows:

Koch's Description of First-Movement Concerto Structure

R-1 (Ritornello 1)	A long statement introducing all the important themes of the movement. The tonal area outlined is most likely to include I–V–I.
S-1 (Solo 1)	A restatement of the main thematic ideas in elaboration, which are idiomatic to the instrument. The harmonic design is I–V.
R-2	Includes the main theme and several other phrases from R-1, ending on a formal cadence in V.
S-2	May start with new material and include some from S-1. The harmonic design is: V–modulatory passage–VI (or some other relative minor key).
R-3	The shortest of the ritornelli, whose primary function is to pave the way to a restatement of the solo in I.
S-3	Repeat of S-1 in I. It leads to a 16/4 chord with a fermata, at which place an instrumental cadenza is improvised.
R-4	A final ritornello, which consists of the closing phrases of R-1 in I.

Koch's view of the overall structure may be summarized as follows: Concerto form is a large-scale structure in which an alternation takes place between two different instrumental textures. While a certain amount of sharing of the musical material occurs, the two groups are structurally independent.

Chamber Music

Varied forms   A wide variety of chamber music forms proliferated during the Preclassic era. There was music in two, three, and four movements (slow–fast, fugal–slow–fast, and so on). Groups of dance movements resembling those in Baroque suites were also commonly used. As the century progressed, the influence of the Baroque dance suite on chamber music diminished, and only the minuet (and, to a lesser extent, the march) was preserved as an integral part of later chamber works. The three-movement structure of the Italian sinfonia gained prominence, and by the last quarter of the century that arrangement, with the addition of a minuet, had become the standard form for trios, quartets, and quintets.

The most popular small chamber genre in the earliest phases of Classicism was the trio sonata. Between 1740 and 1760 most works in this genre still made use of the keyboard continuo, although experiments in texture in which the keyboard was omitted were already in evidence. Consisting of from two to four movements, the trio sonata of this period was known under a variety of names, including even *divertimento* ("diversion"), *notturno* ("nocturne") and *serenata* ("serenade"). The trio, quartet, and quintet attained their structural stability, balance, and independence of parts only in the last quarter of the century, and as such are products of the Classic rather than the Preclassic era.

New forms and styles   From the middle of the century on, as the piano gained in prominence, the balance of instruments within a small ensemble changed. The sound of the piano did not blend with the other instruments so well as the harpsichord did, in its traditional function of providing basso continuo. Therefore composers seem to have chosen one of two directions: omit the continuo part entirely and fill the texture with wind instruments; or emphasize the piano within the ensemble more than the other instruments. The first direction resulted in the development of new chamber types involving small chamber ensembles of from eight to fifteen instruments. The second direction led toward the development of new chamber music combinations such as the piano trio, piano quartet, and, eventually, the piano quintet.

The divertimento, *cassazione* ("cassation"), notturno, and serenata denoted music of a light and entertaining nature performed both indoors and outdoors. An excellent example of this type of music is Mozart's *Eine kleine Nachtmusik* ("A Little Night Music," K. 525). Basically, the four terms were used interchangeably to denote the same types of composition. The serenata or divertimento had no fixed or well-defined form; even the number of movements sometimes varied to include as many as eight. These works used a greater wealth and variety in the treatment of musical ideas than did the contemporary symphony, as well as different combinations of solo instruments. A march frequently opened and concluded a serenata. An allegro movement near the beginning and an Allegro or Presto near the end of the work formed the most substantive musical sections. One or both were generally in sonata form. A slow movement, also part of the overall structure, was usually preceded and followed by a minuet, or a minuet and trio. The actual number of movements fluctuated, but the general compound structure may be represented as follows: March–Allegro–Minuet–slow movement–Minuet–Allegro–March.

Summary

Over a period of approximately seven decades the symphony underwent a gradual metamorphosis, which affected its structure, length, number of movements, and orchestration. The size of the orchestra, performance standards, the skill of composers in directing performances of their own works, the proliferation of public concerts and published music—all affected the nature and structure of a symphony. As a result of superior training, discipline, and musicianship, the Mannheim orchestra excelled in the interpretation of symphonic works. The large orchestras in Paris, and Parisian audiences' demand for new works, directly affected the number of new works composed and performed in that city.

Generally, the Italians imbued the symphony with the freshness and exuberance of their melodic ideas, inspired by their intermezzi and comic operas. The evolving symphonic genre inherited a naturalness and clarity of texture from the Italians. It also acquired its concern for elegance of detail and for orchestral sonority from the French, while the Germans endowed it with a more contrapuntal texture and a more dramatic intensity. The Viennese symphonists introduced the minuet as the third movement, thereby expanding the original three-movement structure to four. Not only was the first-movement sonata form expanded, but in the hands of Dittersdorf the entire symphony became more of an architectonic structure, in which the first and last movements balanced each other.

Symphonists were also active as composers of sonatas, chamber music, and instrumental concertos. The era saw a proliferation of instrumental music due primarily to the utilitarian function of chamber and solo music at the various courts and salons where music was "consumed" on a daily basis by amateur musicians who commissioned and performed much of the repertoire themselves.

The Preclassic solo concerto was considerably more conservative in its stylistic features than the contemporary symphony. Until late in the century the alternation of the orchestral tutti and the instrumental solo still showed the influence of the Baroque concerto grosso structure. The movements generally contained little motivic manipulation, and the symphony seems to have had little influence on the concerto. The concerto assumed the standard number of three movements.

With its music for connoisseurs, amateurs, and professionals, the Preclassic period proved especially conducive to the composition and performance of chamber music. All imaginable instrumental combinations existed to suit every indoor and outdoor occasion: the cassation, serenade, divertimento, and nocturne were but a few of the popular types. The string quartet and quintet in which all instruments shared equally in the texture was established slowly. These forms were to reach their maturity in the Classic era, when the basso continuo was no longer an essential part of the musical texture, and it is to that period and its major stylistic exponents—Haydn and Mozart—that we next turn our attention.

Notes

1. Adam Carse, *The Orchestra in the Eighteenth Century* (Cambridge, England: W. Heffer, 1940), p. 90.
2. In the symphony series issued by Garland Press (see Bibliography).
3. Ibid.
4. Sammartini's symphonies have been catalogued by Newell Jenkins and Bathia Churgin. Each symphony is given a Jenkins-Churgin (J.-C.) number.
5. C. P. E. Bach's works are catalogued by Alfred Wotquenne, much in the same way that Köchel catalogued Mozart's works. Thus, the "W" in front of a number refers to Wotquenne.
6. In *The Mannheim Symphonists: A Collection of Twenty-four Orchestral Works* (2 vols.), eds. Hugo Riemann (New York: Broude Brothers, 1956), vol. I, p. 227.
7. Ibid. Vol II, p. 103.
8. Complete symphony in *Denkmäler der Tonkunst in Österreich,* vol. 81: Carl Ditters von Dittersdorf, *Instrumentalwerke,* ed. Victor Luithen (Graz: Akademishce Druck u. Verlagsanstalt, 1960).

9. Ibid.
10. Ibid.
11. Emily Anderson, ed., *The Letters of Mozart and His Family* (London: Macmillan, 1938), vol. 2, p. 900.
12. Otto Jahn, *The Life of Mozart* (New York: Cooper Square Publishers, Inc., 1970), vol. 1, p. 39.
13. In his *Thematic, Bibliographical and Critical Catalogue of the Works of Luigi Boccherini* (London: Oxford University Press, 1969), Yves Gérard assigns this concerto the catalogue number 482, composed c. 1771. According to Gérard, this work, published by the Eulenburg pocket scores (London, 1949) and edited by Richard Sturzenegger, is the only correct edition of the work. The version published in 1895 by Breitkopf & Härtel, and as revised by Friedrich Grützmacher, while the one most often performed, is nevertheless not based on the original manuscript.

Bibliography

Books and Articles

German Symphonists

GRADENWITZ, PETER. "The Symphonies of Johann Stamitz." *Music Review* 1 (1940): 354–363.

French Symphonists

BROOK, BARRY S. "Simon Le Duc l'aîné, a French Symphonist at the Time of Mozart." *Musical Quarterly* 48 (1962): 498–513.

Form and Structure

CHURGIN, BATHIA. "Francesco Galeazzi's Description (1796) of Sonata Form." *Journal of The American Musicological Society* 21, no. 2 (1968): 180–199.
RATNER, LEONARD. "Eighteenth-Century Theories of Musical Period Structure." *Musical Quarterly* 42, no. 4 (1956): 439–454.
STEVENS, JANE R. "An Eighteenth-Century Description of Concerto First-Movement Form." *Journal of the American Musicological Society* 24, no. 1 (1971): 85–95.

The Sonata and Chamber Music

NEWMAN, WILLIAM S. *The Sonata in the Classic Era.* New York: W. W. Norton, 1971.
WELLESZ, EGON, AND STERNFELD, FREDERICK, eds. *The New Oxford History of Music,* Vol. 7. London: Oxford University Press, 1973. Wellesz and Sternfeld, "The Concerto," pp. 434–494; Günther Hausswald and Friedrich Schiller, "The Divertimento and Cognate Forms," pp. 503–511; Karl Geiringer, "The Rise of Chamber Music," pp. 515–572.

General (*see also Chapter 19*)

CARSE, ADAM. *The Orchestra in the Eighteenth Century.* Cambridge, England: W. Heffer, 1940.

Scores

ABEL, KARL. *Works* (symphonies), ed. Walter Knappe. Cuxhaven, 1962.

BACH, C. P. E. *Symphony No. 3 in C major* (W. 182, No. 3). New York: Kalmus, n.d.

————. *Concerto in D minor* (W. 23), ed. Hans Joachim Moser. *Denkmäler Deutscher Tonkunst,* vols. 29–30.

————. *Vier Orchester-sinfonien,* ed. R. Steglich, in *Das Erbe Deutscher Musik,* vol. 18. Leipzig: Breitkopf & Härtel, 1942.

BACH, J. C. *Fünf Sinfonien,* ed. Fritz Stein. In *Das Erbe Deutscher Musik,* vol. 30. Leipzig: Breitkopf & Härtel, 1956.

BROOK, BARRY S., ed., Barbara B. Heyman, assoc. ed, *The Symphony 1720–1840.* New York: Garland Publishing, Inc. A comprehensive collection of about 600 full scores of eighteenth-century symphonies edited by a large number of people. The projected date of completion is 1982, although several volumes are scheduled to appear each month.

DITTERSDORF, CARL DITTERS VON. *Drei Sinfonien, Eine Serenate,* ed. Victor Luithlen. *Denkmäler der Tonkunst in Österreich,* vol. 81.

————. *Selected Orchestral Works,* ed. Joseph Liebeskind. New York: Da Capo, 1971.

GREEN, DOUGLASS, AND LAZAREVICH, GORDANA, eds. *Neapolitan Opera Overtures* Series A, *The Symphony 1720–1840.* New York: Garland Publishing Inc. Works include Leo's *Amor vuol sofferenze,* Sarro's *Valdemaro, Artemisia, La Ginevra, La Didone,* and Cimarosa's *Il mercato di Malmantile,* among others.

HASSE, JOHANN ADOLF. Overture to *Astarto,* in *L'Artigiano gentiluomo,* or *Larinda e Vanesio,* ed. Gordana Lazarevich. Madison: A-R Editions, Inc., 1979. *Recent Researches in the Music of the Classic Era,* vol. 9.

LEO, LEONARDO. *Concerto for Cello and Strings in F minor,* ed. Felix Schroeder. Leipzig: C. F. Peters.

MONN, MATTHIAS GEORG, AND MANN, JOHANN CHRISTOPH. *Wiener instrumentalmusik vor und um 1750,* ed. Wilhelm Fischer. *Denkmäler der Tonkunst in Österreich,* vol. 39.

MONN, WAGENSEIL, SCHRÖDER, STARZER. *Symphonies.* In *Wiener Instrumentalmusik vor und um 1750,* ed. Karl Horwitz and Karl Riedel. *Denkmäler der Tonkunst in Österreich,* vol. 31.

SAMMARTINI, G. B. *The Symphonies of G. B. Sammartini.* Vol 1, *The Early Symphonies,* ed. Bathia Churgin. Cambridge, Mass.: Publications in Music, 1968.

————. Symphony in D major, J.-C. 15, in F. E. Kirby, ed. *Music in the Classical Period: An Anthology with Commentary,* 12. New York: Schirmer Books, 1978.

RIEMANN, HUGO, ed. *The Mannheim Symphonists: A Collection of Twenty-four Orchestral Works.* 2 vols. New York: Broude Brothers, 1956.

22

The Classic Period

I
N our discussion of the Preclassic period three style variants were detected: Italian, French, and German. Eighteenth-century writers praised Italian music for its expressiveness, lyricism, and seriousness, German music for its compositional craft, and French music for its rhythmic vivacity and pleasing *galant* quality. The Classical epoch, however, witnessed the formation of a universal (European) musical language, embodied in the later works of Mozart, who assimilated these features and combined them into a unique "international" style. This universal language was based on a humanistic ideal: to appeal and be comprehensible to all people, regardless of their social class or national origin. Incorporating folk elements, it aimed to embrace all of humanity. This concept of humanitarianism came to fruition in Schiller's *Ode to Joy,* used as the text for Beethoven's Ninth Symphony (see Chapter 25), and its ideals may be recognized in such masterworks as Mozart's *The Magic Flute* and Haydn's *The Creation* and *The Seasons.*

In order to gain a better understanding of the stylistic transformations and structural features of music in the Classic era, we must study the important genres of the last decades of the eighteenth century as developed by two of the three great composers of Classical works, Haydn and Mozart. The third, Beethoven, will be discussed in the next section, since most of his masterpieces relate to nineteenth-century aesthetics. This chapter, therefore, has two objectives: (1) to define the musical attributes of the Classical style; and (2) to give an overview of the works by Mozart and Haydn, in whose output, from the 1770s on, we can easily trace the metamorphosis of style from the Preclassic to the Classic. Their many contemporaries have already been mentioned in Chapters 18–21 under the specific categories (symphony, concerto, chamber music, etc.) to which each contributed most significantly.

The Concept of "Classic" in Music

Late-eighteenth-century interest in the ideas and ideals of classical Greek and Roman culture was kindled primarily by Johann Winckelmann (1717–

1768), a German archeologist and art historian, who studied antiquity in his search for ultimate perfection. His report on his excavations at the ancient cities of Herculaneum and Pompeii, *Geschichte der Kunst des Altertums* ("History of the Art of Antiquity"), written between 1758 and 1764, fired the imagination of many intellectuals.

The Enlightenment, which corresponded in time to the Preclassic epoch in music, emphasized objectivity and rationalism, which was later replaced by the subjectivity and increasing irrationalism that stemmed from conflicts within Classicism. If the Preclassic style in music is seen as lasting until about 1770, then the Classic period may be seen as beginning in the 1770s and extending to the first two decades of the nineteenth century. The Classic period includes the middle and late works of Mozart and Haydn, as well as the early output of Beethoven and Schubert. The roots of Beethoven's and Schubert's musical styles are to be found in the Classic period: their concern with the structural aspects of a musical composition is typical of this period. The broadened spectrum of their tonal language, however, and the new ideals expressed in their music are features of the Romantic style.

Elements of musical Classicism

The musical language formulated during the Preclassic era enabled Classical composers to give free reign to their imagination and to build on earlier musical structures. Since Haydn, Mozart, Beethoven, and Schubert spent at least part of their creative lives in Vienna, and since certain Viennese elements are recognizable in the Classic style, the term "Viennese Classic" is frequently used to denote the style at the end of the eighteenth and beginning of the nineteenth centuries. Specifically Viennese are the blend of serious with *buffo* (comic) elements, the influence of folk song on instrumental music, and the balance between formal simplicity and highly developed textures.

The transition from Preclassic to Classic style is noticeable in at least five different areas: phrase structure, rhythm, harmony, thematic development, and musical form. Particularly evident is the regularity of the recurrent phrases and periods, the building blocks of larger musical forms. While these elements were already in evidence during the Preclassic era, Haydn and Mozart brought them to levels of greater complexity.

In the Classic period rhythm is refined. Contrasting, contrapuntally interwoven rhythms alternate with rhythmically homophonic sections. Classical symphonies, string quartets, and sonatas demonstrate a closer connection to folk music, which in turn affects their melodic and rhythmic structures. Major keys predominate. The use of a minor key usually implies an impassioned mood, affected by the spirit of the Sturm und Drang. During the Classic era the range of tonality is broadened considerably. We need only look at some of Haydn's symphonies from 1768 to 1772, or the chromatic and enharmonic modulations present in Mozart's late works, to realize that harmonic intensification had by then become part of the Classic aesthetic.

As the musicologist Friedrich Blume wrote: "Melody is the soul of Classic music."[1] Transfer of idiom is quite common, and an instrumental melody frequently resembles an operatic aria. In contrast to the mellifluous, "spun out" melody that is usually confined to a slow movement, the basis for the

Ex. 22.1   *Komm lieber Mai und mache die Wälder wieder grün*

sonata-allegro form of the first movement in a Classic composition is its motive—the smallest compositional unit, a germinal idea capable of being varied and developed. It is strongly defined either through its rhythmic configuration or its melodic contour. Thematic manipulation is based on the principle of motivic development: subjecting the motive to transposition, expansion, contraction, fragmentation, and superimposition.

Sonata-allegro form reaches its structural apogee in the Classic era. As a first-movement form it becomes highly codified and appears in almost all the predominant contemporary instrumental genres: chamber music, the symphony, the instrumental solo sonata, and the concerto. It appears in modified versions in the last-movement rondo, the set of variations, the three-part song form of a slow movement, and at times even in the minuet. In addition, genres that had been evolving during the Preclassic era are standardized during the Classic period. The symphony, for instance, acquires new, larger proportions, with an increased emphasis placed on the balance among its four movements.

An affinity with the popular style seems to be one of the characteristic features of Classical music, and popular and folk tunes were increasingly incorporated into the musical comic genres (such as the Singspiel and opéra-comique). Although the folk-*like* melodies in a symphony or concerto can easily be detected, identifying a real folk melody in Haydn, Mozart, or Beethoven—as opposed to a composer's original melody merely made to sound folk-like—is practically impossible.

The folk element in Classical music

An example of a folk-like theme inspired by an actual folk song is the rondo theme to the finale of Mozart's Piano Concerto in B-flat major, K. 595, which greatly resembles the folk song *Komm lieber Mai und mache die Wälder wieder grün* ("Come, dear May, and make the woods green again"). The folk-song theme and Mozart's rondo theme can be found in Examples 22.1 and 22.2. A different case, however, is the first theme in the finale to Haydn's Symphony No. 104 (*London*) in D major (1797), a rustic theme that may or may not have a folk origin. Its popular, or folk-like, properties are self-evident (see Example 22.3).

Frequently the use of folk-like material in Haydn serves to heighten a humorous moment. Haydn collected folk tunes and actually set a number of

Ex. 22.2   W. A. Mozart, Piano Concerto No. 27 in B-flat major

Ex. 22.3 F. J. Haydn, Symphony No. 104 in D major

Allegro spiritoso

Scottish songs, as did Beethoven. In fact, between 1791 and 1805 Haydn wrote arrangements of several Scottish, Welsh, and Irish songs. In his discussion of the popular style in Haydn, Charles Rosen[2] points out that melodies with a clearly defined popular flavor occur in his works in three specific locations: toward the end of the first-movement expositions, in the Trio sections of the Minuets, and in the opening of Finales.

Franz Joseph Haydn

Haydn's Life

Franz Joseph Haydn (1732–1809), son of poor Austrian parents, obtained his early musical training as a choirboy in the Cathedral of St. Stephen in Vienna. Literally self-taught, Haydn studied the compositional treatises and music of Fux, Mattheson, and C. P. E. Bach. For a short time he even worked as a valet to Porpora in exchange for lessons in musical composition.

The Esterházy years
He obtained his first permanent position in 1761 at the court of Prince Paul Anton Esterházy (1710–1762). Haydn's duties as music director included daily rehearsals with the orchestra and singers, as well as frequent performances. Not only did he have to write music to order and perform as a harpsichordist and violinist, but, as an administrator, he was also librarian, curator of instruments, and supervisor of the music copyists.

The splendor and magnificence of the Esterházy court and the quality of its musical life rivaled those of major European courts. Yet despite the profusion of musical activities under Haydn's direction, he led a rather isolated life during his thirty years of active service at the Esterházy court. Throughout the 1780s Haydn paid frequent visits to Vienna, and his international reputation began to grow. Some of his symphonies were performed at the Concert Spirituel, and he was invited to compose six new symphonies for Paris. This work resulted in the composition of the *Paris* Symphonies, Nos. 82–87, and **Foreign recognition** the three written for Comte d'Ogny, Nos. 90–92. The composer's fame also spread to London, Madrid, and Naples, bringing him invitations to visit all those places.

Despite such recognition, Haydn felt he could not leave his position at the court of Esterházy, and yet his restlessness was becoming more pronounced. Immediately after the death of Prince Nicholas in 1790, therefore, the composer accepted Johann Peter Salomon's invitation to come to London to write an opera for the King's Theatre as well as six symphonies and smaller works for twenty public concerts. In 1791, Haydn was even given an honorary doctorate by Oxford University. He died wealthy and famous in 1809.

Franz Joseph Haydn. The engraving is based on a portrait by Thomas Hardy (1792). (Courtesy, Bildarchiv der Österreichischen Nationalbibliothek)

Symphonic Music

Haydn's 104 symphonies display a great and imaginative variety of moods and structures. They range from the tragic tone of the *Lamentation,* No. 26, to the extreme playfulness and rollicking finale of the Symphony No. 60. Some have a quasi-religious cast resulting from the composer's use of a cantus firmus, such as No. 30, which is based on a Gregorian chant for Eastertime. Others contain exuberant, joyous, yet simple folk-like moments. Some of the folk elements are noticeable in *La Reine* ("The Queen," No. 85), in which the slow movement, a set of variations, is based on a French Romance, while the trio is an Austrian *Ländler* (a folk dance akin to a slow waltz). Noteworthy are Haydn's imaginative use of instruments, innovative structures, predilection for contrapuntal textures, and the intensity of emo-

General charac- teristics

tional expression in the works he composed during the period of his "Romantic crisis," his Sturm und Drang years.

Haydn and the Sturm und Drang

Haydn's Sturm und Drang symphonies are concerned with the expression of intense sentiment, as their descriptive titles indicate: No. 26 (*Lamentation,* 1768), No. 44 in E minor (*The Mourning Symphony,* 1771), No. 45 in F-sharp minor (*Farewell,* 1772), and No. 49 in F minor (*The Passion Symphony,* 1768). These works, however, still share features of Preclassic style. For example, in his Symphony No. 39 in G minor each of the movements is short, and while sonata form is the basis of the first movement, it is presented in a simple, clear-cut manner. Haydn's later tendency to create a tightly knit symphonic structure by basing an entire movement on one theme or motive is already noticeable in this work. This excellent symphony is representative of Haydn's symphonic style prior to the last quarter of the eighteenth century.

An early example of the use of a monothematic idea is the first movement of Haydn's Symphony No. 28, which grows organically out of a single rhythmic motive, thereby generating an inner unity and intense rhythmic energy. The composer's contrapuntal techniques include simple imitation and strict canon. The Minuet of Symphony No. 44, for example, has a canon at the octave between the first and second violins and the cellos and bassoons, while the Finale of the Symphony No. 40 is a fugue.

Uses of instruments

After 1760 Haydn began to use instruments in a more imaginative, virtuosic fashion. Particularly interesting solos are found in the three symphonies composed in 1761—Nos. 6, 7, and 8: *Le Matin* ("Morning"), *Le Midi* ("Noon"), and *Le Soir* ("Evening"). The Finale of *Le Midi* uses flutes, violin, and cello in a *concertante* fashion, while its Adagio employs the violin in an extended cadenza. Haydn's experimentation with horns can be seen in the Symphony No. 31 (*Hornsignal*), in which four solo horns are introduced. High horns, trumpets, and kettledrums are present in Symphonies Nos. 32 and 33, which exude a festive spirit partially because of their use of the C major key.

Instrumental recitative (as already noted in the works of C. P. E. Bach) was a frequent phenomenon in Germany during the period of the empfindsamer Stil and the intense Sturm und Drang (see, for instance, Haydn's Symphony No. 7, in which the second of five movements is actually entitled "Recitativo"). In Example 22.4, the instrumental recitative occurs in measures 6 and 7 and is performed by the solo first violin. The cadential formulas, rests, and expressiveness exhibited in the violin part are direct transfers from vocal recitative. Throughout this movement the tempo fluctuates between *allegro* and *adagio,* as in vocal accompanied recitatives.

Haydn also experimented with differing forms and arrangements of movements. Some symphonies integrate successfully principles of the concertante. In the last movement of No. 38, the idea of the wind-band concerto is integrated into the symphonic style, while the Adagio of Symphony No. 36 employs a solo violin and solo cello in the manner of a double concerto. From a structural point of view, perhaps Haydn's most interesting works from the 1760s and 1770s are Symphony No. 45 (*Farewell*) and the already

Ex. 22.4 F. J. Haydn, Symphony No. 7 in C major, second movement

mentioned trilogy consisting of Nos. 6, 7, and 8. The coda of the *Farewell* Symphony is an *adagio* during which one instrument after another falls silent. In the end, the texture is reduced to one first and one second violin to bring the movement to a close on a *pianissimo* chord in first inversion. Symphony No. 7 is unusual because two of its five movements are related in much the same way as an operatic accompanied recitative and aria; the "recitative" (second movement) functions as an introduction to the third, in which the melody, joined by a solo cello, is very much in the style of a slow-moving, embellished *aria cantabile*.

The *Paris* and *London* symphonies

Between 1785 and 1788 Haydn composed a series of eleven symphonies (Nos. 82–92) for performance and publication in Paris. The *Paris* Symphonies (Nos. 82–87) include such popular works as *L'Ours* ("The Bear," No. 82), *La Poule* ("The Chicken," No. 83), and *La Reine* ("The Queen," No. 85). The last twelve symphonies (Nos. 93–104) were written for performances in London and are known as the *London* or *Salomon* Symphonies. Perhaps the most magnificent of these are the last three, Nos. 102, 103, and 104. The large orchestra of about sixty players available to the composer in London affected the sonority of these compositions. No. 103 employs two flutes, oboes, clarinets, bassoons, horns, and trumpets, plus timpani and strings. Since this work is readily available, we shall use it as an example of Haydn's mature symphonic style. The kernel of the whole first movement is to be found in its introduction, and the feeling of inner unity and cohesion generated by this movement is all the more amazing considering the small number of themes employed by Haydn. The whole texture is motivic, based on: ♪. A second subject, while presenting textural and harmonic contrasts to the first subject, evolves from it. The development section is based entirely on the inversion, contraction, and juxtaposition of the predominant motivic ideas of the exposition, and it also uses the slow introduction's melodic line in diminution. The recapitulation is amazing for the surprise element it incorporates: in the coda Haydn reintroduces part of the introductory Adagio, and the piece finishes by repeating these same ideas in diminution. During the slow movement the art of the variation is shown at its most imaginative and unorthodox.

Haydn's varied, innovative treatment of form makes each work unique. The slow introductions (of the twelve *London* Symphonies only No. 95 is not preceded by one) assume an importance within the thematic web of the whole. First-movement sonata form becomes for Haydn a skillful and monumental structure in which recourse to contrapuntal devices is especially prominent in the development sections, and the codas assume new thematic significance. The second movements show a variety of hybrid forms, including simple strophic (Nos. 94, 95, 97) and double variation (No. 103). The Minuets are robust, far removed from the courtly character of the dance, and the Trios frequently serve as a platform for experimentation with harmonic and orchestral color. The finales parallel the structural imaginativeness of the first movements and are frequently in rondo or sonata form.

Chamber Music

Haydn's contributions to the field of chamber music include composi-**The trios** tions for a variety of instrumental combinations: more than 120 string trios for baryton, viola, and cello; more than 31 piano trios; 21 trio sonatas for two violins and continuo; two sets of trios for two flutes and cello (6 works in 1784 and 3 in 1794); more than 70 string quartets; and 6 duo sonatas for violin and viola (1775), as well as music for the small chamber ensembles—*notturni, Feldparthien, divertimenti,* and so on.

Eighteenth-century chamber music, as we have seen, had a purely utilitar-**Piano** ian function. Haydn's works were therefore usually composed at the com-**trios** mand of his patron and were intended for performances in the prince's private chambers. In his early trios for two violins and cello, written in the 1750s, Haydn demonstrated his debt to the style galant. The use of the basso continuo lends the works the flavor of the more conservative trio sonata. Pieces written in the 1760s have brilliant passages for the first violin, probably because they were intended for the Italian virtuoso Luigi Tomasini (1741–1808), then concertmaster of the Esterházy orchestra. Haydn's finest trios, however, were composed in the 1790s for the combination of violin, cello, and piano.

While his quartets stand along with Beethoven's as masterpieces of the **The** quartet literature, in which the independence of each of the four instruments **quartets** is developed to the fullest, Haydn's piano trios do not exhibit such independence, but are in reality compositions for piano and violin with cello accompaniment. This is especially evidenced in the second movement of Hob. XV, No. 29, in E flat major[3] in which the delightfully simple theme is shared between the piano and the violin, while the cello part resembles that of a basso continuo line.

Best among his twenty-six piano trios are the last (written between 1793 and 1796). The keyboard writing is as technically demanding in these late works as in Haydn's late sonatas and Mozart's piano concertos. Many of the trios have Finales which demonstrate Haydn's flair for the folkish and the dance-like. The last movement of Hob. XV, No. 27, in C major is a symphonic rondo and full of delightfully humorous passages created by the off-beat accents, the unexpected harmonic turns, and a scherzando rhythm. The last movement of Hob. XV, No. 25, in G major is a "Rondo all'Ungarese" (a Rondo in the mode of a Hungarian dance).

As a composer of string quartets, Haydn towers over his contemporaries. Written over a span of half a century, these works demonstrate a stylistic metamorphosis, from the hybrid nature of the earlier ones—a cross between trio sonata texture and divertimento—to the unity of the later ones, which display full technical mastery of the Classic style.

The viola in Haydn's early quartets frequently doubles the cello in a texture dominated by the violins. What a world of difference between these and the later quartets of the 1780s and 1790s, in which a main element is the full equality of all four instruments!

With Op. 17 (1771) and Op. 20 (the *Sun* Quartets, 1772), the four-movement format was standardized. In these pieces Haydn also began to reject rococo figurations, and under the influence of the Sturm und Drang he showed an intensified expressivity, which paralleled that in his symphonies from the same period. Typical of this period is the predilection for minor keys and a gravitation toward the minor mode in his modulations. Rich contrapuntal textures and asymmetrical phrases are also symptomatic of Haydn's "Romantic crisis." In the *Sun* Quartets, for example, three of the six Finales are fugues, while other movements utilize canons and strettos. This set of quartets strongly influenced Mozart's quartet style.

Quartets, Op. 33

With the Op. 33 of 1781 (the *Russian* Quartets, so-called because of their dedication to Grand Duke Paul Petrovich of Russia), Haydn embarked upon a new path. The dynamic force generated in his first movements, and their vivacity and clarity of articulation, could well have resulted from a transfer of idiom from comic opera, which Haydn was writing during the nine years between the *Sun* and *Russian* quartets. Opera buffa influence is strong and may even account for the name *Scherzo* (the Italian word for "joke") given by Haydn to minuet movements.

The whole set is actually subtitled *Gli scherzi* ("The Jokes"). The quartets are bursting with rhythmic vitality, not only in the Finales but also in the Scherzo movements. In Op. 33, No. 3, for example, the Scherzo precedes the slow movement, which is sandwiched between the bubbly movements. In Example 22.5, the very quiet (*sotto voce*) beginning and the sudden *sforzandi*, along with the unequal phrase lengths, add to the joyful, humorous effect. In

Ex. 22.5   F. J. Haydn, Quartet, Op. 33, No. 3, second movement

Ex. 22.6   F. J. Haydn, Trio from Quartet, Op. 33, No. 3, second movement

the Trio section of the same movement (see Example 22.6), bird sounds are created by the two violins (this is why the quartet was subtitled *The Bird*). The last movement is earthy and rustic (see Example 22.7).

The trend toward increasing economy of material in the first movement, already seen in Op. 33, is intensified in the quartets of Op. 50 (1787). Here Haydn shows himself to be a consummate master of the Classical string quartet. Dedicated to Friedrich Wilhelm II of Prussia, who was an amateur cellist (hence the name "Prussian" Quartets), the Op. 50 quartets place a greater emphasis on solo cello passages. Increasingly, one basic motivic idea is elaborated throughout the first movement. An example of this economy may be seen in the first movement of Op. 50, No. 1, in which the main source of energy is the tension between a single-note ostinato and the rhythmic transformation of a six-note motive. **Quartets, Op. 50**

The quartets in Op. 76 (1797), from the same period as the oratorio *The Creation,* include the well-known *Emperor* Quartet (No. 3), the slow movement of which is based on the song that subsequently became the Austrian national anthem: *Gott erhalte Franz den Kaiser* ("God save the Emperor Franz"). The same tune became the German national anthem when its words were changed to *Deutschland über Alles* ("Germany Above All"). The movement—*Poco adagio cantabile*—is an elegant theme with four variations (see Example 22.8).

Among Haydn's compositions for instrumental ensembles are notturni, Feldparthien, and divertimenti, for Haydn contributed his share to the repertoire of outdoor music so much in demand in eighteenth-century Austria. He wrote divertimenti for the wind band of Prince Esterházy—including the Divertimento in B-flat major, which contains the St. Anthony Chorale that the Romanticist Johannes Brahms later utilized as the basis for his own set of **Other ensemble works**

Ex. 22.7   F. J. Haydn, Rondo from Quartet, Op. 33, No. 3

variations. The divertimenti resembled the Feldparthien, outdoor suite music for wind band. On commission from the king of Naples, Haydn also composed a number of notturni for two *lire organizzate* (hurdy-gurdies), two clarinets, two horns, two violas, and bass instruments. The parts for the lire organizzate were later rescored for flute and oboe.

The Sonatas and Concertos

Haydn's keyboard sonatas were written at even intervals over a span of fifty years and reveal his stylistic metamorphosis from Preclassic to Classic tendencies.

The keyboard sonatas   A major influence on the keyboard sonatas of Haydn was C. P. E. Bach. Bach's stamp may be felt in the Sonata No. 34 in E minor,[4] for example, especially in the slow movement, with its improvisatory-sounding runs of 16th- and 32nd-note figures divided between the hands. This influence of the empfindsamer Stil, however, does not extend to the third movement, a rollicking rondo full of humor, exuberance, and childlike naiveté.

Three sonatas (Nos. 40–42) were dedicated in 1784 to Princess Marie Esterházy. These two-movement works, which show the influence of the divertimento, are easy pieces, primarily intended for light diversion, and were therefore suited to Marie's use. Quite in contrast with these works is the great Sonata No. 49 in E-flat major, a technically demanding masterpiece. The *Adagio cantabile* of this sonata contains expressive features indicative of Haydn's "Romantic" style: dark colors created by the introduction of the B-flat-minor triad after the initial statement of the B-flat-major tonality; thick harmonic progressions created by two adjacent diminished chords; accentuation and extension of the dissonance in the appoggiatura unit; motion toward the augmented chord; and, finally, wide leaps in the melodic line (see Example 22.9).

Haydn's lack of interest in the violin and piano sonata resulted in his comparatively unremarkable contributions to that genre. The violin frequently serves as an accompaniment to the piano, playing in unison or in thirds with the melody line. **The violin sonata**

Quite different in character are the sonatas for violin and viola, in which idiomatic writing for the violin prevails, while the viola acts as a basso continuo. This is similar in concept to the Mozart sonata for bassoon and cello (K. 292), in which the cello acts as the continuo instrument.

In the field of concerto writing Haydn did not seem to demonstrate the high degree of workmanship evidenced in his quartet and symphonic output. **The concertos**

Ex. 22.8 F. J. Haydn, *Poco adagio contabile* from Quartet, Op. 76, No. 3

Ex. 22.8   cont.

His activities in this field include several keyboard concertos, as well as one concerto each for cello, horn, and trumpet. Some works have been lost, while the authenticity of others is dubious. For example, of the four violin concertos, two have been attributed to Michael Haydn and one to Cannabich. Haydn also produced a *symphonie concertante* in B-flat major (Hob. I, No. 105) for oboe, bassoon, violin, and cello.

Religious Music

Haydn's religious music includes twelve Masses (at least two others are lost and more than one hundred spurious masses are listed in Hoboken), and a number of smaller church works such as two Te Deums, a Stabat Mater, two Ave Reginas, a Salve Regina, Offertories, and motets. Several cantatas and oratorios were composed in the 1760s and 1770s, including the oratorio *Il ritorno di Tobia* ("The Return of Tobias," 1775), modeled after the Neapolitan *drammi sacri*. His greatest religious works, however, were created toward the end of his life, when, at the request of Nicholas II (Haydn's last Esterházy patron), Haydn returned from England to compose Masses and resume his duties as court Kapellmeister. During that period (1796–1802) he composed his six great Masses: *Missa in tempore belli* ("Mass in Time of War," 1796), also known as the *Paukenmesse* ("Kettledrum Mass"); *Missa Sancti Bernardi* (1796), also known as the *Heiligmesse* ("Holy Mass"); the *Nelsonmesse* ("Lord Nelson Mass," 1798), also known as the *Missa in angustiis* ("Mass of Distress"); the *Theresien-Messe* ("Empress Theresa Mass," 1799); the *Schöpfungs-messe* ("Creation Mass," 1801); and the *Harmoniemesse* ("Wind-Band Mass," 1802).

The dramatic-symphonic idiom Haydn had already developed in his *Lon-*

Masses

Ex. 22.9   F. J. Haydn, *Adagio cantabile* from Sonata No. 49 in E-flat major

don Symphonies and his mastery of sonata form were exploited to the fullest in his later Masses. Vocal solos within the Masses decreased as Haydn intensified the use of the vocal quartet. Tightly knit, contrapuntal passages involving the soloists were contrasted with homophonic portions sung by the full chorus. Solo sections were integrated into the texture of the whole, as, for example, in the *Lord Nelson Mass,* in which the florid soprano line in the second Kyrie functions more as an embellishment of the orchestral music than as an aria supported by the orchestra.

In the great Masses, structural integration matches textural integration as concepts of sonata form are sometimes applied to entire Mass sections, and Classical contrasts of key, tempo, and theme are habitually applied to the liturgical texts. For example, in the Gloria of the *Lord Nelson Mass,* although the text proceeds in an orderly fashion, the musical ideas, tempo, and tonality divide the movement into three sections: (1) *Gloria in excelsis Deo* through *Filius Patris* (D major); (2) *Qui tollis* to *Miserere nobis* (B-flat major, new material); (3) *Quoniam* to *Amen* (D major, based on material from the opening Gloria). The final section, the *Amen,* is a vigorous fugue.

Canonic passages and fugues are frequent in these late Masses. The opening Credo of the *Lord Nelson Mass,* for example, has a canon at the fifth for two sets of voices; *Et incarnatus est* from the *Missa Sancti Bernardi* also contains a canonic section. The Credo in the *Paukenmesse* has a powerful fugal passage.

Haydn is perhaps at his most imaginative in the Masses in the individual treatment of instruments. Witness the menacing drumroll and the wind fanfares at the beginning of the *Dona nobis pacem* in the *Paukenmesse,* or the use of the large wind group in the *Harmoniemesse.* Noteworthy, too, is the passage with the flute solo in the *Et incarnatus est* of the *Schöpfungsmesse,* which is evocative of sounds in nature and presents a pastoral atmosphere. In contrast, the

Lord Nelson Mass uses strings, three trumpets, timpani, and organ obbligato, resulting in a brilliant sound for the only one of Haydn's late Masses that is in a minor tonality.

Haydn's two greatest choral works—*Die Schöpfung* ("The Creation") and *Die Jahreszeiten* ("The Seasons")—were completed in 1798 and 1801, respectively, when the composer was well advanced in age. Both are oratorios of immense breadth, containing a great variety of musical forms, and modeled to a certain extent after the oratorios of Handel. The treatment of the literary topics, musical tone painting, and evocation of scenes from nature continue the Handelian tradition of "secular" oratorios like *Jephtha* and *Susanna*. Although both of Haydn's works are religious in principle, their predominant tone in pastoral—a depiction of various aspects of nature. The large role assigned to the chorus is also reminiscent of the older composer's works.

The Creation is based on a libretto originally compiled for Handel from the first chapter of Genesis and the seventh and eighth books of Milton's *Paradise Lost*. The text was translated for Haydn in Vienna by his friend Baron van Swieten, himself an admirer of Handel. Van Swieten reworked the text and even offered Haydn advice on the musical treatment. The oratorio is in three parts. The first two are narratives, in which three archangels (Gabriel, soprano; Uriel, tenor; Raphael, bass) recount the story of Creation. Through frequent paraphrases of Milton's work, the narrators describe each day of Creation, with the section ending in a majestic chorus. The third part is idyllic in mood: Adam and Eve replace Gabriel and Raphael. Of particular beauty is the descriptive dawn scene, orchestrated for three flutes with pizzicato string accompaniment, and the subsequent duet and chorus, *Von deiner Güt, o Herr* ("By Thee with bliss," No. 30). The last-named is one of the longest numbers in the work. Perhaps the most dramatic numbers, however, are the overture ("Representation of Chaos") in C minor, with its economy of material and ambiguous harmonic progressions, and the ensuing recitative and chorus, *Nun schwanden vor dem Heiligen Strahle* ("And there was light"), which shocks the listener with its sudden, loud turn to C major at the mention of the word "light." Here the composer creates a dramatic contrast between chaos and order (darkness and light) by juxtaposing parallel minor and major keys.

Van Swieten also reworded the libretto to *The Seasons,* based in great part on a poem by James Thompson (1700–1748). Each section deals with one season of the year. Both oratorios attained great popularity in their time. Napoleon Bonaparte himself was present at a performance of *The Creation* in Paris (1800), while in 1808 Haydn was given a medal of honor by the St. Petersburg Philharmonic Society, which specifically cited the greatness of these two works.

Operas

Opera was important at the court of Esterházy and was particularly fostered between 1762 and 1790 during the rule of Prince Nicholas. One of

Haydn's duties as court music director was to prepare and direct performances of operas—his own as well as a large number of works by Italians. Unlike Mozart, who had direct contact with Italian opera composers and singers,
and who was exposed to a variety of performances on his numerous trips to
European musical centers, Haydn was isolated from the mainstream of operatic activity. His primary exposure to the operatic world was through the
many operas that he conducted at the Esterháza palace. These included,
among others, works by Dittersdorf, Sacchini, Piccinni, Paisiello, Guglielmi,
Gazzaniga, Anfossi, and Cimarosa. Haydn's isolation may account for the
small number of performances his operas received during his lifetime.

Haydn's operas (about twenty) include opere buffe (three on a text by
Carlo Goldoni), two of the Italian intermezzo type, several marionette
operas, two Singspiele, and several works in the opera seria category; e.g.,
Orlando Paladino (1782) and *Armida* (1783).

Wolfgang Amadeus Mozart

Mozart's Life

Wolfgang Amadeus Mozart (1756–1791) was an active composer from
the age of six, who wrote his musical masterpieces during a lifetime of only
thirty-five years. His early life was dominated by his father, Leopold, who
acted as the child's agent, traveled with him, and energetically guided his career until 1773. Realizing the extent of Wolfgang's unusual talents, Leopold
undertook a series of concert tours to European musical capitals in an attempt
to show off the prodigy.

Background and early years

Leopold Mozart was himself a composer and performer in Salzburg. As a
court musician he was, in turn, first violinist in the court orchestra, court
composer, and Vice-Kapellmeister. Leopold was conscientious and industri-
ous, as evidenced by the large amount of church music he wrote for the archbishop of Salzburg. He also wrote concertos for solo instruments, including
flute, oboe, bassoon, horn, and trumpet, many of which are now lost. Symphonies, divertimenti, dances, marches, minuets, and a number of string trios
also constitute part of his prolific output.

Leopold Mozart

Overshadowed by his son's works, Leopold's compositions today are
somewhat neglected, perhaps unjustly. He is best known for his violin treatise of 1756, which is one of the important works on eighteenth-century performance practices.

The young Mozart's European travels were highly educational. His exposure to all major musical trends of the day and to other composers and their
works contributed to his musical development. By transcribing and copying
compositions or reading through them with their composer, Mozart assimilated the predominant style variants, and he incorporated into his own musical vocabulary those features that suited him best.

Travels

In 1772 Wolfgang was appointed organist and concertmaster to Arch-

Johann Nepomuk della Croce, *The Mozart Family* (1780–1781), in Salzburg. Nannerl and Wolfgang (now almost 24) are at the keyboard. Their mother, who died in 1778, is represented in the portrait on the wall. Leopold holds his violin to the fore.

bishop Colloredo in Salzburg, but their relationship was to deteriorate because of the young composer's frequent absences from Salzburg and neglect of his duties. His hatred for Salzburg, however, stemmed primarily from his dislike for his patron, and resulted in his eventual resignation from the archbishop's service. The trips to Paris and Mannheim were intended as job-hunting expeditions.

Last years; Baron van Swieten
The last ten years of his life were spent in Vienna as a free agent, since in the summer of 1781 he had formally received his release from the archbishop's service. Perhaps the most important musical influences during this decade were the Baroque polyphony of J. S. Bach and the oratorios of Handel, to which Mozart was exposed at the house of Baron Gottfried van Swieten.

Van Swieten held private weekly concerts, "Sunday musical mornings," that were educational performances intended for the edification and pleasure of a small circle of musicians rather than the entertainment of an audience. The weekly meetings included reading, transcribing, and playing compositions that had not yet been heard in Vienna. For example, Mozart reorchestrated some of Handel's oratorios by substituting wind instruments for the organ.

Mozart's last three years were marked by desperate financial need. His wife's frequent illnesses, a lack of commissions from the emperor (who had appointed Mozart the court composer), his declining popularity as a performer of his own piano concertos, and his poor health contributed to his growing pessimism. The final period of his life was spent under great pressure to complete two commissioned works: the opera seria *La clemenza di Tito* for Prague, and the Requiem. Mozart worked on the Requiem to his dying day, but left it unfinished. His life, which had begun in the glittering splendor of the European courts, ended on the brink of poverty.

Symphonic Music

Mozart's forty-one symphonies serve as examples of the metamorphosis of the composer's style. From the point where, as an eight-year-old child, he learned composition by transcribing other composers' works (the Symphony in E-flat major, K. 18, for example, is a copy of Abel's Symphony Op. 7, No. 6), and passing through a phase where his symphonies were based first on Austrian, then on Italian, models, he attained a very personal solution to the problems of style and structure in the symphonic genre, as seen in his last six symphonies.

His early symphonies, written in 1767 (K. 43, 45, 48), follow the four-movement Viennese tradition of Wagenseil, Holzbauer, and Gassmann. His Italian symphonies, written in 1770 (K. 74, 81, 84), resemble the three-movement Italian opera overture. From J. C. Bach Mozart had absorbed the verve and vitality of the Italian comic idiom, features that were to become an integral part of Mozart's style.

Nearly one-third of Mozart's symphonies were written in the period between 1772 and 1774. Haydn's influence may well have been responsible for the intensification of expression in the "Little" G minor Symphony, K. 183 (written in 1773, after contact with Haydn's music in Vienna). In it the effects of the Sturm und Drang, and, even more specifically, Haydn's Symphony No. 39 in G minor (written between 1768 and 1769), can be felt. Three out of the four movements are in G minor (the slow one is in E-flat major), and both outer movements begin with the strings playing in unison. The syncopations in the first-movement figures and the disjunct melodic motion of the opening intervals add to an impassioned, unsettled feeling characteristic of compositions affected by the Sturm und Drang aesthetic (see Example 22.10).

In 1778, during Mozart's Paris sojourn, the director of the Concert Spirituel in Paris, Jean Le Gros (1739–1793), commissioned a symphony from him. Since the orchestra was one of the grandest in Europe, Mozart welcomed the opportunity to write for the large and virtuosic wind section. The orchestra's potential for rich sound is reflected in the Symphony No. 31 (*Paris*) in D major, K. 297 (1778), which employs flutes, oboes, clarinets, bassoons, horns, trumpets and timpani in addition to the strings, was the first

Stylistic evolution: from Preclassic to Classic

"Little" G minor Symphony

The *Paris* Symphony

Ex. 22.10   W. A. Mozart, Symphony No. 25 in G minor

and one of the few of Mozart's symphonies to include the clarinet. Mozart had previously heard the instrument in England, and was to have contact with it again in Mannheim.

Mozart's impressions regarding the Paris performance of K. 297 were recorded in a letter to his father from Paris on July 3, 1778:

The audience were quite carried away—and there was a tremendous burst of applause. But as I knew, when I wrote it, what effect it would surely produce, I had introduced the (opening) passage again at the close—when there were shouts of "Da Capo." The Andante also found favour, but particularly the last Allegro, because, having observed that all last as well as first allegros begin here with all instruments playing together and generally unisono, I began mine with two violins only [see Example 22.11], *piano* for the first eight bars—followed instantly by a *forte;* the audience, as I expected, said "hush" at the soft beginning, and when they heard the *forte,* began at once to clap their hands.[5]

This passage occurs in the first twelve measures of the third movement.

Le Gros was pleased with the symphony as a whole but felt that the slow movement contained too many changes of key and was generally too long. A month later the symphony was again performed at the Concert Spirituel, this time with a new Andante—a graceful pastoral rondo, shorter than the original Andante. It was much preferred by the Paris audiences.

Another concession to French taste was the opening figure of the first movement, which created an imposing impression through the simultaneous attack on the same note by the entire orchestra—referred to by the idiomatic phrase *Le premier coup d'Archet* (see Example 22.12). The first movement also omitted the customary repeat sign after the end of the exposition, as a repetition of the exposition would have lengthened the symphony. Mozart remarked to his father that the Germans, contrary to the French, had a taste for lengthy performances, while in fact it was better to keep a composition short.

Ex. 22.11   W. A. Mozart, Symphony No. 31 in D major, Mvt. 3

Ex. 22.12   W. A. Mozart, Symphony No. 31 in D major, Mvt. 1

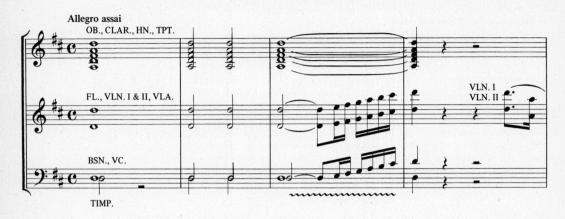

The last six symphonies   Mozart's last six symphonies, composed between 1782 and 1788, are all masterpieces with distinctive characteristics. Their chronology is shown in the table.

Mozart's Last Six Symphonies

Köchel Number	Key	Nickname	Date	No.
385	D major	*Haffner*	1782	35
425	C major	*Linz*	1783	36
504	D major	*Prague*	1786	38
543	E-flat major		1788	39
550	G minor		1788	40
551	C major	*Jupiter*	1788	41

Amazingly enough, the last three were all composed in two months during the summer of 1788. The *Prague* and *Linz* symphonies are named after the cities in which they were premiered, while the *Haffner* (with no musical connection to the *Haffner* Serenade, K. 250) was written for Mozart's Salzburg friend Sigmund Haffner. Originally K. 385 was a second Haffner Serenade, preceded by a march and containing an additional minuet, but in its final version the march and minuet were omitted, making it a four-movement symphony (*Allegro con spirito*, Andante, Minuet, and Presto).

The Symphony No. 40 in G minor, K. 550, exceeds the emotional frame-work of its time. The impassioned tone of the first three movements is counterbalanced by the contrasting merriment of the last movement (ironically, also in G minor), which only seems to intensify the feeling of sorrow that hangs over the whole work.

Symphony No. 40 in G minor

Several unusual features are already noted in the initial measures of the opening movement: (1) the first subject begins *piano,* a rarity for an epoch in which opening statements were generally bold and clearly defined; (2) the first subject delineates the intervals of the minor second and the rising sixth; (3) a three-note rhythmic figure persists throughout the entire movement (see Example 22.13). Even though the more lyrical and relaxed second subject (see Example 22.14) offers a great contrast to the first, the pulsating rhythm resumes in the codetta. The first subject is purely motivic in concept, while the second subject is lyrical. There is also contrasting orchestration since the second subject is segmented and presented as a dialogue between the winds and the strings. The development section is based entirely on the pulsating motive, which is then treated sequentially, contrapuntally, and in inversion.

The intensity of the first movement is not relaxed in the second, which, although in a contrasting tonality, is somber and also has an underlying pulsation. Its serious mood, established immediately through imitative string entrances, creates a tightly knit web heightened by dissonances. The Minuet has an unusual metric irregularity of two three-measure phrases alternating with two four-measure phrases in each period, a far cry from the lighthearted salon dance the minuet had once been.

The Finale introduces a subject to which the emphatic alternation of tutti with solo and *piano* with *forte* lends a dramatic as well as a symmetrical effect (see Example 22.15). In the unison passage that opens the development section any feeling of a tonal center is all but obliterated (see Example 22.16).

Mozart's last symphony, K. 551, the *Jupiter,* contrasts with the passionate and somber preceding work in its choice of the sunny key of C major and in its festive use of trumpets and timpani, instruments omitted in the G minor symphony. Its musical architecture is powerful, and in its last movement fugato passages are integrated into the sonata-form structure.

The Jupiter Symphony

Ex. 22.13   W. A. Mozart, Symphony No. 40 in G minor, opening motive

Ex. 22.14   W. A. Mozart, Symphony No. 40 in G minor, Mvt. 1, second subject

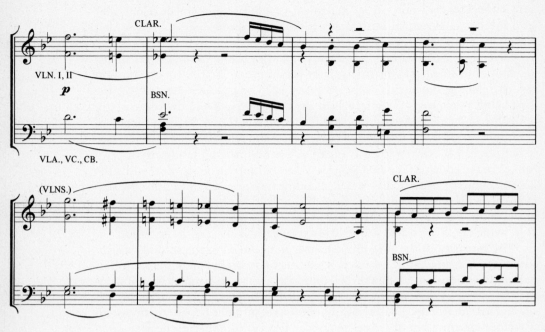

In his last symphonies Mozart raised the genre to a higher plane. Although his symphonies are a synthesis of stylistic elements of his time, the depth of emotion, inherent drama, and structural complexities exhibited in them exceed contemporary limits of musical expectations. It is small wonder, therefore, that these works, along with *Don Giovanni* and the two piano concertos in the minor key (D minor, K. 466, and C minor, K. 499) served as spiritual inspiration to the nineteenth century rather than to Mozart's own generation.

Chamber Music and Smaller Orchestral Works

The quintets

Mozart's contributions to the field of chamber music include both the more intimate categories (quintets, quartets, trios) and such instrumental ensembles as divertimenti, cassations, and serenades. He composed six quintets for strings, two for strings with one wind instrument, and one for piano and winds.

The Horn Quintet, K. 407, was written for Mozart's friend Ignaz Leutgeb, whom Mozart frequently made the butt of jokes. The four horn concertos were also written for him, and as Leutgeb was apparently inclined to drag his tempi, Mozart inscribed the tempo for the horn in one of them as *adagio* while jokingly assigning *allegro* to the orchestra.[6] The Clarinet Quintet, K. 581, was composed, like the Clarinet Concerto, K. 622, for Mozart's friend Anton Stadler.

Ex. 22.15   W. A. Mozart, Symphony No. 40 in G minor, Finale, opening

In his String Quintets K. 515, 516, 593, and 614 Mozart ingeniously wrote two viola rather than two cello parts, thus allowing for greater freedom and independence in each inner voice. Because the inner voices were more active, the outer voices were spread further apart, creating quite novel melodic effects (Example 22.17). Notice the four-octave span of the melody shared by the cello and first violin.

The String Quintets K. 515 (in C major) and 516 (in G minor) share a relationship similar to that of the two Symphonies K. 550 and K. 551, specifically in the contrast between the intense passion of the works in the minor key and the clarity of the two C major works. The Quintet in C major is a marvel of spaciousness in the first movement, in its treatment of sonata form and expansion of the first subject group. Based on motives rather than themes, its sonata-allegro movement has very broad dimensions. The slow movement presents the first violin and the first viola in a duet reminiscent of the middle movement of the Sinfonia Concertante, K. 364. The whole quintet exudes a Classic perfection in its balance of form. The adjacent Quintet in G minor expresses deep emotions, and even the second theme of the first movement remains in the G minor tonality.

The Piano Quintet in E-flat major, K. 452, was performed at a concert in Vienna in 1784 with Mozart himself at the keyboard. He considered it the best composition he had ever written. Thirteen years later Beethoven was to model his Quintet in E-flat major, Op. 16 (for the same instrumental ensemble: piano, oboe, clarinet, bassoon, and horn), on Mozart's K. 452.

Mozart's string quartets may be divided into two distinct groups: (1) the fifteen quartets dating from the early 1770s and (2) the ten mature quartets composed between 1782 and 1790. At least five of the early quartets (K. 155–160) are based on homophonic Italian models, especially those of Sammartini, while the six Viennese quartets of 1773 (K. 168–173) have a more complex texture, enriched with counterpoint. The ten mature quartets include the six

The quartets

Ex. 22.16   W. A. Mozart, Symphony No. 40 in G minor, Finale, development

printed in Vienna by Artaria as Op. 10 (1785), dedicated to Haydn; the *Hoff-meister* Quartet, K. 499; and the three *Prussian* Quartets, K. 575, 589, and 590, dedicated to the cello-playing King Friedrich Wilhelm in Berlin. The six quartets of Op. 10 (K. 387, 421, 428, 458, 464, and 465) may be compared with those of Haydn's Op. 33. The same feeling for inner drama already exhibited in some of Mozart's piano concertos dating from the mid-1780s is recognized in these works, which employ extensive motivic development. K. 465, the so-called *Dissonance* Quartet, derives its name from the fact that in the slow introduction to the first movement (itself a rare occurrence in this genre) the successive entrances of each instrument create some stringent cross-relations. In addition to the string quartets, Mozart also wrote four flute quartets, two piano quartets—K. 478 and K. 493—and an oboe quartet, K. 370, composed for his friend Friedrich Ramm in Munich (1781).

Usually intended for festive occasions, most of Mozart's divertimenti and

Ex. 22.17   W. A. Mozart, String Quintet in C major, K. 515

Ex. 22.18   W. A. Mozart, Divertimento No. 15 in B-flat major, theme from Mvt. 2

serenades were commissioned by friends and rich families in Salzburg and Vienna. The divertimenti may be divided into two groups, according to their instrumental combinations and social functions. One type was written for strings with obbligato winds. This type sometimes incorporated popular Austrian and Bavarian tunes, as, for example, in the Divertimento in B-flat major, K. 287. This work for two violins, viola, bass, and two horns was composed in 1777 and employs folk material in two of its seven movements: in the Theme and Variations, and in the Finale. In the variation movement, the theme is based on the folk song *Heissa, hurtig, ich bin Hans und bin ohne Sorge* (". . . I am Hans and am without worry," see Example 22.18), while the Finale introduces the folk song *D'Bäuerin hat d'Katz verlorn* ("The peasant girl has lost the cat," see Example 22.19). The first violin is the undisputed leader in these works, with displays of virtuosity akin to those found in the concertos.

Smaller or orchestral works

The other main type of divertimento consisted of four pairs of wind instruments (two oboes, horns, bassoons, and clarinets) and was often called a *serenade*. This was exclusively open-air music, performed in a garden or under peoples' windows. Among the best of these works is the *Gran Partita*, Serenade in B-flat major, for thirteen winds, K. 361 (1781). Very much in concertato style, it alternates between tutti and solo forces, with much of the solo work performed by the two clarinets. This composition is noteworthy for its mixture of timbres, idiomatic use of each instrument, and variety of tone color. The *Haffner* Serenade, K. 250, and the Serenade for Strings, K. 525, known as *Eine kleine Nachtmusik,* are among the best-known serenades.

The Instrumental Sonatas

Mozart composed at least nineteen keyboard sonatas, several four-hand piano sonatas (K. 381, 497, 521), a sonata for two pianos (K. 448), forty-four

Ex. 22.19   W. A. Mozart, Divertimento No. 15 in B-flat major, theme from Finale

sonatas for piano and violin, and the seventeen *Epistle* Sonatas. One unusual work stands outside the mainstream of his compositions: a fine sonata for bassoon and cello, K. 196c.

The keyboard sonatas His first group of five keyboard sonatas was composed in Salzburg in 1774. These include K. 279–283 in C, F, B-flat, E-flat, and G major; they are short, three-movement works in which the first movement carries the primary emphasis and structural focus. Preclassic in orientation, they show a variety of influences—Haydn, C. P. E. Bach, and the empfindsamer Stil. Two further sonatas were composed in Mannheim (1777): K. 309 and K. 311 (in C and D major). Both are brilliantly pianistic. Of the Paris sonatas, the one in A minor, K. 310 (1778), stands out for its intense expression, which unifies the work. The development section of the first movement has a passage over a series of pedal points in the bass as the harmony progresses through the circle of fifths. The second movement of the sonata has a beautiful *cantabile*.

In contrast to the somber spirit of K. 310, the next one, K. 330 in C major, is a bright and charming Italianate work with a song-like Finale. K. 331 begins with a Theme and Variations and ends with the rousing *Rondo alla turca*. Both K. 332 and K. 333 show the influence of J. C. Bach, who was in Paris in 1778, and whose Piano Sonatas, Op. 17, were about to be published.

The Fantasy in C minor, K. 475 (1785), and the sonata in the same key, K. 457 (1784), were published in 1785 as a unit. Both works display an intensity that almost exceeds the sensibilities of the Classic era. The Fantasy is even more powerful and dramatic than the sonata. Its kinship to the second movement of J. C. Bach's Symphony in G minor, Op. 6, No. 6, has already been pointed out. True to the improvisatory nature of the fantasy, or fantasia, as a genre, K. 475 has six sections, each of which explores a different tonal area. The notes in this piece extend through the entire range of Mozart's piano (almost a full five octaves), resulting in a new depth of sonority that prefigures Beethoven's middle-period sonatas. The contrasts in the dynamics and character of each section make it highly dramatic. Mozart juxtaposes thematic material and lyrical sections with improvisatory runs and cadential passages.

The sonatas for piano and violin Mozart's sonatas for piano and violin demonstrate the changing relationship of these two instruments during the second half of the eighteenth century. In Schobert's sonatas the piano, not the violin, was predominant. Mozart, however, achieved a balance and a genuine dialogue between the two instruments. His Violin Sonata in E minor, K. 304 (1778), for example, may be viewed as the counterpart of his great A minor piano sonata, in its craft and depth of content.

The Epistle Sonatas The *Epistle* Sonatas, written between 1767 and 1780, are short *sonate da chiesa,* whose instrumentation corresponds to that of the Mass with which each was originally performed. One combination, for example, includes two violins, cello, organ and a bassoon basso continuo.

The Concertos

Mozart's concertos may be divided into several categories: wind concertos, string concertos, sinfonie concertanti, and piano concertos. All of his wind concertos were written on commission, with specific players in mind. The clarinet seems to have held special importance to him among the wind instruments. He wrote the beautiful Concerto in A major, K. 622 (1791) for his friend Anton Stadler, for whom he had earlier composed the clarinet quintet, K. 581.

Sinfonie concertanti were especially popular in Paris and Mannheim in the last quarter of the eighteenth century. Mozart's three works in this category, all written in the late 1770s, include the Concerto for Flute and Harp in C major, K. 299; the Sinfonia Concertante for Flute, Oboe, Horn, and Bassoon, which now remains in a version for oboe, clarinet, horn, and bassoon in E-flat major, K. Anh. 9;[7] and the Sinfonia Concertante in E-flat major for Violin and Viola, K. 364. The last mentioned is perhaps the most outstanding of the three. Mannheim influences are apparent in the first movement, especially in the crescendo over a pedal point just before the end of the opening tutti. The work's middle movement, in C minor, is the longest and most substantive of the three, with extensive expressive passages for the solo instruments supported by repeated chords in the rest of the orchestra. The soloists are treated as equal partners throughout.

The sinfonie concertanti

Mozart composed some of the finest piano concertos of the eighteenth century. Each of his mature works in this genre is unique, filled with unconventional harmonic, melodic, and structural features that show a boundless imagination and wealth of ideas.

The piano concertos

Not counting the early arrangements for piano and orchestra (K. 37, 39–41, 107) of other composers' works—e.g., those of Hermann Friedrich Raupach (1728–1778), Schobert, Johann Gottfried Eckard (1735–1809), and J. C. Bach—Mozart wrote twenty-one concertos for piano and orchestra, one for two pianos (K. 365, in 1779), and one for three pianos (K. 242, in 1776). His most mature concertos date from the Vienna days—six works that all stem from 1784: K. 449, 450, 451, 453, 456, and 459. The last mentioned, a piece of sublime humor, is known as the "Second" *Coronation* Concerto, because Mozart played it along with K. 537, the *Coronation* Concerto, in Frankfurt in 1790 at performances given in connection with the coronation of Leopold II.

The orchestration in his concertos differs from one work to the next. Perhaps the richest orchestration may be encountered in K. 491 in C minor, where oboes and clarinets are used along with other winds in solo and tutti groupings. Clarinets are generally used more frequently in Mozart's concertos than in his symphonies. For example, they are found in the three works of 1785–1786: K. 482, 488, and 491. Trumpets and timpani are used only in brilliant, festive works, such as K. 415 and the two *Coronation* Concertos.

The Concerto in D minor, K. 466 (1785), shows a dualism between the orchestra and the piano that results from the treatment of the two units as opposing entities. The passionate first movement abounds in strong contrasts, especially evident in the development section, in which conflict between the two is presented through an alternation of material, the piano returning several times with its doleful opening strains. Beethoven had a special fondness for this work and wrote cadenzas for its first and third movements.

Mozart is perhaps at his best in passages and movements influenced by operatic style. While the slow movement of K. 482 in E-flat major (1785) stresses operatic conflict and passion, that of K.467 in C major (1785) has the lyrical elements of a flowing aria. The theme first appears in the muted strings with pizzicato accompaniment, then in the piano over an accompaniment of repeated chords. In a letter to his father, Mozart mentions the overwhelmingly favorable response the audience accorded this particular section at the premiere of K. 467 in Vienna: he had to repeat the entire slow movement.

Mozart's last movements frequently have a rondo structure based on folklike themes. Their exuberance breathes the spirit of the opera buffa (see Example 22.20).

Mozart wrote many of these works with the intention of performing them himself. Others were written for and dedicated to individual pupils. K. 271 was composed for a Parisian pianist, Mlle. Jeunehomme, who performed the work in Salzburg. Two (K. 449 and 450) were written for Barbara Ployer, and K. 456 for the blind pianist, composer, and pedagogue Maria Theresa von Paradis (1759–1824). Daughter of one of the empress's councillors, she was a talented Viennese artist whose repertoire included a large number of concertos by her teacher, Leopold Koželuch.

The violin and viola concertos The number and quality of works Mozart wrote for the violin and viola are overshadowed by the music (especially the concertos) he composed for the piano. Five violin concertos, all written in 1775, were created for the Salzburg concertmaster Gaetano Brunetti. Particularly noteworthy are the charming rondos of K. 218 and 219 (D and A major, 1775), as well as the unusual treatment of the solo violin in the first movement of K. 219: after the standard orchestral exposition and before the entry of the soloist in the expected set tempo, the violinist introduces a six-measure *adagio* section. Mozart's other string concertos include the previously mentioned Sinfonia Concertante, K. 364; the Double Concerto for Two Violins, K. 190 (the *Concertone*); and several violin concertos whose authenticity has been questioned in the past, including the Concerto in D major (*Adelaide*), K. Anh. 294a.[8]

Religious Music

Church music in Salzburg was supported by the archbishops who resided in that devoutly Catholic community. Even today, looking at the city from

Ex. 22.20   W. A. Mozart, Piano Concerto in E-flat major, K.482, Mvt. 3

the Hohensalzburg Castle, the most striking landmarks are the church stee-ples that dominate the panorama. Archbishops Sigismund and Colloredo em-ployed a whole contingent of musicians, including such leading Austrian composers of church music as Eberlin, Adlgasser, Michael Haydn, Leopold Mozart, and Wolfgang Mozart. Instruments, including trumpets and other winds, were used in church, and the strict, conservative, Baroque contrapun-tal style mellowed through an admixture of expressive operatic homophony.

Most of W. A. Mozart's church music was composed in Salzburg, and it includes occasional music for the consecration of new buldings and the ordi-nation of priests. He composed two types of Masses: Solemn Masses—bril-liant works displaying alternating solo and choral passages—and the *Missa brevis* for the regular Sunday services. The latter used a modest orchestration in which strings predominated.

The composer's piety and deep feeling for the Mass text itself are evident in his dramatic settings of the various Mass sections. He usually develops the Kyrie into a lengthy movement for soloists and chorus (plus orchestra). In the Gloria of a Solemn Mass the opening musical subject frequently recurs at the word *Quoniam,* where the music functions as a unifying agent. *Laudamus Te* usually begins with a solo, while the nucleus of the Gloria text, the *Qui tollis,* is given to the chorus. The final sentence, *Cum Sancto Spiritu,* presents an ex-treme contrast to the preceding material and is at times treated as an elaborate fugue.

The Masses

Passages that Mozart stresses in the Credo are traditional places of em-phasis, including the words "crucifixion" and "resurrection," which are set for maximum dramatic effect and audience appeal. Here, too, the last words are treated fugally. However, in the three Masses dating from 1776 (K. 257–259) the final fugues in both the Gloria and the Credo are replaced by short, animated choral passages because of Archbishop Colloredo's dislike for fugues.

In his Sanctus settings Mozart observes the natural subdivisions of the text at *Sanctus, Deus sabaoth, Pleni sunt caeli,* and *Benedictus* by creating con-trasting musical passages—a principle he also applied to the last movement of the Mass, the Agnus Dei, with its subdivision at *Dona nobis pacem.*

Increasingly subjective and idiosyncratic, Mozart's Masses were a source of friction between the composer and Archbishop Colloredo, and were a con-tributing factor to his break with the cleric. The latter, unable to appreciate the extent of the composer's genius, demanded traditional and conservative compositions, and Mozart constantly rebelled against these restrictions. The great Mass in C minor, K. 427 (1782–1783), was written for Salzburg after the composer's break with the archbishop, to fulfill a vow in gratitude for his new bride, Constanze Weber (1762–1842). Unfortunately the work was un-accountably never finished. The existing sections include the Kyrie, the Gloria, the first section of the Credo, a sketch for the *Et incarnatus est,* and the Sanctus and Benedictus. Missing are the remainder of the Credo and the en-tire Agnus Dei. The instrumentation is massive: oboes, bassoons, horns, trumpets, four trombones, strings, and an organ continuo. No clarinets are

Mass in C minor

included, and the flute is used only in the *Et incarnatus est,* where three solo wind instruments— flute, oboe, and bassoon—are treated in a concertato fashion with the strings.

The work ranges in style from Italianate aria types (for example, the extremely demanding soprano solo, *Laudamus Te*) to double fugues (the *Osanna* of the Sanctus) and sections in Baroque style (*Qui tollis,* a double chorus in G minor over a chromatically descending bass). Some movements of this Mass show the influence of J. S. Bach and Handel, since a whole new world was opened to Mozart when he became acquainted with their works in Vienna.

The Requiem Mass

Perhaps the greatest mystery surrounding Mozart today involves the Requiem, K. 626, commissioned anonymously by a musical dilettante, Count Franz von Walsegg, and left unfinished at Mozart's death. The composer's pupil Franz Xaver Süssmayr (1766–1803) finished the work, but we don't know how much of what is written in Süssmayr's hand was really his and how much of it had been dictated and guided by Mozart.

Mozart actually completed the Introit and Kyrie and sketched the voice parts and bass line (and some indications as to instrumentation) for the next eight sections (Dies irae to *Hostias*). The last three movements—Sanctus, Benedictus, Agnus Dei—were left untouched by Mozart. It is believed by many that upon Mozart's death, his wife, fearing that the money she needed so desperately would be witheld by Count Walsegg unless the completed Requiem Mass was submitted, gave the manuscript to Süssmayr for completion. Even the publishers of this work—Breitkopf & Härtel—did not know of its incomplete state until 1800, when Süssmayr sent them an explanation.

Operas

Elements of drama are frequently found in Mozart's instrumental as well as religious music, but his dramatic genius found its most complete expression in the comic operas. His keen sense for dramatic characterization, which permeates *Figaro, Don Giovanni,* and *Die Zauberflöte,* brought him to one of the pinnacles of achievement in the history of opera.

It was Italian opera to which young Mozart was most frequently exposed during his early European tours, especially the operas of J. C. Bach, Jommelli, Piccinni, Paisiello, and Hasse. Mozart's major operatic works are listed in the table.

Early works

Most of Mozart's early dramatic output up to 1772 was in the field of serious opera. In addition to the operas, nine Italian concert arias with recitatives were written for London (1764) and Milan (1770–1772), some on Metastasian texts. Some of these concert arias show an affinity with the style of Neapolitan-trained opera composers, particularly Leo and Hasse.

With *Idomeneo,* commissioned by Duke Karl Theodor for a Munich carnival, the composer exhibits a sense of the dramatic. Based on a French tragédie lyrique by Antoine Danchet, the work resembles French opera in spirit, specifically Gluck's *Alceste.* The chorus, which assumes an essential role, the *chaconne* that ends act I, and the introduction of ballet music (K. 367) are all French features.

Mozart's Major Operas

Title	Year	Genre	Librettist	City of First Performance
La finta semplice, K. 51 ("The Fake Simpleton")	1768	*opera buffa*	Marco Cotellini, on a text by Goldoni	Salzburg
Bastien und Bastienne, K. 50	1768	*Singspiel*	F. W. Weiskern's trans. of Favart's parody on Rousseau's *Le Devin du village*	Vienna
Mitridate, rè di Ponto, K. 87 ("Mitridate, King of Ponto")	1770	*opera seria*	Vittorio Amadeo Cigna-Santi	Milan
Ascanio in Alba, K. 111	1771	*serenata*	Abbate Giuseppe Parini	Milan
Il sogno di Scipione, K. 126 ("The Dream of Scipio")	1772	*serenata*★	Metastasio	Salzburg
Lucio Silla, K. 135	1772	*opera seria*	Giovanni de Gamerra	Milan
La finta giardiniera, K. 196 ("The Fake Gardener")	1775	*opera buffa*	Marco Cotellini	Munich
Il rè pastore, K. 208 ("The Shepherd King")	1775	*dramma per musica*	Metastasio	Salzburg
Idomeneo, rè di Creta, K. 366 ("Idomeneo, King of Crete")	1781	*opera seria*	Abbé G. B. Varesco	Munich
Die Entführung aus dem Serail, K. 384 ("The Abduction from the Seraglio")	1782	*Singspiel*	Gottlob Stephanie	Vienna
Le nozze di Figaro, K. 492 ("The Marriage of Figaro")	1786	*opera buffa*	Lorenzo da Ponte after Beaumarchais	Vienna
Don Giovanni, K. 527	1787	*dramma giocoso*	Lorenzo da Ponte	Prague
Così fan tutte, K. 588 ("They All Do It This Way")	1790	*opera buffa*	Lorenzo da Ponte	Vienna
Die Zauberflöte, K. 620 ("The Magic Flute")	1791	*Singspiel*	Emanuel Schikaneder	Vienna
La clemenza di Tito, K. 621 ("The Clemency of Titus")	1791	*opera seria*	C. Mazzolà after Metastasio	Vienna

★ Here, a short operatic work composed in celebration of the birthday of a member of the royal family.

The year 1782 marks the arrival in Vienna of Lorenzo da Ponte (1749–1838), the man who was to be the librettist for three of Mozart's greatest operas: *Le nozze di Figaro, Don Giovanni,* and *Così fan tutte.* With Da Ponte's collaboration, Mozart was to raise the opera buffa genre to unprecedented heights. Da Ponte was a colorful personality whose many impressions of contemporary life are recorded in his *Memoirs.* Teacher, traveler, adventurer, Catholic priest (having converted from Judaism), and friend of Casanova, he settled in Vienna, and, at the invitation of Salieri, accepted the position of theater poet. (For *Die Entführung,* see p. 506.)

Mariage de Figaro.   Acte I.

Ce tour-ci vaut l'autre.

Figaro, an early product of the Da Ponte–Mozart collaboration, was based on the second of the *Figaro* trilogy by Pierre Augustin Caron de Beaumarchais (1732–1799), and was chosen partially to capitalize on the success of the first opera on that subject, namely, Paisiello's *Il barbiere di Siviglia* ("The Barber of Seville," 1782). Although Da Ponte shortened the play and rearranged its five acts into two, a close correspondence exists between the original play and Da Ponte's libretto.[9] *Figaro*

The opera's strength lies in Mozart's skillful musical characterization of each personage. For instance, the scheming and witty Figaro and Susanna propel the music in each act. The Countess is a sad, middle-aged woman, neglected by her husband. Cherubino is an adolescent who suffers the pangs of awakening sexuality; he is especially well portrayed in his simple yet impetuous aria *Non sò più cosa son cosa faccio* ("I no longer know who I am or what I am doing"). This opera, which has fourteen arias and fourteen ensemble numbers (duets, sextet, chorus, finales), shows perhaps the most striking characterization in the finales, through the skillful juxtaposition of the various characters. Especially noteworthy is the first-act finale, with its gradually increasing ensemble of characters, double-entendres, and shifts in situation, each of which is accompanied by a shift of tonality.

Accorded only a lukewarm reception at its Vienna premiere, the opera was so successful in Prague later in the year that Mozart received a commission for another opera to be performed there. He chose Don Juan, or Don Giovanni, as the subject for this new work, a topic that had originated in the seventeenth-century *El burlador de Sevilla* ("The Libertine of Seville") by Tirso de Molina. Molina's work was given many revivals and adaptations throughout the seventeenth and eighteenth centuries. Molière and Goldoni based plays on the story; Gluck wrote a ballet about it; and the librettist Giovanni Bertati (1735–1815) and composer Giuseppe Gazzaniga (1743–1818) collaborated in 1787 on the creation of an opera called *Il convitato di pietra* ("The Stone Guest"). *Don Giovanni*

In contrast with *Figaro,* the plot of *Don Giovanni* is not one of intrigue, but rather concentrates on the misdeeds of a single person. Don Giovanni dominates the story, and his character is revealed in all of its myriad facets through his contact with each personage in the opera. Insolent libertine and seducer, Don Giovanni, the epitome of unscrupulous and unethical behavior—but also the life-force—is presented to us on his road to ruin. At the end the "hero" is engulfed by flames of Hell. Already the overture presents this dichotomy between the sinister elements and the Don's search for pleasure: the slow introduction (D minor) incorporates material and motives that accompany the most dramatic part of the opera, while the main movement, in sonata-allegro form (D major), is wildly ebullient.

Mozart's last opera buffa, *Così fan tutte,* is a piece of buffoonery in the best slapstick tradition. Its plot is based on the model of the Spanish Renaissance comedy. Musicologist Alfred Einstein calls the work "irridescent, like a glorious soap bubble."[10] *Così fan tutte*

A scene from Beaumarchais's comedy *The Marriage of Figaro,* act I (1784). (Courtesy, Bayerische Staatsbibliothek)

Three great works occupied the last year of Mozart's life: *La clemenza di Tito,* written for the coronation of Leopold II, for which Mozart's student Süssmayr composed the secco recitatives; *Die Zauberflöte;* and the Requiem. The librettist for *Die Zauberflöte* was an Austrian actor, comedian, and musician, Emanuel Schikaneder (1751–1812). Steeped in the Singspiel tradition, he was director of the Freihaus Theater auf der Wieden. He even played the

The Magic Flute

comic part of Papageno in the first performance of *The Magic Flute.* Prior to this work, Schikaneder had received acclaim for his libretto for *Oberon, König der Elfen* ("Oberon, King of the Elves"), based on a poem by Wieland. The text was reworked by Ludwig Giesecke and set to music by Paul Wranitzky. This same work was later to be set again by Carl Maria von Weber (1786–1826) as a German fairy-tale opera (see Chapter 28).

Beneath the seeming superficiality of its purely entertaining elements, *The Magic Flute* is full of symbols associated with the brotherhood of Freemasons, by means of which Mozart expressed his philosophy and belief in the goodness of humanity and the brotherhood of man. Mozart and Schikaneder were Freemasons, and the humanitarian spirit propounded by them so influenced the great writer Goethe that he was prompted to begin writing a sequel to *Die Zauberflöte,* a project that he unfortunately never completed.

The Magic Flute masterfully integrates elements of Italian opera seria (for example, the Queen of the Night's coloratura aria *O zitt're nicht*—"O do not tremble"), Austrian and burlesque folk elements from the Singspiel (Papageno's aria *Der Vogelfänger bin ich ja,*—"I am a birdcatcher"), and Italian buffo elements (the trio of Pamina, Monostatos, and Papageno, *Du feines Täubchen* —"You pretty dove"). *The Magic Flute* may be viewed as a milestone in the history of German-language national opera, not only as perhaps the finest work of the genre in the eighteenth century but also as a challenge to the undisputed reign of the Italian opera buffa.

Difficulties for singers

From a performance-practice point of view, Mozart was generally very demanding of his singers, notably the sopranos. This challenge is particularly evident in the concert arias he wrote for Aloysia Weber, Nancy Storace (1765–1817), the first Susanna in the premiere of *The Marriage of Figaro,* and Josepha Dussek (1754–1824). His singers were expected to add their own vocal embellishments and cadenzas. In the Queen of the Night's aria from *The Magic Flute,* he taxes to the utmost a vocal range that spans just over two octaves—from D above middle C to the F two octaves higher. As seen in Example 22.21, ease in the execution of trills, large jumps, staccato notes, and fast runs are also expected of the singer. Mozart even wrote a book of *vocalises* as an aid to the singer in acquiring the desired technique.

The End of an Era: Classicism vs. Romanticism

The passion and subjectivity of the Sturm und Drang created the right atmosphere for Goethe's *Werther* and Schiller's *Die Räuber* ("The Thieves")

Ex. 22.21   W. A. Mozart, *O. Zitt're nicht,* from *Die Zauberflöte,* act I

"And when I see you victorious, then she shall be yours forever."

and *Kabale und Liebe* ("Cabal and Love"). The predominant theme that **The rise**
emerged from this literary movement was the conflict between man's feel- **of Ro-**
ings and contemporary conventions, embodied in the struggle of the artist's **manticism**
spirit to free itself and soar above everyday life. The theme is manifested in
Goethe's *Faust,* the work formulated over fifty years of the playwright's life,
which passed through the varying phases of the Sturm und Drang, Classicism, and Romanticism.

This passion, subjectivity, and appeal to humanity affected European arts,
letters, and music in the last decades of the eighteenth century and the first
decades of the nineteenth. Faustian principles and aspects of this new humani-

tarianism are noticeable in Beethoven's Ninth Symphony, but also earlier in *The Magic Flute*. These were the aspects of the Mozart–Beethoven era that the emerging Romantics singled out, and such nineteenth-century German composers as Robert Schumann and Richard Wagner emphasized these concerns throughout the century. The great German poet E. T. A. Hoffmann saw Mozart's use of minor keys as "demonic," and various works by Mozart, Haydn, and others appealed to the nineteenth-century mind in large part because of their grandiose proportions, chromaticism, and very rich texture.

Operatic develop-ments

Generally, by the last decades of the eighteenth century the Metastasian hold on opera seria was waning, and the comic opera, especially as expounded by Paisiello and Cimarosa, reigned supreme. The powerful impact of the French Revolution of 1789 is mirrored in opera libretti, in which themes of horror, rescue, and passion combine with patriotism. In the early years of the nineteenth century, serious opera was to receive new impetus and develop in new directions under Luigi Cherubini and Gasparo Spontini.

Beethoven and other transi-tional composers

Beethoven's roots were firmly planted in the Classic tradition, and Classic tendencies are especially noticeable in his early instrumental works. Typically Classic is Beethoven's concern with and mastery of symphonic structure, his feeling for logic and order, for proportion, unity, and equilibrium. His motivic workmanship and his use of clearly defined motives as the smallest structural building blocks within the architecture of each symphonic first movement is also a Classic feature. Beethoven's contemporaries, such as Leopold Koželuch, Muzio Clementi, Luigi Cherubini, and especially Franz Schubert, represent along with him the link between the Classic and Romantic eras.

Summary

Mozart and Haydn were the two giants who towered above the mainstream of eighteenth-century Classic musical activity. While the early works of both were steeped in the Preclassic idiom, each man developed the symmetry of phrases, balanced forms, concise use of motivic material, and sense of tonal stability that were typical of the Classic era.

Mozart developed his own style—a masterful synthesis of the existing style variants. Haydn, more isolated from the major centers of musical activity throughout most of his life, was most influenced by the style of C. P. E. Bach. For a time Haydn and Mozart succumbed to the impassioned spirit of the Sturm und Drang. Haydn's encounter with it lasted longer, however, and left its imprint on many different types of his compositions.

As an opera composer, Mozart was the more widely recognized of the two. Although Haydn was exposed to many operas in his capacity as music director for the Esterházys, he saw them performed primarily within the confines of his patrons' circle. Haydn's European fame as an orchestral composer, however, was widespread, and he died, unlike Mozart, a very famous and successful man.

The two geniuses, who crossed paths in the 1780s, developed a deep friendship based on mutual respect. Each influenced the other: Haydn, for instance, learned about melodic lyricism from Mozart; and Mozart, among other things, learned about contrapuntal enrichment of texture from Haydn. Their mature works epitomize Viennese musical Classicism, bequeathing to Beethoven a style and tradition he was to incorporate into the fast-approaching Romanticism of the nineteenth century.

Notes

1. Friedrich Blume, *Classic and Romantic Music,* trans. M. D. Herter Norton (New York: W. W. Norton, 1970), p. 25.
2. Charles Rosen, *The Classical Style: Haydn, Mozart, Beethoven* (New York: W. W. Norton, 1971), pp. 329 ff.
3. Anthony van Hoboken, b. 1887 (Hob.), was a Dutch collector and bibliographer who cataloged and numbered Haydn's works. His numbering system is now in predominant use, much as the Köchel numbers are applied to Mozart's works. His catalogue is cited in the Bibliography.
4. The numbering refers to the original chronological arrangement of the sonatas by Karl Päsler, who in 1918 produced the first complete edition of Haydn's keyboard sonatas. There is some confusion regarding this numbering, since the more readily available Peters edition follows a different order; the two sets of numbers do not coincide. The numbers used in the present text refer to the Päsler edition. For the correct chronological order of these works, consult the Hoboken catalog. This sonata bears the Hoboken number Hob. XVI, No. 34.
5. Emily Anderson, ed., *The Letters of Mozart and His Family* (London: Macmillan, 1938), vol. 2, p. 825.
6. See Otto Jahn, *The Life of Mozart* (New York: Cooper Square Publishers, Inc., 1970), vol. 2, p. 338.
7. K. Anh. (Köchel Anhang) means an appendix or addition to the original Köchel catalog, created when the catalog was revised.
8. For a discussion on authenticity, see H. C. Robbins Landon and D. Mitchell, eds., *The Mozart Companion* (New York: W. W. Norton, 1969), pp. 217–222.
9. *Figaro* is most often performed in four acts now, with the first two equaling the original act I.
10. Alfred Einstein, *Mozart, His Character, His Work* (New York: W. W. Norton, 1962), p. 446.

Bibliography

Books and Articles

The Classic Style

ADLER, GUIDO. "Haydn and the Viennese Classical School." *Musical Quarterly* 13 (1932): 191–207.

BLUME, FRIEDRICH. *Classic and Romantic Music,* trans. M. D. Herter Norton. New York: W. W. Norton, 1970.

NEWMANN, WILLIAM S. "The Recognition of Sonata Form by Theorists of the Eighteenth and Nineteenth Centuries." *Papers of the American Musicological Society,* 1940.

Rosen, Charles. *The Classical Style: Haydn, Mozart, Beethoven.* New York: W. W. Norton, 1971.

Mozart

Anderson, Emily, trans. and ed. *The Letters of Mozart and His Family,* 3 vols. London: Macmillan, 1938.
Badura-Skoda, Eva and Paul. *Interpreting Mozart on the Keyboard.* New York: St. Martin's Press, 1965.
Dent, Edward J. *Mozart's Operas,* 2d. ed. London: Oxford University Press, 1955.
Einstein, Alfred. *Mozart, His Character, His Work.* New York: W. W. Norton, 1962.
Girdlestone, Cuthbert M. *Mozart and His Piano Concertos.* New York: Dover Publications, 1964.
Jahn, Otto. *The Life of Mozart,* 4 vols. Leipzig, 1856–1859. New York: Cooper Square Publishers, Inc., 1970 (3 vols.).
Lang, Paul Henry, ed. *The Creative World of Mozart.* New York: W. W. Norton, 1963.
Robbins Landon, H. C., and Mitchell, Donald, eds. *The Mozart Companion.* London: Rockliff, 1956.

Haydn

Geiringer, Karl. *Joseph Haydn: A Creative Life in Music.* New York: Doubleday (Anchor Books), 1946.
Hoboken, Anthony van. *Joseph Haydn: Thematisch-bibliographisches Werkverzeichnis,* 2 vols. Mainz: B. Schott's Söhne, 1957–1971.
Robbins Landon, H. C. *The Collected Correspondences and London Notebooks of Joseph Haydn (1791–1795).* London: Baine & Rockliff, 1959.
———. *The Symphonies of Joseph Haydn.* London: Universal Editions & Rockliff, 1955.
———. *Haydn: Chronicle and Works,* 5 vols. London: Thames and Hudson, 1977–1978.
Strunck, Otto W. "Haydn's Divertimenti for Baryton, Viola, and Bass." *Musical Quarterly* 18 (1932): 216–251.

Scores

Haydn, Joseph. *Werke.* Published by the Haydn Institute in Cologne. Munich: G. Henle Verlag, 1958.
Mozart, Wolfgang Amadeus. *Neue Mozart Ausgabe sämtlicher Werke.* Published by the Internationale Stiftung Mozarteum Salzburg. Kassel: Bärenreiter, 1955–

PART
FIVE

The Romantic
and Post-Romantic
Eras

23

Music as a Reflection of Nineteenth-Century Society

THE French Revolution and subsequent changes in the European social order directly influenced the place of musicians in the world. Aristocratic patrons of the prerevolutionary period were replaced by a moneyed bourgeois class that supported composers and performers by attending concerts rather than by commissioning new works or employing musicians as household entertainers.

Reason and sobriety, hallmarks of the Classical style, lost their appeal for a new breed of artist. What united nineteenth-century artists most was their firm belief in the rights and importance of the individual, and their works were intended to reveal personal interests and tastes, even if these were considered strange by others. Indeed, the artworks of the time often stressed ideas outside the perimeter of Classical style.

Furthermore, artists began to see themselves as heroes, idols, leaders of their compatriots—in fact, as geniuses deserving of special privileges. Composers were less inhibited than before about expanding the formal and harmonic boundaries of musical works, enlarging their dimensions, and substituting surprises and outbursts of passion for the expectable and restrained. In this chapter we shall trace some of the main trends of Romantic and Post-Romantic life and thought as they affected music.

The Historical and Cultural Background

The Romantic Spirit

The words *Romanticism* and *Romantic* are derived from the term *romance,* a poem or narrative from the Middle Ages written in a Romance language and dealing with heroes and heroic events. A renewed interest in the Middle Ages, heroism, epic tales, and the supernatural led many nineteenth-century artists to include unusual characters and events in a literary or musical piece.

Rousseau's theories and individualism foreshadowed the various kinds of

581

rebellion that became frequent among musical Romantics such as Beethoven, Liszt, and Wagner. Along with their new feelings of emancipation, importance, and rebellion, however, many Romantic composers, including Felix Mendelssohn and Johannes Brahms, preserved certain formal and stylistic elements of the Classical era, although in altered fashion.

Political Developments and Romanticism

The Napoleonic Wars

Together with the ideals of liberty, equality, and fraternity engendered by the French and American revolutions, these upheavals also triggered more than two decades of war between France and the European monarchies, which feared similar revolts in their own countries. Following a series of military victories in Italy during the late 1790s, Napoleon Bonaparte (1769–1821) was made First Consul of France in 1799, after the overthrow of the Directory that had ruled the country since 1795. Soon Napoleon had himself proclaimed Emperor (1804). His persistent attempts to conquer and rule the rest of Europe were not halted until a coalition of European powers defeated his forces at Leipzig (1813) and Waterloo (1815).

After Napoleon's defeat, Vienna became the site of an international diplomatic Congress (1815), which reestablished the European monarchies and ushered in a reactionary period of political repression. Despite censorship, however, the Romantic movements in the arts flourished, and artists retained their liberated status.

Other conflicts

The spread of French revolutionary philosophy, along with economic and social pressures and a growing spirit of nationalism, led to a host of sporadic uprisings and rebellions throughout Europe and the Americas (see Chapter 39). In keeping with the revolutionary spirit of the times, the *Communist Manifesto,* written by Karl Marx (1818–1883) and Friedrich Engels (1820–1895), was published in France in 1848.

Mid-nineteenth-century turmoil

Following the Congress of Vienna, a coalition consisting of England, France, and Turkey ended Russian domination of southeastern Europe (the Crimean War, 1853–1856). Austria was forced out of the German Confederation (the Austro-Prussian War, 1866), and the leadership of the German states was won by Prussia under Otto von Bismarck (1815–1898). After the defeat of Napoleon III of France (reg. 1852–1870) in the Franco-Prussian War (1870–1871), Kaiser Wilhelm I (reg. 1871–1888) founded the German Empire and kept Bismarck as his chancellor.

Italy

Leaders of the *Risorgimento* (Italian unification movement), unsuccessful in their attempt to throw off the yoke of Austrian rule in 1848, sought help from France and England, and gradually loosened Austria's hold. Italy finally achieved unification in 1870, when Rome became its capital and Victor Emmanuel II (reg. 1861–1878) ascended the throne. Contributing to the tremendous popularity of the opera composer Giuseppe Verdi in Italy was the coincidence that the first letters of the words in the patriotic motto *Viva Vittorio Emanuele Re D'Italia!* ("Long live Victor Emmanuel, king of Italy!") combined to spell VERDI.

After the Congress of Vienna, Russia and Austria emerged as the two leading continental European powers. Under Tsars Alexander I (reg. 1801–1825) and Nicholas I (reg. 1825–1855), Russia was severely reactionary. In 1855 Alexander II, a more liberal tsar, came to power, and Russia pursued an aggressive policy of industrialization and territorial expansion throughout the remainder of the nineteenth century. Alexander II freed Russia's millions of serfs in 1861, expanded public education, and lessened censorship. This spirit of change was short-lived, however, for in 1881 he was assassinated. Under Alexander III (reg. 1881–1894) and Nicholas II (reg. 1894–1917) the Russian government reverted to its former restrictive stance, with the populace becoming increasingly frustrated and resistant. Revolution was imminent.

Russia

After Napoleon Bonaparte conquered Spain (1808), he put his oldest brother, Joseph, on the throne. A much-hated ruler, Joseph was forced to abdicate as a result of the Peninsular War (1808–1814). Ferdinand VII, the Bourbon king (reg. 1814–1833), was restored to the throne, but his conservative attitudes antagonized the liberals and nationalists, who had just driven out the French. Under his daughter, Isabella II (reg. 1833–1868), Spain experienced revolutionary movements, military coups d'etat, and a struggle among the republicans, progressives, and reactionaries. Napoleonic Spain was vividly depicted by the Spanish artist Francisco de Goya (1746–1828). His representations of the Spanish struggle against France graphically show the horrors of the time.

Spain

Despite the turmoil on the Continent, England did not experience any violent changes of government during the nineteenth century. In fact, the English monarchy was strengthened under the long and prosperous reign of Queen Victoria (reg. 1837–1901). Another long reign was that of Emperor Franz Joseph of the Austro-Hungarian Empire (reg. 1848–1916). During his lifetime such native-born composers as Bruckner, Johann Strauss, Jr., Mahler, and Schoenberg, and such German composers as Brahms and Richard Strauss, dominated the musical scene in the Imperial capital, Vienna.

Stability in England and Austria

Artistic Currents

In the visual arts, artists strove to "return to Nature" by rejecting the order around them and seeking the unbounded emotional releases that fit their conception of "Nature." Revivals of the distant past, first of ancient Greece and later of the Middle Ages, were tangible expressions of dissatisfaction with the immediate past and the present.

The visual arts

Romanticism in painting is revealed both in the individualism of the artists and in the subject matter of their paintings. Jacques-Louis David (1748–1825) and Goya were stirred by the pressures leading to the French Revolution and its bloody aftermath, and in some of their canvases violence and terror are depicted vividly. Craving truth and naturalness, painters began to imbue scenes of adventure with the violence and elemental forces of Nature. The later style of David was adopted by his pupils Antoine-Jean Gros (1771–1835) and Jean-Auguste Dominique Ingres (1780–1867).

Francisco de Goya (1746–1828), *Dios se lo pague a Usted* ("May God Repay You!,"
c. 1804). In this etching Goya depicts the agony of a blind guitarist impaled on the
horns of a bull, the scene symbolizing the suffering of mankind in a heartless world.
(Prints Division, The New York Public Library; Astor, Lenox and Tilden Foundations)

Nature scenes greatly interested the English masters of landscape painting, John Constable (1776–1837) and William Turner (1775–1851). Constable believed that paintings ought to exhibit a vivid likeness to the actual
world, and his own works reveal his ability to depict real things in a real setting. Turner was interested in literary themes, heroism, history, and the
power of Nature.

The Frenchmen Théodore Géricault (1791–1824) and Eugène Delacroix
(1798–1863) were influenced by Baroque masters. Catapulted to fame by his
scene of Turks slaughtering Greeks in *Massacre de Scio* ("Massacre at Chios,"
1822–1824), Delacroix painted vibrant, colorful canvases of historical and
political events.

Honoré Daumier (1808–1879), whose fame owed much to his satirical
cartoons of French life, tried to capture the reality of human existence. He
presented the poor with compassion and admiration. Daumier was also intrigued by literary themes, especially the story of Don Quixote. The paint-

ings of Gustave Courbet (1819–1877) move from Romantic escapism and imagination to a new realism, exposing programmatic scenes of life.

Literature

The authors Goethe and Schiller, like the composer Beethoven, eventually infused Classical forms with Romantic elements. Such works as Schiller's *Wilhelm Tell* (1804) and Goethe's *Faust* (Part I, 1808) explored humanity's search for truth and its longing for freedom and individual expression. The first wave of German Romantic men of letters included August Wilhelm Schlegel (1767–1845), best remembered for his exquisite German translations (1797–1810) of Shakespeare's plays, a task completed by Ludwig Tieck (1773–1853). All over Europe, Shakespeare's works experienced a revival, and composers such as Berlioz, Verdi, and Robert Schumann were inspired by his words. Composers were also influenced by such early Romantic German writers as E. T. A. Hoffmann (1776–1822; see page 592), Eduard Friedrich Mörike (1804–1875), and Baron Josef von Eichendorff (1788–1857). Achim von Arnim (1781–1831) and Clemens Brentano (1778–1842) collaborated on a collection of folk poems entitled *Des Knaben Wunderhorn* ("The Youth's Magic Horn," 1806–1808), which inspired not only other poets but also composers such as Brahms and Mahler to delve into folklore. Similarly, the brothers Grimm—Jakob Ludwig Karl (1785–1863) and Wilhelm Karl (1786–1859)—did much to revive interest in Germanic folklore with their publication of fairy tales (1812–1815).

After 1815 German literature moved away from descriptions of noble aspirations and depictions of magic and turned its attention more to satire, psychological insight, and mysticism. The chief spokesman of the years 1815–1848 was Heinrich Heine (1797–1856), and his ironic, realistic poems were used as texts for about three thousand art songs.

In post-Napoleonic Germany and Austria the middle classes, stripped of wealth and war-weary, sought simplicity, comfort, and escapist entertainment. During this period (c. 1815–c. 1850) authors wrote vignettes, short stories, almanacs, and ballads—literary forms that inspired such Romantic composers as Schumann and Chopin. Contributing distinction to this era was the Austrian dramatist Franz Grillparzer (1791–1872), whose pessimistic view of the conflict between art and life, between the ideal and real, was shared by a number of his countrymen. German Romanticism waned in the second half of the century, giving way to growing realism and materialism.

England also experienced a flowering of literary Romanticism, led by the poets William Wordsworth (1770–1850), Samuel Taylor Coleridge (1772–1834), George Gordon, Lord Byron (1788–1824), Percy Bysshe Shelley (1792–1822), and John Keats (1795–1821). They believed that words, like music, could evoke emotions in the listener, and their writings served as the basis for songs, operas, and symphonic works by diverse composers.

English literature continued to flourish during the reign of Queen Victoria. Then the works of poets like Alfred Lord Tennyson (1809–1892) and dramatists like Oscar Wilde (1854–1900) were much admired both in En-

The early Romantics

Post-Napoleonic German literature

English literature

gland and on the Continent. Tennyson's poem *The Princess* (1847) was parodied in the operetta *Princess Ida* (1884) by librettist William S. Gilbert and composer Arthur Sullivan, who also combined their talents to spoof Wilde's literary philosophy in *Patience* (1881). Wilde's play *Salomé* (1893), originally written in French, was the basis of Richard Strauss's opera of the same name (1903–1905).

French literature   Rousseau's Romantic philosophy, perpetuated by Germaine de Staël (1766–1817) and François René, Vicomte de Chateaubriand (1768–1848), was brought to fruition in French literature by Alphonse Marie Louis de Lamartine (1790–1869) and Victor Hugo (1802–1885). Like the English poets, Lamartine loved nature and believed in the musical lyricism of verse, as shown in his *Harmonies* (1830); his writings inspired several compositions by Liszt. Hugo's plays *Hernani* (1830) and *Le Roi s'amuse* ("The King Amuses

CROQUIS MUSICAUX   17

L'orchestre pendant qu'on joue une tragédie.

Honoré Daumier (1808–1879), *L'Orchestre pendant qu'on joue une tragédie* ("The Orchestra during the Performance of a Tragedy," 1852). This lithograph exposes tired, bored orchestral players, quite the antithesis of an idealized vision of theatrical glamour and excitement. (Prints Division, The New York Public Library; Astor, Lenox and Tilden Foundations)

Himself," 1832) were the bases of Verdi's operas *Ernani* (1844) and *Rigoletto* (1851), respectively. Among the French Romantic novelists were Stendhal (pseudonym of Marie-Henri Beyle, 1783–1842), who wrote extensively about music and musicians, including a biography of Rossini, and George Sand (pseudonym of Amandine Aurore Lucie Dupin, Baronne Dudevant, 1804–1876), whose love of nature, struggle for women's rights, and social and moral idealism abound in her works. For several years Sand lived with Chopin, and their liaison forms part of the background of her travel account *Un Hiver à Majorque* ("A Winter in Majorca," 1842). Prosper Mérimée (1803–1870) rose to fame as the creator of *nouvelles* (short novels), the best-known of which is *Carmen* (1845), the basis of the 1873–1874 opera by Georges Bizet. Even more influential on Romantic music was Alexandre Dumas fils (1824–1895), whose play *La Dame aux camélias* ("The Lady of the Camelias," 1852), an ultra-Romantic love story known to many a film-goer as *Camille,* was used as the plot for the libretto of Verdi's opera *La traviata* (1853). After the Romanticism of these French writers, various "schools" of French literary thought arose, including the Parnassians and the Symbolists, who, like the Impressionist painters, were to make a tremendous impact on the music of Debussy and early-twentieth-century music in general.

By the end of the nineteenth century, Russia had joined Germany and France as a center of literary activity influencing musicians. During the Napoleonic Wars literary nationalism arose in Russia, and starting in the 1820s Romantic Russian poetry and drama flourished, inspired by Alexander Sergeyevich Pushkin (1799–1837). His long poem *Russlan and Ludmilla* (1820), his drama *Boris Godunov* (1831), his poetic novel *Eugene Onegin* (1825–1831), and his retelling of the folk story *The Golden Cockerel* (1833) became the bases of operas by Mikhail Glinka, Modest Mussorgsky, Peter Ilyich Tchaikovsky, and Nikolai Rimsky-Korsakov, respectively. Russian musicians of the nineteenth and twentieth centuries were also inspired and influenced by the penetrating social and psychological novels of Ivan Sergeyevich Turgenev (1818–1883), Feodor Mikhailovich Dostoyevsky (1821–1881), and Leo Tolstoy (1828–1910).

Russian literature

Perhaps the most influential Romantic Italian man of letters was Alessandro Manzoni (1785–1873), whose literary style and theme of affection for the common people became the model for many future Italian prose authors. Deeply influenced by his works, Verdi composed a Requiem Mass (1874) as a memorial tribute to the writer who was both his national and personal hero.

Italian and Spanish literature

The most important Romantic Spanish playwrights were Angel Pérez de Saavedra, duke of Rivas (1791–1865), and Antonio García Gutiérrez (1813–1884). A play by Rivas was the basis of Verdi's opera *La forza del destino* ("The Force of Destiny," 1862), while García's dramas were adapted by the same composer for his *Il trovatore* ("The Troubadour," 1853) and *Simon Boccanegra* (1857, rev. 1881). A novel by Juan Valera (1824–1905), Spain's great prose stylist, was adapted by his compatriot Albéniz for the latter's opera of the same name, *Pepita Jiménez* (1896).

Composers, Performers, and Audiences

The legacy of Beethoven

For Beethoven and his followers, music became an end in itself. It was considered medicinal for the body and spirit—a vital aspect of a person's life. Circumstances had not generally permitted composers of the Classic era to defy convention or the wishes of their employers, but Beethoven talked back to his patrons and condescended toward princes. In the postrevolutionary era it first became possible for a composer to survive and succeed with eccentric behavior and rude manners. Although the rather uncouth Beethoven succeeded most of all because he was a musician of extraordinary talent, it is also true that the time was right, and that Beethoven dared, and so Romanticism was ushered in.

Romantic vs. Post-Romantic music

Although functional harmony, tonality, and the sonata form were still central to Romantic music, they served as starting points from which composers would depart to varying degrees at different times. Classical contours could be stretched, condensed, and distorted, and such tampering could eventually make the original outlines unrecognizable—which is what happened during the final three decades of the nineteenth century and the early years of the twentieth. In those years, composers such as Wagner, Liszt, and Richard Strauss stressed unprepared and unresolved dissonances, chromaticism, harmonic distortion, shifting tonal centers, a sense of keylessness, the denial or postponement of cadences, and entirely new methods of organizing music. To this transitional era—between the late phase of Romanticism, represented by the mature style of Brahms, and the emergence of clearly defined twentieth-century idioms—the term *Post-Romantic* may be applied.

Diversity of forms and styles

No single stylistic element or group of elements unifies Romantic music in the same way that the basso continuo unifies Baroque or the sonata design unifies Classic music. In fact, Romanticism in music is full of inconsistencies and contradictions. Some composers placed great emphasis on large, theatrical works (e.g., Beethoven's symphonies and Wagner's music dramas). Others lavished care on miniature works (e.g., Schubert's songs and Chopin's preludes). Although many composers rebelled against the confines of Classicism, at the same time they began actively to cherish and perform the music of the immediate past, instead of ignoring and/or criticizing it, as musicians of prior eras had often done.

Importance of instrumental music

Seeking boundless meanings in music, many Romantic composers preferred instrumental to vocal music, as they felt that words tended to limit excessively a composition's meaning. The symphony, with its richly varied medium, the orchestra, had a special appeal for the Romantic artist. On the other hand, most Romantic composers deeply loved the great poetry of their past and present, and were moved to fuse words and music in songs, whose lyrical style also made its way into the symphonies and other instrumental works of the nineteenth century.

Program music

Some maintained the supremacy of instrumental music while still basing their works on extramusical considerations, such as drama or poetry, by writing program music. In the strictest sense these compositions are instrumental music (usually for orchestra) inspired by a poem, novel, play, painting, sculpture, or some other extramusical entity, and meant to suggest the essence of that entity to the listener. The use of program music betrays the Romanticists' interest in the interrelationships of all the arts, and their attachment to suggestion and mystery rather than to the concrete meaning of words.

A basic tenet among Romantic composers was that the aim of music was not merely to please audiences, but to uplift, educate, and arouse them. "[I have] been concerned," said Beethoven in 1806, "with the interests of Art, the ennoblement of taste and the impulse of . . . genius to rise to greater heights of the ideal and of perfection."[1] A musical work of large proportions was art for art's sake. Unlike the music of centuries past, Romantic music was only rarely "occasional." Romantic masterworks seldom served to adorn a church service, to provide entertainment at a wedding, or to accompany men into battle. Music was customarily written in the 1800s for a paying audience assembled in a public hall for the purpose of listening. This audience challenged the composer to provide ever bigger, more original works, and the composer, in turn, challenged the public with subtleties and complexities with which it could not cope.

New functions of music

Locales of Music–Making

Already in the eighteenth century there had been a growing separation between professional and amateur musicians. C. P. E. Bach spelled out the distinction in 1779 when he entitled some of his works *Sonaten für Kenner und Liebhaber* ("Sonatas for Connoisseurs and Amateurs"). In the nineteenth century the rift expanded, since composers made grueling technical demands upon professional performers but knew better than to deflate the pride and spoil the fun of amateurs with music beyond their capabilities.

The largest groups of amateurs were people in their homes who gathered around a piano to play and sing. Composers, no longer supported by wealthy patrons, increasingly depended upon the sales of their compositions to publishers, and so the amateur singers and chamber music players who bought the latest compositions became important sources of revenue. For European families home music-making was a main source of recreation. Thanks to innovations in printing, the price of music came within the reach of average citizens. Furthermore, the Industrial Revolution brought about metallurgical and other technological improvements that enabled more people to purchase musical instruments, now manufactured more cheaply and quickly. Important changes in the structure of instruments made them easier to play, and so more people began to study them.

Music in the home

Another important development was the coming of age of a relatively new keyboard instrument, the piano. During the Classical period the piano gradually supplanted the harpsichord and clavichord. Only in the time of Beethoven did the grand piano, the *Hammerklavier,* which was able to provide gradations of loudness in addition to abrupt changes of dynamics, completely replace its older cousins (see page 602). Both upright and grand

The piano

pianos could be found in the parlors of many European families, where solo piano pieces, as well as piano duets, were often played. Most children were encouraged to take piano lessons, and the piano began on its road to wide and enthusiastic acceptance.

In addition to piano music, composers wrote *Lieder,* or art songs, for home use. The *Lied,* a personal expression of feeling, involving a most intimate medium, voice and piano, was ideally suited to the needs and abilities of family members. Composers had little intention of hearing these delicate, intimate Lieder performed on concert stages. On the contrary, they wrote them for themselves, their friends, and the music-buying public.

Salon music

One important result of the Industrial Revolution was the urbanization of life in Europe, effected partly by improved means of rail and water transportation. More and more people became wealthy, and the public audience became a mass audience. This large group desired entertainment more often than enlightenment, and certain composers—such as Liszt, Chopin, Johann Strauss, Jr., Cécile Chaminade (1857–1944), and Ignacy Jan Paderewski (1860–1941)—wrote great quantities of what came to be called "salon music." The salon itself was usually a spacious chamber in a large house, with room for dancing or for a sizeable audience. Works of visual art were often exhibited there, and music was performed for and applauded by often-pretentious audiences. By means of salon concerts, composers and performers received recognition from wealthy and influential people, and for some artists, like Chopin, the salon was a far more comfortable atmosphere for performing than the concert hall.

Singing groups

The decreasing price of printed music at the end of the eighteenth century and later, along with increasing interest in music among the nouveaux riches, stimulated rapid growth in the number of European singing societies. For instance, the first German choral society, the Berlin *Singakademie,* was founded in 1791 with only about thirty members. By the year 1813 it could boast of more than 300 participants. Amateur choruses often sang at the music festivals that proliferated in Germany and France during the early nineteenth century. In addition, composers wrote oratorios, Masses, and other large choral works because multitudes of singers wanted to perform in them and audiences were eager to hear them.

Public concerts

The development of the public concert in the later eighteenth century, and more especially in the nineteenth, gives evidence of the rise of the conception of music as an aesthetic object whose worth transcended its immediate usefulness. The number of public concert series multiplied vastly in the nineteenth century, when orchestras, choruses, and virtuoso performers were heard. In small halls the public attended intimate recitals of solo and chamber music. With audiences showing greater interest in chamber music, composers wrote increasing numbers of difficult, lengthy works for small ensembles of professional musicians. A turning point in the history of chamber music was reached in the late quartets of Beethoven (1823–1826), which were too difficult for anyone but professional string players to perform. After Beethoven, most composers conceived their chamber works not for a group of players to enjoy in an informal atmosphere but for concert artists to perform before a paying audience.

The Rise of Virtuosity

As long as music served some other purpose—accompanying affairs of Church or state, for example—it was unlikely that most performers would attempt to mesmerize their audiences with technical wizardry. Of course, especially in the world of opera, there had been some exceptions, but never before the nineteenth century did so many performers, knowing that idolizing people were paying to listen to them perform, so completely bewitch their audiences. Instrumentalists and singers alike became international celebrities, and much music was written primarily to *sound* enormously difficult to perform, so that the audience would be thrilled.

During the Romantic era, virtuoso performers, who were often also composers of renown, openly competed with one another for the adulation of the paying public. Opera singers, having inherited a long tradition, enraptured audiences with cadenzas, ornaments, and cantilena. But the nineteenth century brought with it a new emphasis on the acting abilities of singers, and a new breed of performer was born, represented best, perhaps, by the sopranos Giuditta Pasta (1797–1865) and Maria Malibran (1808–1836). Operatic roles were designed to suit the great singers (e.g., Bellini's Norma for Pasta). **The Great Singers**

Piano virtuosos flocked to Paris, with its most receptive middle-class audience. The most internationally respected virtuoso, however, was the Italian violinist Niccolò Paganini (1782–1840). Endowed with an incomparable technique, Paganini performed, with his Guarnerius and Stradivarius violins, musical feats which had previously been considered impossible—including playing triple stops, double harmonics, and simultaneous bowed and pizzicato notes. Paganini inspired Berlioz, Liszt, and others to further the cause of Romantic virtuosity. **Paganini**

In the Classic concerto, composers had tried to maintain a balance between the orchestra and the soloist. In the Romantic period, stressing virtuosity, the composer often gave the soloist more to do than the orchestra. The two forces often fought for supremacy and control of the audience's attention. Composers no longer asked soloists to wait patiently for the orchestra to finish its own exposition, and the orchestra was rarely given sole possession of a theme. **The Romantic concerto**

During this period, also, the notion of the "great conductor" was born. Romantic composer-conductors par excellence, including Weber, Berlioz, Wagner, Mendelssohn, Liszt, and Brahms, were intimately involved with the sound-producing capabilities of the orchestra, and their works display special colors and orchestral subtleties unknown in earlier times. Mendelssohn became the director of the prestigious and influential Gewandhaus concert series in Leipzig (1835). He was then in a position to assist other composers such as Schumann by conducting their orchestral works soon after completion. Similarly, Liszt directed and conducted operas and concerts in Weimar (1848–1861), where he presented the works of such avant-garde composers as Ber- **The Romantic conductor** lioz and Wagner. Despite his flamboyant conducting style, Berlioz, unlike Wagner, believed in strict tempos and was among the first to conduct from a full score. After an extended tour of the podiums of Europe, Berlioz accepted the conductorship of the Drury Lane Theatre in London (1847). But soon afterward the theater failed, and he returned to Paris (1848).

In the Post-Romantic era Mahler and Richard Strauss, who were first-rate conductors, created works with most impressive orchestration. Mahler was so busy conducting (often on tour) that he rarely found time to compose except during the summer, and he referred to himself in frustration as a "summertime composer." Strauss held conducting posts in Munich, Weimar, Berlin, and Vienna, and also toured as a conductor.

The Rise of Music Criticism

Composers as critics   Although the criticism of music is as old as music itself, the art of music criticism—with its direct appeal to a public readership—took on vastly enlarged importance and proportions during the Romantic period. In the nineteenth century, a number of composers themselves became critics, including Weber, Berlioz, Schumann, Liszt, Wagner, and Hugo Wolf. E. T. A. Hoffmann, who spent part of his life as a professional musician and wrote the Romantic fairy opera *Undine* (1816), was another important critic, the first to recognize the greatness of Beethoven. Some of Hoffmann's stories formed the basis for the libretto of Offenbach's opera *The Tales of Hoffmann* (1881).

R. Schumann as critic   Robert Schumann was probably the best and most eloquent spokesman for musical Romanticism. Inspired by his readings of the Schlegels (August and his brother Friedrich [1772–1829]), Tieck, the English Romantics, and his favorite author, Jean Paul (French pseudonym of the German Johann Paul Friedrich Richter, 1763–1825), Schumann founded the influential *Neue Zeitschrift für Musik* ("New Journal for Music") in Leipzig in 1834 and was its chief editor until 1844. In it he published hundreds of reviews of compositions and performances, which set high standards for midcentury musicians. He aimed his acerbic criticism at the untalented, the outmoded, the overly versatile (who spread themselves too thin), the lazy, and the impatient.

Berlioz as critic   Hector Berlioz was a professional music critic and essayist from the mid-1820s to the mid-1860s. Abhorring mediocrity and academicism, he was a most passionate and excitable musician but also one of the fairest critics. His *Mémoires* (1870) and *Soirées de l'orchestre* ("Evenings with the Orchestra," 1852) are among the most interesting musical writings of the century. In his *Mémoires* Berlioz often reveals his disgust with those who tamper with the original version of a work. Here, for instance, is an excerpt from his review of a performance of Weber's opera *Der Freischütz,* which illustrates his major concerns as a critic:

Weber appeared. *Der Freischütz* was performed at the Odéon: not the real thing, but a gross travesty, hacked and mutilated in the most wanton fashion by an arranger. . . .

The young orchestra was excellent, the chorus second-rate, the soloists atrocious. Only one of them . . . knew how to sing; but as she delivered the entire role without a glimmer of intelligence, passion or vitality, it went virtually for nothing.[2]

The poet Heinrich Heine, writing for the *Augsburg Allgemeine Zeitung,* was the first music journalist to write for a nonmusical journal. This literary genius brought to the world of the music review a new pitch of excitement and a large general readership. He is the prototype of our finest contemporary music critics. Demanding the highest standards of performance, he was also merciless in exposing the personal foibles of both performers and composers.

Heine: a poet as critic

Nationalism and Exoticism

Western European music during the Classical and early Romantic eras was of a pan-European character, since the works of a composer would be equally or nearly equally appealing to an audience in any European country. However, in the second half of the nineteenth century, concurrent with nationalistic political movements in various countries, many composers began to emphasize national elements in their works. They incorporated folk tunes and dance rhythms, national anthems, instruments stemming from their homeland (such as the Italian tambourine or the Spanish castanets), and extramusical ideas related to the history, geography, or life-style of their homeland. Among the great nationalistic composers were Smetana and Dvořák of Bohemia; Carl Nielsen (1865–1931) of Denmark; Elgar of England; Sibelius of Finland; Ferenc Erkel (1810–1893) of Hungary; Grieg of Norway; Stanislaw Moniuszko (1819–1872) of Poland: "The Mighty Five" (see page 713) of Russia; and Albéniz and Granados of Spain.

Nation-alism

Many nineteenth-century composers were also attracted to the native music of other lands and tried to incorporate the sounds of the Near and Far East, the Mediterranean area, and other faraway places into their own musical language. Such efforts at what may be called *exoticism* were not new: Mozart's opera *Die Entführung aus dem Serail* is but one earlier example. Nonetheless, it was during the nineteenth century that interest in exoticism became overwhelming. Some examples are: (1) the opera *Der Barbier von Bagdad* ("The Barber of Baghdad," 1855–1858) by Peter Cornelius (1824–1874); (2) Verdi's opera *Aida* (1871); and (3) Rimsky-Korsakov's orchestral suite *Scheherazade* (1888).

Exoticism

Summary

The Romantic era was a time of war and revolution in Europe. Germany and Italy achieved unification only after the middle of the nineteenth century, and such striving for political freedom embodied in so many uprisings had its counterparts in other areas of life. For instance, in the arts (and philosophy), the rights of the individual were stressed. Starting with Beethoven, the artist began to be thought of as a leader or hero, rather than as a servant of the Church, state, or aristocracy. Believing in the notions of genius and superiority, composers became the dictators of musical tastes and fashions.

Lieder, miniature piano pieces, and piano duets were all intended for one or two nonprofessional musicians to perform in an intimate home environment. Composers also provided great numbers of works for amateurs who enjoyed singing in choruses.

On the other hand, music was also created for the entertainment of the growing middle-class audiences at concerts and opera performances, and symphonies, concertos, operas, and other large-scale pieces became longer, louder, and grander in order to excite and impress the public. For similar reasons, the century also witnessed a great number of virtuoso singers and instrumentalists. Since the bourgeoisie was unable to evaluate critically the quality of the music performed, journal and newspaper critics gained considerable influence as guides for the "proper" judging of music and musicians by the paying public.

Each country could boast of its favorite sons and daughters, who in return extolled their homelands through the use of national melodies, rhythms, instruments, anthems, and extramusical associations. Nationalistic and exotic compositions brought such nations as Russia, Norway, and Spain into the limelight of nineteenth-century music history.

Notes

1. Cited in Michael Hamburger, ed. and trans., *Beethoven: Letters, Journals and Conversations* (Garden City, N.Y.: Doubleday & Co., 1960), p. 48.
2. Cited in David Cairns, ed. and trans., *Memoirs of Hector Berlioz* (New York: Alfred A. Knopf, 1969), p. 86.

Bibliography

Books and Articles

The Age

ABRAMS, MEYER HOWARD. *The Mirror and the Lamp: Romantic Theory and the Critical Tradition*. London: Oxford University Press, 1953.
BARZUN, JACQUES. *Darwin, Marx, Wagner: Critique of a Heritage,* rev. 2nd ed. Garden City, N.Y.: Doubleday & Co., 1958.
BRINTON, CRANE. *The Shaping of Modern Thought*. Englewood Cliffs, N.J.: Prentice-Hall, 1963.
COPLESTON, FREDERICK, S. J. *A History of Philosophy,* vol. 7, parts 1 and 2. Garden City, N.Y.: Image Books, 1965.
HALSTED, JOHN B. *Romanticism*. Documentary History of Western Civilization, ed. Eugene C. Black and Leonard W. Levy. New York: Harper Torchbooks, 1969.

HAUSER, ARNOLD. *The Social History of Art,* vols. 3 and 4. New York: Vintage Books [1958].

HONOUR, HUGH. *Romanticism.* New York: Harper & Row, 1979.

LAVRIN, JANKO. *Studies in European Literature.* New York: Richard R. Smith, 1930; reprint, Port Washington, N.Y.: Kennikat Press [1970].

PALMER, ROBERT R., and COLTON, JOEL. *A History of the Modern World,* 5th ed., 2 vols. New York: Alfred A. Knopf, 1978.

Romantic Music in General

ABRAHAM, GERALD. *A Hundred Years of Music,* 4th ed. London: Duckworth & Co., 1974.

BLUME, FRIEDRICH. *Classic and Romantic Music: A Comprehensive Survey,* translated by M. D. Herter Norton. New York: W. W. Norton & Co., 1970.

EINSTEIN, ALFRED. *Music in the Romantic Era.* New York: W. W. Norton & Co., 1947.

19th-Century Music, 1977– . A musicology journal which began publication in 1977.

Writings of Romantic Composers

ANDERSON, EMILY, trans. and ed. *The Letters of Beethoven,* 3 vols. New York: St. Martin's Press, 1961.

BERLIOZ, HECTOR. *Evenings with the Orchestra,* translated, edited, and introduced by Jacques Barzun. Chicago: University of Chicago Press, 1973.

————. *The Memoirs of Hector Berlioz,* translated and edited by David Cairns. New York: W. W. Norton & Co., 1975.

ELLIS, WILLIAM ASHTON, trans. *Richard Wagner's Prose Works,* 8 vols. London: Kegan Paul, Trench, Trübner & Co., 1892–1912; reprint, New York: Broude Brothers, 1966.

HAMMELMANN, HANNS, and OSERS, EWALD, trans. *A Working Friendship: The Correspondence Between Richard Strauss and Hugo von Hofmannsthal.* New York: Random House, 1961; reprint, New York: Vienna House, 1974.

MORGENSTERN, SAM, ed. *Composers on Music: An Anthology of Composers' Writings from Palestrina to Copland,* 2nd ed. New York: Pantheon Books, 1956.

SCHUMANN, ROBERT. *On Music and Musicians,* edited by Konrad Wolff, translated by Paul Rosenfeld. New York: W. W. Norton & Co., 1969.

STRUNK, OLIVER, ed. *Source Readings in Music History: The Romantic Era.* New York: W. W. Norton & Co., 1965.

By and About Music Critics

HANSLICK, EDUARD. *Music Criticisms 1846–99,* rev. ed., translated and edited by Henry Pleasants. Baltimore: Penguin Books, 1963.

PLANTINGA, LEON. *Schumann as Critic.* New Haven: Yale University Press, 1967; reprint, New York: Da Capo Press, 1976.

Nationalism

ABRAHAM, GERALD. *On Russian Music.* London: William Reeves, 1939; reprint, Freeport, N.Y.: Books for Libraries Press, 1970.

COOPER, MARTIN. *French Music from the Death of Berlioz to the Death of Fauré.* London: Oxford University Press, 1961.

HOWES, FRANK STEWART. *The English Musical Renaissance.* London: Secker & Warburg, 1966.

24

The Nature of
Nineteenth-Century Music

MANY Classical elements, devices, and structures prevailed in the music of the Romantic period. In fact, in the history of music, most stylistic periods are more dissimilar to their immediate predecessors than Romanticism is to Classicism. We can indeed speak of a Classic-Romantic era, an age of functional harmony and tonality, enduring from about 1720 to about 1910, with (1) a Classical phase, stressing musical structure (ending during the career of Beethoven, around 1815), and (2) a Romantic phase, emphasizing musical expression and sonority, and leading logically to the music of such later composers as Claude Debussy and Igor Stravinsky.

From the musical vocabulary of the Classical era, Romantic composers took most of their genres, musical forms, and such eighteenth-century procedures as variation, development, fugue, imitation, and ostinato. Nineteenth-century tempos, meters, chord progressions, modulations, phrasing, articulation, and motivic designs had their roots, too, in the Classical style. However, in the nineteenth century, composers put the raw materials of music to new use and interrelated them in novel ways.

Romanticism: Musical Components

Melody

Romantic lyricism   Romantic melody tends to be lyrical, and the word *cantabile* appears very frequently in the tempo indications of purely instrumental works by Beethoven and his successors, instructing the player to aim for the expressive lyricism of a human voice, to play in a "singing" manner. The themes of Romantic sonata-form movements and compositions in a quick tempo are commonly reflective, expressive, or atmospheric, and the unfolding of the melody itself is of prime importance. Folk tunes and melodies constructed to sound like folk tunes abound in the nineteenth century.

596

The most common texture of the period is homophony; that is, the melody is accompanied by chords or patterns providing harmonic support. Though sometimes periodic, the phrasing of both fast and slow melodies is often irregular. Phrases are frequently built of sub-phrases with an odd number of measures (e.g., the opening nine measures of the slow movement in Beethoven's Piano Sonata in D major, Op. 10, No. 3; 1797–1798; *MCP, no.* 24).[1] Motivic development often occurs at the first appearance of a theme, so that the poised periodicity of the late eighteenth century is replaced by a certain restless quality (as in the recurrent motive of Berlioz's *Symphonie fantastique* [1830], first movement, mm. 72–111). In other cases, the denial of a tonic resolution in what would have been a Classical consequent phrase propels the melody forward (e.g., in mm. 27–39 of Mendelssohn's *Rondo capriccioso,* Op. 14, for piano [1824]).

Texture and phrasing

Romantic melodies often consist of long, lyrical lines, which fuse several short motives. Such melodies are propelled by occasional leaps of a sixth or more and often cover a very wide range. Although punctuated by small internal cadences, they flow without a feeling of completion for long periods of time. An example is the opening of the Sonata for Violin and Piano in D minor, Op. 108 (1886–1888), by Brahms (see Example 24.1). The use of "unending" melody becomes extreme in the music of Wagner and his followers, such as Bruckner and Richard Strauss. Their short, energetic motives are continuously developed, enlarged, and contrapuntally combined. Avoiding cadences, they may either crawl along searchingly or press forward relentlessly. Typical of the latter is the first theme of Richard Strauss's *Don Juan* (1888–1889; see Example 24.2).

Length of melodies

Ex. 24.1   Johannes Brahms, Sonata for Violin and Piano in D minor, Mvt. 1, mm. 1–24

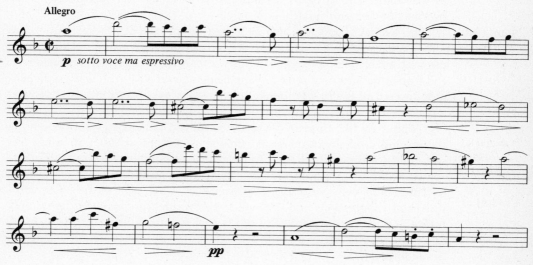

Ex. 24.2   Richard Strauss, *Don Juan*, mm. 9–17

Harmony and Tonality

Chromaticism and modal mixture

Any of the five chromatic neighbors of the seven tones of a diatonic scale can be expected to occur repeatedly during the course of a Romantic composition—more so as we move closer to the end of the century. In addition to chromaticism, modal mixture—the use of parallel major and minor versions of a musical unit in close proximity—is also common in Romantic music. The musical unit may be only a measure or two long, or it can be an entire section, as in Schubert's Impromptu in A-flat major, Op. 90, No. 4 (c. 1827), with its middle portion in C-sharp minor-major.

Prevalence of minor keys

Since the nineteenth century thrived on tense passions, the minor mode rose to a position of unprecedented eminence at this time. One reason was that the minor mode, with its natural, harmonic, and melodic variants, provided the composer with more built-in chromaticism, alterations, and variety. Also, a minor beginning could lead quite dramatically to a major conclusion, with its concomitant suggestion of victory. An important early Romantic composition showing just this type of emotional progression is Beethoven's Fifth Symphony (1807–1808; *MSO* I, p. 313; *NS*, E, I, no. 36; *NS*, S, no. 20),[2] in which the tension of the C-minor scherzo is ultimately resolved by the triumphant C-major finale.

Range of keys

The Romantic era was also an age in which all twenty-four major and minor keys were used regularly. The newly improved musical instruments of the time enabled composers to set down their ideas in any key whatsoever, and Romantic virtuosos took pride in being able to play in all keys with technical surety and agility. In modulating, nineteenth-century composers showed a distinct proclivity for moving up or down a third.

The avoidance of cadences

Composers like Liszt and Wagner employed various ways of preventing the resolution of dissonances and thus increased the sense of yearning and searching for the unattainable. Among their techniques were the use of deceptive cadences, common-tone and enharmonic modulations, rests followed by changes of key, and chains of dissonances. The result of these "endless" dissonant progressions and the avoidance of cadences was a feeling of keylessness, since the predictability of chordal functions was destroyed. More and more, chords were used for coloristic purposes, rather than for their traditional functions.

Modality

A return to the flavors of the medieval and Renaissance modes became increasingly common in the Post-Romantic period, with such composers as Fauré, Mussorgsky, Debussy, and Puccini. The opening of act III of Puccini's opera *La Bohème* (1896) and the Sanctus of Fauré's Requiem (1877, 1887–1890), for example, use modal chord progressions. Composers also altered certain notes of the tonic scale (e.g., raised the fourth tone a half step) in an effort to provide alternatives to the standard major-minor tonality of the period. Many examples can be found in the mazurkas of Chopin—for instance, measures 21–36 of the Mazurka in C major, Op. 24, No. 2, and measures 54–61 of the Mazurka in B-flat minor, Op. 24, No. 4 (both 1834–1835).

Rhythm

Romantic music tends to contain greater rhythmic freedom than does Classical music. Many of the rhythmic intricacies of twentieth-century compositions were introduced in the nineteenth century, when the downbeat was frequently deemphasized. *Cross-rhythms*—the simultaneous use of different or conflicting accents or rhythmic patterns—are common, and the most frequent cross-rhythm of all is *hemiola,* or the use of groups of three (notes, beats, measures) against groups of two. For instance, in Chopin's Etude in F minor, Op. 25, No. 2 (1836), each half measure has two impulses in the right hand against three in the left (see Example 24.3). A similar instance occurs in the same composer's Waltz in A-flat major, Op. 42 (1840), in which the left hand plays in $\frac{3}{4}$ time but the right hand is actually playing in duple time. Brahms is the unparalleled Romantic master of hemiola and other cross-rhythms. Not since the Renaissance had any composer seemed so interested in providing rhythmic multidimensionality.

A more ornamental type of cross-rhythm, favored by Chopin, Liszt, Paderewski, Rachmaninov, and other masters of the piano literature, consists of irregular groups of fairly fast moving notes in the right hand against a steady metrical pattern in the left hand. Almost any Chopin nocturne contains instances of this pattern, but a particularly fine one, which also features all sorts of cross-rhythms (such as five notes in one hand against four in the other), is the Nocturne in E-flat major, Op. 55, No. 2 (1843; see Example 24.4).

In certain passages performers were expected to change the tempo ever so slightly from beat to beat. Each measure was, nevertheless, to have the same overall duration. Similarly, if one or more measures sped along, then the next one or several had to slow down for the sake of balance, so that the total

Cross-rhythms

Ex. 24.3   Frédéric Chopin, Etude in F minor, Op. 25, No. 2, mm. 1–2

Ex. 24.4   Frédéric Chopin, Nocturne in E-flat major, Op. 55, No. 2, mm. 58–62

length of time for the entire group of measures would have a duration equal to what it would have been in a strict tempo. Such a flexible tempo, a prominent feature of the piano works of Chopin and Liszt, for example, is known **Tempo** as *tempo rubato*. It may manifest itself in piano music as an adherence to strict **rubato** tempo by the left hand while the right hand drags or rushes.

Sonority

Favorite   Romantic composers had a penchant for giving primary melodic material
Romantic to instruments that had previously been relegated to providing harmonic and
instru- rhythmic support and for exploiting the timbre of solo instruments. The var-
ments ious characters depicted in such a work as Strauss's *Don Juan* or Berlioz's *Symphonie fantastique* were made consistently identifiable because their themes were assigned to specific single instruments or homogeneous choirs of instruments (e.g., the violas, the oboes, or the entire brass section). German opera composers such as Weber and Wagner carefully matched particular instruments with individual characters, ideas, and scenes. In the overture to Weber's *Der Freischütz* (1821; *NAWM* II, No. 136a),[3] the horn emerges as a mellow, sylvan instrument, just as it does at the start of Mendelssohn's overture to *A Midsummer Night's Dream* (1826; *NS*, E, II, no. 5) and often throughout the nineteenth century. The clarinet became a particular favorite among the Romantics, notably Rossini, Weber, Mendelssohn, Liszt, Berlioz, Richard Strauss, and Mahler. The last four of these exploited each of the different sizes of clarinet to obtain a more richly colored woodwind sound. Toward the end of his life Brahms (like Mozart before him) wrote some of his greatest chamber works—a trio, a quintet, and two duo sonatas—for groups that included a clarinet.

In addition to the horn and the clarinet, the Romanticists' favorite orchestral instruments, which had received far less attention during the preceding era, were the harp, English horn, trombone, tuba, and percussion battery (including triangle, cymbals, tambourine, gong, castanets, wood block, xylophone, and bass drum). Any of Berlioz's orchestral works illustrates his skill as a virtuoso orchestrator. Two especially fine examples are the *Sinfonie fantastique* and *Harold en Italie* ("Harold in Italy," 1834). Noteworthy in the former is the elegant use of the harp in the waltz movement, as well as the evoca-

Berlioz

Charles Joseph Sax (1791–1865), *Clarinet in B-flat* (Brussels, 1830). This ivory clarinet has golden, mellowed brass mountings and keys. Notice the key covers embossed in the shape of lions' heads. (The Metropolitan Museum of Art; Purchase, 1953, Funds from various donors)

tive sound of the English horn in the slow movement. *Harold* shows off the viola's rich dark tone. Berlioz preached what he practiced, and wrote the *Traité de l'instrumentation* ("Treatise on Instrumentation," 1843), the first work of its kind, and still one of the most important bases of orchestration technique.

Wagner   Wagner deliberately emphasized brass and percussion instruments in his music dramas. He made the brasses his fundamental sonority, lending connotations of weightiness, militancy, power, and majesty to his scores. Although Wagner used all instruments imaginatively, he was less interested in orchestral virtuosity than were Berlioz, Richard Strauss, Rimsky-Korsakov, and the later French colorist Maurice Ravel (see Chapter 30). To Wagner the orchestra was primarily a means to one end: the most lucid sounding of the basic harmonic design of the composition. This attitude was shared by Bruckner, whose symphonies depend primarily on an imaginative use of brasses and woodwinds and on his knowledge, as organist, of timbral variety and sub-

Mahler   tleties. His countryman Mahler was far less Wagnerian in his instrumentation than either Bruckner or Richard Strauss. In Mahler's symphonies the trombones and tubas do not attract the listener's attention so much as the flutes, oboes, clarinets, French horns, and violins. Following the precedent set by Berlioz, he used an enlarged orchestra, but the Austrian was reluctant to let all his instruments play together for long periods of time. He used the large group much as a painter might use an immense palette: all the pigments would be available, but only a few would be mixed at a time.

Changes in instrument construction and techniques   One of the reasons for the rise of the virtuoso orchestrator and conductor in the nineteenth century was the tremendous advances made at that time in instrument construction. Along with new technology came new instrumental techniques and the increased use of unusual (although old) ones. Thanks to the efforts of such piano manufacturers as Nannette Streicher (1769–1833) and Conrad Graf (1782–1851) in Vienna, between 1800 and 1820 the range of the piano increased from five octaves to six or six and a half octaves, and pianists also began to be able to employ the various pedals for expressive purposes. Occasional employment of glissandos in the Classical period gave way to their very frequent use during the Romantic, when keyboard actions were much lighter than they are in today's pianos.

The piano   Outside Vienna, some of the most significant piano-manufacturing firms were those founded by Ignace Pleyel (1757–1831) in Paris, John Broadwood (1732–1812) in London, and the Erard brothers, also in London. Sébastien Erard (1752–1831) was the inventor of the repetition action in 1808, and his nephew Pierre Erard (1796–1855) patented the second repetition action in 1821. Known as the double escapement, this action permitted the rapid repetition of a single note, even at a soft dynamic level.

In 1825 Alpheus Babcock (1785–1842) of Boston patented the one-piece cast-iron frame for the square piano. It was also Babcock who first conceived of the cross-stringing of the instrument's treble and bass strings. In 1859 Babcock's ideas were expertly applied to the grand piano, in essentially its modern form, by the manufacturer Steinway & Sons of New York.

Grand Pianoforte by Érard and Co. (London, c. 1830). This lavish piano consists of various types of wood, ivory, and mother-of-pearl inlays. Beethoven was given an Érard piano by its manufacturer in 1803, and it was popular with such pianist-composers as Mendelssohn, Liszt, Thalberg, Hummel, and Moscheles. (The Metropolitan Museum of Art; Gift of Mrs. Henry McSweeney, 1959)

Strings

String players of the Romantic era were asked to produce various sounds that had been used infrequently before. They employed a wide *vibrato,* and played *sul ponticello* (in German, *am Steg;* bowing near the bridge, which creates a brittle kind of sound); *col legno* (drawing the wooden part rather than the hair of the bow across the strings); and *sul tasto* (bowing near the fingerboard, causing a flute-like effect). In the orchestra the strings were often divided into groups that were then assigned different music. In this *divisi* arrangement the first violins, or cellos, or any other section, could produce more than one line at a time. Romantic string players tended to exaggerate the shifts of hand position on the strings, so that the listener could hear them. (Today such audible shifts are frowned upon.) Mention must also be made of the unmeasured *tremolo,* perhaps the most common string effect in dramatic music of the nineteenth century. For this tremolo the player moves the bow up and down on one string rapidly, so that the same note is repeated again and again.

While woodwind technique underwent less modification in the nine-

Winds and brasses

teenth century than did that of other orchestral instruments, the technique of playing brasses was radically altered. With the addition of valves to the French horn and trumpet, these higher-pitched brasses could now play chromatic melodies. Instead of simply providing harmonic support, the horn and trumpet could themselves be harmonically supported by the trombone and tuba. Thus sections of a work could be performed entirely by a brass choir, perhaps alternating with passages for winds or strings.

So many combinations of orchestral instruments were available that Romantic composers never risked running out of possibilities. Add to the more familiar instruments the frequent use of the harp, of all sorts of percussion instruments, and of the human voice in symphonic music (starting with Beethoven's Ninth Symphony), and we sense the richness of the Romantic orchestra. Although the piccolo, English horn (an alto oboe), bass clarinet, contrabassoon, trombone, and tuba had not been customary participants of the Classic symphony, they eventually became regular members of the nineteenth-century orchestra.

The Concept of "Grandness"

Orchestral size

The large size of the orchestra was one manifestation of what Romantic and Post-Romantic composers considered to be "grandness" or "greatness" —often indicated in titles by such words as *grosse* in German and *grande* in French. "Grandness" usually implied large, long, difficult, complex works, with extremes of dynamics and tempo. After Beethoven, "greatness" in the symphony or chamber music could be measured only by Beethovenian standards. As Schubert wrote to a friend in March 1824:

> . . . I have tried my hand at several instrumental works, for I wrote two Quartets . . . and an Octet, and I want to write another quartet, in fact I intend to pave my way towards a grand symphony in that manner. —The latest in Vienna is that Beethoven is to give a concert at which he is to produce his new Symphony, three movements from the new Mass and a new Overture. —God willing, I too am thinking of giving a similar concert next year.[4]

In Schubert's mind "grandness," Beethoven, and success were interconnected, since by 1824 Beethoven had turned the symphony into a long, elevated, richly textured orchestral work intended for a concert-going public at home and abroad—for posterity as well as for his contemporaries.

Structure

The Romantic sonata cycle

The sonata cycle of the Classical era continued to be the foremost structural plan among Romantic composers. A four-movement pattern became customary, but the aristocratic minuet of the Classical period gave way to the *scherzo*. Basically the innovation of Beethoven, the scherzo was a faster dance

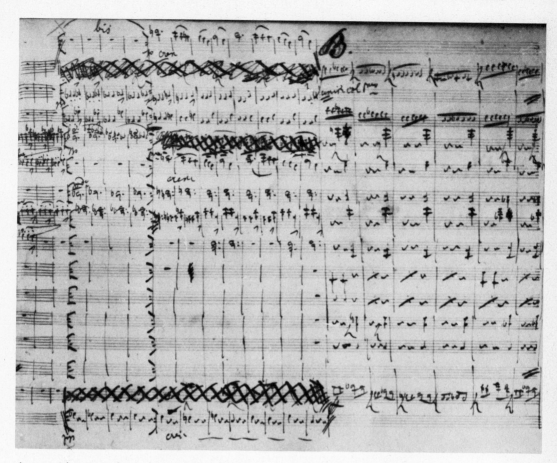

Autograph score of Schubert's *Great Symphony,* D. 944 (1825–1826), folio 67ʳ. This page represents mm. 86–110 of the enormous scherzo movement of Schubert's longest symphony. This scherzo is a vigorous display of contrasting textures and dynamics, daring harmony, and buoyant rhythms. As this page shows, Schubert made radical changes in the score before arriving at a version he considered suitable for performance. (Courtesy, Archives of the Gesellschaft der Musikfreunde, Vienna)

movement in triple meter, of a rambunctious, demoniac, or virtuoso character. Whereas the Classical minuet provided some respite for both the players and the listeners during a long work—after a serious first movement or a long, contemplative slow movement—the Romantic scherzo compounded the difficulties of getting through such a work because of its technical complexities, dramatic tension, and increased length.

For their movements in sonata-allegro form, Romantic composers customarily created different melodic subjects for first and second themes, rather than using a monothematic approach. Furthermore, the closing theme or closing thematic section of the sonata-allegro form was enlarged in the nineteenth century and became a third, very important, melodic idea within the movement. Around 1837 Beethoven's student and Liszt's teacher, the pianist Carl Czerny (1791–1857), wrote his *School of Practical Composition* (published in London in 1848–1849), a treatise on musical form, instrumentation, and other technical aspects of the art. Here he defined sonata form as a compositional design in two large parts (*exposition, development* plus *recapitulation*). The first part consisted of a *principal* subject, its continuation (or amplification) and a modulation (*bridge* section), a *middle* subject, its continuation, and a *final* subject. In other words, the Romantic sonata-allegro movement was described as having three equally important themes, with significant intervening passages.

In observing sonata forms of the Czerny era, we find that an exposition could be quite lengthy. Furthermore, it could contain developmental manipulations of themes, which Classicists had customarily saved for the development section proper, and introduce three or more stressed key-areas. One possible result of these practices was that the development section would contribute little of interest to the movement, since so much had already occurred in the exposition. Sometimes a composer would overcome the problems of the development section by truncating or eliminating it altogether.

Czerny was not the only important writer after Koch to discuss the sonata-allegro and related forms and issues in the music of his era. For example, the Bohemian composer Antoine Reicha (1770–1836) published a *Traité de haute composition musicale* ("Treatise on the Composition of Art Music," 1824–1826), in which he was among the first to provide a clear description of sonata form. The first protracted discussion of sonata form appeared in *Die Lehre von der musikalischen Komposition* ("The Teaching of Musical Composition," 1837–1847) by the German theorist and writer Adolf Bernhard Marx (1795–1866).

Program music

Nineteenth-century formal designs were also suited to the needs of composers of program music. Each movement could represent a different scene or episode in the story, as in the symphonies of Berlioz. Or each section of a single sonata-form movement might be equated with a given character or plot situation in a story, as in the tone poems of Liszt or Richard Strauss. The myriad techniques of development, refined by Haydn, Mozart, and Beethoven, also provided such operatic composers as Wagner and Richard Strauss with the structural foundations for their work.

Sectional forms

The *theme-and-variations* form in the nineteenth century was of two main types. Public audiences, flocking to solo recitals, were eager to listen to virtuosos play dazzling, technically overpowering variations on popular operatic or folk tunes. Such sets of variations were basically ornamental elaborations of the melody on which they were based, and the melody was still recognizable. But there were also more subtle Romantic variation movements in which the melody was heavily disguised: although the main harmonies and overall form of the theme would be preserved, the melody, rhythm, texture, dynamics, and—especially—the emotional expression were often so radically altered that the listener would be hard-pressed to recognize the original theme as the source of the variations. Such pieces are known as *character varia-*

tions, each variation acting like a *character piece.* Examples include the second movement of Beethoven's Sonata in C minor, Op. 111 (1821–1822), and Schumann's *Etudes symphoniques* ("Symphonic Etudes," 1834–1837, rev. 1852).

Ternary form was a favorite among the Romantics for slow movements in multimovement works, for songs, and for character pieces. The B-section in the middle of the piece offered a strong contrast in mood and movement to the surrounding A-sections. Other slow movements were in theme-and-variation form, binary form, or some type of sonata form, with or without a true development section. Such composers as Beethoven and Schubert began to impose sonata form even on their scherzos (e.g., Beethoven's and Schubert's last symphonies), and eventually other composers, too, used it for all the movements of a four-movement work.

Following Beethoven's lead (see p. 613), Romantic composers sometimes concluded multimovement works begun in a minor key with a triumphant finale in a major key. Mendelssohn's Symphony No. 3 (Scotch) in A minor (1842), Brahms's Symphony No. 1 in C minor (1855–1876), and Bruckner's Symphony No. 3 in D minor (1873–1877) are three examples. Beethoven also established the general trend of ending large-scale instrumental works with a rousing finale, as in his Seventh and Ninth symphonies, completed in 1812 and 1824, respectively. Some composers used choruses in their symphonic finales (Beethoven, Mahler), or made use of chorales and hymns (Mendelssohn, Bruckner). Others thickened the texture, increased the dynamic level, and enlarged the size of the orchestra for the final moments of a work (Liszt)—all in a striving for excitement.

Finales

Early Romantic operas were organized as a series of musical *numbers:* arias, ensembles, ballet music, and choruses, just as in the Classical era. But by the 1850s Wagner and Verdi, among others, were writing more continuous music throughout a scene or act (the *through-composed* approach). Recurring musical motives could also be used as unifying elements. Wagner's scenes were frequently a series of short musical forms strung together. The Romantic oratorio similarly moved away from organization by numbers toward a continuous format. The Mass and Requiem remained a series of separate movements, but they grew so long, complex, and difficult to perform that they became concert rather than strictly liturgical works.

Form in dramatic music

Mystery, imagination, improvisation, rhapsody, experimentation, the supernatural, synesthesia, and subjectivity—the elements of fantasy, as the nineteenth century regarded it—fascinated Romantic composers. Their musical fantasies were sometimes tone paintings, atmospheric pieces, improvisatory potpourris, or etudes, and at other times quasi-sonatas and the like, i.e., works bearing a strong resemblance to Classical types but making obvious dramatic departures from them. A few of the most memorable of these fantasy pieces are: Beethoven's *Sonata quasi una fantasia* ("Moonlight" Sonata) in C-sharp minor, Op. 27, No. 2 (1801), Schubert's *Fantasia* ("Wanderer") in C major, Op. 15, D. 760 (1822), Schumann's *Fantasia* in C major, Op. 17 (1836–1838), and his *Phantasiestücke* ("Fantasy Pieces"), Op. 12 (1837), Chopin's

Fantasy in the nineteenth century

Fantaisie in F minor, Op. 49 (1840–1841), and his *Polonaise Fantaisie,* Op. 61 (1845–1846), Berlioz's *Symphonie fantastique,* Liszt's *Hungarian Fantasia for Piano and Orchestra* (c. 1852), and Brahms's *Fantasien,* Op. 116 (1892).

Summary

Between the time of Beethoven and that of Richard Strauss, composers preserved most of the genres and compositional devices of the Classical era. However, the Romantics also added to these, rearranged certain of their elements, took advantage of improvements made in the instruments of the time, and squeezed out of Classicism's raw materials every last bit of musical sound imaginable within the framework of tonality.

Romantic melodies tended to be lyrical and long, and they were often irregularly phrased. In addition to the chords that had formed the harmonic basis of Classical compositions, Romantic composers exploited harmonies that employed chromatic voice-leading and provided the overall sonority of the music with a feeling of sensuousness and shifting colors. Modal mixture, emphasis on the minor mode, and increased use of dissonance were among the other compositional techniques popular throughout the nineteenth century, while a renewal of interest in the medieval modes arose in the Post-Romantic period.

Nineteenth-century composers moved away from the strong downbeat feeling that had been customary in the eighteenth century, and challenged the listener to grasp the new, more complex metrical organization of their music. Cross-rhythms and rubato helped give Romantic music its characteristic shifting rhythmic pulse.

During the Romantic period many instruments came into their own, including the piano, trumpet, horn, harp, and many types of percussion instruments. The sonorities of choirs of brasses, winds, and strings were used in contrast with one another. This was the age of the virtuoso orchestra, large in size and full of subtle nuances.

Some of the genres and forms preferred by Romantic composers were the four-movement sonata, the scherzo, character variations, triumphal finales, and fantasias. Classical sonata-allegro form underwent monumental expansion and, sometimes, extreme truncation. Three main themes became the rule in the exposition, as did thematic development and elaboration. Lieder and short instrumental character pieces tended to be in ternary form, as were most slow movements and dances.

Notes

1. F. E. Kirby, ed., *Music in the Classic Period: An Anthology with Commentary* (New York: Schirmer Books, 1979). (*MCP*)

2. Roger Kamien, ed., *The Norton Scores: An Anthology for Listening,* 3rd ed. (New York: W. W. Norton & Co., 1977). (*NS; S* represents the one-volume Standard edition, and *E* the two-volume Expanded edition)
   William J. Starr and George F. Devine, eds., *Music Scores Omnibus,* 2 vols. (Englewood Cliffs, N.J.: Prentice-Hall, 1964; vol. 1, 2nd ed., 1974). (*MSO*)
3. Claude V. Palisca, ed., *Norton Anthology of Western Music,* 2 vols. (New York: W. W. Norton & Co., 1980). (*NAWM: S* represents the one-volume Shorter edition)
4. Otto Eric Deutsch, *Schubert: A Documentary Biography,* translated by Eric Blom (London: J. M. Dent & Sons, 1946), p. 339.

Bibliography

Books and Articles

Instruments

Berlioz, Hector. *Treatise on Instrumentation,* revised and enlarged by Richard Strauss, translated by Theodore Front. New York: Edwin F. Kalmus, 1948.

Harding, Rosamond E. M. *The Piano-Forte: Its History Traced to the Great Exhibition of 1851.* Cambridge: Cambridge University Press, 1933; reprint, New York: Da Capo Press, 1973.

Romantic Style

Friedheim, Philip. "Berlioz and Rhythm." *The Music Review* 37 (Feb. 1976): 5–44.

————. "A Problem in Nineteenth-Century Musical Structure: The Approach to the Tonic." *The Music Review* 33 (May 1972): 81–92.

Jackson, Roland. "The 'Neapolitan Progression' in the Nineteenth Century." *The Music Review* 30 (Feb. 1969): 35–46.

Ratner, Leonard G. "Key Definition—A Structural Issue in Beethoven's Music." *Journal of the American Musicological Society* 23 (Fall 1970): 472–83.

Read, Gardner. *Style and Orchestration.* New York: Schirmer Books, 1979.

Rosen, Charles. *Sonata Forms.* New York: W. W. Norton & Co., 1980.

Salop, Arnold. *Studies on the History of Musical Style.* Detroit: Wayne State University Press, 1971.

Schenkman, Walter. "Combination of Themes as a Hallmark of Romantic Style." *Music Review* 37 (Aug. 1976): 171–92.

Schoenberg, Arnold. *Style and Idea: Selected Writings of Arnold Schoenberg,* edited by Leonard Stein, with translations by Leo Black. New York: St. Martin's Press, 1975.

Tovey, Donald. *Essays in Musical Analysis.* 7 vols. London: Oxford University Press, 1935–1944.

Scores: Editions of Complete Works of Major Romantic Composers

In instances where modern editions are not as yet complete, available older editions are also provided.

Beethoven, Ludwig van, *Werke,* ed. Selmar Bagge et al. Leipzig: Breitkopf & Härtel, 1864–1890.

————, *Supplemente zur Gesamtausgabe,* ed. Willy Hess. Wiesbaden: Breitkopf & Härtel, 1959–1971.

————, *Werke,* ed. Joseph Schmidt-Görg et al. Munich-Duisburg: G. Henle Verlag, 1961– .

BERLIOZ, HECTOR, *Werke,* ed. Charles Malherbe and Felix Weingartner. Leipzig: Breitkopf & Härtel, 1900–1907.

————, *New Edition of the Complete Works,* ed. Wilfrid Mellers et al. Kassel: Bärenreiter, 1967– .

BRAHMS, JOHANNES, *Sämtliche Werke,* ed. Hans Gál and Eusebius Mandyczewski. Leipzig: Breitkopf & Härtel, 1926–1928; revised Wiesbaden: Breitkopf & Härtel, 1965–

BRUCKNER, ANTON, *Sämtliche Werke,* ed. Robert Haas et al. Vienna: Musikwissenschaftlicher Verlag der Internationalen Bruckner-Gesellschaft, 1930–1944.

————, *Sämtliche Werke,* ed. Leopold Nowak. Vienna: Musikwissenschaftlicher Verlag der Internationalen Bruckner-Gesellschaft, 1951– .

CHOPIN, FRÉDÉRIC, *Complete Works,* ed. Ignacy Paderewski et al. Warsaw: Fryderyk Chopin Institute, 1949–1962.

DVOŘÁK, ANTONÍN, *Complete Edition,* ed. Otakar Šoureck et al. Prague: Czechoslovakian National Music Publishers, 1955– .

LISZT, FRANZ, *Musikalische Werke,* ed. Ferruccio Busoni et al. Leipzig: Breitkopf & Härtel, 1901–1936.

————, *Neue Ausgabe sämtlicher Werke,* ed. Zoltan Gárdonyi and István Szelényi. Kassel: Bärenreiter, 1970– .

MAHLER, GUSTAV, *Sämtliche Werke,* ed. International Gustav Mahler Society. Vienna: Universal-Edition, 1960–

MENDELSSOHN, FELIX, *Werke,* ed. Julius Rietz. Leipzig: Breitkopf & Härtel, 1874–1877.

————, *Leipziger Ausgabe der Werke,* ed. International Felix Mendelssohn Society. Leipzig: VEB Deutscher Verlag für Musik, 1960– .

MUSSORGSKY, MODEST, *Complete Works,* ed. Paul Lamm. Moscow: Soviet National Music Publishers, 1928–1934.

SCHUBERT, FRANZ, *Werke,* ed. Johannes Brahms et al. Leipzig: Breitkopf & Härtel, 1884–1897.

————, *Neue Ausgabe sämtlicher Werke,* ed. Walther Dürr et al. Kassel: Bärenreiter, 1964– .

SCHUMANN, ROBERT, *Werke,* ed. Clara Schumann. Leipzig: Breitkopf & Härtel, 1881–1893.

TCHAIKOVSKY, PETER ILYICH, *The Complete Works.* Moscow: Soviet National Music Publishers, 1940–?

WAGNER, RICHARD, *Musikalische Werke,* ed. Michael Balling. Leipzig: Breitkopf & Härtel, 1912–c. 1929.

————, *Sämtliche Werke,* ed. Carl Dahlhaus. Mainz: B. Schott's Söhne, 1970– .

25

Romantic Music For Orchestra

AYDN and Mozart bequeathed to the nineteenth century nearly 150 symphonies, but these were only rarely provided with extramusical meanings or descriptive titles. Classical composers required listeners to concentrate on the contrasting tempos and moods of the symphony and on its sectional and developmental forms. While many nineteenth-century composers also wrote absolute symphonies, they sometimes provided a text, a title, or both, which revealed the inspirational source or character of the work. Certain symphonies contain local or exotic color, like Borodin's Symphony No. 2 in B minor (1869–1876); others seem to transcend the confines of absolute music through the very intensity of their expression, as in Beethoven's Fifth Symphony, a musical reflection of the struggles and determination of Beethoven himself.

The Absolute Symphony and Its Romantic Extensions

Beethoven

Few sets of works in the history of music have been as successful as the symphonies of the German composer Ludwig van Beethoven, who was born in Bonn in 1770 and died in Vienna in 1827. His Symphony No. 1 in C major (1800) is quite Classical, although even in this he reveals a new spirit by: (1) writing a scherzo for the dance movement, even though he bowed to tradition by calling it a minuet; (2) lengthening the outer movements with substantial codas; and, most of all, (3) postponing the initial tonic chord in the introduction to the first movement (see Example 25.1).

Symphony No. 2 in D major (1801–1802) is closer to the Romantic spirit, with its long introduction to the first movement, sonorous *cantabile* slow movement, full-blooded, confessed "scherzo," and boisterous finale, whose coda is twice the length of its development section. The motivic fragmenta-

Symphonies Nos. 1 and 2

611

Ex. 25.1   Ludwig van Beethoven, Symphony No. 1 in C major, Mvt. 1, mm. 1–4

tion, syncopation, *sforzandi,* trills, and relentless rhythmic drive toward the end all contribute to the humor of the finale.

Beethoven's first two symphonies, dating from what is generally called his first stylistic period, are steeped in the Classical style. However, it was during his second creative stage (c. 1802–c. 1812) that most of his symphonies (Nos. 3–8) were written. They stress certain features in Beethoven's developing style: energetic, fast tempos; syncopation; heavy accentuation; a tendency toward a slow harmonic rhythm when the note-values themselves are extremely short; a preference for scherzos over minuets; extreme dynamic ranges; abrupt changes of mood; a robust sense of humor; elements of suspense and drama (e.g., long rests, outbursts of *tutti* sound, deceptive cadences, false recapitulations); lengthy development sections and codas; and an uncanny ability to develop the most basic motives into large structures.

The *Eroica* Symphony   Never before Beethoven's Symphony No. 3 (*Eroica*) in E-flat major (1803) had a symphony been conceived on such a grand scale (see *MCP,* no. 26; second movement in *NAWM* II, no. 114). We have little doubt that Beethoven intended to dedicate it to Napoleon, the hero who, Beethoven thought, would champion the cause of liberty. However, when Napoleon violated the principles of the French Revolution by having himself crowned emperor, Beethoven apparently "punished" the strongest man in Europe by erasing his name from the title page and giving the symphony a subtitle: "To celebrate the memory of a great man." The music in this symphony speaks of heroism. The preponderance of triadic themes and the prominence of three, rather than the usual two, horns (instruments historically associated with royalty) imbue this work with a feeling of majesty.

Two powerful tonic chords introduce the first movement; then a triadic theme is begun by the cellos. This simple theme becomes for Beethoven the target of kaleidoscopic development and variation treatment. Despite the great length and diversity of the exposition, it is the development section that is the most striking. Nearly 250 measures in length (of a total 691), the intense development is a study in the alternation between tonal equilibrium, on the one hand, and enormous increases in tension, on the other. It also features a theme not heard in the exposition, although comprised of elements that were.

New material in a development section was not Beethoven's innovation (Mozart, for example, had done this often), but its return in the coda was. The slow variation movement of the *Eroica* is grander than any funeral march predating 1803. In a tragic C minor, it can be imagined as a fitting tribute to the victims of the Napoleonic Wars and a lament over lost hopes for a better life. The trio of the restless scherzo highlights triadic fanfares in the horns. In the finale Beethoven invokes a theme that he had used three times previously since 1800—in a ballet, a group of orchestral dances, and a set of variations for piano. In the symphonic finale he unfolds a monumental series of variations with episodes in a fugal style and ends with an extensive coda.

Beethoven's Symphony No. 5 in C minor (1807–1808; *MSO* I, p. 313; *NS*, E, I, no. 36; *NS*, S, no. 20) is probably the most famous symphony ever written. It is also the first symphony to use trombones (three in the finale). The opening four notes of the symphony are a rhythmic and melodic motive unifying not only the first movement but also the symphony as a whole. The designation bestowed upon a work whose movements are related by a recognizable motive is *cyclic* or *cyclical*. In the mysterious scherzo a *pianissimo* dynamic level predominates, and a novel pizzicato string sound is presented after the trio. In this trio the low strings are afforded what was then the rare opportunity of articulating speedy thematic material. In one of the most exciting orchestral crescendos of all time, the scherzo leads directly into the finale (with no pause between them). After Beethoven's "Fifth" it became difficult for composers to avoid concluding minor-mode symphonies *without* turning to the major for an effect of triumph or catharsis.

The Fifth Symphony

The Symphony No. 6 (*Pastoral*) in F major (1808) is the closest Beethoven came to writing a programmatic symphony, but it does not depict specific events or people. Dubbing it a *sinfonia caracteristica* ("characteristic symphony"), the composer insisted in its inscription that it was "more an expression of feelings than tone-painting." He adored the Viennese countryside and wished to suggest its moods in music. With a specific title for each movement, the work has vivid representations of birdcalls at the end of "Scene at the Brook" and a fine thunderstorm in the fourth movement.

The Pastoral Symphony

Beginning with an open fifth, the first movement immediately establishes a rustic atmosphere, further suggested by the slow harmonic rhythm, limited harmonic range, key of F major, and repetitions of simple phrases (e.g., the tenfold reiteration of a gentle little motive in mm. 16–25, all above a pedal on V). In the development section Beethoven prolongs various harmonies for up to twenty-eight measures, creating a sensation of meandering, as if through the countryside. "Scene at the Brook" is also pastoral, with its $\frac{12}{8}$ meter, lingering tunes, unhurried modulation to the second theme, and interruptions in the coda for birdcalls. The third, fourth, and fifth movements are played without interruption. "Merry Gathering of the Country Folk" (movement 3) is a boisterous scherzo, and its trio uses duple meter (unconventional in symphonic dance movements) for a raucous peasant dance. The ensuing "Thunderstorm" makes its effect through massive crescendos, string tremolos, and brass and woodwind outbursts. The fifth movement expresses everyone's feelings of thanksgiving after the storm subsides. The *Pastoral* Symphony was premiered at the same concert as the Fifth: on December 22, 1808.

**The
Seventh
Symphony**

Beethoven's Symphony No. 7 in A major (1811–1812) was called "an apotheosis of the dance" by Wagner. Its compelling rhythmic drive, especially in the relentless finale, is as memorable as the themes themselves, and the continuity in the first movement points to the late nineteenth century. The Allegretto is a haunting example of variation technique.

**The Ninth
Symphony**

The Symphony No. 9 in D minor (1822–1824) is representative of Beethoven's final stylistic period (1816–1827). During these years he showed great interest in fugal procedures, the art of variation, the disruption of continuity (a feature of fantasy), the exhaustive working-out of motivic materials, and the camouflaging of the beginnings and endings of phrases, themes, sections, and, ultimately, entire movements. His late works are often reflective, using improvisatory passages, instrumental recitatives and ariosos, and written-out cadenzas.

Each movement of the "Ninth" is a pinnacle of symphonic expression. The first movement is an immense sonata-allegro, exhibiting a culmination of Beethoven's ability to achieve organic growth. From the first sounds, with their ambiguous mode, tonal center, melodic shape, and rhythmic organization, this gigantic movement relies on the dramatic use of mysterious sonorities, abrupt and extreme changes in dynamics, syncopation, and rhythmic momentum, at the expense of long or well-profiled themes. Furthermore, the multitude of transitional and developmental episodes obscures the "seams" of the sonata form thoroughly, as the musical "connective tissue" that separates themes receives more attention than the themes themselves.

Breaking ground in symphonic history because of its full-fledged sonata-allegro form, the *Molto vivace* second movement is the epitome of the frenzied Beethoven scherzo. It is linked motivically to its trio, whose opening idea is derived from the C-major second theme of the scherzo. The struggle for supremacy between D minor and D major in the first two movements, with the minor persisting in both cases, makes the turn to D major in the finale especially bright and satisfying.

Illustrating the Romantic preference for relating keys a third apart from each other, the *Adagio molto e cantabile* third movement is one of Beethoven's most lyrical pieces. It begins as a double set of variations—i.e., two themes are presented and then varied in turn—but after the second tune is varied just once, it is dropped.

A tour de force for performers and listeners alike, the finale alone is as long as all four movements in a Classical symphony had been just a quarter of a century earlier. This finale uses certain stanzas from Schiller's *Ode an die Freude* ("Ode to Joy," 1785). In this manner Beethoven adds extramusical meaning to the symphony, as a chorus and four solo voices sing the text's messages of love, joy, and brotherhood. Never before had the human voice been employed in a symphony. However, the most unusual aspect of this finale is its formal design, for it can be viewed simultaneously as a theme and variations, a rondo (in either case, with a lengthy introduction and coda), and

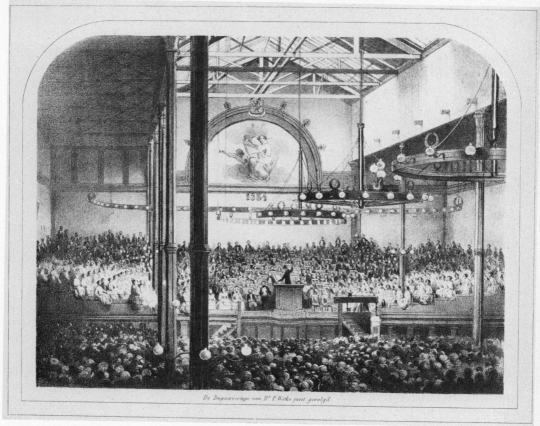

De Daguerreotype van D.ʳ P. Wetke juist gevolgd

C. C. A. Last, *Performance of Beethoven's 9th Symphony under Johannes Verhulst* (1854 lithograph). The choral finale of Beethoven's Ninth, first performed in 1824, involved the largest gathering of instrumentalists and singers in symphonic history to that date. (Collection Haags Gemeentemuseum, The Hague)

a concerto for voices and orchestra. Furthermore, it may be looked upon as a through-composed succession of four movements (a fast opening one, a dance, a slow piece, and a fast finale), serving as the prototype for such later works as Liszt's Concerto No. 1 for Piano and Orchestra in E-flat major (1849, rev. 1853, 1856) and his Sonata in B minor (1852–1853) for piano. We may even regard it as a cantata, with its mix of orchestral, choral, and solo sections, as well as its spiritual and Masonic themes.

Schubert

Vienna at the time of Beethoven and Schubert was exhausted from the Napoleonic Wars and craved peace and pleasure. During this age, many composers merely provided Viennese audiences with lighthearted entertainment music. The native-born Franz Schubert (1797–1828), however, combined the melodiousness and ingenuousness of the popular Viennese style with the profundity of the great Classical symphonists. Like Beethoven, he altered the nature of the symphony, and influenced many future symphonists with his novel approaches to thematic and structural expansion and truncation, and with his colorful use of the orchestra.

The first six symphonies
Between the ages of sixteen and twenty-one, Schubert composed his first six symphonies (1813–1818). They reflect the influence of Haydn, Mozart, Beethoven, Rossini, and such French operatic composers as Cherubini. Themes are lyrical and leisurely, with echo effects and much repetition, and long static passages often create a type of "atmospheric" tension, signifying that something new and important is imminent. Stressing harmonic and tonal variety rather than thematic growth in his sonata-form developments, Schubert often devotes these sections to the second (more tuneful) theme, as in the outer movements of both his symphonies in D major, No. 1 (1813) and No. 3 (1815). In his first six symphonies, he shows relatively little interest in such Classical procedures as thematic inversion, diminution, fragmentation, and recombination. Nor does he tend to take themes apart and then reconstruct them, since motivic ingredients are usually difficult to disengage from lyrical themes. Rather, he extends and expands his already full-blown themes. This practice is largely responsible for the "heavenly length" (a term coined by Robert Schumann in his review of Schubert's last complete symphony) of many of his movements.

In the finale of Schubert's Third Symphony, the tarantella rhythm, along with the restless succession of chords and figurations, repetitions of cadential patterns, crescendos, and *tutti* explosions, brings to mind Rossini's overtures. Extremely popular in Vienna at this time, Rossini's music also influenced Schubert's two overtures "in the Italian style" (D. 590 and D. 591, 1817) and his Symphony No. 6 in C major (1817–1818). Schubert's Symphony No. 5 in B-flat major (1816) has the same instrumentation (no clarinets, trumpets, or timpani) as the original version of Mozart's Symphony No. 40; furthermore, their minuet movements are both in G minor, and Schubert's opening thematic gesture seems modeled on Mozart's. The opening movement of Schubert's Fifth Symphony is very tightly constructed. Its initial four measures, when first heard, sound like a conventional "curtain-raiser," not related thematically to the remainder of the movement. Yet the development section is based in part upon the third and fourth measures of the piece. Such integration of a short opening idea into the further progress of a movement, which reaches a zenith in the first movement of his Symphony No. 7 (*Unfinished Symphony*) in B minor, is one of Schubert's most Romantic traits.

The Unfinished Symphony
In 1822 Schubert approached the symphony in an altogether new way, as an utterly Romantic work, with tuneful melodies, bursts of passion, and poetic uses of the orchestra. The first eight bars of the *Unfinished Symphony*, in which the cellos and basses play a brooding melody *pianissimo*, progress like an introduction in slow-moving note-values, but they are in the *allegro moderato* tempo and present the thematic ideas basic to the development and coda. As such, they are not an introduction but rather a thematic motto (a similar situation occurs in the first movement of Bruckner's Symphony No.

9 in D minor, completed in 1896). Schubert's subtle rhythmic and harmonic manipulations are revealed by the songful first theme of this movement in $\frac{3}{4}$ time. He creates rhythmic intrigue by dividing the $\frac{3}{4}$ measures in half, and skillfully moves away from the tonic after a mere eight bars, only to return to it immediately. The second theme of the movement is one of Schubert's most singable instrumental melodies. In a Romantic vein, however, it is interrupted, first by a warning measure of silence and then by an orchestral outburst that lasts nine measures before yielding to the former state of quietude. These bars are compelling in that although they disrupt the theme in terms of dynamics, texture, and mood, they continue it motivically (see Example 25.2). Unresolved tensions and unstable chord progressions govern the development section, which is as complex harmonically as any other music from the first half of the nineteenth century.

Schubert returned to a more Classical orientation for his Symphony No. 8 (*Great Symphony*) in C major (1825–1826). Yet from the opening horn theme, the work's Beethovenian conceptions of grandiosity and energy are coated with the harmonic and orchestral colors of the nineteenth century. Schubert's love of melody permeates the slow movement, which is related to the corresponding movement of Beethoven's Seventh Symphony in that both of these A-minor pieces move forward slowly but steadily, with marchlike continuity, and reach passionate climaxes. Contributing to the "heavenly length" of Schubert's music is his leisurely enjoyment of harmony, exemplified during the coda of the *Andante con moto.* En route to a tonic cadence, he takes a tangential path, harmonizing an ostinato melodic motive, maintained by the clarinet, in myriad ways (see Example 25.3).

The Great Symphony

Mendelssohn

The symphonies of Felix Mendelssohn (1809–1847) show Classical control of form and proportions, and are largely diatonic, *cantabile,* and periodic, with sections of impressive counterpoint. Mendelssohn's Symphony No. 3 (*Scotch*) in A minor (1842) and Symphony No. 4 (*Italian*) in A major (1833) convey his sentimental and passionate impressions of landscapes. The *Scotch* Symphony is interesting because its four movements are linked thematically and connected without a break. However, the *Italian* Symphony is a more popular work, containing ebullient rhythms in its outer movements, especially the saltarello finale, and great tenderness in the processional *Andante con moto.* Mendelssohn's Symphony No. 5 (*Reformation*) in D minor (1832)

Ex. 25.2 Franz Schubert, *Unfinished Symphony,* Mvt. 1, mm. 60–68

The bracketed motive is derived from the first two notes of the second theme.

Ex. 25.3   Franz Schubert, *Great Symphony*, Mvt. 2, mm. 338–342, schematic

This quality of lingering sets many Romantic compositions apart from the ever-building intensity of most late-eighteenth-century music.

makes use of the Lutheran chorale *Ein feste Burg ist unser Gott* ("A Mighty Fortress Is Our God").

Schumann

Robert Schumann (1810–1856) came to the symphony in 1841, after composing dozens of piano works and Lieder. He was so much a pianistic thinker that his orchestration fell short of the breathtaking levels reached by Schubert, Mendelssohn, and Berlioz. Nonetheless, Schumann's symphonies show inspired themes and rhythmic energy, as in the opening theme of the Symphony No. 3 (*Rhenish*) in E-flat major (1850), with its magnificent opposition of $\frac{3}{4}$ and $\frac{3}{2}$ meters. This work, depicting scenes of life in the Rhineland, is modeled on the Mendelssohnian notion of the landscape. Schumann's Symphonies No. 1 (*Spring*) in B-flat major (1841), No. 2 in C major (1845–1846), and No. 4 in D minor (1841, rev. 1851) are fashioned after Beethoven's motivic, cyclical approach. The *Spring* Symphony was inspired by a poem about springtime by Adolph Böttger (1815–1870).

The Fourth Symphony of Schumann is a masterpiece of motivic manipulation and cyclical form, and the four movements are played without intervening pauses. The first motive heard in the slow introduction returns to propel the first theme of the opening movement's much truncated sonata-allegro form (the movement has no discrete recapitulation). Furthermore, this same motive governs the middle section of the ternary *Romanza*, gives birth to the trio in the third movement, and yields the finale's slow introduction, as well as some of the accompaniment figures in the first theme (see Example 25.4).

Schumann considered calling this work a symphonic fantasia, probably because of its deviations from Classical symphonic form.

Bruckner

Symphonic activity continued in Vienna with the work of the Austrian Anton Bruckner and the German-born Johannes Brahms, and later with the Austrian Gustav Mahler. A professor of organ and counterpoint, Bruckner (1824–1896) was influenced profoundly by Wagner, Beethoven, and Schubert. From his idol, Wagner, he adopted the huge orchestra, as well as a late-Romantic harmonic language. From Beethoven—especially the Ninth Symphony—he learned of the immense proportions the symphonic genre could sustain, the cyclical approach, and the value of an ambiguous opening and an uplifting finale. Yet the greatest influence on Bruckner was his compatriot

Ex. 25.4   Robert Schumann, Symphony No. 4 in D minor

(a) **Ziemlich langsam** (first movement, introduction, mm. 2-5)

(b) **Lebhaft** (first movement, first theme, mm. 29-32)

(c) (second movement, middle section, mm. 26-30)

Ex. 25.4   cont.

(d) **Trio** (third movement, mm. 65-73)

(e) **Langsam** (fourth movement, introduction, mm. 1-3)

(f) **Lebhaft** (fourth movement, first theme, mm. 17-18)

Schubert, for both emphasized the use of folk-like and attractive tunes, sequential repetitions of themes in development sections, modulations to keys a whole tone away, and long melodies.

Starting with his Symphony No. 2 in C minor (1871–1872), Bruckner seems to have adopted a "method" for writing symphonies. In addition to the mysterious opening, a Bruckner symphonic movement in sonata form tends to possess a first theme based on a triad or open fifth, a $\frac{4}{4}$ rhythmic pattern in which two quarter notes are followed by three quarter-note triplets, a song-like second theme, a chorale-like closing theme, and a coda combining all the themes. His hymn-like slow movements are also in a variant of sonata form, and his dance movements consist of a weighty but energetic scherzo and a trio steeped in Austrian dances and popular tunes. Bruckner's Symphony No. 4 (*Romantic*) in E-flat major (1874, rev. 1878–1880, 1886) at one time contained some programmatic descriptions, but in the Beethoven-Schubert vein he deleted them. His last three symphonies, Nos. 7–9 (1881–1896), use the Wagner tuba, a special brass instrument created for use in Wagner's *Ring,* whose tone quality lies somewhere between a horn's and a tuba's.

Brahms

Stymied for years by his fear of falling below the standards set by Beethoven, Johannes Brahms (1833–1897) ultimately completed four symphonic masterpieces within a decade. These absolute works display Brahms's deliberate, painstaking approach to the genre. Like Beethoven, he was a master of motivic development, and his music sounds even more concentrated than Beethoven's. For example, the motive D–C#–D permeates his Symphony No. 2 in D major (1877). The symphonies all demonstrate Brahms's combination of Romantic expressiveness, harmony, and instrumental color with Classical proportions and meticulousness of formal design. The last movement of his Symphony No. 4 in E minor (1884–1885), a magnificent chaconne, is a contrapuntal tour de force.

The hallmarks of Brahms's style include: (1) long, often asymmetrical melodies; (2) subtle manipulations of rhythm; (3) a somber orchestration, featuring the lower instruments, and doubled thirds in these low voices, resulting in a dense texture; and (4) a predilection for mediant, submediant, and especially subdominant chords and tonal regions, secondary dominants, modal mixture, chromatic alteration, and, on occasion, Church modes (as, for example, in his Symphony No. 4, whose slow movement uses Phrygian relationships). One of his contributions to symphonic history is the lyrical and graceful third movement, found in each of his first three symphonies; these movements are similar to some of his intermezzos for piano. Brahms also relates the keys of the movements in an original way; for example, in the stormy Symphony No. 1 in C minor (1855–1876; *MSO* II, p. 116) the keys proceed by major thirds: C minor, E major, A-flat (enharmonic G-sharp) major, and C minor and major.

Symphony No. 3 in F minor (1883; *NS*, E, II, no. 15; *NS*, S, no. 33) is an example of Brahms's style. It contains a broad, passionate first movement, employing much major-minor mixture and cross-rhythm, as at the very opening; an idyllic second movement; a wistfully graceful third; and an energetic, sometimes turbulent, finale, using a chorale-like theme near the end as a prelude to the return of the symphony's opening theme. The main motive in this symphony consists of the notes F–A♭–F, derived from Brahms's philosophical motto: "*frei aber froh*" ("free but happy").

Tchaikovsky

Without actually joining the nationalistic movement, Peter Ilyich Tchaikovsky (1840–1893) filled his symphonies with traces of Russian folk songs, as in his Symphony No. 2 (*Little Russian*) in C minor (1872, rev. 1879–1880) and Symphony No. 4 in F minor (1877–1878). He also employed such Russian traits as motivic repetition and frequent melodic leaps. Nonetheless, Tchaikovsky's symphonies are steeped in the Western European tradition and give evidence of their composer's emotional, lyrical impulse and his seemingly limitless melodic inventiveness. As an orchestrator Tchaikovsky was very sensitive and skilled. His grouping of allied tone colors, his fondness for

pizzicato strings and octave doubling in strings (and winds), and his preference for the lower register of the wind instruments are all in evidence in the
scherzo of the Fourth Symphony. This work, plus No. 5 in E minor (1888)
and No. 6 (*Pathétique*) in B minor (1893), are his most popular. The first two
possess a motto theme and therefore a cyclical structure. The *Pathétique,* a
hauntingly poignant work, is unusual in containing a waltz movement in $\frac{5}{4}$
time and in concluding with an Adagio fourth movement. Five of Tchaikovsky's six symphonies are in a minor key, and all create tension as much
from accented melodic dissonance as from harmonic progression.

Dvořák

Championed enthusiastically by Brahms, the Bohemian Antonín Dvořák
(1841–1904) was another symphonist who created beautiful melodies and
subtle orchestrations, as in the slow movement of his Symphony No. 6 in D
major (1880). His forms are more Classical than Tchaikovsky's, but his nationalistic spirit was stronger. For example, his symphonies contain such Bohemian elements as dance (e.g., furiant and polka) rhythms; rhythmic figures
in which an accented short note is followed by a much longer note; and scales
with notes omitted. Dvořák is best known for the Symphony No. 9 in E
minor (1893), which he composed while in residence in the United States.
Entitled *From the New World,* it is, however, as much influenced by Czech
music as by Negro spirituals or American Indian tunes (Dvořák was interested in Indian and Black history and culture at this time). The themes in
this piece are tuneful, making an immediate and lasting appeal. Add to this
fine melodic sense a facility with cross-rhythms (e.g., in the furiant-scherzo
of the Sixth Symphony), modal mixture, and chromatic and enharmonic harmony, and we have the special Dvořák sound. It is nowhere more poignant
than in the waltz-like scherzo and trio from his Symphony No. 8 in G major
(1889), a piece imbued with a sense of rhapsodic improvisation.

Sibelius

The seven symphonies of the Finnish composer Jean Sibelius (1865–
1957), composed between 1899 and 1924, vary greatly, since his interests and
the influences on him underwent great changes during these years. From an
absorption with Russian music and Finnish folklore in the 1890s, he became
fascinated with Beethoven and the notion of organic development in the next
decade, the time of his most popular symphony, No. 2 in D major (1901–
1902). His later music became more subjective and abstract, though no less
expertly constructed. His exquisitely designed symphonies are scored with
preferences for the bass register (like Brahms) and allied timbres (like Tchaikovsky). Free of actual Finnish folk melodies, they do, however, contain
some modality, a Finnish trait. One by one Sibelius introduces his motives;
they then gradually become intertwined to produce finally an immense, often
solemn, mass of sound, whose texture is heavy but clear.

Sibelius felt himself a slave to his themes, and in this regard he was a spiritual descendant of Beethoven and Brahms. However, more like Schubert and Berlioz, Sibelius designed themes in terms of timbre, and his orchestration is successful in suggesting landscapes, as it emphasizes soft sustained chords in the brasses, mixed string harmonies, long pedal points, the lower register of the oboe for melodies, muted tremolo strings, and solo trombone or trumpet passages.

Mahler

From Bruckner, his teacher, Gustav Mahler (1860–1911) learned how to handle the large dimensions of the symphony. Bruckner may also have inspired Mahler to include marches in his works, to build up slowly to great climaxes, and to change tonalities abruptly. But unlike Bruckner, Mahler was a great conductor, a director of the New York Philharmonic and the Metropolitan Opera Orchestra during his final years. Mahler knew exactly what an orchestra could do well, and as a composer he demanded much of both or-

Richard Jack, *Arthur Nikisch at a Rehearsal with the London Symphony* (1912). The age of great conductors like Nikisch (1855–1922) witnessed a new emphasis on painstaking rehearsals, necessitated by the orchestral complexities in the scores of such composers as Mahler and Richard Strauss. (The Tate Gallery, London)

chestra and conductor. His scores are full of indications for dynamics, phrasing, and tempo. Furthermore, Mahler never found a pattern for the symphony that satisfied him for long. Throughout his career he experimented with its design and nature, resorting at various times to texts, human voices, and extramusical ideas. All of these occur in his monumental Symphony No. 8 (*Symphony of a Thousand*) in E-flat major (1906), whose two long choral movements use as texts the plainsong hymn *Veni creator spiritus* and the closing scene of Part II of Goethe's *Faust,* respectively.

Mahler represents a coalescence, in a sense a recapitulation, of the entire nineteenth century. His orchestration is large and colorful, his music is governed by melodic invention, and a folk influence is readily apparent. His works contain chorales, marches, and Ländler, as well as eerie, diabolical, melancholy, and brooding moments (the latter, perhaps, having to do with Mahler's fascination with and enormous fear of death). As a student and admirer of the music of Beethoven, Liszt, and Wagner, Mahler knew well how to vary, develop, and transform themes and how to interrelate the various movements of a symphony. And no one was better than Mahler in fusing the elements of song and symphony.

We find a bittersweet taste to Mahler's harmonizations of melodies, and sometimes to the melodies themselves. He distorts melody for special effect, mixing major and minor versions and harmonizations continuously. A memorable example is the slow movement of his Symphony No. 1 (*Titan*) in D major (c. 1884–1888, rev. 1893–1896), a distortion of the French round *Frère Jacques.* In the scherzo of his intimate Symphony No. 4 in G major (1892, 1899–1900, rev. 1901–1910; fourth movement in *NS, E,* II, no. 20; *NS, S,* no. 37) he even uses a scordatura tuning for solo violin to suggest a medieval fiddle playing an eerie Dance of Death. Symphony No. 4, with its song-finale, is of further interest in that it begins and remains primarily in the key of G major but ends in E major; in several of his other symphonies, too, Mahler ends in a different key from the original.

Symphony No. 2   Symphony No. 2 (*Resurrection*) in C minor (1888–1894, rev. 1903) clearly illustrates Mahler's style. The opening *Allegro maestoso,* proceeding like a funeral march, with a heavy beat, oppressive rhythms, tremolo string passages, and orchestral outbursts, is a sonata-form movement with a concentrated development section and a compressed recapitulation. After a lilting Ländler comes a busy scherzo, whose melody is derived from a sardonic Mahler song, *Des Antonius von Padua Fischpredigt* ("St. Anthony's Sermon to the Fishes," 1893), one of his settings of *Des Knaben Wunderhorn.* Another setting from this collection of folk poetry gives rise to the fourth movement, *Urlicht* ("Original Light"), for alto solo and orchestra. The music used to set the words *Ich bin von Gott* ("I am from God") becomes part of the texted finale, inspired by a resurrection ode of the German poet Friedrich Gottlieb Klopstock (1724–1803). Set for soprano and alto soloists, chorus, and orchestra, these words of salvation and belief dispel the earlier abandon of the finale, and the C-minor symphony ends peacefully in E-flat major.

Extramusical Influences from Beethoven to Richard Strauss

Programmatic music is as old as music itself. Yet only during the nineteenth century did it become common for instrumental music to attempt to convey a story or a scene vividly to an audience. Then, as a full-fledged type of composition, program music rose to a position of great importance.

Beethoven was the fountainhead of Romantic program music. His programmatic concert overtures set a trend for such future works as Mendelssohn's overture to *A Midsummer Night's Dream* (1826; *NS*, E, II, no. 5). Often such works served as the first number in a set of pieces performed before and between the acts of a play and during some of its scenes, and they were therefore known as *incidental music*.

Concert overtures and incidental music

Berlioz

Hector Berlioz (1803–1869) was really the "father" of the *program symphony,* that is, an orchestral work in several movements, roughly parallel in form and tempo to those of an absolute symphony, with each reflecting one portion of the extramusical "program." The well-read Berlioz, a fine writer himself, especially liked the plays of Shakespeare, Goethe's *Faust,* Vergil's epics, and English Gothic novels. He believed in the supremacy of instrumental music, the incomparable greatness of Beethoven's symphonies, and the necessity of tying a musical composition to a literary idea. His doctrine was that a program helps listeners understand a symphony just as spoken dialogue helps them comprehend the musical numbers in an opera.

Berlioz wrote a literary program for the 1830 audience to read before listening to the music of his *Symphonie fantastique* (fourth movement in *NS,* E, II, no. 4; *NS*, S, no. 24; fifth movement in *MSO* II, p. 74). In this highly subjective work the hero clearly represents the composer himself. At this time Berlioz was infatuated with the English actress Harriet Smithson (1800–1854; later to become his wife), and similarly, the hero in the symphony, under the influence of opium, is lovesick for an elusive woman. This work deserves the modifier *fantastique* because it contains: (1) a program, written by Berlioz; (2) five full-fledged, separate movements; and (3) a recurrent musical motive, termed an *idée fixe* by the composer, which represents the beloved woman pursued by the hero, and which appears in every movement of the work, thereby unifying it in a wholly new manner.

The *Symphonie fantastique*

The *Symphonie fantastique* is a striking example of Berlioz's colorful and virtuoso use of the orchestra. Equally striking in this respect are his symphony-concerto *Harold in Italy* (1834), with its part for solo viola, and the seven-movement *Roméo et Juliette* (1839). The former contains many impressive moments, including the slow introduction in a double-fugue style; the pilgrims' march, in which serene harmony contrasts with dissonant pedal points and harmonic friction; and the finale, whose opening section is patterned structurally after the beginning of the finale of Beethoven's Ninth

Berlioz's style

Symphony. *Roméo et Juliette* (scherzo in *NAWM* II, no. 125) uses a chorus, but its most poignant moments, such as Romeo's solo meditation, the ball, and the love and death scenes, are reserved for the orchestra alone.

Among Berlioz's most important characteristics are long, asymmetrical melodies, often reharmonized at their return; contrapuntal combinations of themes, including fugal sections; rhythmic elasticity, achieved through syncopation, cross-rhythms, unusual meters, and an avoidance of downbeat stress; formal organization based as much on rhythm, tempo, and melodic activity as on tonality; and a predilection for bass motion by a third and for modulation accomplished by means of diminished-seventh chords. The imaginative Berlioz occasionally shocked his audiences, as during the vulgarly varied *Dies irae* (the Requiem sequence) in the Underworld scene of the *Symphonie fantastique*.

Liszt

Hungarian-born Franz Liszt (1811–1886)—who was influenced greatly by Berlioz—developed the *symphonic poem,* or *tone poem,* a single, through-composed movement that relates extramusical ideas. It was no doubt an outgrowth of the overture. Whereas Berlioz, who could not play the piano, was a master orchestrator, Liszt, a piano virtuoso, needed outside help in orchestrating his works. Although he was in the mainstream of Romantic composers who organized their works around key relationships, Liszt nonetheless altered the nature of harmonic and tonal organization so drastically that his music, along with Richard Wagner's, became known as "the new music" or "the music of the future."

Liszt's thirteen tone poems are based on such works as Goethe's play *Tasso* (1789), Hugo's poem *Mazeppa* (1828), Shakespeare's *Hamlet* (c. 1600), and a fresco by Wilhelm von Kaulbach (1805–1874) entitled *Hunnenschlacht* ("The Battle of the Huns," 1834–1837). The composer's best-known tone poem is *Les Préludes* (1848, rev. before 1854), whose original version was to have been an actual prelude to one of his own uncompleted choral works. The score of the revised version, marked "after Lamartine," contains a line from the Frenchman's collection of poems *Méditations poétiques* ("Poetic Meditations," 1820): "What is our life but a series of preludes to that unknown song the first solemn note of which is sounded by Death?" This tone poem is an account of life's stages, each represented by a musical section: youth and young love (mm. 1–108), the problems of youth (mm. 109–99), the serene joys of maturity (mm. 222–343), and finally death's call and the ultimate triumph of the soul (mm. 344–419). These four sections correspond roughly in tempo and character to the four movements of a symphony. However, the entire piece can be considered a single sonata-form movement with a slow introduction and with a recapitulation in which the second thematic group precedes the first. The influence of the finale of Beethoven's "Ninth" is undeniable.

An important Romantic aspect of *Les Préludes* is that its changes of tempo, thematic entries, and establishment of new keys do not coincide. Another is

Les Préludes

that Liszt depends on just a few short motives, which he varies, develops, and—most individually—transforms as the piece progresses. This *transformation of theme,* namely, altering a subject so as to change its personality, involves tailoring the rhythm, tempo, harmonization, melodic inflection, mode, articulation, and timbre of the theme to fit ever-changing emotional demands. In *Les Préludes* a descending semitone and an ascending perfect fourth are the intervallic motives from which Liszt develops the entire composition (see Example 25.5).

Liszt composed two program symphonies. The first theme of the *Faust Symphony* (1854–1857) is unusual in that it contains all twelve tones of the chromatic scale, arranged in a series of augmented triads, a favorite Liszt chord. The three movements are called "Faust," "Gretchen," and "Mephistopheles," and they are meant to represent, respectively, earthly, heavenly, and hellish realms. The final *chorus mysticus* from Goethe's play, set for tenor, men's chorus, and orchestra, ends the work. The *Dante Symphony* (1855–1856) creates visions of "Inferno" and "Purgatorio" in its two movements with those titles and concludes with women's voices singing the words of the Magnificat.

Program symphonies

Richard Strauss

The Post-Romantic composer who raised the tone poem to new heights was a German, Richard Strauss (1864–1949), a magnificent orchestrator and

Tone poems

Ex. 25.5   Franz Liszt, *Les Préludes*

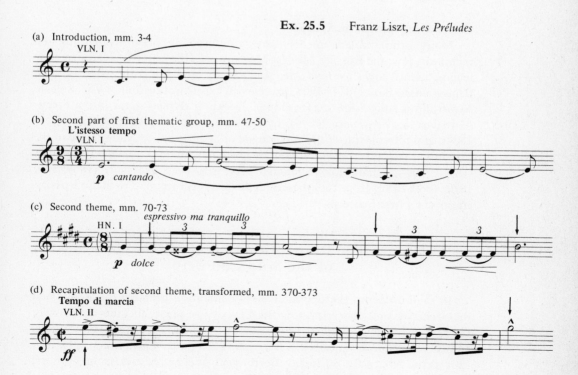

(a) Introduction, mm. 3-4

(b) Second part of first thematic group, mm. 47-50

(c) Second theme, mm. 70-73

(d) Recapitulation of second theme, transformed, mm. 370-373

conductor who demanded absolute precision from his players. In his compositions Strauss favors the brasses, especially the horns, and provides climaxes featuring *fortissimo* string sound and the contrapuntal combination of themes. His melodies are accompanied by active inner voices.

Whereas Liszt's tone poems were, for the most part, atmospheric and unattached to *specific* events or pictures, Strauss aimed at vivid and realistic descriptions in several of his tone poems. He wanted his listeners to hear windmills and bleating sheep in *Don Quixote* (1896–1897), swordplay in *Don Juan* (1888–1889), and the cackling of music critics in his autobiographical *Ein Heldenleben* ("A Hero's Life," 1897–1898). Nonetheless, Strauss also wrote tone poems that substitute reflection and meditation for action and story, such as *Tod und Verklärung* ("Death and Transfiguration," 1888–1889) and *Also sprach Zarathustra* ("Thus Spake Zarathustra," 1895–1896), inspired by the prose poem of Friedrich Nietzsche (1844–1900).

Strauss used the Classical forms. *Don Juan,* for instance, is in sonata form, the hero being portrayed by the first theme, and one of his lady loves by the second. *Don Quixote* is a theme and variations, with each adventure producing new thematic manipulations. *Till Eulenspiegels lustige Streiche* ("Till Eulenspiegel's Merry Pranks," 1894–1895; *MSO* II, p. 276), about a likeable rascal who meets his death by hanging, is a rondo in which the two themes representing Till keep returning in greatly varied guises; quite naturally, Strauss includes elements of theme-and-variations form and also of the sonata-allegro.

Other Programmatic Works

Many programmatic pieces were composed by other Romantics. To mention a few, the Russian Modest Mussorgsky (1839–1881) creates an eerie feeling in his *Night on Bald Mountain* (1867), and his compatriot Nikolai Rimsky-Korsakov (1844–1908) presents an exotic impression of *The Arabian Nights* in his suite *Scheherazade* (1888). Trickling rivulets grow into a turbulent river in *The Moldau* (1874), by the Bohemian Bedřich Smetana (1824–1884), and the colorful sights and sounds of Spain seem to come to life in the exciting travelogue *España* (1883) by the Frenchman Emmanuel Chabrier (1841–1894). Tchaikovsky's fantasy overture *Romeo and Juliet* (1869, rev. 1870, 1880; *MSO* II, p. 166), based on the Shakespeare play, was the Russian composer's first masterpiece.

The Romantic Concerto: Rise of the Solo Concerto

In the nineteenth century the idea of contention between the soloist and the orchestra in a concerto grew markedly. The piano and the violin were the two instruments preferred by Romantic audiences and performers alike, and therefore most concertos were written for these. Composers of significant piano concertos included Beethoven, Weber, Mendelssohn, Robert

Schumann, Chopin, Liszt, Brahms, Saint-Saëns, Grieg, Tchaikovsky, and Rachmaninov. Among the important violin concertos were those composed by Beethoven, Paganini, Mendelssohn, Brahms, Sibelius, Saint-Saëns, Tchaikovsky, Dvořák, Louis Spohr (1784–1859), Henri Wieniawski (1835–1880), Henri Vieuxtemps (1820–1881), Edward Elgar (1857–1934), Edouard Lalo (1823–1892), Max Bruch (1838–1920), and Alexander Glazunov (1865–1936). Among the celebrated concertos for other instruments were those for cello by Robert Schumann, Dvořák, and Saint-Saëns, the clarinet and bassoon concertos by Weber, the horn concertos by Richard Strauss, and the double concerto for violin and cello by Brahms. By writing concertos, many composers provided themselves with music that could impress and excite an audience. Composers frequently came to the public's attention by performing their own or someone else's concerto.

Dating from the early part of his career, Beethoven's first three piano concertos are similar in many respects to Mozart's late piano concertos. Beethoven's Concerto No. 3 in C minor, Op. 37 (c. 1800), seems closely linked in spirit to Mozart's Piano Concerto No. 24 in the same key, K. 491, despite Beethoven's unorthodox use of E major for the slow movement. However, Beethoven was also a trend-setter for the Romantic concerto. By connecting the middle and final movements in his last two piano concertos, No. 4 in G major, Op. 58 (1805–1806), and No. 5 (*Emperor*) in E-flat major, Op. 73 (1809), Beethoven paved the way for similar designs in concertos by such composers as Spohr, Weber, and Mendelssohn. Beethoven's last two piano concertos also display a truly symphonic orchestra more than capable of competing with the piano that attempts to overpower it. Beethoven was innovative in the *Emperor* Concerto in writing out the final cadenza in the first movement, rather than leaving it to the soloist to improvise. Furthermore, this cadenza is accompanied by the orchestra after its first eighteen measures. Despite their elements of virtuosity Beethoven's concertos are serious, expressive works in which there is cooperation, interplay, and mutual musical development between the soloist and the orchestra. Finest among them in this respect is the Violin Concerto in D major, Op. 61 (1806).

Beethoven

Whereas Beethoven preserved the Classical format of a double exposition in the first movements of his concertos, Felix Mendelssohn presented his themes only once in a combined exposition by soloist and orchestra. In the Violin Concerto in E minor, Op. 64 (1844; first movement in *NS*, E, II, no. 6; *NS*, S, no. 25; finale in *MSO* II, p. 9), Mendelssohn assigns to the cadenza of the first movement the role of providing a transition from the development section to the recapitulation. On the other hand, no cadenza is provided or even permitted in Mendelssohn's two piano concertos (1831 and 1837). All three works sound smooth, effortless, and continuous, and all possess glittering, mirthful finales typical of their composer.

Mendelssohn

The concertos of Robert Schumann—one each for piano, violin, and cello—are more serious, avoiding virtuoso display. His best is the Piano Concerto in A minor, Op. 54 (1841, 1845; first movement in *MSO* II, p. 41), a poetic, heartfelt work. Beautiful and intimate dialogues occur between the

R. Schumann

soloist and the orchestra. Schumann wrote out the long and strenuous cadenza at the end of the first movement. By this point Romantic composers, who considered themselves geniuses and leaders, seemed reluctant to permit performers to improvise or compose cadenzas. Wanting complete control over their works, composers did not risk having their music weakened by the ineptitude or tastelessness of performers. Because of this attitude and the nature of the repertory it inspired, the art of musical improvisation began to fade until its rebirth in jazz in the twentieth century (see Chapter 40).

Liszt and others   Franz Liszt applied his cyclical approach and notion of thematic transformation to his two piano concertos (1849, rev. 1853, 1856; and 1839, rev. 1849–1861). In altering themes that recur throughout the connected movements, Liszt followed the tradition of Beethoven's Ninth Symphony by superimposing one huge continuous sonata-allegro form on top of the individual shapes of the several movements. Liszt's approach to concerto form was adopted by such composers as Saint-Saëns and the Englishman Frederick Delius.

Brahms   In the tradition of his idol, Beethoven, and his benefactor, Robert Schumann, Brahms wrote two piano concertos, one violin concerto, and his double concerto, all of which are difficult, serious, and essentially symphonic works. This is especially true of his tragic, stormy Piano Concerto No. 1 in D minor, Op. 15 (1854–1858), which originated as a symphony, and his four-movement Piano Concerto No. 2 in B-flat major, Op. 83 (1878–1881). Brahms reverted to the Classical design of double exposition and of separation between movements.

Virtuoso concertos   Unlike Brahms, most Romantic composers used the concerto for virtuoso display. Among those who were also performers are Mendelssohn, Weber, Chopin, Liszt, Grieg, Tchaikovsky, Rachmaninov, Paganini, Wieniawski, and Vieuxtemps. In some cases, such as the two early piano concertos of Chopin (1830 and 1829–1830), the orchestral players do little more than provide a frame and an accompaniment for the spotlighted soloist. The piano concertos of Liszt, Tchaikovsky, and Rachmaninov offer more of a battle for ultimate domination. These are among the most *bravura* concertos, filled with chordal pounding, octave passages, and elaborate virtuoso figurations. Liszt consciously stressed virtuosity, for he knew that the public audience in the concert hall craved it. "Fireworks" displays of technique remained the norm for the rest of the century.

Summary

In the Romantic era both absolute and programmatic orchestral music were written. The absolute symphony, championed by such composers as Beethoven, Schubert, Brahms, and Bruckner, challenged listeners to use their own imagination, intelligence, and musical literacy to discover meaning in a composition. However, even basically absolute symphonies were often endowed with titles, subtitles for movements, texts, or biographical connections with events in their composers' lives. The program symphony, tone poem, program overture, and incidental music favored by such composers as Berlioz, Liszt, and Richard Strauss were inextricably tied to some literary, pictorial, nationalistic, or philosophical idea, with which their listeners were expected to be familiar.

Piano and violin concertos were extremely popular among Romantic composers. Some, like those of Beethoven and Brahms, were imbued with seriousness and symphonic proportions. Others, like those of Chopin and Paganini, were vehicles for showing off the technical capabilities of the solo player. In either case, audiences flocked to hear the great virtuosos perform concertos and the great conductors lead the orchestras of the time.

Bibliography

Books and Articles

Orchestral Music

GROVE, SIR GEORGE. *Beethoven and His Nine Symphonies,* 3rd ed. London: Novello, Ewer & Co., 1898; reprint, New York: Dover Publications, 1962.

HARRISON, JULIUS. *Brahms and His Four Symphonies.* London: Chapman & Hall, 1939; reprint, New York: Da Capo Press, 1971.

SIMPSON, ROBERT, ed. *The Symphony,* 2 vols. Baltimore: Penguin Books, 1966.

STEDMAN, PRESTON. *The Symphony.* Englewood Cliffs, N.J.: Prentice-Hall, 1979.

TEMPERLEY, NICHOLAS. "The *Symphonie fantastique* and Its Program." *The Musical Quarterly* 57 (Oct. 1971): 593–608.

ULRICH, HOMER. *Symphonic Music: Its Evolution Since the Renaissance.* New York: Columbia University Press, 1952.

VEINUS, ABRAHAM. *The Concerto.* New York: Dover Publications, 1963.

Studies on Major Symphonists

ABRAHAM, GERALD, ed. *The Music of Schubert.* New York: W. W. Norton & Co., 1947; reprint, Port Washington, N.Y.: Kennikat Press, 1969.

————. *The Music of Tchaikovsky.* New York: W. W. Norton & Co., 1974.

————. *Schumann: A Symposium.* New York: Oxford University Press, 1952; reprint, Westport, Conn.: Greenwood Press, 1977.

ARNOLD, DENIS, and FORTUNE, NIGEL, eds. *The Beethoven Reader.* New York: W. W. Norton & Co., 1971.

BARZUN, JACQUES. *Berlioz and the Romantic Century,* 3rd ed., 2 vols. New York: Columbia University Press, 1969.

BIBA, OTTO. "Schubert's Position in Viennese Musical Life." *19th-Century Music* 3 (Nov. 1979): 106–113.

BLAUKOPF, KURT. *Gustav Mahler,* translated by Inge Godwin. New York: Praeger Publishers, 1973.

BROWN, DAVID. *Tchaikovsky: The Early Years 1840–1874.* New York: W. W. Norton & Co., 1978.

BROWN, MAURICE J. E. *Schubert: A Critical Biography.* New York: St. Martin's Press, 1961; reprint, New York: Da Capo Press, 1977.

CHISSELL, JOAN. *Schumann.* New York: Collier Books, 1962.

CLAPHAM, JOHN. *Antonín Dvořák: Musician and Craftsman.* London: Faber & Faber, 1966.

DEL MAR, NORMAN. *Richard Strauss: A Critical Commentary on His Life and Work,* 3 vols. Philadelphia: Chilton Book Co., 1962–1972.

DICKINSON, A. E. F. *The Music of Berlioz.* New York: St. Martin's Press, 1972.

FORBES, ELLIOT, ed. *Thayer's Life of Beethoven.* Princeton, N.J.: Princeton University Press, 1970.

GEIRINGER, KARL. *Brahms: His Life and Work,* 2nd rev. ed. New York: Oxford University Press, 1947.

PERÉNYI, ELEANOR. *Liszt: The Artist as Romantic Hero.* Boston: Little, Brown & Co., 1974.

SEARLE, HUMPHREY. *The Music of Liszt,* 2nd ed. New York: Dover Publications, 1966.

SIMPSON, ROBERT. *The Essence of Bruckner.* New York: Crescendo Publishers, 1967.

SOLOMON, MAYNARD. *Beethoven.* New York: Schirmer Books, 1977.

TAWASTSTJERNA, ERIK. *Sibelius,* vol. I: *1865–1905,* translated by Robert Layton. Berkeley, Cal.: University of California Press, 1976.

WERNER, ERIC. *Felix Mendelssohn: A New Image of the Composer and His Age,* translated by Dika Newlin. New York: Free Press, 1963.

Scores

For symphonies, concertos, and other orchestral works by Beethoven, Berlioz, Brahms, Bruckner, Chopin, Dvořák, Liszt, Mahler, Mendelssohn, Mussorgsky, Schubert, R. Schumann, Tchaikovsky, and Wagner, see the bibliography for Chapter 24.

The Symphony 1720–1840, ed. Barry S. Brook. New York: Garland Publishing, 1979–.

In Dover Music Books —Complete Scores Series
(New York: Dover Publications)

BEETHOVEN, LUDWIG VAN, *Nine Symphonies in Full Orchestral Score,* 4 vols., ed. Max Unger. 1976 reprint of the edition published by Ernst Eulenberg, London, c. 1936–1938; text of finale of the Ninth Symphony translated into English.

BRAHMS, JOHANNES, *Complete Symphonies in Full Orchestral Score,* ed. Hans Gál. 1974 reprint of the edition published by Breitkopf & Härtel, Leipzig, 1926.

MENDELSSOHN, FELIX, *Major Orchestral Works,* ed. Julius Rietz. 1975 reprint of the edition published by Breitkopf & Härtel, Leipzig, 1874–1877.

SCHUBERT, FRANZ, *Four Symphonies in Full Score,* ed. Johannes Brahms. 1978 reprint of the edition published by Breitkopf & Härtel, Leipzig, 1884–1885.

SCHUMANN, ROBERT, *Complete Symphonies in Full Score,* ed. Clara Schumann. 1980 reprint of the edition published by Breitkopf & Härtel, Leipzig, 1881–1887.

STRAUSS, RICHARD, *Tone Poems,* series I and series II, 2 vols. 1979 reprint of the editions published by Jos. Aibl Verlag, Munich, and (for part of series II) Verlag von F. E. C. Leuckart, Leipzig, 1890–1899.

TCHAIKOVSKY, PETER ILYICH, *Fourth, Fifth, and Sixth Symphonies in Full Score.* 1979 reprint of the edition published by Breitkopf & Härtel, Leipzig, n.d.

In Norton Critical Scores Series
(New York: W. W. Norton & Co.)

BEETHOVEN, LUDWIG VAN, *Symphony No. 5 in C minor,* ed. Elliot Forbes. 1971.

BERLIOZ, HECTOR, *Fantastic Symphony,* ed. Edward T. Cone, 1971.

BRAHMS, JOHANNES, *Variations on a Theme of Haydn,* Op. 56a and 56b, ed. Donald M. McCorkle. 1976.

SCHUBERT, FRANZ, *Symphony in B minor,* rev. ed. Martin Chusid. 1971.

26

Nineteenth-Century Song and Choral Music

IN the nineteenth century many people could afford a piano at home, and the cultivation of the art song became a favorite pastime. Romantic poems, expressing personal feelings, attracted the attention of many composers, and thousands of art songs were written in the 1800s, especially in Germany, Austria, and France. Balancing lyricism and drama, composers such as Mahler provided songs with active orchestral parts in creating the hybrid genre known as the song-symphony. The Romantic era was also an age of choral music, which not only fulfilled the needs of amateurs participating in singing societies and choral festivals but also provided composers with opportunities to set inspiring sacred and dramatic texts and to write in a grandiose vocal style.

The Art Song in German-Speaking Lands

The Early Romantic Era

At the end of the eighteenth century, many German poets wrote Romantic poems actually intended for singing, in opposition to the preceding attitude that a poet's words were self-sufficient and invited no musical accompaniment. The young poets, such as Heine, Eichendorff, and Mörike, welcomed the addition of music that turned their poems into art songs (*Lieder;* singular, *Lied*).

Known as the *volkstümliches Lied* (national or popular song), the late-eighteenth-century German art song was simple and folk-like, as its composers reacted against the bravura style in the operas of the time. Two writers of such songs were Johann Friedrich Reichardt (1752–1814) and Carl Friedrich Zelter (1758–1832), the teacher of Felix Mendelssohn. *Volkstümliche Lieder* were often dry and pedantic, but Reichardt and Zelter, like Haydn, Mozart, and Beethoven, were able to inject them with new lyricism. Nonetheless, most Classicists were relatively uninterested in the Lied, since miniature genres were not in vogue at that time.

The volkstümliches Lied

**Beetho-
ven's
Lieder**

Even though Beethoven composed more than sixty Lieder, most of his important compositions were in other genres. Many of his songs are *volkstümlich* in style, but a few, such as *Adelaide,* Op. 46 (1794–1795; poem by Friedrich von Matthison, 1761–1831), are operatic. His most important songs are the group entitled *An die ferne Geliebte* ("To the Distant Beloved," Op. 98; 1815–1816), which are settings of poems by Alois Jeitteles (1794–1858). Connected by modulatory interludes played by the piano, these six Lieder are further related through keys and harmonies. Such a group of Lieder, related to one another both poetically and musically, and forming one larger musical entity, is known as a *song cycle,* or, in German, *Liederkreis.*

Ballades

One type of Lied that arose in the late eighteenth century was a setting of the ballades of German poets, inspired by similar works (ballads) of English and Scottish authors. Ballades (in German, *Balladen*) were lengthy works with contrasting sections that paralleled the events in the narrative or historical text. Long ballades might be in several movements of varying tempo and character. The form of such Lieder tended to be through-composed (a literal translation of the German *durchkomponiert*), meaning that just as the text proceeded from beginning to end, the music would flow accordingly, ever changing as the text might demand. Two outstanding composers of ballades were Johann Rudolf Zumsteeg (1760–1802), whose works were much admired by Schubert, and Carl Loewe (1796–1869).

**Schubert's
Lieder**

The first master of Lieder was Franz Schubert, who devoted himself to songs, composing more than six hundred in a space of about fifteen years. Fortunate in growing up during the heyday of German poetry, Schubert worked with poems by such writers as Goethe, Schiller, the Schlegel brothers, Tieck, and Heine, as well as the recent translations into German of Shakespeare, Scott, and others. In addition, he was inundated by the poetry of such friends as Johann Mayrhofer (1787–1836) and Franz von Schober (c. 1798–1883). Setting great and less important poems alike, Schubert turned them into compelling Lieder, maintaining a careful balance between voice and piano, words and music, melodic line and accompaniment, and unity and variety.

Schubert looked for a definite feeling, a clear subject, and a specific setting in a poem. Often the piano sets the scene and conveys the emotions or images inherent in the poem, while the voice utters the words of the personages present or expresses the poetic sentiments involved. Schubert was extremely sensitive to the various dimensions of a poem: its meter and accent, formal construction, imagery, ideas, affective state, and verbal acoustics. Nonetheless, he took liberties with the text, such as repeating words and lines, when he thought the music demanded them. Most often he matched the musical form to the poetic structure. For a poem not divided into stanzas, or strophes, he would tend to use the through-composed format. For one that had such divisions, he would often employ a strophic arrangement, in which the same music is used for each stanza. Sometimes, in order to reflect changes of mood and meaning in the poem from one stanza to the next, he would make appro-

Leopold Kupelwieser, *Gesellschaftsspiel in Atzenbrugg* ("Party Game in Atzenbrugg," 1821). Franz Schubert, seated by the piano, and some friends at a musical party are shown in this watercolor. Of all the great Romantic composers, Schubert wrote the most Lieder and four-hand piano music, ideal for home entertainment. (Photographic Archives of the Österreichische Nationalbibliothek, Vienna)

priate musical alterations, whether obvious or subtle, while preserving the essence of the first stanza's music throughout. As exemplified in *Der Linden-baum* ("The Linden Tree") from the song cycle *Winterreise* ("Winter Jour-ney," D. 911; 1827), this form is known as *modified strophic*. Schubert also took advantage of other forms: e.g., ternary form, used in *Der Atlas* ("Atlas") from the posthumous (1829) collection its publisher dubbed *Schwanengesang* ("Swan Song," D. 957; 1828; poem by Heine); and arch form (e.g., ABCBA), as in *Aufenthalt* ("Abode"; poem by Ludwig Rellstab, 1799–1860) from the same set. Even a ground bass is used in a Schubert Lied, *Der Doppelgänger* ("The Double"; poem by Heine; *AMA*, p. 341),[1] also from *Schwanengesang*.

Schubert possessed a wealth of melodic ideas, often lyrical but sometimes declamatory (*Aufenthalt*) or recitative-like (*Der Doppelgänger*). Furthermore, the tuneful Lieder range from the simple, folk-like, and strophic *Heidenröslein* ("Little Heather Rose," 1815; poem by Goethe; *MSO* II, p. 8) to the spiritual *Ave Maria* (1825) and the tender *Ständchen* ("Serenade," from *Schwanengesang;* poem by Rellstab). The appealing melodies of Schubert are supported by sen-sitive harmonic progressions (see Example 26.1), featuring chromatic chords, modal mixture, and enharmonic, chromatic, and common-tone modulations. The modulation shown in Example 26.1, typical of Schubert's harmonic fi-

Ex. 26.1   Franz Schubert, *Der Neugierige* ("The Curious One"), mm. 40–43, from *Die schöne Müllerin*

"(the two little words enclose) the whole world for me. O little brook. . . ."

nesse, serves a dramatic as well as a musical purpose. This change in key occurs when the singer's recitative-like thoughts about unrequited love yield to a warm and tender song addressed to the brook that is comforting him.

Gretchen am Spinnrade ("Gretchen at the Spinning Wheel," 1814), one of Schubert's greatest Lieder, was written when he was only seventeen. It is a scene from Goethe's *Faust,* whose textual refrain is: *Meine Ruh' ist hin,/Mein Herz ist schwer,/Ich finde sie nimmer/Und nimmermehr* ("My rest is gone, my heart is heavy, I will never ever find rest again"). The musical refrain occurring whenever these words appear serves as a rondo theme, implying, perhaps, the circular nature of the spinning wheel. More obviously representing this motion is the piano's treble line, while the left hand's rhythm serves a dual purpose, symbolizing not only the sound of Gretchen's foot upon the treadle but also her beating heart. Thinking about her beloved Faust, Gretchen becomes more and more excited, and her vocal line rises amidst sequential harmonies, quickens, and increases in volume. At the remembrance of his kiss, she is so overwhelmed that she stops spinning. Schubert provides a fermata over a diminished-seventh chord, while the girl collects herself and prepares to resume her work. The highest vocal pitch is reserved for her wish to die in Faust's embrace.

A Lied like *Erlkönig* ("Erlking," 1815; *AMA,* p. 343; *NS,* E, II, no. 1; *NS,* S, no. 21), set to Goethe's 1782 ballade, requires four different timbres of the singer for portraying the narrator and three characters. Here the piano represents the galloping horse upon which a father and son ride, as well as the father's fear that his boy will perish in the sinister Erlking's grip. The agitation of *Rastlose Liebe* ("Restless Love," 1815; poem by Goethe) is shown not only by the rushing sixteenth-note figure, which unifies this through-composed Lied, but also by the appoggiaturas and ambiguous tonality. The slippery motion of a fish is suggested by the piano part of *Die Forelle* ("The Trout," final version 1821; poem by C. D. Schubart, 1739–1791; *MSO* II, p. 6).

Schubert's two song cycles are setting of poems by the German Wilhelm

Müller (1794–1827). Whereas *Die schöne Müllerin* ("The Fair Miller-Girl," D. 795; 1823; excerpts in *ML* I, p. 91)[2] is a love story, *Winterreise* is a reflection on life and death, and both are sung by just one character, a wanderer. The first song of *Die schöne Müllerin,* entitled *Das Wandern* ("Wandering"), demonstrates Schubert's use of strophic form. Perfect for the imagery of the miller's wheels (third stanza) and dancing stones (fourth stanza), this music fits the meaning of the other stanzas less comfortably, and the singer must vary his inflection, timing, dynamics, and color to make the musical repetition effective. This seemingly easy vocal line, full of rests and sixteenth notes, would be uncomfortable to sing without the support of the piano, which represents the turning wheels, the heavy stones, and the continuity of the life cycle. Only when the voice and the piano jointly interpret the words does the Lied spring to life. Schubert was the first to make this fusion effectively and consistently.

In the generation after Schubert the finest Lied composer was Robert Schumann. A well-read man, he found inspiration in the subjective poems of Heine, Mörike, Eichendorff, Friedrich Rückert (1788–1866), and Adalbert von Chamisso (1781–1838), to mention just a few. Unlike Schubert, Schumann was almost exclusively interested in setting great poems by great poets (the Chamisso works are the primary exception).

Schumann's Lieder

Possessing unusual talent for adapting music to poetry, Schumann preferred cycles to isolated, individual Lieder. As a pianist, he often approached the song as a duet for voice and piano, in which the piano provides the continuity while the voice enters and exits freely. Contributing rich sonority and technical brilliance, the piano further offers preludes, interludes, and postludes within a song, and transitions from one song to the next in the cycles. The dialogue between piano and voice in which Schumann specializes is present in *Er, der Herrlichste von Allen* ("He, the Most Marvelous of All") from the Chamisso cycle *Frauenliebe und -leben* ("Woman's Love and Life," 1840; see Example 26.2). This fervent, sweeping Lied also shows the composer's

Ex. 26.2   Robert Schumann, *Er, der Herrlichste von Allen,* from *Frauenliebe und -leben,* mm. 21–28

Ex. 26.2   cont.

Schein,   nur in De - muth ihn be - trach - ten,

ritard.

se - lig nur und trau - rig sein!

ritard.

"Wander, wander on your paths; only let me view your brilliance, only view it in humility, only be blessed and sad."

penchant for chains of dissonant chords, many of them diatonic, and of secondary dominant chords. The continuity and sonority of the piano part would permit the first song from *Dichterliebe* ("Poet's Love," 1840), entitled *Im wunderschönen Monat Mai* ("In the Marvelously Beautiful Month of May"; *CAMF* I, no. 18),[3] to stand as a piano miniature, were the voice omitted. The longing and desire expressed in the text are realized musically by the ascending patterns in the piano and the music's inability to arrive at a tonic cadence. In *Das ist ein Flöten und Geigen* ("There Is Playing of Flutes and Fiddles"), from the same cycle, the piano plays a restless waltz, while the singer (the poet) laments on the marriage of his beloved to another; when emotional strife prevents the singer from continuing, the piano carries on alone until the final cadence. And when *Dichterliebe* ends, the piano has a long, poignant epilogue.

Schumann's *Eichendorff Songs,* Op. 39 (1840), show Nature in sympathy with mankind. In this group the piano and voice support one another throughout. *Mondnacht* ("Moon-Night"; *MSO* II, p. 40; *NS*, E, II, no. 10;

NS, *S*, no. 29) consists mainly of one repeated phrase, ever increasing in intensity. A moonlit atmosphere is created by slow, controlled, gently dissonant music, featuring a dominant pedal point; the arpeggiation at the outset represents the sky's descent to "kiss" the earth. In *Im Walde* ("In the Forest"), whose melody is divided between the voice and piano, the zestful joy of the opening contrasts vividly with the grievous chill of the end.

Other composers of Lieder in the first half of the nineteenth century include Weber, Mendelssohn, and the German pianists and composers Clara Schumann (1819–1896) and Fanny Mendelssohn Hensel (1805–1847). Clara Schumann is actually the composer of three songs in her husband Robert's Op. 37 collection, Nos. 2, 4, and 11 (1840). Similarly, Fanny Hensel, who was Felix Mendelssohn's sister, wrote Nos. 2, 3, and 12 of his Op. 8 set of songs (1828) and Nos. 7, 10, and 12 of his Op. 9 (1830). Felix, in fact, did not approve of Fanny's publishing her own music, but, despite his objections, she published some solo songs, part-songs, piano pieces, and a piano trio.

Other Romantic Lied composers

Later Lied composers included Liszt, Wagner, and Robert Franz (1815–1892). Liszt's songs have rich, sometimes intrusive, piano parts, but they are unusually beautiful fusions of words and music, such as *Die Loreley* ("The Lorelei," 1841; poem by Heine), richly harmonized in a chromatic way that simply had to work its influence on Richard Wagner. In *Fünf Gedichte von Mathilde Wesendonk* ("Five Poems of Mathilde Wesendonk," 1857–1858), Wagner reveals some of the sentiments and music found in *Tristan und Isolde* (see pp. 711–712), as he sets the words of the poetess with whom he was madly in love during these years. Representing a blend of Schubert's lyricism and Robert Schumann's passion, Robert Franz wrote approximately 350 Lieder, which stress grace and charm and possess striking piano parts. Among his most famous Lieder are *Die Lotosblume* ("The Lotus Flower," 1843; poem by Heine) and *Wonne der Wehmut* ("Delight of Melancholy," 1864; poem by Goethe).

The Late Romantic Era

Johannes Brahms, who adored the works of Franz Schubert and Robert Schumann and was fascinated by German folk music, was himself a masterful Lied composer. Like Schubert, Brahms disliked empty display and devoted himself to Lieder throughout his career. Also like Schubert, he set some second-rate poems to music. What Brahms sought from a text was an evocative atmosphere, an overall idea that could be embodied in music. In the Lieder of Brahms the voice is dominant; the piano provides an accompaniment featuring harmonic support and permitting dialogue with the voice, which, however, always preserves the clarity and continuity of the vocal line.

Brahms's Lieder

Although attracted to poems about love and nature, Brahms was most interested in the topic of death, especially in his later years. Death is the subject of *Feldeinsamkeit* ("Loneliness in the Field," c. 1877–1879; *AMA*, p. 423), *Der Tod, das ist die kühle Nacht* ("Death—That Is the Cool Night," 1884; poem by Heine), and *Immer leiser wird mein Schlummer* ("My Slumber Grows Ever More Quiet," 1886; *MSO* II, p. 114), as well as of the cycle *Vier ernste*

Gesänge ("Four Serious Songs," 1896), which are set to biblical texts. *Feldein-samkeit* illustrates Brahms's fondness for gently arpeggiated melodies, rich harmonic support, long pedal points, strophic form, and a texture in which the vocal line is enclosed between the treble and bass of the piano (see Example 26.3). In *Der Tod, das ist die kühle Nacht,* the night and nightingale are symbols of death; here modal mixture, mild dissonance, emphasis on the bass register, pedal point, arpeggiation, and an iambic rhythm combine to create an ethereal, otherworldly aura.

The folk and folk-like songs of Brahms are among his most original contributions to Romantic music. Adding interesting harmonies and sonorities to these tunes, he never violated the spirit of folk music. For example, *Sonntag* ("Sunday," 1860), taken from a folk-song collection of the German poet Johann Ludwig Uhland (1787–1862), is notable for its plain periodicity, clear harmonies, repetition, slight variation, sequence, and an echo effect in the last

Ex. 26.3   Johannes Brahms, *Feldeinsamkeit,* mm. 1–9

"I lie quietly in the high, green grass, and for a long time direct my glance upward, upward."

line. Even simpler is the famous *Wiegenlied* ("Cradle Song," 1868), a lullaby illustrating Brahms's fondness for pedals, open fifths, and beautiful melody.

A generation later than Brahms was the German Hugo Wolf (1860–1903), whose compositional career was devoted to Lieder, created in bursts of activity, mostly between 1887 and 1897. Eager to translate every ambiguity and connotation of a text into music, Wolf conceived of Lieder as poems for voice and piano. He set only great poetry, by such masters as Mörike, Goethe, and Eichendorff. He also used German translations of Spanish and Italian poetry in his *Spanisches Liederbuch* ("Spanish Songbook," 1889–1890) and *Italienisches Liederbuch* ("Italian Songbook," Part I in 1890–1891, Part II in 1896). Like Schumann, Wolf died young after suffering the tortures of insanity.

Wolf's Lieder

Wolf disliked the artificialities of strophic form, periodicity, and pretty tunes, and favored a through-composed design unified by the piano accompaniment, which frequently contained ostinato patterns. His piano parts are often extremely complex and technically demanding, and his harmonies are customarily dissonant and chromatic, sometimes even strident. Commonly declamatory, his vocal lines correspond to the rhythm of the poetry and therefore tend to be asymmetrical. Leaps to dissonances, ambiguous tonalities, and chromatic voice-leading combine to make Wolf's Lieder difficult for singers.

Among the fifty-three Mörike songs set by Wolf in 1888 is *Auf einer Wanderung* ("Roaming"), in which the daydreaming and wandering of the protagonist are translated musically as constantly changing keys. When the wanderer stops to enjoy certain sights and sounds, the piano carries on alone with a long interlude. Later, as the wandering youth acknowledges the inspiration of the Muse, a broad chordal climax is reached, and then a postlude assures us that he is scampering home. In *Das verlassene Mägdlein* ("The Forsaken Maiden"; *AMA,* p. 443; *ML,* I, p. 116), from the same collection, a sparse, dactylic figure in the piano and a descending, unresolved vocal line combine with the very soft dynamic level and the minor mode to depict the falling tears and shattered dreams of a young girl.

Wolf's concentrated, intense style is shown in *Auf ein altes Bild* ("On an Old Picture"), also from the Mörike set. This song is governed throughout by the progression of fourteen chords in the four-bar piano introduction. Also showing Wolf's economy of means is *In dem Schatten meiner Locken* ("In the Shade of My Curls," 1889; *AMA,* p. 446) from the *Spanisches Liederbuch.* Rhythmic devices point out the textual contrast between the sleeping and the passionate lovers, and the ascending musical lines for the repeated question ("Should I wake him up now?") are poignantly interrogatory. Among Wolf's greatest settings of Goethe poems (1888–1889) are *Ganymed* (1889) and *Anakreons Grab* ("Anacreon's Grave," 1888; *MSO* II, p. 252).

Another Post-Romantic composer of Lieder was Gustav Mahler. He wrote the poems for his *Lieder eines fahrenden Gesellen* ("Songs of a Wayfarer," 1883–1885, rev. c. 1891–1896) himself. Using either an orchestral or piano accompaniment, this cycle is related in spirit to Schubert's *Winterreise.* The third of its four songs, *Ich hab' ein glühend Messer* ("I Have a Glowing

Mahler's Lieder

Dagger"), is a tempestuous song of pain and anguish. About half of Mahler's songs use poems from *Des Knaben Wunderhorn,* and many contain folk elements (such as Ländler), military fanfares, and tone painting. Dated 1887–1890 and 1892–1898, these simple songs use only a piano accompaniment.

In Mahler we find a fusion of song and symphony. Just as most of his symphonies are based on themes from his songs, many of his Lieder are large-scale, dramatic pieces. *Das Lied von der Erde* ("The Song of the Earth," 1908–1909), a cycle of six songs for tenor and contralto soloists (three for each) and orchestra may be considered a song-symphony. The texts are German translations by Hans Bethge (1876–1946) of Chinese poems on the forces of life and death. The pentatonic scale (a musical exoticism inspired by the source of the poems), a large and richly variegated orchestra, and symphonic architecture contribute to the impact of this work.

More delicate and melancholy are the incomparably sorrowful *Kindertotenlieder* ("Songs on the Death of Children," 1901–1904) for low voice and orchestra. Subtle phrasing and restrained emotions permeate these songs to texts by Rückert.[4] The vocal line in the first song, *Nun will die Sonn' so hell aufgeh'n* ("Now the Sun Wants to Rise as Brightly"; *NAWM* II, no. 132), reflects the rising sun as well as the sinking spirits of the parent (see Example 26.4). Furthermore, the lyrical tenderness of this line is complemented by a transparent orchestration and poignant harmonic progressions.

R. Strauss's Lieder   Like his contemporary Mahler, the young Richard Strauss devoted much of his attention to the art song. Most of Strauss's Lieder were written before 1900, when he was also writing tone poems. Dealing with such issues as time, the seasons, love, ribaldry, and sentimentality, they feature florid melodies, soaring vocal lines, brilliant climaxes, and richly textured piano parts. Strauss's Lieder are often somewhat pretentious in their emotional outbursts and technical intricacies, and many are settings of poor poetry. Yet their

Ex. 26.4   Gustav Mahler, *Nun will die Sonn' so hell aufgeh'n,* from *Kindertotenlieder,* mm. 5–15

"Now the sun wants to rise as brightly as if no disaster, no disaster had occurred during the night."

chromatic dissonances, unexpected modulations, undulating melodies, and fluctuating tessitura often lead to gloriously fervent music. Two of Strauss's finest Lieder in this vein are *Allerseelen* ("All Soul's Day," 1885) and *Cäcilie* (1894). Some of Strauss's songs show the declamatory style of Wagner—for instance, *Ruhe, meine Seele* ("Rest, My Soul," 1894). Others are much more subdued and lyrical, such as *Traum durch die Dämmerung* ("Dream Through the Twilight," 1895) and the well-liked *Ständchen* ("Serenade," 1885–1887). His final works for high voice and orchestra, *Vier letzte Gesänge* ("Four Last Songs," grouped and titled by the publisher, 1948; first three poems by Hermann Hesse, 1877–1962; fourth poem by Eichendorff), are extremely moving, upholding the Post-Romantic Austro-German musical tradition that ended with Strauss's death the following year.

The Art Song in France

Early Songs

During the French Revolution patriotic songs, such as *La Marseillaise* by Claude-Joseph Rouget de Lisle (1760–1836), were very popular. Two leading composers of such songs were Etienne Nicolas Méhul (1763–1817) and François-Joseph Gossec (1734–1829). Also in vogue was the simple, folk-like *romance,* whose text frequently concerned unrequited love. The piano sometimes communicated the setting or sentiment expressed in the texts of these often strophic works. Méhul composed romances of this type, as did Hippolyte Monpou (1804–1841), whose selection of poetry by Alfred de Musset (1810–1857) and Victor Hugo gained him fame.

Patriotic songs and romances

The French art song closest in essence to the German Lied is the *mélodie,* characterized by subtle phrasing, delicate and curvaceous melodic lines, supple rhythms, sonorous harmonies, and nuances related to the poetry. Hector Berlioz, the first Frenchman to call his songs *mélodies,* was the master of this style in the early Romantic period. Dedicated to his beloved Harriet Smithson, his *Elégie en prose* ("Elegy in Prose") from *Neuf mélodies irlandaises* ("Nine Irish Songs," between 1827 and 1829), to words based on a poem by Thomas Moore (1779–1852), shows the same Romantic fervor expressed in the *Symphonie fantastique.* Berlioz's exquisite song cycle *Les Nuits d'été* ("Summer Nights," 1840–1841) brilliantly translates into music six Romantic poems by his compatriot Théophile Gautier (1811–1872). Berlioz originally wrote the accompaniments for piano but later orchestrated them. The melodic lines in these songs of grace, mournfulness, and tempestuousness are long, asymmetrical, and rhythmically free.

The mélodies of Berlioz

Later Songs

Most French opera composers of the second half of the nineteenth century also wrote art songs, which were frequently performed in French homes and salons. Among these were Charles Gounod (1818–1893), Ambroise Thomas (1811–1896), Camille Saint-Saëns (1835–1921), Georges Bizet (1838–1875),

Late Romantic mélodies

LA MODE ILLUSTRÉE

This fashion plate from *La Mode illustrée* of 1865 shows an elegant presentation of art songs in the intimate environment of a home. (The Metropolitan Museum of Art, The Costume Institute Library)

and Jules Massenet (1842–1912). Gounod's mélodies stressed the simplicity of the romance style. He created many songs of grace, charm, and directness, such as *Sérénade* (1857; poem by Hugo) and *L'Absent* ("The Absent One," 1877). Massenet, who popularized the song cycle in France, combined Gounod's qualities with his own sensitivity to the meanings of words, emphasis on the importance of the accompaniment, and voluptuousness in the vocal line. One of his best sets of songs is the *Poème d'avril* ("Poem of April," 1866) to words by Armand Silvestre (1837–1901). Other composers of mélodies included the Belgian César Franck (1822–1890), who was greatly influenced by contemporaneous German composers; Léo Delibes (1836–1891), who was more famous for his ballet music, such as *Coppélia* (1870); Emmanuel Chabrier (1841–1894), a witty composer who took delight in choosing texts about animals, such as the *Ballade des gros dindons* ("Ballad of the Big

Turkeys," 1890); and Cécile Chaminade (1857–1944), the Frenchwoman whose pianistic talents and agreeable salon style gained her extreme popularity in England, the United States, and her native land.

Although Franck did not excel in song composition, his interest in it inspired several of his students, including Vincent d'Indy (1851–1931), Guillaume Lekeu (1870–1894), Ernest Chausson (1855–1899), and Henri Duparc (1848–1933). Chausson, like his teacher, was very much affected by Wagner's late works—as is evident in the song cycle for voice and orchestra *Poème de l'amour et de la mer* ("Poem of Love and the Sea," 1882–1890, rev. 1893)—but his refinement, spontaneity, and predilection for modality mark him as a Frenchman. Duparc's sixteen songs (1868–1884) have achieved immortality for him. Each one matches the moods, words, and even the sounds of its poem with perfectly suited music, filled with exquisite, evocative melody and floating harmonies free of any angularity. Carefully choosing his texts from the poetry of such masters as Charles Baudelaire (1821–1867) and Charles Marie Leconte de Lisle (1818–1894), the self-critical Duparc labored long over every one of his works. Among his enchanting mélodies are *Chanson triste* ("Sad Song," c. 1868, rev. 1902), *Soupir* ("Sigh," c. 1869, rev. 1902; poem by R. F. A. Sully-Prudhomme, 1839–1907), and *L'Invitation au voyage* ("Invitation to the Voyage," 1870; poem by Baudelaire).

The most prolific composer of the late Romantic mélodie is Gabriel Fauré (1845–1924). At first influenced by Gounod, he developed his own unmistakable style, noted for its undulating piano accompaniments, ever-changing harmonies, elegant and restrained vocal lines, and very supple rhythms. Disliking virtuosity and emotionalism, Fauré favored modality, sequential harmonies, long melodic lines, and, above all, a feeling of repose. His own chromaticism is coloristic, mildly embellishing the melodic line and harmonic direction rather than building tension and pulling toward a tonic chord. Two of his songs using delicate patterns of swift arpeggiation and rolling harmonies in the piano are *Nell* (1878; poem by Leconte de Lisle) and *Notre Amour* ("Our Love," c. 1879; poem by Silvestre). His nonjarring chromaticism and syncopation fill *Au bord de l'eau* ("At the Edge of the Water," 1875; poem by Sully-Prudhomme; see Example 26.5). Like Duparc, Fauré was skilled at evoking the nostalgic, exotic, and aromatic atmospheres of such poets as Leconte de Lisle and Paul Verlaine (1844–1896).

Franck and his students

Fauré's mélodies

The Romantic Art Song in Russia and Elsewhere

Mikhail Glinka (1804–1857), noted for his operas, combined his cosmopolitan musical education and enormous talent with the wealth of Russian folk music to call attention to the art song in Russia. Glinka's songs, usually in ABA form, are similar in style to the French romances of the time. Two of his outstanding works are *The Night Review* (1836), a declamatory ballade, and *The Lark,* part of the collection entitled *A Farewell to St. Petersburg* (1840).

Glinka

Ex. 26.5   Gabriel Fauré, *Au bord de l'eau,* mm. 1–6

"For us both to sit down at the edge of the stream which passes, to see it pass. . . ."

**Mussorg-
sky**

The greatest and most influential Post-Romantic Russian song composer was Modest Mussorgsky (1839–1881). Respecting the inflections and intonations of the Russian language, his roughly hewn songs are generally declamatory, with discontinuous, asymmetrical, motivic melodies, and changeable, irregular meters. Although Mussorgsky provides a tonal center, the customary harmonic functions are often weakened or ignored, and there is much modality and chromaticism, as in Russian folk music. The composer uses relatively few note-values in a given work and prefers small melodic intervals to wide ones.

Some of Mussorgsky's songs are very lyrical. These include *Hebrew Song* (1867), with a text from the *Song of Solomon,* and *A Child's Song* (1868). Others are more realistic and objective, such as the song cycle *The Nursery* (1868–1872), in which the composer tries to capture the characteristics of a child's speech. Very different, again, is the dramatic cycle *Songs and Dances of Death* (1875–1877), dealing with various grim images, such as Death riding across a moonlit battlefield, in the last song (*Field Marshal Death,* 1877). Whereas Mussorgsky's songs are vigorous and natural, those of Tchaikovsky and Rachmaninov are sentimental and sensuous.

Art songs were written in all the musical centers of Europe during the nineteenth century. Among the composers whose songs have a universal appeal are Dvořák in Bohemia, Edvard Grieg (1843–1907) in Norway, and Frederick Delius (1862–1934) in England. Dvořák's *Gypsy Songs* (1880) possess colorful harmonies, lyrical melodies, irregular and dance rhythms, some bravura piano accompaniments, and unabashed sentimentality, as in the well-known *Songs My Mother Taught Me*. Unlike Dvořák, Grieg was more at home in the miniature than in the theatrical side of Romanticism, and his best-liked songs include *I Love Thee* (1863–1864; poem by Hans Christian Andersen, 1805–1875) and *A Swan* (1876; poem by Henrik Ibsen, 1828–1906). Grieg's song style is spontaneous, lyrical, and overflowing with Norwegian folk music, modal melodies, sudden modulations to distant keys, and irregular resolutions. He exhibits a strong preference for simple strophic form. Grieg was a major influence on Delius, who dedicated two sets of songs (twelve in all) on Norwegian texts (1888–1890) to Grieg's wife, the soprano Nina Grieg (1845–1935); two of these are *Secret Love* and *Twilight Fancies* (both 1889–1890). Delius went on to set poems of Verlaine, Shakespeare, Tennyson, and others, some with piano accompaniment and some with orchestra. His style is elegant, delicate, and harmonically sensual.

Songs in other countries

Religious Choral Music in the Nineteenth Century

Romantic composers used the chorus in symphonies and operas, and also wrote much music expressly for chorus, usually with orchestral support and often with vocal soloists. Composers of the nineteenth century called upon the chorus primarily in sacred music, according to the traditions that were well established in the history of Western music. Many of their sacred works, however, were too long, grandiose, or difficult for performance in a religious service. Beethoven's *Missa solemnis,* Op. 123 (1819–1823), for example, has symphonic proportions, and Berlioz's Requiem, or *Grande Messe des morts* ("Great Mass of the Dead," 1837), ideally requires at least four hundred performers. These pieces demand countless hours of rehearsal, professional performers, and an audience willing to spend two hours listening to subtle, complex music. The synesthetic experience of hearing such music in a cathedral is indeed awe-inspiring, but it is more a concert experience than a devotional one.

Most of those who wrote music intended for performance in local churches were trained in Renaissance and Baroque music. The study and resuscitation of past styles were concerns of the nineteenth century, and churches—strongholds of tradition and conservatism—emerged as loci for much music in older styles. A cappella choral music, chant and chant-like melodies, modal harmonies, and strict counterpoint were demanded by many Catholics and others, who resented what they considered the excrescences of the Classical and Romantic eras. These people admired Palestrina's style, and

Conservative religious attitudes

in the mid-nineteenth century there was a Catholic effort to restore to current use the ideals of Gregorian chant and of Palestrina.[5] Similar to the Nazarene movement in painting, this one came to be known as the *Cecilian movement.* As observed in the works of such composers as the German Johann Kaspar Aiblinger (1779–1867), the movement produced little of enduring value. Perhaps the happiest compromise between the purity of the Cecilians and the fervor of the Romanticists came in the Masses of Anton Bruckner.

Many Protestants also looked to the past and viewed Palestrina and J. S. Bach as their musical heroes. Believing that Palestrina's music was genuinely fitting for churches, King Friedrich Wilhelm IV of Prussia (reg. 1840–1861) called for a reactionary musical style. Such German composers as Eduard August Grell (1800–1886) wrote church music in this vein, but it is largely uninspired and no longer performed. Two composers of Protestant music who reached a happy medium between the propriety of their music for churches and their own needs as original, inspired artists were Mendelssohn[6] and Brahms.

The Mass

Beethoven and Schubert

Beethoven's Mass in C major, Op. 86 (1807), follows the traditions of the orchestral Masses of Haydn and Mozart. The *Missa solemnis,* however, transcends the liturgical function of the Mass and uses a symphonic style to communicate a universal avowal of faith and ethical behavior. Dependent upon the orchestra for continuity, development, and interaction with the four solo voices and the chorus, the *Missa solemnis* is also symphonic in its organic growth and use of forms like the sonata. It shows off, too, Beethoven's wide dynamic range, expert orchestration, and contrapuntal abilities, as in the great fugues that conclude the Gloria and the Credo (a double fugue). When Beethoven began this Mass, he intended it for the enthronement of Archduke Rudolph (1788–1831)—the younger brother of the emperor of Austria and the composer's patron, student, and friend—as archbishop of Olmütz in 1820. However, Beethoven's devotion to the significance of the Mass outweighed his commitment to the archduke, and he labored over the piece for three additional years.

Schubert's first four Masses (1814–1816) are melodious and simple in design, with little counterpoint. Far more overpowering are his last two. The Mass No. 5 in A-flat major (1819–1822), reflective and lyrical, shows Schubert's great gift for melody but also impresses with its harmonic twists and key changes, and with its brilliant fugue at the end of the Gloria. More dramatic, the Mass No. 6 in E-flat major (1828) depends less on the solo voices, more on the chorus, and much more on the orchestra. It is about one hour long and contains extended fugal sections. Because Schubert took extreme liberties with the text, his Masses cannot be considered liturgical. He omitted and transposed words, repeated them out of context, and telescoped phrases. Such practices became common in the Romantic era.

Cherubini and Rossini

Luigi Cherubini (1760–1842), who met Beethoven in Vienna and was influenced by the Viennese Classical style, wrote a Mass in D minor (1811). Its influence is felt in the *Missa solemnis* of Beethoven, who openly expressed admiration for Cherubini's music. Long after Gioacchino Rossini (1792–1868) retired from operatic composition, he composed his *Petite Messe solennelle* ("Little Solemn Mass," 1863, rev. 1867). Although it started out as a "little" piece, scored for harmonium and two pianos rather than orchestra, the final version was long and grand, showing off Rossini's beautiful melodies, bold harmonic strokes, exceptional orchestration, and command of imitative counterpoint. Instrumental sections and a cappella movements contrast effectively with operatic numbers and huge fugues.

At first Franz Liszt showed his sympathy with the reform movement in his 1848 Mass, using only men's voices, an organ, chant-like melodies, and modal, as well as chromatic, harmonies. However, his Festival Mass (1855, rev. 1857–1858) for the consecration of the cathedral at Gran (Esztergom) in Hungary, resplendent with Romantic exuberance and emotionalism, requires a great number of singers, an organ, and an orchestra, and abounds in fanfares, rich harmonies, and thematic transformation. Yet after this attempt to unite the worlds of symphony, opera, and Mass, Liszt reverted to the Cecilian style for his *Missa choralis* (1865), composed during his decade in Rome (the 1860s), where he took minor orders in the Catholic Church.

Liszt and Gounod

Like Liszt, Charles Gounod was torn between the secular and sacred sides of life. He composed fifteen Masses, some a cappella and some accompanied

Jean-Auguste-Dominique Ingres (1780–1867), *Portrait of M. Charles Gounod* (1841). Ingres's pencil drawing shows Gounod at the piano, but the composer's preferred keyboard instrument was the organ. (Courtesy of The Art Institute of Chicago; Gift of Messrs. Charles Deering McCormick, Brooks McCormick, and Roger McCormick)

only by organ or by full orchestra, and he even wrote one for orchestra alone, with voices optional. His most famous Mass, however, is the *Messe solennelle de Sainte-Cécile* ("Solemn St. Cecilia Mass," 1855), which contains his characteristic lyricism and sentimentality.

Bruckner   In the late Romantic era Anton Bruckner raised the Mass to heights not reached since Schubert. Some of the themes of Bruckner's Masses occur also in several of his symphonies, and the general method of composition is the same in both genres. One of the best organists of the century, Bruckner was also a deeply devout Catholic, who believed that music ought to serve religion.

Of Bruckner's three mature Masses, No. 1 in D minor (1864, rev. 1876, 1881–1882) and No. 3 in F minor (1867–1868, rev. 1876, 1881) are symphonic, making use of large sonata designs. Moreover, they contain plainsong fragments, chorale tunes, contrapuntal agility, Romantic harmony, and a large Wagnerian orchestra. Failing to realize Bruckner's devotion to the liturgy, the Cecilians were aghast at these Masses. Their beliefs, however, must have influenced Bruckner when he wrote his neo-medieval Mass No. 2 in E minor (1866, rev. 1876, 1882), scored for eight-part chorus and wind band.

The Romantic Requiem Mass: Cherubini, Berlioz, and Verdi

The Requiem, with its allusions to the terror and wrath of the Day of Judgment and with its pleas for deliverance and eternal peace, inspired several Romantic composers to great heights of creative expression. Among them were Cherubini, Berlioz, and Verdi. Berlioz explained the impact of this text upon him in his *Mémoires:* "The text of the Requiem was a quarry that I had long coveted. Now at last it was mine, and I fell upon it with a kind of fury. My brain felt as though it would explode with the pressure of ideas."[7]

Cheru-   A dramatic Requiem in C minor (1816) by Cherubini, for orchestra and
bini's   four-part choir, shows the influence of Beethoven's C-minor compositions,
Requiem   as it features chromatic chordal progressions, energetic motives, sharp accents, extremes of dynamics, and a balance between homophony and counterpoint. Cherubini's Requiem in D minor (1836) is scored for orchestra and a three-part men's choir, because the archbishop of Paris forbade the use of women's voices in church. It juxtaposes a dramatic orchestra with a cappella passages.

Cherubini's music owes much to the era of the French Revolution, when gigantic music festivals were organized by the revolutionaries to boost the public morale and arouse republican fervor. Odes and songs of praise were written to honor dead and living heroes, and to extol the abstract virtues of the period. These works had to command the attention of a huge audience, and therefore they were colossal; among the composers were François-Joseph Gossec and André-Modeste Grétry (1741–1813).

Berlioz's   A more famous Requiem than Cherubini's that also stemmed from the
Requiem   colossal French tradition is Berlioz's *Grand Messe des morts.* The audacious composer brought this big outdoor style into the concert hall, where the acoustics were far superior. He scored his Requiem for a huge orchestra,

with sixteen kettledrums and ten pairs of cymbals, four extra brass ensembles, a tenor soloist, and an immense chorus. However, master orchestrator that he was, Berlioz used the entire body only for special portions of the text, such as the *Tuba mirum* ("A trumpet . . . wondrous") chorus. Much of this score is poetic and subtle, and the *Quaerens me* ("Seeking me") portion of the Sequence (*Dies irae*) is set for a cappella chorus (see Example 26.6).

Repeating portions of the text out of context and out of order, Berlioz was typically Romantic in going beyond the confines of the liturgy. His main motivations were musical, and he even repeated music from one movement to another. For example, part of the music for the Introit recurs during the Agnus Dei. The work is basically homophonic; yet it contains impressive fugal writing for orchestra in the Offertory, complementing a choral part confined to a two-note alternation in octaves. This Requiem is truly a great dramatic symphony for instruments and voices, which Berlioz liked best among all his works.

The Berlioz Requiem greatly influenced Giuseppe Verdi (1813–1901). **Verdi's** Three years after *Aida,* Verdi finished his Requiem (1874; opening of *Dies irae* **Requiem** in *NS*, E, II, no. 14; *NS*, S, no. 32). Although written in memory of Manzoni, it may also be considered a tribute to Rossini, whose death in 1868 had prompted Verdi to make plans for a Requiem in that master's honor. The

Ex. 26.6   Hector Berlioz, *Quaerens me,* from the Requiem, mm. 1–17

Ex. 26.6   cont.

"Seeking me, Thou didst sit down weary, Thou didst suffer the Cross to redeem me. Let not so great a labor be in vain."

Libera me ("Deliver me"), or Responsory, was, in fact, composed at that earlier time. A profound religious faith permeates the work, even though portions sound like recitatives, arias, or ensembles from Verdi's operas. Scored for orchestra, chorus, and four solo singers, the Verdi Requiem is one of the composer's supreme masterpieces.

At the opening the chorus prays in a declamatory fashion, while muted strings provide exquisite harmonies. After an agitated a cappella section in imitative counterpoint, the initial music returns to complete the ternary form. Then the four soloists enter in turn with a melodic phrase of great power and beauty, which governs the entire Kyrie (see Example 26.7).

The *Dies irae* ("Day of wrath") or Sequence, which follows, is well-known for its terrifying opening chords, the bass drum pounding out the unaccented beats, and the chromatic screams and wails of the chorus. The longest movement of the Requiem, the Sequence is divided into contrasting sections such as the *Tuba mirum,* which contains trumpet fanfares showing the influence of Berlioz; the majestic *Rex tremendae* ("King of dread"); the lyrical and serene *Recordare* ("Remember"), a duet for the two women soloists; and the concerted *Lacrymosa* ("Weeping"), which contains a simple, heartfelt melody and an ingenious contrapuntal design.

After the Offertory in an arch (ABCBA) form, Verdi uses the double-fugue procedure for the Sanctus, in which his choir is split into two halves. The peaceful Agnus Dei provides three varied statements of a sustained, narrow-ranged melody for the soprano and mezzo-soprano, with choral refrains. After the somber *Lux aeterna* ("Eternal light") for mezzo-soprano, tenor, and bass, the soprano sings the *Libera me* ("Deliver me"). The monotone at the beginning of this prayer for deliverance is chant-like, and the arioso section expresses fear of the Last Judgment. There follows a return of the clamorous *Dies irae*, and then a return of the opening *Requiem aeternam* ("Eternal rest"), as thoughts of fear and peace are juxtaposed. More chanting by the soprano gives way to a magnificent fugue, but the work ends with quiet, solemn, homophonic music.

Other Requiems

Other composers of large-scale Romantic Requiems include Saint-Saëns (1878) and Dvořák (1890). On the other hand, Fauré wrote a delicate and subdued Requiem (1877, 1887–1890) in memory of his father. Wishing to convey only restfulness and faith, and neither fear nor trepidation, Fauré omitted most of the Sequence and most references to the Last Judgment from his Requiem, which is scored for soprano and baritone soloists, chorus, organ, and a small orchestra. Representative of this contemplative work, the Sanctus contains short melodic phrases that are narrow in range and harmonies that are mildly dissonant and at times modal. Most of the movement is *pianissimo,* but at the words *Hosanna in excelsis* there is a *fortissimo* exclamation. The ensuing *Pie Jesu* ("Blessed Jesus") for soprano solo and organ (with strings doubling the organ after the initial pair of phrases) is ethereal and totally unpretentious. As a whole, the work's clear melodies and textures, transparent orchestration, including harp and organ, rolling arpeggiation, restraint, and simplicity render it unmistakably French.

Fauré's Requiem

Quite different is *Ein Deutsches Requiem* (1857–1868) by Brahms, the first work that gained him international recognition. "A German Requiem" is not an ideal title for this piece, since it is not the use of the German language but

Brahms's Requiem

Ex. 26.7   Giuseppe Verdi, Kyrie, from the Requiem, mm. 1–5

"Lord, have mercy on us." As in his operas, Verdi's effective vocal writing and sensitive harmonizations are apparent throughout his Requiem.

rather the expression of a Lutheran attitude toward death which sets the work apart from the Catholic Requiems discussed above. This Requiem is addressed to the living. Moved by the death of his mother in 1865, Brahms determined to write the Requiem that had first occurred to him when Robert Schumann died in 1856. Selecting verses from the Old and New Testaments, Brahms, a devoted student of J. S. Bach's works, chose words of consolation, faith, humility, and hope. In spirit the text is close to many a Bach cantata text, and a chorale tune by the Lutheran Georg Neumark (1621–1681), used also by Bach in his Cantata No. 27 (1726), is the basis for much of the "German Requiem." This tune appears at the start of the first movement and in the alto part at the beginning of the choral section of the second movement.

The entire piece is in an arch design (ABCDCBA). The outer movements are in F major, use a slow tempo, and deal with the concept of holiness. The second and sixth movements have gloomy openings that give way to triumphant fugal conclusions. Movements 3 and 5 make use of the soloists, a baritone in the responsorial third movement and a soprano in the fifth. In the center is the serene, fluid, lyrical *Wie lieblich sind Deine Wohnungen* ("How lovely are Thy tabernacles"), similar in style to some of Brahms's symphonic slow movements.

The somber, peaceful first movement uses no violins and takes full advantage of a tonic pedal and deceptive cadences. Quite different is the haunting second movement, *Denn alles Fleisch es ist wie Gras* ("For all flesh is as grass"), a funereal procession in triple meter with elemental power in its big block chords, dynamic growth, and many reiterations. The harmonic progressions point up Brahms's penchant for modal mixture, plagal motion (IV–I), secondary triads, suspensions, and syncopation (see Example 26.8).

The Oratorio in the Nineteenth Century

After Handel and Haydn the oratorio fell into a period of decline and conservatism in the hands of such composers as Ludwig Spohr and Carl Loewe, whose works were popular only in the nineteenth century. Even Beethoven's *Christus am Ölberge* ("Christ on the Mount of Olives," 1803, rev. 1804) suffers from a deficiency of musical interest. The composer who restored the oratorio to a high level was Felix Mendelssohn, who wrote appealing melodies much admired by choral singers of his time. *Paulus* ("St. Paul," 1836) is a dramatic oratorio in the Handelian tradition. Set in two parts, it contains forty-five numbers and begins with an overture based on the chorale *Wachet auf!* ("Sleepers, awake!"), made famous by J. S. Bach in his Cantata No. 140. More than five hundred people took part in the first performance of this oratorio in Düsseldorf, and its success in Germany and England helped make Mendelssohn an international figure.

Mendelssohn

However, Mendelssohn's finest choral work is his other oratorio, *Elias* ("Elijah," 1846), written for a festival performance in Birmingham, England.

As usual, Mendelssohn exhibits flawless technique, pictorial orchestration, and a refined musical taste, and the biblical text here inspired him to great heights. In reestablishing the Protestant spirit of J. S. Bach, Mendelssohn created renewed interest in the four-part chorale style and in Baroque *Fortspinnung* (the continuous spinning-out of a motivic idea), as heard in the overture, which is played after an introductory recitative sung by Elijah.

Ex. 26.8   Johannes Brahms, *A German Requiem,* Mvt. 2, mm. 22–42

Ex. 26.8   cont.

"For all flesh is as grass, and all the glory of man as the flower of grass. The grass has withered, and the flower has fallen away."

Part 1 of *Elijah* is the story of Israel's anguish and the drought brought on by Elijah when his people forsook the Lord and turned to the false god Baal. Part 2 tells of the attempts of Elijah's enemies to destroy him and ends with his ascension to Heaven in a fiery chariot. Among the most beautiful arias in *Elijah* are *If with all your hearts,* No. 4, for tenor; *It is enough,* No. 26, for baritone; and *O rest in the Lord,* No. 31, for alto. *He, watching over Israel,* No. 29, is a sweet, fluid chorus; and the delicate trio for women's voices, *Lift thine eyes,* No. 28, exhibits a pastel timbre that was then in vogue (see Example 26.9).

The two oratorios (alternately referred to as cantatas or dramatic choral **R. Schumann** works) of Robert Schumann are secular. *Das Paradies und die Peri* ("Paradise and the Peri," 1843) and *Der Rose Pilgefahrt* ("The Pilgrimage of the Rose," 1851) are no longer popular, but the former was quite successful in Schumann's time. Based on an exotic poem by Thomas Moore called *Lalla Rookh* (1817), *Das Paradies und die Peri* tells of an angel's (Peri's) expulsion from Heaven and the trials she must pass in order to be reinstated. A narrator relates the story, in arioso and aria styles. The largely homophonic choruses

Ex. 26.9   Felix Mendelssohn, *Lift thine eyes,* from *Elijah,* mm. 1–16

Ex. 26.9   cont.

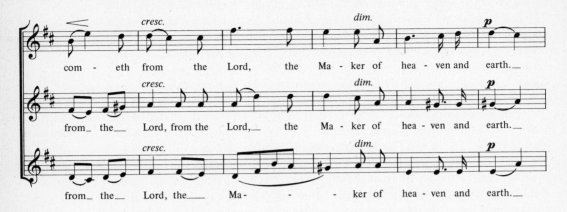

com - eth from the Lord, the Ma - ker of hea - ven and earth.__

from_ the__ Lord, from the Lord,__ the Ma - ker of hea - ven and earth.__

from_ the__ Lord, the__ Ma - - - ker of hea - ven and earth.__

lack dramatic power, but the orchestral accompaniments and the pseudo-Oriental coloring provided in Choruses Nos. 11 and 18 are effectively Romantic.

The Late Romantic Oratorio

Liszt, Berlioz, and others   In the late Romantic era many composers, including Liszt, Berlioz, Franck, Gounod, and Elgar, turned their attention to the oratorio. During his years as court music director in Weimar, Liszt worked on much choral music, such as *Die Legende von der heiligen Elisabeth* ("The Legend of St. Elizabeth," 1857–1862), which contains folk and chant melodies and thematic transformation. Chant is the basis of *Christus* (1862–1867), which also has several a cappella numbers. The Liszt of these oratorios is not the virtuoso but the religious mystic.

In his great oratorio, *L'Enfance du Christ* ("The Childhood of Christ," 1850–1854), Berlioz, too, renounced grandiloquence for charm and restraint. Except for a few operatic moments, this work displays great intimacy and reverence. In trying to resurrect the spirit of the biblical world, and the seventeenth-century oratorio, Berlioz prepared the text himself and used some modality. One of the tenderest numbers is the chorus of shepherds bidding farewell to the Christ child. Later French composers, such as Franck in *Les Béatitudes* (1869–1879), Gounod in *La Rédemption* (c. 1882), and Saint-Saëns in *The Promised Land* (1913), responded to the needs of the many amateur singers who formed choral societies and established choral festivals.

The Romantic oratorio in England   The widespread acceptance of Handel's oratorios led to the continuing popularity of this genre in nineteenth-century Britain. Mendelssohn's sacred oratorios were so much admired there that the English adopted him as one of their own, and London became his favorite residence. However, the English also produced their own oratorios, such as *The Prodigal Son* (1869) by Arthur Sullivan (1842–1900), *Judith* (1888) by Charles Hubert Hastings Parry (1848–1918), and *The Crucifixion* (1887) by John Stainer (1840–1901). The Irishman Charles Villiers Stanford (1852–1924) epitomizes the era of great choral festivals in such places as Norwich, Cardiff, Hanley, and Leeds. Among his oratorios was *Eden* (1891).

One English oratorio from the late Romantic era that is still performed occasionally is *The Dream of Gerontius* (1899–1900) by Sir Edward Elgar (1857–1934). A large-scale work organized to a great extent on the principles of Richard Wagner (see Chapter 28), it communicates Catholic thoughts on death, the Last Judgment, Purgatory, and salvation. Elgar was able to free English music from its rather parochial attitudes and came to symbolize England during its nationalistic movement in music.

Other Types of Religious Choral Music

Psalm Settings

Romantic composers often set the texts of biblical psalms to music. Schubert's setting of Psalm 23, D. 706 (1820), for four-part women's chorus and piano, was intended as a pedagogical work, but his Psalm 92, D. 953 (1828), for a cappella chorus and baritone, written for use by the cantor in the synagogue in Vienna, employs the Hebrew text. Liszt's Psalm 13 (1855, rev. 1859), for tenor, chorus, and orchestra, and Bruckner's Psalm 150 (1892), for soprano, chorus, orchestra, and organ, are outstanding settings by Catholic composers. On the Protestant side, Mendelssohn composed several choral and orchestral psalm-settings, including Psalm 95 (with tenor soloist, 1838, rev. 1841), which uses recitatives as well as unison, responsorial, and antiphonal singing, and Psalm 114 (1839), with its prominent contrasts of dynamics and mood, caustic harmonies, and magnificent counterpoint. Another Protestant setting is Brahms's Psalm 13 (1859), for three-part women's chorus and organ.

Te Deums and Other Sacred Pieces

In the nineteenth century the hymn of thanksgiving *Te Deum laudamus* ("We praise thee, O Lord") inspired music for the celebration of military victories, anniversaries, and other special occasions. The Berlioz Te Deum (1849), originally planned as a memorial to Napoleon Bonaparte, was first performed at the Paris Exhibition of 1855. For a large orchestra, organ, two choirs, and a children's chorus, this massive work contains eight numbers, including a prelude (No. 3) and a march (No. 8) for orchestra alone. It is a showcase of Berlioz's genius in orchestration, counterpoint, rhythmic finesse, and patriotic fervor. Bruckner's Te Deum (1881–1884) for four soloists, chorus, organ, and orchestra is one of his most brilliant works, resplendent with fugal power, massive chords, and motivic development.

Berlioz and Bruckner

Dvořák's symphonic Te Deum (1892) for soprano, bass, chorus, and orchestra shows imaginative orchestration and dramatic climaxes, and reflects the influence not only of Beethoven and Schubert but also of J. S. Bach and Handel. Verdi's Te Deum, from his *Quattro pezzi sacri* ("Four Sacred Pieces," 1889–1897), is scored for double choir and orchestra. Using plainsong and

Dvořák and Verdi

similar melodies for this reverential setting, Verdi achieved a variety of harmonies, textures, dynamics, and feelings.

Also in Verdi's *Quattro pezzi sacri* are an Ave Maria and a Stabat Mater, two of the most inspirational texts of the Catholic liturgy. Other Romantic settings of the Stabat Mater include those by Rossini (1832, rev. 1841) and Dvořák (1876–1877).

Other Romantic Works for Chorus

Schubert

Mendelssohn

Brahms

The nineteenth century witnessed the composition of numerous works that are variously called secular oratorios, dramatic choral works, or cantatas, since none of the conventional designations seems to fit them. Schubert wrote such fine works as the unfinished religious drama *Lazarus* (1820), for chorus and orchestra, and *Mirjams Siegesgesang* ("Miriam's Song of Triumph," 1828), for chorus and piano. Mendelssohn's very imaginative *Die erste Walpurgisnacht* ("The First Walpurgis Night," 1832, rev. 1843), a setting of a Goethe text, combines humor and charm, grotesqueness and elfin lightness, sweetness and harsh dissonance.

Brahms, especially, contributed much to the choral repertoire. His Rhapsody (1869), for alto, male chorus, and orchestra, also uses a text by Goethe. In the first stanza the alto sings in a recitative style, and the second is an aria in three parts. Only in the third stanza, speaking of love and optimism, does the chorus support the soloist, as the C minor of the desolate opening yields to a tranquil C major. Quite the opposite kind of mood change takes place in the *Schicksalslied* ("Song of Destiny," 1868–1871), for chorus and orchestra, to a poem of the German poet Friedrich Hölderlin (1770–1843). The *Triumphlied* ("Song of Triumph," 1870–1871), for baritone, double choir, and orchestra, celebrates the end of the Franco-Prussian War and the establishment of the German Empire. Brahms himself selected the text from the Bible, and he used such traditional choral techniques as a cantus firmus and an anthem-like handling of the two choirs.

Coleridge-Taylor

Delius

Samuel Coleridge-Taylor (1875–1912), the son of a white Englishwoman and a black physician from Sierra Leone, achieved renown for his *The Song of Hiawatha,* for solo voices, chorus, and orchestra. This trilogy consists of *Hiawatha's Wedding Feast* (1898), the most successful of the three parts; *The Death of Minnehaha* (1899); and *Hiawatha's Departure* (1900). The overture to *Hiawatha's Wedding Feast* is based on the Black spiritual *Nobody Knows de Trouble I've Seen;* Coleridge-Taylor enjoyed incorporating folk music into his works. Among his other choral compositions is the exotic *Kubla Khan* (1906), a rhapsody for mezzo-soprano, chorus, and orchestra, based on the poem of S. T. Coleridge. Coleridge-Taylor also composed for orchestra without voices, organ, piano, and chamber groups, and his works include songs, church music, two operettas, and an opera—all abounding in charming melodies and richly hued orchestration. Another important composer in England was Delius, whose large-scale, dramatic *A Mass of Life* (1904–1905), based on Nietzsche's *Also sprach Zarathustra,* is a poetic work of ethereal beauty for soloists, chorus, and orchestra.

Mention should also be made of the profusion of part songs composed for men's, women's, and mixed choruses throughout the century. Such works came to be in demand because of the emergence of amateur singing groups and choral festivals, which, in turn, were related to contemporary feelings of nationalism and fraternity. These homophonic songs, a cappella or accompanied, with the melody in the top voice, dealt with all types of subject matter, but patriotic and convivial poems were favorites. Among the nineteenth-century composers of part songs were Weber, Schubert, R. Schumann, Mendelssohn, Liszt, Gounod, Parry, Stanford, and Elgar.

Part songs for chorus

Summary

The Romantic era was the great age of the art song for voice and piano, as composers tried to communicate in music the words and emotions of the poetry of their time. Especially in Germany and Austria, the art song, or Lied, became one of the primary concerns of most composers. Schubert established it as a musical genre of lasting importance, and his influence was felt by those who followed, such as Robert Schumann, Brahms, Wolf, Mahler, and Richard Strauss.

In France the art song, or mélodie, was cultivated by such masters as Berlioz, Duparc, and Fauré. Mussorgsky developed a Russian song style, which was faithful to the intonations and inflections of his spoken language. Similarly, composers in other countries developed art songs expressive of their nation's poetry, philosophy, and geography.

Choral music of diverse types was composed during the Romantic era. Although the Church had lost its former control over the arts, few Romantic composers resisted the temptation to set inspiring liturgical and sacred texts to music. The three most important Romantic choral genres were the Mass, Requiem, and oratorio, although many hymns, prayers, secular dramatic works, and part songs were also composed. Among the greatest Masses of the period are the *Missa solemnis* of Beethoven, Schubert's last two Masses, and Bruckner's last three. The Requiems by Berlioz, Verdi, Fauré, and Brahms also stand as pinnacles of choral writing. In the field of oratorio Mendelssohn was best able to approach the greatness of Handel and Haydn, but such other composers as Liszt, Berlioz, and Elgar also made significant contributions.

Notes

1. Charles Burkhart, ed., *Anthology for Musical Analysis,* 3rd ed. (New York: Holt, Rinehart and Winston, 1978). (*AMA*)
2. Gordon Hardy and Arnold Fish, eds., *Music Literature: A Workbook for Analysis,* 2 vols. (New York: Harper & Row, 1963–1966). (*ML*)

3. David Ward-Steinman and Susan L. Ward-Steinman, eds., *Comparative Anthology of Musical Forms,* 2 vols. (Belmont, Calif.: Wadsworth Publishing Co., 1976). (*CAMF*)

4. Rückert had lost a child before writing these poems, but Mahler suffered the death of a daughter only after he had completed this cycle.

5. The first biography of Palestrina, written by Giuseppe Baini (1775–1844), was published in 1828. In 1825, A. F. Thibaut of Heidelberg (1772–1840) published his tract *Über Reinheit der Tonkunst,* issued in English in 1877 as *On Purity in Musical Art.*

6. Felix Mendelssohn was born Jewish, and was, in fact, the grandson of Moses Mendelssohn (1729–1786), one of the foremost Jewish philosophers of all time. Felix, his brother, and his two sisters were converted to Christianity in 1816 by their parents.

7. Cited from David Cairns, trans., *The Memoirs of Hector Berlioz* (New York: Alfred A. Knopf, 1969), chap. 46, p. 228.

Bibliography

Books and Articles

Translations of Song Texts

FISCHER-DIESKAU, DIETRICH, comp. *The Fischer-Dieskau Book of Lieder,* translated by George Bird and Richard Stokes. New York: Alfred A. Knopf, 1977.

MILLER, PHILIP L., trans. and comp. *The Ring of Words: An Anthology of Song Texts.* New York: W. W. Norton & Co., 1973.

The Art Song in General

IVEY, DONALD. *Song: Anatomy, Imagery, and Styles.* New York: Free Press, 1970.

MEISTER, BARBARA. *An Introduction to the Art Song.* New York: Taplinger Publishing Co., 1980.

STEVENS, DENIS, ed. *A History of Song.* New York: W. W. Norton & Co., 1970.

Studies of the Art Songs of Individual Composers

CAPELL, RICHARD. *Schubert's Songs,* 2nd ed. New York: Macmillan, 1957; reprint of the 1928 ed., New York: Da Capo Press, 1977.

MEISTER, BARBARA. *Nineteenth-Century French Song: Fauré, Chausson, Duparc, and Debussy.* Bloomington, Ind.: Indiana University Press, 1980.

NOSKE, FRITS. *French Song from Berlioz to Duparc,* 2nd ed., revised by Rita Benton and Frits Noske, translated by Rita Benton. New York: Dover Publications, 1970.

PETERSEN, BARBARA A. *Ton und Wort: The Lieder of Richard Strauss.* Studies in Musicology, ed. George Buelow. Ann Arbor, Mich.: UMI Research Press, 1980.

SAMS, ERIC. *The Songs of Hugo Wolf.* London: Methuen & Co., 1961.

STEIN, JACK M. *Poem and Music in German Lied from Gluck to Hugo Wolf.* Cambridge, Mass.: Harvard University Press, 1971.

WALSH, STEPHEN. *The Lieder of Schumann.* New York: Praeger Publishers, 1971.

WENK, ARTHUR B. "The Composer as Poet in *Das Lied von der Erde.*" *19th-Century Music* 1 (July 1977): 33–47.

Choral Music

HUTCHINGS, ARTHUR. *Church Music in the Nineteenth Century*. New York: Oxford University Press, 1967; reprint, Westport, Conn.: Greenwood Press, 1977.
JACOBS, ARTHUR, ed. *Choral Music: A Symposium*. Baltimore: Penguin Books, 1963.
PRITCHARD, BRIAN W. "Mendelssohn's Chorale Cantatas: An Appraisal." *The Musical Quarterly* 62 (Jan. 1976): 1–24.
ROBERTSON, ALEC. *Requiem: Music of Mourning and Consolation*. New York: Frederick A. Praeger, 1968; reprint, Westport, Conn.: Greenwood Press, 1976.

Scores

For art songs and choral music by Beethoven, Berlioz, Brahms, Bruckner, Chopin, Dvořák, Liszt, Mahler, Mendelssohn, Mussorgsky, Schubert, R. Schumann, Tchaikovsky, and Wagner, see the bibliography for Chapter 24.

STRAUSS, RICHARD, *Lieder. Gesamtausgabe,* ed. Franz Trenner. London. Boosey & Hawkes, 1964.
WOLF, HUGO, *Sämtliche Werke,* vols. 1–7, ed. Hans Jancik. Vienna: Musikwissenschaftlicher Verlag, 1963–1966.

In Dover Music Books—Complete Scores Series
(New York: Dover Publications)

BRAHMS, JOHANNES, *Complete Songs for Solo Voice and Piano,* series I–IV, 4 vols., ed. Eusebius Mandyczewski. 1979 (series I–II) and 1980 (series III–IV) reprints of the edition published by Breitkopf & Härtel, Leipzig, c. 1926; texts trans. Stanley Applebaum.
Fifty Art Songs by Nineteenth-Century Masters, ed. Henry T. Finck. 1975 reprint of the edition published by Oliver Ditson Co., Boston, 1902.
French Art Songs of the Nineteenth Century: 39 Works from Berlioz to Debussy, ed. Philip Hale. 1978 reprint of *Modern French Songs (for High Voice)*, published by Oliver Ditson Co., Boston, 1904.
LISZT, FRANZ, *Thirty Songs (for High Voice)*, ed. Carl Armbruster. 1975 reprint of the edition published by Oliver Ditson Co., Boston, 1911.
SCHUBERT, FRANZ, *Complete Song Cycles: Die schöne Müllerin, Die Winterreise, Schwanengesang,* ed. Eusebius Mandyczewski. 1970 reprint of the edition published by Breitkopf & Härtel, Leipzig, 1895.
————, *Schubert's Songs to Texts by Goethe,* ed. Eusebius Mandyczewski. 1979 reprint of the edition published by Breitkopf & Härtel, 1884–1897.
VERDI, GIUSEPPE, *Requiem,* ed. Kurt Soldan. 1978 reprint of the edition published by C. F. Peters, Leipzig, n.d.

In Norton Critical Scores Series
(New York: W. W. Norton & Co.)

SCHUMANN, ROBERT, *Dichterliebe,* ed. Arthur Komar. 1971.

27

Piano and Chamber Music in the Nineteenth Century

THE importance of the piano in nineteenth-century homes and salons and as a medium for virtuoso display has already been discussed. During the nineteenth century, chamber music, often involving the piano, also took on larger, more virtuoso dimensions than before. Frequently demanding a performing technique beyond the capabilities of amateur players, nineteenth-century chamber music moved away from the home and into the concert hall. In this chapter we shall investigate the nature of Romantic piano and chamber music and the achievements of some of the composers in these fields.

Types of Romantic Piano Music

Traditional genres   Romantic piano music may be divided into six major categories: traditional genres (e.g., sonata, rondo, theme and variations, fantasia, fugue), character pieces, dances, etudes, program music, and piano transcriptions. Beethoven wrote thirty-two piano sonatas and several sets of variations. Schubert, Weber, Mendelssohn, Brahms, and Scriabin are among the other Romantic and Post-Romantic composers who emphasized traditional types of piano music.

Character pieces   A *character piece* is a relatively short work, whose title suggests a mood, feeling, or personality for the piano. Character pieces, usually in ternary form, include the *bagatelle, moment musical, impromptu, ballade, scherzo, nocturne, capriccio, intermezzo,* and *prelude.* Some of these titles are misleading, even meaningless. For instance, *moment musical* suggests a piece that takes but a moment, and an example such as Schubert's *Moment musical* in F minor, Op. 94, No. 3 (1823), is indeed very short. On the other hand, the second and sixth similarly named members of the same set are relatively slow and leisurely. An *impromptu* (the word in French means extempore, or without preparation) is a composition supposedly suggestive of improvisation, but the impromptus of Schubert and Chopin are straightforward in style; the title, therefore, appears to be fanciful. An *intermezzo,* which we would expect to be played between two other pieces, is simply an atmospheric work, whose character is sometimes revealed by its tempo and expressive indications. Examples are Brahms's Intermezzo in A-flat major, Op. 76, No. 3 (1878), marked *Grazioso* ("Gracefully"), and his Intermezzo in B-flat minor, Op. 117, No. 2 (1892), marked *Andante non troppo e con molto espressione* ("Moving along but not too fast and with a great deal of expression"). And a Romantic piano *prelude,* unlike the similarly named works of J. S. Bach in his *Well-Tempered Clavier,* is not something that precedes or is paired with another composition, but a piece that stands alone as a graceful, reflective, fleeting, passionate, or melancholy pianistic expression. Chopin's Preludes, Op. 28 (1836–1839; excerpts in *AMA,* p. 370), a set of two dozen in a sequence defined by the circle of fifths (C, a, G, e, D, etc.), are the best-known Romantic examples, and Debussy's ushered in the twentieth century (see Chapter 30).

Some character-piece titles are easier to comprehend. *Bagatelle* means "trifle," or a very short piece, like all of Beethoven's bagatelles. A *capriccio* tends to be either humorous, like Brahms's Capriccio in B minor, Op. 76, No. 2 (1878), or energetic and agitated, like the same composer's Capriccio in D minor, Op. 116, No. 7 (1892). The word *ballade* is used when a piece seems particularly narrative, dramatic, or descriptive of some unrevealed story. Chopin composed four ballades, and Brahms wrote five. The same two composers wrote *scherzos* for the piano—dramatic developments of one motivic idea interrupted in the middle by a more lyrical section. Related in spirit and in form to the scherzo movement of the Romantic sonata cycle, these piano pieces are in a fast, agitated triple meter.

A *nocturne* (derived from the Latin word for "night") is usually a slow, dreamy *cantabile* melody accompanied by rolling arpeggios and chordal patterns. The Irish composer John Field (1782–1837) was the first to use the term "nocturne" for piano pieces. After studying with Clementi in London, he spent most of his career in Russia, where his influence was great. Chopin, impressed by Field's nocturnes and piano concertos, composed twenty-one nocturnes himself.

Among the favorite nineteenth-century dances written for piano were the **Dances** *waltz, Ländler, mazurka, polonaise,* and *écossaise.* The Austrian Ländler was **for piano** like the slow waltz, which eventually superseded it, but the dance steps involved a gliding motion of the foot on the first beat of each measure rather than the stomping motion of the slow waltz. Schubert composed dozens of Ländler and waltzes. Chopin and Brahms later added many waltzes to the repertoire.

The *polonaise* and *mazurka* are both Polish dances immortalized by that country's greatest Romantic composer, Frédéric Chopin (1810–1849). His majestic, robust polonaises, like the two by Liszt and many written for piano duet by Schubert, are based on the rhythmic figure $\begin{smallmatrix}3\\4\end{smallmatrix}$ ♫ ♩♫♫ ♩. For Chopin the polonaise represented Polish chivalry and patriotism. The several different varieties of mazurkas are shown by the diverse speeds and moods of Chopin's examples for piano. They are all in $\frac{3}{4}$ time, however, and have the unusual characteristics of stressing weak beats and varying the accentuation pattern. Many contain alterations of the diatonic scale, modal passages, and clouded tonalities (e.g., the contemplative introduction to the Mazurka in A minor, Op. 17, No. 4; c. 1831). Like the nocturnes and preludes, the mazurkas reveal Chopin at his most poetic, intimate, and innovative.

Unlike the other dances mentioned, the *écossaise* is in duple meter. A type of English country dance in a quick tempo, it is not related to authentic Scottish dance music. Beethoven and Schubert wrote collections of écossaises.

The piano étude

An *étude* is a composition designed to improve and display the performer's technique. A given étude tends to concentrate on one particular problem, such as playing octaves, arpeggios, or leaps, or acquiring digital independence, dexterity, or strength. Although études as finger exercises were composed by Clementi, Czerny, Ignaz Moscheles (1794–1870), and others, it was Chopin who turned the étude into a work of fine art. His études Op. 10 and Op. 25 (twelve in each set, 1829–1836) develop the technique of the pianist but also make their appeal to an audience as serious music. Liszt, Brahms, Scriabin, and Debussy also composed concert études for the piano. Liszt went to the extreme of writing twelve excruciatingly difficult études that he entitled *Etudes d'exécution transcendante* ("Transcendental Etudes," 1851), indicating that these works were too hard to be played—that is, except by Liszt himself.

Program music for piano

Program music for the piano, like that for orchestra, has extramusical associations. Robert Schumann frequently wrote this kind of piano music. For instance, his *Papillons* ("Butterflies"), Op. 2 (1829–1831), is a musical setting of the final, masked-ball episode in Jean Paul's novel *Flegeljahre* ("Years of Adolescence," 1804–1805). And, although we know of no program for Schumann's *Carnaval,* Op. 9 (1833–1835), the waltz and polonaise rhythms, and the characters named in the titles of some of the numbers, imply another ballroom scene, in which people meet, dance, and reveal their identities to varying degrees. In many of his piano works, such as *Kinderszenen* ("Scenes of Childhood," 1838), Schumann expresses musically the images that a child might see in a picture book, e.g., a hobby horse, a fireplace, and a game of hide and seek.

Liszt's collections entitled *Années de pèlerinage* ("Years of Pilgrimage," three volumes, 1835–1877) are his impressions of Switzerland and Italy. Among the pieces are *Les Cloches de Genève* ("The Clocks of Geneva," 1835–1836, rev. 1855), *Tre Sonetti del Petrarca* ("Three Petrarch Sonnets," c. 1839–1846; no. 104 in *NS*, E, II, no. 11), and *Les Jeux d'eaux à la Villa d'Este* ("The Fountains of the Villa d'Este," 1877). The *Années* include many tender works that contrast well with Liszt's more typically virtuoso pieces.

In *Pictures at an Exhibition* (1874) Mussorgsky created three pieces inspired by paintings of the Russian artist Victor Hartmann (1834–1873) that were displayed at a memorial exhibition in St. Petersburg in January 1874. They are *The Ballet of Chicks in Their Shells, A Hut on Chicken Legs,* and *The Great Gate of Kiev.* The other seven numbers in the collection, however, are splendid products of Mussorgsky's imagination.

In the Romantic era, listeners enjoyed hearing symphonic works and numbers from cantatas and operas played on the versatile and ubiquitous piano. Liszt made piano transcriptions of such works and also of songs, simple piano pieces, and organ and violin compositions, in which he captured the spirit of the original but usually transformed it into a bravura showpiece. His titles often reveal how far afield Liszt's versions were from the original; two such instances are the *Grand Fantasy on "La Sonnambula"* (1839, rev. 1840–1841) and the *Paraphrase on Themes from Verdi's Opera "Rigoletto"* (1859). Other transcribers include the virtuoso pianist Sigismond Thalberg (1812–1871); Carl Tausig (1841–1871), a student of Liszt; Ferruccio Busoni (1866–1924), essayist and composer of several operas, including *Doktor Faust* (1916–1924) and *Turandot* (1917); and the pianist and editor Louise Farrenc (1804–1875), whose operatic potpourris are derived from works by Rossini, Bellini, Weber, Donizetti, and Meyerbeer.

Piano transcriptions

Compositional Styles in Nineteenth-Century Piano Music

Beethoven

Beethoven's thirty-two piano sonatas demonstrate his stylistic metamorphosis from student of Haydn to idol of the Romantics. In addition to Haydn and Mozart, Clementi and Jan Ladislav Dušek (1760–1812) are among the influences on Beethoven's piano works. The outer movements of his first sonata, Op. 2, No. 1, in F minor (1793–1795; first and third movements in *AMA*, p. 270) are reminiscent of *Sturm und Drang* and of Haydn's pieces in the same key, and the finale of Op. 2, No. 2, in A major (1794–1795) is in the *style galant*. Several of Beethoven's slow movements are *empfindsam*, as in Op. 2, No. 1, and Op. 7 in E-flat major (1796–1797; second movement in *AMA*, p. 279). The *Largo appassionato* in Op. 2, No. 2, is reminiscent of a Baroque saraband, with its second-beat accents and its "walking" bass line. In his selection of themes, motivic development, extremely slow second movements, quick dance movements, and frequent touches of humor—especially in finales, e.g., Op. 10, No. 2, in F major (1796–1797) and Op. 10, No. 3, in D major (1797–1798; *MCP*, no. 24)—Beethoven is very much like Haydn.

Early sonatas

Nonetheless, Beethoven always showed individuality: for example, in his extensive use of the minor mode, his unexpected modulations, and his exhaustive motivic manipulations, as in the Presto of Op. 10, No. 3, in which the opening four-note descent governs all the other themes in the exposition. Beethoven also combined *cantabile* lyricism with gravity and weight in his *adagio* movements, which proceed ever so slowly and often rise passionately to great climaxes.

With the *Sonate Pathétique* in C minor, Op. 13 (c. 1797–1798; *NS*, E, I, no. 35; *NS*, S, no. 19; second movement in *ML* I, p. 169; third movement in *AMA*, p. 288), Beethoven began to search for ever-new ways of expressing himself at the keyboard. The work's introductory Grave, in the style of a

French overture, recurs strategically at the juncture of the exposition and the development, and just before the final stormy measures in the coda. This sonata also has an *Adagio cantabile,* in which the piano must stimulate the singing quality of less percussive instruments, and a finale whose rondo theme is derived from the second theme of the first movement.

Op. 13 has pathos, and the *Moonlight* Sonata (1801) contains violence, in its *Presto agitato.* Never before had the piano been used for such emotional outbursts. The effect is even greater because the sonata's first movement is slow and introverted. Beethoven titled this work *Sonata quasi una fantasia,* and the word "fantasia" implies that the sonata is unusual in the nature, form, and order of its movements. It is also unusual that the first movement of Op. 26 in A-flat major (1800–1801) is a theme with five variations, and its third (slow) movement is a funeral march. Beethoven's Op. 31, No. 1, in G major (1802) contains a second theme in the opening movement that is not only in the unorthodox key of B major but is also in the style of Italian comic opera of the time. The Sonata (*Tempest*) in D minor, Op. 31, No. 2 (1802), is remarkable in having recitative-like passages in its first movement (this movement is in *AMA,* p. 297, and in *MCP,* no. 25).

Middle sonatas   Beethoven's two monumental sonatas dating from his middle period are the so-called *Waldstein* Sonata in C major, Op. 53 (1803–1804; dedicated to Beethoven's patron Count Ferdinand Waldstein, 1762–1823; first movement in *AMA,* p. 304), and the emotionally charged *Appassionata* Sonata in F minor, Op. 57 (1804–1805; *MSO* I, p. 300). The most unusual aspects of these works are their extreme length, expansive developments and codas, rhythmic drive, and the virtuosity necessitated by their inherently musical demands. The second theme in the *Allegro con brio* of Op. 53 is in the key of E major (as in Op. 31, No. 1, a I–III relationship) and proceeds in a relatively slow chordal fashion. Such hymn-like sonority, which is also stressed, for instance, in the trio section of the Allegretto of Op. 10, No. 2, is quite frequent in Beethoven.

The *Allegro ma non troppo* of the Sonata in F-sharp major, Op. 78 (1809), is a fusion of a fast sonata-allegro form and a warm, lyrical melodic content. The second movement of Op. 90 in E minor (1814) is an E-major sonata-rondo which has the leisurely lyricism of Schubert.

Last sonatas   Beethoven's last five sonatas, his most esoteric and difficult, baffled his audiences. These works stress counterpoint, variation technique, great length, rhythmic complexity, and the blurring of demarcations between successive thematic areas and sometimes between movements. Fugues occur in the finales of Op. 101 in A major (1816), Op. 106 in B-flat major (*Hammerklavier,* 1817–1818), and Op. 110 in A-flat major (1821–1822; *MCP,* no. 29). Theme and variations is the format for the last movements of Op. 109 in E major (1820) and Op. 111 in C minor (1821–1822). These long, contrapuntal finales shift the center of gravity in the sonata cycle from its more traditional location in the first movement to the last movement. Beethoven's variation technique is also seen in his *Thirty-Three Variations on a Waltz by Diabelli,* Op.

120 (1819, 1822–1823), the largest and most imaginative set of keyboard variations since J. S. Bach.

Schubert, His Contemporaries, and Mendelssohn

The piano music of Carl Maria von Weber (1786–1826) is brilliant and at times poetic—for example, his *Aufforderung zum Tanz* ("Invitation to the Dance," 1819)—but it sometimes tends toward superficiality. On the other hand, many of the piano pieces by the Bohemians Dušek, Václav Jan Tomašek (1774–1850), and the latter's student Jan Hugo Voříšek (1791–1825) are elegant. Their character pieces, with such poetic titles as *eclogue* and *rhapsody,* influenced Schubert greatly.

Along with almost two dozen sonatas, the last three of which are especially fine blends of lyricism and drama, Schubert composed many piano miniatures. Whether on a large or small scale, Schubert's piano works are tuneful and tasteful, and generally avoid virtuosity. An outstanding exception is his virtuoso *Wanderer Fantasy,* D. 760 (1822), which foreshadows Liszt's thematic transformation and uninterrupted sequence of movements. Schubert's title reveals his work's derivation from the eighteenth-century fantasia and its use of a theme from his own Lied *Der Wanderer,* D. 489 (1816).

Schubert

Like Schubert, Felix Mendelssohn was averse to bravura music, preferring moderation and clarity. His interest in J. S. Bach led him to compose preludes and fugues. Mozart was the model for many of Mendelssohn's works, and it may be said of Mendelssohn that he preserved the composure, restraint, and elegance of the Classical style in an age of subjective experimentation, emotion, and rebellion. One of Mendelssohn's finest concert pieces is the *Variations sérieuses* ("Serious Variations") in D minor, Op. 54 (1841). However, Mendelssohn's most popular piano pieces are his *Lieder ohne Worte* ("Songs Without Words," 1830–1845; excerpts in *AMA,* p. 353; *ML* I, p. 52), miniatures that show their composer's ability to capture a scene or sentiment in music.

Mendelssohn

Robert Schumann

Robert Schumann epitomizes the new Romantic spirit of the early nineteenth century. Writer, critic, editor, and dreamer, he was an intellectual subject to extremes of ecstasy and despair. His life was plagued by syphilis, which brought on the mental disorders that eventually killed him. From 1828 to 1839 Schumann devoted himself to the piano, for which he published his first twenty-three works. As a youth he had hopes of becoming a concert pianist, and some of his early works are of a virtuoso nature. Starting with the *Carnaval,* however, Schumann put his aesthetic theories into practice and avoided empty, flashy display.

Schumann's piano music is sonorous and dynamic. Except for a few nearly "impossible" passages, such as the "Paganini" section of the *Carnaval,* his music can be said to be pianistic, that is, comfortable for the fingers while still taking full advantage of the instrument. Schumann uses a wide range,

Musical style

lingers on nonharmonic tones, favors the appoggiatura, and avoids strident dissonances. He masterfully juggles such rhythmic effects as syncopation, hemiola, and bar-line displacement. Schumann's frequent use of loud chords alternates with contrapuntal part-writing and delicate, often harmonically ambiguous, sections.

Literary titles and intellectualism

Many of Schumann's piano works have literary titles (e.g., "novellette"), indications (e.g., "in the tone of a legend"), and programs (e.g., *Papillons*). His scores even contain citations from literature (e.g., from Goethe's *Faust,* Gretchen's words *Meine Ruh' ist hin* in the second intermezzo from Op. 4; 1832). What is more intriguing, however, is Schumann's enjoyment of musical games, anagrams, and connections among pieces that can be understood fully only by people familiar with his total output. His first published work is a theme and variations based on the name of a woman whom he had met at a ball, Meta von Abegg. Since the German letters ABEGG represent the tones A–B-flat–E–G–G, this five-note motive becomes the theme of Schumann's composition (1829–1830). Similarly, the *Carnaval* (excerpts in *MSO* II, p. 38) is derived from the tones A–E-flat–C–B (in German, A–Es = S–C–H), or A-flat–C–B (in German, As–C–H) because Asch was the name of his girlfriend's hometown. Also, a–S–c–h is the quartet of letters in Schumann's name which can be turned into musical tones. Schumann also composed fugues on the name of Bach, i.e., on the motive B-flat–A–C–B.

Some pieces share interrelationships. For instance, *Papillons* and *Carnaval* both deal with masked-ball scenes. Therefore, perhaps, the "butterfly theme" which opens the first number in *Papillons* returns in the "Florestan" movement of *Carnaval,* and the D-major *Grossvatertanz* ("Grandfather dance") theme from the finale of *Papillons* reappears in the finale of the *Carnaval* to represent the archaic Philistines. Another carnival scene occurs in Schumann's *Faschingsschwank aus Wien* ("Carnival Jest from Vienna"), Op. 26 (1839–1840); note the "asch" in *Faschingsschwank*. In the opening rondo of Op. 26, the four untitled episodes are musical references to four composers popular at the time; Schumann in turn imitates a nocturne of Chopin, a Venetian boat-song (as in the "Songs Without Words") of Mendelssohn, the third movement from Beethoven's Sonata in E-flat major, Op. 31, No. 3 (1802), and a Ländler of Schubert. When the "Schubert" episode ends, Schumann plays a musical joke by quoting *La Marseillaise,* the playing of which was strictly forbidden for political reasons in post-Napoleonic Vienna, the setting of this carnival.

Clara Schumann

Although many musicians realize that Clara Schumann (1819–1896) edited her husband's works, very few are familiar with her own exquisite piano music, including dances, variations, preludes and fugues, and such character pieces as romances, scherzos, and an impromptu. This magnificent pianist and champion of her husband's works, as well as those of Brahms, also composed a stirring Piano Concerto in A minor, Op. 7 (c. 1835), and a Piano Trio in G minor, Op. 17 (by 1846).

Chopin, Liszt, and Brahms

Most of Frédéric Chopin's music is for piano solo, and all of his other works use the piano, too. He himself was a successful pianist, making Paris his home from 1831 on, but he avoided extremes of showmanship, especially loud playing, and much preferred the salon to the concert hall. Chopin's piano music is designed to fit the player's fingers in a natural, relatively comfortable manner (except for some of the etudes and other purposely problematic pieces), and much of it exploits the full range of the keyboard. An admirer of the lyricism of Bellini's operas, Chopin created the most appealing melodic ideas and graceful pianistic embellishments imaginable. His rich harmonic language makes much use of chromaticism, modality, enharmonic modulations, excursions into unexpected keys, chords with added tones, all kinds of seventh chords, and many nonharmonic tones, often unprepared and sometimes unresolved. A typically colorful sequence by Chopin is found in his *Fantaisie* in F minor, Op. 49 (1840–1841; see Example 27.1).

Chopin

Ex. 27.1 Frédéric Chopin, *Fantaisie in* F minor, mm. 21–28

As these measures show, Chopin was adept at making brief excursions to unexpected tonalities.

Occasionally, Chopin's harmonic and tonal schemes are quite ambiguous, and avant-garde for their time; examples are the Prelude in A minor, Op. 28, No. 2 (1838; *AMA*, p. 371; *MSO* II, p. 29), and the opening of the Scherzo in C-sharp minor, Op. 39 (1839). It would not be unfair to say that in Chopin's music one finds forebodings of the end of the tonal era in music history, and that had he lived longer he would have been an able partner of Liszt's in bridging the gap between Romanticism and the twentieth century.

Rubato is called for in almost every Chopin composition, for his music breathes in a rhapsodic, passionate manner and engages in introspective and improvisatory sections, as in the *Polonaise-Fantaisie,* Op. 61 (1845–1846). Furthermore, frills and flourishes often create interesting cross-rhythms. Although his pieces, especially the miniatures, tend to be in ternary or rondo form, Chopin reveals himself as a master of musical architecture and capable

Grandville (pseudonym J. I. I. Gérard), *Galop chromatique* (1843). Liszt's unbridled virtuosity at the piano was a natural target for caricaturists such as Grandville. (Courtesy, photographic services of the Bibliothèque Nationale, Paris)

of great climaxes in such works as the four ballades, each a complex rear-
rangement of the tonal and thematic relationships in the sonata form.

Chopin's piano style was the basis for that of Liszt. However, Liszt's fiery   **Liszt**
Hungarian temperament, extreme virtuosity, Viennese training with Czerny,
and fascination with literary Romanticism and the programmatic approach of
Berlioz all contributed to his own very individual style. Liszt's piano music
abounds in climaxes, chromaticism, scales, octaves, leaps, ornamented melodic lines, free rhythms, and improvisatory, cadenza-like passages. He also
favors full chords in both hands, chordal scales, arpeggiation, strident dissonances, hand crossings, trills in double notes, and lightning-fast passagework.

Idolized by women, students, and the public, Liszt provided a link between the early Romanticism of Robert Schumann and Mendelssohn and the
Post-Romantic language of Mahler, Richard Strauss, and even Debussy. On
the one hand, Liszt composed salon music and sentimental works like the
Hungarian Rhapsody No. 13 in A minor (1853). On the other hand, he wrote
lugubrious, stark pieces such as the *Sunt lacrymae rerum* ("There Are Tears for
Misfortune," 1869), from the third set of the *Années de pèlerinage,* and the dissonant *Pensée des morts* ("Thought of the Dead"), from the *Harmonies poétiques
et réligieuses* ("Poetic and Religious Harmonies," 1845–1852), which opens
in $\frac{5}{4}$ time (see Example 27.2) but is as free of metrical regularity as it is of a
key signature. Employing whole-tone scales, altered chords, and severe harmonic clashes, Liszt's late works eroded the foundations of functional harmony
and influenced such later composers as Mahler, Debussy, Ravel, Stravinsky,
Schoenberg, Prokofiev, and Shostakovich. Some of his late works, such as
Nuages gris ("Gray Clouds," 1881; *NAWM* II, no. 124), contain features of

Ex. 27.2   Franz Liszt, *Pensée des morts,* mm. 1–14

Ex. 27.2 cont.

the Impressionistic style and of Schoenberg's pre-twelve-tone works. Moreover, the diabolical spirit of Liszt's Third Mephisto Waltz (1883) and *Totentanz* ("Dance of Death," 1849, rev. 1853, 1859), a set of variations on the plainsong *Dies irae* for piano and orchestra, influenced such composers as Mahler and Stravinsky. And the bombastic heroism and passionate rhetoric of such passages as that shown in Example 27.3 from the most impressive Sonata in B minor (1852–1853) promise things to come in the music of Mahler, Puccini, and others.

Brahms   Brahms's piano music is Romantic in its rich harmonizations, long and lyrical melodic lines, and myriad rhythmic complications. However, Brahms turned his back on both sentimentality and virtuosity, and his piano pieces are primarily serious, absolute works, usually thickly textured, contrapuntal, and modeled on the piano music of Beethoven, Schubert, and Robert Schumann. Brahms probably first impressed Schumann, who introduced him to musical society as a "young eagle," with his sprawling piano sonatas, especially Sonata No. 3 in F minor, Op. 5 (1853). Later in life Brahms turned away from long sonatas and sets of variations to short, poetic character pieces, his favorites being intermezzos and capriccios. In these little pieces Brahms takes one basic motive and exploits its possibilities at length. For instance, see Example 27.4, showing Brahms's motivic manipulation in the Intermezzo in E minor, Op. 119, No. 2 (1892).

Post-Romantic Piano Music in France, Spain, and Russia

In Post-Romantic Germany and Austria, piano music received less attention than before, as Wagner, Bruckner, Mahler, Wolf, and Richard Strauss were more interested in voices and the orchestra. However, in France such composers as Franck, Fauré, and Saint-Saëns wrote many piano works, as did

France and Spain

Ex. 27.3   Franz Liszt, Sonata in B minor, mm. 105–112

Ex. 27.4   Johannes Brahms, Intermezzo in E minor, Op. 119, No. 2

Debussy and Ravel. In French Romantic piano music, we find restraint, elegance, colorful harmonies and sonorities, and Classical orderliness; as is usual among the French, the emphasis is on color and linear design. Spanish composers also wrote for the piano during this period; two of the most outstanding were Isaac Albéniz (1860–1909) and Enrique Granados (1867–1916). The former, whose most famous work is *Iberia* (1906–1908), a set of twelve evocative pieces, was a child prodigy greatly admired by Liszt (who was briefly his teacher).

In Russia, Tchaikovsky, Scriabin, and Rachmaninov lavished much effort on piano music. The most intriguing of these three was perhaps the concert pianist Alexander Scriabin (1872–1915), whose earliest works sound like John Field and Chopin. Under the influence of Liszt and Wagner, Scriabin's style became more dissonant, chromatic, and even Impressionistic, to the point of his abandoning the tonal system entirely in the last five of his ten sonatas (1912–1913). Scriabin became a mystic and theosophist, and such a piece as *Vers la flamme* ("Toward the Flame," 1914; *NAWM* II, no. 148) conjures up a mystical, demonic picture of darkness gradually yielding to a dazzling light that ultimately devours everything around it. The piano style of Sergei Rachmaninov (1873–1943) includes flurries of notes up and down the keyboard in both hands, octave passages, sentimental and languishing melodies, sensitive harmonizations, and heroic chordal climaxes in the tradition of Liszt.

Russia

Organ Music in the Romantic Era

While the piano flourished during the Romantic era, with its increased emphasis on secularism, the importance of the organ declined drastically. The devotion of Mendelssohn to the Protestant musical tradition, and especially to J. S. Bach's music, was exceptional for his time, and he wrote many solo compositions for the organ, including Three Preludes and Fugues, Op. 37 (1837), and Six Sonatas, Op. 65 (1844–1845). Mendelssohn's model was the organ style of J. S. Bach, but he added his own Romantic sense of color, dynamic shading, and the singing line.

Mendelssohn

Even more colorful is the output of Liszt, who began writing organ music as early as the 1850s, well before his years as a cleric in Rome (1861–1868). For Liszt the organ provided a palette comparable to that of the orchestra. Among his organ pieces are a Prelude and Fugue on B–A–C–H (1855, rev. 1870) and the litany *Ora pro nobis* ("Pray for Us," 1864). Other composers who looked upon the organ as a one-man orchestra were the French virtuoso organists Charles Marie Widor (1844–1937) and Louis Vierne (1870–1937). The founder of this new school of French organ composition was César Franck, who wrote many short pieces and is represented often in recital by his Three Chorales (1890). His *Grande pièce symphonique* (c. 1860), which combines its four movements into one continuous work, betrays its composer's

Liszt and French organ music

attitude in its title. Another French work that uses the organ very effectively, together with the orchestra, is Saint-Saëns's mighty Symphony in C minor, Op. 78 (1886), especially impressive in its thunderous finale.

Brahms   Like Mendelssohn, Brahms revived the organ genres of the Protestant Baroque tradition. Most impressive are his Eleven Chorale Preludes, Op. 122 (1896), exhibiting his consummate contrapuntal skill and Romantic emotionalism. Providing a link between Brahms and twentieth-century organ composers in Germany is Max Reger (1873–1916), whose music in general abounds in chromaticism, complex harmonies, unusual modulations, and fullness of texture.

Romantic and Post-Romantic Chamber Music

Extremists that they were, most Romantic composers preferred both the intimacy of the piano and the grandiosity of the orchestra to the small chamber music group. Furthermore, at concerts people wanted virtuosity, and at home, songs and easy piano pieces. Amateurs did play chamber music, but in this area they favored the treasures from the Classical period, because Romantic chamber music tended to make technical demands beyond their capabilities. Beethoven and Schubert, who grew up during the Classical era, devoted much time to writing chamber music. After them, however, composers showed less interest in it until Brahms restored it to a position of great importance.

The popularity of the piano in the nineteenth century extended to the domain of chamber music, and composers frequently wrote for various combinations of strings and piano. Sonatas for piano and one other instrument, usually violin or cello, were fairly common, as were string quartets, ever the symbol of the ideal ensemble.

The String Quartet of the Romantic Era
Beethoven   Beethoven, who composed sixteen string quartets, did not complete his first set of six (Op. 18) until 1800. The main influences on Beethoven's Op. 18 included Mozart, Haydn, and Emanuel Aloys Förster (1748–1823), an Austrian teacher of harmony and composition and the author of four dozen string quartets. From these composers Beethoven learned grace and elegance, as in No. 5 in A major, modeled after Mozart's K. 464; the possibilities of thematic development, as in the first movement of No. 1 in F major (*MSO* I, p. 276; *NS*, E, I, no. 34); and humor and playfulness, as in the Haydnesque finale of No. 4 in C minor. From them all Beethoven also learned how to employ the instruments in a contrapuntal manner and how to treat each as an important voice.

The set of three quartets dedicated to the Russian ambassador to Vienna, Count Andreas Rasumovsky (1752–1836), Beethoven's Op. 59 (1805–1806), considerably enlarged the dimensions of the string quartet. In these works Beethoven unleashed his dramatic talents by employing ambiguous har-

This woodcut taken from the *Illustrated London News* of 1872 shows the great violinist Wilma Neruda (c. 1838–1911) in a string quartet performance. A reporter for the *News* wrote (p. 199): "Perhaps no lady violinist has ever equalled Madame Norman-Neruda in calm repose of manner and graceful use of the bow arm. Certainly no player of her sex has commanded a purer tone, a truer intonation, or more neat and finished mechanism." (Courtesy, Southampton University Library)

monies (e.g., the opening of Op. 59, No. 1, in F major on a tonic second-inversion chord, or some of the irregular resolutions in that work's second movement; complete work in *MCP,* no. 27) and by writing fugatos and fugues (e.g., the double fugato in the development section of the first Allegro in Op. 59, No. 1, and the fugue that serves as the finale of Op. 59, No. 3, in C major; see Example 27.5). He also injected drama by using varied recapitulations and by concealing the structural demarcations between sections of a movement and between themes within a section. In tribute to Rasumovsky, Beethoven used Russian melodies in each of the first two of these quartets.

Beethoven's Quartet in F minor, Op. 95 (1810), was called *Quartetto serioso* by the composer himself. In a key then considered "uncomfortable" for string players, this piece is highly concentrated, tense, and passionate, with a minimum of bridge or cadential materials. It also features extreme changes of emotion, severe dissonances, chromaticism, fugal sections (in the second movement), a connection between the inner movements, a chorale-like trio in its march-like scherzo, a false recapitulation in its finale, and an ironically merry ending, which sounds like the finale of an opera buffa. For fourteen years after Op. 95, Beethoven completed no more string quartets.

The last five of Beethoven's string quartets (1823–1826), which appeared in relatively quick succession despite his illness, were rarely performed until the time of Brahms. Having abandoned the piano, Beethoven felt a string quartet more capable of playing the counterpoint and the shifting sonorities

Ex. 27.5   Ludwig van Beethoven, String Quartet in C major, Mvt. 4, mm. 1–35.

Ex. 27.5 cont.

he wished to use. However, these quartets were incomprehensible to the audiences of Beethoven's era, and too difficult for most string players at the time. Few liked the *Grosse Fuge,* Op. 133 (1825–1826)—originally the finale of Op. 130 in B-flat major—because of its tautness, exhaustive treatment of one motive, disagreeable dissonance, and enormous length.[1] And not many could cope with the Renaissance modality and metrical patterns in the slow movement of Op. 132 in A minor (1825); the subtlety of the variation movements in Op. 127 in E-flat major (1823–1824) and Op. 131 in C-sharp minor (1826); or the eerie, ethereal endings in Opp. 127 and 132. All of these elements are features of Beethoven's late style. (Op. 130 is in *MSO* I, p. 280; its second movement is in *CAMF,* I, no. 48, Op. 131 is in *MCP,* no. 30; its first and second movements are in *NAWM* II, no. 108; its first movement is also in *ML* II, p. 281.)

Austrian and German quartets after Beethoven

Like Mozart, Beethoven, and Dvořák, Schubert played the viola in chamber music groups, and his early string quartets (1812–1817) were mainly entertainment pieces for himself, his family, and friends. The finest among Schubert's fifteen quartets, however, are the last three: in A minor, D. 804 (1824); in D minor, D. 810 (*Death and the Maiden,* 1824), with a second-movement set of variations on Schubert's song of the same title, D. 531 (1817; *MSO* II, p. 8); and in G major, D. 887 (1826). These late works are tuneful, warm (the cello has much melodic material), and clear. The Quartet in A minor is the most singable, although the song is sad and delicate, until the happy gypsy-like finale breaks this mood. D. 887 is a study in modal mixture, especially in its first movement.

While Mendelssohn wrote his six string quartets with the same skilled craftsmanship shown in his symphonies, the absence of the colors of the orchestral palette makes his quartets far less remarkable. Robert Schumann's three string quartets are more passionate and unorthodox in form. Like Beethoven, Schumann wrote long, contrapuntal developments, very slow *cantabile* movements, and music in which whimsicality and ferocity alternate. Unlike Beethoven, however, Schumann is repetitive in his developments and has difficulty in making recapitulations sound climactic. He is most comfortable in scherzos (e.g., the great one in theme-and-variations form in his Quartet No. 3 in A major, 1842) and slow movements, sections which allow for imagination and moodiness.

Brahms

Even more impressive are the three string quartets of Johannes Brahms, one of the greatest chamber music composers of all time. Severely self-critical, Brahms is said to have destroyed dozens of works, and once reported that he had written twenty string quartets before deeming one good enough to publish. In 1873 he completed two well-integrated, motivically economical quartets. For example, in the Quartet in A minor, Op. 51, No. 2, the initial nine measures give rise to all the other themes of the *Allegro non troppo,* and in the Quartet in C minor, Op. 51, No. 1, the first eight notes generate themes in all four movements. Brahms's last string quartet, Op. 67 in B-flat major (1876), is a lighter, more bucolic work, which features the combination of $\frac{2}{4}$ and $\frac{6}{8}$ meters. Another German composer who preserved various features of the Baroque and Classical styles was Max Reger. His six string quartets contain much chromaticism, full texture, and the increased length common in the Post-Romantic era.

Outside Germany and Austria some of the finest string quartets were written by the Bohemians Smetana and Dvořák and the Frenchmen Fauré and D'Indy. Smetana's two string quartets are autobiographical program pieces, the first such works conceived for this medium. The Quartet in E minor (1876) is entitled *From My Life* and expresses Smetana's Romantic youth (first movement), penchant for dancing (polka in the second movement), love for his first wife (third movement), and patriotic pride (folk-like finale). Toward the end, however, a sustained high tone symbolizes the whistling sound in Smetana's ears that accompanied his growing deafness.

Bohemian and French quartets

Dvořák's Quartet in E-flat major, Op. 51 (1878–1879), contains a polka, a *dumka,* a *furiant,* and a *skočna,* all Bohemian dances. And along with the *New World* Symphony, Dvořák composed a string quartet and string quintet during his brief sojourn in the United States. The *American* Quartet in F major, Op. 96 (1893), contains pentatonic themes (as does the symphony), a sweet songfulness, and strong dance rhythms. This composer's last two quartets, in A-flat major, Op. 105, and G major, Op. 106 (both 1895), are magnificent works, showing the spirit of Brahms.

Dvořák

Gabriel Fauré's one string quartet, Op. 121 (1923–1924), adds to the Classical French qualities of clarity, grace, and balance several harmonic innovations, such as modality, enharmony, frequent use of nonharmonic tones, and much chromaticism. However, the tonal center is always clear, and the sound is never harsh or disturbing. Vincent d'Indy's three string quartets (1890, 1897, and 1928–1929) include melodic references to Gregorian chant, French folk songs, some Wagnerian harmonies, and an architectonic approach to structure.

Fauré

Several Romantic composers better known for their work in other genres also wrote string quartets. These include Cherubini, Donizetti, Verdi, Spohr, Borodin, Tchaikovsky, and the Russian Anton Arensky (1861–1906).

The Duo Sonata in the Nineteenth Century

Beethoven, whose violin sonatas were published as "Pianoforte Sonatas with Violin Accompaniment," inherited the Classical attitude that the duo sonata was a work for keyboard accompanied by another instrument, such as the violin or flute. However, the Romantic impulse was too passionate and dramatic for nineteenth-century composers to adhere to this notion for long. Beethoven's Sonata in C minor, Op. 30, No. 2 (1801–1802), is already a study in the equality of the two instruments, which share thematic material. His ten violin and five cello sonatas occupied him in the middle of his career (1796–1815) and demonstrate the essential features of his early and middle styles. For instance, the Sonata for Violin and Piano No. 4 in A minor, Op. 23 (1800), reveals his urgently driving power, whereas No. 5 (*Spring*) in F major, Op. 24 (1800–1801), for the same instruments, exemplifies his warmth and relaxed lyricism. As Beethoven remarked, No. 9 (*Kreutzer*) in A major, Op. 47 (1802–1803), also for violin and piano, is "written in a highly concerted style, just like a concerto," and it was dedicated to the renowned French violinist Rodolphe Kreutzer (1766–1831). This virtuoso never played it, however, because he deemed it outrageously difficult, even unmanageable. In

Beethoven

Henri Fantin-Latour (1836–1904), *Un Morceau de Schumann* ("A Piece by Schumann," 1864). In this etching Fantin-Latour, often inspired by musical compositions, depicts the English artists Edwin Edwards and Mrs. Edwards performing a chamber work by Robert Schumann—certainly an arrangement, as Schumann wrote nothing for flute and piano. (Prints Division, The New York Public Library; Astor, Lenox and Tilden Foundations)

1803 Beethoven himself performed it for the first time, with the mulatto violinist George Bridgetower (1779[?]–1860). The *Kreutzer* Sonata's first movement is unusual in having a slow introduction in A major followed by a sonata-allegro in A minor. While Beethoven's first two cello sonatas are diffuse, his third, in A major, Op. 69 (1807–1808; first movement in *CAMF* II, no. 153), is a robust and tightly knit work with wonderful dialogues between the piano and cello in the second themes of the outer movements.

Other duo sonatas before 1870   Schubert's most interesting duo sonata is an 1824 work making use of a short-lived instrument called the *arpeggione,* which combined the features of a cello and a guitar. Far better music, however, are Robert Schumann's two sonatas for violin and piano (1851), which tend toward cyclical form and contain highly expressive slow movements. Chopin's Sonata for Cello and Piano in G minor, Op. 65 (1845–1846), provides the cellist with glorious melodies and the pianist with a powerful supportive role, and the sonata form in the *Allegro moderato* is handled expertly. In Norway Grieg produced three violin sonatas (1865, 1867, 1886–1887) and one cello sonata (1883), all well balanced between the two instruments, melodically appealing, and rich in chromatic, Chopinesque harmonies.

Brahms composed three violin, two cello, and two clarinet (or viola) sonatas. Each is a masterpiece, reflecting the composer's Classical control and restraint, Romantic melodies and harmonies, and a wide range of emotions. In the Sonata for Violin and Piano in D minor, Op. 108 (1886–1888), the development section of the Allegro retains a dominant pedal throughout its forty-six measures. The Adagio is an instrumental song, the frisky intermezzo-like third movement is a series of variations on a small motive, and the finale is stormy. In the tradition of Schubert, Brahms used the theme of a song (*Regenlied,* or "Rain Song," Op. 59, No. 3; c. 1871) in the finale of the Sonata for Violin and Piano in G major, Op. 78 (1878–1879), a peaceful and gentle work.

Brahms

Brahms's emotional Sonata for Cello and Piano No. 1 in E minor, Op. 38 (1862–1865), emphasizing the lower register of the cello, culminates in a fugato finale. His No. 2 in F major, Op. 99 (1886), is especially melodious, brilliant, and colorful. The two clarinet sonatas—the more passionate F minor work and the more delicate one in E-flat major (Op. 120; 1894)—can also be played by viola and piano; Brahms himself made the few necessary alterations.

In France such composers as Fauré, Franck, and Saint-Saëns wrote beautiful duo sonatas. Fauré created long, supple, and asymmetrical melodic lines in the tradition of Berlioz, as can be heard in his Sonata for Violin and Piano in A major, Op. 13 (1875–1876), a work whose structure is quite Classical. Franck's Sonata in A major for the same two instruments (*MSO* II, p. 231; first movement in *AMA,* p. 411) is much more popular today. This cyclical work is full of wonderful sonorities and contains instrumental recitatives, fantasias, cadenzas, and, in its rondo-finale, imitative canon. The opening violin melody, spelling out a dominant-ninth chord, provides the motivic material from which Franck weaves much of the sonata. In works such as this, Franck combined the structural control of the German style and the voluptuousness and broadened harmonic language of the French.

French Post-Romantic duo sonatas

Nineteenth-Century Music for Other Small Instrumental Combinations

Romantic and Post-Romantic composers wrote music for many small ensembles, usually with three to eight players. Although the piano was often involved, much music was written for string groups and mixed string and wind ensembles. One composer who emphasized the woodwind quintet (flute, oboe, clarinet, bassoon, and French horn) was Antoine Reicha, who wrote two dozen works for this combination. Reicha composed a prodigious amount of chamber music, including a decet for five strings and five winds.

Reicha

Three piano trios (i.e., works for piano, violin, and cello) constituted Beethoven's first publication, and Op. 1, No. 3, in C minor (c. 1794–1795) already reveals the composer's dramatic flair and expert handling of all three instruments. The most famous of his nine piano trios is No. 6 (*Archduke*) in

Beethoven's trios and septet

B-flat major, Op. 97 (1810–1811), dedicated to Archduke Rudolph. As a middle-period work in the composer's career, this trio breathes freely, is lyrically expansive, and enjoys a sweeping opening theme (see Example 27.6). The trio continues with a scherzo, a set of ornamental variations, and (without a pause) a rondo. Beethoven's piano had a more limited range of dynamics than today's concert grand, so that the violin and cello together were then more evenly matched with the piano.

    The work that first brought Beethoven into the public eye was his Septet in E-flat major, Op. 20 (1799–1800), for violin, viola, cello, bass, clarinet, French horn, and bassoon. In the style of a divertimento, it nonetheless contains symphonic dimensions and a richness of sonority. Annoyed that the public preferred this work to his more serious pieces, Beethoven took a dislike to it and wrote no more compositions of this kind.

Schubert's octet, trios, and quintets

    Beethoven's septet was the prototype for Franz Schubert's Octet in F major, D. 803 (1824), for the same seven instruments plus a second violin, with the same number of movements (six) in the same sequence. A nobleman in the service of Archduke Rudolph commissioned the work and requested something like the Beethoven piece. Despite its cheerfulness, the Schubert

Ex. 27.6   Ludwig van Beethoven, *Archduke* Trio, Mvt. 1, mm. 1–8

octet is a serious work, as indicated by the chromatic harmonies in the slow introduction and the ominous opening of the finale. The theme of its variation movement is from Schubert's opera *Die Freunde von Salamanka* ("The Friends from Salamanca," 1815). The composer's two piano trios in B-flat major, D. 898 (c. 1827), and E-flat major, D. 929 (1827), exploit the upper registers of the piano to balance the low register of the cello. So does the entertaining *Trout* Quintet in A major (for violin, viola, cello, bass, and piano, c. 1819), whose theme-and-variations movement is based on the composer's song *Die Forelle* ("The Trout"), D. 550 (1816–1817, rev. 1818; the variation movement is in *MSO* II, p. 1, and in *NS*, E, II, no. 3; *NS*, S, no. 23).

Although Mozart's string quintets contained two violins, two violas, and one cello, Schubert followed Boccherini's lead in using two violins, one viola, and two cellos. The added richness and warmth of the low strings helps make this Quintet in C major, D. 956 (1828), one of Schubert's greatest creations. Its *Allegro ma non troppo* uses a nonfunctional diminished-seventh chord in the second measure and is colored throughout by wonderful harmonic strokes. For instance, the closing, march-like idea demonstrates Schubert's finesse in shifting tonal planes (see Example 27.7). This theme is also the basis for much of the development section. In the Adagio the ethereal, contemplative opening theme moves slowly and serenely but with soaring lyricism and inexorable forward thrust. As in many ternary movements, its middle section provides a stormy, emotional mood. The gloomy trio of the scherzo movement is a disturbing foreboding of the severity with which the finale ends. When this final movement (an Allegretto) begins, as an entertaining rondo, it is imbued with the joyful aura of the Viennese café, but near its end the C-minor theme begins to speed up tremendously, and then a harsh, dissonant attack seems to choke it off.

Mendelssohn's best-liked chamber works are his Octet in E-flat major, Op. 20 (for double string quartet, 1825), and his Piano Trio in D minor, Op. 49 (1839). This music glitters with rhythmic drive, especially in the scherzos, and abounds in pleasant, tuneful themes. Written when its composer was only sixteen, the octet is a model of Classical craftsmanship; its finale contains a cyclical reference to the main theme of the scherzo and exhibits highly complex counterpoint, including some fugatos.

Mendels-sohn's octet and D-minor trio

The cyclical Piano Quintet in E-flat major, Op. 44 (1842), of Robert Schumann, the first piece ever composed for this medium (piano plus string quar-

Schumann's quintet

Ex. 27.7   Franz Schubert, String Quintet in C major, Mvt. 1, mm. 138–142

tet), sparkles with spontaneity and charm, and contains splendid motivic development. The slow movement in C minor has the character of a funeral march; the scherzo makes effective use of ascending and descending scales; and in the finale the main theme of the brilliant first movement, in augmentation, initiates a fugato whose countersubject is the main theme of the finale. Schumann also composed a piano quartet and three piano trios.

Various chamber works by Brahms

Of the two dozen chamber pieces by Brahms, only the Trio in E-flat major, Op. 40 (for French horn, violin, and piano, 1865), forgoes the sonata-allegro form in its first movement, whose design is ABABA. His slow movements are gloriously lyrical ternary works, and his scherzos range from the healthy open-air sound of the Op. 40 horn trio to the mysterious whisperings of the Piano Trio in C major, Op. 87 (1880–1882). His finales are usually sonatas or rondos, sometimes evocative of gypsy music, e.g., in the Piano Quartet in G minor, Op. 25 (1861).

Among Brahms's most exciting works is the Piano Quintet in F minor, Op. 34A (1864), originally intended as a string quintet with two cellos, then as a work for two pianos, before reaching its final medium. The *Allegro non troppo* is in a clear sonata form, except that the initial music heard seems to double as the first theme proper and as introductory material—as in Schubert's *Trout* Quintet or Brahms's own Piano Quartet in C minor, Op. 60 (1855–1875). The *Andante, un poco adagio* is very similar to Schubert's *cantabile* Andantes in ABA form, although the chordal piano writing and the syncopation are truly Brahmsian. The quintet's scherzo contains a motor rhythm, pizzicato articulation, syncopation, a victorious chordal theme, cross-rhythms, and a certain diabolical quality. The finale is a sonata-allegro whose carefree, dancelike nature is in sharp contrast to the frenzy of the scherzo.

Another great quintet by Brahms is that for clarinet and string quartet, Op. 115 (1891; first movement in *MSO* II, p. 159), in which the composer effectively contrasts the timbres of the high strings, the low strings, and the clarinet. This cyclical work's finale is a lyrical theme and variations (at the same time a rondo), resisting all temptations to be virtuoso or agitated.

Other chamber works of Dvořák, Franck, Fauré

Also during the late nineteenth century, Dvořák, Franck, and Fauré were among those who composed superior chamber music combining strings with piano. Dvořák's Piano Quartet in E-flat major, Op. 87 (1889), has a resolute opening movement, an emotional Lento, a Ländler-like *Allegro moderato, grazioso,* with a glittering piano sound, and a march-like finale. His better-known Piano Quintet in A major, Op. 81 (1887), contains much modal mixture, ebullient rhythms, beautiful timbres, and emotional melodies. The entertaining *Dumky* Trio in E minor, Op. 90 (1890–1891), presents a series of six dance movements, including slow *dumky* (elegies and laments), fast *furiants,* marches, and a scherzo.

The Piano Quintet in F minor (1878–1879) by César Franck is an imaginative, chromatic, sensuous, rhapsodic work. Alternately gentle and energetic, this quintet is cyclical, like many of Franck's other pieces. Its recurring theme is similar to that in Franck's Symphony in D minor (1886–1888); the rise and fall of the chromatic, modulatory melody has an almost mesmerizing effect upon the listener.

Fauré's chamber music with piano is delicate and graceful, and he has a way of making the piano sound like a harp, as in the scherzo of his Piano Quartet No. 1 in C minor, Op. 15 (1876–1879). The Adagio, one of the most expressive pieces of the late nineteenth century, has a funereal sound but sets forth its tension and tragedy in a noble manner. A later work by Fauré, which possesses profound sentiments, larger proportions, broad melodies, and powerful expression—the characteristics of his later style—is his Piano Quintet No. 2 in C minor, Op. 115 (1919–1921).

Summary

Romantic composers wrote many kinds of pieces for solo piano. These included sonatas, themes and variations, character pieces, dances, études, program works, and transcriptions. Beethoven's piano sonatas set many standards for future composers of piano music. Some of the most idiomatic and imaginative Romantic music for the piano was composed by Robert Schumann, Chopin, and Liszt. Schumann created the piano cycle—short, related pieces—with its frequent extramusical connotations, and played intellectual games with the players and auditors of his piano music. Chopin brought to the instrument a thorough understanding of its sonorous, emotional, and technical capabilities. Liszt demanded that extremes of delicacy and violence, simplicity and subtlety, passion and spiritualism be communicated through his piano music. In the later nineteenth century Brahms and Scriabin were among those who took advantage of the expressive possibilities of the piano. As interest in secularism and the piano increased in the 1800s, there was a correlative decrease in emphasis on the organ, although Mendelssohn, Brahms, and Franck were among those who produced masterworks for that instrument.

Chamber music at this time continued to reflect composers' abilities to write serious absolute music, stressing the purity of musical ideas, contrapuntal dialogue among the players, thematic development, and cyclical relationships. Virtuosity and the complexity of Romantic harmonies and rhythms led to chamber music that was too difficult for all but professional musicians to play. String quartets, duo sonatas, piano trios, and other Classical types of chamber music continued to be composed. However, in the nineteenth century there were also other combinations, such as the piano quintet and the trio for horn, violin, and piano.

Note

1. Beethoven was persuaded to disengage the fugue from the rest of the Op. 130 quartet, publish it separately, and write a simpler finale for the quartet. There was, however, a tradition of fugal finales, inherited from Haydn, e.g., in three of his Op. 20 quartets.

Bibliography

Books and Articles

Piano Music in General

DALE, KATHLEEN. *Nineteenth-Century Piano Music: A Handbook for Pianists.* London: Oxford University Press, 1954; reprint, New York: Da Capo Press, 1972.

NEWMAN, WILLIAM S. *The Sonata in the Classic Era,* 2nd ed. New York: W. W. Norton & Co., 1972.

————. *The Sonata since Beethoven,* 2nd ed. New York: W. W. Norton & Co., 1972.

Studies of the Piano Music of Individual Composers

See also Bibliography for Chapter 25, "Studies on Major Symphonists."

ABRAHAM, GERALD. *Chopin's Musical Style.* London: Oxford University Press, 1946.

BLOM, ERIC. *Beethoven's Pianoforte Sonatas Discussed.* London: J. M. Dent & Sons, 1938; reprint, New York: Da Capo Press, 1968.

DRAKE, KENNETH. *The Sonatas of Beethoven as He Played and Taught Them.* Bloomington: Indiana University Press, 1981.

HEDLEY, ARTHUR. *Chopin,* revised by Maurice J. E. Brown. Master Musicians Series. Totowa, N.J.: Littlefield, Adams & Co., 1978.

WALKER, ALAN. "Liszt and the Schubert Song Transcriptions." *Musical Quarterly* 67 (Jan. 1981): 50–63.

Chamber Music

FERGUSON, DONALD N. *Image and Structure in Chamber Music.* Minneapolis: University of Minnesota Press, 1964; reprint, New York: Da Capo Press, 1977.

KERMAN, JOSEPH. *The Beethoven Quartets.* New York: Alfred A. Knopf, 1971.

ROBERTSON, ALEC, ed. *Chamber Music.* Baltimore: Penguin Books, 1970.

See also the two volumes by William S. Newman listed above.

Scores

For piano and chamber works by Beethoven, Brahms, Chopin, Dvořák, Liszt, Mendelssohn, Schubert, R. Schumann, Tchaikovsky, and Wagner, see Bibliography for Chapter 24.

In Dover Music Books—Complete Scores Series
(New York: Dover Publications)

BEETHOVEN, LUDWIG VAN, *Complete Piano Sonatas,* 2 vols., ed. Heinrich Schenker. 1975 reprint of the edition published by Universal-Edition, Vienna, 1923.

————, *Complete String Quartets and Grosse Fuge.* 1970 reprint of the edition published by Breitkopf & Härtel, Leipzig, n.d.

BRAHMS, JOHANNES, *Complete Chamber Music for Strings and Clarinet Quintet,* ed. Hans Gál. 1968 reprint of the edition published by Breitkopf & Härtel, Leipzig, c. 1927.

————, *Complete Shorter Works for Solo Piano,* ed. Eusebius Mandyczewski. 1971 reprint of the edition published by Breitkopf & Härtel, Leipzig, c. 1927.

————, *Complete Sonatas and Variations for Solo Piano,* ed. Eusebius Mandyczewski. 1971 reprint of the edition published by Breitkopf & Härtel, Leipzig, c. 1927.

————, *Complete Transcriptions, Cadenzas and Exercises for Solo Piano,* ed. Eusebius Mandyczewski. 1971 reprint of the edition published by Breitkopf & Härtel, Leipzig, c. 1927.

FRANCK, CÉSAR, *Selected Piano Compositions,* ed. Vincent d'Indy. 1976 reprint of the edition published by Oliver Ditson Co., Boston, 1922.

MENDELSSOHN, FELIX, *Complete Chamber Music for Strings,* ed. Julius Rietz. 1978 reprint of the edition published by Breitkopf & Härtel, Leipzig, 1874–1877.

————, *Complete Works for Pianoforte Solo,* 2 vols., ed. Julius Rietz. 1975 reprint of the edition published by Breitkopf & Härtel, Leipzig, 1874–1877.

Nineteenth-Century European Piano Music: Unfamiliar Masterworks, ed. John Gillespie. 1977, original Dover publication.

SCHUBERT, FRANZ, *Complete Chamber Music for Pianoforte and Strings,* ed. Ignaz Brüll. 1973 reprint of the edition published by Breitkopf & Härtel, Leipzig, 1886.

————, *Complete Chamber Music for Strings,* ed. Eusebius Mandyczewski and Joseph Hellmesberger. 1973 reprint of the edition published by Breitkopf & Härtel, Leipzig, 1890–1897.

————, *Complete Sonatas for Pianoforte Solo,* ed. Julius Epstein. 1970 reprint of the edition published by Breitkopf & Härtel, Leipzig, 1888.

————, *Shorter Works for Pianoforte Solo,* ed. Julius Epstein. 1970 reprint of the edition published by Breitkopf & Härtel, Leipzig, 1888.

SCHUMANN, ROBERT, *Chamber Music of Robert Schumann,* ed. Clara Schumann. 1981 reprint of the edition published by Breitkopf & Härtel, Leipzig, 1880–1887.

————, *Piano Music of Robert Schumann,* series I–III, 3 vols., ed. Clara Schumann and (part of series III) Johannes Brahms. 1972 (series I–II) and 1980 (series III) reprints of the edition published by Breitkopf & Härtel, Leipzig, 1879–1893.

SCRIABIN, ALEXANDER, *The Complete Preludes and Etudes for Pianoforte Solo,* ed. K. N. Igumnov and Y. I. Mil'shteyn. 1973 reprint of the edition published by "Music" Publishing House, Moscow, 1966–1967.

In Norton Critical Scores Series
(New York: W. W. Norton & Co.)

CHOPIN, FRÉDÉRIC, *Preludes,* Op. 28, ed. Thomas Higgins. 1973.

28

Nineteenth-Century Opera
and Music Drama

IN the Romantic era the mixing of Italian, French, and German operatic styles that began in the Classical period continued. At the same time certain opera composers took pains to refine their own national styles, and areas such as Russia, Bohemia, and Poland began to develop their own varieties of opera. Operetta and light opera also took on great importance.

Romanticism affected opera enormously. The large, virtuoso orchestra and the emphasis on grandiosity inspired composers to write long and spectacular works requiring many performers. Such Romantic characteristics as increased dissonance, chromaticism, new key relationships, and asymmetrical melodies gave composers new opportunities for writing continuous musical scenes rather than arranging them as series of independent numbers. Employing development, variation, and thematic transformation, composers unified scenes, acts, and entire operas thematically, and dramatized the music so as to parallel the actions and thoughts of the characters on stage.

Opera in Italy

Bel Canto and the Italian Tradition

Created and nurtured in Italy, opera remained that nation's primary musical preoccupation during the nineteenth century. The traditions of *opera seria* and *opera buffa* were the backbone of Italian Romantic opera. As always, this was a singer's art, and the Romantic *bel canto* singing style stressed a well-rounded legato tone, good intonation, pure vowels, evenness of tone in various registers, the improvisation of ornaments, virtuosity, and the avoidance of vulgarity. As such, it prevailed throughout the century. Audiences flocked to hear great singers perform, and composers designed roles especially for those who would sing them.

Romantic opera seria adopted several stylistic tendencies of Mozartian opera buffa, including greater dependence on ensembles, the orchestra, and

The notion of bel canto

Romantic opera seria and Mayr

692

chorus; the use of tenors and basses in primary roles; and the climactic function of the finales of acts. One composer who linked Classical and Romantic opera was Donizetti's teacher, Johann Simon Mayr (1763–1845); he often drew on French sources for his serious librettos, as was common during the Napoleonic era. Mayr's best-known works are *Lodoïska* (1796) and *Medea in Corinto* ("Medea in Corinth," 1813), and his characteristic operatic style includes the orchestral crescendo (later the hallmark of Rossini's style), colorful instrumentation, and the use of a dramatic chorus. He also wrote concerted numbers with continuous action and music, and emotional recitatives and arias that provide effective character delineation.

Gioacchino Rossini (1792–1868) was the operatic leader in the early nineteenth century. Between 1810 and 1820 he wrote thirty operas, for such opera houses as the Teatro San Carlo in Naples and La Scala in Milan. Through his

Rossini

The most famous number in Rossini's *Otello* is the heroine Desdemona's *Willow Song* in the last act, shown in this lithograph. Unlike Verdi's *Otello,* based entirely on Shakespeare's *Othello,* Rossini's opera is derived from historic chronicles, some of which were probably used by Shakespeare as well. (Courtesy, Kenneth Stern Collection)

music Rossini could move people to laughter and tears with equal ease, as demonstrated by two works composed in the same year (1816): *Il barbiere di Siviglia* ("The Barber of Seville"; excerpt in *NAWM* II, no. 133; *NAWM, S,* no. 73) and *Otello* ("Othello"). One of the greatest operatic comedies of all time, Rossini's *Barber* sparkles with inexhaustible melodies, lightning-fast *parlando* (patter singing), vigorous tempos, brilliant ensembles, and colorful orchestration. And his tragic opera *Otello* was so highly acclaimed in the nineteenth century that Verdi had to think twice about creating another opera based on the same story.

Rossini gave the public what it demanded: loud and fast music, virtuoso singing, and the military rhythms that were popular during the Napoleonic era. Using garlands of fast-moving triplets and sixteenth notes, Rossini made dramatic use of the "steamroller" and crescendo that had risen to prominence in Mannheim years earlier. His overtures possess drive, tunefulness, and color, and are often performed in orchestral concerts.

Rossini wrote out ornamentation in his scores in an effort to prevent singers from interfering with the drama of the opera. His choral parts are quite simple because the chorus singers of the time could not read music. On the other hand, his orchestration tends to be noisy and heavy, especially in the brasses and at the ends of numbers, scenes, and acts. This effect was calculated to stimulate loud applause.

Sometimes Rossini wrote a melody for the orchestra, while having the singers provide declamatory dialogue above it (*parlante*). In stringing together recitatives, arias, ariosos, parlante sections, choral interjections, and climactic ensembles—mainly in his serious operas—Rossini built large operatic scenes that departed from pure number opera. His tragic masterpiece, *Semiramide* (1823), failed in Venice, and shortly afterward he left Italy permanently to settle in Paris. There he created two French operas, *Le Comte Ory* ("Count Ory," 1828), an opéra-comique, and *Guillaume Tell* ("William Tell," 1829), a grand opera. For nearly forty years thereafter, Rossini refrained from writing opera.

Donizetti   Composer of about seventy operas, Gaetano Donizetti (1797–1848) had a flair for the theater. His vocal rhythms and melodies stem from the accent and flow of spoken words. The great singer-actors of the period were able to impress audiences with their interpretations of Donizetti roles, especially because the composer's vocal lines reflected all kinds of nuances of characterization. He provided opera with a new, vivid realism, and refined the architectural design that dominated Italian opera throughout most of the century: the *scena ed aria*. This format has four sections: (1) recitative; (2) a *cavatina,* a slow, lyrical aria (or duet); (3) *materia di mezza,* an interruption caused by the entrance or discourse of another character or group, supplying new dramatic information; and (4) a *cabaletta,* a faster, more brilliant aria.

Donizetti liked melodramatic stories, such as *Lucrezia Borgia* (1833, rev. 1840) and the extremely popular *Lucia di Lammermoor* (1835), whose librettos stemmed from literary works by Victor Hugo and Sir Walter Scott (1771– 1832), respectively. The composer conveyed heightened emotions musically by means of such devices as syncopation and embellishment. A specialty of his was the "mad" scene, in which a primary character (usually a soprano) would put on a virtuoso exhibition of bel canto singing. In ensembles, such as the famous sextet from *Lucia,* the characters would each sing different words and melodies, maintain their own personalities by means of the music, and create jointly a harmonious and dramatic musical climax.

As a man of the theater, Donizetti made liberal use of the chorus, sometimes just to provide more sound and contribute to the *mise en scène,* or total stage picture. Furthermore, his harmonies, rhythms, instrumental interjections, embellishments, vocal lines, tessituras, and key changes shed light on the characters involved. For instance, in *Maria Stuarda* (1834, rev. 1835), adapted from Schiller, Queens Elizabeth and Mary are consistently differentiated through music, and their confrontation in Act II is an unforgettable clash of personalities.

Like Rossini, Donizetti wrote first-rate opera buffa, such as *Don Pasquale* (1843), and French opéras-comiques, such as *La Fille du régiment* ("The Daughter of the Regiment," 1840). Furthermore, Donizetti helped create the genre of *opera semiseria,* which combined a serious plot with elements of comedy, lightheartedness, and Romantic scenery and pathos. An example is his *Linda di Chamounix* (1842).

Less forceful drama but more consistently engaging lyricism is found in the ten operas of Vincenzo Bellini (1801–1835), who tried to infuse his works with Classical elegance, clarity, and expressivity. A slower worker than Donizetti, Bellini aimed at a perfect union between music and words, in which he was ably assisted by his librettist Felice Romani (1788–1865). Bellini's recitative style is conversational, and his arias have flexible, flowing lines leading to poignant climaxes. His most dramatic work is *Norma* (1831; excerpt in *NAWM* II, no. 134; *NAWM,* S, no. 74), whose title role is one of the most difficult soprano parts in opera. The influence of Bellini's melancholy, elegiac, subtly harmonized melodies on Chopin, Liszt, and even Wagner, who loved *Norma* in his youth, should not be overlooked.

Bellini and Mercadante

A fellow pupil of Bellini's at the conservatory in Naples was Saverio Mercadante (1795–1870). In his best-known operas, *Il giuramento* ("The Oath," 1837; based on a work by Hugo) and *La vestale* ("The Vestal Virgin," 1840), we find long, asymmetrical vocal lines, melodramatic recitatives, rhythmic and harmonic variety, and rich orchestration. Mercadante also avoided cabalettas and other soloistic extravagances, as well as very loud orchestral dynamics.

Verdi

Throughout his long career Giuseppe Verdi (1813–1901) tried to uphold the traditions of Italian opera and preserve his art from the influence of German Romanticism, as expressed by Wagner. A proud Italian, Verdi subtly incorporated patriotic choruses and a brass-band sound into many of his early operas, such as *Nabucco* ("Nebuchadnezzar," 1842). The young Verdi wrote music for great singers to perform in the bel canto style, and he supported the

Verdi's approach

LA FILLE DU REGIMENT.

The title role of Donizetti's *La Fille du régiment* was often performed by Jenny Lind (1820–1887), the "Swedish Nightingale," shown in this lithograph of c. 1850. (Courtesy, Kenneth Stern Collection)

vocal part with the orchestra, especially with a warm, vibrating string sound. Containing wide vocal ranges and some uncomfortable tessituras, his major roles were ideal for singers who possessed heavy voices with powerful projection.

Early opera plots　　During his early years Verdi liked violent, even brutal, melodramatic plots, involving such subject matter as seduction, assassination, torture, the cruelty of Fate, hatred, and vengeance.[1] His characters—often vicious, lustful, and decrepit—were subordinated to the situation. The plot itself could be improbable or even impossible, lacking in subtlety, logic, and consistency.

Opera structure　　Verdi was, however, consistent about the way in which he constructed operas. Most Verdi operas have four acts, or three acts and a prologue. The leading singers each have two or more impressive arias, perform duets with one another, and take part in larger ensembles at critical moments. The final act tends to open with some kind of solo, such as a *preghiera* (prayer scene), usually for the heroine. And one inner act probably has a grandiose male duet (e.g., a friendship pact). At least one important chorus is to be expected, and so are choral interpolations during various concerted numbers. Declamatory singing over a continuous orchestral melody is common, as is accompanied recitative and arioso, depending on the dramatic needs of the moment. Verdi adhered to the number-opera format until his last two works.

Rigoletto (1851), *Il trovatore* ("The Troubadour," 1853; excerpt in *NAWM* II, no. 138; *NAWM, S,* no. 76), and *La traviata* ("The Lady Gone Astray," 1853) are the three operas which earned Verdi great fame. Based on a work by Hugo, *Rigoletto* provides a story of lechery, sarcasm, curses, kidnapping, deformity, and assassination. The hunchbacked court jester, Rigoletto, is one of Verdi's favorite creations, because the title character is a study in contrasts: external deformity and callousness, and internal sensitivity and fatherly devotion. In fact, the libretto deals with the Romantic opposites of good and evil, beauty and ugliness, and opulence and squalor.

Rigoletto

By the mid-nineteenth century Italian composers frequently replaced the full-length overture with a brief, atmospheric prelude. In the prelude to *Rigoletto* the brass instruments present the recurring motive of the curse (cast upon the title character by the father of one of the victims of the duke of Mantua, a Lothario at whose court Rigoletto works). This bleak music gives way to a bright scene at the duke's court, in which the duke sings, in a popular Neapolitan style, of his love of life and women. His strophic aria *Questa o quella per me pari sono* ("This one or that one—they're the same to me") has a catchy melody, bouncing rhythm, and simple harmonization, but near the final cadence Verdi demonstrates his harmonic finesse by moving briefly to the flatted mediant (see Example 28.1).

Rigoletto's daughter, Gilda, is a young girl who loves her father but becomes infatuated with the rakish duke. In her aria *Caro nome* ("Dear name") in act II, Gilda's music alternates between the simplicity of slowly descending scales and the showiest type of *coloratura,* allowing the soprano to display her technical prowess even though the dramatic situation does not call for it. Rigoletto's deformity is shown throughout the opera by convoluted, turning orchestral figures, the best example of which comes in his second-act monologue, *Pari siamo!* ("We are the same!"), written as an accompanied recitative. The duke's aria *La donna è mobile* ("Woman is fickle") in the last act and the great quartet that follows (*MSO* II, p. 253) are show-stoppers.

In *La traviata* (excerpt in *NS, E,* II, no. 13; *NS, S,* no. 31), which was based on a play written by Alexandre Dumas the younger, Verdi placed on stage a contemporary plot and characters. Instead of looking at gods, sorceresses, or the like, the audience watched people like themselves with problems like their own. The sensitive topics of physical illness (tuberculosis) and social vice (the love affairs of a courtesan) were new in opera and looked ahead to the future, as did the expressively declamatory melodic style.

La traviata

For about twenty years after *La traviata,* Verdi composed more slowly

Ex. 28.1   Giuseppe Verdi, *Questa o quella per me pari sono,* mm. 30–42 from
Rigoletto, act I, scene 1

"If this one finds favor with me today, perhaps another, perhaps another will tomorrow—another, perhaps another will tomorrow."

**Later
style**
and experimented often. Influenced by Meyerbeer's grand operas and wishing to impress French audiences, Verdi lengthened his operas, added more
ballet music and spectacle, and looked for librettos with subplots and powerfully dramatic scenes. His works of the late 1850s and 1860s employ varied
and rich orchestration, a wide tonal and harmonic range, many concerted
scenes, and arias (especially for soprano) with soaring climaxes. *Don Carlos*

(1867, rev. 1884), based on a Schiller play, is an example of this period in Verdi's career, which culminates in the opera *Aida* (1871), commissioned by the Khedive of Egypt to celebrate the opening of the Suez Canal.

Shakespearean dramas provided the now rich and famous composer with the subjects of his last two operas, *Otello* (1887) and *Falstaff* (1893). The librettist for both was Arrigo Boïto (1842–1918), himself the composer of the striking opera *Mefistofele* (1868). *Falstaff* sparkles with effective comic ensembles, a quick pace, continuity, and clear orchestral delineation of character. In the great tragedy *Otello,* composer and librettist condensed and telescoped Shakespeare's drama without sacrificing its emotional impact. Although the opera contains duets, arias, choruses, and large ensembles, there are no breaks in the action; the music is continuous in each act, with transitions linking the numbers together. Iago seems to be Verdi's focal character in this opera, and Iago's music—for example, his first-act *brindisi* (drinking song) and his second-act *Credo* ("I believe")—is vehement, embellished, chromatic, and serpentine, to match his villainous character (see Example 28.2). Iago's *Credo* is

Otello and
Falstaff

Ex. 28.2   Giuseppe Verdi, Iago's *brindisi,* mm. 43–51 of the *Allegro con brio,* from *Otello,* act I, scene 1

"Drink, drink, drink, drink, drink."

one of the strongest, most chilling affirmations of evil in all art. The love duet at the end of act I, and the "Willow Song" and *Ave Maria* that Desdemona sings in act IV, are unforgettable moments of lyrical warmth, orchestral radiance, and unostentatious, beautiful melody.

Verismo Opera and Puccini

It was not until the Post-Romantic period (approximately 1870–1910) that Italian operas depicted everyday people behaving violently or in the heat of lust and passion. In Post-Romantic librettos, sections dealing with sex and violence were often set with loud, heavy-textured music, soaring melodic lines, strident dissonance, and orchestral outbursts in what is known as the *verismo* style. Two such Italian operas that are still popular are *Cavalleria rusticana* ("Rustic Chivalry," 1890) by Pietro Mascagni (1863–1945) and *I Pagliacci* ("The Clowns," 1892) by Ruggiero Leoncavallo (1857–1919).

Tosca   *Tosca* (1899) by Giacomo Puccini (1858–1924) is also a veristic opera, but Puccini's sense of theater surpassed that of his Italian contemporaries. Few composers have known better how to communicate a theatrical situation and characters' feelings to an audience through direct, vivid music. Puccini also thoroughly understood the human voice and wrote for it with great skill, as is amply demonstrated in his ever-popular *La Bohème* (1896; excerpt in *NS*, E, II, no. 19; *NS*, S, no. 36).

Puccini's interest in exoticism is manifested in such works as *Madama Butterfly* (1904), set in Japan; *La fanciulla del West* ("The Girl of the Golden West," 1910), set in California; and *Turandot* (completed in 1926, after Puccini's death, by Franco Alfano, 1875–1954), set in China. His operas also make extensive use of recurrent and transformed musical motives, in the tradition of Wagner, whom he admired greatly.

Opera in France

Opéras-comiques

Paris emerged as the most important operatic center in the first half of the nineteenth century. To be considered a great success in opera, a composer had to appeal to the middle-class Parisian audience. These people, who had themselves experienced oppression and liberation, were especially partial to operas in which a loyal spouse or lover would risk anything to liberate an imprisoned hero or heroine. Such *rescue operas,* as they were called, featured charac-

operas   ters who were easy to admire or loathe, large choruses, and, very often, spoken French dialogue and musical *melodrama* (in which characters speak their lines above or in alternation with the orchestra). Among the best was *Les Deux Journées* ("The Two Days," 1800) by Luigi Cherubini. Beethoven, who considered Cherubini the best living composer of opera, patterned certain aspects of his only opera, *Fidelio* (1804–1805, rev. 1805–1806, 1814), on Cherubini's works.

Rescue operas using spoken dialogue instead of recitative were considered *opéras-comiques* and were automatically ineligible for performances at the Paris Opéra. Nonetheless, they continued to be popular during the early nineteenth century. Although some of these relatively short, unpretentious works were indeed "comic," others tended toward sentimentality or even seriousness. They all were characterized by charming and melodious music, strophic songs with refrains, and interesting ensembles. They required relatively few singers, players, and "extras" on the stage and used simpler scenery and costumes than did *grand opera*.

Romantic opéras-comiques

Among the prominent composers of opéras-comiques during the early Romantic period were Etienne Nicolas Méhul (1763–1817), François Adrien Boïeldieu (1775–1834), Daniel François Esprit Auber (1782–1871), and Louis Joseph Ferdinand Hérold (1791–1833). Boïeldieu's *La Dame blanche* ("The White Lady," 1825) was especially popular because of its sweet melodies and dramatic use of French popular songs. A more Italianate melodic style was practiced by Hérold in such operas as *Zampa* (1831), full of variety, contrasting moods, and dramatic interest. Auber, who was Cherubini's pupil, had a long and extremely successful career. He relied heavily on the librettos of Augustin Eugène Scribe (1791–1861), the most prolific French librettist of the time. Auber's best-known comic works include *Fra diavolo* ("Brother Devil," 1830) and *Les Diamants de la couronne* ("The Crown's Diamonds," 1841). The more Classical Méhul, who excelled in serious and dramatic operas, had a special talent for depicting local color, as can be seen in his biblical *Joseph* (1807). Méhul's overtures and symphonies, popular in Germany and Austria, influenced such composers as Beethoven and Schubert.

Large-scale French Opera

When the new French Republic and subsequent Empire were established, many public ceremonies took place in which the masses gathered to celebrate their liberation in word and song. Opera composers such as Cherubini and Méhul provided them with patriotic music, much of which was massive in sonority but simple enough for the citizens to sing. Intended for hundreds of people and large bands of instruments performing in the open air, this music was grandiose, as were many of the French operas of the time. Cherubini's *Médée* ("Medea," 1797) bridged the calmness of the Classical age and the emotionality of the Romantic. In it, Cherubini wrote poignant arias and ensemble parts for the passionate Medea, expressive of her jealousy, hatred, and grief. Intensely dramatic, her music taxes the soprano, because of its dynamic range, intervallic content, and uncomfortable tessitura. Like Cherubini, Gaspare Spontini (1774–1851) moved from Italy to make a great name for himself in France. In *La Vestale* (1807) he blended the solemnity of Classical French opera, a spectacular rescue plot, and the dimensions and rich orchestration of the emerging grand operatic style. The work has marvelous crowd scenes and a huge climax culminating in a fire brought on by Divine intervention. Spontini's *Fernand Cortez* (1809, rev. 1817) was even more successful, influencing the next generation of composers of grand opera.

Cherubini and Spontini

A *grand opera* is a long, large-scale work, involving huge choruses, numer-

French grand opera and Meyerbeer

ous ballets, and spectacle-filled crowd scenes. It has a historical plot and employs symphonic, vocal, and dance styles. In this genre composers tended to abandon the logical unfolding of the drama for unbridled sensationalism and maudlin sentimentality. Auber established a model for the genre in *La Muette de Portici* ("The Mute Girl of Portici," known also as *Masaniello,* 1828), and one of the best scores in this style is *La Juive* ("The Jewish Girl," 1835) by Jacques Fromental Halévy (1799–1862).

The extreme popularity of grand opera in the Paris of the 1830s was due mainly to the efforts of Giacomo Meyerbeer (1791–1864). Born Jakob Beer in Berlin, he studied French history and art, and joined the librettist Scribe and the impresario Louis Véron (1798–1867) at the Paris Opéra to form one of the most successful teams in operatic history. They turned opera into a mass commercial enterprise and affected the creative impulses of such foreigners as Bellini, Verdi, and Wagner.

Giving careful thought to every detail, Meyerbeer breathed new life into the grand opera style. His huge orchestra impressed even Berlioz and Wagner, and his vocal lines were among the most florid of the early Romantic era. Favoring keys with many sharps or flats, Meyerbeer frequently resorted to enharmonic modulations. The opera that brought Meyerbeer into the limelight was *Robert le diable* ("Robert the Devil," 1831, rev. 1839), one of

The Opéra in Paris was the most important opera house in the world for Romantic composers. This lithograph by J. Arnout shows the interior of this remarkable theater, and, on the stage, the Nuns' Scene from Meyerbeer's grand opera *Robert le diable* (1831), starring the great French tenor Gilbert-Louis Duprez (1806–1896). Notice that the audience is more concerned with talking and gazing at one another than watching the opera. (Courtesy, Kenneth Stern Collection)

the first in a long line of Romantic operas to include a church scene with an organ on the stage. Another big success was *Les Huguenots* ("The Huguenots," 1836; excerpt in *NAWM* II, no. 135), whose exciting overture makes use of the Lutheran chorale *Ein' feste Burg* ("A Mighty Fortress"), amply demonstrating the composer's contrapuntal skill. *Le Prophète* ("The Prophet," 1836, 1849, rev. c. 1850) and the exotic *L'Africaine* ("The African Girl," begun in 1837 and given a first performance a year after the composer's death, in 1865) were Meyerbeer's final grand operas.

Lyric Opera

Taking elements from both grand opera and the sentimental type of opéra-comique, French composers of the second half of the nineteenth century created a new type of serious musical drama, *opéra-lyrique*. With stories that tug at the audience's heartstrings, these works are filled with appealing melodies, which are often chromatic and frequently in compound meter. Composers of lyric opera include Ambroise Thomas (1811–1896), Charles Gounod (1818–1893), Jules Massenet (1842–1912), and Camille Saint-Saëns (1835–1921). They retold great love stories: of Goethe's Mignon and Wilhelm Meister (Thomas' *Mignon,* 1866), Goethe's Faust and Gretchen (Gounod's *Faust,* 1859), Shakespeare's Romeo and Juliet (Gounod's *Roméo et Juliette,* 1867), Goethe's Werther and Charlotte (Massenet's *Werther,* 1892), and the Old Testament's Samson and Delilah (Saint-Saëns's *Samson et Dalila,* 1877). The last-named work, like Massenet's *Hérodiade* (1881) and *Thaïs* (1894), is a study in voluptuous sound. One of the best composers ever for the human voice, Massenet understood well what could and what could not be sung effectively. He was also versatile, and his operas range from the most delicate sentimentality (*Manon,* 1884) to epic heroism (*Le Cid,* 1885) and verismo (*Sapho,* 1897, rev. 1909).

Carmen (1873–1874) by Georges Bizet (1838–1875), not very successful at first, is now the most popular French opera from this period. A veritable showcase of "hit tunes," *Carmen* contains exoticism (local Spanish color), realism and a tough-minded attitude (pointing toward verismo), brilliant orchestration, invigorating rhythms, exquisite contrapuntal ensembles, melodic verve, and a passionate human story.

Bizet's Carmen

The Operas of Berlioz

In the domain of opera, as elsewhere, Hector Berlioz showed his remarkable individuality. He called for complicated sets and costumes, large casts, a multitude of choral singers and dancers, and a huge orchestra. Many of his roles, such as that of Aeneas in the monumental *Les Troyens* ("The Trojans," 1856–1858), are excruciatingly difficult to sing, and Berlioz was certainly not catering to popular taste in devising long, asymmetrical melodies, syncopated rhythms, displaced bar-lines, and unusual forms. In the great length of his works, the richness of his orchestration, and the use of recurrent motives, his work is akin to Wagner's.

Benvenuto Cellini (1834–1837) and *La Damnation de Faust* ("The Damnation of Faust," 1845–1846), the latter called a "dramatic legend" and not in-

Edouard Manet (1832–1883), *Emilie Ambre dans le rôle de Carmen* ("Emilie Ambre in the Role of Carmen," c. 1880). Like his compatriot Bizet, the French artist Manet was attracted by the exotic appeal of Spain. (Philadelphia Museum of Art; Given by Edgar Scott; photograph by A. J. Wyatt, Staff Photographer)

tended for stage performance, are series of scenes or tableaux rather than gradually unfolding dramas. *Cellini* was conceived in the spirit of Auber's comedies, but is much subtler. Berlioz uses the number-opera format, but provides for continuity by avoiding recitatives, linking set pieces to ariosos and orchestral passages, and connecting musical ideas from one section to another. The best-known parts of this opera are its overture and the "Roman Carnival" scene, which ends act II. Another comedy by Berlioz, *Béatrice et Bénédict* (1860–1862), based on Shakespeare's *Much Ado About Nothing,* is a shorter opera with a delicate sense of humor.

Les Troyens   *Les Troyens* brings the noble tradition of Gluck and Spontini to its final culmination. Since the opera was considered too long by Berlioz's contemporaries, he divided it into two parts: *La Prise de Troie* ("The Capture of Troy") and *Les Troyens à Carthage* ("The Trojans in Carthage"). Much of the libretto, prepared by Berlioz himself, is a literal translation of Vergil's *Aeneid*. In this opera music and drama are inextricably intertwined, and the French words give rise to appropriate vocal lines. One of the loveliest numbers in the work is the rapturous fourth-act duet of Dido and Aeneas, *Nuit d'ivresse et d'extase infinie* ("Night of intoxication and boundless ecstasy"). In *Les Troyens* Berlioz created a French music drama that realized many of the theories expressed by the master of German music drama, Richard Wagner.

Opera in German Centers

Romantic *Singspiele*

German opera composers in the early 1800s tried to portray the same feelings and evoke the same responses as their literary colleagues. They looked upon Mozart's *The Magic Flute* as the model of German opera. Its supernatural elements were retained in such early-nineteenth-century works as *Undine* (1816) by E. T. A. Hoffmann, *Zemire und Azor* (1818–1819) by Louis Spohr, and *Die Zauberharfe* ("The Magic Harp," 1820) by Franz Schubert, and its ethical concern and use of spoken German dialogue were adopted by Ludwig van Beethoven in *Fidelio*.

Although Schubert wrote about a dozen operas, half of them *Singspiele,* his extremely lyrical and repetitive vocal style seems not to have found a proper home in the opera house. Nonetheless, when cleverly staged, such a piece as *Die Verschworenen* ("The Conspirators," 1823) is highly entertaining. Not only Schubert, but, in fact, most of the great German and Austrian composers of the nineteenth century had enormous difficulties in putting together any opera, let alone a successful one. The list of such people includes Beethoven, Mendelssohn, Robert Schumann, Wolf, and Mahler.

Fidelio's original French libretto by Jean-Nicolas Bouilly (1763–1842) appealed to Beethoven because of its themes of courage, sacrifice, endurance, loyalty, and unselfish love. *Fidelio* failed at its first performance in November 1805 because French armies had just occupied Vienna a week earlier and the Theater an der Wien was almost empty, and also because some considered the work too long and not altogether well organized. In 1806 a revised and shortened version received a performance, but Beethoven, sensing that his cuts had been made ruthlessly and inartistically, withdrew it again and did not release a final version of it until 1814, when the opera became a success.

Fidelio is a curious work that strings together three types of dramatic musical events: (1) a comic Singspiel, in the flirtation between Marzelline and Jacquino; (2) a rescue opera in the French tradition, in the main body of the work, in which Leonora frees her husband, Florestan, from the villainous clutches of the prison governor, Pizzaro; and (3) a final cantata in celebration of the triumph of Good over Evil. Beethoven's sketchbooks show at least ten versions of the final chorus, and the composer produced no fewer than four overtures for the opera. No work gave him more trouble, but opera as a genre was dear to him, and he wanted to succeed with this one. The greatness of *Fidelio* comes when Beethoven is moved by the lofty aspects of the text, as in Leonora's recitative and aria in act I beginning with the words *Abscheulicher! Wo eilst du hin?* ("Despicable man! Where are you hurrying to?").

Beethoven's *Fidelio*

German Romantic Opera

Carl Maria von Weber (1786–1826) firmly established German *romantische Oper* (Romantic opera), a genre characterized by the supernatural, magic, legends, tales from the Middle Ages, and the workings of Fate and Nature. Characters seem to be controlled by the supernatural forces of Good and Evil. Good always triumphs in the end, and this victory is symbolic of redemption or salvation. Forests, animals, water, and sky adorn the stage and play a role in the plot. The music in these German Romantic operas contains melodies that resemble German folk songs and uses colorful orchestration, including such special effects as tremolo, to accompany and further the action on the stage.

Weber's *Der Freischütz* and other works

Weber's landmark opera was *Der Freischütz* ("The Freeshooter," 1817–1821; excerpts in *NAWM* II, no. 136), about a youth who sells his soul to the devil for some magic bullets that will permit him to win the hand of his lady love. Her pure and unfailing love ultimately releases the lad from his bargain with the forces of evil. The central "figure" of this work, however, is the

This steel engraving provides a portrait of Carl Maria von Weber surrounded by miniature scenes from his greatest opera, *Der Freischütz,* in which Nature and the supernatural play prominent roles. (Courtesy, Kenneth Stern Collection)

German forest, capable of beneficence but also of malevolence. Such evil is dramatized in the unforgettable Wolf's Glen scene in act II, which contains melodrama and some of the most startling orchestral effects of the century. Weber uses the horns to symbolize the out-of-doors, the low register of the flute to accompany the evil Samiel, and the clarinet to represent Agathe, the heroine. Alongside such forward-looking uses of instruments and Weber's application of recurring motives are marches, dances, polonaise rhythms, Italianate arias, and German folk-like songs.

Only after finishing an opera did Weber compose its overture. He then took a few of the main themes from the opera and built a sonata-like form around them. Among his best-liked overtures are those of *Abu Hassan* (1810–1811), *Euryanthe* (1822–1823), and *Oberon* (1825–1826), in addition to that of *Der Freischütz*. *Abu Hassan* is Weber's contribution to the "Turkish," i.e., pseudoexotic, Singspiel repertoire. With *Euryanthe,* his only opera without spoken dialogue, Weber's designs were more grandiose, as he tried to provide musical continuity and unity by means of recurrent musical themes, timbres, and tonalities, paving the way for Wagner.

Two of the best composers of German opera between Weber and Wagner were Heinrich Marschner (1795–1861) and Albert Lortzing (1801–1851). Marschner rose to fame by composing the supernatural *Der Vampyr* ("The Vampire," 1827) and the adventurous *Der Templer und die Jüdin* ("The Templar and the Jewish Girl," 1829), the latter with a libretto based on Scott's *Ivanhoe* (1820). Lortzing was most successful in comedy. His *Zar und Zimmermann* ("Czar and Carpenter," 1837) contains pretty arias, similar to the simple airs of Weber, and a magnificent buffo bass character, the bumbling mayor, Van Bett. Lortzing's *Der Wildschütz* ("The Poacher," 1842) is a more elegant comedy. Three other durable comic operas from this period are *Martha* (1847) by Friedrich von Flotow (1812–1883), *Die lustigen Weiber von Windsor* ("The Merry Wives of Windsor," 1849) by Otto Nicolai (1810–1849), and *Der Barbier von Bagdad* ("The Barber of Baghdad," 1855–1858) by Peter Cornelius (1824–1874).

Marschner, Lortzing, and others

Richard Wagner and Music Drama

The music and writings of the controversial composer Richard Wagner (1813–1883) dominated the late Romantic period. He intrigued philosophers, poets, writers, and composers, and feelings about him ran high. As his letters and treatises indicate, he felt an irrepressible need to dominate everything. A curious blend of arrogance and charm, Wagner was irresponsible in matters of love and money. He believed in the superiority of the German people and considered himself a king among champions.

Wagner, the man

For Wagner, music was to serve as a vehicle for dramatic expression, and, more than any of his predecessors, he aimed at a fusion of the arts. Therefore he wrote his own librettos, composed the music, designed the sets and costumes, choreographed the ballets, rehearsed the musicians, conducted the orchestra, and ultimately designed the opera house that would show his work to best advantage, the *Festspielhaus* (Festival House) in Bayreuth, Germany.

Wagner's Romantic operas

In the years 1833–1839 Wagner was a conductor, chorus trainer, and opera-house manager in Germany. He then went to Paris, where he was influenced by the grand operas of Spontini and Meyerbeer, a period which resulted in his own grand opera, *Rienzi* (1838–1840, rev. 1843). However, his devotion to things German led him to compose the German Romantic opera *Der fliegende Holländer* ("The Flying Dutchman," 1841, rev. 1846, 1852, 1860), and the successful performances of *Rienzi* and *Dutchman* in Dresden led to his appointment as the director of the opera house there. *The Flying Dutchman,* based on a legend by Heine, is a psychological drama that deals with the mysterious sea, the supernatural, and the self-sacrificing love of a woman. Its overture, as is customary with Wagner, contains important themes of the opera.

Leitmotifs

As early as *Dutchman,* Wagner revealed his skill in using recurring musical motives, or *leitmotifs.* These highly malleable short themes or motives represent a character, place, event, object, mood, or situation, and are capable of musical development and transformation to parallel the subject's dramatic development onstage. Thus a motive can be made more or less dissonant, chromatic, or the like; it can be subjected to augmentation, diminution, inversion, fragmentation, and all the other operations of symphonic development. Leitmotifs of related people, things, or feelings are similarly related musically. The orchestra plays a leitmotif the first time that the entity in question is mentioned, and whenever this motive is brought back, some character on stage is assuredly thinking of whatever or whomever it represents. The orchestra can thereby reveal the thoughts of the characters.

Wagner came to depend on leitmotifs in his works after 1850. In *Tannhäuser* (1845, rev. 1845–1846, 1847, 1860–1861, 1865, 1875), a German Romantic story is wedded to the French grand operatic style, including great ballets specifically intended for Parisian performances. Symbolizing the battle between Good and Evil are the two sopranos, Elisabeth and Venus, respectively. Representing Wagner's own thirst for superiority is the plot element of the song contest.[2] The chorus sometimes comments on the action and sometimes participates in it, but the role of the orchestra is overwhelming, as the composer starts weaving the voice into the orchestral texture. Furthermore, he goes beyond Weber in breaking down the symmetry of the aria and in arriving at an ideal fusion between recitative and song.

Lohengrin

The culmination of German Romantic opera was Wagner's *Lohengrin* (1846–1848), retelling an old Teutonic legend about a knight's search for the Holy Grail. Legend proved to be the perfect dramatic subject for Wagner, because it is timeless, concentrated, inexhaustible, and more intense and elevated than everyday life. *Lohengrin* again pits brightness against darkness. Specific keys and instrumental colors represent the various characters. For instance, F-sharp minor and the bass clarinet are consistently associated with the evil conspirators. The vocal lines are more arioso than before, and wide leaps serve expressive ends (see Example 28.3). In this opera Wagner uses such leitmotifs as the "forbidden question" and the Holy Grail. But the most impressive aspect of the score is the refined treatment of the orchestra, especially in the Preludes to acts I and III. In the former Wagner represents the Holy Grail's descent to Earth and return to Heaven with some of the most shimmering string effects in all of music.

Wagner's political involvement in the abortive Revolution of 1848 forced him to flee from Germany. He settled in Zurich, where he fell in love with the poetess Mathilde Wesendonk (1828–1902) and wrote his three greatest essays: *Die Kunst und die Revolution* ("Art and Revolution," 1849), *Das Kunstwerk der Zukunft* ("The Artwork of the Future," 1849), and *Oper und Drama* ("Opera and Drama," 1851, rev. 1868). In them he criticized the opera of his own era as debased, superficial entertainment, catering to a decadent society, which was in need of redemption through new great art. After reaching its pinnacle in ancient Greece, said Wagner, drama had deteriorated for the next two thousand years, partly because the dogmas of the Church had conflicted with art. Wagner went on to preach that art, springing from nature as the mirror of civilization, could free the self-conscious society and ennoble those who aspired to high ideals. German mythology, understandable to German people, wrote Wagner, could teach eternal truths; and music, as the servant of drama, could convey what words alone could never express. Wagner therefore set out to reassemble the components of tragedy—to fuse the arts—in achieving a new kind of opera.

Wagner's writings

Ex. 28.3   Richard Wagner, *Lohengrin,* act II, scene 4, mm. 82–94

Ex. 28.3   cont.

"Stand back, Elsa! No longer will I suffer to follow you like a servant! You should let me go before you everywhere; before me you should bow down humbly." (In this scene Ortrud, the heathen and evil sorceress, is confronting the heroine, Elsa.)

Wagner spent the rest of his life trying to accomplish his ideal of the *Gesamtkunstwerk,* or total artwork. In the seven masterpieces that occupied him for over thirty-five years, he moved away from the traditions of opera and

The music drama

created what he called "music drama." Wagner's theories of the legend, the fusion of the arts, and music's service to drama are realized through various means in his music dramas. Leitmotifs abound, intertwining with one another to create symphonic webs of continuous music, in which cadences are avoided, keys are in flux, arioso melody flows endlessly, and periodicity succumbs to a freely floating rhythm. Wagner's German poetry stresses alliteration and assonance in an effort to unify speech and song.

In the music drama, Wagner worked on a monumental formal scale. He thought of each of his scenes (and, in turn, acts) as a series of musical units in such patterns as ABA (arch form) or AAB (bar form). Each group of small units could in turn become one larger unit on a higher formal plane, until ultimately an entire act might turn out to be one colossal A-section or B-section of the whole music drama. Woven around the small units are introductions, variations, codas, developmental stretches, and transitional material, so that only painstaking analytical study of the score can reveal Wagner's scheme.[3]

Wagner's largest achievement was the tetralogy based on the Norse myth entitled the *Nibelungenlied* ("Song of the Nibelung"; the Nibelungs were a race of dwarfs). He envisaged the four dramas as one huge work, which he called *Der Ring des Nibelungen* ("The Ring of the Nibelung"). Wagner's *Ring* consists of: (1) *Das Rheingold* ("The Rhine-gold," 1853–1854); (2) *Die Walküre* ("The Valkyrie," 1854–1856); (3) *Siegfried* (1856–1871); and (4) *Götterdämmerung* ("Twilight of the Gods," 1869–1874). These four music dramas demand elaborate staging and scenery, and in 1876 Wagner had the Festspielhaus built according to his own specifications, including a sunken orchestral pit. The story of the *Ring* shows how all beings, mortals and gods alike, fight to control the world. Greed and power are weighed against love and obedience. In the ultimate destruction of the world at the end of the *Ring,* Romantic monumentalism is exposed at its most extreme. The *Ring* is a showcase for brass and percussion instruments. The agile Wagner tuba was designed for the *Ring,* which also shows off the bass trumpet, contrabass trombone, and regular tuba. However, Wagner also made wonderful use of the bass clarinet, English horn, and the upper ranges of the strings. He divided his string section into more than the conventional five parts, used valved brasses, expanded the range of the orchestra, increased the number of woodwinds and brasses, and used such effects as muted sounds, tremolos, and metallic noises, in these ways turning the opera house into a showcase of orchestral sonority, subtlety, and splendor. **The *Ring***

The singers of Wagnerian music drama have to cope with a heavy orchestral fabric, shifting tonalities, suspensions, chromaticism, difficult leaps, wide vocal ranges, and uncomfortable tessituras. Yet they must sing with the greatest beauty and convey every nuance of the text and drama. Brilliance and volume must be balanced by sensitivity and subtlety. It is not surprising, therefore, that a tenor able to overcome these problems is known as a *Heldentenor,* or heroic tenor. Life is no easier for Wagnerian sopranos.

One of the most famous pieces of the nineteenth century is the Prelude to *Tristan und Isolde* (1857–1859; *AMA,* p. 397; *CAMF* II, no. 163; *MSO* II, p. 205; *NS,* E, II, no. 12; *NS,* S, no. 30), because of its harmonic audacity. In this work Wagner depends upon the allure of nonharmonic tones, chromatic chords, and ceaseless modulation—to the point of preventing the emergence of a clear tonic key. In an overall ABA form, the Prelude presents the opera's primary leitmotifs, including the themes of love's yearning, the power of love, and destiny. Entering singly, the leitmotifs eventually combine to create great climaxes in the B-section. Irregular, asymmetrical rhythms are wedded to the continuous melodic unfolding, all of which is beautifully colored by the subtle shadings of Wagner's orchestration. Fluid tonality fills the pages of this story of passion, magic, and Fate. The emotional intensity of such scenes as the love duet in act II (*NS,* E, II, no. 12) and the final moments of the work—when Isolde sings of the eternal love that only death can bring, in her *Liebestod* ("Love-Death"; *AMA,* p. 402; *MSO* II, p. 214) aria—is rare in all of **Tristan** music. In capturing the ill-fated lovers' passions and tensions in his unstable and ambiguous harmonic progressions, Wagner opened the door to the demise of the tonal system. After the first performance of *Tristan* in 1865, the great majority of composers felt compelled to respond to it somehow—in most cases by employing various elements of its style in their own works. Undeniably, the seeds of early-twentieth-century musical style were sown in *Tristan*.

Die Meister-singer

In *Die Meistersinger von Nürnberg* ("The Mastersingers of Nuremberg," 1862–1867) Wagner compromised many of his theories. This great comic work contains set pieces, such as Walther's *Prize Song* in act III, choruses, rhymed verse, historical characters, and magnificent counterpoint, which Wagner had once called a musical artifice that impeded drama. Nevertheless, this opera is based on leitmotifs, bar forms, and continuous melodic and dramatic flow, and is as genuinely Wagnerian as anything else he wrote.

Parsifal

Wagner expressed strong anti-Semitic sentiments in his writings, and his theories as well as his music were much admired by Adolf Hitler decades later. The composer was also an outspoken adversary of the Christian Church. It was therefore surprising to his contemporaries when he brought forth his final work, *Parsifal* (1877–1882), preaching Christian faith and love. Wagner called it a "Festival Dedication Play" and ordered that it be performed only at Bayreuth.

The influence of Wagner

Primarily because of his avoidance of complete cadences through the use of chromaticism, enharmony, deceptive cadences, shifts of tonality, and suspensions and appoggiaturas, Wagner invited the demise of the era of tonality and, therefore, of the Romantic musical style. However, what makes Wagner special is not the harmonic language itself, which can be shown to have begun with Liszt, but its interaction with symphonic development, leitmotifs, and continuous drama, and the amazing—often ridiculous, crude, or vicious—intellectual and philosophical ideas of this master composer.

Post-Wagnerian German Opera

Few German opera composers after Wagner were willing or able to resist the spell of his influence. Even in a work based on a fairy tale, *Hänsel und Gretel* (1893) by Engelbert Humperdinck (1854–1921), one encounters Wagnerian leitmotifs, orchestration, and counterpoint. One genius who revitalized the German music drama in the early years of the twentieth century was

Richard Strauss

Richard Strauss (1864–1949). He was similar to Wagner in his use of leitmotifs, textual and dramatic nuances, and declamatory and arioso vocal styles. But while Wagner's works contain philosophical messages, Strauss aimed to entertain and even shock his audiences with raw, intense music drama.

Strauss turned Oscar Wilde's lustful, brutal one-act play *Salomé* into a frenzied one-act music drama, which created a scandal at its first performance in 1905. People were revolted by the strident dissonances and angular, exaggerated vocal writing, as well as by its cast of despicable characters and the vulgarity of Salomé's dance and actions. Strauss's next work, *Elektra* (1906–1908), dealing with unbridled hatred and vengeance, began his long and fruitful collaboration with the outstanding Viennese librettist and playwright Hugo von Hofmannsthal (1847–1929). With its extreme dissonance, *Elektra* is an eerie mixture of diatonic, chromatic, and polytonal passages.

Strauss and Hofmannsthal moved from Greek tragedy to eighteenth-century Vienna in their next work, an opulent comedy of manners entitled *Der Rosenkavalier* ("The Rose Cavalier," 1909–1910). This work contains sections of tuneful, diatonic music and the charm of the Viennese waltz. The luxuriance of Strauss's orchestral and harmonic language, the lyrical beauty of his vocal writing (as in the final trio), and his dramatic use of intricate ensembles make this a great comic opera. In the revised version of *Ariadne auf Naxos* ("Ariadne on Naxos," 1911–1912, rev. 1916) Hofmannsthal and Strauss combined the styles of opera buffa and music drama. A Neoclassic chamber opera, *Ariadne* employs an orchestra of only thirty-six players and returns in part to the Classical system of set pieces. Starting with *Der Rosenkavalier* and *Ariadne,* Strauss became more conservative, and this was the direction he took throughout the rest of his long career.

Romantic Opera in Other Centers

Russia

Russia produced a number of important operas during the nineteenth century. Mikhail Glinka (1804–1857) began the nationalistic movement in Russian music with his rescue opera *A Life for the Tsar* (1834–1836), which aroused patriotic feelings by using melodies and harmonies common in Russian folk songs and by making Russian peasants its central figures. Glinka followed with a fairy-tale opera, *Russlan and Ludmilla* (1837–1842), which has more musical continuity. A very original composer was Alexander Dargomyzhsky (1813–1869), who set Pushkin's treatment of the Don Juan legend in *The Stone Guest* (1860s; completed by Cui and orchestrated by Rimsky-Korsakov for the first performance in 1872). This linear, dissonant work makes constant use of recitatives, allowing speech inflection to dictate melodic outlines.

Glinka

Three members of the so-called "Mighty Five," the great quintet of Russian nationalists—Mily Balakirev (1837–1910), Borodin, César Cui (1835–1918), Mussorgsky, and Rimsky-Korsakov—contributed several fine operas. To the oriental exoticism in *Prince Igor* (1869–1870, 1874–1887), Alexander Borodin (1833–1887) added especially lyrical melodies. Nikolai Rimsky-Korsakov (1844–1908) wrote fifteen operas, the best known of which is *The Golden Cockerel* (1906–1907), a political satire. *The Snow Maiden* (1880–1881, rev. c. 1895) and *Sadko* (1894–1896) are other operas by this masterful orchestrator, who enjoyed alternating modal diatonicism with delicate chromaticism.

The greatest of the Russian nationalistic operas is *Boris Godunov* (1868–1869, rev. 1871–1872, 1873; excerpt in *NS*, E, II, no. 16) by Modest Mussorgsky (1839–1881). A succession of tableaux, it is a psychological study of

Mussorgsky's Boris Godunov

all layers of Russian society and examines the relationship between the ruler and the ruled. The original version contained no great female roles, and so Mussorgsky added two scenes set in Poland and created the role of Marina, a Polish princess, for a performance in 1874. Following the lead of Dargomyzhsky, Mussorgsky constructed vocal lines that reflect ordinary Russian speech and are therefore asymmetrical. Yet the opera contains some very lyrical music, as shown in Example 28.4.

    Boris impresses with its brilliant sonorities, massive and colorful effects, fluctuating metrical patterns (including measures of $\frac{5}{4}$ time), ostinato figures, and long pedal points, all of which are contained in the great "Coronation Scene" of the Prologue. Also present is a Russian folk song style, featuring a narrow range, reiteration of motives, modality, and a cadence in which the line descends a fourth. Although Mussorgsky gives each character a musical motive, he does not use Wagnerian methods of thematic transformation and development, nor does he permit the orchestra to overpower his singers. In *Boris* the music serves the text in a clear and direct manner.

Tchaikov-
sky
    Although Tchaikovsky's ballets *Swan Lake* (1875–1876), *The Sleeping Beauty* (1888–1889), and *The Nutcracker* (1891–1892; excerpts in *NS*, *E*, II,

Ex. 28.4   Modest Mussorgsky, Love duet, mm. 1–12, from *Boris Godunov*, act III

Ex. 28.4   cont.

love — that drove me to speak thus; jeal - ous am I for thy fame — and thine hon - or!

Now hear me, love, when night — is dark — and si - lent.

poco cresc.

no. 18; *NS, S,* no. 35) are well known, his operas are not, despite their sensitive delineation of character, orchestral beauty, and lyricism. The two most popular are based on Pushkin stories: *Eugene Onegin* (1877–1878), a picture of Russian country life; and *The Queen of Spades* (1890), an intense tragedy.

Other Countries

Like Russia, other nations produced operas steeped in patriotic plots and folk music. The best known folk opera from Central Europe is Smetana's **Central** *The Bartered Bride* (1863–1866, rev. 1869–1870); in the style of an opéra-   **Europe** comique, it is alive with interesting rhythms, warm lyricism, and a robust sense of humor. Less popular but just as interesting is Smetana's historical opera *Dalibor* (1865–1867, rev. 1870), based on a Bohemian legend spiritually related to Beethoven's *Fidelio,* and influenced by Wagner in its musical continuity and excellent orchestration.

In Felipe Pedrell (1841–1922), Spain produced a composer whose philos-   **Spain** ophy was that a country's folk songs should be the basis for all its music. One of his best works illustrating this tendency is *La celestina* ("The Procuress," 1904). As a composer and musicologist, Pedrell had some illustrious students, including Albéniz, Granados, and Manuel de Falla (1876–1946). Although these composers are known mostly for their colorful piano music, they all wrote operas, and Granados' *Goyescas* (1916), whose music is based on his piano suite of the same name (1911), is a good example of the verismo style.

England   Sometimes called the English Rossini, Henry Rowley Bishop (1786–1855) was a prolific opera composer; among his works are such ballad operas as *Clari, or The Maid of Milan* (1823) and the exotic *The Fall of Algiers* (1825), both derived from plays by John Payne (1791–1852). Irish-born Michael Balfe (1808–1870), who sang such roles as Mozart's Figaro and Papageno, also composed operas, including *The Maid of Artois* (1836) and *The Bohemian Girl* (1843).

Lighter Operatic Types in the Romantic Era

France

French opéras-comiques and German comic Singspiele may be said to be the progenitors of nineteenth-century light opera and *operetta,* works having great audience appeal. By "operetta" is meant a light and entertaining theatrical work with spoken dialogue, dancing, a sentimental plot, and very lyrical musical numbers.

Offen-bach's operettas   The principal advocate of the French operetta, or *opéra-bouffe,* was the German-born Jacques Offenbach (1819–1880). His works glisten with wit, parody, and political and social satire, clothed in music that is graceful, ebullient, and melodious. In *Orphée aux enfers* ("Orpheus in the Underworld," 1858) and *La Belle Hélène* ("The Beautiful Helen," 1864), Offenbach parodied the French reverence for the theatrical conventions of Greek antiquity, which he had come to know as a conductor of entr'acte music during performances of French Classical tragedies. In *La Vie parisienne* ("Parisian Life," 1866) he took aim at the corrupt contemporary life under Napoleon III. The texts contain puns and jokes, and the musical parody is aimed largely at Meyerbeer's grand operas and Italian *opera semiseria,* as in Offenbach's hilarious *Ba-ta-clan* (1855), set in China. Yet Offenbach's attacks tend to be amusing rather than caustic or invidious. He poked fun at all kinds of people, and his audiences laughed heartily, even when it was at themselves. Offenbach's most enduring work, however, has been the serious opéra-comique entitled *Les Contes d'Hoffmann* ("The Tales of Hoffmann," 1881), whose orchestration was completed after the composer's death by Ernest Guiraud (1837–1892).

Vienna

The Viennese operetta   Offenbach's popularity spread to Vienna during the 1860s, where it inspired a spate of operettas. The Viennese were less interested in satire than in sheer escapist entertainment and sentimentality, and the Viennese operetta tradition began to take shape in the works of Franz von Suppé (1819–1895), including his *Boccaccio* (1879) and the burlesque of Wagnerian opera, *Der Tannenhäuser* (1852). Karl Millöcker (1842–1899) followed with such works as *Der Bettelstudent* ("The Beggar Student," 1882), his enduring operetta. However, the leading figure in this realm was Johann Strauss, Jr. (1825–1899), the "waltz king" of Vienna. The waltz, polka, *csárdás* (a Hungarian gypsy dance), scintillating use of the orchestra, and silly, sentimental stories fill his stage works, including the ever-popular *Die Fledermaus* ("The Bat," 1874) and *Der Zigeunerbaron* ("The Gypsy Baron," 1885). Franz Lehár (1870–1948) continued this tradition in *Die lustige Witwe* ("The Merry Widow," 1905) and other operettas. A similar style in the United States involved such composers as Victor Herbert, Rudolf Friml, and Sigmund Romberg (see Chapter 40).

England

In London, Arthur Sullivan (1842–1900) applied some of the Offenbachian brand of parody and satire to English life, and did so with even merrier music than Offenbach's. In collaboration with the brilliant librettist William S. Gilbert (1836–1911), Sullivan created some of the best operettas in the English language, for he was a highly skilled composer and a true craftsman, and had a flair for the theater. He knew the music of the past and was able to allude musically to the works of Verdi, Wagner, Gounod, Rossini, Bizet, and Schubert, and to English patriotic songs, nautical tunes, and glees (simply harmonized, unaccompanied songs for three or more solo men's voices). His command of counterpoint was remarkable, too, leading to the great ensemble scenes in his works. We can find no better examples of patter song than those in the operettas of Gilbert and Sullivan, e.g., the *Model of a Modern Major General* from *The Pirates of Penzance* (1879). The two most popular works by Gilbert and Sullivan are *H.M.S. Pinafore* (1878) and *The Mikado* (1885).

Gilbert and Sullivan

Spain

During the nationalistic movements of the mid-nineteenth century, the Spanish *zarzuela,* which had fallen into a period of dormancy during the Classical era, was revived by such composers as Francisco A. Barbieri (1823–1894) and Pascual Arrieta y Correra (1823–1894). In the 1840s and 1850s the zarzuela exhibited a lightness characteristic of the French opéra-comique, and many French librettos were adapted for Spanish musical settings. An example of this popular nationalistic style is Barbieri's *Gloria y peluca* ("Glory and Wig," 1850). Like Offenbach in France, Barbieri composed more than seventy light operas, the best known of which is *Pan y toros* ("Bread and Bulls," 1864). Alongside the light and comic *zarzuelita* in one act, there developed the *zarzuela grande* in three acts, often possessing more of the dramatic seriousness of French grand opera, as well as Italianate orchestration, harmony, and vocal writing. An early example is *Marina* (1855) by Arrieta y Correra, and one from the end of the century is *La bruja* ("The Witch," 1887) by Ruperto Chapí y Lorente (1851–1909).

The Spanish zarzuela

Summary

In the nineteenth century the great traditions of Italian opera were preserved by such composers as Rossini, Donizetti, Bellini, Verdi, and Puccini. At the same time, however, Italian domination of opera in Europe declined, as France, Germany, and other nations developed and refined their own operatic styles. Paris became the center of operatic activity, and success there was a goal for most opera composers.

Italian audiences wanted to hear great bel canto singing. The French wanted lighthearted, sentimental entertainment, such as Auber's opéras-comiques, or else spectacular scenes, choruses, and ballets, as found in Meyerbeer's grand operas. In Germany audiences flocked to enjoy folk songs and dances, stories from folklore, tales about nature and the supernatural, and symphonic use of the orchestra. These ideals were embodied in the German Romantic operas of such composers as Weber and Wagner. Similar nationalistic purposes were envisaged by Russians, Bohemians, Spanish, and others.

Opera as music drama was a great concern to many Romantic composers. In France the ideals of nobility and simplicity were preserved in many operas by such composers as Cherubini and Berlioz. In Italy bel canto composers continually increased the role of the orchestra and provided more continuity between and unity within their scenes. Every nuance of the singing voice was put to dramatic use, and composers created for it music appropriate to the character and dramatic situation at hand. The pinnacle of this style was reached in the last works of Verdi.

Wagner's music dramas were envisioned as total artworks, in which the various arts cooperated to make the symbolic meaning of the drama as clear as possible. In developing his system of leitmotifs and in applying the formal procedures of symphonic development to his works, Wagner arrived at a continuous operatic style, almost devoid of set pieces. Avoiding full cadences and periodicity, Wagner led the way to Post-Romanticism.

Late Romantic opera composers in France, such as Gounod and Massenet, combined elements from the opéra-comique and grand opera in achieving the new style of lyric opera, stressing appealing melodies and sentimental stories. In Italy a new kind of opera arose, depicting sex and violence with loud dynamics and dissonance. This style, known as verismo, was handled most effectively by Puccini.

Alongside the serious operas of the nineteenth century were hundreds of operettas and other light types of musical theater. Especially memorable are the French opéras-bouffes of Offenbach, the Viennese operettas of Johann Strauss, Jr., and the English operettas of Gilbert and Sullivan.

Notes

1. Such topics seem not to have irked the censors of the time very much. They were intolerant, however, of allusions to the Church, sacred subject matter, the acting out of political conspiracies, and criticism of rulers, past or present.
2. Who could write the best, or prizewinning, song would also be the problem facing the characters of a later Wagner work, *Die Meistersinger,* which is, in a way, the comic counterpart to *Tannhäuser.*

3. These views of form in Wagner's music drama are derived from the findings of the Viennese musicologist Alfred Lorenz (1868–1939). Although Lorenz's systematic, often forced analyses and opinions are open to question, they do provide the student with some good guidelines for further study.

Bibliography

Books and Articles

General Books on Opera

CONRAD, PETER. *Romantic Opera and Literary Form.* Berkeley, Cal.: University of California Press, 1977.

DENT, EDWARD J. *The Rise of Romantic Opera,* edited by Winton Dean. Cambridge: Cambridge University Press, 1976.

GROUT, DONALD J. *A Short History of Opera,* 2nd ed. New York: Columbia University Press, 1965.

KERMAN, JOSEPH. *Opera as Drama.* New York: Vintage Books, 1959.

PLEASANTS, HENRY. *The Great Singers from the Dawn of Opera to Our Own Time.* New York: Simon & Schuster, 1966.

Italian Opera

AYCOCK, ROY E. "Shakespeare, Boito, and Verdi." *Musical Quarterly* 58 (Oct. 1972): 588–604.

BALDINI, GABRIELE. *The Story of Giuseppe Verdi: Oberto to Un ballo in maschera,* edited by Fedele d'Amico, translated and edited by Roger Parker. Cambridge: Cambridge University Press, 1980.

BUDDEN, JULIAN. *The Operas of Verdi,* vol. I: *From Oberto to Rigoletto;* vol. II: *From Il Trovatore to La Forza del Destino.* New York: Oxford University Press, 1978.

CARNER, MOSCO. *Puccini: A Critical Biography,* 2nd ed. New York: Holmes & Meier, 1977.

OSBORNE, CHARLES. *The Complete Operas of Verdi.* New York: Alfred A. Knopf, 1970; reprint, New York: Da Capo Press, 1977.

WALKER, FRANK. *The Man Verdi.* New York: Alfred A. Knopf, 1962.

WEINSTOCK, HERBERT. *Rossini: A Biography.* New York: Alfred A. Knopf, 1968.

French Opera

COOPER, MARTIN. *Opéra Comique.* New York: Chanticleer Press, 1949.

CROSTEN, WILLIAM L. *French Grand Opera: An Art and a Business.* New York: King's Crown Press, 1948; reprint, New York: Da Capo Press, 1972.

PENDLE, KARIN. *Eugène Scribe and French Opera of the Nineteenth Century.* Studies in Musicology, ed. George Buelow. Ann Arbor, Mich.: UMI Research Press, 1979.

German Opera

BAILEY, ROBERT. "The Structure of the *Ring* and Its Evolution." *19th-Century Music* 1 (July 1977): 48–61.

DONINGTON, ROBERT. *Wagner's Ring and Its Symbols: The Music and the Myth,* 3rd ed. London: Faber & Faber, 1974.

GARLINGTON, AUBREY S. "German Romantic Opera and the Problem of Origins." *Musical Quarterly* 63 (April 1977): 247–263.

GARTEN, H. F. *Wagner: The Dramatist*. Totowa, N.J.: Rowman & Littlefield, 1978.

GUTMAN, ROBERT. *Richard Wagner: The Man, His Mind, and His Music*. New York: Harcourt, Brace & World, 1968.

MANN, WILLIAM. *Richard Strauss: A Critical Study of the Operas*. London: Cassell & Co., 1964.

NEWMAN, ERNEST. *Wagner as Man and Artist*. New York: Vintage Books, 1960.

———. *Wagner Operas*. New York: Alfred A. Knopf, 1949.

WARRACK, JOHN. *Carl Maria von Weber*, 2nd ed. Cambridge: Cambridge University Press, 1976.

WESTERNHAGEN, CURT VON. *Wagner: A Biography*, 2 vols., translated by Mary Whittall. Cambridge: Cambridge University Press, 1978.

Russian Opera

TARUSKIN, RICHARD. "Glinka's Ambiguous Legacy and the Birth Pangs of Russian Opera." *19th-Century Music* 1 (Nov. 1977): 142–162.

Scores

For operatic works by Beethoven, Berlioz, Dvořák, Mendelssohn, Mussorgsky, Schubert, R. Schumann, Tchaikovsky, and Wagner, see Bibliography for Chapter 24. Piano-vocal scores of all the operas in the standard repertoire are published primarily by G. Schirmer and Belwin-Mills Publishing Corp.

Early Romantic Opera, ed. Philip Gossett and Charles Rosen. New York: Garland Publishing, 1978–   .

In Dover Music Books —Complete Scores Series
(New York: Dover Publications)

VERDI, GIUSEPPE, *Falstaff*. 1980 reprint of the edition published by G. Ricordi & Co., Milan, 1893.

WAGNER, RICHARD, *Die Meistersinger von Nürnberg*. 1976 reprint of the edition published by C. F. Peters, Leipzig, c. 1910.

———, *Tristan und Isolde*. 1973 reprint of the edition published by C. F. Peters, Leipzig, c. 1911.

———, *Die Walküre*. 1978 reprint of the edition published by C. F. Peters, Leipzig, c. 1910.

WEBER, CARL MARIA VON, *Der Freischütz*. 1977 reprint of the edition published by C. F. Peters, Leipzig, n.d.

PART SIX

The Twentieth Century

29

The Twentieth Century:
An Overview

URING the twentieth century traditional values have come again under attack. The immense changes brought about by rapidly developing technology and two global wars have helped create ideas and attitudes toward life and art that are vastly different from those of preceding centuries. The past no longer seems to provide reliable models for many composers. More often than not, then, each generation searches for its own solutions, a struggle mirrored by novel trends in the arts.

Diversified assumptions about the aesthetics of creativity have accompanied these shifts. The seventeenth through nineteenth centuries had been dominated by the idea of progress. The nineteenth century especially had nurtured the notion of the individual genius, and its correlative concept of art as personal expression. Some artists have retained this belief, and see their work as the continuation of a great musical tradition. For others, this ideal has dissolved in favor of a new objectivity, bringing with it an escape from the personal. Sometimes referred to as Formalists, the artists sharing this belief view themselves as craftsmen rather than inspired beings, and their artistic works as unique solutions to problems rather than as expressions of feelings. They see the past as relevant for the problems raised but not for the solutions offered. Yet other creators believe that all traditions and systems are harmful because they limit our freedom of thought and action. They tend to seek novelty. They deem each creation valid simply by virtue of its existence.

In this chapter, the discussion of the multiple trends of our century has been divided chronologically into three parts. The first era, beginning in the late nineteenth century and ending with World War I, is characterized by the breakdown of traditional musical procedures and a search for new approaches to compositional problems. The second era, culminating in World War II, sees an attempt to consolidate the pre–World War I experiments, as well as the new beginnings and developments that arise as natural outgrowths of earlier trends. The most recent era shows a renewed interest in experimentation followed by further attempts at consolidation in the 1970s and 1980s.

723

During the last decades of the nineteenth century, it became increasingly evident that the limits of an internationally accepted musical style had been reached. The orchestra grew enormously, many works assumed unprecedented proportions, and the harmonic language became increasingly dense, approaching harmonic chaos. Simultaneously, ways of thinking about music were slowly changing.

**Impres-
sionism**

A distinctive direction was taken by French composers. In reaction against Wagner and the Germanic tradition, Claude Debussy and Maurice Ravel, among others, wrote music labeled *impressionistic.* Works in this style often borrowed scales from the ancient modes as well as from non-Western traditions, and used nonfunctional harmonies. Color, or timbre, was important, assuming a status independent of melody and harmony (see Chapter 30).

**Expres-
sionism**

Just as painting moved away from perspective, so music moved away from tonality and the melodic-harmonic hierarchy. In German-speaking countries the gradual dissolution of tonal boundaries under the impact of the fluid chromaticism of Wagner and Strauss led to the expressionist atonal works of the Viennese composer Arnold Schoenberg and his famous disciples Alban Berg and Anton Webern (see Chapter 31).

**Stravinsky
and
rhythm**

The early works of Russian-born Igor Stravinsky point to yet a third direction. While German-speaking composers concentrated on inner expression through extensive use of dissonance, large leaps, fragmented melodies, and other pitch-related changes, Stravinsky and others turned to rhythm. His early works, which show some indebtedness to the nineteenth-century Russian nationalist composers, use primitive, driving rhythms that helped to free rhythm from its comparatively subordinate role in the Western music tradition (see Chapter 32).

**Nation-
alism**

From the beginning of the twentieth century until the end of World War II, there was a resurgence of musical nationalism. Unlike many nineteenth-century composers, however, the twentieth-century nationalists did not smooth out unconventional aspects of folk and traditional music. The Hungarian-born Béla Bartók's strongly rhythmic music was especially influential in this regard, and the careful fieldwork during which he collected authentic folk melodies set an example for countless others (see Chapter 33).

**Neo-
classicism**

Igor Stravinsky was probably the most influential composer of the between-the-wars period (1918–1945). His work has often been compared with that of Picasso because his style changed from work to work, and because each change inspired many imitators. Although Stravinsky's early style was nationalistic and his post–World War II style eventually turned to serialism, most of his works written between the World Wars have been considered Neoclassical, since he uses stylistic elements of past epochs with modern inflections and techniques superimposed (see Chapter 34).

**"Acces-
sible"
music**

A combination of leftist political beliefs and the resurgence of nationalism served to make composers feel that experimental trends in music had created too large a gap between composer and audience. These composers, who sought to create an art that was fresh yet more easily accessible, included Kurt

Weill in Germany and Darius Milhaud in France during the 1920s, and Aaron Copland in the United States during the 1930s. Other composers, such as Berlin born and trained Stefan Wolpe, diverged briefly from an experimental style to write songs "for the people." Two outgrowths of this trend surfaced after World War II: politically committed art, but with a more experimental musical language, grew especially during the politically active 1960s, while an "accessible" style, although never disappearing from the work of composers such as Benjamin Britten in Britain, gained additional followers in the 1970s and 1980s from the ranks of composers who had been working with other musical languages (see Chapter 33).

But not all composers were interested in either accessibility or the past. Schoenberg's expressionist phase led to the development of *serialism,* a system that determined the pitch choices of each musical work by precompositional procedures. Serialism did not gain widespread acceptance, however, until after World War II. **Serialism**

Timbral or coloristic experimentation, impressively demonstrated in the compositions of Debussy, was an important feature in the works composed by French-born Edgard Varèse during the 1920–1930 period—the first decade of his permanent residence in the United States. In France this experimental trend was further explored by Olivier Messiaen beginning in the 1930s. Varèse was more abstract, working with planes of sound, while Messiaen developed a highly personalized, mystical language. This coloristic trend, too, remained relatively isolated until after World War II (see Chapter 30). **Coloristic experiments**

By the early 1950s two different directions became discernible in music: total control and its opposite, total freedom. The former grew out of serialism, which was originally created as a system of pitch organization. Composers such as the American Milton Babbitt, the French Pierre Boulez, and the German Karlheinz Stockhausen extended this system to include the organization of rhythm, dynamics, timbre, and sometimes form (see Chapter 34). **Total serialism**

The opposite point of view, which produced chance or aleatoric music, was advanced by the Americans John Cage and Morton Feldman. Cage, who was influenced by Erik Satie, abstract expressionist painting, and Zen Buddhism, made musical decisions by random techniques meant to free the composer from traditional modes of thought. The musical movements known as *minimal art* and *conceptual art* arose from this school. Minimalism has grown in prominence since the late 1970s, especially in the United States (see Chapter 35). **Chance music and related trends**

Wartime technology has led to the development of the tape recorder and magnetic tape, which in turn made possible the development of electronic music. Such music had already been envisaged in the theoretical writings of Ferruccio Busoni and Edgard Varèse. Advances in technology also made possible the development of computer music. The latter had fewer adherents, due both to the expense of purchasing computer time and the need for the composer to be familiar with mathematics as well as music (see Chapter 34). **Electronic and computer music**

In addition to creating new sound sources with machines, composers also were interested in obtaining new sounds from traditional instrumentation.

Andy Warhol (b. c. 1930), *Green Coca-Coca Bottles* (1962). Warhol's use of a small unit repeated many times without change parallels simultaneous developments by minimalist composers. (Courtesy, the Whitney Museum of American Art, New York; Gift of the Friends of the Whitney Museum of American Art)

Further coloristic experiments   Some followed the Debussy-Varèse tradition, using sounds as a primary method of organizing their works. The Rumanian-born Greek composer Iannis Xenakis followed certain mathematical laws, while Krzysztof Penderecki and Witold Lutoslawski, who form part of what is referred to as the "Polish school," achieved somewhat similar sound results without a mathematical basis (see Chapter 34).

Tonality and Rhythm

The twentieth century has seen the dissolution of traditional functional harmony along with the traditional duple and triple meter schemes associated with the Classical–Romantic style. This is not to say that remnants do not exist. Rather, diversified trends, including continuations of traditional practices, have replaced the formerly prevailing sense of a common rhythmic and harmonic language. Many of the various trends that coexist today have roots in the practices of the nineteenth century, as will be shown in subsequent discussions.

Approaches to tonal centers

Many twentieth-century compositions still retain a tonal center or multiple temporary tonal centers. Functional harmony, however, based on the importance of the dominant and dominant-tonic relationship, has largely been abandoned. Thus these centers are necessarily established by new means, the central note or chord itself, which is asserted repeatedly, often as a pedal point or as part of an ostinato pattern. This technique can be seen, for instance, throughout the works of Debussy. Other compositions combine two or more tonal centers simultaneously, a practice referred to as *polytonality,* as illustrated in some of the compositions of Milhaud. Yet in other music, such as the atonal pieces of Schoenberg and Webern, as well as several post–World War II serial works, composers have tried to avoid entirely the sense of tonal center. Another possibility is that a composition may be atonal or polytonal in some passages, while tonal in others.

Harmony

Twentieth-century harmony has been forced to expand. Parallel chords, forbidden in functional harmony, are often used as a way of thickening a line. This technique can be found in the music of Debussy and the early works of Stravinsky. In addition to chords built by thirds, composers used chords built by seconds (as in the famous tone clusters of Henry Cowell), and in fourths and fifths. Composers also formed polychords by combining two or more triads or other simple chords. An example, taken from the opening of the second movement of William Schuman's *Three-Score Set* for piano solo (1943), is given in Example 29.1. Experiments with different types of scales—pentatonic, modal, and microtonal—have also led to new vertical possibilities.

Counterpoint

Counterpoint has regained prominence in most twentieth-century music due, in part, to the influence of Neoclassicism. Some composers, including Paul Hindemith, have adopted traditional Baroque forms such as canon and fugue. Other composers, including Elliott Carter and Roger Sessions, have

Ex. 29.1   William Schuman, *Three-Score Set*

created counterpoint with independent, nonimitative parts. The sonorities produced by free linear textures are often explainable only as the outcome of line against line, a contrast with the Baroque practice that had a harmonic underpinning.

Rhythm   Just as composers have explored new avenues of melody and harmony, they have also experimented with rhythm. Twentieth-century rhythmic practices include regular groupings of irregular numbers of beats, such as $\frac{5}{8}$ and $\frac{7}{8}$; *additive meters,* in which larger groups are formed by the addition of smaller, unequal ones (e.g., $\frac{8}{8}$ as [2 + 3 + 3]/8 rather than [4 + 4]/8); *polymeters,* in which two or more meters are used concurrently, although not necessarily notated with separate time signatures; and changing meters, changing accents within a given meter, or both. The changing meters of this last category are illustrated in Example 29.2 in an excerpt from the opening of Igor Stravinsky's *Danse sacrale* (1943 revision) from *Le Sacre du printemps* ("The Rite of Spring," 1913) for orchestra. Many works not only combine the above-listed metrical possibilities, but also alternate between metrical and nonmetrical sections.

Twentieth-Century Performance Practices

Background   The twentieth century has witnessed continual expansion in instrumental and vocal technique, so that many new demands are now imposed on performers. They are expected to execute large leaps of pitch quickly, to feel comfortable with dissonant intervals and extreme ranges, and even to coordinate precisely with a prerecorded tape. *Tempo rubato,* so characteristic of nineteenth-century music, is often frowned upon, and today's performers are generally expected to follow all of the composer's indications precisely.

New music has been written for all instruments, with preference given to instruments and instrumental combinations ignored in earlier centuries. Chamber music has become the norm, partially because orchestral performances are hard to obtain and rehearsal time is expensive.

Wind instruments   Woodwind players have had to learn additional ways of producing sounds, since they, unlike string players or percussionists, have traditionally played only one note at a time. Now, however, a combination of overblowing and special fingerings makes it possible to play *multiphonics* — chords of two to four notes. Several examples of such sounds are included in the Italian composer Bruno Bartolozzi's book *New Sounds for Woodwind.*[1] Wind players, including brass, are sometimes required to blow into the instrument without pressing the keys, or, conversely, to press the keys without blowing (producing a clicking sound). Other twentieth-century techniques include "flutter tonguing" (rolling the tongue while playing a note) and whistling or singing into the instrument while playing. It is interesting to note that, as in past centuries, compositional demands for new techniques have led to new instrument designs. In 1978, at IRCAM (in Paris, France), Arthur Benade, with the

Ex. 29.2   Igor Stravinsky, *Danse sacrale,* from *Le Sacre du printemps*

This excerpt is taken from Stravinsky's 1943 revision. In this version, sixteenth notes have been changed to eighths, and some rescoring has occurred.

Copyright 1945, 1973 by Associated Music Publishers, Inc., New York. Used by permission.

collaboration of Alfred Cooper (of London), devised a new flute to simplify the playing of multiphonics.

In earlier style periods, percussion instruments had been used mainly to build orchestral crescendos and to add dramatic intensity to *forte* passages. Only a few of these instruments were generally required for any composition. In modern music, however, the percussionist often plays a battery of different instruments and may be required to change rapidly from one to the other. Then, too, the use of percussion is no longer limited to bands and orchestras. Many contemporary works have been written for percussion soloists and percussion ensembles. Since World War II the vibraphone, originally used only in dance bands, has become prominent in serious music.

Contemporary piano music often avoids the virtuoso style of the nine-

Percussion

Piano

teenth century. Instead, the piano is sometimes used as a percussive instrument. Bartók was one of the first composers to employ the piano in this manner, and such music is often as technically demanding as the works of Liszt and Chopin.

Composers have also begun to explore the inside of the piano. Today pianists are sometimes asked to pluck the piano strings with their fingernails. In such instances, the necessary strings are marked with colored masking tape. In other instances, the piano is "prepared": strips of cardboard and other materials are inserted between the strings, a technique whose invention is attributed to John Cage. The pianist plays the keys, but each sound has a modified timbre. One variation of this technique occurs in Lukas Foss's *Ni bruit ni vitesse* ("Neither Noise nor Speed," published 1972). Here two percussionists modify the sounds while playing inside the piano, while the two pianists play on the keys.

Vocal techniques   Singers wishing to perform twentieth-century repertory have also had to master special techniques. Where *Sprechstimme* ("speech song") is required, as in several of the works of Arnold Schoenberg, singers must find a way of producing notes that have a spoken quality rendered on approximate pitches with rhythmic precision. At times singers must be willing to disregard the idea of expressing emotions through words, since coherent texts are sometimes replaced by parts of words or just sounds, such as hissing. The sounds themselves often require the vocalists to experiment with new means of vocal production, as in Iannis Xenakis' *Nuits* ("Nights," 1967) for twelve mixed solo voices. Vocal multiphonics (the production of two notes simultaneously) are also used on occasion.

The composer-performer relation-ship   In addition to such changes in instrumental and vocal technique, the twentieth century has seen a reevaluation of the composer-performer relationship. Because of the development of electronic music (following World War II), some composers have felt that performers are no longer needed. From this it follows that if live performers are to be used, their abilities as thinking human beings rather than their purely mechanical abilities to produce sounds should be utilized. Therefore, performers of the music in question are given tasks that involve them in the creative process, such as making specific choices during each performance from a set of verbal instructions. Not all performers, of course, wish to learn such new techniques, nor do they wish to use a musical language that may seem foreign to them. This situation has encouraged among performers a degree of specialization unique to our time.

The New Notation

As ways of thinking about music have changed, many composers have found that the system of notation inherited from previous centuries no longer suffices. Existing notations have had to be extended and new notations invented. During the first half of the twentieth century, composers sought to notate with even greater precision than in the past (observe, for instance, Schoenberg's dynamic markings in his piano works) and often chose to use more complex rhythms within their works. The traditional symbols continued to be used, with some additions (e.g., for quarter tones), but the resultant score was often quite complex and hence difficult to perform.

In the 1950s, some composers reacted against the rhythmic and other complexities in the music of many of their colleagues. In certain passages, such as fast runs, individual note choices seemed unimportant to the musical concept. In these instances a simplified notation could be used, one merely indicating the nature of the passage, while allowing the performer to choose the actual pitches during the performance. This made the composition somewhat easier for the performer to read and interpret. Additionally, it provided performers with a small role in the compositional process.

Composers who wished to include the performer actively in the creative process had to invent notations that allowed the latter to make choices. One solution, used by Morton Feldman in his early piano music, is to specify the notes but to leave the rhythmic choices up to the performer. Conversely, the rhythmic choices might be specified and the pitch choices left free. Or performers might be given several possibilities for the same moment in time and told to choose one during the performance. If such choices occur in an established, regulated framework, as in *controlled chance* music, they are often notated within boxes (referred to as *frame notation*).

Notation allowing for choice

Frame notation

The increased freedom made possible by such techniques soon led to musical graphics, in which musical symbols are replaced by visual ones. These drawings are meant to free performers from traditional thought patterns, enabling them to discover new sound possibilities spontaneously.

Musical graphics

Another of the notational problems facing twentieth-century composers has involved the creation of symbols for nontraditional instrumental techniques. Because this notation is not standardized (sometimes the techniques are newly invented for each composition), they are usually explained at the beginning of a musical work. One such page of explanation, taken from Henry Cowell's *The Banshee* for piano (1925), is reproduced below.

Notation of non-traditional instrumental techniques

"The Banshee" is played on the open strings of the piano, the player standing at the crook. Another person must sit at the keyboard and hold down the damper pedal throughout the composition. The whole work should be played an octave lower than written. R.H. stands for "right hand." L.H. stands for "left hand." Different ways of playing the strings are indicated by a letter over each tone, as follows:

Ⓐ indicates a sweep with the flesh of the finger from the lowest string up to the note given.
Ⓑ sweep lengthwise along the string of the note given with flesh of finger.
Ⓒ sweep up and back from lowest A to highest B-flat given in this composition.
Ⓓ pluck string with flesh of finger, where written, instead of octave lower.
Ⓔ sweep along three notes together, in the same manner as Ⓑ.
Ⓕ sweep in the manner of Ⓑ but with the back of finger-nail instead of flesh.

Ⓖ   when the finger is halfway along the string in the manner of Ⓕ, start a sweep along the same string with the flesh of the other finger, thus partly damping the sound.

Ⓗ   sweep back and forth in the manner of Ⓒ, but start at the same time from both above and below, crossing the sweep in the middle.

Ⓘ   sweep along five notes, in the manner of Ⓑ.

Ⓙ   same as Ⓘ but with back of finger-nails instead of flesh of finger.

Ⓚ   sweep along in manner of Ⓙ with nails of both hands together, taking in all notes between the two outer limits given.

Ⓛ   sweep in manner of Ⓒ with flat of hand instead of single finger.

Proportional notation

Traditional music tends to divide the beat in a limited manner and to group these divisions of beats into regular units. Many modern composers have increased these rhythmical resources, either through the use of irregular groupings or by employing a freer notation that bypasses the beat. The latter is called *proportional* notation. In such notation, distances between marked-off units express time duration, and the length of each tone is shown by a continuous line of proportionate length. At the beginning of a work or subsection, a basic unit of time is indicated, in either seconds or metronome units. The units are often either indicated on graph paper or represented by dotted lines. Thus if each unit represents five seconds, a note placed one-fifth of the distance beween the two lines would enter after one second.

Summary

The decades following 1870 saw the emergence of the values of the twentieth century—the elevation of timbre and rhythm to structural roles, and the dissolution of functional tonality. As technology developed, rapid innovation became an all-important goal. Thus began the continuous search for the new, which has led to so many different styles and trends. Each of these has spread rapidly, aided by improved means of transportation and new inventions in communication.

Artists had hoped that World War I would pave the way to a brighter future. Such hopes were dashed by World War II, which left artists even more disillusioned, with ever-greater feelings of skepticism and isolation. Some reacted by trying to create their own order and their own reality out of the chaos surrounding them. This attempt may have been partially responsible for the development of totally serialized music. Others believed only in the present moment and created chance music.

As time has passed, the divergent trends of the 1950s have continued to merge. New syntheses have been achieved, and new freedoms won. Dogmatism has faded; what remain are the newly opened possibilities of sounds and techniques.

Throughout the contemporary period, the trends and their underlying philosophies have led to the development of new procedures. For composers, this progress has often meant the invention of new notational symbols and even new systems of notation. Performers wishing to play their pieces have had to learn the new musical languages and have frequently had to master new instrumental or vocal techniques. Gradually, however, the new has merged with the more traditional language to form the unique *lingua franca* of the twentieth century.

Note

1. Translated and edited by Reginald Smith Brindle (London and New York: Oxford University Press, 1967).

Bibliography

Music Reference Books

ANDERSON, E. RUTH. *Contemporary American Composers: A Biographical Dictionary.* Boston: G. K. Hall, 1976.

EWEN, DAVID. *The World of Twentieth-Century Music.* Englewood Cliffs, N.J.: Prentice-Hall, 1968.

FINK, ROBERT, and RICCI, ROBERT. *The Language of Twentieth-Century Music: A Dictionary of Terms.* New York: Schirmer Books, 1975.

SLONIMSKY, NICHOLAS. *Music Since 1900,* 4th ed. New York: Charles Scribner's Sons, 1971.

VINTON, JOHN, ed. *Dictionary of Contemporary Music.* New York: E. P. Dutton & Co., 1974.

General Books and Articles on Music

AUSTIN, WILLIAM W. *Music in the Twentieth Century.* New York: W. W. Norton & Co., 1966.

BRINDLE, REGINALD SMITH. *The New Music: The Avant-Garde Since 1945.* New York: Oxford University Press, 1975.

COOPER, MARTIN, ed. *The New Oxford History of Music.* Vol. 10. *The Modern Age, 1890–1960.* London, New York: Oxford University Press, 1974.

COPLAND, AARON. *The New Music, 1900–1960,* rev. and enl. ed. New York: W. W. Norton & Co., 1968.

DALIN, LEON. *Techniques of Twentieth Century Composition,* 3rd ed. Dubuque, Iowa: William C. Brown Co., 1974.

DELONE, RICHARD; KLIEWER, VERNON; REISBERG, HORACE; WENNERSTROM, MARY; WINOLD, ALLEN; WITTLICH, GARY E., coordinating ed. *Aspects of Twentieth Century Music.* Englewood Cliffs, N.J.: Prentice-Hall, 1975.

DERI, OTTO. *Exploring Twentieth-Century Music.* New York: Holt, Rinehart, & Winston, 1968.

GRIFFITHS, PAUL. *A Concise History of Avant-Garde Music, from Debussy to Boulez.* New York: Oxford University Press, 1978.

HANSEN, PETER S. *An Introduction to Twentieth Century Music,* 4th ed. Boston: Allyn & Bacon, Inc., 1978.

LANG, PAUL HENRY, and BRODER, NATHAN, eds. *Contemporary Music in Europe: A Comprehensive Survey.* New York: W. W. Norton & Co., 1968.

MACHLIS, JOSEPH. *Introduction to Contemporary Music,* 2nd ed. New York: W. W. Norton & Co., 1979.

MARTIN, WILLIAM R., and DROSSIN, JULIUS. *Music of the Twentieth Century.* Englewood Cliffs, N.J.: Prentice-Hall, 1980.

MELLERS, WILFRID. *Romanticism and the Twentieth Century.* Man and His Music, Part 4. New York: Schocken Books, 1969.

MEYER, LEONARD B. *Music, the Arts, and Ideas: Patterns and Predictions in Twentieth-Century Culture.* Chicago: University of Chicago Press, 1967.

PERSICHETTI, VINCENT. *Twentieth-Century Harmony.* New York: W. W. Norton & Co., 1961.

PEYSER, JOAN. *The New Music: The Sense Behind the Sound.* New York: Delacorte Press, 1971.

SALZMAN, ERIC. "'Modern' Music: The First Half Century." *Stereo Review,* October 1970, pp. 75–83.

———. *Twentieth Century Music: An Introduction,* 2nd ed. Prentice-Hall History of Music series, ed. H. Wiley Hitchcock. Englewood Cliffs, N.J.: Prentice-Hall, 1974.

SCHWARTZ, ELLIOT, and CHILDS, BARNEY, eds. *Contemporary Composers on Contemporary Music.* New York: Holt, Rinehart & Winston, 1967.

STUCKENSCHMIDT, H. H. *Twentieth-Century Music,* trans. Richard Deveson. World Universal Library. New York: McGraw-Hill Book Co., 1969.

New Musical Notations and Techniques

KARKOSCHKA, ERHARD. *Notation in New Music: A Critical Guide to Interpretation and Realisation,* trans. Ruth Koening. New York: Praeger Publishing Co., 1972.

READ, GARDNER. *Contemporary Instrumental Techniques.* New York: Schirmer Books, 1976.

Musical Anthologies

BRANDT, WILLIAM; CORRA, ARTHUR; CHRIST, WILLIAM; DELONE, RICHARD; and WINOLD, ALLEN. *The Comprehensive Study of Music.* Vol. IV. *Anthology of Music from Debussy through Stockhausen.* New York: Harper's College Press, 1976.

WENNERSTROM, MARY H. *Anthology of Twentieth Century Music.* Englewood Cliffs, N.J.: Prentice-Hall, 1969.

30

New Uses of Timbre:
Impressionism and Its Outgrowth

THE twentieth century has seen the emergence of composers in whose works instrumental color plays a major structural role. Many of these composers were born and trained in France, and they have often resided there, perhaps because French music has always been somewhat outside the Italo-Germanic tradition, or perhaps because Paris at the turn of the century, when this trend originated, was a major European center.

This chapter will trace the background of this new emphasis on timbre and texture, as well as describe the development of this movement and its effect on a number of twentieth-century composers. It will also attempt to show how such thinking, beginning with Debussy, contributed to the break with the past.

Before World War I:
Impressionism in the Arts

Impressionism, a movement prominent at the end of the nineteenth and the beginning of the twentieth centuries, produced the last unified international style. Those that have followed have existed simultaneously with other "new" developments—a splintering unique, perhaps, to the twentieth century. Impressionism looked both forward and backward, culminating the developments of the nineteenth century, yet breaking new ground. Originating in Paris, it developed first in painting, then in literature, and finally in music. Central to the movement was a belief in the dominance of the moment over permanence and continuity—the certainty that every phenomenon was fleeting and never to be repeated. Art, once based on the stable and the coherent, was now concerned with the unfinished and fragmentary.

Historians disagree on the year that marked the beginning of impressionism in the visual arts. Some place it as early as 1856, while others prefer a later date. General agreement, however, dates the label from 1874. In that year, the

The visual
arts

735

Berthe Morisot (1841–1895), *Portrait of a Child with Hat* (1883), oil painting. Morisot, a student of Corot and also a close friend, was a member of the Impressionist movement, which paid special attention to the play of light and use of color. (Courtesy, The Baltimore Museum of Art; The Cone Collection)

French art critic Louis Leroy applied the term derogatorily in his review of the first show of a group of nonacademic painters who had banded together, taking the term from the title of one of the paintings exhibited in the show: Claude Monet's *Impression: Soleil levant* ("Impression: Sunrise," 1872). In addition to Monet, painters considered to be impressionists include the Frenchmen Edouard Manet, Camille Pissarro, and Auguste Renoir, as well as a few Americans who studied in Paris or moved there, such as Mary Cassatt. The movement gradually lost its currency in painting after 1886.

Impressionism developed logically from naturalism, but departed from the past by separating the visual elements of experience from the conceptual and then by elaborating on the former. The subjects treated, such as boating and swimming resorts, a café, a visit, or a walk on a pebbly beach, had previously been considered banal and insignificant. The impressionist painters were committed to spontaneity and expressed this in a seemingly casual style, thus angering both critics and a public that wanted artistic creations to reflect both technical facility and hard work.

Impressionism treated color in a new way, attempting to turn the whole canvas into a harmony of color and light. The subjects were used more for the tones embodied than for themselves, a development that helped pave the way for abstract art. The evenly colored surface was dissolved into spots and dabs of color applied with abrupt strokes of the brush, resulting in a play of reflected light and illuminated shadows.

Symbolism in literature was a reaction against naturalism, and in many ways a move toward greater abstraction in poetry and drama. The movement included poets Stéphane Mallarmé, Paul Verlaine, and Arthur Rimbaud and dramatists Maurice Maeterlinck and Henrik Ibsen. The term "symbolism," first defined by the poet Jean Moréas, refers to the use of symbols in place of openly stated ideas, thus permitting various interpretations.

The symbolists

Impressionism in Music

Claude Debussy (1862–1918) pioneered a new musical style that attempted to avoid the obvious and to create vague, shimmering, veiled sounds. In such impressionist music the manipulation of color and atmosphere tended to replace thematic development and dramatic buildups and releases.

In impressionist music, ninth, eleventh, and thirteenth chords are often used, as are triads and seventh chords and triads with added seconds, sixths, or both. Such chords are often chosen for color rather than function. Parallel or *gliding* chords of the same content, both consonant and dissonant, are often found, in defiance of the oft-cited harmonic rule recommending contrary motion in outer voices. This technique is often referred to as either *chord streaming* or *planing*. Triads are sometimes used with the third absent, and the resultant parallel fifths and octaves produce an effect similar to medieval organum. The traditional pedal point is sometimes expanded into a pedal chord, sustained in piano music by the middle pedal, with other melodies and harmonies surrounding it.

Chords

Scales not in the major-minor system are borrowed to add color to the traditional major and minor keys. These include the whole-tone scale and the medieval modes, with preference for those that avoid the leading tone. In addition, non-Western scales, such as the Chinese pentatonic, may be used. (Pentatonic, as the name suggests, is a five-note scale. The Chinese form has no semitones and may be reproduced on the black keys of the piano.)

Scales

Some of the impressionist techniques discussed above may be observed in Example 30.1, an excerpt from Debussy's *La Cathédrale engloutie* ("The Sunken Cathedral"), from *Douze Préludes* ("Twelve Preludes," Book I, 1910). The first measure of this excerpt uses the pentatonic scale. The bass

Ex. 30.1   Claude Debussy, *La Cathédrale engloutie*, mm. 5–10

and treble contain a widely spaced, sustained chord, and within it progressions of parallel fifths and octaves. The second measure serves as a short transition to the third through sixth measures, which use the Lydian mode transposed to E.

Composers and influence

Composers whose works incorporate impressionist techniques include the French Maurice Ravel (1875–1937), Paul Dukas (1865–1935), and Lili Boulanger (1893–1918); English-born Frederick Delius (1862–1934), who spent his latter years in France; the American Charles Griffes (1884–1920); and the Italian Ottorino Respighi (1879–1936), especially in works such as his *I pini di Roma* ("The Pines of Rome," 1924). Additionally, impressionist influence may be seen in the works of many nationalists, including Karol Szymanowski, Béla Bartók, and the early compositions of Igor Stravinsky.

Debussy

Debussy's music serves as a culmination of the nineteenth century in its programmatic titles, large orchestra, preference for rich chords, use of functional harmony, and freedom of form and rhythm. At the same time, it lays the basis for the twentieth century in its structural use of timbre, avoidance of traditional developmental procedures, and employment of chords in nonfunctional, coloristic ways.

Many of the characteristics of Debussy's music have already been described. In addition, however, the following features may be noted: (1) melodies are likely to be brief and are often repeated immediately; (2) rhythms often mask the beat with irregular subdivisions and syncopations; (3) phrase structure is determined more by the shape, character, and timbral value of the motives than by the demands of tonal progression; (4) ostinatos are used for coherence; (5) pedal points and frequent returns to the primary chords of the key create a sense of tonality; (6) chordal structures are often masked by figuration, and, in the piano music, blurred by use of the damper pedal.

Orchestration

Debussy generally uses a large orchestra, with a preference for divided and muted strings, harps, solos by a low flute, oboe, or English horn; soft horns and trumpets, at times muted; and many kinds of percussion. Woodwinds and brass are used with balance and delicacy. Many of these characteristics may be observed in his *Prélude à l'Après-midi d'un faune* ("Prelude to the Afternoon of a Faun," 1894), usually cited as the first impressionist orchestral work. For example, the opening (shown below in Example 30.2) and final section use the solo flute in its lower range, accompanied by harp and a lightly scored orchestra. The return of this timbre, as well as restatements of thematic material, contributes to the form of the composition.

Works

Debussy's principal piano works are those published in collections between 1903 and 1913, including *Estampes* ("Prints," 1913), two books of *Images* (Book I, 1905; Book II, 1907), and two books of *Douze Préludes*

Ex. 30.2   Claude Debussy, *Prélude à l'Après-midi d'un faune*

("Twelve Preludes," Book I, 1910; Book II, 1913). His orchestral works include the previously mentioned *Prélude à l'Après-midi d'un faune; Nocturnes* (1899), and *La Mer* ("The Sea," 1905). Several of his works, however, are not impressionistic. These include his *Sonates pour divers instruments* ("Sonatas for Different Instruments"), which consist of *Sonate pour violoncello et piano* ("Sonata for Cello and Piano," 1915), *Sonate pour flûte, alto, et harpe* ("Sonata for Flute, Viola, and Harp," 1915), and *Sonate pour violin et piano* ("Sonata for Violin and Piano," 1917). Such compositions are more concerned with classical values and are free from extramusical associations.

La Mer   *La Mer* is a symphonic work in three movements: *De L'Aube à midi sur la mer* ("From Dawn to Midday at Sea"), *Jeu de vagues* ("Play of the Waves"), and *Dialogue du vent et de la mer* ("Dialogue of the Wind and the Sea"). The work is united by several motifs that are presented in the opening measures. The orchestration calls for strings that are often muted and divided, frequently muted horns and trumpets, and much percussion, and uses a low-register flute as well as an oboe and English horn as solo instruments.

The beginning of the first movement exemplifies Debussy's sensitivity to color. It starts with a soft drumroll and a pedal note in the double basses, and uses the pentatonic scale. This introduction presents two important motifs in shimmering settings—the first in low winds, over tremolo violins, and the second in the English horn and muted trumpet over tremolo cellos and double basses. The first main section consists of characteristic pentatonic woodwind patterns, arpeggiated harp parts, and moving strings, over which horns present the main theme, which is related to the second motif of the introduction. A contrasting middle section using triplets builds to a climax, then diminishes before a reminiscence of an earlier idea returns. A chordal passage ensues; it will be developed further near the end of the third movement, but here it is followed by a return to the opening motif.

The second movement, a kind of scherzo, is built of shifting textures and lacks traditional developmental procedures. Instead we have a sense of section flowing into section. Impressionistic techniques in this movement include the use of whole-tone harp glissandi, ostinato, and a long pedal note (G-sharp in the double basses). The music builds to a climax above the latter, which in turn reverts to the statement of a fragment of the main motif of the movement. The last movement includes a return to motivic material of the first. The work ends in D-flat major, but with a hint of Lydian mode (raised fourth degree) in the approach to the cadence.

Ravel

Compared
with
Debussy   While the works of Maurice Ravel are often grouped with those of Claude Debussy, and while his music does contain many elements considered impressionistic, his inclinations were more elegant and Classical than those of his colleague. His language can be considered a mixture of impressionism and Classicism.

Ravel used the "new" vocabulary of his time, including pentatonic and modal elements, parallel intervals, and complex chords. Yet his works are often more clearly tonal and his harmonies more functional than Debussy's. His concern for clear structure, which contrasts with Debussy's more rhapsodic approach, shows even in his most impressionistic compositions, such as *Jeux d'eau* ("Play of Water," 1901), written in sonata form. His rhythms are often strong and uncomplicated, in contrast with Debussy's more fluid approach. He often uses dancelike rhythms, and his late works incorporate basic elements of jazz, as in his Sonata for Violin and Piano (1927), the second movement of which is entitled *Blues.*

Many of these characteristics may be seen in Ravel's Quartet in F major (1902). This work is similar to the Debussy String Quartet in G minor (1893) in its cyclical form and use of special effects (pizzicato and mutes). It differs from the latter in both its materials and their development. A comparison of the opening measures of both quartets, for instance, shows Ravel's tendency to use longer melodic lines than Debussy.

Quartet in F

The quartet has the traditional four movements. The first is clearly in sonata form, with two distinct themes. Theme I is in F major while Theme II is in D minor. The development section varies clearly recognizable parts of both themes. As in the Classic sonata form, the recapitulation brings back both themes in F major. The second movement, a scherzo in sonata–allegro form, also presents two contrasting main themes. The first, stated pizzicato, is in Aeolian mode. The movement uses simple rhythmic patterns enlivened by cross-rhythms. Rhythmic interest in the third movement is obtained by several changes in meter and tempo. This slow fantasia has three contrasting themes, the second of which is related to the main theme of the first movement. The last movement, rondo-like in form and character, also uses themes based on the first movement of the quartet.

Between the Wars

In the years between World War I and World War II, most composers became less interested in timbre as a prime structural factor in composition. Two highly individualistic composers, however, continued to explore the relationship between timbre and form. The first was French-born American Edgard Varèse (1883–1965), whose major works, apart from a few electronic compositions written after World War II, were composed in the 1920s and 1930s.

The second composer is Olivier Messiaen (b. 1908). His musical theories were formulated during the late 1930s and early 1940s, although many of his important works have been written since World War II. Like many twentieth-century composers, Messiaen can be classified in several ways. His works may be considered in relation to new methods of pitch and rhythmic organization. Yet he is discussed here because of his concern for harmonic color and unique instrumental timbres. Despite his complex theories about pitch and rhythm, he is primarily a mystic, and thus differs from the purposely abstract Varèse.

Varèse

Compared with Debussy

Varèse rejected the traditional post-Renaissance view of music as expression and communication. He went further than Debussy in rejecting the musical language of Romanticism, however, by doing away with the conventional materials of diatonic and chromatic melody and harmony and with rhythmic patterns related to harmonic tensions and releases. Instead, he worked with unified wholes involving timbre, accent, and rhythm.

Musical techniques

His music starts from the sound characteristics of each instrument—its density or timbral properties apart from pitch relationships. Each is then assigned its own unique figure or rhythmic pattern, which either remains the same or changes slowly. These patterns are built into blocks of sound, each characterized by its own intervallic and rhythmic content. Thus masses of shifting planes replace linear counterpoint. The masses of sound are treated as spatial objects held together by rhythmic energy. On colliding, they appear either to penetrate or to repel each other. Zones of intensity are established by using different timbres at varying volumes.

Crystallization

Varèse, whose early training had been in mathematics and engineering. compared his process of composing to crystal formation, with no composition made to fit a known container (i.e., musical form). Crystallization involves taking a simple idea or sound mass, possibly based on pitch, timbre, or rhythm, and expanding the idea, splitting it into different parts, varying its shape, speed, or direction, and interlocking or superimposing other ideas. A good example of this process is the beginning of *Hyperprism* (1923) for woodwinds, brass, and percussion. Here the first sound mass is the pitch C-sharp, which changes timbrally by the use of different attacks and instrumentation, and finally becomes the interval D–C-sharp with the addition of the bass trombone. The major seventh, or its semitone inversion, forms an important crystal in the work, splitting into two major sevenths in measures 12–13 and then undergoing further change. Examples of this process involving rhythmic sound masses are found in *Ionisation* (1933) for thirteen percussionists. Here two important sound masses are the metallic sound of the gong, tam-tams, and cymbals of measure 1, and the rhythmic idea presented by the *tambour militaire* (snare drum) in measures 8–12.

Messiaen

Compared with Varèse

Messiaen's works are similar to and perhaps influenced by those of Varèse in their use of both static, spatial forms and planes of sound. In many other ways, however, Messiaen's music is the opposite of Varèse's. It is subjective rather than objective, having at its core Messiaen's strong religious convictions. His compositions reflect the composer's symbolic interpretation of Catholic dogma, and these extramusical associations often lead to unique timbres, as in the last variation of the second movement of *L'Ascension* ("The Ascension," 1933), where trilled chords and sliding harmonies contribute to a representation of "a Soul desiring Heaven." His works incorporate techniques derived from his studies of: (1) non-Western rhythm, especially

Hindu; (2) plainsong, including its procedures for rapid syllabic text setting; and (3) the songs of birds, which he has cataloged. He has developed all three extensively and has used the first two as a basis for his individual system of rhythms and modes.

Messiaen has created a set of rhythmic procedures in which *nonretrogradable rhythms* and the *valeur ajoutée* ("added value") play an important role. Nonretrogradable rhythms are those that sound the same both backward and forward. The term "valeur ajoutée" has been invented by Messiaen to refer to nonsymmetrical increases of duration values by adding a short value—a note, a rest, or a dot—to any rhythm. The device is often used to avoid the emergence of a rhythmic pedal point. Other rhythms favored by the composer include patterns taken from Greek meters. Rhythm becomes a structural device through the use of ostinato patterns that may involve literal or highly decorated repetitions, or changing time and space relationships in the manner of isorhythmic motets.

Rhythm

Messiaen has also adopted a systematic approach to pitch, deriving new scales of six to ten notes (which he refers to as "modes") from the twelve semitones of the tempered chromatic scale. These modes are limited in their ability to be transposed. For example, one of his modes is simply a whole-tone scale, while another consists of a strict alternation of semitones and whole tones. These modes are associated in Messiaen's mind with visual colors. For instance, in the program notes for the second movement of *L'Ascension,* he states that he used the second and third transposition of the "third mode of limited transposition," which represents the colors "gray and mauve with a little pale yellow, then blue and green." Although use of the whole-tone scale can be traced back to Liszt and Glinka, among others, and the whole-step half-step alternation to Rimsky-Korsakov, Messiaen was the first to study these scales methodically and to derive a harmonic system from them. His systemized approach to pitches and rhythms led him to write his *Mode de valeurs et d'intensités* ("Mode of Durations and of Dynamics"), with pitch, durations, dynamics, and types of attack following a pattern of organization determined prior to the actual composition of the work. (For further discussion of this piece, see Chapter 31.)

Pitch system

Many other musical influences are seen in Messiaen's style, although such sources may be traced in only a limited number of works. For instance, the *Turangalila-Symphonie* ("Turangalila Symphony," 1948), for piano, ondes Martenot, and orchestra, uses the curves of Indian melody in the creation of a lengthy ten-movement work.

The Post–World War II Generation

The renewed interest in timbral organization among the post–World War II composers discussed below has influenced even those who also use other organizational means and who will, therefore, be discussed in subsequent chapters. The latter have become increasingly sensitive to new possibilities of sound combinations, and some have even joined the constant search for new uses of both instruments and voices.

Xenakis

Iannis Xenakis (b. 1922 in Rumania of Greek parents), who has resided in France since the end of World War II, is one of the most unusual as well as one of the most influential members of this group. A composer who has always rejected serialism, he makes music with sounds and sound masses rather than with individual notes. Believing that music should be an expression of human intelligence through sonic means, he tries to reduce certain sound sensations to their scientific bases in order first to dominate these sounds and then use them in desired constructions. This approach, he feels, will give his art a reasoned support less perishable than the impulse of the moment. In spite of the highly scientific nature of his work, however, Xenakis still believes that instinct and subjective choice are the only guarantors of a work's value, and that science and logic serve to verify truths glimpsed intuitively.

Xenakis works to order and justify his sounds by discovering and clarifying their relation to universal laws. Like the ancient Greek philosophers Pythagoras and Aristoxenus, he finds these universal laws in mathematics and the physical sciences. Perhaps because of his training in engineering and architecture, Xenakis finds that mathematics is a systematic expression of internal order and that, as such, it provides a way of using existing structures of thought to find a new more universal way of communicating. Thus the act of composition necessarily becomes abstracted and formalized.

Xenakis has codified some of his compositional innovations as follows: **Stochastic music** *stochastic music,* which uses probability theory and chain reactions; *strategic music,* which involves game theory; and *symbolic music,* which utilizes set theory and mathematical logic. In his stochastic works, Xenakis uses the laws of probability to insure that his music is neither more nor less structured than the physical world. He has considered the problem of boredom resulting from repeated hearings of his works, and tries to compensate for this possibility mathematically by modifying the relative distances of statistical frequencies at the moment of programming, striving for balance between details and form at all levels of structure. In many of his works, form is viewed as a sequential programming tied to the entropy (decay) or nonentropy (lack of decay) of sonorous events.

The stochastic works make use of chance, but in a way completely different from that of John Cage and his followers. For Xenakis, chance is a scientific concept. "Chance" activities in his music apply the Law of Large Numbers of seventeenth-century Swiss mathematician Jacques Bernoulli; this law states that as the number of repetitions of a given "chance" trial, such as flipping a coin, increases, the probability that the results tend to a determinate end approaches certainty. Thus Xenakis has used the term "stochastic," which he derives from the Greek word *stochos,* meaning "target." One such stochastic work is *Pithoprakta* ("Actions by Probabilities," 1956), which calls for fifty instruments, each playing a separate part. The musical material is organized by various laws of large numbers, and the density and structure of the "clouds" of sound are controlled by the Scottish James Clerk Maxwell's and the German Ludwig Boltzmann's nineteenth-century Kinetic Theory of Gases. *Pithoprakta* was composed on graph paper, then transcribed in traditional notation. In this composition, as in some of his architectural works, Xenakis is concerned with confrontations of continuity, represented by sustained sounds and individually calculated glissandi; and discontinuity, represented by pizzicatos and *col legno* (on the wood) bow strokes.

 Duel (1959), *Stratégie* ("Strategy," 1962), and *Linaia-Agon* (1971) are examples of his strategic music. In these works, the composer has taken into account the fact that play is one of the principal elements of human activity. *Linaia-Agon,* inspired by a Greek legend, is a game between Linos, represented by the trombone, and Apollo, represented by the French horn or the tuba. It proceeds by complex rules that involve mathematically provided decision matrices. An excerpt of the work is given in Example 30.3. This short passage shows much timbral diversity, including "rapid pizzicato glissandi" indicated by ⅃), and irregular vibrato. The passage also uses quarter tones.

Strategic music

Ex. 30.3 Iannis Xenakis, *Linaia-Agon,* mm. 34–44

Symbolic music

In symbolic works such as *Herma*—*musique symbolique pour piano* ("Connection—Symbolic Music for Piano," 1961), sounds are used as signs or symbols, which are treated independently of traditional contexts with their set time frames. *Terrêtektorh* (1966) shows the composer's interest in spatial music by scattering eighty-eight musicians throughout the audience so that the sound surrounds the people. (The title of this work derives from the words "earth" [*terre*], "tectonic" [*tekt*], and the action suffix *orh*.) Finally, *Polytope* ("Many Loci," 1967) shows his interest in synthesizing sound and visual art. In this work, the same principles control both the light show and the music.

The Polish School

Many works composed in Poland after World War II also have structures based on musical color. They use many new sounds, including dense, fluctuating clouds of sonority and the exploitation of glissandi (both of which were also used by Xenakis) and tone clusters. These composers have been labeled "the Polish school." The two most famous members, discussed below, are Witold Lutoslawski (b. 1913) and Krzysztof Penderecki (b. 1933). Other noteworthy composers include Henryk Górecki (b. 1933), Boguslaw Schaeffer (b. 1929), Wlodzimierz Kotonski (b. 1925), Kasimierz Serocki (b. 1922), and Grazyna Bacewicz (1913–1969).

Lutoslawski

Several of Lutoslawski's early works incorporated Polish folk music. In the late 1950s, however, he revised his compositional techniques, experimenting first with serialism, then with aleatory techniques. Throughout his works, a sense of form and construction is evident, perhaps reflecting his mathematical training.

Aleatory counterpoint

One of the characteristic techniques of his later music is what he calls *aleatory counterpoint*. In the first movement of *Jeux vénitiens* ("Venetian Play," 1961), the first of his works to employ this technique, the aleatory counterpoint is created as follows: The instrumentalists each have separate lines, with pitches and rhythmic values indicated. The rhythms, however, are meant to be approximate, and the tempo is flexible. With the exception of the first aleatory section, players choose a starting point at any phrase except at the beginning, then repeat the section if time permits. The beginning and the ending of each of these sections is signaled by the conductor, in accordance with time limits established by the composer. These freer sections alternate with clearly laid out ones.

Other techniques

Lutoslawski believes that in order fully to utilize coloristic possibilities, intervallic and harmonic choices must also be considered. Since 1958 he has been working with twelve-note chords, and has been especially interested in those in which the adjoining sounds have a limited number of interval types (i.e., a twelve-note chord constructed from only minor seconds would have only one interval type). He finds that chords with one, two, or three types of intervals have distinct characteristics, while those with all types of intervals are colorless. For similar reasons, he prefers families of instruments playing together instead of mixed timbres, since, to him, accentuating the pure colors deepens the contrasts.

Penderecki

Penderecki's music, like that of Lutoslawski, combines a wide variety of techniques and influences that make his work fresh and accessible. Some of his music grows from a religious outlook and creates a dramatic effect, as in one of his most famous works, *Passio et mors Domini nostri Jesu Christi secundum Lucam* ("The Passion According to St. Luke," commonly referred to as the "St. Luke Passion," 1965). A clearly structured work calling for the unconventional use of string instruments and human voices, this composition uses a twelve-note series that includes a motive based on B–A–C–H (the pitches B-flat, A, C, B-natural) among other materials, as well as quasi-Gregorian melismas, vocal and instrumental clusters, and choral whispering and hissing.

St. Luke Passion

Penderecki is perhaps best known for his inventive orchestral and choral textures. One of his typical devices is the cluster of string instruments, separated from one another by a semitone or a quarter tone, thus forming dense bands of sound. They either remain static or else expand and contract by means of glissandi. This technique is used in his well-known *Threnody for the Victims of Hiroshima* (1960). Penderecki often freely combines ostinati or ostinati-like passages that are repeated by instrumental groups and spread throughout the orchestra with a cumulative effect, as in *De Nature Sonoris #1* ("On the Nature of Sound," 1966). The latter work also contains controlled improvisation.

Musical techniques

Penderecki's sounds are not limited, however, to the newly invented. Sometimes, short melodies or triadic harmonies emerge briefly.

Ligeti

Like Lutoslawski, Hungarian-born György Ligeti (b. 1923) studied both his native folk music and the implications of Webernian serialism. After leaving Budapest in 1956 he began to experiment, creating dense yet precisely calculated textured works. This method of composing is similar to that of the Polish school, but it developed from experiments in electronic music.

A typical Ligeti approach is heard in *Atmosphères* (1961), for orchestra, which uses bands of sound that change in pitch, density, and length. The work's interest lies not in new instrumental effects but rather in the way in which the parts combine. The timbres are absolute in themselves, and they project little sense of contour or form—an idea carried still further in Ligeti's *Volumina* for organ (1962, revised 1966).

Atmosphères

Crumb

The American composer George Crumb (b. 1929), like the European composers discussed above, uses timbres as an initial part of his compositional conception. His atmospheric works often contain small melodic units that contribute to the structure. His sounds, interspersed with silences that draw the listener closer, create their own microcosmic world. This music shows the influence of many traditions—electronic music, Webern, and Bartók, for instance—yet the total effect is uniquely Crumb's. It conveys a sense of ritual and of time suspended.

Timbres

Crumb is constantly experimenting with and inventing new sounds, many of which are beautifully fragile. Such sounds include rapid tremolos played on the violin, the banjo, or the piano strings with thimble-capped fingers in order to produce a ghostly effect; and piano harmonics produced with a small chisel. At times, the performer may be called upon to whistle or sing while playing.

Use of nonmusical art forms

Crumb's works incorporate aspects of other art forms. For instance, his music is often printed in such visual patterns as a circle or a cross. Additionally, many of his works are performed theatrically, e.g., on darkened stages and by players wearing masks.

Ancient Voices of Children

Ancient Voices of Children (1970), one of Crumb's most popular works, is written for soprano, boy soprano, and seven instruments. Like many of his compositions, it is based on a work by the great Spanish poet Federico García Lorca (1899–1936). One of the unusual sound effects of this piece is produced by the amplified soprano soloist, who vocalizes over open piano strings, causing them to vibrate and echo.

Summary

The Italo-Germanic tradition of the Baroque, Classical, and Romantic eras was challenged by the French impressionist composer Claude Debussy. His music, the first to elevate timbre and texture to a major role in composition, avoids standard "common practice" harmonic progressions in favor of chords that move in parallel motion. He thus bypasses the traditional concern for musical tension and release. His works not only paved the way for the other composers discussed in this chapter, but also influenced almost every other composer of the twentieth century because they freed the individual elements of music to function independently. Elements of impressionist techniques are found in the music of Debussy's well known but more classically oriented French colleague Maurice Ravel, as well as the music of other composers working at the turn of the century, including the early ballets of Igor Stravinsky.

Between the World Wars, most composers turned to the Neoclassical style of Stravinsky. In contrast to this trend, two very different, nonconformist French-born composers, Edgard Varèse and Olivier Messiaen, continued the tradition of the impressionistic concern with color. Messiaen's unique style of composition arises from religious beliefs, which are often expressed symbolically through his own personalized system of modes and rhythms; through striking instrumental timbres, including those that are imitations of birdcalls, often used structurally; and through harmonic color. Varèse, whose music forms a direct link between Debussy and the post–World War II composers, created masses of sounds that he juxtaposed in space.

After World War II, a widespread interest in pure structured sound again became evident, due in part to the influence of Iannis Xenakis, a student of Messiaen. The music of Xenakis, like that of Varèse, uses masses of sound. But while Varèse used science in a general way in creating and explaining his music, Xenakis usually applies specific mathematical laws in structuring his sounds. His timbres have influenced many composers. Similar timbral concerns have been found among the composers referred to as "the Polish school," including Witold Lutoslawski and Krzysztof Penderecki.

Bibliography

Books and Articles

CHOU, WEN-CHUNG. "Varèse: A Sketch of the Man and His Music." *Musical Quarterly* 52 (1966): 151–170.

DEBUSSY, CLAUDE. "Monsieur Croche the Dilettante Hater," in *Three Classics in the Aesthetics of Music.* New York: Dover Publications, 1962.

ERHARDT, LUDWIK. *Music in Poland.* Warsaw: Interpress Publishers, 1975.

FLEURET, MAURICE. "Xenakis: A Music for the Future." *Music and Musicians* 20 (April 1972): 20–27.

JOHNSON, ROBERT SHERLAW. *Messiaen.* Berkeley: University of California Press, 1975.

LEWIS, ROBERT HALL. "George Crumb: 'Night Music I.'" *Perspectives of New Music* 3, no. 2 (1965): 143–151.

LIGETI, GYÖRGY; LUTOSLAWSKI, WITOLD; and LINDHOLM, INGVAR. *Three aspects of New Music: From the Composition Seminar in Stockholm.* Stockholm: The Royal Academy of Music and the Royal College of Music. Publication #4 (Nordiska Musikforlaget), 1968.

LOCKSPIESER, EDWARD. *Debussy: His Life and His Mind,* 2 vols. New York: Macmillan, 1962–1965.

MESSIAEN, OLIVIER. *Technique of My Musical Language,* 2 vols., trans. John Lutterfield. Paris: Alphonse Leduc & Cie., 1956.

SALZMAN, ERIC. "Edgard Varése." *Stereo Review* 26 (June 1971): 56–61.

STUCKENSCHMIDT, H. H. *Maurice Ravel: Variations on His Life and Work,* trans. Samuel R. Rosenbaum. Philadelphia: Chilton Book Co., 1968.

VARGA, BÁLINT ANDRÁS. *Lutoslawski Profile: Witold Lutoslawski in Conversation with Bálint András Varga,* English trans. prepared with the help of Stephen Walsh. London: Chester Music, 1976.

XENAKIS, IANNIS. *Formalized Music.* Bloomington: Indiana University Press, 1971.

Scores

The main publisher of George Crumb is C. F. Peters (New York).

The main publisher of Claude Debussy is Durand & Cie. (Paris), although many of the works are in the public domain and have been reprinted by other publishers.

The main publishers of Olivier Messiaen are Leduc (Paris) and Durand & Fils (Paris).

Most of the works of Witold Lutoslawski are published by Polski Wydawnictwo Muzyczne (Polish Music Publishers, Cracow and Warsaw).

The earlier works of Krzysztof Penderecki are mainly available from Herman Moeck Verlag (Celle, Germany) and Polski Wydawnictwo Muzyczne (Polish Music Publishers, Cracow and Warsaw). Many works since 1968 are available from B. Schott's Söhne (Mainz).

Maurice Ravel's works are published primarily by Durand & Cie. (Paris).

The works of Edgard Varèse are mainly published by Colfranc (c/o Belwin-Mills Publishing Corp., New York).

Most of the earlier works of Iannis Xenakis are published by Boosey & Hawkes (London and New York), and the later ones by Salabert (Paris).

31

Expressionism and Serialism

XPRESSIONISM, a movement that was, in some ways, a logical outgrowth of German Romanticism, expressed a distorted, Freudian world filled with pain. Musically foreshadowed in the operas of Richard Strauss, especially *Salome* (1905) and *Elektra* (1909), two violent, dramatically powerful works, it found musical realization in the works of Schoenberg, Berg, and Webern. Such works could not rely on an accepted common musical language or its implied musical procedures.

Schoenberg was led to the concept of serialism by his desire both to renew the orderliness of old classical tradition and to make a new form of classicism possible. Although much of the music produced by his method sounds alien to an untrained ear, serialism developed logically from some of the most traditional aspects of Western music. In order to understand this method of pitch organization, therefore, we must reexamine the basic concepts underlying tonality.

Beyond the Tonal System

In tonality, the tones of the scale exist in a hierarchical relationship to the tonal center. Tonal music creates tension and motion by moving away from the central triad (modulation), and release and stability when the tonic returns. In the process of modulation pivotal chords are used, creating a moment of uncertainty for the listener. This tonal ambiguity can be extended to longer phrases and passages, either by successions of chords that lack clear tonal associations or by movement through a series of keys so rapidly that none achieves tonal stability.

The basis of tonality

During the nineteenth century, chords were increasingly inflected with chromatic nonharmonic tones, and color chords were used with greater frequency. The resultant chromaticism veiled the sense of key and thus eventually eroded the hierarchical structure of tonal chord progressions.

Changes in harmonic concepts

By the end of the nineteenth century, many composers were writing

Toward atonality

highly dissonant music that was often in a definite key but lacked the sense of direction traditionally associated with tonal movement. It is hard to perceive whether their music is moving toward or away from a given tonality, and even clearly tonal sections seem to lack a logical connection with the overall tonal-harmonic plan. The moment that Schoenberg refers to in his writings as "the emancipation of the dissonance"[1] had nearly arrived.

At first Schoenberg wrote in the Austro-Germanic style of Wagner and Strauss. However, his music became increasingly chromatic until he consciously abandoned all tonal references, finding them meaningless in a

Atonality

nonstructural context. He thus arrived at *atonality*, a term Schoenberg disliked, and one that has been the subject of much theoretical controversy. Many theorists question whether it is possible to avoid totally momentary tonal implications. The ambiguity of this terminology also results from differing definitions of tonality. Contemporary compositions have shown that triadic structures may be retained without a tonal center, while nontraditional harmonies have been made to function referentially.

The atonal works of Schoenberg and his two famous disciples, Alban Berg and Anton Webern, will be discussed in the section on expressionism. We will point out here, however, that Schoenberg soon sensed the dangers and problems inherent in this new freedom from tonality. The absence of the dissonance-consonance distinction removed a traditional source of tension and release, and put an additional burden on other musical elements in creating musical coherence. And the lack of an underlying system, hitherto provided by tonality, necessitated a more intuitive manner of pitch choice that appears to have made the construction of large-scale works difficult except when they were unified by a text.

Schoenberg's preference for order, which he equated with comprehensibility, and his desire to maintain the supremacy of pitch as a principle of organization led him to codify the results of the experiments in his expressionist works. In 1923, after several years of silence as a composer, he presented his

The birth of serialism

"method of composing with twelve tones which are related only to one another,"[2] which became known as serialism. (Although the first serial work appeared in 1923, Schoenberg formed his theories earlier, possibly in 1921.)

Expressionism in the Arts

Background

Expressionism, like impressionism, is a term derived from painting. This movement developed in music, theater, and poetry, as well as in the visual arts. Whereas impressionism was French in origin, expressionism was Teutonic. The aim of the impressionists was to represent objects in the external world as experienced at a given moment; the expressionists saw inner experience as the only reality.

The typical subject matter of expressionism was emotional intensity verging on hysteria. It was undoubtedly related to an awareness of the desperate

Karl Schmidt-Rottluff (1884 –1976), *Houses at Night* (1912). An example in oil of twentieth-century Expressionism, with shapes distorted to heighten the intensity of the work. (Courtesy, The Museum of Modern Art, New York; gift of Mr. and Mrs. Walter Bareiss)

state of the world. Its emotional subjectivity and obsession with the grotesque link it to the nineteenth century. But the irrational, subconscious inner experience that was expressed, and its means of portrayal, clearly establish expressionism as a twentieth-century movement, for it arose from the same cultural climate that produced Sigmund Freud. Expressionist art portrays the inner conflicts and fears of the isolated individual in ways that defied established order and accepted form.

The twentieth-century expressionist movement in painting is generally **Painting** considered to have begun in 1905, when the group *Die Brücke* ("The Bridge") was founded in Dresden, Germany, by the painters Ernst Ludwig, Karl Schmidt-Rottluff, Erich Heckel, and Fritz Bleyl. The final style of the group, which disbanded in 1913, combined cubist fragmentation, fauvist color, and expressionist intensity. Another important group was the *Blaue Reiter* ("Blue Rider," 1911–c. 1914), whose members included the Russian Vassily Kandinsky, the Germans Franz Marc and August Macke, and the Swiss Paul Klee. The composer Arnold Schoenberg, who was also a painter, exhibited with this group. Many other painters, including the German Paula Modersohn-Becker and the Austrian Oskar Kokoschka, worked independently in the expressionist style.

Theater   Expressionism flourished in the theater mainly between 1910 and 1925. Dreams, especially nightmare fears and obsessions, were used to dramatize inner life, clearly revealing the influence of Freud. Expressionist plays relied on nontraditional means—including sound, movement, and color—to build to a climax, and the deliberate break with realism was reflected also in the set design, which used leaning walls and roofs that seemed to hang unsupported. Typical expressionist plays are the German Georg Kaiser's *Gas I* (1918) and Bertolt Brecht's *Baal* (1918); the Swedish August Strindberg's *Elt Drönspel* ("The Dream Play," 1902); and the American Elmer Rice's *The Adding Machine* (1923).

Expressionism in Music

Expressionism in music is mainly associated with the Austrian composers Arnold Schoenberg, Alban Berg, and Anton Webern, and the music they wrote between 1908 and 1923. These composers are often referred to as the "second Viennese school." Works by other composers which exhibit similar characteristics, including some after 1923, are also part of this movement.

General characteristics   Expressionism found an appropriate language in atonality. It is a music whose expressive violence is conveyed by wide leaps, fragmented melodies, the use of instruments in their extreme ranges, jagged rhythmic contours, thick and complex textures, and violent contrasts. In vocal music the texts, often dealing with violence and neurosis, are set with a disregard for natural speech rhythms in order to heighten tension. This music is, in sum, an intense experience in which no note is expressively neutral.

Musical structure   Expressionist composers tended to renounce forms based on thematic repetition, which in turn led to problems of organization. One solution was to develop highly concentrated miniatures. This approach characterizes the music of Webern. The second of Webern's *Drei kleine Stücke* ("Three Little Pieces," Op. 11; 1914) for cello and piano, for instance, is only thirteen and a half seconds long. The number of motifs in a movement were few, and the movement ended when they had been sufficiently elaborated. Another solution to the problem of formal organization, especially in longer works, was to use a text. Here compositional size and shape were established by the divisions of the text and its changes of character and mood.

Schoenberg's *Pierrot lunaire*   Two of the most influential examples of expressionist works with texts are Schoenberg's *Pierrot lunaire* ("Moonstruck Pierrot," 1912) and Berg's opera *Wozzeck* (1921; orchestration finished 1922). The former, a work for instrumental quintet and voice, sets twenty-one poems by the Belgian writer Albert Giraud (pseudonym for Marie Emile Albert Kayenbergh) as three groups of seven "songs." The instruments—flute (doubling on piccolo), clarinet (doubling on bass clarinet), violin (doubling on viola), cello, and piano—are used in ever-changing combinations with the voice, a continuation of the principle of perpetual variation. The vocal part is famous for its use of *Sprechstimme,* also referred to as *Sprechgesang.* This was first used by Schoenberg in his *Gurre-Lieder* ("Songs of Gurre," 1901; orchestration finished 1911; Gurre is the name of a castle in Sjaelland in Denmark). Each individual movement of *Pierrot lunaire* has a harmonic consistency. Contrapuntal techniques, typical of Schoenberg's style, are present here. Nos. 17 and 18 contain canons.

Berg's *Wozzeck* is considered to be one of the masterpieces of twentieth-century opera. While expressionistic in its subject, mood, and much of its language, it is atypical of the trend in that it also combines features of other styles. It unites the pre-Wagnerian technique of division into sections with the Wagner leitmotif technique and Baroque and Classical (Neoclassical) instrumental forms. At the same time, it is a typical Berg work in its careful planning and in the expressiveness of its vocal lines.

Berg's Wozzeck

Wozzeck, based on a drama by Georg Büchner, is about a soldier, a representative of the *arme Leute* ("poor people"), who becomes a symbol of human oppression and misfortune. He is destroyed by the forces around him, a victim of circumstances beyond his control. The tight construction of the three-act opera, with five scenes in each act, enhances rather than hinders the dramatic flow. The form can be considered ABA, since the middle act is longer and in closed symphonic form, while the outer two acts are looser in construction.

The first act, an exposition, consists of five character pieces (each scene comprising one piece), each of which introduces a person important in Wozzeck's life. The first scene, between Wozzeck and the Captain, is in the form of a suite. Scene 2, involving Wozzeck and his friend Andres, is a rhapsody. Scenes 3, 4, and 5 successively present Marie (Wozzeck's common-law wife and the mother of his child), the Doctor, and the Drum Major (Marie's new boyfriend), and are in the forms of a military march and a lullaby, a passacaglia ground with twenty-one variations, and a rondo.

In act II, Wozzeck becomes more and more convinced of Marie's infidelity. The music develops act I material and uses the following forms: sonata, fantasy and fugue on three subjects, a Largo for chamber orchestra, a scherzo, and a rondo. Act III ends in the inevitable catastrophe. Wozzeck is driven by jealousy to murder Marie, and by a sense of hopelessness to his own suicide. The five scenes of act III comprise a series of six inventions, with the fifth found as the orchestral interlude between scenes 4 and 5. The inventions are on: (1) a theme (seven variations on a seven-bar theme, followed by a double fugue); (2) a note (the pitch B); (3) a rhythm; (4) a hexachord—the pitches B-flat, C-sharp, D-sharp, E, F, and A-flat—in which the tones are presented with changed register and in inversion; (5) a tonality (B minor); and (6) continuous eight-note motion (*perpetuum mobile*).

The opera is further unified by leitmotifs that represent situations (e.g., the fear motif, heard in act II, scene 1), characters, and actions. Wozzeck, for instance, is represented by a descending whole-tone fragment. The opera uses many types of text setting. Although it has no traditional recitative, it uses ordinary speech, popular songs, and Sprechstimme, as well as conventional singing. Different situations and individuals are represented by the various styles of vocal writing. Additionally, although the musical language is unifyingly atonal, certain tonal passages are used, as in the invention on a key.

Serialism

Definition

Serial music uses *serial* or *twelve-tone* (*dodecaphonic*) techniques, involving a succession of one or more elements of music ordered in a predetermined way. The terms "serial" and "twelve-tone" should not be used interchangeably, because it is possible to have an ordered succession (series) of more than or fewer than twelve tones. While most serial music is *atonal,* it is possible to have music that contains one or several tonal centers but follows serial rules.

Predecessors

Even before the invention of serialism, twelve-note melodies and chords had appeared. Perhaps the earliest example of a theme incorporating all twelve notes is that of the B minor fugue in J. S. Bach's *Well-Tempered Klavier,* Book I. Another example occurs in the "Wissenschaft" fugue of Richard Strauss's *Also Sprach Zarathustra* ("Thus Spake Zarathustra," 1896); and the third song of Berg's *Fünf Orchester-Lieder nach Ansichtskarten-Texten von Peter Altenberg* ("Five Orchestral Songs on Picture Postcard Texts of Peter Altenberg," 1912; commonly referred to as the "Altenberg Lieder") opens on a twelve-note chord. An earlier attempt at a twelve-tone system had been made by the Austrian composer Josef Matthias Hauer (1883–1959), who singled out certain basic types from all the possible twelve-note combinations and listed them as forty-four *tropes.* Each trope had two six-note groups of mutually exclusive pitches in which the content, but not the order, was specified. Schoenberg, however, was the first to use the twelve notes in a universally applicable technique.

As conceived by Schoenberg, serialism is a precompositional method of pitch organization designed to build musical structures from one unifying idea. It uses all twelve notes of the chromatic scale in various arrangements, but is totally unrelated to the traditional use of this scale.

Compositional procedures

Serialism makes constant and exclusive use of a *set* (also referred to as a *row* or *series*) made up of all twelve pitches of the chromatic scale. These pitches are arranged linearly in an order that is chosen anew by the composer for each composition. When the set is notated during this planning stage, all the pitches are generally stated within the span of a single octave. They are really *pitch-classes* rather than individual pitches, since they do not specify octave position. No note is repeated within the set, and no note may be repeated (except immediately) until all of the other pitches have been stated. All twelve notes should have equal emphasis in order to avoid having any pitch function, even temporarily, as a tonic.

Manipulations of the set

Schoenberg believed that musical space is multidimensional. A musical idea, therefore (which he considered as an entity comparable to a knife or a bottle), can be perceived whether it appears horizontally (melodically), vertically (harmonically), forward, backward, or upside-down. Thus in his system the set may be presented in any of four forms. The original form of the plan, although not always the first to be stated in the actual composition, is called the *prime* (or, on occasion, the *basic set*). When the prime is stated backward, it is called the *retrograde*. When the set is stated in mirror image (both versions begin on the same note, but an interval that goes up in the original version goes down by the same distance in the new one), this new form is known as the *inversion*. When not only is the prime inverted but the inversion is stated backward, we have the *retrograde inversion*. The above techniques, referred to as the *transformations* of the set, are illustrated in Example 31.1. These techniques extend earlier contrapuntal practices.

Since each of these transformations may be stated as *transpositions* on any degree of the chromatic scale, forty-eight *set-forms* (versions of the original set) are available to the composer. They may be used separately or in combination.

Often the set is constructed so that it naturally or functionally divides, a process known as the *segmentation,* or division into *subsets*. The most usual groupings are two groups of six notes (hexachords), three groups of four notes (tetrachords), or four groups of three notes. One way of creating unity within a segmented set is to construct the row symmetrically. This technique is illustrated in Example 31.2. In this row, used for all the movements of Schoenberg's *Suite für Klavier,* Op. 25 (1923), the first two tetrachords end with a tritone. A tritone also exists between the first and last notes of the row. In order to take advantage of the interval that is characteristic of this series, Schoenberg used the transposition of an augmented fourth.

Segmentation

One special kind of set construction results in *combinatoriality,* a device discovered by Schoenberg and further developed by the American composer Milton Babbitt. Combinatoriality results when the first hexachord of at least

Combinatoriality

Ex. 31.1   Transformations of the basic set

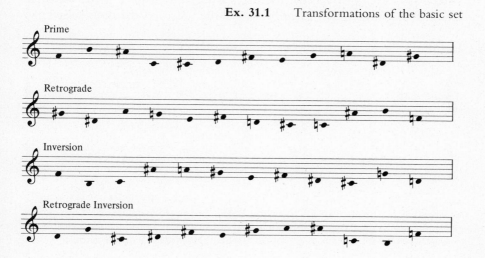

Ex. 31.2   Prime form of the row of Schoenberg's Piano Suite, Op. 25

Brackets indicate tritones.

one of the transformations of the set (excluding its retrograde) can be transposed so that its first six notes are the same, with regard only to content and not to order, as the last six notes of the prime set. The first six notes of both these sets will then jointly contain all twelve notes (referred to, in analytical writings about serialism, as a twelve-pitch *aggregate*). A *semi-combinatorial* set has this relation to any transformation, while an *all-combinatorial* set relates in this manner to all its transformations and at least one of its own transpositions. An example of the former is shown in Example 31.3. It presents the set used semi-combinatorially by Schoenberg in his *Klavierstück* ("Piano Piece," Op. 33b; 1932). The advantage of combinatoriality is that it provides a more logical means of organizing and unifying twelve-tone music.

Uses of sets in forming compositions   A mere description of the set and the transpositions and transformations to which it has been subjected does not explain a serial work. It only exposes the substructure—the system of tone relations that forms the basis of the work. The set is merely an abstract concept (in the sense that a major or a minor scale with its implied internal relationships is an abstract concept), which must be given rhythm, texture, timbre, dynamics, and form. The texture may be either homophonic or polyphonic, with some adjacent notes of the set forming the melody and others forming chords. Two or more forms of the set, usually stated contrapuntally, may be used at the same time.

The basic set acquires the character of a theme when consistently separated from its background by rhythm, texture, or dynamics. Even when the entire set is not used as a theme, it is still the source of the motifs used in a

Ex. 31.3   Semi-combinatorial row of Schoenberg's Piano Piece, Op. 33b

Pitches 7–12 of the original row are the same six pitches (although in a different ordering) as pitches 1–6 of the inversion transposed up five semitones. The first six pitches of the original plus the first six pitches of inversion 5 produce twelve different notes, as do the second six of the original plus the second six of inversion 5.

serial composition. By partitioning certain carefully chosen set-forms into well-defined motifs and by retiring melodically extraneous notes to the background, many of the functions of tonality can be reconstituted. Thus Berg was able to insert the opening of Wagner's Prelude to his opera *Tristan und Isolde* into his *Lyrische Suite für Streichquartett* ("Lyric Suite for String Quartet," 1926) and to insert a Bach chorale setting into his *Violinkonzert* ("Violin Concerto," 1935).

In books and articles dealing with serialism, certain symbols are generally used. P stands for prime (or, sometimes, O for original), R for retrograde, I for inversion, and RI for retrograde inversion. They are generally followed by an arabic numeral between 0 and 11. These numbers indicate the level of transposition relative to the original set. Thus P^0 (also written P–0) is the original set, while P^1 is the same set stated a half tone higher.

Symbols

Serialism has been attacked as an arbitrary and cerebral procedure—one that reverses the traditional procedure of deriving theory from the practice of composers. While it may be viewed as intellectually attractive, some musicians question whether the row will be perceived even subconsciously by a listener who has never studied the score. Others view the whole theory as irrelevant, since they feel that serialism does not really offer a fundamentally new approach to musical composition. Still others fear that it will encourage young composers to work mechanically.

Criticisms of serial music

The music of Schoenberg has also been criticized from within the serialist ranks by the post–World War II generation of young composers who felt that there was a dichotomy between Schoenberg's use of traditional forms and his twentieth-century technique. They felt that new forms were required so that structure and content would correspond.

Proponents of serialism argue that serialism is a system similar in function to the tonal system. Hence it is not serialism itself, but the way in which it is used, that determines its validity. The most successful serial works are not cerebral, but reveal great sensitivity in the handling of musical materials.

The Serialist Composers: Before World War II

Schoenberg

Arnold Schoenberg (1874–1951) was influenced by several late-nineteenth-century composers of the Austro-Germanic tradition. From Brahms he assimilated developing variation technique, asymmetrical phrase structure, and a penchant for counterpoint; from Mahler, a style of orchestration that sometimes uses a large orchestra as chamber groups of constantly changing timbres; from Wagner, harmonic fluidity; and from Strauss, as from Wagner, the increased use of chromaticism. His early music, which includes the famous *Verklärte Nacht* ("Transfigured Night," for string sextet, Op. 4, 1899; string orchestra version, 1917), shows increasing harmonic complexity, until tonality disappears in the later, expressionist works.

Serial works

In his serial works, which start with the last movement of [*Fünf*] *Klavierstücke* ("Five Piano Pieces," Op. 23; 1923), Schoenberg's rhythm and phrasing and the contour of his melodies show the influence of the past. The composer also depended on traditional forms, since he viewed these forms as an ideal set of proportions with expressive potentials that transcend musical language and style. He generally begins his compositions with the basic set, and uses transpositions to build subordinate ideas (such as second themes) in a way parallel to the modulations of tonal music. After 1930 he was concerned with semi-combinatorial rows—especially those that align the prime form with the inversion transposed a fifth below.

Use of tonality with serialism

After his arrival in the United States in 1933, Schoenberg created several works in which tonality was incorporated into his serial procedures. One such work is his *Ode to Napoleon Buonaparte,* Op. 41 (1942).

String Quartet No. 4

Schoenberg's String Quartet No. 4, Op. 37 (1936), is another work from his American period. All four movements are based on the same row, which is presented homophonically at the opening of the first movement. This work makes free use of the forms of a Classical string quartet, while the row is used to form themes through the application of rhythm and dynamics. The first movement is in sonata-allegro form; the second movement is a Ländler; the third movement is a Largo in large binary form, with both main sections opening with unison statements of the row; and the last movement is a free rondo with varied repetitions of the opening theme. The work combines a Classical transparency of texture with an intensity of expression. Both homophonic and contrapuntal textures are present. This quartet incorporates many of Schoenberg's favored string devices, such as harmonics, pizzicato, sul ponticello, and col legno, some of which may be seen in the excerpt from the second movement shown in Example 31.4.

Berg

Alban Berg (1885–1935), in his few twelve-tone pieces (he wrote only a handful of works during the last several years of his life), ignored the principle of using only one series, and did not feel obliged to follow strict serial ordering. In his opera *Lulu* (short score 1934; act III orchestration unfinished at the composer's death in 1935 but subsequently completed by George Perle), the motifs that he derives from the series are often used independently of their original twelve-tone milieu. The work has a general harmonic background that unites different sets. Berg's pitch materials are expanded by certain mathematical operations. For example, the row used for the character Alwa appears to have been derived from the basic row by using the first pitch, skipping the next six, using the eighth pitch, skipping the next six, and so on. Additionally, a motive of fourths is drawn from the original row and becomes the *Erdgeist* ("Earth Spirit") theme used throughout the opera, while the remaining eight pitches are used as part of the musical development. And a motif of four three-note chords, associated with Lulu, is also drawn from the original series (see Example 31.5).

Lulu

Ex. 31.4   Arnold Schoenberg, String Quartet No. 4, Mvt. 2, mm. 558–562

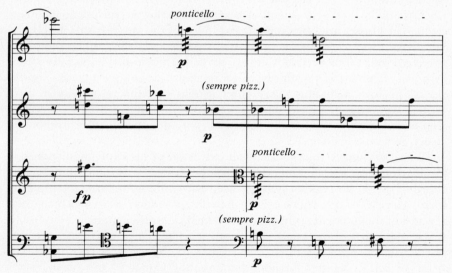

Webern

Anton von Webern (1883–1945) also progressed from Romanticism to atonality (beginning with *Fünf Lieder* ["Five Songs," Op. 3, for medium voice and piano; 1908]) to serialism (beginning with *Drei Volkstexte* ["Three Sacred Folksongs," Op. 17, also translated as "Three Traditional Rhymes,"

Ex. 31.5   Some of the rows used in Alban Berg's *Lulu*

(a) The basic row of the opera, assigned to Lulu

(b) Chords associated with Lulu

(c) Alwa's row

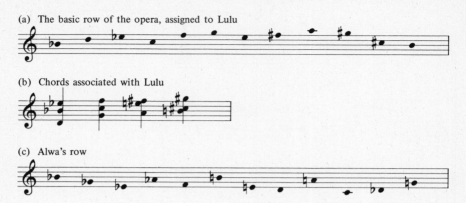

for voice, violin/viola, clarinet, and bass clarinet; 1924]). His works, almost equally divided between vocal and purely instrumental compositions, show similarities of style throughout these changes.

Webern's music is marked by a chamber music quality even in works for large orchestra. His pointillistic use of instruments is reminiscent of medieval hocket techniques, and suitable for his highly motivic approach to composition. Many unusual instruments appear in his orchestra, including the mandolin. The brasses are often muted, and much of the music is soft, rarely rising above forte. Tempos fluctuate, with ritards and rubato often indicated. Preferred intervals are seconds, thirds, sevenths, and ninths (especially minor seconds, major and minor thirds, major sevenths, and minor ninths). Contrapuntal devices, including many strict canons, abound, especially in later works. Webern is best known for his economy of means, extreme concentration of style even in the serial works, and spare and open textures containing many intervening silences.

Webern's twelve-tone music is an extension of his expressionist works. His love of order is seen in his preference for series in which the second hexachord of the set possesses a symmetrical relationship to the first (often in the form of a palindrome, which exists when the second half of an idea is an exact reversal of the first half, as in the name Anna). It is also apparent in his use of rows that transform a small serial unit or *cell* (usually consisting of three notes) in such a way that these units relate to one another. Such a row, taken from Webern's *Konzert für neun Instruments* ("Concerto for Nine Instruments," Op. 24; 1934), is shown in Example 31.6. This row, like all of Webern's rows, is constructed predominantly of semitones, with some thirds, allowing him considerable use of his preferred intervals.

Symphonie   Webern's *Symphonie* ("Symphony," Op. 21; 1928) illustrates many of the characteristics discussed. It has two movements, the first in a much-modified sonata form, and the second a theme and seven variations plus a coda. The whole composition is based on the row shown in Example 31.7. It should be

Ex. 31.6   Prime form of the row used in Anton Webern's *Concerto for Nine Instruments,* Op. 24

P-0   RI-7   R-6   I-6

Brackets indicate cells. The second group is a retrograde inversion of the original three pitches (transposed), and so on.

noted that the second half of the row is a palindrome of the first half. Thus only twenty-four forms of the row are available for use in the composition, since the basic series is the same as the transposed retrograde, and so, then, are the inversions of both.

The first movement is especially fascinating structurally. Its sonata form is created by row usage rather than relationships of key. The beginnings of the main sections—exposition, development, and recapitulation—are marked by new row forms presented without overlap. The exposition is a double canon in contrary motion. The transpositions of the series used here have been chosen so that the eleventh and twelfth notes of one form become the first and second notes of the next. This overlap is accomplished by having a prime form of the row followed by an inversion and vice versa. Such interlocking is built into the construction of the series. Some use is also made of pitches found in specific octave positions. The same forms of the row, in the same order, appear in the recapitulation, although the register is changed. The development, by contrast, is a four-part canon that uses limited interlocking of rows. The development splits into symmetrical halves, with the second half a retrograde of the first.

The texture of the movement is sparse, with many rests. Each instrument has only a few notes, outlining—much of the time—a seventh or a ninth. The instrumental lines contain wide leaps, which remain a prominent feature of Webern's music. The notation of dynamics is extremely precise.

Other Early Serialists

In the United States, early serialists included Wallingford Riegger (1865–1961), George Perle (b. 1915), Carl Ruggles (1875–1971), and Ruth Crawford Seeger (1901–1953). Riegger created works that unite twelve-tone technique and Classical forms, although several of his compositions use the technique only in sections. His earliest serial piece is *Dichotomy* (1932) for chamber orchestra; it uses two opposing tone rows. Perle, who also turned to serialism in

Riegger

Ex. 31.7   Row for Anton Webern's *Symphony,* Op. 21

Perle and Ruggles

the 1930s, was attracted to the method of the Viennese school because of its systematic nature. In about 1939 he developed a "twelve-tone modal system" that incorporates tonality into serial procedures. Ruggles adapted serial ideas to his own stylistic needs.

Crawford Seeger

Ruth Crawford Seeger, too, adapted the principles of Schoenberg to a personal style. Her mature compositions, most of which date from the late 1920s and early 1930s, combine expressivity with clarity of organization. Sprechstimme, tone clusters, and other experimental devices are present in her works, which also make much use of counterpoint. Characteristic, too, are the use of short, narrow-range motifs and a utilization of aspects of serial technique without Schoenberg's precision in the ordering of the twelve tones. Her *String Quartet* (1931) foreshadows techniques that gained wider acceptance only after World War II.

Křenek

Still another important early adherent of serialism is the Viennese-born Ernst Křenek (b. 1900). Křenek emigrated to the United States in 1938. His first work to use the twelve-tone technique throughout was his opera *Karl V* (1953). His *Lamentatio Jeremiae prophetae* ("Lamentation of the Prophet Jeremiah," 1941) uses *row rotation* (exchanging pitches within a given row in a systematic manner), which he applied to several subsequent works.

Lutyens

In Britain, Elizabeth Lutyens (b. 1906) and Humphrey Searle (b. 1915) were among the few pre–World War II serialists. The former's works have long, evolving melodies and harmonies of differing densities, with harmony and melody unified through the use of sustained melodic notes that assume a harmonic function. This is seen, for instance, in her *Six Tempi for Ten Instruments* (1953).

Dalla-piccola

A combination of expressivity and serial technique is found in the works of Italian composer Luigi Dallapiccola (1904–1975), who adopted serialism in the 1930s. His music includes tonal and modal elements, and his instrumental lines form smooth curves that show the influence of the Italian vocal tradition.

Serialist Composers after World War II

Growing influence of serialism

Between World Wars I and II, the most prominent style of composition was Neoclassical. At that time, the modern music world was sharply divided between the followers of Arnold Schoenberg and the more numerous ones of Igor Stravinsky (1882–1971). After World War II serialism, which had been banned in European countries under Naziism, briefly became a dominant trend, not only in Europe but in the United States as well. Many postwar composers were, at least briefly, serialists. American composers include George Rochberg (b. 1918), Ross Lee Finney (b. 1906), Roger Sessions (b. 1896), who first used the twelve-tone technique in his Violin Sonata (1953), and Ralph Shapey (b. 1921), whose works combine an individualized approach to serialism with the Varèse idea of sounds as sculptural forms.

Even those who did not fully embrace the technique of serialism, such as the Swiss composer Frank Martin (1890–1974), did integrate parts of it within their overall style. Nonserial composers, such as the American Leon Kirchner (b. 1919), often used in his early works a harmonic language related to that of Schoenberg and Berg. With the rise of serialism and the fading of Neoclassicism, the Schoenberg-Stravinsky controversy became meaningless. Illustrative of this circumstance is the fact that starting in the early 1950s Stravinsky's works use elements of serialism, and beginning in 1958 with his *Threni; id est Lamentationes Jeremiae prophetae* ("Dirges; that is, the Lamentations of the Prophet Jeremiah"), they are completely serial.

Threni is a three-movement work, with the middle movement subdivided into three parts. As the subtitle indicates, this work sets excerpts from the biblical text of the Lamentations of Jeremiah. The somberness of the text is reflected in Stravinsky's orchestration, which makes considerable use of trombones and other low winds including the tuba, bass clarinet, alto clarinet, and sarrusophone. The row used is shown in Example 31.8. (Some analysts prefer to think of this as the retrograde form.) **Stravin-sky's *Threni***

Just as Webern's rows contain his favorite intervals (sevenths and ninths), Stravinsky's row here reflects consonant intervals that have fascinated him throughout his career. Stravinsky used row technique freely. For example, internal segments of the row are repeated, and in the last section of the second movement, the pitches of his original row appear in the order 1–3–5–7–9–11–12–10–8–6–4–2 to form a new row.

The influence of Webern can be seen in the use of canons and double canons in the work (for instance, the canons that begin the second movement). But throughout, the work is permeated by the energy and unusual orchestration that are so much a part of the Stravinsky tradition.

Total Serialism

After World War II, several composers became interested in carrying serialism to what they considered its logical conclusion. They therefore extended the organization of pitch to all other elements of music, including rhythm, dynamics, and color. These developments occurred almost simultaneously in the United States and Europe. In the United States, however, interest in these serial experiments continued, while in Europe the movement faded after a few years.

The first totally organized works were those created by the American composer Milton Babbitt (b. 1916): *Three Compositions for Piano* (1947), *Composition for Four Instruments* (1948), and *Composition for Twelve Instruments* (1948). For Babbitt, the row becomes not only a structure but also **Babbitt**

Ex. 31.8   Row for Igor Stravinsky's *Threni*

an operational process representing all possible relationships of every aspect of the music. Along with the highly individualistic serial composer Stefan Wolpe (who lived in the United States from 1939 until his death in 1972), Babbitt has influenced a whole generation of American serialists, including Charles Wuorinen (b. 1938). (See Chapter 40.)

Babbitt, whose theoretical writings on total serialism are as important as his compositions, used scientific, philosophical, and linguistic studies in arriving at his conclusions. He relates these disciplines to musical thought, viewing the act of composing as a grouping of interdependent, rational choices made valid by experience and experimentation. Thus, for him, the invention of musical systems is integral to the act of composition.

Three Compositions for Piano, No. 1

The complexity of Babbitt's thought may be observed by examining one of his simpler pieces, No. 1 of *Three Compositions for Piano.* The eight row forms used have an all-combinatorial relationship. The horizontal succession of row forms arises from the *secondary sets* (the second hexachord from one form followed by the first hexachord from another, or vice versa, resulting in a new group containing all twelve pitches) created by using combinatorial rows. This short work, which is divided into six sections, arranges the set-forms to construct a large-scale structure of a canon in retrograde in which sections 4 and 5 reverse the order of the reversed row forms (sections 3 and 2) at the original levels of transposition, while section 6 reverses section 1 transposed by a tritone. The rhythm is also serialized. The original form of the rhythm is in the ratio $5:1:4:2$ (e.g., five sixteenths, one sixteenth, etc.), the retrograde is $2:4:1:5$, the inversion is $1:5:2:4$, and the retrograde inversion is $4:2:5:1$. Each section has its own rhythmic articulations. The dynamics correlate simply—the prime is *mezzo piano,* the retrograde is *mezzo forte,* the inversion is *forte,* and the retrograde inversion is *piano.* This scheme is modified only in the closing section, where each form is two degrees less intense (e.g., the prime is *pianissimo*).

Wolpe

Wolpe, who studied briefly with Webern, was an early advocate of serialism. His music generates motifs from small cells and relies on development by variation. It often uses cumulative forms.

Messiaen's *Mode de valeurs* . . .

The first totally organized piece of music in Europe was *Mode de valeurs et d'intensités,* one of a set of piano pieces written by Olivier Messiaen in 1949. This piece uses a mode, not a series, but carefully prescribes all parameters of sound. Its mode has thirty-six different sounds in its melody, twenty-four rhythmic durations, seven different dynamic intensities, and twelve different keyboard attacks. Each sound always appears with the same rhythmic duration, the same intensity, and the same attack.

Boulez; other post-Webern serialists

Messiaen was the teacher of both the French Pierre Boulez (b. 1925) and the German Karlheinz Stockhausen (b. 1928). These two composers, along with the Italians Luigi Nono (b. 1924), Luciano Berio (b. 1925), and Bruno Maderna (1920–1973), were the leading young proponents of post-Webern serialism. They used twelve-tone technique as a total generating principle for achieving new materials, structure, and expression. This technique is seen in

Boulez's first book of *Structures* for two pianos (1952), in which all parts of the musical event undergo perpetual transformation. For each particular pitch, the same attack, the same intensity, and the same duration never recur.

During these years, Stockhausen's works were possibly even more organized than those of Boulez. The former was concerned with extending serial control even to such domains as chord density, the number of events in given time segments, the size of intervals and the choice of register, the types of attack and articulation, and the rate of change of texture and tone color. These concerns are illustrated, for example, in Stockhausen's *Klavierstücke I–IV* ("Piano Pieces I–IV," 1953).

Stock-hausen

Summary

By the beginning of the twentieth century, the viability of tonality seemed exhausted to Schoenberg, Berg, and Webern, and they chose to abandon it. Their music became atonal in those emotionally intense works categorized as expressionistic.

Gradually, however, these composers realized the limitations of their atonal style. Schoenberg developed a method of choosing pitches that was independent of traditional tonality. His system is universal rather than personal, in that each composer can adapt it to his own use.

In the period between the World Wars, there were few serialists. In the early 1950s, however, interest in serial techniques flourished. Many of the postwar serialists preferred total organization. However, relatively few composers now use these techniques as a sole means of organization.

Notes

1. Arnold Schoenberg, *Style and Idea: Selected Writings of Arnold Schoenberg,* ed. Leonard Stein, with translations by Leo Black (London: Faber & Faber, 1975), p. 216.
2. Ibid., p. 218.

Bibliography

Books and Articles

Background

RAABE, PAUL, ed. and annotator. *The Era of Expressionism,* trans. J. M. Ritchie. Woodstock, N.Y.: Overlook Press, 1974.

Music

BASART, ANN PHILIPS. *Serial Music: A Classified Bibliography of Writings on Twelve-Tone and Electronic Music.* Berkeley: University of California Press, 1961.

BOULEZ, PIERRE. *Notes of an Apprenticeship.* Texts collected by Paule Thévenin, trans. Herbert Weinstock. New York: Alfred A. Knopf, 1968.

KOLNEDER, WALTER. *Anton Webern: An Introduction to His Works,* trans. Humphrey Searle. Berkeley: University of California Press, 1968.

MOLDENHAUER, HANS, AND MOLDENHAUER, ROSALEEN. *Anton von Webern: A Chronicle of His Life and Work.* New York: Alfred A. Knopf, 1978.

PAYNE, ANTHONY. "Lutyens' Solution to Serial Problems." *The Listener* (BBC publication) 70 (Dec. 5, 1963): 961.

PERLE, GEORGE. *Serialism and Atonality,* 5th rev. ed. Berkeley: University of California Press, 1981.

———. *The Operas of Alban Berg. Vol I: Wozzeck.* Berkeley: University of California Press, 1980.

REICH, WILLI. *Alban Berg,* trans. Cornelius Cardew. London: Thames and Hudson, 1965.

ROSEN, CHARLES. *Arnold Schoenberg.* Modern Masters series, ed. Frank Kermode. New York: Viking Press, 1975.

SEEGER, CHARLES. "Ruth Crawford." In *American Composers on American Music: A Symposium,* ed. and with an introduction by Henry Cowell. New York: Frederick Ungar Publishing Co., 1962.

STUCKENSCHMIDT, H. H. *Arnold Schoenberg: His Life, World, and Work,* trans. Humphrey Searle. New York: Schirmer Books, 1977.

WEBERN, ANTON. *The Path to New Music,* ed. Willi Reich, trans. Leo Black. Bryn Mawr: Theodore Presser, 1963.

WÖRNER, KARL H. *Stockhausen: Life and Work,* introduced, trans. and ed. by Bill Hopkins. Berkeley: University of California Press, 1973.

Periodicals

Perspectives of New Music. Published in Annandale-on-Hudson, N.Y. (formerly, New York and Princeton) since 1962.

Die Reihe, edited by Herbert Eimert and Karlheinz Stockhausen. Vol. 1–8. German edition: Universal Edition (Vienna), 1955–1962. English edition: Theodore Presser (Bryn Mawr, Pa.) 1958–1968.

Scores

The works of Milton Babbitt are mainly published by Associated Music Publishers (New York).

The works of Alban Berg are published by Universal Edition (Vienna and London).

Since 1952, the works of Pierre Boulez have been published by Universal Edition (Vienna and London).

Until 1932 Arnold Schoenberg was mainly published by Universal Edition (Vienna and London), excluding Ops. 23 and 24, published by Hansen (Vienna). His main publisher for subsequent works was G. Schirmer (New York).

The works of Karlheinz Stockhausen are mainly published by Universal Edition (Vienna and London).

The works of Anton Webern were mainly published by Universal Edition (Vienna and London).

32
Nationalism and Neoclassicism

MOST twentieth-century composers have faced the dual problems of finding new musical materials and of discovering the means of structuring them. The composers discussed in this chapter solved the former problem by using conventional tonal materials in new ways (Neoclassicism) or by introducing new scales and rhythms (nationalism). Nationalism and Neoclassicism offered different solutions to the problems of content and form. Both shared, however, a belief in the supreme importance of pitch in the musical hierarchy.

Nationalism

As in the nineteenth century, contemporary musical works considered "nationalistic" incorporate folk materials. Musical nationalism has occurred in almost every country of the world. A few of the better-known nationalists are discussed below.

Hungary

The Hungarian-born composers Zoltán Kodály (1882–1967) and Béla Bartók (1881–1945) were both interested in integrating rhythmically complex Eastern European modal melodies with the Western musical tradition. Although their knowledge of Hungarian folk music was acquired firsthand through extensive field trips, each composer achieved the East-West synthesis in a different way. Kodály's music, including such works as his *Psalmus Hungaricus* ("Hungarian Psalm," Op. 13; 1923) for tenor, chorus, and orchestra, remained closer to its Hungarian roots than Bartók's; it was more tonally and triadically oriented, and more songlike. Bartók, in transcending his regional materials, developed an international style.

Kodály's melodies incorporate pentatonic scales and a limited chromaticism. His music, with its abrupt tempo changes and mood shifts, has an improvisational quality. Repeated patterns of simple rhythms, rhythmic vitality, and orchestral color are other features of his style.

Kodály

Bartók   Bartók's music consciously merges the devices of Bach's counterpoint with Beethoven's use of form and Debussy's coloristic harmony and pentatonic and modal melodies. From folk music, Bartók took unconventional scales, thematic materials that often oscillated around a central pitch, and an emphasis on the tritone. He also used asymmetrical rhythms with measures of five, seven, and nine beats, and within measures he varied rhythmic groupings—including 3 + 2 + 3 and 1 + 3 + 1 + 3—many of which were derived from folk dances. Folklike melodies are found in several of his works, including his String Quartet No. 5 (1934); String Quartet No. 6 (1939); Divertimento for Strings (1939); and Music for String Instruments, Percussion, and Celesta (1936).

Bartók's output can be divided into three style periods. Early Bartók clearly shows diverse influences, such as impressionism, German Romanticism (Strauss and Liszt), and some folk music. As Bartók developed artistically, some of these influences disappeared, while the rest were integrated into his style. In the 1920s and early 1930s, Bartók's music entered his "advanced period," in which tonal centers are present but obscure, and the compositional techniques are more complex. By the late 1930s and early 1940s, Bartók had returned to a simpler, more tonal style, with easily perceived forms and recognizable melodies. These latter works have great audience appeal.

Musical   Certain characteristics are common throughout Bartók's various style pe-
style   riods. A sense of tonality pervades all works in varying degrees. As is true of most twentieth-century composers, Bartók's tonality is manifested in the establishment of temporary tonal centers rather than in the use of traditional functional harmony. His work abounds in free imitations, formal canons, and fugatos, and many of his novel harmonies result from his contrapuntal adventures. His works are often fashioned from limited musical materials; the opening motif frequently contains the substance that will be developed throughout the movement, with subsequent themes related to the first. Ostinato patterns are also present in many works. But perhaps the salient feature of Bartók's music is his incorporation of folk materials, resulting from his extensive ethnological research in Rumania, Hungary, Bulgaria, and North Africa.

Bartók used traditional forms, although always inventively. He makes frequent use of the sonata–allegro, for instance, but the recapitulation is never exact, themes are not generally defined by conventional key relationships, and material is developed continuously throughout the movement, not just in the development section. Other favored structural devices are arch form and the use of multisectional movements.

Bartók orchestrated sensitively, particularly in his string writing, which reveals coloristic techniques developed in the string quartets. These include such devices as glissandi (including glissandi that end in harmonics), pizzicati (including the "snap pizzicato," sometimes referred to as the "Bartók pizzicato," in which the string rebounds from the fingerboard), and triple and quadruple stops.

Bartók's evolution can be traced by comparing and examining three works: String Quartet No. 1 (c. 1908, an early work), String Quartet No. 4 (1928, a middle-period work), and Concerto for Orchestra (1943, a late work, written when Bartók was living in the United States). String Quartet No. 1 is in three movements: the first in ABA' form, and the second and third in modified sonata-allegro form. The entire work exhibits the rhythmic vitality so characteristic of Bartók's music. Its texture, like that of all Bartók's quartets, is complex in its independence of parts. Folk influences, so prominent in much of Bartók's music, are found chiefly in the last movement.

The first movement opens with a freely developed double canon, beginning with a descending sixth followed by an ascending fifth—intervals that remain important throughout the movement (see Example 32.1). These intervals are prominent not only in the A section, but in the B section as well, where the interval of the fifth becomes a double pedal point in the cello, above which the viola has the descending sixth, horizontally stated but rhythmicized and filled in. The unfolding of the A section is marked by interval expansion, another common developmental technique of Bartók. This may also be seen, for example, in the measure after rehearsal no. 5, where the descending sixth of the first violin becomes a descending seventh in violin II.

The second movement begins with an introduction, which functions as a transition from the previous movement. The first theme (rehearsal no. 1) is a four-note ostinato pattern, coupled with a descending three-note countermotif. (This main motif can be related to the semitonal appoggiatura-like figures that pervade movement 1, and will, in turn, generate the first theme of the third movement.) The waltzlike second theme is also surrounded by an ostinato. In the third movement, folk influences may be discerned in the cello passage in the cadenza-like introduction, and the insistent repeated notes of the first theme. The second theme is characterized by syncopated fourths and interrupted by an impressionistic episode (rehearsal no. 11). The development section contains a fugato. The work ends with chords on A, the tonal center of the piece.

String Quartet No. 4, regarded as one of Bartók's greatest works, is in arch form, with the first and fifth, and second and fourth movements sharing related materials. (The materials of the latter two movements grow out of a germinal motif presented in movement 1.) The third movement, which forms the center of the arch, is itself in ABA form, with the A sections based on a Hungarian-flavored motif. Thus B is the center of the entire arch. The composition ends with the germinal motif of the beginning.

The string writing in this work is advanced. The players are required to perform such techniques as snap pizzicato, pizzicato sul ponticello, pizzicato glissando, numerous wide-range glissandi, col legno chords, and difficult multiple stops. Canons and free imitation abound (as do ostinatos). Bitonality is used. Also characteristic of Bartók is the "Night Music" figuration in the third movement (so named after its use in the *Musiques Nocturnes* ["Night Music"] movement of Bartók's 1926 *Out of Doors* piano suite).

The Concerto for Orchestra, in five movements, uses the instruments of

String Quartet No. 1

String Quartet No. 4

Ex. 32.1 Béla Bartók, String Quartet No. 1

Concerto
for
Orchestra the orchestra as soloists. The movements are less strongly related than in the
fourth quartet, although the introduction to the first movement furnishes the
thematic material of the third. The first movement is in modified sonata-
allegro form, with the main motif of the first theme anticipated in an ostinato
pattern (the last eighteen measures of the introduction). This theme is typical
of Bartók—a five-note scale that spans a tritone and is immediately altered.

The second movement is a series of folk-influenced dance sections, presented by instruments in pairs, which form the A sections of an ABA' form. The B section is a brass interlude. The third movement is in five main sections in arch form (ABCB'A'). It, too, has several highly appealing folk-influenced themes. The A sections use a "Night Music" theme. The fourth movement is a free rondo: ABA, Interruption(C), B'A'. The themes of the A and B sections are based on Bulgarian rhythms. The Interruption is a harsh parody of the marchlike crescendo theme of Shostakovich's Seventh Symphony, as shown by the brass and woodwind passages that interrupt and distort the original theme. The finale, with its dance rhythms, incorporates a complex fugue, which integrates quadruple stretti and augmentation techniques into the overall sonata form.

Great Britain

The British composers Gustav Holst (1874–1934) and Ralph Vaughan Williams (1872–1958) were musically influenced by the revival of English folk music and of sixteenth- and seventeenth-century English Tudor music. Both wrote music containing bitonality resulting from contrapuntal combinations. Holst's music from about 1900 to 1912 shows his interest in Hindu subjects and scales, as in his opera *Sāvitri* ("The Revivifier," Op. 25; 1908; based on an episode from the *Mahābhārata,* an ancient epic poem of India describing war). In general, his music uses modal melodies, and his harmonies sometimes lack a sense of progression. Holst thus often relies on rhythm, especially ostinatos, to create larger forms. Throughout his life Ralph Vaughan Williams was interested in the symphony, and his symphonic works incorporate modal and pentatonic melodies, cross-relationships, and nontraditional modulatory patterns. His harmony is essentially triadic, and incorporates the impressionist technique of chord streams. His rhythms vary from complex patterns that seem to disregard the bar line (Tudor influence) to more regular patterns (folk-influenced passages). Contrapuntal techniques include the use of fugue, passacaglia, ostinato, and free counterpoint.

Holst and Vaughan Williams

Russia

Stravinsky's early ballets, which established his reputation, had roots in the music of the nineteenth-century Russian nationalists but showed great originality in their treatment of folk material. By the time he composed *Le Sacre du printemps* ("The Rite of Spring," 1912), the boldness with which he used rhythm had a lasting effect on several generations of composers. *The Rite of Spring* was the composer's third work for the Russian ballet company of Serge Diaghilev (1872–1929), the first two being *L'Oiseau de feu* ("Firebird," 1910) and *Petrouchka* (1911). When the *Rite* was first performed in Paris in 1913, Stravinsky's then-novel instrumentation, including the bassoon solo in the extreme upper register that opened the composition, and what was at that time considered to be the immoral theme of the ballet (human sacrifice), combined to produce a scandalized riot in the audience.

These early works foreshadow his Neoclassical techniques in their asym-

Early Stravinsky

metrical rhythms, juxtaposition of ideas rather than traditional motivic developmental techniques, and unusual and striking orchestrations. *Firebird* uses contrasting materials that are suddenly stopped, fragmented, and interchanged. *Petrouchka,* which incorporates Russian folk songs and popular songs and dances (e.g., the barrel-organ tune of scene 1), uses polyrhythms, irregular rhythms, and rapidly changing meters. The work contains sections of conventional tonality, percussive parallel chords, and polytonality. Notable, too, is the famous "Petrouchka chord" consisting of the combination of C against F-sharp triads, creating an important tritone relationship.

Rite of Spring   The *Rite* is regarded as one of the masterpieces of twentieth-century music. It is divided into two large parts, each of which begins with a slow introduction and ends with a climactic dance. The primitive subject matter (a virgin who dances herself to death as a sacrifice to spring) is reflected in a carefully controlled musical primitivism, created by relentless simple, driving repetition. The significance of the *Rite* lies in the fact that it treats rhythm as an independent force, a form-building element as important as melody and harmony.

The *Rite* still uses folk and folk-influenced motifs—brief diatonic fragments that are repeated and varied—and the melody that opens the work is a Lithuanian folk tune. Ostinato patterns, a Stravinsky trademark, abound. The rhythm makes use of constant shifts: asymmetry (e.g., *Jeu de rapt,* or "Game of Abduction"); polyrhythm (e.g., *Glorification de l'elue,* or "Glorification of the Chosen Maiden"); and "hammered" style (insistently repeated rhythms). The rhythm falls into two basic types: regular metric patterns upset by irregular accents (e.g., *Danse de la terre,* or "Dance of the Earth") and measures in which the meter constantly changes (e.g., *Danse sacrale*). The orchestration includes the following unusual effects: the high bassoon solo that was already noted, basses divided into six parts, and bass and flute harmonics.

Jazz-Influenced Composition

Early jazz, a unique American style with worldwide influence, arose as a synthesis of the march or dance beat overlaid with syncopations taken from ragtime (a style of American popular music that reached its peak between 1910 and 1915); syncopated dance rhythms of Afro-Caribbean origin; basic harmonies from European art music; and various Negro songs such as the responsorial work song, field holler, spiritual, and secular blues. It fascinated composers both with its rhythmic vitality and its unique blend of Afro-American folk culture with the Western harmonic tradition. (For a more detailed discussion of jazz, see Chapter 40.)

Numerous European composers experimented with jazz, including Claude Debussy. His *Golliwog's Cakewalk* is from the *Children's Corner* suite for piano (1908), an excerpt from which can be seen in Example 32.2.

Other works include Ernst Křenek's opera *Jonny spielt auf* ("Johnny Strikes Up," 1926); Paul Hindemith's *Shimmy* and *Ragtime* from the Suite for Piano (1922), and Darius Milhaud's *La Création du monde* ("The Creation of the World," 1923). The last-named work uses "blue" notes. (These are

Ex. 32.2   Claude Debussy, *Golliwog's Cakewalk,* from *The Children's Corner,* mm.
             10–13

pitches with intonation falling somewhere between the normal major and minor intervals. This is particularly true of the third and seventh degrees of the scale.)

The influence of ragtime is seen in three of Stravinsky's works: Piano Rag-music (1919), Ragtime for Eleven Instruments (1918, piano reduction 1919), and the ragtime dance from his *L'Histoire du soldat* ("The Soldier's Tale," 1918). The latter work uses a seven-piece chamber ensemble, including percussion, in an instrumentation close to that of a New Orleans jazz band. A much later work, the Ebony Concerto (1945), uses jazz within a Neoclassical style.

Jazz in Stravinsky's music

Some composers in the United States attempted to use jazz in ways similar to those in which the European nationalists employed their native folk music. These Americans aimed for a synthesis of jazz and traditional Western music. John Alden Carpenter (1876–1951) and George Gershwin (1898–1937), in the 1920s, and Gunther Schuller (b. 1925), in the 1950s, stand as leading exponents of this effort. Carpenter used ragtime rhythms in his concertino for Piano and Orchestra (1915), and created a jazz pantomime with his ballet *Crazy Cat* (1921). Gershwin's jazz-influenced concert pieces include his *Rhapsody in Blue* (1924) for piano and orchestra.

Jazz elements in American works

In 1957, Schuller applied the term "Third Stream" to his jazz-Classical mixture. In works such as *Concertino* (1959), which sets a jazz quartet against a symphony orchestra, the styles are juxtaposed rather than blended. Other works, such as the *Seven Studies on Themes of Paul Klee* (1959), move closer to a synthesis. (Chapter 40 has further discussion of these composers and trends.)

Schuller

Nationalism in the United States

In the 1930s, several American composers began to write works that used American folk themes. Among these composers was Aaron Copland (b. 1900), who changed from an abstract style to a more accessible one. Copland's music has, in fact, gone through several style changes. He began with Neoclassicism in the early 1920s and then wrote abstract music, the most extreme example of which is to be found, perhaps, in his Piano Variations of 1930. Moving through the use of jazz and then other American sources, Cop-

Copland

Edward Hopper (1882–1967), *Early Sunday Morning* (1930), oil on canvas, 35 × 60 inches. Aaron Copland, Roy Harris, and Virgil Thomson, in rejecting the complex language and syntax of early twentieth-century European music, created a distinctly American mood and setting evidenced in Hopper's painting from the same period. (Collection of the Whitney Museum of American Art, New York)

land later incorporated serial principles into his harmonic language. Through most of these changes, Copland's music has remained essentially diatonic, with some polytonality, major-minor conflicts, and modal flavor; simple, direct melodies; strong rhythms, some of which make use of syncopation; and an uncluttered texture. These qualities may be seen in *Billy the Kid* (1938), a ballet suite that utilizes traditional cowboy melodies such as *I Ride an Old Paint* and *The Dying Cowboy,* but without literal quotation. The work uses parallel modal harmonies in the prologue, and polymodality and polyrhythm in the scene that follows.

Harris   Roy Harris (1898–1979), one of the most frequently performed American composers of the 1930s, used popular American hymn tunes and cowboy songs. His music—with its long-lined melodies that sometimes incorporate modality and chromaticism, sometimes use bichordal harmony, and frequently use contrapuntal devices—expresses the exuberance of American life.

Thomson   The work of Virgil Thomson (b. 1896) is marked by sophisticated simplicity, as in the two operas he wrote with Gertrude Stein as librettist: *Four Saints in Three Acts* (1928) and *The Mother of Us All* (1947), the latter of which deals with suffragette Susan B. Anthony. The excerpt from *The Mother of Us All,* taken from near the end of act II, scene 2 (see Example 32.3), is typical of Thomson's calculated simplicity of style. (For more extended discussions of these composers, see Chapter 40.)

Czechoslovakia

Two important Czechoslovakian nationalists are the composer Leoš Janáček (1854–1928) and his successor, Bohuslav Martinů (1890–1959), whose works exhibit a classical sense of form. In his late works Janáček, known especially for operas such as *Věc Makropulos* ("The Makropulos Affair," 1924), developed a style in which modality and pentatonicism are blended with harmonies built on whole tones and fourths as well as on triads. He was influenced by his studies of Czechoslovakian and Moravian folk music, bird songs, and speech rhythms. This combination of influences led him to use small figures, repeated over and over in blocklike sections that were then juxtaposed and contrasted.

Janáček

Spain

The music of the Spanish composer Manuel de Falla (1876–1946) is especially close to the *flamenco* and *hondo* of the Andalusian region of Spain. He often uses the *polo* form, which alternates $\frac{3}{4}$ and $\frac{6}{8}$ meters. *El amor brujo: gitaneria* ("Love, the Magician," 1915) is a ballet inspired by gypsy folk songs. Other works that use the Andalusian style are *Noches en los jardines de España* ("Nights in the Gardens of Spain," 1915) for piano and orchestra, which also incorporates elements of French impressionism, and the ballet *El sombrero de tres picos* ("The Three-Cornered Hat," 1919). De Falla's late works employ national elements in a more stylized way.

De Falla

Ex. 32.3   Virgil Thomson, *The Mother of Us All*

Copyright 1947 by Associated Music Publishers, Inc., New York. Used by permission.

Latin America

Villa-Lobos

Two important Latin American nationalists whose works have gained international stature are the Brazilian Heitor Villa-Lobos (1887–1959) and the Mexican Carlos Chávez (1887–1979) (for further discussion, see Chapter 40). Although the Romanticist Villa-Lobos rarely quoted Brazilian folk music except in choral and piano works, his native music nonetheless influenced his style. This is seen especially in his melodies, which display a predilection for falling lines; his rhythms, which make much use of syncopations; and his use of percussion instruments native to Brazil. His best-known works include his nine *Bachianas Brasileiras,* written between 1930 and 1944.

Chávez

Chávez, too, uses the atmosphere of the Aztec Indian folk music rather than direct quotation, and incorporates native percussion instruments. Unlike the Romanticism of Villa-Lobos, however, he employs Neoclassical conciseness of ideas and clarity of texture. A salient characteristic is his use of clearly separated linear textures. In his later works, his melodies are predominantly diatonic and his rhythms have a continuous flow reminiscent of the Baroque era.

Other Nationalists

Bloch

Other nationalists are the Polish composer Karol Szymanowsky (1883–1937), who began to use Polish folk materials in the 1920s; the Greek composer Mikis Theodorakis (b. 1925); and the Swiss-born composer Ernest Bloch (1880–1959). Bloch sometimes used the cantillation and melismatic embellishments of Jewish melodies in his intense, richly scored works. The Jewish influence is especially evident in his works inspired by the Scriptures, which include *Schelomo* ["Solomon"]: *Hebraic Rhapsody for Cello and Orchestra* (1916), perhaps his most widely performed work. This composition uses repeated notes and the intervals of the perfect fourth and augmented fourth to produce melodic lines that somewhat resemble the call of the shofar (an ancient Jewish instrument made from a ram's horn) on the Jewish high holy days. The free rhythmic flow of his melody, similar to traditional chant, may be seen in the solo cello line that opens the work (Example 32.4).

Neoclassicism in Music

Definition

Neoclassicism in music is a twentieth-century movement that adapted features derived from the seventeenth and eighteenth centuries. The influence of J. S. Bach is seen in the new importance given to counterpoint and in the revival of Baroque forms. This return to the models and principles of the past is not unique to the twentieth century. What distinguishes this attempt from prior movements, however, is that it grew from a detailed knowledge of past styles, a result of the growth of historical musicology.

A reaction against the emotionalism of German Romanticism, Neoclassicism adheres, instead, to the Classical ideals of balance, objectivity, and non-

Ex. 32.4   Ernest Bloch, *Schelomo*

programmatic works. It is also a reaction against Impressionism, replacing the rich orchestral colors with precise lines stated by smaller, simpler instrumental combinations, resulting in economy of musical forces and clarity of texture. Additionally, it is a reaction against Richard Wagner's idea of musical progress.

The forerunners of Neoclassicism can be traced back to Johannes Brahms, **Forerunners** who included passacaglia forms, modal harmonies, and Baroque techniques of rhythm and phrase structure within what was then a new (nineteenth-century) language. German-Italian composer Ferruccio Busoni was influential in reviving interest in J. S. Bach. For instance, his *Fantasia contrappuntistica* ("Contrapuntal Fantasy"; four versions published between 1910 and 1912) includes fugues on subjects from Bach's *Art of the Fugue.* In a letter first published in Frankfurt (February 7, 1920),[1] he advocated a return to a new classicism and a departure from thematicism and subjectivity, putting these ideas into practice in his opera *Arlecchino oder die Fenster* ("Harlequin or the Windows," 1916) and in his late piano works.

Neoclassical elements are found in the works of Maurice Ravel, especially **Early** his *Le Tombeau de Couperin* ("The Tomb of Couperin," 1917); and these ele- **works** ments are also found in the Classical Symphony (1917) of Sergei Prokofiev (1891–1953). However, the dominating Neoclassical influence has been that of Stravinsky.

Stravinsky

Stravinsky's Neoclassical works grew out of his nationalistic compositions. Many musicologists believe that this phase, which ended with his opera *The Rake's Progress* (1951), can be considered to start with his post–World War I ballet *Pulcinella* (1919), based on music by Pergolesi. As in the earlier works, the driving rhythms remain the essential feature. Stravinsky overcomes the regularity imposed by the bar line by introducing irregular rhyth-

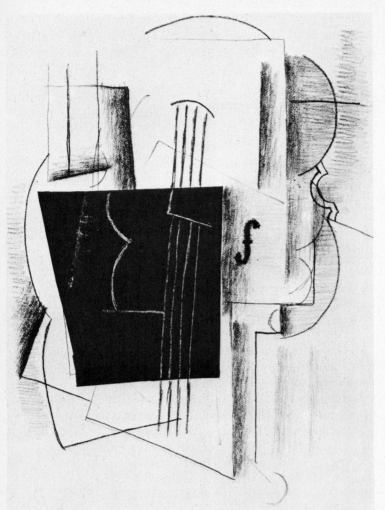

Georges Braque (1882–1963), *Still Life* (1913). (Philadelphia Museum of Art: Louise and Walter Arensberg Collection)

These two painters parallel facets of Stravinsky's style. Matisse's use of the representational within new concepts parallels Stravinsky's roots in tonality and his attempts to give new meaning to classicism, while Braque's Cubism parallels Stravinsky's juxtaposition of materials in place of traditional developments.

mic patterns. Different rhythms may be combined simultaneously, a technique known as *polyrhythm*. Finally, rhythmic motives are frequently shifted in position within a measure. This technique may be seen in an excerpt from *Scherzo à la Russe* ("Scherzo in the Russian Style," 1944), of which the first solo violin's line is shown in Example 32.5. Here the repeated five-note pattern on F-sharp first begins on beat 2, then on beat 1, and is next heard on beats 2 and then 4.

Stravinsky's music is tonal, even when it becomes serial. Especially characteristic is the conflict between major and minor thirds, either stated simultaneously or juxtaposed. Melodic ideas are usually brief, and are put into new contexts or used as ostinatos rather than traditionally developed. At times, different ideas advance on separate levels of musical space (often stated by different timbres), interrupting one another until a final synthesis is reached.

Henri Matisse (1869–1954), *The Music Lesson* (1922). (Baltimore Museum of Art: The Cone Collection, formed by Dr. Claribel Cone and Miss Etta Cone of Baltimore, Maryland)

Characteristic, too, is Stravinsky's striking use of color both in his careful spacing of chords and in the choice and use of instruments.

Stravinsky's *Symphony of Psalms* (1930) was written for chorus and for an orchestra lacking clarinets, violins, and violas. This work is Neoclassical in its affirmation of tonality, its use of major and minor triads, and its fugal second movement. The opening of the first movement strikingly contrasts a carefully spaced E-minor triad and a melodic line that outlines B-flat and G dominant-seventh chords. These linear chords establish a B–B-flat conflict. The chord and the line abruptly interrupt each other. The work abounds in metric shifts, and as the movement unfolds, ostinato patterns are established, contributing to a sense of rhythmic drive. The choral part sounds "medieval," as is appropriate to the Latin version of its biblical text. This archaic quality is created by the use of a chantlike vocal part, the Phrygian mode, and unique instrumental-vocal doublings. The movement ends on a G-major chord, in effect a cadence on the dominant, since the next movement is in C.

Symphony of Psalms

Ex. 32.5   Igor Stravinsky, *Scherzo à la Russe*

The second movement is a double fugue, with the first subject stated by the instruments and the second by the voices. The third movement, after the introduction, makes use of four basic motifs, simple in structure and distinctive in their rhythmic formation. These motifs are combined in many interesting juxtapositions. The final section of this work reveals Stravinsky's use of polyrhythm in its opening bars. The harp, pianos, and timpani have an ostinato pattern lasting four beats, while the choral parts conform to a three-beat time signature. The work ends on a C-major chord.

Hindemith

Of all the composers who changed styles in the late 1920s and early 1930s in an effort to bridge what they perceived to be an alarmingly wide gap between the public and the composer, perhaps the most influential has been Paul Hindemith (1895–1963). His Neoclassical style evolved from a Post-Romantic language that included dissonant harmony and counterpoint which sometimes obscured tonality. Hindemith's contrapuntal procedures (fugue, canon, passacaglia, and ostinato) show the influence of Bach. Other Neoclassical or Neo-Baroque elements include a clarity of form and texture, economy of means, and a firm tonal basis. Hindemith's music is also marked by the use of diatonic melodies, some chromaticism, modes, a prominence of perfect intervals (fourths and fifths), and rhythmical freedom that may incorporate polymeters or frequent metrical change.

Mathis der
Maler   Hindemith's mixture of elements from past styles can be seen in his opera *Mathis der Maler* ("Mathias the Painter," 1934), which combines medieval modality, folk songs, and elaborate counterpoint, all on a firm tonal basis. The opera's structural framework derives from Baroque and Classical vocal and instrumental forms.

Philosophy   Hindemith believed that music should be a medium of communication between composer and audience. He felt that the composer should consider the needs and capacities of the audience for whom he writes, the place where the music will be performed, and the technical capacity of the performers for whom the piece will be written.

These beliefs inspired the composition of *Gebrauchsmusik*—that is, "music for use" or "utility music," intended to satisfy the demand of a particular medium or occasion, as opposed to music composed for its own sake. Such music includes Hindemith's vocal and instrumental compositions for amateurs and schoolchildren, among them his *Schulwerk für Instrumental-Zusammenspiel* ("School Work for Instruments to Play Together," 1927). All these compositions were written in a simplified style designed to be attractive to performers. Many of Hindemith's later works may also be considered "useful" in that they were written for particular players or as additions to the repertoire of certain instruments for which there had been little prior literature.

Gebrauchsmusik

Hindemith's desire to replace what he considered the confusion of the twentieth-century tonal-harmonic practice with a more systematic method led him to develop a theory of tonality broader than the traditional one of the eighteenth and nineteenth centuries. His ideas were codified in *The Craft of Musical Composition* (1937–1939, first appearing in German as *Unterweisung im Tonsatz*). He became convinced that tonality is as inevitably a part of music as the law of gravity is of the physical world, and that ignoring tonality would lead to musical decline. His harmonic theory, especially influential in the 1930s and 1940s, begins with the overtone series. He derives the ordering of the twelve tones of the tempered scale in relation to a "progenitor" or central tone. He controls all harmonic materials by a system of root progressions, chord categories, and harmonic fluctuations between greater and lesser degrees of dissonance.

Theoretical system

Les Six

Les Six was the name given to six young French composers—Georges Auric (b. 1899), Louis Durey (1888–1979), Arthur Honegger (1892–1955, a Swiss national), Darius Milhaud (1892–1974), Francis Poulenc (1899–1963), and Germaine Tailleferre (b. 1892, currently living in the United States)—six friends somewhat arbitrarily grouped together by the French critic Henri Collet in 1920. Although not strictly Neoclassicists, they opposed impressionism and favored instead the simplicity, directness, and economy characteristic of Neoclassicism. The group, which had existed prior to its official designation, remained together for only a short time.

These composers, many of whose concepts were summarized by Jean Cocteau in his writings of that period, gradually developed some similar ideas. They viewed composition as an everyday affair rather than as a special event requiring the spark of inspiration. They admired music-hall music for its simplicity and lack of pretentiousness, and their own works were characterized by impertinence and an element of farce. Their individual compositional styles, however, varied greatly.

Satie

All of these characteristics may be found in the works of Erik Satie (1866–1925) who, along with Cocteau, was an important influence on *Les Six*. Satie's paradoxical music passed through several phases. Many of his earlier works, influenced by his Rosicrucian mysticism, have nonmetrical, Gregorian chant–like melodic lines and use harmonies that extend the concepts of Debussy by becoming tonally directionless. These attributes are most apparent in his *Messe des Pauvres* ("Mass of the Poor," 1894), for voices and piano or organ. His acquaintance with cafe music comes from the cafe concerts he gave during this period to earn a living. Throughout his life he produced mainly short works, including many for piano. Most of these piano pieces contain elements of parody in their whimsical titles, instructions, and program notes.

He became famous with the ballet *Parade* (1916), created for Diaghilev in collaboration with Cocteau, Massine, and Picasso. The work, which deals with the relationship of reality to illusion, is musically similar to cubist art in its juxtaposition of undeveloped materials. It incorporates rhythms from popular music, as seen in Example 32.6. Such melodies appear suddenly and disappear just as rapidly. The work also employs repetitive ostinatos, a technique utilized in *Socrate* (1918), a setting of fragments of three Platonic dialogues. Both Satie's musical outlook and this use of repetition (found even in some early works) has had a great influence on Cage and on the minimalist composers after World War II.

After *Les Six* Disbanded

Of the original six, Tailleferre shifted to a simpler style with Classical forms. Durey became a Communist and wrote many political compositions, while Auric turned to film music. Poulenc continued to compose a series of small, witty, elegant, melodious pieces, including many songs and piano works, as well as some large operas. Both Honegger and Milhaud developed individual styles with a tonal basis.

Ex. 32.6   Erik Satie, *Il-Petite Fille Americaine,* from *Parade,* reh. #23

Ex. 32.7   Francis Poulenc, *Chanson d'Orkenise*, from *Banalités*, mm. 13–16

Et les gar - des   de la vil - le   Cou-rant sus   au   va - nu - pieds:___

"And the guards of the city fell upon the barefoot tramps."

In Poulenc's works melody is the predominant factor. Harmony is simple   **Poulenc**
and diatonic, with triadic structures colored by added sixths or dissonances.
The texture is basically homophonic, and rhythms are simple and may include perpetual motion. These qualities may be seen in the excerpt, given in
Example 32.7, from *Chanson d'Orkenise* ("Orkenise Song"), from the song
cycle *Banalités* ("Banalities," 1940).

In his later years, Poulenc turned to opera. His three completed operatic
works are: *Les Mamelles de Tirésias* ("The Breasts of Tiresias," based on a play
by Guillaume Apollinaire, 1944), a comic opera that contains Spanish dances
and other popular elements; the religious *Dialogues des Carmélites* ("Dialogues
of the Carmelites," 1956); and *La Voix humaine* ("The Human Voice," based
on a play by Cocteau, 1958), a monodrama that incorporates a conversational
vocal style. *Dialogues des Carmélites,* based on a play by Georges Bernanos,
connects scenes within an act by orchestral interludes, and uses leitmotifs for
unity. It also contains chorale-like harmonizations and has quasi-melodic declamatory vocal lines.

Milhaud's music is written in a personal language, subjective and lyrical in   **Milhaud**
inspiration, yet maintaining a Classical sense of balance and clarity within his
preferred forms of sonata and fugue. His melodies are strongly characterized
in both shape and rhythm, and his works frequently show the influence of
Brazilian folk music. (Milhaud served as a cultural attaché in Brazil during
World War I.)

Milhaud is best known for his use of *polytonality* (two or more keys used   **Milhaud's**
at the same time). Although he did not invent the technique—it had been   **poly-**
used prior to World War I by several composers including the Italian Alfredo   **tonality**
Casella (1883–1947), the American Charles Ives (1874–1954), and Béla
Bartók—he is the composer who applied the technique most consistently.
His music reflects an awareness that the successful combination of different

keys depends on their separation in space, the timbre and intensity of the instruments to which they are assigned, and the character of the melodic lines involved. The brief excerpt given in Example 32.8 from *Le Boeuf sur le toit* ("The Steer on the Roof," 1919) uses Brazilian folk songs and Carnival tunes from Rio de Janeiro in different tonalities. Only simple tonic, dominant, and subdominant cadences are used on each tonal plane, but the composite effect is dissonant and original.

Honegger   Honegger's originality consists chiefly in using novel harmonies with his tonal-centered, goal-oriented works. His *Le Roi David* ("King David," 1921) has become a model for pieces in a popular choral style built on simple modal tonality, counterpoint, and small, easily understood forms. His harmonies, both diatonic and modal, consist of accumulations of thirds with added chromatic tones.

Other Neoclassicists

Roussel and Casella   Other important Neoclassicists were Albert Roussel (1869–1937), Alfredo Casella, and Grażyna Bacewicz. Both Roussel and Casella were committed to a new Classicism that they regarded as part of an evolutionary continuum. Many of Casella's mature works include a dissonant diatonicism in

Ex. 32.8   Darius Milhaud, *Le Boeuf sur le toit*

which contrapuntal lines move against each other at intervals of a second and a seventh without conventional resolution.

Bacewicz was one of Poland's few important Neoclassicists. Her work may be divided into four style periods, the first three of which are Neoclassical. In her first period (from her Wind Quintet of 1933 until 1945) she is concerned with Neoclassical forms. Her second period (1945–1954), which includes her Symphony No. 3 (1952) and her Violin Concerto No. 4 (1951), shows extensive use of Neoclassical counterpoint. Her third phase (1955–1960), which includes her Violin Concerto No. 6 (1957), is characterized by an interest in Neo-Baroque, used within an individualized style, coupled with a preference for dramatic themes, massive sounds, and extended formal developments. In some of the works of her last phase she merges Neoclassicism with the new Polish trends of sound and color experimentation. This may be seen in *Pensieri notturni* ("Nocturnal Thoughts," 1961) for chamber orchestra. After 1965 she abandoned Neoclassicism, creating instead in an independent style with works such as *In una parte* ("In One Part," 1967) for orchestra. **Bacewicz**

Many composers espoused Neoclassicism in the years between World War I and World War II. Some, such as Paul Hindemith, arrived at the style independently. Others followed the example of Igor Stravinsky, often influenced in this direction by the enthusiasm of the great French pedagogue Nadia Boulanger (1887–1979), herself a composer in her youth. These composers, most of whom later changed to more individualistic styles, include Boulanger's American student Elliott Carter (b. 1908), who is better known for his later works. His later compositions include rhythmic complexity and the technique of *metrical modulation* (changing tempos by setting up a cross-rhythm in the old tempo that becomes the basic beat in the new one). **Carter**

Although Neoclassicism faded after World War II, several recent developments have occurred that reveal similar aesthetic principles. One is the use of *collage* technique, in which works of many styles, including those of pre–twentieth-century composers and popular music, are juxtaposed. A prominent exponent of this technique is the American George Rochberg (b. 1918), who changed several years ago from serialism to this more accessible style. Another trend is the "new Classicism," a term coined by Gunther Schuller to indicate attempts (including his own) to find an accessible yet new style. **Collage**

Summary

Nationalism was a movement based upon folk traditions. The synthesis of these native traditions with Western thinking is perhaps best exemplified by the music of Bartók. His solutions, arrived at after many years of experimentation, drew upon Hungarian and other Eastern European folk musics for their unique rhythms and novel harmonies.

Neoclassicism was based on a reevaluation of the past. In reaction to the richness of nineteenth-century homophony, which appeared excessive to many twentieth-century musicians, Neoclassicists returned to Baroque counterpoint, clearer textures, and the idea of the composer as craftsman rather than "artist." Neoclassicism is most clearly identified with Stravinsky, whose music retained the strongly rhythmical character of his earliest works.

Note

1. Quoted in *The Essence of Music and Other Papers,* translated by Rosamond Ley (New York: Dover Publications, 1957), pp. 19–22.

Bibliography

Books and Articles

BERGER, ARTHUR. *Aaron Copland*. New York: Oxford University Press, 1953.

CHASE, GILBERT. *The Music of Spain*. 2nd rev. ed. New York: Dover Publications Inc., 1959.

EÖSZE, LASZLÖ. *Zoltán Kodály: His Life and Work,* trans. István Farkas and Gyula Gulyás. London: Collet's, 1962.

HELL, HENRI. *Francis Poulenc,* trans. Edward Lockspieser. New York: Grove Press Inc., 1959.

HOLLÄNDER, HANS. "The Music of Leoš Janáček: Its Origin in Folklore." *Musical Quarterly* 41 (April 1955): 171–176.

KEMP, IAN. *Hindemith*. London: Oxford University Press, 1967.

KENNEDY, MICHAEL. *The Works of Ralph Vaughan Williams*. London and New York: Oxford University Press, 1964.

LANG, PAUL HENRY, ed. *Stravinsky: A New Appraisal of His Work*. New York: W. W. Norton & Co., 1963.

LENDVAI, ERNÖ. *Béla Bartók: An Analysis of His Music*. London: Kahn & Averill, 1971.

MILHAUD, DARIUS. *Notes Without Music*. New York: Alfred A. Knopf, 1953.

MYERS, ROLLO. *Erik Satie*. New York: Dover Publications Inc., 1968.

PAYNE, ELSIE M. "Vaughan Williams and Folk Song." *Musical Review* 15 (May 1954): 103–126.

SKELTON, GEOFFREY. *Paul Hindemith*. London: Victor Gollancz Ltd., 1975.

STEVENS, HALSEY. *The Life and Music of Béla Bartók,* 2nd ed. New York: Oxford University Press, 1964.

STRAVINSKY, IGOR and CRAFT, ROBERT. *Conversations with Igor Stravinsky*. New York: Doubleday & Co., 1959.

TURUSKIN, RICHARD. "Russian Folk Melodies in *The Rite of Spring*." *Journal of the American Musicological Society* 33, no. 3 (Fall 1980): 501–543.

VAUGHAN WILLIAMS, RALPH. *National Music and Other Essays*. London: Oxford University Press, 1963.

WHITE, ERIC WALTER. *Stravinsky: The Composer and His Works*. 2nd ed. Berkeley: University of California Press, 1979.

WILKINS, NIGEL, ed. and trans. *The Collected Writings of Erik Satie*. London: Edition Eulenberg Ltd., forthcoming.

Scores

The works of Béla Bartók are published mainly by Universal Edition (Vienna and London) and Boosey & Hawkes (London and New York).

The works of Paul Hindemith are published mainly by B. Schott's Söhne (Mainz).

The works of Igor Stravinsky are published mainly by Boosey & Hawkes (London and New York).

33

Traditionalists, Eclectics, and the Art of Political Commitment

NOT all twentieth-century composers have been concerned with novelty; some have remained convinced that the heritage of the past has not yet worn itself out. A few carry on the Romantic tradition, while others have evolved a style that combines this tradition with later developments. The former have often been labeled traditionalists (or Neoromantics) and the latter eclectics, but the two categories sometimes overlap.

In the first twenty-five years of the twentieth century several new styles developed, and the rift between composers, and a public that preferred popular music, or Classical music from past centuries, became greater than ever. The extent of this gulf can be seen in the fact that even today, after more than three-quarters of this century has elapsed, a large number of works from the early part of the century remain problematical to many listeners.

Many of the composers discussed in previous chapters either ignored this problem or reacted to it by continuing to write for themselves and a select audience, often in the belief that their ideas would be proven valid sometime after their deaths. Most of the composers discussed in this chapter, however, whether coming from a belief in the traditions of the past, or out of a desire to contribute to society by influencing audience understanding of social problems through the medium of art, are united by their concern with music as communication.

Continuing Traditions

Instrumental Music: Symphonies

Despite the proclamations of many twentieth-century composers that the symphony is a dead form, the twentieth century has probably produced as many symphonies as have prior centuries. In addition to the many traditionalist and a few eclectic composers discussed in this chapter, several of the nationalists were symphonists, including the Polish composer Karol Szyman-

790

owski. Bartók wrote no symphonies, but his concertos were symphonic in scope. Many Neoclassicists, who purposely sought to utilize the forms of the past, also wrote symphonies. Among them are Paul Hindemith and Igor Stravinsky.

France and Its Influence

In France, the symphonic tradition was carried on in the 1920s by Arthur Honegger, Darius Milhaud, and Albert Roussel. Their works display characteristics common to many twentieth-century symphonies: fine craftsmanship, driving rhythms, dissonance, and unusual orchestration. Symphonies have also been created by other French composers such as Elsa Barraine (b. 1910), whose style is close to that of Roussel; Henri Dutilleux (b. 1916); and Charles Koechlin (1867–1950). These composers have influenced the symphonic style of many others, including the German-born Israeli composer Paul Ben-Haim (b. 1897).

Koechlin's works prior to 1947, when he became interested in serialism, are characterized by long melodies that span a large tessitura. Koechlin tends to begin his works with dronelike accompaniments, and seems to prefer widely spaced chords, many of which are built on fourths. He also uses freely imitative counterpoint, which often becomes elaborate and polytonal, and his dynamics fluctuate within a soft range. Many of his rhythms start from the patterns of the jig or the siciliano, but then add extra measures or beats. His large-scale works include the Seven Stars Symphony (1933) and *Hymne au soleil* ("Hymn to the Sun," also from 1933).

Charles Koechlin

American Symphonists

The United States has produced many symphonists who have created works in diverse styles. In addition to the composers discussed below, a partial listing includes Charles Ives, Aaron Copland, William Schuman (b. 1910), Howard Hanson (1896–1981), Vincent Persichetti (b. 1915), William Grant Still (1895–1978), and Roy Harris. All of the composers discussed below can be considered traditionalists, with the exception of Sessions, who, in the broad definition of the term, may be considered eclectic.

Walter Piston (1894–1976) was a Neoclassicist who used Baroque counterpoint and Classical developmental techniques. His tonal language incorporates dissonance, and his music displays rhythmic energy. Peter Mennin (b. 1923) writes tonal music that combines lyrical diatonic melodies with flexible and sometimes asymmetrical rhythms. His works are characterized by a flowing polyphonic texture within a strongly rhythmical framework.

Piston and Mennin

Samuel Barber (1910–1981)—better known for his operas *Vanessa* (1958; libretto by Gian-Carlo Menotti) and *Antony and Cleopatra* (1966; revised 1975), as well as his chamber music—has also written for orchestra. These orchestral works include Essay for Orchestra No. 1 (1937) and Essay for Orchestra No. 2 (1942). Barber is usually considered to be a Neo-Romantic. His music is basically tonal, but the degree to which tonal organization prevails varies from work to work. Formal counterpoint is prominent.

Barber

Bernstein   Although not primarily known as a symphonist, Leonard Bernstein (b. 1918) has written several symphonies. Bernstein's style, while traditional, is also eclectic in that it consolidates different trends, including occasional twelve-tone technique within tonality and the use of jazz. He uses syncopation and cross-rhythm. Symphony No. 1 (*Jeremiah*) (1944) includes traditional Jewish music, as does Symphony No. 3 (*Kaddish*) (1963), for female narrator, soprano, boys' chorus, chorus, and orchestra.

Sessions   Roger Sessions (b. 1896) employs various styles in his compositions. His Symphony No. 1 (1927), the first of eight symphonies, is quite diatonic and Neoclassic, while his No. 2 (1946) and No. 3 (1957) employ serial techniques. Throughout his works he uses dense, highly contrapuntal textures and long melodic lines. (See Chapter 40 for further discussion of these composers.)

Great Britain

Britain, too, has produced many twentieth-century symphonists. In addition to the nine symphonies of the nationalist Ralph Vaughan Williams, we find examples by Gustav Holst, Michael Tippett (b. 1905), Elizabeth Maconchy (b. 1907), and William Walton (b. 1902). Walton's style shows the influence of the Post-Romantic English composer Edward Elgar. His earlier works attempted to fuse the nineteenth-century symphonic poem with elements derived from earlier English traditions, such as Handelian dance music.

Scandinavia

Two of the greatest symphonists of Scandinavia were the Danish Carl
Nielsen   Nielsen (1865–1931) and the Finnish Jean Sibelius (1865–1957). Nielsen's symphonic works, which incorporate techniques of sixteenth-century counterpoint, have clear forms and logical developments in the Brahmsian tradition. Nielsen creates drama with conflicting tonalities that battle until one
Sibelius   emerges, often in simple, hymn-like triads. Sibelius's works display a unique symphonic style. Beginning with the second symphony, he evolves a method of organic growth that uses short fragments that are eventually brought together, in contrast to traditional symphonic practice in which ideas are first stated and then fragmented. His melodies are sometimes modal, an outgrowth of Finnish folk traditions, and often in a minor tonality. Triplets are a favored rhythmic figure.

The Soviet Union

Many Soviet composers have written symphonies, both because of the Russian tradition inherited from such nineteenth-century composers as Tchaikovsky and because the symphonic genre conforms to the "Socialist realist" philosophy of creating music accessible to large numbers of listeners. The works of Sergei Prokofiev and Dmitri Shostakovich will be treated in the discussion of Socialist realism at the end of this chapter.

Vocal Music: Opera

As the reader may have gathered from the operas mentioned and discussed in other chapters of this section, operas have been created in most of the styles of twentieth-century music. Important impressionist operas are Claude Debussy's *Pelléas et Mélisande* (1902), with a libretto by Maurice Maeterlinck, which breaks with its nineteenth-century predecessors to return to natural speech rhythms in its text settings, and Maurice Ravel's opera buffa *L'Heure espagnole* ("The Spanish Hour," 1907), based on a comedy by Franc-Nohain. In addition to the works discussed in Chapter 31, Schoenberg's monodrama *Erwartung* ("Expectation," Op. 17; 1909), with a libretto by Marie Pappenheim, is a further example of expressionism, while his *Moses und Aron* (first two acts 1932, third act unfinished), with a libretto by the composer, further illustrates operas incorporating serialism. Additional nationalist operas include Janáček's *Jenufa* (1903, revised 1906, 1911, 1916), with libretto by Gabrielá Preissova, and Gershwin's folk opera *Porgy and Bess* (1935), with a libretto by Du Bose Heyward; another influential Neoclassical opera is Stravinsky's comic opera *Mavra* (1922), with the original Russian libretto by Boris Kohno after a story by A. Pushkin. Post-Wagnerianism continued in the operas of Richard Strauss, several of which have become part of the operatic repertoire. Traditionalist operas were written by the American Douglas Moore (1893–1969), whose style established roots for the operas of the Americans Jack Beeson (b. 1921), Ezra Laderman (b. 1924), and Robert Ward (b. 1917). And eclecticism may be found in the works of the American composers Dominick Argento (b. 1927). Hugo Weisgall (b. 1922 in Czechoslovakia), and Thea Musgrave (b. 1928 in Scotland). Musgrave's *Voice of Ariadne* (1973), with a libretto by Amalia Elguera, for instance, displays aleatory elements and a harmonic language ranging from diatonicism to atonality.

Additionally, two traditionalist composers, the British Benjamin Britten (1913–1976) and the Italian-American Gian-Carlo Menotti (b. 1911), and two eclectic composers, the German Hans Werner Henze (b. 1926) and Alberto Ginastera of Argentina (b. 1916), have made substantial contributions to the field of opera. Some of their works are discussed below.

Britten

Britten's operas tend to have humanitarian subjects. The consistency of his lyrical vocal lines, as well as the texts themselves, serve to integrate the operas. Although the composer's musical language contains conservative diatonic elements, it is, nevertheless, fresh and individual within these limits. He uses basically familar material in novel and unexpected ways. His timbral and harmonic combinations, as well as his rhythms, are a highly inventive synthesis of early Stravinsky (rhythm), Mahler (orchestral lyricism), Berg (expressionism), and the English tradition.

Even when Britten eclectically uses more modern techniques, as in *The Turn of the Screw* (1954), an opera in the form of a twelve-note theme with **Musical style** variations (theme and variations are a favored form), he adapts them to his own, basically tonal, needs. *Arioso,* adapted to the English language, forms the core of his operas. His unique, expressive melodic lines have occasional wide leaps, especially those of a sixth or a seventh. Britten's chords are often triadic in nature, including triads with added notes and plain triads divorced from their traditional contexts. He is interested in a classical approach to opera, hence his forms are tightly constructed. Counterpoint is also used extensively; several of the operas, for instance, contain fugal passages. Some of these qualities can be seen in the excerpt given in Example 33.1 from one of Britten's many songs—the beginning of *Echo* from *The Poet's Echo* (1966), for high voice and piano, which sets poems by Pushkin translated by Peter Pears. Note the opening leap of a seventh, balanced by a descending scalar passage. The accompaniment contains chords built by thirds with an added note and uses imitation based on rhythmic variants of the vocal line.

Operas   Some of Britten's best-known operas are *Peter Grimes* (1945), with a libretto by Montagu Slater, after George Crabbe's poem "The Borough"; *Albert Herring* (1947), with a libretto by Eric Crozier, after a story by Guy de Maupassant; *Billy Budd* (1951, revised 1960), with a libretto by E. M. Forster and Eric Crozier, after Herman Melville's novel; and *A Midsummer Night's Dream* (1960), with a libretto by the composer and Peter Pears, after William Shakespeare's play. *Peter Grimes,* with its separate musical numbers joined by orchestral interludes, uses some recurring themes in a musical idiom suggestive of English folk song. *Albert Herring* shows a distinctive handling of varied types of recitative. It uses counterpoint, including several fugues, to build tension. In *Billy Budd,* the hatred of master-of-arms Claggert for Budd is represented by the use of bitonality, with two keys whose tonics are a semitone apart. *A Midsummer Night's Dream* is Britten's satire on nineteenth-century Romantic opera. It makes extensive use of ostinato, and contains an opera buffa in the third act within the framework of the larger work. All of these compositions illustrate Britten's skill at characterization through music and his ability to create the moods required by the dramatic action.

Menotti

Born in Italy, Gian-Carlo Menotti came to the United States at the age of seventeen and settled in this country. His operatic style may be considered traditional, although he employs atonality, dissonance, and other techniques to heighten dramatic effects. Menotti's operas have enjoyed widespread popularity, both with opera devotees and the general public. *Amahl and the Night Visitors* (1951) has long been a favorite television special during the Christmas season, and *The Medium* (1945), concerned with the world of spiritualists, enjoyed a highly successful Broadway run.

A strong religious sense runs through Menotti's operas, particularly evidenced by *The Saint of Bleecker Street* (1954) and one of his most recent works, *La Loca* (1979), based on the life of the unhappy sixteenth-century Spanish

Ex. 33.1   Benjamin Britten, *Echo,* from *The Poet's Echo*

figure Juana the Mad. In addition to writing his own librettos, which have been praised for their dramatic effect, Menotti has penned the texts for operas of other composers, including Samuel Barber's *A Hand of Bridge* (1959) and *Vanessa* (1957).

Henze

Henze's music synthesizes all the major styles of the twentieth-century. While many of his techniques are borrowed rather than invented, his works contain melodies, textures, and instrumental colors uniquely his own. Forms emerge naturally from ideas established in the first several measures of the work, and the kinds of texts he chooses vary as widely in dramatic style as does his music.

Henze's operas, especially those of the 1950s, combine Neoclassical and serial tendencies. This mixture can be observed in *Elegie für junge Liebhaber* ("Elegy for Young Lovers," 1961). Like Stravinsky's *The Rake's Progress,* this work is a "number" opera. At the same time, it is unified by row procedures. Characterization is obtained by using motifs derived from the row and by assigning special instrumental timbres to each of the six principal characters.

"Elegy for Young Lovers"

Henze's more recent works, mostly smaller-scale dramatic compositions with politically oriented texts, further compound the mixture of musical and dramatic elements typical of his style. Some sections are tonally clear and are notated traditionally, while others are completely aleatory.

Ginastera

Ginastera's music falls into several style categories. He changed from a nationalistic to a more "advanced" style in about 1960—a development that may be seen especially in his operas. In general, his compositions are characterized by traditional forms, dense orchestration, and strong rhythms, and sometimes incorporate microtonal elements. Some of his works use serial techniques, as in his opera *Bomarzo* (1967), which contains an eclectic mixture of large intervallic leaps, Sprechstimme, twelve-tone rows, microtones, and complex rhythms, as well as aleatory elements.

Vocal Music: Religious Works

Twentieth-century works with religious texts form a smaller percentage of the total number of compositions than in earlier eras. This trend is consistent with the increasing secularization of society. A few twentieth-century composers, such as the Russian-born American Lazar Weiner (b. 1897), write mainly religious works (that is, works specifically designed for liturgical use or works incorporating church or synagogue melodies, texts, or both). These composers tend to have a conservative musical style. Others, including some of the most prominent composers of our century, have expressed some degree of spiritual conviction in works written in their own musical language. Such compositions include Stravinsky's *Symphony of Psalms* (1930) and *Canticum sacrum ad honorem Sancti Marci nominis* ("Holy Song in Honor of the Holy Name of St. Mark," 1956); Anton Webern's *Fünf geistliche Lieder* ("Five Sacred Songs," Op. 15; 1923) and *Fünf canons, nach lateinischen Texten* ("Five Canons After Latin Texts," Op. 16; 1924); Krzystof Penderecki's *Stabat Mater* (1962) and *Passion According to St. Luke* (1965), and many of the works of Messiaen.

Political Commitment in the Arts

Throughout the ages, artists have attempted to express their political beliefs through their works. Mozart's *Marriage of Figaro,* for example, criticizes the behavior of the aristocracy, while the choral movement of Beethoven's Symphony No. 9 expresses the composer's belief in the brotherhood of man. In the twentieth century, events such as the Depression and the rise of fascism have been so overpowering that many artists have felt the need to react in the way they know best—through their art. One of the earliest examples of twentieth-century political music can be found in the work of the British composer Dame Ethel Mary Smyth (1858–1944). Best known as a composer of opera, she became a leader of the English women's suffrage movement prior to World War I. Her *March of the Women* (1911) became the battle song for the Women's Social and Political Union, the first and largest militant suf-

Smyth

Renato Guttuso (b. 1912), *The Mafia*. A post-World War II painting that uses a deliberately simplified style to express a Marxist message. (Collection of Nelson A. Rockefeller, photograph by Soichi Sunami)

frage group in England. Founded in 1903 by Emmaline Pankhurst and her daughters Christabel and Sylvia, it disbanded during World War I.

The Arbeiter-Sängerbund

After World War I, left-wing political movements realized the value of the arts in furthering their aims. In Germany, the *Arbeiter-Sängerbund* ("Workers Choral Society") attracted several composers, including Stefan Wolpe, who created several works for them in a popular style.

Brecht's Collaborators and Influence

Bertolt Brecht (1898–1956), founder of the politically motivated Epic Theater in the 1920s, collaborated directly with the German-born composers Kurt Weill (1900–1950), Hanns Eisler (1898–1962), Paul Hindemith, and, after World War II, Paul Dessau (1894–1979). Possibly as a result of Brecht's influence, Weill's music developed into a style characterized by simple and aggressive melodies and rhythms. This music became a model for left-wing music in Germany, and, somewhat ironically, influenced the American musical theater from the 1930s onward. Two of Weill's best-known operas on Brecht librettos are his *Aufstieg und Fall der Stadt Mahagonny* ("The Rise and Fall of the City of Mahagonny," 1927, extended 1930), and *Die Dreigroschenoper* ("The Threepenny Opera," 1928).

Weill's Threepenny Opera

Especially influential is Weill's *Threepenny Opera,* a work adapted by Brecht from John Gay's eighteenth-century ballad-opera, *The Beggar's Opera.* It deliberately rejects the complexities of modern music. Its message is that food for the poor must come before preaching. The work, which incorporates jazz elements, is Neoclassical in its use of an eighteenth-century libretto and a French overture. Scored for an ensemble resembling a dance band, it uses simple melodies accompanied by primitive tonal harmonies and basic dance rhythms. The vocal parts are deliberately designed to be easy enough for performance by actor/singers, but the music is unconventional in that it jumps from key to key instead of modulating.

Eisler

Like Weill, Hanns Eisler also changed styles and aims in the late 1920s. The musical development of this former pupil of Schoenberg became linked to his political beliefs. In 1930 he collaborated with Brecht on *Die Massnahme* ("The Measures Taken," a Brecht *Lehrstück,* or teaching piece). The setting is for mixed choir, usually in two parts, and an orchestra of brasses and percussion; the piano is used as a symbol of bourgeois culture.

Blitzstein

Another of Schoenberg's pupils (who had also studied with Nadia Boulanger), the American composer Marc Blitzstein (1905–1964), experienced a similar stylistic change. His Brecht-like opera *The Cradle Will Rock* (1937) shows the strong impression made on him by Weill's *Threepenny Opera.* Blitzstein's work, which deeply influenced the American musical stage, is a morality play written from a trade-unionist point of view. The scenes blend spoken dialogue and precisely notated rhythmic speech with songs containing vocal lines written in the style of American popular music but accompanied by fresh harmonies. Blitzstein's radio song-play *I've Got the Tune* (1937) was also pro-labor.

His early music, like that of many pupils of Boulanger, was influenced by French music of the 1920s and, especially, the music of Stravinsky. His style changed in the early 1930s, as he became politically oriented. The later works use diatonic melodies, dissonant harmonies that include polychords and polytonality, and, at times, some elements of jazz or popular music. (See also Chapter 40.)

Reactions to the Nazi Ascendancy

The rise to power of the Nazis had an enormous impact on the musical world. Many composers fled to the United States, thus influencing American music. These included Arnold Schoenberg, Paul Hindemith, Béla Bartók, Kurt Weill, Ernst Křenek, Stefan Wolpe, and Darius Milhaud. Numerous anti-Fascist works were created by British composers (England had become a leader in the production of left-wing vocal music during the 1930s). They were also created by émigré composers. One of the best-known examples of World War II–inspired music is Arnold Schoenberg's serial work, *A Survivor from Warsaw* (1947).

Several British anti-Fascist works were heard at the 1939 London "Festival of Music for the People," including compositions by Alan Bush (b. 1900), Lutyens, Vaughan Williams, and Britten. Britten has written many political and humanist works, including *The Ballad of Heroes* (1939), which commemorates the British members of the International Brigade killed while fighting in the Spanish Civil War.

British reactions

Also falling within this category is Sir Michael Tippett's oratorio *A Child of Our Time* (1941), which deals with war, oppression, persecution, and isolation through his dramatization of a true story of Nazi terror. This work substitutes Negro spirituals for Bach's Lutheran chorales, thus making symbolic use of the music of an oppressed people. As in other of Tippett's earlier works, the rhythm is syncopated (influenced by jazz), and much use is made of half-step motion within polyphonic lines.

Tippett's *A Child of Our Time*

After World War II

After World War II, many artists of political commitment dissociated themselves from the Weill-Eisler idea of writing didactic, simplified music to fill the needs of the working people and began, instead, to incorporate recently evolved compositional techniques. Some are seen, for example, in the activities of the Scratch Orchestra, a British group founded in the 1960s as an experimental orchestra for the common people. In the same vein, too, are several works of the American composer Frederic Rzewski (b. 1938), the Japanese born composer Yuji Takahashi (b. 1938), and the French-born American Christian Wolff (b. 1934).

The first movement of Wolff's *Accompaniments* (1972) for piano illustrates this new merger of political content and avant-garde techniques. The composer draws his text for the movement from Jan Myrdal's book *China: The Revolution Continued,*[1] which, as the title implies, deals with the progress

Wolff's *Accompaniments*

achieved by the People's Republic of China. The musical structure derives from the piano chords that accompany the text. The four-note chords are arranged in groups of sixteen, although not all of these chords are played during every performance. Each sequence of chords is based on one chord that generates the next fifteen by allowing each of the original four notes to be read either in the bass or treble clef. During the performance the pianist can choose either to use the entire text or to make selections from it, as long as the excerpts make sense.

Italy: Dallapiccola and Nono

Since 1945, composers like Luigi Dallapiccola and Luigi Nono have helped make Italy a leader in the field of politically oriented vocal works. Several of Dallapiccola's works center around the idea of liberty, including his serial opera *Il prigioniero* ("The Prisoner," 1948). Nono's works are more specifically political. His *Il canto sospeso* ("The Suspended Song," 1956) is based on the last letters of resistance fighters, while his *La fabbrica illuminata* ("The Lighted Factory," 1964) is a sound study of an imaginary factory of the future. In the former work, the composer experiments with vocal techniques, including the breaking of texts into syllables and even into phonemes to be sung separately. The latter work uses an electronic tape containing factory sounds and electronically processed choral singing, over which a live or recorded soprano protests the inhuman existence of industrialized labor.

France: Durey and Nigg

In France Louis Durey, one of *Les Six,* espoused communism. After seven years of artistic silence (1937–1944), he became the leading French musician of various Communist organizations. His postwar works, mainly unknown since most are unpublished, include his *Grève de la faim* ("Hunger Strike," 1950) and *Deux Poèmes d'Ho Chi-Minh* ("Two Poems of Ho Chi-Minh," 1951). Other French postwar works of political commitment include those of the twelve-tone composer Serge Nigg (b. 1924), including his oratorio *Le Fusillé inconnu* ("The Unknown Soldier," 1949) and his *Chant des mineurs* ("Song of the Miners," 1952).

Germany: Henze

Since about 1967, the works of Hans Werner Henze have reflected his commitment to socialism. These compositions consist of many smaller theater pieces and dramatic concert works, as well as the opera *We Come to the River* (1976), with libretto by Edward Bond, which has one hundred twenty-six characters and requires three separate orchestras in three separate locations.

Typical of the varied compositional techniques found in these works are those used in Henze's *Il difficile percorso verso la casa di Natascha Ungeheuer* ("The Tedious Way to the House of Natasha Ungeheuer," 1971), with text by Gastón Salvatore. The instrumentation is used symbolically. A "Classical" quintet, the same instrumental group used by Schoenberg in *Pierrot lunaire,* represents the old, diseased bourgeoisie; a brass quintet signifies music sounded by guards on a fortress; a jazz quartet with a Hammond organ symbolizes a false Utopia; a percussionist playing sounds made from the wreckage of an automobile represents the means by which humanity can finally take command of the technology of production which has controlled him;

and an electronic tape made from street noises and bits of older music stands for false, quasi-religious support.

Various performance techniques are used, with the procedures changing continuously. Sections in which all of the music is determined by the composer alternate with others in which rhythm and phrasing are left to the performers' improvisation. One section specifies the rhythmic and metric durations but leaves the pitch choices to the performers. In other parts, durations are indicated, but graphic symbols are used to suggest otherwise free improvisation.

Greece has long had a tradition of politically active artists; an outstanding contemporary exponent is composer Mikis Theodorakis. Although some of his earlier pieces use mathematical calculations, his post-1959 works turn to the Greek folk culture as a way of reaching his people. This stylistic simplification is similar to the path adopted by the politically committed composers of the 1930s. It is also linked, however, with the post–World War II emergence of nationalism in countries that had not yet undergone this phase of cultural renewal. **Greece: Theodorakis**

Theodorakis' music uses the traditional *bouzouki,* a pear-shaped instrument with three or four sets of double strings, and has incorporated Greek dances, such as the *rebeticos,* which is in $\frac{9}{8}$ meter, divided into the rhythmic pattern $2 + 2 + 2 + 2 + 1$. He also established the popular song cycle as a serious art form. Typical of his music is his *I Ballada Tis Romiosynis* ("The Ballad of Romiossini," 1965), with texts by the Greek poet Yannis Ritsos. The piece deals with the themes of courage, deprivation, bitterness, and hope in the story of Greek revolutionaries from the ninth century through World War II.

Socialist Realism in the Soviet Union

Immediately after the Russian Revolution of 1917, experimentation in all the arts was both encouraged and actively pursued. Gradually, however, the government realized that in order to build a new society of workers it needed the arts as an educational tool. The theater, for instance, could function as a lecture platform by presenting realistic rather than experimental plays. Thus by the early 1930s the idea of using the arts to serve the needs of the general public became formalized into the policy known as "Socialist realism." Specific guidelines were then issued for all the arts.

In music this doctrine was formulated in 1934. It encouraged a synthesis of the tradition of Tchaikovsky and Rimsky-Korsakov with a more modern, popular style. The favored genres were those that could convey concrete rather than abstract images. These included opera, songs, oratorio, cantata, and instrumental program music. Soviet opera, for instance, was expected to treat Socialist subjects, to use a realistic (i.e., easily accessible) musical language, and to describe the new, positive hero who represented the new, Socialist age. The influence of these requirements is seen in the works of Sergei Prokofiev (1891–1953), who returned to the Soviet Union in the 1930s after several years abroad, and Dmitri Shostakovich (1906–1975). Both were considered Formalists in relation to other Soviet composers such as Aram Khachaturian (1903–1978) and Dmitri Kabalevsky (b. 1904).

Prokofiev

Prokofiev's music grows out of the heritage of the "Russian five" and Tchaikovsky. Within a basically conservative style, he has created music with a unique blend of sarcasm and lyricism. The originality of his bold harmonies and driving rhythms was already pronounced in his early works. A certain similarity between his musical language and that of Shostakovich is evident in the use of ostinatos; motoric or toccata-like rhythms; some dissonance and polytonality; major-minor third conflicts; orchestration that places heavy emphasis on bass lines by doubling lower strings, lower brass or winds, piano, and harp; grand, festive build-ups to finales; and a clarity of form rooted in the Classical tradition.

In Prokofiev's music, folk influence can be seen in the diatonicism, modality, and contours of some of his melodies and his use of folk and dance rhythms. His harmonic style is unique in its sudden modulations to unrelated keys within a phrase, as in the opening of *Petia ee Volk* ("Peter and the Wolf," 1936), a work for narrator and orchestra. His works also contain unexpected shifts of tonality by half step. Tchaikovsky's influence can be seen in the doubling of strings at the octave and double octave.

Early compositions   Prokofiev's early compositions are modernistic, full of vitality, wit, irony, striking dissonances, and motoric rhythms. The piano, when present, is used in a new, percussive way. These qualities can be seen in his operas *Ngrok* ("The Gambler," Op. 24; 1916, revised 1927) and *Liubov'k trëm apel'sinam* ("The Love for Three Oranges," Op. 33; 1919). On his return to the Soviet Union in 1932 (after an absence of fourteen years) the scherzo-like element of his work, often stretched to the grotesque, became subordinate to his lyricism, as in his ballet *Romee ee Djulieta* ("Romeo and Juliet," Op. 64; 1936).

Classical Symphony   One of his most popular early works is his Classical Symphony, cast in four movements. The themes follow the Classical tradition with running scales, arpeggios, appoggiaturas, and other devices, yet contain the Prokofiev sense of irony, as in the second theme of the first movement. Later stylistic devices of ostinato and unexpected modulations are also present, as are angular lines and motoric rhythms.

Symphony No. 5   Perhaps his best-known symphony is Symphony No. 5, Op. 100 (1944). The first movement is in sonata-allegro form. As the first, somewhat more angular theme unfolds, the characteristic low bass doubling may be observed at rehearsal no. 3 (Kalmus pocket score edition), where bass clarinet, bassoon, contrabassoon, horn, tuba, cello, and double bass double the bass line. The second movement, a Scherzo and Trio, shows folk influence. The strong motoric rhythms characteristic of his style, seen throughout the movement, are established at the beginning of the scherzo with an ostinato-like pattern of a minor third in the first violin, which, by the third measure, begins characteristic half-step modulations. The scherzo theme itself, stated by the clarinet, is typically playful. On its return at the end of the scherzo, it appears in two variations, the first of which (rehearsal no. 32) shows the angularity of line used by Prokofiev in some of his melodies. The trio has a marchlike rhythm. (The incorporation of march movements is another characteristic of Prokofiev's style.) The return of the A section uses low-register trumpets, an orchestration device frequently found in Prokofiev.

The third movement can be considered as ABA with Coda. The opening and the last eight measures of the movement emphasize the typically Russian major-minor third contrasts found in many works. Within the A section there are many half-step key relationships. The movement opens in F major, for instance, and the next key signature (rehearsal no. 60) is E major. This change of key also illustrates Prokofiev's use of octave doublings in the strings; first and second violins and divisi cellos state the theme in four octaves. The basically diatonic theme is given interest by the contrasting use of narrow range in the first part and wide leaps in the second, and by the insertion of a $\frac{4}{4}$ measure within the predominant $\frac{3}{4}$ meter. The last movement, in sonata allegro form, quotes the first theme of the first movement in the introduction (change to $\frac{3}{2}$ meter at rehearsal no. 79). The theme that appears at the opening of the introduction is a clear illustration of the tonal ambiguity created by Prokofiev through modulations within the phrase. The fast tempo and strong motoric rhythms, especially prominent at the beginning of the exposition and in the coda, show folk influence. The long coda builds to a triumphant, typically Russian ending.

In an effort to fill the needs of various Soviet institutions, Prokofiev wrote operas, cantatas, and occasional pieces with political texts. His opera *Semyon Kotko,* Op. 81 (1939), with libretto by J. Katanyev and the composer, for instance, tells the story of a Ukranian soldier who has just returned from fighting for the revolution. In order to win his bride, he must stop her father's antirevolutionary acts. This work includes folklike Ukranian choruses. Probably his most outstanding work along these lines is his opera *War and Peace,* Op. 91 (1943, revised 1952), with a libretto by the composer and M. Mendelson-Prokofieva after the novel by Leo Tolstoy, a historic grand opera with thirteen scenes and a choral prologue. As in previous operas, themes recur as a unifying device. The work contains many expressive melodies.

Semyon Kotko

War and Peace

Shostakovich

Shostakovich firmly established his claim as a contemporary composer with his first symphony, written when he was only nineteen years old. There is both stylistic consistency and diversity through the large body of his works, which include fifteen symphonies, operas, ballets, and a large number of chamber compositions. His slow movements are intensely lyrical; long-flowing, often modal melodies are characteristically preferred, at times reminding one of Gustav Mahler. Stylistic extremes exist both within and among works, and a great contrast may be found between passages of extended lyricism and those that are grotesque, dissonant, and witty. In his earlier works this disparity is partially due to his use of parody techniques, as in his operas *Nos* ("The Nose," Op. 15; 1928), with a libretto by A. Price after Gogol, and the controversial *Katerina Izmailova,* Op. 29, originally known as *Ledi Makbet Mtsenskogo Uezda* ("Lady Macbeth of Mtsensk," 1932, revised 1962), with libretto by A. Price after a story by Leskov. Throughout his career Shostakovich used traditional forms, including the sonata, the fugue, and the passacaglia, but treated them imaginatively.

"Leningrad" Symphony

Many of his works are programmatic, as is often reflected in their form. In his Symphony No. 7 ("Leningrad"), Op. 60 (1941), for instance, which lasts for more than seventy minutes, the development section of the first movement is replaced by a new, marchlike theme that is repeated eleven times, with an increase in volume for each restatement. This theme is intended to represent the invading Nazis.

Later works

The composer's later symphonies, most of which are programmatic works on revolutionary subjects, often use a mosaic of themes, sectional structures, and orchestrations that exploit the highest and lowest registers of the instruments. In Symphony No. 14, Op. 135 (1970), as well as in a few chamber works such as Violin Sonata, Op. 134 (1967), and String Quartet No. 12, Op. 133 (1968), Shostakovich uses twelve-tone rows with their transpositions and mirror forms, albeit motivically and in a tonal context.

Summary

While new developments may be important in any branch of study, a musical approach concerned only with novelty may overlook many fine traditional compositions, as well as those that are eclectic and therefore not supported by any particular faction or ideology. This chapter has discussed such works, giving a general overview of contemporary developments within traditional genres, especially the opera and the symphony, and examining the styles of composers such as Henze and Ginastera, who have merged traditional and contemporary techniques into unique, personal styles. Also considered were composers who consciously chose to put aside the "avantgarde" style, in order to convey a political message (e.g., Weill) and those who combined their messages with more contemporary techniques.

Note

1. Translated by Paul B. Austin (New York: Pantheon Books, 1970).

Bibliography

Books and Articles

ABRAHAM, GERALD, ed. *The Music of Sibelius*. New York: W. W. Norton & Co., 1947.

BAKST, JAMES. *A History of Russian-Soviet Music*. New York: Dodd, Mead, & Co., 1966.

DALLAPICCOLA, LUIGI. "The Genesis of the *Canti di prigionia* and *Il prigioniero:* An Autobiographical Fragment." *Musical Quarterly* 39 (July 1953): 355–372.

GIANNARIS, GEORGE. *Mikos Theodorakis: Music and Social Change*. New York: Frederick A. Praeger, 1972.

HINES, ROBERT STEPHAN, ed. *The Orchestral Composer's Point of View: Essays on Twentieth Century Music by Those Who Wrote It,* introduction by William Schuman. Norman: University of Oklahoma Press, 1970.

MARTIN, GEORGE WHITNEY. *The Opera Companion to Twentieth Century Opera*. New York: Dodd, Mead, & Co., 1979.

NORTHOUSE, CAMERON. *Twentieth Century Opera in England and the United States: A Reference Guide* (ser. seventy). Boston: C. K. Hall, 1976.

POLYAKOVA, LYUDMILA. *Soviet Music,* trans. Olga Shartse. Moscow: Foreign Languages Publishing House.

ROUTH, FRANCIS. *Contemporary British Music: The Twenty-Five Years from 1945–1970*. London: Macdonald & Co., 1972.

SIMPSON, ROBERT WILFRED LEVICK. *Carl Nielsen, Symphonist, 1865–1931,* biographical appendix by Torben Meyer. London: J. M. Dent, 1952.

WHITE, ERIC WALTER. *Benjamin Britten: His Life and Operas*. Berkeley: University of California Press, 1970.

Scores

Most of the works of Benjamin Britten through Op. 69 were published by Boosey & Hawkes (London and New York). With Op. 70, Faber Music, Ltd. (London), became Britten's publisher.

The works of Hans Werner Henze are published by B. Schott's Söhne (Mainz).

The works of Sergei Prokofiev are available from Boosey & Hawkes (London and New York) or Mezhdunarodnayakniga (Soviet Music Export Agency, Moscow).

The works of Dmitri Shostakovich are available from Mezhdunarodnayakniga (Soviet Music Export Agency, Moscow).

34

Electronic and Computer Music

THE twentieth century is a machine-oriented era. Machines are used for the manufacture of goods, for the production of food, for transportation, and for communication, to cite but a few obvious examples. They have taken the place of men and animals, resulting in increased efficiency and hence a greater speed of labor. Not only have such developments had an enormous influence on everyday life, but an impact has also been felt in the arts.

In 1909 Futurism—one of the first artistic movements to recognize consciously and to incorporate directly the implications of the machine through painting, literature, and music—was started in Italy under the leadership of the poet Emilio Filippo Tommaso Marinetti. It included the Italian painters Giacomo Balla, Umberto Boccioni, Gino Severini, and Luigi Russolo (who was also a musician). In painting the Futurists found ways of portraying the movement and speed of a technological society. In music they created works consisting of noises, including howls, roars, and gurgles, for they viewed the sounds of factories, railways, and battleships—sounds others considered "unacceptable"—as a way of presenting the musical soul of the masses. This genre of composition with noises, termed *Bruitism,* invented by Russolo (1885–1947), is described in his manifesto *L'Arte dei Rumori* ("The Art of Noises," 1913).[1]

During the 1920s artists were intrigued by the sensation of the gleaming machine and the rational arrangement of its parts, a fascination shared by many composers. This interest is seen in such compositions as Arthur Honegger's *Pacific 231* (1924), a musical representation of a locomotive; and the American George Antheil's (1900–1959) *Ballet mécanique* ("Mechanical Ballet," 1924; revised 1953), which incorporated car horns, airplane propellers, saws, and anvils as part of its instrumentation.

In the 1920s there was also increased experimentation with machines that could produce music. At the same time, experiments were conducted at the Bauhaus in Weimar, Germany, where records were deliberately played backward, scratched to alter rhythms, and cut in their grooves to produce glissandi. Meanwhile, the Austrian composer Ernst Toch (1887–1964) and Paul

Fernand Léger (1881–1955), *The City* (1919), oil. Léger, who had been in close contact with workers, mechanics, and engineers during the war, created paintings that drew themes from modern industrialism. (Philadelphia Museum of Art: Louise and Walter Arensberg Collection)

Hindemith conducted related experiments in Berlin during the years 1929 and 1930. All these activities were further manifestations of an interest that grew, after World War II, into the fields of electronic and computer music.

Electronic Music

Mechanical and Philosophical Predecessors

The term *electronic music* refers to music that uses electroacoustical devices to produce, modify, and record sounds. This term does not specify either compositional style or technique. Electronic music, which uses mechanical equipment to produce sounds, has many forerunners, including such instruments as mechanical trumpets, organs, musical clocks, and glass harmonicas.

Mechanical precursors

These instruments, produced through the centuries beginning with the Middle Ages, gained great popularity during the Classical era. We should also consider as predecessors instruments like the *clavecin électronique* (electrical harpsichord), invented by the French pastor R. P. Delaborde (d.c. 1777), which, according to a description published in 1761, had bells electrically stimulated under the control of a keyboard; and the Electroharmonic piano invented by the American scientist Elisha Gray (1835–1901) in 1876.

In the early twentieth century, many instruments were invented to generate pitches electronically. The first was probably the Dynamophone of Thaddeus Cahill (1867–1934), also called the Telharmonium, which was demonstrated to Leopold Stokowski in 1906. The Dynamophone used a method of tone generation similar to that employed over thirty years later in the Hammond organ. A series of precisely scaled rotating gears induced proportionate changes in the electromagnetic fields varying the current used to produce individual tones. The Dynamophone was played as a keyboard instrument, and the music it produced was intended for transmission to homes via telephone wires. Other monophonic instruments began to appear in the 1920s and 1930s. These include the Trautonium (1930) of the German Friederich Trautwein (1888–1956), in which tones generated by a thyratron tube and controlled by a row of moveable tabs could be arranged to produce microtonal scales; the Theremin (c. 1920), invented by the Russian engineer Leon Theremin (b. 1896); and the *ondes Martenot* (1928) of the Frenchman Maurice Martenot (b. 1898).

Philo-sophical precursors

Years before the suitable equipment was invented, a few farsighted composers envisioned the possibility of electronic music and did whatever was possible to advance its development. Two of its most dedicated advocates were Ferruccio Busoni and his student Edgard Varèse.

Busoni

Busoni felt that the lack of freedom found in the music of his time was partially due to the limitations of existing instruments, which, with their equal-tempered scales, functioned in contradiction to the infinite gradations found in nature. Busoni foresaw that machines would be necessary to create newer, freer music, and correctly predicted that industry would play a role in the development of such machines.

Varèse

Varèse, a trained engineer, was very much influenced by Busoni. But Varèse's interest in electronic machines was closely related to his compositional ideas. The development of such machines would have enabled him to write the works he imagined—works containing planes of sound with complex rhythms that could only be approximated with conventional instruments. They would also have freed him from the tempered system he found paralyzing, and would have made available hitherto unsuspected possibilities of high and low ranges and new timbres.

Production

In electronically generated music, all aspects of the sound must be planned. To understand the process employed in the production of electronic music, therefore, it is necessary to have a basic comprehension of acoustics and psychoacoustics—that is, the physical and psychological attributes of sound.

Sound consists of vibrations in the air and travels in waves (periodic alternations in atmospheric pressure). Each musical sound, except for the electronically produced *sine* tone, is not one pitch but a blend of many. The basic tone is called the *fundamental,* and the higher tones are called the *overtones.*

Properties of sound

Each sound has a beginning, a middle, and an end, referred to respectively as the *attack, steady state,* and *decay,* and the entire shape of the sound—how it begins, how it ends, and its characteristics during the intervening time—is referred to as the *envelope.* The differing timbres of conventional instruments are partially due to the different envelope shapes created by them, as well as to the relative strengths or weaknesses of their overtones.

The production of electronic music involves three steps: the generation of materials, the transformation of materials, and the recording of the results. Sounds can be produced and recorded on magnetic tape one at a time or in variously determined patterns. The sounds originate either as electronically generated signals or as concrete materials (live sounds picked up by a microphone and recorded on tape). In the former case, the units that initiate the signals, referred to as the *signal generators,* are of two types. One is the *oscillator,* which produces wave forms, such as the sine wave, at various pitches. The other is the *white-noise generator,* which produces a band of sound consisting of all possible frequencies. This noise, resembling the sound of a jet of steam, is rarely used in its raw state.

Electronic sound production

Sound generators

In order to modify pitch, timbre, duration, or loudness and thus obtain more complex, interesting sounds, the sound can be processed in several ways. One category of electronic processing devices includes various types of *filters,* which can be used to suppress partially or eliminate selected overtones or pitches. A bank of filters in a device called a *vocoder* makes possible rapid and subtle changes in timbre. Very radical changes in timbre are produced by the use of *ring modulators* and *frequency shifters* (also referred to as *klangumwandlers*). A mechanical change of the original pitches can be obtained on tape recorders through *tape-speed variation;* timbre and dynamic quality are also affected. *Reverberation,* a way of simulating mechanically the natural echo quality of music performed in a room or concert hall, may also be added.

Sound-modifying devices

Sound-generating and sound-modifying electronic devices of the studio are normally connected through *patch cords*—wires that carry the signal between the generators and the processors. When the quality of the sound has been chosen and the patches are set, the sound is recorded on tape. Once a number of different sounds have been recorded, they are distributed among two or more tapes. Such tapes are likely to contain a number of precut sections spliced together. Blank tape can be inserted between recorded sections of tape, used either to construct rhythmic patterns from isolated recorded sounds or to bring into precise alignment the tapes being mixed through several tape recorders. The attack and decay of sounds may also be controlled by

Other electronic procedures

splicing, although this is more frequently accomplished with *envelope genera-tors* during the processing of the sound.

The various tapes are then mixed, usually by passing the taped material through a *mixing panel* in order to control the volume during the process. This process may occur once or several times until the composition is completed.

Synthe-sizers   A *synthesizer* is a unit that combines sound generators, modifiers, and mixers in one package. That is, with the exception of the tape recorders, it contains everything needed to produce electronic music. The synthesizer may either be used to produce one sound at a time, as described above, or it may be preset and then used to produce a series of sounds, employing a device called a *sequencer*. Many synthesizers have keyboards and can thus be "performed" live in concerts. The more popular models include the Buchla, the Moog, the Putney, and the Serge Modular.

Notational problems   Because electronic music is generally composed by means of experimentation with sounds on tape, it poses notational problems for the creator. Individual solutions to these problems range from extremely general indications, specifying mainly timings, to a precise score with all rhythms, pitches, and dynamics calculated.

History

Electronic music began almost simultaneously in three separate locations: France, Germany, and the United States. The possibility of using magnetic fluctuations for recording and reproducing had been discovered in 1898 by the Danish electrical engineer Valdemar Poulsen (1869–1942). The first magnetic tape recorder, the Magnetophone, which used a metal tape, was invented in 1935. The invention of plastic tape shortly after World War II, however, made the tape recorder a manageable tool and thus paved the way for a full-scale development of electronic music.

France: musique concrète   The first center was Paris, where the Musique Concrète group was established in 1948 by the French engineer Pierre Schaeffer (b. 1910). He chose the term *musique concrète* for his experiments in order to distinguish the physical presence of this music, which existed in permanent form—that is to say, its "concreteness"—from the momentary sounds produced by live instrumentalists. Schaeffer and his colleagues worked with recordings of actual sounds and noises, which they then modified by playing them backward, by cutting off attacks, resonances, or decays, or by changing the speed. Schaeffer's early experiments, which began as a revival of the Futurists' attempts to find applications for everyday noises, used phonograph records because plastic tape was not yet available. His work differed from similar German experiments of the 1920s in that it showed greater freedom in the selection of sounds and noises.

The RDF studio   In 1949 Schaeffer joined with the French composer Pierre Henry (b. 1927), and in 1951 they established the first studio especially designed for tape composition at the Radio-Diffusion Française (RDF) in Paris. Between 1951 and 1954, many well-known composers worked there, including Pierre Boulez, Olivier Messiaen, Karlheinz Stockhausen, Edgard Varèse, and Darius Milhaud.

The Cologne studio was started in 1951 at the West German national radio station by the Germans Werner Meyer-Eppler (1913–1960) and Robert Beyer (b. 1901), both experts in mathematics, acoustics, physics, and electronics, and the German composer Herbert Eimert (1897–1972). Many theoreticians and acousticians worked there, and the first composers to use the studio were also familiar with electronics and acoustics.

Germany

Perhaps the most famous member of the group is Karlheinz Stockhausen (b. 1928). In 1953 he produced (*Elektronische*) *Studie I*—"(Electronic) Study No. 1"—the first European work to use only sine tones (pure musical sounds without overtones) as the basic material of an entire composition. "Pure" electronic music, that is, music created by sound generators alone, as opposed to the French montages of manipulated natural sounds, became the new avenue explored by the German school. Stockhausen's most famous electronic work, however, is probably *Gesang der Jünglinge* ("Song of Youths," 1956). It combines sounds produced by skillfully manipulating a single boy's voice with a complex texture of electronically generated materials, and it uses the movement of sound to create form. Many of the words are used for their timbral properties.

Stock-hausen

The third pioneering group was formed in New York City by the American composers Vladimir Ussachevsky (b. 1911 in China of Russian parents) and Otto Luening (b. 1900). In 1951 Ussachevsky (without prior knowledge of parallel European experiments) began to experiment with a tape recorder purchased by Columbia University to record concerts. He discovered new sound possibilities by recording musical instruments, transforming the recorded sounds by tape-speed variation and electronic feedback, and creating patterns for use in tape compositions, then superimposing these sounds on tape. These experimental works were presented in concert in May 1952. This same year Luening (a former student of Busoni) became interested in Ussachevsky's experiments, and the two composers worked together to produce several works based on live instrumental sounds modified by simple portable electronic equipment. These pieces often mixed electronic sections with conventional live instruments, a technique illustrated in *Rhapsodic Variations* (1954), the first composition ever for tape recorder and orchestra. The home-based portable electronic equipment served as the nucleus of the Experimental Music Studio at Columbia.

U.S.A.: Luening and Ussachev-sky

In 1959 funding was finally secured to establish a permanent home for the electronic equipment—the Columbia-Princeton Electronic Music Center, directed jointly, at first, by Luening and Ussachevsky of Columbia University and Milton Babbitt and Roger Sessions of Princeton. Composers with long-term association with the studio have included the Americans Alice Shields (b. 1943), Pril Smiley (b. 1943), Bülent Arel (b. 1919 in Turkey), and Mario Davidovsky (b. 1934 in Argentina).

Columbia-Princeton Center

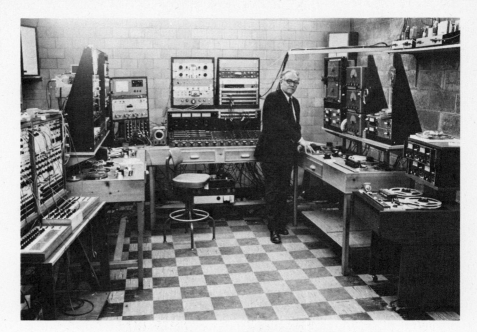

The Columbia–Princeton Electronic Music Center. These two photos compare a large, classical electronics studio (including a synthesizer on the extreme right) with a small (Buchla) synthesizer. The synthesizer alone can be used to create electronic works if tape recorders are added to the equipment shown. The composer pictured in these photos is Vladimir Ussachevsky, a founder of the Center. (Courtesy of the Columbia–Princeton Electronic Music Center)

As the three permanent centers discussed above were being established, John Cage was organizing the short-lived Project for Magnetic Tape in New York City (1951–1953) to produce his electronic works and those of his close associates: the Americans Morton Feldman, Earle Brown, and Christian Wolff. The first completed composition was Cage's *Imaginary Landscape No. 5* (1952). Like his instrumental works, the piece uses random, or chance, techniques, and in this case requires the taping of any forty-two phonograph records. The score, composed by chance operations based on the *I-Ching,* is a set of instructions for splicing together the recorded material.

Cage's music for Magnetic Tape project

Beginning in the mid-1950s, electronic studios began to appear in all parts of the world, including Poland, Japan, Holland, Sweden, and Italy. The Milan Studio of Musical Phonology of the Italian radio station was the home base of Luciano Berio and Bruno Maderna (its cofounders), Luigi Nono, and the Belgian composer Henry Pousseur (b. 1929), all of whom have used electronic techniques for dramatic or theatrical effects. Although the physical equipment of the 1950s was far less sophisticated than that in use today, many of the works produced then remain classics in the field of electronic music. These include Varèse's *Déserts* ("Deserts," 1954) for orchestra and tape, his *Poème électronique* ("Electronic Poem," 1958) for tape, and Ussachevsky's *Piece for Tape Recorder* (1956).

Diffusion of electronic music: the 1950s

A subfield of electronic music, called *live electronics,* began in the early 1960s. It involves the use of electronic equipment, including microphones, amplifiers, filters, and modulating devices, to produce or transform sounds from conventional or amplified instruments. Experiments in this field have been carried out mainly by composers of minimal music, including the Americans Pauline Oliveros (b. 1932), Steve Reich (b. 1936), Alvin Lucier (b. 1931), and Annea Lockwood (b. 1939 in New Zealand). Live electronic ensembles have been formed in Europe as well as in the United States. The development of such ideas has been encouraged by John Cage, whose *Cartridge Music* (1960), for amplified "small sounds" or amplified piano and cymbal, is the first substantive example of live electronics. Another important influence has been Karlheinz Stockhausen, who began touring with his live electronic ensemble in 1964. One of his many live electronic works is *Sternklang* ("Starsound," 1971), designed to be performed in a park.

Live electronics

The difference between electronic music produced in a studio and live electronics is that the former can be reworked until the composer is satisfied with the results while the latter exploits the variability and unpredictability of the moment. Live systems may involve special circuitry to interact with live instruments during performance, or the use of acoustical *feedback.* (Acoustical feedback occurs when sound levels of an amplified instrument/speaker system are so high that when the instrument is too close to the speaker, a continuous circuit is set up that feeds back on itself, producing a continuous roar.) Some composers perform live concerts on a synthesizer, adjusting the settings that control timbre, dynamics, and other variables during the performance.

Studio vs. live electronics

The compositions of the 1960s and beyond show that interest in studio-produced tape music has continued, and that the tape medium has been incorporated into the varied trends of the post–World War II era. Milton Babbitt's *Philomel* (1964), for soprano and tape, with a text by the poet John Hollander based on Ovid's origin of the nightingale, uses serial techniques for pitch, rhythm, dynamics, and tone color. Steve Reich's *Come Out* (1966) is an electronic example of minimalism. This work uses his much-copied "phase" technique, in which identical lines of music, text, or both gradually move apart in time until they obliterate the original phrase and thus produce new combinations. Vladimir Ussachevsky's *Colloquy* (1976) for orchestra and tape, a dialogue between the tape recorder and the orchestra, combines humor and a tonal lyricism. The American composer Jacob Druckman's (b. 1928) *Animus II* (1967), for mezzo-soprano, two percussionists, and tape, shows off the virtuosity of the performers in a theatrical work.

The electronic tape may exist alone, as in Alice Shield's *The Transformation of Ani* (1970), which gradually transforms a text from the Egyptian *Book of the Dead,* or in the American composer Morton Subotnick's (b. 1933) *Silver Apples of the Moon* (1967), the first electronic work commissioned for a record rather than a live performance. Or the prerecorded tape may form an adjunct to an instrumental work, as in Norwegian composer Arne Nordheim's (b. 1931) *Epitaffio* ("Epitaph," 1963), where the tape provides sounds for the orchestra to mimic; in Canadian composer R. Murray Schaffer's (b. 1933) opera *Toi Loving* ("Loving You," 1965) for singers, narrators, dancers, chamber orchestra, and band; or in Swedish composer Karl-Birger Blomdahl's (1916–1968) spaceship opera *Aniara* (1959) with libretto by Erik Lindegren after Harry Martinsson, which used tape to symbolize tension between the technological and spiritual realms. Often, however, the tape and the instrument(s) are given equal roles, as in Mario Davidovsky's *Synchronisms #1–8* (1963–1977). The tightly organized works in this series of pieces for solo instruments or instrumental groups and tape "synchronize" or merge the two contradictory media by common musical gestures.

While composers remain fascinated by the still unexplored possibilities of the electronic medium, interest has shifted from creating solo tape works, which give the composer complete control over the musical realization of his work, to instrumental-electronic mixtures. Recently, too, some composers have started using small computers to gain more precise control over the analog studio equipment.

The impact of electronic music has been widely felt. It has influenced almost all twentieth-century composers, even those who have never themselves worked in the medium. It has been used to create background music for television commercials and numerous short and feature-length films, such as *Apocalypse Now.* In secondary schools in the United States and elsewhere, the synthesizer has moved into the classroom, both to encourage creativity and to teach the basic elements of music. Many rock musicians have used electronic techniques, including the Beatles (who were influenced by Stockhausen) and the Mothers of Invention (influenced by Varèse).

The Computer and Music

Production and Mechanical Precursors

A computer can aid the composer in constructing a score or in generating actual sounds by following a set of instructions written in a mathematically based computer language. These instructions are referred to as a *program*. The idea of a stored program dates back to the mechanical musical instruments that used barrels or cylinders programmed by a series of appropriately placed pins or punched paper tape. One of the earliest examples is the carillon, which was brought to Europe from China during the Middle Ages. The first actual use of cards with holes punched for storing information comes from a non-musical activity–the mechanical weaving of cloth patterns that was begun around 1800.

Mechanical precursors

The idea of using a machine to write music dates back to the Baroque era. At that time, Baroque scholars speculated on the possibility of the dispensibility of man in the creation of music. In 1622 Athanasius Kircher wrote a treatise that included an outline of an apparatus called the "Arca Musarithmica," which could turn out compositions by a mathematical process. A more recent speculation occurred in the nineteenth century, when the English mathematician Charles Babbage (1792–1871) made the first attempt to develop a large mechanical computer. His "Analytical Machine," never completed, has both a stored program and a means of encoding information. His British colleague Lady Augusta Ada Lovlace (1815–1852) foresaw that such a machine might someday be used for writing music.

When the computer is used to help create a musical score, it is programmed with a set of rules that are stored in its memory banks. It may also be called upon to produce a set of random numbers, which, through programmed interpretation, can refer to pitch, rhythm, or any other parameter of music, accepting those numbers that conform to the stored set of rules and rejecting those that violate them. The numerical output can then be translated into conventional notation.

Musical composition

The computer may also be used to produce sounds, since the shape of any sound wave can be described as a series of numbers. This digital representation of the sound can be put through a digital-to-analog converter, which changes the numbers into analogous series of electrical oscillations, which in turn can activate a loudspeaker. The composer can use this process in connection with computer-aided compositional choices, or can predetermine the choice of pitch, rhythm, or other sound parameters and use the computer only as a source of unique timbres.

Many works of the last-named type use a computer program, such as Music V, designed by the American Max Mathews (b. 1926), which in some ways simulates the set-up of an electronic studio. Such programs generally have two parts: an "orchestra" consisting of "instruments" (timbres) designed by the composer, and a "score" of "notes" that tell the computer when and how to play the "instruments." The data are in numerical terms.

Most composition of computer music involves a time delay between the

"Real time" equipment

moment of programming, when the compositional instructions and relevant data are fed to the computer from a typewriter terminal, and the moment, after digital-to-analog conversion, when the tape is heard. There have been systems developed, however, that involve "performance" in "real time" (that is, sounds that can be heard as they are programmed).

Computer vs. electronic music

One advantage of computer music over electronic music is that all kinds of sound waves can be invented and used, rather than the few limited shapes produced by electronic oscillators. Thus the potential exists for producing a greater variety of sounds. Another point in its favor is that the computer has a precision of pitch and rhythm often missing from the electronic equipment. Additionally, the computer eliminates the tedious task of splicing together small bits of tape. And not to be overlooked is the fact that the change of a few instructions can create several different versions of the same composition. In its current stage of development, however, computer music also has its shortcomings. These include the necessity for precise, mathematical instructions; the need for yet more experimentation in order to construct interesting sounds by means of programming; the expense of renting computer time or of buying computers; and the usual time delay between conception and realization of a musical idea.

These problems, however, are gradually being solved. Graphic inputs to the computer have been and are still being developed; acoustical research into the nature of sound is continuing; and the development of micro-processors has brought the cost of a small computer into the price range of synthesizers and more conventional musical instruments. And at M.I.T., programs have been developed to allow composers to communicate with the computer in a musical language. With their specially developed "Score Editor," the composer puts in his information for the computer on an organ-like keyboard. He can thus create a large, complex score, then rewrite and modify his results.

History

Some of the earliest studies in computer music were conducted at the University of Illinois. There, beginning in 1955, the Americans Lejaren A. Hiller (b. 1924) and Leonard M. Isaacson (b. 1925) conducted a series of experiments using the computer to compose scores based both on conventional rules of music theory and on mathematical probability distributions. Together, they created Illiac Suite for String Quartet, published in 1957.

University of Illinois

In 1958 Hiller established the Experimental Music Studio at the University of Illinois to carry on a program of research, composition, and teaching in the areas of computer music, electronic tape music, and acoustics. Several other schools, such as Stanford University in California, the University of California at San Diego, M.I.T. in Boston, and Colgate University in Hamilton, N.Y., have developed studios in computer music. Their faculty members continue to create works involving new methods of synthesis of sounds.

Bell Telephone

At the Bell Telephone Laboratories in New Jersey, Max Mathews, the American J. R. Pierce (b. 1910), and their associates began generating music by computer in 1958. Such research had been supported by the Bell Laboratories for decades, growing out of attempts to analyze the electrical quality of speech and hearing in order to improve articulation over the telephone lines. The program developed by Mathews for generating sound was expanded at Princeton University by the Englishman Godfrey Winham (1934–1975) and the American Hubert S. Howe, Jr. (b. 1942), while the experiments in synthetic speech were taken up by Charles Dodge (b. 1942), who has explored these techniques in several works, including *The Story of Our Lives* (1974).

In Europe, much innovative work was done by the Paris-based Iannis Xenakis, who also spent several years working concurrently at the University of Indiana in the United States. Xenakis originally turned to the computer in 1960 as a way of rapidly calculating the mathematical formulas needed for his instrumental compositions, a usage continued in works such as *N'shima* ("Breath," 1975). However, he soon also became interested in the problem of using the computer to generate unique sounds.

Xenakis

At the same time as Xenakis began his computer experiments, French composer Pierre Barbaud (b. 1911 in Algeria), in collaboration with Roger Blanchard, began systematic investigation of the use of the computer in aleatory music. A well-known film composer, Barbaud has used his results in his commercial work. The early and mid-1960s were also a time of computer experiments in other European countries. In Holland, the German composer Gottfried Michael Koenig (b. 1926), who had worked with Stockhausen and others at Cologne (1954–1964) before becoming director of the Utrecht University studio, wrote a program to use the computer in composing works. He later established computer music sound synthesis at his studio. Other early experiments were carried out in Stockholm, Sweden, in 1963 by the Norwegian Knut Wiggen (b. 1927), while still other composers were active in computer music in England, Germany, and other countries.

Other European experiments

An important new center for computer research was established in Paris, France, in the 1970s. In 1971, at the request of then-President Georges Pompidou, Pierre Boulez agreed to establish IRCAM (Institute de Recherche de Coordination Acoustique-Musique [Institute of Research and Coordination for Acoustics and Music]). Shortly thereafter, Boulez chose a team consisting of the composers Luciano Berio, the American Gerald Bennett (b. 1942), and the French Vinko Globokar (b. 1934), Jean-Claude Risset (b. 1938), and Michel Decoust (b. 1936), to establish goals for this large-scale, government-sponsored project. The actual building, however, was not completed until 1978.

IRCAM

The purpose of IRCAM is to bring together scientists and musicians for interdisciplinary work. Research is being carried out in computers, electroacoustics, and the properties of instruments and the human voice. This has led, for instance, to the development of a machine that can synthesize sound in real time and can be used both for music composition and as a musical instrument in concert; new methods of music and speech synthesis; and the simulation of acoustical spaces on the computer (thus making synthesized sound seem closer to that of a live performance). Some of the research undertaken has been in cooperation with the personnel of Stanford University (U.S.). Additionally, compositions have been realized, including Jean-Claude Risset's *Mirages* (1978) for sixteen instruments and electronic tape.

The computer and other branches of music

In addition to its usefulness in music composition, the computer has shown potential as an analytical tool for music theorists, musicologists, and ethnomusicologists. Because the computer can calculate, sort, and compare data one hundred million times faster than human beings, it is invaluable for processing data and testing hypotheses. This phenomenon was demonstrated as early as 1949, when the American Bertrand H. Bronson (b. 1902) used the computer in a comparative study of British and American folk songs. The use of the computer to analyze and then to synthesize folk materials has had wide application in Eastern Europe, with the earliest such experiment conducted in the U.S.S.R. by Rudolf Khafizovich Zaripov. The computer may also aid in the publication of music, since it can be programmed both to print scores, using a computer-controlled plotter, and to extract the parts, transposing whenever necessary. One such system has been worked out at Stanford University by the American composer Leland C. Smith (b. 1925). A different system, which closely approximates an engraved score, was developed by another American composer, Mark Zuckerman (b. 1948) of Columbia University.

Summary

Electronic music and computer music, both of which developed after World War II, when war research had led to the invention of the necessary equipment, are expressions of a machine-oriented society. They are logical outgrowths of twentieth-century artistic trends.

Both trends reflect increased sensitivity to timbre, which, in turn, has encouraged the development of new musical resources. This progress has led to the adoption, for musical purposes, of equipment originally designed for nonmusical uses. In the process, many engineers have turned to composition, and many composers have acquired some knowledge of science and mathematics. Thus a new hybrid has appeared: the composer/scientist.

Note

1. Included in Nicholas Slonimsky's *Music Since 1900*. 4th ed. New York: Scribner's, 1971.

Bibliography

Electronic Music

Books and Articles

Note: Some of the books listed below also contain information on computer music.

APPLETON, JON H., and PERERA, RONALD C., eds. *The Development and Practice of Electronic Music.* Englewood Cliffs, N.J.: Prentice-Hall, 1975.

EIMERT, HERBERT, and STOCKHAUSEN, KARLHEINZ, eds. *Die Reihe 1* ("Electronic Music"). Bryn Mawr: Theodore Presser Co., German edition 1955, English edition 1958.

ERNST, DAVID. *The Evolution of Electronic Music.* New York: Schirmer Books, 1977.

GRIFFITHS, PAUL. *A Guide to Electronic Music.* London: Thames and Hudson, 1979.

HOWE, HUBERT S., JR. *Electronic Music Synthesis: Concepts, Facilities, Techniques.* New York: W. W. Norton & Co., 1975.

KEANE, DAVID. *Tape Music Composition.* London: Oxford University Press, 1980.

KONDRACKI, MIROSLAW, STANKIEWICZ, MARTA, and WEILAND, FRITZ C. *International Electronic Music Discography.* Mainz: B. Schott's Söhne, 1979.

RUSSCOL, HERBERT. *The Liberation of Sound.* Englewood Cliffs, N.J.: Prentice-Hall, 1972.

USSACHEVSKY, VLADIMIR. "Notes on a Piece for Tape Recorder." *Musical Quarterly* 46, no. 2 (1960): 202–209. Also in Lang, Paul Henry, ed., *Problems of Modern Music.* New York: W. W. Norton & Co., 1962.

———. "The Processes of Experimental Music." *Journal of the Audio Engineering Society* 6, no. 3 (July 1958):202–208.

WELLS, THOMAS. *The Technique of Electronic Music.* New York: Schirmer Books, 1981.

Periodicals

Electronic Music Review 1–7. Trumansburg, N.Y.: Jan. 1967–July 1968.

Computer Music

Books and Articles

CHOWNING, JOHN. "The Stanford Music Project." *Numus West* 1: 12–14.

KOSTKA, STEFAN M. *A Bibliography of Computer Applications in Music.* Clifton, N.J.: European-American Music, 1974.

LINCOLN, HARRY B., ed. *The Computer and Music.* Ithaca, N.Y.: Cornell University Press, 1970.

MATHEWS, MAX V. *The Technology of Computer Music.* Cambridge, Mass.: M.I.T. Press, 1969.

REICHARDT, JASIA. *Cybernetic Serendipity: The Computer and the Arts.* New York: Frederick A. Praeger, 1968.

VON FOERSTER, HEINZ, and BEAUCHAMP, JAMES W., eds. *Music by Computers.* New York: John Wiley & Sons, 1969.

Periodicals

Computer Music Journal. Menlo Park, Calif.: Feb. 1977–present.

35

Non-Western Influences and New Principles of Form

THE twentieth century has seen a renewed interest in non-Western music and philosophy, and many of the composers discussed in this chapter have turned to the East in an attempt to develop a new musical language. Some, such as the microtonal composers, have adopted non-Western scales. Others, such as the chance composers and the minimalists, have been influenced by Eastern philosophy.

Many of the works discussed in this chapter challenge the idea of form arising from the demands of the musical materials and attempt, instead, to involve the performer, the audience, or both in the compositional decision-making process, or at least in the perception of the results. Even in totally planned multimedia events, for example, the audience can shift its focus from one simultaneous event to another. Quite often a new notation, graphic or, at times, verbal, is necessary for these works. Such compositions are often created by composers who wish to return to the anonymity of ancient times, either by removing their personalities from their creations or by becoming part of a group. This approach, which originated in the United States and spread to Europe, gained recognition for the innovative potential of America's artists.

Microtonal Experiments

Microtones are intervals smaller than a semitone, the smallest division of the tempered scale. Intervals smaller than a semitone have long been used in the music of many parts of the world. For centuries they have been a feature of traditional Asian music—in India, for example, where the interval of a *śrutis,* by means of which the octave is divided into twenty-two microtonal parts, was described in theoretical writings dating to approximately 200 B.C.

Historical Background
In Western tradition, the use of microtones dates back to ancient Greek music that used an enharmonic tetrachord in which two of the four tones

820

were microtonally altered. In about the fifth century, Martianus Capella mentioned third-tones and quarter-tones in his treatise *De nuptiis Mercurii et Philopiae* ("Of the Marriage of Lyricism and the Love of Learning"). Several of the decorative neumes of Gregorian chant probably used quarter-tones, and quarter-tones were used in the eleventh-century Gradual of Montpellier.

In the late Renaissance, harpsichords were built that tried to recreate the Greek modes. These included the Arcicembalo (c. 1550), a harpsichord with thirty-one microtones to the octave, invented by the Italian composer and theorist Don Nicola Vicentino (1511–1572) and built by Vicenzo Colombo, and one built by the Italian Vito Trasuntinis (fl. 1560–1606) in 1606. Additionally, the Italian Domenico Pesarese built, in 1548, a harpsichord with nineteen divisions to the octave to the specifications of the Italian theorist Gioseffa Zarlino.

At the end of the seventeenth century the Dutch mathematician, physicist, and astronomer Christian Huygens (1629–1695) proposed dividing the octave into thirty-one parts, a system revived in the twentieth century by the Indonesian-born Dutch physicist Adriaan Fokker (1887–1972), and used by several Dutch composers, including the Indonesian-born Henk Badings (b. 1907). During the eighteenth and nineteenth centuries, however, microtonal experiments were generally abandoned.

The Twentieth Century

In 1895 the Mexican composer Julián Carrillo (1875–1965) began to experiment with microtones, and in 1903 he wrote his Quartet in E-flat, the first of his works to incorporate microtonal elements. He also devised a microtonal theoretical method that he called *Sonido trece* ("The Thirteenth Sound," published in 1948 after over fifty years of formulation). In most of his compositions after 1922 he used third-tones, quarter-tones, eighth-tones, and sixteenth-tones.

Carrillo

Between 1903 and 1914 Charles Ives wrote a quarter-tone Chorale for strings that later became the third piece of Three (Quarter-Tone) Pieces for Two Pianos (c. 1914). In these works Ives used quarter-tone harmonies both to support the melody and to generate it. (For more on Carrillo and Ives, see Chapter 40.)

Ives

In 1907 Ferruccio Busoni published his *Entwurf einer neuen Aesthetik der Tonkunst* ("Sketch for a New Aesthetic of Music"), in which he discussed a possible expansion of the system of semitones to a 36-note scale by combining two 18-step third-tone scales.

Busoni

Beginning in 1918 the Russian-born composer Ivan Wyshnegradsky (1893–1979), who moved to Paris in 1920, wrote several quarter-tone pieces. Even more prolific was the Czechoslovakian composer Alois Hába (1893–1972). Starting in approximately 1919 he wrote a series of works for quarter-tones and sixth-tones and even used twelfth-tones, dividing the octave into seventy-two steps. In 1923 he established a class in quarter-tone composition at the Prague Conservatory.

Wyshne-gradsky and Hába

In the United States Harry Partch (1901–1974) devoted his life to micro-

Partch

tonal composition. His musical language is based on a division of the octave into forty-three parts and requires specially constructed instruments of fixed pitch.

Microtones as coloration

Microtones have gradually become part of the sound resources available to every twentieth-century composer. They are used by many composers as additional coloring rather than as part of an overall theoretical system, especially in electronic music, where the equipment makes such pitches readily available. A few of the many works for traditional instruments incorporating microtones are Ernest Bloch's Quintet for Strings and Pianoforte (1923), Béla Bartók's Sixth String Quartet, and the String Quartet No. 2 (1964) of American composer Ben Johnston (b. 1926).

Microtonal instruments

Since standard keyboard instruments were unable to play microtonal compositions, new instruments had to be developed. In 1892 the German G. A. Behrens-Senegaldens patented the first quarter-tone piano. In 1924 the Czechoslovakian firm of August Foerster designed and built a grand piano with two manuals, the second of which was a quarter-tone higher than the first, and the German-born composer Hans Barth (1897–1956) built a similar instrument in the United States in 1928. Some composers have designed and built their own instruments. Julián Carrillo, for instance, manufactured special pianos tuned to the intervals required by his works, and a harp-zither with strings for ninety-six divisions within the octave. An even larger collection of instruments was designed and constructed by Partch. More recently, the American composer Lucia Dlugoszewski (b. 1931) has devised over one hundred percussion instruments for her compositions.

Multimedia Works

Multimedia compositions are those that combine two or more art forms. Such works may be the result of an artistic desire to express or control all aspects of human sensation within a performance situation. Historically, they can be viewed as an extension of composite art forms such as ballet and opera. A more immediate stimulus, however, may have been the need to provide a visual activity to accompany electronic music, which in its pure form lacks the presence of live performers.

Musical precursors

The multimedia movement of the mid-twentieth century that began after World War II was anticipated by Scriabin in his late work *Prometheus, The Poem of Fire* (1911). The Russian mystic called for the projection of colored lights, which he listed in a table that pairs them with specific chords. He also planned, but never completed, a work to be entitled *Mysterium,* a mass dance of ecstasy with audience participation, combining light, color, scents, and physical contact. Working independently of Scriabin, Kandinsky and Schoenberg created effects similar to those of *The Poem of Fire* in Schoenberg's dramatic work *Die glückliche Hand* ("The Lucky Hand" or "The Hand of Fate," 1913).

Some multimedia events are completely planned, while others result from choices made during the performance itself. An example of the former is *Poème électronique* ("Electronic Poem," 1958) by Edgard Varèse. Written for performance at the Phillips Pavillion of the Brussels World's Fair in a building especially designed for it by the architect-composer Iannis Xenakis under the overall direction of Le Corbusier, the work was a unique union of architecture and music. The music was played from several hundred speakers inserted within the walls and ceiling so as to surround the audience, while slides were projected. **Varèse's *Poème électronique***

The *Happening* is a multimedia event carried out partially or entirely in a random way. The first Happening occurred at Black Mountain College in North Carolina in the summer of 1952. Composer John Cage and some of his friends—American pianist/composer David Tudor (b. 1926), painter Robert Rauschenberg (b. 1925), and dancer/choreographer Merce Cunningham (b. c. 1922)—jointly played records, read lectures from stepladders, danced, used projections, and displayed "white" paintings (paintings in which the painted white surface has been compartmentalized by scratched lines, often outlining inscriptions or numbers). The materials used—the lectures, projections, paintings, and records—were preestablished, while the sequence of events was random. **Happenings**

The concept of multimedia influenced some composers to create "theatrical" works, nonoperatic compositions that require acting or other movements on the part of the performers. Examples of this trend may be found in works by Luciano Berio and Thea Musgrave, both of whom have resided in the United States. In Berio's *Circles* (1960) for voice and percussionists, and Musgrave's Horn Concerto (1971), the movements of the performers are part of the effect of the piece. In the last section of the Musgrave work, for example, the orchestral horn players are scattered around the hall to surround the soloist. **"Theatrical" works**

Berio and Musgrave

A later work by Berio exhibiting theatricality is his *Sinfonia* (1968) for orchestra, organ, harpsichord, piano, chorus, and reciters. It is a four-movement work, the second movement a tribute to Martin Luther King. Like *Circles,* the *Sinfonia* uses the structure and sound of the language of its texts, and voices and instruments interchange roles. The work incorporates scat singing and many musical quotations, both from other composers and from Berio himself. The third movement has a background based on the third movement of Mahler's Second Symphony, but with references to many other composers, over which are parts of a Samuel Beckett play and student slogans from then-current political confrontations. In general this work, with its texts derived from many sources, is a commentary on the politically turbulent late 1960s. **Berio's *Sinfonia***

Improvisation

Improvisation, the spontaneous creation of a composition or an unrehearsed modification of the same by one or more performers, differs from *controlled chance,* to be discussed shortly, in that it requires interaction among performers. Improvisation challenges traditional musical directions more by reason of the absence of precise notation than by its philosophy.

This technique dates back to Gregorian chant, in which certain details were improvised. It was an essential part of Baroque music, which depended on the player of the chordal instrument to realize spontaneously the figured bass, as well as Classical music, where it was used to create cadenzas for concertos. Even in the twentieth century, it has always been an integral part of jazz.

Foss's ensemble

In the late 1950s, and early 1960s, a number of groups dedicated to improvisation were created. The first of these was probably the Improvisation Chamber Ensemble at the University of California at Los Angeles, established in 1957 by Lukas Foss. The group worked from charts that showed only the initial ideas—such as motif, rhythm, and pattern—needed to create a work. They rehearsed until a polished group composition resulted. Participation in these experiments helped to free Foss from his previous Neoclassical style. Although most of Foss's later compositions use controlled chance rather than improvisation, one work that does use the latter is his Four Etudes for Organ (published in 1968).

Other improvisation groups

Foss disbanded his group because he felt that the results of improvisation were too predictable. Performers tended to rely on known finger patterns rather than their improvisatory gifts. Other improvisation groups formed during the 1960s, including the Michigan "Once" group, QUAX (Prague), the AMM (London), the Italian-American Musica Elettronica Viva (MEV, Rome), the University of Illinois Chamber Players, and the MW 2 Ensemble (Poland). As in the case of multimedia, these group experiments also influenced individual composers. One instance of this, an excerpt of which is shown in Example 35.1, is Trio for Flute, Percussion, and String Bass (1963) by Pauline Oliveros.

Indeterminacy

The interchangeable terms *indeterminate, chance,* and *aleatory* are used to describe music that relies on the elements of randomness in its compositional procedures, performance, or both. Such works are part of a general movement in science, philosophy, and the arts that sees the world in terms of possibility rather than necessity.

The aim of chance music is to free sounds from the composer's control and thus to eliminate his ego. This concept is related to oriental philosophy, especially to Zen Buddhism, and constitutes rejection of the past several centuries of Western musical tradition.

In such works, the sounds are to be enjoyed for their own sake; all sound and nonsound events are of equal importance. The music is directionless, with no concern about time as a measure of distance from a moment in the past to one in the future. Such a concept of indeterminacy is very different

Ex. 35.1   Pauline Oliveros, Trio for Flute, Percussion, and String Bass

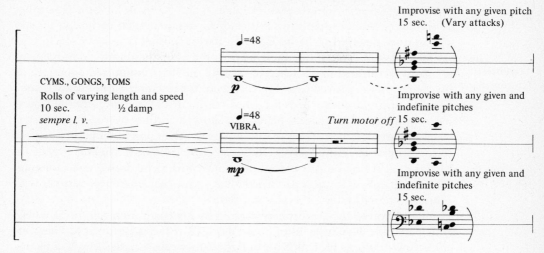

The rhythms and durations are improvised where there is no time signature.

from the stochastic works of Iannis Xenakis, for whom chance is a mathematical process that produces a desired scientific result.

Indeterminacy treats art as a process, different for each new performance, rather than as a fixed creation. There is no beginning, no middle, no end; musical "objects" no longer exist. The composer no longer creates compositions with precalculated materials, structures, and relationships that will remain the same for each performance. Instead he merely outlines a situation in which sound may occur or action may be generated. Thus the composer avoids subjective decisions. For such works, compositional rules rather than completed compositions are presented, and within these limits anything produced is acceptable, since the philosophy of chance music allows for no value judgments.

Musical Precursors

In music, indeterminate techniques, which may have been attempted as early as the eleventh or twelfth centuries, date at least as far back as 1751, when the British composer William Hayes (1706–1777) described a technique of composition by splattering notes onto staff paper in *The Art of Composing Music by a Method Entirely New, Suited to the Meanest Capacity*.

Music composed by rolling dice is the subject of *Musikalisches Würfelspiel* ("Musical Dice Game," K. 294d), published in London in 1806, a work attributed to Mozart. It consists of a set of first measures, second measures, and so forth. A throw of the dice determines which measure of each set is to be used, thus providing a simple way to compose rondos, waltzes, hornpipes, and reels. An earlier surviving example of this type of entertainment is Joseph

Early works

Phillip Kirnberger's *Der allezeit fertige Polonaisen-und-Minuettenkomponist* ("The Ever-Ready Composer of Polonaises and Minuets," 1756). A number of similar publications followed, including one attributed to Joseph Haydn and another believed to be by C. P. E. Bach.

The twentieth century In the twentieth century the Dadaists, members of an artistic movement formally established in Zurich, Switzerland, in 1916, conducted experiments involving chance procedures. Tristan Tzara, for instance, would draw from a hat slips of paper with words inscribed on them, and then present the resulting combinations as a poem. Hans Arp allowed cutouts of free or geometric shapes to arrange themselves in random order, then pasted them on a surface to form a picture. And Marcel Duchamp created *Erratum Musicale* ("Musical Mistake," 1913), a set of random notes intended to be drawn out and sung. This Duchamp work was patterned after a proposal by Lewis Carroll, with musical intervals taking the place of words.

In addition to the atmosphere created by Dadaism, many musical works anticipated the development of post–World War II indeterminacy. These include certain works by Erik Satie and the Americans Charles Ives and Henry Cowell (1897–1965), discussed below.

Satie Some of the works of Erik Satie lack conventional transitions, as in *Parade,* where short melodies appear without preparation and then disappear. This view of music as succession rather than progression became an important part of indeterminate aesthetics. A few Satie works foreshadowed certain indeterminate developments. Satie had a proposal, for example, for a *musique d'ameublement* ("furniture music") that he presented in 1920, with Darius Milhaud, at the Galéries Barbezanges, a Paris art gallery. Musicians played unrelated melodies in different sections of the concert room, while the audience was urged to move around and talk. In such an atmosphere, music was considered a utilitarian object like furniture.

Ives and Cowell In a few works of Charles Ives and Henry Cowell the performer is encouraged to participate in the creative process—an important principle behind many aleatory works. Ives's *Hallowe'en* (c. 1906) for piano quintet, with drum ad libitum, is eighteen measures long and may be played either three or four times, leaving out or changing the various parts according to written instructions. If a third repetition is taken, the tempo becomes "as fast as possible without disabling any player or instrument." And in Henry Cowell's *Mosaic Quartet* (1935), the performers are supposed to put together a composition from the blocks of material provided by the composer.

Also influential was Ives's "Postface" to *114 Songs* (1922). Here the composer described his vision of a person sitting in a rocking chair, smoking a pipe, and viewing the landscape from his porch. The man he envisioned would be sitting quietly, hearing his own symphony, an idea that foreshadowed Cage's *4' 33"* (1952) by thirty years.

After World War II

In the early 1950s chance music originated in New York City with composers John Cage, Morton Feldman, and Earle Brown, and then spread to

Marcel Duchamp (1887–1968), *Bride Stripped Bare by Her Bachelors Even* (1915–1923), oil and lead wire on glass. This uses chance techniques in the determination of some of the lines and points of the pattern and in the preservation of dust allowed to accumulate. Duchamp influenced composer John Cage. (Philadelphia Museum of Art: bequest of Katherine S. Dreier)

Europe. These composers were friendly with and influenced by several visual artists: John Cage by Marcel Duchamp, Morton Feldman by Philip Guston, and Earle Brown by Alexander Calder and Jackson Pollack. The young composer Christian Wolff was also closely associated with this group.

Cage (b. 1926) is considered by many to be the father of post–World War II chance music. His works encompass every aspect of "experimental" music between 1950 and the present time, but his experiments with new sounds date back to his compositions of the 1930s and 1940s, when he developed the

Cage

prepared piano (see Chapter 29) as an extension of his experiments with all-percussion works.

Cage's use of the *I-Ching*

In 1950 and 1951 Cage, as former Schoenberg student, had been using serial squares to set out his musical material, somewhat in the manner of Pierre Boulez. At the same time, he had been introduced by Christian Wolff to the *I-Ching* ("The Book of Changes"). The *I-Ching,* attributed to Fu Hsi (c. 3000 B.C.), is the first written book of wisdom, philosophy, and oracle. It is used to make decisions on possible courses of action. To use it, three yarrow sticks, or, more recently, three coins are tossed six times, and the resulting combination is then sought in the book in order to find corresponding paragraphs of advice. In the course of trying to get from square to square without using serial procedures, Cage decided to use the *I-Ching* in making compositional choices, thus arriving at musical chance. The first work to use these procedures was his *Music of Changes* (1951), although two pieces written earlier in the same year—Sixteen Dances (for chamber ensemble) and Concerto for Prepared Piano and Chamber Orchestra—were transitional works also containing chance elements. In *Music of Changes,* for piano solo, the piano produces scattered sound-noises that are precisely notated, with the frequency and duration of their occurrence dictated by the *I-Ching.*

Later Cage experiments

Cage's later experiments, which aim to dissociate the artist from the work, include using the imperfections in sheets of paper as a basis for pitch choices. In these later works the silences between sounds are often longer than the sounds themselves, which thus seem to be present merely to emphasize the silences. He also has created works that have an unlimited capacity to combine with other of his compositions, thus allowing him to eliminate the distinguishing characteristics of each individual piece as a self-contained unit.

Feldman

Morton Feldman (b. 1926) creates his works instinctively, working directly with sounds, which he thinks of in painterly terms as colors on a surface. In both his chance works and the later, fully composed ones his sounds are generally very soft, delicate, and carefully spaced. His sense of spacing parallels his way of talking, with sentences stopped midway to force listener concentration before the thought is continued. The habitual lack of contrasting dynamic levels, except in rare instances, focuses attention on the quality of the sounds themselves. This approach to sound may also be partially influenced by the third of Arnold Schoenberg's *Fünf Orchesterstücke,* Op. 16 ("Five Orchestra Pieces," 1909), in which subtle changes of orchestral color occur without the listener's being aware of individual instrumental entrances and exits.

Pieces for Four Pianos

During the 1950s Feldman was the first composer to create music that is indeterminate in respect to performance, as well as the first to use nonrepresentational graphic notation. Pieces for Four Pianos (1957) allows performers to play through the notated materials at their own speed. Here Feldman has created a single part consisting of delicate chords. All four players start together, then choose their own durations for each sonority within an agreed-upon tempo. This technique creates irregularly spaced repetitions as each of the players reaches the same chord.

By the end of the 1950s Feldman had abandoned graphic notation. The graphic experiments had made it possible for him to gain the effect of freely spaced timings even in his later, completely notated works. Like the graphic works, the nongraphic ones continue to be sensitive to the needs and possibilities of the performers and of the instruments themselves.

The name of Earle Brown (b. 1926) is most often associated with his development of *open form* (a piece without a set beginning or a set ending or both). He developed this idea after looking at the mobiles of Alexander Calder and may have been influenced by similar experiments of Henry Cowell. In open-form works, the actual compositional materials are preestablished, but their order and the amount of material used is chosen during the performance. Thus a new form, and at times a new length, is determined during each performance of the piece. Open form, which enabled Brown to find a balance between total control and total lack of control, involves the acceptance of all possible orderings of the material. Although Brown started

Brown's open form

Alexander Calder (b. 1898), *Mobile*. Mobiles by Calder, such as this one, create new juxtapositions of elements as the wind shifts. This idea of ever-new combinations from unchanging materials influenced the composer Earle Brown in his development of open-form works. (Philadelphia Museum of Art: Louise and Walter Arensberg Collection)

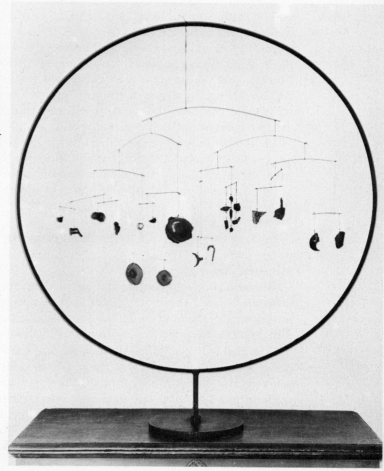

these experiments in the 1950s, perhaps the most often performed of these works are the two he wrote in 1961 and 1962 respectively, *Available Forms I* and *Available Forms II*.

Controlled chance

In Europe, most composers had abandoned total serialism by the middle or late 1950s in favor of *controlled chance:* music in which the performers can make choices within limits set by the composer. The limitations imposed differ from composer to composer and even from work to work. This change was due in part to the influence of Karlheinz Stockhausen and Pierre Boulez, both of whom had formerly been strong advocates of total serialism. Controlled-chance techniques often adapt indeterminate freedoms to more traditional structures.

Boulez

Pierre Boulez (b. 1925) tends to limit choice to such details as the partial ordering of precomposed sections; whether to play the complex or simple version of a piece; and whether to include or omit ornaments. Several of his works of the late 1950s contain related but freestanding sections which fit within preplanned forms that are often related to literary ideas.

Stock-hausen

Boulez had begun to use controlled chance with his *Troisième Sonate pour piano* ("Piano Sonata No. 3," 1957). Slightly earlier, Stockhausen had made a similar move in his *Zeitmasse für fünf Holzbläser* ("Tempos for Five Woodwinds," 1956) and *Gruppen für drei Orchester* ("Groups for Three Orchestras," 1957). Stockhausen, however, has allowed his performers more freedom than Boulez. This can be seen in Stockhausen's *Klavierstücke XI* ("Piano Pieces XI," 1956), which consists of nineteen "events," or fragments, to be played in whatever order meets the eye of the pianist during the performance. The first group is played with any of six possible tempos, dynamics, and types of touch, but the following group must then be played with whatever directions are given at the end of the first group. When a group is chosen for a second time, the instructions given in parentheses must be observed. The piece ends as soon as one fragment has been spotted by the performer for the third time.

Other Movements

Minimal Art

Minimal and *conceptual* art may involve indeterminacy. Often, however, these works are determinate—that is, their outcomes are predictable. Both movements permit the composer to remain impersonal and thus, aesthetically, may be regarded as outgrowths of indeterminacy.

Minimal works are those that use the simplest possible means. A poem of only a few words (as in the writings of Gertrude Stein), a painting of only one color (such as the "white" painting of Robert Rauschenberg), and a musical composition containing only one or two notes would fall into this category. The term itself is believed to have originated in 1965 with the American art critic Richard Wollheim, who used it to describe simple examples of pop art.

Minimal music has been especially popular in the United States and Great Britain since the mid-1960s. This movement was foreshadowed by Satie's

Vexations (c. 1893) for piano, consisting of a series of dissonant chords to be repeated 840 times, and influenced by the repetitiveness of non-Western religious ritual music. In many works, the minimal sound activity consists of carefully chosen, mainly tonal elements. Thus a sense of direction leading to arrival points is eliminated, and the listener's attention is directed from the pitches themselves, which are predictable after the first few repetitions, to minute timbral and other differences.

Four well-established minimal composers are the Americans Terry Riley (b. 1935), Philip Glass (b. 1937), Steve Reich, and La Monte Young (b. 1935). Glass, Reich, and Young have established touring ensembles to perform their works.

Riley Riley emphasizes pulse in his works. Unlike the more controlled scores of Reich and Young, Riley's pieces allow each performer individual judgment. The work *In C* (1964), for example, permits the performer to decide when to begin and whether to keep an old figure going or to move on to the next.

Glass In many of Glass's works, the opening establishes a melodic unit that is repeated several times. The next unit is a melodic extension of the first, and this process continues throughout the work, although musical material may be subtracted instead of added. This process may be seen in *Music in Fifths* (1969). Some works give players the freedom of changing parts at certain points, as in *Music with Changing Parts* (1971). Perhaps his most famous work is his opera *Einstein on the Beach* (1977), which has lyrics and music by Philip Glass and spoken text by Christopher Knowles, Lucinda Childs, and Samuel M. Johnson.

Reich Reich's music uses gradual, slow changes, a process that Reich himself has compared to sands running through an hourglass. Reich has been influenced by non-Western musics and, thus, sometimes uses African rhythms. *Drumming* (1971), which uses bongos, marimbas, and glockenspiels respectively in the first three sections and all three in the last, produces complex cross-rhythms by combinations of simple rhythmic patterns.

Young Some of Young's works use a modal system and rely on the establishment of a drone, above which he articulates harmonically related tones. The importance of harmonic concurrences (as opposed to the melodic successions guiding Glass and others) may be seen in his *The Tortoise, His Dreams and Journeys,* a continuing performance work begun in 1964, usually played in two two-hour sessions with projections by Marian Zazeela.

Conceptual Art

Conceptual works are those in which the underlying idea is more important than the actual realization. These works have been created by artists who are trained in music, dance, and the visual arts but transcend the boundaries of any one discipline. Such pieces range from the completely indeterminate to those that outline a specific action. One example of the latter is La Monte Young's *Composition 1960 No. 2* (1960), which consists of four paragraphs of instructions for building a fire before an audience.

Anti-Art

Anti-art, as the term implies, intends to negate all traditional ideas about art, aiming for the ultimate effect beyond whose borders no avant-garde or post-avant-garde movement can pass. In such "works," boredom and danger play important roles. The movie *Sleep* (1963) by the American Andy Warhol (b. 1931), an eight-hour film of a man sleeping, belongs in this category.

Anti-music is indeterminacy taken to its ultimate conclusion; it is philosophy rather than sound. The ultimate freedom has ironically become the ultimate restriction, since the lack of boundaries makes it impossible to create a purposeful work. To those involved in this line of thought, music must become part of the world situation since humanity is part of the world. This includes thinking about suicide, death, and danger. Sounds, lights, and actions are only important in conception, then, since the arts have merged with reality.

Anti-art works can also be considered minimal or conceptual art, although the converse is not always true. The two "musical" works most often cited as examples of anti-music are John Cage's *4'33"* (an instance of conceptual art) and La Monte Young's *Composition 1960 No. 7* (1960, an instance of minimal art). The former work, intended to make the listener aware of the sounds around him, merely specifies a length of silence (four minutes and thirty-three seconds) to be divided into three movements, each of a specified length. The latter work consists only of the pitches B and F-sharp and of the instructions to hold them "for a long time."

The group FLUXUS, consisting of composers, poets, and visual artists, has created numerous compositions along these lines. The original movement was based in New York City, but other FLUXUS movements have also arisen in other countries, including Japan and Germany. Their works involve danger and violence, in order to make simple tasks more exciting; boredom; and environmentalism (in which the environment becomes part of the work).

The "New" Tonality

In the mid-1960s, experimental music began to move away from abstraction, discontinuity, and discord in order to return to the "beautiful," often tonal or modal sounds. This trend has been seen in the works of minimal artists like Riley, who have avoided the problem of a new tonal language, however, by emphasizing process over materials.

Summary

In addition to tracing microtonal developments, this chapter has surveyed the ideas of composers who have challenged both traditional definitions of music and, at times, questioned even the existence of music as a separate art form. Some of these composers have blurred the boundaries of music by combining it with the other arts, as in multimedia works (including Happenings), or by creating works not definitively part of any one branch of the arts, as in conceptual art. Many have challenged the definition of music as movement in time by eliminating perceived motions through the use of silences or constant repetition, as in minimal music. Even the idea of a composer as a controller of sounds has been questioned by experiments with chance techniques and, to a limited extent, improvisation. By their defiance of convention, such works raise important aesthetic questions.

Bibliography

Books and Articles

BATTCOCK, GREGORY, and NELSON, CYRIL I., eds. *Breaking the Sound Barrier: A Critical Anthology of New Music.* New York: E. P. Dutton, 1981.

BEHRMAN, DAVID. "What Indeterminate Notation Determines." *Perspectives of New Music* 3, no. 2 (1965): 58–73.

CAGE, JOHN. *Silence* (*Lectures and Writings*). Middleton, Conn.: Wesleyan University Press, 1961.

COPE, DAVID. *New Directions in Music.* 2nd ed. Dubuque, Iowa: William C. Brown Co., 1976.

FOSS, LUKAS. "The Changing Composer-Performer Relationship: A Monologue and a Dialogue." *Perspectives of New Music* 1, no. 2 (1963): 45–53. Also in Schwartz, Elliott, and Childs, Barney, eds. *Contemporary Composers on Contemporary Music.* New York: Holt, Rinehart and Winston, Inc., 1967.

KIRBY, MICHAEL. *Happenings.* New York: E. P. Dutton, 1965.

NYMAN, MICHAEL. *Experimental Music.* New York: Schirmer Books, 1974.

PARTCH, HARRY. *Genesis of a Music,* 2nd ed., enlarged. New York: Da Capo Press, 1974.

Periodicals

Source: Music of the Avant-Garde. Davis and Sacramento, Calif.: 1967–1973.

Scores

JOHNSON, ROGER, selector and commentator. *Scores: An Anthology of New Music.* New York: Schirmer Books, 1981.

Many of Luciano Berio's early works are published by Edizioni Suvini-Zerboni (Milan), and the later ones by Universal Edition (Vienna and London).

Many of the early works of Earle Brown are published by Associated Music Publishers (New York), and the later ones by Universal Edition (Vienna and London).

John Cage's works are published by C. F. Peters Corp. (New York).

The earlier works of Morton Feldman are published by C. F. Peters Corp. (New York), and the later ones by Universal Edition (Vienna and London).

PART
SEVEN

*The
New
World*

36

Renaissance Music and the New World

THROUGHOUT this book we have seen how various European musical traditions have influenced and enriched each other. Just as the discovery of the New World opened up vast territories for man to explore and develop, so, too, in music the myriad influences at work in the Americas led to the development of new forms and styles.

To the already existing cultural heritage of the American Indians were added the traditions of the European nations and those of West Africa, as all these peoples intermixed. The results of these artistic cross-currents have yet to be completely studied and analyzed, but various major elements will be explored in this and the following chapters.

Indian Civilizations before Columbus

The cultural and artistic life of the New World dates back some twenty thousand years, when Asians are believed to have migrated to the American continents across a land bridge that existed in what is now the Bering Strait. Once the migrants reached North America, they spread out until their numbers were distributed throughout the Americas. Christopher Columbus called them "Indians" when he first saw them in 1492, because he mistakenly thought he had landed in what we today call the East Indies.

A succession of highly developed urban civilizations evolved in the New World, especially in Mexico, Guatemala, and the western portion of South America. Greatest of these were the Aztec, in the area around what is today Mexico City; the Maya, in the sections now called Yucatán, Guatemala, and Honduras; and the Inca, whose territories at one time extended from present-day southern Colombia on the north to Bolivia on the south. A smaller but also important civilization was that of the Chibcha, who lived in what we know as the highlands of Colombia. Able astronomers, surgeons, and mathematicians were found among the Mayas, Aztecs, and Incas. Their concepts and numerical systems often attained such complexity that even today not

The great empires

837

every aspect of the Aztec Calendar Stone, for example, has been deciphered. Astronomer-priests made extremely accurate astronomical predictions and descriptions, using special observatories built for these purposes.

The arts
The great Indian civilizations developed both useful and ornamental metalwork, and their artists and artisans also produced elaborate textiles and ceramics of all types. Often these showed scenes and actions taken from everyday life, including depictions of music making, dancing, and musical instruments.

Indian Music at the Time of the Discovery

Instruments and performance practice
Musicians of the Indian empires used trumpets and drums in battle and religious ceremonies. Giant conch shells, which served both the Aztecs and the Incas as trumpets, were so highly prized by the Incas that they sent out emissaries on balsa rafts as far away as Panama to barter for them. Metal and wooden trumpets also existed, as did many varieties of large and small drums.

With the exception of war music and the activities of groups of court musicians, Aztec music was firmly tied to religious functions. In Mexico the households of the important *caciques* (chiefs) employed groups of singers and instrumentalists similar to the court musicians attached to the establishments of European nobles. Precision was demanded in the performance of complicated religious music learned by rote. A mistake on the part of a musician carried the death penalty, because it was believed that imperfection angered rather than appeased the gods. On the other hand, court musicians were highly valued for their abilities to compose new songs glorifying the wealth, power, and family history of their employers.

Among the Incas, different varieties of festive dancing and singing were designated for each social class and for different occasions. Consorts of *antaras* (clay or bone panpipes consisting of from three to fifteen tubes held together with glue or cord) serenaded the Inca ruler. Groups of *antara* players were usually small compared to the large numbers of instrumentalists assembled by the Inca nobles to play the *pincollo* (a bone or cane flute).

The more personal and private uses of music among the Incas were admirably described by Garcilaso de la Vega:

The performers were Indians trained to provide music for the king and the great lords, and although their music was simple, it was not common, but learned and mastered by study. . . . [Their songs] were composed in measured verse and were mostly concerned with the passion of love.[1]

Music was important too in the lives of other American Indian groups. Dancing, singing, and the playing of musical instruments served both social and religious purposes throughout the Americas. The hundreds of Indian tribes had literally thousands of different chants, rituals, dances, and ceremonials in which music figured significantly.

The Heritage and Influence of Indian Music and Folklore

American Indian folklore, customs, and language, and the history of the tribes' dealings with Europeans, have served as the bases for songs, chamber music, program music, operas, and, in fact, every type of Western art music. During the nineteenth and twentieth centuries the use of subjects relating to Indians increased dramatically in the works of both Old World and New World composers, reflecting a general trend toward exoticism and the rediscovery of a legendary past, forming part of the movement known in all the arts as Romanticism. Composers such as Carlos Chávez of Mexico and Arthur Farwell (1872–1952) of the United States have attempted to use either the "spirit" of Indian music or themes transcribed from actual performances of this music.

The Discovery of America

Explorers before Columbus

The fifteenth and sixteenth-century explorers sent out by Spain, Portugal, and other European nations were not the first voyagers from the Old World to see the American continents. Some historians believe that sailors from Carthage in North Africa and Cádiz on the southern coast of what is now Spain (both settlements were then parts of the Phoenician Empire) were in contact with North, Central, and South America as early as the sixth century B.C. Others maintain that a Chinese ship carrying a Buddhist monk and a crew of five men landed on the western shore of Mexico in 459 B.C. Still others claim that some Irish monks, driven from their Iceland outposts by invading Vikings early in the ninth century, sought sanctuary on the shores of North America. *Early voyagers*

Leif Ericson and other Norsemen did set up temporary colonies in coastal North America (c. A.D. 1000). Norse sagas (epic poems describing their early history and the exploits of their greatest heroes) give us the little information we have about Norse music. From them we know that trumpets were used in Iceland, and that the Norsemen enjoyed dancing and played both pipes and drums. *The Norsemen*

These groups brought to the Americas their culture, traditions, and music. But because their settlements were short-lived, they seem to have had no permanent impact on the development of music in the New World.

Explorers after Columbus

The Italian explorer Christopher Columbus (1451?–1506) and his multinational crew had served Ferdinand and Isabella of Spain. Because their successor, Charles V (reg. 1519–1554), ruled over so many different cultural groups and was so heavily in debt to German bankers, not all of the Spanish-sponsored explorers and conquerors (*conquistadores*) of the New World were Spaniards.

When Charles V abdicated his throne in the mid-1550s, he gave his son Philip the Netherlands and his Italian possessions, along with Spain and its New World colonies. The rest of the Holy Roman Empire became the property of Charles's younger brother, Ferdinand. Thereafter the development of Ibero-America was tied to that of Spain.

The race for New World lands

By 1494 Spain and Portugal had already concluded agreements with the help of the pope, dividing all of the not-yet-explored lands of the world between them. Brazil was part of the area originally granted to Portugal under the terms of the Treaty of Tordesillas (1494). At first, Portugal was Spain's greatest rival in the race for riches and empire in the Americas, but before long, the English, the rebellious Dutch, and the French had also entered the struggle.

The Age of Discovery and New World Music: Music at Sea

Shipboard life

Music and musicians were part of the sailors' daily experience. The departure of a seagoing expedition was itself a ceremonial occasion. When Columbus departed on his second voyage to the New World in 1494, one Italian reported that

> streamers wound about the rigging and the colors of the sovereigns adorned the stern of every ship. The musicians, playing the flute and the lyre, dumbfounded the very nereids, sea-nymphs and sirens with their mellifluous strains. The shores rang with the blare of trumpets and the blast of horns.[2]

A day aboard a sixteenth-century ship was broken up into "watches" of four hours each and was filled with organized, formalized rituals, observed with particular diligence by Spanish and Portuguese crews. Time was told by means of a Venetian hourglass filled with sand, which held enough sand for half an hour. Each time it was turned by the ship's boy, he sang a ditty appropriate to the hour. The practice of using the youngest members of the crew to sing and recite devotional material was continued throughout the day and night. Not all of the mariners were accomplished singers, however. One Spaniard who made the crossing in 1573 describes the performance practice as follows:

> . . . the eight tones of music they distribute into thirty-two other and different tones, perverse, resonant, and very dissonant, as if we had today in the singing of the *Salve* and *Litany* a tempest of hurricanes of music, so that if God and his glorious Mother and the Saints to whom we pray should look down upon our tones and voices and not on our hearts and spirits, it would not do to beseech mercy with such a confusion of bawlings.[3]

When no priest was present, the captain or master of the ship led morning and evening prayers. The *Salve* sung by these sailors after their own fashion was the plainsong shown in Example 36.1.

Ex. 36.1   *Salve Regina*

Sal - ve Re - gi - na mi-se - ri - cor - di - ae *etc.*

"Hail, O Queen!"

Prayer and song aboard ship were not confined to Catholic vessels. Religious ritual accompanied by music was also a part of Protestant seamen's everyday life. The English captain John Smith (1580–1631) wrote of religious ritual aboard an English ship: "At six a-clocke [they] sing a Psalme, say a Prayer, and the Master with his side begins the watch . . . till midnight; and then his Mate with his larboard men with a Psalm and a prayer releeves them."[4]

On larger ships, orders had to be sounded on a whistle or pipe so all the crew could hear. The ship's trumpeter signaled passing ships, sounded general quarters, recalled ships, and sometimes heralded the changing of the watch.

Once having reached the New World, captains often used music and dancing to attract the sometimes reticent Indians, not always with predictable results. On his third voyage (1498–1500) Columbus tried to induce some Indians from Trinidad to come closer to his ship by ordering

Shipboard diplomacy

that a tabor player get up on the poop [deck] and that the ships' boys dance, thinking it would please them. But they did not feel that way about it; on the contrary, when they saw the playing and dancing, they took it as a sign of war . . . dropped their oars and seized their bows and arrows [and shot at the crew]. . . . When he saw this the Admiral ordered the song-and-dance show to cease.[5]

Many other Indians found European music more to their liking. The chief of the Indians of Puerto Rico, for example, after being "piped aboard with great pomp, welcomed by the beating of drums, the clashing of cymbals, and the flashing bombardment of the ship's canon,"[6] sat down to banquet with the Spaniards.

Many ships also carried instruments of other types, such as recorders and shepherds' pipes. No Elizabethan expedition sailed without a four-piece consort, and, as the captain of a ship in the Sir Humphrey Gilbert expedition of 1583–1585 wrote: "For the solace of our people, and allurement of the Savages, we were provided of Musike in good variety not omitting the least toyes, as Morris dancers . . . and Manylike conceits to delight the Savage people."[7]

Shipboard entertainment

Most of the many captains who traveled the Atlantic, and the officers who served under them, were either well respected and successful members of the middle class or members of the petty nobility (*hidalgos* in Spanish) who had endured genteel poverty in their homelands. All were conversant with the arts, including music. A Spanish captive aboard Sir Francis Drake's *Golden*

Hind, for example, reported that fiddlers played background music while the admiral dined on gold-rimmed plates.

Music, Missionaries, Conquest, and Settlement

As early as 1502, Columbus had asked the pope to send missionaries to accompany him on his fourth and final voyage to the New World (1502–1504). Only one missionary, Brother Alexander, accepted this invitation. On August 14, 1502, he celebrated what was probably the first Mass in the continental New World, on the shores of Honduras. Soon priests (and later Protestant ministers) joined many expeditions, and they often used music as an aid in the conversion of the natives.

Within two years of the discovery of Hispaniola (the island on which the present-day Dominican Republic and Haiti are located), Columbus had established a colony there. Before 1600 only the Spanish and the Portuguese had managed to set up permanent settlements in the Americas. Most friendly Indian groups were quickly demoralized or succumbed to European diseases against which they had no immunity. Warlike tribes and the great Indian empires, on the other hand, offered organized resistance to the Europeans. Some of these Indians held out successfully for many years before capitulating.

By the beginning of the seventeenth century, a similar process was taking place in North America, with the conquests made this time mainly by the English, French, and Dutch. Parts of what are today states in the southern coastal and southwestern United States were part of the Spanish territory, so their political and artistic fortunes were bound up with those of Spain. Iberian control extended as far north as the Carolinas, and eventually expanded as far west as California. Indian uprisings and wars occurred well into the sixteenth century in Latin America. In North America, the Indians continued their wars against white domination until the late nineteenth century.

Musicians accompanied both exploratory expeditions and armies of conquest. Contemporary depictions of these groups show *ministriles* (minstrels) performing the same functions for their employers as they did in Europe.

Economic Organization

The Spanish crown had decided to run its new American territories on a medieval model, granting land to Catholic settlers, who were then considered by Spain to be entitled to the labor of those Indians living on "their" territory. When the Indians proved unsuited to hard labor, the new American landowners began to import black slaves to replace them. Although black slavery had been officially sanctioned in the New World as early as 1500, it was not until after 1518 that blacks arrived in ever-increasing numbers. In almost all areas of the Spanish-American territories, blacks outnumbered whites before the end of the sixteenth century, sometimes as much as seven to one.

Because the Brazilian Indians had neither great cities nor rich mines to lure treasure-seeking, Portuguese-supported armies into the interior, and because the land itself was fertile, Brazil had developed a plantation system by the mid–sixteenth century. Black slaves worked on the sugar plantations, which were the mainstay of the Brazilian economy. Both a rising middle class and the wealthy hereditary landowners were supported by this plantation economy. French attempts to wrest Brazil from the Portuguese occurred throughout the sixteenth century but were unsuccessful. The Inquisition, which meted out harsh punishment to heretics in the Spanish colonies, was absent from Brazil during its early formative years. Thus English, Germans, Italians, and recently converted Jews (*maranos*) all found a welcome in Brazil. Even during the years when the Spanish king also ruled Portugal (1580–1620), he did not alter the Brazilian system, which differed radically from that of the Spanish colonies in its total lack of dependence on various forms of tribute collected from the Indians.

The West African Heritage

Many aspects of the West African cultural heritage were preserved for more than two centuries among the blacks of Latin America. An example is the founding of *confradías* (religiously based fraternal organizations) among the elite of the urban blacks and Indians, which was actively encouraged by both local clergy and missionaries of the Catholic Church during the colonial period. West Africans had been captured and sent to Spain and Portugal as slaves from the fifteenth century on, and confradías had existed in Europe for decades preceding the discovery and conquest of the New World. Many blacks brought to Latin America were the descendants of the West Africans who had been slaves in Europe, so the setting up of confradías in the New World was for them the continuation of a tradition. American confradías were often organized among blacks who could trace their ancestry to the same tribe, or at least to the same region of Africa. Usually each black confradía had as its patron saint a black person important in Church history. The confradías sponsored charitable activities and parades with floats, dancing, singing, and music on the day of their saint, and money was set aside to pay outside singers and instrumentalists.

Confradías and music

That both European and New World composers were very much interested in the music of the blacks is amply documented. One of the earliest European composers of *negros* (*villancicos* written in Negro dialect, also called *guineos*), Philippe Rogier (1560/61–1596), was a member of the Madrid *capilla flamenca* of Philip II. The first known composer of *negros* in the Americas was a Portuguese, Gaspar Fernandes (c. 1566–1629), who first became chapelmaster in Antigua, Guatemala, and ended his life as chapelmaster and organist in Puebla, Mexico (1606–1629). The *guineos* are festival pieces in which hemiolas dominate the rapid triple meter, causing frequent changes in meter from $\frac{6}{8}$ to $\frac{3}{4}$. They are almost always in F major, and the texture is that of a soloist or soloists answered by a chorus. The rhythmic pattern itself is remi-

Black influence on music

niscent of similar pieces recorded in West Africa. Fernandes's *Guineo a 5*, of which one section is transcribed in Example 36.2, is in the form of a sung *sarabande*. This dance form, which originated in early-sixteenth-century Mexico, soon became very popular in Europe, where its lascivious nature led Philip II to attempt to ban it around 1590. As with other *negros,* it is written in the dialect Spanish spoken by the New World black slaves.

Ex. 36.2   Gaspar Fernandes, *Guineo a 5*

"Play little drum, dear black man; sing, brother."

Translation by Robert Stevenson; copyright by the Regents of the University of California. Example copyright 1964 by *The Musical Quarterly*. Used by permission.

The New World Influences the Old

The sarabande is only one example of an early artistic development in the New World. Ever since the Renaissance the Americas have played an important role in the history and development of European civilization. Not only have their vast territories conjured up visions of limitless riches in the minds of Europeans, but the manners and customs of their inhabitants—Indian, African, European, and the various racial mixtures that sprang from them—have also fired the imagination of writers, philosophers, social historians, artists, and musicians.

Indians brought to Europe

No descriptions of the Indian musicians taken to Europe in 1527 have been found in the writings of distinguished European musicians of that era. But we do know that Cortés himself sent a company of Aztec dancers and musicians to Charles V that year, and that they spent a full morning performing before the emperor in his palace at Valladolid, while the entire court marveled at the rhythmic precision of their music making and dancing. This was only one of a series of Indian groups from various parts of the Americas taken to Europe, as part of the spoils of war, to prove that people other than Europeans did exist, or to "educate" the Indians in European ways.

During the sixteenth century European travelers to the New World commonly wrote about their experiences. An ill-fated attempt to set up a French king in Brazil (1555–1567) gave rise to the publication by one of the Calvinist settlers, Jean de Léry, of a book entitled *L'Histoire d'un voyage fait en terre du Brésil autrement dit l'Amérique* ("History of a Voyage Made to the Land of Brazil, Otherwise Called America," 1578). It not only provided Europeans with a glowing account of the Indian inhabitants, but also transcribed several melodies of the Tupinambá tribe. Two of those printed in the 1586 edition of this book were later used by the Brazilian composer Heitor Villa-Lobos as a part of the first of his *Trois poèmes indiens*.

Positive attitudes toward Indians

Michel de Montaigne, the French essayist and social critic who wrote about the visit of Guaraní Indians from Paraguay to the court of Charles IX at Rouen in 1562, was also deeply influenced by Léry and other Europeans who had spent time in the New World. Montaigne decided that the Indians had a better social organization than that of the European conquerors, and a far superior ethical code. In idealizing the first inhabitants of the Americas, he echoed sentiments expressed by Europeans as far back as the Italian explorer Giovanni da Verrazzano (1485?–1528?) and Columbus himself.

Music for the Church and the State

In the Spanish colonies important population centers fostered the development of music. Spaniards not only captured Indian cities and superimposed their culture on the inhabitants, but they also founded no fewer than twenty-five new cities, from Florida to Paraguay, between 1494 and 1565. To rule the

American territories, the Spanish crown sent viceroys. In the rich cities of Mexico City and Lima, where these important functionaries lived, the music compared with that in major European courts. Until the eighteenth century there were only two viceroyalties in Spanish America—that of New Spain (including Mexico, the southwestern United States, and the Philippines) and that of Peru. But lesser governmental centers (*audiencias,* or high courts) also existed. Even before 1600 such centers were founded in Santo Domingo, Guadalajara (Mexico), Bogotá (Colombia), Charcas (Bolivia), and Quito (Ecuador).

Immigrant musicians and music education

In addition to the opportunities provided for music making by the government, the church invited and encouraged European musicians to teach, to compose, and to perform in American churches. Then, too, Indians, *mestizos* (offspring of Spanish and Indian parents), and *creoles* (American-born offspring of Spanish parents) were trained as performers and composers of European music. The Church established schools to instruct the Indians in religion, the arts, and manners, and the Franciscan lay missionary Peter of Ghent (Pedro de Gante, 1480?–1572), a cousin of Charles V himself, founded an extremely successful school in Mexico that emphasized music in order to attract Indian students. Gante's fame as a protector of music was so great that it earned him renown among later generations of Indians, to the extent that a number of Indian composers even adopted his name as their own.

Large churches, cathedrals, and missions were also musical centers—especially those run by the Jesuits, a religious order created in 1534 to further the interests of the Church. By the middle of the sixteenth century the Jesuits had arrived in Brazil, and by 1583 they were performing *autos* (religious dramas containing many interludes of music, dancing, and the singing of native airs) for the Indians of northeastern Brazil. The *auto* became popular throughout both the Spanish and Portuguese New World colonies, just as similar plays by Juan del Encina, Gil Vicente, and Lope de Vega had found favor in Spain and Portugal.

As a result of the activities of European missionaries, major centers of religious music developed during the sixteenth century in such places as Guatemala, Mexico, Peru, Ecuador, Bolivia, and Colombia. Members of religious orders were frequently teachers of music. All missions in the Valley of Mexico, for example, had music teachers and gave instruction in singing, the playing of instruments, and instrument building.

Printed and manuscript music

The diffusion of European music in the New World was aided not only by the accomplished composers and teachers who traveled from one city to another, but also by the establishment of a printing press in Mexico City (1525). When music printing became available in 1556, the first book containing music was published there, an *Ordinarium Missae.* In all, the Mexico City press published some thirteen liturgical books with music between 1558 and 1589, twelve more than appeared in Madrid itself during the same period.

Both printed and manuscript music reached the colonies by ship from Europe. As in the case of some published music by Cabezón, the music had appeared in the mother country only a few years earlier, and so was fairly up-

Ca.5. De benedictionibus & absolutionibus.

gnat in secula seculorum:Et a vinculis peccatorum nostrorum ab-
soluat nos omnipotens, & misericors dominus:semper suis locis,&
diebus dicantur,& cantentur in tono capitulorum,verso sacerdote
ad altare.Benedictiones vero in tono lectionis dicantur. Lectiones
verolegantur sub hoc tono.

¶ Lectiones vero mortuorum, &
prophetie: simili modo dicuntur.
¶ Terminantur autē sicut sex lectiones,quę leguntur in secundo,
& tertio nocturno in cęna domini
& parasceue, & sabbato sancto, q̃
in seipsis terminātur,sub hoc tono.

u be dõ ne be ne dic e re.

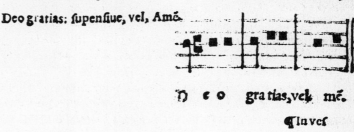

¶ In fine vero lamentationū prę-
dictorum triū dierum dicitur hye-
rusalem:hyerusalem: cõuertere ad
dominum Deum tuum:in tono la-
mentationum.In fine autem alia-
rū omniū lectiõum,quę infra annū
dicūtur:dicatur.Tu aūt dñe misere
re nobis. ¶ Tonus aūt capitulorū si-
nitur sicut patebit in suo loco.
¶ Orationes vero per horas diei
prętercq̃ in vesperis, & matutinis:
terminantur in tono capitulorū.
¶ Et tunc sacerdos quando dicit
Dominus vobiscum, dicit orationes,& bñdicamus domino, in eo-
dem tono. Cui respondetur.

Nõ sub si stam.

I n se cula se cu lo rū.

Deo gratias: supensiue, vel, Amē.

Ð e o gra tias,vel mē.

¶ In ves

First page containing music
from the first book with
music printed in the New
World, the Mexico City
Ordinarium Missae (1556).
(Courtesy New York Pub-
lic Library, Rare Books Division)

to-date by sixteenth-century standards. After music had been brought into
the colonies it could easily be copied by scribes, and this circulation of manuscript versions facilitated performances. We know that Spanish music was
performed in the colonies. The Spanish composer Victoria once directed his
New World agent to collect the 900 reales due him for the performance and
sale of his music in the Americas. Although no Portuguese music from this
period has yet been found in Brazil, evidence indicates that the Spanish and
Portuguese sacred and para-liturgical repertories (the latter had music with
religiously inspired texts but did not form part of the official order of a worship service) had much in common.

Composers in Spanish America: "Neo-Hispanic" Polyphony

The viceregal centers, Mexico City and Lima, proved hospitable to a number of sixteenth-century composers. In Mexico City both Hernando Franco (1532–1585) and Juan de Lienas (fl. 1550) were active, although Franco had previously spent time in Guatemala after migrating to the New World from his native Spain in 1573. The third important composer of this era, often considered the first major South American composer, was the Peruvian Gutierre Fernández Hidalgo (c. 1533–1520), who worked in Lima as well as in Bolivia, Colombia, and Ecuador.

Franco   Franco's liturgical style is entirely dependent upon the usage of the New World, which, in turn, derived from that of Seville. The two halves of the choir sat facing each other, and the antiphonal effects derived from this arrangement were as common in colonial music as in the music of the mother country. Like its Spanish counterpart, almost all extant Neo-Hispanic liturgical music requires the singing of alternate verses in plainsong and polyphony. Half the choir sang the plainsong, the other the polyphony. In the use of polyphony, and in inventiveness, word-painting, and other aspects of late-Renaissance style, the works of Franco compare favorably with those pro-

The first two pages of the celebrated manuscript known as the Franco Codex (copied c. 1610). (Photo courtesy Thomas Stanford)

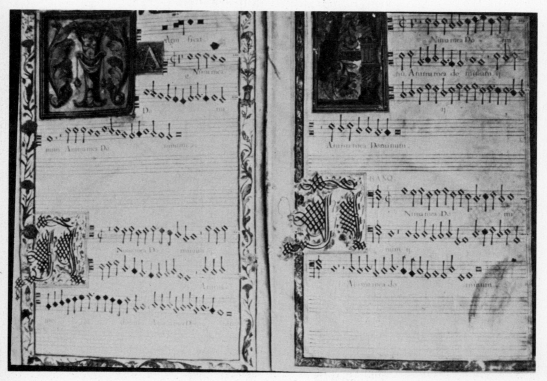

duced by his Spanish contemporaries Morales and Guerrero. It was customary for the composer to create melodies from existing plainsong formulas, and the table in Example 36.3 shows how the opening *cantus* parts of five of Franco's seven extant Magnificats were created from rhythmically and melodically manipulated plainsong formulas.

Other examples of alternative plainsong and polyphony are to be found in the works of Fernández Hidalgo. In his *Laudate pueri,* the composer set alternate verses of the text (Psalm 112, the second psalm of Vespers) in polyphony for four voices. The work is in the second tone, which Fernández Hidalgo transposed a fourth higher. The composer's mastery of counterpoint has often been credited with establishing his reputation as "the best South American composer of the sixteenth century."[8]

Fernández Hidalgo

In existing records of churches dating from this period, there are many references to their "orchestras." Because these churches also had organs, it is almost certain that most—if not all—of the church music performed in the New World during this era was accompanied by instruments. Colonial church musicians most likely followed European practice, especially since so many of the chapelmasters during the early years of European dominion in the New World came from the Old World.

Performance practice

Ceremonial and Secular Music in Spanish America

Music was also performed during times of public mourning and public rejoicing (the welcoming of a new viceroy, ceremonies to congratulate major public officials, and royal births, deaths, or weddings). The more solemn the

Ex. 36.3   Hernando Franco's manipulation of plainsong formula

(a) Plainsong formula: Tone I

a - ni - ma me - a Do - mi - num

Franco: Magnificat Tone I

a - ni-ma me - a Do - mi - num

(b) Plainsong formula: Tone II   Franco: Magnificat Tone II

a - ni - ma me - a Do - mi - num   a - ni - ma me - a Do - mi - num

(c) Plainsong formula: Tone IV   Franco: Magnificat Tone IV

a - ni - ma me - a Do - mi - num   a - ni - ma me - a Do - mi - num

occasion, the more varied, complex, and "learned" was the music, and the more people of different social classes were likely to be present. A friend of the Spanish music theorist Juan Bermudo was on hand to hear the music accompanying the elaborate memorial pageant performed in Mexico City on St. Andrew's Day, November 30, 1559, in honor of Charles V. After a two-and-a-half hour procession, during which over two hundred chieftains, two thousand prominent locals, and many other dignitaries had marched past a crowd of forty thousand, the vigil began in the cathedral with the chapel-master

directing one of his two antiphonal choirs in the singing of the invitatory, *Circumde-derunt me,* by Cristóbal de Morales; and then the other in the singing of the psalm, *Exultemus,* also by Morales. Since both settings are polyphonic throughout and the choirs sang them with the utmost sweetness, the vigil began with a devotional fervor that elevated the minds of everyone present.[9]

The role of blacks and Indians

Indians and blacks were prominent in public celebrations, both sacred and secular. Fray Toribio Benavente de Motolinía (1490–1569) documents the participation of large groups of Mexican Indian musicians in such festivals as Corpus Christi Day and Easter Week. By the 1530s some outlying districts had choristers capable of singing complex polyphonic music in processions. Flutes doubled the treble and were accompanied by trumpets, drums, and bells. Traditionally garbed Indians, dancing and singing (generally in their native tongue), often to the accompaniment of indigenous instruments, were also on hand to welcome new government officials. Bands of musicians playing European music were common.

Black drummers were hired to welcome the viceroy of New Spain when he paid a visit to Lima in 1551. Within twelve years of this occasion black drumming and dancing in the streets of the city had brought traffic to a standstill so frequently that the council ordered that such entertainments be confined to the public square. Similar restrictions were also imposed in Mexico City.

Geographic Diffusion and Stylistic Changes

Lay musicians and music teachers

Princes, adventurers, and secular musicians all sought their fortunes in the New World. By 1530 so many European music teachers were in Mexico that the authorities spread them among the Indian villages, lest a concentration in one town result in economic hardship. Some were teachers of the shawm, rebec, viol, harp, fife, and drum, to name a few. At least twenty-one secular musicians are known to have been active in Peru before 1553. As in Mexico, they spread through the countryside, introducing European music to the Indians.

Conservatism vs. innovation

Music in the New World retained its Renaissance characteristics in varying degrees, just as stylistic traits associated with Renaissance music in Europe persisted to different extents in different places and in different musical genres. The persistence of these traits in both the Old and New Worlds depended upon two major conditions. First, the remoteness of an area from the major centers of culture sometimes created a time lag between the development of a new style in the urban centers and its adoption in more rural settings. Second, liturgical music itself tended to be more conservative than para-liturgical forms, such as the villancico, or secular music in general.

Examples of the second principle can be found throughout Latin America, but let us examine just one: Mexico. Although Baroque elements in para-liturgical music—the two-voice texture over a bass line, for instance—had appeared far earlier, Renaissance elements retained their currency in Mexican church music for more than a century longer than in Europe. Composers active in Puebla and Mexico City, like Juan Gutiérrez de Padilla (c. 1590–1664) and Francisco López Capilla (c. 1612–1673), conserved Renaissance practices to such an extent that López Capilla not only wrote a hexachord Mass in the tradition of Brumel, Morales, and Palestrina, but also interested himself so much in mensural devices that he has been called "the Ockeghem of Mexico."[10] Both of these men lived well into the period normally considered the "Baroque era."

Prima prattica survivals

Summary

This chapter has traced some of the main musical elements brought to the Americas before 1600. The American Indians arrived thousands of years before Columbus. Each different tribe had its distinctive culture, and, of course, its own music. The most complex Indian civilizations had musical organizations and activities that in many ways paralleled those in Europe. Song-and-dance festivals were held, and musicians played for sacred and secular ceremonial functions as well as for the entertainment of nobles.

The coming of Europeans and their subsequent conquest of much of the Americas imposed Old World musical elements on the existing indigenous musical culture—when that culture and its supporting civilization were not totally destroyed. Both *ministriles* and missionaries became teachers, thus transmitting their musical heritage to the colonies. Many Indians and mestizos became extremely proficient in the new musical styles.

Finally, the importation of African and African-descended slaves to serve the Europeans and Creoles provided another important source for the development of music in the Americas. Such compositions as the *negros* found in both Europe and Latin America attest to the black influence on European composers, and many references to black musicians playing for public celebrations as well as for their own entertainment show that they were highly prized as performers.

Notes

1. Garcilasco de la Vega, *Royal Commentaries of the Incas,* trans. Harold V. Livermore (Austin and London: University of Texas Press, 1966), p. 125.

2. Samuel Eliot Morison, ed. and trans., *Journals and Other Documents on the Life and Voyages of Christopher Columbus* (New York: Heritage Press, 1963), p. 230.
3. Samuel Eliot Morison, *The European Discovery of America: The Southern Voyages, A.D. 1492–1616* (New York: Oxford University Press, 1974), p. 179.
4. John Smith, quoted in Morison, *The European Discovery . . . Southern Voyages,* p. 182.
5. Morison, *Journals,* p. 267.
6. Ibid., p. 241.
7. Cited in Samuel Eliot Morison, *The European Discovery of America: The Northern Voyages* (New York: Oxford University Press, 1971), p. 573.
8. Samuel Claro Valdés, *Antología de la música colonial en América del Sur* (Santiago de Chile: Universidad de Chile, 1974), p. xxvii. (Claro)
9. Francesco Cervantes de Salazar, cited in Robert Stevenson, *Music in Aztec and Inca Territory* (Berkeley and Los Angeles: University of California Press, 1968, rev. 1976), p. 201.
10. Lincoln Spiess and Thomas Stanford, *An Introduction to Certain Mexican Musical Archives* (Detroit: Information Coordinators, 1969), p. 37.

Bibliography

Books and Articles

ARCINIEGAS, GERMÁN. *Latin America: A Cultural History*. New York: Alfred A. Knopf, 1967.

BÉHAGUE, GERARD. *Music in Latin America*. Englewood Cliffs, N.J.: Prentice-Hall, 1979.

CASTEDO, LEOPOLDO. *A History of Latin American Art and Architecture from Pre-Columbian Times to the Present*. New York and Washington: Frederick Praeger, 1969.

CHASE, GILBERT. *A Guide to the Music of Latin America*, 2nd ed., rev. and enl. Washington, D.C.: Library of Congress and the Pan American Union, 1962; reprint, New York: AMS Press, 1972.

———. *America's Music*, 3rd ed. Urbana, Ill.: University of Illinois Press (in press).

ESTRADA, JESUS. *Música y músicos de la epoca virreinal*. Mexico: Secretaría de Educación Pública, 1973.

HITCHCOCK, H. WILEY. *Music in the United States: A Historical Introduction*, 2nd ed. Englewood Cliffs, N.J.: Prentice-Hall, 1974.

KALLMANN, HELMUT. *A History of Music in Canada, 1534–1914*. Toronto: University of Toronto Press, 1960.

KELEMEN, PÁL. *Art of the Americas, Ancient and Hispanic*. New York: Thomas Y. Crowell, 1969.

MORISON, SAMUEL ELIOT. *The European Discovery of America: The Northern Voyages*. New York: Oxford University Press, 1971.

———. *The European Discovery of America: The Southern Voyages*. New York: Oxford University Press, 1974.

SPIESS, LINCOLN, and STANFORD, THOMAS. *An Introduction to Certain Mexican Musical Archives*. Detroit Studies in Music Bibliography, 15. Detroit: Information Coordinators, 1969.

STEVENSON, ROBERT. "European Music in Sixteenth-Century Guatemala." *Musical Quarterly* 50, no. 3 (1964):341–52.

———. *A Guide to Caribbean Music History*. Lima: Ediciones Cultura, 1975. (From the beginning, but particularly good on the later period, especially the eighteenth century.)

————. *Music in Aztec and Inca Terrritory*. Berkeley and Los Angeles: University of California Press, 1968 (reprint, with revisions, 1976).

————. *Renaissance and Baroque Musical Sources in the Americas*. Washington, D.C.: General Secretariat, Organization of American States, 1970.

————. "The Western Hemisphere: From the beginning to 1600." In *Music from the Middle Ages to the Renaissance,* ed. F. W. Sternfeld. New York: Praeger, 1973.

THOMPSON, ANNIE FIGUEROA, comp. *Annotated Bibliography of Writings about Music in Puerto Rico*. MLA index and bibliography series, 12. Ann Arbor, Mich.: Music Library Association, 1974.

Scores

The Latin American Music Center of the School of Music, Indiana University, Bloomington, Indiana, maintains an extensive score, record, and tape library. Many of these materials circulate outside the university community. Those works by a particular composer desired by students may be found by consulting:

ORREGO-SALAS, JUAN A., ed. *Music from Latin America Available at Indiana University*. Bloomington, Indiana: Latin American Music Center, School of Music, Indiana University, 1971.

Two more recent score anthologies contain Latin American music up to c. 1800. These are important collections:

CLARO VALDÉS, SAMUEL. *Antología de la música colonial en América del Sur*. Santiago de Chile: Ediciones de la Universidad de Chile, 1974.

STEVENSON, ROBERT. *Latin American Colonial Music Anthology*. Washington, D.C.: Organization of American States, General Secretariat, 1975.

37

Baroque Music and the New World

IN the Americas the Baroque era found expression in painting, the building of elaborate structures, and the composition of ceremonial music. Art, literature, and music usually flourished in wealthy colonies with comparatively stable governments, adequate protection from the incursions of other nations, and the ability to resist rebellions from within. In this chapter we will discuss the development of musical styles in such areas as Peru, Mexico, Argentina, Puritan New England, and French Canada.

Music in Spanish Colonial Life

Secular Music: Spanish American Baroque Opera

Early works
Opera may have begun in Lima as early as 1672, when *El arco de Noé* ("Noah's Ark") was presented under the patronage of the viceroy of Peru. Elaborately staged in the Baroque manner, this sacred play was set to musical recitative.

Torrejón y Velasco
As a page to a Spanish grandee, Tomás de Torrejón y Velascó (1644–1728) probably witnessed the first Spanish operas, *La púrpura de la rosa* ("The Blood of the Rose") and *Celos aun del aire matan*. When his employer became viceroy of Peru (1667), Torrejón and his wife sailed for the New World. In 1676 Torrejón became chapelmaster of Lima Cathedral.

La púrpura de la rosa
Commissioned by the then-viceroy of Lima to write an opera celebrating Philip V's eighteenth birthday, Torrejón chose *La púrpura de la rosa* as his subject. The five-hour opera had a libretto with seventeen characters, and the text is itself typically Spanish, in that it intersperses a comic plot developed by a trio of jealous peasants with the myth of Venus and Adonis. As in the operas of Monteverdi, musical refrains portray psychological states and differentiate among characters. However, the use of each such motto is limited to one scene. Torrejón gives each new emotion new music, but if the affect

854

Ex. 37.1   Tomás de Torrejón y Velasco, *La púrpura de la rosa*

5 times
(ending on D*)

remains the same he repeats the music for each succeeding similar quatrain. For instance, when Mars and Bellona talk of war, the composer introduces a repeating bass in dotted rhythms to depict the martial mood (Example 37.1). Cross-relations, conflicts of major and minor, and imitation among solo voices and continuo parts also emphasize the meaning of the text.

Spreading Italian Influence

After the coming to power of the House of Bourbon, the Spanish taste for Italian music spread to Hispano-America. The careers of numerous musicians mirror this development, but we will limit our discussion of Italian Baroque elements in New World secular music to one representative composer active in each viceregal capital: Roque Ceruti and Manuel de Zumaya.

Roque Ceruti

Milan-born Roque Ceruti (d. 1760) became director of music and leader of the nine European musicians employed by the Marquis Castell dos Rius in Spain. He followed his employer to the New World when the Marquis was appointed viceroy of Peru by Philip V (1707). The court of Madrid was fond of the Italian style and particularly favored Neapolitan opera. With the dominance of this music came the eclipse of the Spanish style exemplified by Torrejón. Ceruti's arrival in Peru is generally accepted as the beginning of Italian musical hegemony in the Hispanic New World.

Ceruti was probably the first composer in Lima to use recitativo accompagnato. One admiring contemporary compared Ceruti's works to those of Arcangelo Corelli. Ceruti's vigorous rhythmic style and preference for tonic, dominant, and subdominant harmonies was not shared by later Lima composers. From the time the viceroy asked him to compose the incidental music for *El mejor escudo de Perseo* ("Perseus' Best Shield," 1708), Italian elements were evident in both Ceruti's secular and sacred music. As with many successful composers in Latin America, Ceruti was equally adept at composing church, theater, and popular-style devotional music.

Manuel de Zumaya

The creole Manuel de Zumaya (c. 1678–1756) seems to have spent his entire life in Mexico. Beginning his musical training in the customary way, as a *seise* (choirboy) at Mexico City Cathedral, Zumaya came under the tutelage of Spanish-trained Antonio de Salazar (fl. 1690), who became *maestro de capilla* (chapelmaster) there in 1679.

In addition to fulfilling his Cathedral duties, Zumaya found time to compose music for the secular stage. The viceregal court itself was probably the only institution wealthy enough to subsidize the production of full-scale music dramas. Zumaya's first opera, *El Rodrigo* (1708), dealing with Roderick, king of the Visigoths, is presumed to have had music similar to that in contemporary Spanish comedies, but only its text is now extant. When the new viceroy, an aficionado of the newly popular Neapolitan opera style, arrived in Mexico City, Zumaya, too, came under this influence. He translated Italian libretti into Spanish and set them to music. The only one of Zumaya's efforts in this genre that we know by name is *La Parténope* (1711), of which the music is not extant. Produced the same year that Handel's first opera was presented in England, it was the first three-act opera composed and presented in North America. The text, a Spanish translation of Silvio Stampiglia's 1699 Neapolitan libretto of the same name, was later revised and set to new music by Handel (1730).

Other Secular Music

Chamber music   Although instrumental music often accompanied church worship, some was essentially secular in intent. Corelli was represented in New World instrumental collections, and an important Mexican manuscript dating from the first half of the eighteenth century (Mexico City, National Library MS 1560, olim 1686) lists his compositions and works by several other composers as well as some anonymous works. Dutch, French, Jewish, and black influences were also felt in Mexico. Black entertainers enjoyed great popularity. **"Oratorios"**   Their productions were called *oratorios,* but these had nothing in common with the oratorio of the Old World. They began as expressions of homage to the Virgin, the Holy Cross, or a saint, but evolved into essentially secular festivities, including music, dancing, refreshments, and eventually poetry reading to musical accompaniment. They were banned by edict on December 5, 1643, but blacks and mulattoes continued to be arrested for organizing such performances. All races and social classes enjoyed these presentations, and by 1746 when a citizen of Guadalajara complained about such goings-on, the Court of the Inquisition itself refused to intervene. The judges' argument: if the best citizens of the town considered it harmless entertainment, why should the Inquisition interfere?

Liturgical and Church-Related Music

The Peruvian Masters

Araujo   Three Baroque composers in Peru are preeminent: Tomás de Torrejón y Velasco, Juan de Araujo (1646–1712), and Roque Ceruti. Their works will be discussed in the order of the composers' accession to the post of maestro de capilla of Lima Cathedral.

Arriving in Lima from Spain in 1667, Araujo may have studied with Torrejón. Although Torrejón's works are dramatic, Araujo's are marked by polychoral effects, contrapuntal subtlety, sprightly rhythms, and melodic inventiveness. Araujo was peripatetic, acting as maestro de capilla in Lima (1670–1676), then traveling to Panama and possibly to Guatemala as well (c. 1676–1679), serving briefly in Cuzco Cathedral, and ending his days in the then-wealthy Cathedral of La Plata (today Sucre), Bolivia. In La Plata (1680–1712) he had at his disposal about fifty vocalists and instruments, a large force in those days, even for Europe.

Among Araujo's compositions for the musicians of La Plata's cathedral is *Fuego de amor* ("Love's Fire"), a polychoral work for four choirs with basso continuo played by the harp (a favored continuo instrument in Hispano-America). Consisting of four verses (*coplas*) and a refrain (*texto*), the work alternates between homophonic and contrapuntal textures and uses polychoral effects and solo-choral dialogue as well. Considerable interplay takes place between modality and the key of F major. *Fuego de amor* is a para-liturgical villancico with a text in Spanish, written in honor of the Most Holy Sacrament. Its opening demonstrates Araujo's contrapuntal and homophonic styles, as well as his juxtaposition of binary and ternary rhythms.

Fuego de amor

An illustration showing the disposition of various types of instruments within a church setting. From an eighteenth-century *Libro de Canto Llano, II.* (Photo courtesy Thomas Stanford)

Torrejón   Araujo's successor and the last maestro de capilla in the Spanish tradition to work in Lima Cathedral, Torrejón held the post until his death. An example of his polychoral technique is his *Lamentation* No. 2, a setting for two choirs and basso continuo of the first Lection for the first Nocturne of Matins for Holy Thursday (Claro, pp. 165–67).

Ceruti   The Italian Ceruti succeeded Torrejón as chapelmaster in 1728. His liturgical and para-liturgical music generally adheres closely to central-Baroque musical style. Frequently, as in his Christmas villancico entitled *A cantar un villancico* ("To Sing a Villancico"), for two singers, two violins, and basso continuo, the piece is a miniature cantata of the type so popular in Spain in the early eighteenth century.

The Mexican Masters

As we saw in Chapter 36, many *prima prattica* elements survived in Neo-Hispanic Baroque music, and they coexisted with Baroque tendencies and techniques. Works by Juan Gutiérrez de Padilla and López Capilla are in this category. Major musical centers of Baroque Mexico included Mexico City, Jalisco, Michoacán, Oaxaca, and Puebla. The last-named had musical resources rivaling those in the viceregal capital itself. The double choir of the Puebla Cathedral provided musical forces adequate for the performance of polychoral works, such as those by Padilla.

Other Centers

Elaborate religious music required support by rich organizations and individuals. Areas such as Argentina and Colombia became increasingly important and were able to attract many able musicians and composers. The Jesuit **Argentina:** organist-composer Domenico Zipoli (1688–1726) was born near Florence, **Zipoli** studied with Alessandro Scarlatti in Naples, and completed his musical education under Pasquini in Rome. He published his *Sonate d'intavolatura per organo e cimbalo* ("Sonatas in Tablature for Organ and Harpsichord," Rome, 1716) and left for the New World the following year. He settled in Córdoba, Argentina, where he was organist of the Jesuit church until his death. Melodic invention, counterpoint, and (especially in his keyboard music) imaginative figurations combine with Baroque sequences and link his work both to the Baroque and to the Preclassic style of another Pasquini pupil, Domenico Scarlatti.

Colombia: Starting in 1690, Juan de Herrera served as chapelmaster in the Convent of **Herrera** Santa Inés in Bogotá. His thirty-five-year service as chapelmaster of Bogotá Cathedral was a mixed blessing. Although Herrera was a distinguished composer, he was not a disciplinarian, and as the quality of the cathedral's music itself improved, the quality of performance deteriorated. Yet despite protests, Herrera maintained his position until his death. The majority of Herrera's works are in Latin, but he did write some in Spanish, usually for two or three voices with continuo. Religious works predominate, including six Masses.

Portuguese America

Brazil's art-music tradition developed far more slowly than that of Hispano-America. For the first two centuries of Portuguese rule, Brazil lacked the formidable system of church organization that had provided such a spur to musical production in the Hispanic New World. Art-music activities were concerned primarily with performances of church music, but none of the actual music from this period has been found. We have only written documents that mention instances of music-making and composers in such Brazilian cities as Olinda and Recife in Pernambuco State, and Bahia in Salvador State. Even less material is available on musical life in São Paulo and Rio de Janeiro prior to the mid-eighteenth century.

Bahia

As the capital of Brazil until 1763, Bahia was important both politically and musically. Its cathedral, in which music played a major role at all times, had maintained an official chapelmaster as early as 1559. Such posts required the chapelmaster to compose music as well as to teach, sing, play at least one instrument well, and conduct the choir. In addition, he controlled all music performed in his area, and was able to grant or deny permission to anyone who wished to conduct a musical group.

Frei Agonstinho de Santa Monica (1633–1713) became *mestre de capela* in Bahia during the 1680s and held the post until about 1703. He is reported to have written many polychoral Masses and other liturgical works, but they have not yet been found.

The first archdiocesan council, which met in Bahia in 1707, enjoyed performances by local musicians, according to an account published in Lisbon in 1719. We have also a written reference to the 1728 performance of a Te Deum, whose singers and musicians were divided into four choruses, and to the practice of having three alternating choirs for psalmody.

Early performances of secular music in Bahia date back to the seventeenth century. In 1662, in honor of the wedding of the Portuguese infanta Dona Catarina to Charles II of England, a stage work with music was given. The performance of Spanish plays with incidental music was the rule in Brazil, and works by Calderón are known to have been presented in this way.

Rio de Janeiro

Prior to 1763, when it became the capital city of Brazil, Rio de Janeiro was a less important center than Bahia. However, there as well we have evidence of considerable musical activity during the seventeenth and early eighteenth centuries. Among the seventeenth-century monks associated with the Mosteiro São Bento were the organists Frei Plácido Barbosa, Frei Plácido das Chagas, and Frei Francisco da Cruz. Two priest-chapelmasters were active in Rio de Janeiro during the mid-seventeenth century—Padre Cosme Ramos de Moraes, named mestre da capela in 1645, and Padre Manoel da Fonseca, named to that post in 1653. Between then and the mid-eighteenth century, the name of São Paulo–born chapelmaster Antônio Nunes de Siqueira (1692–1759) is the only one known to us.

Fonseca   One Brazilian composer spent time in Italy. Born in Rio de Janeiro in 1681, João Seyxas da Fonseca studied in Bahia. From there he went to Italy, where his dedication written for the work entitled *Sonatas de Gravo compostas por Ludovico Justini de Pistoya* ("Keyboard sonatas composed by Ludovico Justini de Pistoya") was published in Florence in 1732. Printed also the same year, the same collection was given another, very significant title: *Sonate Da Cimbalo* [sic] *di piano, e forte detto volgarmente di martelleti . . . composte Da D. Lodovico Giustini da Pistoya,* Op. 1 ("Sonatas for the keyboard pianoforte, popularly called the one with the little hammers . . . composed by D. Lodovico Giustini da Pistoya"). As has been shown by musicologists William S. Newman and Robert Stevenson, this publication is of great importance: it marks the first time in the history of music that a composition that can be accurately dated calls specifically for performance by a pianoforte.[1]

Pernambuco

Pernambuco also had important musicians. Among them was the seventeenth-century mestre da capela at the cathedrals of Bahia and Olinda, Father João de Lima. None of his works can be found today, but even half a century after he died his music was still considered a valuable teaching aid. Born in 1688 in Recife, Father Inácio Ribeiro Noya (also spelled Nóia), whose date and place of death are unknown, was famous during his lifetime as both composer and performer. His works, like those of Father João, have been lost. During the seventeenth and eighteenth centuries, about six hundred musicians—including singers, instrumentalists, composers, and organ builders— were active in Pernambuco.

São Paulo

The Cathedral of São Paulo was established in 1611. It always had a chapelmaster, and the names of the men who served in that capacity during the Baroque era have been preserved in cathedral records. Not until the late eighteenth century, however, did São Paulo Cathedral encourage the composition of elaborate sacred music which has survived to the present day.

Music in the English and German Colonies

Jamestown

There were English settlers in the Americas before 1607, but their efforts at colonization were both unsuccessful and short-lived. It is not until the founding of Jamestown, Virginia, in 1607 that we can speak of permanent English settlements in the New World. The Jamestown colonists—as distinguished, for example, from the Puritans who were to arrive in 1620 and from the convicted debtors who were to be Georgia's settlers in 1733—were a heterogeneous although basically Anglican group, united in their mercantile interests and controlled by Puritans living in England.

Coming to the New World at a time when England was in the midst of an artistic golden age, the Jamestown settlers had a heritage that was rich in literature and in music by such composers as Dowland, Bull, and Morley. The colonists were doubtless familiar with this culture and preserved it as well as they could in their new environment. Just as they did in the Old World, the Jamestown colonists used drums and trumpets on state occasions and in battle. The lack of mention of psalmody in Virginia before 1624 may simply have resulted from such practices being taken for granted by the colonists. Other forms of music were certainly present, as is proved by John Smith's description of a celebration in Bermuda (then considered part of the Virginia colony) in 1609: "neither was the afternoone without musicke and dancing."[2] The types of music heard in Virginia were the same as those later found in Puritan New England.

The Puritans

Contrary to some earlier, erroneous impressions of their lifestyle, Puritans enjoyed the good things of life—among them, eating, drinking, dressing up, socializing, reading, and making music well. The Puritan refugees who sought religious asylum in Holland continued these practices. A contemporary account describes the festivities before one contingent of Puritans left Holland to found their first New World colony:

When the ship was ready to carry us away, the bretheren . . . that stayed at Leyden feasted us that were to go, at our pastor's house, being large; where we refreshed ourselves, after tears, with singing of psalms, making joyful melody in our hearts as well as with the voice, there being many of our congregation very expert in music; and indeed it was the sweetest melody that ever mine ears heard.[3]

The psalms referred to are those of the Sternhold and Hopkins Psalter and the Ainsworth Psalter. (The Sternhold and Hopkins Psalter was used in Jamestown as well.)

Although the Puritans disapproved of the use of instruments during worship, they never legally banned instrumental music. Musical instruments and music books were mentioned before 1700, both in the wills of American Puritans and in their diaries. One diary entry indicates not only that keyboard instruments, specifically the virginal, were popular in New England, but that the region even boasted an instrument tuner and repairer.

Anglo-American Secular Music

The early eighteenth century marked the beginning of opera and concert life in Anglo-America. But this secular music was certainly not the first in the Anglo-American tradition to be heard in the New World. Not only could cultured colonists perform and listen to Elizabethan and later English and continental secular music, but all social classes could also enjoy the "popular music" of the day.

Popular music

Anglo-American popular music consisted in part of hundreds of songs that formed the English, Scottish, and Irish repertoire. These had been passed down by rote from generation to generation, and thus have been called "the oral tradition" by modern scholars. Because the first colonial music printers were generally connected with the Church, they did not bother to record such popular music, which was useless for their purposes. Since the words and the music were not written down during the early years, the more than one hundred Anglo-American songs that still survive in the United States and Canada do so in varying versions.

Not all the Anglo-American songs brought to the New World survived the voyage for very long. Among the casualties were songs with aristocratic and chivalric texts, which were alien to the colonists' experiences. However, songs like *Barbara Allen,* and others that dealt with sexual frustration, pain, and rivalry, were perennial favorites, especially those that related events from the woman's point of view. Other popular songs, such as *Captain Kidd,* had historical texts describing New World events. Some texts were changed to reflect colonial experiences. An example is the Anglo-Irish ballad *The Red Herring Song* (also known as *My Jolly Herring*), which became a comic tale of Yankee ingenuity, receiving the New World title *The Sow Took the Measles.*

British popular and traditional musical publications, as mentioned above, were also available in the colonies. Secular collections published in England by Ravenscroft, Playford, d'Urfey, Watt, and Walsh, spanning the period 1609–1731, also influenced colonial tastes.

Religious Music in the New England Colonies

Perhaps the best-known Baroque music in the New World is the religious repertory brought to Massachusetts by the Puritans. What had once been a culturally knowledgeable group of people, however, became in succeeding generations progressively less sophisticated musically. By the time music was

Bay Psalm Book

included in the *Bay Psalm Book* (1698), only thirteen tunes with basses were given. To these melodies, the Puritans were expected to sing all 150 psalms. It was possible to do so because the psalms had only three types of metric structure:

Metric Structure of Puritan Psalms

Type	Metric Structure
common meter	syllables per line: 8, 6, 8, 6, etc.
long meter	syllables per line: 8
irregular meter	syllables per line: 6, 6, 8, 6, etc.

This reliance on codification reflected a desire to simplify the repertory. It was now considered too difficult for congregations to sing these pieces by rote (most members could no longer read music), and even some precentors (members of the congregation whose special job was to sing each line of the melody before the other members) were having difficulty. (Using a lead singer to "line out" a tune was by no means confined to Puritan New England. We find this practice again in southern black congregations during the nineteenth century.)

As the quality of congregational performance deteriorated during the eighteenth century, the educated clergy began to call for reform, propagandizing the practice of singing by note ("regular singing") rather than by rote ("the common way" or "the usual way"). The latter had become the norm, especially in rural areas where most churchgoers were illiterate, and led to results that Cotton Mather (1663–1728) disapprovingly described as "an odd noise"[4] in 1721.

The call for "regular singing"

Ephrata Cloister

In 1732 a group of German religious refugees founded a celibate community based on Seventh-Day Baptist (Dunker) principles in Pennsylvania, the Quaker colony that had long since become a haven for the persecuted. Ephrata Cloister, as it was known, was directed by the indefatigable Conrad Beissel (1690–1768). Not only did he lead the choir—which he trained until it could sing eight-part music—but he also found time to write more than a thousand religious works.

Beissel was almost entirely self-taught. His style is marked by direct modulation, parallel perfect intervals, and a rhythm that follows the text. He may have used instrumental doubling of vocal parts, and the bass part itself may have been entirely instrumental. His *Gott ein herrscher aller Heyden* ("God, Ruler of All Lands," 1754) is representative of his compositions (*MA*, pp. 64–66),[5] containing no evidence of sophisticated counterpoint and using dissonances only as passing tones. Although colonial leaders such as Benjamin Franklin were aware of Ephrata's activities, its music did not influence America's musical mainstream.

French Settlements

As early as the 1530s, the French had begun to explore New France, which came to include parts of what is now central and eastern Canada and the Mississippi River basin. But it was not until 1608 that Quebec, France's first permanent American settlement, was established by Samuel de Champlain (c. 1570–1635). Despite efforts to attract colonists to the Canadian portion of this territory, reports of severe winters discouraged many. In addition, the Huguenots, who might willingly have emigrated to escape religious persecution at home, were expressly forbidden to do so by French law. Before 1730 the French New World possessions extended from Labrador on the north to Louisiana on the south, bordering the English Atlantic colonies on the east, and the as-yet-unsettled western portion of what is now the United States and Canada on the west.

Nonliturgical and Secular Music in New France

Port Royal (now Annapolis Royal), Nova Scotia, was the scene of the first known performance of a masque in New France. On November 14, 1606, only a year after the founding of this settlement, Marc Lescarbot's *Le Théâtre de Neptune* ("The Theater of Neptune") was performed in honor of the safe return of the colony's leader, Baron de Pontrincourt. Written especially for this occasion, the work was presented on floating barges. Its musical interest lies in its trumpet cue and in a short verse designated for four-part singing. According to the distinguished Canadian ethnomusicologist and folklorist Marius Barbeau, this part-song was sung to the tune of the sixteenth-century French song *La Petite Galiotte de France* ("The Little French Schooner").

Use of French folk songs

French folk songs were often used by the missionaries in their work with the Indians. When the original liturgical and para-liturgical melodies did not fit the Indian-language translations they had made, these men fitted the words to other music. An example of this hybridization is *Jesous Ahatonhia* (also known as the *Noël Huron*), which has been called "America's first Christmas carol."[6] Père Juan de Brebeuf is credited with writing the Huron words that relate the story of Christmas in a manner that reflects the Huron environment and experience. A slightly modified version of the French six-teenth-century song *Une Jeune Pucelle* ("A Young Maiden") was used for the music. This work was written down in approximately 1641.

As in Anglo-America, the colonists of New France had brought with them secular folk songs that were an established part of their oral tradition. The French missionaries refused to consider this heritage of any special importance, except as it might occasionally help them in their work. Ninety percent of the seven to ten thousand songs that have been collected in Quebec Province predate 1673, and it has been established that most entered Canada during a great wave of French immigration to New France between 1665 and 1673.

As for other secular music in New France, the powerful Jesuits frowned on it. They roundly condemned the first formal ball (1667), and they suppressed seventeenth-century theatrical performances that included incidental music, a genre that did not thrive again until the late eighteenth century.

Religious Music in New France

Those who were best organized and able to preserve whatever they could were the missionaries, who considered the Catholic Church and the propagation of the faith their major concern. Thus it is not surprising that the first extant composition written in Canada was a prose for the Mass of the Holy Family composed by Charles-Amador Martin (1648–1711), the second Canadian to be ordained a priest (1671). He studied at the Jesuit college in Quebec and later became a canon of Quebec Cathedral. The melodic line of this plainchant (probably composed in 1674 or later) shows the fluidity with which Martin treated the voice.

The Anglo-French wars that raged during the seventeenth and early eighteenth centuries in what is now Canadian territory caused unrest and conse- **Political** quently inhibited the development of music. Records show that new organs **unrest** were installed in churches in new communities, and we might logically as- **and music** sume that music continuously functioned in secular as well as sacred contexts, but comparatively little is known about music in Canada during the early eighteenth century.

Summary

Musical activities in the various centers of the New World are not equally well documented, but surviving evidence indicates that music everywhere formed an important part of sacred and secular occasions.

A strong emphasis on professionalism and the conservation of tradition existed in the wealthier Spanish colonies, where sacred and secular music following the tastes of the mother country continued to be written. Before 1701 musical practices were almost exclusively Iberian, but with the arrival of Roque Ceruti, the balance quickly shifted in favor of Italian forms and practices both in church-related and in non–church-related compositions.

Because of the many Protestant sects that arrived in the English-owned New World territories, religious and musical customs varied among the different groups, and within the same group in different generations. A trend toward simplification and codification is evident in the practices advocated by the *Bay Psalm Book* (1698) and a generation later by Cotton Mather (1721). Within the English sphere of influence, other musical traditions, such as that of Ephrata Cloister, also flourished.

The highly unsettled quality of life in disputed areas like the Caribbean and Quebec inhibited the growth of the kinds of formal structures and associations that fostered musical life on the European model elsewhere in the New World.

Notes

1. William S. Newman, *The Sonata in the Baroque Era,* 3rd ed. (New York: W. W. Norton, 1972), pp. 194–195, 404.
2. Cited in Victor Yellin, "Musical Activity in Virginia before 1620," *Journal of the American Musicological Society* 22, no. 2 (Summer 1969): 289.
3. Cited in Percy A. Scholes, *The Puritans and Music* (New York: Russell and Russell, 1962), p. 3.
4. Cited in ibid., p. 37.
5. W. Thomas Marrocco and Harold Gleason, *Music in America* (New York: W. W. Norton, 1964, reprint 1974). (*MA*)
6. Helmut Kallmann, *A History of Music in Canada, 1534–1914* (Toronto: University of Toronto Press, 1960), p. 13.

Bibliography

Books and Articles

For general books spanning the entire period covered by the New World section, consult Bibliography of Chapter 36. Other especially useful studies include these general works:

GIBSON, CHARLES. *Spain in America.* New York: Harper Colophon Books, 1967.

KELEMEN, PÁL. *Baroque and Rococo in Latin America,* 2 vols. New York: Dover, 1967.

LEONARD, IRVING A. *Baroque Times in Old Mexico.* Ann Arbor, Mich.: Ann Arbor Paperbacks, 1966.

WRIGHT, LOUIS B. *The Cultural Life of the American Colonies, 1607–1763.* New York: Harper Torchbooks, 1962.

For Anglo-American music, the following are representative of the best scholarly studies:

AMTMANN, WILLY. *Music in Canada, 1600–1800.* Montreal: Habitex Books, 1975.

LOWENS, IRVING. *Music and Musicians in Early America.* New York: W. W. Norton, 1964.

SOUTHERN, EILEEN. *The Music of Black Americans: A History.* New York: W. W. Norton, 1971.

———, ed. *Readings in Black American Music.* New York: W. W. Norton, 1971.

STEVENSON, ROBERT. *Protestant Church Music in America.* New York: W. W. Norton, 1966.

Special studies of Latin American Baroque subjects may be added to the more general ones listed in the Bibliography of Chapter 36:

AYESTARÁN, LAURO. "El barroco musical hispanoamericano." *Yearbook of the Inter-American Institute for Musical Research,* vol. 1 (1965), pp. 55–93.

———. "Domenico Zipoli y el barroco musical sudamericano." *Revista musical chilena* 16, nos. 81–82 (July–Dec. 1962): 94–124.

CATALYNE, ALICE RAY. "Manuel de Zumaya (c. 1678–1756): Mexican Composer for Church and Theater." *Festival Essays for Pauline Alderman,* ed. Burton L. Karson. Provo, Utah: Brigham Young University Press, 1976.

DINIZ, JAIME C. *"Músicos pernambucanos do passado,* 2 vols. Recife: Universidade Federal de Pernambuco, 1969–1971.

STEVENSON, ROBERT. "The South American Lyric Stage to 1880." *Inter-American Music Bulletin* 87 (July–Oct. 1973): 1–25.

———. "Opera Beginnings in the New World." *Musical Quarterly* 45, no. 1 (Jan. 1959): 8–25.

———. "Some Portuguese Sources for Early Brazilian Music History." *Yearbook of the Inter-American Institute for Musical Research,* vol. 4 (1968), pp. 1–43.

Scores

In addition to the anthologies mentioned in the list of scores for Chapter 36, the following are particularly relevant to Chapter 37.

Anglo-America

APPEL, RICHARD G. *The Music of the Bay Psalm Book: 9th Edition (1698).* Brooklyn, N.Y.: Institute for Studies in American Music, 1976.

MARROCCO, W. THOMAS, and GLEASON, HAROLD, eds. *Music in America, An Anthology.* New York: W. W. Norton, 1964 (reprint, 1974).

WIENANDT, ELWYN A. *The Bicentennial Collection of American Music: Vol. I (1698– 1800).* Carol Stream, Ill.: Hope Publishing Co., 1974.

Latin America

STEVENSON, ROBERT. *Christmas Music from Baroque Mexico.* Berkeley and Los Angeles: University of California Press, 1974.

————. *Foundations of New World Opera.* Lima: Ediciones "Cultura," 1973. (Includes the first modern edition of Torrejón y Velasco's *La púrpura de la rosa,* along with performance indications.)

VON GAVEL, ARNDT, ed. *Investigaciones musicales de los archivos coloniales en el Peru.* Lima: Associación Artística y Cultural Jueves, 1974.

38

Preclassic and Classic Music
in the Americas

TTEMPTS to classify and popularize existing knowledge, a gradual codification of new artistic forms, and a strong desire for rational explanations of natural phenomena are all hallmarks of the eighteenth-century Enlightenment. During this Age of Reason, many Europeans left their native lands to settle more or less permanently in the New World, while some Americans traveled, studied, and lived in Europe. The political ferment of this age culminated in numerous successful revolts against long-established governments in the New World (the independence movements in the Americas) as well as in the Old (the French Revolution). Dissension at home and armed conflicts abroad had already weakened the Spanish, French, and English monarchies.

Throughout this period of radical change, music continued to be the pastime of both aristocrats and common people, and to serve both religion and the state. In this chapter we will discuss Preclassic and Classic music as exemplified by representative New World composers and compositions of this era.

Hispano-American Music

Women performers

Many Latin American convents, like the Venetian *ospedaletti,* placed great emphasis on training their young female novices in music. Especially during the eighteenth century, the Spanish-American nunnery on a holy day was likely to play host to a public concert at which specially chosen young nuns could be heard singing and playing instruments behind curtained grilles. Frequently these nuns were orphans, whose education was subsidized by wealthy patrons. Large archives of eighteenth-century cantatas, arias, masses, sonatas, suites, fugues, and overtures have been found, which show that they performed secular as well as sacred music. Little solo organ music has been found, however.

Outdoor music

Outdoor music was performed at public and private celebrations. Military music was heard everywhere during the revolutionary period of the early nineteenth century, when the armies of such liberators as Simón Bolívar (1783–1830), Francisco de Miranda (1750–1816), José de San Martín (1778–1850), Miguel Hidalgo y Costilla (1753–1811), José Gervaisio Artigas (1774–1850), and Bernardo O'Higgins (1776–1842) clashed with those of Napoleonic Spain, which was determined to keep Hispano-America under its control.

European musicians arrived in the New World, bringing with them their expertise. Africans, too, were brought over in ever-increasing numbers, and their music was heard in the streets, taverns, and public squares, sometimes discussed at length in colonial periodicals, and even collected and transcribed by interested outsiders. Occasionally an exceptionally gifted black performer achieved lasting fame. One of these was the Peruvian troubadour Galindo (d. c. 1800), who almost half a century after his death was still honored by the Peruvian press as an outstanding instrumentalist. **Music and musicians**

Hispano-American art music continued to follow European models throughout this period. Two centers, Cuba and Venezuela, achieved prominence. Music in such other previously important centers as Argentina, Colombia, and Mexico experienced a period of decline, as second-rate foreign musicians or dynasties of uninspired American-born musicians occupied all the important posts.

Hispano-American Composers

Despite its small population (the whole of Cuba had only some 170,000 inhabitants in 1774), Havana became a thriving cultural center during the late eighteenth century. Private performances of works by Calderón and Lope de Vega and public performances by amateur mulatto players preceded the creation of Havana's first public theater (1776), which soon became the site of concert, ballet, opera, and *zarzuela* presentations. The Teatro Principal's resident Spanish theatrical company even gave a New World premiere of Grétry's *Zémire and Azor* in Spanish translation (1791). In these and other performances the theater orchestra usually was supplemented by instrumentalists from the cathedral. Havana's musical taste retained Preclassic and Classic elements until the 1830s. **Cuba**

Cuba's first composer of art music whose works are still extant is Esteban Salas y Castro (1725–1803), who raised music-making in Santiago Cathedral to new artistic heights. While maestro de capilla (1764–1803), he founded a conservatory of music so that both instrumentalists and vocalists could receive professional training. Salas also organized the first Cuban ensemble ever to play symphonies by such composers as Haydn, Pleyel, and Gossec, and religious compositions by Paisiello and Porpora. **Salas y Castro**

All of Salas' extant works are either liturgical or para-liturgical, showing elements of the Classical style as manifested by Haydn, Pergolesi, and Soler. His music exhibits clarity of line and interest in both counterpoint (especially fugue and canon) and varied instrumental timbres. His thirty villancicos (1783–1802) are perhaps the most intimate expression of the composer's musical thought. Written for one, two, three, four, or six voices, these works

Ex. 38.1   Esteban Salas y Castro, *Pues la fábrica de un templo*

Copyright by Alejo Carpentier. Used by permission.

often have instrumental accompaniment and are generally divided into three vocal sections, frequently following this model: *Obertura* (instrumental prelude similar to an Italian overture), *Recitativo, Pastorela* (containing the melody in the instruments, supported by the voice or voices), and *Allegro.* This structure differs radically from the traditional Spanish villancico form of alternating *coplas* and *estribillos.* Salas' *Pues la fábrica de un templo* ("Building a Temple," 1783) begins with an instrumental prelude that resembles Domenico Scarlatti (see Example 38.1). In his larger works Salas shows a concern not only for counterpoint and timbre within movements but also for contrast between them, as in his *Misa de Navidad* ("Christmas Mass") and his *Stabat Mater* (1790).

The Venezuelan Classic School

The late eighteenth century saw the development of the Venezuelan Classic school, whose influence continued into the early nineteenth century. Pedro Ramón Palacios y Sojo (Padre Sojo, 1739–1799) established the Academy of the Oratorio of San Felipe Neri in 1784. Padre Sojo, who had studied in Europe, held musical soirees on his coffee plantation near Caracas which profoundly impressed his guests. Simón Bolívar's teacher, the Venezuelan poet-patriot Andrés Bello (1781–1865), called Padre Sojo "the founder of music in Venezuela."[1]

Musicians who met at Padre Sojo's estate are called the Chacao school (after the region) or the school of Padre Sojo, but the mulatto Juan Manuel

Olivares   Olivares (1760–1797), a violinist, composer, and pianist, was actually their teacher. Only a few of Olivares' works survive, but these show a mastery of the Preclassical and Classical styles. His *Salve* (for three voices and orchestra)

and his *Stabat Mater* (for four voices and orchestra) are among the finest Venezuelan compositions. Olivares' *Dúo de violines* ("Violin Duet") is the only extant secular chamber music of the Venezuelan Classic school.

Another extraordinary musician was José Angel Lamas (1775–1814), whose liturgical music shows supple melodies and careful musical craftsmanship. Among his more than forty extant works is the *Misa en re* ("Mass in D"), of which the *Qui tollis* and *Et incarnatus* are especially effective.

Lamas

We may reach a number of general conclusions about extant Venezuelan Classic works: (1) with the exception of one piece of chamber music and a few patriotic songs, all compositions are either liturgical or para-liturgical; (2) although most works are composed for three or four voices with orchestral accompaniment, a few are still for the old Baroque texture of one or two voices with basso continuo; (3) many works were based on European compositional models, e.g., masses follow the forms typical of those of Haydn and Mozart; (5) composers frequently set Lessons, to which they generally gave the form of cantatas, as Couperin had done before them; (6) works with Spanish texts were more popular in style; in this category are the villancicos and similar compositions.

Venezuelan Classic style

Four-part orchestration was the rule, and the instrumentation is typical of the Mannheim school. The use of instruments follows stereotyped procedures, so that the first violin usually has the melody, and the rest accompany except when the first and second violins are supporting a vocal duet. Tremolos or pizzicatos are rare.

Choral passages frequently contain syncopated sixteenth-note violin figuration. Voices are used homophonically, rarely in imitation, but sequences are common. In three-part choruses (SAT), the tenor does not usually go down to the root of the chord until the end. Primary triads, dominant and diminished-seventh chords, and fairly simple modulations are the rule.[2]

Other Trends and Composers

In the Catholic missions of Texas and California, music followed the rhythm of both secular and religious life and formed an integral part of it. Indians were taught to chant the *Pater noster,* the *Salve,* and the *Ave Maria.* They could also speak Spanish, play instruments, sing, and dance, "perhaps even more beautifully and gracefully than the Spaniards,"[3] according to an account of 1767 from San Antonio. Life in California's twenty or so missions was similar, and we are fortunate that numerous compositions from this period (most of them anonymous) have been found and classified. Some have even been recorded.

In Lima, José de Orejón y Aparicio combined Neapolitan cantata and Spanish villancico techniques, and Baroque with Preclassic elements, as can be seen in his *Ah del gozo!* ("Oh, the Joy!"; Claro, pp. 30–45). The dramatic music of Fray Esteban Ponce de León (c. 1692–175?), an Augustinian monk active in Cuzco, shows similar stylistic mixtures—his opera-serenade *Venid, venid, Deydades* ("Come, Come, O Gods," 1749), for example (Claro, pp. 108–133).

Classical style is reflected in the works of at least nine composers active in Mexico City, but among them Francisco Delgado (fl. c. 1786–1826) was the most important composer of sacred music. His most representative work, the *Missa a quatro voces* ("Mass for Four Voices"), is in a meticulous and fully developed Classical idiom. Delgado's work is further testimony to the internationalism of the Classical style. Although his compositions show many similarities to Haydn's in instrumentation, form, melody, and harmony, no direct influence has yet been proved.

The Portuguese Viceroyalty

Great estates and convents were cultural centers in Brazil, and subversive literature frequently circulated from one intellectual to another as it traveled either from hand to hand in printed form or from teacher to pupil (the ideas of the *Encyclopédistes* were transmitted by the latter method in the seminaries). But the major population centers fostered the greatest development of the arts and music. Performance standards were not always high, however. One French visitor, Louis-Antoine de Bougainville, wrote in 1771:

[The viceroy] reserved a box for us at the opera. We were able to see the master works of Metastasio played by a cast of mulattoes in a very beautiful hall and to listen to divine excerpts from the Italian masters performed by a poor orchestra that a hunch-backed priest in clerical garb was directing at that time.[4]

The plays and operas of Brazilian Antonio José da Silva (1705–1739) continued to be as popular in the second half of the eighteenth century as they had been earlier. It was during a performance of one of his comedies that the Rio opera house in which it was being given burned down in 1776.

The school of Minas Gerais The arts underwent a great flowering in the state of Minas Gerais during the late eighteenth century. Settlement and the building of churches brought with them musical instrument-making and organ-building. Musicians associated with the great growth of art music during this period, however, were mulatto members of local *irmandades* (confraternities) in the cities of Minas Gerais, where such guilds were practically free of Church control. Most musicians received social, monetary, and musical benefits from their irmandades, and these groups produced an important number of eighteenth-century composers.

About a thousand musicians were active in Minas Gerais between 1760 and 1800. As early as 1734, one observer described an elaborate ceremonial procession that had taken place in Vila Rica, complete with singers and instrumentalists. Blacks as well as whites and mulattoes formed the complement of musicians. The inland cities of Minas Gerais knew the latest Preclassical and Classical music, as did those on the coast. Pastimes there included the playing of chamber music by Pleyel, Boccherini, and Haydn. The extraordinary importance of mulattoes to Brazil's cultural and spiritual life can be seen in the fact that the Vila Rica Irmandade de São José dos Bem-Casados (Confraternity of St. Joseph of the Well-Married) eventually changed its name to Irmandade de São José dos Homens Pardos (Confraternity of St. Joseph of the Colored Men [i.e., the mulattoes]).

Among the most important composers between 1760 and 1808 are José Joaquim Emerico Lobo de Mesquita (c. 1740–1805), Marcos Coelho Netto (d. 1823), Francisco Gomes da Rocha (d. 1808), and Ignacio Parreiras Neves (c. 1730–c. 1793). Active in Minas Gerais, they were associated with mulatto musical irmandades there. Of the hundreds of works produced by the Minas Gerais school that have come down to us, all but one composition thus far discovered is in Latin, and all are either liturgical or paraliturgical. Their common stylistic elements include the following Classical traits: (1) extensive use of orchestral strings; (2) harmonic emphasis on tonic, dominant, and subdominant key relationships; (3) clearly articulated modulations, with first and second violins independent melodically; and (4) the presence of a classically balanced chorus (prevalence of the vocal quartet). The only specifically Baroque trait still in evidence is the use of a basso continuo, and that survived into the early nineteenth century even in Europe. Most works of the Minas Gerais school are for four-part string orchestra, with reeds, brasses, and occasionally timpani used as they would have been in Europe. Typical musical forces for them ranged from seven to thirty-seven musicians—a combination of vocalists and instrumentalists that varied from year to year and according to the solemnity of the occasion.

The composition of both organ and chamber music throughout the century in Brazil has not yet been documented, although musicians fully acquainted with works in these genres by contemporaneous Europeans might logically be assumed to have written some of their own. On the other hand, the writing and performance of liturgical and paraliturgical music surpassed all else in the lives of these Brazilians. It was as church musicians that they earned their livelihood.

Instrumental music and opera

Did they also write operas? In Minas Gerais, as in Rio de Janeiro and other Latin American centers, the opera was popular. Mulatto troupes were fairly common throughout the colonial areas of Brazil. However, no Brazilian operatic works dating from this period have yet been found.

Even before the Minas Gerais school flourished, the works of at least one native Brazilian composer combined Baroque and nascent Classic elements. This mulatto composer, Luiz Alvares Pinto (1719–1789), who became the chapelmaster of the Church of São Pedro dos Clérigos in Recife, also founded there the famous irmandade of Santa Cecília dos Músicos. Pinto is credited with writing one of the two oldest extant Brazilian-composed musical works that can be attributed to a specific composer, a Te Deum (c. 1760) for four voices and orchestral accompaniment. In it, the composer shows a clear sense of structure and a preference for binary forms. Most harmonic complications occur in the B sections. The results of Pinto's study with one of the finest teachers in Portugal, as well as his own inventiveness, can be seen in his han-

Other Brazilian centers

dling of double fugue and expressive dissonance. Unfortunately, only the voice, continuo, and horn parts are extant, so it is impossible to analyze Pinto's instrumentation in this work.

André da Silva Gomes

Pinto was only one of a number of composers who worked in Brazil outside of the Minas Gerais district during the late eighteenth and early nineteenth centuries. Brazil's growing prosperity also encouraged the arts in seaports like Bahia, Recife, and nearby Olinda. A slightly more conservative trend held sway in São Paulo. Portuguese-born André da Silva Gomes (1752–1844), brought in by the bishop of São Paulo to moderate the very blatant Italianization and secularization in the works of his predecessors, became chapelmaster at the cathedral there in 1774. A prolific composer of sacred music (at least seventy-six of his works are known), Gomes was famous also as a teacher, and as such he affected later Brazilian music. Typical of his works is the *Missa a 8 vozes e instrumentos* ("Mass for 8 Voices and Instruments"), which shows his command of contrapuntal techniques and his use of expressive harmony.

Rio de Janeiro and J. M. Nunes Garcia

In November 1808, the entire Portuguese court, along with all of its servants and attendants, fled to Brazil to evade capture by Napoleon's armies. After the court's arrival, Brazilian performance standards improved, gifted foreigners were imported by the emperor, promising Brazilians were subsidized and sent abroad to study, and the cultural life of Rio de Janeiro, where the court lived, experienced an era of enormous growth. It was in Rio de Janeiro that Brazil's first acknowledged major composer, José Mauricio Nunes Garcia (1767–1830), was active, and the presence of the emperor's court there was particularly important to his development. José Mauricio (as he is generally referred to in Brazil) was a transitional figure like Beethoven, in both his dates and his musical style. Because the major part of his musical activity and production came after 1800, and particularly after 1808, a more detailed discussion of this composer has been reserved for the next chapter.

Anglo-America: The United States to the War of 1812

Political, economic, intellectual, religious, and artistic ferment sparked by the Enlightenment was widely diffused throughout Anglo-America, and in the other territories that were later to become part of the United States of America. Disagreements and rivalries among the Spanish, English, French, Indians, and Anglo-American colonists often led to armed conflict.

Religion and music

Religious counterparts of the political upheavals were the revival movements that swept Anglo-America periodically during the eighteenth century. Just as the regular-singing movement was promulgating a return to a simpler, more codified way of singing, so, too, did fundamentalist preachers like John Wesley (1703–1791), founder of Methodism, crisscross the colonies decrying the distracting influences of commerce and urbanization on devoutness and urging a return to older, stricter moral codes. Both attitudes were manifestations of the end of ostentatious, ornate late-Baroque sensibilities and the onset of a desire for directness and clarity typical of Classicism.

Little is known about musical composition in Anglo-America prior to 1761, when Peter Pelham, a New York City–based organist, offered to train people in his art. The main emphasis, however, was always on performance rather than on composition, and public performances were generally given by itinerant musicians. In the home, harpsichords and "spinets" (actually small harpsichords) were common, and were played by both men and women. Men generally played violins and flutes; women usually became proficient singers and guitarists. Itinerant musicians offered private instruction in the pupil's home or in special schools set up for the purpose. One even taught in a Philadelphia coffeehouse! A music teacher—or "professor of music" as he was usually called—had a social standing below that of the most important portrait painter but above that of the actor. He was considered a tradesman and commanded the same respect as any other skilled workman. Women, too, taught music as well as other "useful arts," including dancing and needlework.

Stress on performance

A knowledge of music was a status symbol for gentlemen and gentle-

Robert Feke (fl. 1740–1748), *Mrs. Barlow Trecothick* (c. 1748). A woman's role as a singer is shown in this portrait of the wife of a well-to-do colonial gentleman. (Courtesy, Wichita Art Museum: The Roland P. Murdock Collection)

**Music and
gentility**
women, an expected and necessary accomplishment in polite society. One
suitor praised his lady love's ability to play the spinet this way:

> Corelli, Handel, Felton, Nares
> With their concertos, solos, airs
> Are far less sweet to me![5]

Colonials were thoroughly familiar with art music by such composers as Vivaldi, Domenico Scarlatti, Geminiani, Corelli, and Arne, but Handel's compositions had outstripped all others in popularity by the 1760s, and their fame continued to grow throughout the rest of the century in Anglo-America, just as they did in England.

Cultivated colonials played and sang throughout their lives. They passed on the genteel tradition by hiring music teachers for their children. Among those who conformed to this pattern were the notable amateurs Thomas Jefferson, Benjamin Franklin, and Francis Hopkinson. Jefferson was not only an accomplished violinist but also amassed a large and impressive music library, as well as an excellent collection of instruments. All three men provided for the musical education of their sons and daughters.

Southern plantation owners like Jefferson sometimes created a concert life on their estates, just as did those in Brazil and Venezuela. In all three places, blacks played an important part in musical life. Many slaves played for their masters' amusement and for dancing. Freedmen, Indians, and mulattoes were also expected to be musical. Virginia, for instance, was the first colony to require members of all the above groups to serve in its militia as either drummers or trumpeters (1738). The black presence in music extended also to the northern colonies. Even among the Yankee psalmodists, one of the best known, Andrew Law (1748–1821), found that the extraordinary success of one of his black former pupils as a singing-school master was depriving him of students. On October 1, 1786, Law complained to his brother that "Frank the Negro who lived with me . . . takes the bread out of my mouth."[6] (Some local instrument makers, mostly itinerants from Europe, were available, but the majority of colonial instruments were imported from France, Spain, Italy, and Germany.)

**English
theater
music**
In addition to the art-music tradition as such, English theater music continued to be popular. Song collections appeared that contained the "latest hits" from the London stage. Sometimes American-printed books excluded the bawdier favorites from Vauxhall and other theaters in acknowledgment of less boisterous colonial tastes.

The development of operatic performances centered in the area from New York southward. Two active and respected troupes performed eighteenth-century ballad opera in Anglo-America: William Hallam's London
**Ballad
operas**
Company of Comedians and Thomas Wignell and Alexander Reinagle's New Company. The former first performed in Williamsburg (1752), renamed itself the American Company after its move to New York, and then became the Old American Company. Returning to England during the Rev-

olutionary War, it settled once again in New York after the war. The New Company (established in New York in 1792), with its lavish 2,000-seat hall and large stage, vied with the Old American for the loyalty of the New York public. Both presented ballad operas intended to entertain general audiences rather than a small number of cognoscenti. (Similar emphasis was evident, too, in the singing school, with its "masters" and composers.)

Philadelphia

After 1790 New York assumed new importance as a musical center, as did Philadelphia, which, from its early days, had enjoyed an active intellectual and artistic life. George Washington enjoyed musical performances there, first as a delegate to the Constitutional Convention (1787) and later as the first president. On June 12, 1787, Washington attended a concert given by the English musician Alexander Reinagle, who had arrived in the United States in 1786. Reinagle included his own works on the program, together with an overture by J. C. Bach. Reinagle taught music to Washington's adopted daughter.

During Philadelphia's years as the nation's capital (1790–1800), the riotous behavior of theatergoers was inhibited by the presence of military guards stationed in the theater whenever President Washington attended. Otherwise, the audience in the cheaper seats might have resorted to their usual habits, such as throwing food, bottles, or other objects at any time. Generally, theater regulations were ignored, especially the prohibitions against smoking and drinking alcoholic beverages. Prostitutes used theater boxes as their headquarters until 1795, when a new law forbade such persons to take seats in already occupied boxes. Such were the customs at all theaters, including the New Theatre in Chestnut Street (established in 1792 by Thomas Wignell), of which Reinagle was musical director beginning in 1794. Theaters were generally closed during epidemics of yellow fever and other contagious diseases.

Theaters

Joseph, Thomas, and Benjamin Carr were leaders in Philadelphia musical life. They published and sold music, beginning with a music shop in the city (1793), until they branched out, opening similar establishments in Baltimore and New York. Benjamin made a lasting reputation, not only as a singer in ballad operas, arranger, pianist, organist, and composer, but also as an editor and publisher, taking over and renaming the *Musical Journal* (1800) founded by Joseph. Significantly, he deliberately chose to publish both European and American works. In the first issue of his *The Gentleman's Amusement,* Carr published an American composition, a march that with new words by Francis Hopkinson's son Joseph became famous as *Hail Columbia* (1798).

The Carrs

Boston

Not until after 1790 did Boston become a force in opera performances. In fact, it was there that a visiting opera troupe gave the American premiere of a European hit, Grétry's *Richard Coeur de Lion* ("Richard the Lion-hearted," 1797), before taking the production to Philadelphia. (The work, in fact, was performed as far away as Halifax, Nova Scotia, in 1798.)

Charleston

Despite its comparatively small population of ten thousand, colonial Charleston had grown rich on trade in rice and indigo. (Cotton was not to become a major southern crop until the 1790s.) With its reputation as the richest, most artistically and socially conscious Anglo-American urban area, Charleston was a magnet for professional musicians.

Charleston had been a musical and dramatic center as early as the 1730s. The city developed a thriving cultural life, and especially before the Revolution of 1775 was the home of a large community of professional musicians. The St. Cecilia Society, the oldest musical society in the United States, was founded there in 1762. Its private subscription concerts offered a genteel social atmosphere where many elegant colonial ladies mingled with well-born gentlemen—both American and European. The musical fare consisted primarily of works by then-living composers: J. S. Bach's sons, Haydn, and Stamitz, in addition to local musicians and recently arrived immigrants. Society members were extremely eager to hear great quantities of the best available music and to know as soon as possible of the latest European developments. After the Revolutionary War, Charleston's importance as a musical center declined. Its musicians began to move further north, especially to Philadelphia.

New Orleans

In 1792 the public balls for white people, held in New Orleans since the late 1770s, were moved into a specially built hall of their own, the Conde Street Ballroom. Parallel black activities took place at the Coquet Theatre. Legalized by the governor in 1799, these black dances theoretically admitted slaves only with their master's written consent. Soon, however, these balls acquired a bad reputation. Public outdoor dancing by slaves was a frequent sight in New Orleans. In 1786 slaves were forbidden to dance in the public square before the end of the evening church service on Sundays and holy days, but could often be seen dancing on the levees.

Grétry's opera *Sylvain* was given in New Orleans in 1796. Although certainly not the first operatic performance in that city, it was the first for which we have both a definite date as well as the name of the work. The presence of French opera in New Orleans is one more evidence of the territory's intellectual and artistic ties to France.

Anglo-American "Popular" and "Art Music" Traditions

"Popular" and "art music" traditions coexisted in various ways in Anglo-America. Prior to the American Revolution, little of what we would today call original composition existed, because most of the colonists' inventiveness was concentrated instead on composing new verses to already existing tunes. In doing so they were following a longstanding British broadside tradition, typified by Gay's *The Beggar's Opera*.

From the British and other European army detachments, the colonists learned yet another type of music. *Harmoniemusik* was the name given to music played by the bands of six or eight instrumentalists, generally wind players, hired by army officers. They played serenades, chamber music, and other standard eighteenth-century "concert" music in addition to military music, and were considered separate from the enlisted men who played the fife, drum, and trumpet to signal the troops in the field. Typical eighteenth-century Harmoniemusik had pairs of oboes, horns, bassoons, and sometimes clarinets. If the officers were very interested in music, the organization would be more elaborate, and its members sometimes played keyboard or string instruments as well. In Boston in 1771, for example, the band of the 64th Regiment performed songs, violin music, overtures by Handel and K. F. Abel, and symphonies by J. C. Bach and Stamitz. Psalmodist Josiah Flagg was the concert's organizer and director.

Other groups also cultivated the European art-music tradition in Anglo-America, among them Moravians and musical émigrés. The latter influenced American musical development after the Revolution. Although it is impossible to examine all of the complex influences and trends in depth, we can at least consider a few of the most important here: psalmody, secular music, and the Moravian heritage.

Psalmody

Anglo-American psalmody descended from sixteenth-century English psalmody. Style changes during the Baroque era have already been mentioned, but with the growth of the regular-singing movement, new emphasis was placed on the ordinary congregant's learning to read the tunes rather than relying on his musical memory. Between 1720 and 1760 psalm and hymn tune collections appeared, containing harmonized melodies (usually for three voices) but no words. Books were also published on how to sing. These went hand in hand with the rise of the singing-school movement. Typically, these volumes contained an introduction explaining the "rudiments of music," including solfege and rhythm. Their purpose was to reinstitutionalize the practice of adhering to the printed notes.

The singing-school movement

Major figures in the early singing-school movement included Thomas Symmes (1667–1725), a minister whose pamphlet "The Reasonableness of Regular Singing" (1720) was the first practical plea for singing by note. In 1721 Thomas Walter (1696–1725) published *The Grounds and Rules of Musick Explained, or An Introduction to the Art of Singing by Note.* This book was the first in Anglo-America to be printed with bar-lines. By 1764 at least eight editions of the book had been issued. John Tufts (1689–1750), a minister from Newbury, Massachusetts, wrote the first textbook on music in the United States, *An Introduction to the Singing of Psalm-Tunes* (1721), which includes a preface on the fundamentals of music and a plea for singing by note rather than by rote.

The musical style of the thirty-seven psalm tunes in the Tufts volume reflects contemporary British psalmody, but the *100 Psalm Tune New* (which

Early eighteenth-century psalm tune style

appears in its first-known extant version dating from 1726) is different. Some claim it to be the first Anglo-American composition, in part because it has not been found in earlier publications. Tufts himself may have written it. The work shows the use of parallel perfect intervals and spare and angular melody in the treble (*cantus*) (score in *MA,* no. 23). Similar in style are Walter's 1721 tunes *Litchfield* and *100 Psalm Tune* (*MA,* nos. 24 and 26). Later in the century, such features had become common in the music of Yankee tunesmiths like Lyon, Billings, Read, and Morgan.

Singing schools served both religious and social functions throughout Anglo-America, providing edification and a means of communal entertainment in a colonial setting where religion was part of everyday Protestant life. The lessons were usually taught by itinerant singing masters, who probably composed some of the tunes themselves but who also took some from the collections of others. This "borrowing" without payment or credit, which we would today consider infringement of copyright, was common before the late eighteenth century, because no Anglo-American law protected either music or literary works. The tunebooks themselves, generally oblong volumes, contained instructions in the rudiments of singing, theory, notation, and performance practice, along with a collection of three- or four-part tunes for mixed voices. By the later eighteenth century, these books included not only psalm tunes but also anthems, hymn tunes, and sometimes secular songs as well. Following the long Calvinist tradition, no instrumental parts were printed, but by the 1790s instruments such as organ or bass viol, or occasionally clarinet, did begin to find a place even in the Congregational churches.

Fuging tunes   *Fuging tunes* became an important type of Yankee psalmody, and the anthem, with its sectional structure, was a perennial favorite for imitation. The fuging tune generally consisted of the following elements: (1) a four-part, homophonic section; (2) a second, imitative section (called "fuging section" or "fuge," it was based on a point of imitation); and (3) a closing homophonic section, usually followed by a repeat of the second section. American works in this genre tended to be more modal and folkish, less rounded melodically, and less rhythmically complex than their European counterparts, often creating stark effects, and sometimes humorous ones. Billings' *Modern Musick* (Example 38.2), taken from *The Psalm-Singer's Amusement* (1781), shows the composer's awareness of both musical and social functions to be served by his music. The text explains exactly how composer, performers, music, and audience were expected to interact.

Billings   As can be seen from Example 38.2, Billings was a master of the fuging tune, capable of using both word-painting and humor. (It is important to remember that these works were never "fugues" in the strict sense, but rather pieces containing imitative counterpoint.) Awareness of the rules of composition did not stop Billings from deliberately ignoring them for reasons that would have pleased the nineteenth-century Romantics, and later made him attractive to many historians as an iconoclast. Already in *The New England Psalm-Singer* (1770), he had stated his position:

Ex. 38.2   William Billings, *Modern Musick*

N. B. After the Audience are seated and the Performers have taken the pitch slyly from the Leader the Song begins.

Ex. 38.2   cont.

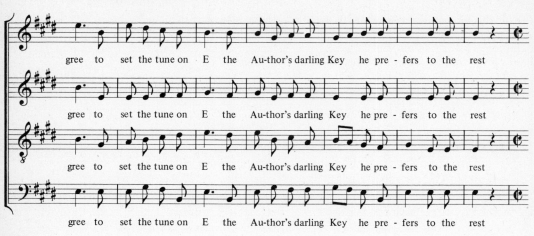

gree to set the tune on E the Au-thor's darling Key he pre - fers to the rest

gree to set the tune on E the Au-thor's darling Key he pre - fers to the rest

gree to set the tune on E the Au-thor's darling Key he pre - fers to the rest

gree to set the tune on E the Au-thor's darling Key he pre - fers to the rest

Let the Tre -ble in the

Let the Coun - ter in - spire the

Let the Te - nor suc - ceed and fol - low the

Let the Bass take the Lead and firm - ly pro - ceed till the

rear no long - er fore - bear but ex - press - ly de -

rest of the Choir in flam'd with de - sire

Lead till the parts are a - greed

parts are a - greed to fugue a - way

Nature is the best Dictator. . . . Nature must lay the foundation. . . . I don't think myself confin'd to any rules for composition, laid down by any that went before me, neither should I think (were I to pretend to lay down Rules) that any one who came after me were any ways obligated to adhere to them, any further than they should think proper . . . in some forms of Composition, there is dry Study required . . . For instance, in a *Fuge,* where the parts come in after each other, with the same notes; but even there, Art is subservient to Genius, for Fancy goes first, and strikes out the Work roughly. And Art comes after, and polishes it over.[7]

Among Billings' many excellent works are the four-part canons *When Jesus Wept* and *Canon of 4 in 1* (from *The New England Psalm-Singer*), and humorous compositions such as *Consonance* and *Jargon* (from *The Psalm-Singer's Amusement* and *The Singing Master's Assistant,* respectively; *Jargon* is in *MA,* no. 44). His extremely popular *Chester* (1770) was reprinted (1778) in the midst of the Revolutionary War. Its patriotic words and martial music helped make it a rallying song of the American insurgents.

William Billings, Daniel Read, Timothy Swan, Supply Belcher, Justin Morgan, Andrew Law, Jacob French, Jeremiah Ingalls, and other "Yankee tunesmiths" make up what may be called the "first New England school." Their music reveals such common traits as placement of the melody in the tenor, parallel perfect intervals (especially fifths), modal rather than chromatic melodies, unorthodox voice leading, and cadential chords with the third omitted. In addition, the four-part texture of this music was customar-

The Yankee tunesmiths

Frontispiece from William Billings, *The New England Psalm-Singer* (1770), which shows the singing of psalms around a table in a secular setting. (Courtesy, The New York Public Library, Music Division)

ily expanded in performance by doubling the soprano an octave lower and the tenor an octave higher, thereby creating a six-part rather than a four-part composition.

Two remaining groups played a role in Anglo-America's "serious" musical life—the Moravians and European émigrés.

The Moravians

The Moravians (members of the *Unitas Fratrem* movement) were a German-speaking Protestant sect in which music played an important part. Count Nicholas von Zinzendorf (1700–1760), who had homes in Saxony and England, originated the idea of sending members of the group to Anglo-America, and it was he who financed the project. His plan called for carefully organized new communities, in which each individual was fully qualified for the specific job he or she would be called upon to do.

In 1732 the first Moravians reached the West Indies. Later (1741), as fugitives from Georgia's Indian Wars, they settled in Bethlehem, in the Quaker-dominated Anglo-American colony of Pennsylvania, an area noted for its religious toleration. Here they established a *collegium musicum* (in this instance, a small orchestra) in 1744, and the group remained active and famous for its performances for more than fifty years. Many other Moravians—including sect members who founded settlements in Lititz, Lancaster, and Nazareth, Pennsylvania, and in Salem (later Winston-Salem), North Carolina—were trained in musical performance. Moravians were extremely fond of trombone music and imported a four-part trombone choir from Europe in 1751. Their practice of having groups of trombones perform from the local church's bell tower has remained a part of Moravian life to the present day. Other instruments were used, too: violins, flutes, and horns accompanied the voices in song services, and spinets and organs were used both in church and in the social halls set up for the amusement of the settlers and the conversion of the Indians.

We cannot be sure which music was performed on a given occasion, but all the music that survives in written form was performed for spiritual enrichment rather than for purely secular purposes. The comparative paucity of secular music can be explained by the fact that those who led the music-making and those whose compositions are still extant were members of the Moravian church hierarchy. However, the existence of home tutoring manuals, and books of exercises for the spinet and organ, as well as a harmony textbook, suggests a secular music tradition, even though it is much less well documented than the sacred one. Fine organs were installed by Moravian organ builders, including those of David Tannenberg (1728–1804), who was responsible for the design and construction of about fifty in Moravian, Lutheran, and Roman Catholic churches.

Benjamin Franklin lived in Bethlehem for a few weeks in 1755, and in his diary Franklin wrote that he had heard Moravian music-making. Before 1762 most Moravian musical performances consisted of Reformation-era chorales and antiphonal liturgical singing, so this is the type of music Franklin most likely heard.

In the records of Bethlehem mention is made of religious music having been composed there as early as 1747. The first extant Moravian work composed in America is the *Liturgy* (1766) of Jeremiah Dencke (1725–1795). In 1767 he composed two sets of music, the first for the "Choir Festival of the 'Older Girls,'" the second for Christmas services. After Dencke came Johannes Herbst (1734–1812), John Antes (1741–1811), Johann Friedrich (also called John Frederick) Peter (1746–1813), and David Moritz Michael (1751–1825). All served the Moravian Church actively as administrators, missionaries, or members of the clergy.

Herbst was the most prolific, with some 125 sacred songs and anthems to his credit. Arriving in the New World in 1786, he first became pastor at Lancaster, then at Lititz (1791). By 1812 he had been promoted to pastor and bishop of Salem, where his library of some five hundred scores was amassed, much of it copied out by hand from European and American originals. He carefully cataloged the contents of his own library, and his personal diaries provide important source material on performance practice in the sung liturgies. Such works as *Praise the Lord, O Jerusalem* (c. 1800) are typical of his musical style. Bishop Herbst wrote a treatise on harmony that is also preserved in manuscript in the Moravian library collections. **Herbst**

American-born Antes was a maker of stringed instruments. After becoming a pastor, he was sent to Egypt as a Moravian missionary. There he wrote the first chamber music to be composed by a native of Anglo-America, three trios for two violins and cello (1799–1801; see *MA*, nos. 32–34). **Antes**

Peter was perhaps the most gifted Moravian composer. Among his nearly one hundred sacred and secular works are six string quintets, written in Salem (1789). His *Quintet V* (see excerpt in *MA*, no. 35) and sacred songs such as *Ich will mit euch einigen ewigen Bund machen* ("I Will Make an Everlasting Covenant with You," 1782; *MA*, no. 36) are representative. **Peter**

European-born D. M. Michael worked in Nazareth, Pennsylvania (1795), then in Bethlehem, returning to Europe in 1814. Perhaps the finest Moravian instrumentalist, he played the violin and most wind instruments. His *Parthia No. 1* (Bethlehem, c. 1807), a suite for six wind instruments, is typical (see *MA*, no. 37, for an excerpt). Some of Michael's wind music was composed specifically for outdoor performance. Although he also wrote anthems and sacred ariettas, he is best known for his instrumental works, and for having led the first United States performance (1811) of Haydn's *Creation*. **D. M. Michael**

Moravian composers in America produced hundreds of works, eventually amassing a music library at Bethlehem that included more than two thousand items relating to musical life in the various New World Moravian settlements. Twentieth-century musicologists rediscovered this collection and the five hundred scores in Herbst's library in Salem, North Carolina. Those musicologists best known for this work are Hans T. David and Donald McCorkle. Since 1956 the Moravian Music Foundation in Winston-Salem,

North Carolina, has been active in fostering performances of music by eighteenth- and early-nineteenth-century Moravian musicians.

European Emigrés

They worked in many different ways, and their impact was cumulative. French émigrés brought with them French traditions, Englishmen reinforced already present English elements, the Italians imported Preclassic and Classic music from Italy, and the Germans introduced North Americans to the music of the Viennese and North German schools. Examples drawn from the works of Tuckey, Eckhard, Selby, Reinagle, Taylor, Carr, Hewitt, Pelissier, Gram, Van Hagen, and Jackson may be found in *MA* (nos. 70–82). They wrote music in genres—from chamber music, opera, and symphonic music to occasional music such as Van Hagen's *Funeral Dirge on the Death of General Washington* (1799; *MA,* no. 81). Of all resident composers, Reinagle is probably the best composer of sonatas. The full force of these musicians' influence was not felt in the United States until after the War of 1812 (1812–1814), and therefore will be discussed further in the next chapter.

Other Centers

Canada

Music in French and English Canada

The development of urban entertainment proceeded more slowly in French Canada. Primarily agrarian and subject to the constant uncertainties of war, its sparse population (70,000 in 1760) seems not to have been able to support the grander forms of musical entertainment consistently until after the English takeover (1763). By 1800 the total Canadian population was only about 300,000, compared to about 5,000,000 in the United States and about 17,000,000 in Latin America. Most Canadians were still not city dwellers: major settlements, such as Quebec, Montreal, Halifax, and Saint John, each had fewer than 15,000 inhabitants. European refugees sought asylum in Canada from the French Revolution and other European upheavals, and North American loyalists took up residence there during and after the Revolutionary War. The early nineteenth century brought with it Canada's first printed music; previously it had all been imported. Public music was provided by military bands, pick-up orchestras, and part-time professionals, as well as by itinerant troupes, but Canadian population centers lacked the organization and comparative stability of the important cities in the United States and Latin America.

In Canada, the singing-school tradition spread, as did the fuging tune. Its Anglo-American heritage also gave it military bands, but its French heritage is well served, too, by what remains of the works of French-born Joseph Quesnel (1749–1809). An educated and widely traveled man, Quesnel had sailed as far as Pondicherry, Madagascar, and Brazil before coming to North America as captain of a ship trying unsuccessfully to carry contraband weapons to the American rebels. Captured by the British, Quesnel settled in Canada, where his operas such as *Colas et Colinette* (1788) were written in the style of the comic operas of Grétry, Philidor, and Monsigny.

Guadeloupe and Haiti

Although France had lost its colonial territories on the North American continent, it still retained other New World possessions. Of these, Guadeloupe and Haiti are of interest during this period. The former was the birthplace of the mulatto violinist-swordsman-conductor-composer, the Chevalier de St. Georges, who spent most of his adventurous life in Paris. The latter supported a thriving operatic culture in the last half of the eighteenth century, in the course of which works by Grétry, Favart, Gluck, Monsigny, Dalayrac, and J. J. Rousseau were performed in a highly professional manner. Rousseau's *Le Devin du village* was so popular in Haiti that it inspired a New World parody, *Les Amours de Mirabelais* ("The Loves of Mirabelais"). When the Haitian Revolution (1796–1799) caused many professional and talented amateur musicians to flee the island, some sought refuge in North America. Wherever they settled, from the Louisiana Territory to Canada, they brought with them a new taste for Preclassic and Classic French music.

Summary

During the eighteenth and early nineteenth centuries, Preclassic and Classic elements entered the music of the New World. In Latin America this process was a logical development of the reciprocal attitude long evident between the Iberian countries and their colonies. The growth of art music was bound up with the development of groups with adequate leisure to perform this music or patrons wealthy enough to support them. Therefore the longer-established, generally more stable Latin American colonies fostered such activities sooner than their northern neighbors.

Musicians from Europe continued to leave their homes to work in North and South America, bringing with them music, ideas, and instruments. In Latin America these people often served to stifle local talent, but in the United States and Canada they increased the impetus toward further artistic development on the part of native-born composers. Whereas Latin American composers tended to be identified with one area or even one city, the North American journeyman tradition and economic necessity encouraged both Yankee tunesmiths and émigré musicians to travel. Furthermore, the greater availability of music printing in Anglo-America encouraged the diffusion of music by Lyon, Billings, Morgan, and others. On the other hand, the music of the Chacao school, of Salas, and of the Minas Gerais school remained in manuscript until the twentieth century. In all cases, however, art music in the New World during this period developed from European styles and forms (the villancico, Te Deum, sonata, and fuging tune, for example), but contained techniques of composition and sometimes called for performance practices different from those prevailing in Europe.

Later in the nineteenth century still more Europeans settled in America, and Americans in increasing numbers went abroad to study. The effects of this continuing intellectual and artistic interpenetration will be discussed in the next chapter.

Notes

1. Cited in Juan Bautista Plaza, "Music in Caracas During the Colonial Period (1770–1811)," *Musical Quarterly* 29, no. 1 (1943): 201. Plaza was responsible for studying and classifying all of the known extant manuscripts of the Venezuelan Classic school.
2. For a more detailed discussion of the Venezuelan Classic school, see Plaza, ibid., and José Calcaño, *La ciudad y su música* (Caracas: Conservatorio Teresa Carreño, 1958), pp. 55 ff.
3. Cited in Lota M. Spell, *Music in Texas* (Austin, Texas: n.p., 1936), p. 9.
4. Ibid., p. 410.
5. Cited in Kenneth Silverman, *A Cultural History of the American Revolution* (New York: Thomas Y. Crowell, 1976), p. 31.
6. Cited in Robert Stevenson, "The Afro-American Musical Legacy to 1800," *Musical Quarterly* 54, no. 4 (1968): 475.
7. Portions of this essay are reprinted in Gilbert Chase, ed., *The American Composer Speaks* (Baton Rouge: Louisiana State University Press, 1966), pp. 29–31. (*ACS*)

Bibliography

Books and Articles

General

SILVERMAN, KENNETH. *A Cultural History of the American Revolution.* New York: Thomas Y. Crowell, 1976.
WHITAKER, ARTHUR P., ed. *Latin America and the Enlightenment,* 2nd ed. Ithaca, N.Y.: Cornell University Press, 1961.

Anglo-America

The following are cited in addition to books and articles mentioned in the bibliographies to previous chapters.

CRAWFORD, RICHARD. *Andrew Law: American Psalmodist.* Evanston, Ill.: Northwestern University Press, 1968.
DESAUTELS, ANDRÉE. "The History of Canadian Composition, 1610–1967." In *Aspects of Music in Canada,* ed. Arnold Walter. Toronto: University of Toronto Press, 1969.
LAWRENCE, VERA BRODSKY. *Music for Patriots, Politicians, and Presidents.* New York: Macmillan, 1976.
McCORKLE, DONALD. *The Moravian Contribution to American Music.* Winston-Salem: Moravian Music Foundation, 1956.

McKay, David, and Crawford, Richard. *William Billings of Boston*. Princeton: Princeton University Press, 1975.

Murray, Sterling E. "Timothy Swan and Yankee Psalmody." *The Musical Quarterly* 61, no.3 (July 1975): 433–63.

Sonneck, Oscar George Theodore. *A Bibliography of Early Secular American Music (18th-Century)*, rev. and enl. by William Treat Upton. Washington, D.C.: Library of Congress, 1945 (reprint, Da Capo Press, 1964).

Tawa, Nicholas E. "Secular Music in the Late-Eighteenth-Century American Home." *Musical Quarterly* 61, no. 4 (Oct. 1975): 511–27.

Wagner, John W. "James Hewitt, 1770–1827." *Musical Quarterly* 58, no. 2 (Apr. 1972): 259–76.

Latin America

Among the few important English-language sources are the following, in addition to more general works mentioned in earlier chapters.

Carpentier, Alejo "Music in Cuba (1523–1900)." *The Musical Quarterly* 33, no. 3 (July 1947): 365–80.

————. *La música en Cuba*. Mexico: Colección Tierra Firme, 1946 (reprint, 1972).

Plaza, Juan Bautista. "Music in Caracas During the Colonial Period (1770–1811)." *The Musical Quarterly* 19, no. 1 (Jan. 1943): 198–213.

Lange, Francisco Curt. "La música en Minas Gerais. Un informe." *Boletín latino americano de música* 6 (1946): 408–494.

Scores

In addition to the relevant scores mentioned in previous chapters, and to the Earlier American Music Series (Da Capo Press, 1972–, ed. H. Wiley Hitchcock), which has issued facsimile editions of Belcher's *Harmony of Maine* and Billings's *The Psalm-Singer's Amusement,* the following are representative of available music from Anglo-America during this period.

Billings, William. *Continental Harmony*. Cambridge: Harvard University Press, 1961.

————. *Complete Works,* ed. Hans T. Nathan. Charlottesville, Virginia: University Press of Virginia, 1977–   .

Clark, J. Bunker. *Anthology of American Keyboard Music, 1787–1830,* 2 vols. Madison, Wisc.: AR Editions, 1976.

Johannes Herbst Collection. Fort George Station, N.Y.: University Music Editions, 1976.

Kroeger, Karl, ed. *A Moravian Music Sampler*. Winston-Salem: Moravian Music Foundation, 1974.

Tufts, John. *A Very Plain and Easy Introduction to the Singing of Psalm Tunes* (1726). Reprint, Philadelphia: Musical Americana, 1954.

The general anthologies of Latin American music mentioned in earlier chapters continue to be useful. To them may be added the following more specialized publications.

Brazil (all modern editions)

Lange, Francisco Curt, ed. *Archivo de músico religiosa de la Capitania Geral das Minas Gerais (siglo XVIII)* . . . Mendoz, Argentina: Universidad Nacional de Cuyo, 1951.

Gomes, André da Silva. *Missa a 8 vozes e instrumentos,* ed. Regis Duprat. Brasília: Universidad de Brasília, Instituto Cultural de Artes, 1966.

PINTO, LUIS ALVARES. *Te Deum laudamus a 4 vozes*. Recife: Secretaria de Educação e Cultura de Pernambuco, 1968.

Cuba: scores available from Bloomington, Latin American Center.

Venezuela

MOREIRA, SERGIO. *Música religiosa de maestros venezolanos de la colonia*. Caracas: Ediciones del Congreso de la Republica, 1973.

39
Romantic Music and the New World

D URING the first three quarters of the nineteenth century the New World underwent a series of radical political, economic, and artistic transformations. National boundaries and the legitimacy of governments were often in hot dispute. Romantic nationalism manifested itself even in areas that remained under colonial rule. The concept of grandness invaded the political sphere, leading to coalitions and enormous territorial expansion in the United States. Some areas experienced rapid increases in population and the burgeoning of new organizations and institutions to serve the artistic preferences of their populace.

Not only did many European-born musicians tour or emigrate to the Americas, but also increasing numbers of American-born musicians traveled, studied, and concertized in Europe, thus bringing more prestige to their native lands and contributing to national pride. At the same time, citizens of the Americas were able to hear and appreciate more accomplished classically trained musicians than before, and in general performance standards improved. Composers active in the New World during the Romantic era show the same varied stylistic tendencies and wide range of personal characteristics as their European contemporaries.

In this chapter we shall first trace some of these new developments in the Americas and their relationships to music. Then we shall discuss representative composers active in the New World, with emphasis on the Romantic elements in their music.

Hispano-America in the Romantic Era

Performances of symphonies and other orchestral works took place from Mexico to Argentina, especially after the Wars of Independence, during the first decades of the nineteenth century. Italian opera, which had already gained some supporters, quickly became so popular that Manuel García, who toured the United States and Mexico from 1825 to 1827 with his opera com-

891

pany, presented his works in Mexico City with their librettos in Italian! Composers of both sacred and secular music proliferated throughout Spanish America, as did New World performers of international repute, most of whom also composed.

Two primary influences are evident in most Spanish-American music of this period—Italian opera and French salon music. New World variants of the songs, waltzes, tarantellas, and other dance, programmatic, and genre pieces of the day made their appearance in the cultivated salons of Hispano-America. Italianate opera was widely performed and composed throughout the Latin American countries. Earlier composers who exemplified these trends are the Mexican Cenobio Paniagua (1821–1882) and the Spanish-born, French-trained Chilean Isadora Zegers de Huneeus (1803–1869).

Especially after 1850, a growing musical nationalist movement with its deliberate use of folk elements coexisted within otherwise fairly standard forms. European Romantic composers shared this interest. Early Spanish-American nationalist composers included Aniceto Ortega (1823–1875) of Mexico and Juan Morel Campos (1857–1896) of Puerto Rico.

Opera and Operetta

Italian influence dominated operatic production for the first three-quarters of the century, and even longer in places like Argentina. In Spanish America the *zarzuela* and *zarzuelita* provided comic opera fare.

García   Manuel García's troupe had popularized Italian opera. Such works had been sung before in Spanish translation, but after García's tour they began to be sung in Italian instead. Furthermore, operas written in Latin America customarily had Italian-language librettos. Mexico during the 1830s gave operas only in Italian, to the annoyance of some local critics, and often the only performers available were troupes of resident or itinerant Italians. This vogue of Italian opera, especially among the elite, led to the idolization of Italian performers regardless of their abilities. Performers were trained primarily for opera, and Italian opera elements found their way into other musical genres.

Mexico   After Mexico achieved independence, its first native-born opera composer, Luis Baca (1826–1855), was encouraged in his work by Donizetti. Unfortunately, Mexico City's local Italian troupe would perform only works with Italian libretti, so his works went unperformed. Paniagua solved this problem by writing a Donizetti-like opera with an Italian libretto, *Catalina di Guisa* (written 1845; premiered 1859), as did his pupil Melisio Morales (1838–1908). Morales's *Ildegonda* (premiered in Mexico City, 1866; Florence, 1869) won its composer as much acclaim as Paniagua's first opera did for him, but both men's careers declined thereafter. A doctor who also composed, Aniceto Ortega wrote a patriotic opera, based loosely on the story of the last Aztec prince, *Guatimotzín* (1871). Its great success was based largely on nationalistic appeal rather than musical merit.

Other   Operatic life had begun in Chile with the immigration (1844) of Bavarian-
centers   born Aquinas Ried (1810–1869). Extremely active in Chilean musical circles after his arrival, Ried has the distinction of having composed the first

opera ever written in Chile, *La Telésfora* (1846). The vocal style in this and his later opera *Il granatiere* ("The Grenadier," 1857) have much in common with that of his *Missa Solemne* (1844), for all are Italianate. Based on the biblical story, *Ester* (1874), the first Colombian opera, written by José María Ponce de León (1846–1882), reflected its composer's studies at the Paris Conservatory under Gounod and Thomas. This opera and the same composer's *Florinda* (1880) were the only works by a native-born Colombian produced in Colombia during this period.

Early Peruvian nationalist composers included the Italian immigrant Claudio Rebagliati (1843–1909). Italianate elements abound in the works of the Cuban Gaspar Villate (1851–1912) and in those of the Guatemalan violinist José Escolástico Andrino (fl. mid-nineteenth century), who moved to El Salvador in 1845. The latter's opera *La Mora generosa* ("The Generous Moorish Girl," date unknown) and his two symphonies and three Masses are especially Italianate. In Venezuela, Italian influence is found in the works of José Angel Montero (1839–1881), a member of a well-known family of Caracas musicians, who composed zarzuelas and Venezuela's first opera, *Virginia* (1873), in addition to church music.

Two composers are known primarily for their zarzuelas. José María Arredondo (1840–1924) of the Dominican Republic applied Italian lyricism to Spanish zarzuela form. So did Venezuelan Federico Villena (1835–c. 1900), perhaps the most prolific Caracan composer of this era, who also wrote instrumental works, chamber music, religious music, and songs.

Choral and Instrumental Music

Composers rarely confined themselves to one genre. An example is Amancio Alcorta (1805–1862) of Argentina, who wrote songs, chamber music, and piano works along with his sacred music. Known also as a politician and economist, Alcorta was active as a composer after 1822, and was one of a number of semiprofessional composers of the era, as was his countryman Juan Pedro Esnaola (1808–1878), who wrote church music and two symphonies in addition to his works for piano and solo voice. Antonio Raffelín (1796–1882) and Laureano Fuentes (1825–1898) of Cuba wrote sacred and symphonic music, and in Fuentes's case, chamber music as well. Puerto Rican–born Juan Bautista Alfonseca (1810–1875) led the development of art music in the Dominican Republic, composing both sacred music (two Masses) and popular instrumental works, as did his pupil José Reyes (1835–1905), composer of the Dominican national anthem (1883). In addition to two books on music theory, the Mexican José Mariano Elízaga (1786–1842) wrote Masses, Lamentations, other church music, and piano music. Paniagua also composed two oratorios, *Siete palabras* ("Seven Last Words," 1869) and *Tobias* (1870), as well as several Masses. Juan Morel Campos, the most famous Puerto Rican composer of the past century, was similarly versatile, writing for church, theater, and chamber and choral groups with equal facility.

Many religious compositions as well as secular orchestral works with and without chorus fall within this category. In those works for soloists and orchestra, the same stress on virtuosity that prevailed in contemporaneous Europe is evident. Sometimes such pieces went unperformed for years for lack of competent personnel. This music was intended for public occasions, requiring so many vocalists, instrumentalists, or both that they could only be performed in a large auditorium, church, or palace ballroom, or in the open air.

Religious music

The Church's temporal power had waned considerably during the late eighteenth century, but Spanish America continued to have strong ties to Roman Catholicism. Music written for church, however, differed little if at all from that performed on the operatic stage and in concert, as was true generally in the eighteenth century. In 1841 the wife of Spain's first diplomatic envoy to Mexico commented that during a Good Friday Night procession "a military band struck up an air from *Semiramide*."[1] Later, describing the ceremonies accompanying a girl's becoming a nun, she was surprised that the entry music for the guests was a Strauss waltz. Finally, she complained that at a Mass for the gentry "the music was beautiful, but too gay for a church. There were violins and wind instruments, and several amateur players."[2] Since secular compositions were often used in church and since church music incorporated secular styles, the primary difference between these genres is that the text of sacred music was generally in Latin, or the composer designated certain of his works as "church" music.

Some composers were known for their ability in one specific genre. The precocious but short-lived Mexican Joaquín Beristaín (1817–1839) is known primarily as the composer of an overture and an orchestral fantasy. Although the reputation of Colombian composer Julio Quevedo Arvelo (1829–1897) rests mainly on his church music, he also wrote a considerable number of virtuoso show pieces.

Dance music

Dance music was extremely popular throughout Spanish America— above all the *contradanza*. It consisted of sets of eight-measure phrases that could be repeated indefinitely and, as a semipopular form, was just as at home in the ballrooms of the elite as in the social gatherings of the less affluent. It had developed from the French *contradanse* during the late eighteenth century and spread throughout Europe. Indeed, Beethoven used a contradanse as the basis for the final movement of his *Eroica* Symphony. Thousands of contradanzas and other dance forms were composed from Mexico to Chile, generally for piano. In Cuba the outstanding composer of contradanzas was Manuel Saumell (1817–1870); in Puerto Rico Manuel Gregorio Tavárez (1843–1883) and Morel Campos shared this distinction; in Chile it was Isadora Zegers de Huneeus. Originally dance music without lofty artistic pretensions, the contradanza became increasingly stylized as the century progressed, particularly in the works of Saumell, Tavárez, and Morel Campos.

Salon and virtuoso music

Salon and virtuoso music were written by composers like Alcorta, Esnaola, the Chileans Juan Bautista Alberdi (1810–1884) and Federico Guzmán (1837–1885) (the latter a pianist-composer who wrote more than two hundred piano works), as well as Morales and Ortega. Most of these pieces show evidence of European Romanticism. Composers cultivated such national dance forms as the *járabe* (a Mexican binary form of moderate tempo with shifts from $\frac{3}{4}$ to $\frac{6}{8}$ meter) and the *cueca* (a Chilean quick dance with alternating $\frac{3}{4}$ and $\frac{6}{8}$ meter). Such use of rural and traditional materials was part of an important international trend toward the exploration of folk heritages.

Other chamber music combinations, above all Italianate or French-influenced solo songs, were also very popular. Most composers of piano pieces also wrote songs—Alcorta, Alberdi, Esnaola, and Zegers, for example. In the area of "serious" chamber music, however, less material has come to light. The Cuban José White (fl. 1875) wrote a string quartet (1872) and other chamber works, in addition to *Six Grandes Etudes* for violin solo (1868), which won him an award from the Paris Conservatory. Possibly the closest to the German Romantic ideal is the work of the internationally famous Venezuelan piano virtuoso Felipe Larrazábal (1816–1873). His *Trio No. 2,* Op. 138, for violin, cello, and piano is one of his few compositions that survived an Atlantic shipwreck.

Chamber music

Portuguese America in the Romantic Era

With the arrival of the Portuguese court (1808), an entirely new intellectual, political, and artistic climate was created in Brazil. Trade, education, science, the arts, in short all the things that had not previously been encouraged, were actively fostered by the court. The 10,000 Portuguese émigrés needed goods and services in order to maintain their accustomed lifestyle. Independence came to Brazil in four stages: (1) loyalty to the Portuguese rulers after their move to Brazil (the King of Portugal was also Emperor of Brazil); (2) Emperor João VI's pact with Crown Prince Pedro (1798–1834) that the latter would rule Brazil after João's return to Portugal (1821); (3) Pedro I's proclamation of independence (1822); and finally (4) the peaceful abdication of Dom Pedro II (1825–1891) after Brazil was declared a republic (1889).

For the first time, during the reign of João VI foreign artists and scientists were allowed to enter and travel freely throughout Brazil. Through diplomatic channels the personnel of Brazil's new Academy of Fine Arts of Rio was selected in France. The group of outstanding French artists included painters, a sculptor, and an architect. Jean-Baptiste Debret (1768–1848), one of the painters, also served for seven years as stage manager for the newly created Teatro São João (royal theater). Collectively, the members of this artistic colony were known as the French Artistic Mission of 1816.

Most musicians holding important court posts were Europeans hired specifically for that purpose by the emperor. Some, however, like José Maurício Nunes Garcia (1767–1830), mestre da capela to Emperor João VI (1808–1821), were Brazilians. During the same period, Portuguese-born Marcos Portugal (1762–1830) obtained the post of general director of music in Rio de Janeiro, where he helped to found the Teatro São João, which became a glittering center for the production of grand opera (1813–1889). Many salon pieces, operettas, and operas were written, and foreign virtuosos also added luster to the musical scene.

The predominant influences on Brazilian musical life during the Empire were Italian and French—and later German, after the accession of Pedro II, a scholar, patron of the arts, and Wagner enthusiast.

Opera   Opera began to flourish in Rio de Janeiro after Marcos Portugal settled there (1811). Italian opera was the officially sanctioned form, and the government subsidized performances of repertory ranging from Rossini to Verdi. Attempts to encourage the production of Portuguese-language opera by Francisco Manuel da Silva (1795–1865), composer of Brazil's national anthem, were unsuccessful at first. Then Pedro II supported the idea with his patronage, and the Imperial Academy of Music and National Opera was founded (1857). Thereafter operas by Brazilians were presented, among them works by Elias Alvares Lôbo (1834–1901) and especially the mulatto

Gomes   Antônio Carlos Gomes (1836–1896).

After studying music in Brazil, Gomes applied to the emperor for support and was given a scholarship to the Milan Conservatory. He subsequently received international acclaim as Brazil's finest composer of operas in the Italian style. His compositions combine fluid lyric melody with solid drama. His most famous work, *Il Guarany* (based on Alençar's novel *O Guaraní*, premiered in Rio de Janeiro in 1870 and met with enormous success for nationalistic as well as musical reasons. It was also well received in Europe, with performances in Italy (1870), England (1872), and Russia (1879), and finally had its North American premiere in 1884. The opera is written in the style of Verdi's *Aida,* while Gomes's later compositions show the influence of Richard Wagner.

Religious   Along with grand opera, the royal court also demanded religious music in
music   the grand manner. The two best-known composers of sacred and concert music—and probably the finest as well—were two friends: Austrian-born Sigismund Neukomm (1778–1858) and João VI's chapelmaster Garcia.

Neukomm   Neukomm, a former pupil of both Michael and Joseph Haydn, wrote more than two thousand works in all musical genres. He was in the employ of Prince Talleyrand in Paris when Louis XVIII reestablished diplomatic relations with the Portuguese court in Brazil (1816). When the French king's chosen ambassador invited Neukomm to join him, Neukomm accepted and spent five productive, influential years in the New World. Part of this pleasant experience was traceable to his powerful patrons, part to his success as composer, conductor, and teacher. Neukomm also participated in the work of the French Artistic Mission of 1816, which had not initially included a musician.

While in Brazil, Neukomm had as students some of the most aristocratic Brazilian residents, among them the royal family. Dom Pedro, later the emperor, studied music "in a princely way [i.e., as a dilettante],"[3] as Neukomm put it, but nevertheless learned enough to compose dance music and patriotic songs that attained great popularity. Neukomm's other pupils included Francisco Manuel da Silva, later founder of the Conservatory of Rio de Janeiro.

During his years in Rio, Neukomm wrote letters to the Viennese *Allgemeine Musik Zeitung* describing musical life there. In relating a major event of 1819, a performance of Mozart's *Requiem,* he said that under Garcia's direction "the performance of Mozart's masterpiece left nothing to be desired."[4]

Neukomm's compositional style was conservative. His work was praised by Mendelssohn, who said, "I do not know what I could do better than to follow his example."[5] Nevertheless, Romantic temperament is evident in his programmatic music, much of which was for piano or chamber music combinations and will be discussed later. Several of his works in the larger forms were for specific public celebrations—his *L'Allégresse publique* ("Public Rejoicing," a symphonic march celebrating Dom João's coronation in 1816), *Misa pro die acclamationis* ("Mass for the Day of Acclamation," i.e., the coronation), and *Grand Te Deum* (for the same occasion). Although his *Symphony in E-flat,* Op. 37, and other orchestral and band compositions date from his Brazilian period, the number of Neukomm's church-related pieces dwarfs his orchestral production from that era. His considerable influence in Brazil continued after his return to Europe (1821).

J. M. Nunes Garcia

Garcia's mother was of Guinean extraction; his father was Brazilian. His father's death in 1773 placed a financial burden on his mother and aunt, but they supported Garcia until he could earn his own way by performing locally as violinist, pianist, and singer of both the art and popular music of the day. He was ordained a priest in 1792. Only 30 of this cleric's 419 works are secular.[6] Among his secular pieces there is only one opera, but there are three choral works with orchestra and four for orchestra alone.

The finest Brazilian composer of his era, Garcia's career bears witness both to his abilities and to the variable quality of musical life in Brazil. Even before the arrival of the court, he had attained status, if not wealth, as a composer. But his position was greatly enhanced when he was named mestre da capela to the crown. This financial aid ceased, however, when João VI returned to Lisbon in 1821.

One of Garcia's finest sacred works is his *Requiem,* M. 185. Written in 1816 at João VI's request for his mother's funeral, this piece undoubtedly had special meaning for the composer, coming as it did in the year of his own mother's death. The work, for orchestra, soloists, and chorus, shows the stylistic influences present in Brazilian music of this epoch. It ranges from Mozartean echoes in the Kyrie and Gradual to a strong infusion of Italian operatic elements in the *Dies irae,* which combines dramatic shifts of mood with lyrical solos and homophonic choral passages. Garcia sums up this era in Brazil. His Classicism recalls the school of Minas Gerais, while his Romantic characteristics make him a product of his time.

Salon music

Brazilian salon music of this period is exemplified by the piano works Neukomm wrote while in Rio. The influence of Brazilian forms and styles makes Neukomm's piano and chamber music not just works composed in Brazil, but in an important way "Brazilian," serving in part as the basis of the later nationalist tradition. His interest in Brazilian dances can be seen in his use of the Afro-Brazilian *lundú* (originally a lively triple-meter rural harvest

Ex. 39.1   Sigismund Neukomm, *Amor brasileiro*

Ex. 39.2   Sigismund Neukomm, *La Mélancolie,* from *L'Amoureux*

dance) in his piano caprice *Amor brasileiro* ("Brazilian Love"), Op. 40 (see Example 39.1).

Neukomm's fascination with the urban popular song of Rio, the *modinha* (a lyrical, sentimental song with chamber music accompaniment that developed from the mingling of Italian opera and Portuguese folksong), is shown in his still-unpublished collection of twenty modinhas. One by the famous Brazilian mulatto popular singer Joaquim Manuel (fl. c. 1800–c. 1820), whose works are otherwise lost to us, was preserved by Neukomm in the section *La Mélancolie* ("Melancholy") from his fantasy for flute and piano called *L'Amoureux* ("The Lover"), Op. 41 (see Example 39.2).

The United States in the Romantic Era

After the United States had proved its political viability in the War of 1812, a sense of nationhood and a strong expansionist spirit took root among the majority of citizens. Precursers of this attitude can be found in such actions as the Louisiana Purchase, which later evolved into the idea of "Manifest Destiny"—the belief that the United States was "destined" to rule all the North American land between the Atlantic and Pacific Oceans. This doctrine induced many adventurous people to make the trek westward.

Lifestyles and music   Three different lifestyles coexisted in the United States during this period—that of the frontier, the rural pioneer town, and the city. Life in the first two places left little leisure for the cultivation of the arts, particularly music. As in earlier times, only urban areas could support professional musicians, who were primarily immigrants from Europe. During the nineteenth century many arrived from Germany, bringing with them the German Romantic tradition and a distaste for the popular and folk music they encountered. In most frontier and rural areas of the United States, music as a full-time occupation was nonexistent. It was considered a frill, an unnecessary amusement fit only for foreigners, itinerant "professors," women, and men unsure of their manhood or unfit for heavy labor.

Until the final decades of the century, Italian music dominated the operatic and vocal spheres, as, for example, in the works of William Henry Fry (1813–1864). Germanophiles who espoused the German Romantic idealism that stressed the edifying of "good" (i.e., serious) music, while condemning all other types as "bad," gained in number and increased the rift between the popular and "cultivated" traditions. Nevertheless, they were unable to contain the spread of salon and virtuoso music, as seen in the works of Stephen Foster (1826–1864) and Louis Moreau Gottschalk (1829–1869), although "cultivated" United States citizens, bent on "improving" the popular taste, tried their best. Among these latter were the hymnodist Thomas Hastings (1784–1872) and the extremely influential critic John Sullivan Dwight (1813–1893).

Musical prefer- ences

Thomas Hicks (1823–1890), *The Musicale, Barber Shop, Trenton Falls, N.Y.* (1866). (Collection of the North Carolina Museum of Art, Raleigh)

Blackface Minstrelsy

Ballad opera gave way to operatic parodies such as those found in the blackface minstrel shows. In fact, an early American ballad opera, *The Disappointment* (1767), contains the first known written song that imitates black speech patterns. During the final decade of the eighteenth century, other so-called "Negro songs" were made public by Carr and Graupner, white men who produced on stage their impressions of the sounds and actions of their black compatriots. Some British comedians also blackened their faces for such performances. These "Negro songs" were generally sentimental and condescending.

Matthews

One early-nineteenth-century blackface comedian is credited with helping to establish the minstrel show tradition. The English actor Charles Matthews, with his "Negro" (i.e., blackface) act, toured the United States in 1822. While traveling, he carefully observed and transcribed black speech, using in his performance the parts that interested him most. This approach added some authenticity to his popular acts, even though the old attitudes toward blacks still prevailed.

Dixon

In the northern United States, so-called Negro sketches were much in vogue during the 1820s and 1830s. During that era George Washington Dixon (1808–1861) is considered to have been the first song-and-skit writer to popularize the two stereotypical black characters of the minstrel-show genre: the poor but eternally cheerful southern plantation hand and the citified man-about-town who feigned sophistication. These oversimplified and exaggerated characterizations were also found in the performances of other American blackface comedians, such as Thomas Dartmouth ("Daddy") Rice (1808–1860). While playing in Louisville in 1828, Rice observed a black stable groom, the model for his famous character Jim Crow.

Minstrel shows

The minstrel show, also called "the Ethiopian opera," had much in common with the ballad opera. Stage comedy, including jokes, speeches, comic dialogues, and dances, was bound together with music gleaned from any available source and employed whenever and wherever convenient. In the minstrel show, however, the actors appeared in blackface, dressed stereotypically either as rural or exaggeratedly dandified urban blacks. In illustrations of the period they are often shown singing, accompanied by a banjo, tambourine, bones (castanets), and violin.

Minstrel songs

Minstrel songs were usually based on a solo-chorus form with a simple accompaniment. Refrains, when repeated, could be sung in unison, in three parts or in four parts with a simple accompaniment. Most minstrel songs were in a major key; the sung tune was preceded by an instrumental introduction (*vamp*) and was ended with another instrumental section (*tag*). Neither instrumental section necessarily bore any relationship to the tune of the song itself. The final number of the minstrel show (*walk-around*) began fairly simply as a dance, but after 1858 it became far more elaborate. After the whole company had arranged themselves onstage in a semicircle, some of their number stepped forward and tried to sing a stanza, only to be interrupted by other members of the company (*end-men*). This scene was followed by a final chorus in which some members of the troupe kept time to the music by clapping their hands and stomping their feet, while others danced and still others sang.

Traveling troupes such as Bryant's Minstrels, the Ethiopian Serenaders, and the Christy Minstrels were immensely popular during this period (1830s–1860s). A song used in performance by one of these groups could become an international commercial success for its composer, a fact well known to composers like Stephen Foster. (Typical minstrel songs like *Jim Crow, Zip Coon*—also known as *Turkey in the Straw*—and *Dixie's Land* may be found in *MA,* nos. 104, 105, 106, and 109, respectively.)

Opera

Inroads made by Italian opera helped hasten the demise of ballad opera by providing more "cultivated" entertainment for the elite. After the success of Manuel García, other troupes continued to intensify the Italian opera mania sweeping the Americas. One such group, which also made occasional tours of Mexico and Cuba from its home base in New York City, was that of Czech-born Max Maretzek (1821–1897), who left Europe after having served as chorus master under Berlioz in England (1847–1848). He arranged performances of the Italian Opera Company for nearly forty years, presenting premiers of works by Gounod, Verdi, Donizetti, and Meyerbeer.

Success of Italian opera

Perhaps the two finest United States opera composers at this time were Philadelphia-born William Henry Fry and English-born George Frederick Bristow. Considerable Italian influence is evident in their works. Fry, also a journalist who loudly supported the rights of American composers to American performances of their works, composed the first grand opera in the manner of Bellini and Donizetti native to the United States: *Leonora,* which premiered in Philadelphia in 1845. (Two of its arias are available in a modern edition: *MA,* nos. 128 and 129.) Bristow, however, became the first to write an opera on an American subject. Based on the story by Washington Irving, the libretto of *Rip Van Winkle* (1855, revised 1882) was given music less Italianate than *Leonora*'s; in fact, it betrays a thorough study of German instrumental music. *Rip*'s chromatic, Germanic harmonic devices contrast with its blocklike phrases so that the two rarely seem of a piece. It was performed with considerable success (modern editions of two arias and a chorus are in *MA,* nos. 130 and 131), but Bristow never finished *Columbus,* his second opera on an American subject. Example 39.3 shows Bristow's typical style.

Fry and Bristow

Others, including Gottschalk, also composed operas, but these usually went unperformed. Given the great vogue of Italian opera during this period, it is not surprising that musicians such as Gottschalk should have tried their hand at the genre.

Choral Music

Most frontier and pioneer areas still had inadequate leisure for or interest in large musical spectaculars, so the cultivation of art music remained a pri-

Ex. 39.3 George Frederick Bristow, *Alas, They Know Me Not,* from *Rip Van Winkle*

Ex. 39.3   cont.

marily urban activity. The nearest most non–city dwellers came to the "cultivated" tradition of music was in church, where the music used depended both on the denomination for which each work was intended and on the musical forces available for performance.

Protestant music

In the late eighteenth century some of the Protestant musical elite already thought fuging tunes were dated and destructive of the clarity of the text. The result was a school of Protestant church music emphasizing greater simplicity and homophony, closer in style to German Classicism and early Romanticism than to Monumental Romanticism. Harmony, not melody, reigned supreme. Chorales and such composers as Beethoven, Handel, Haydn, Gluck, and Mozart all influenced the Protestant composers.

The shape-note music of the eighteenth-century Yankee tunesmiths (discussed below) left its original urban setting to travel south and west with the new settlers. Denounced as "unscientific" by Hastings, Massachusetts-born Lowell Mason (1792–1872), and others, it continued to flourish in areas with fewer artistic pretensions, and still serves as the foundation of a vital tradition.

In the United States during the early nineteenth century, "west" meant west of the Appalachians, and "south" began below Pennsylvania. Both German- and English-speaking Pennsylvanians used this music. John Wyeth (1770–1858), a Harrisburg printer, published *Der leichte Unterricht* ("The Easy Instructor," 1810), *Die Franklin Harmonie* ("The Franklin Harmony," 1821), *The Repository of Sacred Music* (1810), and *Repository of Sacred Music, Part Second* (1813), the last of which has been called "the first really influential anthology of spiritual folksong."[7] The musicologist Dr. George Pullen Jackson (1874–1953) coined the term "spiritual folksong" to describe religious texts set to vernacular music such as songs and dances.

Revival hymns   Beginning with Kentucky's Great Revival (1800), the southern and western United States underwent a religious renaissance. Baptist, Methodist, and Presbyterian camp meetings were prayer marathons that sometimes lasted all day and all night for four or five consecutive days. Participants often numbered in the tens of thousands. Out of these shared communal experiences developed a new type of religious verse-and-refrain song: the revival hymn, also called the "spiritual song." As early as 1819, some observers noticed similarities between these hymns as sung by white people and the performance practices of black camp-meeting worshippers, who were quartered separately from the whites.

Early published collections such as *A Collection of the Most Admired Hymns and Spiritual Songs, with the Choruses* [i.e., refrains] *Affixed, as usually sung at camp-meetings* (published by John C. Totten in New York, 1809) contained the texts but not the music to the songs. Tune books later published in the South included music. Of these, perhaps the two most famous collections are *The Southern Harmony* of William ("Singin' Billy") Walker (1809–1875), which was published in Spartanburg, South Carolina, in 1835, and *The Sacred Harp* (printed in Philadelphia, 1844), compiled by Benjamin Franklin White (1800–1879) and E. J. King (d. 1844?). Both of these were "shape note" hymn books. That is, they employed a notation with four musical symbols, ◻ (fa), ○ (sol), ◻ (la), and ◇ (mi), which had already been popularized by the Yankee tunesmiths. The sources of these songs varied widely, ranging from *Hail Columbia* (in Walker's collection) to newly written down pieces like *Wayfaring Stranger* and *The Old Ship of Zion* (in White and King). The last-named song exists in both white and black versions. The one used in *The Sacred Harp* has been described as being a North Carolina variant. *The Sacred Harp* was phenomenally successful, going through numerous revisions and republications, one as recently as the 1970s! Recent editions have been published by the Sacred Harp Publishing Company of Cullman, Alabama. (For examples of *Sacred Harp* revival hymns, see *MA,* nos. 102 and 103.)

Gospel hymns   By the last quarter of the nineteenth century, revival hymns coexisted with a new form of devotional music, the gospel hymn (or gospel song, as it was also called). While the revival hymn had grown up in rural America, the gospel hymn was an urban development, reflecting the changing residence patterns of the last half of the century. Harmonically, devotional songs were "correct," according to established rules. They followed the lead of Mason and Hastings, but were generally more chromatic. Other influences may also be discerned in them, ranging from North American transplantations of German *Volkslieder* as performed by *Männerchore* (male choruses) to combinations of revival song form and barbershop quartet harmony. The texts of these works tend to be sentimental.

Composers of successful gospel songs had much in common with today's successful Broadway composers, in that publicity campaigns were launched for their works, which enjoyed enormous commercial success. The best-known composers of gospel hymns are Philip D. Bliss (1838–1876), Ira D. Sankey (1840–1908), and Rev. Robert Lowry (1826–1899). Of these, Lowry is mainly known as the author of *Beautiful River* (*Shall We Gather at the River,* 1878), which Charles Ives used in the Allegro movement of his *Violin Sonata No. 4,* "Children's Day at the Camp Meeting" (1914–1915). Sankey collaborated with Bliss on his *Gospel Hymns,* published in New York (1875). This collection and later volumes of gospel songs published by Bliss and other collaborators after Sankey's death were enormously popular, and in 1894 Sankey brought out a cumulative volume, *Gospel Hymns Nos. 1 to 6 Complete.* From these collections have come songs to which new words have been added, such as *O Happy Day* from the 1894 collection (No. 543), known to us today in a parody form as *How Dry I Am!* From an earlier edition (1883), the song by Bliss entitled *Hallelujah, 'Tis Done* (No. 2) acquired new words and is now sung under the title *Hallelujah, I'm a Bum.* Some phrases taken from the words to these songs—for example, "hold the fort," "sweet by-and-by," and "arise and shine"—have entered our everyday vocabulary.

The German Influence

John Knowles Paine (1839–1906) partook of the growing German influence in North American music during this period. Groups of German musicians, fleeing unrest at home, had settled primarily in the northern states. Paine, in his hometown of Portland, Maine, studied with one such immigrant, Hermann Kotzschmar (1829–1909). He pursued advanced studies in Germany (1858–1861), coming under the influence of Schumann, Mendelssohn, and other early Romantics, and conducting a performance of his own *Mass in D,* Op. 10, at the Berlin Singakademie (1867). Paine's setting of Whittier's *Hymn* as his *Centennial Hymn,* Op. 27 (for the Centennial Exposition, Philadelphia, 1876), reflects Mendelssohn's choral style, just as his symphonies, performed to much acclaim in New England, reflect Schumann's.

After considerable struggle against the prevailing American attitude that music was an unnecessary frill in college life, Paine managed to attain a professorship at Harvard University (1875), thus becoming the first university music professor in the country. Until his retirement (1905) he taught men who later carried on the tradition of the "university composer," among them Arthur Foote, Daniel Gregory Mason, and John Alden Carpenter. Paine passed on the values he himself had internalized, especially the German Ro-

Paine

mantic stress on the moral and educational functions of music—in part perhaps in reaction against his detractors at Harvard, who were forever attempting to prove music a frivolity that could easily be cut from the curriculum.

Music for Large Groups

Three composers may be considered representative of North American
Romanticism: Anthony Philip Heinrich, Louis Moreau Gottschalk, and Stephen Foster. Heinrich was a model of the successful musical immigrant
steeped in the Austro-German tradition. Gottschalk, one of the first United
States–born performers of international repute, was deeply influenced by the
French style. Foster, despite his private study of German masters, remained a
self-taught composer and an American original.

Heinrich and Gottschalk, more classically trained than Foster, produced
works in the larger and smaller forms. Foster, however, is known as a composer and arranger only of miniatures. Heinrich and Foster, who were trying
to earn money from their compositions, customarily published collections
containing arrangements or transcriptions for home use.

Heinrich   Bohemian-born Anthony Philip Heinrich (1781–1861), who settled initially in Philadelphia (c. 1810), wrote dozens of works in the larger forms. He
was the first Romantic composer in the United States, known to some of his
contemporaries as "The Beethoven of America." Heinrich turned to composition about 1817 while living in the wilds of Kentucky. (His first major accomplishment there was to bring together musicians for a large-scale benefit
band concert under his direction. At the same concert he also played both
violin and piano. Such a program was highly unusual for its host town, Lex-
ington, Kentucky, which was then a frontier settlement.)

Heinrich's orchestral works include all manner of program music, much
of it inspired by the landscape, legends, or history of his adopted country.
The composer's style throughout his 60 known symphonic works is extrava-
gantly Romantic in its use of extreme contrasts of texture, ranging from
dancelike homophony to wildly chromatic counterpoint, and from four-
square phrases to hyper-extended phrase structure on one hand and general
pauses on the other. Added to this Romanticism of opposites is the composer's imaginative use of orchestral color and exotic instruments not considered part of the standard orchestra of his day. Heinrich has the additional distinction of having been the first composer to gather and use music of the
American Indian in his large-scale works, thus presaging a major interest of
many later composers. The characteristics of his large works are evident also
in his many piano works, chamber-music works, and songs.

Fry   William Henry Fry, too, entered the Romantic Grandness sweepstakes.
For his hour-long Belliniesque *Stabat Mater* (finished in 1855 but never performed during the composer's lifetime), Fry required the services of 372 musicians playing 8 flutes, 8 piccolos, 8 horns, 24 saxhorns, 24 kettledrums, 100
violas, 100 cellos, and 100 double basses.

Gottschalk   Louis Moreau Gottschalk grew up in the New Orleans French tradition,
fully conversant with the music of the Louisiana and Haitian French and with

that of the West Indies and Creole blacks. In 1809–1810 more than ten thousand black, white, and mulatto refugees from West Indian strife had arrived in Louisiana, bringing their music and customs with them. These West Indian elements attracted Gottschalk throughout his creative life, first as a child prodigy, then during his years of study in Paris, and finally during his distinguished career as a traveling virtuoso pianist. However, he also composed Romantic symphonic works on the same grand scale as Berlioz, with whom he has been compared. For one performance in Havana (1860) of his *Marcha triumfal y final de ópera* ("Triumphal and Final Opera March"), he claimed to have had 882 performers—650 in the orchestra; 87 in the chorus; 80 drums; 50 trumpets; and 15 vocal soloists—or, as he put it, "nearly nine hundred persons bellowing and blowing to see who could scream the loudest."[8] For an 1869 concert in Rio de Janeiro, the composer managed to find about 650 musicians to perform the Andante of his symphony *La Nuit des tropiques* ("Night in the Tropics," 1858–1859). Gottschalk's recently rediscovered one-movement work, the *Montevideo* Symphony (subtitled *Romantique*, 1868?), is in the same tradition of full-blown Romanticism.

Salon and Solo Piano Music

The piano was just as much the instrument of the general public in North America as in Latin America and Europe, and songs with piano accompaniment as well as music for piano solo flourished. Dances, themes with variations, operatic medleys, and light program pieces intended as music for home entertainment were especially popular. Of this salon music, some works were virtuoso variations, intended to be brilliant and difficult, and to sound as if they were being improvised on the spot, as appropriate to the concert stage as to the drawing room. But most can best be characterized by the title of a waltz by the prolific German-born Charles Grobe (c. 1817–?): *Amusement de salon* ("Salon Entertainment," c. 1850?). The same spirit, fed by the sentimental temperament of the times, was prevalent in the vocal music of such composers as English-born Henry Russell (1812–1900), who wrote *Woodman, Spare That Tree* after his arrival in the United States (1833). The texts for these songs are maudlin, the vocal range is limited, the phrase structure simple, the form generally strophic, and the chromaticism sparing and applied for affect.

Whatever the musical medium, most works were meant both for home use and for the girls attending the female seminaries sometimes called "colleges" (approximately equivalent to latter-day finishing schools) that were then flourishing in North America. These generally were church-related, Protestant institutions, designed to prepare middle-class girls to become wives and mothers, and music—especially the sentimental and not too technically demanding variety—was considered ideal for these purposes. Grobe was a music teacher at just such a female seminary, Wesleyan Female College in Wilmington, Delaware. The lack of division between "home" and "concert" repertory can be seen in the fact that Russell's songs and other vocal and instrumental "salon" music enjoyed frequent public performances.

William Mason

Lowell Mason's third son, William (1829–1908), was a gifted, German-trained pianist. Despite his professed high musical ideals, the pieces he wrote (e.g., his *Lullaby,* Op. 10, in *MA,* no. 26) were derivative, essentially predictable, and catered to the popular taste. The left-hand ostinato figuration in Mason's *Lullaby* sounds Chopinesque because it is—it is modeled on Chopin's *Berceuse.*

Heinrich

Heinrich also composed piano music (e.g., his *Yankeedoodle,* a section of *The Hickory,* c. 1849, in *MA,* no. 127) and chamber music. His works differ markedly from Mason's in their wild chromaticism and erratic nature, elements of Romantic unpredictability that mark all his compositions. In his 1820 collection called *The Dawning of Music in Kentucky* (Preface in *ACS,* pp. 42–43) are songs, dances, and variations. The anthology ends with a piano fantasy-quintet, *The Yankee Doodleiad,* based variously on its title tune, trumpet calls, and finally fourteen variations on *Yankee Doodle.* In the midst of the final variations is a paraphrase of *The President's March* by Philip Phile (1734–1793)—hardly the sort of composition that would be considered "serious" by German Romantic standards. In the same anthology, however, is an extraordinary piano work entitled *A Chromatic Ramble, or the Peregrine Harmonist.* This piece, with its labyrinthine modulations and enharmonic musical puns, is clearly the work of an inventive musical mind (see Example 39.4).

Ex. 39.4   Anthony Philip Heinrich, *A Chromatic Ramble, or the Peregrine Harmonist*

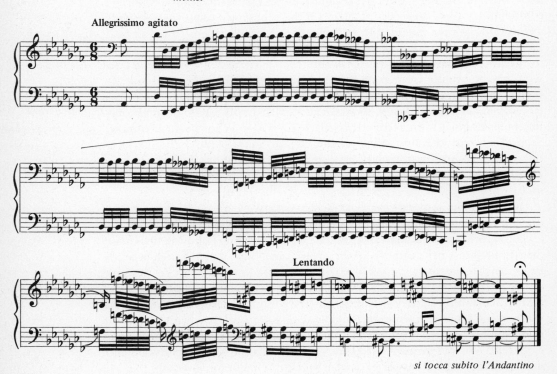

Ex. 39.4   cont.

Gottschalk's pianistic prowess earned him glowing reviews, both in the Americas and in the European press, which compared him to Paganini and Liszt. Welcomed to the ranks of distinguished musicians by both Chopin and Berlioz, Gottschalk studied with the latter and presented concerts with him in Paris (1846–1847). Some of Gottschalk's earliest Afro-Caribbean-influenced music was written in France, when the composer was in his teens. The various musical influences drawn from the composer's youth are clearly shown in his *Bamboula* (c. 1845), a piano work based on Creole melodies in which a variant of the Cuban *habanera* rhythm plays a role (see Example 39.5).

Gottschalk

In Gottschalk's more than one hundred piano pieces there is great stress on virtuosity, in keeping with the Romantic idolization of the virtuoso. Flurries of octaves and other parallel passagework embroider the melodies. But a fidelity to the spirit and rhythmic characteristics of the original musical model is also evident, as in *Le Bananier* ("The Banana Tree"), Op. 5, and his ever-popular show stopper *Le Banjo* ("The Banjo"), Op. 15 (*MA,* no. 125). Gottschalk's ear was, in typical Romantic fashion, well attuned to local color wherever he found it. His *Midnight in Seville* and *Jota Aragonesa,* Op. 14 (1851–1852), are as faithful to Spanish elements as are his Creole and Caribbean works to their origins. He also wrote for the sentimental fashions of the day, as his most successful bathetic composition, *The Last Hope,* Op. 16

Ex. 39.5   Louis Moreau Gottschalk, *Bamboula: Danse des Nègres*

Copyright 1908 by G. Schirmer, Inc., New York. Used by permission.

(1854), readily attests. Its lyrical, artfully graceful melody is given an emotional expression through deft use of chromaticism which plays the melody off against the accompaniment. Gottschalk's other works of this type include *The Dying Poet* (1863–1864), a favorite Romantic subject, and *Morte!!* ("She is Dead," 1868?).

Foster   Stephen Foster has been called "America's Troubadour." His youth was spent in a middle-class Anglo-Irish environment in Pittsburgh, thus making him the only one of the three composers to come from the "West." Since Foster came neither from the Austro-German tradition of Heinrich nor from the aristocratic Creole-French tradition of Gottschalk, he encountered the traditional North American prejudice against the choice of music as a man's career. His family accepted it as a hobby—after all, his father played the violin, his sister the piano—but Foster was largely self-taught. Although he analyzed much of the music of the Austro-German masters, he lacked a thorough grounding in the classical fundamentals of composition; consequently much of his music fails to conform to the then-accepted European "rules." His primary gift is beyond doubt a Romantic rather than an academic one—the sensuous and facile melodies that flowed through almost every page of his music.

Primarily a song composer, Foster wrote about 150 of what have been called "household songs,"[9] but his *Social Orchestra* (1854), which enjoyed enormous sales until the late 1880s, contained primarily transcriptions and arrangements of European masters, among them Bellini, Donizetti, Boïeldieu, Mozart, Schubert, and Weber. The collection's few original instrumental works show Foster to have been influenced sometimes by Italian opera (as in *Anadolia*) and sometimes by the nineteenth-century dance music tradition (as in *Jennie's Own Schottisch* and *Plantation Jig*).

Foster's genius, however, lay in his songs. Their sentimentality was rarely as extravagant as that of comparable works by Russell, George Frederick Root (1820–1895), and Henry Clay Work (1832–1884). Work's *Marching Through Georgia* (1865; *MA, no.* 121) and Root's *The Battle Cry of Freedom* (1863) and *Tramp! Tramp! Tramp!* (1864) were, however, superior to Foster's own Civil War–inspired songs, such as *We Are Coming, Father Abraham, 300,000 More* (1862). As a comic poet (*Oh! Susanna*, 1847), a balladeer (*Jeanie with the Light Brown Hair*, 1854), and a purveyor of pathos and nostalgia for idealized times gone by (*The Old Folks at Home*, 1851), Foster was unsurpassed in conveying the spirit of his age.

Foster had first learned the songs of the blackface minstrels during his boyhood. By the time he began to write such works (1847–1848), he was already thoroughly familiar with all the conventions of this type of entertainment. He excelled at broad humor, so much a part of the minstrel shows, in his *Oh! Susanna*. Nostalgia for the white man's concept of rural black life is expertly depicted in his *Old Folks at Home* and *My Old Kentucky Home* (1853). These and other Foster minstrel songs (also called "Ethiopian songs") were introduced by the then internationally famous Christy Minstrels during the 1840s and 1850s. Such works were commercial successes, but the composer himself remained less well known than the performers who sang his music. When Foster turned to sentimental songs outside the minstrel tradition, his commercial success waned during the 1850s. He died poor, having produced only a few successful songs in the "Ethiopian" tradition, all in 1860—the nostalgic *Old Black Joe* and *Down Among the Canebrakes,* and the humorous *The Glendy Burk* and *Don't Bet Your Money on de Shanghai.* (Reprints of Foster's *Oh! Susanna* and *Old Folks at Home* are in *MA,* nos. 107 and 108, respectively.)

The texts of many of Foster's minstrel songs (e.g., *Old Black Joe* and *The Old Folks at Home*) have sometimes caused the charge of bigotry to be raised against him. Nevertheless, a few of his songs, such as *Camptown Races* (1850) and *Oh! Susanna,* have enjoyed enormous currency—so much so that they have frequently been mistaken for folk songs. Foster's songs have been adopted by people all over the world, and have served as the bases of both art and popular music adaptations by composers as diverse as Dvořák, Charles

Foster and minstrelsy

Antoine Plamondon (1804–1895), *Portrait of Madame Papineau and Her Daughter Ezilda* (1836). The rich dress of both mother and child show that the family was extremely well-to-do, and the child's place at the piano shows the common conception of music as both a leisure-time activity and a children's amusement. Contrast with Hicks's *The Musicale* (p. 899), in which the men are not playing keyboard instruments. (Courtesy, The National Gallery of Canada, Ottawa)

Ives, Ray Charles, and Ornette Coleman (see Chapter 40). Are Stephen Foster's songs "art" music or "folk" music or "popular" music? In some ways they belong to all three categories. Once again, as with much other New World music, perhaps the function they fulfill in the lives of the people who sing and enjoy them is the most important element.

Canada

Musical life In Canada, the number of public concerts increased throughout the first half of the nineteenth century. True to their different heritage, the French had a musical ideal which was more passionate and virtuoso than that prevalent in North America and England—or so wrote a German traveler in the 1850s. The French also showed a preference for opera and song, whereas the English favored oratorio and choral music.

Before the 1840s, little systematic music education was available. Considering Canada's relatively small population (Montreal, its largest city, had a population of only 19,000 in 1800) and the rural nature of most of the country, this situation is hardly surprising. By midcentury, however, Canada had begun to be part of the international concert circuit.

Opera performances were rare in Canada. Amateur societies presented parts of operas or ran through French or Italian works in concert form, but even as late as the 1860s the majority of operas heard in Canada were given by visiting troupes. Under such circumstances it is natural that Canada's comic opera composer of the era, Calixa Lavallée (1842–1891), lived and worked outside the country most of his life, primarily in the United States.

Opera

Other currents in North American music flowed from the Catholic and Anglican churches. Between 1819 and 1845 French-Canadian collections of sacred music appeared, among them *La Lyre sainte* ("The Holy Lyre," 1844–1845), a two-volume set of hymns compiled by German-born Catholic convert Theodore Frederic Molt (c. 1796–1856), an acquantance of Beethoven, Moscheles, and Czerny. The English fondness for large-scale choral forms was brought to Quebec in 1834 with a three-and-a-half-hour concert of sacred music at the Anglican cathedral. With an orchestra of 60 and a chorus of 111, it was a spectacular extravaganza. Along with works by Haydn, Mozart, and Rossini, the *Invocation* for organ by the Cathedral's organist Stephen Codman (1792?–1852?) received hearty public approval.

Catholic and Anglican music

Summary

Romanticism was an integral part of many nineteenth-century New World developments. Nationalism, idealism, and the cults of the individual and of emotion combined with constant population shifts to produce a society in a state of flux. The social status of music and musicians also varied, depending upon the cultural heritage of a given area at a particular time.

In Latin America the major influences were Italian opera and French salon music. The arrival of Italian opera troupes nourished this trend, as did the longstanding popularity of France as the "philosophical home" of New World revolutionaries. Romantic interest in the cultivation of folk forms and their use in art music also encouraged the growth of nationalist schools of composition.

The United States and Canada, with their sparse population and predominantly northern European heritage, also felt the influence of Italian opera and French salon music. But they had, as well, a long tradition of English musical practice. To that was added the influx of German forms, styles, and ideas brought by the many German-speaking immigrants who settled in large urban areas and small towns, especially in the United States.

Music education was growing in the New World, as were the number of musical organizations. Most "serious" musicians still went abroad to study, thereby achieving credibility and prestige. At the same time, traveling virtuosos of the era set new, higher performance standards.

During this period, the New World was becoming simultaneously more nationalistic and more cosmopolitan. The implications of these developments will be discussed in the next chapter.

Notes

1. Cited in Stevenson, *Music in Mexico* (New York: Crowell, 1970), p. 195. From Mme. Calderón de la Barca, *Life in Mexico* (London: Everyman, 1841), p. 137.
2. Ibid. (from Calderón, op. cit., p. 286).
3. Cited in Luiz Heitor Correa de Azevedo, "Sigismund Neukomm, An Austrian Composer in the New World," *Musical Quarterly* 45, no. 4 (Oct. 1959): 477.
4. Ibid., p. 478.
5. Ibid., p. 473.
6. This figure, which includes works of doubtful authenticity, arrangements, and lost works, is based on the *Catálogo tematico das obras do Padre José Maurício Nunes Garcia* (Rio de Janeiro: Ministério da Educação e Cultura, 1970) by Cleofe Person de Mattos. Because Mattos was the first to compile a catalog of this composer's works, his compositions are referred to by "M" numbers just as Mozart's are by their "K" numbers.
7. Irving Lowens, *Music and Musicians in Early America* (New York: W. W. Norton, 1964), p. 134.
8. Cited in H. Wiley Hitchcock, *Music in the United States: A Historical Introduction* (Englewood Cliffs, N.J.: Prentice-Hall, 1974), p. 91.
9. Ibid., p. 69.

Bibliography

Books and Articles

United States

AUSTIN, WILLIAM. *"Susanna," "Jeanie," and "The Old Folks at Home."* New York: Macmillan, 1975.

GOTTSCHALK, LOUIS MOREAU. *Notes of a Pianist,* ed. Jeanne Behrend. New York: Alfred A. Knopf, 1964.

HOWARD, JOHN TASKER. *Stephen Foster, America's Troubadour,* 2nd rev. ed. New York: Thomas Y. Crowell, 1962.

KMEN, HENRY. *Music in New Orleans: The Formative Years, 1791–1841.* Baton Rouge: Louisiana State University Press, 1966.

SHANET, HOWARD. *Philharmonic: A History of New York's Orchestra.* Garden City, N.Y.: Doubleday, 1975.

UPTON, WILLIAM TREAT. *Anthony Philip Heinrich.* New York: Columbia University Press, 1939.

———. *William Henry Fry, American Journalist and Composer-Critic.* New York: Thomas Y. Crowell, 1954.

WOLFE, RICHARD J. *Secular Music in America, 1801–1825,* 3 vols. New York: New York Public Library, 1964.

Latin America

Other, more general works have been cited in the Bibliographies of earlier chapters. As was true in preceding chapters, few published English-language materials exist. Useful studies, in addition to those already mentioned, include:

CORREA DE AZEVEDO, LUIZ HEITOR. "Sigismund Neukomm, An Austrian Composer in the New World." *Musical Quarterly* 45, no. 4 (Oct. 1959): 471–78.

LANGE, FRANCISCO CURT. "Sobre las difíciles huellas de la música antigua del Brasil: La 'Missa abrevia da' del Padre José Maurício Nunes Garcia." *Yearbook of the Interamerican Institute for Musical Research* 1 (1965): 15–40.

MATTOS, CLEOFE PERSON DE. *Catálogo tematico das obras do Padre José Maurício Nunes Garcia.* Rio de Janeiro: Ministério da Educação e Cultura, 1970.

MIKOWSKY, SOLOMON. "The Nineteenth-Century Cuban 'Danza.'" Ph.D. dissertation, Columbia University, 1973.

URRUTIA BLONDEL, JORGE. "Doña Isadora Zegers, 1803–1869." *Revista musical Chilena* 25 (Jan.–June 1971): 3–17.

VEGA, CARLOS. "La musique en Amérique latine au XIXe siècle." *Revue musicale* 242 (1958): 101–104.

Scores

The Earlier American Music Series (Da Capo Press) has reprinted Heinrich's *The Dawning of Music in Kentucky* (1973) and *Western Minstrel* (1973); Foster's *Household Songs, 1844–1864* (1973) and *Minstrel Show Songs* (1979); and Henry Clay Work's *Songs* (1974). Dover has produced facsimile reprints (with excellent introductory notes) of works of Foster and Gottschalk. Two other collections are important:

GOTTSCHALK, LOUIS MOREAU. *The Piano Works of Louis Moreau Gottschalk,* 5 vols. New York: Arno Press and The New York Times, 1969.

HEINRICH, ANTHONY PHILIP. *Songs and Choral Music,* ed. David Barron. Madison, Wisc.: AR Editions (in press).

The Instituto de Cultura Puertorriqueña has published a selection of works by Juan Morel Campos. Reproductions of manuscript scores are available from the Latin American Music Center, Bloomington, and from the Instituto de Musicología, Montevideo, Uruguay.

40

Contemporary Music in and of
the Americas

ROMANTICISM and its offshoots have remained part of the fabric of New World life well into the present century and now coexist with other more recently developed ideas, attitudes, and modes of perception. Nationalism has created many American intra-hemispheric tensions, while concurrently regionalism has developed. Emphasis on ethnic origins has led to a rediscovery of the cultural heritages of the various peoples of the Americas, as political and artistic organizations have developed on a Pan-American and global scale. Political theory, philosophy, population shifts, new scientific discoveries, and the growth of technology have combined to alter the quality of life.

The New World in the twentieth century has become an acknowledged artistic center for the creation of new musical forms and styles, which have been diffused throughout the world. In this century also, many composers of the Americas have become part of the international mainstream of music, and so their "international" works have been discussed in detail in Part 6. This chapter will therefore concentrate on those genres and movements that are identified mainly with the New World: e.g., nationalist trends, jazz, rock 'n' roll, and the musical.

Music and Society

The cultured New World elite in the late nineteenth century looked to France and Italy or to Germany and Austria for artistic models. Composers and performers flocked to the Americas in search of both political asylum and greater economic opportunity. Ethnic groups in the New World often sought the continuity of artistic traditions they had known before emigrating. Frequently New World musical organizations contracted for the services of musicians, including conductors, in Europe.

The Austro-German Romantic tradition, which stressed the elevated moral purpose of "serious" music, induced many people in the New World

916

Winslow Homer (1836–1910), *Amateur Musicians.* (Courtesy, The Metropolitan Museum of Art: Samuel D. Lee Fund, 1939)

to scorn such genres as operetta, popular music, salon music, and folk music. This attitude is still with us to some extent, although composers like Leonard Bernstein (b. 1918) have successfully written works in both "classical" and "popular" genres. To take just one example, Bernstein's *Prelude, Fugue, and Riffs* for large dance band (1949) shows the interpenetration of jazz and Classical form and procedure.

Modern popular music groups of the New World often enjoy some of the same status as the medieval troubadours, and they arrive in many different cities to heroes' welcomes. But then, so do some star performers of art music. Less often is such public acclaim accorded to composers of serious music.

American Originals

Perhaps the two types of music most consistently and internationally considered to be "American" are jazz and rock music. Of these, jazz is the more readily accepted by "serious" musicians, in part, perhaps, because it has tenaciously remained in the public eye, and because some of its elements have been in existence for more than three-quarters of a century. Evolving in the southern United States from a combination of influences, jazz first flowered in and around New Orleans at the turn of the century. Much of its early development took place in the black districts of American cities, and it was accepted by society at large only after years of protest by groups who did not deem it "respectable." A major step in the international acceptance of jazz came when Paul Whiteman's band first toured Europe (1920). Today jazz fans are to be found on every continent of the world.

Rock 'n' roll in the 1950s represented a stripping away of the sometimes elaborate nuances and improvisations of the complex jazz of that era in favor of simpler melody and harmony, and insistent rhythms. This extreme rhythmic emphasis, often known as the "big beat," frequently became intentionally both loud and hypnotic. Critics of rock music dismissed it as a barbaric tribal rite, much as many had also dismissed the early stages of jazz. Yet it, too, persisted, and has acquired disciples and imitators in the form of rock groups all over the world. As we have already observed, growing confusion exists in the minds of many about where "serious" music stops and "popular" music begins. This uncertainty has resulted in part from the fact that just as in earlier eras, musicians listen to what is happening around them. Contemporary composers and exotic music exercised a great influence on modern European rock groups, and a similar interpenetration of styles took place in such American groups as The Mothers of Invention (est. 1964), who were influenced by the works of "serious" and avant-garde composers like Bartók, Stravinsky, Stockhausen, Ives, and, above all, John Cage. Like jazz, rock 'n' roll was first adopted and accepted among American blacks, and only after time acquired "respectability" in the eyes of the rest of society. Musicians trained in classical music have also found their way to rock, both to praise its innovators (as Leonard Bernstein did The Beatles in the 1960s) and to perform it (the New York Rock and Roll Ensemble, for example).

Jazz

Origins and character   Several traditions and styles contributed to the birth of jazz. West African drum rhythms and Afro-Caribbean rhythms combined with European functional harmony. To these were added the gospel song, born of the urban Protestant revival movement of the 1850s. With melodies and forms borrowed from the popular music of the day, gospels added an improvisatory call-and-response style. The final element in jazz, and one whose origin is not yet clear, is the blues scale, three variants of which are given in Example 40.1.

Jazz, then, has the above characteristics, along with standard harmonic

Ex. 40.1   The blues scale

schemes, a continuo-like rhythm section, special intonation, and distinctive timbres. Each of its subcategories resulted from modifications of one or another of these component parts, and therefore the history of jazz can be traced here only in its broadest possible outline.

The name "jazz" was not widely used until 1913–1915. However, before that time both instrumental and vocal forms evolved that were later considered aspects of jazz: ragtime (c. 1890–1920), originally an instrumental style, and blues (c. 1900–   ), originally a vocal style.

Ragtime

The piano was the quintessential ragtime instrument, and ragtime piano performance required a percussive touch with no pedal. A typical rag has duple meter, primary chords (with secondary dominants in the major keys), and song-form structures comprised of 16-bar or 32-bar periods. It may also have brief introductory and transitional sections (called *vamps*), codas, and syncopated melodies in the right hand over nonsyncopated harmonic bass lines. Melodies generally move at twice the speed of the bass, with primary syncopations falling in $\frac{4}{4}$ on the second and fourth eighth-notes. Typical of ragtime is the even performance of eighth notes, a practice not generally used in other forms of jazz.

Brass bands were also very popular for playing ragtime. In the bands, treble melody instruments fulfilled the same functions as the pianist's right hand, and mid-range instruments provided the harmony with a brass bass and bass-drum rhythmic accompaniment.

The ragtime revival of the late 1960s–1970s brought with it a great resurgence of interest in the music of such composers as Scott Joplin (1868–1917, "King of Ragtime"); James Sylvester Scott (1886–1938); Thomas Million Turpin (1873–1922, "Father of St. Louis Ragtime"); and James Hubert "Eubie" Blake (b. 1883).

Scott Joplin grew up in Texarkana, Texas. His family was musical, and Joplin's early evidence of pianistic talent was recognized locally and en-   **Joplin**

Thomas Eakins (1844–1916), *Negro Boy Dancing*. White artists frequently interested themselves in black subjects, just as white musicians did. (Courtesy, The Metropolitan Museum of Art: Fletcher Fund, 1925)

couraged. After teaching himself to play, he received free instruction in piano, theory, and appreciation of European music from a local German immigrant musician.

By 1885 Joplin had played his way through the Mississippi Valley towns and settled in St. Louis, then a frontier town. There he played in the Silver Dollar saloon, one of a number owned by the Turpin family, who encouraged the development of ragtime in these tenderloin clubs. Joplin remained in Missouri until the 1890s.

These years were a watershed period in Joplin's development. One of many black musicians who had gone to Chicago hoping to find work, he played at the World's Columbian Exposition there in 1893. Joplin had already begun to write down his musical ideas, but not until after 1895 was he able to find publishers interested in printing his compositions. His first five works (1896–1898) consisted of two sentimental songs, two piano marches, and a piano waltz. All were pale and lacking in the character and verve of his later rags. Although he played in a syncopated style, these early pieces were not so written since the "rag" style did not become popular until 1898, and no publisher would yet accept such music.

After settling in Sedalia, Missouri, in 1896, Joplin performed at the Maple Leaf Club in the town's red light district and studied advanced harmony and composition at the George Smith College for Negroes. In 1898 he finally found a publisher for his ragtime works.

Joplin's most famous composition—during his life as well as after his death—was his *Maple Leaf Rag* (published 1899), named for the club where he worked. It was the second of his piano rags. Joplin's first, *Original Rags* (sometimes called *Original Rag*), had been published earlier that same year. But these were only the first two of his thirty-nine rags, some of which were written in collaboration with other musicians. These pieces included such favorites as *Sugar Cane Rag* (1908) and *Wall Street Rag* (1909). Of all his rags, only two have fewer than the traditional four themes, and only two have more. Those works written before the last few years of Joplin's life are generally considered the model for ragtime composers. Most have the following form: introduction—ABACD. However, at the end of his life Joplin entered into an experimental phase in which he varied this form. For example, his *Euphonic Sounds* (1909) is a rondo, while the *Magnetic Rag* (1914) proceeds directly through the introduction and all four strains, then repeats the first strain before ending with a coda. Joplin also wrote a self-tutor entitled *School of Ragtime* (1908). Between 1906 and 1909, Joplin toured regularly with vaudeville shows and made piano-rolls for the then-popular Pianola Player Piano.

The *Maple Leaf Rag*—a virtuoso showpiece that has become a standard test for ragtime pianists—was both a popular and a financial success, selling hundreds of thousands of copies by 1909. Joplin's publisher, John Stilwell Stark, had given Joplin $50 plus royalties for this composition. Its success allowed Joplin to stop playing piano in clubs and instead dedicate himself entirely to composing and teaching.

In 1903 Joplin produced two long musical works—an opera and a folk ballet with narration. His *A Guest of Honor, a Ragtime Opera* was given a single concert performance in St. Louis. Although it made a very favorable impression on its audience, we cannot hear it today because the manuscript has been lost. Sedalia's Opera House was the scene of the premiere of Joplin's twenty-minute *The Ragtime Dance*, which used the cakewalk, the "slow drag" (a black dance to ragtime music), and other popular dances of the time, performed to a sung narration describing the dances.

Joplin eventually settled in New York City in 1909. Despite the continuing success of his published rags, he became increasingly obsessed with work on his second ragtime opera, *Treemonisha* (1911), a story of how the forces of evil attempt to thwart the forces of good (personified by the black heroine, Treemonisha, who wants to save her black neighbors with the learning she has acquired with the help of her white adoptive parents).

Unable to find a publisher, Joplin himself assumed the expense of publishing the 230-page score. After orchestrating the work, in collaboration with Sam Patterson (1881–?), Joplin underwrote all the costs of a Harlem rehearsal run-through (1915), training all the performers himself and playing a piano reduction of the orchestral score in the performance in a last, desperate, unsuccessful attempt to attract financial support for his venture. Under the strain of this failure, Joplin's mental health was destroyed and he died in an institution two years later. His orchestrations were lost, and not until Gunther Schuller reorchestrated *Treemonisha* and conducted a revival of it in 1975 did the public at large have a chance to enjoy it.

Although ragtime is essentially an instrumental form, songs were also written in this style, and some were extremely well received by the public. The popularity of ragtime is attested to by the early publication of a self-tutor—the appearance in New York in 1897 of *The Ragtime Instructor* by Benjamin (Ben) Harney (1871–1938).

Blues

Origins and character

The term *blues* was first used c. 1900 to refer to music unified in style by a combination of performance practice, form, and a melancholy emotional state. In contrast to ragtime, the blues was born of the black vocal tradition as revealed in work songs and spirituals. A recurring twelve-bar harmonic structure in common time ($\frac{4}{4}$ meter) is typical of the blues, as is its division into three groups of four measures, in which the chord progression is generally as follows:

Measure: 1 2 3 4 5 6 7 8 9 10 11—12
Chord : I——— IV —I—V—— I ——

Strikingly characteristic of the blues is the use of the "blues scale," combining both major and minor modalities with nontempered scale intervals, as we saw in Example 40.1. Many nuances of vocal inflection (including *portamento* [bent pitch], the nontempered scale, and various types of vibrato) apply to the blues and are an integral part of the style.

Standard blues rhythm consists of a steady stream of strong pulses, as opposed to the alternating strong and weak patterns found in ragtime. Blues performers frequently create syncopation by missing beats rather than by accenting them, as had been customary in ragtime. The newer form allows enormous flexibility for the performer. Blues was at first performed by a solo voice accompanied by a piano or guitar. Later, instrumental ensembles replaced the voice with a melodic instrument, imitating or expanding on its original capabilities in the varieties of timbres, envelopes (rate of growth and decay of sounds), and *portamenti* so characteristic of the blues style. The country blues often used a period length that varied from eight to fifteen bars, as contrasted with the twelve-bar structure typical of city blues. One of the most famous examples of the genre—and coincidentally one of the first blues pieces to become widely popular—was the *St. Louis Blues* (1914), written by the "Father of the Blues," William Christopher Handy (usually called simply W. C. Handy, 1873–1958).

Jazz Styles

The "big-band sound" developed in the 1920s. Edward Kennedy "Duke" Ellington (1899–1974) in Harlem and Earl ("Fatha") Hines (b. 1905) in Chicago were among those who enlarged their bands to include two trumpets, a trombone, and three saxophones. **The big-band sound**

In earlier jazz forms individual solo instruments were used, and in Dixieland jazz no more than two sections, rhythm and melody, were found. But the big-band sound relied on at least three sections—reeds, brass, and rhythm—and sometimes as many as five. The existing brass section might be divided into trumpet and trombone choirs, and violins might also be added. As the size of the bands increased, improvisation was no longer possible, and the composer-arranger became ever more important. The length of individual solos was decided by the arranger, and "group solos" were handled by choirs of instruments. The bands themselves were racially segregated then, but musicians often ignored color lines by playing together during after-hours "jam" sessions. Among the most famous black big bands were those of Louis Armstrong (1900–1971) and Joseph "King" Oliver (1885–1938). Examples of the white big-band sound may be found in the work of Ferde Grofé (1892–1972), Don Redman (1900–1964), and Paul Whiteman (1900–1967).

By 1936 both black and white big bands had become famous throughout the Americas and Europe. Much of the big-band sound had been reduced to such formulas as the use of mutes; four- and five-note chords (rather than triads); antiphony among the various sections; and close harmony among players in a single section. By 1939 this type of music, rather than improvisational jazz, was flooding the commercial market.

The 1930s saw the emergence of "swing," of Kansas City style, and of Duke Ellington's orchestral style. In swing, the drummer provided a basic pulse by striking the bass drum on each beat ("driving") and hitting the cymbals with a stick on all beats, accenting the second and fourth beats of the measure ("riding"). Except during brass solos, syncopated, staccato brass chords accompanied the sax section melody to complete the style. Improvisation in a swing band was rare, and solos seldom exceeded one chorus in length. Such leaders as Benny Goodman (b. 1909), Jimmy Dorsey (1904–1957), and Gene Krupa (1909–1973) were known for their virtuosity on their own instruments. During the same period Ellington combined swing techniques with solos emphasizing the abilities of his players, thus focusing on the soloist to a much greater extent than did typical swing bands. In Kansas City style, pioneered by William "Count" Basie (b. 1904), a big band playing blues repertory improvised in four or five parts, using short repeated figures ("riffs") played either in unison or in harmony, and percussive, syncopated brass chords. The melody was often improvised in this style, and the full arrangement might not be written down at all. **Swing** **Kansas City style**

"Be-bop," "re-bop," or simply "bop," as it was also called, developed **Be-bop** during the 1940s, generally among smaller groups. Bop instrumentation called for four or five rhythm instruments and one or two solo instruments. "Scat-singing" (singing nonsense syllables to the instrumental line) was an integral part of the style. To earlier blues patterns were added increasing chromaticism, instrumental virtuosity, and more complex chord sequences using ninth, eleventh, and thirteenth chords as well as added tones, tonal ambiguity, and frequent modulation. Charlie Parker (1920–1955) and John Birks "Dizzy" Gillespie (b. 1917) are outstanding exponents of bop, an introspective style in which only the string bass and cymbals still maintained the beat, thus requiring more concentration from the audience.

Bop of the 1950s, with a new soft, breathy sound and slow, narrow vibrato or even none (rather than the fast, wide one that had marked 1940s bop), was called "cool jazz." Its originators included Stan Getz (b. 1927) and Miles Davis (b. 1926). Harmonically, however, this music was still bop, as was "hard bop" (also called "funky jazz"). During this period, swing maintained its popularity, and Dixieland and Armstrong experienced revivals.

Free jazz   With the 1960s came "free jazz," often considered a vehicle for the expression of black nationalism in the United States. It avoided traditional forms and a constant metric pulse, and embraced instead surprise, chance, and atonality. Early explorers of this idiom were Ornette Coleman (b. 1932) and John Coltrane (1926–1967).

Non-Western elements   Two other innovations of the 1960s and 1970s emerged: non-Western ideas and electronics. The first included the use of nonstandard instruments, tunings, scales, and harmonies, as well as a different harmonic framework and philosophy, leading to such manifestations as "raga jazz" and "raga rock." The use of new electronic devices of various kinds to alter timbre and **Electronic jazz** create new effects for both soloists and groups has been more widespread, gaining acceptance in jazz as well as in other branches of music.

The Rise of Rock Music

Rhythm-and-blues   "Rhythm-and-blues," a combination of blues, jazz, and gospel, was a form of black urban folk music, which grew from the "sepia," or "race," music that existed before and just after World War II. Based on simple harmonic progressions (I–IV–V), it had simple melodies and insistent, repetitive rhythmic patterns in duple meter. The singer was backed by a rhythm group featuring a wailing tenor saxophone. Before the mid-1950s such songs were performed primarily by black musicians such as Little Richard (b. 1935), Antoine "Fats" Domino (b. 1928), and Chubby Checker (b. 1941).

Early rock 'n' roll (also called "hard rock"), however, resulted from a mixture of black rhythm-and-blues and hillbilly ("bluegrass," or "country-and-western") songs. The term "rock 'n' roll" originally was a euphemism for sexual intercourse, and for years music bearing this designation was considered highly improper, unfit for polite society. The first phenomenally successful **Presley** white exponent of the style was Elvis Presley (1935–1977).

By the 1960s, rock music had developed into electronically amplified forms including the "psychedelic," played by such groups as the Jefferson Airplane (est. 1965) and The Doors (fl. 1964–1973). The sensational British quartet, The Beatles (fl. 1961–1970), learned enough about this American form to achieve as great a success as Presley. They integrated into their music new stylistic developments from psychedelic rock to raga rock, expanding their horizons toward the East and abandoning the drug culture for oriental philosophy during the late 1960s. The group officially disbanded in 1971.

Rock groups

Not until April 28, 1968, with the production of Galt MacDermot's *Hair,* was rock successful on the Broadway stage. (The show had opened off-Broadway a year earlier.) It was followed by such Broadway phenomena of the 1970s as the controversial *Jesus Christ, Superstar* (1971).

Since the mid-1950s, new forms and the hybridization of old ones have created constantly shifting patterns, and rock has combined with folk music, light shows, and other musical styles. Electronic effects such as hyperamplification pervaded "hard rock," as played by Cream (disbanded 1972). Even more interested in the marriage of rock and electronics was Frank Zappa (b. 1940), whose performances with his group, The Mothers of Invention (est. 1964), were iconoclastic and freewheeling. He also made a much-publicized attempt to combine rock and classical music: a joint concert with the Los Angeles Philharmonic in which excerpts from Zappa's *200 Motels* were performed to mixed critical reception. The nostalgia craze of the 1970s brought with it a revival of early rock music—a retrospection further heightened by the death of such rock stars as Elvis Presley.

Hybrid rock forms

The Musical Comedy

Another New World development that has found wide international acceptance is the "musical." Related in its early stages to the Viennese operetta the United States musical (or "musical comedy," as it is sometimes called) can also trace its ancestry to eighteenth-century American stage shows with music, as well as to such nineteenth-century American works as *The Black Crook* (1866). The existence of both professional and amateur operetta troupes throughout the United States and Canada, even in places that were not major urban centers, attests to the widespread popularity of operetta as a genre during the last quarter of the nineteenth century. *Leo, the Royal Cadet* (1889), for instance, was written by a German-born Canadian immigrant, Oscar F. Telgmann (1853–1945). Its first performance was in Kingston, Ontario, but it also was given in Ottawa and Toronto, and in Utica, New York. As far west as Winnipeg, only twenty-two years later, two English-born composers, Dr. Ralph Joseph Horner (1849–1926) and William Dichmont (1882–1943), were actively writing operettas. Sheet music of popular music and of songs from revues and operettas circulated widely—so much so, in fact, that it has always accounted for the bulk of music published in the United States and Canada as well as for the single largest segment of the record industry.

Early efforts

Nothing before the late nineteenth century has the peculiar blend of strong plots and dialogue (the "book"), and the balancing of a variety of song types (song program), that twentieth-century audiences have come to expect from this genre.

A milestone in the history of the musical was reached in Victor Herbert's *Babes in Toyland* (1903), when both connecting and incidental music were used, elements that became integral parts of the modern musical. Four years later, the American success of Franz Léhar's *The Merry Widow* (originally produced in Europe in 1905) brought with it a new emphasis on the dance that was later explored in ballroom sequences in the 1920s and 1930s. More sophisticated music was added by Rudolf Friml (*High Jinks,* 1913) and Sigmund Romberg (*The Passing Show,* 1914). At the same time, ragtime began to enter the musical in the works of George M. Cohan (1878–1942; *Hello Broadway,* 1914) and Irving Berlin (b. 1888; *Watch Your Step,* 1914).

A deep interest in the integration of musical and dramatic elements was a trait of composers like George Gershwin (1898–1937; note especially *Of Thee I Sing,* 1931, and *Porgy and Bess,* 1934–1935) and Jerome Kern (1885–1945; note especially *Showboat,* 1927). This new emphasis, coupled with the genre's growing complexity, finally produced a whole notable for its intricately related elements of design, book, music, direction, and expense (a single show may cost well over $1 million to produce). Prominent composers of modern musicals include Richard Rodgers, Cole Porter, Meredith Willson, Frank Loesser, and Leonard Bernstein.

Rodgers   Richard Rodgers (1902–1979) composed the music for some of the finest American musical comedies. The following were all written in collaboration with Lorenz Hart (1895–1943): *A Connecticut Yankee* (1927, based on a novel by Mark Twain, and source of the song *Thou Swell*); *On Your Toes* (1936, source of the ballet *Slaughter on Tenth Avenue*); *The Boys from Syracuse* (1938, source of the songs *This Can't Be Love, The Shortest Day of the Year,* and *Sing for your Supper*); and *Pal Joey* (1940, a daring story at the time, dealing with the fortunes of a gigolo). After Hart's death, Rodgers's successful Broadway musicals included *Oklahoma!* (1943), *Carousel* (1945), *South Pacific* (1949), and *The Sound of Music* (1959), all created with lyricist Oscar Hammerstein II (1895–1960). These works reflect a growing concern with the integration of plot, action, character, and music into one coherent whole.

Porter   Born in Peru, Indiana, Cole Porter (1893–1964) studied at Yale, Harvard, and the Schola Cantorum in Paris. The musicals he wrote reflected the urbane, sophisticated life of the elegant social set to which he himself belonged. His works show Porter's command of compositional techniques. Although he wrote a number of well-received musicals, his best known is *Kiss Me, Kate* (1948), with a libretto by Sam and Bella Spewack based on Shakespeare's *The Taming of the Shrew.* The show successfully integrated elements of music, drama, and characterization in the same way that Rodgers and Hammerstein did in *South Pacific. Kiss Me, Kate* has become one of the classics of the American musical theater.

Willson   Beginning his New York career as a radio conductor of popular music, Iowa-born composer-librettist Meredith Willson (b. 1902) achieved a resounding Broadway success with *The Music Man* (1957), for which he wrote both music and lyrics—a nostalgic, idealized view of Iowa in 1912.

Frank Loesser (1910–1969) began his career in Hollywood, where he wrote words and music for such World War II–era popular tunes as *Praise the Lord and Pass the Ammunition*. Following his initial Broadway success with *Guys and Dolls* (1950, with Abe Burrows, b. 1910), he continued to enjoy successes, including *The Most Happy Fella* (1956, adapted from Sidney Howard's 1924 play, *They Knew What They Wanted*) and *How to Succeed in Business Without Really Trying* (with Abe Burrows and others, 1961). *Guys and Dolls,* and above all, *How to Succeed . . .* , are wittily satirical comments on elements of American society—the first reflecting New York low life, the second the competitive world of big business.

Loesser

Leonard Bernstein came to the attention of Broadway audiences with his musical comedy *On the Town* (with book by Adolph Green and Betty Comden, 1944), based on *Fancy Free,* a ballet which Bernstein had written for choreographer Jerome Robbins earlier that year. Its plot concerned three American sailors on leave in New York City. Robbins himself provided additional choreography that was both entertaining and an integral part of the plot development. Bernstein's next musical comedy success was *Wonderful Town* (1953), again in collaboration with Comden and Green. Although *Candide* (1956) was not itself a hit in its initial production, Bernstein's overture to the work became quite popular on concert programs, as did a revised version of the show (1975). The book was based on Voltaire's *Candide,* for which Bernstein created music ranging from eighteenth-century style to jazz and tangos. Perhaps his greatest popular success was the fiercely evocative portrayal of gang warfare in the slums, *West Side Story* (1957). This extraordinarily realistic work marked the Broadway debut as lyricist of Stephen Sondheim (b. 1930). At the time, the use of street language in the production was considered shocking by some. The play, like Bernstein's other Broadway successes, has been a perennial favorite, and has given the public such songs as *Maria, Somewhere, Tonight,* and *I Feel Pretty.* Bernstein has managed to couple his extensive knowledge of classical music with a flair for dramatic gesture, and in the process he has created some memorable moments in the history of the American musical theater.

Bernstein

Latin American Popular Music

The influence of European theater and popular music showed in Latin America in the popularity of European-derived genres, notably variations of the waltz, polka, and other dance forms.

Dance music

One of the best-known Latin American composers of semipopular and popular music was the Cuban Ernesto Lecuona (1896–1953), whose best-known song, *Siboney,* transcended not only his own nation's borders but those of Ibero-America as well. So, too, did the compositions of the Mexican Augustín Larra (1900–1970), who died a national hero, with numerous songs and operettas to his credit. Operetta found its adherents as far south as Ecuador and Uruguay. In Ecuador, Luis H. Salzado (b. 1903) wrote in all genres, including his operetta *Ensueños de Amor* ("Dreams of Love"). In Uruguay, Ramón Rodríguez Socas (1893–1957) was active as a writer of both serious and comic operas.

European dance music found its way into the working musical vocabulary of many Latin Americans. In the New World, waltzes by composers including Mexicans Ernesto Elorduy (1853–1912), Ricardo Castro (1866–1907), and Felipe Villanueva (1863–1893) provided entertaining diversions for home listening. Perhaps the most famous waltz written in Latin America was that by another Mexican, Juventino Rosas (1868–1894), whose *Sobre las olas* ("Over the Waves"), written for piano as most dance music was then, created an international sensation.

The tango   The tango is a special case. Some experts consider it to be a descendant of the contradanse, while others contend it is Afro-Hispanic in origin. All agree, however, that it was codified in the Río de la Plata region during the last years of the nineteenth century. Popular first in Argentina and Uruguay, it later spread both northward and eastward. It became the most popular ballroom dance of the Western world about the time of World War I and was danced in the movie *The Four Horsemen of the Apocalypse* (1921) by Italian-born actor Rudolph Valentino, who played the part of a gaucho. Tangos can also be found in "serious" music, such as Stravinsky's *L'Histoire du soldat* ("The Soldier's Tale"), and in the theater of social comment, in such works as Weill's *The Threepenny Opera*. Other, more popular North American uses of this form are exemplified by Leroy Anderson's *Blue Tango* (1951).

The Legacy of Romanticism

During the final decades of the nineteenth century and the entire twentieth century, different approaches to music were evident among composers in the Americas. Those who based their works on European models looked for inspiration to France, Italy, the German-speaking lands, or the Slavic countries. Eventually, however, these trends not only coexisted but even intermingled.

The Second New England School

The group that has come to be known as the Second New England school (the Yankee psalmodists were the first)—among them Arthur W. Foote (1853–1937), Daniel Gregory Mason (1873–1953), George W. Chadwick (1854–1931), Horatio W. Parker (1863–1919), and Mrs. H. H. A. Beach (née Amy Marcy Cheney; 1867–1944)—were all influenced by German Romantic music for at least part of their careers. The first three composers were all pupils of John Knowles Paine. At the outset they adhered to the ideals of the Austro-German symphonic tradition as exemplified by works from Haydn to Schumann, but around the turn of the century they incorporated Wagnerian and Brahmsian aesthetic principles as well. Chadwick taught at the New England Conservatory (est. 1867), while Parker was a professor of music at Yale University (1895–1919).

Mrs. Beach is the maverick of the group. Trained primarily as a pianist rather than as a composer, she was widely acclaimed in both Europe (especially Germany) and the United States for her performances. Many of her more than 150 songs belong to the sentimental variety so popular at the turn of the century. These—above all her *Ah, Love, but a Day* and *The Year's at the Spring* (to Browning's poetry)—have so far remained the best known of her works, but Beach's more ambitious compositions, such as her *Gaelic Symphony* (based on Gaelic folk tunes) and her *Piano Concerto,* have acquired their share of devotees. **Beach**

Foote assimilated influences primarily from Brahms and Wagner. Unlike most American composers of his period, who had high artistic aspirations, Foote did not study in Europe. On the other hand, through his teachers and his own predilection, he used Brahmsian textures in much of his chamber music—his *Piano Quartet,* Op. 23 (1891), *Quintet for Piano and Strings* (1898), and *Piano Trio in B-flat* (1909), for example. In his large-scale works such as *The Wreck of the Hesperus* (1888) and *The Skeleton in Armor,* for chorus and orchestra (1893), Wagnerian harmonies and textures are particularly evident, above all in storm scenes. **Foote**

Scion of a musical family, Chadwick was originally taught music as a desirable leisure activity. But his unquenchable desire to become a professional musician led him to Germany, where he studied in Berlin, Leipzig, and finally Munich. From his return to Boston (1880) until his death, he taught music—first privately, then (1882) at the New England Conservatory, where he became director in 1897. His symphonic poem *Aphrodite* (1913) reflects his interest in ancient mythology. Most of Chadwick's music is descriptive, consisting either of programmatic instrumental works or choral settings of narrative poetry. Many of his pieces in the latter category belong to what has been called "the Victorian cantata," a genre no longer in favor. His operas were not notably successful, but his music drama *Judith* was given a concert performance (1901). In his five string quartets and piano quintet, Chadwick generally shows the contemporaneous German preoccupation with contrapuntal textures. **Chadwick**

Another German-trained New Englander was Parker, who had been one of Chadwick's first private pupils in 1880, before studying in Munich (1882–1885). Parker began his studies with his mother, an amateur organist, when he was fourteen. After returning to the United States, he first worked in New York, but spent his last twenty-five years as professor of music at Yale (1894–1919). Even before returning to the United States, Parker had had public success in Munich, but his international reputation was established by his *Hora Novissima* ("Cometh Earth's Latest Hour") for chorus and orchestra (New York premiere, 1893). Its English premiere (1899) brought its composer other choral commissions and growing fame, crowned when Parker was awarded the Doctor of Music degree by Cambridge University (1902). **Parker**

The composer also won United States competitions for both choral and operatic music, receiving a $10,000 prize from the Metropolitan Opera for his opera *Mona* (1912). It became the third American opera ever to be produced by that organization, but did not remain in the repertory beyond 1912. Most of Parker's music, including his opera *Fairyland* (1915), is well crafted but in no way innovative.

Daniel Gregory Mason

Mason joined the other "Boston Classicists" in a dislike for his contemporaries Ravel and Debussy. A student of Paine, Chadwick, and Percy Goetschius (1853–1943) in New York, he finally went to study with D'Indy in Paris. This German-influenced Frenchman became Mason's model, and he generally kept his music within the bounds set by his teacher. Mason has been roundly criticized by Gilbert Chase for his imitation of European forms and styles, and the consequent production of music that cannot be readily identified as "American." This same complaint can be—and in fact has been—lodged against other members of the Second New England school.

Impressionists

Few American composers wrote music wholly in the impressionist style. However, it is possible to isolate and identify impressionistic elements as they apply to specific works by particular composers, including Charles Griffes, Edward MacDowell, and Charles Loeffler.

Griffes

Charles Tomlinson Griffes (1884–1920), perhaps the most famous exponent of impressionism in the United States, was born in New York. Despite his years of study in Germany, he was attracted to the music of Debussy and dismissed his own earlier German-inspired compositions as unimportant. Many of Griffes's best pieces are Debussyesque in harmony but show a melodic style similar to that of Ravel. This combination forms part of *Symphony in Yellow* and *La Fuite de la lune* ("The Flight of the Moon"), both settings of poems by Oscar Wilde, from Griffes's *Tone Images,* Op. 3 (1912), for mezzo-soprano and piano. "The White Peacock," Griffes's best-known composition, is one movement of the *Roman Sketches,* Op. 7 (1916), which Griffes originally wrote for piano, but later orchestrated along impressionist lines. A portion of this work is given in Example 40.2.

MacDowell

Edward MacDowell (1861–1908) has sometimes been described as an impressionist, not because of his technique, but rather because of the names he gave to his compositions. On the other hand, novelist Upton Sinclair, who took MacDowell's music appreciation course at Columbia University in 1899, has said that MacDowell challenged his students to attempt (however unsuccessfully) to guess at the extramusical associations in his music. A staunch individualist, MacDowell was never happy with academic constraints, and he left Columbia University unhappy with his lack of influence on policymaking.

MacDowell has often been compared to Grieg. Each has his own distinctive musical style, and each is important to the later development of music in

Ex. 40.2   Charles Griffes, *The White Peacock*

Copyright 1917 by G. Schirmer, Inc., New York. Used by permission.

his native land. MacDowell is more ambitious in his use of sonata form, but shows less mastery of form than the European composer. However, the music of both composers is lyrical and episodic, with frequent climaxes. In later life, MacDowell often claimed that he deliberately avoided hearing other composers' works so that he would not be influenced by them.

Trained in France and Germany, MacDowell explicitly denied the existence of "national" music, claiming that music's meaning lay in its context. He would have denied that his use of American Indian themes in his *Second (Indian) Suite,* Op. 48 (1897), made the work "American," any more than his *Norse Piano Sonata,* Op. 57 (1900), dedicated to Grieg, was specifically "Norwegian." MacDowell's first published work, his *First Modern Suite,* Op. 10, for piano (1883), remains popular, although it is not as individual as his later compositions, especially those written after 1890. Of all MacDowell's works, perhaps the best-known are his exquisite piano pieces. Beginning with *Twelve Virtuoso Studies* (1894)—of which *Novelette, Improvisation,* and *Polonaise* are among his finest works—the composer continued with his most famous collection, *Woodland Sketches* (1896), which included the ever-popular *To a Wild Rose* and *To a Water Lily.* MacDowell's *Sea Pieces,* Op. 55 (1898), for piano, and his song *Menie,* Op. 34 (1889; text by Robert Burns), are also

Loeffler

worthy of mention. With the exception of his *Indian Suite,* he generally seemed less at ease in the larger forms than in the smaller ones.

Charles Martin Loeffler (1861–1935), born and trained in France, did not arrive in the United States until 1881. His works are "American" in that he lived first in New York and then in Massachusetts, but he retained his impressionistic tendencies, as can be seen in his best-known work, *A Pagan Poem,* based on Vergil's eighth Eclogue. First written in 1901, this piece was later orchestrated, provided with a piano obbligato by the composer, and premiered by the Boston Symphony (1907). His *Music for Four Stringed Instruments* (published 1923) and *Evocation* (1931) for orchestra, women's chorus, and speaking voice are among his other representative works. Other impressionist-influenced composers of the United States and Canada include E. B. Hill (1872–1959), John Alden Carpenter (1876–1951), Clarence Cameron White (1880–1960), and Claude Champagne (1891–1965).

Latin America and the Caribbean

Those who looked to France for artistic inspiration included Alberto Williams (1862–1952) of Argentina. Trained extensively in Paris, he was a precursor of the nationalist school in his native land after he returned to Buenos Aires. Nevertheless, impressionist textures, harmonies, and instrumentation are evident in many of his works. In Brazil, Francisco Braga (1868–1945) drew on both German Romantic and French impressionist models, the latter a reflection of the time he spent studying with Massenet in Paris. Pedro Humberto Allende-Sarón (1885–1959) of Chile combined impressionism with the use of native rhythms, while Colombian composer Guillermo Uribe-Holguín (1880–1971) mixed nationalist, Wagnerian, and impressionist elements in his music. The nationalist-impressionist combination is also evident in works by the Cubans Alejandro García Caturla (1906–1940) and Amadeo Roldán (1900–1939). Manuel M. Ponce (1882–1948) of Mexico began as an impressionist, but later turned to nationalism and Neoclassicism. In Panama, that country's first important professional composer and strong proponent of contemporary music, Hubert de Castro (b. 1906), also wrote in the impressionist manner. Impressionism also gained adherents in Venezuela, where some composers continued to mix impressionist and folkloric elements in their works until midcentury and even beyond. Enrique de Marchena-Dujaric (b. 1908) of Santo Domingo wrote consistently in a primarily impressionist idiom.

Early Radical Innovators

The United States has been the New World leader in avant-garde trends, especially since the 1950s. During the first decade of the century, however, composers like the New Englander Charles Ives (1874–1954) had to some extent already declared artistic independence from European models, embracing techniques which extended from the choice among variant versions of passages that Ives sometimes allowed performers, and the use of microtones and noise in his scores, to the incorporation of various contrasting layers of harmonic and rhythmic elements. This last characteristic of his music has led to its being called "the first extensive musical application of collage techniques."[1]

In Mexico during the first thirty years of this century, Julián Carrillo (1875–1965) was also at work codifying his own elaborate microtonal system (see Chapter 35). All his adult life he espoused the cause of innovation in music, concentrating on the type and quality of sound. Carrillo's aesthetic approach has gained adherents among younger Latin American composers. Although Ives and Carrillo were temperamentally and musically entirely different personalities, their common characteristics were an emphasis on new combinations of sounds and on the importance of new ideas to serious music-making.

What was considered avant-garde music before World War II is now generally regarded in retrospect as the work of "radical innovators"—such composers as Ives, Henry Cowell, Harry Partch, Carl Ruggles, and Carrillo. Their compositions may be classified into three general categories: those exploiting fully and expanding the resources of traditional instruments outside of tonal harmony; those requiring the construction of new instruments or the development of new technology; and those combining elements of both traditional and innovative systems.

Charles Ives, usually regarded as the first radical innovator in the United **Ives** States, falls into the first category. He credited his father, a bandmaster in Danbury, Connecticut, and general musician in the town, with shaping his own experimental attitude toward the new uses and combinations of sounds that are so characteristic of Ives's style. Greatly influenced also by the New England Transcendentalist writers, Ives strove to find a musical counterpart to their thought, to express in music the sound qualities of life itself.

Although he used such traditional instruments as piano, orchestra, and voice, he often wrote for them in what were then extremely innovative ways. Another curious aspect of his personal musical philosophy was that he tended to equate dissonance with virility, and ridiculed "nice" (i.e., traditional, harmonious) music. His disdain for traditional harmony simply because it was traditional can be seen in many of his works, among them *The Unanswered Question* (1906), a piece for chamber orchestra that combines tonality and atonality until rhythm and harmony reach a state of confusion that the composer does not resolve. (Hence the "question" of the title remains unanswered.) Another characteristic of Ives is the use of musical quotations to add to the atmosphere, as in his songs *Evening* (1921) and *Charlie Rutlage* (1920–1921). These two works contrast in terms of temperament and style. *Evening* is a tone picture with impressionistic elements; *Charlie Rutlage,* which makes use of noise, requires the singer to recite unpitched sounds and the pianist to strike the piano with his fists. Ives's compositions in other genres are equally innovative for his time period and include the use of quarter tones (*Three Pieces,* for two pianos, 1923–1924). Since he made his living in the insurance business, Ives was free to experiment in his compositions without the worry of producing "practical" music for immediate performance.

Ruggles   Ruggles (1876–1971) also pushed the potential of conventional instruments to the limit and was concerned with creating new textures and timbres. A quintessential individualist, he wrote music that used all twelve chromatic tones as equally as possible, creating nontonal (yet not Schoenbergian) dodecaphonic music. Harmony in his works is frequently formed by melodic suspensions. His best-known composition is probably *Sun-Treader* (1931–1932), for orchestra. Like his other, comparatively few, mature works, it is an instrumental piece that embodies his artistic tenets.

Cowell   Henry Cowell (1897–1965), who had known of Ives's work since 1927, provided a vital link between the ideas of Ives and more recent avant-garde music, as did musicologist Charles Seeger (1887–1979), a prominent avant-garde theorist during the 1920s. In the process, Cowell assimilated and reinterpreted much ethnic music of both East and West and experimented with new methods of notation. His other innovations included the use of tone clusters, leading him to be known for this practice, which scandalized audiences when he first introduced it in his piano work *The Tides of Manaumaun* (1912). Among his earliest works in which the piano strings themselves had to be manipulated directly by the performer, either with the hands or in some other manner, is *The Banshee* (1925; *AMA,* pp. 564–565). The combination of these innovative elements, first applied by Cowell between 1912 and 1930, has served as the basis of later interest in the mingling of different musical traditions. He was one of a group of California innovators that also included Partch and Cage.

Partch and Carrillo   Partch developed not only a new system of tuning but also special musical instruments on which his conceptions could be realized. His was essentially an isolated stand, away from the mainstream of musical thought, much as Carrillo's was in Mexico. Their work with microtones is discussed in detail in Chapter 35.

Americanism and *Americanismo* in Music

Aaron Copland, Gershwin, and similar composers in the United States, like their Latin American and Caribbean counterparts, were concerned with making the works they wrote distinctly "American," if not specifically identifiable with a particular country. Often, as we will see later in the discussion of Neoclassicism, traditional folk elements were mixed with Neoclassicism, but the purpose behind their inclusion in "serious music" was the same as that which had inspired the Russian nationalists during the nineteenth century: to create a combination of traits that fostered a sense of ethnic, national, or even continent-wide unity and hence to provide a means of artistic identity.

Copland   After studying in New York City with composer Rubin Goldmark (1872–1936), Brooklyn-born Aaron Copland (b. 1900) went to Paris to continue his work. In France he found a music teacher who was all but unknown in the New World—Nadia Boulanger. Copland polished his compositional technique under her guidance, receiving from her entree into elite musical circles. At her request, Copland wrote a concerto for organ and orchestra to serve as Mlle. Boulanger's American debut work in January 1925. The controversial composition launched Copland's career.

Copland had gone to Europe to study at a time (1921–1924) when the United States, indeed the entire New World, sought a unique artistic voice that could be accepted as worthwhile. The composer felt that Mlle. Boulanger had helped him to find his own way toward this goal and recommended her as the ideal teacher of musical composition. By November of 1925, Copland had decided to try to create music that could be recognized immediately as distinctly "American."

The first of his compositions to adhere to this artistic doctrine was *Music for the Theater* (1925), which employed jazz elements in its second movement (*Dance*). Copland's *Piano Concerto* (1927) also used jazz in the second movement within an overall Neoclassic symphonic framework. Even more ambitious, and still jazzier, was his *Symphonic Ode* (1928, rev. 1955). Ceasing his attempts at symphonic jazz, the composer turned to material from American folklore, using folk music. To this style belong his ballets *Billy the Kid* (1938), *Rodeo* (1943), and *Appalachian Spring* (1945), as well as his instrumental works *Music for Radio* (1937, commissioned by CBS Radio and later retitled *Saga of The Prairie*), *John Henry* (1940, for small orchestra), and *Lincoln Portrait* (1942, for narrator and orchestra). Copland also wrote music for *Twelve Poems of Emily Dickinson* (1950), for voice and piano, and arranged two groups of *Old American Songs* (i.e., folk songs; 1950 and 1954, respectively). His fascination with Latin American rhythms and dances can be seen in his *El Salón México* ("Mexico Dance Hall," 1936) and *Danzón Cubano* ("Cuban *Danzón,*" 1942; originally written for two pianos; transcribed for large orchestra, 1945).

In his film music, Copland avoided Hollywood clichés, while contributing appropriately to the setting and atmosphere of such movies with American subjects as *The City* (1939), *Of Mice and Men* (1939), *Our Town* (1940), *The Red Pony* (1948), and *The Heiress* (1948).

Another Brooklyn-born composer who has made significant contributions to "Americana" in music is Morton Gould (b. 1913). Among Gould's many works a large number of the earlier ones use elements drawn from jazz, popular music, and folksongs. His *Chorale and Fugue in Jazz* (1932) is one such orchestral work. Later, Gould's works became abstract rather than programmatic, and his style incorporated more counterpoint and dissonance, e.g., his dodecaphonic *Prisms* (1962). In 1976 he showed his interest in American musical sources again. All of the movements of his *American Ballads for Orchestra* (1976) are settings of American tunes, including *The Star-Spangled Banner; Taps;* and *America the Beautiful.*

Gould

New York-born Ferde Grofé (1892–1972) spent ten years as a violist with the Los Angeles Symphony Orchestra before Paul Whiteman hired him as an arranger (1919). Grofé made a name for himself in the field of symphonic jazz, especially after he orchestrated George Gershwin's *Rhapsody in Blue* (1924). Not until then did Grofé attempt composition on his own, in works

Grofé

that are usually American in program and that use "popular" musical ideas in a symphonic manner. Among these are his *Mississippi Suite* (for Whiteman, 1924), *San Francisco Suite* (1960), *Niagara Suite* (1961, written for the opening of the Niagara Power Company's new plant), and *World's Fair Suite* (1964, written for that year's New York World's Fair). His most famous original composition is the *Grand Canyon Suite* (1931), which was conducted by Toscanini and other serious conductors. Grofé himself often conducted both popular and classical orchestras in live and broadcast performances.

Harris   Roy Harris (1898–1979) was born in Nebraska. He did not decide on a composing career until he was twenty-four. After that, he studied first on the West Coast with Arthur Farwell. In 1926 the twenty-eight-year-old Harris set out for Paris to work with Nadia Boulanger, by then famous in the United States as a composition teacher.

During his years with Mlle. Boulanger (1926–1929), Harris produced works such as his *Piano Sonata Op. 1* (1928–1929), typical of his style in its "Americanism," including a scherzo theme that resembles *Turkey in the Straw*. Harris's *Symphony No. 3* (1939) remains the composer's most frequently played work. Like most of Harris' production, it uses open fourths and fifths, in ways derived from rural American folk music and Anglo-American hymns. This tradition is especially characteristic of his *Folk Song Symphony* (Symphony No. 4, 1939). Harris, although a prolific composer in other forms, wrote no operas or film music.

Chávez   Carlos Chávez (1899–1978) was one of a generation of composers who repudiated nineteenth-century Mexican compositions as a mere imitation of European music. Ideologically, this rejection and the concurrent search for a specifically "Mexican" character in music, as in the other arts, was tied both to the goals of the Mexican Revolution of 1910 and to the larger movement known as *americanismo musical*.

Mexican *indigenismo* ("Indianism") found in Chávez a vigorous proponent, primarily during the 1920s and 1930s, and Copland saw in Chávez the ideal Indianist. Chávez was the most outstanding theorist and practitioner of Mexican musical nationalism, and was Mexico's most influential composer between the 1920s and the 1950s.

In 1928 Chávez enunciated the credo of Mexican nationalist music. He believed that music should search for its roots in the pre-Conquest past, and asserted that Indian, especially Aztec, music used primarily minor thirds and perfect fifths, and the pentatonic scale. Therefore, in order to recapture the spirit of Indian music, he felt that these elements should be maintained. To ears trained in traditional European harmony, this texture created the feeling of polytonality (in this case polymodality, since the pentatonic scale has no leading tone). Despite his emphasis on these seemingly esoteric musical resources, Chávez later consciously attempted to create works understandable to the general public. In his latter aim, he agreed not only with the goals of the Mexican Revolution but also with the ideals of other American nationalist composers, among them Copland and Villa-Lobos.

Even before he had studied Indian music, Chávez wrote a ballet, *El fuego nuevo* ("The New Fire," 1921, rev. 1927), that uses Aztec percussion instruments among its large percussion battery and employs the pentatonic scale. His contribution to Indianist music in this piece is in his evocation of its mood and spirit rather than through a literal recreation of the music of the vanished past.

Perhaps the composer's best-known Indianist works are his *Sinfonía India* ("Indian Symphony," 1935–1936) and his ballet *Xochipilli-Macuilxóchitl* (1940). The former, written while Chávez was in New York City, again uses Indian percussion instruments and authentic, although in this instance nonpentatonic, melodies. These are coupled with other, newly composed pentatonic melodies, sections in which a constant beat is kept but in which the meter varies, and extensive use of repetition of both melodies and segments of melodies. In the *Sinfonía India,* symphonic form has been compressed into one movement, using repeated patterns in which timbre and texture vary in place of sonata-allegro development. In this work Chávez incorporated an authentic Yaquí Indian melody, and accompanied it with woodwind and percussion instruments in a manner akin to the instrumentation of traditional Central and South American Indian music. Although ideologically a strongly Indianist work, this composition shows impressionist parallelism, Neoclassical formal concerns, and the use of hemiolas typical of mestizo (as opposed to Indian) music.

His ballet *Xochipilli-Macuilxóchitl* was written for a group of Indian instruments that formed three percussion sections: Yaquí drum, clay rattle, Yaquí metal rattle, water gourd, tenabari (a string of butterfly cocoons), two teponaxtles (replacing a xylophone), grijutian (a string of deer hoofs), Tlapanhuchuetl (replacing the bass drum), and raspador Yaquí (replacing the ordinary rasping stick). These the composer called his "Mexican Orchestra" in the score, although he did not mind if they were replaced in performance by similar modern instruments if the original Indian instruments or replicas of them were unavailable. The ballet itself takes its name from the Aztec god of love, dance, and flowers, and bears the subtitle "An Imagined Aztec Music." In the first and last (third) movements, Chávez attempts to evoke the pomp of Aztec ceremony through pentatonic polyphony and polyrhythm.

Active in Mexico as a teacher, government official, writer on music, and conductor, as well as a composer, Chávez had incalculable influence. He was director and permanent conductor (1928–1948) of the OSM (Orquesta Sinfónica de México, est. 1928) and directed the National Conservatory (1928–1933 and much of 1934), continuing to teach composition there until 1964. After the 1940s, Chávez's musical production centered less on Indianist motifs, although such later compositions as his *Sinfonía No. 3* (1951–1954) also contain some Indian elements.

Heitor Villa-Lobos (1887–1959) was an intensely prolific and creative composer, whose most original compositions belong to the tradition of folkloric nationalism. His approach to music was intuitive, combining elements of Brazilian popular music and culture with aspects of European compositional technique. As a youth, he had played guitar among the Rio de Janeiro

**Villa-
Lobos**

street musicians (*chorões*), learned cello from his father, and later spent years traveling throughout Brazil listening and learning, but he never studied composition in a formal academic way.

Of the composer's approximately fifty-five compositions before 1913, his *Suite dos cânticos sertanejos* ("Suite of Songs of the Backlands," 1910) is probably his first work with folk-music themes. Villa-Lobos introduced popular and folk elements and native subjects into such pieces as *Amazonas* (1917) and *Lenda do caboclo* ("Mestizo Legend," 1920). His works were controversial in Brazil for years.

Between 1910 and 1920 the composer's production, including his landmark series of piano works, *Choros* (1920–1929) and *A Prole do Bebê* ("The Baby's Family," 1918), showed impressionist influence, although it remained strongly Brazilian in character. By the time of his *Cirandas* (1926), his nationalism is even more clearly evident, in that he bases each of these sixteen piano pieces on a Brazilian children's folk song, combined with percussive effects, syncopation, double-dotted figures, and sometimes impressionistic harmony.

Villa-Lobos was inspired by the various meanings of the word *chôro:* (1) urban ensemble music, with a specially designated soloist set apart from the others; (2) a group of late-nineteenth-century serenading musicians (*chorões*), usually playing winds, plucked strings, and percussion; and (3) a syncopated binary dance-form (*chôro* or *chorinho*) of the 1920s and 1930s, closely related to the *samba* and other urban dances, which differ from each other primarily in tempo. Probably his greatest contributions to Brazilian nationalist music are his fourteen *choros* (not counting the *Introducão* ("Introduction") and *Choros bis* ("Choros reprise"). These vary widely in medium, from a single soloist (guitar, in *Choros No. 1*) to massed vocal and instrumental forces (mixed chorus and large orchestra in *Choros No. 10,* 1926, and chorus, band, and orchestra, in *Choros No. 14,* 1926). In his larger-scale *Choros,* typical Brazilian instruments are added to the ensemble, and, along with pentatonicism and narrow-range melodies, extensive use of dissonance and parallelism, and brilliantly conceived timbral shadings, create the exotic effect that is characteristic of, for example, *Choros No. 10.*

The same composer's nine *Bachianas brasileiras* (1930–1945), although written in homage to J. S. Bach, share many stylistic elements with the *Choros.* As with the *Choros,* the *Bachianas* are a series of pieces, and are always cited in the plural. In these later works, Villa-Lobos has successfully captured the contrapuntal and rhythmic procedures that Brazilian popular music shares with Bach's music. To functional harmony, considerable independence of the various voices, and arpeggiated and repeated-note patterns are added the regular sixteenth-note pulsation so typical of both Afro-Brazilian dance music and many of Bach's instrumental dance movements. Almost all of the individual movements of the *Bachianas* are in ABA form, with the A section more elaborate and extensive than the B. They also carry a double designation, with a European name such as "introduction," "prelude," or "fugue" coupled with a specifically Brazilian one such as *modinha* (a lyrical Brazilian song developed from the Italian aria) or *chôro.* The number of movements varies from two in Nos. 5, 6, and 9 to four in Nos. 2, 3, 4, 7, and 8, with only No. 1 having three movements. Perhaps the most famous of these works are Nos. 1, 2, and 5.

Among Villa-Lobos's compositions are many other currently less famous nationalistic works: his thirteen *Canções típicas brasileiras* ("Typical Brazilian Songs," 1919–1935) and his thirteen *Modinhas e Canções* ("Modinhas and Songs," 1933–1943). Although Villa-Lobos was not Brazil's first nationalist composer, he became the most enthusiastic proponent and one of the most original exponents of Brazilian nationalist music.

Ginastera

Before the mid-1950s, Alberto Ginastera (b. 1916) had earned his reputation as the leader of the Argentine nationalist school. In 1937, while still a student at Argentina's National Conservatory, he wrote the ballet *Panambí* and a set of three works for piano, *Danzas argentinas* ("Argentine Dances"). He was given the national prize for music in 1940 after *Panambí* was premiered in Buenos Aires, and was then commissioned by American Ballet Caravan to write a ballet on an Argentinian theme. The result was *Estancia* ("Farm," 1941), which made him the acknowledged head of the Argentine nationalist music movement. *Estancia,* perhaps the composer's most obviously nationalistic work in the larger forms, was followed by other tonal pieces based on *gauchesco* (the *gaucho* is the cowboy of the Argentine *pampas*) literary tradition, combining local subjects with occasional use of folk music and sometimes very dissonant passages. To Ginastera's early, objective nationalistic period (1937–1947) belong his *Obertura para el "Fausto" criollo* ("Overture for the Creole 'Faust,'" 1943), his *Cinco canciones populares argentinas* ("Five Popular Argentinian Songs," 1943), and his piano work entitled *Suite de danzas criollas* ("Suite of Creole Dances," 1946). By 1947 Ginastera had begun to enter a new phase, in which he made reference to, rather than directly stated, Argentine rhythms and tunes. This second category includes his transitional composition *Pampeana No. 1* ("Music of the Pampas, No. 1," 1947) and later works such as his first *String Quartet* (1948), *Piano Sonata* (1952), and *Variaciones concertantes* (1953). Ginastera's *Pampeana No. 3* (1954), although still nationalist, shows his gradual abandonment of nationalism. (For further discussion of Ginastera's later musical style, see Chapter 33.)

Neoclassicism

Outstanding nationalists such as Villa-Lobos, Chávez, and Copland have also written works that combine national elements with Neoclassicism. But Neoclassically oriented composers were also active elsewhere in the Americas. Their music varied from seminationalism to conscious avoidance of anything that might compromise the "internationalism" they were seeking. Members of this group in Argentina included Roberto García Morillo (b. 1911), José María Castro (1892–1964), and Roberto Caamaño (b. 1923), whose *Bandoneón Concerto,* Op. 19 (1954), refers in its title to an Argentinian instrument related to the accordion that was traditionally used for playing

Latin America

tangos. Like Aaron Copland, Ginastera underwent a Neoclassic phase in the late 1940s and 1950s. Brazilian composer Oscar Lorenzo-Fernândez (1897–1948) also cast folk and popular materials within sonata form, a procedure especially evident in such works as his *Trio brasileiro* ("Brazilian Trio," 1923). Another prominent Brazilian Neoclassicist is Camargo Guarnieri (b. 1907), who has attempted a similar fusion of elements, as can be seen in his *Symphony No. 4,* "Brasilia" (1963). Neoclassicism has influenced such Chilean composers as Domingo Santa Cruz (b. 1899) and his pupil Gustavo Becerra-Schmidt (b. 1925). Perhaps the most internationally famous Chilean composer of his generation is Juan Orrego-Salas (b. 1919), now residing in the United States. His Neoclassic phase is well represented by his *Canciones castellanas* ("Spanish Songs"), Op. 21 (1947).

The U.S. and Canada Neoclassicism was an important trend in the United States and Canada from 1925 to about 1950. Hindemith, Stravinsky, and those who propounded their tenets of musical composition are primarily responsible for these developments. Hindemith himself taught at Yale (1940–1953). Probably a more important source for the promulgation of Neoclassicism was the teaching of Nadia Boulanger in Paris, and, during World War II, in the United States, where she was then living and working. To her came such American composers as Aaron Copland, Virgil Thomson, Roger Sessions (b. 1896), and Walter Piston (1894–1976), who was most consistent of all in spreading the gospel of Neoclassicism in his capacity as professor of music at Harvard from 1926 to 1959. Other Boulanger students—Louise Talma (b. 1906), Ingolf Dahl (1912–1970), and Andrew Imbrie (b. 1921), among others—went through a Stravinskian phase during the 1940s. Some representative Neoclassic works of United States composers are Thomson's *Sonata da chiesa* (1926) and Piston's *Three Pieces* (1926), for clarinet, flute, and bassoon. All of Talma's pre-1953 works are Neoclassic, as are the pre-1945 works of another Boulanger student, Elliott Carter (b. 1908).

Most Canadian Neoclassicists received their musical training either with Mlle. Boulanger or with one of her students. The first case is perhaps exemplified by the noted French-Canadian composer Jean Papineau-Couture (b. 1916), who studied with Boulanger in California during World War II. His works at that point—and, in fact, until 1948—are firmly rooted in Neoclassicism. During her studies in France, Winnipeg-born Barbara Pentland (b. 1912) absorbed the influences of Franck, but later her work with Copland at Tanglewood (1941, 1942) deeply affected her compositionally, as seen, for example, in her *Violin Concerto* (1942).

Dodecaphony, Atonality, and Serialism

World War II was, in a sense, a dividing line for music in the Americas. It marked the beginning of a period when twelve-tone music and serialism began to gain ascendancy—due at least in part to the large-scale emigration of European musicians during the years immediately before, during, and after that war. Just as nationalism had come to characterize the generally isolation-ist stance of the New World with respect to the Old earlier in the century, so Neoclassicism and then twelve-tone techniques seemed to go hand-in-hand with greater internationalism (see Chapter 31 for a complete discussion of twelve-tone developments).

Among those Europeans whose twelve-tone music and/or teaching has been extremely influential in the development of such music in the New World since the 1930s are Ernest Křenek, Stefan Wolpe, and Arnold Schoen-berg in the United States, and Hans Joachim Kollreutter in Brazil. Then, too, some American-born composers turned toward a twelve-tone music idiom independently. Even Copland had made an attempt in this direction as early as 1927 (his *Song*), but did not take it up consistently until almost thirty years later. An early North American twelve-tone composer was the Canadian John Weinzweig (b. 1913), whose works appear to have made him the first Canadian to espouse these techniques (his *Suite No. 1, 1939*). His early works still have a tonal center, something Weinzweig abandoned later when he turned to serialism.

Some composers have actively sought to reconcile twelve-tone tech-niques with tonality. Of these, Ross Lee Finney of the United States (b. 1906) is a good example. In keeping with the generally international character of dodecaphony and serialism, such composers as the Brazilian Cláudio Santoro (b. 1919) turned to it after the war. He and the Panamanian Roque Cordero (b. 1917) were among the earliest Latin Americans to abandon nationalism for dodecaphony.

During the 1950s both dodecaphony and serialism became major musical trends in the Americas, by which time such early United States exponents of these procedures as Wallingford Riegger, George Perle, and Milton Babbitt had long been applying them. Not all composers using twelve-tone elements adopted the orthodoxy of the Schoenbergian canon. Roger Sessions, for ex-ample, combined Neoclassical and twelve-tone techniques beginning with his *Violin Sonata* (1953), but has not used dodecaphony as a determining prin-ciple of structure. Instead he has employed it as a textural principle.

The late 1950s saw the conversion to twelve-tone techniques of two com-posers born in Latin America, Ginastera and Chilean-born Claudio Spies (b. 1925), now a United States citizen. Ginastera came to serialism from national-ism. Spies approached dodecaphony from the Neoclassicism he had absorbed from his studies with Boulanger, Fine, Hindemith, and Piston, and from his close personal association with Stravinsky.

Electronic Music

In Chapter 34 we saw the general international development of electronic and computer music. In this section we shall explore the composers and cen-ters that were especially important to such music in the Americas. Com-posers such as Milton Babbitt, who were concerned with total control of all musical parameters, are discussed in detail in Chapter 34.

Studios   Electronic music has also interested composers of the Americas greatly. Because of the great expense involved in establishing and maintaining complex electronic and computer equipment, most electronic music laboratories were initially owned by large institutions such as radio stations and universities. Among the most important New World electronic studios during the 1950s and 1960s were the Columbia-Princeton Electronic Music Center (est. 1958), the one at the California Institute of Arts in Valencia (est. 1970), and the studio at the Instituto Torcuato di Tella in Buenos Aires (est. 1962). The largest such studio in the Caribbean is located at the University of Puerto Rico at Río Piedras.

Composers   Among composers of the Americas working with live electronics are Robert Ashley (b. 1930), Roger Reynolds (b. 1934), and Steve Reich (b. 1936) of the United States; Cuban-born Aurelio de la Vega (b. 1925); Argentine-born Mario Davidowsky (b. 1934); and the Canadian R. Murray Schafer (b. 1933). Some composers are known for their use of either electronic or computer music in only certain pieces. These include Wendy (formerly Walter) Carlos (b. 1939) and Charles Wuorinen (b. 1938) of the United States. Carlos's *Switched-on Bach* and *The Well-Tempered Synthesizer* brought electronic music to a wider audience than ever before. Wuorinen's electronic work *Time's Encomium* (1968–1969) won a singular distinction: It was the first piece in that genre (and the first piece that existed only on records) to win a Pulitzer Prize (1970).

The confluence of interest in machine sounds and experimental music can be found in individual composers, including John Cage, Maurício Kagel, and Pauline Oliveros (b. 1932). Born in Buenos Aires (b. 1932), Kagel has produced compositions in both electronic and experimental media, among them his landmark electronic work *Transición I* ("Transition I," 1958–1960), composed in the Cologne studio after Kagel moved to that city in 1957. Oliveros, born in the United States, has also been active in both experimental and electronic music, and has combined them in her mixed-media works, such as *To Valerie Solanas and Marilyn Monroe in Recognition of Their Desperation* (1970), for orchestra, chorus, electronics, and lights.

Third-Stream Jazz, Romanticism, and Eclecticism

Third-stream jazz (a term coined during the 1950s by Gunther Schuller) is a movement that uses both jazz and other methods of composition. It developed in the 1950s and grew to encompass works by such United States composers as Hall Overton (1920–1970) and Francis Thorne (b. 1922). Thorne's *Six Set Pieces* (1967), for example, incorporates elements of both jazz and serialism. Jazz influence extends to the title of the work itself, since "set" refers to a unit of performance in jazz consisting of several pieces, each set separated from the next by a period of rest for the performers. This meaning, in combination with the twelve-tone meaning of "set" in music, makes the title a double pun.

The composition of third-stream music has not been confined to the United States. In Toronto there worked a group of Canadian third-stream composers, of whom the best known is probably Norman Symonds (b. 1920); his *Concerto grosso* (1968) is written for jazz quintet and symphony orchestra.

Romanticism, in the forms commonly known as "Neo-Romanticism" and "Schoenbergian Romanticism," has persisted, although this trend seems to be declining. Among the first generation of Neo-Romantics in the United States are Virgil Thomson, Roger Sessions, Howard Hanson (1905–1981), Samuel Barber (1910–1981), and Leon Kirchner (b. 1919); the latter carried Neo-Romanticism into the 1960s. Other United States composers, notably Ben Weber (b. 1916), George Rochberg (b. 1918), and Ralph Shapey (b. 1921), have incorporated various twelve-tone principles without forfeiting the emotional intensity commonly associated with Romanticism, and sometimes have even preserved some aspects of tonality.

Perhaps the largest single remaining category of musical composition is that called "eclectic," which encompasses various styles. Eclectic composers are to be found throughout the Americas. United States composer Ned Rorem (b. 1923), in his early songs, uses diatonicism in the voice and chromaticism in the piano accompaniments. Many of his instrumental works of the 1960s, however, employ modified serial procedures, while later lyrical works have retained their simple charm, with a less chromatic piano accompaniment than before. George Crumb, also of the United States, is another well-known eclectic composer (see Chapter 34 for an extended discussion of his works). Successful Latin American eclectics include Juan José Castro (1895–1968) of Argentina; Miguel Letelier-Valdés (b. 1939) and Juan Orrego-Salas (b. 1919) of Chile; Fabio González-Zuleta (b. 1925) of Colombia; and Lan Adomián (1905–1979), who was born in the Ukraine, emigrated to the United States, and toward the end of his life became a Mexican citizen.

Summary

In this chapter we have traced some of the more important trends in contemporary music. During the early years of the century, radical innovators produced music that was to influence later generations of avant-garde composers. Ives, Ruggles, Cowell, and Carrillo helped to provide the impetus for the development of new concepts of form, style, time, space, and aesthetics, which were later developed in the works of Cage, Kagel, Partch, and Oliveros.

Important electronic music centers were established in the Americas after World War II. In Argentina and the United States, composers such as Babbitt, Oliveros, Carlos, Wuorinen, and Davidowsky have helped to develop the possibilities inherent in these new musical media, and to bring the result-ant compositions to the attention of a wider audience.

Nationalist composers such as Chávez, Copland, Villa-Lobos, and Ginas-tera struggled during the first half-century to create music clearly identifiable as "American." Finney, Sessions, Cordero, and Ginastera are some of the composers who had been nationalists during the 1920s–1940s, but who em-braced twelve-tone and serial techniques to varying degrees during the 1950s. Despite the general trend toward dodecaphony among serious composers, traditional and eclectic composers such as Thomson, Barber, Rorem, Crumb, Adomián and González-Zuleta have chosen to adapt elements from various different styles to form a personal amalgam.

The Americas have made particularly significant contributions to world popular music during the twentieth century. Rock 'n' roll, jazz, and the tango are three of the forms that grew up in the New World and have received in-ternational acceptance in both Europe and the Americas. A specifically North American type, the musical comedy, evolved from loosely organized skits interspersed with songs, or alternately Americanized Viennese operetta, to become a popular but sometimes extremely complex musico-dramatic whole in the hands of such composers as Gershwin, Rodgers, and Bernstein.

During the twentieth century the Americas have become a force to be reckoned with in world music, with major centers of musical culture scat-tered throughout the New World and New World composers receiving worldwide recognition. In this era of questioning and the reexamination of long-held aesthetic assumptions, many different styles and philosophies exist side by side. It is this heterogeneity that perhaps best characterizes twentieth-century music of the Americas and, indeed, of the entire world.

Note

1. Laurence Wallach, "Charles Ives," in *Dictionary of Contemporary Music,* ed. John Vinton (New York: E. P. Dutton, 1974), p. 360.

Bibliography

Books and Articles

Macmillan has published a Jazz Masters series, written by authorities, with one vol-ume devoted to each decade. Among other excellent studies are:

ANDERSON, DONNA KAY. *The Works of Charles T. Griffes: A Descriptive Catalogue.* Ph.D. dissertation, Indiana University, 1966.
ANSON, GEORGE. "Contemporary Piano Music of the Americas." *Inter-American Music Bulletin,* no. 13 (Sept. 1959): 4–24.
BÉHAGUE, GERARD. *The Beginnings of Musical Nationalism in Brazil.* Detroit Mono-graphs in Musicology, 1. Detroit: Information Coordinators, 1971.

BELLAMY, LAURETTE. *The Sonido Trece Theoretical Works of Julián Carrillo: A Translation with Commentary*. Ph.D. dissertation, Indiana University, 1972.

BENJAMIN, GERALD R. "Julián Carrillo and 'Sonido Trece.'" *Yearbook of the Interamerican Institute for Musical Research* 3 (1967): 33–68.

BERGER, ARTHUR. *Aaron Copland*. New York: Oxford University Press, 1953.

CAGE, JOHN. *Silence*. Middletown, Conn.: Wesleyan University Press, 1961.

————. *A Year from Monday*. Middletown, Conn.: Wesleyan University Press, 1969.

CASO, FERNANDO H. *Hector Campos Parsi in the History of Twentieth-Century Music of Puerto Rico*. Masters essay, Indiana University, 1972.

COWELL, HENRY, ed. *American Composers on American Music*. Stanford, Ca.: Stanford University Press, 1933; reprint, New York: Frederick Ungar, 1962.

————, and COWELL, SYDNEY. *Charles Ives and His Music*. New York: Oxford University Press, 1955.

EDMUNDS, JOHN, and BOELZNER, GORDON, comps. *Some Twentieth Century American Composers*. 2 vols. New York: New York Public Library, 1959–1960.

GILMAN, LAWRENCE. *Edward MacDowell: A Study*. New York: John Lane and Co., 1908; reprint, New York: Da Capo Press, 1969.

IVES, CHARLES E. *Charles E. Ives: Memos,* ed. John Kirkpatrick. New York: W. W. Norton, 1972.

KEIL, CHARLES. *Urban Blues*. Chicago: University of Chicago Press, 1966.

KUSS, MALENA. *Nativistic Strains in Argentine Operas Premiered at the Teatro Colón, 1908–1972*. Ph.D. dissertation, University of California, Los Angeles, 1976.

LOWENS, IRVING. "Edward MacDowell." *Hi Fi/Stereo Review* 19, no. 12 (Dec. 1967): 61–72.

LUPER, ALBERT T. "Lorenzo Fernândez and Camargo Guarnieri: Notes Toward a Midcentury Appraisal." *Conference on Latin-American Fine Arts, Proceedings*. Austin, Texas: University of Texas, Institute of Latin American Studies, 1952, pp. 98–114.

MALMSTRÖM, DAN. *Introduction to Twentieth-Century Mexican Music*. Ph.D. dissertation, Uppsala, Sweden, Institute of Musicology, 1974.

MARIZ, VASCO. *Villa-Lobos: Life and Work*. 2nd ed. Washington, D.C.: Brazilian American Cultural Institute, 1970.

ORREGO-SALAS, JUAN. "The Young Generation of Latin American Composers: Backgrounds and Perspectives." *Interamerican Music Bulletin* (English edition), no. 38 (Nov. 1963): 1–10.

PARTCH, HARRY. *Genesis of a Music*. 2nd ed., enl. New York: Da Capo Press, 1974.

REISNER, ROBERT. *The Literature of Jazz: A Selective Bibliography,* 2nd ed. New York: New York Public Library, 1959.

ROSSITER, FRANK. *Charles Ives and His America*. New York: W. W. Norton, 1975.

RUSSELL, ROSS. *Jazz in Kansas City and the Southwest*. Berkeley: University of California Press, 1971.

SCHULLER, GUNTHER. *Early Jazz: Its Roots and Musical Development*. New York: Oxford University Press, 1968.

STEARNS, MARSHALL. *The Story of Jazz*. New York: Oxford University Press, 1956; reprint Mentor Books.

THOMSON, VIRGIL. *Virgil Thomson*. New York: Alfred A. Knopf, 1966; reprint New York: Da Capo Press, 1977.

Scores

The Pan American Union has issued bilingual catalogues listing the works and publishers of most of the composers mentioned in this chapter (in *Composers of the Americas,* 18 vols.), along with short biographies. The musical supplements to volumes I, III, IV, and VI of the *Boletín latinoamericano de música* contain works by Castro, Gianneo, Isamitt, Paz, Villa-Lobos, Mignone, Mortet, García Morillo, Santa Cruz, Posada Amador, Uribe Holguín, Sas, Braga, Santoro, and Cosme. *New Music* has also published many new scores, among them its volume 16, no. 1, devoted to Brazilian piano music. The publishers of individual composers' works may generally be found in John Vinton's *Dictionary of Contemporary Music.* Da Capo Press's Earlier American Music Series has reissued Paine's *Symphony No. 1,* Parker's *Hora Novissima,* and Chadwick's *Judith* and *Symphony No. 2* (1972). Other useful collections include:

Blesh, Rudi. *Classic Piano Rags.* New York: Dover, 1974.

Cage, John, and Knowles, Alison, eds. *Notations.* West Glover: Something Else Press, Inc., 1969.

Escobar, Luis Antonio, ed. *Obras polifónicas, autores colombianos.* Bogotá: Imprenta Nacional, 1972.

Guenther, Feliz, ed. *Collection espagnole (Colección de obras españolas e iberoamericanas) . . . for piano solo.* New York: Edward B. Marks, 1941.

Handy, W. C. *Blues: An Anthology.* New York: A & C Boni, 1926.

Joplin, Scott. *The Collected Works of Scott Joplin,* ed. Vera Brodsky Lawrence. New York: New York Public Library, 1971.

Lange, Francisco Curt, ed. *Latin American Art Music for the Piano by Twelve Contemporary Composers.* New York: G. Schirmer, 1942.

Lawrence, Vera Brodsky. *Wa-Wan Press, 1901–1911,* ed. R. Jackson. Reprint edition, with introduction by Gilbert Chase. New York: Arno-New York Times, 1970.

About the Contributors

Léonie Rosenstiel studied violin with Louis Persinger and Sandor Végh and earned her Ph.D. in historical musicology from Columbia University. A former special project editor of *Current Musicology* and consulting editor for Da Capo Press, she has written biographies of Lili and Nadia Boulanger and was honored by UNESCO and the Mexican government for her work in Latin American Music. She wishes to thank the following teachers and scholars for their insights, comments, and suggestions: Professors William Austin, Cornell; Robert Stevenson, UCLA; Raoul Camus, Queensborough Community College; Samuel Claro, Universidad Nacional de Chile; Carleton Sprague Smith, Rutgers; Eve R. Meyer, Temple; Thomas Stanford, University of North Carolina, Greensboro; Aurelio de la Vega, California State University, Northridge. Special acknowledgment is due Professor Roque Cordero, University of Illinois, Normal, for his constant encouragement.

Charlotte Roederer received her Ph.D. in music history from Yale University. A student of medieval chant, she has researched manuscript collections in Paris and other European cities and has taught at Bryn Mawr College and the State University of New York at Buffalo. She wishes especially to thank a colleague, Professor Roger Evans; two thoughtful assistants, Myrl Hermann and Roger Parris; and three students, Sharon Kerman, Jean Sutherland, and Thomas Witakowski.

Alejandro Enrique Planchart received his Ph.D. in music history from Harvard University. The conductor of an early-music ensemble and a composer, he is a professor of music at the University of California at Santa Barbara. He wishes to thank the staff of the music department at the University of California, Santa Barbara, who helped with the preliminary typing of his manuscript.

Lowell Lindgren received his Ph.D. in musicology from Harvard University, where he also taught for many years. A student of Italian opera of the late Baroque era, he has written for *Studi Musicali, Music and Letters, The Musical Quarterly,* and other publications and is an associate professor at the Massachusetts Institute of Technology. He gratefully thanks the following professors for their critical comments: Michael Gillespie, University of Chicago; David Grayson, Amherst; Winston Kaehler, College of St. Catherine; Susan McClary, University of Minnesota; Martin Marks, MIT. He also acknowledges the generous help of his former colleagues at Harvard University: Professors Louise Litterick (now at Mt. Holyoke), Luise Vosgerchian, and Christian Wolff.

Gordana Lazarevich received her M.S. in piano from the Juilliard School of Music and her Ph.D. in musicology from Columbia University. The editor of critical editions of four intermezzi of Johann Adolf Hasse and a contributor to the forthcoming *New Pergolesi Edition,* she heads the graduate program in music at the University of Victoria in Victoria.

L. Michael Griffel received his M.S. in piano from the Juilliard School of Music and his Ph.D. in historical musicology from Columbia University. A former editor-in-chief of *Current Musicology,* he is an associate professor at Hunter College and at the Graduate Center of The City University of New York. He wishes to thank several colleagues and friends: Professor William B. Kimmel, Hunter College (Emeritus); Professor Elliott Kaback, Hunter College; Dr. Steven M. Cahn, The Rockefeller Foundation; Mr. Kenneth Stern, Hunter College; and Ms. Jeannie G. Pool.

Faye-Ellen Silverman is a composer and pianist who holds advanced degrees in music composition from Harvard University and the Columbia University School of the Arts. She has taught at Goucher College and is a member of the department of music history and literature of the Peabody Conservatory of Johns Hopkins University. She gratefully acknowledges the assistance and encouragement of Maurice Edwards; Iannis Xenakis; Professor Robert Hall Lewis, Goucher College and Peabody Conservatory; and Professor Vladimir Ussachevsky, Columbia-Princeton Electronic Music Center.

Margaret Ross Griffel received her Ph.D. in historical musicology from Columbia University. A former editor of *Current Musicology,* she has conducted research for Oxford University Press and Novello and is a consulting editor for G. Schirmer.

Index

Page numbers in **boldface** refer to musical examples.

A cantar un villancico, Ceruti, 858
A Prole do Bebê, Villa-Lobos, 938
Abaco, Evaristo Felice dall', 368
Abel, Carl Friedrich, 529, 531, 557, 879
Abelard, Peter, 4
Absent, L', Gounod, 644
Absolute symphony, 611–24
Abu Hassan, Weber, 707
Académie Royale de Musique, 460
Accentualists, 33
Accompaniments, Wolff, 799–800
Achille in Sciro (Metastasio), Sarro, 492
Achtliederbuch, 248
Achtzehn Probestücke, C. P. E. Bach, 480
Acis and Galatea, Handel, 413
Ad organum faciendum, 80
Adam de la Halle, 143
Adam und Eva (Theile), 401
Adelaide, Beethoven, 634
Adew, Adew, Cornysh, 227
Adlgasser, Anton, 511, 569
Adomián, Lan, 943
Adveniam pervenian—Tamquam, 99
Aeneid, Vergil, 704
Aesthetics, 311–12, 478, 486–87
Affektenlehre, 312, 478
Africaine, L', Meyerbeer, 703
Agincourt, François d', 474
Agnus Dei, 54–55, **56**
Agricola, Alexander, 193, 199–200, 279
Agricola, Johann Friedrich, 463, 480
Aguilera de Heredia, Sebastian, 432
Ah del gozo!, Orejón, 871
Ah, Robin, Gentle Robin, Cornysh, 227
Aiblinger, Johann Kaspar, 648
Aida, Verdi, 593, 651, 699, 896
Ainsi qu'on oit, Goudimel, 251, **251**
Air, 357–58
Air de cour, 216, 317–18, 358
Alba, 69
Albéniz, Isaac, 587, 593, 677, 715
Alberdi, Juan Bautista, 894, 895
Albert, Heinrich, 360
Albert Herring, Britten, 794
Alberti, Domenico; Alberti bass, 473
Albinoni, Tomaso, 369, 370
Alceste, Gluck, 495, 496, 497, 570
Alcestis, Schweitzer, 494
Alcina, Handel, 412
Alcorta, Amancio, 893, 895
Alcuns Pseaulmes et cantiques, 249–50

Aleatory music, 725, 746
Alençar, J. de, 896
Alexander's Feast, Handel, 413
Alfano, Franco, 700
Alfonseca, Juan Bautista, 893
Algarotti, Francesco, 488
Alidoro, Leo, 501
Allégresse publique, L', Neukomm, 897
Allegri, Gregorio, 418, **419**
Allegro ed il Penseroso, L' (Milton), Handel, 413
Alleluia, 51–52
Alleluia celebranda, **62**
Alleluia Dies sanctificatus, 82
Allemande, 282
Allende-Sarón, Pedro Humberto, 932
Allerseelen, R. Strauss, 643
Allezeit fertige Polonaisen, Der, Kirnberger, 826
Allgemeine Theorie der schönen Künste, Sulzer, 463, 477, 524
Alma redemptoris mater, 44
Alma redemptoris mater, Ockeghem, 180–81, **181**
Alpha vibrans—Coetus—(Contra)—Amicus, 143
Also sprach Zarathustra: Nietzsche, 661; R. Strauss, 628, 756
Altenberg Lieder, Berg, 756
Alypian tables, 12–13
Amahl and the Night Visitors, Menotti, 794
Amans ames, Cordier, 153
Amati, Nicola, 304
Ambrosian chant, 24
American Ballads for Orchestra, Gould, 935
American Quartet, Dvořák, 683
Americanism, 934–36
Americanismo in music, 936–39
Amfiparnaso, L', Vecchi, 237, 325
Amor brasileiro, Neukomm, 898
Amor brujo, El, Falla, 777
Amor vuol sofferenze, Leo, 521, **522**
Amour courtois, l', 68
Amoureux, L', Neukomm, 898
Amours de Bastien et Bastienne, Les, Favart, 504
Amours de Mirabelais, Les, 887
Amours dont sui espris, L', Blondel de Nesle, 72–73, **73**
Amours partes, Sermisy, 214, 215, **217, **284
An die ferne Geliebte, Beethoven, 634
Ana, Francesco d', 208
Anadolia, Foster, 911

Anakreons Grab (Goethe), Wolf, 641
Anchieta, Juan de, 221
Ancient Voices of Children (García-Lorca), Crumb, 748
Andersen, Hans Christian, 647
Anderson, Leroy, 928
Andrea dei Servi, 151, 154, **156**
Andrino, José Escolástico, 893
Andromeda, Manelli, 393
Anerio, Giovanni Francesco, 427
Anfossi, Pietro, 555
Anglebert, Jean Henri d', 376
Anglican church music, 252–53
Animus II, Druckman, 814
Années de pèlerinage, Liszt, 666, 673
Anonymous IV, 86, 92n
Antes, John, 885
Antheil, George, 806
Anthems, 447–48
Anthoni usque ad limina, Busnois, 184
Anti-art (music), 832
Anti-Fascist movement, 799
Antiphonale missarum, 45–46, 61
Antiphonale officii, 46
Antiphons, Marian, 44
Antonius von Padua Fischpredigt, Des, Mahler, 624
Antony and Cleopatra, Barber, 791
Appalachian Spring, Copland, 935
Appassionata Sonata, Beethoven, 668
Apt manuscript, **156**
Aquil'al tera—Creatura gentil—Uccel di dio, Jacopo da Bologna, 149
Araujo, Juan de, 856
Arbeau, Thoinot, 129
Arbeiter-Sängerbund, 798
Arcadelt, Jacob, 208, 211, 216, 255
Archduke Trio, Beethoven, 685
Archilei, Antonio and Vittoria, 386
Arco de Noé, El, 854
Arel, Bülent, 811
Arensky, Anton, 683
Argento, Dominick, 793
Arias: Baroque, 315–44; bel canto, 327–34; buffo types, 500–501; French, 505; monody, 324–27; seria types, 486
Aria da cantar, 315–17
Aria di Passacaglia, Frescobaldi, 331
Ariadna auf Naxos, Benda, 494
Ariadne auf Naxos, R. Strauss, 713
Ariadne musica, Fischer, 431
Arianna, L', Monteverdi, 236, 325–26, **326,** 387

949